T0140075

Lecture Notes in Networks and Systems

Volume 223

Series Editor

Janusz Kacprzyk, Systems Research Institute, Polish Academy of Sciences, Warsaw, Poland

Advisory Editors

Fernando Gomide, Department of Computer Engineering and Automation—DCA, School of Electrical and Computer Engineering—FEEC, University of Campinas—UNICAMP, São Paulo, Brazil

Okyay Kaynak, Department of Electrical and Electronic Engineering, Bogazici University, Istanbul, Turkey

Derong Liu, Department of Electrical and Computer Engineering, University of Illinois at Chicago, Chicago, USA; Institute of Automation, Chinese Academy of Sciences, Beijing, China

Witold Pedrycz, Department of Electrical and Computer Engineering, University of Alberta, Alberta, Canada; Systems Research Institute, Polish Academy of Sciences, Warsaw, Poland

Marios M. Polycarpou, Department of Electrical and Computer Engineering, KIOS Research Center for Intelligent Systems and Networks, University of Cyprus, Nicosia, Cyprus

Imre J. Rudas, Óbuda University, Budapest, Hungary

Jun Wang, Department of Computer Science, City University of Hong Kong, Kowloon, Hong Kong

The series "Lecture Notes in Networks and Systems" publishes the latest developments in Networks and Systems—quickly, informally and with high quality. Original research reported in proceedings and post-proceedings represents the core of LNNS.

Volumes published in LNNS embrace all aspects and subfields of, as well as new challenges in, Networks and Systems.

The series contains proceedings and edited volumes in systems and networks, spanning the areas of Cyber-Physical Systems, Autonomous Systems, Sensor Networks, Control Systems, Energy Systems, Automotive Systems, Biological Systems, Vehicular Networking and Connected Vehicles, Aerospace Systems, Automation, Manufacturing, Smart Grids, Nonlinear Systems, Power Systems, Robotics, Social Systems, Economic Systems and other. Of particular value to both the contributors and the readership are the short publication timeframe and the world-wide distribution and exposure which enable both a wide and rapid dissemination of research output.

The series covers the theory, applications, and perspectives on the state of the art and future developments relevant to systems and networks, decision making, control, complex processes and related areas, as embedded in the fields of interdisciplinary and applied sciences, engineering, computer science, physics, economics, social, and life sciences, as well as the paradigms and methodologies behind them.

Indexed by SCOPUS, INSPEC, WTI Frankfurt eG, zbMATH, SCImago.

All books published in the series are submitted for consideration in Web of Science.

More information about this series at http://www.springer.com/series/15179

Nancy L. Black · W. Patrick Neumann ·
Ian Noy
Editors

Proceedings of the 21st Congress of the International Ergonomics Association (IEA 2021)

Volume V: Methods & Approaches

 Springer

Editors
Nancy L. Black
Département de génie mécanique
Université de Moncton
Moncton, NB, Canada

W. Patrick Neumann
Department of Mechanical and Industrial
Engineering
Ryerson University
Toronto, ON, Canada

Ian Noy
Toronto, ON, Canada

ISSN 2367-3370   ISSN 2367-3389   (electronic)
Lecture Notes in Networks and Systems
ISBN 978-3-030-74613-1   ISBN 978-3-030-74614-8   (eBook)
https://doi.org/10.1007/978-3-030-74614-8

This Springer imprint is published by the registered company Springer Nature Switzerland AG
The registered company address is: Gewerbestrasse 11, 6330 Cham, Switzerland

Preface

The International Ergonomics Association (IEA) is the organization that unites Human Factors and Ergonomics (HF/E) associations around the world. The mission of the IEA is "to elaborate and advance ergonomics science and practice, and to expand its scope of application and contribution to society to improve the quality of life, working closely with its constituent societies and related international organizations" (IEA, 2021). The IEA hosts a world congress every three years creating the single most important opportunity to exchange knowledge and ideas in the discipline with practitioners and researchers from across the planet. Like other IEA congresses, IEA2021 included an exciting range of research and professional practice cases in the broadest range of Human Factors and Ergonomics (HF/E) applications imaginable. While the conference was not able to host an in-person meeting in Vancouver, Canada, as planned by the host Association of Canadian Ergonomists/*Association canadienne d'ergonomie*, it still featured over 875 presentations and special events with the latest research and most innovative thinkers. For this congress, authors could prepare a chapter for publication, and 60% chose to do so. The breadth and quality of the work available at IEA2021 are second to none—and the research of all authors who prepared their publication for this congress is made available through the five volumes of these proceedings.

The International Ergonomics Association defines Human Factors and Ergonomics (HF/E) synonymously as being:

the scientific discipline concerned with the understanding of interactions among humans and other elements of a system, and the profession that applies theory, principles, data and methods to design in order to optimize human well-being and overall system performance.

Practitioners of ergonomics and ergonomists contribute to the design and evaluation of tasks, jobs, products, environments and systems in order to make them compatible with the needs, abilities and limitations of people.

Ergonomics helps harmonize things that interact with people in terms of people's needs, abilities and limitations. (https://iea.cc/definition-and-domains-of-ergonomics/)

The breadth of issues and disciplines suggested by this definition gives one pause for thought: what aspect in our lives is not in some way affected by the design and application of HF/E? For designers and managers around the world, a similar realization is growing: every decision made in the design and application of technology has implications for the humans that will interact with that system across its lifecycle. While this can be daunting, the researchers and professionals who participated in IEA2021 understand that, by working together across our disciplines and roles, we can achieve these lofty ambitions. This is especially relevant as we continue our collective journey into an increasingly "interconnected world"—the theme for the 21st IEA Congress. With the rise of a myriad of technologies as promulgated by Industry 4.0 proponents, we need now, more than ever, the skills and knowledge of HF/E researchers and practitioners to ensure that these tools are applied in a human-centric way towards resilient and sustainable systems that provide an enduring and sustainable road to prosperity—as advocated in the new Industry 5.0 Paradigm (Breque et al. 2021). Where the trend of Industry 4.0 aims primarily at encouraging technology purchasing and application, Industry 5.0 includes goals of resiliency and sustainability for both humans and our planet. These proceedings provide examples of research and development projects that illustrate how this brighter, human-centred future can be pursued through "*Ergonomie 4.0*", as stated in the French theme of the Congress.

While the theme of the Congress concerns human interactions within a rapidly evolving cyber-physical world, the devastating impact of the COVID-19 pandemic has given an added dimension to the Congress theme and its delivery model. As the pandemic began to engulf the world, the traditional in-person Congress became increasingly less viable and gave way to the creation of a hybrid model as a means to enhance international participation. In early 2021, it became clear that holding an in-person event would not be possible; hence, the Congress was converted to a fully virtual event. The uncertainty, mounting challenges and turbulent progression actually created new possibilities to engage the global HF/E community in ways that were never previously explored by the IEA. Indeed, one of the scientific tracks of the congress focuses explicitly on HF/E contributions to cope with COVID-19, and readers will find some submissions to other tracks similarly focus on what HF/E practitioners and researchers bring to the world during this pandemic period. This journey epitomizes broader transformative patterns now underway in society at large and accentuates the urgency for resilience, sustainability, and healthy workplaces. No doubt, the notion of globalization will be redefined in the wake of the pandemic and will have far-reaching implications for the connected world and for future society, and with new paradigms emerge a host of new human factors challenges. The breadth of topics and issues addressed in the proceedings suggests that the HF/E community is already mobilizing and rising to these emerging challenges in this, our connected world.

IEA2021 proceedings includes papers from 31 scientific tracks and includes participants from 74 countries across 5 continents. The proceedings of the 21st triennial congress of the IEA—IEA2021—exemplify the diversity of HF/E, and of the association, in terms of geography, disciplines represented, application domains, and aspects of human life cycle and capability being considered. Our diversity mirrors the diversity of humans generally and is a strength as we learn to weave our knowledge, methods, and ideas together to create a more resilient and stronger approach to design than is achievable individually. This is the strength of the IEA congresses, in the past, in the current pandemic-affected 21st occasion, and in the future. There is no other meeting like it.

A substantial number of works were submitted for publication across the Scientific Tracks at IEA2021. This gave us the happy opportunity to group contents by common threads. Each volume presents contents in sections with papers within the track's section presented in alphabetical order by the first author's last name. These proceedings are divided into five volumes as follows:

VOLUME 1: SYSTEMS AND MACROERGONOMICS (ISBN 978-3-030-74601-8)

Activity Theories for Work Analysis and Design (ATWAD)
Systems HF/E
Ergonomic Work Analysis and Training (EWAT)
HF/E Education and Professional Certification Development
Organisation Design and Management (ODAM)

VOLUME 2: INCLUSIVE AND SUSTAINABLE DESIGN (ISBN 978-3-030-74604-9)

Ageing and Work
Ergonomics for children and Educational Environments
Ergonomics in Design for All
Gender and Work
Human Factors and Sustainable Development
Slips Trips and Falls
Visual Ergonomics

VOLUME 3: SECTOR BASED ERGONOMICS (ISBN 978-3-030-74607-0)

Practitioner Case Studies
Aerospace Ergonomics
Agricultural Ergonomics
Building and Construction Ergonomics
Ergonomics in Manufacturing
HF/E in Supply Chain Design and Management
Transport Ergonomics and Human Factors

VOLUME 4: HEALTHCARE AND HEALTHY WORK (ISBN 978-3-030-74610-0)

Health and Safety
Healthcare Ergonomics

HF/E Contribution to Cope with Covid-19
Musculoskeletal Disorders

VOLUME 5: METHODS & APPROACHES (ISBN 978-3-030-74613-1)

Affective Design
Anthropometry
Biomechanics
Ergonomics in Advanced Imaging
Human Factors in Robotics
Human Modelling and Simulation
Neuroergonomics
Working with Computer Systems

These volumes are the result of many hours of work, for authors, Scientific Track Managers and their reviewer teams, student volunteers, and editors. We are grateful to Springer for making it available to you in book form and are confident you will find these works informative and useful in your own efforts to create a better, more human-centred future.

References

Breque, M., De Nul, L., Petridis, A., 2021. Industry 5.0: Towards More Sustainable, Resilient and Human-Centric Industry, in: Innovation, E.D.-G.f.R.a. (Ed.), Policy Brief. European Commission, Luxembourg, p. 48. https://ec. europa.eu/info/news/industry-50-towards-more-sustainable-resilient-and-human-centric-industry-2021-jan-07_en

International Ergonomics Association (2021) Definitions and Domains of Ergonomics. https://iea.cc/definition-and-domains-of-ergonomics/; accessed March, 2021

Nancy L. Black
W. Patrick Neumann
IEA2021 Scientific Co-chairs

Ian Noy
IEA2021 Conference Chair

The original version of the book was revised: The author name in part VI has been amended. The book have been updated with the changes. The correction to the book is available at https://doi.org/10.1007/978-3-030-74614-8_105

IEA2021 Acknowledgements

The IEA Congress organizing committee acknowledges many individuals whose contributions to the event have been invaluable to its success.

First and foremost, we acknowledge with deep appreciation the tremendous work of Steve Marlin, CEO of Prestige Accommodations, International Inc. His firm, hired to assist with organizing and executing the Congress, delivered unparalleled service throughout the planning process. Tragically, Steve passed away in early 2021. He provided outstanding support and wise counsel, always with a smile. He is sorely missed. We remain indebted to the Prestige staff, whose expertise and outstanding professionalism guided us through the planning process. In particular, we are grateful to Laurie Ybarra, Sr. Meetings Manager, who oversaw the many diverse aspects of our ever-changing plans and Christine Reinhard, Director of Operations, who skilfully managed the budget, website and registration system. Laurie and Christine's friendly approach, and their unique combination of technical and interpersonal skills, made it a pleasure to work with them. Marie-Hélène Bisaillon, Executive Director of the Association of Canadian Ergonomists/ *Association canadienne d'ergonomie*, supported their work.

The Organizing Committee is also indebted to those contributors who were instrumental in developing and promoting IEA2021. Joanne Bangs, our freelance Communications Specialist, provided engaging news blogs and other promotional collateral to help get the word out about the Congress. Sadeem Qureshi (Ryerson University), Elizabeth Georgiou, Elaine Fung, and Michelle Lam (Simon Fraser University) helped to create widespread awareness of the Congress as well as the HF/E field and profession through creative use of digital and social media. We are also grateful to those who worked diligently to ensure that the Congress provided meaningful opportunities for students and early career researchers, including Daniel P. Armstrong and Christopher A.B. Moore (University of Waterloo), Owen McCulloch (Simon Fraser University), Dora Hsiao (Galvion, Inc.), Chelsea DeGuzman and Joelle Girgis (University of Toronto), and Larissa Fedorowich (Associate Ergonomist, self-employed). The ePoster presentation option, new to IEA triennial congresses in 2021, was defined with care by Anne-Kristina Arnold (Simon Fraser University). Colleen Dewis (Dalhousie University) was key to interpreting our technical submission software and adapting its capacities to our needs. Hemanshu Bhargav (Ryerson University), Rachel Faust (Université de Québec à Montréal), Myriam Bérubé (Université de Montréal), Charlotte Bate, Vanessa DeVries, Caleb Leary, and Marcelo Zaharur (Fanshawe College), Tobi Durowoju (EWI Works), Issa Kaba Diakite, Mariam Keita, Mouhamadou Pléa Ndour, Shelby Nowlan, Faouzi Mahamane Ouedraogo, Jenna Smith, and Israël Muaka Wembi (Université de Moncton), and the aforementioned Larissa Fedorowich assisted with technical submission database verification and clean-up. We are particularly grateful that so many came to us through the Association of Canadian Ergonomists/Association canadienne d'ergonomie, witnessing to the active and motivated ergonomics and human factors community in IEA2021's host country.

The organizers are especially grateful to our sponsors, whose generous contributions made the Congress possible and readily accessible to the global HF/E community. Their recognition of the Congress as a valuable opportunity to advance the field of HF/E, as well as their steadfast support throughout a very trying planning period, was critical to the success of the Congress. The IEA 2021 sponsors include:

Benefactor Level:
    Amazon.com, Inc.

Platinum Level:
    Anonymous

Diamond Level:
    Healthcare Insurance Reciprocal of Canada

Gold Level:
    Huawei Technologies Canada
    Institute for Work and Health (Ontario)
    WorkSafe BC

Silver Level:
    Fanshawe College
    Simon Fraser University
    Aptima, Inc.

Organization

IEA2021 Organizing Committee

IEA2021 Congress Chair

Ian Noy — HFE Consultant and Forensic Expert, Toronto, Ontario, Canada

Technical Program Committee Co-chairs

Nancy L. Black — Department of Mechanical Engineering, Faculté d'ingénierie, Université de Moncton, Canada

W. Patrick Neumann — Human Factors Engineering Lab, Department of Mechanical and Industrial Engineering, Ryerson University, Canada

Media Outreach

Hayley Crosby — Options Incorporated, Canada

Developing Countries

Manobhiram (Manu) Nellutla — Actsafe Safety Association, Canada

ePosters Coordinator

Anne-Kristina Arnold — Ergonomics, Simon Fraser University, Canada

Exhibits Coordinator

Abigail Overduin — Workplace Health Services, The University of British Columbia, Canada

Early Career Researcher Program Coordinator

Sadeem Quershi   Human Factors Engineering Lab, Department
                                        of Mechanical and Industrial Engineering,
                                        Ryerson University, Canada

Media Relations

Heather Kahle   Human Factors Specialist/Ergonomist,
                                        WorkSafeBC, Canada
Jenny Colman   Human Factor Specialist, Risk Analysis Unit,
                                        WorkSafeBC, Canada

Events/Social

Gina Vahlas   Human Factors Specialist/Ergonomist,
                                        Risk Analysis Unit, WorkSafeBC, Canada
Era Poddar   Specialist Safety Advisor-Ergonomics,
                                        Manufacturing Safety Alliance of BC, Canada
Alison Heller-Ono   CEO, Worksite International, USA

French Language Coordinator

François Taillefer   Faculté des sciences, Université de Québec
                                        à Montréal, Canada

Communications Coordinator

Joanne Bangs   Free-lance consultant, USA

EasyChair Platform Technical Liaison

Colleen Dewis   Department of Industrial Engineering,
                                        Dalhousie University, Canada

Scientific Committee of IEA2021

Nancy L. Black (Co-chair)   Université de Moncton, Canada
W. Patrick Neumann   Ryerson University, Canada
  (Co-chair)
Wayne Albert   University of New Brunswick, Canada
Sara Albolino   Director Centre for Patient Safety Tuscany region
Thomas Alexander   Federal Institute for Occupational Safety
                                        and Health (BAUA), Germany
Anne-Kristina Arnold   Simon Fraser University, Canada

Pascal Béguin	Institut d'Études du Travail de Lyon (IETL)—Université Lumière Lyon 2, France
Tommaso Bellandi	Northwest Trust - Regional Health Service of Tuscany, Italy
Klaus Bengler	Technische Universität München, Germany
Yuval Bitan	Ben-Gurion University of the Negev, University of Toronto, Israel
Ivan Bolis	Universidade Federal da Paraíba, Brazil
Tim Bosch	TNO, Netherlands
Richard Bowman	Intertile Research Pty Ltd, Australia
Guy André Boy	CentraleSupélec (Paris Saclay University), ESTIA Institute of Technology, France
Karen Bredenkamp	Magic Leap, USA
Ole Broberg	Technical University of Denmark, Denmark
Katie Buckley	University of Melbourne, Australia
Robin Burgess-Limerick	University of Queensland, Australia
Peter Burns	Transport Canada, Canada
Chien-Chi (Max) Chang	National Tsing Hua University, Taiwan
Andy S. K. Cheng	Hong Kong Polytechnique University, Hong Kong
Pieter Coenen	Amsterdam UMC (VUmc location), Netherlands
Teresa Cotrim	University of Lisbon, Portugal
Ann Marie Dale	Washington University in St. Louis, USA
Jonathan Davy	Rhodes University, South Africa
Enrique De la Vega	TECNM/Instituto Technologico de Hermosillo, Mexico
Catherine Delgoulet	CRTD, Conservatoire National des Arts et Métiers (CNAM), France
Michiel de Looze	TNO, Netherlands
Colleen Dewis	Dalhousie University, Canada
Clark Dickerson	University of Waterloo, Canada
Francisco José de Castro Moura Duarte	Federal University of Rio de Janeiro, Brazil
Tamsyn Edwards	San Jose State University, NASA Ames Research Center, USA
Georg Effenberger	AUVA-Hauptstelle, Austrian Ergonomics Society, Austria
Echezona Nelson Dominic Ekechukwu	University of Nigeria, Nigeria
Antonella Frisiello	LINKS Foundation, Italy
Carlos Manuel Escobar Galindo	University of Nottingham, Universidad Peruana Cayetano Heredia, Peru
Anindya Ganguli	Bureau of Indian Standards (BIS), Bharat Heavy Electricals Ltd. (BHEL), India
Richard Gardner	Boeing Research & Technology, USA

Rafael E. Gonzalez	Bolivarian University, Petróleos de Venezuela, S.A. (PDVSA), Venezuela
Ewa Górska	University of Ecology and Management in Warsaw, Poland
Maggie Graf	International Ergonomics Association - Professional Standards and Education, Certification Sub-committee, Switzerland
Alma Maria Jennifer Gutierrez	De La Salle University—Manila, Philippines
Jukka Häkkinen	University of Helsinki, Finland
Gregor Harih	University of Maribor, Slovenia
Veerle Hermans	Vrije Universiteit Brussel, Belgium
Dora Hsiao	Revision Military, Canada
Laerte Idal Sznelwar	Universidade de São Paulo, Brazil
Rauf Iqbal	National Institute of Industrial Engineering (NITIE), India
Nicole Jochems	University of Luebeck, Germany
Marie Laberge	Université de Montréal, Centre de recherche du CHU Ste-Justine, Canada
Fion C. H. Lee	UOW College Hong Kong, Hong Kong
Yue (Sophia) Li	KITE, Toronto Rehabilitation Institute—University Health Network, Canada
Peter Lundqvist	SLU - Swedish University of Agricultural Sciences, Sweden
Neil Mansfield	Nottingham Trent University, UK
Márcio Alves Marçal	Universidade Federal dos Vales do Jequitinhonha e do Mucuri, Brazil
Blake McGowan	VelocityEHS, USA
Ranjana Mehta	Texas A&M University, USA
Marijke Melles	Delft University of Technology, Netherlands
Marino Menozzi	Swiss Federal Institute of Technology, ETH Zurich, Switzerland
Francisco Octavio Lopez Millan	TECNM/Instituto Tecnológico de Hermosillo, Mexico
Karen Lange Morales	Universidad Nacional de Colombia, Colombia
Ruud N. Pikaar	ErgoS Human Factors Engineering, Netherlands
Dimitris Nathanael	National Technical University of Athens, Greece
Yee Guan Ng	Universiti Putra Malaysia, Malaysia
Jodi Oakman	La Trobe University, Australia
Udoka Arinze Chris Okafor	University of Lagos, Nigeria
Paulo Antonio Barros Oliveira	Federal University of Rio Grande do Sul, Brazil
Vassilis Papakostopoulos	University of the Aegean, Greece
Maria Pascale	Uruguayan Association of Ergonomics (AUDErgo), Uruguay

Gunther Paul	James Cook University, Australia
Chui Yoon Ping	Singapore University of Social Sciences, Singapore
Jim Potvin	McMaster University, Canada
Valérie Pueyo	Université Lumière Lyon 2, France
Sadeem Qureshi	Ryerson University, Canada
Sudhakar Rajulu	NASA - Johnson Space Center, USA
Gemma Read	University of the Sunshine Coast, Australia
David Rempel	University of California Berkeley; University of California San Francisco, USA
Raziel Riemer	Ben-Gurion University of the Negev, Israel
Michelle M. Robertson	Office Ergonomics Research Committee, Northeastern University, University of Connecticut, University of California, Berkeley, USA
Martin Antonio Rodriguez	Universidad Tecnológica Nacional Buenos Aires FRBA, Argentina
Gustavo Rosal	UNE (Spanish Association for Standardisation), Spain
Patricia H. Rosen	Federal Institute for Occupational Safety and Health (BAUA), Germany
Ken Sagawa	AIST, Japan
Paul M. Salmon	University of the Sunshine Coast, Australia
Marta Santos	Universidade do Porto, Portugal
Sofia Scataglini	University of Antwerp, Belgium
Lawrence J. H. Schulze	University of Houston, USA
Rosemary Ruiz Seva	De La Salle University, Philippines
Fabio Sgarbossa	Norwegian University of Science and Technology, Norway
Jonas Shultz	Health Quality Council of Alberta, University of Calgary, Canada
Anabela Simões	University Lusófona, Portugal
Sarbjit Singh	National Institute of Technology Jalandhar, India
John Smallwood	Nelson Mandela University, South Africa
Lukáš Šoltys	Czech Ergonomics Association, Czech Republic
Isabella Tiziana Steffan	STUDIO STEFFAN—Progettazione & Ricerca (Design & Research), Italy
Daryl Stephenson	Occupational Health Clinics for Ontario Workers, Canada
Gyula Szabó	Hungarian Ergonomics Society, Hungary
Shamsul Bahri Mohd Tamrin	Universiti Putra Malaysia, Malaysia
Andrew Thatcher	University of the Witwatersrand, South Africa
Giulio Toccafondi	Center for Clinical Risk Management and Patient Safety GRC, WHO Collaborating Center, Florence, Italy

Contents

Part I: Affective Design (Edited by Rosemary Ruiz Seva)

**Design for UX in Flexible Offices – Bringing Research
and Practice Together** 3
Antonio Cobaleda-Cordero and Maral Babapour

**Outlining Experience and Well-Being in the Interaction
with Social Media Apps** 12
Beatriz de Paulo and Manuela Quaresma

Affective Trash Bin Signage to Promote Waste Segregation 20
Arvidas Kio Dy, Margarita Lazo, Andreana Gabrielle Santos,
and Rosemary Seva

**Analysis of Geometric Features of 3D Shapes on Perception of Product
Appearance for Visual Brand Affiliation** 31
Matthias Sebastian Fischer, Daniel Holder, and Thomas Maier

**Affective – Cognitive – Usability (ACU) Model Incorporating
Eye Tracking Analysis for Redesigning the e-Commerce Website** 39
Markus Hartono, Argo Hadi Kusumo, and Dwilita Aprilin Asikin

**The Functions of Computer-Mediated Touch at a Distance:
An Interactionist Approach** 45
Robin Héron, Stéphane Safin, Michael Baker, and Françoise Détienne

**Merging Total Design and User Centered Design for Designing
a Mountable Toy: Achieving a Useful, Functional
and Desirable Product** 54
Julieta María Covarrubias Cruz, María Fernanda De La Rocha Barbosa,
Fernanda Santos Rivera, and Pilar Hernández-Grageda

**Behavioral and Cognitive Methods to Assess Users and Assist Physical
Point of Sale Experience Design** 62
Paulo Eduardo Hauqui Tonin

**Design Process of a Mountable Toy Based on Total Design
and User Centered Design Methodologies** 71
Ana Sofía Olivares Jiménez, María Inés Ibarra Caballero,
Lilia Atziri Urías Dueñas, and Pilar Hernández-Grageda

Part II: Anthropometry (Edited by Karen Bredenkamp)

**Anthropometric Indices and Nutritional Status of Infants
in Nigeria – A Preliminary Study** 81
Echezona Nelson Dominic Ekechukwu, Chiamaka Chinyere Anyaene,
Ogechukwu Ikefuna, Emmanuel Nwabueze Aguwa,
Israel Chijioke Iroezindu, Theodora A. Okeke, and Susan U. Arinze-Onyia

**Mexican Older-Adult Sitting and Standing Anthropometric
Dimensions. Comparison with Other Populations** 96
Elvia Luz González-Muñoz, Rosalio Avila Chaurand,
John A. Rey Galindo, and Gabriel Ibarra Mejia

**Firefighters' Anthropometrics: A Comparison Between Two
Portuguese Fire Brigades** 105
Anna S. P. Moraes, Miguel A. F. Carvalho, Rachel S. Boldt,
Fernando B. N. Ferreira, Susan P. Ashdown, and Linsey Griffin

A Motion Capture System for Hand Movement Recognition 114
Graciela Rodríguez-Vega, Dora Aydee Rodríguez-Vega,
Xiomara Penelope Zaldívar-Colado, Ulises Zaldívar-Colado,
and Rafael Castillo-Ortega

Hand Shape Modeling for the Mexican Population 122
Graciela Rodríguez-Vega, Xiomara Penelope Zaldívar-Colado,
Ulises Zaldívar-Colado, Enrique Javier De la Vega-Bustillos,
and Dora Aydee Rodríguez-Vega

Part III: Biomechanics (Edited by Rauf Iqbal)

**Effects of a Back-Support Exoskeleton on Pelvis-Thorax Kinematics
and Coordination During Lifting** 131
Sivan Almosnino, Rong Huangfu, and Jessica Cappelletto

**Measurement of Work-Related Physical Workloads - Proposal
for a Body Region-Related Categorization System** 139
Rolf Ellegast, Britta Weber, Christoph Schiefer, Kai Heinrich,
and Ingo Hermanns-Truxius

**Optimization of Product Handle Material Mechanical Properties
for Improved Ergonomics Using Finite Element Method
and Subjective Response** 148
Gregor Harih, Andrej Cupar, Jasmin Kaljun, and Bojan Dolšak

Evaluation of Force Exertion Strategies During Repetitive Lifting/ Lowering Tasks Based on Time-Frequency Analysis 155
Kazuki Hiranai, Miho Yaji, and Akihiko Seo

A Wearable Device to Assess the Spine Biomechanical Overload in a Sample of Loggers 162
Federica Masci, Giovanna Spatari, Concetto Mario Giorgianni,
Sara Bortolotti, John Rosecrance, and Claudio Colosio

Relationship of Floor Material and Fall Risk Assessment During Descending Stairs 171
Takeshi Sato, Mizuki Nakajima, Ryota Murano, Macky Kato,
and Kimie Nakajima

PEPPA - Exchange Platform for Measurements of Occupational Physical Activity and Physical Workload 175
Christoph Schiefer, Vera Schellewald, Stefan Heßling,
Ingo Hermanns-Truxius, Kévin Desbrosses, Marjolein Douwes,
Francesco Draicchio, Henrik Enquist, Mikael Forsman, Nidhi Gupta,
Andreas Holtermann, Reinier Konemann, Norbert Lechner, Peter Loewis,
Satu Mänttäri, Svend Erik Mathiassen, Andrew Pinder, Peter Schams,
Marianne Schust, Michaela Strebl, Kaj Bo Veiersted, Britta Weber,
and Rolf Ellegast

Biomechanical Simulation and a Detailed Analysis of the Roadside Cleaning Activity 183
Neelesh K. Sharma, Mayank Tiwari, Atul Thakur,
and Anindya K. Ganguli

Kerbside Waste Collection Round Risk Assessment by Means of Physiological Parameters: sEMG and Heart Rate 191
Alessio Silvetti, Lorenzo Fiori, Antonella Tatarelli, Alberto Ranavolo,
and Francesco Draicchio

Using Complex Biomechanics Models to Communicate Simple Messages 200
Carrie Taylor and Josie Blake

Overview of Measurement-Based Assessment Approaches from the MEGAPHYS Project 206
Britta Weber, Kai Heinrich, David H. Seidel, Ingo Hermanns-Truxius,
Ulrike Hoehne-Hückstädt, Dirk Ditchen, Matthias Jäger, Lope H. Barrero,
and Rolf Ellegast

Part IV: Ergonomics in Advanced Imaging (Edited by Jukka Häkkinen)

Effects of Avatars on Street Crossing Tasks in Virtual Reality 215
Philipp Maruhn and Simon Hurst

Estimating Time to Contact in Virtual Reality:
Does Contrast Matter?   224
Sonja Schneider, Mariam Salloum, Katharina Gundel, and Annika Boos

Part V: Human Factors in Robotics (Edited by Sascha Wischniewski
and Patricia H. Rosen)

Three-Stage Evaluation for Defining the Potential of an Industrial
Exoskeleton in a Specific Job   235
Michiel de Looze, Aijse de Vries, Frank Krause, and Saskia Baltrusch

Human-Robot Collaboration During Assembly Tasks: The Cognitive
Effects of Collaborative Assembly Workstation Features   242
Federico Fraboni, Luca Gualtieri, Francesco Millo, Matteo De Marchi,
Luca Pietrantoni, and Erwin Rauch

Evaluation of Physiological Costs Using Standardized Analysis
Methods During Simulated Overhead Work with
and Without Exoskeleton   250
Sandra Groos, Nils Darwin Abele, Petra Fischer, Michael Hefferle,
and Karsten Kluth

Development of a Multifunctional Test Station and a Reproducible
Test Design for the Evaluation of Stress and Strain During Overhead
Work with and Without Upper Body Exoskeletons   258
Sandra Groos, Nils Darwin Abele, Kevin Kruse, Petra Fischer,
Michael Hefferle, and Karsten Kluth

Evaluation of Variables of Cognitive Ergonomics in Industrial
Human-Robot Collaborative Assembly Systems   266
Luca Gualtieri, Federico Fraboni, Matteo De Marchi, and Erwin Rauch

Optimizing Force Transfer in a Soft Exoskeleton Using
Biomechanical Modeling   274
Christina M. Harbauer, Martin Fleischer, Cerys E. M. Bandmann,
and Klaus Bengler

How User Presence Impacts Perceptions and Operation Routines
of Robotic Vacuum Cleaners – a 'Stay at Home' Experiment   282
Shanee Honig and Tal Oron-Gilad

Evaluation of Different Degrees of Support in Human-Robot
Cooperation at an Assembly Workstation Regarding Physiological
Strain and Perceived Team Fluency   291
Verena Klaer, Hendrik Groll, Jurij Wakula, and Tim Steinebach

Field Study to Objectify the Stress and Strain on Male Workers
During Car Wheel Changes in the Course of Using an Active
Exoskeleton   300
Karsten Kluth and Michael Hefferle

Contents

Using Multimodal Data to Predict Surgeon Situation Awareness 308
Aurelien Lechappe, Mathieu Chollet, Jerome Rigaud,
and Caroline G. L. Cao

**Preliminary Requirements of a Soft Upper-Limb Exoskeleton
for Industrial Overhead Tasks Based on Biomechanical Analysis** 317
Dario Panariello, Stanislao Grazioso, Teodorico Caporaso,
Giuseppe Di Gironimo, and Antonio Lanzotti

**A Pilot Study on Auditory Feedback for a Lower-Limb Exoskeleton
to Increase Walking Safety** 325
Jing Qiu, Yilin Wang, Hong Cheng, Lu Wang, and Xiao Yang

**Human-Robot Collaboration (HRC) Technologies for Reducing
Work-Related Musculoskeletal Diseases in Industry 4.0** 335
Alberto Ranavolo, Giorgia Chini, Francesco Draicchio, Alessio Silvetti,
Tiwana Varrecchia, Lorenzo Fiori, Antonella Tatarelli,
Patricia Helen Rosen, Sascha Wischniewski, Philipp Albrecht, Lydia Vogt,
Matteo Bianchi, Giuseppe Averta, Andrea Cherubini, Lars Fritzsche,
Massimo Sartori, Bram Vanderborght, Renee Govaerts,
and Arash Ajoudani

**Results from the Third European Survey of Enterprises
on New and Emerging Risks on Human-Robot Interaction** 343
Sascha Wischniewski, Eva Heinold, and Patricia Helen Rosen

**Part VI: Human Modelling and Simulation (Edited by Gunther Paul,
Gregor Harih and Sofia Scataglini)**

**A Digital Human Modelling-Based Optimization Framework
to Minimize Low Back Cumulative Loading During Design
of Lifting Tasks** 349
Sivan Almosnino

**Assessing the Efficiency of Industrial Exoskeletons with Biomechanical
Modelling – Comparison of Experimental and Simulation Results** 353
Lars Fritzsche, Christian Gärtner, Michael Spitzhirn, Pavel E. Galibarov,
Michael Damsgaard, Pauline Maurice, and Jan Babič

**Current Trends in Research and Application of Digital
Human Modeling** 358
Lars Hanson, Dan Högberg, Erik Brolin, Erik Billing,
Aitor Iriondo Pascual, and Maurice Lamb

**Validation of an Inverse Kinematic VR Manikin in Seated Tasks:
Application in Ergonomics Training** 367
Mohammad Homayounpour, Dorien Butter, Saaransh Vasta,
and Andrew Merryweather

**Multi-objective Optimization of Ergonomics and Productivity
by Using an Optimization Framework** 374
Aitor Iriondo Pascual, Dan Högberg, Anna Syberfeldt, Erik Brolin,
Estela Perez Luque, Lars Hanson, and Dan Lämkull

**Demographic Effects on Mid-Air Gesture Preference for Control
of Devices: Implications for Design** 379
Haoyan Jiang, Mark Chignell, Sachi Mizobuchi, Farzin Farhadi Niaki,
Zhe Liu, Wei Zhou, and Wei Li

**A Human-Centered Design Procedure for Conceptualization Using
Virtual Reality Prototyping Applied in an Inflight Lavatory** 387
Meng Li, Doris Aschenbrenner, Daniëlle van Tol, Daan van Eijk,
and Peter Vink

**Automated Segmentation of 3D Digital Human Model for Area
and Volume Measurement** 394
Flavia Cristine Hofstetter Pastura, Tales Fernandes Costa, Gabriel de
Aguiar Mendonça, Thatiane dos Santos Lopes,
and Maria Cristina Palmer Lima Zamberlan

A Conceptual Framework of DHM Enablers for Ergonomics 4.0 403
Gunther Paul and Leyde Briceno

**Characterizing Adaptive Display Interventions
for Attentional Tunneling** 407
Kayla Pedret and Greg A. Jamieson

**Digital Production Planning of Manual and Semi-automatic Tasks
in Industry Using the EMA Software Suite** 415
Michael Spitzhirn, Lars Fritzsche, and Sebastian Bauer

**Probabilistic Human-System-Integration (HSI) Models: Review
and Extension** 420
Ephraim Suhir and Gunther Paul

**Assessment of Biomechanical Risk Factors During Lifting Tasks
in a Spacesuit Using Singular Value Decomposition** 429
Linh Q. Vu, Han K. Kim, and Sudhakar L. Rajulu

**A Preliminary Study on the Effects of Foam and Seat Pan Inclination
on the Deformation of the Seated Buttocks Using MRI** 434
Xuguang Wang, Léo Savonnet, and Sonia Duprey

Tool Development for Ergonomic Design of Automated Vehicles 439
Hans-Joachim Wirsching and Martin Fleischer

Simplifying Ergonomic Assessment for Designers: A User-Product
Interaction-Modelling Framework in CAD   447
Alexander Wolf, Yvonne Wagner, Marius Oßwald, Jörg Miehling,
and Sandro Wartzack

Usability Study on a New Assembly of 3D Interactive Gestures
for Human–Computer Interaction   453
Bohan Wu, Gang Zhang, Xuegang Zhang, Shibo Mei, Jinduo Wu,
Hongting Li, and Zhen Yang

Combining a Wearable IMU Mocap System with REBA and RULA
for Ergonomic Assessment of Container Lashing Teams   462
Sander Zelck, Stijn Verwulgen, Lenie Denteneer, Hanne Vanden Bossche,
and Sofia Scataglini

Development of Guidelines for the Ergonomic Evaluation of Human
Work in Digital Factory Tools   466
Gert Zülch

Part VII: Neuroergonomics (Edited by Echezona Nelson Dominic
Ekechukwu)

Cognitive Aspects in Control Rooms: Anticipated Response
to Adverse Situations   473
Juan Alberto Castillo-M and Maria Constanza Trillos Ch.

Independent Driving Improved the Self-esteem and Health Related
Quality of Life of a Polio Survivor   481
Olumide Olasunkanmi Dada, Femi Abolaji Ogundapo,
Olusegun Adeyemi Adejare, Chidozie Emmanuel Mbada,
and Echezona Nelson Dominic Ekechukwu

Disability and Community Reintegration Among Community
Dwelling Persons Living with Stroke, Spinal Cord Injury
and Limb Amputation – A Comparative Study   487
Echezona Nelson Dominic Ekechukwu, Chinwendu Obi Nwokocha,
Blessing Chiagozikam Atuenyi, Antoninus Obinna Ezeukwu,
and Olumide Olasunkanmi Dada

Virtual Reality, a Neuroergonomic and Neurorehabilitation Tool for
Promoting Neuroplasticity in Stroke Survivors: A Systematic Review
with Meta-analysis   495
Echezona Nelson Dominic Ekechukwu, Ikenna Collins Nzeakuba,
Olumide Olasunkanmi Dada, Kingsley Obumneme Nwankwo,
Paul Olowoyo, Victor Adimabua Utti, and Mayowa Ojo Owolabi

Are the Psychosocial and Physical Disabilities of Stroke Survivors
Ageing Related?   509
Echezona Nelson Dominic Ekechukwu, Nelson Okogba,
Kingsley Obumneme Nwankwo, Nmachukwu Ifeoma Ekechukwu,
Amaka Gloria Mgbeojedo, Olusegun Adeyemi Adejare,
Uchenna Prosper Okonkwo, and Victor Adimabua Utti

Analyzing the Effect of Visual Cue on Physiological Hand Tremor
Using Wearable Accelerometer Sensors   517
Vishal Kannan, K. Adalarasu, Priyadarshini Natarajan,
and Venkatesh Balasubramanian

Perceived Barriers and Facilitators of Return to Driving Among
a Sample of Nigerian Stroke Survivors - A Qualitative Study   537
Kingsley Obumneme Nwankwo, Olubukola Adebisi Olaleye,
Tal'hatu Kolapo Hamzat, and Echezona Nelson Dominic Ekechukwu

VR Application for Vestibular System Training (Pilot Study)   552
Daria Plotnikova, Aleksandr Volosiuk, Gleb Tikhonov,
Aleksandr Tsynchenko, Anastasiia Luneva, and Artem Smolin

Determination of the Influence of Music on Working Memory
Performance Using EEG Analysis   559
Minerva Rajendran, Tanya Malaiya, and Venkatesh Balasubramanian

Part VIII: Working with Computer Systems
(Edited by Nicole Jochems)

Empirical Comparison of the Effects of Symmetrical and
Asymmetrical Video Game Console Controllers on Players
Performance   569
Asma Alfargani and Ahamed Altaboli

A Novel 3D Editor for Gesture Design Based on Labanotation   577
Kathleen Anderson, Börge Kordts, and Andreas Schrader

Advancing Towards Automated Ergonomic Assessment:
A Panel of Perspectives   585
Daniel P. Armstrong, Christopher A. B. Moore, Lora A. Cavuoto,
Sean Gallagher, SangHyun Lee, Michael W. Sonne,
and Steven L. Fischer

From Globalization to Circular Economy, Which Issues for Health
and Safety at Work?   592
Agnès Aublet-Cuvelier, Michel Hery, and Marc Malenfer

**Collaborative Robotics and Industry 4.0: An Engineering, Sociology
and Activity-Centered Ergonomics Cross-Experience** 597
Flore Barcellini, Willy Buchmann, Richard Béarée,
Tahar-Hakim Benchekroun, Mouad Bounouar, Gérard Dubey,
Caroline Moricot, Anne-Cecile Lafeuillade, Celine Rosselin-Bareille,
Marco Saraceno, and Ali Siadat

**Trade-offs of Users and Non-users of Life-Logging – Desire for
Support vs. Potential Barriers** 605
Laura Burbach, Chantal Lidynia, Philipp Brauner, and Martina Ziefle

**Enabling Collaborative Situations in 4.0 Industry: Multiple
Case Study** 614
Nathan Compan, Fabien Coutarel, Daniel Brissaud,
and Géraldine Rix-Lièvre

**The Impact of Expertise on Query Formulation Strategies During
Complex Learning Task Solving: A Study with Students in Medicine
and Computer Science** 621
Cheyenne Dosso, Lynda Tamine, Pierre-Vincent Paubel,
and Aline Chevalier

**Artificial Intelligence (AI) in the Workplace: A Study of Stakeholders'
Views on Benefits, Issues and Challenges of AI Systems** 628
Tamari Gamkrelidze, Moustafa Zouinar, and Flore Barcellini

**The Remanufacturing Activity: Skills to Develop and Productive
Organizations to Rethink** 636
Kevin Guelle, Sandrine Caroly, and Aurélie Landry

**Steady Hands - An Evaluation on the Use of Hand Tracking in Virtual
Reality Training in Nursing** 643
Tino Hentschel and Jan A. Neuhöfer

**Supporting Pain Management for Mechanically Ventilated Intensive
Care Patients Using a Novel Communication Tool** 650
Jan Patrick Kopetz and Nicole Jochems

**Users' Error Recovery Strategies in the Interaction with Voice
Assistants (VAs)** 658
Isabela Motta and Manuela Quaresma

**User Needs for Digital Creativity Support Systems in an
Occupational Context** 667
Lorenz Prasch, Lena aus dem Bruch, and Klaus Bengler

**An Empirical Study on Automation Transparency (i.e., seeing-into)
of an Automated Decision Aid System for Condition-Based
Maintenance** 675
Fahimeh Rajabiyazdi, Greg A. Jamieson, and David Quispe Guanolusia

A User Study to Evaluate the Customization of Automatically
Generated GUIs 683
David Raneburger, Roman Popp, and Hermann Kaindl

A Framework for Future Navigation Aids 691
Adam J. Reiner, Greg A. Jamieson, and Justin G. Hollands

Explainable AI for Entertainment: Issues on Video
on Demand Platforms 699
Cinthia Ruiz and Manuela Quaresma

Reliability of Heuristic Evaluation During Usability Analysis 708
Thomas J. Smith and Cindy Kheng

Clinical Usability Studies – Clash of Cultures? Study Design Proposal
from Lessons Learned 715
Thomas Stüdeli and Limor Hochberg

Collaborating with Communities in Participatory System
Development 725
Torben Volkmann, Michael Sengpiel, and Nicole Jochems

Making Tax eForms Less Taxing—Comparing Evaluation Measures
of User-Experience, Usability, and Acceptance in Public Sector
eForms 735
Mourad Zoubir, Daniel Wessel, Tim Schrills, Thomas Franke,
and Moreen Heine

Part IX: Ergonomic Work Analysis and Training (EWAT) –
Addendum (Edited by Catherine Delgoulet and Marta Santos)

Learning Scenarios for the Improvement of Operating Safety
of Machine Tools 749
Leif Goldhahn and Robert Eckardt

Developing a Training Action for Primary School Teachers by Doubly
Considering (Their) Work 758
Ana Rodrigues, Maria Cadilhe, Filipa Ferreira, Cláudia Pereira,
and Marta Santos

Part X: HF/E Education and Professional Certification Development –
Addendum (Edited by Chien-Chi (Max) Chang and Maggie Graf)

Applications and Implications of the Brazilian Ergonomics Regulatory
Standard (NR17) 767
Lia Buarque de Macedo Guimarães, Marcia Gemari Derenevich,
and Rosimeire Sedrez Bitencourt

Part XI: Organisation Design and Management (ODAM) – *Addendum*
(Edited by Laerte Idal Sznelwar)

**Occupational Safety and Protection Against Infection in Times
of the Pandemic: Challenges for Human Factors and Regulation** 777
Thomas Alexander, Lars Adolph, and Stefan Voss

Presenteeism and Voice: Ergonomic Factors for Sports Coaches 783
Katie Buckley, Jennifer Oates, Paul O'Halloran, Mandy Ruddock-Hudson,
and Lindsay Carey

Ergo@Large: Collaborating for the Benefits of HF/E 791
Jeanne Guérin

**A Synthesis of Subjective Scales Which Assess Worker Fatigue:
Building a Simple, Reliable, and Effective Evaluative Instrument** 797
Gabriella M. Hancock, Mira Gruber, Uyen D. Bui, Jessica Blay-Moreira,
Yvette Apatiga, Christian E. Schmitz, and Peter A. Hancock

**Heat Stress Management in the Construction Industry:
A Socio-technical Systems Perspective** 804
Damithri Gayashini Melagoda and Steve Rowlinson

Attitude Towards Artificial Intelligence in a Leadership Role 811
Deborah Petrat

**Macroergonomics-Based Approach for a Management Trainee
Program in the Utilities Industry** 820
Yogi Tri Prasetyo and Johnamae Khow

Part XII: Systems HF/E – *Addendum* **(Edited by Paul M. Salmon)**

**Human Factors Effects on a Human-Robot Collaboration System:
A Modelling Approach** 829
Guilherme Deola Borges, Paula Carneiro, and Pedro Arezes

Part XIII: Slips, Trips and Falls – *Addendum*
(Edited by Richard Bowman)

The Future of Footwear Friction 841
Kurt E. Beschorner, Yue (Sophia) Li, Takeshi Yamaguchi, William Ells,
and Richard Bowman

**Effects of Foot–Floor Friction on Trip-Induced Falls During Shuffling
Gait: A Simulation Study** 856
Takeshi Yamaguchi, Kenichi Nakatani, Tomoki Hirose, Takashi Yoshida,
and Kei Masani

**Correction to: Proceedings of the 21st Congress of the International
Ergonomics Association (IEA 2021)** C1
Nancy L. Black, W. Patrick Neumann, and Ian Noy

Author Index 861

Part I: Affective Design (Edited by Rosemary Ruiz Seva)

Design for UX in Flexible Offices – Bringing Research and Practice Together

Antonio Cobaleda-Cordero[1]([✉]) [iD] and Maral Babapour[1,2] [iD]

[1] Chalmers University of Technology, Gothenburg, Sweden
cobaleda@chalmers.se
[2] Institutet för Stressmedicin, Gothenburg, Sweden

Abstract. A growing number of organisations are relocating from traditional office environments to flexible office environments (FOEs) such as 'combi' or 'activity-based' offices. Research efforts are being dedicated to understanding the challenges and benefits that these office designs represent. Yet, there is a gap between design research and practice that limits innovations in FOE design and smears the overall user experience at work. This paper addresses the exploration of design opportunities for artefacts and spaces enabling positive user experience (UX) in FOEs together with experts from a relevant European actor in the office furniture sector. First, an explorative workshop was conducted to understand practitioners' perspective and priorities when designing for FOEs. Findings from previous research work by the authors plus the workshop results were used to propose and discuss four 'Design for UX' areas worth of further exploration. Among these, the UX of control in FOEs was chosen, and a subsequent workshop was conducted to deepen into the matter. The last session concluded with the formulation of a specific UX proposal to be developed in the near future. The value and originality of this paper reside in two aspects: (i) a UX approach that relies on the 'innovation of meaning' and splits from a creative problem-solving mainstream; and (ii) a collaboration between user-centered design research and product development practice that enable the alignment of resources and strategies in the benefit of users and innovation.

Keywords: User experience · Design for UX · Exploratory sessions · Design opportunities · Flexible offices · User research · Product development

1 Introduction

Flexible office environments (FOEs) where employees can switch between different types of workstations and spaces depending on the activity at hand have become increasingly popular [1]. Further, many organisations plan and dimension their flexible offices assuming that not everyone will be at the office every day, nor need a desk at the same time [2]. In comparison to traditional offices, this represents a paradigmatic change in terms of design qualities that determine the preconditions for distinct user experiences (UXs) at work. However, whether these experiences are meaningful or taxing for users remains debatable [3].

© The Author(s), under exclusive license to Springer Nature Switzerland AG 2022
N. L. Black et al. (Eds.): IEA 2021, LNNS 223, pp. 3–11, 2022.
https://doi.org/10.1007/978-3-030-74614-8_1

The increasing research efforts in relation to FOEs that occurred in recent years has brought a richer understanding of the associated challenges and benefits, although research evidence shows discrepant findings between cases [4, 5]. The discrepancies signal relevant unresolved issues, among others, artefacts such as chairs with sub-optimal design qualities for intense shared use [6]. Moreover, the fact that the design of most office artefacts for individual use remain the same for both traditional and flexible offices indicates a gap between design research and practice [ibid]. Exploring design opportunities from a UX perspective demands to close this gap. UX in FOEs should benefit from the alignment of researchers' in-depth understanding of users and their (anticipated/present/past) experiences, and practitioners' expertise on translating complex user needs into tangible solutions.

This paper is based on a series of exploratory sessions about UX in FOEs carried out in collaboration with a leading European office furniture manufacturer. The aims of this paper are to (i) explore design opportunities for positive UX in FOEs, and (ii) provide insights on the experience of a collaboration between user-centered design researchers and practitioners from the office furniture industry.

2   Exploring Design Opportunities for Positive UX in FOEs

According to Marc Hassenzahl, *"User Experience is not about good industrial design, multi-touch, or fancy interfaces. It is about transcending the material"* and *"experiences emerge from the integration of perception, action, motivation and cognition into an inseparable, meaningful whole"* [7]. This suggests that 'User Experience' is a narrower idea than experiences in general and that the exploration of design opportunities requires a thorough understanding of users and situations of use. In this case, the understanding of FOE users and situations of using FOEs from two perspectives, i.e., research and practice, have deliberately come together for discussion and convergence along three exploratory sessions. The three sessions that are reported in this paper belong to a larger interactive research project in which the authors and a group of company representatives are involved. Table 1 provides an overview of the participants at each of the sessions and their roles and responsibilities.

Table 1. Roles and backgrounds.

Expertise	User-Centered Design Research	Product Design & Development	Marketing	Office Planning
Roles	Researchers as **facilitators**	Company representatives as participating **experts**		
Session 1	f1 f2	e1 e2	e3 e4	e5 e6
Session 2	f1 f2	e1 e2		
Session 3	f1	e1 e2 e7 e8	e3 e4	e5

2.1 Session 1. Understanding Practitioners' Standpoint

A 3-h exploratory workshop was held in the headquarters of the furniture company with the authors of this paper as facilitators and six company experts as participants - see Table 1. The session was organised in three blocks with breaks in between and a final discussion on findings and next steps. The first block focused on sensitising, the second on exploring and the third one on ideating.

The goal of this workshop was to explore design opportunities for office artefacts and spaces that enable the experience of 'security blanket' in flexible offices. Security blanket, also known as 'comfort object' refers to familiar artefacts that individuals, usually toddlers, carry with them and provide with psychological comfort against stress [8]. Thus, it was a metaphorical reference. The intended outcomes of the session were twofold: (i) gain a richer understanding of practitioners' perspective on flexible offices, and (ii) find ideas/areas of mutual interest for further collaboration.

Method

The sensitising block consisted of two activities. First, as an icebreaker activity, participants presented and discussed each other results from a sensitising assignment prior to the session. The assignment consisted of collecting pictures of artefacts and spaces that they experienced as their particular 'security blanket'. Next, participants were requested to write down on sticky notes the identified 'security blankets' plus others that may have come to their minds along the discussion and map them on a wall according to a set of generic themes: indoor climate comfort, adjustments, auditory comfort, visual comfort, safety, privacy, and preferences. Participants had the possibility to add new themes if needed.

The activity for the explorative block consisted of an office walkthrough [9]. In two groups of three, the participants walked around their own flexible office showing each other the spaces and artefacts that they experienced either positively or negatively, marking these with green or pink sticky notes respectively. After the walking tour, the two groups returned to the workshop room to share their insights. To conclude the activity, the participants -as experts in different fields- were invited to list areas of interest for the exploration of design opportunities in flexible offices.

The ideation block consisted of a 6-3-5 [10]. The participants were requested to generate ideas departing from the areas of interest identified in the previous block. The participants were provided with A1 templates, colour pens and markers, play dough, glue, tape, scissors, sticky notes of different colours and shapes, and printed miniatures of human figures and furniture pieces for collages. The entire session was audio-recorded, and the outcomes of the activities were collected for a thematic analysis. A summary of the session was shared with the participants.

Findings

The sensitising assignment helped participants to reflect on experiences of, with, and through artefacts and spaces, both in their flexible office environment (e.g., their laptops) and out of it (e.g., a car). The sticky notes helped participants to deepen the discussion initiated with the sensitizing assignment and narrow down the focus to the physical office environment. The theme 'social environment' was added to the default set provided to map the sticky notes. Examples of 'security blankets' identified by the participants featured smartphones, plants, a cup of coffee, colours and materials, colleagues, teams, etc. as 'things' that elicited the feeling of a security blanket -psychological comfort- . Participants also elaborated on, for example, a notebook that *"helps me focus and organise my tasks" (e4)*, workstations *"with no one behind peeking on what one does" (e2)*, or personal outfits that *"make us feel that we are ready for an important meeting" (e3)*. Abstract 'security blankets' were also referred, for example, the possibility to choose among diverse office settings to meet personal needs and preferences for lighting, temperature, ventilation or background sound.

During the office walkthrough, recurrent observations made by the participants related to zoning; zones that are clearly defined are experienced positively and vice versa. Also, the diversity of open and private settings for meetings influenced positively the perceived flexibility of the office. However, participants pointed out that *"many times the problem is not a product, but where it is placed" (e1)* and that this is more evident when they, as a company, are allowed late in an office project where *"many decisions are already taken and you have to work with many limitations" (e5)*, although *"it could be interesting to think on products that are less sensitive to their placement" (e3)*. To conclude the activity, the participants listed areas of interest to be further explored in the last block -ideation- and the results were clustered as: possibility to adjust environmental conditions -climate, lighting, sound, etc.-; clear zoning; the right furniture/function in the right place; technology that works seamlessly; internalisation of flexible working; and colour/finishing.

The last block consisted of a 6-3-5. A total of 90 collaborative ideas were generated that corresponded to: (i) experiences such as recreating a coffee shop feeling or enabling a seamless docking to shared workstations; (ii) spaces such as an outdoor or outdoor-like office; (iii) products such as connected furniture or different seating solutions and for diverse postures; and (iv) properties of spaces and products such as textures, colours, functions, and parts.

2.2   Session 2. Discussing Alternative UX Scenarios

An online follow-up session was held to continue the discussions initiated in the workshop. The goal of this session was to narrow down the design opportunities in flexible offices to a relevant UX scenario within the area of product design and development that could be explored in collaboration. The intended outcome was the selection of a particular UX scenario among different proposals elaborated by the authors, as the input for a subsequent explorative workshop.

Method

The outcomes from the first workshop plus key findings from previous research work conducted by the authors [6, 11] were compared, compiled, and presented as four proposals of UX scenarios in FOEs for debate:

(i)   Experience of purpose while sharing: in relation to the need for meaningful and pleasurable spaces/artefacts for individual use that are shared in FOEs.

(ii) Experience of community: in relation to the need for visibility, face-to-face encounters, and sense of belonging of individuals and groups.
(iii) Experience of autonomy: in relation to the need of deciding and acting according to own standards, being able to deal with the (social) context.
(iv) Experience of control: in relation to the need for managing and adapting the surrounding office environment to suit personal needs and values.

Findings

These scenarios related to unresolved issues in flexible offices that were discussed from both researchers' and practitioners' angle, and finally the experience of control was selected. Representative examples discussed for each scenario were:

(i)   The conflict between users' motives to use a workstation and the need to set up every workstation before use.
(ii) The anonymity experienced by users who may often work next unknown colleagues, have difficulties locating teammates, and/or identifying groups.
(iii) The misuse of zoning that result from ambiguous rules and design cues.
(iv) The lack of control over environmental stimuli causing distractions.

2.3   Session 3. Formulating a UX Proposal for Further Exploration

A 2-h online workshop was held with seven participants -see Table 1-. The goal was to explore and discuss suboptimal experiences of control over FOEs and choose one to be solved. The intended outcome of the workshop was the formulation of a proposal for positive UX that were the opposite of the chosen suboptimal experience.

Method

The session started with a brief seminar on the concepts of 'UX' and 'personal control' to level-up participants' understanding before the activities. Following, a group activity was carried out on online platform Mural, for which a quick test was shared in advance to allow the participants becoming familiar with the interface. This group activity consisted of the following steps:

(i)   The participants read seven text boxes with examples from user studies that related to seven different suboptimal experiences of control -see findings-.
(ii) Second, each participant placed three sticky notes on the three boxes considered to be the most relevant for the design of a positive UX of control. Participants wrote the reason for their choices on each of the sticky notes.
(iii) Third, the boxes were reviewed one by one and the authors of the notes, as experts in different fields, had three minutes to convince the other participants of the pertinence of their choice. Responses and additional comments were allowed.
(iv) Next, the participants voted for the box -suboptimal experience- that should be considered as top priority for a new and meaningful UX design.

Finally, the most voted suboptimal experience was taken as a reference to formulate the opposite positive UX of control over the environment. Such UX proposal was discussed, refined, and validated by the participants.

Findings
The seven boxes, each related to a suboptimal experience of control collected attention from the participants and were discussed, although control over sound/noise and control over privacy received more notes justifying their relevance for a redesign. Below are representative comments from the discussion on the control over:

- Lighting/Daylight: *"I consider this fundamental in terms of ergonomics. [...] If you are older you may need more light and vice versa" (e2).*
- Indoor climate/air quality: *"It can be cold by the windows in old buildings [...] and after the weekends or weather changes, there is a delay until the system adjusts" (e8); "We should be able to choose this individually" (e4)*
- Sound/Noise: *"When you are involved in adjusting your workplace, the perception of noise and sound is different [...] This is very individual [...] and yet at the core of ergonomics in an office" (e1); "Noise is one of the biggest reasons for stress" (e3).*
- Visual distractions: *"I want more than a desktop screen [...] we should look somewhere else for new solutions, for example, in nature" (e8) Is it really the noise or this [visual stimuli] that causes distraction? Or both? It is essential to understand this" (e1).*
- Privacy: *"We have different tasks [...] and we may need privacy for an hour [...] it is important to have it when we need it" (e5); "Sometimes you need it for yourself and sometimes to avoid bothering others" (e4); "The possibility to work secluded is very important to be able to focus" (e3)*
- Furniture adjustments: *"It is very important to provide adjustments for different body types, especially when you use it for a long time" (e4); "This affects the long-term wellbeing and also the perceived quality of the product" (e1)*
- Shared workstations: *"I think that activity-based working is good and you should try it [...] but it doesn't work for everyone [people can feel stressed if forced to be flexible] [...] So it is always important to have choices" (e7).*

Following the discussion, the participants voted on the suboptimal experience to be redesigned, and the control over sound/noise was chosen by the majority. This was followed by furniture adjustments -instead of privacy-, meaning that the discussions may have changed participants' priorities to some extent. According to the voting, the suboptimal experience of control over sound/noise was taken as a reference to formulate the opposite positive UX. The initial formulation was discussed and refined by the participants, who validated the following:

"We want the users of a flexible office to have a positive experience of control over the sound stimuli and the distractions caused by this".

Such proposal is meant to be addressed in a 'research through design' collaborative project in the near future, and it should culminate in a concrete conceptual solution with the potential to break through to the market.

3 Reflections and Conclusion

This paper elaborates on the collaboration between user-centered design researchers and office furniture experts in the exploration of design opportunities for a positive UX in flexible office environments. In particular, three sessions are reported here that provide with insights on design and practical aspects of the collaboration. The sessions were planned to: (i) understand the experts' perspective on flexible office design and user needs from a practitioner viewpoint, (ii) compare and contrast their view with key findings from the authors' research perspective, and (iii) combine both perspectives into the decision making for a specific proposal of positive UX in FOEs.

The validated UX proposal on the user control over sound stimuli relates to two subjects of great relevance attending to the available body of research: personal control [12] and sound stimuli in office environments [13]. Personal control over the environment has been found fundamental for office users' wellbeing [11, 14, 15] and clearly linked to how positively or negatively users experience the office environment [16–18]. Regarding sound stimuli in offices -not only flexible offices, but any office type-, research shows that it is among the most recurrent issues determining satisfaction with offices [19–21]. Further, exposure to stimuli and acoustics is highlighted as one of the most common reasons behind preference and non-preferences for the use of spaces in FOEs [3]. Thus, the UX proposal formulated here is relevant and pertinent from a research perspective and aligned with the interests and views of a leading office furniture manufacturer. The proposal delimits a potential solution space that will be explored in follow-up sessions.

The methodology and activities helped participants reflect on experiences of use on a wide sense and diversity of affective outcomes. Further, the sessions provided with a common space for engagement and co-creation through concrete strategies highlighted in previous research [22–24]: sensitising activities, introductory seminars on key concepts and research findings, a Mural trial prior to the session, frequent opportunities for discussion, and involvement of a fixed team of experts over time.

This convergence between research and practice is consistent with previous evidence showing that collaboration between different actors of a problem area is not only desirable, but necessary [22]. However, offices are complex systems with a notable diversity of actors aboard. The experts explicitly noted that during the first session when they highlighted the challenges that may entail a late arrival to an office development project. Further, other actors such as organizational decision-makers, facility managers, architects, procurement officers, etc. depart from disparate briefs and perspectives that may not have the user in focus [6, 25]. The knowledge and practice gaps across disciplines have been identified as barriers for successful collaboration in previous research [22, 26]. This paper exemplifies a way to bridge such gaps, although extending this kind of initiatives to new actors is highly advisable to bridge further gaps. In this particular case, the actors involved share a customer/user-centered approach, which opened up for a rich understanding of the complex nature of UX in FOEs and meaningful UX design proposals.

The role of a UX approach in guiding the exploration of design opportunities has been central, as traditional design processes depart from the ideation of solutions, while in this case such ideation belongs to the last stage of a thorough funnelling process.

Previous research has referred to similar approaches as a transition from 'creative problem solving' to the 'innovation of meaning' [27]. In relation to this, future work entails, first, the exploration of design strategies to deliver the proposed UX of control and, only afterwards, the exploration of concrete design solutions that can realise the proposed experience with the chosen strategy.

Acknowledgements. The authors would like to express their gratitude to MariAnne Karlsson for her precious support and feedback, and to the workshop participants for their valuable time and insights. This research work is part of a doctoral project and it has been developed in collaboration between Chalmers University of Technology and Kinnarps.

References

1. Brunia, S., De Been, I., van der Voordt, T.J.M.: Accommodating new ways of working: lessons from best practices and worst cases. J. Corp. Real Estate **18**, 30–47 (2016)
2. Wohlers, C., Hertel, G.: Choosing where to work at work–towards a theoretical model of benefits and risks of activity-based flexible offices. Ergonomics **60**, 467–86 (2016)
3. Babapour, M., Harder, M., Bodin, D.: Workspace preferences and non-preferences in activity-based flexible offices: two case studies. Appl. Ergon. **83**, 102971 (2020)
4. Cobaleda-Cordero, A., Babapour, M.: Discrepancies between intended and actual use in activity-based flexible offices-a literature review. In: Joy at Work' Nordic Ergonomics Society Conference Proceedings, NES 2017, Lund, Sweden, 20–23 August 2017, p. 56 (2017)
5. Engelen, L., Chau, J., Young, S., Mackey, M., Jeyapalan, D., Bauman, A.: Is activity-based working impacting health, work performance and perceptions? A systematic review. Build. Res. Inf. **47**, 468–479 (2019)
6. Babapour, M.: The quest for the room of requirement why some activity-based flexible offices work while others do not. Chalmers University of Technology (2019)
7. Hassenzahl, M.: Encyclopedia entry on user experience and experience design. In: Soegaard, M., Dam, R.F. (eds.) Interaction-Design.org, 2nd edn, pp. 1–14. The Interaction Design Foundation, Aarhus (2011)
8. Merriam-Webster dictionary. https://www.merriam-webster.com/dictionary/security_bla nket. Accessed 21 Jan 2021
9. Babapour, M., Cobaleda-Cordero, A.: Contextual user research methods for eliciting user experience insights in workplace studies. In: Transdisciplinary Workplace Research (TWR) Conference, pp. 1–10 (2020)
10. van Boeijen, A., Daalhuizen, J., van der Schoor, R., Zijlstra, J.: Delft Design Guide, 4th edn. BIS, Amsterdam (2014)
11. Cobaleda-Cordero, A.: Office Landscapes for Well-being. Chalmers University of Technology (2019)
12. Skinner, E.A.: A guide to constructs of control. J. Pers. Soc. Psychol. **71**, 549–70 (1996)
13. Oseland, N., Hodsman, P.: A psychoacoustical approach to resolving office noise distraction. J. Corp. Real Estate **20**, 260–80 (2018)
14. Clements-Croome, D.: Creating the Productive Workplace, 3rd edn. Routledge, New York (2018)
15. Ulrich, R.S.: Effects of interior design on wellness: theory and recent scientific research. J. Health Care Inter. Des. **3**, 97–109 (1991)
16. Lee, S.Y., Brand, J.L.: Effects of control over office workspace on perceptions of the work environment and work outcomes. J. Environ. Psychol. **25**, 323–33 (2005)

17. Kwon, M., Remøy, H., van den Dobbelsteen, A., Knaack, U.: Personal control and environmental user satisfaction in office buildings: results of case studies in the Netherlands. Build. Environ. **149**, 428–35 (2019)
18. Boerstra, A.C., Loomans, M.G.L.C., Hensen, J.L.M.: Personal control over temperature in winter in Dutch office buildings. HVAC R Res. **19**, 1033–50 (2013)
19. Haapakangas, A., Hongisto, V., Eerola, M., Kuusisto, T.: Distraction distance and perceived disturbance by noise-an analysis of 21 open-plan offices. J. Acoust. Soc. Am. **141**, 127 (2017)
20. Kim, J., de Dear, R.: Workspace satisfaction: the privacy-communication trade-off inopen-plan offices. J. Environ. Psychol. **36**, 18–26 (2013)
21. Appel-Meulenbroek, R., Steps, S., Wenmaekers, R., Arentze, T.: Coping strategies and perceived productivity in open-plan offices with noise problems. J. Manag. Psychol. (2020)
22. Eriksson, S., Wallgren, P., Karlsson, M.: Facilitating users and designers towards a shift of perspective for true participation in co-creation in health care: a holistic activity theoretical approach. In: Proceeding 6th International Conference on Design, Amsterdam, pp. 1–8 (2020)
23. Broberg, O., Andersen, V., Seim, R.: Participatory ergonomics in design processes: the role of boundary objects. Appl. Ergon. **42**, 464–472 (2011)
24. Andersen, S.N., Broberg, O., Havn, E.C.: Participatory simulation in hospital work system design. Technical University of Denmark Department (DTU) (2016)
25. Cobaleda-Cordero, A., Babapour, M., Karlsson, M.: Feel well and do well at work. J. Corp. Real Estate. **22**, 113–37 (2019)
26. Pirinen, A.: The barriers and enablers of co-design for services. Int. J. Des. **10**, 27–42 (2016)
27. Dell'Era, C., Magistretti, S., Cautela, C., Verganti, R., Zurlo, F.: Four kinds of design thinking: from ideating to making, engaging, and criticizing. Creat. Innov. Manag. **29**, 324–44 (2020)

Outlining Experience and Well-Being in the Interaction with Social Media Apps

Beatriz de Paulo$^{(\boxtimes)}$ ⓘ and Manuela Quaresma ⓘ

LEUI | Laboratory of Ergodesign and Usability of Interfaces, Department of Arts and Design, PUC-Rio University, Rio de Janeiro, Brazil

Abstract. Social media apps (SMAs), like Instagram or Facebook, are actively used by one-in-three people in the world. The vast adoption of these technologies is changing multiple aspects of peoples' lives. Through the means of meaning and emotional experiences, the products people use every day have the potential of influencing their happiness and wellbeing. The present work points and discusses which themes are more prominent and relevant regarding how users engage with SMAs and how it can relate to their wellbeing. Through the discussion of a systematic literature review and other seminal works, the study proposes four main channels the interaction with SMAs can relate to users' wellbeing: interpersonal relationships, information consumption, self-image, and relationship with technology. The study also hypothesizes on how SMAs as interactive products can deliver experiences that nurture users' wellbeing, on top of being pleasurable and usable.

Keywords: Social media · Experience · Design for wellbeing · Social connection · Positive design · Digital wellbeing

1 Introduction

Intentionally or not, designers always have the potential of affecting the lives and well-being of users through the products they conceive. For massively adopted interactive products like social media apps, this potential is considerably higher, once that small decisions in these products can impact the lives of billions of people. Social media apps can be described as "web-based services that allow individuals to a. construct public profiles within a bounded system, b. articulate a list of other users with whom they share a connection, and c. view and traverse their list of connections and those made by others within the system" [1]. As interactive products, SMAs are evolving from communication tools to entertainment and information platforms as well. While making peoples' lives easier by connecting them with dear ones and providing curated entertainment, the relationships between SMA use and wellbeing can not be stated as thoroughly positive or negative. Users can interact with SMAs in diverse contexts, with numerous intents and behaviors. Considering that experiences are shaped by personal and contextual factors, it would be unworkable to map out specific aspects of each experience. However, SMAs are products acting upon fundamental human tendencies and needs, like the need to

N. L. Black et al. (Eds.): IEA 2021, LNNS 223, pp. 12–19, 2022.
https://doi.org/10.1007/978-3-030-74614-8_2

belong and relate or to nurture bonds. SMAs provide a new and evolving context where widely studied relationships and tendencies can happen. Emotions and meaning in experiences are closely related to the way a product can affect its users' well-being [2, 3]. The current studies in the fields of Human-Computer Interaction, Design, and Psychology provide various known associations between emotions, behaviors, and interaction with SMAs. However, research on the relationship between well-being and interaction with SMAs can be considered equivocal [4, 5]. We believe that a discussion of the existing literature can provide a structured approach to the understanding of how the experience of interacting with SMAs can relate to peoples' wellbeing.

We conducted a Systematic Literature Review, using Booleans for the intersections between social media use, human-computer interaction, user experience and wellbeing. The results, after the application of Inclusion, Exclusion and Quality criteria, consisted in 24 full-text articles, published between January 2010 and October 2020. The search was conducted in the following Digital Libraries: Taylor and Francis Online, Scopus, ACM and ScienceDirect.

2 Four Touchpoints Between Social Media Use and Wellbeing

Whilst the study of the relationship between SMA use and wellbeing is still a transforming topic, there is a group of variables that seem to mediate its polarity. Prominent examples are self-esteem, which is positively related to better life satisfaction [6], and social comparison, which can function as a mediator in the negative relationship between SMA use and well-being [7]. The role of social connection and belonging was also an occurring theme in the discussed works, associating SMA use as a catalyzer for positive connection feelings [8]. It can be observed that while a series of mediators are associated with the relationship between SMA use and well-being, it remains unclear which psychological constructs or individual particularities are involved in this relationship. The following section will approach the matter in a broader sense, discussing the four hypothesized paths where SMA use can connect to users' well-being and how.

2.1 Social Media Use and Technology-Related Behavioral Patterns

In the process of creating any product or service, designers can, intentionally or not, influence the well-being and emotions of their users [9]. When analyzing the meaning and emotional experience that comes from SMA use and its relationship with well-being, it is paramount to observe the behaviors and habits that are formed by this continued interaction. The discussion of the relationship between technology use and well-being is better defined as a net with multiple points and connections and less as a single path. Therefore, the present section will discuss a few relationships between aspects of SMA use and behavioral patterns.

A social app like Facebook or Instagram has a diverse set of functionalities. The analysis of the relationship between behavioral patterns and well-being focuses on specific aspects of the apps, like the "infinite" feeds, notifications, or direct messages. Salehan and Negahban [10] present findings where social media use intensity can function as a predictor for smartphone addiction. The concept of addiction is an unusual and repetitive dependency of something, where the sum of the consequences for the individual is negative [10]. This addictive behavior, which is by definition harmful for one's well-being, does not come from SMA use in general, seems to come from a few aspects of how these apps and smartphones are conceived.

The consequences of compulsive behavior in SMA use, like any excess, are associated with several negative outcomes for one's well-being. Hartshorne et al. [11] observed that SMA compulsive use harms the academic, physical, and social performance of college students. In the workplace context, Srwilai and Charoensukmongkol [12] have found out that SMA addicted workers had less focused attention on their tasks and lesser problem-solving skills. Regarding push notifications, a widely used artifice by SMAs to recover users' attention, Kushlev et al. [13] also point out that constant notification exposure is related to ADHD-analogue symptoms and hyperactivity. It is important to note that the adoption of a compulsive behavior towards SMA use also depends on external factors, like personality or life events. However, it is questionable if the way SMAs are designed provides tools for users to perceive and mitigate those behaviors.

The mere realization that technology can module certain aspects of our life does not mean necessarily we lack the freedom to control that mediation. Dorrestjin and Verbeek [9] point out that the role of design for wellbeing in technology is to provide the tools to develop a critical and active relationship with them. Therefore, when we observe the ways SMA uses mediates the relationship with technology in general, it is relevant to question what kind of opportunities these products create: for a passive and potentially compulsive use or a critical, conscious use pattern.

2.2 Interaction with Social Media Apps and Interpersonal Relationships

The main premise of most social apps is to connect the user with other people in an easier and dynamic way. Nowadays, these connections can range from dear relatives to potential clients or complete strangers. While apps like Facebook and Instagram are no longer limited to that function, interpersonal connections are still a central theme when discussing social media.

Social media apps act upon the way we connect and form bonds with other people, creating a new context where known and repeated phenomena and tendencies can happen. However, technological advances will inherently influence on how we communicate [14]. SMAs work actively upon our innate need to belong, communicate, and recognize ourselves in others. Humans are naturally oriented to form and foster social bonds, even in adverse conditions. For most people, the search for belonging and connection is associated with better mental health and well-being [15]. This habit finds a new context in social media. If before their invention we had to create opportunities for connection through visits, letters, or phone calls, SMAs bring the potential of a seemingly constant and quick connection. In some cases, the app can even encourage certain bonds, in the form of curated notifications or the prioritization of one's content in others' feeds. Roberts and David [4] found that the relationship between the "fear of missing out" (FoMO) and social media is negatively related to wellbeing. The FoMO can be described as the anxiety coming from the feeling that one is "missing" things are happening or is uninformed. SMAs act upon these fundamental tendencies, but the consequences for the users' wellbeing depend heavily on how users themselves deal with those stimuli.

Considering the human need to belong and maintain bonds, we can think about SMAs as a new means to this end, like the phone or a visit. A tool with unique features, that can be employed in different ways. The SMAs allows users to maintain bonds even with their distant acquaintances. A very important construct SMAs can help building and maintaining is the social capital, defined as the compound of accumulated resources from the relationships with other people (emotional support, the possibility of having help in emergencies, and others) [16]. When used in an active manner and for strengthening ties that find ground in "real" life, SMA use can be beneficial to well-being. That positive relationship comes from the feeling of belonging and social support [17, 18]. Even the FoMO, which by itself is negative for wellbeing, can be positive when motivates social connection [4]. Ultimately, when applied to strengthen bonds that find ground in other forms of connection, SMAs can be positive for well-being.

As previously stated, social media apps are not limited to social connections anymore. Users are invited through algorithm-curated feeds to interact with celebrities, distant people, brands, and various information sources The way and with whom one interacts in SMAs can be divided into "passive" and "active" use [17, 18]. Active use means creating content and engaging with other users' content, as posting pictures, writing, and answering comments. On the other hand, passive use is characterized by only consuming and not interacting with other users' content.

Considering the active and passive use patterns, while a predominantly active use is associated with feelings of belonging and social support, passive use is associated with feelings of rejection, loneliness, and negative comparison [18]. The predominantly passive use can promote a false sense of social connection, bringing interactions that do not contribute to interpersonal bonds. The persistence of this behavior can generate a "social resources deficit" [19]. Chou and Edge [20] argue that users with more strangers added on their social media and are passive users are more prone to negative comparison with others. The intimate interaction with bonds that do not find ground in the "real" world is pointed by Sbarra [14] as prejudicial for the actual close relationships. The use of smartphones and SMAs in contexts where face-to-face interactions are also happening, like a dinner or a meeting, can undermine the pleasure that comes from these interactions. In what is behind, the use type and context can be perceived as relevant variables in the emotional and meaning-related experiences with social media, and are closely related to wellbeing.

2.3 Social Media Apps as Information Sources

From the moment we wake up, we are offered multiple opportunities for consuming information, even without a clear reason or motivation. When checking a news feed from any SMA, we are delivered all the information "lost" since the last session. From an evolutive point of view, humans have an innate need of searching for information [4]. SMAs act upon this drive, delivering a seemingly infinite source of content and information.

When observing the escalade of the COVID-19 pandemic worldwide, this phenomenon intensified. The search and spread of information about an unknown and new disease became a necessity for one's protection. During the pandemic, the constant information flow was pointed by Gao et al. [21] and Rosenberg et al. [22] as sources of stress and fatigue. The World Health Organisation recommended conscious information consumption about COVID, limited in closed sessions with clear goals and trusted sources [23]. However, the endless and indiscriminate way social apps deliver information to their users seems to go directly against these recommendations, leaving it on the users' responsibility to break those cycles.

Infinite feeds and automatic content transitions, like on Instagram or TikTok, have become design patterns in the most popular social apps. While these patterns provide a more fluid experience, they also bring a massive flow of information, rising the potential of a mental overload [24] and putting a barrier on conscious consumption. Information overload is pointed by Zhang et al. [25] as a source of stress in SMA use. The design patterns present in most SMAs seem to go on the opposite way of a healthy relationship with content and information, leaving on the users' side to identify and avoid prejudicial behaviors.

2.4   The Tense Relationship Between Social Media and Self-image

As interactive products, SMAs provide the tools for presenting a curated and fine-tuned self-image of ourselves to the world. While not every user behaves the same way, the segmentation of circles, filters, and avatars provided by social apps emerge as a catalyzer for this phenomenon. As with any tool, choosing exactly how we are going to present ourselves to the world has both advantages and disadvantages. There is a certain lure to the ability to play with different images of ourselves and others through social apps. However, the constant exposition to curated, numerous, and mutable images of others can bring negative consequences to how we see ourselves. Healthy and positive self-esteem and self-image are directly related to one's well-being [6].

Social apps provide us with a novel and constant offer of information about others, what they do, where they eat, and how they dress for a day of work. In the first popular social sites like MySpace, this group normally consisted of close friends and family. As SMAs became more complex and diverse, the group was expanded to public figures, celebrities, and digital influencers, figures whose fame is solely based on their online presence. The way SMAs handle this flow can bring two fundamental consequences to how we perceive ourselves: the formation of our self-image and the ability to be in solitude, which influences self-esteem.

Self-esteem and social comparison are strong mediators of the relationship between social media and well-being [5, 18]. Since SMAs provide a curated exposure of who we are, the possibility of social comparison increases [5]. When consuming those ideal images of others, users tend to perceive themselves negatively and feel less satisfied with their own lives [20]. Considering the possible positive outcomes of that configuration, the possibility of experimenting with different identities is pointed as an important actor for teenagers building their self-image [16, 26]. Self-esteem acts as an important mediator between SMA use and well-being: users that are already prone to negative comparison will tend to feel negatively affected [17].

Another important component of the construction of self-image and self-esteem is loneliness periods. With a world of information and interaction at the distance of a few taps, solitude starts to seem like a problem to be quickly solved by SMAs. However, solitude is a fundamental practice for an individual to develop new skills, self-evaluate, and transform [27, 28]. Turkle [29] argues that solitude moments are crucial to the building of self-image. A moment of loneliness is crucial for an individual to decide if their interactions should come from the anxiety of a push notification or a real desire for connection. The way SMAs are designed seems to go on the opposite way of a healthy relationship with solitude, favoring quick interactions to solve the "problem" of solitude. Considering that self-esteem and self-images are important actors in well-being, it becomes relevant to question how the interaction with SMAs acts upon these two compounds.

3 Final Considerations

The current studies in the fields of Human-Computer Interaction and Psychology provide various known associations between emotions, behaviors, and interactions with SMAs. Variables like self-esteem, use type, and the decision of consuming information in a conscient way are relevant mediators between how SMA use affects our well-being. However, most of these mediators are heavily dependent on the users' own choices, predispositions, and capability to adapt themselves. The path to a healthy and free relationship with any influencing technology can be seen as a critical, well-informed, and active use, where every influence and consequence is known by the user. It is the role of the designers and stakeholders involved in the project of any product to provide the necessary tools, but a look at SMAs current design patterns leaves doubt if these tools are being provided. Given that SMAs are apps made by and for people, we can argue that they should adapt themselves to provide healthy and pleasurable interactions to their massive user base.

References

1. Boyd, D.M., Ellison, N.B.: Social network sites: definition, history, and scholarship. J. Comput.-Mediat. Commun. **13**(00), 210–230 (2007)
2. Hassenzahl, M., Eckoldt, K., Diefenbach, S., Laschke, M., Lenz, E., Kim, J.: Designing moments of meaning and pleasure. Experience design and happiness. Int. J. Des. **7**(3), 21–31 (2013)
3. Casais, M., Mugge, R., Desmet, P.: Objects with symbolic meaning: 16 directions to inspire design for well-being. J. Des. Res. **16**(3–4), 247–281 (2018)
4. Roberts, J.A., David, M.E.: The social media party: fear of missing out (FoMO), social media intensity, connection, and well-being. Int. J. Hum.-Comput. Interact. **36**(4), 386–392 (2020)
5. Faelens, L., Hoorelbeke, K., Soenens, B., Van Gaeveren, K., De Marez, L., De Raedt, R., Koster, E.H.W.: Social media use and well-being: a prospective experience-sampling study. Comput. Hum. Behav. **114**, 106510 (2020)
6. Diener, E., Diener, M.: Cross-cultural correlates of life satisfaction and self-esteem. J. Pers. Soc. Psychol. **68**(4), 653–663 (1995)
7. Verduyn, P., Ybarra, O., Résibois, M., Jonides, J., Kross, E.: Do social network sites enhance or undermine subjective well-being: a critical review. Soc. Issues Policy Rev. **11**(1), 274–302 (2017)
8. Sheldon, K., Abad, N., Hinsch, C.: A two-process view of Facebook use and relatedness need-satisfaction: disconnection drives use, and connection rewards it. J. Pers. Soc. Psychol. **100**(4), 766–75 (2011)

9. Dorrestjin, S., Verbeek, P.P.: Technology, wellbeing, and freedom: the legacy of utopian design. Int. J. Des. **7**(3), 45–56 (2013)
10. Salehan, M., Negahban, A.: Social networking on smartphones: when mobile phones become addictive. Comput. Hum. Behav. **29**(6), 2632–2639 (2013)
11. Benson, V., Hand, C., Hartshorne, R.: How compulsive use of social media affects performance: insights from the UK by purpose of use. Behav. Inf. Technol. **38**(1), 549–563 (2018)
12. Sriwilai, K., Charoensukmongkol, P.: Face it, don't Facebook it: impacts of social media addiction on mindfulness, coping strategies and the consequence on emotional exhaustion. Stress Health **32**(4), 427–434 (2016)
13. Kushlev, K., Proulx, J., Dunn, E.W.: "Silence your phones": smartphone notifications increase inattention and hyperactivity symptoms. In: Conference on Human Factors in Computing Systems 2016 on Proceedings, pp. 1011–1020. Association for Computing Machinery, New York (2016)
14. Sbarra, D.A., Briskin, J.L., Slatcher, R.B.: Smartphones and close relationships: the case for an evolutionary mismatch. Perspect. Psychol. Sci. **14**(4), 596–618 (2019)
15. Zukauskiene, R., Baumeister, R.F., Leary, M.R.: The need to belong: desire for interpersonal attachments as a fundamental human motivation. Interpers. Dev. **117**(3), 57–89 (1995)
16. Ellison, N.B., Steinfield, C., Lampe, C.: The benefits of Facebook "friends:" social capital and college students' use of online social network sites. J. Comput. Mediat. Commun. **12**(4), 1143–1168 (2007)
17. Clark, J.L., Algoe, S.B., Green, M.C.: Social network sites and well-being: the role of social connection. Curr. Dir. Psychol. Sci. **27**(1), 32–37 (2018)
18. Frison, E., Eggermont, S.: Exploring the relationships between different types of Facebook use, perceived online social support, and adolescents' depressed mood. Soc. Sci. Comput. Rev. **34**(2), 153–171 (2016)
19. Gardner, W.L., Pickett, C.L., Knowles, M.: Social snacking and shielding. In: Williams, K.D., Forgas, J.P., von Hippel, W. (eds.) The Social Outcast: Ostracism, Social Exclusion, Rejection, and Bullying, pp. 227–242. Psychology Press, New York (2005)
20. Chou, H.T.G., Edge, N.: "They are happier and having better lives than I am": the impact of using Facebook on perceptions of others' lives. Cyberpsychol. Behav. Soc. Netw. **15**(2), 117–121 (2012). https://doi.org/10.1089/cyber.2011.0324
21. Gao, J., Zheng, P., Jia, Y., Chen, H., Mao, Y., Chen, S., Wang, Y., Fu, H., Dai, J.: Mental health problems and social media exposure during COVID-19 outbreak. PLoS ONE **15**(4), 1–10 (2020)
22. Rosenberg, H., Syed, S., Rezaie, S.: The Twitter pandemic: the critical role of Twitter in the dissemination of medical information and misinformation during the COVID-19 pandemic. CJEM **22**(4), 418–421 (2020)
23. World Health Organization: Facing mental health fallout from the coronavirus pandemic. https://www.who.int/news-room/feature-stories/detail/facing-mental-health-fallout-from-the-coronavirus-pandemic. Accessed 07 July 2020
24. Bright, L.F., Kleiser, S.B., Grau, S.L.: Too much Facebook? An exploratory examination of social media fatigue. Comput. Hum. Behav. **44**(3), 148–155 (2015)
25. Zhang, K.Z.K., Chen, C.: Understanding the role of motives in smartphone addiction. In: 2014 Pacific Asia Conference on Information Systems (PACIS) in Proceedings (2014)
26. Wood, M.A., Bukowski, W.M., Lis, E.: The digital self: how social media serves as a setting that shapes youth's emotional experiences. Adolesc. Res. Rev. **1**(2), 163–173 (2014)
27. Koch, P.: Solitude: A philosophical encounter. Open Court Publishing (1994)

28. Long, C.R., Averill, J.R.: Solitude: an exploration of benefits of being alone. J. Theory Soc. Behav. **33**(1), 21–44 (2003)
29. Connected, but alone? https://www.ted.com/talks/sherry_turkle_alone_together?language=en. Accessed 10 Feb 2020

Affective Trash Bin Signage to Promote Waste Segregation

Arvidas Kio Dy, Margarita Lazo, Andreana Gabrielle Santos, and Rosemary Seva[✉]

De La Salle University, 2401 Taft Avenue, Malate, Manila, Philippines
rosemary.seva@dlsu.edu.ph

Abstract. Signages that elicit guilt is an effective strategy in influencing segregation behaviour especially if it includes a statement of action and an appropriate picture to illustrate the consequence of bad behavior. This paper examines the direct effect of signage design factors: type of guilt statement and pictorial component to guilt. Clarity of purpose was considered as a mediating variable between the design factors and guilt, while guilt proneness was considered as moderating variable between guilt and segregation behavior. The evaluation of the model was done through a Structural Equation Model (SEM) with a data set count of 404. There was no significant effect in the use of actual picture and cartoon in promoting the clarity of purpose of a signage. The mediating effect of clarity of purpose was established between the design factors and guilt, while guilt proneness also moderated the relationship between guilt and segregation behavior.

Keywords: Affective design · Sustainability · Waste segregation · Emotion · Structural equation modeling

1 Introduction

Proper trash segregation is one common solution to manage waste in urban areas. However, there are many barriers for its successful implementation such as public apathy, lack of awareness regarding its environmental benefits [1] and the lack of intention to segregate [2]. One possible way to promote waste segregation behavior is providing information through proper use of signage. Signage, in this paper, is defined as a prompt that contains pictorial and verbal components (images and texts) that are used to communicate information to the public. Several studies showed that signage is effective in influencing behaviour, such as in the case of smoking [3], health [4–6], and sustainable behaviour [7–9].

A signage can include an emotional message to promote certain behaviors. Fear appeals, or persuasive messages that are aimed at eliciting fear, are commonly used in advertising in order to divert certain behaviours that are harmful to oneself such as smoking [3] and unsafe sex practices [4]. The use of guilt appeals have also been widely used in behavioural change interventions, particularly when the target behaviours are prosocial, such as in the case of donation behaviour [8, 10, 11] and environmental behaviours [9]. Batson [12] and Tangney [13] have demonstrated that both empathy

N. L. Black et al. (Eds.): IEA 2021, LNNS 223, pp. 20–30, 2022.
https://doi.org/10.1007/978-3-030-74614-8_3

and guilt enhance prosocial behavior. However, in presenting information, one must also recognize that one of the significant factors in determining the effectiveness of a signage is clarity of purpose [14]. Verdonk, Chiveralls, and Dawson [15] discovered that signage that embody positive messages to promote waste segregation behaviour were unsuccessful because they were not motivational enough. Waste segregation behaviour is classified as prosocial behaviour because protecting the environment requires a person to think beyond themselves and consider the repercussions of their actions in relation to others and the planet. As such, Batson [12] and Tangney [13] have demonstrated that both empathy and guilt enhance prosocial behavior.

There are other factors that influence guilt arousal such as guilt proneness as people who have a high level of guilt proneness tend to feel more compelling feelings of guilt in a situation and respond to consequences with guilty responses across a wider scope of situations [16].

Overall, there is still a lack of research regarding the effect of negative affect, specifically guilt, to waste segregation behaviour. The role of guilt in influencing environmental behaviours has gained attention in the past years, however, the factors that come into play in guilt arousal and decision-making have not yet been studied in the context of waste segregation behaviour. Thus, this study aims to examine the following relationships:

1. mediating effect of clarity of purpose in the relationship between the signage factors (textual and pictorial components) and guilt
2. guilt response and segregation behaviour
3. moderating effect of guilt proneness in the relationship between guilt and segregation behavior.

The research framework is shown in Fig. 1.

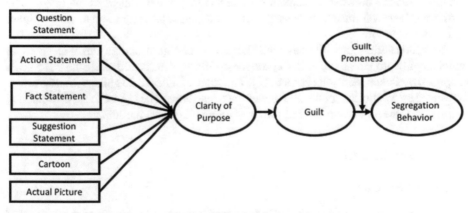

Fig. 1. Research framework

2 Method

2.1 Participants

Participants of the study are students, faculty, staff alumni and community members of a local university in the Philippines that are of 16–60 years of age. Quota sampling was used to gather 404 participants that are either students or staff of the university and regularly purchase food from establishments within the campus or from food stalls around the school.

2.2 Variables and Measurements

There were two independent variables considered in the experiment: textual and pictorial component of the signage. The textual component had four levels, which are statement of action, statement of question, suggestive statement, and factual statement. The pictorial component had two levels, which are photo and cartoon. A total of 8 different combinations were tested by matching each type of verbal component to each type of picture in the signage. These variables were considered binary variables in the structural equation model.

The dependent variables are guilt and behavior. A 7-point scale was used to measure the intensity of guilt (G) patterned after Wonneberger [17] and reworded to fit the context of segregation. Guilt was measured with three items that composed a reliable scale ($\alpha =$ .92). Self-reported perceived segregation behaviour was measured by two questions that were patterned after the measure of perceived effectiveness using a scale from 0 (not likely at all) to 10 (very likely) [14].

Clarity of purpose (COP) was considered a mediating variable between the signage design and guilt. A section on understanding was part of the post-observation questionnaire to know the participant's understanding of the context of the image. The participant's answer must be consistent with the actual context for them to have a higher understanding score.

One moderating variable was considered between guilt and sustainable behavior which is guilt proneness (GP). Guilt proneness (GP) was measured using the GP-5 scale proposed by Cohen, Kim, and Panter [18]. The score of the 5-scale guilt proneness tool is measured by computing for the average of the 5 questions. The higher the score obtained in the GP-5, the higher the level of the guilt proneness of the participant.

3 Signage Design

3.1 Photo Selection

The appropriate photo to be included in the signage was chosen following the method of the Categorized Affective Pictures Database (CAP-D) [19]. A photo database that depicts the consequences of improper waste segregation were collected from the Internet. Top five photos per consequence were selected and narrowed down by asking 97 people in a preliminary survey to identify the context of the photos. The responses were classified into three unique contexts: dirty/contaminated water, water near trash area, and a person placing water in a bottle. These three contexts were used to search top photos in the Internet to use in the second survey. The top five photos obtained after the search were paired with a "statement of action" to create a "signage." Each participant rated the strength of guilt felt from the provided image through a Likert scale that was adapted from Basil, Ridgway, and Basil [20] in the second survey. The intensity of guilt was measured to determine the photo that will elicit the highest guilt. The photo that obtained the highest score in terms of the intensity of guilt was used in the final experiment.

3.2 Pictorial Component

The photo chosen was animated or in other words, turned into a cartoon version. The animation of the photo was done to provide the levels for the independent variable, which are PHOTO and CARTOON. The animation of the photo was done by a graphic designer.

3.3 Textual Component

After selecting the final photo from the second survey, guilt appeal statements were generated to be placed on the signage. Since the context that was chosen was "water pollution", the guilt appeal statements were framed in the context of water pollution and can be seen in Table 1. The statements were carefully formulated by following the method of constructing each of the four statement types presented by Huhmann and Brotherton [21]. This was done to ensure that each type of statement conveys the essence of the message.

The text of signage was in font style Sans Serif, a font recommended because it is easy to read [22]. It was also recommended that the font color be either black or white.

It was ensured that both the photo signage and the cartoon signage had consistent font styles, font sizes and placement of the texts to avoid any external bias. The Sample signage are shown in Fig. 2.

3.4 Questionnaire

The first section of the questionnaire collected background information. The list of questions are summarized in Table 2.

3.5 Procedure

The social media platform "Facebook" was used in order to invite participants to join the study. The invitation to participate was posted on Facebook containing the information regarding the schedule, qualifications and compensation were given to those who joined.

A screening process was conducted via video call. They were asked about their status at the University and if they purchase food from establishments within the campus or from food stalls surrounding/nearby the school to ensure that the participant has interacted with the segregation bins when he/she disposes of food purchased from food stalls inside and outside the university. Since segregation bins are always present where people can

Table 1. Guilt appeal statements

	Definition	Statement formulated
Statement of action	The statement of action reports personal behaviour that should or should not occur	Your failure to segregate trash contributes to the pollution of our waters
Statement of fact	The statement of fact reports circumstances or information that may produce guilt	In the Philippines alone, there are 595,248 tons of garbage getting leaked into our oceans yearly
Suggestion	A suggestion recommends future action or proposes that one should participate/engage in a certain behavior	You should segregate your trash to lessen the pollution leaking into our waters
Question	Asks about one's thoughts, feelings, or behavior	When did you last segregate your trash and think about how you contribute to the pollution of our waters?

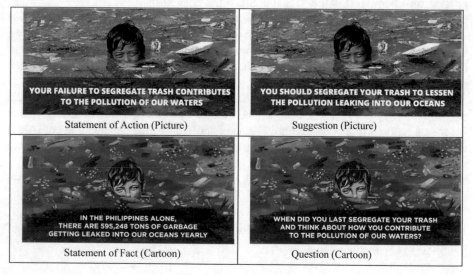

Fig. 2. Sample signage

buy food, and sit down and eat their food, it is assumed that they dispose of their trash in these bins. Furthermore, segregation bins are present almost everywhere inside the university which means that they interact with the segregation bins one way or another.

When all screening requirements are passed, an email containing a link to the questionnaire was sent to the participant. A between-subject design was used where one participant was only exposed to one of the eight signage. To make sure that there was no repetition of respondents, access to the survey was only through a unique link sent via

Table 2. Survey questions

Variable	Question
G1	I felt guilty about the thought of carrying out improper waste segregation after seeing the signage
G2	I felt sorry regarding my possible contribution to the effect of improper waste segregation after seeing the signage
G3	I felt regretful if I did not follow proper waste segregation after seeing the signage
COP1	When I saw the signage while disposing my trash, I depicted the image show in the signage as "Water Pollution"
COP2	It was clear in the signage that water pollution is an effect of improper waste segregation
GP1	At a coworker's house warming, you spill red wine on their new cream-colored carpet. You cover the stain with a chair so that nobody notices your mess. What is the likelihood that you feel that the way you acted was pathetic?
GP2	You lie to people but they never find out about it. What is the likelihood that you would feel terrible about the lies you told
GP3	Out of frustration, you break the photocopier at work. Nobody is around and you leave without telling anyone. What is the likelihood that you would feel bad about the way you acted
SB1	How likely are you to segregate your trash after seeing the signage above?
SB2	The signage has an impact on your segregation behavior

email. Once the participant passed the screening process, an email containing a unique link was sent to the participant on their chosen schedule. Each link only accepts one response.

3.6 Data Analysis

Data collected were analyzed using structural equation modeling (SEM). The moderating effect of guilt proneness was analyzed by investigating the direct and interaction effect of guilt (G) and guilt proneness (GP) to segregation behavior (SB). Double mean centering in data transformation of interaction. Results of the SEM were used to derive model parameter estimates. Model fit was evaluated using several fit indices. The SEM was analyzed using the AMOS software.

4 Results

4.1 Participant Demography

A total of 404 participants were included in the study of which 56% are females. The minimum age of participants is 16 while the maximum is 54 years. The median age is 23 years.

4.2 Structural Model

A covariance structure analysis was conducted by constructing the paths of each factor using maximum likelihood method. Based on the goodness-of-fit of the basic measurement model, the model was improved by using a modification index (MI) that was based on theory. The goodness-of-fit index (GFI = 0.81), adjusted goodness-of-fit index (AGFI = 0.75), and RMSEA = 0.10 of the revised model showed fair fit.

The results of the analysis of the structural model is shown in Table 3. Significant results were highlighted with asterisk.

Table 3. Path coefficients of structural model

		Estimate	S.E	P
COP	Question	−0.20	0.09	**
COP	Fact	−0.25	0.09	***
COP	Suggestion	−0.19	0.09	**
COP	Picture	0.08	0.06	0.24
GUILT	COP	1.09	0.19	***
GUILT	Question	−0.08	0.15	0.57
GUILT	Fact	−0.18	0.15	0.22
GUILT	Suggestion	−0.19	0.15	0.19
GUILT	Picture	0.17	0.10	0.09
SB	GPRONE	0.27	0.11	*
SB	GUILT × GPRONE	0.57	0.19	**
SB	GUILT	1.17	0.08	***

The type of statements was binary coded in the model with statement of action as reference. The results show that the statement of action has a stronger effect compared to all the other types of statements as indicated by the negative coefficients. It also shows that the statement is the one creating the feeling of guilt as all the pictures are the same.

There was no significant difference in the use of cartoon or actual picture in eliciting guilt feelings. This is probably because the picture had already been screened and was found to elicit guilt. The same picture was cartoonized but was able to preserve the important aspects of the picture.

The mediation effects of clarity of purpose to guilt are statistically significant across all guilt appeal statements. The path coefficient estimate indicated that the paths between clarity of purpose and guilt response are significant and positive. When the message of the signage is clear the guilt response is also high. The respondents had to understand the context or the purpose of the sign in order to feel guilt and had they not inferred from the sign that improper waste segregation leads to water pollution, the emotional response would have not been triggered as strongly.

The moderation effect of guilt proneness was also established in this study. Guilt, guilt proneness and the interaction of the two are significant which are the necessary conditions for moderating effect.

The path between guilt and segregation behaviour are significant and positive and also is the interaction between guilt and guilt proneness. People who experienced higher guilt through the signage reported a higher value of self-reported perceived segregation behaviour. This is expected as many studies have proven repeatedly that guilt elicited in the presence of a transgression increases commitment to subsequent helping behavior [23].

5 Discussion

The current study proposed two ways of presenting guilt appeals, through cartoon visuals and photos (realistic images) which are important components in eliciting guilt [21]. Although the result was statistically insignificant, it can be inferred that the use of the photo may have a little advantage in eliciting guilt when influencing segregation behaviour. The cartoon illustration could have been interpreted in multiple ways especially since the visual is not as concrete as photos. Similar to the current study, Rodriguez [24] compared using cartoons and real photos in presenting information, and it was found that more time is required when identifying the meaning of a cartoon illustration in a given situation. The variation in the time it took for participants to imagine themselves disposing of their trash may have resulted in different interpretations of the situation presented by the cartoon illustration.

Upon interviewing the participants, those that observed the photo stated that the situation presented is easy to empathize with because it is something that they are able to visualize in real life. Rodriguez [24] found that between actual and cartoon photographs, actual photos are more reliable while cartoon photographs can be more persuasive, meaning they could compare it better to real-life situations. Therefore, it would be valid for the photo to elicit higher guilt because the photo allows the participant to see what is truly happening in real life. On the other hand, when a photo is animated, it loses certain elements of reality; it loses detail and it becomes difficult to appreciate it for what it truly is. The quality of the cartoon doesn't mirror real life unlike the photo.

Though there were a number of studies present in literature that examined guilt appeals, it was not previously known what factors make up an effective and successful guilt appeal. This study was able to identify which guilt appeal statement is most effective for eliciting guilt. The 'statement of action' was found to be the most effective in eliciting guilt. The statement of action informs the audience of whether they should follow or avoid certain behaviours by supporting or rejecting the idea of doing them [25]. It tells them that they disobeyed or potentially disobey a rule or guideline through their actions [21]. Somehow, such information allow them to have some kind of reflection and motivate them to do what is right.

Clarity of purpose was found to have mediating effects on the relationship between the signages and guilt. In eliciting guilt to influence waste segregation behaviour, the audience must understand the context and message of the signage. The results suggest that the users understood that the photo is depicting water pollution, and the signage shows that water pollution is an effect of improper segregation. The novelty of the sign prompted the viewer to "infer" the intended meaning in order to act on the behaviour that the signage is suggesting.

The results of the current study also found that the general population's segregation behaviour was significantly affected by the guilt that was elicited through the signages. Literature showed that one of the major reasons why people do not segregate was due to lack of awareness of the consequences of improper segregation. People do not see the importance of properly segregating their trash. Hence, the current study proved that when people are informed about the consequences of improper segregation, the awareness provided by the signage motivates them to act on their misbehaviour. Such as is in the case of smoking advertisements that show ill-effects of smoking on user's health; a number of studies have found that showing graphic images and showing the negative effects of smoking on a person's health led to increased willingness to quit [26]. Similarly, placing a signage that gave information on AIDS and death rates directly above a box of condoms actually encouraged users to take them. This goes on to give more evidence that when people are informed about the consequences of a certain behaviour, they are more willing to change their behaviour in a positive way.

The study also gives insights on the use of guilt for encouraging environmental behaviour. The current study proposed that guilt would be the most appropriate emotion to use for environmental behaviour. This is because environmental behaviour is actually classified as a prosocial behaviour, and guilt is one of the most powerful motivators for behaviours of the same type. Guilt is an emotion that arises after a moral transgression [27] and what follows is the tendency to make up for the wrongdoing and to undertake actions to lessen the damage caused by the individual [28]. The findings of the current study provide more evidence of the Negative-State Relief Model of Batson, which states that people have an innate drive to reduce negative feelings. The guilt elicited upon seeing the signages was able to improve willingness to segregate. For future studies, it may be worthwhile to test actual behaviour using these signages.

Guilt proneness was also found to be a significant determinant of guilt. However, when creating guilt appeals, it is best to use the photo instead of a cartoon especially when considering guilt proneness. Furthermore, it is also best to use the 'statement of action when creating guilt appeals, and only on the basis of guilt proneness as a determining factor.

6 Conclusion

Signages eliciting guilt is an effective strategy in influencing segregation behaviour especially if it includes a statement of action and an appropriate picture to illustrate the consequence of bad behavior. Clarity mediated the relationship between the signage factors and guilt response. Guilt was found to be an effective predictor of self-reported perceived segregation behaviour across all signages. Guilt proneness was also found to moderate the effects of the signage factors to guilt.

The findings of the study can serve as a substantial guide for those who are looking to create proper waste segregation signages, or signages aimed at encouraging environmental behaviour. It will prove useful to those who are designing a waste disposal system and are looking for a simple yet effective solution to the problem of waste management.

References

1. Bom, U., Belbase, S., Lila, R.: Public perceptions and practices of solid waste recycling in the city of Laramie in Wyoming, U.S.A. Recycling **2**, 11 (2017)
2. Atthirawong, W.: Factors affecting household participation in solid waste management segregation and recycling In Bangkok, Thailand. In: Claus, T., Herrmann, F., Manitz, M., Rose, O. (eds.) 30th Conference on Modelling and Simulation (2016)
3. Manyiwa, S., Brennan, R.: Fear appeals in anti-smoking advertising: how important is self-efficacy? J. Mark. Manag. **28**(11–12), 1419–1437 (2012)
4. Honnen, T.J., Kleinke, C.L.: Prompting bar patrons with signs to take free condoms. J. Appl. Behav. Anal. **23**(2), 215–217 (1990)
5. Burt, C.D., Henningsen, N., Consedine, N.S.: Prompting correct lifting posture using signs. Appl. Ergon. **30**(4), 353–9 (1999)
6. Yoon, A., Choi, S., Mun, J., Hong, J., Hahn, D., Kang, M., Lee, S.: Motivational signage increases stair usage on a Hispanic serving institution. J. Am. Coll. Health **68**(3), 236–241 (2018)
7. Gifford, R., Sussman, R.: The Oxford Handbook of Environmental and Conservation Psychology. Oxford University Press, Oxford (2012)
8. Hibbert, S., Smith, A., Davies, A., Ireland, F.: Guilt appeals: persuasion knowledge and charitable giving. Psychol. Mark. **24**(8), 723–742 (2007)
9. Jiménez, M., Yang, K.C.C.: How guilt level affects green advertising effectiveness. J. Creative Commun. **3**(3), 231–254 (2008)
10. O'Malley, M.N., Andrews, L.: The effect of mood and incentives on helping: are there some things money can't buy? Motiv. Emot. **7**(2), 179–189 (1983)
11. Lwin, M., Phau, I.: Effective advertising appeals for websites of small boutique hotels. J. Res. Interact. Mark. **7**(1), 18–32 (2013)
12. Batson, C.D.: The handbook of social psychology. McGraw-Hill, Boston (1998)
13. Tangney, J.P.: Self-Conscious Emotions: The Psychology of Shame, Guilt, Embarrassment, and Pride. Guilford Press, New York (1995)
14. Meis, J., Kashima, Y.: Signage as a tool for behavioral change: direct and indirect routes to understanding the meaning of a sign. PLoS ONE **12**(8), e0182975 (2017)
15. Verdonk, S., Chiveralls, K., Dawson, D.: Getting wasted at WOMADelaide: the effect of signage on waste disposal. Sustainability **9**(3), 344 (2017)
16. Flynn, F.J., Schaumberg, R.L.: When feeling bad leads to feeling good: guilt-proneness and affective organizational commitment. J. Appl. Psychol. **97**(1), 124–133 (2012)
17. Wonneberger, A.: Environmentalism—a question of guilt? Testing a model of guilt arousal and effects for environmental campaigns. J. Nonprofit Public Sector Mark. **30**(2), 168–186 (2018)
18. Cohen, T.R., Kim, Y., Panter, A.T.: The Five-Item Guilt Proneness Scale (GP-5). Carnegie Mellon University, Pittsburgh (2014)
19. Moyal, N., Henik, A., Anholt, G.E.: Categorized affective pictures database (CAP-D). J. Cogn. **1**(1), 41 (2018)
20. Basil, D., Ridgway, N., Basil, M.: Guilt and giving: a process model of empathy and efficacy. Psychol. Mark. **25**(1), 1–23 (2008)
21. Huhmann, B.A., Brotherton, T.P.: A content analysis of guilt appeals in popular magazine advertisements. J. Advert. **26**(2), 35–45 (1997)
22. Kasperek, S.: Sign redesign: applying design principles to improve signage in an academic library. Pennsylvania Libr. Res. Pract. **2**(1), 48–63 (2014)
23. O'Keefe, D.J.: Guilt and social influence. Commun. Yearb. **23**(1), 67–101 (2000)

24. Rodriguez, L., Lin, X.: The impact of comics on knowledge, attitude and behavioural intentions related to wind energy. J. Vis. Lit. **35**(4), 237–252 (2016)
25. Wen, T.: A content analysis of guilt appeals in animal welfare campaigns. Graduate Theses and Dissertations. Iowa State University (2016)
26. Durkin, S., Biener, L., Wakefield, M.: Effects of different types of antismoking ads on reducing disparities in smoking cessation among socioeconomic subgroups. Am. J. Public Health **99**(12), 2217–2223 (2009)
27. Baumeister, R.F., Stillwell, A.M., Heatherton, T.F.: Guilt: an interpersonal approach. Psychol. Bull. **115**(2), 243–267 (1994)
28. Tangney, J.P., Miller, R.S., Flicker, L., Barlow, D.H.: Are shame, guilt, and embarrassment distinct emotions? J. Pers. Soc. Psychol. **70**(6), 1256–1269 (1996)

Analysis of Geometric Features of 3D Shapes on Perception of Product Appearance for Visual Brand Affiliation

Matthias Sebastian Fischer[(⊠)], Daniel Holder, and Thomas Maier

Department of Industrial Design Engineering, Institute for Engineering Design and Industrial Design, University of Stuttgart, Pfaffenwaldring 9, 70569 Stuttgart, Germany
matthias.fischer@iktd.uni-stuttgart.de

Abstract. Products can be assigned to a brand by their visual similarity. An important factor here is the shape of the products. Previous methods for determining similarity for brand affiliation can only be applied to products with the same layout. For products with different structures (e.g. power tools), no methods exist for the 3D shape. Here, there is a need for research in order to be able to specifically design products similarly (or dissimilarly) for brand affiliation. The shape parameters that are independent of layout and are highly relevant for this purpose are determined on the basis of the perception (evoked feelings) of shapes. The approach implies that the communication of the corporate identity also takes place via the product appearance. Similar perceptions of the products lead to a perceived similarity. The results are based on a literature review of research in the field of affective design, emotional design and kansei engineering. The following 3D shape parameters were determined as important in descending order: edge/corner type, line and surface type, element amount (number of lines/edges and surfaces). Furthermore, the shape parameters are specified in 3D space.

Keywords: Affective design · Perception · 3D shape · Brand affiliation · Industrial design

1 Introduction and State of the Art

The product appearance has significant influence on the consumer acceptance and success on the market [1]. It is very important to be competitive with other products within the same category [2]. An important part of product appearance is brand recognition and affiliation. Aesthetic product design leads to positive brand evaluations and serves to categorize products and brands, influencing customers' opinions of the product and brand [3]. The visual assignment to a brand can be abstracted based on a high degree of similarity between the products [4].

In addition to color, graphics, and logos, brand affiliation can be achieved through similar shape language. Previous research regarding shapes mainly considers products with the same layout (e.g. cars) [5]. Relevant shape features for brand affiliation are identified and compared between products. Mostly, only outlines and contours of the

N. L. Black et al. (Eds.): IEA 2021, LNNS 223, pp. 31–38, 2022.
https://doi.org/10.1007/978-3-030-74614-8_4

shape features are considered in 2D representations (e.g. [4, 6]). This assumes that the same shape features are found in largely identical positions in all products. For product portfolios with products of different layouts (e.g. power tools) these procedures are not possible. Here, the complete use of 3D shapes (specific freeform surfaces) must be considered. With this knowledge about relevant shape parameters and their characteristics and weighting, products can be designed in a targeted, efficient and brand-specific manner. There is a need for research in this area. Only Wallace and Jakiela [7] mention the importance of corner design in this context.

In order to determine relevant shape parameters, an approach based on research in affective design, emotional design and kansci engineering is presented. This is based on the fact that products have an impact on the user through their physical attributes [2]. In addition, brands have identities (corporate identity), which in turn are ideally also communicated through the brand's product appearance [8]. Accordingly, it is assumed that similar (or dissimilar) product perceptions have an impact on brand affiliation. From this, it is concluded that shape parameters, which have a large influence on the product perception, are at the same time relevant for brand affiliation.

The paper presents an approach to the relationship between shape and perception of product shapes for brand affiliation based on a literature review of research. From this, recommendations for the use of shape parameters for brand affiliation are derived and specified.

2 Approach

The direct link between product shape and brand affiliation has already been discussed in many studies [5]. In some cases, the product perception has also been mentioned [6]. One research uses shape perception as a bridge between geometric properties and the determination of brand recognition and design freedom [9]. An important factor for the perception of products on users is the product shape [2]. According to Norman's model [10], emotional design consists of three parts: visceral design (appearance), behavioral design (pleasure and effectiveness of use) and reflective design (self-image, personal satisfaction, memories). In this context, the visceral response is particularly relevant as the first impression of the product design. Kim et al. [11] summarizes that affect is an object-oriented impression of the product, while emotion is an introspective feeling to external or internal events. Since the two terms are closely related, they are used interchangeably in research [12]. Part of kansei engineering is to design the product in such a way that intended feelings are evoked [13]. The corporate identity, or the character of a brand, is intended to create a unified impression among the products of a brand for brand affiliation [8].

Accordingly, the direct link between shape and brand affiliation can be used on the one hand, and the indirect link via the perception of shapes on the other (see Fig. 1). However, previous methods for the direct link between shape and brand affiliation are largely layout-dependent and based on single shape elements [5]. In order to determine structure-independent shape parameters for brand affiliation, the indirect link is used backwards. The identified layout-independent shape parameters (influencing product perception) can then be used to subsequently influence brand affiliation. The specific perceived properties of the shapes are not important for the time being. The two ways from the shape to the brand affiliation and this approach are visualized in Fig. 1. With the new approach it is possible to influence the relevant shape parameters on the basis of the findings on the perception of shape and in this way to establish characteristics for brand affiliation.

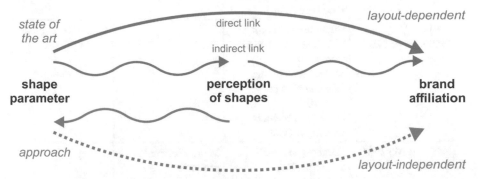

Fig. 1. Visualization of the direct and indirect link between shape parameters and brand affiliation (layout-dependent) and the approach (layout-independent)

3 Literature Review on Product Perception of 3D-Shapes

Publications are analyzed which deal with the perception of 3D product shapes by means of structure-independent shape parameters. Independent shape parameters are functionally neutral and describe mainly the general (global) surface usage. This overall shape definition already has meaningful effects [14]. Further requirements for the publication are that the products are shown in 3D surface form and not only in line form. The context of industrial design is also important. Accordingly, size, volume, composition (including symmetry) and orientation are not relevant. Also the combination of several shape parameters to terms like "organic" or "geometric/angular" are not purposeful (e.g. [15–17]). The overview (Table 1) is structured according to author, year, naming (terms instead of perception), example product, studied shape parameters (including mentioned shape characteristics) and type of research. In the case of the shape parameters, it is also indicated which shape parameters were found to be particularly significant within a study. Only the relevant shape parameters are mentioned in the overview. Most studies have also investigated a variety of other non-shape factors, which are not the focus of this paper.

Table 1. Overview of determined shape parameters and their characteristics

Author, year and *naming*	Shape Parameter and characteristics	Product	Type
Chen and Owen 1998 [18] *Stylistic description*	Edge type (sharp, step, fillet, bevel, round) Corner type (sharp, step, fillet, bevel, round) Face type (radii)	Cube, (furniture)	Proposed method
Pham 1999 [19] *Aesthetic properties*	Curvature (smoothness of transitions, change) Convexity Surface type (plane, single/double curved, warped) Number of features Line/curve type	-	Literature analysis
Chuang and Ma 2001 [20] *Product image*	Corner type (small, large rounded) Convex curvature surface	Micro-electronic products	Survey
Hsiao and Tsai 2005 [21] *Product image*	Line (different arcs) Surface (different arcs (convex)) Fillet radius (different radii or sharp)	Electronic Door lock	Proposed method
Hsiao and Chen 2006 [22] *Affective responses*	Corner type (sharp, large arc)** Surface type (flat, curve)* Line type (straight, curve)* Element amount (less, more)*	Kettle, sofa, automobile	Survey and experts
Perez Mata et al. 2017 [23] *Product perception*	Lines ratio (straight/curved)* Complexity level (number of modules)* Corner ratio (curved/sharp)	Vase	Survey
Kapkın and Joines [24] *Perceived meaning*	Edge roundness (radii)* Edge and corner roundness (radii)*	External hard drive, soap dispenser	Survey

* & ** [22]: high ranked by experts; * [23, 24]: significant impact

4   Results and Discussion

Based on the number of mentions and the characteristics, a tendency can be determined. The corner type is named most frequently, distinguishing between sharp and curved with different radii. Only one publication mentions further corner types [18]. Subsequently, surface type and line type are mentioned by most authors. Characteristics are flat and different curvatures for the surface type and straight and curved for the line type. Third most frequently the number of elements and the edge type are mentioned. In addition, one publication mentions convexity and curvature in general [19].

The authors of the researches from Table 1 only partially use the same terms for the shape parameters and vary in their number. It should be emphasized that only in two publications [18, 24] corner and edge are mentioned at the same time. All other publications use only one of the terms. Moreover, it becomes clear that edge and corner type are usually identical [18]. Therefore, a suitable 3D shape description model is developed for the interpretation of the results.

4.1   Model for the Description of 3D Geometric Shape Parameters

The description of 3D freeform surfaces can be done locally based on the curvatures at each point [25]. Globally a distinction between surface and edges (surface boundary) is necessary. A surface is characterized by a largely monotonous curvature [26]. In contrast, an edge is characterized by high relative curvature changes. Edges can be visually perceived by shading with large gray differences [27]. In extreme cases, an edge is not rounded at all, or is rounded to such an extent that it no longer exists as an edge and no longer represents a surface boundary. The differentiation of line and edge refers to the creation of surface patches with lines as boundary [28]. Thus, the surface contains properties of the lines. If two surface patches do not have a continuous transition, a hard edge is created along the separating line. If this non-continuous transition is rounded, the edge along the line becomes softer (see Fig. 2). In the case of a continuous surface transition, the separating line between the surfaces is not visible. The edge is, so to speak, the cross section along the line. The smaller the rounding of the edge, the more clearly the underlying line is recognizable. A corner is created when three or more edges meet.

Among other things, the 2D description of a corner leads to ambiguities in the interpretation. Here the combination of two lines is sufficient. Thus, an edge that runs along a line in the direction of view can also be interpreted as a corner. This ambiguity and the 3D shape description model are visualized in Fig. 2.

4.2   Interpretation of the Results with the 3D Shape Description Model

If we assume that corner type and edge type are mostly identical [18] and that edges are often interpreted as corners according to chapter 4.1, edge and corner can be combined into one parameter "edge/corner". This is supported by the largely identically named characteristics of edge type and corner type (sharp, curved/radius/arc: roundness). Accordingly, this shape element would also be the most important for shape perception. This is supported by the studies of Kapkın and Joines [24], according to which even small changes in the roundness of the edges already have an effect on the

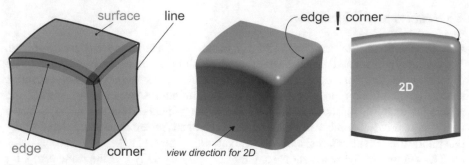

Fig. 2. Visualization of 3D line, face, edge, corner and the ambiguity of interpreting corners in 2D view.

perceived meanings. Wallace and Jakiela [7] also confirm this high relevance for brand affiliation. In the following, line type and surface type can be mentioned as the next important shape parameters. These are also described by Hsiao and Chen [22] as almost equivalent. In the case of surface patches, they cannot be considered completely separately, since they may influence each other. Line and surface types are described mainly by their curvature. Only two publications go into further details of curvatures of surfaces (especially convexity [19, 20]). As last relevant factor the number of elements can be described. Here the number of edges or lines and surfaces on the product is relevant.

In general, the research does not provide any information on the extent to which these shape parameters influence each other. Moreover, only the simpler shape characteristics have been researched so far (e.g. different radii). Further details of the edges, lines and surfaces, such as the style properties mentioned by Giannini et al. [26] (e.g. tension, acceleration) have not been investigated in this context so far. It should also be noted that the relationships between the geometric factors and their perception do not have to be linear [24].

5   Conclusion and Outlook

This paper describes an approach to determine relevant shape parameters for the brand affiliation of products with different layouts. For this purpose, the assignment to a brand by similar shape perception of the products is used. For the determination of relevant shape parameters, research in the field of affective design, emotional design and kansei engineering was analyzed. For the interpretation of the results, a general model for the 3D shape parameters was created. As a result, the following shape parameters are relevant for the product perception with their characteristics in descending order: edge/corner type (sharp, different radii), line and surface type (straight, different curvatures and flat, different curvatures), element amount (number of edges/lines and surfaces). This order also corresponds to the recommendation of the shape parameters for the generation of brand affiliation or differentiation on the market.

As a next step, the shape parameters determined should be validated in the context of brand affiliation. It is also interesting to see to what extent the shape parameters influence each other and how large geometric changes may be for assignment to a brand. It should also be investigated whether further details of the shape characteristics according to Giannini et al. [26] (such as tension and acceleration) can be used for brand affiliation.

References

1. Bloch, P.H.: Seeking the ideal form: product design and consumer response. J. Mark. **59**(3), 16–29 (1995)
2. Crilly, N., Moultrie, J., Clarkson, P.J.: Seeing things: consumer response to the visual domain in product design. Des. Stud. **25**(6), 547–577 (2004)
3. Kreuzbauer, R., Malter, A.J.: Embodied cognition and new product design: changing product form to influence brand categorization. J. Prod. Innov. Manag. **22**(2), 165–176 (2005)
4. Ranscombe, C., Hicks, B., Mullineux, G.: A method for exploring similarities and visual references to brand in the appearance of mature mass-market products. Des. Stud. **33**(5), 496–520 (2012)
5. Fischer, M.S., Holder, D., Maier, T.: Evaluating similarities in visual product appearance for brand affiliation. In: Fukuda, S. (eds.) Advances in Affective and Pleasurable Design. AHFE 2019. Advances in Intelligent Systems and Computing, vol. 952, pp. 3–12. Springer, Cham (2019)
6. McCormack, J.P., Cagan, J., Vogel, C.M.: Speaking the Buick language: capturing, understanding, and exploring brand identity with shape grammars. Des. Stud. **25**(1), 1–29 (2004)
7. Wallace, D.R., Jakiela, M.J.: Automated product concept design: unifying aesthetics and engineering. IEEE Comput. Graph. Appl. **13**(4), 66–75 (1993)
8. Schmitt, B.H., Simonson, A.: Marketing Aesthetics: The Strategic Management of Brands, Identity, and Image. The Free Press, New York (1997)
9. Burnap, A., Hartley, J., Pan, Y., Gonzalez, R., Papalambros, P.Y.: Balancing design freedom and brand recognition in the evolution of automotive brand styling. Des. Sci. **2** (2016)
10. Norman, D.A.: Emotional Design: Why We Love (or Hate) Everyday Things. Basic Books, New York (2004)
11. Kim, H.K., Han, S.H., Park, J., Park, J.: Identifying affect elements based on a conceptual model of affect: a case study on a smartphone. Int. J. Ind. Ergon. **53**, 193–204 (2016)
12. Khalid, H.M.: Embracing diversity in user needs for affective design. Appl. Ergon. **37**(4), 409–418 (2006)
13. Nagamachi, M.: Kansei/Affective Engineering. CRC Press, Boca Raton (2011)
14. Fontana, M., Giannini, F., Meirana, M.: A free form feature taxonomy. Comput. Graph. Forum **18**(3), 107–118 (1999)
15. Van Breemen, E.J.J., Sudijono, S.: The role of shape in communicating designers' aesthetic intents. In: Proceedings of the 1999 ASME Design Engineering Technical Conferences, Las Vegas (1999)
16. Hsu, S.H., Chuang, M.C., Chang, C.C.: A semantic differential study of designers' and users' product form perception. Int. J. Ind. Ergon. **25**(4), 375–391 (2000)
17. Fischer, M.S., Holder, D., Maier, T.: Brand affiliation through curved and angular surfaces using the example of the vehicle front. In: ASME 2020, Volume 8: 32nd International Conference on Design Theory and Methodology (DTM). American Society of Mechanical Engineers, Virtual, Online (2020)
18. Chen, K., Owen, C.L.: A study of computer-supported formal design. Des. Stud. **19**(3), 331–359 (1998)
19. Pham, B.: Design for aesthetics: interactions of design variables and aesthetic properties. In: SPIE IS&T/SPIE 11th Annual Symposium - Electronic Imaging 1999, pp. 364–371. SPIE, San Jose (1999)

20. Chuang, M.-C., Ma, Y.-C.: Expressing the expected product images in product design of micro-electronic products. Int. J. Ind. Ergon. **27**(4), 233–245 (2001)
21. Hsiao, S.-W., Tsai, H.-C.: Applying a hybrid approach based on fuzzy neural network and genetic algorithm to product form design. Int. J. Ind. Ergon. **35**(5), 411–428 (2005)
22. Hsiao, K.-A., Chen, L.-L.: Fundamental dimensions of affective responses to product shapes. Int. J. Ind. Ergon. **36**(6), 553–564 (2006)
23. Perez Mata, M., Ahmed-Kristensen, S., Brockhoff, P.B., Yanagisawa, H.: Investigating the influence of product perception and geometric features. Res. Eng. Des. **28**(3), 357–379 (2017)
24. Kapkın, E., Joines, S.: An investigation into the relationship between product form and perceived meanings. Int. J. Ind. Ergon. **67**, 259–273 (2018)
25. Koenderink, J.J., van Doorn, A.J.: Surface shape and curvature scales. Image Vis. Comput. **10**(8), 557–564 (1992)
26. Giannini, F., Monti, M., Podehl, G.: Styling properties and features in computer aided industrial design. Comput.-Aided Des. Appl. **1**(1–4), 321–330 (2004)
27. Mallot, H.A.: Sehen und die Verarbeitung visueller Information – Eine Einführung, 2nd edn. Vieweg, Wiesbaden (2000)
28. Salomon, D.: Curves and Surfaces for Computer Graphics. Springer, New York (2006)

Affective – Cognitive – Usability (ACU) Model Incorporating Eye Tracking Analysis for Redesigning the e-Commerce Website

Markus Hartono[✉], Argo Hadi Kusumo, and Dwilita Aprilin Asikin

Department of Industrial Engineering, University of Surabaya, Surabaya, Indonesia
markus@staff.ubaya.ac.id

Abstract. This study discusses the investigation of how both cognitive and affective factors bring significant impact on the usability in e-commerce website selling consumer products. It raises a question of which one is more dominant, whether it is cognition or affect for consumer experience? It is a critical thing to investigate. Eye tracking analysis is utilized to emphasize concerns related to comfortable display. A case study on a popular e-commerce website of consumer products in Indonesia was taken to validate the proposed model. Through Structural Equation Modeling (SEM), it shows that affect was found to be more dominant than that of cognition in affecting to usability. In order to provide more applicable improvement strategy related to efficiency of display, eye tracking analysis was used. The analysis referred to metrics that have been designed in the research of Ehmke and Wilson [1] which focuses on the number of fixations and revisits in the Area of Interest (AOI). The most critical proposed improvement was that to change the location of the product price ordering menus so that they are adjacent to where the search results filter elements are located in that e-commerce website. Practical and theoretical implications were discussed as well.

Keywords: Affective · Cognitive · Usability · e-Commerce website · Kansei

1 Introduction

1.1 Background and Research Motivation

Both cognitive and affective process have been taken into account for both product and service interaction. It leads to the usability of product and service. Not only cognitive based, the product and service usability also consider the affect or emotional needs of customer. The cognitive aspect of usability is shown through ease of use, identification, download delay and trust, whereas the affective one is through colors, images, shapes, and perception of information system. Hence, a unified cognition and affect provides a comprehensive human information and processing system which leads to any forms of customer intention as a consequence.

Cognition alone is insufficient in representing a whole experience of customer interaction with product and services. Affect will complement this human-system interaction.

© The Author(s), under exclusive license to Springer Nature Switzerland AG 2022
N. L. Black et al. (Eds.): IEA 2021, LNNS 223, pp. 39–44, 2022.
https://doi.org/10.1007/978-3-030-74614-8_5

As a result, both affective and cognitive evaluation will bring more complete information for product and service development. According to Khalid and Helander [2], affect or Kansei will make judgement faster than cognition. For instance, affect will be responsible for assessing whether the environment is safe or dangerous. Cognition is quite related to formulation of meaning and beliefs due to perceived information.

As discussed earlier, usability is positioned to be a consequence due to complex process of cognition and affect in service or product interaction. A recent study by Prastawa et al. [3] tried to build a comprehensive model of affective process, cognitive process, and usability taking into account e-learning as the empirical study involving undergraduate students as respondent. However, the opportunities for conducting this study are still prospective. Limitations on the diverse of service settings and also the number of respondents motivate this current study. Hence, it is still quite interesting to explore more the interaction of affective-cognitive-usability (known as ACU model) incorporating different service settings as a way to investigate the generalization of the proposed model.

1.2 Problem Statement

Studies on the relationship between affective, cognitive, and usability (ACU) is still relatively rare. Recent study by Hartono and Raharjo [4] shows that affect (as represented by Kansei) and cognition have proportional weight on customer loyalty. Cognition here is represented by overall satisfaction due to rational assessment of perceived service quality. More specifically, Kansei and cognition account for 24% and 28%, respectively.

E-commerce website is a vital feature of online business information platforms, and it is full of complex customer mental process experience. Study by Prastawa et al. [3] shows that cognition is still found to be the primary determinant of usability. Once it is replicated to other product experience or service settings, the results could be different. Nevertheless, a study on ACU model in services is very potential to explore. Which one is more dominant whether cognitive or affective process in influencing the usability performance, is deemed to be quite interesting. It is especially for product or service designer in tackling issues on which product or service attributes are critical to customer.

1.3 Objective and Question

This study has two main objectives as follow. First, it is to examine and analyze the relationship among the constructs of affect, cognition, and usability (ACU) for e-commerce website of consumer products incorporating eye tracking analysis. A modified model of ACU (i.e., modification from [3] and an empirical study on a very popular e-commerce website in Indonesia) are reported. The second is that to formulate the improvement strategies for e-commerce website services based on the findings of path model above. Study on the investigation of e-commerce service attributes or components is interesting nowadays, especially in the pandemic since many people are involved in Work-from-Home (WfH) activities. It is so obvious the use of internet or online platform including e-commerce transaction is very intensive.

2 Methodology

This study applied survey interview and face-to-face questionnaire as a powerful research method in exploring framework [5] and proven effective [6, 7]. Convenience sampling was used. Adopting the previous A-C-U framework [3], there were 3 hypotheses:

H1: Cognition has positive impact on Affect at the e-commerce website transaction
H2: Affect has positive impact on Usability at the e-commerce website transaction
H3: Cognition has positive impact on Usability at the e-commerce website transaction

The respondents aged 19–24 years old with number of 56 subjects and were deemed sufficient for the Structural Equation Model Partial Least Square (SEM-PLS) [8] and with minimum of 39 sample [9]. The rationale is as follows. This is obtained from the average range of the number of samples needed to perform the analysis using the Structural Equation Model Partial Least Square (SEM-PLS) based on previous research. Based on previous research conducted by the Nielsen Norman Group, the minimum number of respondents in an eye tracking study in order to get stable results is 39 people. Thus, the determination of the number of samples of 56 people is deemed correct in conducting this research. This has also taken into account the possibility of failure in the recording of respondents in collecting eye tracking data.

The user being researched was given a task to do when the user accesses the e-commerce website which can be called a task. This task represents the core activity of e-commerce. The task is designed to create uniformity for all respondents who are tested using either the questionnaire method or eye tracking. The results of the questionnaire in the form of a Likert scale were analysed using the Structural Equation Model Partial Least Square (SEM-PLS) with the help of SmartPLS software. The results of data processing using the SmartPLS software answered the designed hypotheses.

3 Results

Using the SEM-PLS, the validity and reliability tests for the survey instrument were done. Through several iterations, the final path model was set, valid and reliable. It is shown in Fig. 1. The Goodness of Fit (GoF) of 0.8594 showed that the cognition and affect can explain 85.94% of the usability. All t-statistics values at all alternative hypotheses were greater than the significant value at the alpha of 5% (i.e., 1.96). The relationship between X1 and X2 is 10.59; between X1 to Y is 3.97; and between X2 to Y is 4.42, where these three values were greater than 1.96. This means reject H0. Thus, based on these results it can be concluded that the cognitive and affective aspects had a significant effect on user usability in using the e-commerce website.

Hence, both cognition and affect had a significant effect on the usability. It shows that affect was more dominant than cognition in affecting usability. In other words, in a case of e-commerce, affect was more important than that of cognition.

Through quadrant analysis, subjected to user perception and factor loading of structural model, there were two critical attributes, i.e., (i) The user is aware of any errors occurred, and (ii) The user can cancel any orders made. In formulating improvement

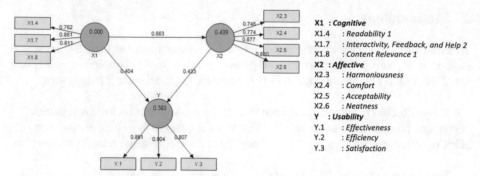

Fig. 1. A significant structural model Affective-Cognitive-Usability (ACU) in e-commerce website

strategy, eye tracking analysis was used according to the number of fixations and revisits in the Area of Interest (AOI). Both are related to error prevention.

4   Discussion

According to the findings of path model and hypotheses testing, cognition was proven significantly as the antecedent of affect. This confirms the previous study by Hartono and Tan [6]. Comparing the effect on usability, the affect construct was more dominant than that of the cognition. It was shown by the path coefficient of affect (0.433) which was higher than that of the cognition (0.404) on usability. It was unique and interesting since the respondents' rationale and feeling was proportional when it came to the case of e-commerce website.

More specifically, in the usability attribute "Efficiency – I can achieve my goals quickly and economically when using the e-commerce website" was critical. Indeed, both rationale and emotion were merged and equally important when it was dealing with e-commerce website experience. Afterward, through eye tracking, the details of problem related to fixations and revisits on area of interest (AOI) and how to solve it were formulized. The average fixations and revisits were deemed to be sufficient input for improvement. An example of AOI for a certain task related to variable "error prevention" is provided in Fig. 2.

The error prevention issue was becoming the prominent concern. Some proposed improvement strategies were as follow. First, to change the location of the product price ordering elements so that they are adjacent to where the search results filter elements are located. Second, to provide a list entry containing words that are close to the keyword when the user types the keyword in the search box. Third, to provide word suggestions in the error description in the form of correcting keywords that can be clicked directly to go to the search for that word. Fourth, to remove the "Other" element and position the order cancellation element which can be directly selected in the order list view. One example of a comparison between the existing and proposed condition is shown in Fig. 3.

This study has limitations at the relatively small sample size, service setting, and previous research studies on the similar topic.

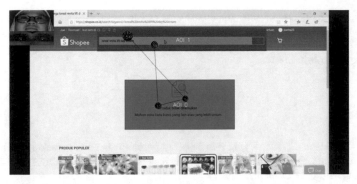

Fig. 2. AOI for task related to error prevention

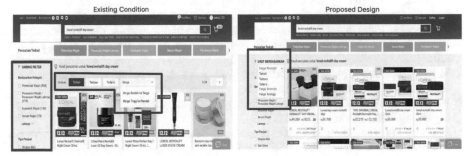

Fig. 3. A comparison between the existing condition and proposed design related to change of ordering and filtering product

5 Conclusion

This study has proposed and validated the model of affect, cognition, and usability (ACU) by taking into account an empirical study on e-commerce website of a popular business in Indonesia. It is hoped that the e-commerce service provider may use this study as a practical guidance for making their business more effectively and efficiently.

This research is expected to be useful for e-commerce companies and academics. For e-commerce companies, this study provides an illustration that the usability aspect of an e-commerce website is also part of the quality of the website, so it is important to pay attention to the website's performance in accordance with customer expectations as a user. The results of this study are also expected to provide guidelines or references for designers and developers of e-commerce websites in designing, developing and improving website designs so that they meet the usability aspect by paying attention to the cognitive and affective aspects. For the academic community, this research is expected to provide a reference on usability testing by considering cognitive and affective aspects which refer to the indicators of the Affective-Cognitive-Usability integration model through questionnaire instruments and eye tracking methods.

Acknowledgment. This study was supported by the research grant from the Ministry of Research and Technology/National Research and Innovation Agency of Republic Indonesia 2020 under scheme of Basic Research of Higher Education Excellence (PDUPT) with theme of Kansei Engineering for Robust Design.

References

1. Ehmke, C., Wilson, S.: Identifying web usability problems from eye-tracking data. In: People and Computers XXI HCI.But Not as We Know It - Proceedings of HCI 2007: The 21st British HCI Group Annual Conference (2007)
2. Khalid, H.M., Helander, M.G.: Customer emotional needs in product design. Concurr. Eng. Res. Appl. **14**(3), 197–206 (2006)
3. Prastawa, H., Ciptomulyono, U., Laksono-Singgih, M., Hartono, M.: The effect of cognitive and affective aspects on usability. Theor. Issues Ergon. Sci. **20**(4), 507–531 (2019)
4. Hartono, M., Raharjo, H.: Exploring the mediating role of affective and cognitive satisfaction on the effect of service quality on loyalty. Total Qual. Manag. Bus. Excell. **26**(9–10), 971–985 (2015)
5. Voss, C., Tsikriktsis, N., Frohlich, M.: Case study research in operations management. Int. J. Oper. Prod. Manag. **22**(2), 195–219 (2002)
6. Hartono, M., Tan, K.C.: How the Kano model contributes to Kansei Engineering in services. Ergonomics **54**(11), 987–1004 (2011)
7. Hartono, M.: The modified Kansei Engineering-based application for sustainable service design. Int. J. Ind. Ergon. **79**, 102985 (2020)
8. Ulum, M., Tirta, I.M., Anggraeni, D.: Analisis structural equation modeling (SEM) untuk sampel kecil dengan pendekatan partial least square (PLS). Prosiding Seminar Nasional Matematika Universitas Jember, pp. 1–15 (2014)
9. Nielsen, J.: How many test users in a usability study? (2012). https://www.nngroup.com/articles/how-many-test-users/

The Functions of Computer-Mediated Touch at a Distance: An Interactionist Approach

Robin Héron[(✉)], Stéphane Safin, Michael Baker, and Françoise Détienne

i3, UMR-9217 CNRS, Télécom Paris, Institut Polytechnique de Paris, Palaiseau, France
robin.heron@telecom-paris.fr

Abstract. Touch is essential in our relationships and social interactions. Our study aims at understanding the functions of touch as they are co-constructed in computer-mediated interaction. We observed three couples interacting during one hour at distance with a simple touch device. On the basis of an interactionist approach, we identified correspondences between touch occurrences and (a) the structure of the dialogue and (b) the emotional tonalities of the interaction. Our results highlight three types of functions of touch: interaction management (e.g., turn taking), emotional communication (e.g., emphasis) and behavioural touches (e.g., mimicry).

Keywords: Social touch · Affective communication · Emotion · Remote communication

1 Introduction

Touch is essential in our relationships and social interactions. In face-to face communication, touch can support several functions (positive affect, interaction rituals, etc.), depending on the context of interaction (Jones and Yarbrough 1985). Integrating touch and its emotional dimension has become an important issue in computer-mediated interaction research. So far, an "encoding-decoding paradigm" (positing direct relations between touch physical characteristics and its functions, such as the expression of particular emotions) has been dominant in the study of mediated social touch (van Erp and Toet 2015). Only a few studies have tested social touch devices in the context of human-human interaction (e.g. Park et al. 2013). Our research aims to understand the uses of touch devices and more specifically the functions of touch in computer-mediated interactions at a distance. The originality of our study is to adopt an interactionist approach according to which the meaning of touch emerges from social interaction. Our research questions concern the functions of touch related to (1) interaction structuring (e.g. turn-taking) and (2) the emotional tonalities of the interaction.

2 Social Touch and Mediated Touch

Social touch is crucial for our wellbeing. Evidence from different fields highlights the correlation between social touch behaviours and lower stress levels, heart rate, blood

© The Author(s), under exclusive license to Springer Nature Switzerland AG 2022
N. L. Black et al. (Eds.): IEA 2021, LNNS 223, pp. 45–53, 2022.
https://doi.org/10.1007/978-3-030-74614-8_6

pressure, and pain (Ditzen et al. 2007; Henricson et al. 2008). The lack of affective touch has also been correlated with depression, stress, and emotional awareness for adults (Floyd 2014). Given the important role of social touch, touch deprivation may have negative impact on psychological wellbeing (Field 2010).

Touch supports several functions in communication which can be grouped into 7 categories (Jones and Yarbrough 1985): Positive Affect, Playful, Control, Ritualistic, Hybrid, Task-related and Accidental. Nevertheless, even more so than for speech, the meaning of touch behaviours, is highly contextual. Personality, previous experiences, social conventions, the object or person providing the touch, all these factors and more are necessary to establish the meaning of touch behaviours (Huisman 2017). This means that the link between the forms and the functions of touch is not univocal: a given touch form (e.g., stroking, tapping, holding) can have various functions (see above), and a given touch function can be supported by various forms (Jones and Yarbrough 1985).

Research on touch often focusses on its ability to convey and elicit emotions, especially since the discovery of specialised afferents directly connected to the insular cortex where emotions are processed (McGlone et al. 2014). Touch is an effective medium to express a wide range of emotions: from positive emotions such as love, support and affection, to negative emotions such as anger, disappointment or frustration (Hertenstein et al. 2009; Bianchi-Berthouze and Tajadura Jimenez 2014).

Research on integrating touch into computer mediated communication, to support affective communication (e.g., Tsalamlal et al. 2013; Wilson and Brewster, 2017), has mostly investigated properties of communication in the laboratory. Only a few studies have tested prototypes of social touch in the context of human-human interaction. Chang et al. (2002), with ComTouch and Park et al. (2013), with POKE analysed phone interactions with the addition of the tactile modality. They identified different touch functions in interaction such as *emphasis* (touch patterns supporting speech to emphasise certain parts of the verbal message), *turn-taking* (particular tactile patterns were used, such as vibrations prior to speaking) and *mimicry* (exchange of similar vibrotactile patterns). They also reported the co-elaboration of vibrotactile codes.

To go further, we aim to explore the functions of touch emerging in the interaction with respect to the structure of the interaction, in particular interaction management, and to the content of the interaction, in particular its emotional tonalities.

3   An Interactionist Approach to Computer-Mediated Touch

In an "interactionist paradigm", the function (or meaning) of touch is contextual in an extended sense. It takes into account the dynamic evolution of the interaction context. Whereas this paradigm has been extensively used to understand the communicative functions of various modalities of communication (verbal, gestural...) it has not been developed for the tactile modality. We propose to adopt this approach to understand the functions of social touch co-constructed in the interaction. The meaning-making of touch can be viewed as interactively constructed through (1) interactive alignment (Garrod and Pickering 2009) – automatic alignment of para-verbal behaviour in the interaction (e.g., alignment of posture or speech rate) – and (2) grounding (Clark and Brennan 1991) – the interactive process by which communicators exchange evidence about what they do (not) understand over the course of a conversation, as they accrue common ground by a collaborative effort. – These processes are involved at different levels of communication, from the interaction itself (are the interactants willing or not to communicate) to meaning and language itself (e.g., construction of shared codes).

On the basis of this theoretical approach, we conducted a study to explore the functions of touch developed by three couples interacting at a distance. Couples were chosen as subjects given the broader range of touch functions that are possible and relevant for them, in comparison with acquaintances or strangers. Our focus is on the functions related to interaction management and to emotional content of the interaction. To do so, we developed a method to analyse the articulation between touch behaviours, paraverbal behaviours – in particular, indicators of emotion –, the structure of interaction (verbal turns) and the verbal content of the interaction.

4 Methodology

The study was carried out with three romantically involved couples communicating through a video call, with a simple touch device, *Sphero mini* (vibration and colour) that can be grasped in their hands and a smartphone used to control their partner's touch device at a distance (e.g., by making the partner's device vibrate, spin or change its colour: see Fig. 1). The experimentation took place at the participants' homes. Prior to the experimentation, the procedure was explained to the participants, they each read and filled out an informed consent form. They were then separated in different rooms sitting each in front of a desk with the laptop with the video call software open, the Sphero mini and a smartphone.

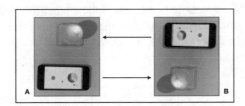

Fig. 1. Sphero mini and smartphone for participants A and B. Smartphone A is connected to Sphero mini B and Smartphone B to Sphero mini A.

The experimentation was divided into two phases (see Fig. 2). During the familiarisation phase, participants alternatively told the (abridged) story of their lives in no more than 10 min each. Participants could see and 'touch' each other with Sphero. However, only the storyteller could speak in order to encourage the participants to experiment with the device in a communication manner. During the collaborative remembering phase, both participants could speak and use the Sphero device to communicate. They alternatively presented artefacts related to past shared events to discuss for 20 to 30 min. These tasks (life story and collaborative remembering) were chosen given their potential for being emotionally heightened and thereby for stimulating touch interaction. During the week following the experiment, each participant was interviewed separately in an auto-confrontation setting (Mollo and Falzon 2004) to obtain his/her feedback on the meanings of touches in the exchanges.

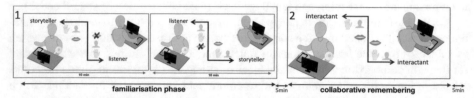

Fig. 2. Experimental setting – (1) the familiarisation and (2) the collaborative remembering phase, as well as two five-minute breaks to discuss the use of the touch device.

We selected excerpts (ranging from 60 to 120s) of the interaction following five principles: (1) recurring use of device in similar context, (2) intensive use of the device, (3) apparent understanding or misunderstanding of the use of the device, (4) rare way of using the device, and (5) verbalisation around the use of the device.

The video recordings were annotated with ELAN (a multimedia annotator, see https://tla.mpi.nl/tools/tla-tools/elan/). The annotations were done according to behavioural indicators, in order to identify the touch occurrences and the structure of the interaction: speech turns (temporal structure of the dialogue); and touch behaviours (occurrence and duration). Furthermore, we used verbal contents (transcript of the verbal exchange) and para-verbal behaviours to identify the content and emotional tonalities of the interaction. The follow-up interviews completed the analysis with participants' points of view on the interaction.

We then identified correspondences between touch occurrences and (a) the structure of the dialogue and (b) the emotional tonalities of the interaction. These analyses allowed the identification of touch functions within the excerpts. In this paper we only take account of the fact that touch behaviour has been produced or not (colour, intensity and duration are not reported).

5   Results

Overall, we identified various functions of touch belonging to the categories of interaction management, emotional interaction and behavioural (see Table 1).

The results of our analyses as well as the points of view of the participants highlighted specific ways of appropriating the touch expression device over time. Couple 1 appeared to be mostly using the device to convey positive affect and playfulness. Couple 2 mainly focused on behavioural touches – mainly doodle and the feeling of closeness. Couple 3 briefly constructed meanings around touch behaviours on which they had implicitly agreed as the interviews show a common understanding of the meaning of touch behaviour. Furthermore, all participants mentioned a stronger feeling of connectedness while using the device.

In the following subsections we present and illustrate those functions with verbatims. In the transcripts, '.' indicates a pause, '-' a lengthening, '[]' an overlap, and '()' gives further paraverbal information. Touch behaviours are represented by + in a grey line.

Table 1. Touch functions distribution for the 388 touch occurrences analysed (98 for C1, 149 for C2, 141 for C3). One touch occurrence can support more than one function (the total percentage by participant can be over 100%).

Interaction management	%C1	%C2	%C3	Emotional communication	%C1	%C2	%C3	Behavioural Touches	%C1	%C2	%C3
Turn-taking*	1,0	5,4	12,8	Emotional emphasis*✛	10,2	14,1	25,5	Doodle✛	–	29,5	–
Turn-giving*	4,1	2,0	5,0	Positive affect*✛	30,6	10,1	19,1	Mimicry✛	15,5	14,8	7,1
Continuer*	9,2	4,7	–	Playful interaction*✛	17,3	3,4	18,4	Closeness✛	3,1	20,1	4,3
Beat*	11,2	8,1	5,7	Treading carefully*✛	4,1	1,3	0,7				
Understanding*	2,0	1,3	5,7								

* correspondence analysis ✛ auto-confrontation interviews

5.1 Interaction Management

These touch functions are identified by making correspondences between touch occurrences and the structure of the interaction.

Turn-Taking. These touch behaviours are used by interactants to take the turn. Therefore, they are observed either before or at the beginning of their turns. They can overlap with the other interactant's turn.

> A   It was the first time I met your parents, who, surprisingly didn't make any joke.
> B   They were timid at the beginning. You didn't make any joke either did you ?
>   [Oddly]
> A   [Er-   ] no . I think I did not make any joke.
>   +++++

Turn-Giving. Speakers indicate that their turn is ended. Either they expect an answer to their question or they indicate that they do not have anything to add on the matter.

> A   Well yes but it was an exception
> B   Er no no . . you think so?
>   +++

Continuer. The listener gives backchannels to the speaker on his/her presence. The touch behaviours follow the rhythm of the speaker's verbal communication and occur mostly during his/her pauses and marks of hesitation.

> A   I don't know we had been in the flat for one month . A little less . An I don't know why I absolutely
> B   ++++++++++
> A   wanted us to- . Take a picture and immortalise this-
> B   ++++++++++++

Beat. These are rhythmic touch behaviours linked to the prosodic structure of speech, which do not convey any semantic information. Speakers touch at the rhythm of their own speech, mostly during pauses and marks of hesitation.

> B   It was the day when we found your- . polaroid camera I think . You took the well you found the
>   +++++++++++++++   ++
> B   polaroid camera and we had opened a box and you absolutely wanted to use it

Understanding. Sometimes interactants touch each other to manifest their agreement or common understanding. These touches are co-occurrent with moments of understanding or agreement marked with verbalisation or vocalisation such as "Oh right!" or "Ah!".

> B   It was like a sort of suit, er like with small shorts but in a rigid fabric you know
> A   Ah yes OK
>   +++++++
> B   Yes there so you see
>   +++++++

5.2 Emotional Communication

These touch functions are identified by making correspondences between touch occurrences and the emotional tonalities of the communication, as revealed by verbal content and para-verbal behaviours. In addition, the participants' points of view helped us disambiguate or render more precise certain functions.

Emotional Emphasis. Interactants tended to emphasise certain words or phrases bearing a strong emotional content, which can be positive (e.g., happiness, excitement) or negative (e.g., anger, sadness). Interactants can also emphasised laughs.

```
B    Since the beginning I think of all the first
B    times . But like it was also the first time a girl really . pissed me off you know!
     +++++++++++++++++++++++++++++++++++++++++++++++++++++++++++++++++++++
```

Positive Affect. Intentional communication of affect such as love, tenderness, support, etc. These touch behaviours can occur any time, and the meaning is accessed by paraverbal indicators, such as smile, gaze or prosody.

```
B    Actually, it's- a lot of memories with you. So it's cool
A    Ye-s
     (slow and rising intonation)
B    There's also Brazil . No it's not this one . There must be Cairo too
A    +++++++++++++
A    Ye-s
     (slow and rising intonation)
     ++++
```

Playful Interaction. Interactants highlight jokes, irony, teasing or play with touch behaviours.

```
A    Er let me talk . and I admit that I felt a little bit down
B    It's false . It's false . It's false
     (        robot voice        )
     ++++++  ++++++  ++++++
```

Treading Carefully. When the interactants broach a sensitive subject, especially when one of them feel guilty about their behaviour, touch is used simultaneously to speech while advancing cautiously into the conversation.

```
B    You were really angry with me. But for me it was well-intentioned . Not to- not to give any news
                                  +++++++++++++  ++++
B    Well it was not a good feeling but it was an impossibility you know
                                  +++++++
```

5.3 Behavioural Touches

We observed three other well-represented touch behaviours (see Table 1): mimicry – where participants touch alternatively or simultaneously in response to one another – 'doodle' – where participants use the device to scribble, as they would do with a pen or any other object, in a self-oriented manner – and closeness – touch behaviours maintaining a feeling of closeness between the participants, often explained as mimicking caresses. These functions emerge from our analysis of the interaction, combined with the participants' points of view on touch occurrences from the auto-confrontation interviews.

6 Discussion

In this article we highlighted a variety of functions supported by mediated touch which can be grouped into three categories: (1) interaction management touch, with functions such as turn-taking, beating time and continuer; (2) emotional communication touch, such as positive affect, emotional emphasis and playful interaction; (3) behavioural touch, such as doodle, mimicry and closeness. Our interviews allowed a better understanding of certain functions, especially regarding emotional communication, while participants were mostly not conscious of interaction management behaviours. Furthermore participants reported a better sense of connectedness with touch being included in distant computer-mediated interactions. They envisioned that they could use such a device when apart for a long period of time (e.g., work trip, holidays) as well as with close family members living far away (e.g., parents).

It is interesting to notice the transfer of functions from other modalities onto touch in mediated communication. Indeed we observed beat touch behaviours, which are usually supported by gestures in face-to-face communication. Similarly, turn management mechanisms usually rely on non-verbal behaviour (e.g., gaze) to succeed while our participants also used touch (Jokinen et al. 2010; Wagner et al., 2014).

While analysing the form of touch was not the focus of this paper, we noticed cases where the rhythm of touch and of speech aligned. Furthermore, the form of touch appears to be important for understanding certain functions: intensity, pace and colour were often reported by the participants in the interviews to explain their intentions. This was the case for *iconic* uses of the touch device. Participants took into account behavioural or emotional properties of the related stories and illustrated them with particular forms of touch. For instance, they could illustrate a dance move by vibrating at a certain rhythm and intensity, or anger by changing the colour to red and vibrating intensively. Participants also illustrated physical characteristics of scenes (e.g., changing the colour to green when talking about a story taking place in a wood). For these behaviours, colour choice appears to be central.

In future research, we aim to better understand the processes by which interactants co-construct these functions, by analysing the evolution over time of forms and functions in their dynamic contexts.

References

Bianchi-Berthouze, N., Tajadura Jimenez, A.: It's not just what we touch but also how we touch it. In: Workshop on Tactile User Experience Evaluation Methods, CHI 2014 (2014)

Chang, A., O'Modhrain, S., Jacob, R., Gunther, E., Ishii, H.: ComTouch: design of a vibrotactile communication device. In: Proceedings of the 4th Conference on Designing Interactive Systems: Processes, Practices, Methods, and Techniques, pp. 312–320, June 2002

Clark, H.H., Brennan, S.E.: Grounding in communication. In: Resnick, L.B., Levine, J.M., Teasley, S.D. (eds.) Perspectives on Socially Shared Cognition, pp. 127–149. American Psychological Association (1991)

Ditzen, B., Neumann, I.D., Bodenmann, G., von Dawans, B., Tuner, R.A., Ehlert, U., et al.: Effects of different kinds of couple interaction on cortisol and heart rate responses to stress in woman. Psychoneuroendocrinology **32**, 565–574 (2007)

Field, T.: Touch for socioemotional and physical well-being: a review. Dev. Rev. **30**(4), 367–383 (2010)

Floyd, K.: Relational and health correlates of affection deprivation. Western J. Commun. **78**(4), 383–403 (2014)

Garrod, S., Pickering, M.J.: Joint action, interactive alignment, and dialog. Top. Cogn. Sci. **1**(2), 292–304 (2009)

Henricson, M., Ersson, A., Määttä, S., Segesten, K., Berglund, A.L.: The outcome of tactile touch on stress parameters in intensive care: a randomized controlled trial. Complement. Ther. Clin. Pract. **14**(4), 244–254 (2008)

Hertenstein, M.J., Holmes, R., McCullough, M., Keltner, D.: The communication of emotion via touch. Emotion **9**(4), 566 (2009)

Huisman, G.: Social touch technology: a survey of haptic technology for social touch. IEEE Trans. Haptics **10**(3), 391–408 (2017)

Jokinen, K., Harada, K., Nishida, M., Yamamoto, S.: Turn-alignment using eye-gaze and speech in conversational interaction. In: Eleventh Annual Conference of the International Speech Communication Association, pp. 2018–2021, June 2010

Jones, S.E., Yarbrough, A.E.: A naturalistic study of the meanings of touch. Commun. Monogr. **52**(1), 19–56 (1985)

McGlone, F., Wessberg, J., Olausson, H.: Discriminative and affective touch: sensing and feeling. Neuron **82**(4), 737–755 (2014)

Mollo, V., Falzon, P.: Auto- and allo-confrontation as tools for reflective activities. Appl. Ergon. **35**(6), 531–540 (2004)

Park, Y.W., Baek, K.M., Nam, T.J.: The roles of touch during phone conversations: long-distance couples' use of POKE in their homes. In: Proceedings of the SIGCHI Conference on Human Factors in Computing Systems, pp. 1679–1688, April 2013

Tsalamlal, M.Y., Ouarti, N., Martin, J.C., Ammi, M.: EmotionAir: perception of emotions from air jet based tactile stimulation. In: 2013 Humaine Association Conference on Affective Computing and Intelligent Interaction, pp. 215–220, September 2013

van Erp, J.B.F., Toet, A.: Social touch in human-computer interaction. Front. Digital Humanit. **2**, 2 (2015)

Wagner, P., Malisz, Z., Kopp, S.: Gesture and speech in interaction: an overview. Speech Commun. **57**, 209–232 (2014)

Wilson, G., Brewster, S.A.: Multi-moji: combining thermal, vibrotactile & visual stimuli to expand the affective range of feedback. In: Proceedings of the 2017 CHI Conference on Human Factors in Computing Systems, pp. 1743–1755, May 2017

Merging Total Design and User Centered Design for Designing a Mountable Toy: Achieving a Useful, Functional and Desirable Product

Julieta María Covarrubias Cruz, María Fernanda De La Rocha Barbosa,
Fernanda Santos Rivera, and Pilar Hernández-Grageda(✉)

Universidad Panamericana Campus Guadalajara, Calzada Circunvalación Poniente N. 49,
Zapopan, Mexico
{0196289,0198763,0200515,phernand}@up.edu.mx

Abstract. Through a hybrid design model that fuses key elements of the Total Design and User Centered Design approach and focusing on the safety of the child in and out of the water, cooperative socialization and a timeless life cycle as main design aspects, we developed a terrestrial-aquatic ride on toy proposal which generates feelings of attachment, unforgettable memories and an emotional bond with the product. Playing is extremely essential for fulfilling early childhood development needs and ride on toys promote a complete socialization in early stages. We accomplished all design requirements with this new hybrid design methodology centered both in the user and in the functional value of the product; resulting in a product that enhances a strong emotional bond and a better life cycle, achieving a desirable, useful and valuable product.

Keywords: User Centered Design · Total design · Ride on toy · Socialization through play · Product life cycle · Design methodology

1 Introduction

Technology has represented a great change for society, which has generated the need to solve new design problems through creative, innovative, viable and sustainable solutions [1]. When talking about possible design methods to consider when creating a new product, it is known that when used separately they can have their own limitations.

The Total Design method is based on systematized activities that help to detect market needs in order to turn them into required specifications that the new product must meet, generating a variety of alternatives through conceptual proposals whose value will be calculated using an evaluation matrix, which will determine the one that provides the greatest functional value, detailing it later to reach the manufacturing stage and delivery to the final user [2, 3]. The User Centered Design approach provides guidelines so that the product or system being designed reaches usability standards based on the understanding of the users, the context in which the product will be used and the tasks that will promote interaction between the user and the product [4]. In addition, User Centered Design promotes a co-creation process or a participatory process, where the user is taken into account during the design process [5].

Taking into account the best of both methodologies, a hybrid model is proposed in which the technical and the empirical are merged, counteracting the limitations of each method and causing "the stimulation of creativity in design solutions" [1].

The objective of this work is to structure and test a new replicable design methodology for future projects with a user-centered approach and functional value, through the unification of key elements of already established design processes, with the aim to achieve a product that is desirable, useful and valuable.

To evaluate the proposed hybrid model, a current problem that arises from the impact of new technologies on traditional or "non-digital" toys was considered, since these have been left aside because children are changing at the same rate as technology. A traditional toy provides cognitive and emotional learning that technology cannot replace. These toys are essential to promote social relationships, by sharing moments and emotions, a complete socialization process is generated [6]. By promoting cooperative social interaction, the user will associate his product with different people or events; in such a way that, over time, it will become inseparable for the owner until it becomes irreplaceable [7]. That is why we have focused on the development of a mountable toy with two modes of use, which does not include advanced technology for the performance of its functions, but is capable of providing the necessary innovation to ensure user fun. In our design process, the principles of social integration, emotional value of the product and life of the product were taken as the guiding principle.

2 Method

The hybrid design model that was followed throughout this work is made up of seven main stages, as seen in Fig. 1, merging the key elements of Total Design's engineering approach and the focus on users through the co-creation of the User Centered Design methodology. The main stages are: *Empathy*: delimits the final user; *Define*: market determination and design specifications; *Ideate*: conception of multiple conceptual designs that comply with the list of specifications to qualify them through the Evaluation Matrix and identify the "ideal" proposal; *Prototype*: presentation of preliminary design proposal; *Feedback*: validation of the preliminary design proposal through usability tests; *Reflection*: identify and prioritize problems in the user experience to make adjustments in the product design. And, as a result of the previous six steps, the hybrid design process ends with a *final Prototype*, which is a design ready for manufacture and delivery to its end user.

2.1 Empathy: Define the Final User

Based on three known empathy tools, IDEO Method Cards, personal interviews and an Empathy map, it was possible to define who the final user would be.

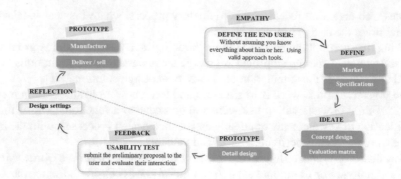

Fig. 1. Hybrid design model. The steps proposed by User-Centered Design are highlighted in yellow and the stages proposed by Total Design are highlighted in blue.

Two main categories of the IDEO Method cards were used in order to get to know our user: Learn and Look. For the Learn category, findings were obtained through Secondary research, which consisted of researching articles based on four keywords: design of aquatic toys, socialization through play, emotional bonding and longevity of toys. In addition, with Character profiles, a group of children was observed: Paula (7 years old), Matías (5 years old), Nicolás (10 years old), Sebastián (4 years old), Vannya (5 years old), to develop worksheets of possible users. Finally, Activity Analysis gave us a list of actions that a child could carry out when interacting with a rider: visual attraction, approaching, touching it, looking for extra elements, mounting it, handling it, getting off and leaving the rider anywhere. As for the Look category, the findings were obtained from A day in the life, Rapid Ethnography, and Fly on the wall. These observation methods highlighted the children's interest in collaborative games, without influencing their performance despite their difference in age and preferences.

Personal interviews were conducted with Paula, Nicolás and Matías, with questions mainly focused on their opinion about aquatic environments, highlighting the social relations that can be achieved when playing among friends. At this point, it was clear that what makes an aquatic experience memorable for the kids is the presence of their friends and having aquatic toys to play. Figure 2 shows the Empathy map created at the end of the previously mentioned observing exercises. This tool is known for helping to detect opportunity areas that can be taken into account through the design process, in this case for improving social abilities and personal skills.

The ideal user of our product is a child between 4 to 7 years old, with an interest in the use of toys that promote cooperative social interaction and physical activity, who has basic skills in the practice of swimming and recreational activities in pools and with a developed level of gross motor skills that allows it to execute muscular movements necessary to propel the product in the aquatic and terrestrial environment.

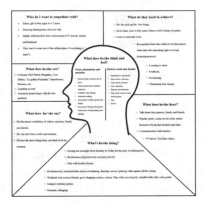

Fig. 2. Empathy Map, through which we answered the question "Who is the user who will interact with my mountable toy?"

2.2 Define

A benchmark analysis was conducted by comparing ten mountable toys that already exist in the market, including physical stores and online selling (see Fig. 3). Even though the selected products were the ones that best met the characteristics of our final users, at this point it was noticed that there are no mountable toys for children between 4 and 7 years' old that can be used in different environments, that can be shared at the same time among users and that can be customized.

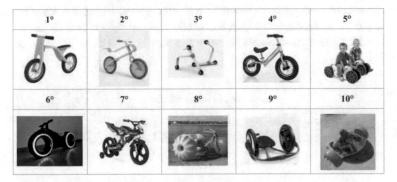

Fig. 3. The 10 mountable toys selected for Market Analysis and Specification Identification are displayed.

A list of the main fifteen characteristics or requirements identified among the ten selected products from the market was determined; this list pretends to become a baseline for the future design proposal: height, handling or support for the hands, seat, resistant materials, nontoxic materials, an easy to clean surface, intuitive, anatomic adjustments, technological implementation, customizable, easy or safe to ride on, propitiate socializing, thematic, not so heavy and curved edges.

2.3   Ideate: Conceptual Proposals and Evaluation Matrix

Nine proposals for mountable toys were created including all the characteristics and specifications that we seek for our product, selecting the ideal one from among those nine. This ideal proposal was compared with the rest and they were evaluated using the following criteria for each requirement: if it is better than the ideal product (+), or less than the ideal product (−) and the S was used to indicate that it is similar to the ideal product. At the end of the evaluation, a total sum of each aspect (+, −, S) was made in order to obtain the results. The toys that reflected high scores in the sum of more and similar represent strong characteristics to implement in our preliminary design proposal. This objective method is optimal for making decisions that, by comparing against an ideal, help the designer to consider the most useful properties for product design.

2.4   Prototype: Preliminary Proposal

Three "hybrid" proposals were created by combining some of the conceptual models, together with the ideal model and with the results of the evaluation matrix. These proposals served as a starting point to reach the preliminary proposal.

   Yellow Marine is a mountable toy that can be used in double terrain, land and water, and allows the transport of two children. Its shape is inspired by submarines and it was sought to be something attractive for children 4–7 years old.

2.5   Feedback

As the conceptual proposal continued to improve, a redesign stage was reached focused on user experience, design requirements, and user needs. Using the User Experience Map tool, the possible emotions that the product could arouse and its usability were analyzed and the interaction points between the user and the conceptual proposal were validated (Fig. 4).

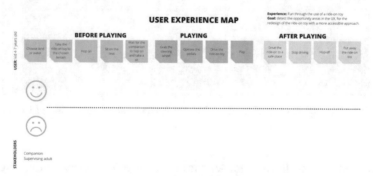

Fig. 4. User Experience Map. Its objective was to detect the opportunity areas in the interaction with our preliminary proposal, for the redesign of the mountable.

   It was also necessary to validate the user experience, and it was done through seven important factors given by Peter Morville's honeycomb model [8]. The first one refers to the purpose or benefits that our product offers; make it useful. The second is that it is usable, which indicates that the product through its efficiency and effectiveness allows the user to meet the expected objectives. The third is that it is usable; the elements and instructions should be easy to identify. The fourth factor is to be credible, build trust in the product and that it lasts for a reasonable time. The fifth one is to make our product preferable over others; desirable. The sixth covers accessibility; allowing the experience to be enjoyed by users with broad abilities and even disabilities. Finally, the seventh, is to deliver value to the user. Knowing the objective of each of these seven factors is a great starting point to ideate seven questions focused on obtaining the information that ensures an improvement in the interaction of the user and our product. These questions were used as a reminder to later validate that the final product answered each of them.

2.6 Reflection

The Lightning Decision Jam tool was used with the intention of detecting those details where the product still had opportunities for improvement, which is displayed in Fig. 5. In this particular case, the tool was used to analyze interaction aspects and the user experience. Once the areas of opportunity have been identified, they are prioritized and then turned into challenges and possible solutions. Finally, they are categorized by priority level, thus establishing the tasks and actions to be carried out within the design team.

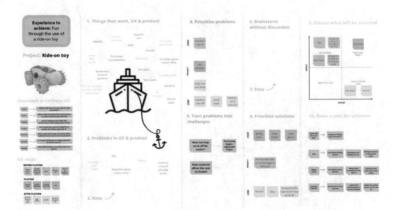

Fig. 5. Lightning Decision Jam. It shows the procedure we followed to analyze the areas of opportunity and prioritize their importance.

3 Results

As a result of extensive research and application of the hybrid design method, a final proposal of *Yellow Marine* was reached.

Yellow Marine is a submarine-inspired mountable toy, with capacity for one or two users from 4 to 7 years old. It has a bioplastic structure (PLA) that allows it to be used in double areas: land and water. Its main components are: a rudder to give direction, a brake lever, two pairs of pedal boats, four wheels that combine the shape of a tire and the propellers of a hydraulic mill to ensure use in double terrain, two aligned seats of waterproof fabric, two steps, an adjustable surface anchoring mechanism and a customizable plate that allows the user to create a broad bond with the product (Fig. 6).

After evaluating the areas of opportunity for the ride-on toy, it was decided to keep the concept and the modalities of use: off-road. It was also decided to follow the line of the intuitive and desirable, so that, through the experience, an emotional bond, social interaction and longevity of the product could be achieved. The added value of the proposal is that currently no mountable can be used in double terrain and most only allow the individual use of the product; they do not contribute to socialization.

Yellow Marine works with a hydro-pedal mechanism and is given direction through a rudder. The materials used in its structure such as plastic and waterproof fabric guarantee safety and thus extend the longevity of the toy. It has four tires, two seats, two pairs of pedals, the rudder and a customizable plate that allows the user to create a broad bond with the product.

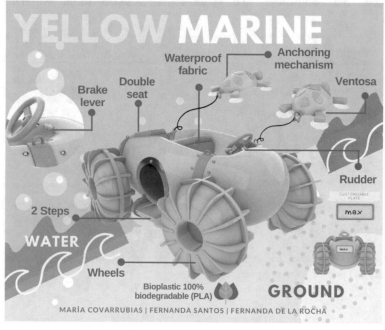

Fig. 6. The final proposal of *Yellow Marine* with its components and main features.

4 Conclusion

By carrying out the proposed hybrid methodology, designers obtain global knowledge about their user and the user experience offered by their product, and at the same time this methodology provides the tools to develop a product with a functional value greater than that obtained by using a non-hybrid methodology.

Therefore, we can suggest that this hybrid model could be used in the design of other products, as long as the purpose of the designer is based on the understanding of its user through the application of different tools, to satisfy their needs adequately. It is extremely important to take into account that, throughout the process, nothing is taken for granted, but rather that each stage is carried out consciously and being open to the different possibilities that may arise during the design process.

References

1. Cantú Hinojosa, L.: Desgin methods and their limitations in the creative phase from Portsmouth to the Design Thinking (2014). https://eprints.uanl.mx/5859/1/metodos_de_diseno.pdf
2. Pugh, S.: Integrated Methods for Successful Product Engineering. Addison-Wesley, New Jersey (1990)
3. Flaschner, A.: Creating innovative products using total design: the living legacy of Stuart Pugh. J. Prod. Innov. Manag. **3**, 233–235 (1997)
4. Huang, P.-H., Chiu, M.-C.: Integrating user centered design, universal design and goal, operation, method and selection rules to improve the usability of DAISY player for persons with visual impairments. Appl. Ergon. **52**, 29–42 (2016)
5. Veryzer, R., Borja de Mozota, B.: The impact of user-oriented design on new product development: an examination of fundamental relationships. J. Prod. Innov. Manag. **22**, 128–143 (2005)
6. De la Rosa, A.B.: El juguete tecnológico transporta a los niños a una falsa realidad (2019). https://www.magisnet.com/2019/el-juguete-tecnologico-transporta-a-los-niños-a-una-falsa-realidad/
7. Mugge, R., Schoormans, J.P., Schifferstein, H.N.: The value of toys: 6–8 year-old children's toy preferences and the functional analysis of popular toys. Int. J. Play **5**, 11–27 (2016)
8. Morville, P., Sullenger, P.: Ambient findability: libraries, serials, and the internet of things. Serials Librarian **58**, 33–38 (2010)

Behavioral and Cognitive Methods to Assess Users and Assist Physical Point of Sale Experience Design

Paulo Eduardo Hauqui Tonin$^{(\boxtimes)}$ ⏺

Universidade do Estado de Santa Catarina, Florianópolis, Brazil

Abstract. The rise of digital stores and new shopping formats require designers and retailers to rethink the role of physical point of sale and the experience they offer to users. According to some reports on consumer behavior, carried out by Global Data in 2017, physical stores, when compared to the digital ones, have been losing significant space in people's daily lives in the last decade, seen by many as the era of the customer. Inadequate to the current users' needs, many brands that still offer traditional experiences at their stores and not take into account, for instance, sensory stimulation and technology, end up becoming obsolete and having difficulty navigating in the current fast-moving market. Now with the recent Coronavirus pandemic situation, consumers seem to have drastically shifted to e-commerce since online shopping appears to be the safest and fastest way to purchase goods or services. This exploratory research seeks to investigate and compare, in the existing literature, both in human factors and in related areas, the main cognitive and behavioral methods that can be applied in the evaluation of users as in the process of designing experience at the physical point of sale.

Keywords: Cognitive ergonomics · Experience design · Human centered design · Retail · User experience

1 Introduction

1.1 Problem Statement

Attracting and retaining customers, in this new consumption scenario, is a difficult task for companies, which still seek to understand the best way to work with the concept of Omnichannel, an expression used for the multichannel shopping experience, which crosses physical and virtual environments [1]. According to a report on consumer habits prepared in 2017 by Global Data, only 5.8% of customers, in 2011, preferred virtual stores. In 2016, the number increased to 9.2% and in 2021, the estimate was 13.3% However, the estimate did not take into account an important aggravating factor: the Covid-19 pandemic. Numerous articles have been showing the impact of the event on consumer behavior, so the previous estimate of 13.3% is expected to increase considerably, since the event has limited and modified consumption patterns throughout the world [2, 3].

© The Author(s), under exclusive license to Springer Nature Switzerland AG 2022
N. L. Black et al. (Eds.): IEA 2021, LNNS 223, pp. 62–70, 2022.
https://doi.org/10.1007/978-3-030-74614-8_8

1.2 Objective/Question

For many reasons, such as convenience, users who used to buy at physical points of sale seem to have migrated to digital. In order to guarantee permanence and interest in physical stores in the midst of a precisely digital moment, any and all design practices must be entirely aimed to users [4]. Understanding, therefore, the best methods to evaluate users and assist the experience design of the physical point of sale is of utmost importance. What are the best ergonomic methods for understanding user behavior in retail environments and, therefore, offering an experience aligned to their real needs?

1.3 Methodology

The present study is characterized as an exploratory research, which intends to raise information and formulate problems regarding the phenomenon. Bibliographic research, as a data collection technique, seeks to provide the necessary theoretical framework to understand what the experience design at the physical point of sale consists of, usability (satisfaction) and decision-making (purchasing) as well as the ergonomics and its cognitive and behavioral methods. Based on the methods presented by Stanton et al. [5], those with relevance for application in this specific case are selected. Subsequently, the information obtained is crossed with two studies involving human factors and the evaluation of users in the retail environment. The methods with a strong indication are then discussed and compared, as well as possible future investigations on the subject are suggested.

2 Human Factors in the Retail Environment

2.1 Experience Design and Its Relations Between Store Image, Usability and Decision Making

By analyzing the complexity of consumer behavior throughout their shopping journey, Experience Design works with the store's image and allows them to develop strategies that involve winning over users during their stay at physical or virtual points of sale, increasing the possibility of conversion or purchase and satisfaction (see Fig. 1). In order to compete with online retailers, physical stores have to focus on their main advantages and emphasize what they do best, that is, highlight their positive attributes in their image. The image of a store consists of a complex of attributes such as layout and architecture, symbols and colors, advertising and sales people. Consumers frequent stores whose image is congruent with their self-perceptions and unconscious needs and therefore the store's image influences their shopping behavior [6].

In its ISO 9241, the International Organization of Standardization defines usability as the effectiveness, efficiency and satisfaction with which specific users can achieve certain objectives in a given context. The levels of effectiveness and efficiency of a product or service directly influence the degree of user satisfaction; and despite this influence, satisfaction can be treated independently [7]. Satisfaction concerns the degree of comfort that users feel when they use the product or service, how much they consider it appropriate as a means to achieve their goals and therefore determines customer loyalty; in other words, it is what makes them come back or not.

Certain factors such as intuition, rationality and perception can influence a decision. Intuition is born out of experience and feelings about sensory stimuli. The main difference between digital and physical point of sale is precisely the possibility that the second one has of offering shopping experiences capable of exploring the senses and consequently influencing (purchasing) decision-making [8]. For ergonomics, decision-making is the process of choosing one among a set of alternatives and it is up to the decision maker: 1 - to recognize and diagnose the situation; 2 - generate alternatives; 3 - evaluate the alternatives, 4 - select the best alternative, 5 - implement the chosen alternative and 6 - evaluate the results [9, 10].

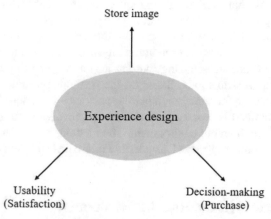

Fig. 1. Relations between experience design, usability and decision-making. Source: Elaborated by the Author.

2.2 Behavioral and Cognitive Methods

Cognitive and behavioral methods have their original foundation in the disciplines of psychology. These user assessment methods or techniques provide information about the perceptions, cognitive processes and potential responses of individuals. The information obtained is perceived through sensory systems, which influence the way the user interacts with the task, its decision-making and satisfaction [11]. The fifteen cognitive and behavioral methods listed by Stanton et al. are classified into four groups: 1 - General Analysis Methods, 2 - Cognitive Task Analysis Methods; 3 - Error Analysis Methods; 4 - Methods of Situational Analysis and Mental Load. For the present study, the groups of General Analysis Methods and Cognitive Task Analysis Methods were considered. Groups 3 and 4 despite being flexible and adaptable to the investigations that are intended, refer much more specifically to users as workers and their relations with the workplace, their tasks and tools [5].

From the groups considered, the methods related to usability and decision-making were selected, assuming that these, as they deal with consumer satisfaction and the conversion or purchase at the physical point of sale, are the most relevant in investigations involving retail environments. Taking into account the characteristics that determined the selection, the methods that were analyzed in this study are: 1 - Interview, 2 - Verbal Protocol, 3 - Repertory Grid, 4 - Focus Groups, 5 - HTA (Hierarchical Task Analysis), 6 - CDM (Critical Decision Method) and 7 - ACWA (Applied Cognitive Work Analysis). The first four belonging to the General Analysis Methods group and the last three to the Cognitive Task Analysis Methods group.

2.3 Former Studies on the Phenomenon

Palací et al. [12], in a systematic review of research approaches for the assessment of cognitive and affective antecedents related to consumer satisfaction in retail environments, gathered 104 studies involving different ways of measuring user satisfaction in both physical and virtual environments. Studies, published between 1975 and 2014, show that both cognitive and affective aspects are statistically significant precursors of satisfaction. For the present exploratory research, the instruments used to measure consumer satisfaction in the studies presented were analyzed. Among the 104 articles considered, approximately 80% refer to questionnaires developed especially for each specific case. Involving different retail areas, the questionnaires were applied to users and employees from shoe stores and dealerships to restaurants and gyms. The other 20% concentrate on studies in which it was not possible to identify the tool used for data collection and also two cases where the information was obtained from user reviews on digital platforms, such as *TripAdvisor*. These services have a comment section for consumers, who are encouraged to openly share their impressions and opinions about products and services.

In a review of the contribution of the discipline of human factors in the physical and digital commercial environment, Kim and Kim [13] brought together 49 studies in a state-of-the-art summary table dealing with factors related to man and retail. From the information obtained through the studies gathered by the authors, between 1975 and 2011, the research methods used in each case were considered. The methods that stood out in number of applications were experiments (21 studies) and questionnaires (17 studies). Experiments are surveys in which the researcher manipulates and controls one or more variables to capture cause and effect relationships. In the retail environment, the experiments can be applied as market tests, where researchers go to the field to understand consumer behavior in real situations. These experiments can bring together a set of other methods and tools, which were not specified in the synthesis presented by Kim and Kim. Questionnaires are commonly used in the evaluation of the consumer experience, as we saw in the other study previously presented, especially because they mainly reach a wide spectrum of people in a short period of time. Other methods, such as focus groups and interviews, have been applied in only two studies. Conceptual framework and observation, one study each (see Fig. 2).

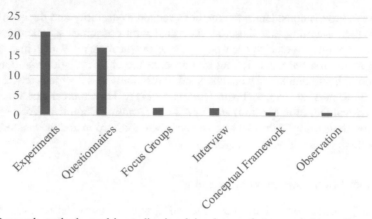

Fig. 2. Research methods used in studies involving human factors and the retail environment. Source: Elaborated by the author based on the synthesis presented by Kim and Kim [13].

3   Results

As existing behavioral and cognitive methods were raised, it was realized that some of them focus on the relationship between humans and their jobs, meaning that they were originally created to understand users as workers or operators. The fact that some methods were not created based on the users' understanding as consumers did not prevent them from being considered relevant for this study. In fact, some methods, such as focus groups, are multidisciplinary and commonly used in other areas of knowledge and research, for instance, marketing and social sciences. From the research, it was possible to highlight methods that can significantly contribute to the process of designing experiences in physical commercial spaces. Some methods with strong indication, others with less. It was also realized that no single method could collect all the necessary information from these relationships with consumers and physical stores.

To achieve significant results it would be interesting to carry out a combination of methods, personalized and related to the brand, its target audience and the product it sells. The following methods have no indication for usability (satisfaction) evaluation: Observation, Verbal Protocol, HTA and CDM. For decision-making (conversion into purchase), the Observation and Repertory Grid methods are not indicated. The focus group and ACWA method are strongly indicated for the investigation of usability while for the decision-making the CDM is indicated [5]. Table 1 shows a comparison between the cognitive and behavioral methods considered in the present study, containing their advantages and disadvantages. When crossing the information obtained by surveying the existing methods and those that are commonly used in research involving the evaluation of users as consumers and the presence of human factors in the retail environment, we realize that few are explicitly applied. Although they may be present in some way in the experiments conducted, it is still undetermined how they are contributing to user experience investigations at physical points of sale. Questionnaires remain a multidisciplinary method with easy application and relevant validity, however, for the most part, they are unable to establish empathy with the user as the ergonomic methods that deal with mental processes and responses are capable of.

Table 1. Advantages and disadvantages of cognitive and behavioral methods for the assessment of factors related to usability and decision-making.

Method	Advantages	Disadvantages
Interview	Commonly known by the participants, flexible, consistent and meticulous when structured	Analysis can be time-consuming. If the characteristics of the demand are not well defined, they can lead to misleading results
Verbal Protocol	Rich source of data in quantity and content. Especially good at investigating behaviors in natural environments and sequentially analyzing activities	Data collection and analysis is often time consuming. Some theoretical issues related to verbal reports do not necessarily correlate with the knowledge used in performing tasks
Repertory Grid	Structured and comprehensive procedure. Manual analysis does not require statistics, but it does provide "reasonable" results	Analysis can be tedious and time-consuming for large sets of items. The procedure does not always produce considerable factors
Focus Groups	Group interviews allow researchers to gather a large number of opinions quickly. In focus groups, respondents can also provide support to each other to say things that they would not otherwise be willing to discuss on their own with an interviewer	Conducting group interviews and analyzing the data can be time consuming. Requires extensive planning and an experienced moderator. The lack of standardization raises concerns about reliability
Hierarchical Task Analysis (HTA)	In addition to being an adaptable method, it allows the analysis of the task at different levels, depending on the purpose. When used correctly, HTA provides a thorough analysis of the problem addressed	It requires treatment by a well-trained analyst in a variety of methods of data collection and in relevant human factor principles, as well as full collaboration of stakeholders

(continued)

Table 1. (*continued*)

Method	Advantages	Disadvantages
Critical Decision Method (CDM)	Detailed interactive structure of real critical incidents that allows to identify influences and strategies in subtle aspects of the experience. Cognitive surveys and hypothetical queries used to capture and recognize decision-making processes	Uncertain reliability because it deals with retrospective incidents, which may change due to evidence of memory degradation over time for critical events and details of those events
Applied Cognitive Work Analysis (ACWA)	Perspective centered on the decision and, therefore, able to offer support in unforeseen situations and also in expected situations. It guarantees the traceability of the design elements to the cognitive requirements they must support, that is, to understand how one thinks during the decision-making and planning process	It requires comprehensive analysis and documentation of domain demands and decision support system requirements, as well as specific training to apply the method

Source: Elaborated by the author based on Stanton et al. [5]

4 Discussion

Since ergonomics is the science that studies the relationship between human beings and a specific object (product, service, environment and others), cognitive ergonomics, an emerging branch of ergonomics, is related to the emotional performance and responses or mental processes of users to a particular situation [14, 15]. That is exactly why the understanding of cognitive ergonomics and its methods combined with the concept of user experience are relevant to this research. Much is known about consumer behavior when exposed to virtual shopping environments, such as e-commerce and websites; however, the same is not true for physical stores. The bibliography lacks applications for the type of situation and interface that this research seeks, which is ergonomics as a basis for understanding human beings as consumers and their relationship with physical stores. Human factors' behavioral and cognitive methods can be of great value in evaluating users' experiences at physical points of sale, mainly because this environment often involve sensory stimuli that cannot be transmitted through a computer or a smartphone screen [16].

In e-commerce, although visually stimulated through laws and principles of good design, such as the laws of Hick and Fitt, the senses are not captured in the way that physical retail environments do. If only questionnaires are applied or observations are conducted to collect information, the user is not being involved in the process of creating the shopping experience offered at the store. Even though the questionnaires statistically fulfill what is expected in a consumer behavior survey and use scales, such as Likert's, which allow a closer approximation to users' cognitive responses; they do not establish the empathy that other methods, previous presented in this study, are capable of [17]. Although the collection of information on the cognitive and behavioral methods is lower in numbers and may be time consuming, they certainly have a higher quality of information, since they bring the user to the center of the process of understanding their behavior.

With a strong indication for the investigation of usability (satisfaction), the focus group is an extension of the individual interview with a long tradition in market research and product design [5]. This method recreates scenarios and investigates behavior using other activities as support, including storyboarding and brainstorming, just as Design Thinking does. The critical decision method or CDM can clearly map and identify the decision-making (purchasing) process. It is known that the method was developed to analyze specialists and novices when dealing with tasks and critical incidents related to their jobs; however, one cannot help but notice its potential for use in investigations involving consumers in retail environments. As the method makes a temporal and sequential recap of real incidents, with some adaptations it can understand crucial factors in the user's journey inside the store. Other methods, such as the verbal protocol and the hierarchical task analysis (HTA), can also deal with the consumers' journey, because together with observation they can assume the creation of hypothetical scenarios that help in understanding the real mental processes of the evaluated users. As they basically require a pen, paper and some audio/video recorder, all the methods presented can be easily applied. However, some of the methods require specific training, such as the cognitive work analysis method (ACWA); which can make it difficult to access users and consequently obtain the necessary information for the design of the experience.

5 Conclusion

Based on the assumption that this study understands users as consumers, the choice of relevant methods has become easier, since some of them are preferably used in the investigation of man-work relationships, which is commonly attributed to ergonomics. As there is no ideal method of collecting information from users for this type of situation and interface, it is advisable to carry out further research on the topic. Such research can address, for instance, the contribution of psychophysiological methods (not covered in this study) as well as suggest new methods for the analysis of human factors in the retail environment. These studies can effectively contribute to the understanding of users' needs and behavior at physical stores, helping to create relevant and memorable shopping experiences, thus ensuring the importance and relevance of physical points of sale in the digital age.

It is important to note that most of the relationships that are intended to be investigated, not only in what applies to the theme of this study, require not only one but a combination of two or more methods. This combination of methods is based on the advantage of data crossing and its validation based on the variety, since different methods can generate different results and consequently contribute to the quality of the information collected. Selecting the appropriate set of methods requires the analyst to carefully define the purpose of the analysis. With this study it can be concluded that, although they need to be adjusted to the reality of phenomena, cognitive and behavioral methods can be of great contribution in assessing people's behavior in commercial environments, since they access consumers' thoughts with empathy and ethic. Understanding the purchase journey and its satisfaction and decision-making processes is essential to offer an experience aligned to the current consumers's needs. Design is about people, and especially in environments that involve their senses, as is the case with physical stores, it is extremely important that users are at the center of the process of creating the shopping experience that the brand wants to offer its customers [18].

References

1. Kent, T.: Creative space: design and the retail environment. Int. J. Retail Distrib. Manag. **35**(9), 734–745 (2007)
2. Solanki, A., Nelson, A., Saunders, N.: As shopping behaviors evolve, the retail experience must follow best practices for shifting to an experience-per-square-foot business strategy. Colliers International & Global Data, Toronto (2017)
3. Solanki, A., Nelson, A., Saunders, N.: Why online isn't the end of the physical retail store: myths, misconceptions and opportunities. Colliers International & Global Data, Toronto (2017)
4. Lewis, R., Dart, M.: The New Rules of Retail: Competing in the World's Toughest Marketplace. Palgrave Macmillan, New York (2014)
5. Stanton, N.A., Hedge, A., Brookhuis, K., Salas, E., Hendrick, H.: Handbook of Human Factors and Ergonomic Methods. CRC Press, Boca Raton (2006)
6. Mondal, S., Mall, M., Mishra, U.S., Sahoo, K.: Investigating the factors affecting customer purchase activity in retail stores. Revista Espacios **38**(57), 22–44 (2017)
7. Jordan, P.W.: An Introduction to Usability. CRC Press, Boca Raton (1998)
8. Chater, N., Huck, S., Inderst, R.: Consumer decision-making in retail investment services: a behavioural economics perspective. Online Interactive Research Ltd., London (2010)
9. Bertoncini, C.O., Brito, A., Silva, I., Leme, E.: Processo decisório: a tomada de decisão. Revista Eletrônica de Administração **5**(9), 01–10 (2012)
10. Kotler, P., Kartajaya, H., Setiawan, I., Pyka, P.: Marketing 4.0: der leitfaden für das marketing der zukunft. Campus Verlag, Frankfurt (2017)
11. Wickens, C.D.: Engineering Psychology and Human Performance, 2nd edn. HarperCollins Publishers, New York (1992)
12. Palací, F., Salcedo, A., Topa, G.: Cognitive and affective antecedentes of consumers' satisfaction: a systematic review of two research approaches. MDPI Sustain. J. **11**(431), 2–35 (2019)
13. Kim, J.-E., Kim, J.: Human factors in retail environments: a review. Int. J. Retail Distrib. Manag. **40**(11), 818–841 (2012)
14. Cañas, J.J., Waerns, Y.: Ergonomía cognitiva: Aspectos psicológicos de la interacción de las personas con tecnología de la información. Editorial Médica Panamericana, Madrid (2001)
15. Cybis, W., de Betiol, A.H., Faust, R.: Ergonomia e usabilidade: conhecimentos, métodos e aplicações. Novatec, São Paulo (2010)
16. Lindstrom, M.: Brand Sense: Sensory Secrets Behind the Stuff We Buy. Free Press, New York (2010)
17. Manzano, A.R.: Marketing sensorial: Comunicar con los sentidos en el punto de venta. Pearson, Madrid (2012)
18. Lowdermilk, T.: User-centered design: a developer's guide to building user-friendly applications. O'Reilly & Associates, Sebastopol (2013)

Design Process of a Mountable Toy Based on Total Design and User Centered Design Methodologies

Ana Sofía Olivares Jiménez, María Inés Ibarra Caballero, Lilia Atziri Urías Dueñas, and Pilar Hernández-Grageda(✉)

Universidad Panamericana Campus Guadalajara, Calzada Circunvalación Poniente N. 49, Zapopan, Mexico
{0196245,0197536,0199886,phernand}@up.edu.mx

Abstract. In this work we start from the idea that an isolated design methodology cannot be used with the purpose of simultaneously ensure usability outcomes and technical feasibility results. Since mountable toys are among the most used by young children nowadays, they were chosen to be the product that serves to validate how to apply a hybrid design method, using both User Centered Design and Total Design methodologies combined in an orderly and systematic process that can be replicated in future product design or redesign processes that seek, at the same time, to generate desirable products that match the needs of users, and that meet functionality standards.

Keywords: Mountable toy · Ergonomics · Children · Interaction · Long lasting products

1 Introduction

The project presented in this article consists of the creation of a new mountable toy for children that met certain characteristics described later on through the paper. The development process for the new toy was hard, the team could not find one single methodology to follow, reason for mixing two of them and having a hybrid design method. One of these methodologies is mostly based on ergonomic principles while the second one helps us assure a functional final product.

Nowadays, consumerism and planned obsolescence of products is a reality. This generates a vast amount of waste and brutal pollution worldwide. The toy industry is a high consumer sector as it produces products that will only last a few years. This is mainly due to several reasons; children are rapidly growing, their bodies and needs are constantly changing and they will always be always looking for something new because trends are constantly changing and they aren't emotionally attached to their toys. Through our proposal we seek to achieve the opposite: a non-disposable product that will accompany the user throughout its childhood while creating a strong bond. By doing so, we will reduce the environmental impact and promote a circular economy.

© The Author(s), under exclusive license to Springer Nature Switzerland AG 2022
N. L. Black et al. (Eds.): IEA 2021, LNNS 223, pp. 71–77, 2022.
https://doi.org/10.1007/978-3-030-74614-8_9

While designing a toy, it's really important to consider the stage in which the child is in, since this determines in great part the ability it has to explore the surrounding environment [1]. Likewise, an adequate interaction with the toy can influence the child's experience towards it, impacting positively on the emotions triggered by its use and resulting in an increased longevity of the product [2]. In other words, the fonder they grow towards the toy, the longer they'll keep it. Furthermore, since the object to design is a toy, the material should be strong yet suitable for children, meaning it should not be toxic or flammable. Also, because the texture, stiffness and colors directly influence the impression that the product generates, they should be appealing for our target user [3].

2 Methodology

Since it was found that non suitable methodology could be used isolated to achieve "the ideal proposal", two known design methodologies were chosen in order to merge them into a hybrid method.

The first one, Total Design, was proposed by Stuart Pugh in 1990. This methodology parts from an engineering approach, it produces a series of systematized activities to help detect market needs and further on convert them into specifications that work as a base for possible design solutions. Using an evaluation matrix, the best ideas are defined and those alternatives that do not add enough value are discarded. Finally, the ideal design is selected to begin the refining, redesigning, manufacturing and delivery stage [4, 5].

On the other hand, User-Centered Design provides guidelines so that the product or system being designed reaches the highest usability standards based on the understanding of the users, the context in which the product will be used and the tasks that will promote interaction between the user and the product [6]. In addition, it promotes a co-creation procedure where the user's point of view and ideas are taken into account during the process [7]. Hence, we implemented both approaches by combining their elements in a hybrid design process, as shown in Fig. 1.

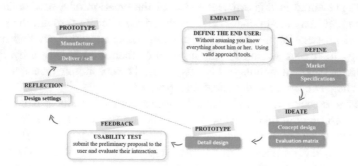

Fig. 1. The steps proposed by the User Centered Design Method are shown in yellow while the Total Design Method in blue.

2.1 Final User Delimitation

Our design is intended to be used by 4–6 year olds. To devise a toy that suits them best, the first step is to get to know the user, in this case, these children. To do so, we spoke with some parents and created an Empathy Map, shown in Fig. 2, which points out their preferences, frustrations, dreams, and really lets un get inside their minds.

Fig. 2. User empathy map.

2.2 Market Analysis

For research purposes, we went to several toy stores where existing toys were analyzed, along with children's behavior towards them. Using, "…A toy which children can ride on and push themselves with; either using their own strength or through mechanisms such as pedals…" as a definition of a mountable toy, we kept certain characteristics that must of the toys had in common and an Attribute List was made, which our proposal will have to meet at the best possible way. This List is shown in Table 1.

Table 1. Margins required for Springer book chapters.

Attribute	Attribute	Attribute
(1) Hand bar for support	(6) Intuitive design	(11) Lightweight
(2) Easy to clean	(7) Safe structure	(12) With an added value
(3) Stable/Safe	(8) Attractive	(13) Easy to manufacture
(4) Weight resistant materials	(9) Customizable	(14) Height
(5) Nontoxic materials	(10) Comfortable seating	(15) Variety of colors

2.3 Conceptual Proposals and Evaluation Matrix

Once the Attribute list was completed, an "ideal" toy was chosen from the market, which fulfilled all the aspects that we were looking for the best possible way. Then, our own proposals were created and used latter in an Evaluation Matrix. The main purpose of this matrix is to compare the products with each other in order to identify their strengths and weaknesses. Sketches of the new design proposals were placed on the "X" axis of the matrix, and the Attribute list was written on the "Y" axis. Each proposal was compared with the ideal toy, and a ranking was created based on how the proposals complied with each specification in comparison to the ideal toy, as shown in Fig. 3. Positive, negative and similar (+, −, S) symbols were used to show the results. For example, if proposal No. 1 was safer than the ideal, a + sign was placed in the corresponding place. Once we were done ranking all the proposals, the highest ranked one was chosen as our winning design.

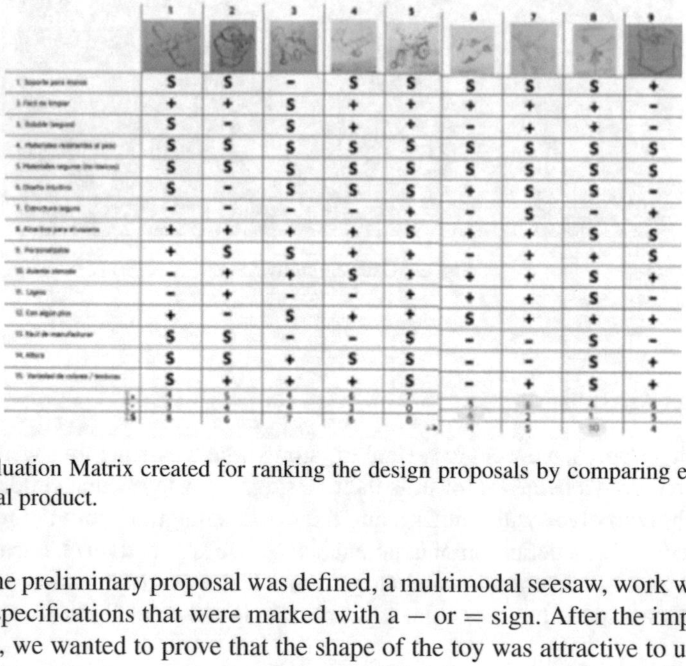

Fig. 3. Evaluation Matrix created for ranking the design proposals by comparing each of them with the ideal product.

Once the preliminary proposal was defined, a multimodal seesaw, work was done on fixing the specifications that were marked with a − or = sign. After the improvements were made, we wanted to prove that the shape of the toy was attractive to users. To do this, an online survey was created and sent to mothers of young children asking them to record their children's responses to the following three questions: gender, age and the object or animal they liked the most. For the last question, four possible figures were presented to the children; all of them had a curvy bottom that allowed the toy to fulfill the desired rocking movement.

2.4 Initial Prototype

The first prototype is shown in Fig. 4. Initially, the toy works as a simple rocker for one or two users; but it can be easily transformed into a tricycle by adding the gadgets that are stored inside of it. The dual mode allows the toy to accompany the user during its different development stages. The seesaw is intended to be used when the user is younger, and the tricycle later, as he grows older. One of the advantages of this product is that it enhances social interaction, when children coexist, they establish bonds, reinforce their trust and develop respect for others. The proposed material is injected polypropylene and the toy consists of six parts: the main body (with two interior compartments in the seats), a handlebar, the front wheels and two rear wheels (left and right).

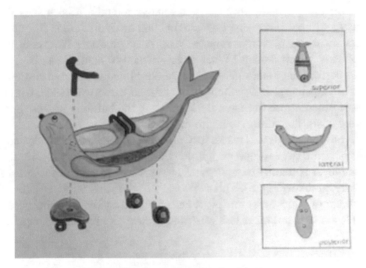

Fig. 4. First prototype sketch with views.

2.5 Feedback

Finally, to ensure that the user had the best possible experience using the toy, a series of questions that validate the seven usability factors, proposed by Peter Morville's honeycomb model [8], were developed and used as a guide during the re-designing process.

Useful: What benefit is my user getting from my product?
Usable: Is my product both effective and efficient?
Believable: Is my product reliable for the users? Does it promise a long useful life?
Desirable: Why should the customer choose my product over others in the market, would it recommend it?
Findable: Will the user be able to find all the information needed to understand how my product works?
Accessible: Can the experience generated by my product be enjoyed by the widest variety of users possible?
Valuable: What the product offers, is it more than what I am giving for it?

3 Results

For the proposal's redesign, the *Lightning Decision Jam* tool was used, where strengths and weaknesses of the toy were defined. Two main aspects that needed improvement were found, the first being an easier design to manufacture and the second, an increase in the emotional bond between the product and the user so that our toy would not be just another toy, but his/her favorite one. To achieve this, Value Engineering methods and Emotional design were used as a guide.

Value engineering's main purpose is to remove anything that makes the product more expensive without increasing its main function but maintaining its quality. This is accomplished by asking questions such as: What is the product? What does it do? What should it do? How much it costs? What other material or method can be used without modifying its performance and safety? We concluded that the material chosen in the first proposal should be changed. A switch from plastic to wood was made, with the aim of having a more efficient use of materials, facilitating the building process and reducing manufacturing costs, in addition to improving it aesthetically. With this modification, a change in the product shape was made, leaving the structure hollow inside and removing excess material from the original design. In addition, the final toy is easy to assemble and disassemble. It is mainly composed of two wooden boards on the sides and some crossbars that join them (Fig. 5). This allows any of the parts to be replaced if they get damaged or wear out, just order that piece and change it easily. By being able to replace a single piece, the user produces less waste and assures the product's longevity.

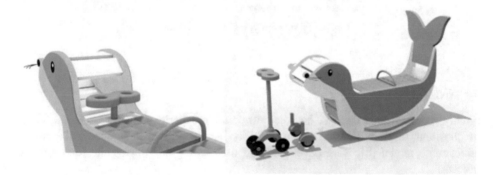

Fig. 5. Final proposal for the mountable toy.

Roni, the seal shaped toy, is the perfect toy for a child aged 4 and older, as it provides fun for them and their parents from the moment they begin assembling it. It is an interactive toy that encourages coexistence and helps kids explore their abilities.

4 Conclusion

We found that by using two methodologies, the 'User-Centered Design' and 'Total Design', more about the user could be understood and therefore it is possible to create a better and more successful design. Our initial idea for the mountable was a plastic toy, completely solid and quite colorful. By doing deeper research in children's emotions, materials, manufacturing processes, we decided to redesign the product in order to obtain a simple assemblable and disassemblable toy, mainly made out of wood, with attractive colors and two modalities, a seesaw and a tricycle, that could be shared by two users. In addition, after researching about emotional attachment of children to toys, a storybook for the children and a name for the mountable were implemented, bringing *Roni* to life.

References

1. Eka Rizki, A., Salis, K.: Effective learning activities to improve early childhood cognitive development. Al-Athfal J. Pendidikan Anak **4**, 103–112 (2018)
2. Gulden, T., Ahram, T., Karwowski, W., Marek, T.: Toys and product longevity. Hum. Factors Ergon. 19–23 (2014)
3. Friso, V., Silva, J., Landim, P., Paschoarelli, L.: Ergonomic analysis of visual and tacticle information of materials used in the manufacture of toys. Procedia Manuf. 6161–6168 (2015)
4. Pugh, S.: Integrated Methods for Successful Product Engineering. Addison-Wesley, New Jersey (1990)
5. Flaschner, A.: Creating innovative products using total design: the living legacy of Stuart Pugh. J. Prod. Innov. Manag. 233–235 (1997)
6. Huang, P.-H., Chiu, M.-C.: Integrating user centered design, universal design and goal, operation, method and selection rules to improve the usability of DAISY player for persons with visual impairments. Appl. Ergon. **52**, 29–42 (2016)
7. Veryzer, R., Borja de Mozota, B.: The impact of user-oriented design on new product development: an examination of fundamental relationships. J. Prod. Innov. Manag. **22**, 128–143 (2005)
8. Morville, P., Sullenger, P.: Ambient findability: libraries, serials, and the internet of things. Serieals Librarian **58**, 33–38 (2010)

Part II: Anthropometry (Edited by Karen Bredenkamp)

Anthropometric Indices and Nutritional Status of Infants in Nigeria – A Preliminary Study

Echezona Nelson Dominic Ekechukwu[1,2,3](✉) ⓘ, Chiamaka Chinyere Anyaene[1],
Ogechukwu Ikefuna[1], Emmanuel Nwabueze Aguwa[2,4], Israel Chijioke Iroezindu[5],
Theodora A. Okeke[2,4], and Susan U. Arinze-Onyia[6]

[1] Department of Medical Rehabilitation, FHST, College of Medicine, University of Nigeria,
Nsukka, Nigeria
nelson.ekechukwu@unn.edu.ng
[2] Occupational and Environmental Health Unit, IPH, College of Medicine,
University of Nigeria, Nsukka, Nigeria
[3] Lancet Physiotherapy, Wellness and Research Centre, Enugu, Nigeria
[4] Department of Community Medicine, FMS, College of Medicine, University of Nigeria,
Nsukka, Nigeria
[5] Occupational Health International SOS West Africa, Port Harcourt, Nigeria
[6] Department of Community Medicine, Enugu State University College of Medicine, Parklane,
Enugu, Nigeria

Abstract. Paediatric anthropometric database is important for child product design and their public health plans. This is unavailable in Nigeria and most developing nations. This study aims to provide a preliminary anthropometric database of infants in our environment and determine how they relate with their nutritional status. This cross-sectional survey was conducted among 108 infants recruited from a health centre in Enugu East LGA. Anthropometric variables (body weight; head, abdominal, chest, wrist, forearm, mid arm and mid-thigh circumferences; shoulder breadth; crown-to-rump, crown-to-sole, rump-to-sole, shoulder-to-elbow lengths etc.) were assessed using standard procedures. Nutritional status was assessed using the Weech formula and the Mid Upper Arm Circumference (MUAC) index. Data obtained were analyzed descriptively, while chi-square test was used to determine the association between variables at $\alpha = 0.05$. A total of 53 females and 55 males participated in this study. Their mean age, birth weight, and total body weight were 10.64 ± 5.46 weeks, 3.30 ± 0.59 kg, and 5.61 ± 1.00 kg respectively. Their mean head, abdominal, mid-arm, and mid-thigh circumferences were 40.01 ± 1.92 cm, 42.21 ± 3.22 cm, 13.01 ± 1.22 cm, and 19.50 ± 2.47 cm respectively. The (75th, 95th) percentile of their chest circumference, mid arm circumference, shoulder breath and total body weight were (42.00 cm, 44.50 cm), (13.88 cm, 15.11 cm), (17.38 cm, 19.00 cm) and (6.30 cm, 7.56 cm) respectively. There was significant association between nutritional status [(Weech), (MUAC)] and each of chest circumference [$(x2 = 52.42, p < 0.0001)$, $(x2 = 95.88, p = 0.010)$], abdominal circumference [$(x2 = 68.25, p < 0.0001)$, $(x2 = 115.58, p = 0.010)$], foerarm circumference [$(x2 = 45.19, p < 0.0001)$, $(x2 = 151.90, p < 0.0001)$], and wrist circumference[$(x2 = 46.94, p < 0.0001)$, $(x2 = 146.19, p < 0.0001)$]. The protocol is pragmatic and some selected anthropometric variables of infants can relied upon to determine their nutritional status.

N. L. Black et al. (Eds.): IEA 2021, LNNS 223, pp. 81–95, 2022.
https://doi.org/10.1007/978-3-030-74614-8_10

Keywords: Anthropometry · Nutritional status · Infants · Database · Nigeria

1 Introduction

Anthropometry is the science dealing with the physical measurements of the human individual, such as the person's size, form and functional capacities [1]. It is the study of the measurement of the human body in terms of the dimensions of bone, muscle, and adipose tissue [2]. Anthropometry is a key component of nutritional status assessment in children and adults [3]. The anthropometric data for infants and children reflect general health status [4], and dietary adequacy [5]; and can therefore be used to track trends in their growth and development over time. For infants, some important anthropometric measurements include weight, head circumference, and length/height. Head circumference is known to be positively correlated with brain growth and volume [6]. Also, the weight of a child can be used to assess the presence of malnutrition [7], while their length/height are used to assess creatinine height index (an index of protein nutrition), and basal energy expenditure [8, 9].

The physical characteristics of anthropometry are dimensions of hands and feet and other body members and are subject to variations according to sex, age and built. A large bank of this data (database) is utilized by ergonomists, government, medical engineers, and health practitioners for the designing of physical facilities, decision making and general manufacturing [10]. Since the 1940s, several developed countries have been working on the establishment of anthropometric databases of their military, workforce or citizens in general. Worldwide, there are at present more than 90 large scaled anthropometric databases, and most of them are for Western populations. In Asia [11–13], and America [14–16]; there exist several anthropometric databases. With the exception of very few sizing and fits studies in South Africa [17, 18], there appear to be no anthropometric database for the African population; more so, for Nigeria, the most populous nation in Africa.

It is a known fact that differences in nutrition and life style, as well as hereditary and ethnic factors can lead to difference in body sizes and dimensions [19], thus underscoring the need for an African anthropometric database. Also, most of the databases world over was built only for adults with the aim of increasing industrial safety, and much less attention has been paid to adolescents and children. Hence, this study seeks to provide anthropometric indices of infants in an African environment and establish their relationship with the nutritional status of this population.

2 Material and Methods

2.1 Study Area

Enugu East Local Government Area Health Centre, located in Abakpa close to the market, mostly inhabited by low income earners.

2.2 Subjects

One hundred and eight infants participated in this cross-sectional preliminary survey (53 females, 55 males). All participants lived within the study area.

2.3 Eligibility Criteria

Only infants between 6 and 36 weeks, live in Enugu East Local Government Area, whose parents gave their consent participated in this study. However, babies that met the above criteria but presented to the health centre for other medical treatment other than immunization were excluded.

2.4 Outcome Measures

Nutritional Status This was done using the Mid Upper Arm Circumference (MUAC) index and the Weech index.

The Mid-Upper Arm Circumference is the circumference of the left upper arm, measured at the mid-point between the tip of the shoulder (the acromium) and the tip of the elbow (olecranon process). It is a good predictor of mortality and in many studies, MUAC predicted death in children better than any other anthropometric indicator. By the World Health Organisation standard (WHO, 2010), MUAC less than 110 mm indicates Severe Acute Malnutrition (SAM), and the child should be immediately referred for treatment. MUAC between 110 mm and 125 mm indicates Moderate Acute Malnutrition (MAM), and the child should be immediately referred for supplementation. MUAC of between 125 mm and 135 mm, indicates that the child is at risk for acute malnutrition and should be counseled and followed-up for Growth Promotion and Monitoring (GPM). MUAC over 135 mm indicates that the child is well nourished [20].

WEECH Index is a frequently used formula for estimating weight and height using age of children in developing countries [21]. For children less than 12month like participants in this study, the following formula was used:

$$Estimated\ Weight(Kg) = Age(months)\ 2 + 9$$

Participants were classified as underweight and malnourished when the observed weight was found to be less than the estimated weight [22].

Anthropometric Measurements. Participants were weighed and their lengths and circumferences (weight, height, head circumference, head length, chest circumference, abdominal circumference, mid arm circumference, forearm circumference, wrist circumference, hand length, crown-to-sole, crown-to-rump, rump-to-sole, rump-to-knee, mid thigh circumference, calf circumference, ankle circumference, foot length, foot breath) were assessed using standard procedures as described below and illustrated in Fig. 1.

Head Circumference. Babies were position comfortably in supine lying on the assessment board, parents were asked to remove any of the child's hair ornaments or braids. Measurement was done by placing the measuring tape around the child's head so that the tape lies across the frontal bones of the skull, slightly above the eyebrows, perpendicular to the long axis of the face, above the ears, and over the occipital prominence at the back of the head. The tape was moved up and down over the back of the head to locate the maximal circumference. The insertion tape was tightened so that it fits snugly around the head and compresses the hair and underlying soft tissues. The measurement was taken twice to the nearest 0.1 cm and the average of the two measurements calculated and recorded.

Body Weight. Electronic Infant weighing scale (MTB, UK) was used to assess the body weight of the participants. The caregiver undressed the participant down to light clothing (e.g. onesie or T-shirt and a clean dry diaper) and gently placed on the scale already covered with disposable table paper that was changed for each participant. The weight of the participant was read to the nearest kilogram.

Recumbent Lengths. A Recumbent board was used for these measurements. It was covered with a disposable scale liner that was changed for each participant, then their caregiver undressed them to light clothing and a clean, dry diaper. Also, any hats, hair barrettes, or anything in the crown of the hair that would prevent an accurate measurement was removed. The participant was placed supine on the recumbent board. The caregiver was asked to hold the participant's head so that the crown touches the head of the board and he/she looking straight up. Participant's legs were held lightly together just above the knees and gently pushed down against the recumbent board to ensure that he/she is in full extension. The vortex of the crown and each of the rump, knee and sole were marked off. Thereafter, the crown-to-rump, Crown-to-Sole, Rump-to-Sole and Rump-to-Knee, Knee-to-Sole lengths were measured. Measurement were taken twice to the nearest 0.1 cm, the average was calculated and recorded.

Body Circumferences. Body circumferences such as the Chest, Abdominal, Waist, Mid Arm, Forearm, Wrist, Mid-thigh, Calf, and Ankle Circumferences were assessed with the participants in supine lying on the recumbent board. Tape rule was used to measure the body circumference at specific landmarks. Chest, Abdominal, and waist circumferences were taken at the level of the nipple, umbilicus, and the narrowest part below the umbilicus respectively. Mid-arm, forearm, and wrist circumference were taken at the midpoint between the shoulder and the elbow, mid point between the elbow and the wrist, and over the radial styloid respectively. In the same vein, the mid-thigh, calf, and ankle circumferences were taken at the mid-point between the hip and the knee, the bulkiest part of the gastrocnemius, and over the lateral malleolus respectively as illustrated in Fig. 1. The above measures were taken twice in their nearest 0.1 cm and their average calculated and recorded.

Limb Lengths/Breadths. Measures such as Hand, Shoulder, and foot Breadths, as well as Elbow-to-Hand, Shoulder-to-Elbow, Hand, and Foot Lengths were also assessed on the recumbent board. The participants were also positioned as described above. The hand breadth was measured from the widest surface of the palm between the index and little fingers, and similar measurement was equally done for the foot breadth. Shoulder breadth was assessed as the length between the left and right acromium posteriorly. The shoulder to elbow and elbow to hand lengths were defined as the distance between the acromium

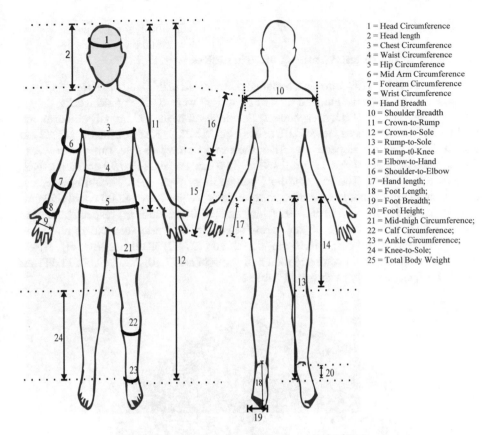

1 = Head Circumference
2 = Head length
3 = Chest Circumference
4 = Waist Circumference
5 = Hip Circumference
6 = Mid Arm Circumference
7 = Forearm Circumference
8 = Wrist Circumference
9 = Hand Breadth
10 = Shoulder Breadth
11 = Crown-to-Rump
12 = Crown-to-Sole
13 = Rump-to-Sole
14 = Rump-t0-Knee
15 = Elbow-to-Hand
16 = Shoulder-to-Elbow
17 = Hand length;
18 = Foot Length;
19 = Foot Breadth;
20 = Foot Height;
21 = Mid-thigh Circumference;
22 = Calf Circumference;
23 = Ankle Circumference;
24 = Knee-to-Sole;
25 = Total Body Weight

Fig. 1. Infant anthropometric measures and their sites

and the olecranon, and between the olecranon and the radial styloid respectively. The hand and foot lengths were measured as the distance between the midpoint of the radial and ulna styloids and the index finger, and between the calcaneus and the longest toe respectively. All measurements were taken twice to the nearest 0.1 cm, the average calculated and recorded.

Data Analysis. Data obtained was cleaned and analysed using Statistical Package for Social Sciences (SPSS) version 21.0. Descriptive statistics of frequency, percentages, mean and standard deviation were used to summarise participants variables in tables and pie charts. Chi-square inferential statistics was used to determine the association between the participants' anthropometric variables and nutritional indices. Level of significance was set at $\alpha = 0.05$.

3 Results

3.1 Summary of Infants' Anthropometric Indices

A total of 108 infants (53 females, 55 males) participated in this study as shown in Fig. 2. Their mean age, birth weight, and total body weight were 10.64 ± 5.46 weeks, 3.30 ± 0.59 kg, and 5.61 ± 1.00 kg respectively. Their mean head, abdominal, mid-arm, and mid-thigh circumferences were 40.01 ± 1.92 cm, 42.21 ± 3.22 cm, 13.01 ± 1.22 cm, and 19.50 ± 2.47 cm respectively. Also, their mean crown-to-sole, rump-to-sole, and foot lengths were 58.97 ± 4.13 cm, 24.90 ± 3.29 cm, and 9.22 ± 0.90 cm respectively as shown in Table 1. The 75th and 95th percentile of their chest circumference, mid arm circumference, shoulder breath and total body weight were (42.00 cm, 44.50 cm), (13.88 cm, 15.11 cm), (17.38 cm, 19.00 cm) and (6.30 cm, 7.56 cm) respectively. Also, the 75th and 95th percentile of their crown-to-rump, crown-to-sole and rump-to-sole were (36.00 cm, 39.00 cm), (61.15 cm, 66.00) and (27.00, 30.00) respectively. Again, that of hand length, foot length and total body weight are (7.10, 7.50), (9.00, 11.11) and (6.30, 7.56) respectively as shown in Table 1.

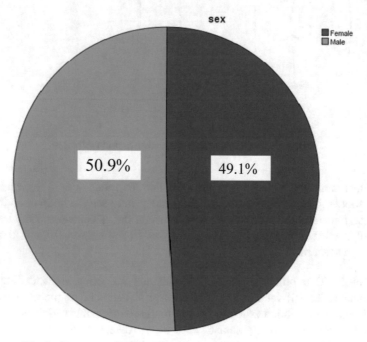

Fig. 2. Frequency distribution of the sex of participants (N = 108)

Table 1. Mean anthropometric indices of the participants and their percentiles

Anthropometric variables	N	Min	P5	P25	P50	P75	P95	Max	X	SD
Birth weight (kg)	85	1.80	2.33	2.90	3.30	3.70	4.10	5.40	3.30	0.59
Age (weeks)	108	5.00	6.00	6.00	10.00	12.00	22.20	36.00	10.64	5.46
Head circumf (cm)	108	33.60	37.00	38.60	40.00	41.00	43.78	44.00	40.01	1.92
Head length (cm)	105	1.00	11.00	11.50	12.00	13.00	13.35	14.00	11.96	1.36
Chest circumf (cm)	108	35.00	36.00	38.10	40.00	42.00	44.50	46.00	40.22	2.52
Abdominal circumf (cm)	108	30.00	36.64	40.00	42.00	44.38	47.78	48.50	42.21	3.22
Mid-arm circumf (cm)	108	10.50	11.00	12.00	13.00	13.88	15.11	16.50	13.01	1.22
Forearm circumf (cm)	108	10.00	11.00	11.50	12.50	13.00	14.78	15.50	12.51	1.16
Wrist circumf (cm)	108	0.50	8.10	9.28	10.00	10.15	11.00	12.00	9.73	1.24
Hand breath (cm)	106	3.50	3.89	4.00	4.20	4.50	5.00	5.50	4.26	0.32
Shoulder breath (cm)	108	13.50	15.00	16.00	17.00	17.38	19.00	20.00	16.78	1.18
Crown-to-rump (cm)	108	27.50	30.00	32.50	34.00	36.00	39.00	43.00	34.38	2.80
Crown-to-sole (cm)	108	47.00	52.45	56.50	58.50	61.15	66.00	71.50	58.97	4.13
Rump-to-sole (cm)	108	13.00	20.00	23.00	25.00	27.00	30.00	34.50	24.90	3.29
Rump-to-knee (cm)	108	6.50	9.50	11.50	12.75	14.00	16.78	19.50	12.74	2.12
Elbow-to-hand (cm)	108	10.00	14.50	15.50	16.50	17.50	19.00	21.00	16.54	1.57
Shoulder-to-elbow (cm)	108	8.00	8.50	9.50	10.00	11.00	12.78	16.00	10.40	1.38
Hand length (cm)	108	6.00	6.23	7.00	7.00	7.10	7.50	8.00	7.00	0.35
Foot length (cm)	108	7.50	8.00	8.50	9.00	9.50	11.11	12.00	9.22	0.90
Foot breath (cm)	108	3.50	3.80	4.05	4.50	4.50	5.00	6.00	4.41	0.43
Mid thigh circumf (cm)	108	14.00	15.73	18.00	19.00	21.00	24.00	26.00	19.50	2.47
Calf circumf (cm)	108	11.50	12.00	13.50	14.50	15.88	17.77	19.00	14.63	1.59
Ankle circumf (cm)	108	8.50	9.50	10.00	11.00	12.00	13.00	14.50	10.97	1.10
Knee-to-sole (cm)	108	10.50	12.80	14.00	15.00	15.00	17.00	18.00	14.78	1.20
Total body weight (kg)	108	3.50	4.19	4.90	5.00	6.30	7.56	8.20	5.61	1.00

Key: Cirumf = Circumference, Min = Minimum value, P = Percentile, Max = Maximum value, X = Mean, SD = Standard Deviation.

3.2 Summary of the Association Between Nutritional Status and Anthropometric Indices of Infants

Using the Weech index, 39.8% of the participants were underweight and 60.2% of them were normal weight as shown in Fig. 3, with the MUAC index, 1.9% were classified as having severe acute malnutrition, 26.9% as moderate acute malnutrition, 32.4% as having the risk of acute malnutrition, and 38.9% as being well nourished as shown in Fig. 4. There was significant associations between nutritional status using WEECH and MUAC indices with each of chest circumference [$(x^2 = 52.42, p < 0.0001)$, $(x^2 = 95.88, p = 0.010)$], abdominal circumference [$(x^2 = 68.25, p < 0.0001)$, $(x^2 = 115.58, p =$

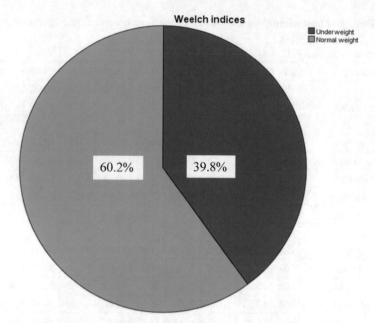

Fig. 3. Frequency distribution of Weech Score of the participants (N = 108)

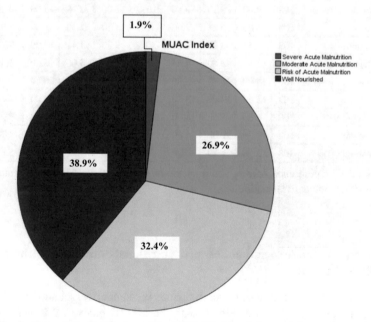

Fig. 4. Frequency distribution of the MUAC index of the participants (N = 108)

0.010)], forearm circumference [($x^2 = 45.19$, p < 0.0001), ($x^2 = 151.90$, p < 0.0001)], and wrist circumference[($x^2 = 46.94$, p < 0.0001), ($x^2 = 146.19$, p < 0.0001)]. However, rump-to-sole length ($x^2 = 102.53$, p = 0.033), elbow-to-hand length ($x^2 = 77.32$, p = 0.02) and total body weight ($x^2 = 216.88$, p < 0.0001) were only significantly associated with nutritional status assessed using the MUAC index as shown in Table 2. On the other hand, there was no significant association between sex and nutritional status assessed with both the WEELCH index ($x^2 = 2.35$, p = 0.125) and the MUAC index ($x^2 = 6.67$, p = 0.0.083) as shown in Figs. 5 and 6 respectively.

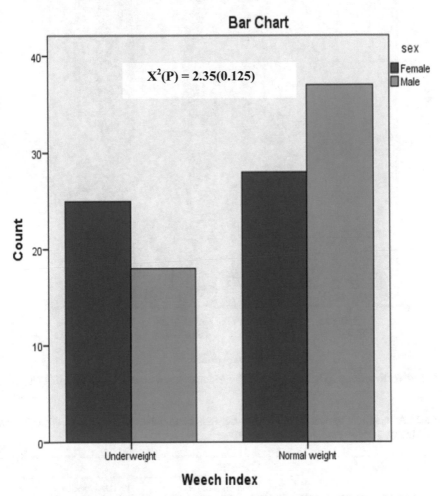

Fig. 5. Relationship between sex and Nutritional Status assessed with Weech's Index

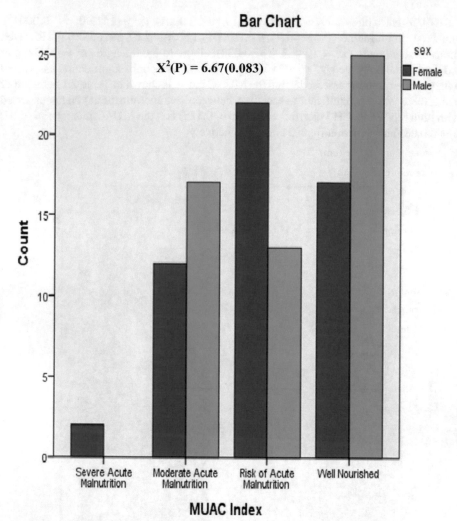

Fig. 6. Relationship between sex and Nutritional Status assessed with MUAC index

Table 2. Association between anthropometric Indices and Nutritional Status (Weech's and MUAC Indices) of the Participants (N = 108)

Anthropometric indices	X^2 (p)	
	Weech's index	MUAC index
Head circumference (cm)	30.43 (0.047)	72.15 (0.085)
Head length (cm)	16.06 (0.188)	34.46 (0.542)

(*continued*)

Table 2. (*continued*)

Anthropometric indices	X^2 (p)	
	Weech's index	MUAC index
Chest circumference (cm)	52.42 (<0.0001)*	95.88 (0.010)*
Abdominal circumference (cm)	68.23 (<0.0001)*	115.58 (0.04)*
Mid-arm circumference (cm)	47.90 (<0.0001)*	N/A
Forearm circumference (cm)	45.19 (<0.0001)*	151.95 (<0.0001)*
Wrist circumference (cm)	46.94 (<0.0001)*	146.19 (<0.0001)*
Hand breath (cm)	14.50 (0.151)	19.25 (0.935)
Shoulder breath (cm)	16.90 (0.204)	45.28 (0.226)
Crown-to-rump (cm)	35.98 (0.055)	80.43 (0.232)
Crown-to-sole (cm)	40.11 (0.184)	111.99 (0.175)
Rump-to-sole (cm)	24.51 (0.547)	102.53 (0.033)*
Rump-to-knee (cm)	20.83 (0.470)	74.56 (0.151)
Elbow-to-hand (cm)	21.18 (0.131)	77.32 (0.02)*
Shoulder-to-elbow (cm)	14.42 (0.567)	30.79 (0.975)
Foot length (cm)	17.94 (0.118)	57.16 (0.014)*
Foot breath (cm)	31.64 (0.002)*	90.52 (<0.0001)*
Mid thigh circumference (cm)	45.75 (0.003)*	152.26 (<0.0001)*
Calf circumference (cm)	59.36 (<0.0001)*	143.01 (<0.0001)*
Ankle circumference (cm)	41.35 (<0.0001)*	143.14 (<0.0001)*
Knee-to-sole (cm)	23.72 (0.096)	107.81 (<0.0001)*
Birth weight (kg)	23.68 (0364)	74.46 (0.222)
Total Body Weight (Kg)	N/A	216.88 (<0.0001)*

Key: X^2 = Chi-square value, * = Significant, N/A = Not Applicable.

4 Discussion

The mean birth weight was of the infants in this study was 3.30 kg which is considered normal given that the average birth weight of full term babies ranges between 2.5 kg and 4.5 kg [23]. This range is approximately the 5th and 95th percentiles of the birth weight of the infants in this study (2.33 kg to 4.1 kg) which could be considered a normative value for new born babies in this environment. Studies [24–27], have shown that African babies have lower birth weights than their Caucasian counterparts. Poor maternal nutrition [28, 29], hypertension [30], glucose intolerance obesity [31], and socioeconomic status [32, 33]; have been fingered to be partly responsible for this differences. It was however observed in this study that the mean body weight (5.61 kg) was considered normal for the mean age of the participants (10.62 weeks) going by the WHO's infant weight chart that estimated the body weight of 3 month old babies between 5.4 kg and 6 kg [34].

The mean head circumference in this study and its 5th and 95th percentiles are within the ranges stipulated in the WHO Child Growth standard [35]. According to the WHO standards, for 11months old infants, the average head circumference for boys and girls are 39.90 cm and 38.97 cm respectively; while the 5th–95th percentiles for boys and girls are 38.0–41.8 cm and 36.9–41.0 cm respectively. The finding is also consistent with the reports of Neyzi et al. [36], that found the average head circumference of male and female children (3 months old) to be 41.1 cm and 40.0 cm respectively. The clinical implication of head circumference appears unsettled in literature. Wright and Emond [37], argued that extreme head size is neither specific nor sensitive for detecting neurocognitive disorders and went further to opine that routine measurement of head circumference was unhelpful. On the other hand, Sacco et al. [38], argued that macrocephaly and megalencephaly (brain overgrowth) are associated with autism spectrum disorder and further corroborated by Menounou [39], who also argued that the head size, the growth rate and the shape are important pointers towards benign or more sinister medical conditions; thu, suggesting that this be routinely examined in children. However, from an ergonomic viewpoint, the head circumference of infants would be useful to manufacturer and suppliers of baby clothings, caps and hat. Data from this study may therefore be useful for babies in this environment for the purpose of standardization.

Majority of the participants in this study were classified as being underweight using the Weech formula whereas using the MUAC index most the participants were classified as being well nourished. However and worrisome as well is the fact that a good number of the participants 26.9% were classified as having moderate acute malnutrition. This appears to be of public health concern as this implies that one of every four infants in this environment may have moderate acute malnutrition. According to a research by Black et al. [40], and Pelletier et al. [41] in rural Malawi, Moderate acute malnutrition (MAM) affects 11% of children worldwide under the age of 5 years. Children with MAM are not only at 3 times' greater risk of death than well nourished children but also face greater risk of morbidity from infectious diseases and delayed physical and cognitive development. This calls for urgent attention of the government and health workers on the need for nutritional education and availability of nutritional supplements at reduced prices or no price at all as poor financial state of the parents could be a major cause of malnutrition.

There was a significant association between the nutritional status assessed using Weech and MUAC index with some selected anthropometric variables such as chest circumference, abdominal circumference, calf circumference and wrist circumference. This implies that these measurements in an infant may be used to assess their nutritional status. This is in line with the study by Ferretti et al. [42], who posited that calf circumference is a good indicator for monitoring nutritional status of children and adolescents with malignant neoplasm. Also, there was no significant association between sex and nutritional status in this study, this goes contrary to a report by National Family Health Survey in 2016 in India stating that female children are more malnourished than their male counterparts [43], although the only 2 severe acute malnourished cases that presented in this survey were females. There appear to be conflicting reports on the effects of gender on nutritional status of a child. Dereń et al. [44], found more boys to be underweighted than girls and in the same study found more boys to be obese than girls. Pandev [45], appears to support the option of more girls being underweight than boys in India. He attributed this to parental bias, as parents with no male child tend to breastfeed their female children less longer as they keep attempting to have a male child. In Nigeria, there is an unverified belief that male children suckle better than female children and they tend to continue breastfeeding for a more prolonged period of time than female children. This belief is however not supported by the result of this study that found no relationship between sex and nutritional status. It is pertinent to state that this is a preliminary study, given the limited sample size and sample recruitment from a single location that may affect the external validity of the result. It should therefore be interpreted with caution.

5 Conclusion

This approach is pragmatic for developing an anthropometric database of infants in Nigeria. The head circumference and body weight of an infant in Enugu Metropolis are within the normal ranges reported by WHO. Finally, anthropometric variables like chest, abdominal, calf and wrist circumferences are useful determinants of infant's nutritional status.

Acknowledgment. We wish to acknowledge and appreciate the mothers and caregivers that presented their infants as participants in this study.

References

1. Abd Rahman, N.I., Dawal, S.Z., Yusoff, N., Kamil, N.S.: Anthropometric measurements among four Asian countries in designing sitting and standing workstations. Sādhanā **43**(1), 1–9 (2018)
2. Stewart, A., Ackland, T.: Anthropometry in physical performance and health. Body Compos. Health Perform. Exerc. Sport **20**(1), 89–108 (2017)
3. Madden, A.M., Smith, S.: Body composition and morphological assessment of nutritional status in adults: a review of anthropometric variables. J. Hum. Nutr. Diet. **29**(1), 7–25 (2016)
4. Sandell, A., Baker, R.D., Maccarone, J., Baker, S.S.: Health status and anthropometric changes in resettled refugee children. J. Pediatr. Gastroenterol. Nutr. **65**(5), 569–73 (2017)
5. Perkins, J.M., Jayatissa, R., Subramanian, S.V.: Dietary diversity and anthropometric status and failure among infants and young children in Sri Lanka. Nutrition **55**(1), 76–83 (2018)
6. Treit, S., Zhou, D., Chudley, A.E., Andrew, G., Rasmussen, C., Nikkel, S.M., Samdup, D., Hanlon-Dearman, A., Loock, C., Beaulieu, C.: Relationships between head circumference, brain volume and cognition in children with prenatal alcohol exposure. PLoS ONE **11**(2), 15–37 (2016)
7. Bhutta, Z.A., Berkley, J.A., Bandsma, R.H., Kerac, M., Trehan, I., Briend, A.: Severe childhood malnutrition. Nat. Rev. Dis. Primers **3**(1), 17–67 (2017)
8. Medhat, A.S., Ahmed, A.O., Thabet, A.F., Amal, M.: Creatinine height index as a predictor of nutritional status among patients with liver cirrhosis. J. Public Health Epidemiol. **8**(10), 220–228 (2016)
9. Agostoni, C., Edefonti, A., Calderini, E., Fossali, E., Colombo, C., Battezzati, A., Bertoli, S., Milani, G., Bisogno, A., Perrone, M., Bettocchi, S.: Accuracy of prediction formulae for the assessment of resting energy expenditure in hospitalized children. J. Pediatr. Gastroenterol. Nutr. **63**(6), 708–712 (2016)

10. Qutubuddin, S.M., Hebbal, S.S., Kumar, A.C.: Significance of anthropometric data for the manufacturing organizations. Int. J. Eng. Res. Ind. Appl. (IJERIA) **5**(1), 111–126 (2012)
11. Kim, J.Y., You, J.W., Kim, M.S.: South Korean anthropometric data and survey methodology: 'Size Korea' project. Ergonomics **60**(11), 1586–1596 (2017)
12. Raveendran, M.: The South Asian facial anthropometric profile: a systematic review. J. Cranio-Maxillofacial Surg. **47**(2), 263–272 (2019)
13. Virani, N.: Reference curves and cut-off values for anthropometric indices of adiposity of affluent Asian Indian children aged 3–18 years. Ann. Hum. Biol. **38**(2), 165–174 (2011)
14. Snyder, R.G.: Anthropometry of Infants, Children, and Youths to Age 18 for Product Safety Design. Final Report (1977)
15. Granberry, R., Duvall, J., Dunne, L.E., Holschuh, B.: An analysis of anthropometric geometric variability of the lower leg for the fit & function of advanced functional garments. In: Proceedings of the 2017 ACM International Symposium on Wearable Computers, pp. 10–17. Association for Computing Machinery, New York (2017)
16. Kuebler, T., Luebke, A., Campbell, J., Guenzel, T.: Size North America–the new North American anthropometric survey. In: Proceedings of the 2019 International Conference on Human-Computer Interaction, pp. 88–98. Springer, Cham (2019)
17. Hunter, L., Harlock, S.C., Pandarum, R.: Empirical study exploring sizing and fit of apparel for South African women consumers. J. Family Ecol. Consum. Sci. **2**(1), 40–54 (2017)
18. Muthambi, A., De Klerk, H.M., Mason, A.M.: Sizing for ethnicity in multi-cultural societies: development of size specifications for young South African women of African descent. J. Consum. Sci. **24**(1), 43–52 (2015)
19. Deurenberg, P., Deurenberg-Yap, M., Foo, L.F., Schmidt, G., Wang, J.: Differences in body composition between Singapore Chinese, Beijing Chinese and Dutch children. Eur. J. Clin. Nutr. **57**(3), 405–409 (2003)
20. Mother and Child Nutrition Homepage. Early detection and Referral of Children and Manutrition. MUAC Resources. https://motherchildnutrition.org/early-malnutrition-detect ion/detection-referral-children-with-acute-malnutrition/interpretation-of-muac-indicators. html. Assessed 01 Feb 2021
21. Haq, I., Shah, M.S., Bachh, A.A., Ansari, M.A.: Validity of Weech's formulae in detecting undernutrition in children. Nepal Med. Coll. J. **12**(4), 229–233 (2010)
22. Brahmbhatt, K.R., Hameed, S., Naik, P.M., Prasanna, K.S., Jayram, S.: Role of new anthropometric indices, validity of MUAC and Weech's formula in detecting under-nutrition among under-five children in Karnataka. Int. J. Biomed. Adv. Res. **3**(12), 896–900 (2013)
23. Healthwise Staff – MyHealth Alberta. Physical Growth in Newborn: Topic Overview. https://myhealth.alberta.ca/Health/Pages/conditions.aspx?hwid=te6295. Accessed 01 Feb 2021
24. Coutinho, R., David, R.J., Collins, J.W., Jr.: Relation of parental birth weights to infant birth weight among African Americans and whites in illinois: a transgenerational study. Am. J. Epidemiol. **146**(10), 804–809 (1997)
25. Braveman, P.A., Heck, K., Egerter, S., Marchi, K.S., Dominguez, T.P., Cubbin, C., Fingar, K., Pearson, J.A., Curtis, M.: The role of socioeconomic factors in black–white disparities in preterm birth. Am. J. Public Health **105**(4), 694–702 (2015)
26. Catov, J.M., Lee, M., Roberts, J.M., Xu, J., Simhan, H.N.: Race disparities and decreasing birth weight: are all babies getting smaller? Am. J. Epidemiol. **183**(1), 15–23 (2016)
27. Burton, W.M., Hernandez-Reif, M., Lian, B.: Addressing the racial disparity in birth outcomes: implications for maternal racial identity on birth-weight. J. Health Disparities Res. Pract. **10**(2), 9–13 (2017)
28. Gebremedhin, M., Ambaw, F., Admassu, E., Berhane, H.: Maternal associated factors of low birth weight: a hospital based cross-sectional mixed study in Tigray Northern Ethiopia. BMC Pregnancy Childbirth **15**(1), 1–8 (2015)

29. Zerfu, T.A., Umeta, M., Baye, K.: Dietary diversity during pregnancy is associated with reduced risk of maternal anemia, preterm delivery, and low birth weight in a prospective cohort study in rural Ethiopia. Am. J. Clin. Nutr. **103**(6), 1482–1488 (2016)

30. Lackland, D.T., Egan, B.M., Ferguson, P.L.: Low birth weight as a risk factor for hypertension. J. Clin. Hypertens. **5**(2), 133–136 (2003)

31. Ju, A.C., Heyman, M.B., Garber, A.K., Wojcicki, J.M.: Maternal obesity and risk of preterm birth and low birthweight in Hawaii PRAMS, 2000–2011. Matern. Child Health J. **22**(6), 893–902 (2018)

32. Martinson, M.L., Reichman, N.E.: Socioeconomic inequalities in low birth weight in the United States, the United Kingdom, Canada, and Australia. Am. J. Public Health **106**(4), 748–754 (2016)

33. Rahman, N.I.A., Dawal, S.Z.M., Yusoff, N., Kamil, N.S.M.: Anthropometric measurements among four Asian countries in designing sitting and standing workstations. Sādhanā **43**(1), 1–9 (2018)

34. World Health Organization: WHO child growth standards: head circumference-for-age, arm circumference-for-age, triceps skinfold-for-age and subscapular skinfold-for-age: methods and development. WHO, Geneva (2007)

35. WHO Homepage. World Health Organization Standards: Child Growth Standards – Head Circumference-for-Age. https://www.who.int/childgrowth/standards/hc_for_age/en/. Accessed 01 Feb 2021

36. Neyzi, O., Bundak, R., Gökçay, G., Günöz, H., Furman, A., Darendeliler, F., Baş, F.: Reference values for weight, height, head circumference, and body mass index in Turkish children. J. Clin. Res. Pediatr. Endocrinol. **7**(4), 1–28 (2015)

37. Wright, C.M., Emond, A.: Head growth and neurocognitive outcomes. Pediatrics **135**(6), 1393–1398 (2015)

38. Sacco, R., Gabriele, S., Persico, A.M.: Head circumference and brain size in autism spectrum disorder: a systematic review and meta-analysis. Psychiatry Res. Neuroimaging **234**(2), 239–251 (2015)

39. Menounou, A.: Head size: Is it important. Adv. Clin. Neurosci. Rehabil. **11**(2), 16–20 (2011)

40. Black, R.E., Allen, L.H., Bhutta, Z.A., Caulfield, L.E., De Onis, M., Ezzati, M., Mathers, C., Rivera, J.: Maternal and child undernutrition study group. Maternal and child undernutrition: global and regional exposures and health consequences. Lancet **371**(9608), 243–260 (2008)

41. Pelletier, D.L., Low, J.W., Johnson, F.C., Msukwa, L.A.: Child anthropometry and mortality in Malawi: testing for effect modification by age and length of follow-up and confounding by socioeconomic factors. J. Nutr. **124**(1), 2082–2105 (1994)

42. Ferretti, R.L., Maia-Lemos, P.S., Guedes, K.J., Caran, E.M.: Malnutrition in children and adolescents with malignant neoplasms under antineoplastic treatment: is there any method of identification that has a good correlation with other valid methods? Clin. Nutr. ESPEN **40**(1), 6–14 (2020)

43. Iips, I.: National Family Health Survey (NFHS-4), 2015–16. International Institute for Population Sciences (IIPS), Mumbai, India (2017)

44. Dereń, K., Nyankovskyy, S., Nyankovska, O., Łuszczki, E., Wyszyńska, J., Sobolewski, M., Mazur, A.: The prevalence of underweight, overweight and obesity in children and adolescents from Ukraine. Sci. Rep. **8**(1), 1–7 (2018)

45. Pandey, K.: Why are boys more malnourished than girls in India? Down to Earth. https://www.downtoearth.org.in/ blog/health/why-are-boys-more-malnourished-than-girls-in-india-59734. Accessed 26 July 2019

Mexican Older-Adult Sitting and Standing Anthropometric Dimensions. Comparison with Other Populations

Elvia Luz González-Muñoz[1](✉) ⓘ, Rosalio Avila Chaurand[1] ⓘ,
John A. Rey Galindo[1] ⓘ, and Gabriel Ibarra Mejia[2] ⓘ

[1] Universidad de Guadalajara, Guadalajara, Jalisco, México
elvia.gmunoz@academicos.udg.mx
[2] University of Texas at El Paso, El Paso, USA

Abstract. The results of an anthropometric study carried out with 425 older adults of both sexes are presented. The research was carried out in a Social Center for Older Adults by Day in the Metropolitan Area of Guadalajara. The sample consisted of 319 female and 106 male subjects. Thirty-nine anthropometric parameters were measured, and tables were built with the collected data. The anthropometric measures were compared to previous studies on Mexican older-adult populations. Those from other countries, as part of the overarching goal for improving the interactions between the older-adult user population, their environment, and the objects themselves. By applying a t-test to compare the dimensions between men and women, we found statistically significant differences ($p < 0.001$) in the analyzed measurements, except for maximum body depth and thigh height. Likewise, it was possible to verify the secular trend of weight and height in the studied population, finding that the older the age, the smaller these dimensions are. The data obtained were compared with those of studies of older adults of other nationalities. Statistically significant differences were found ($p = 0.01$) with women from Italy [1], Brazil [2], and Sweden [3].

Keywords: Anthropometric · Older-adult · Design · Mexican population

1 Introduction

At present, Mexico has an aging population trend. This phenomenon is repeated both in Latin America and in the rest of the world. By the year 2050, data and projections of the National Population Council indicate that almost 30% of Mexico's population will be older adults [4]. This situation represents a significant challenge for society. It is necessary to guarantee an accessible and coherent context with the characteristics and requirements of the elderly population. Based on this, it is essential to begin transforming spaces and objects to favor more inclusive environments.

Although it is not the only aspect, reference anthropometric population dimensions are essential to adjust the environments to their characteristics. These are fundamental for identifying differences among populations, defining the dimensions, and improving

N. L. Black et al. (Eds.): IEA 2021, LNNS 223, pp. 96–104, 2022.
https://doi.org/10.1007/978-3-030-74614-8_11

the interaction between people, spaces, and products, considering possible vulnerable populations. Having updated and complete anthropometric data is essential for making the right design decisions regarding the environment and products' dimensions.

Older Mexican adults' reference anthropometric data are necessary to design coherent and inclusive systems that account for diversity between populations and age generations. Having these reference values will allow for more suitable conditions that will minimize risks while using spaces, improve usability, and allowing greater independence for older adults in their daily activities.

The purpose of the present study is to delineate an anthropometric profile of the elderly Mexican population to provide reference data for designers of spaces and objects. We analyzed the collected data to identify anthropometric variability and other differences associated with gender in this specific age group. Several dimension parameters were compared to reference parameter values from a previous study of a sample of the elderly Mexican population and reference parameters from foreign populations, such as Holland, Italy, Brazil, and Sweden, to find variations.

2   Methodology

The research was carried out in a senior daycare social center in the Guadalajara, Mexico Metropolitan Area. The study included 425 adults, 319 females, and 106 males. According to a previous screening questionnaire, their age ranged between 60 and 93 years, and they were all able to carry out their daily activities. The sample size was considered representative of the population, according to ISO 15535 [5].

The instruments used were a Martin-type Anthropometer, model U. of G, two calipers (Glissier type), a small 45 cm, and a large 70 cm; a depth gauge and a wooden handle cone graduated with 1 mm diameter scale increases. Weight was measured using a Seca weight scale model 803, with a ± 100 g precision.

2.1   Procedure

Thirty-nine anthropometric dimensions were measured; 29 considering the guidelines and definitions of ISO 7250-1, [6] and 10 using the technique described by Avila, Prado, and González [7]. The latter were considered since they are necessary to design various objects of everyday use for the elderly.

The standing position measurements were taken in the Frankfort Plane, with shoulders relaxed and both at the same height, arms alongside the body, with the hands gently touching the thighs, heels together, and the balls of the feet apart, forming an angle of 45°.

We used an adjustable-height chair and flat seat pan to collect anthropometric measures in the seated position. The subject was sitting with the head oriented in the Frankfort plane, with shoulders and arms relaxed, hands resting on the first third of the thighs. The seat height was adjusted so that the thighs will form a 90-degree angle with the leg and the feet resting entirely on the floor.

3 Results

Descriptive data were obtained for all individual variables. The data normality was checked to employ the variation coefficient; kurtosis and skewness were also estimated. The Table 1, 2, 3 and 4 were developed, including the estimated mean, standard deviation, and 5th and 95th percentiles of the anthropometric measures. The reported data show normal behavior, except for weight in both sexes and height of the sitting elbow and thigh height in women.

Table 1. Standing measurement of older females (F) and males (M)

Measurement	Sex	Mean	sd	Percentiles		t-test
				P5	P95	
Weight	F	66.09	12.12	49	87	5.62***
	M	75.03	14.78	51	103	
Stature	F	1506	64.26	1408	1614	16.25***
	M	1639	76.25	1505	1767	
Eye height	F	1399	62.29	1298	1502	16.62***
	M	1531	73.27	1399	1653	
Shoulder height	F	1243	57.70	1156	1344	16.52***
	M	1368	70.36	1248	1475	
Elbow height	F	930	50.16	856	1004	14.53***
	M	1023	57.31	916	1110	
Knee height	F	430	29.38	382	478	13.22***
	M	473	30.25	419	523	
Chest depth	F	298	32.21	247	354	5.66 ***
	M	277	29.08	229	341	
Body depth	F	316	38.64	251	375	1.33
	M	310	43.63	249	402	
Chest breadth	F	323	35.01	267	380	4.42***
	M	341	34.78	286	407	
Max. body breadth	F	490	46.69	421	566	6.30***
	M	523	50.34	445	620	

***$p \leq 0.001$

Table 2. Sitting measurements of older females (F) and males (M)

Measurement	Sex	Mean	sd	Percentiles		t- test
				P5	P95	
Height. sitting	F	780	45.08	714	844	12.96***
	M	844	42.51	768	918	
Shoulder height. sitting	F	519	40.07	453	573	11.36***
	M	569	36.73	509	632	
Elbow height. sitting	F	206	42.22	144	265	2.62**
	M	218	32.78	160	277	
Thigh clearance	F	144	37.59	113	177	1.85
	M	149	18.60	118	177	
Knee height. sitting	F	456	41.64	412	503	10.68***
	M	503	32.79	449	557	
Popliteal height. sitting	F	364	34.96	316	412	11.08***
	M	405	26.95	362	455	
Shoulder-elbow length	F	331	22.54	300	365	6.12***
	M	363	19.95	326	398	
Bideltoideal breadth	F	465	51.87	392	562	2.26*
	M	479	61.40	372	574	
Elbow-to-elbow breadth	F	481	52.73	400	575	1.60
	M	491	57.60	401	586	
Hip breadth. sitting	F	392	43.43	325	474	1.17
	M	387	35.24	328	449	

*$p \leq 0.05$ **$p \leq 0.01$ ***$p \leq 0.001$

Table 3. Functional measurements of older females (F) and males (M)

Dimension	Sex	Mean	sd	Percentiles		t-test
				P5	P95	
Grip diameter	F	35	4.28	28	41	7.25***
	M	38	4.15	32	46	
Fist height	F	664	41.95	595	725	11.58***
	M	726	49.82	642	803	
Foward reach	F	715	39.64	644	774	11.51***
	M	767	42.78	695	839	
Side arm reach	F	688	35.44	631	751	16.37***

(*continued*)

Table 3. (*continued*)

Dimension	Sex	Mean	sd	Percentiles		t-test
				P5	P95	
	M	755	38.11	696	817	
Maximum vertical reach	F	1830	85.78	1690	1972	16.81***
	M	2004	108.40	1803	2180	
Chest breadth	F	323	35.01	267	380	4.42***
	M	341	34.78	286	407	
Max. body breadth	F	490	46.69	421	566	6.30***
	M	523	50.34	445	620	
Buttock-popliteal length	F	444	38.07	391	511	3.58***
	M	455	27.93	402	500	
Buttock-knee length	F	541	55.06	440	605	6.50***
	M	577	31.31	520	626	
Elbow-wrist length	F	327	24.61	295	358	8.99***
	M	357	21.07	322	388	

***$p \leq 0.001$

Table 4. Measurements on specific body segments of older females (F) and males (M).

Measurement	Sex	Mean	sd	Percentiles		t-test
				P5	P95	
Head breath	F	150	7.60	140	160	6.43***
	M	155	8.47	143	170	
Face length	F	126	9.06	111	142	10.16***
	M	137	10.15	121	158	
Head length	F	183	13.62	172	196	6.11***
	M	191	7.21	179	205	
Hand breadth at the thumb	F	90	7.82	80	103	11.89***
	M	100	7.44	86	111	
Hand breadth at metacarpals	F	74	4.20	68	81	18.13***
	M	83	4.62	76	92	
Hand length	F	165	9.43	149	179	14.14***
	M	180	10.54	162	196	

(*continued*)

Table 4. (*continued*)

Measurement	Sex	Mean	sd	Percentiles		t-test
				P5	P95	
Palm length perpendicular	F	94	7.66	82	102	10.23***
	M	102	.6.82	90	114	
Thickness hand	F	29	3.88	24	36	9.61***
	M	34	3.65	27	40	
Foot length	F	226	13.51	204	247	14.89***
	M	249	14.78	223	271	
Foot breadth	F	87	6.46	75	97	10.35***
	M	94	5.96	86	106	
Heel foot breath	F	64	7.72	53	76	8.40***
	M	71	7.01	60	84	

$*p \leq 0.05 **p \leq 0.01 ***p \leq 0.001$

3.1 Comparison by Gender and Secular

When comparing the male and female groups using a t-test, a statistically significant difference was found between both groups for all measures, except for maximum body depth and thigh height.

The results were compared with a sample obtained by Ávila et al. [7] in the same locality and using the same technique to establish the secular trend. We compared the weight and height data obtained in both studies; no statistically significant differences were found (Figs. 1 and 2).

Statistically significant differences were found between the age groups. An inverse relationship between age and weight and height dimensions was identified by logistic regression analysis. The dimensions of the participants were smaller as age increased.

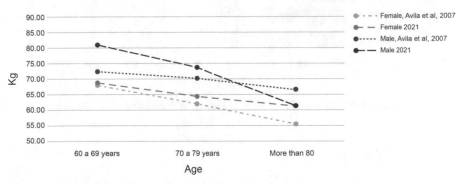

Fig. 1. Comparison of the weight of male and female with Avila et al. [7]

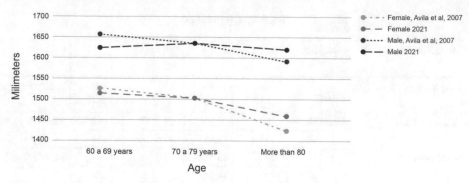

Fig. 2. Comparison of the height of male and female Avila et al. [7]

3.2 Comparison with Other Populations

We compared the height data obtained in this study with other published data from older adults of different nationalities. Height is a dimension measured in all studies and with the same technique. Statistically significant differences were found ($p = 0.01$) with women from Italy [1], Brazil [2], and Sweden [3]. Furthermore, men's height was also compared with previous studies from Italy and Sweden, yielding statistically significant differences.

Both sexes' data were compared with the study results in Australia [8], showing no statistically significant differences. Recognizing these differences is essential since it implies the need for older adults' objects to be designed or chosen according to their dimensions (Figs. 3 and 4).

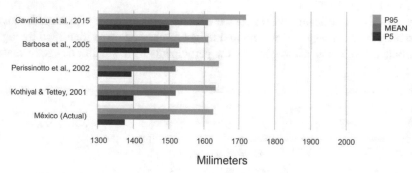

Fig. 3. Comparison of the height of female from different populations.

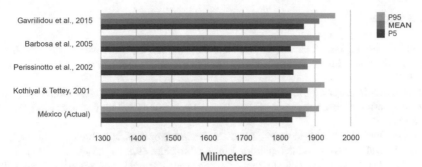

Fig. 4. Comparison of the stature of male from different populations

4 Discussion

Rapid population changes show the importance of having up-to-date data on user dimensions. These changes are even more relevant if we consider that populations such as the elderly have seldom focused on anthropometric studies and population distribution changes. This situation has begun to put older adults at the center of the built environment's development.

Although no significant differences were found between the older adults reported by Ávila et al. and the results of the present study, in the groups of 60 to 69 and 70 to 79, differences in weight between populations are similar to those reported by Dey et al. [9] who found 1.5 and 6.3 kg heavier to the later-born cohort in comparison to an earlier-born cohort. Differences between age and gender groups in the present study match other studies in Latinamerica [10].

It is essential to develop anthropometric reference data considering sitting and standing postures. One of the limitations in indirect methods such as scanners is registering body dimensions in sitting posture. Using scanners for anthropometry represents a problem. Designers need baseline parameters to design different spaces and workstations for sitting posture [11], which is not feasible using 3-D scanners. Also, scanners have shown less accuracy for measuring body areas when there are small posture variations, e.g., shoulders, head, and neck [12]. In this case, the direct 1-D method used in the present study has the advantage of allowing to collect data in both postures.

5 Conclusions

The data obtained were representative of the Mexican population in the western part of the country. Statistically significant differences were found in comparing men and women in the study population and data from other countries.

The use of 1D measurements is advantageous due to the cost that it implies, especially for studies carried out in developing countries. Having anthropometric data on older adults, representing this population, will allow both designers and architects to build better housing and consumer goods that fit the elderly.

References

1. Perissinotto, E., Pisent, C., Sergi, G., Grigoletto, F., Enzi, G., ILSA Working Group: Anthropometric measurements in the elderly: age and gender differences. Br. J. Nutr. **87**(2), 177–186 (2002)
2. Barbosa, A.R., Souza, J.M., Lebrão, M.L., Laurenti, R., Marucci, M.D.F.N.: Anthropometry of elderly residents in the city of São Paulo, Brazil. Cadernos de Saúde pública **21**(6), 1929–1938 (2005)
3. Gavriilidou, N.N., Pihlsgård, M., Elmståhl, S.: Anthropometric reference data for elderly Swedes and its disease-related pattern. Eur. J. Clin. Nutr. **69**(9), 1066–1075 (2015)
4. CONAPO (Consejo Nacional de Población): Proyecciones de la población de México 2010–2050 Documento metodológico (2012)
5. ISO (International Standardisation Organisation): ISO 15535:2012 General Requirements for Establishing Anthropometric Databases. International Organization for Standardization, Geneva, Switzerland (2012)
6. ISO (International Standarisation Organisation): ISO 7250–1:2008 Basic Human Body Measurements for Technological Design - Part 1: Body Measurement Definitions and Landmarks. International Organization for Standardization, Geneva, Switzerland (2008)
7. Avila, R., Prado, L.R., Gonzalez, E.L.: Dimensiones Antropométricas de Población Latinoamericana. Universidad de Guadalajara, México (2007)
8. Kothiya, K., Tettey, S.: anthropometry for design for the elderly. Int. J. Occup. Saf. Ergon. **7**(1), 15–34 (2001)
9. Dey, D.K., Rothenberg, E., Sundh, V., Bosaeus, I., Steen, B.: Height and body weight in elderly adults: a 21-year population study on secular trends and related factors in 70-year-olds. J. Gerontol. Ser. A Biol. Sci. Med. Sci. **56**(12), 780–784 (2001). https://doi.org/10.1093/gerona/56.12.m780
10. Canaan, F., Queiroz, A., Priore, S., Castro, S.: Anthropometric differences related to genders and age in the elderly. Nutr. Hosp. **32**(2), 757–764 (2015)
11. Bragança, S., Arezes, P., Carvalho, M., Ashdown, S.: Current state of the art and enduring issues in anthropometric data collection. DYNA **83**(197), 22–30 (2016)
12. Tomkinson, G., Shaw, L.: Quantification of the postural and technical errors in asymptomatic adults using direct 3D whole body scan measurements of standing posture. Gait Posture **37**(2), 172–177 (2013). https://doi.org/10.1016/j.gaitpost.2012.06.031

Firefighters' Anthropometrics: A Comparison Between Two Portuguese Fire Brigades

Anna S. P. Moraes[1](✉) ⓘ, Miguel A. F. Carvalho[1] ⓘ, Rachel S. Boldt[1] ⓘ,
Fernando B. N. Ferreira[1] ⓘ, Susan P. Ashdown[2] ⓘ, and Linsey Griffin[3] ⓘ

[1] University of Minho, Guimaraes, Portugal
[2] Cornell University, Ithaca, USA
[3] University of Minnesota, Minneapolis, USA

Abstract. In firefighting, fit and sizing of personal protective equipment are directly related with the protection level, work performance, and comfort of firefighters. Furthermore, proper fit and sizing depend on appropriate sizing systems and the validity of the data from which they were constructed. Thus, anthropometric data are paramount for personal protective equipment design. Despite recent studies, anthropometric databases on firefighters are still very limited. Aiming to fulfill this shortcoming as well as to understand if Portuguese firefighters' protective equipment is adjusted to their anthropometrics, a study designated as *Size FF Portugal – Anthropometric Study of Portuguese Firefighters* is currently underway. This paper presents a preliminary comparison of anthropometric data of firefighters from two different fire brigades: a mixed brigade and a professional brigade. Results of an initial analysis show that participants from the professional brigade were on average 29 mm taller than participants from the mixed brigade. Moreover, participants from the mixed brigade were on average 6.93 kg heavier. Further, results of inferential ANOVA test at a 95% confidence level revealed statistically significant differences of the stature and weight between career-volunteer firefighters from the mixed brigade and career firefighters from the professional brigade. Furthermore, an examination of Body Mass Index revealed that 71.88% of all participants from the mixed brigade as well as 41.58% of participants from the professional brigade were considered above the normal weight range. Differences of anthropometric measurements between the two fire brigades reveal the relevance in developing a more comprehensive yet detailed anthropometric database of Portuguese firefighters.

Keywords: Anthropometric data · Body mass index · Firefighting · Fit and sizing · Personal protective equipment

1 Introduction

Anthropometric data are essential for applying ergonomic principles to the design of a wide range of products and are paramount when developing personal protective equipment (PPE). In the case of occupations that deal with extreme circumstances, as is the

N. L. Black et al. (Eds.): IEA 2021, LNNS 223, pp. 105–113, 2022.
https://doi.org/10.1007/978-3-030-74614-8_12

case of firefighting, fit and sizing of PPE is not only related with protection level but also with work performance, mobility, and comfort.

A proper fit of PPE depends on appropriate sizing systems. This, in turn, depends on the methods used for developing the sizing system and the validity of the data from which it was constructed. As stated by Zakaria and Gupta [1], an accurate sizing system must be built based on actual anthropometric data as the understanding of body sizes and shapes is the only way to cater to the needs of consumers.

In the last decades, studies have been finding significant anthropometric differences among specialized occupational groups [2–4]. Hsiao *et al.* [2], for example, compared data of a US anthropometric database and identified that both men and women serving in protective service occupations[1] have different body dimensions and configurations when compared to other occupational groups as well as to the general population.

The importance of PPE fit and sizing for the firefighting profession, allied to the specificity of occupational groups anthropometrics justify the need for a better understanding of firefighters' body dimensions.

1.1 Firefighters' Anthropometric Surveys

Anthropometric databases on firefighters are still very limited, despite the growing interest of researchers on this topic. Comprehensive anthropometric surveys including large sample sizes were conducted in the USA, in New Zealand and in the United Kingdom. To the best of found knowledge, the most thorough firefighters anthropometric survey was conducted at the National Institute for Occupational Safety and Health (NIOSH), comprised of a sample of 951 US firefighters, including male and female professionals from different types of commitment [5]. Another broad study was conducted in New Zealand, involving a sample size of 691 male participants including both professional and volunteer firefighters [6]. Furthermore, a survey focused on a sample of about 310 female firefighters was conducted in the United Kingdom [7]. Types of commitment were not mentioned in the study [7]. Other studies with smaller sample sizes were also identified in a literature search [8–11].

1.2 The Study *Size FF Portugal*

Since 2017, a consortium of US Universities has been conducting an anthropometric study of firefighters named *Size FF*, under the scope of a larger project[2]. In 2018, the Centre for Textile Science and Technology (2C2T), in the Department of Textile Engineering at the University of Minho, took the study to Portugal. The study *Size FF Portugal – Anthropometric Study of Portuguese Firefighters* was launched.

The main goals of the *Size FF Portugal* study are to understand if Portuguese firefighters' PPE is adjusted to their anthropometrics and to present Ergonomic redesign solutions to better improve the fit and sizing of such equipment. Anthropometric data,

---

[1] Including firefighting and fire prevention occupations, police, detectives, and guards.

[2] NC170 Multistate Project – Personal Protective Technologies for Current and Emerging Occupational Hazards.

socio-demographic information as well as the perceptions and experiences of firefighters when selecting and wearing their current PPE are collected following the same procedures and materials used in the US study.

In an initial stage of the study, data were collected in two fire brigades located in the North of Portugal. This paper presents a comparative analysis of anthropometric data of participant firefighters from these two fire brigades.

2   Materials and Methods

2.1   Data Collection

The process of gaining access to participants initiated with a formal request to the fire brigades' chiefs-in-command. After obtaining authorization, all firefighters from both brigades were invited to participate in the study. Once willing to participate, subjects were fully informed about the study protocols. On agreement to participate, subjects were requested to sign an informed consent form. Data were collected in fire brigades' facilities, in private rooms especially assigned for the study. Data were individually collected, and all data collection stages lasted for about 2 h. In some cases, data collection was completed in two sessions.

Initially, participants were requested to answer an online questionnaire. A semi-structured interview was also administered. Socio-demographic information and participants' perceptions about their current PPE was gathered. Subsequently, participants' body, hands, and feet were scanned using a handheld 3D body scanner. Additionally, measurements of calf circumference, calf height, crotch height, weight, and stature were manually obtained. Measurements were acquired with participants barefoot and wearing underwear. In this paper, stature and weight data will be presented. Data acquisition protocols followed standardized protocols [12].

2.2   Data Treatment and Analysis

Participants' data were anonymously and confidentially treated and analyzed. Data were analyzed using descriptive and inferential statistics.

Initially, basic descriptive statistics analysis on participants' stature and body weight were performed for the arithmetic mean, standard deviation, as well as minimum and maximum. Moreover, data were prepared as suggested in the EN-ISO 15535:2012 standard: measurements over ± 3 SD from the mean were reviewed [13]. Coefficients of variation were calculated for each measurement and compared to the literature. Moreover, body mass index (BMI) was estimated according to the BMI equation[3]. BMI results were analyzed using reference values suggested by the World Health Organization [14].

Later, statistical hypothesis tests were performed aiming to verify differences between measurements of firefighters from both brigades. Participant firefighters were divided considering different types of commitment. For the application of the One Way ANOVA inferential test, assumptions of independent samples, normal distribution of the analyzed population, and equal standard deviations were verified. Firstly, normality of

---

[3] $BMI = weight/height^2$ (kg/m^2).

data was assessed using the Shapiro-Wilk test. Secondly, the Levene test was applied to verify if the difference between the variances of two or more groups was significant. Finally, the ANOVA test (right tailed) was applied for each dimension, taking into consideration the type of commitment. Later, the post-hoc Tukey HSD test was performed for multiple comparisons between each 2 groups. All tests were applied considering a 95% confidence level.

3 Results

As aforementioned, data were collected in two Portuguese fire brigades[4]. First, a pilot study was conducted in a mixed fire brigade (MB[5]) that has both career-volunteer[6] firefighters and volunteer[7] firefighters. Next, data was collected in a professional fire brigade (PB[8]) in which all members are career firefighters.

3.1 Descriptive Statistics Analysis

A total of 32 male firefighters from the MB agreed to participate in the pilot study and completed all data collection stages[9]. Considering the type of commitment, from the 32 participants, 24 (75.00%) were career-volunteer firefighters and 8 participants (25.00%) were volunteer firefighters. Considering the PB, 101 male firefighters agreed to participate[10].

Results show that all firefighters from the MB were on average 1723.47 mm tall. The mean stature of career-volunteer firefighters (MB) was 1720.71 mm while the mean stature of volunteer firefighters was 1731.75 mm. The mean stature of participants from the PB was 1752.57 mm. Furthermore, participants from the PB presented a wider stature range, varying from 1576.00 mm to 1921.00 mm. For the MB, stature ranged from 1610.00 to 1812.00 mm, being the shortest participant a career-volunteer firefighter and the tallest one a volunteer firefighter.

Participants from the MB presented an average weight of 83.65 kg, compared to 76.72 kg of participants from the PB. Considering the two types of commitment of the

---

[4] According to the Decree-Law no. 247/2007 [19], Portuguese fire brigades are classified into 4 types: professional fire brigades, mixed fire brigades, volunteer fire brigades, and private fire brigades. Professional fire brigades have exclusively career firefighters and depend on a municipality. Mixed fire brigades depend on a municipality or an association of firefighters and have both career firefighters and volunteer firefighters.

[5] Hereafter referred to as MB.

[6] Career firefighters serving in mixed brigades may also offer their services on a volunteer basis. In this fire brigade, career firefighters usually volunteer during night shifts and weekend shifts.

[7] Part-time firefighters who voluntarily offer their services in firefighting. In this brigade, volunteer firefighters serve during night and weekend shifts.

[8] Hereafter referred to as PB.

[9] Some participants decided to interrupt their participation and others were not available to conclude all data collection stages.

[10] However, many participants of the PB did not complete all data collection stages. Due to this limitation, some data were not discussed in this paper, such as participants' average age and years of experience in firefighting.

MB, the mean weight was greater in the case of career-volunteer participants (86.14 kg) than for volunteer participants (76.18 kg).

Coefficients of variations for considered dimensions were in the characteristic value range proposed by Pheasant and Haslegrave [15]: 3–4% for stature and 10–21% for weight. During data preparation, one measurement was identified as an outlier[11].

Descriptive statistics for both stature and weight are summarized in Table 1.

Table 1. Descriptive statistics of stature and weight data for each fire brigade and type of commitment.

	Sample size	Sample mean	Standard deviation	Range	Coefficient of variation
Stature (mm)					
MB participants	32	1723.47	48.91	1610–1812	2.84%
Career-volunteer	24	1720.71	45.93	1610–1794	2.67%
Volunteer	8	1731.75	59.65	1619–1812	3.44%
PB participants	101	1752.57	61.27	1576–1921	3.50%
Weight (kg)					
MB participants	32	83.65	13.81	58.0–112.6	16.51%
Career-volunteer	24	86.14	12.78	61.6–112.6	14.84%
Volunteer	8	76.18	14.93	58.0–102.3	19.60%
PB participants	101	76.72	9.96	50.8–109.7	12.98%

3.2 Hypothesis Testing Analysis

Prior to the application of the ANOVA test, normality of data and equality of variances were verified. The Shapiro-Wilk test accepted the hypothesis of data normality of considered measurements for all groups of participants. Moreover, Levene test results revealed that the population's variances were considered to be equal, for both stature (p-value = 0.542) and weight (p-value = 0.228).

Results of the ANOVA test for mean stature rejected the null hypothesis, which indicates that that the difference between the average stature of the population of firefighters from the three types of commitment was big enough to be statistically significant (p-value = 0.04897)[12]. Similarly, the null hypothesis for the mean weight was rejected, meaning that weight averages of some of the firefighters' populations from different types of commitment were not equal (p-value = 0.00081)[13].

---

[11] Weight, PB: 109.7 kg > 76.72 + 3*9.96 kg.

[12] Statistic F for mean stature was 3.08767 (not in the 95% critical value accepted range: $[-\infty: 3.0658]$).

[13] Statistic F for mean weight was 7.52212 (not in the 95% critical value accepted range: $[-\infty: 3.0658]$).

The post-hoc Tukey HSD test identified that the mean stature of career-volunteer firefighters from the MB and career firefighters from the PB are significantly different[14]. Statistically significant differences were not found when comparing mean stature of career-volunteer firefighters and volunteer firefighter from the MB[15] as well as when comparing career firefighters from the PB and volunteer firefighters from the MB[16]. Similar results of the Tukey HSD test were found considering the mean weight: significant differences between career-volunteer firefighters from the MB and career firefighters from the PB[17], no significant differences between career-volunteer firefighters and volunteer firefighters from the MB[18] as well as between career firefighters from the PB and volunteer firefighters from the MB[19].

3.3 Body Mass Index Analysis

The average Body Mass Index was higher for the participants from the MB than from the PB (28.2 kg/m^2 and 24.9 kg/m^2, respectively). An analysis of the BMI ranges revealed that 58.42% (n = 59) of participants from the PB were considered in the Normal Weight category. The same category summed 28.13% (n = 9) of total participants from the MB. Thirteen (40.63%) participants from the MB were in the Pre-obesity range (11 career-volunteers and 2 volunteers) and 7 (21.88%) were considered in the Obesity Class I category. Furthermore, the BMI of 3 (9.38%) career-volunteer participants from the same brigade was in Obesity Class II category. Table 2 presents the number of participant firefighters in each BMI category.

Table 2. Number of participant firefighters according to BMI (kg/m^2) range

	Under-weight	Normal weight	Pre-obesity	Obesity Class I	Obesity Class II	Obesity Class III
BMI range*	**<18.50**	**18.50–24.99**	**25.00–29.99**	**30.00–34.99**	**35.00–39.99**	**≥40.00**
MB participants	0 (0.00%)	9 (28.13%)	13 (40.63%)	7 (21.88%)	3 (9.38%)	0 (0.00%)
Career-volunteer	0 (0.00%)	4 (16.67%)	11 (45.83%)	6 (25.00%)	3 (12.50%)	0 (0.00%)
Volunteer	0 (0.00%)	5 (62.50%)	2 (25.00%)	1 (12.50%)	0 (0.00%)	0 (0.00%)
PB participants	0 (0.00%)	59 (58.42%)	36 (35.64%)	6 (5.94%)	0 (0.00%)	0 (0.00%)

*According to the WHO [14].

[14] Difference 31.87 mm; p-value = 0.04789.
[15] Difference 11.04 mm; p-value = 0.88988.
[16] Difference 20.82 mm; p-value = 0.60026.
[17] Difference 9.42 kg; p-value = 0.00057.
[18] Difference 9.97 kg; p-value = 0.06593.
[19] Difference 0.55 kg; p-value = 0.98967.

4   Discussion

Anthropometric databases are usually built from stratified samples. Stratification variables such as age and gender are commonly found. Furthermore, according to the purpose of the investigation, other stratification variables such as race/ethnicity and geographical regions may also be taken into account. Preliminary results presented in this study suggest that type of commitment may be a relevant stratification variable to be exploited in the ongoing study as well as in other firefighting anthropometric studies.

Some research has explored the differences among different types of commitment of firefighters in what regards the satisfaction with their turnout ensembles [16] or BMI differences [17]. However, not many studies were found concerning anthropometric differences relevant to the design of PPE. Furthermore, results of studies were not consensual. Significant differences in means of key dimensions[20] between career[21] and volunteer firefighters were noted in the Laing *et al.* [6] study. Contrarily, significant differences between career and volunteer firefighters in some key dimensions[22] were not found in the survey conducted by Hsiao *et al.* [5]. However, the later authors [5] mention that volunteer firefighters were underrepresented in their sample and suggest the inclusion of strata considering different types of commitment in future research.

The presented results revealed differences between stature and weight of participant firefighters from the two fire brigades: participants of the MB were heavier and participants of the PB were taller. In a subsequent analysis, participants of the MB were divided according to their type of commitment. Inferential statistics test revealed that differences of both stature and weight of career firefighters from the PB and career-volunteer firefighters from the MB were statistically significant at a 95% confidence level. In contrast, significant differences were not found when comparing volunteer firefighters and career-volunteer firefighters from the MB as well as volunteer firefighters from the MB and career firefighters from the PB, considering the same confidence level. However, they demonstrate that a special attention must be given to potential differences of Portuguese firefighters' anthropometrics considering their types of commitment.

Furthermore, it is worth mentioning that a further investigation with larger samples may assist to clarify if anthropometric differences may be more related to the type of commitment or to the type of fire brigade which is served. Moreover, an analysis of other key dimensions relevant to firefighting PPE design may also improve this assessment and a better characterization of Portuguese firefighters' anthropometrics.

Despite the fact that no significant differences were found between volunteer firefighters and other types of commitment, this topic deserves further attention. It is worth mentioning that the majority of firefighters serving in Portuguese fire brigades are volunteers, corresponding to 63.10% of Portuguese firefighters [18]. Results may have been affected by the small sample size of participants from the MB, especially in the case of volunteers (n = 8).

---

[20] According to the study: stature, body weight, acromiale height, crotch height, and some circumference measurements (hip girth and chest girth).

[21] Referred as permanent firefighters and including both active and non-active firefighters.

[22] According to the study: stature, body weight, and some circumference measurements.

Not surprisingly, differences between participant firefighters reflected in the BMI results. The analysis of BMI revealed a prevalence of participants from the MB in and over the Pre-Obesity category. Hsiao *et al.* [5] found similar results in the US firefighting population and emphasized that despite the fact that firefighters predominantly have larger body builds than the general population, they are not immune from the overweight prevalence. Ode *et al.* [17] point out that BMI should be used cautiously to identify obesity in this occupational group, in whom muscle mass may be higher.

5   Conclusions and Final Considerations

For anthropometric data to be useful, it must accurately represent the dimensions of the population to which the design is intended. In the case of the firefighting profession, different types of commitment may influence anthropometrics. In this paper, results of statistical analyses evinced the anthropometric differences between firefighters from two different brigades. Statistically significant differences were found for average stature and weight of career-volunteer firefighters from a mixed brigade and career firefighters from a professional brigade. The preliminary results hereby presented will have a significant impact on the definition of the *Size FF Portugal* study sample size and stratification.

Given the limited amount of literature assessing anthropometric differences in both career and volunteer firefighters, the continuation of the study throughout regions of Portugal should focus on larger and diverse samples considering different types of commitment and different types of brigades. Considering this, the development of the study *Size FF Portugal* will allow to develop a more comprehensive yet detailed anthropometric database of Portuguese firefighters. In the end, it is expected to contribute to their protection, performance, and comfort.

Acknowledgments. We would like to acknowledge the 2C2T-Centre for Textile Science and Technology of the University of Minho. This work is financed by FEDER funds through the Competitive Factors Operational Program (COMPETE) POCI-01-0145-FEDER-007136, by national funds through the FCT-Portuguese Foundation for Science and Technology under the project UID/CTM/000264, by Fundo de Apoio às Vítimas dos Incêndios de Pedrógão, and by ICC/Lavoro.

References

1. Zakaria, N., Gupta, D.: Apparel sizing: existing sizing systems and the development of new sizing systems. In: Gupta, D., Zakaria, N. (eds.) Anthropometry, Apparel Sizing and Design, pp. 3–33. Woodhead Publishing, Cambridge (2014). https://doi.org/10.1533/978085709689 0.1.3
2. Hsiao, H., Long, D., Snyder, K.: Anthropometric differences among occupational groups. Ergonomics. **45**, 136–152 (2002). https://doi.org/10.1080/00140130110115372
3. Zhuang, Z., Landsittel, D., Benson, S., Roberge, R., Shaffer, R.: Facial anthropometric differences among gender, ethnicity, and age groups. Ann. Occup. Hyg. **54**, 391–402 (2010). https://doi.org/10.1093/annhyg/meq007
4. Stewart, A., Ledingham, R., Williams, H.: Variability in body size and shape of UK offshore workers: a cluster analysis approach. Appl. Ergon. **58**, 265–272 (2017). https://doi.org/10.1016/j.apergo.2016.07.001

5. Hsiao, H., Whitestone, J., Kau, T.Y., Whisler, R., Routley, J.G., Wilbur, M.: Sizing firefighters: method and implications. Hum. Factors **56**, 873–910 (2014). https://doi.org/10.1177/001872 0813516359
6. Laing, R.M., Holland, E.J., Wilson, C.A., Niven, B.E.: Development of sizing systems for protective clothing for the adult male. Ergonomics **42**, 1249–1257 (1999). https://doi.org/10.1080/001401399184929
7. Stirling, M.: National Anthropometry Survey of Female Firefighters - Designing for safety, performance and comfort. Tamworth (2002)
8. Boorady, L.M.: Bunker gear for fire fighters: does it fit today's fire fighters? J. Text. Apparel Technol. Manag. **9**, 1–15 (2015)
9. Langseth-Schmidt, K.: Anthropometric fit evaluation of structural firefighters' protective pants: a gender comparision study (2014). https://search-proquest-com.proxy.library.cornell.edu/docview/1651620916?pq-origsite=summon&accountid=10267
10. Veghte, J.H.: Field Evaluation of Chemical Protective Suits. Beavercreek (1991)
11. McQuerry, M.: Effect of structural turnout suit fit on female versus male firefighter range of motion. Appl. Ergon. **82**, 102974 (2020). https://doi.org/10.1016/j.apergo.2019.102974
12. Lohman, T.G., Roche, A.F., Martorell, R. (eds.): Anthropometric Standardization Reference Manual - Abridged Edition. Human Kinetics Books, Champaign (1991)
13. International Organization for Standardization: EN-ISO 15535:2012 - General Requirements for establishing anthropometric databases (2014)
14. World Health Organization: Obesity: preventing and managing the global epidemic: report of a WHO consultation, Geneva (2000)
15. Pheasant, S., Haslegrave, C.M.: Bodyspace: Anthropometry, Ergonomics and the Design of Work. CRC Press - Taylor & Francis Group, Boca Raton (2006)
16. Park, H., Hahn, K.H.Y.: Perception of firefighters turnout ensemble and level of satisfaction by body movement. Int. J. Fash. Des. Technol. Educ. **7**, 85–95 (2014). https://doi.org/10.1080/17543266.2014.889763
17. Ode, J., Knous, J., Schlaff, R., Hemenway, J., Peterson, J., Lowry, J.: Accuracy of body mass index in volunteer firefighters. Occup. Med. (Chic. Ill) **64**, 193–197 (2014). https://doi.org/10.1093/occmed/kqt143
18. Statistics Portugal - InstitutoNacional de Estatística: Firemen (N.o) by Geographic localization (NUTS-2013), Sex, Age group and Type of link (2019)
19. Ministério da Administração Interna: Decreto-Lei no. 247/2007 de 27 de Junho do Ministério da Administração Interna, Portugal (2007)

A Motion Capture System for Hand Movement Recognition

Graciela Rodríguez-Vega[1,3]([⊠]), Dora Aydee Rodríguez-Vega[2],
Xiomara Penelope Zaldívar-Colado[1], Ulises Zaldívar-Colado[1],
and Rafael Castillo-Ortega[3]

[1] Facultad de Informática, Universidad Autónoma de Sinaloa, Culiacán, Sinaloa, México
[2] Unidad Académica de Mecatrónica, Universidad Politécnica de Sinaloa, Mazatlán, Sinaloa, México
[3] Departamento de Ingeniería Industrial, División de Ingeniería, Universidad de Sonora, URC, Hermosillo, Sonora, México

Abstract. One of the most frequently-used body regions in daily activities is the upper limbs, and many of the work-related musculoskeletal disorders occur in this area, mainly the hands. We highlight the importance of studying hand movements executed at work, and how they affect workers' health and productivity. Data were collected from a hand-motion capture system conformed by six inertial measurement units and six resistive force sensors from hand and fingers movements. Two common hand movements were analyzed using wrist flexion-extension with a small ($-15°$ to $15°$) and medium ($<-15°$ and $>15°$) range of motion and flexion-extension movement with the hand pronated-supinated. Data were classified by traditional methods. A more complex movement involving a 3-finger spherical grip was also recorded. It was found that the lectures from the six inertial sensors and the six force resistive sensors showed a pattern that facilitates the recognition of basic and more complex movements (flexion-extension and spheric handgrip) through visual analysis of the plotted data, even at different ranges of motion.

Keywords: Wrist flexion-extension · Wrist pronation-supination · Spherical grip · Inertial measurement units · Resistive force sensors

1 Introduction

One of the human body regions that is frequently used in daily and work activities are the upper limbs, mainly the hands [1]. Most manual-work at factories is highly repetitive and requires huge force and awkward postures to be executed, sometimes exceeding the workers' capacities [2]. This behavior can be the cause of many work-related musculoskeletal disorders, which represent a third of the injuries at work, a quarter of lost time, and one-fifth of permanent disabilities [3]. As a result, it is important to study the hand movements executed at work to see how they can affect workers' health and productivity.

Human Activity Recognition (HAR) has been widely used to analyze human–machine interactions [4, 5]. The main goal of RAH is to identify activities based on

N. L. Black et al. (Eds.): IEA 2021, LNNS 223, pp. 114–121, 2022.
https://doi.org/10.1007/978-3-030-74614-8_13

the information obtained through a sensory network, which has been possible by the development of low-cost, small-size, and high-computational-capacity technologies [6].

When handling the object, the subject can independently decide how to grasp it, increasing the complexity of the activity recognition [7]. Xue et al. [7] recommended that motion capture systems used in object handling recognition should include tactile and force sensors in addition to inertial sensors.

This study relies on the analysis of data collected by a hand-motion capture system conformed by inertial and force resistive sensors to determine its use in the classification of the hand and fingers movements.

2   Method

2.1   Motion Capture System and Data Collection

A data glove motion-capture system (MoCap) adapted from six inertial sensors with 9 degrees of freedom located on the proximal phalanges and the dorsal side of the hand, and six force resistive sensors, collocated on each fingertip and palm, were used to generate data regarding hand and fingers movements.

Data collected included ten variables for each finger and hand: triaxial acceleration (m/s^2), triaxial angular velocity (rad/s), triaxial magnetic field (μT), and the force exerted by each fingertip described by the voltage (V) measured by the master–slave system. Data processing used Matlab 2019b software in a laptop running Windows 10. The lectures from the inertial sensors were calibrated using *zero motion* and *zero rate* methods before data collection [8].

A simple validity procedure for the inertial and force resistive sensors was performed prior the measurements to assure the correct MoCap system-computer communication.

2.2   Experimental Design

Two movements using the dominant hand were performed to analyze the capability of the data glove in the recognition of the hand and fingers movement: wrist flexion-extension and spheric hand grip. The flexion-extension movement was based on the Rapid Upper Limb Assessment (RULA) criteria [9]. Movements within the range $-15°$ to $15°$ and movements in a wider range ($< -15°$ and $> 15°$) were performed (Fig. 1a). A goniometer with 1° resolution was placed on the dorsal side of the hand to assure the movement was in the correct range.

Additionally, flexion-extension movement was recorded when the wrist was pronated, supinated, and in a neutral position (Fig. 1b). Both datasets were classified using the Classification Learner application from Matlab 2019b. Data were segmented based on a sliding window with size $= 30$ observations and step $= 10$ observations. Accuracy of k-nearest neighbors (k-NN), the support-vector machine (SVM), decision trees, and Naïve–Bayes algorithms were obtained as performance metrics [10].

The spheric hand grip was performed using five fingers. A compressible ball was used to reproduce the movement.

The results obtained for the two experimental movements were plotted and graphically analyzed to determine if it was possible to identify a movement pattern that could be used in classification methods.

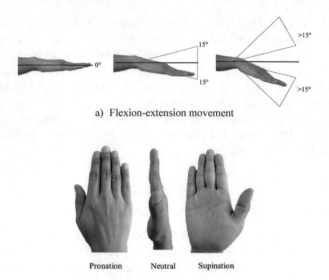

a) Flexion-extension movement

Pronation   Neutral   Supination

b) Pronation-supination movement

Fig. 1. Hand movements

3   Results

Data collected from the Mocap system while performing the wrist flexion-extension in the $-15°$ to $15°$ range of movement are presented in Fig. 2a, while the data collected from a wider range are presented in Fig. 2b. Only the readings obtained by the inertial sensor located on the dorsal side of the hand are presented because the fingers are not involved in the flexion-extension wrist movement considered in this study. The differences in the lecture's amplitude for all the variables can easily be appreciated.

Figure 3 presents the accelerometer, gyroscope, and magnetometer readings obtained from the sensor positioned on the dorsal side of the hand, when the wrist was in a neutral, pronated, and supinated position (lectures 1–500, 500–1000, and 1000–1500, respectively).

Results obtained when classifying both datasets are shown in Table 1. The accuracy value indicates that in both cases, most of the time data can be classified correctly.

Figure 4 shows the confusion matrix obtained for the tree classifier. Figure 5 and 6 show the data obtained for the spherical grip movement. Figure 5 presents the readings obtained by the inertial sensors located on the proximal phalange of each finger and the dorsal side of the hand. In Fig. 6, there is a clear pattern corresponding to each spherical grip exerted from each force-resistive sensor by the lectures.

4   Discussion

In the case of the small wrist flexion-extension movement, the acceleration components x and y obtained by the inertial sensor located at the dorsal side of the hand was near to 0,

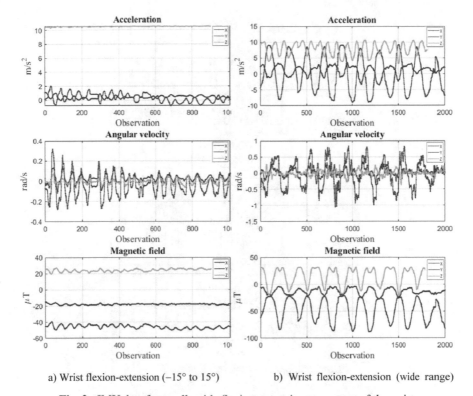

a) Wrist flexion-extension (−15° to 15°)   b) Wrist flexion-extension (wide range)

Fig. 2. IMU data for small–wide flexion-extension movement of the wrist

while the z-axis acceleration was near 9.81 m/s^2 (Fig. 3a). Even though the component of acceleration along the x-axis was near to 0, it was the only variable that let us identify the small movements of the hand graphically. Due to the small range of movement, the angular velocity was close to 0 rad/s (Fig. 3b). In the wider wrist flexion-extension movement analysis, the lectures behaved differently: the full set of acceleration, angular velocity, and magnetic field components present a patron according to movement that can be easily identified. Even though data read from the magnetometer present a cyclical pattern corresponding to each movement exerted, careful interpretation of the movement recognition is necessary due to variations in the readings that can be obtained from the different object materials and the same movement.

When performing the flexion-extension movements in combination with pronation-supination of the wrist, patterns can also be identified from the accelerometer, gyroscope, and magnetometer data. The results obtained by analysis of the corroborated data from the different common classifiers can be categorized correctly, which could be associated with the isolation of the movements performed in a theoretical work environment. This study limitation could be solved by testing the hand mocap in common activities performed in real industrial work.

In the case of the spheric 3-finger handgrip movement, the dorsal side of the hand values do not allow an easy way to identify a patron due to the movement characteristics

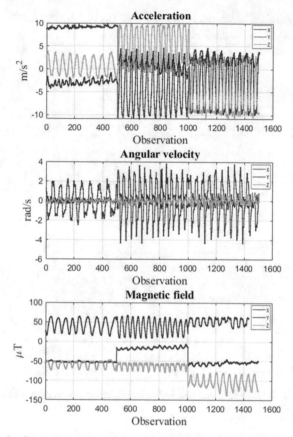

Fig. 3. IMU data for flexion-extension of the wrist with a neutral, pronated, and supinated wrist

Table 1. Classical classifiers accuracy

Classification method	Accuracy (%)	
	Small-wide FE	Pronation-supination + FE
Decision tree	**95.9**	**98.1**
Naïve-Bayes	92.4	97.6
SVM	94.5	81.9
kNN	93.5	97.5

(hand opening and closing). On the contrary, the thumb, index, middle, ring, and little finger lectures show an easy-to-identify patron in the data plot. Due to the fingertip contact with the manipulated object, the voltage measures enable identification of the

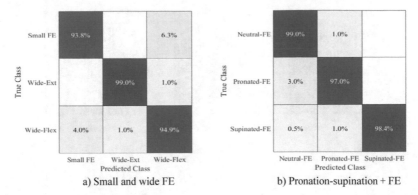

a) Small and wide FE   b) Pronation-supination + FE

Fig. 4. Confusion matrix of the decision tree classifiers

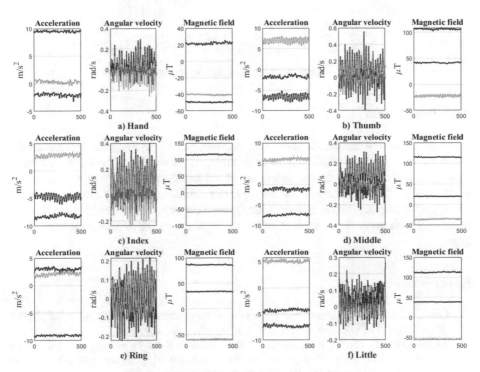

Fig. 5. IMU data for the 3-finger spherical grip

time when the force resistive sensors placed at the thumb tip and index and middle fingertips were used, and the palm, ring finger, and little finger force sensors were not.

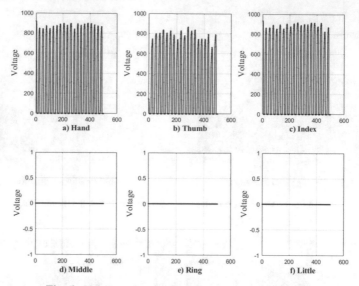

Fig. 6. Voltage value for the FSR and the spherical grip

5   Conclusions

It was demonstrated that the use of only six inertial sensors with 9 degrees of freedom and six resistive sensors are required to identify the basic movement of flexion-extension in small and large ranges of motion, as well as when identifying a pronation and supination position when flexion-extension movement is executed. Data patterns can also be found when performing a 3-finger spherical handgrip. This study can be extrapolated to the other two wrist movements, such as lateral movements, and to the common hand grasp types.

References

1. Lee, K.S., Jung, M.C.: Ergonomic evaluation of biomechanical hand function. Saf. Health Work **6**(1), 9–17 (2015). https://doi.org/10.1016/j.shaw.2014.09.002
2. Armstrong, T.J., Foulke, J.A., Joseph, B.S., Goldstein, S.A.: Investigation of cumulative trauma disorders in a poultry processing plant. Am. Ind. Hyg. Assoc. J. **43**(2), 103–116 (1982). https://doi.org/10.1080/15298668291409433
3. Marty, J., Porcher, B., Autissier, R.: Traumatismes de la main et accident du travail, Statistiques et prevention. Annales Chirurgie de la main **2**(4), 17–19 (1983)
4. Wang, J., Chen, Y., Hao, S., Peng, X., Hu, L.: Deep learning for sensor-based activity recognition: a survey. Pattern Recogn. Lett. **119**, 3–11 (2019). https://doi.org/10.1016/j.patrec.2018.02.010
5. Nweke, H.F., Teh, Y.W., Al-garadi, M.A., Alo, U.R.: Deep learning algorithms for human activity recognition using mobile and wearable sensor networks: state of the art and research challenges. Expert Syst. Appl. **105**, 233–261 (2018). https://doi.org/10.1016/j.eswa.2018.03.056

6. Lara, D., Labrador, M.A.: A survey on human activity recognition using wearable sensors. IEEE Commun. Surv. Tutor. **15**(3), 1192–1209 (2013)
7. Xue, Y., Ju, Z., Xiang, K., Chen, J., Liu, H.: Multimodal human hand motion sensing and analysis—a review. IEEE Trans. Cogn. Dev. Syst. **11**(2), 162–175 (2019). https://doi.org/10.1109/TCDS.2018.2800167
8. Papafotis, K., Sotiriadis, P.P.: Accelerometer and magnetometer joint calibration and axes alignment. Technologies **8**(1), 11 (2020). https://doi.org/10.3390/technologies8010011
9. Lynn, M., Corlett, N.: RULA: a survey method for the investigation of work-related upper limb disorders. Appl. Ergon. **24**(2), 91–99 (1993)
10. Saez, Y., Baldominos, A., Isasi, P.: A comparison study of classifier algorithms for cross-person physical activity recognition. Sensors **17**(1), 66 (2016). https://doi.org/10.3390/s17010066

Hand Shape Modeling for the Mexican Population

Graciela Rodríguez-Vega[1,2]([✉]), Xiomara Penelope Zaldívar-Colado[1],
Ulises Zaldívar-Colado[1], Enrique Javier De la Vega-Bustillos[3],
and Dora Aydee Rodríguez-Vega[4]

[1] Facultad de Informática, Universidad Autónoma de Sinaloa, Culiacán, Sinaloa, México
[2] Departamento de Ingeniería Industrial, División de Ingeniería, Universidad de Sonora, URC,
Hermosillo, Sonora, México
[3] División de Estudios de Posgrado e Investigación, TECNM/Instituto Tecnológico de
Hermosillo, Hermosillo, Sonora, México
[4] Unidad Académica de Mecatrónica, Universidad Politécnica de Sinaloa, Mazatlán, Sinaloa,
México

Abstract. Anthropometric characteristics should be considered in the hand tools,
workstations, and product design to diminish the risk of work-related musculoskeletal disorders. Even though univariate approaches disadvantages when used
in multivariate analysis, most designs are based on the traditional percentile anthropometric data. This study obtained hand models through the univariate percentile
values (1–99%) and two multivariate approaches: Principal Components Analysis
(PCA) and Archetypal Analysis (AA) based on four hand dimensions. Fourteen
hand models were obtained by the PCA, while three, five, and nine archetypal
analysis k-value were selected after a root sum of squares analysis for $k = 1,..., 12$
archetypes. Results suggest that AA models could provide higher accommodation
levels, followed by PCA models and percentile values.

Keywords: Anthropometry · Percentiles · Principal Components Analysis ·
Archetypal analysis

1 Introduction

Poor anthropometric design can lead the individual user to assume awkward postures that
can reduce their capacity at work and increase the risk for work-related musculoskeletal
disorders [1, 2]. It is well known that most anthropometric workstation and hand tools
designs are based on univariate anthropometric data [3]. It has also been demonstrated
that the use of percentiles can be inappropriate since percentile values are not additive
unless they are equal to 50% [4–6]. Several studies in the literature have investigated
representative human models for different populations and anatomical regions across
the world by using multivariate approaches such as Principal Components Analysis
(PCA) and Archetypal Analysis (AA) [5, 7–9]. These study authors found no evidence
of research that has analyzed human/hand models in the Mexican/northwestern Mexican
population.

N. L. Black et al. (Eds.): IEA 2021, LNNS 223, pp. 122–127, 2022.
https://doi.org/10.1007/978-3-030-74614-8_14

The primary aim of this study is to model the dominant hand dimensions of the current northwestern Mexican male population. The study's second goal is to provide useful dominant hand models of the northwestern Mexican population that can be applied in the ergonomic design of workstations, hand tools, and products.

2 Materials and Methods

2.1 Anthropometric Data: Participants and Data Collection

To obtain the anthropometric information a total of 2,613 males were randomly selected for the survey. Subjects included healthy university professors, graduate and postgraduate students, and industrial workers between 18 and 61 years-old, who resided in northwestern Mexico at the time of the survey. Four hand measurements were taken from the dominant hand (Table 1).

Hand length, palm length, and palm width were taken with a caliper with a 1 mm accuracy; values were registered in centimeters. Grip diameter was measured with a plastic cone and the value measured was registered in millimeters.

Table 1. Anthropometric dimensions

Anthropometric dimension	Description	Measurement unit
Hand Length	Length of the dominant hand between the stylion landmark of the wrist and the tip of the middle finger	cm
Palm length	The length of the dominant hand between the landmarks of metacarpal 2 and metacarpal 5	cm
Palm width	Width of the palm measure below the knuckles, excluding the thumb	cm
Handgrip diameter	The maximum circumference of the circle drawn by the index finger and thumb of the dominant hand	mm

2.2 Data Analysis

Percentiles 1, 5, 10, 25, 50, 75, 90, 95, and 99 were calculated on each dimension. The mean, standard deviation, maximum and minimum values were also calculated.

The anthropometric dimension values were standardized using the normal distribution. Then, two boundary methods were considered in this study, Principal Components Analysis (PCA) and Archetypal Analysis (AA).

A 99% sphere was adjusted to the data. A total of 14 theoretical boundary cases were identified on the sphere contour. From the theoretical boundary cases the real boundary subjects were identified by selecting the closest subject to the boundary case point within the ellipsoid, based on the Euclidean distance. The PCA was performed using Matlab 2020a.

AA was performed using the Anthropometry Package developed by Vinue in RStudio [10]. AA assumes that there are several "pure" individuals who are on the "edges" of the data, and all other individuals are considered a mixture of these pure types. The analysis was performed for k = 1,..., 11 archetypes. The best k-value was determined by a graphical analysis of the root sum squared values (RSS). The real boundary cases were defined by the nearest neighbors to the archetypes, based on the Euclidean distance.

The percentile corresponding to each anthropometric dimension value was obtained, based on the complete database.

3   Results

The univariate percentile values, mean, standard deviation, and minimum and maximum values are presented in Table 2.

Table 2. Male percentiles, mean and standard deviation

AD	Percentile									Mean	SD	Min	Max
	1	5	10	25	50	75	90	95	99				
Hand length	16.8	17.4	17.7	18.3	18.8	19.4	19.9	20.2	20.8	18.81	0.85	15.50	22.00
Palm length	9.4	9.8	10.1	10.4	10.7	11.1	11.5	11.7	12.1	10.75	0.60	8.20	13.30
Palm width	7.6	8	8.2	8.4	8.7	9.1	9.4	9.6	10.04	8.77	0.50	7.00	10.70
Handgrip diameter	39	42	43	45	48	51	53	54	57	47.93	3.84	36.00	60.00

Table 3 shows the PCA scores for the four-hand anthropometric dimensions. The first three PCs were used to define the body models, as the first three components accounted for 95.19% of the total variance [11]. PC1, which was positive and accounted for 60.95% of the total variation, predicted the overall hand size. PC2, accounting for 19.24% of the variation, contrasted the dimensions correlated with hand length and handgrip diameter, and those correlated with palm length and palm width. PC3, accounting for 15.01% of the variation, contrasted the measurements of hand length and palm length with the rest of the dimensions.

Table 4 show the percentile values for the 14 boundary cases obtained by PCA. It can be assumed that models 1 and 3 are similar to the 99 a 1 percentile models, respectively.

In the case of AA results, Fig. 1 shows the RSS for the archetypal models obtained for k = 2,..., 11. It can be seen three inflection points at k = 3, k = 5, and k = 9. Percentile values for AA are shown in Tables 5, 6, and 7. The AA results obtained for k = 3 indicates that model 2 and 3 are the most similar to 1 and 99 percentile models,

Table 3. PCA scores for the hand dimensions

AD	PC1	PC2	PC3	PC4
Hand length	0.5880	−0.0996	−0.2508	0.7626
Palm length	0.5479	0.0043	−0.5724	−0.6101
Palm width	0.3996	0.7975	0.4485	−0.0564
Hand grip diameter	0.4410	−0.5951	0.6390	−0.2077
% Explained variance	60.95	19.24	15.01	4.81
Cumulative %	60.95	80.19	95.19	100.00

Table 4. Percentile values for the boundary cases obtained by PCA

AD	Model													
	1	2	3	4	5	6	7	8	9	10	11	12	13	14
Hand length	>99	49	<1	54	20	59	8	68	40	40	8	72	20	49
Palm length	>99	72	<1	18	10	77	5	77	60	60	22	90	72	92
Palm width	95	98	3	3	75	13	6	75	86	53	18	95	13	37
Hand grip diameter	99	10	2	86	91	6	22	98	40	22	15	71	61	10

whereas models 3 and 5 are the closest to the percentile models in the $k = 5$ AA. For the AA when $k = 9$, the most extreme models are archetypes 5 and 6 for the $k = 9$ analysis, similar to the 1 and 99 percentile models.

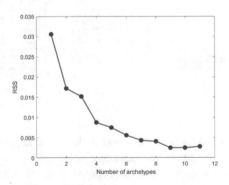

Fig. 1. RSS for the $k = 1,..,11$ archetypes

126 G. Rodríguez-Vega et al.

Table 5. Percentile values for the boundary cases obtained by AA, k = 3

AD	Model		
	1	2	3
Hand length	49	1	99
Palm length	72	<1	100
Palm width	100	1	86
Hand grip diameter	10	10	100

Table 6. Percentile values for the boundary cases obtained by AA, k = 5

AD	Model				
	1	2	3	4	5
Hand length	68	82	<1	20	99
Palm length	92	46	<1	28	98
Palm width	100	75	13	1	97
Hand grip diameter	6	100	4	31	97

Table 7. Percentile values for the boundary cases obtained by AA, k = 9

AD	Model								
	1	2	3	4	5	6	7	8	9
Hand length	12	95	6	99	98	<1	4	75	40
Palm length	2	96	33	100	77	<1	2	53	100
Palm width	23	93	100	86	100	2	18	<1	75
Hand grip diameter	61	2	10	100	94	<1	100	61	71

4 Conclusions

Hand models were obtained by univariate and multivariate approaches. Although hand models for the northwestern Mexican male population obtained by multivariate accommodation methodologies (i.e., AA and PCA) can be used in workstations design due to their similar univariate percentiles, AA models could provide a higher accommodation level.

The models presented in this study can be used to develop hand tools and design workstations for 99% of the northwestern Mexican male population. The different models can also be used to create hand tools and personal protective equipment sizes. Despite the utility of these models, they can be improved by considering additional hand descriptors.

References

1. Hanson, L., Sperling, L., Gard, G., Ipsen, S., Olivares Vergara, C.: Swedish anthropometrics for product and workplace design. Appl. Ergon. **40**(4), 797–806 (2009). https://doi.org/10.1016/j.apergo.2008.08.007
2. Wichansky, M.: Usability testing in 2000 and beyond. Ergonomics **43**(7), 998–1006 (2000). https://doi.org/10.1080/001401300409170
3. Das, B., Sengupta, A.K.: Industrial workstation design: a systematic ergonomics approach. Appl. Ergon. **27**(3), 157–163 (1996)
4. Robinette, K.M., McConville, J.T.: An alternative to percentile models (1981). https://doi.org/10.4271/810217
5. Zehner, G.F., Meindl, R.S., Hudson, J.A.: A multivariate anthropometric method for crew station design: abridged (U) (AL-TR-1992-0164). Wright-Patterson Air Force Base (1993)
6. Albin, T.J., Vink, P.: An empirical description of the dispersion of 5th and 95th percentiles in worldwide anthropometric data applied to estimating accommodation with unknown correlation values. Work **52**(1), 3–10 (2015). https://doi.org/10.3233/WOR-141899
7. Bittner, A.C.: A-CADRE: advanced family of manikins for workstation design. In: Proceedings of the XIVth Triennial Congress of the International Ergonomics Association and 44th Annual Meeting of the Human Factors and Ergonomics Association. Ergonomics for the New Millennium, pp. 774–777 (2000). https://doi.org/10.1177/154193120004403824
8. Epifanio, I., Vinué, G., Alemany, S.: Archetypal analysis: contributions for estimating boundary cases in multivariate accommodation problem. Comput. Ind. Eng. **64**(3), 757–765 (2013). https://doi.org/10.1016/j.cie.2012.12.011
9. Young, K., Margerum, S., Barr, A., Ferrer, M.A., Rajulu, S.: Derivation of boundary manikins: a principal component analysis. SAE Tech. Pap., no. 724 (2008). https://doi.org/10.4271/2008-01-1879
10. Vinué, G.: Anthropometry: an R package for analysis of anthropometric data. J. Stat. Softw. **77**(6), 1–39 (2017). https://doi.org/10.18637/jss.v077.i06
11. Jolliffe, I.T.: Principal component analysis, second edition. Encycl. Stat. Behav. Sci. **30**(3), 487 (2002). https://doi.org/10.2307/1270093

Part III: Biomechanics (Edited by Rauf Iqbal)

Effects of a Back-Support Exoskeleton on Pelvis-Thorax Kinematics and Coordination During Lifting

Sivan Almosnino, Rong Huangfu$^{(\boxtimes)}$, and Jessica Cappelletto

Amazon.Com, Inc., Seattle, WA 98109, USA

Abstract. We assessed the effects of a commercially available passive back support exoskeleton device on pelvis thorax kinematics and coordination. Eight male participants performed randomized block trials of 8 freestyle, symmetrical lifting tasks of a 13 kg container with or without use of the device. We obtained whole body kinematic data using an inertial motion capture system. We used Principal component analysis (PCA) to discern angular position and velocity waveform variations between conditions and assessed inter-segmental coordination using continuous relative phase measures. For joint angular position, only 1 PC exhibited statistical significance across conditions. This PC, which explained 10% of the loading vector variation, was interpreted as a phase shift feature. For joint angular velocity profiles, 2 PCs statistically differed between conditions. We interpreted these PCs as local magnitude difference features, particularly at the initial portion of the lift cycle. We did not detect a significant main effect of device usage or lifting phase on pelvis-thorax coordination. Our preliminary results suggest that use of a passive back support exoskeleton changes joint kinematics, but not inter-segment coordination during performance of a lifting task. These results may help understand device usability and interaction.

Keywords: Exoskeleton · Low back · Kinematics · Biomechanics · Principal component analysis

1 Introduction

Exoskeletons are receiving considerable interest for adoption in industrial settings as a control to ease physical demands. Recently, Kazerooni et al. [7] show proof of concept of a passive, low back support exoskeleton aimed at generating a moment between the torso and thigh that counteracts the moment generated by the upper body and external load. The device uses gas springs for energy storage and force generation. The device incorporates an engagement mechanism only when the user bends their trunk, thus likely allowing unconstrained performance of other tasks (e.g., carrying, driving, etc.). In support of the device effectiveness, the authors report reductions in erector spinae muscular raw voltage ranging between 51% and 76% in a group of eight participants when performing a static stoop-style task.

© The Author(s), under exclusive license to Springer Nature Switzerland AG 2022
N. L. Black et al. (Eds.): IEA 2021, LNNS 223, pp. 131–138, 2022.
https://doi.org/10.1007/978-3-030-74614-8_15

A follow up study report that using the device results various reductions in erector spinae electromyographic measures and a 52% increase in endurance time following performance of a continuous lifting task [11]. The authors also report no statistically significant changes in energy consumption rates between the device/no device conditions, which they partially attributed to the participant's fitness level and lifting technique. In specifics to the latter, the authors elaborate that some of their participants elected to lean forward into the device (instead of pushing/crouching into the device), thereby letting gravity initiate trunk flexion and reduce the force required to compress the gas springs. These latter observations raise queries about how users interact with the device and whether it changes lifting technique because of device usage. Knowledge regarding how participants adjust their lifting strategy (or not) when using exoskeletons may aid in decisions pertaining to device usability and possibly guide standard instructions and training of new users. In addition, since different exoskeleton designs may induce different coordination patterns, it is important to assess such devices individually. Thus, this study assesses the effect of a passive, back assist exoskeleton on pelvis-thorax joint kinematics and inter- segment coordination during performance of a symmetrical lifting task.

2   Methods

2.1   Participants and Experimental Procedures

Eight male participants (mean ± SD age: 34 ± 5 yrs., height: 1.81 ± 0.10 m, weight: 85 ± 15 kg.) not affiliated with our worker population were recruited for this study. Testing took place in a climate-controlled laboratory setting and took place between August and November 2019. The participants performed randomized block lifting tasks with and without use of a back-support passive exoskeleton (BackX, model S, SuitX, Emeryville, CA, USA). We adjusted the exoskeleton to each participant's dimensions per the manufacturer's guidelines. We set the support setting to "standard mode", which engages the device with a forward bend of 30° to 45° and provides a 9 kg support strength. The participants were familiarized with the tasks and device through instructions and practice. The participants were then asked to perform eight non-continuous free style lifting and lowering trials of a fixed sized 13 kg plastic container. Lifting occurred from floor level to a table surface height set at 50% of individual stature. During trial performance we recorded full body joint kinematic data from a 17-sensor inertial motion unit system sampling at 60 Hz. (Xsens, Enschande, the Netherlands).

2.2   Data Analysis

Three-dimensional segment angles of the trunk and pelvis and corresponding joint angle were calculated using a ZXY Euler sequence. Note the thorax segment angle was calculated at the T8 segment level. We then calculated joint angular velocities using a central difference method.

We subsequently divided the signals into cycle start and end points using the following procedure: Initially, we converted the position signals to energy signals using the

Teager-Kaiser Energy Operator shown in Eq. 1 [6]:

$$\Psi x(t) = x2(t) - x(t - 1)x(t + 1) \tag{1}$$

Movement initiation to movement termination in a standing posture was defined by the time stamps exceeding three standard deviations from baseline. We verified these visually and manually adjusted if deemed appropriate. Segmental position and velocity time series were then interpolated using a shape preserving spline to 101 data points corresponding to 0%–100% of the lift or lowering cycle.

We quantified inter-segment coordination of the pelvis-trunk using continuous relative phase (CRP) for both ascent and descent phase, which were determined based on the first instant of the trunk or pelvis local maximum. The CRP was calculated following the guidance of Lamb and Stöckl [8]: first; we centered the normalized time series amplitude around zero according to Eq. 2:

$$X_{center}(ti) = x(ti) - \min(x(t)) - (\max(x(t)) - \min(x(t)))/2 \tag{2}$$

We then transformed the angular position signal into a complex, analytical signal $z(t)$, where H(t) of x(t) provide the imaginary part of the analytical signal (Eq. 3):

$$z(t) = x(t) + iH(t) \tag{3}$$

Following, the segmental phase angle (φ) at time point t_i was calculated using the inverse tangent per Eq. 4:

$$\emptyset(t_i) = \tan^{-1}(H(t_i)/x(t_i)) \tag{4}$$

Where of the H(t) is the transformed signal and x(t) is the original signal. The pelvis-trunk CRP is calculated according to Eq. 5:

$$CRP_i = \emptyset_{i,pelvis} - \emptyset_{i,thorax} \tag{5}$$

Waveform principal component analysis (PCA) was used to identify kinematic amplitude and timing differences through the entire task cycle and objectively extract the major contributing variance forms [2]. We first arranged the pelvis-trunk joint position and velocity data into two 128 × 101 matrices where the number of rows correspond to 8 participants × 8 individual trials × 2 conditions. The data were mean centered and subsequently used to calculate the covariance matrix. We then decomposed the covariance matrix according to the model $Z = U^T X$, where U is a transformation matrix which converts the original data into a new coordinate system, and whose columns are the principal component loading vectors. We used a 90% trace criterion for retainment of PCs for further analysis and interpretation. Mean differences between conditions were assessed using paired, two tailed t-tests with alpha level present at 0.05 and adjusted using a Bonferroni correction. Identification of amplitude, difference, and temporal phase shift features was achieved via visual inspection of loading vector plots and single component reconstructions [2].

To compare inter-segment coordination across condition and movement phases (i.e., ascend/descend, or vice versa) we computed the mean absolute relative phase (MARP), where a value equal to $0°$ shows a completely synchronized pattern between the segments, and values of $180°$ point to an out-of-phase pattern [1, 5]. We assessed differences across lifting conditions and phases using a 2-way, repeated measures analysis of variance with alpha a priori set at 0.05 and effect sizes quantified using eta squared.

3 Results

We present descriptive statistics of key principal component models in Table 1. For joint angular positions, 2 PCs explained >90% of the variance between the no device and exoskeleton condition.

Table 1. Key principal component models for pelvis-thorax angular position and velocities.

Task	Kinematic variable	PC #	Explained variance (%)	PC score no device	PC score exoskeleton	p value
Lifting	Angular position	1	80.1%	4.1 ± 122	-4.1 ± 109	0.53
		2	10.0%	-16.9 ± 31.2	16.9 ± 42.6	<0.001
	Angular velocity	2	20.9%	-51.9 ± 105	51.9 ± 172	<0.001
		3	10.5%	25.7 ± 66.3	-25.7 ± 132	0.0015

Evaluation of the corresponding loading vector and single PC reconstruction plots (Fig. 1) show PC1 being a measure of overall magnitude where those with higher PC scores exhibited a larger joint angle throughout the entire task cycle. Examination of individual joint angle time series between and within conditions exhibited reveal large variations, which likely contributed to PC1 not reaching statistical significance level. PC2, which explained 10% of the variance between conditions and was statistically significant (Fig. 1), shows a clear phase shift in which those with lower PC scores reached peak angular position at approximately 60%–70% of the cycle, while those with higher PC scores reached peak angular position at approximately 40%–50% of the cycle.

For joint angular velocity profiles (Fig. 2), 10 PCs reached the 90% trace criteria. However, statistical significance across conditions was detected by only PC2 which explained 20.9% of the variance, and PC3, which explained 10.5% of the variance. Examination of the PC2 loading vector and corresponding single PC reconstruction plots suggest that in the no device condition, local peak angular velocity is achieved at approximately 10% of the cycle. On the other hand, when wearing the device, the angular velocity magnitude at that time point exhibits a local minimum. The PC2 loading vectors also suggest a local minima difference in joint angular velocity amplitude at about 85% of the cycle where use of the exoskeleton resulted in a slightly higher angular velocity at this period. PC3 appears to reinforce a local difference in joint angular velocities between conditions at approximately 25% and 65% of the cycle where those with higher PC scores exhibit a larger velocity magnitude profile.

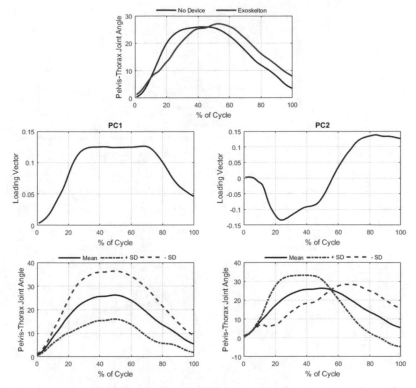

Fig. 1. Pelvis-thorax joint angle principal component analysis. *Top row:* mean time series across participants in each condition. *Middle row:* loading vector plots of PC1 and PC2. *Bottom row:* Mean waveform across both conditions bounded by ±1 SD of the loading vector variation.

Descriptive statistics of MARP values are presented in Table 2. On average, the no device conditions yielded smaller MARP values for both lift descent and ascend phases compared to exoskeleton usage. In addition, the no device condition showed less variability between participants compared to the exoskeleton condition. However, the results of the two-way repeated measures ANOVA revealed no significant main effect of device usage on the participant's pelvis-thorax coordination ($F (1,7) = 2.0$, $p = 0.19$, $\eta_p^2 = 0.22$). There was also no significant main effect of lifting phase ($F (1,7) = 0.0$, $p = 0.98$, $\eta_p^2 = 0.05$). Last, device by phase interaction was not statistically significant ($F (1,7) = 0.66$, $p = 0.44$, $\eta_p^2 = 0.11$).

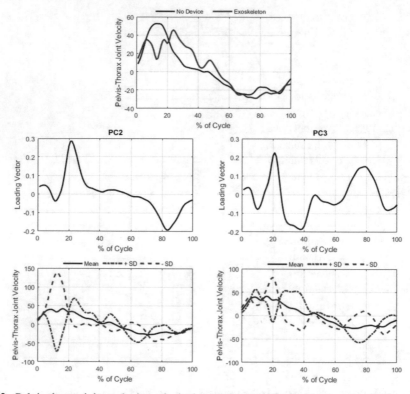

Fig. 2. Pelvis-thorax joint velocity principal component analysis. *Top row:* mean time series across participants in each condition. *Middle row:* loading vector plots of PC2 and PC3. *Bottom row:* Mean waveform across both conditions bounded by ±1 SD of the loading vector variation.

Table 2. Mean ± SD mean absolute relative phase scores for each condition and task phase.

Condition	No device		Exoskeleton	
Lifting phase	Descend	Ascend	Descend	Ascend
MARP	10.6 ± 6.0	9.7 ± 6.9	16.6 ± 11.5	17.6 ± 19.3

4   Discussion

Previous investigations assessing kinematic differences during lifting with and without a back-support exoskeleton using PCA include that performed by Sadler et al. [12]. In their investigation, the authors report a significant decrease in trunk flexion throughout the entire lift cycle when using the device, irrespective of gender. Our results show this trend as well, however, lack statistical significance. We also identified a phase shift phase shift in reaching peak trunk flexion. The differences might be explained by our protocol involving single task freestyle lift performance while the participants in [12] performed continuous lifts at a set pace. In addition, we used a fixed external load, while [12] adjusted the external load to correspond to 10% of maximal back strength. Last, [12] used a table surface with a cutout portion and a smaller container size which perhaps allowed their participants to be positioned closer to the lift destination location and perform continuous lifting tasks while avoiding a collision between the lift destination surface and the container.

The joint angular velocity profiles in our study show the instance at which the exoskeleton is engaged, resulting in a momentary reduction in angular velocity at the beginning of the lift cycle. During this period, the device support counteracts the inertial effects of the upper body mass. These observations are interesting since the participants are likely activating their abdominal muscles to compress the springs. The stability of the lumbar spine is influenced by a complex interaction of abdominal and back muscle magnitude and timing [10]. Further investigations are warranted to assess whether the likely activation of the abdominal muscles when compressing the spring, with the documented reduction in back muscular activity levels [7] influence spinal stability.

Pertaining to pelvis thorax coordination measures, the lack of statistically significant results in our study are naturally attributed to the small sample size. However, another contributing factor are the large variations observed between participants when using the device. These variations may be a function of individual control strategies when engaging and controlling the device support. In our study, we used a constant 9 kg support based on participant preference. However, maybe a more refined decision on the provided support, for example based on torso strength capabilities, would be more optimal for some individuals. Although requiring further investigation, this may practically necessitate measurement of muscle strength capabilities prior to usage. Another aspect that may have contributed to MARP variations may be our decision to use a self-selected freestyle lifting technique. We perceive this to be most valid for extrapolation of results to real-world settings. Last, inter-segmental pelvis-thorax coordination seems to be affected by the magnitude of the external load handled [1], and we tested only one external load condition. On a more fundamental level, we should note that it is not clear whether a pelvis-thorax coordination being more in-phase or out-of-phase is beneficial (or not). Previously, some have suggested that injury risk is thought to be partially influenced by the coordination of spinal components [3, 4, 9]. Pertaining to exoskeletons, Graham et al. [4] report that inter-joint coordination patterns are more synchronous compared to no device freestyle lifting (albeit affected by the external mass handled), and although reserved in their argument, suggest the results provide some evidence of device safety. We cannot directly compare our study results because of measuring *inter-segmental* coordination, while the mentioned studies quantified *inter-joint* coordination, as well report different coordination measures. In any case, the results of our investigation can serve as an initial baseline which can be re-evaluated once more information is available on the association between pelvis-thorax coordination, performance, and injury risk.

Further investigation on the topic is warranted regarding the effects of different lifting scenarios, including multi-axis movements using different external loads in order to assess a range of possible work requirements.

References

1. Armstrong, D.P., et al.: Is deep squat movement strategy related to floor-to-waist height lifting strategy: implications for physical employment testing. Ergonomics **63**(2), 152–162 (2020)
2. Brandon, S.C., et al.: Interpreting principal components in biomechanics: representative extremes and single component reconstruction. J. Electromyogr. Kinesiol. **23**(6), 1304–1310 (2013)
3. Burgess-Limerick, R., et al.: Self-selected manual lifting technique: functional consequences of the interjoint coordination. Hum. Factors **37**(2), 395–411 (1995)
4. Graham, R.B., et al.: Interjoint coordination and the personal lift-assist device. J. Appl. Biomech. **29**(2), 194–204 (2013)
5. Hamill, J., et al.: A dynamical systems approach to lower extremity running injuries. Clin. Biomech. **14**(5), 297–308 (1999)
6. Kaiser, J.F.: On a simple algorithm to calculate the 'energy' of a signal. In: International Conference on Acoustics, Speech, and Signal Processing, pp. 381–384. IEEE (1990)
7. Kazerooni, H., et al.: Evaluation of trunk-supporting exoskeleton. In: Proceedings of the Human Factors and Ergonomics Society Annual Meeting, vol. 63, no. 1, pp. 1080–1083. SAGE Publications, Los Angeles (2019)
8. Lamb, P.F., Stöckl, M.: On the use of continuous relative phase: review of current approaches and outline for a new standard. Clin. Biomech. **29**(5), 484–493 (2014)
9. Maduri, A., et al.: Lumbar–pelvic range and coordination during lifting tasks. J. Electromyogr. Kinesiol. **18**(5), 807–814 (2008)
10. McGill, S.M., et al.: Coordination of muscle activity to assure stability of the lumbar spine. J. Electromyogr. Kinesiol. **13**(4), 353–359 (2003)
11. Poon, N., et al.: Evaluation of a trunk supporting exoskeleton for reducing muscle fatigue. In: Proceedings of the Human Factors and Ergonomics Society Annual Meeting, vol. 63, no. 1, pp. 980–983. SAGE Publications, Los Angeles (2019)
12. Sadler, E.M., et al.: The personal lift-assist device and lifting technique: a principal component analysis. Ergonomics **54**(4), 392–402 (2011)

Measurement of Work-Related Physical Workloads - Proposal for a Body Region-Related Categorization System

Rolf Ellegast[✉], Britta Weber, Christoph Schiefer, Kai Heinrich,
and Ingo Hermanns-Truxius

Institute for Occupational Safety and Health of the German Social Accident Insurance (IFA),
Sankt Augustin, Germany
rolf.ellegast@dguv.de

Abstract. In this article a proposal for categorization of measurement systems for recording and assessing of work-related musculoskeletal workloads and disorders (MSD) for body region-related risk assessments is presented. It consists of three categories according to the different user groups: operational practitioner (Cat 1), ergonomic expert (Cat 2) and scientist (Cat 3). Principal characteristics of measuring systems in the categories 1, 2 and 3 are derived from common measurement setups and application cases. For the body regions upper extremities, spine, lower extremities implementations for the associated risk factors, measurement technique and parameters as well as assessment approaches are presented.

Keywords: MSD · Risk assessment · IMU (inertial measurement unit) · EMG · Categorization

1 Introduction

With advancing digitalization and technical development, more and more measurement systems are available for recording and evaluating physical workloads. In order to make the measurement data comprehensively usable, e.g. for databases of work-related MSD risk factors or as input exposure data for epidemiological studies, a systematic approach to categorize both the types of measurement systems and the related processed exposure data is necessary. EU-OSHA's risk assessment system for work-related musculoskeletal workloads is widely used in practice. It is a five-step scheme, divided into observation-based (entry screening, screening, expert screening) and measurement procedures (field measurements, laboratory measurements/simulations) [1]. Observation-based methods are here used by practitioners in the workplace, while measurement methods are intended exclusively for ergonomics experts and scientists for very specific, more complex risk assessments.

N. L. Black et al. (Eds.): IEA 2021, LNNS 223, pp. 139–147, 2022.
https://doi.org/10.1007/978-3-030-74614-8_16

In recent years, measurement systems for physical risk assessment have become more practicable and therefore more accessible to the user group of practitioners [2]. Since measurement techniques allow a more objective and detailed assessment of MSD risk factors, there is a chance to use qualitatively better exposure data for epidemiological studies by pooling exposure data. A wider use of technical measures to improve the quality of work-related musculoskeletal workloads is also more and more demanded in epidemiological MSD literature reviews (see e.g. [3]). A prerequisite for the aggregation of MSD exposure data is a categorization of measurement techniques used and a standardized assessment of measured exposure data. Therefore, the aim of this paper is to propose a categorization of measurement recording and assessment of physical exposures with reference to body regions.

2 Methods

2.1 Update Categorization of Work-Related MSD Risk Assessments

For the specific case of the measurement-based assessment of sedentary work there is a further development of the existing EU-OSHA's risk assessment categorization [4, 5]. In this categorization three different categories and user groups for the application of measurement-based assessments (1: practitioners, 2: ergonomists, 3: measurement expert/scientist) are distinguished (see Fig. 1). This updated categorization therefore represents an expansion of the user group of measurement systems to include the target groups of operational practitioners.

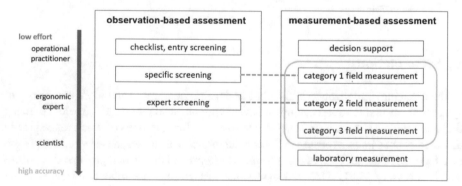

Fig. 1. Principle categories of tools for recording and assessing work-related physical workloads (observation-and measurement-based), summarized and based on [1, 4, 5]

Within the framework of this article the updated categorization was principally transferred to the recording and assessment of work-related musculoskeletal workloads in the body regions of the spine, upper extremities and lower extremities. In this context, measurement-based registration of associated biomechanical risk factors using physical (e.g. inertial measurement units – IMU, accelerometer) and physiological (e.g. electromyography-EMG) techniques as well as standardized associated assessment approaches for all measurement categories 1, 2 and 3 were developed. The principal characteristics of measuring systems in the categories 1, 2 and 3 are described across the workload types and body regions.

2.2 Assignment of Body Region-Related Measurement Concepts to Categories and Associated Assessment Protocols

For the body regions upper extremities (hand, elbow, shoulder), spine (cervical spine, lumbar spine) and lower extremities (hip, knee) standardized recording and assessment approaches based on the results of the MEGAPHYS project [6] were compiled and generalized. As a result, for each of the categories 1 to 3, body localization-related physical (e.g. IMU) and physiological (e.g. EMG) sensor constellations and corresponding standardized assessment protocols were derived. The assessment protocols are based on the four-level risk concept of the MEGAPHYS project (1: low workload, long-term MSD unlikely; 2: moderately increased workload, long-term MSD for persons with reduced resilience possible; 3: substantially increased workload, long-term MSD possible even for persons with normal resilience; 4: high workload, long-term MSD likely for all persons) [6]. In this article, principle systematics and body region-related assessment approaches for the above-mentioned body regions are summarized.

3 Results

3.1 Principal Characteristics of Measurement Categories

Sensor systems of category 1 consist of 1–2 mostly IMU sensors and are characterized by a high practicability. Herewith, specific biomechanical risk factors for one body localization can be quantified and assessed. Measurement category 2 addresses related larger body regions, e.g. in the shoulder-elbow-hand area. IMUs, if necessary combined with EMG measurements, provide here input data for biomechanical models of partial body regions. For the shoulder/elbow/hand region, these include, for example, time components in unfavorable joint angle positions, micropauses, repetition parameters (e.g. mean power frequencies of joint movements). Measurement category 3 includes complex 3D motion analysis of several joints/body regions with IMUs, supplemented by physiological (EMG) and possibly other physical measurements, for complex biomechanical model calculations.

Table 1 shows the general characteristics of measuring systems for recording and assessing work-related musculoskeletal loads in the categories 1, 2 and 3.

Table 1. Characteristics of measuring systems for recording and assessing work-related musculoskeletal loads in the categories 1, 2 and 3, summarized after [Lit], Legend: "+" applicable, "o" partly applicable, "−" not applicable

		Category 1	Category 2		Category 3
		1-2 sensors, attachment to one body location	Integrated sensors in smart textiles	few sensors, attachment to a partial body area	multi sensor systems, complex sensor attachment
Accuracy requirement (measurement data)	low	+	+	-	-
	moderate	-	o	+	-
	high	-	-	-	+
Data accessibility	No access to raw data required	+	o	-	-
	limited access to raw data required	-	+	+	-
	full access to raw data required	-	-	o	+
Expert knowledge on data analysis	Not required	+	o	-	
	partly required	+	+	o	-
	required	+	+	+	+
Measuring and power supply duration	≤ 1 work day	+	+	+	+
	2 - 3 work days	+	o	o	-
	4 or more work days	+	o	-	-
size of subject collective /number of subjects	Small	+	+	+	+
	medium high	+	+	o	o
	high	+	o	-	-
Cost/effort per subject	low	+	-	-	-
	moderate	+	+	o	-
	high	+	+	+	+
Effort calibration / attachment	low	+	o	-	-
	moderate	-	+	o	-
	high	-	-	+	+

3.2   Risk Assessment Upper Extremity Workloads

The risk factors posture, repetition, muscular load, force exertion and hand arm vibration are well known for the development of work-related musculoskeletal disorders

Table 2. Upper extremity workloads: joints, risk factors (*measurement technique/sensor*) and corresponding measurement parameters and assessments (evaluable with MEGAPHYS risk concept [6] in 4 risk areas ⌷1⌷2⌷3⌷4⌷). The gray colors of the matrix fields refer to the measuring system category class: acquisition/assessment possible from Cat 1 □, from Cat 2 ▣und from Cat 3 ◼.

joint/body region risk factor (sensor)	wrist/hand measurement parameter	assessment 1 2 3 4	elbow measurement parameter	assessment 1 2 3 4	shoulder measurement parameter	assessment 1 2 3 4
Posture (IMU)	Joint angles [°] wrist: flexion/extension, radialduction fore arm pronation/supination	Percentage of working time [%] in neutral, moderate and extreme joint angle positions, in awkward static postures	Joint angle [°] elbow flexion/extension	Percentage of working time [%] in neutral, moderate and extreme joint angle positions, in awkward static postures	Joint angles [°] shoulder flexion/extension abduction/adduction anterior/posterior internal/external rotation	Percentage of working time [%] in neutral, moderate and extreme joint angle positions, in awkward static postures, overhead work
Repetition (IMU)	Joint angles [°] : flexion/extension, radialduction fore arm pronation/supination	Median angular velocities [°/s], mean power frequency MPF [Hz], micro pauses [% time]	Joint angle [°] elbow flexion/extension	Median angular velocities [°/s], mean power frequency MPF [Hz], micro pauses [% work time]	Joint angles [°] shoulder, flexion/ extension , abduction/ adduction anterior/ posterior, internal/external rotation	Median angular velocities [°/s], mean power frequency MPF [Hz], micro pauses [% time]
muscular activity (EMG)	electrical activity eA [RMS µV] e. g. m. finger flexor/extensor	Median, 90th percentile [% MVC] muscle fatigue, median frequency [Hz/s]	electrical activity eA [RMS µV] m. elbow flexor/extensor	median, 90. Perz. [% MVC]	electrical activity eA [RMS µV] e. g. m. trapezius, m. deltoickus	median, 90th percentile [% MVC] muscle fatigue, median frequency [Hz/s]
Force + biomechanical modelling (3D force measuring system+ IMU)	hand force [N]	wrist joint moment [Nm], dose [Nmh]	hand force [N]	elbow joint moment [Nm], dose [Nmh]	hand force [N]	shoulder joint moment [Nm], dose [Nmh]
hand arm vibration (3D accelerometer)	acceleration [m/s²]	frequency and direction weighted acceleration [m/s²]				

of the upper extremities and must therefore be quantified and evaluated in associated risk assessments. Ambulatory measurement systems usually use IMU sensors attached to the corresponding body locations hand, forearm upper arm, shoulder to record the risk factors posture and repetition. Muscular activity can be quantified by EMG and hand forces by hand force measuring systems. 3D accelerometers are used to quantify hand-arm vibration exposures. Category 1 applications are limited to the detection and evaluation of selected risk factors of one body location. Here, mainly IMU sensors can be applied, as the other measurement techniques mentioned above are too complex for use by operational practitioners. Assessments are mostly limited to posture assessments, e.g. of the wrist, in category 1. Other simple applications are the assessment of overhead work and upper arm flexions in category 1 [7]. Category 2 includes IMU applications at more than one body location (e.g. in smart textiles or with direct sensor attachment) as well as surface EMG applications at selected muscle groups. This allows for more accurate assessments considering the risk factors posture, repetition and muscular activity. In category 3, all the above-mentioned measurement methods are used [8]. A complex assessment of all areas of the upper extremities is possible, also using complex biomechanical models to estimate joint moments and workload doses.

Table 2 summarizes joints, risk factors and corresponding measurement/assessment parameters proposed for measurement based assessments in the categories 1, 2 and 3. All assessment results can principally be categorized in four risk areas defined by MEGA-PHYS [6]. Thus, for each risk factor, a need for action for deriving preventive measures can be derived and, by combining the results, also a standardized overall risk assessment is possible. The assignment to measurement categories allows a comparability of the measurements in different application scenarios.

3.3 Risk Assessment Spinal Workloads

Analogous to Chapter 3.2, Table 3 summarizes risk factors, measurement/assessment parameters for the assessment of work-related lumbar and cervical spine workloads. Again, an assignment to the measurement categories 1, 2 and 3 is illustrated. The assessment results can principally be categorized in four risk areas defined by MEGAPHYS [6].

Table 3. Spinal workloads: location, risk factors (measurement technique/sensor) and corresponding measurement parameters and assessments (evaluable with MEGAPHYS risk concept [6] in 4 risk areas [1][2][3][4]). The gray colors of the matrix fields refer to the measuring system category class: acquisition/assessment possible from Cat 1 □, from Cat 2 □und from Cat 3 □.

joint/body region	lumbar spine		Cervical Spine	
risk factor (sensor)	measurement parameter	assessment [1][2][3][4]	measurement parameter	assessment [1][2][3][4]
posture kinematic activity *(IMU)*	Joint angles [°] trunk: flexion/extension, lateral flexion, torsion lumbar spine kyphosis/lordosis	Percentage of working time [%] in neutral, moderate and extreme joint angle positions, in awkward static postures, angular velocities [°/s],	Joint angles [°] Cervical spine: flexion/extension, lateral flexion, torsion	Percentage of working time [%] in neutral, moderate and extreme joint angle positions, in awkward static postures, angular velocities [°/s]
muscular activity (EMG)	electrical activity eA [RMS µV] musculature low back, e. g. m. erector spinae	median, 90. Perz. [% MVC] muscle fatigue, median frequency [Hz/s]	electrical activity eA [RMS µV] musculature upper back, e. g. m. trapezius	median, 90. Perz. [% MVC] muscle fatigue, median frequency [Hz/s]
Force + biomechanical modelling *(3D force, ground reaction force measuring system+ IMU)* whole body vibration *(accelerometer)*	hand force, ground reaction force [N] acceleration [m/s²]	lumbar spinal moment [Nm], dose [Nmh] lumbar disc compression force [N], dose [Nh] cumulative handled load weights [kgs] frequency and direction weighted acceleration [m/s²]	hand force, ground reaction force [N]	cervical spinal moment [Nm], dose [Nmh] cervical disc compression force [N], dose [Nh]

3.4   Risk Assessment Lower Extremity Workloads

Analogous to Chapter 3.2, Table 4 summarizes risk factors, measurement/assessment parameters for the assessment of work-related lower extremity workloads. The assignment to the measurement categories 1, 2 and 3 is illustrated. The assessment results can principally be categorized in four risk areas defined by MEGAPHYS [6].

Table 4. Lower extremity workloads: location, risk factors (measurement technique/sensor) and corresponding measurement parameters and assessments (evaluable with MEGAPHYS risk concept [6] in 4 risk areas ⊡ 1 | 2 | 3 | 4 ⊡). The gray colors of the matrix fields refer to the measuring system category class: acquisition/assessment possible from Cat 1 □, from Cat 2 ◻ und from Cat 3 ◼.

joint/body region risk factor (sensor)	knee joint measurement parameter	assessment 1 | 2 | 3 | 4	hip joint measurement parameter	assessment 1 | 2 | 3 | 4
posture (IMU)	Joint angles [°] Knee joint: flexion/extension,	Percentage of working time [%] in neutral, moderate and extreme joint angle positions, in asymmetrical kneeling, in awkward static postures, number of posture changes (into/out kneeling)	Joint angles [°] Hip joint: flexion/extension, abduction/adduction	Percentage of working time [%] in neutral, moderate and extreme joint angle positions, in awkward static postures
muscular activity (EMG)	electrical activity eA [RMS µV] musculature knee, e. g. m. quadriceps	median, 90. Perz. [% MVC] muscle fatigue, median frequency [Hz/s]	electrical activity eA [RMS µV] musculature hip, e. g. m. gluteus	median, 90. Perz. [% MVC] muscle fatigue, median frequency [Hz/s]
Force + biomechanical modelling (3D ground reaction force measuring system+ IMU)	ground reaction force [N]	Knee joint moment [Nm], dose [Nmh]	ground reaction force [N]	Hip joint moment [Nm], dose [Nmh], cumulative handled load weights [kgs]

4 Discussion

The proposed categorization represents a first proposal for the systematic recording and assessment of work and body region-related workloads. In the following, the proposed assessment strategies have to be evaluated especially with regard to category 1 and 2 systems in practice, e.g. in use by laboratory inspectors. Data protection requirements must be followed when using wearable technology. In principle, this approach enables more precise measurements of MSD risk factors also in the target group of company practitioners. Measurement results from different measurement categories can be compared with each other.

5 Conclusion

The described category system seems to be suitable for a comprehensive classification of existing measurement techniques for recording physical workloads. This offers a chance to generate a good starting point for the compilation of exposure data sets for pooled epidemiological evaluations in combination with standardized procedures for body region-related risk assessments.

References

1. EU OSHA OSHWIKI: Assessment of physical workloads to prevent work-related MSDs (2020) https://oshwiki.eu/wiki/Assessment_of_physical_workloads_to_prevent_work-related_MSDs
2. Lin, J.-H., et al.: New technologies in human factors and ergonomics research and practice. Appl. Ergon. **66**, 179–181 (2018)
3. Wærsted, M., et al.: Work above shoulder level and shoulder complains: a. systematic review. Int. Arch. Occup. Environ. Health **93**, 925–954 (2020)
4. Holtermann, A., et al.: A practical guidance for assessments of sedentary behavior at work: a PEROSH initiative. Appl. Ergon. **63**, 41–52 (2017)
5. Boudet, G., et al.: How to measure sedentary behavior at work? Front. Public Health **7**, 1–11 (2019)
6. DGUV: MEGAPHYS Mehrstufige Gefährdungsanalyse physischer Belastungen am Arbeitsplatz. Bd 2. DGUV, Berlin (2020). https://www.dguv.de/ifa/fachinfos/ergonomie/megaphys-mehrstufige-gefaehrdungsanalyse-physischer-belastungen-am-arbeitsplatz/index-2.jsp
7. Yang, L., et al.: An iPhone application for upper arm posture and movement measurements. Appl. Ergon. **65**, 492–500 (2017)
8. Seidel, D.H., et al.: Assessment of work-related hand and elbow workloads using measurement-based TLV for HAL. Appl. Ergon. **92**, 1–11 (2021)

Optimization of Product Handle Material Mechanical Properties for Improved Ergonomics Using Finite Element Method and Subjective Response

Gregor Harih[1]([⊠]), Andrej Cupar[2], Jasmin Kaljun[1], and Bojan Dolšak[1]

[1] Laboratory for Intelligent CAD Systems, Faculty of Mechanical Engineering,
University of Maribor, Maribor, Slovenia
gregor.harih@um.si
[2] Laboratory for Product Design, Faculty of Mechanical Engineering, University of Maribor,
Maribor, Slovenia

Abstract. Finite element method (FEM) is being increasingly used in ergonomics and biomechanics lately, since it can provide various quantitative results, which are otherwise not obtainable, however, it does not provide any results in terms of subjective rating. Therefore, in this paper we investigated to what extent the quantitative results of FEM can be used to predict the subjective comfort rating. We focused on the optimization of the product handle material parameters to lower the contact pressure while maintaining the stability of the handle in hands. Basic criterion of pressure discomfort threshold has been used for the FEM approach. Deformable meta-material interface layer of a product handle has been manufactured using 3D printing technology based on the obtained results. Additionally, one handle with higher stiffness, one with lower stiffness and handle made from hard plastic have been manufactured for comparison. A sawing task has been utilized for the evaluation of the subjective comfort rating. Results have shown the material properties of the deformable handle obtained by FEM with optimization yielded in higher comfort rating when compared to the hard-plastic handle while maintaining same stability. Stiffer deformable handle showed slight increase in comfort rating with similar perceived stability, while softer deformable handle was rated lower in terms of subjective comfort and provided less stability. Results indicate FEM can be successfully used for initial material parameter identification; however subjective response needs to be considered for fine tuning of the material behavior.

Keywords: Product handle · Subjective comfort rating · Material properties · Finite element method

1 Introduction

When considering the ergonomics of the handheld products, besides its main functionality, the most important aspect is the product gripping surface i.e. handle [1]. Powered

N. L. Black et al. (Eds.): IEA 2021, LNNS 223, pp. 148–154, 2022.
https://doi.org/10.1007/978-3-030-74614-8_17

and non-powered hand tools and different handheld products can result in high contact pressures on the hands due to high grip, push, pull or torque exertion on the handle. This has been shown to be one of the major factors for the development of cumulative trauma disorders [2].

In order to investigate the quantitative aspect of the loads on the hand, several researchers focussed on determining the mechanical behaviour of the biological materials, such as skin, subcutaneous tissue, etc. [3]. Soft tissue in humans generally exhibits non-linear viscoelastic mechanical properties, with low stiffness regions at small strains and sudden increase in the stiffness when a certain amount of strain is achieved. Based on the soft tissue mechanical behaviour and subjective response, researchers tried to quantify the maximum allowable contact pressures on the hands. Different methods and subjective perception of the load on the hand resulted in different reported values ranging from 104 kPa to 188 kPa [4, 5].

Most of the researchers focussed on the sizes and shapes of the tool-handle, however they neglected the handle materials, which could further improve the ergonomics [6–8]. The distinctive mechanical behaviour of the skin and subcutaneous tissue has suggested the handle interface material should be deformable during grasping to lower the contact pressure. In this regard foam rubber interface material has been already used to provide more uniform distribution of contact pressures on the hand resulting in higher comfort ratings [9]. However, on the other hand foam rubber grips produced a loss of control feeling due to excessive softness and thickness of the foam. Measurement of stresses, strains and especially contact pressures at the hand-handle interface is not possible due to the complex geometry of the handles and human hands.

Several researchers tried to overcome mentioned limitations using finite element method (FEM), which can provide results in terms of stresses, strains, displacements, and contact pressures. FEM has become an established method in biomechanics and also ergonomics lately [10–12]. We already explored the biomechanical aspect of use of foam materials for tool-handles using finite element method [13]. Results have shown that correct foam material can provide a more uniform distribution of the contact pressure and overall lower value of contact pressure. Based on the provided maximum allowable contact pressure and FEM, we proposed handle interface foam material properties using optimisation with genetic algorithm [14]. Results have shown that the developed composite hyper-elastic foam material can lower the contact pressure whilst keeping the low deformation rate of the product handle material to maintain a sufficient stability while grasping the product. However subjective response has not been measured yet.

Therefore, the main goal of this research was to investigate to what extent the quantitative results of the biomechanical analyses using FEM and optimization of the material properties can be used to predict the subjective comfort rating.

2 Methods

2.1 Determination of the Optimal Handle Material Properties Based on FEM

The deformations of the handle interface material should be as small as possible till the allowable contact pressure is achieved and should rise as slow as possible with smallest possible deformation of the handle material to provide stability. To find the optimal material properties of the hyper-elastic cellular material we decided to use 100 kPa (0,1 MPa) for the contact pressure threshold [14]. Mathematical optimization using genetic algorithm with elitism was performed using a validated fingertip finite element model. Results have shown the optimal material should have following material parameters $\varepsilon_2 = 0.064$, $\varepsilon_3 = 0.486$, $\varepsilon_4 = 0.9$, $\sigma_2 = 59$ kPa, $\sigma_3 = 116$ kPa and $\sigma_4 = 796$ kPa.

2.2   Manufacturing of the Deformable Handles

Deformable handle interface materials have been manufactured using 3D printing technology. Material properties were set that one interface material matched the material properties resulting from optimization (10% density), one was softer (6% density), and one was stiffer (14% density) (Fig. 1). Additionally, one handle was made from hard plastic for reference. Hereby the effect of material properties and stiffness of the handle interface material could be assessed using the proposed task and subjective comfort rating questionnaire as described in the following subsection.

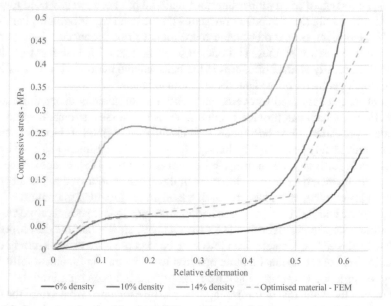

Fig. 1. Mechanical response of the three different 3D printed deformable interface layer materials compared to material properties obtained by optimization.

2.3   Measurement of Subjective Response

A sawing task consisting of various loading cases on the hand (grasping, pushing, pulling, twisting) has been utilised to be able to evaluate the subjective comfort of the different handle interface layer materials. Ten healthy subjects with average age of 24 years were recruited for the task. Subjects were given a random saw with its corresponding handle and they had to perform five sawing tasks with each saw. Afterwards subjects had to evaluate each saw and its corresponding handle using subjective rating questionnaire with a scale ranging from 1 to 7, where 1 was "totally disagree" and 7 was "totally agree".

3 Results

Results in terms of subjective comfort rating were collected and statistically analyzed (Fig. 2). Results have shown that the hard-plastic handle was rated the worst with comfort rating of 3.78 and SD of 1.7. On the other hand, the handle with 3D printed meta-material density of 10% was rated 5.0 with SD of 1.4, which was lower than the stiffer 14% dense meta-material handle (comfort rating of 5.8 with SD of 1.0). Significance levels show that there is no statistically significant difference between saws with handles utilizing the optimal – 10% dense material and the 14% dense meta-material. However, there was a statistically significant difference (at $p < .05$) between the saw with 14% and with 6% dense meta-material handle, which was rated 4.4 with SD of 1.7. Statistically significant difference could be also observed between the hard-plastic handle and the 14% dense meta-material handle (at $p < .001$) and between hard-plastic handle and the 10% dense meta-material handle (at $p < .05$).

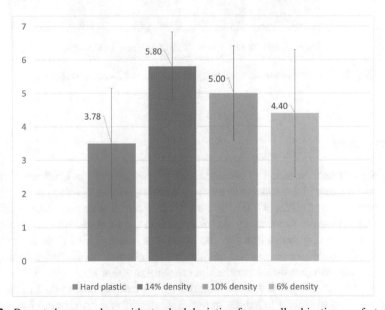

Fig. 2. Reported mean values with standard deviation for overall subjective comfort rating.

To measure the subjective response in terms of stability of the saws and handles in the hands during the sawing task, we also evaluated the subjective rating of the stability descriptor "Allows good transfer of forces and moments". Results have shown that the handle with the deformable meta-material interface handle with the 14% density was rated the highest with value of 5.44 with SD of 1.32, next was the saw with hard-plastic handle with value of 5.33 and SD of 1.07, followed by 10% dense meta-material handle with value of 5.00 and SD of 1.45 and finally 6% dense meta-material handle with value of 4.22 and SD of 1.10 (Fig. 3). The softest 3D printed meta-material handle (6%) was statistically significant different with all other handles (hard-plastic, 14% dense and 10% dense meta-material handle) at p < .05.

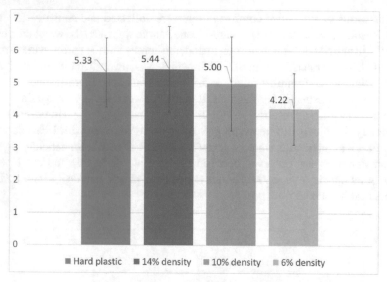

Fig. 3. Comfort descriptor "allows good transfer of forces and moments".

4 Discussion

The desired response in terms of biomechanical behaviour of the hand soft tissue has been evaluated using FEM. Results in terms of stresses, strains, displacements, and contact pressure are obtainable, which can be used in the optimisation of the mechanical response. Optimisation in our study was focussed on the minimisation of contact pressure while maintaining the stability of the product in hands. This has been done using deformable 3D printed meta-material handles, which allowed controlled deformation of the handle under compression, hence while grasping the handle.

The deformable 3D printed meta-material shows inverse mechanical behaviour to soft tissue. In this manner, the handle material stays stiff and firm during low grasping forces and deforms only when the set critical contact pressure is reached to provide higher contact area and lower the contact pressure in hands, since higher contact pressures have been shown to increase the likelihood of discomfort and pain and also cumulative trauma disorder development. Based on the literature review we set the pressure threshold to 100 kPa (0,1 MPa), despite several authors proving also higher values. To cover higher values, we also introduced a denser meta-material handle (14%), which deforms at more than twice the value of compression stress (0,25 MPa) when compared to the handle with 10% density (0,1 MPa). Additionally, a less dense deformable handle (6%), which deforms at about half the value of the optimal material, has been manufactured for reference. To be able to directly compare the results of subjective comfort rating, a handle hard plastic handle has been also manufactured.

Results have shown that the deformable 3D printed meta-material handles were rated significantly higher in terms of overall comfort. Since the size and shape of all handles were the same, the difference in subjective comfort rating can be attributed solely to the material and the fact that the 3D printed meta-material handles deform when the critical contact pressure is achieved during grasping and hereby provide higher contact area and hence lower the contact pressure and provide more uniform distribution.

The 3D printed meta-material handle with highest density of 14% has been rated highest, despite the 10% dense handle was closest to the material properties from the optimization. This can be most likely explained by the fact that the pressure discomfort and pressure pain threshold are more likely higher and are task and product dependent. Additionally, it is more likely the users prefer slightly higher contact pressure while maintaining the stability of the handle and product in hands due to the low deformation rate of the material. This can be explained by the results of overall subjective rating for the 6% dense handle, which was rated lowest among the handles using deformable meta-material. On the other hand, the hard-plastic handle was rated even lower indicating that the peak contact pressure and its distribution has greater impact on the subjective comfort rating than stability.

Analysis of the comfort predictor referring to stability (Allows good transfer of forces and moments) showed that the deformable handle with lowest density (6%) was too soft, since it was rated significantly lower compared to stiffer deformable handles. There was no statistically significant difference between other two deformable handles (14%, 10%) and the handle made from hard plastic indicating all handles provided same or similar stability.

In this paper we have shown that FEM and optimization can be successfully utilized to develop, and manufacture deformable handles, which are more comfortable than traditional hard-plastic handles and provide same stability. Results from the analysis of the subjective comfort rating have shown that FEM and optimization approach can only provide the basis for identification of material parameters and the final parameters should be determined based on subjective response using target population and task.

5 Conclusion

Quantitative results in terms of biomechanical numerical analyses using FEM can be used as a foundation for development and manufacturing of deformable handle material for improved comfort rating. Comfort is highly subjective and optimal material mechanical properties can be identified only using combination of quantitative results of the numerical analyses and extensive comfort measurements.

References

1. Kong, Y.K., Kim, D.M., Lee, K.S., Jung, M.C.: Comparison of comfort, discomfort, and continuum ratings of force levels and hand regions during gripping exertions. Appl. Ergon. **43**, 283–289 (2012)
2. Rempel, D.M., Harrison, R.J., Barnhart, S.: Work-related cumulative trauma disorders of the upper extremity. JAMA: J. Am. Med. Assoc. **267**, 838–42 (1992)
3. Joodaki, H., Panzer, M.B.: Skin mechanical properties and modeling: a review. Proc. Inst. Mech. Eng. Part H: J. Eng. Med. **232**, 323–343 (2018)
4. Aldien, Y., Welcome, D., Rakheja, S., Dong, R., Boileau, P.E.: Contact pressure distribution at hand–handle interface: role of hand forces and handle size. Int. J. Ind. Ergon. **35**, 267–286 (2005)
5. Fransson-Hall, C., Kilbom, Å.: Sensitivity of the hand to surface pressure. Appl. Ergon. **24**, 181–189 (1993)
6. Rossi, J., de Monsabert, B.G., Berton, E., Vigouroux, L.: Does handle shape influence pre-hensile capabilities and muscle coordination? Comput. Methods Biomech. Biomed. Eng. **17**, 172–173 (2014)
7. Seo, N.J., Armstrong, T.J.: Effect of elliptic handle shape on grasping strategies, grip force distribution, and twisting ability. Ergonomics **54**, 961–970 (2011)
8. Garneau, C.J., Parkinson, M.B.: Optimization of tool handle shape for a target user population. In: Proceedings of the Asme International Design Engineering Technical Conferences and Computers and Information in Engineering Conference, San Diego, California, USA, pp. 1029–1036 (2009)
9. Fellows, G.L., Freivalds, A.: Ergonomics evaluation of a foam rubber grip for tool handles. Appl. Ergon. **22**, 225–230 (1991)
10. Dallard, J., Merlhiot, X., Duprey, S., Wang, X., Micaelli, A.: Fingertip finite element modelling–on choosing the right material property. Comput. Methods Biomech. Biomed. Eng. **17**, 30–31 (2014)
11. Wu, J.Z., Wimer, B.M., Welcome, D.E., Dong, R.G.: An analysis of contact stiffness between a finger and an object when wearing an air-cushioned glove: the effects of the air pressure. Med. Eng. Phys. **34**, 386–393 (2012)
12. Yoshida, H., Tada, M., Mochimaru, M.: A study of frictional property of the human fingertip using three-dimensional finite element analysis. Mol. Cell. Biomech.: MCB **8**, 61–71 (2011)
13. Harih, G., Dolšak, B.: Recommendations for tool-handle material choice based on finite element analysis. Appl. Ergon. **45**, 577–585 (2014)
14. Harih, G., Borovinšek, M., Ren, Z., Dolšak, B.: Optimal product's hand-handle interface parameter identification. Int. J. Simul. Model. **14**, 404–415 (2015)

Evaluation of Force Exertion Strategies During Repetitive Lifting/Lowering Tasks Based on Time-Frequency Analysis

Kazuki Hiranai[1]([✉]) [iD], Miho Yaji[1], and Akihiko Seo[2]

[1] Graduate School of Systems Design, Tokyo Metropolitan University, Hino, Japan
hiranai-kazuki@ed.tmu.ac.jp
[2] Faculty of Systems Design, Tokyo Metropolitan University, Hino, Japan

Abstract. This study aimed to evaluate the force exertion strategies during repetitive luggage lifting/lowering tasks based on time-frequency analysis. Right-handed male subjects participated in this experiment and repetitively performed a sequential task including luggage lifting and lowering for 25 times. To vary the workload on the right and left hands, the luggage used in this experiment was designed to enable the modification of the location of additional heavy goods. The experimental conditions included scenarios wherein heavy goods were installed to the right side, center, and left side on the top of the luggage and scenarios without additional heavy goods. In the experiment, the handling force on each hand was measured using two six-axis force-torque sensors at a sampling frequency of approximately 50 Hz. The measured handling forces were analyzed using a short-time Fourier transformation, and the median frequency was calculated. In the scenario where additional heavy goods were installed, the median frequency of handling force on the left hand increased whereas that on the right hand decreased with time. In conclusion, the present study clarified that participants adopted different force exertion strategies with the left and right hands or under experimental conditions and that the applied strategies can be evaluated based on time-frequency analysis.

Keywords: Repetitive tasks · Physical workload · Handling force · Manual material handling tasks · Time-frequency analysis

1 Introduction

Manual work in the modern industrial workplaces mainly consists of repetitive tasks with a low physical workload [1]. However, muscle fatigue may be caused by performing repetitive tasks [2–4]; therefore, evaluation of the tasks is important to improve comfort for workers. As the working posture or handling force varies during repetitive tasks, muscle fatigue or physical workload may differ according to these variations. For example, to reduce the physical workload on the upper limbs or lower back during the repetitive task of luggage lifting/lowering, workers skillfully adjust their handling forces or working postures. The efficacy of movement or working posture variations to prevent musculoskeletal disorders in repetitive tasks has been reported [5, 6]. As many previous studies which evaluates the handling force in manual material handling tasks or other tasks focuses on the magnitude or orientation of handling forces [7, 8], few studies have investigated the variability of handling forces during repetitive tasks.

To evaluate the variability of handling forces, this study focuses on time-frequency analysis. The time-frequency analysis has often been used to evaluate muscle fatigue based on measured electromyography (EMG) data [9, 10]. Applying time-frequency analysis to the evaluation of the variability in handling forces may clarify the force exertion strategies. For example, if the handling force signal mainly consists of the low-frequency band, the minute or unexpected changes are not incorporated into the handling force signal. Therefore, the handling force signal that mainly consists of the low-frequency band can suggest that the worker adopted smooth force exertion strategies. This study aimed to evaluate the changes in force exertion strategies during repetitive luggage lifting/lowering tasks based on a time-frequency analysis.

2 Material and Method

2.1 Participants

In this experiment, five healthy, right-handed male students without any self-reported upper limb and lower back disorders were recruited. All participants provided written informed consent after they were briefed about the research protocol, which follows the principles outlined in the Declaration of Helsinki and was approved by the Research Safety Ethics Committee of Tokyo Metropolitan University. The mean ± standard deviation (SD) of participants' age, height, and weight were 24.0 ± 1.9 years, 169.4 ± 4.6 cm, and 66.2 ± 12.0 kg, respectively.

2.2 Experimental Condition and Procedure

In the experiment, the participants repetitively performed a sequential task including luggage lifting and lowering. To vary the workload on the right and left hands, the luggage used in this experiment was designed such that the location of additional heavy goods could be modified. Moreover, to measure the handling force on each hand separately, two six-axis force-torque sensors (FFS080YS102U6, Leptrino Inc.) were installed on the luggage. The weights of luggage and the additional heavy goods were 3 and 2 kg, respectively. Experimental conditions included scenarios where locations of heavy goods were changed and scenarios without additional heavy goods (non-loaded condition). The heavy goods were installed to the right side, center, and left side on the top of the luggage. These experimental conditions were defined as right-loaded, center-loaded, and left-loaded.

The participants were instructed to maintain a standing posture at the beginning of the experiment. After maintaining the standing posture for 10 s, participants lifted the luggage within 5 s. After maintaining the standing posture for 5s again, participants lowered the luggage within 5 s. A sequential task from luggage lifting to lowering was repeated 25 times. The effect of residual fatigue on their working motion was eliminated by providing sufficient rest before the next experimental conditions.

2.3 Measured Data and Analysis

In the experiment, the handling force on each hand was measured using two six-axis force-torque sensors at a sampling frequency of approximately 50 Hz. The work period for which participants performed the luggage lifting and lowering tasks were extracted from the sequential motion data. Subsequently, the mean handling force at each trial was calculated by averaging the handling force in each extracted work period. In the end, the mean handling force at each trial under each experimental condition was calculated for all participants.

Figure 1 shows the procedure for handling force analysis. The measured handling forces were analyzed using a short-time Fourier transform (STFT); then the median frequency (MF), at which the power of power spectrum corresponding to the fast Fourier transform was halved, was calculated. However, as the MF of handling force includes the frequency component at maintaining the standing posture, the MF of handling force repetitively increased or decreased with time. To clarify the trend of the MF of handling force, the MF was smoothed using exponential smoothing. The smoothing coefficient was set to 0.10. However, the smoothed MF of handling force up to 100 s was affected by the initial value. Therefore, in this study, the smoothed MF values of handling force until 100 s was eliminated from the analysis, and the MF values after 100 s were used to

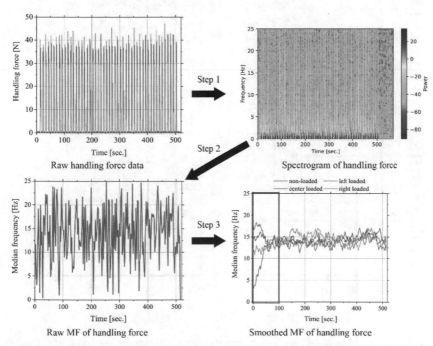

Fig. 1. Procedure for handling force analysis. Step 1: Obtain spectrograms of handling force from raw handling force data using STFT. Step 2: Calculate the MF of handling forces at each time based on obtained time, frequency, and power spectrum. Step 3: Smooth the MF of handling force using exponential smoothing. The smoothed MF of handling force inside the red frame in the figure has been affected by an initial value.

evaluate the trend of MF. For all participants, the trends of MF with time were obtained as a linear approximation and evaluated.

3 Results

3.1 Change in Mean Handling Force

Figure 2 shows the change in mean handling force during the repetitive lifting/lowering tasks. In the left-loaded condition, the mean handling force on the left hand was larger than that on the right hand. In contrast, under the right-loaded condition, the mean handling force on the right hand was larger than that on the left hand. In the center-loaded condition, the mean handling force on the right and left hand increased in repeated trials.

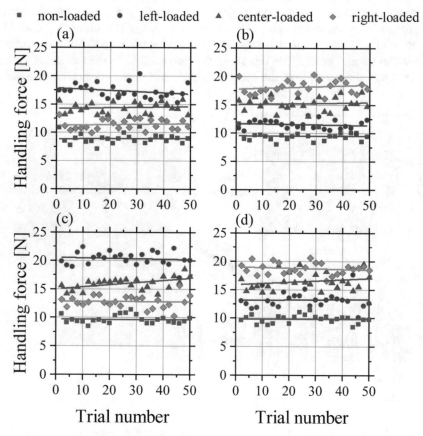

Fig. 2. Change in mean handling force during repetitive lifting/lowering tasks. Mean handling force on the (a) left hand and (b) right hand in lifting motion; mean handling force on the (c) left hand and (d) right hand in lowering motion.

3.2   Trend of MF of Handling Force

Figure 3 shows the trend of the MF of handling force on each hand under each experimental condition. The trends of the MF obtained were approximately linear. In the
non-loaded condition, the MF of handling force on the left hand decreased with time,
and that on the right hand slightly increased with time. In the left-, right-, and center-
loaded conditions, the MF of handling force on the left hand increased with time, and
that on the right hand decreased with time. The final score of MF of the handling force
for the left and right hands in the right-loaded condition was greater than and less than
that of the other experimental conditions, respectively.

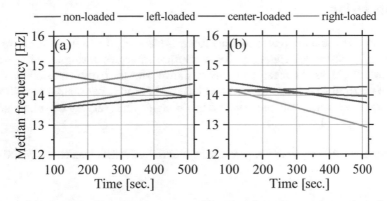

Fig. 3. Trend of the MF of handling force on each hand under each experimental condition. MF
on the (a) left hand and (b) right hand.

4   Discussion

According to experimental results, the mean handling force on hands, corresponding to
the location of additional heavy goods, was larger than that on the other hand, regardless
of lifting/lowering motion. In the left-, center-, and right-loaded conditions, the MF of the
handling force on the left hand increased with time, and that on the right hand decreased
with time. The difference between trends the in MF of handling force on the left and right
hands might be due to the effect of the participant's dominant hand. As all participants
were right-handed, they most likely found it easier to control the exertion of handling
force on the right hand. Thus, with the repetition of lifting/lowering motion, participants
learned the smooth force exertion, and the variation in handling force decreased.

To maintain the balance of luggage during lifting/lowering motion, the handling force
on the left hand might adopt the different force exertion strategies to that on the right
hand. In the right-loaded condition, the final score of MF on the left hand was larger than
in other conditions, and that on the right hand was smaller than in other conditions. As
mentioned before, the participants were able to learn the smooth handling force exertion
by repetitively performing the lifting/lowering tasks. However, even if the participants
learned the smooth force exertion, the variation of the handling force may occur in the

lifting/lowering motion. To achieve a stable lifting/lowering motion, participants exerted the handling force on the left hand to adjust the error, which is difficult to control by the handling force on the right hand.

The experimental conditions in this study had several limitations. Note that the results obtained in this study were biased to the right-handed male participants, and the number of participants was relatively small. The individual differences such as age, gender, physical size, and dominant hand might have affected the change of force exertion strategies in repetitive lifting/lowering tasks. Therefore, the influence of these characteristics should be investigated in subsequent studies with significantly more participants.

5 Conclusion

To evaluate the variability of handling forces, this study focuses on time-frequency analysis and evaluate the change in force exertion strategies during repetitive luggage lifting/lowering tasks. As a result, this study showed that the participants adopted different force exertion strategies the right and left hands or in experimental conditions and that the applied strategy can be evaluated based on the time-varying MF obtained in the time-frequency analysis.

Acknowledgement. This work was supported by JSPS KAKENHI Grant Number 19K04922.

References

1. Mathiassen, S.E.: Diversity and variation in biomechanical exposure: what is it, and why would we like to know? Appl. Ergon. **37**, 419–427 (2006)
2. Hansson, G.Å., Balogh, I., Ohlsson, K., Pålsson, B., Rylander, L., Skerfving, S.: Impact of physical exposure on neck and upper limb disorders in female workers. Appl. Ergon. **31**, 301–310 (2000)
3. International Organization for Standardization: ISO/TR12295 Ergonomics–Application document for International Standards on manual handling (ISO11228-1, ISO11228-2, and ISO11228-3) and evaluation of static working postures (ISO11226) (2014). https://www.iso.org/obp/ui/#iso:std:iso:tr:12295:ed-1:v1:en
4. Kinali, G., Kara, S., Yildirim, M.S.: Electromyographic analysis of an ergonomic risk factor: overhead work. J. Phys. Ther. Sci. **28**, 1924–1927 (2016)
5. Falla, D., Farina, D.: Periodic increases in force during sustained contraction reduce fatigue and facilitate spatial redistribution of trapezius muscle activity. Exp. Brain Res. **182**, 99–107 (2007)
6. Madeleine, P., Madsen, T.M.T.: Changes in the amount and structure of motor variability during a deboning process are associated with work experience and neck-shoulder discomfort. Appl. Ergon. **40**, 887–894 (2009)
7. La Delfa, N.J., Potvin, J.R.: The 'Arm Force Field' method to predict manual arm strength based on only hand location and force direction. Appl. Ergon. **59**, 410–421 (2017)
8. De Looze, M.P., van Greuningen, K., Rebel, J., Kingma, I., Kuijer, P.P.F.M.: Force direction and physical load in dynamic pushing and pulling. Ergonomics **43**(3), 377–390 (2000)

9. Coorevits, P., Danneels, L., Cambier, D., Ramon, H., Vanderstraeten, G.: Assessment of the validity of the Biering-Sørensen test for measuring back muscle fatigue based on EMG median frequency characteristics of back and hip muscles. J. Electromyogr. Kinesiol. **18**, 997–1005 (2008)
10. Politti, F., Casellato, C., Kalytczak, M.M., Garcia, M.B.S., Biasotto-Gonzalez, D.A.: Characteristics of EMG frequency bands in temporomandibullar disorders patients. J. Electromyogr. Kinesiol. **31**, 119–125 (2016)

A Wearable Device to Assess the Spine Biomechanical Overload in a Sample of Loggers

Federica Masci[1(✉)], Giovanna Spatari[2], Concetto Mario Giorgianni[2], Sara Bortolotti[3], John Rosecrance[4], and Claudio Colosio[1]

[1] Department of Health Sciences of University of Milan and International Centre for Rural Health of the Santi Paolo e Carlo ASST of Milan, Milan, Italy
Federica.masci@unimi.it
[2] Department of Biomedical, Dental and Morphological and Functional Imaging, University of Messina, Messina, Italy
[3] University of Milan, Milan, Italy
[4] Department of Environmental and Radiological Health Sciences, College of Veterinary Medicine and Biomedical Sciences, Colorado State University, Fort Collins, CO, USA

Abstract. Forestry workers are exposed to harsh environmental conditions, awkward postures, and high intensity load handling that might lead to low back injuries. The objectives of our study were 1) to define the trunk postures associated with risk of low back injury in a sample of forestry workers involved in tree felling, delimbing and bucking tasks and 2) to identify prevention strategies that reduce the risk of low back injury. Forty loggers were selected among the population of forestry workers in the province of Enna, Sicily-Italy. Each worker was required to perform for a period of 30 min the three main tasks: felling, delimbing and bucking for a total of 90 min of working activity. All subjects involved in the study wore a Zephyr Bioharness device on their trunk, which enabled the recording of sagittal inclination of the trunk, heart rate, breathing rate, and an estimate of body temperature. The results indicated that the felling task required loggers to work more time in awkward postures. Additionally, sagittal inclination of the trunk was greater than 60° for the 13% of the time, compared with delimbing (3%), and bucking (11%). The percentage of time spent with the trunk in sagittal inclination greater than 60° was correlated with the use of heavy (>7,2 kg) chainsaws during the felling and in the delimbing tasks. The study results indicated that the trunk posture during tree delimbing and felling tasks contributed significantly to the risk of biomechanical overload among the loggers. Preventive strategies should focus on specific interventions that reduce biomechanical stress including worker training and implementation of ergonomic designed tool.

Keywords: Biomechanical overload · Spine · Loggers

1 Introduction

According to official statistics from the Eurostat Labour Force Survey, musculoskeletal disorders (MSDs) are currently the most prevalent work-related diseases in Europe [1].

The primary reported clinical outcomes are back pain/injuries and work-related upper limb disorders, followed by lower limbs diseases. Recent studies provide substantial evidence that heavy loads lifting, awkward and prolonged posture, repetitive movements and lack of pauses are among the causes of these disorders, that also represent one of the most important reason of long-term sickness absences [2].

In Italy, the incidence of MSDs has systematically grown across all industries and especially in forestry sector, where low back injuries are reported to be the 60% of the total occupational diseases claimed to the Italian compensation authority (INAIL), in the period between 1999–2012 [3]. In particular, among the Italian regions, Sicily have registered in the same period a percentage of 35% of low back occupational disease among forestry workers [4].

The literature indicates that combined exposure to vibration, biomechanical overload and awkward postures is mainly characteristic of many tasks performed in silviculture [5]. Moreover, high intensity work rhythm and lack of training may increase the incidence of musculoskeletal diseases in forestry workers required to carry heavy loads for a long period [6]. Spasms, muscular pain and sleep diseases are among the most common disorders workers refer about [7], that also contribute to accidents or near miss.

Studies have also shown that felling, delimbing and bucking tasks (Figs. 1, 2 and 3 respectively) require a considerable effort, which increases with hardwood harvesting [8].

Fig. 1. Tree felling task   **Fig. 2.** Tree delimbing task

Fig. 3. Tree bucking task

In order to evaluate the biomechanical overload, different methods such as OWAS [9], RULA, RIBA [10] and OCRA [11] were successfully used in the forestry industry. Nevertheless, there are few original studies in literature that quantify low back biomechanical overload among forestry workers using a wearable technology.

Assessing the risk of spine injuries among forestry workers is the first step in the development of prevention strategies. Therefore, the aim of our study was to a) determine the trunk postures associated with risk of low back injury in a sample of forestry workers involved in tree felling, delimbing and bucking tasks; b) investigate the strength of correlations between biomechanical risk and personal as well as chainsaw characteristics; and c) identify prevention strategies to reduce the risk of low back injury.

2   Material and Methods

Forty male loggers were selected among the population of forestry workers in the province of Enna (Sicily), Italy. Participant study selection criteria were least eighteen years old, but not older than 65 and to have at list three years of working experience in logging activities. All the workers involved in the study were informed about the aims of the research and signed informed consent.

Each worker was required to perform the tasks of felling, delimbing and bucking for a period of 30 min each. All subjects wore a Zephyr Bioharness (Fig. 4) around their chest to detect and store the following information: sagittal inclination of the trunk, activity level (static, walking, running), heart rate, breathing rate and estimated body temperature.

Fig. 4. A worker equipped with Zephyr Bioharness 3

Before the data collection in the field, each worker was asked to stand straight next to a wall for 30 s in order to normalize the individual's natural anatomical inclination of the trunk to their upright posture.

Trunk posture data were processed after the data collection and were classified in inclination:

– <0°

- 0°–30°
- 30°–60°
- >60°.

Based on this criterion, the percentage of time spent in the different posture was calculated.

Personal data (age, working experience, secondary job), anthropometric measurements (height and weight) and the characteristics (model and weight) of the chainsaws during the task performance were collected.

The average weight of the chainsaw (about 7.39 kg.) was used as cutoff to classify them as "light" or "heavy".

2.1 Statistical Analysis

Data processing and statistical analyses were performed using the program SPSS PC version 23. The differences among the tasks and trunk inclination of the workers were investigated using a repeated measures ANOVA, with statistical significance set at p ≤ 0.05. We also investigated the role of the personal variables (age, BMI and working experience) in the performance of the different tasks and trunk inclination using an ANOVA, with statistical significance set at p ≤ 0.05.

3 Results

3.1 Study Population

The study involved a sample of 40 male chainsaw operators recruited from the population of forestry workers in the province of Enna (Sicily). Anthropometric measurements (height and weight) and personal data (age, sport, working experience, secondary job) were collected and are shown in Table 1.

Table 1. Characteristics of the population

	Min	Max	Mean	SD
Height (cm)	152	187	172,00	7,582
Weight (kg)	60	110	81,95	13,814
Age (years)	47	63	52,60	4,534
Body mass index	21,2	35,9	27,6	3,7
Working experience (years)	6	41	27	6

The average age of the workers recruited to the study was 53 years, with a minimum age of 47 and a maximum age of 63 (D.S. 4.53). As shown in Table 1, average height was 172 cm with a minimum of 152 cm and a maximum high of 187 cm (D.S. 7.852);

the average weight was about 82 kg with a minimum of 60 kg and a maximum of 110 (D.S. 13.814). From these data we obtained the Body Mass Index (BMI). The average BMI was 27.61. Fourteen workers were normal weight, 16 overweight, 9 suffer from mild obesity and 1 of medium obesity. The sample recruited had an average of 27 years of work experience, with a minimum of 6 years and a maximum of 41. Only three persons declared to perform sports: football, trekking and volleyball respectively. The sport variable was therefore not considered in the analyses.

Out of 40 workers, 13 declared they did not perform any secondary job, 15 declared they were employed in other agriculture activities, 9 in the construction sector and 3 in food market (2) and transport sectors (1). The minimum weight of the chainsaws used by the workers was about 3.1 kg, while the maximum was 8.3 kg. Therefore, average weight of the chainsaws (about 7.39 kg) was used as cut off to define a heavy or light chainsaw. In particular, most workers (n = 31) used a "heavy" chainsaw, while only 9 workers used "light" chainsaws.

3.2 Trunk Inclination

Our results indicated that the forestry workers spent approximately the same proportion of time (18%) in sagittal trunk inclination less than 0° in the three tasks (Fig. 5). Moreover, the felling task required loggers to work more time in awkward postures: the sagittal inclination of the trunk resulted greater than 60° for the 13% of the data collection time, compared with delimbing (3%), and bucking (11%) (Fig. 6).

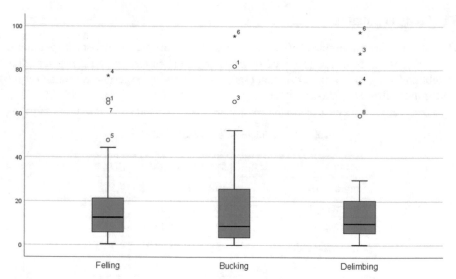

Fig. 5. Percentage of time spent with a sagittal inclination of the trunk less than 0° during felling, bucking and delimbing

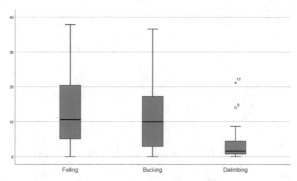

Fig. 6. Percentage of time spent with a sagittal inclination of the trunk greater than 60° during felling, bucking and delimbing

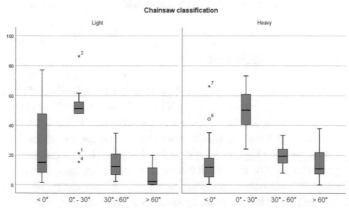

Fig. 7. Comparison among the percentage of time spent with a sagittal inclination of the trunk respectively less than 0°, 0°–30°, 30°–60° and greater than 60° and chainsaw's weight used during the felling task ($P < 0,05$).

In the felling (Fig. 7) and in the delimbing tasks (Fig. 8) the percentage of time spent with a sagittal inclination of the trunk greater than 60° is correlated with the use of heavy chainsaws (>7,2 kg).

No statistically significant differences were found among the working posture in the 3 tasks in relation to age, BMI and working experience and secondary job.

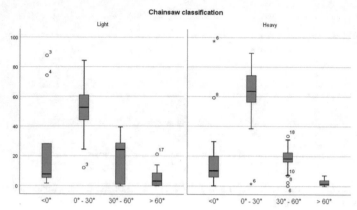

Fig. 8. Comparison among the percentage of time spent with a sagittal inclination of the trunk respectively less than 0°, 0–30°, 30°–60° and greater than 60° and chainsaw's weight used during the delimbing task (P < 0,05).

4 Discussion and Conclusions

The Zephyr BioHarness 3 device was used to assess the trunk inclination in a sample of loggers while performing the tasks of trees felling, delimbing and bucking. The results of the data analysis assisted in the development of prevention strategies to mitigate the risk of low back disorders among forestry workers in the region of Sicily. Our results suggest the felling trees is a high-risk task for low back injuries, which requires workers to spend a high percentage of time with a trunk inclination greater than 60°.

These findings are consistent with Grzywinski et al. who analyzed 10 expert chainsaw operators and noted that using a chainsaw requires a great effort to the musculoskeletal system especially during the felling phase, where the condition of bent legs and back are very common [12]. Moreover, Sawastian [13] assessed the awkward postures of two loggers using different chainsaws with the OWAS (Ovako Working Posture Analysis System) method. Sawastian [12] reported that the loggers postures were in the high risk category of the OWAS system. Unfortunately, occupational exposure to such awkward postures and repetitive motions are primarily related to low back pain (LBP) [14], especially if performed wearing wet clothes in harsh environment [15].

Our study also tried to investigate if personal factors such as age and BMI could affect awkward postures. Interestingly, no differences were found when comparing the trunk inclination data of older workers (>55 years) to the youngest. Conversely, we noted in the present study, that during the felling task, those suffering from mild obesity spent more time with an inclination of the trunk between 30° and 60° compared to normal weight workers, which spend most of their time in not awkward trunk postures. Nevertheless, this difference was not statistically significant.

Miranda (2001) conducted a study of 7000 employees in a large forestry industry in Finland that completed a questionnaire related to musculoskeletal pain and potential risk factors, such as age, sex, BMI, sport and mental stress. The study demonstrated that the risk of shoulder pain increased with both age and body mass index and the awkward sagittal inclination (>60°) represent an additional risk factor [16]. Interestingly

Miranda also noted that dancing slightly increases the risk of shoulder pain, while running decreases the risk [16]. Unfortunately, we couldn't explore the correlation of our results to sport, since only few workers declared to play sport.

Lastly the study results indicated that the trunk posture during tree delimbing and felling tasks contributed significantly to the risk of biomechanical overload among the loggers in association to heavy chainsaw. A study supporting this finding indicated that working postures that involve trunk flexion during felling task with chainsaw may lead to increased loading of the lumbar paraspinal muscles, suggesting a relationship between low back pain and the use of a chainsaw [17].

The Zephyr Bioharness demonstrated to be a useful wearable exposure assessment tool to characterize the postures associated with biomechanical overload in the low back among forestry workers. Safety training initiatives have been successful in reducing injuries and increasing workers' awareness of health and safety issues among loggers [18]. Additionally, others have reported that if adequate work training is associated to a good working environment, which includes safety tools, the physical workload decreases and productivity improves [19]. Strategies to prevent biomechanical overload in the trunk of loggers should focus on specific interventions such as worker training in order to promote the adoption of proper postures and implementation of ergonomic designed tools.

Acknowledgments. The authors want to thank the forestry department of the province of Enna, the Health and Safety manager and the Occupational Physician of the company who helped in the study population selection.

References

1. EUROSTAT: Exposure to risk factors. Health and safety at work in Europe (1999–2007), 103 p. (2010)
2. European Agency for Safety and Health at Work - Annual Report 2017 Luxembourg: Publications Office of the European (2018). Print ISBN 978-92-9496-815-9 ISSN 1681-0155. https://doi.org/10.2802/680079
3. Rapporto Inail Infortuni e malattie professionali 1 Luglio (2012)
4. INAIL: MALPROF 2011–2012 - Rapporto INAIL_Nessi causali positivi Malattie del rachide (2016)
5. Blombäck, P.: Improving occupational safety and health: the international labour organization's contribution FAO (2002)
6. Lewark, S. (ed.): Institutionen för skogens produkter och marknader Scientific reviews of ergonomic situation in mechanized forest operations, no. 2 (2005)
7. Ashby, L., Bentley, T., Parker, R.: Musculoskeletal disorders in silviculture and logging 1995 – 1999. OHFE (2001)
8. Blombäck, P., Poschen, P., Lövgren, M.: Employment trends and prospects in the European forest sector 2003 Geneva Timber and Forest Discussion Papers. United Nations
9. A. C. Innovation Technology to Empower Safety, Health and Welfare in Agriculture and Agro-food Systems: Musculoskeletal disorders (MSD) risks in forestry: a case study to propose an analysis method. DEIAFA, Italy (2008)

10. Micheletti Cremasco, M., Giustetto, A., Caffaro, F., Colantoni, A., Cavallo, E., Grigolato, S.: Risk assessment for musculoskeletal disorders in forestry: a comparison between RULA and REBA in the manual feeding of a wood-chipper. Int. J. Environ. Res. Public Health **16**(5) (2019). https://www.ncbi.nlm.nih.gov/pubmed/30841494
11. Jones, T., Kumar, S.: Comparison of ergonomic risk assessment output in four sawmill jobs. Int. J. Occup. Saf. Ergon. **16**(1), 105–11 (2010)
12. Grzywiński, W., Jelonek, T., Tomczak, A., Jakubowski, M., Bembenek, M.: Does body posture during tree felling influence the physiological load of a chainsaw operator? Ann. Agric. Environ. Med. **24**(3), 401–405 (2017)
13. Sawastian, K., Grzywiński, W., Turowski, R.: Analysis of postural strain of loggers during timber harvesting in a spruce stand analysis of postural strain of loggers during timber harvesting in a spruce stand (January 2015)
14. Petit, A., Roquelaure, Y.: Low back pain, intervertebral disc and occupational diseases. Int. J. Occup. Saf. Ergon. **21**(1), 15–19 (2015). https://www.ncbi.nlm.nih.gov/pubmed/26327258
15. Skandfer, M., Talykova, L., Brenn, T., Nilsson, T., Vaktskjold, A.: Low back pain among mineworkers in relation to driving, cold environment and ergonomics. Ergonomics **57**(10), 1541–1548 (2014). https://www.tandfonline.com/doi/abs/10.1080/00140139.2014.904005
16. Miranda, H., Martikainen, R., Takala, E., Riihimäki, H.: Miranda-2001-a prospective study.pdf, pp. 528–534 (2001)
17. Kawahara, D., Urabe, Y., Maeda, N., Sasadai, J., Fujii, E., Moriyama, N., et al.: The effect of different working postures while felling a tree with a chain-saw on trunk muscles' activity. Sangyo Eiseigaku Zasshi **57**(4), 111–116 (2015). https://www.ncbi.nlm.nih.gov/pubmed/25995000
18. Nkomo, H., Niranjan, I., Reddy, P.: Effectiveness of health and safety training in reducing occupational injuries among harvesting forestry contractors in KwaZulu-Natal. Workplace Health Saf. **66**(10), 499–507 (2018). https://www.ncbi.nlm.nih.gov/pubmed/29962302
19. Caliskan, E., Caglar, S.: An assessment of physiological workload of forest workers in felling operations. Afr. J. Biotechnol. **9**(35), 5651–5658 (2010)

Relationship of Floor Material and Fall Risk Assessment During Descending Stairs

Takeshi Sato[1]([⊠]) [iD], Mizuki Nakajima[1], Ryota Murano[2], Macky Kato[2], and Kimie Nakajima[3]

[1] Jissen Women's University, Tokyo 191-8510, Japan
`sato-takeshi@jissen.ac.jp`
[2] Waseda Univeristy, Tokorozawa 359-1192, Japan
[3] Junior College of Kiryu, Midori 379-2392, Japan

Abstract. Japan is facing an aging population. A ten-fold increase in the incidence of falls was reported in the elderly (over 65 years) compared to younger individuals. Just as the risk for slips and falls increases with age, so too does the severity of the outcome of these accidents. Falls are often listed among the leading causes of serious unintentional injuries. Especially risk during stair negotiation. Stair falling accidents the multiple, interacting environmental and human factors involved. Among the environmental factors are properties of the walking-surface and shoe or foot (e.g. material properties, tread). Human factors include gait, expectation, the health of the sensory systems and the health of the neuromuscular system. In short stair design and environmental conditions may play a role in slip accidents. The objective of the present study the environment of the feet which are easy to operate and more secure during stair descent. Sixteen healthy volunteers (age range 20–24; 14 female, 2 male) participated in this study. Each subject performed stair descent and walking on a force plate (Kistler, 9286BA) in all 12 conditions. Measured knee joint angle and ankle angle by reflective markers respectively. There were 4 parts of surface reflective markers below: Greater trochanter (GT) Lateral malleolas (LM) Distal phalanges (DP). Measurement of trunk accelerometer, parts of surface trunk accelerometer below third cervical spine. It was that barefoot, two slippers (simple slippers (SS) or slippers (S)), nurse Shoes × three types of flooring (solid wood (SW) or carpet (C) or solid wood with non-slip (NS)). The trials were performed that three steps stair descent or walking was right stance phase. All signals were collected of 1 kHz sampling. All statistical analyses were performed the SAS University Edition and significance levels were set at p < 5%. The results of this study revealed that descending stairs barefoot reduces posture upset and body burden on the landing area. Collectively. The risk of falling increased because the use of the elderly experience kit was painful to bend the joint and the sense of balance decreased. Risking stair descent is related not only to remove slippers. The results of this study will help you develop appropriate renovations and foot environments tailored to the living environment.

Keywords: Force plate · Knee joint angle · Ankle angle · Trunk accelerometer · Stair descent

N. L. Black et al. (Eds.): IEA 2021, LNNS 223, pp. 171–174, 2022.
https://doi.org/10.1007/978-3-030-74614-8_20

1   Introduction

Balance instability is a common condition in older people. Falls are a major determinant of poor quality of life, immobilization, and reduced life expectancy in people affected by older adults more generally [1, 2]. However, vibratory devices are expensive, complex, and difficult to use an effective intervention in the mass market to reduce postural sway. The Japanese people have a custom of taking their shoes off before they enter a house. Japanese houses are built of wood and they catch well-ventilated building. Therefore, they put on slipper into the front door. Stair falling accidents the multiple, interacting environmental and human factors involved. Among the environmental factors are properties of the walking-surface (such as surface roughness, topography) and shoe/slipper or foot (e.g. material properties, tread down floor). Human factors include gait, expectation, the health of the sensory systems and the health of the neuromuscular system. In short stair design and environmental conditions may play a role in slip accidents. The objective of the present study the environment of the feet which are easy to have combination floor and more safety foot during stair descent.

2   Methods

Sixteen healthy volunteers (age range 20–24; 14 female, 2 male) participated in this study. Subject performed three stair descent (Fig. 1) and walking on a force plate (Kistler, 9286BA) in all conditions to measure the grand reaction force. It was 20 cm typical Japanese home stair difference level with solid wood, carpet and solid wood with non-slip rim. Measured knee joint angle and ankle angle by reflective markers respectively. There were 4 parts of surface reflective markers below: Greater trochanter (GT) Lateral malleolas (LM) Distal phalanges (DP). It was measured knee joint and ankle joint from each three points of 2D coordinates. Measurement of trunk accelerometer (Logical

A	B	C
Solid wood	Carpet	Solid wood with non-slip rim

Fig. 1. Three experimental stair conditions as typical Japanese residence A: Solid wood, B: Carpet, and C: Solid wood with resistance rim, each rising steps 20 cm.

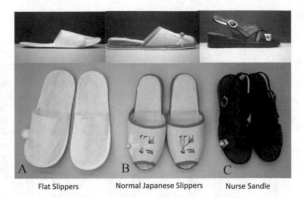

Flat Slippers   Normal Japanese Slippers   Nurse Sandle

Fig. 2. Three experimental foot conditions, A: simple, B: typical Japanese residence use, C: Nurse Sandle

Product, LP-WS1215), parts of surface trunk accelerometer below third cervical spine. It was that barefoot, two slippers (simple slippers (SS) or slippers (S)), nurse Shoes × three types of flooring (solid wood (SW) or carpet (C) or solid wood with non-slip rim as resistance tape (NS)). The trials were performed that three steps stair descent or walking was right stance phase (Fig. 1). It was performed randomly for each subjects with wearing slippers (Fig. 2). It was analyzed the data period from foot contact to toe off on the force plate. Jissen Women's University's Ethics Committee was approved this study (AC_2019_13). All signals were collected of 1 kHz sampling. All statistical analyses were performed the SAS University Edition and significance levels were set at $p < 5\%$.

3   Results

The results of this study revealed that descending stairs barefoot reduces posture upset oscillation and body moving load on the landing area from ground reaction force. Figure 3 was illustrated the landing area from GRF, there was no significant difference in these experimental trials. It was the lowest average GRF value in nurse shoes with carpet condition. On the other side, it was the largest average GRF value in simple slipper with non-slip rim as a resistance tape, because of stance phase longer by using slippers. Moreover, there was no significant difference in knee angle, foot angle and the acceleration.

In addition, it was revealed that it was not only the foot environment but also the flooring environment influenced the cause of the thing which increased load at the time of the stair descenting (Fig. 3).

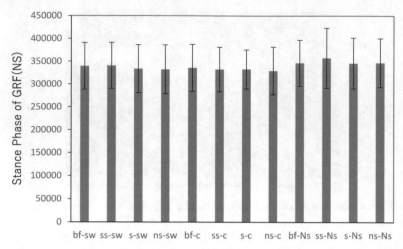

Fig. 3. Ground reaction force in each experimental conditions, bf: Bare foot, ss: Simple slipper, s: normal slipper, and ns: nurse sandle.

4   Discussion

Risking stair descent was related to remove simple slipper. It was appeared to decrease the value of the acceleration in nurse sandal than slippers. It was contributed stepping down stability to keep capability of foot angle rather than slippers. However, it was not appropriately to wear the nurse sandal in Japanese residence. It was considered, important of home mobility was not only between the foot and the step environment but also construct renovations highly airtight and highly heat insulating.

References

1. Fasano, A., Canning, C., Hausdorff, J., Lord, S., Rochester, L.: Falls in Parkinson's disease: a complex and evolving picture. Mov. Disord. **32**(11), 1524–1536 (2017)
2. Nagano, H., Sparrow, W.A., Begg, R.K.: Biomechanical characteristics of slipping during unconstrained walking, turning, gait initiation and termination. Ergonomics **56**(6), 1038–1048 (2013)

PEPPA - Exchange Platform for Measurements of Occupational Physical Activity and Physical Workload

Christoph Schiefer[1]([✉]), Vera Schellewald[1], Stefan Heßling[1],
Ingo Hermanns-Truxius[1], Kévin Desbrosses[2], Marjolein Douwes[3],
Francesco Draicchio[4], Henrik Enquist[5], Mikael Forsman[6], Nidhi Gupta[7],
Andreas Holtermann[7], Reinier Konemann[3], Norbert Lechner[8], Peter Loewis[9],
Satu Mänttäri[10], Svend Erik Mathiassen[11], Andrew Pinder[12], Peter Schams[9],
Marianne Schust[9], Michaela Strebl[8], Kaj Bo Veiersted[13], Britta Weber[1],
and Rolf Ellegast[1]

[1] Institute for Occupational Safety and Health of the German Social Accident Insurance,
Sankt Augustin, Germany
christoph.schiefer@dguv.de

[2] French National Research and Safety Institute for the Prevention of Occupational Accidents
and Diseases, Vandoeuvre, France

[3] Netherlands Organisation for Applied Scientific Research (TNO), Leiden, The Netherlands

[4] National Institute for Insurance Against Accidents at Work, Rome, Italy

[5] Occupational and Environmental Medicine, Lund University, Lund, Sweden

[6] Karolinska Institutet and KTH, Stockholm, Sweden

[7] National Research Centre for the Working Environment, Copenhagen, Denmark

[8] Austrian Workers' Compensation Board, Vienna, Austria

[9] Federal Institute for Occupational Safety and Health, Berlin, Germany

[10] Finnish Institute of Occupational Health, Helsinki, Finland

[11] University of Gävle, Gävle, Sweden

[12] Health & Safety Executive, Glasgow, UK

[13] National Institute of Occupational Health, Oslo, Norway

Abstract. Technical measurements allow an objective assessment of MSD risk factors at work. There is a need for common standards regarding data collection and processing, as well as an exchange platform storing measurement data of occupational physical activity and workload for further analysis. Several research institutes started a feasibility study to work on developing standards for assessment of risk factors and implement them in an exchange platform prototype.

The first prototype already demonstrates a technical feasibility. Coordination and structure of the contents, as well as estimates of costs and efforts needed for further development need more examination in order to arrive at a final platform with good feasibility.

Keywords: Physical workload · Physical activity · Measurement-based assessment · Accelerometer · Inertial measurement unit

© The Author(s), under exclusive license to Springer Nature Switzerland AG 2022
N. L. Black et al. (Eds.): IEA 2021, LNNS 223, pp. 175–182, 2022.
https://doi.org/10.1007/978-3-030-74614-8_21

1 Problem Statement

Occupational workloads, including physical activity, can have a two-way effect on the worker´s health. On one hand, high occupational physical activity and musculoskeletal workloads are generally acknowledged as important risk factors for the development of musculoskeletal disorders [1]. On the other hand, physical inactivity at work has been identified as a main determinant for "lifestyle" diseases such as overweight, diabetes type II and hypertension [2].

In recent years, wearable systems for assessing physical activity, postures and movements have become more practicable and therefore more accessible to practitioners [3]. Since techniques using wearable sensors allow a more objective assessment of MSD risk factors compared to methods based on observations or self-report [4, 5], epidemiological studies of load and health could be greatly enhanced by pooling data [6]. Therefore, epidemiologic MSD literature reviews increasingly call for more extensive use of directly measured data to improve the quality of assessment of work-related musculoskeletal load [7].

Common standards for measurement procedures to guarantee their comparability would simplify the pooling of measurement data. A common platform on which such measurements can be stored and exchanged would simplify the collection for larger datasets. Thus, several research institutes set out in a PEROSH (Partnership for European Research in Occupational Safety and Health) initiative to define common standards and implement them in a prototype for an exchange platform.

2 Objective/Question

The PEROSH group has already developed recommendations on how to objectively assess sedentary behavior and arm elevation at work with wearable technical measurement systems [5, 8]. Based on these recommendations, 13 OSH research institutes from 10 different European countries are working together in a feasibility study to develop a first prototype of an exchange platform: PEPPA – PEROSH Exchange Platform for measurements of occupational Physical Activity and physical workload.

The main aim of this feasibility study is to build a prototype of an exchange platform allowing collection, analysis, and sharing of data on occupational physical activity and workload by the participating institutes. In this context, one challenge is to construct harmonized data sets, considering that the different institutes involved apply similar, yet in detail different, measurement methods and analysis procedures. As a proof of concept, the results of the feasibility study could validate whether such a platform appears technically and organizationally possible.

This requires the development of a standardized data documentation as a prerequisite for an eventual analysis of merged data sets, and includes the definition of common criteria for documentation of data and the structure of the sharing platform.

The most important questions within the project are:

- Which measurement scenarios are to be considered and what kind of measurement technology will be used?

- What kind of data is to be collected?
- Who are the different user groups and what kind of tasks do they want to perform? Which functions are the platform required to offer?
- What technical, content-related, organizational, or statutory framework conditions must be taken into account?

The feasibility of the exchange platform can be examined by addressing these questions.

3   Methodology

First, the requirements for the exchange platform are collected from the participating institutes and analysed. The requirements relate to functional, technical and content aspects, as well as aspects of common terms of use.

In this phase, we aim at finding a consensus of the partners involved about the type of data collected, how it should be processed and analysed, and what information and criteria are required to arrive at a standardized data documentation. The development of the prototype is based on the application scenarios described in the previous PEROSH recommendations regarding sedentary behavior at work and arm elevation at work.

By collecting user stories and user roles, the necessary functions for the exchange platform are determined. The requirements are discussed with the project partners. Potential problems are to be identified from previous comparable database projects and solution strategies adopted (Nano exposure and contextual information database – NECID [9]).

On this basis, a prototype platform is developed and tested to determine the amount of data and technical requirements for future use. This allows an estimation of the effort and costs for the implementation of a full-scale platform in practice.

In a final phase of the project, the participating institutes should be able to enter example measurement data sets into the platform, according to the defined standards.

4   Results

A first database prototype has been developed, which is now developed further in an iterative process. A first test data set has been imported and processed. The agreement between participants on measurement and analysis standards as well as the construction of interfaces for data import and export are progressing, with thorough documentation. Initial results of the feasibility study, which is an ongoing project, are reported below.

4.1   Initial Concept of the Exchange Platform

Based on discussions within the project group, a rough idea of the exchange platform structure was created (Fig. 1).

The initial concept proposes a database separated into three different levels: a project level, a subject level, and a measurement level. On the project level, the information describes the subject collective and the objective of a study or measurement project.

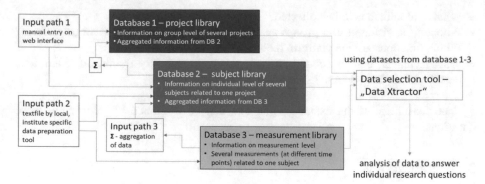

Fig. 1. Initial prototype structure of the exchange platform PEPPA

On the subject level, the characteristics of the participants involved in measurements are stored, including, e.g. height, weight, health, and other relevant characteristics. On the measurement level, time courses of measured values, calculated results or labels of classified data as well as summary statistics on those values are stored. For example, the time course of arm elevation, the label "supported posture when elevated", percentiles of arm elevation, and time proportion of unsupported arm elevation above a certain level.

In addition, three different input paths are available; i.e. to enter data manually into a web interface, to load data files into the databases, and to automatically aggregate input data to form certain parameters like number of subjects in a study or percentiles on the time course of measurements. For joint analysis and merging of datasets, a data selection tool allows users to seek relevant datasets based on a fine-tuned filter system, download them and perform special analysis of the data according to own preferences.

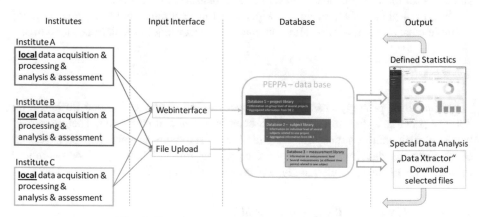

Fig. 2. Interface structure for data input and output

The participating institutes should be able to continue to work with their measurement infrastructure independently of the data requirements of the platform. The interface concept (Fig. 2) shows how standardized data can be processed. On the one hand, by entering information on a web interface, on the other hand by specifying a format and a structure for upload files. On the output side, universal analyses can be viewed directly in the web interface, while for special analysis questions the relevant data sets can be downloaded in the standardized data format.

4.2 User Groups and Functional Requirements

Various user roles are defined with different tasks and authorizations, as follows:
Administrators manage the platform as a whole and its use at the various institutes. They should be able to create, update or delete users at their home institute.
Project leaders are assigned by each institute and manage their own projects/studies. They should be able to create and edit new studies and assign staff members to a study.

Staff members manage the study subjects and measurements. They should be able to create, update or delete data on subjects and measurements.

Members of the participating institutes are only able to view shared project information, filter projects according to certain criteria, and download the accessible information. They are not able to modify shared data from other institutes.

These and other functions were defined in the requirements analysis for user and rights management and implemented in the prototype.

4.3 Exchange Platform Contents

Occupational physical activity and physical workload can be recorded using many different approaches, in terms of measurement methods and strategies. In the context of the present project, an approach as simple as possible should be chosen, since the complexity for finding common standards is expected to be high even for simple measurement approaches and the requirements for the platform also increase with increasing complexity.

Based on the recommendations in the group, the focus was set on rather simple measurement systems containing just one type of wearable sensor and a single or few sensors applied at the body (category 1 and 2 [5]); specifically accelerometers and inertial measurement units. In a later phase, after the present project, the platform could be extended to other body localizations, sensor technologies, or measurement systems of higher complexity.

Information and data to be collected at the three data levels were described in detail for the two measurement scenarios, in the process of specifying the database contents. Mainly on the level of project and subject descriptions and for single measurement parameters, the required information can be described as a draft for a common standard of documentation. On the measurement level, a collection of statistical analysis and their assessment exists from which the most useful procedures must be selected, depending on the specific research questions. A generally valid preselection as a standard could not be made yet, therefore recommendations for one possible way of evaluation and assessment are given. The participating institutions can do additional analyses or invent additional variables, depending on their research questions.

4.4 General Conditions of Use

Various technical and organizational solutions and principles have been developed, such as arriving at a decision that only finally processed data and results are uploaded. Thus, no data processing of raw data from the measurement level takes place within the platform.

There is no version control of uploaded data planned. A change notification would log a change of the data in the database and inform all users who have downloaded that data. Users can then decide whether they need to update an analysis based on PEPPA data, for example.Additionally, a disclaimer will be added to the webpage saying that PEPPA provides only the most up to date version of the uploaded data.

Institutes that upload data have the permission to share those data with all partners. Every user of the platform must be willing to share their own data and to indicate the data source when using data from other users. Statutory aspects, such as copyright and data protection, were taken into account as far as possible and reasonable in the current study phase. For example, only anonymized data should be uploaded into the database to avoid issues with processing and storing personal data.

Furthermore, there are is a proposal to implement two types of ownership: The ownership of the data itself and the ownership of responsibility of the data. The first ownership belongs to the uploading institution while the second ownership will be transferred to whoever is in possession of the data, meaning the ownership of responsibility is first with the host of the database, and it will be transferred to the downloader of the data.

Finally, cost and effort estimates are to be carried out based on the prototype and the conditions of use.

5 Discussion

The technical feasibility already appears to be confirmed. Whether the financial and human resources are available to implement the platform can only be assessed once the cost and effort estimates have been completed.

There are still questions to be answered regarding the contents of the intended platform. Issues concerning possible evaluation and assessment parameters go beyond the previous PEROSH recommendations regarding sitting and arm elevation and require further discussion.

The definition of standard analysis and assessment standards proves to be difficult since different research questions at the different institutes require different research approaches. Where possible, a draft of standards has been developed. Where a definition was not yet possible, recommendations for data collection and analysis are given. These can be further developed in future work until a standard can be agreed about. To promote research freedom, the concept of the data selection tool enables answering individual research questions and increases the flexibility of analysis approaches by providing relevant data sets for independent evaluation by the researcher.

The current concept and prototype of PEPPA, when put into practice, can be used as a kind of library that allows users to compare their measurement approaches with those of the partners in the PEROSH group. In addition, it is possible to provide measurement data to create larger data sets for analysis. Thus, in the current phase of the project, both main objectives of PEPPA appear achievable with some limitations.

If the exchange platform cannot be put into operation for technical, financial, data protection or other reasons, the present feasibility study has lead to progress anyway towards the development of common standards, necessary to create uniform data sets for pooled data analyses.

In case it is feasible to put the intended exchange platform into operation, it will considerably simplify scientific exchange and collaboration with respect to collection, analysis, and evaluation of MSD risk factors. If the exchange platform can be launched successfully, a next step could be to do a similar joint effort on the outcome/health side to analyse the relation of exposition and health outcome.

6   Conclusions

Wearable sensor technology allows for a more objective assessment of MSD risk factors than methods based on observation or self-report [4, 5]. There is a need for common standards for collecting and analysing data, and an exchange platform to collect measurement data of occupational physical activity and workload for further analysis. Several research institutes joined in a feasibility study to try developing common standards and implement them in a prototype for an exchange platform.

The implementation of the first prototype already shows good technical feasibility. Coordination and structure of the contents, as well as estimates of costs and efforts needed for further development need more examination in order to arrive at a final platform with good feasibility. Further examination will indicate whether the platform is a suitable initiative in collecting, exchanging and jointly analysing data from measurements of occupational physical activity and physical workload, and whether it shows a potential to be transferred into practical operation in a follow-up project.

References:

1. Van der Beek, A., Dennerlein, J., Huysmans, M., Mathiassen, S.E., Burdorf, A., Van Mechelen, W., Van Dieën, J., Frings-Dresen, M., Holtermann, A., Janwantanakul, P., Van Der Molen, H., Rempel, D., Straker, L., Walker-Bone, K., Coenen, P.: A research framework for the development and implementation of interventions preventing work-related musculoskeletal disorders. Scandinavian J. Work Environ. Health **43**(6), 526–539 (2017)
2. Lakerveld, J., Loyen, A., Schotman, N., Peeters, C., Cardon, G., Van Der Ploeg, H., Lien, N., Chastin, S., Brug, J.: Sitting too much: a hierarchy of socio-demographic correlates. Prevent. Med. **101**, 77–83 (2017)
3. Lin, J.-H., Kirlik, A., Xu, X.: New technologies in human factors and ergonomics research and practice. Appl. Ergon. **66**, 179–181 (2018)
4. Lowe, B.: Accuracy and validity of observational estimates of shoulder and elbow posture. Appl. Ergon. **35**, 159–171 (2004)
5. Holtermann, A., Schellewald, V., Mathiassen, S.E., Gupta, N., Pinder, A., Punakallio, A., Veiersted, K.B., Weber, B., Takala, E.P., Draichio, F., Enquist, H., Desbrousses, K., Sanz, M.P.G., Malinska, M., Villar, M., Wichtl, M., Strebl, M., Forsman, M., Lusa, S., Tokarski, T., Hendriksen, P., Ellegast, R.: A practical guidance for assessments of sedentary behavior at work: a PEROSH initiative. Appl. Ergon. **63**, 41–52 (2017)

6. Stamatakis, E., Koster, A., Hamer, M., Rangul, V., Lee, I.M., Bauman, A.E., Atkin, A.J., Aadahl, M., Matthews, C.E., Mork, P.J., Askie, L., Cistulli, P., Granat, M., Palm, P., Crowley, P.J., Stevens, M., Gupta, N., Pulakka, A., Stenholm, S., Arvidsson, D., Mishra, G., Wennberg, P., Chastin, S., Ekelund, U., Holtermann, A.: Emerging collaborative research platforms for the next generation of physical activity, sleep and exercise medicine guidelines: the Prospective Physical Activity, Sitting, and Sleep consortium (ProPASS). Br. J. Sports. Med. **54**(8), 435–437 (2020). https://doi.org/10.1136/bjsports-2019-100786
7. Wærsted, M., Koch, M., Veiersted, K.B.: Work above shoulder level and shoulder complaints: a. systematic review. Int Arch of Occupational and Environmental Health, **93**, 925–954 (2020)
8. Weber, B., Douwes, M., Forsman, M., Könemann, R., Heinrich, K., Enquist, H., Pinder, A., Punakallio, A., Uusitalo, A., Ditchen, D., Takala, E.P., Draicchio, F., Desbrosses, K., Wichtl, M., Strebl, M., Wærsted, M., Gupta, N., Lechner, N., Bayona, T., Hoehne-Hueckstaedt, U., Mathiassen, S.E., Holtermann, A., Veiersted, K.B.: Assessing arm elevation at work with technical systems. Partners. Eur. Res. Occupat. Saf. Health (PEROSH) (2018). https://doi.org/10.23775/20181201
9. PEROSH project homepage: Nano exposure and contextual information database (NECID); https://perosh.eu/project/9387. Accessed 09 Jan 2021

Biomechanical Simulation and a Detailed Analysis of the Roadside Cleaning Activity

Neelesh K. Sharma[1](✉) ⓘ, Mayank Tiwari[1] ⓘ, Atul Thakur[1] ⓘ, and Anindya K. Ganguli[2] ⓘ

[1] Mechanical Engineering Department, Indian Institute of Technology, Patna 801106, Bihar, India
1821me12@iitp.ac.in
[2] Faculty in Ergonomics, PG Section, Rammohan College, University of Calcutta, Kolkata 700009, West Bengal, India

Abstract. Purpose: The commercial cleaning sector workers are prone to musculoskeletal disorders because of the monotonous burden and overexertion with awkward posture for an extended period. This study presents a detailed biomechanical approach for analyzing the roadside manual cleaning activity, which can help introduce suitable ergonomic interventions for workers' comfort.

Method: Anthropometric information of ninety-two cleaning staff was utilized to generate the population for the Three-Dimensional Static Strength Prediction Program (3DSSPP) software. The videography of the roadside cleaning activity is then analyzed in a frame-by-frame manner and replicated on the humanoid in software. The workers' cleaning activities were classified into three categories, namely a) sweeping activity- collecting waste through the long broomstick; b) dumping activity- unloading gathered waste through dustpan, and c) scraping activity- removing mud and grass with a spade.

Results: Analysis of the frames in 3DSSPP software of sweeping activity revealed that there were significant variation among back compression force (BCF) values but consistent for shear force (SF) values. Erector spinae muscle group, hand-load, and upper body weight contributed to BCF in the dumping activity. SF in the frontal plane was found in sweeping activity only and was most noticeable in the sagittal plane during scraping activity. 'Strength percent capable' values identified knee and hip as the limiting joints for dumping and scraping activity, respectively.

Conclusion: Software-based analysis helped identify the prominent body parts under the influence of biomechanical overexertion during cleaning activity. It can also provide initial guidance for introducing interventions in the workspace.

Keywords: Ergonomics · Musculoskeletal disorders · Ergonomic assessment · Biomechanical modeling · Waste management

1 Introduction

In a world with a population of approximately 7.7 billion, around 3.46 billion constitutes the workforce [1]. Routine tasks of material handling, repair, and maintenance are done

N. L. Black et al. (Eds.): IEA 2021, LNNS 223, pp. 183–190, 2022.
https://doi.org/10.1007/978-3-030-74614-8_22

manually in developing and developed countries. There is evidence of workload-based overexertion among waste collection workers in Brazil [2], Netherlands [3], USA [4], India [5], Denmark [6], Great Britain [7]. Laborers in this waste management sector experience the ill effects of respiratory illnesses, dermatological issues with high frequency of musculoskeletal morbidities [8]. Musculoskeletal disorders (MSDs) are the pain or disturbance in the muscles, joints, ligaments, and nerves and are commonly found in the lower back, neck, and limbs [9].

A proactive approach is preferred over a reactive approach by inducing the software-based biomechanical analysis [10]. Several software have been developed for ergonomic assessment purposes like MINTAC, ErgoSHAPE, HUMAN, RAMSIS, Mannequin, ANYBODY, and 3DSSPP. The three-Dimensional Static Strength Prediction Program (3DSSPP) is a software-based assessment tool created to determine spinal compression forces, joint static strength capabilities and quantify the biomechanical risk [11]. In this assessment technique, the subject is recorded continuously from different angles while being occupied with a real working condition. The video is then studied in a frame-by-frame pattern and imitated in 3DSSPP. At that point, the software helps to recognize awkward poses by assessing the workforce's population deemed fit for working in such an unnatural stance.

The danger of WMSDs even exacerbates for nations with low income because of work-intensive frameworks, insignificant administrative structure, young specialists, lacking instruments, and heavier burdens to lift [12]. More studies involving such workers are warranted in developing nations, like India, to incorporate customized interventions. Also, the strategies utilized for the ergonomic assessment often rely on feedback of the workers, that suffer from response bias [13, 14]. To recognize, assess, and give due accentuation to the welfare hazards related to the cleaning occupations, this study is initiated. A biomechanical approach for the manual task simulation is presented in this study, which will help in the ergonomic assessment of the roadside cleaning activity. This investigation will help arrange and execute ergonomic mediations that could help to upgrade working tools and work environments to uplift of the working condition for the manual laborers.

2 Methodology

A total of ninety-two cleaning workers in the Patna region (Bihar) took an interest in the investigation. The Indian Council of Medical Research's Ethical Guidelines were followed for conducting tests on human subjects [15]. Workers' weight was estimated using a weighing scale (HealthSense, India) with a measuring capability of 180 ± 0.1 kg. The height was measured using a stadiometer (PrimeSurgicals, India) with a measuring capability of 200 ± 0.1 cm.

The workers' cleaning activities were classified into three categories, namely a) sweeping activity, b) dumping activity, and c) scraping activity (Fig. 1). The sweeping activity included clearing the pathways with the long broomstick for the assortment of waste on the sides of the road and was repeated continually for at least two hours a day. The dumping activity includes transferring gathered dust and solid waste materials, through the dustpan, to the dumpsite and necessitates typically bending or squatting posture for approximately 20 min a day. The scraping activity includes scratching off mud, dried bird droppings, and grass from the pathway using a spade, floor scrubber, or hand scraper.

(a) Sweeping   (b) Dumping   (c) Scraping

Fig. 1. Categorization of the cleaning activity

The 3DSSPP software was utilized for generating the humanoid based on the physical measurements. Seven of the workers engaged in the road cleaning activity were video recorded (Nikon J7 camera). The video recording was examined frame-by-frame for repetitive activities (Fig. 2), and the awkward posture was identified by mimicking the posture on the humanoid in the 3DSSPP software simulation [16].

The software's 3D human structure can be articulated around eleven significant joints of the body and comprises sixteen straight, rigid links. The 3DSSPP program utilizes the measured height and weight to determine the link lengths and loads, while the body shape used to wrap the stick figure can be altered by selecting the subject's appropriate BMI.

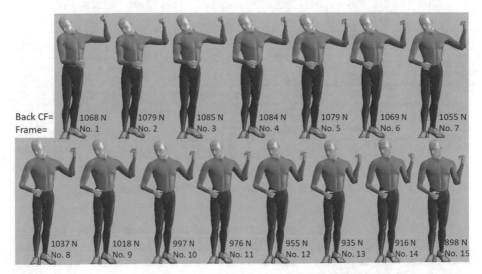

Fig. 2. A frame-by-frame distribution of Back Compression Force (BCF) in sweeping activity

The biomechanical study evaluates the percentage of subjects, with the selected anthropometry, expected to achieve the task's strength requirements. 3DSSPP computes the back-compression force (BCF) and shear forces (SF) at the L5/S1 vertebral disc and the subject's balance for the comprehensive analysis of the biomechanical models.

Table 1. Output of the demographic study (n = 92)

	Count	Age	Height		Weight	
		Mean	Mean	SD	Mean	SD
Male	57	38.9	161.3	5.3	56.7	7.5
Female	35	41.6	149.2	3.6	54	8.9

*SD = Standard deviation

Table 2. Variation of forces in the spine during the biomechanical analysis

Fr No.	Sweeping activity				Dumping activity				Scraping activity			
	Male		Female		Male		Female		Male		Female	
	BCF	SF	BCF	SF	BCF	SF	BCF	SF	BCF	SF	BCF	SF
1	1068	273	874	202	3228	252	2296	197	2028	329	1402	239
2	1079	273	884	202	3241	252	2308	197	2064	333	1436	242
3	1085	273	889	202	3256	252	2320	197	2098	337	1468	244
4	1084	273	889	202	3273	252	2334	197	2131	341	1498	247
5	1079	273	885	202	3290	252	2349	197	2162	344	1526	250
6	1069	273	876	202	3308	252	2363	197	2191	348	1552	253
7	1055	273	864	202	3325	252	2378	197	2219	352	1576	256
8	1037	273	849	202	3343	252	2393	197	2246	356	1599	258
9	1018	273	833	201	3359	252	2406	197	2271	359	1620	261
10	997	273	815	201	3374	252	2418	197	2295	363	1641	264
11	976	273	797	201	3387	252	2429	197	2319	367	1661	267
12	955	273	780	201	3398	252	2437	197	2341	370	1681	269
13	935	272	763	201	3406	252	2443	197	2363	374	1700	272
14	916	272	748	201	3411	252	2446	197	2385	377	1721	275
15	898	272	733	201	3412	252	2446	197	2405	381	1741	277

* All the back-compression force (BCF) and shear force (SF) are in Newton

The analysis is backed by the experiments and the National Institute for Occupational Safety and Health (NIOSH) guidelines for back compression design limits (BCDL), strength percent capabilities (SPC), and muscles' maximum voluntary contraction (MVC) for the joints.

3 Results

The output of the demographic investigation of ninety-two workers is presented in Table 1. The mean and standard deviations were used in software to perform the biomechanical study. The frame-by-frame analysis helped identify the critical frame, like frame 3 in Fig. 2 with BCF as 1085 N.

The data in Table 2 shows the variation in the BCF and SF at the L5/S1 level of the spine during the three cleaning activities for the 50th percentile male and female member. The sweeping movement caused a significant variation among BCF values (range = 187 N for male and 156 N for female) but was consistent for SF values. The member's dumping movement analysis revealed that the BCF generated was too close to the NIOSH BCDL of 3400 N [17] and even crossed it in a few frames. The average BCF value for the dumping activity was 3334 N for males and 2384 N for females. There was no variation found in the SF values for dumping activity. The force variations were highest during the scraping activity, with the range of 377 N and 339 N in BCF, and 52 N and 38 N in SF, for the male and female members, respectively.

Table 3. Components of BCF and SF for the cleaning activities

		Sweeping activity		Dumping activity		Scraping activity	
		Male	Female	Male	Female	Male	Female
BCF	Erector spinae	729	612	2960	2446	2311	1741
	Rectus abdominus	0	0	0	0	0	0
	Abdominal	−20	−12	0	0	−76	−37
	Hand loads	31	31	61	61	0	0
	Upperbody weight	344	258	392	294	170	127
SF	Sagittal plane	272	201	252	197	381	277
	Frontal plane	−21	−21	0	0	0	0

[*] All the back-compression force (BCF) and shear force (SF) are in Newton

The BCF's significant contributors were; erector spinae and rectus abdominus muscle group, abdominal pressure, hand-loads, and upper body weight (Table 3). Scraping activity had a significant opposing impact of the abdominal pressure on the BCF. Erector spinae muscle group, hand load, and upper body weight contributed to BCF in the dumping activity. Components of the SF were recorded in sagittal and frontal planes. SF in the frontal plane was found in sweeping activity only and was most noticeable in the sagittal plane during scraping activity.

The SPC and MVC for key joints were listed in Table 4. SPC was restricted mainly by the wrist and hip joints during the sweeping activity. The knee joint appeared to be under

Table 4. Strength Percent Capable (SPC) and Maximum Voluntary Contraction (MVC) for the joints

Joint position	Sweeping activity				Dumping activity				Scraping activity			
	Male		Female		Male		Female		Male		Female	
	SPC	MVC	SPC	MVC	SPC	MVC	SPC	MVC	SPC	MVC	SPC	MVC
Wrist	96	55	94	63	94	65	90	74	100	20	99	23
Elbow	100	10	100	13	100	20	100	33	100	17	99	33
Shoulder	100	42	95	70	97	63	73	102	100	7	99	13
Torso	99	24	99	29	98	41	96	49	97	51	96	53
Hip	97	33	95	50	95	48	90	69	93	58	BC*	BC
Knee	100	10	100	16	36	147	13	182	99	35	BC	BC
Ankle	98	40	98	50	97	47	97	59	100	11	BC	BC

* BC- Balance critical; All the SPC and MVC values are in percentage.

the troublesome condition for the dumping activity. Scraping activity was delimited by hip and torso joints and even resulted in critically balanced circumstances for the female member.

4 Discussion

The unorganized workers in developing nations get low importance and limited clinical provision for medical problems [18]. The diversified workplaces and working techniques cause hindrance in applying standardized protocols for risk assessments. A detailed ergonomic consideration while redesigning equipment and customizing the workplace can improve the physical and mental condition of the worker population [19]. The present biomechanical study endeavors to highlight the cleaning workers' unnatural working conditions that warranted photo and video-based observations only. The analysis helped to identify alarming postures, like BCF above the NIOSH thresholds and unacceptable balance, during the cleaning activities.

The force analysis of the sweeping activity presented a substantial variation in the BCF and steady SF. The variation can be due to the repetitive motion of the upper extremities (hands, forearm, and upper arm) and the trunk and waist regions' stationary posture. Most of the compressive load was the impact of erector spinae muscle groups and upper body weight. Here, erector spinae muscle groups are utilized for maintaining the erect posture, which causes the direct stacking of the body weight onto the spine (L5/S1). Shear forces in the frontal plane indicated a twisting movement of the trunk, which was absent in other cleaning activities. A slight decrease in SPC in the wrist and hip joint can be because of the guiding action required for the broomstick sweep and twisting motion of the trunk, respectively. MVC was maximum in the wrist and shoulder joints, as the muscle groups in these areas are comparatively weaker than the hip joint. So, even though the SPC indicated the hip joint as the restricting joint, MVC was lower in that area.

The dumping activity's biomechanical study uncovered the massive spinal BCF required to maintain this activity's squatting posture. SPC and MVC revealed the location of the stress concentration in the posture as the knee joint. The posture was suitable for less than 36% of the population, which could be the reason that the dumping activity was not performed for more than 20 min in the whole 8 h shift of the day.

Both BCF and SF values fluctuated heavily due to the stooping to bending stance acquired while performing the scraping activity. The erector spinae muscle group had a major contribution in BCF in this activity, but the role of upper body weight was greatly reduced when compared with the dumping activity. The variation could be contemplated from the forward bent posture that took away the direct compressive burden on the spine and slightly increased the shear force in the sagittal plane. SPC and MVC indicated an increase in shear stress in the torso and hip joints, which could be dangerous as the spine's SF capacity is lesser than the BCF capacity [20]. Also, the balance changes from acceptable to critical during scraping activity for the female member, which can be credited to the female body structure's unique weight distribution.

The current study highlights the significance and capability of a software-based study in ergonomically assessing the manual task. Such type of study additionally opens the scope for detailed analysis of the work and workspace in the developing countries with low-income category as this approach doesn't require any costly setups [21]. Observation-based research can also help eradicate interaction-related biases and don't hamper the worker's work cycle or efficiency.

5   Conclusion

Manual labor, in the under-developed and developing countries, work under antagonistic ergonomic conditions. Analyzing and quantifying this adversity generally require expensive gear and arrangements. Software-based analysis can assist in recognizing prominent body areas under the influence of biomechanical overloading. It is useful in reducing overall analysis time by experimenting with humanoids with varying anthropometry or tool alternatives. It can also provide initial guidance to the designer or administration for introducing reasonable interventions for the improvement of the working condition for roadside cleaning workers. So, as the posture prediction and biomechanical models will improve, the designers and analysts will become successively better equipped to prevent the risk of MSDs.

References

1. Labor Force Total: World development indicators. https://data.worldbank.org/indicator/SL. TLF.TOTL.IN. Accessed 04 Oct 2020
2. Do Carmo Cruz Robazzi, M. L., Murakawa Moriya, T., Favero, M., Sicchiroli Lavrador, M. A., Villar Luis, M.A.: Garbage collectors: occupational accidents and coefficients of frequency and severity per accident. Ann. Agric. Environ. Med. 4(1), 91–96 (1997)
3. Kuijer, P.P.F.M., et al.: Effect of a redesigned two-wheeled container for refuse collecting on mechanical loading of low and back and shoulders. Ergonomics 46(6), 543–560 (2003)
4. Dorevitch, S., Marder, D.: Occupational hazards of municipal solid waste workers. Occup. Med. State Art. Rev. 16(1), 125–133 (2001)

5. Sharma, N.K., Tiwari, M., Thakur, A., Ganguli, A.K.: Ergonomic study of the cleaning work-ers to identify the prevalence of musculoskeletal disorders in India. In: 18th International Conference of Indian Society of Ergonomics on Humanizing Work and Work Environment, p. 32. Theem College of Engineering, Boisar, Palghar (2020)
6. Poulsen, O.M., et al.: Collection of domestic waste Review of occupational health problems and their possible causes. Sci. Total Environ. **170**(1–2), 1–19 (1995)
7. Oxley, L., Pinder, A.D., Cope, M.T.: Manual handling in kerbside collection and sorting of recyclables Report No. HSL/2006/25 (2006)
8. Jayakrishnan, T., Jeeja, M., Bhaskar, R.: Occupational health problems of municipal solid waste management workers in India. Int. J. Environ. Health Eng. **2**(1), 42 (2013)
9. Sanders, M., McCormick, E.: Human factors in engineering and design. McGraw-Hill Companies, US (1987)
10. Feyen, R., Liu, Y., Chaffin, D., Jimmerson, G., Joseph, B.: Computer-aided ergonomics: a case study of incorporating ergonomics analyses into workplace design. Appl. Ergon. **31**(3), 291–300 (2000)
11. University of Michigan: 3D Static Strength Prediction Program TM Version 7.0.4 User's Manual. Center for Ergonomics, Ann Arbor, Michigan (2018)
12. Cointreau, S.: Occupational and environmental health issues of solid waste management. The World Bank, No. 33779, 57 (2006)
13. Schwartz, A., et al.: Janitor ergonomics and injuries in the safe workload ergonomic exposure project (SWEEP) study. Appl. Ergon. **81**, 102874 (2019)
14. Ziaei, M., Choobineh, A., Abdoli-Eramaki, M., Ghaem, H.: Individual, physical, and organi-zational risk factors for musculoskeletal disorders among municipality solid waste collectors in Shiraz. Iran. Ind. Health **56**(4), 308–319 (2018)
15. Mathur, R., Swaminathan, S.: National ethical guidelines for biomedical and health research involving human participants. Ind. J. Med Res **148**(3), 279 (2017)
16. Chaffin, D. B., & Erig, M.: Three-dimensional biomechanical static strength prediction model sensitivity to postural and anthropometric inaccuracies. IIE Trans. (Institute Ind Eng **23**(3), 215–227 (1991)
17. American Conference of Governmental Industrial Hygienists (ACGIH) Worldwide: Thresh-old Limit Values for chemical substances and physical agents in the work environment. Cincin-nati, OH (2002)
18. Khan, M.R., Singh, N.K.: Prevalence of musculoskeletal disorders among Indian railway sahayaks. Int. J. Occup. Environ. Health **24**(1–2), 27–37 (2018)
19. Sharma, N.K., Tiwari, M., Thakur, A., Ganguli, A.K.: A systematic review of methodolo-gies and techniques for integrating ergonomics in development and assessment of manually operated equipment. Int. J. Occup. Saf. Ergon. 1–25 (2020)
20. Gallagher, S., Marras, W.S.: Tolerance of the lumbar spine to shear: a review and recommended exposure limits. Clin. Biomech. **27**(10), 973–8 (2012)
21. Sain, M., Meena, M.L.: Occupational health and ergonomic intervention in Indian small scale industries: a review. Int. J. Recent. Adv. Mech. Eng. **5**(1), 13–24 (2016)

Kerbside Waste Collection Round Risk Assessment by Means of Physiological Parameters: sEMG and Heart Rate

Alessio Silvetti[✉], Lorenzo Fiori, Antonella Tatarelli, Alberto Ranavolo, and Francesco Draicchio

DIMEILA, INAIL Research Area, Monte Porzio Catone, Rome, Italy
{al.silvettio,l.fiorio,a.tatarelli-sg,a.ranavolo,
f.draicchio}@inail.it

Abstract. The occupational health risks in waste collection workers have been widely investigated. Many studies show that workers are exposed to several risk factors.

Aim of the study is biomechanical risk assessment of kerbside waste collection workers. The paper focused on the task that literature showed as the most overloading, that is emptying the bin in the lorry. Simulations were made in a rubbish dump where upper limbs and trunk muscles activity were recorded through surface electromyography (sEMG) to verify the biomechanical load for the four emptying techniques usually adopted. It was also recorded heart rate of workers during the collection round to determine their Relative Cardiac Cost (RCC).

sEMG results for the task of emptying the bin, showed a significant effort of the paravertebral muscles for each techniques. About upper limbs, sEMG showed that emptying the bin directly into the collection lorry from the back was the most overloading technique. This is due to the workers arms raise well over shoulder height. The lightest technique was the emptying of the bin inside a certified container but, due to its small volume, this led to an increase in collection round time. RCC results showed moderate activity, according to the Chamoux scale, in three of the four workers, only one of them showed a quite heavy activity.

A redesign of the collection lorries with certified and larger containers would reduce the risk. It would be also desirable a turnover of employees to allow them to work alternatively in areas of high population density, with higher risk, and in low-density areas with lower risk.

Keywords: Biomechanical overload · MSDs · Fatigue · 3DSSPP · Awkward posture

1 Introduction

Our way of life causes a growing waste problem. Besides representing an ecological problem, this leads to increased workloads in waste collection workers.

© The Author(s), under exclusive license to Springer Nature Switzerland AG 2022
N. L. Black et al. (Eds.): IEA 2021, LNNS 223, pp. 191–199, 2022.
https://doi.org/10.1007/978-3-030-74614-8_23

Health and safety in this sector have been widely investigated. An early paper from Cimino [1] highlighted how this activity, in New York City, was one of the most hazardous. Lifting and walking with heavy loads were among the tasks with the highest injury frequency. Lower back injuries represented about a quarter of all injuries reported in working hours and more than 50% of injuries occurred during non-working hours. Cimino highlighted that these latter could be also related to biomechanical overload during working time.

Similar findings are also in a review from Pereira [2]. He claims that kerbside workers are exposed to several hazards: chemical, physical, biological, psychosocial, injury, and ergonomic.

In developing countries, due to the lack of hygienic conditions, chemical/biological risks remain the main ones, whereas in developed countries these are decreasing, being replaced by biomechanical risk [2–7].

Evidence on musculoskeletal disorders (MSDs) in developing countries is shown in two other studies from India and Iran [8, 9]. Reddy [8] showed that, in the past 12 months, 70% of workers reported MSDs in one of the 9 joints considered; the percentage reached 91.8% considering the last week. The most affected joints were knees, shoulders, and lower back. Finally, the research highlighted a strong correlation among MSDs and gender (women were the more affected), low cultural level, poor economic/social status, high Body Mass Index and limited body activity. Ziaei [9] observed similar data. Results showed that MSDs affected 92.5% of the population in the past 12 months. The most affected joints were knees and trunk. Major risk factors included age, weight, working time, job type, and low decision-making authority.

University of Florida [10] did a comprehensive biomechanical overload analysis of kerbside workers. Using several methods are presented in this report: RULA, REBA, JACK, 3DSSPP, Borg scale, heart rate. Results showed that, as in our earlier research [11], orthogonal forces at L5/S1 level were close to the NIOSH threshold of 3400 N. These results were obtained with a heavier load (19 kg Vs 10 kg) and with a bigger bin compared to our one. The comparison between our results and those of the University of Florida showed that the handling technique and the lorries used could vary based on the contexts investigated and significantly impacted on biomechanical load.

Lastly, Botti [12], did an ergonomic risk assessment of the task of emptying the bins into the lorry through NIOSH Variable Lifting Index (VLI) at the origin and at the destination. Results showed that VLI at the destination fell within the red zone (64% of obs) or purple zone (36% of obs) in the summer season. VLI fell in red zone 13% of obs in autumn/spring seasons and 7% of obs in winter season. VLI at the origin was always in the green zone in all seasons except for the summer were VLI was in red zone (14% of obs) or in the yellow zone (21% of obs). Authors highlighted that, according to Cimino, the wrong design of the pick-up lorry, is one of the main issues. For risk mitigation, authors suggest organizational action such as increasing the employed workforce. It would be helpful in particular in summer when more biodegradable waste is generated.

The aim of our study is an ergonomic risk assessment of kerbside waste collection workers particularly in the task of unloading the bins in the lorry. Surface electromyography, that has never been applied in this context, will be used. Recordings of trunk and shoulders muscles were made during simulations of this task in a rubbish dump.

Meanwhile, the Relative Cardiac Cost (RCC) of the workers throughout the collection round will be analyzed by means of heart rate monitors to quantify their activity over the entire shift. Findings will be useful both for the improvement of vehicle designs and for the health and safety specialists to reduce biomechanical risk.

2 Material and Methods

Heart rate monitors, to record heart rate (HR), and surface electromyograph (sEMG), to record electrical muscle activity from trunk and shoulder muscles, were used.

The collection round was assessed by using heart rate monitors (Polar s510) on two workers in both inspections. From HR recordings RCC was determined for each worker based on the following Frimat's formula [13]:

$$FCmax = 220 - age$$
$$RCC = (FCmean - FCrest)/(FCmax - FCrest) * 100\%.$$

Table 1 shows the work activity level based on the RCC values [14].

Table 1. Activity level categorization based on RCC values according to Chamoux

Relative Cardiac Cost %
0-9 very light
10-19 light
20-29 moderate
30-39 quite heavy
40-49 heavy

The task of emptying the bin in the lorry was investigated by sEMG through simulations in the rubbish dump. Bin weight was 10 kg, it was lower than the 11.38 kg recommended by Oaxley [15] as the maximum weight limit for eight consecutive working hours with two lifts per minute. Our load is close to Botti's [12] mean weight (9.4 kg). The lorry used in the simulation was the standard one (Iveco Daily).

Measurements were taken on a subject with no clinical history of MSDs (height 171 cm, weight 70 kg). They included lifting phase, transport, and the unloading of the bin. Three acquisitions have been made for each of the four emptying techniques:

1) in the lorry by a side window at 135 cm (WIN);
2) in the lorry from the back at 200 cm (POST);
3) in a certified container to be mechanically unloaded in the lorry at 90 cm (HOM);
4) in a non-certified container to be mechanically unloaded in the lorry at 110 cm (NHOM).

Images show the four emptying techniques analyzed (Fig. 1, 2, 3 and 4) and the start of the lifting (Fig. 5) which was the same for each technique.

Fig. 1. NHOM **Fig. 2.** HOM **Fig. 3.** REAR

Fig. 4. WIN **Fig. 5.** Lifting start

Bilateral mean muscle activities, as a percentage of Maximum Voluntary Contraction (MVC), from Anterior Deltoideus (DAdx, DAsx), Lateral Deltoideus (DLdx, DLsx), Upper Trapezius (TSdx, TSsx) and Erector Spinae (ESdx, ESsx) muscles have been calculated. MVC exercises and probes placement were in according to the Atlas of Muscle Innervation Zones [16].

Muscle activity was recorded by a Wi-Fi surface electromyograph (FreeEMG 300, BTS SpA) at a sampling rate of 1 kHz. After skin preparation, the electromyographic signals were acquired by two disposable Ag/AgCl electrodes for each muscle (H124SG, Kendall ARBO). Electromyographic signals were processed through rectification, integration with a sliding window of 125 ms, filtered with a low-pass filter at 5 Hz, and then normalized to the mean peak of two MVC acquisitions peaks for each muscle.

3 Results

Heart Rate
Hereafter are the results of heart rate monitors recordings in wintertime (temperature around 0 °C) and in late summer (temperature around 25 °C). Topography of the two places was similar, with an historical center with narrow streets with steep and short climbs, whereas peripheral wide and with slight slopes.

Figure 6 shows the Poincaré plot of the first worker in winter. Worker aged 64, average HR was 115 bpm, and rest HR was 85 bpm. The Frimat formula results in a

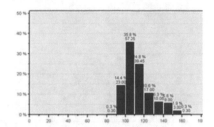

Fig. 6. Poincaré plot of the first worker acquired in winter.

Fig. 7. Percentage distribution, in 10 bpm bands, of the HR of the first worker in winter

RCC value of 42%. This corresponds to "heavy" activity on the Chamoux scale. Figure 7 shows the HR percentage distribution. For 71.2% of the working time, the worker had an HR between 100 and 130 bpm.

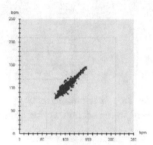

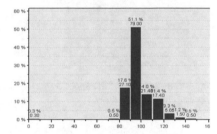

Fig. 8. Poincaré plot of the second worker acquired in winter

Fig. 9. Percentage distribution, in 10 bpm bands, of the HR of the second worker in winter.

Figure 8 shows the Poincaré plot of the second worker in winter. Worker aged 35, average HR was 97 bpm, and rest HR was 75 bpm. His activity mainly consisted of driving, occasionally he got out from the lorry. The Frimat formula results in a RCC value of 20%. This corresponds to "moderate" activity on the Chamoux scale.

Figure 9 shows the HR percentage distribution. For 76.5% of the working time, the worker had an HR between 90 and 120 bpm.

Figure 10 shows the Poincaré plot of the first worker in summer. Worker aged 42, average HR was 109 bpm, and rest HR was 75 bpm. He used to work alone. The Frimat formula results in a RCC value of 33%. This corresponds to "quite heavy" activity on the Chamoux scale. Figure 11 shows the HR percentage distribution. For 74.5% of the working time, the worker had an HR between 100 and 130 bpm.

Figure 12 shows the Poincaré plot of the second worker of summer recordings. Worker aged 56, average HR was 108 bpm, and rest HR was 90 bpm. He used to work alone. The Frimat formula results in a RCC value of 25%. This corresponds to "moderate" activity on the Chamoux scale. Figure 13 shows the HR percentage distribution. For 73.5% of the working time, the worker had an HR between 90 and 120 bpm.

Fig. 10. Poincaré plot of the first worker acquired in summer

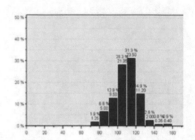

Fig. 11. Percentage distribution, in 10 bpm bands, of the HR of the first worker in summer

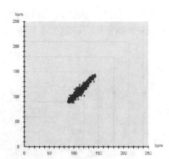

Fig. 12. Poincaré plot of the second worker acquired in summer

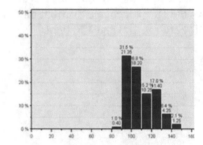

Fig. 13. Percentage distribution, in 10 bpm bands, of the HR of the second worker in summer

sEMG

Trunk muscles do not show clear differences among the four techniques. The right side showed values between 22% of MVC (HOM and NHOM) and 25% of MVC (WIN); the left side showed values of MVC from a minimum of 19% (REAR) to a maximum of 26% (HOM).

Shoulders muscles of the left side were generally more involved than right side ones. The most overloading technique was REAR while the less overloading was HOM technique.

DAsx showed the highest values in REAR (35% MVC) and WIN (23% MVC) techniques; DAsx was scarcely used with NHOM (8% MVC) and HOM (4% MVC) techniques. DAdx was less involved with values from a maximum of 8%MVC (WIN) to a minimum of 6%MVC in the other techniques.

The highest value of the DLsx was with REAR technique (9% MVC); DLsx was less engaged in the other techniques: 4%MVC (WIN), 3% MVC (HOM and NHOM).

Muscle DLdx was more activated than the DLsx; the lowest values was found in HOM technique (8% MVC). All the other techniques showed values above 10% MVC (11% REAR; 12% NHOM; 14% HOM).

TSsx had the maximum value in the REAR technique (22% MVC), this is followed by WIN (19% MVC), NHOM (14%MVC) and HOM (11% MVC).

TSdx showed smaller values of MVC compared to TSsx. In detail, values were: 10% (HOM), 13% (NHOM), 14% (REAR), and 17% (WIN).

Figure 14 below summarizes the mean values of %MVC for the three acquisitions made, for each of the eight muscles recorded, and for each of the four handling techniques analyzed.

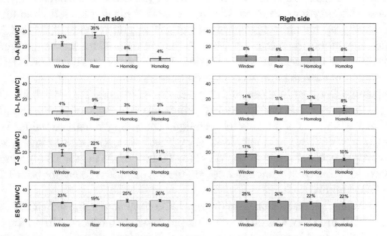

Fig. 14. Image shows mean sEMG values of the three recordinde, for the four techniques investigated and for the four muscles investigated (ES, TS, DL, DA).

4 Discussion

As Teerioja claimed [17], nowadays kerbside waste collection system is six times more economic than pneumatic waste collection system.

Kerbside waste collection, however, implies a high biomechanical load for workers.

In our study biomechanical load has been assessed through HR monitors and sEMG.

Heart rate is a physiological parameter that can significantly change within the work shift due to several factors. Among those the main ones, in this activity, are: extreme temperatures, age, anthropometry, health status, distance and slope of the paths, weight of handled bins, and frequency of getting in and out of the lorry. Results from heart rate monitor of waste collection rounds, assessed with the RCC, showed moderate levels of intensity according to Chamoux's scale. One of the four workers showed an RCC value of 42% ranking the work as "quite heavy". Heart rate distributions showed that over 70% of the activity fell within a range of 90 to 130 bpm for all workers. Those values are reached because of the type of activity in which the workers continuously jump in and out of the lorry.

Electromyographic data shows that, in our scenario, REAR technique was the most demanding one, followed by WIN and NHOM; HOM was the less overloading one.

An analysis of the data showed that the only trunk muscles (ESsx and ESdx) where always over 20% MVC. The highest recorded value (26% MVC) was in the ESsx while handling the bin in HOM technique. The trunk sagittal and lateral bending might have been the cause. Similar results were found for the NHOM technique. Also, the WIN technique had high levels of %MVC not only due to trunk flexion but also caused to twisting and lateral bending. REAR was the less overloading technique for trunk muscles.

DAdx activity was low, between 6 and 8% of MVC, for all techniques. DAsx, by contrast, showed high levels of activity in REAR (35%MVC) and WIN (23%MVC) techniques. This may have been caused by the worker placing his left hand under the bin and moving up his arms beyond his shoulders height. In both HOM and NHOM techniques, this motion did not occur. Indeed, the worker used his left hand to guide the bin to the edge of the containers for pivoting. Furthermore, in HOM and NHOM the worker should not elevate his arms over shoulder height.

Comparable findings to those of DA were found in both TSs. For both TSs, the handling technique contributed to reach significant percentages of MVC, in particular for WIN and REAR techniques. WIN technique showed symmetrical values between the right (17% MVC TSdx) and left (19% MVC TSsx) side. REAR technique was found to produce asymmetrical values (14% MVC for TSdx; 22% MVC for TSsx). Since arms did not have to be raised over shoulder height, the lowest values found for both TSs were found in HOM and NHOM.

DL showed higher mean values on the right side compared to the left side for all four techniques. This probably was due to the first phase where the worker lifted the bin and placed it on his right side to allow his left hand to be placed on the bottom of the bin.

Electromyographic results confirm our previous 3DSSPP findings [11]. REAR was the most overloading technique for the upper limb, whereas HOM was the best one.

HOM technique unloading presents the drawback that, due to the reduced container size, as previously explained [11], it would delay the collection round to be complete. This downside was also emphasized by Ziaei [9] and Camada [18].

The collection round, by analyzing RCC levels, showed moderate workloads and sporadic peaks depending on local morphology, worker's health status, and load handled. Also seasonality is of great importance, not just from the metabolic point of view, but even in terms of overall weight lifted. As Botti [12] highlighted, organic waste weighs more than double in summer, in the same collection round, as compared to winter. Although it was not quantified as in [12], it was confirmed in our workers interviews.

Results may vary considerably depending on workers' anthropometric, equipment characteristics (bins and lorry), and morphological characteristics of the area where the collection is carried out.

As Battini suggested [19] it would be advisable, as well as a re-design of the collector lorries, to alternate activities in high-density and low-density areas. Because of technical limitations, it was impossible to evaluate, with sEMG, the throwing of the plastic bags directly into the lorry.

Finally, it would be desirable to obtain sEMG data on a larger sample of workers. This was not possible in this study because we investigated small rural towns with few workers.

Aknowledgements. We would like to thank Rubes Triva foundation for promoting this study and [11].

References

1. Cimino, J.A.: Health and safety in the solid waste industry. AJPH **65**(1), 38–46 (1975)
2. Pereira-de-Paiva, M.H., et al.: Occupational hazards of Brazilian solid waste workers: a systematic literature review. Rev. Bras. Med. Trab. **15**(4), 364–371 (2017)
3. Eskezia, D., Aderaw, Z., Ahmed, K.Y., Tadese, F.: Prevalence and associated factors of occupational injuries among municipal solid waste collectors in four zones of Amhara region Northwest Ethiopia. BMC Pub. Health **16**, 862 (2016)
4. Jerie, S.: Occupational risks associated with solid waste management in the informal sector of Gweru, Zimbabwe. J Environ Public Health (2016). Article ID 9024160, 14 pages
5. Ravindra, K., Kaur, K., Mor, S.: Occupational exposure to the municipal solid waste workers in Chandigarh India. Waste Manag. Res. **34**(11), 1192–1195 (2016)
6. Korley, T.N., Fianko, J.R.: Solid waste management in households: a case of Sekondi-Takoradi, Ghana. J. Environ. Waste Manag. **4**(3), 224–234 (2017)
7. Thakur, P., et al.: Occupational Health Hazard Exposure among municipal solid waste workers in Himachal Pradesh India. Waste Manag. **78**, 483–489 (2018)
8. Reddy, E.M., Yasobant, S.: Musculoskeletal disorders among municipal solid waste workers in India: A cross-sectional risk assessment. J. Family Med. Prim. Care **4**, 519–524 (2015)
9. Ziaei, M., et al.: Individual, physical, and organizational risk factors for musculoskeletal disorders among municipality solid waste collectors in Shiraz Iran. Ind. Health **56**, 308–319 (2018)
10. McCauley Bush, P., et al.: 2012. Ergonomic & Environmental Study of Solid Waste Collection Final Report. https://erefdn.org/wp-content/uploads/2015/05/EREF-Ergonomics-in-Waste-Collection-Final-Report-PDF.pdf. Accessed 27 June 2020
11. Silvetti, A., et al.: Back and shoulder biomechanical load in curbside waste workers. AHFE 2020, AISC 1215, pp. 237–243 (2020). https://doi.org/10.1007/978-3-030-51549-2_31
12. Botti, L., et al.: Door-to-door waste collection: Analysis and recommendations for improving ergonomics in an Italian case study. Waste Manag. **109**, 149–160 (2020)
13. Frimat, P., et al.: Le travail à la chaleur (verrerie). Etude de la charge de travail par ECG dynamique. Applications de la Méthode de VOGT Arch. Mal. Prof., 40 (1–2), 191, 201 (1979)
14. Chamoux A, Catilina P. Le système Holter en pratique Medicine du Sport **58**(5), 43–273, 54–284 (1984)
15. Oxley, L., Pinder, A., Cope, M.: Manual handling in kerbside collection and sorting of recyclables. HSL/2006/25 (2006)
16. Barbero, M., Merletti, R., Rainoldi, A.: Atlas of Muscle Innervation Zones. Springer, Italia (2012). ISBN 978-88-470-2462-5
17. Teerioja, N., et al.: Pneumatic vs. door-to-door waste collection systems in existing urban areas: a comparison of economic performance. Waste Manage. **32**, 1782–1791 (2012)
18. Camada, I.: Heavy physical work under time pressure: the garbage collection service: a case study. Work **41**(Suppl 1), 462–469 (2012)
19. Battini, D., Persona, A., Sgarbossa, F.: Innovative real-time system to integrate ergonomic evaluations into warehouse design and management. Comput. Ind. Eng. **77**, 1–10 (2014)

Using Complex Biomechanics Models to Communicate Simple Messages

Carrie Taylor[✉] and Josie Blake

Taylor'd Ergonomics Incorporated, Cambridge, ON, Canada
carrie@taylordergo.com

Abstract. Most people understand that lifting with the knees bent is better than lifting from the waist, but they have trouble comprehending how much better it is, or why. Using biomechanical analysis tools to provide objective proof that one specific method is better than another can help people understand the how and why. Unfortunately, biomechanical models output very complex information. Therefore, a way to succinctly express the difference between the two methods is needed. This presentation reviews the use of data from biomechanical analyses to help workers to choose biomechanically advantageous work methods, and suggests how to present these concepts effectively.

Keywords: Ergonomics · Biomechanics · Biomechanical modeling · Best practices · Ergonomic training

1 Introduction and Problem

Ergonomics training tends to be very generic, and workers have difficulty applying it in the workplace. We often see posters of "safe lifting techniques" that show a worker lifting a small box using a perfect squat posture, when in reality, few jobs require workers to lift compact loads, perfectly positioned between their feet.

Ergonomics training for material handling, even when done in person, is often general in nature, and uses examples that are not relevant in the workplace. Researchers have often concluded that on-the-job "ergonomics" training is an ineffective control measure, although recent research suggests that practical, "hands-on" training is more effective (Beach and Dutta 2020).

As practitioners, we constantly aim to improve training and find new ways to make ergonomics concepts "stick". Using workplace-specific visuals such as posters, bulletins, and monitor displays, with photographs and videos of current employees, real workstations, tools, and materials found in the workplace are ways to help workers see how ergonomics *can* be applied to their specific line of work. Relevant visuals may increase the likelihood of workers trying out a "new" ergonomic technique or method during their regular duties.

N. L. Black et al. (Eds.): IEA 2021, LNNS 223, pp. 200–205, 2022.
https://doi.org/10.1007/978-3-030-74614-8_24

2 Context

Biomechanical models (for example, University of Michigan's 3D Static Strength Prediction Program [3DSSPP], 2019) form an important part of an ergonomist's toolbox.
However, ergonomists often struggle to explain the results to employers and employees
in terms they can understand. We often focus on the numbers and provide wordy reports
to explain the results. These models often include a visual in the form of a mannequin
positioned in the same posture as the worker, which is often the only part that resonates
with the people who review our technical reports as they can see precisely which task
we were assessing and confirm that the model has predicted the posture accurately.

Based on these observations, we expected that workers may also be more easily
persuaded to follow our recommendations for safe lifting techniques if we showed them
this "scientific" visual in the context of their own workplace.

3 Actions

A client asked us to "prove" best practices that employees had discovered through experience. To start, we worked with small groups of employees, to identify the "best practices" for each task. We chose to work with small-statured employees, previously injured
employees, and highly experienced employees who often adopted unique, specific work
methods that offered a biomechanical advantage.

We used biomechanical modeling (3DSSPP) to compare the "best practices" identified by the workers, with the more "common practices" used by their co-workers. Where
an advantage could be shown, we created a report to compare the methods, and to offer
instructions, suggestions, and constraints around the use of the method.

The visuals in the report included photographs of a worker using the "common practice" and the "best practice" with the 3DSSPP mannequin positioned in the same posture
directly beside each photograph. We also showed the percent maximum voluntary contraction (%MVC) for each body part in a table under the photographs (see Fig. 1), with
a description explaining how to interpret the results: "lower numbers mean that the task
is easier for that body part".

Over time, we discovered that the reports were still too difficult to interpret (in
particular the table of %MVCs), and we developed simpler formats. Currently, the visual
only shows the %MVC for the body parts that the "best practice" is aiming to protect.
An example of this simpler version is shown in Fig. 2, showing that this best practice is
primarily protecting the shoulders.

4 Outcomes

After creating the best practice reports, clients have used the reports for several initiatives
including:

– Worker training. The training typically includes an overview of the general ergonomics
   principles, and then follows-up with workplace-specific examples. This is particularly
   effective for workers in jobs where manual handling is the primary way to get things

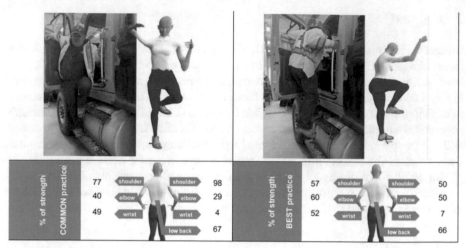

Fig. 1. An example of a visual aid showing a "common practice" vs. a "best practice" and the %MVC for each body part

Fig. 2. An example of a simpler visual aid showing a "common practice" vs. a "best practice".

done. For example, teaching outdoor workers to "maintain the low back curve" is more effective when we can show a commonly used tool or piece of equipment in a workplace setting (e.g. two operators lifting a plate tamper, as shown in Fig. 3), instead of a chair that might otherwise be used as a "prop" in a training facility (shown Fig. 4).

– Coaching plans for supervisors. Creating a "package" of best practices for supervisors can allow workplaces to facilitate their own "custom" training without the ergonomist being present during pre-shift meetings. A supervisor who has experience on the job before becoming a supervisor can be a more effective trainer, as the workers respect the supervisor's work experience. The visual aids with %MVCs can help the workers *and* the supervisor "see" the science behind the technique.

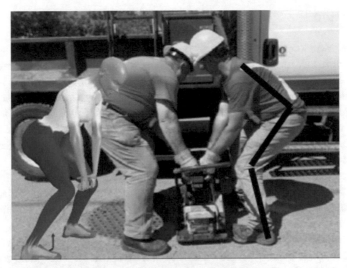

Fig. 3. A photo showing two outdoor workers "maintaining the low back curve" while lifting a plate tamper

Fig. 4. A photo showing an example of "maintaining the low back curve" in an office or training setting

– Social media content images. We use these visuals to promote ergonomics awareness amongst the general public. For example, showing a common practice vs. a best practice applied in a household setting can get people thinking about ergonomics *all* the time, not just at work. If ergonomics is constantly being reinforced, we hope that people will apply it in all scenarios and reduce their risk of non-work-related MSDs as well. We also hope that the general public will become more aware of what ergonomists do, and how they do it.

5 Discussion

Initially, we were concerned about a "best practice" showing an advantage for one body part, while adversely affecting other body parts, and this does occur from time to time. We were concerned that our simplified visuals might obscure these results, and therefore felt compelled to report on all body parts (as in Fig. 1 above). A newer report template highlights only the most significant improvements (Fig. 2 above). However, the ergonomist is still required to review all body parts, to avoid misleading the reader. We report all body parts on "page 2" of the best practices document, to ensure transparency to our client.

Initial versions of the best practices report explained how the analysis was done, using 25th percentile female strength, and 50th percentile height and weight. This, naturally, created some confusion amongst readers, and eventually, we softened the language and moved this information to page 2 of the report as well.

We experimented with formats that included only photographs, and only the biomechanical mannequins, and decided that both were important. The photograph shows the "real world" application, but the postures are easier to compare when viewing the mannequins.

The ergonomist is required to think critically through the entire task, to ensure that s/he does not promote work methods that minimize one hazard, at the expense of another. When viewing the simplified visual aids, workers will pick up on these "compromises" as they know the job very well, and will be able to identify when the ergonomist has not done the work necessary to confirm that the best practice is truly "the best". For example, sitting on a stool to unload a machine might reduce back flexion demands by allowing work to be performed with the torso upright. However:

- This "best practice" also requires lifting, carrying, and placing a stool. If a lightweight stool is not available, or if storage space is not available and the stool needs to be carried a long distance, overall the use of a stool might not be advantageous. Using a stool in this case would also be very inefficient.
- The knees may be strained when sitting and arising from a low stool.
- The forward reach into the machine while sitting may place the shoulders at higher risk than they would be while standing bent.

We also work with the employer safety resources to ensure that the best practice does not promote a "shortcut" that might expose the worker to another hazard.

Best practice reports have formed the basis for effective employee MSD prevention training for specific tasks such as shoveling (outdoor workers), wrenching (utility service), wiping (custodial work), driving snow plows, and transferring large, awkward, items (distribution). We have developed coaching plans so that supervisors, safety coordinators, or JHSC representatives can facilitate training. Non-ergonomists tend to feel more confident delivering training that is based on objective analyses, with very specific workplace examples, rather than broad "textbook" statements.

We have used the best practices to develop clear visual aids to be posted in the workplace, or at a specific workstation. These visual aids reinforce hands-on training, or fill gaps when the employer cannot take all employees offline for training. Posted best practices also help to communicate with multiple shifts. Care should be taken to ensure that workers who are photographed in the "common practice" photographs do not feel as though they are doing the *job* wrong, but rather that there may be a better technique to use in terms of protecting the body, while still achieving the same productivity. Often, the workers who tell us about the best practice also show us the common practice.

Finally, when creating visual content for social media, we found that the process of identifying and evaluating best practices in everyday activity formed a useful training exercise for ergonomics interns who were completing their studies during the pandemic. Unable to go into workplaces, we challenged them to explore their home environment to identify best practices, and then use the biomechanics program to compare best and common practices. The social media campaign aimed to make the technical aspects of ergonomics interesting, relatable, and practical, just as we try to do in the workplace.

6   Conclusion

Biomechanical tools offer a way for ergonomists to communicate ergonomics principles more effectively using numbers, photographs and illustrations, instead of long narratives. Keeping the message as simple as possible appears to be a key to successfully promoting safer work practices.

References

1. Beach, T., Dutta, T.: Training for Manual Materials Handling Tasks: Strategies for First Responders and Healthcare Workers CREMSD Webinar (2020)
2. University of Michigan: 3D Static Strength Prediction Program, Version 7.0.7 (2019)

Overview of Measurement-Based Assessment Approaches from the MEGAPHYS Project

Britta Weber[1]([✉]), Kai Heinrich[1], David H. Seidel[1], Ingo Hermanns-Truxius[1], Ulrike Hoehne-Hückstädt[1], Dirk Ditchen[1], Matthias Jäger[2], Lope H. Barrero[3], and Rolf Ellegast[1]

[1] Institute for Occupational Safety and Health of the German Social Accident Insurance (IFA), Sankt Augustin, Germany
`britta.weber@dguv.de`
[2] Leibniz Research Centre for Working Environment and Human Factors at Dortmund University of Technology (IfADo), Dortmund, Germany
[3] School of Engineering, Department of Industrial Engineering, Pontificia Universidad Javeriana, Bogotá, Colombia

Abstract. Technical systems are being used more and more frequently to analyze physical workloads. However, suitable approaches to evaluate the measured exposures with regard to their health hazards are lacking.

New exposure indicators have been developed and evaluated, which allow a body region-specific risk assessment based on technically measured exposure parameters. The development and testing of the indicators was part of the MEGAPHYS project (multilevel risk assessment of physical exposures). Required exposure parameters were determined by kinematic, electromyography and heart rate recordings at 186 workplaces. Simultaneously, medical examinations of musculoskeletal complaints and diseases of 808 employees at these workplaces were conducted. Validity of the exposure indicators was checked by linking them to the results of the medical examinations.

Numerous plausible associations were identified between the exposure indicators and specific body region-related health outcomes. A comprehensive and evaluated concept for measurement-based risk assessment is now available. The exposure indicators are applicable for measuring systems at different levels of complexity.

Keywords: Risk assessment · Physical workload · Measurement-based assessment · CUELA system · Exposure indicators · Musculoskeletal complaints and diseases

1 Introduction

Increasingly, measurement-based methods are being used to quantify physical workloads. Compared to observation-based methods, measurement-based methods are characterized by their objectivity and accuracy. Moreover, they allow the analysis of parameters that cannot be captured by simple observation, such as time courses of joint angles,

N. L. Black et al. (Eds.): IEA 2021, LNNS 223, pp. 206–212, 2022.
https://doi.org/10.1007/978-3-030-74614-8_25

forces or physiological parameters. Observation-based methods are sufficient for crude surveys; technical methods are recommended for risk assessments, e.g., before and after an intervention [1–4]. Advances in technology are making ambulatory measurement systems more and more feasible and affordable. This offers good conditions for widespread application, not only by scientists and measurement experts but also by practitioners.

Of central importance is the assessment of physical workload with regard to possible health hazards for the musculoskeletal system. Often, guidelines or assessment procedures originally developed for observational methods are used to assess exposures quantified by measurement [e. g. 5–9]. However, these do not exploit the full potential of technically measured exposures because they usually take into account body postures but rarely, for example, velocities of movements. To date, few assessment approaches have been published that have been explicitly developed for technically measured data. Balogh et al. [10], for example, propose limit values for upper arm and wrist movement velocities based on epidemiological evidence. However, there is still a need for more suitable approaches assessing technically measured exposures in terms of their health risks.

The following describes a new approach in which many parameters were measured simultaneously and assessment procedures were derived for different body regions. This paper gives an overview of the developed procedures. Methods and main results of the validation are briefly outlined.

2 Methodology

Within the German joint project MEGAPHYS (multilevel risk assessment of physical workload), body region-specific assessment procedures for the measurement-based analysis of musculoskeletal workload were developed and evaluated [11].

2.1 Exposure Measurement

To obtain the required exposure parameters, the CUELA system [12] was used in the MEGAPHYS field study. In addition to body posture and movement recordings, heart rate (model M400, Polar Electro, Finland) and forearm muscle activity were determined using 4-channel surface electromyography (OEMG; BioMed, Germany). Each subject performed isometric maximal contractions on a power grip (PABLO®, Tyromotion, Austria), which were used to normalize EMG data [13].

2.2 Exposure Indicators

Based on occupational science and medical findings, exposure indicators were defined for the body regions cervical spine, shoulders, elbows, wrists, lumbar spine, hips, and knees. In addition, indicators were determined to assess the loading of the cardiovascular system and energy metabolism. Including the differentiation between left and right side of the body, 28 exposure indicators were applied. The indicators include established methods, revised procedures as well as newly developed assessment approaches. The workload assessment is based on biomechanical and physiological measurement parameters.

The Kinematic Assessment Index (KAIx) provides the time proportion [%] of non-recommended postures and movements with regard to kinematic aspects such as angular velocity, joint angle, duration of static postures and support of body parts [11]. The KAIx records the kinematic load of the body regions cervical spine, shoulders, elbows, wrists and lumbar spine.

To estimate the compressive force (CF) acting on the lowest lumbar spine disc, the simulation model *The Dortmunder* [14] was integrated into the CUELA software. With the *CUELA-Dortmunder* continuous CF can be estimated for the intervertebral disc L5-S1. The dose calculation is based on a quadratic weighting of the CF (doseCF L5-S1 [kNh]). The CF is included in the dose calculation if it reaches or exceeds the threshold of 1.8 kN or if the trunk posture is in a non-neutral range (trunk flexion $\geq$ 20° or trunk extension $\geq$ 5° or trunk lateral flexion (left or right) $\geq$ 10° or trunk torsion (left or right) $\geq$ 10°). Another indicator of biomechanical lumbar load is the number of operations exceeding recommended values (ExcOp) according to the *Revised Dortmund Recommendations* [15].

The Repetition Score (RS) evaluates the repetitive kinematics of wrist and elbow considering mean angular velocity, mean power frequency of the angular data and kinematic micropauses of wrist flexion/extension respectively forearm supination/pronation [13].

Forearm force exertion was evaluated based on the percentage of maximum voluntary contraction (%MVC). The 90th percentile of the %MVC values is considered the peak load (P90%MVC). Another muscle activity indicator of the distal upper extremities that was incorporated is the proportion of EMG micropauses (MP [%]) based on [16, 17].

The dose of shoulder moments (ShMom [Nmh]) is used to express the load in the shoulder joint. The joint moments are determined using an inverse kinematic approach, taking into account anthropometric characteristics and handled loads.

The hip load is determined via the dose of the CF in the hip joint during activities in which high pressure values are to be expected (doseCF hip [% body weight]). Lifting and carrying heavy loads ($\geq$20 kg) and climbing up and down stairs and ladders are considered as hip-loading activities [18].

The load in the knee joint is indicated by the proportion of knee-loading activities [%], and the number of postural changes to knee-loading postures.

The strain on the cardiovascular system and the energy metabolism is reflected by mean working heart rate [bpm], mean heart rate reserve [%], time above steady-state level (t > SS [%]) and working energy expenditure (EEwork [kJ]).

2.3 Health Risk Assessment

The assessment of risk to musculoskeletal health is based on the MEGAPHYS risk concept [19]. The concept defines four risk categories (RC) which assign exposure levels to probabilities of physical overload:

RC 1: low exposure – physical overload is unlikely to occur.
RC 2: slightly increased exposure – physical overload may occur for workers with limited physical capacity
RC 3: substantially increased exposure – physical overload may occur for all workers

RC 4: high exposure – physical overload is likely to occur.

The determined exposure was transferred to the risk categories based on established assessment approaches, frequency distributions or subjectively perceived exposure [11].

2.4 Evaluation

In the MEGAPHYS field study, physical workloads were investigated in 44 companies from various industries throughout Germany. Exposures were measured by CUELA at 186 workplaces and assessed using the new exposure indicators. In each case, representative sections of the workload were recorded, which were then extrapolated to a typical work shift. At the same time, physicians examined a total of 808 employees at these workplaces with regard to musculoskeletal complaints and diseases [19, 20].

The CUELA indicators were tested for validity by linking them to the results of the medical complaint survey and diagnostics. For this purpose, association analyses were performed between the shift-related workload level determined by the CUELA indicators and the prevalence of typical musculoskeletal complaints and diseases. Associations were analyzed with generalized estimating equations (GEE), adjusting for the confounders age, gender, BMI, smoking habits, exercise, job satisfaction, and comorbidity (number of additional diseases or complaints).

3 Results

The exposure levels determined in the field study using the CUELA indicators show a mixed picture with regard to the different body regions and target systems. Rather low proportions (<20%) in RC 3 and 4 were found for indicators of the body regions cervical spine, elbow, wrist (KAIx), lumbar spine (KAIx, ExcOp) hip, knee, and for energy expenditure. Higher proportions (>30%) in RC 3 and 4 were obtained for indicators of the body regions shoulder, wrist (RS, %MVC, MP), lumbar spine (doseCF L5-L1) and for all heart rate indicators.

Numerous and mostly plausible associations were identified between several CUELA exposure indicators and specific body-region-related health outcomes. For example, positive associations were found between:

– carpal tunnel syndrome and KAIx wrist,
– osteoarthritis of the distal joints of the upper extremities and RS wrist/elbow, KAIx elbow, P90%MVC,
– wrist complaints and RS wrist, KAIx wrist, P90%MVC,
– shoulder complaints and ShMom, KAIx elbow, RS elbow,
– lumbar facet syndrome and KAIx lumbar spine, doseCF L5-S1, ExcOp, doseCF hip
– lumbar spine complaints and ExcOp, KAIx lumbar spine, t > SS.

There were also some negative associations, e. g., between lumbago and doseCF L5-S1 and EEwork. Relatively few associations were found overall for the cervical spine and lower extremity body regions.

4   Discussion

A comprehensive concept for objective quantification of physical workload and its assessment based on technically measured exposure data has been developed. For most body regions, the exposure indicators correspond to an increasing prevalence of typical musculoskeletal complaints and diseases. These exposure indicators can be assumed to be valid with respect to the related health outcomes.

The evaluation was performed on a relatively large sample regarding the effort for exposure measurement and medical data collection. Both the quality of the exposure data and the health data are considered to be of high quality.

A limitation is the cross-sectional study design, which does not allow conclusions on the causality of associations and is often associated with the "healthy worker effect". It can be assumed that the negative associations between lumbago and some exposure indicators are due to this effect. Another limitation is a possible selection bias (sampling bias). The selection of the workplaces and of workers could not be done randomly, because participation was voluntary. Thus, certain industries as well as occupations that are typically performed in smaller companies may be underrepresented.

In the past, technical measurements were often considered impractical because they required a lot of time and expertise and were deemed to be invasive. Thanks to miniaturization and (partial) automation, today's recording systems allow increasingly simple and non-reactive analysis. Thus, the CUELA system has also evolved in the meantime to minimize all these limitations.

The CUELA risk assessment concept represents an initial approach that can be further examined, adapted and supplemented. There may be a need to revise the indicators for the cervical spine and lower extremities, for example, as hardly any associations with the health outcomes could be found here. A useful addition to the presented assessment concept is, for example, the combined consideration of force expenditure determined via EMG and kinematic parameters. A combined assessment approach has already been developed and tested for the body regions wrist and elbow [13]. Another valuable addition to the assessment could be the extension by or combination with external forces.

The work presented focuses on loads that can lead to health impairments due to physical overload. It must be taken into account that a healthy musculoskeletal system requires a certain amount of load for optimal performance. Accordingly, a complete lack of load or too little load (physical underload) can also lead to damage to the musculoskeletal system. In the future, the CUELA assessment concept should therefore be supplemented by procedures to assess physical underload, e.g. due to prolonged sitting or standing.

5   Conclusion

The presented exposure indicators are suitable for the objective quantification of body region-related exposures and for risk assessment with regard to musculoskeletal diseases and complaints.

For the first time, such a comprehensive and evaluated concept for risk assessment of measurement-based exposure data is available. The CUELA assessment concept represents an initial approach that can and should be expanded and further tested beyond the evaluation carried out. The concept constitutes a new step towards a measurement-based risk assessment of physical workload, which can serve as a valuable basis for deriving target-specific preventive measures.

The methods presented are applicable for measurement systems of varying complexity. In addition to comprehensive analyses with expert measurement systems, it is also possible to analyze individual body regions using simple systems with a few sensors. This enables a simpler use in operational practice in order to be able to establish a broader application of measurement-based risk assessment approaches in the occupational safety and health area in future.

References

1. Ranavolo, A., Draicchio, F., Varrecchia, T., Silvetti, A., Iavicoli, S.: Wearable monitoring devices for biomechanical risk assessment at work: current status and future challenges-A systematic review. Int. J. Environ. Res. Public Health **15**(9), 1–26 (2018)
2. Rhén, I.M., Forsman, M.: Inter- and intra-rater reliability of the OCRA checklist method in video-recorded manual work tasks. Appl. Ergon. **84**, 103025 (2020)
3. Spielholz, P., Silverstein, B., Morgan, M., Checkoway, H., Kaufman, J.: Comparison of self-report, video observation and direct measurement methods for upper extremity musculoskeletal disorder physical risk factors. Ergonomics **44**(6), 588–613 (2001)
4. Weber, B., Douwes, M., Forsman, M., Könemann, R., Heinrich, K., Enquist, H., Pinder, A., Punakallio, A., Uusitalo, A., Ditchen, D., Takala, E.P., Draicchio, F., Desbrosses, K., Wichtl, M., Strebl, M., Wærsted, M., Gupta, N., Lechner, N., Bayona, T., Hoehne-Hueckstaedt, U., Mathiassen, S.E., Holtermann, A., Veiersted, K.B.: Assessing Arm Elevation At Work With Technical Systems. Partnership for European Research in Occupational Safety and Health (PEROSH) (2018). https://doi.org/10.23775/20181201
5. ISO 11226: Ergonomics – Evaluation of static working postures. Beuth, Berlin (2000)
6. EN 1005–4: Safety of machinery - Human physical performance - Part 4: Evaluation of working postures and movements in relation to machinery. CEN, Brussels (2005)
7. ACGIH: 2018 TLVs® and BEIs®: based on the documentation of the threshold limit values for chemical substances and physical agents & biological exposure indices. In: American Conference of Governmental Industrial Hygienists (ACGIH), Cincinnati, pp. 182–213 (2018)
8. Peppoloni, L., Filippeschi, A., Ruffaldi, E., Avizzano, C.A.: A novel wearable system for the online assessment of risk for biomechanical load in repetitive efforts. Int. J. Ind. Ergon. **52**, 1–11 (2016)
9. Vignais, N., Bernard, F., Touvenot, G., Sagot, J.C.: Physical risk factors identification based on body sensor network combined to videotaping. Appl. Ergon. **65**, 410–417 (2017)
10. Balogh, I., Arvidsson, I., Björk, J., Hansson, G. Å., Ohlsson, K., Skerfving, S., Nordander, C.: Work-related neck and upper limb disorders - quantitative exposure-response relationships adjusted for personal characteristics and psychosocial conditions. BMC Musculoskeletal Disord. **20**(1), 139:1–19 (2019)
11. DGUV: MEGAPHYS - Mehrstufige Gefährdungsanalyse physischer Belastungen am Arbeitsplatz. Volume 2. Deutsche Gesetzliche Unfallversicherung e.V. (DGUV), Berlin (2020). https://publikationen.dguv.de/widgets/pdf/download/article/3635
12. Ellegast, R.P., Hermanns, I., Schiefer, C.: Workload assessment in field using the ambulatory CUELA system. In: Duffy, F. (ed.) DIGITAL HUMAN MODELING, HCII 2009, LNCS 5620, pp. 221–226. Springer, Berlin (2009)

13. Seidel, D.H., Heinrich, K., Hermanns-Truxius, I., Ellegast, R., Barrero, L.H., Rieger, M.A., Steinhilber, B., Weber, B.: Assessment of work-related hand and elbow workloads using measurement-based TLV for HAL. Appl. Ergon. **92**, 1–11 (2021)
14. Jäger, M., Luttmann, A., Göllner, R., Laurig, W.: The Dortmunder – Biomechanical model for quantification and assessment of the load on the lumbar spine. In: SAE Digital Human Modeling Conference Proceedings, paper 201–01–2085. Society of Automotive Engineers, Arlington VA (2001)
15. Jäger, M.: Extended compilation of autopsy-material measurements on lumbar ultimate compressive strength for deriving reference values in ergonomic work design: The Revised Dortmund Recommendations. EXCLI J. **17**, 362–385 (2018)
16. Hansson, G., Balogh, I., Ohlsson, K., Skerfving, S.: Measurements of wrist and forearm positions and movements: effect of, and compensation for, goniometer crosstalk. J. Electromyogr. Kinesiol. **14**(3), 355–367 (2004)
17. Hansson, G., Balogh, I., Ohlsson, K., Granqvist, L., Nordander, C., Arvidsson, I., Akesson, I., Unge, J., Rittner, R., Strömberg, U., Skerfving, S.: Physical workload in various types of work: Part I. Wrist and forearm. Int. J. Ind. Ergon. **39**(1), 221–233 (2009)
18. Glitsch, U., Ditchen, D., Varady, P., Augat, P.: Analyse der Hüftgelenksbelastung bei beruflichen und außerberuflichen Tätigkeiten (IFA-Report 03/2016). Deutsche Gesetzliche Unfallversicherung e. V. (DGUV), Berlin (2016). https://publikationen.dguv.de/widgets/pdf/download/article/3113
19. BAuA: MEGAPHYS - Mehrstufige Gefährdungsanalyse physischer Belastungen am Arbeitsplatz. Volume 1. Bundesanstalt für Arbeitsschutz und Arbeitsmedizin (BAuA), Dortmund/Berlin/Dresden (2019). https://www.baua.de/DE/Angebote/Publikationen/Berichte/F2333.pdf?__blob=publicationFile&v=11
20. Klussmann, A., Liebers, F., Brandstaedt, F., Schust, M., Serafin, P., Schaefer, A., Gebhardt, H., Hartmann, B., Steinberg, U.: Validation of newly developed and redesigned key indicator methods for assessment of different working conditions with physical workloads based on mixed-methods design: a study protocol. BMJ Open, 7 (8/e015412), 1–12 (2017).

Part IV: Ergonomics in Advanced Imaging (Edited by Jukka Häkkinen)

Effects of Avatars on Street Crossing Tasks in Virtual Reality

Philipp Maruhn$^{(\boxtimes)}$ (iD) and Simon Hurst (iD)

Technical University of Munich, 85748 Garching, BY, Germany
philipp.maruhn@tum.de

Abstract. Head-mounted displays (HMDs) are a commonly applied tool to analyze pedestrian behavior in virtual environments. However, compared to reality,
one's own body can only be represented in the form of a virtual replica. The present
study examined the effects of displaying different virtual self-representations, or
avatars, in a street crossing task on presence, virtual body ownership, gap acceptance and virtual collisions. 29 participants were instructed to cross a one-lane
street with varying gap sizes between vehicles ranging from 1 to 6 s. Two different avatar concepts (with or without hand and finger tracking) were compared
to a baseline without any visual body self-representation. Crossing was repeated
ten times in each avatar condition, resulting in a total of 30 trials per participant.
There was no difference in presence scores between the conditions. The illusion
of virtual body ownership was stronger for an avatar that featured hands and finger tracking compared to an avatar in which only the position of the hands was
displayed based on two hand-held controllers. In trials in which any avatar was
present, participants accepted significantly smaller gaps to cross the street. An
equal number of virtual collisions was observed for both avatars and the baseline
without an avatar.

Keywords: Virtual reality · Pedestrian simulator · Avatar · Street crossing

1 Introduction

The rapid technological advancements of head-mounted displays (HMDs) led to an
increasing number and variety of pedestrian simulator setups [1]. In contrast to Cave
Automatic Virtual Environments (CAVEs) [2], the own body is usually invisible when
wearing an HMD. Additional tracking of the extremities allows the display of a virtual
self-representation in the form of an avatar [3]. However, this is often associated with
additional technical and methodological efforts. Thus, HMD based pedestrian simulators
often lack any form of body representation [1].

2 Avatars in Virtual Environments

Effects of avatars on perception and immersion in virtual environments have been studied
from the beginning of research on the sense of presence [4]. Displaying an avatar is

© The Author(s), under exclusive license to Springer Nature Switzerland AG 2022
N. L. Black et al. (Eds.): IEA 2021, LNNS 223, pp. 215–223, 2022.
https://doi.org/10.1007/978-3-030-74614-8_26

reported to increase spatial presence, affect an individual's behavior and trigger certain physiological responses (e.g. heart rate) [5].

Distance compression marks a commonly reported phenomenon related to virtual environments and HMDs. Especially in experiments related to pedestrian safety, a realistic distance perception is crucial. Participants tend to underestimate egocentric distances in comparison to the real world. In the context of natural walking, the feeling of not moving far enough in the virtual world relative to real movement is often reported. The presentation of a dynamic avatar seems to positively influence distance perception. However, the feeling of embodiment also appears to play a significant role. [6].

This raises the question of how the presence of avatars influences experiments such as common gap acceptance studies.

3   Methodology

3.1   Virtual Environment and Avatars

The virtual scenario was created with Unity 2018.3, modeled after a typical Munich city center environment (Fig. 1) and rendered on an HTC Vive Pro. This HMD features a resolution of 1440×1600 pixels per eye with a 110° field of view. The HMD and Leap Motion sensor (mounted on the HMD) were connected to the PC via a 6-m cable. The scene featured one way traffic on a 3.5 m wide single lane. Vehicles appeared around the corner at the end of the street and traveled at a constant speed of 30 km/h. The gap size between the vehicles increased from 1 to 6 s during the trials. The rate of increase was predefined for each trial and varied between .25 and 1 s, increasing either with each or every second car. The available physical space was sufficient to easily cross the street. Nonetheless, a blue guardian mesh was displayed for safety reasons as soon as subjects approached the physical boundaries of the room. The participants were instructed to cross the street as soon as they felt the gap size was sufficient. Once they reached the other side of the street, they turned around; the gaps of the current trial were filled with additional cars (making another safe crossing impossible) and the new set of cars for the next trial was spawned. This resulted in a seamless connection of trials and continuous traffic. In each experimental condition, participants crossed five times in each direction, resulting in ten trials per block.

The display of an avatar was varied between experimental blocks. There was either: (1) no avatar as a baseline, (2) an avatar based on Vive trackers or (3) an avatar with Vive trackers and Leap Motion tracking for the hands. In all conditions, participants were equipped with Vive trackers on both feet and the waist. For conditions (1)–(2), Vive controllers were held in both hands. The Leap Motion sensor was mounted on the HMD's front and enabled rendering of the participant's hand and finger gestures on the virtual avatar. The avatar's movements were based on an inverse kinematics model [7]. A unisex monochrome blue dummy (Fig. 1) was used as the avatar model to avoid possible mismatches related to gender and ethnicity and the associated uncanny valley effect [8].

3.2   Dependent Measures

The goal of pedestrian simulators is to observe behavior as close to reality as possible, while making use of the safety and controllability of a simulated environment. In this

Fig. 1. The virtual environment, featuring a one-way street with one lane. On the left, the avatar is visible displayed in the two conditions of Vive Controller and Leap Motion.

context, the feeling of immersing oneself in a virtual world, which is also described as presence [9], is of high interest [10]. In this study, the German version of the Igroup Presence Questionnaire (IPQ) [11] was used. The IPQ consists of 14 items that are measured on a seven-point Likert scale and assess presence in the dimensions of general presence, spatial presence, involvement, and realism.

In addition to presence, the particular focus of this study was on the examination of the subjective perception of two different avatar concepts. The German version of the Alpha IVBO [12] was used to measure the Illusion of Virtual Body Ownership (IVBO). The questionnaire features 13 items on a 7-point Likert scale and measures the dimensions Acceptance (of the virtual body), Control (feedback of motion), and Change (in self-perception).

Analyzing the gap size during street crossing tasks is an often used objective metric in pedestrian simulators [1]. For that, the positional data for cars, HMD, controllers, and trackers was continuously logged. Additionally, when crossing the middle of the street, the participant triggered a ray cast function to calculate the gap size, i.e., the difference in meters from the rear bumper of the gap opening car to the front bumper of the gap closing car. This distance was then divided by the cars speed (30 km/h) to obtain the gap size in seconds.

Besides gap sizes, virtual collisions are of core interest in street crossing simulators. This is especially relevant in this case, where research revolves around the question of whether the presence of a body representation influences the number of collisions. Invisible sphere colliders (10 cm diameter) were located on the participants virtual head, waist, hands, and feet. A collision was logged as soon as one of these triggers entered the collider encompassing each vehicle. Due to this implementation, it was possible to get hit multiple times but with different body parts (e.g., with the left foot and the waist) during the same crossing.

3.3 Study Protocol

A standardized greeting and consent form was followed by a demographics questionnaire and a measurement of the participants interpupillary distance (IDP). Three Vive trackers were attached to the feet and waist, the HMD was put on and adjusted to the individual's IDP. This was followed by a familiarization with the virtual environment including four practice road crossings without traffic and two to four crossings (until participants felt confident) with traffic featuring 6 s gaps. The participants were asked to explore their virtual body in experimental blocks in which an avatar was displayed. At the beginning of the trials, they were instructed to cross the street, after the first car had passed if they considered the gap to be large enough to do so safely. They were further informed that vehicles travelled with a constant velocity and would not brake. Each experimental block featured 10 crossings. Subsequently, the IVBO (in case an avatar was displayed) and presence questionnaire were presented in VR with the HMD on. Participants were asked to verbalize their answers before continuing with the next block after a short break to adapt the hardware for the next avatar concept and provide some rest outside the virtual environment. In total, each participant crossed the street 3 × 10 times, while order of conditions (No Avatar, Vive Controller and Leap Motion) was randomized. The overall duration of the experiment was approximately 30 to 40 min. This study design was approved by the university's ethics committee.

4 Results

A total of $N = 29$ subjects between 18 and 33 years ($M = 25.59$, $SD = 3.05$) participated in the study. The sample was predominantly composed of students (82.76%) with an overall gender distribution of 13 female and 16 male participants. 13 participants indicated they already had experience in VR due to gaming ($N = 5$), participation in other VR studies ($N = 4$), their own research ($N = 2$), for work ($N = 1$), or from exhibits ($N = 1$).

4.1 Presence and IVBO

Figure 2 displays the IVBO questionnaire's results. Shapiro Wilk's test indicated a deviation from the normal distribution for the differences between the Leap Motion and Vive Controller avatars in the IVBO subcategory Control. Subsequently, and to account for outliers, a Wilcoxon signed rank test was used for pairwise comparisons (Table 1). The Leap Motion avatar scored higher in all IVBO dimensions, with significant effects in Acceptance and Control.

Presence scores are summarized in Fig. 3. Shapiro Wilk's tests indicated multiple significant deviations from the normal distribution based on a $p \leq .05$ level for the groups No Avatar – General Presence, No Avatar – Spatial Presence, Vive Controller – General Presence, Leap Motion – General Presence and Leap Motion – Spatial Presence. Friedman's tests showed that there were no significant differences between the three avatar levels (No Avatar, Vive Controller and Leap Motion) for any of the presence subscales: General Presence ($X^2{}_F(2) = .419$, $p = .811$), Spatial Presence ($X^2{}_F(2) = .544$, $p = .762$), Involvement ($X^2{}_F(2) = 5.029$, $p = .081$) and Realism ($X^2{}_F(2) = 2.490$, $p = .288$).

Table 1. Descriptive and statistical results for IVBO. For pairwise comparison, a Wilcoxon signed rank test was calculated.

	Leap Motion	Vive Controller	W	p	Rank-Biserial Correlation
Acceptance	$M = 4.54$ $SD = 1.314$	$M = 3.871$ $SD = 1.548$	334.0	0.003**	0.645
Control	$M = 6.052$ $SD = 0.683$	$M = 5.638$ $SD = 1.028$	211.0	0.006**	0.668
Change	$M = 2.344$ $SD = 1.022$	$M = 2.190$ $SD = 0.828$	163.0	0.455	0.181

$** p \leq .01$

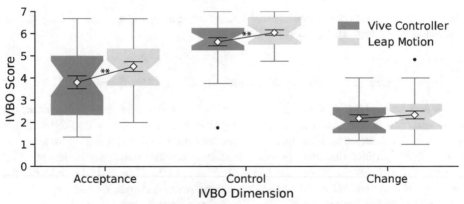

Fig. 2. IVBO scores for the Vive Controller and Leap Motion avatar. Mean values are represented by white diamonds, caps connected to the means represent the standard error. Boxplot whiskers extend up to 1.5 of the interquartile range. Notches indicate the 95% confidence interval of the median. $** p \leq .01$

4.2 Gap Size and Virtual Collisions

Figure 4 renders gap size (in seconds) grouped by avatar. Five values were excluded since the participants crossed the street after the last experimental gap (which resulted in gap sizes > 6 s) in the respective trials. A linear mixed effects model was created in R [13] with lme4 [14]. Avatar served as fixed effect (with No Avatar as baseline) and participant as random effect (Eq.*Gap Size ~ Avatar + (1|Participant)* (1). An ANOVA with Satterthwaite's method was used to analyze the model. It revealed a significant effect of the displayed avatar on gap size when crossing the street $F(2,834) = 22.454$, $p < .001$ $\eta_p^2 = .05$. Visual inspection of QQ-plots indicated a normal distribution of residuals. Bonferroni corrected post hoc pairwise comparisons (least-squares means) revealed that smaller gaps were taken when displaying either the Vive Controller avatar ($p < .001$) or Leap Motion avatar ($p < .001$) compared to No Avatar. There was no significant difference regarding gap sizes between the two avatars ($p = .239$).

$$Gap\ Size \sim Avatar + (1|Participant) \tag{1}$$

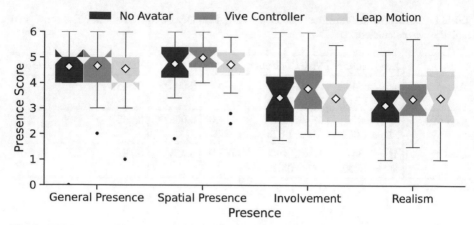

Fig. 3. IPQ Presence Scores for the three conditions No Avatar, Vive Controller and Leap Motion. The same boxplot aesthetic rules apply as in Fig. 2.

$$Gap\ Size \sim Avatar * Condition\ Order + (1|Participant) \qquad (2)$$

A second model (Eq. *Gap Size ~ Avatar * Condition Order + (1|Participant)* (2) was created to account for possible learning effects. The order in which the different avatars were displayed and the interaction between order and avatar type were added as fixed effects, with the first condition as a baseline. Comparing the two models revealed that order significantly affected the gap size ($X^2(6) = 67.727, p < .001$), reducing the gap size by -0.53 s ($SD = 0.12$ s) for the second presented condition and by -0.29 s ($SD = 0.12$ s) for the last block. The effect size of order was $\eta_p^2 = .07$. Again, an ANOVA with Satterthwaite's method was used to analyze the model. There was no significant interaction ($F(4,847) = 1.031, p = .390$) between avatar and condition order. Bonferroni corrected post hoc pairwise comparisons showed a significant reduction of gap size between the first and the second trial block ($p < .001$), and the first and the third blocks ($p < .001$), but no difference between the latter two ($p = 1.0$).

Collisions were detected when any of the tracked body parts collided with a vehicle. Since the head was located too high to collide with the cars and collisions with the Leap Motion avatar's hands were not tracked, further analysis is based on the two foot and waist trackers. Overall, 245 collisions of these three trackers were recorded. 53.5% of these collisions were created by only three individuals. Lowest number of collisions per condition was recorded with the Leap Motion avatar ($M = 2.034, SD = 4.204$) followed by No Avatar ($M = 2.931, SD = 4.729$) and the Vive Controller avatar ($M = 3.483, SD = 6.133$) as depicted in Fig. 5. Similar distributions were observed when only the waist tracker was considered: Leap Motion avatar ($M = 1.000, SD = 1.871$), No Avatar ($M = 1.379, SD = 2.351$) and the Vive Controller avatar ($M = 1.724, SD = 2.776$).

Due to the deviation from normal distribution for all three levels of Avatar (based on a Shapiro Wilk test, $p < .001$), differences were analyzed with Friedman's test. There was no significant effect of the different avatar displays on the number of recorded collisions ($X^2_F(2) = 1.680, p = .432$). Excluding the three individuals with the most collisions showed similar results ($X^2_F(2) = 1.365, p = .505$).

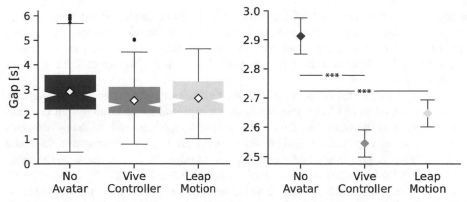

Fig. 4. Left: Overall gap acceptance values for the three conditions No Avatar, Vive Controller and Leap Motion. The same boxplot aesthetic rules apply as in Fig. 2. Right: Mean values with standard error as whiskers. For better comparability, the Y axis is limited to the relevant section. *** $p \leq .001$

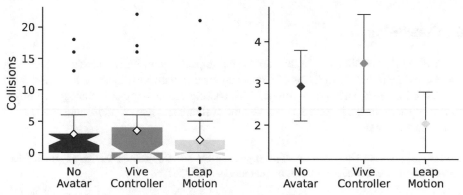

Fig. 5. Left: Number of overall collisions (sum of feet and waist tracker) in each of the three conditions No Avatar, Vive Controller and Leap Motion. The same boxplot aesthetic rules apply as in Fig. 2. Right: Mean values with standard error as whiskers. For better comparability, the Y axis is limited to the relevant section.

5 Discussion

Smaller gaps were accepted by the participants in VR when displaying avatars. Although the virtual body might increase spatial awareness and facilitate crossing decisions, spatial presence scores remained equally high for all conditions. Particularly noteworthy is the high number of collisions, which also go hand in hand with the high acceptance rates of small gaps. This also calls into question the transferability of this and other simulator studies into reality. One possible reason could be the relatively young sample of participants, that perceives VR as a game and who are therefore more likely to display risky behavior. However, it should be noted that this demographic composition is not uncommon for VR studies [1]. One might further argue that the avatar's resemblance with a crash test dummy enforced risky behavior, especially in relation to the Proteus effect [15]. This effect describes that the appearance of the avatar, for example the avatar's age or size, can influence the behavior of the user. However, due to the first-person perspective, the participants mainly experienced the avatar's hands and feet and not its overall appearance.

There are only minor differences between the two avatar conditions. The participants were encouraged to test hand gestures in the "Leap Avatar condition during familiarization, but this did not significantly affect presence scores, gap decisions or collisions during the actual experiments. Only differences in IVBO ratings compared to the avatar without hand tracking could be found. One reason might be that the hands were rarely visible when walking due to the Vive Pro's restricted field of view (110°). In other applications, where more hand interaction is required, larger differences could possibly be found.

There are also technical limitations to be mentioned: due to the leap motion controller, a wired connection to the HMD was necessary. Especially during the practice trials, participants struggled with the handling of the cable when turning around after each crossing. Whenever possible, a wireless connection should be preferred.

6 Conclusion

It could be shown that displaying an avatar impacts quantitative metrics describing street crossing behavior in terms of gap acceptance as well as subjective measures such as IVBO. However, an avatar without hand tracking seems to be sufficient for common gap acceptance tasks. Future studies should evaluate the use of additional trackers to represent an avatar.

Acknowledgments. This research was supported by the Deutsche Forschungsgemeinschaft (German Research Foundation/DFG, project number 317326196).

References

1. Schneider, S., Bengler, K.: Virtually the same? Analysing pedestrian behaviour by means of virtual reality. Transp. Res. Part F: Traff. Psychol. Behav. **68**, 231–256 (2020). https://doi.org/10.1016/j.trf.2019.11.005
2. Cavallo, V., Dommes, A., Dang, N.-T., Vienne, F.: A street-crossing simulator for studying and training pedestrians. Transp. Res. Part F: Traff. Psychol. Behav. **61**, 217–228 (2019). https://doi.org/10.1016/j.trf.2017.04.012
3. Feldstein, I., Dietrich, A., Milinkovic, S., Bengler, K.: A Pedestrian simulator for urban crossing scenarios. IFAC-PapersOnLine **49**(19), 239–244 (2016). https://doi.org/10.1016/j.ifacol.2016.10.531
4. Slater, M., Wilbur, S.: A Framework for Immersive Virtual Environments (FIVE): speculations on the role of presence in virtual environments. Presence: Teleoper. Virtual Environ. **6**(6), 603–616 (1997). https://doi.org/10.1162/pres.1997.6.6.603
5. Biocca, F.: Connected to my avatar. In: Social computing and social media: 6th international conference, SCSM 2014, held as part of HCI International 2014, Heraklion, Crete, Greece, June 22–27, 2014, proceedings, Cham, pp. 421–429 (2014)

6. Renner, R.S., Velichkovsky, B.M., Helmert, J.R.: The perception of egocentric distances in virtual environments - a review. ACM Comput. Surv. **46**(2), 1–40 (2013). https://doi.org/10.1145/2543581.2543590

7. Rootmotion, Final IK v.1.8: Rootmotion, 2018. https://root-motion.com/. Accessed 24 Jan 2021

8. Schwind, V., Wolf, K., Henze, N.: Avoiding the uncanny valley in virtual character design. Interactions **25**(5), 45–49 (2018). https://doi.org/10.1145/3236673

9. Slater, M.: Measuring presence: a response to the Witmer and singer presence questionnaire. Presence Teleoper. Virtual Environ. **8**(5), 560–565 (1999). https://doi.org/10.1162/105474699566477

10. Witmer, B.G., Singer, M.J.: Measuring presence in virtual environments: a presence questionnaire. Presence: Teleoper. Virtual Environ. **7**(3), 225–240 (1998). https://doi.org/10.1162/105474698565686.

11. Schubert, T., Friedmann, F., Regenbrecht, H.: The experience of presence: factor analytic insights. Presence: Teleoper. Virtual Environ. 10(3), 266–281 (2001). https://doi.org/10.1162/105474601300343603.

12. Roth, D., Lugrin, J.-L., Latoschik, M.E., Huber, S.: Alpha IVBO - construction of a scale to measure the illusion of virtual body ownership. In: Proceedings of the 2017 CHI Conference Extended Abstracts on Human Factors in Computing Systems, Denver Colorado USA, 2017, pp. 2875–2883 (2017)

13. R. Core Team: R: A Language and Environment for Statistical Computing. Vienna, Austria. https://www.r-project.org/

14. Bates, D., Mächler, M., Bolker, B., Walker, S.: Fitting linear mixed-effects models using lme4. J. Stat. Software **67**(1), 1–48 (2015). https://doi.org/10.18637/jss.v067.i01

15. Reinhard, R., Shah, K.G., Faust-Christmann, C.A., Lachmann, T.: Acting your avatar's age: effects of virtual reality avatar embodiment on real life walking speed. Media Psychol. **23**(2), 293–315 (2020). https://doi.org/10.1080/15213269.2019.1598435

Estimating Time to Contact in Virtual Reality: Does Contrast Matter?

Sonja Schneider$^{(\boxtimes)}$ (iD), Mariam Salloum(iD), Katharina Gundel, and Annika Boos(iD)

Department of Mechanical Engineering, Chair of Ergonomics, TU Munich, Boltzmannstr. 15, 85748 Garching, Germany
sae.schneider@tum.de

Abstract. Virtual reality (VR) is increasingly used in the research of pedestrian behavior. At the same time, empirical evidence suggests that perceptual processes in VR may deviate from real world. Such perceptual biases may affect the estimation of the time until a moving object reaches an observer (time to contact, TTC) - a parameter which is crucial to collision avoidance in the frequent use case of pedestrian street crossing.

While several factors appear to influence TTC estimates, the present study focused on the effects of reduced visual contrast and a potential interaction with speed effects. In a virtual street environment, participants indicated the moment at which they expected an approaching vehicle to pass them. In line with earlier findings, TTC estimates tended to increase at higher speed, whereas effects of contrast were insignificant. While also the interaction term turned out insignificant, the descriptive data suggest that limited visibility at large distances should be considered in the context of speed effects. Questionnaires revealed that estimation accuracy was related neither to the feeling of presence, nor to the participants' assessment of their own performance.

Keywords: Virtual reality · Visual perception · Time to contact · Road traffic

1 Background

In urban traffic, collisions with motorized vehicles usually occur when pedestrians attempt to cross a street [1]. In this context, the risk of an accident is likely to increase if individuals fail to correctly anticipate the time that remains until an approaching vehicle reaches their crossing line. Such estimates, however, are often inaccurate: During the past decades, participants in both virtual and non-virtual environments were reported to underestimate the temporal gap to an approaching object by approximately 25% [2]. This finding may be explained by a "tendency to err in the direction of safety", at least in environments that encompass detailed contextual stimuli [2]. In comparison to physical environments, however, the use of virtual reality (VR) may induce additional biases. Since this methodology is increasingly used to investigate pedestrian behavior [3], more information is needed about the perceptual biases that arise in simulated traffic in general and during street crossing in particular.

N. L. Black et al. (Eds.): IEA 2021, LNNS 223, pp. 224–231, 2022.
https://doi.org/10.1007/978-3-030-74614-8_27

Their relevance for traffic safety has stimulated research on TTC estimates, producing a list of factors that presumably influence their accuracy. At high vehicle speeds, for instance, pedestrians tend to overestimate the remaining time, resulting in the acceptance of smaller and thus riskier time gaps [4]. Since speed effects appear largest for impoverished visual conditions [2, 5], they are likely more pronounced in virtual environments, in which properties such as the visual resolution and the field of view (FOV) are usually restricted [6]. As VR is used not only to predict real-world actions, but also to illuminate perceptual processes [7], it is important to know how the quality of the visual representation may influence the experimental findings.

A number of technological parameters have been reported to influence human perception in virtual environments. In addition to stereoscopy and the size of the FOV, the evaluation of an object's approach may be affected by the visual contrast [2]. Low contrast may alter the perceived distance by reducing or distorting the available depth cues [8]. In the domain of traffic simulation, changes in contrast are mostly discussed as a result of foggy weather [9, 10]. When visibility was reduced in a fog chamber, Cavallo [8] found participants to rate egocentric distances as larger under both nighttime and daytime conditions. These findings, however, seemed to depend on whether or not the outline of a vehicle was visible, and were not replicated for moderate fog levels in a driving simulator.

While the impression of larger distances may lead participants to overestimate TTC, the estimates can be expected to additionally depend on the perceived velocity. In an early experiment, Stone and Thompson [11] observed that higher contrast led participants to perceive the upward movement of horizontal gratings as faster. In both simulated and recorded traffic scenes, reduced contrast not only caused participants to perceive approaching vehicles as slower, but also impaired their ability to differentiate between speed levels [9]. The underestimation of velocities was more pronounced for a reference speed of 40 km/h than for a higher speed of 60 km/h. The range of displayed speeds, however, was related to distinct mechanisms for generating the visual stimuli in this case [9].

Snowden et al. [10] demonstrated that biases in speed perception were not limited to the movement of external objects. Instead, they found participants in a driving simulator to underestimate also their own speed as contrast declined. Their findings, however, partially conflict with later research by Owens et al. [12] as well as by Cavallo [8], who found speed perception to be similarly reliable for different contrast levels. While Owens et al. [12] attached plastic filters to the car windows, Cavallo [8] explains differences in comparison to Snowden et al. [10] by the mechanism employed to represent fog. She thereby suggests that speed perception may be more biased by uniform changes in contrast than by actual fog, which causes an exponential attenuation as a function of distance. This assumption is supported by Pretto et al. [13], who reported speed to be underestimated when contrast was reduced regardless of distance, but overestimated when the decline in visibility was consistent with actual fog. Hence, when relating previous findings to the quality of visual displays, attention must be paid to the mechanism that was used for generating different contrast levels.

It is yet unclear whether the impact of speed effects translates to TTC estimates. If low contrast indeed causes humans to perceive movements as slower, this may result in an overestimation of TTC. Such a conclusion, however, relies on two assumptions. First, it requires TTC estimates to arise from a combination of speed and distance information, whereas previous research indicates that humans more commonly rely on changes in angular size [2]. Second, although unlikely according to the findings of Cavallo [8], contrast-induced changes in perceived physical distance may counteract the effects of speed on TTC estimates: If estimates of both distance and velocity declined at a similar rate, this would result in a constant TTC across contrast levels.

Currently, empirical evidence regarding the relationship between contrast and TTC estimates is scarce. For simplistic laboratory stimuli, Landwehr et al. [14] observed TTC estimates to be unaffected by changes in contrast and luminance. The lack of three-dimensional information and contextual stimuli, however, renders the transferability to VR pedestrian simulation questionable [2]. In the present study, we therefore evaluated if contrast-induced changes in perceived velocity propagate to TTC estimates in virtual traffic scenarios displayed via an HMD. To account for possible interactions [9], we manipulated the vehicle speed in addition to image contrast.

2 Methodology

In a within-subject experiment, 27 participants (12 females, 24.3 ± 2.49 years) esti-mated the TTC of vehicles, which approached sequentially from the left and at a constant speed of either 30, 40, or 50 km/h. The virtual scene represented an urban street envi-ronment modelled in Unity3D, which was displayed via an Oculus Rift DK2 HMD. The OLED display provided stereoscopic vision at 1920 × 1080 pixels and a 100° nominal FOV. Contrast was adjusted by a white overlay of 100%, 87.5%, or 75% transparency, which uniformly affected all surroundings (Fig. 1). Our approach to manipulate contrast was thus similar to Horswill and Plooy [9] and Snowden et al. [10]. Acoustic stimuli mimicking the engine sounds were present while vehicles were visible.

Fig. 1. Sample scene of the virtual environment with a white overlay of 100% (left), 87.5% (center), or 75% (right) transparency.

Depending on their speed, vehicles started from a distance between 55 and 76 m. The screen turned black after 3 to 3.2 s, when the vehicle had reached a location between 30 and 32 m from the observer (Fig. 2). Slight variations in the duration of the simula-tion and the point of disappearance were intended to prevent participants from basing their estimates primarily on the position of the vehicle. The car model, in contrast, was identical for all trials to avoid any confounding effects due to its size and appearance [7]. A white horizontal line marked the hypothetical crossing trajectory perpendicular to the vehicle's direction of approach.

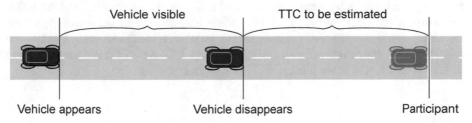

Fig. 2. Depiction of an experimental trial. The approach of each vehicle was visible for 3 to 3.2 s, before the scene turned black. Participants were instructed to indicate the moment when they expected the vehicle to reach their crossing line under the assumption that it maintained a constant speed.

Participants indicated the moment in which they expected the vehicle to pass them by pushing a button. Since the distance at which the virtual scene disappeared was relatively constant, the actual TTC at this point primarily depended on the vehicle speed, resulting in values between 2.16 and 3.84 s. Estimation error was calculated by dividing the difference between estimated and actual TTC by the actual TTC. Hence, overestimations resulted in positive, underestimations in negative values. Estimation error was predicted by a mixed linear regression including vehicle speed, contrast, and their interaction as fixed effects and random intercepts to model interpersonal differences between participants. One observation was removed from the analysis because of a particularly large Cook's distance. In this case, the observed estimation error corresponded to 361% of the actual TTC and was more than twice as large as the second highest error for the respective individual. Speed and contrast levels were considered categorical and ordered.

After providing informed consent, participants completed a total of twelve practice trials. In the first six of them, the scene remained visible to ensure that the instructions had been understood. Apart from that, participants did not receive any feedback about the accuracy of their judgements. Repeating each speed/contrast combination six times, they completed a total of 54 experimental trials. Speed and contrast levels were permuted according to a Latin Square. After the first 27 trials, a short break was allowed, in which participants provided information on demographic properties. Additionally, they answered questions on their feeling of presence [15] and the perceived effort associated with the estimation task after the second block of experimental trials. Overall, participants needed approximately half an hour to complete the experiment, of which they spent a maximum of 20 min in VR. To incentivize accurate estimates, they were informed that the best performance would be rewarded by a voucher.

3 Results

Contrary to previous findings [2], TTC generally tended to be over- rather than under-estimated, resulting in an overall mean error of 6.1%. At the same time, variance was high, as indicated by a standard deviation of 45.8%. The descriptive distribution of errors appeared relatively similar across speed and contrast levels (Fig. 3). Accounting for interpersonal variation by means of random intercepts, a mixed linear regression revealed a significant effect of vehicle speed ($b = 0.035, t(1422) = 2.95, p = .003$). The coefficients for both contrast ($b = -0.019, t(1422) = 1.57, p = .117$) and the interaction term ($b = 0.012, t(1422) = 0.60, p = .549$) were insignificant.

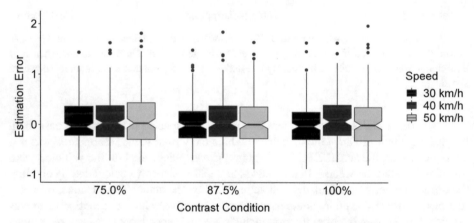

Fig. 3. Estimation error as a function of vehicle speed and contrast. Notches represent the 95% confidence interval of the median.

While higher TTC estimates at increasing speed are consistent with previous research [2], the mean values in the present study suggest a potential quadratic relationship: For all contrast levels, estimates increased with speed from 30 to 40 km/h, but declined again from 40 to 50 km/h, albeit to a lesser extent. Although this observation may be a statistical artefact, it may also indicate the existence of further perceptual biases, such as difficulties with judging the speed at large distances, which reduce the de facto observation time. In line with the lack of statistical significance, no clear pattern emerged with respect to changes in contrast.

Averaged presence scores had a median of 4.91 on a 7-point Likert scale, with 95.7% ranging above the mid value of 3.5. The extent of subjective presence was unrelated to the accuracy of TTC estimates (Spearman's rho $= -.155, t(25) = 0.78, p = .440$). Furthermore, participants tended to think they had underestimated the actual TTC (median $= 3$ on a 7-point Likert scale ranging from "too short" to "too long"). The average estimation error, in contrast, was small but positive and did not correlate significantly with the extent of perceived underestimation (Spearman's rho $= .263, t(25) = 1.36, p = .185$). The latter finding indicates a limited ability to judge one's own performance.

4 Discussion

To our knowledge, the present work represents the first experiment to systematically evaluate effects of image contrast on TTC estimates in a high-fidelity pedestrian simulator. In line with a more simplistic laboratory task [14], TTC perception in a detailed traffic environment did not seem to be distorted by a decline in contrast of up to 25%. This finding conflicts with previous studies that demonstrated speed to be underestimated at low contrast [2], which should, all other things being equal, result in an overestimation of TTC.

Differences to previous research may be explained by a number of methodological factors. First, we investigated a relatively narrow range of contrast levels and effects may be more pronounced if visibility was further reduced [8]. Although we cannot rule out that TTC estimates will be biased below some threshold, however, the relevance of extensive changes in contrast seems questionable for recent HMD applications. Second, a number of participants complained about the difficulty of the task, and 17 out of 27 individuals expected that they had clearly underestimated the actual TTC. Five of them stated that they thought changes in contrast to impair their performance, highlighting that the differences between the experimental conditions were noticeable. In this context, the relatively large standard deviation of the error term reflects interpersonal variation, but also implies some uncertainty associated with the estimation task. Although the time during which vehicles were presented was similar to other studies [4, 9], difficulty may be reduced by extending observation times, as some researchers suggest that accuracy increases with them [2]. The insignificant effect of contrast is nonetheless unlikely to result from guessing at chance, since estimates averaged close to the actual TTC and common effects of speed variations were replicated. Finally, although there is some agreement that low contrast results in an underestimation of speed [2], this finding appears to be mediated by further variables [12], such as the mechanism that is used to manipulate visibility [8, 13].

Earlier research mostly focused on the processing of speed rather than TTC. Consequently, the absence of a more pronounced effect may also indicate that different perceptual processes apply to the two parameters. If distances, for instance, would shorten rather than expand at low contrast, this might compensate for an underestimation of speed. Even if the two mechanisms do not completely balance each other, net effects may be too small to become evident in the current experiment. Although previous findings suggest opposite effects with regard to distance perception [8], it is unclear to which extent they apply to the present use case. Alternatively, if TTC estimates are primarily based on changes in angular size [2], neither speed nor distance perception may impact them directly. Instead, visual resolution may be crucial in this case, in particular at larger distances.

While the increase in TTC estimates between 30 and 40 km/h is consistent with previous research, it did not seem to generalize to higher speed in the present study. Since vehicle speed was related to the actual TTC, either of the two parameters may be responsible for the observed pattern. Apart from the possibility of a statistical artefact, our observations may indicate that virtual environments put further restrictions on perceptual processes. For instance, vehicles driving at a higher speed cover a wider spatial range during a given amount of time, which may facilitate estimates. If, however, motion becomes hard to distinguish at large distances due to limited resolution, any such advantage may disappear. Future research should clarify related differences between virtual and physical environments.

Generally, TTC in the present study tended to be over- rather than underestimated. This result is particularly noteworthy, because an overestimation of TTC is likely to compromise traffic safety: It may cause pedestrians to cross in front of a vehicle [4], although the available time gap is objectively insufficient. In the present experiment, the magnitude of overestimations exceeded 0.8 s in 29.2% of the trials, and 1.2 s in 20.7% of them. The latter two values represent average safety margins observed on a busy intersection in Shanghai, China [16]. If pedestrians deem such relatively short time gaps as sufficient, the observed misjudgment would result in a higher number of collisions. If any feature of the simulation triggered this kind of bias, it may thus cause researchers to observe riskier behavior in simulators due to a perceptual distortion. Considering the relevance of TTC estimation for common crossing scenarios [4], future research should therefore clarify the influence of alternative technological parameters.

5 Conclusion

In summary, we did not find evidence that moderate changes in contrast influence TTC estimates in VR pedestrian simulators. This suggests that either technological advancements mitigate biases which were previously reported for speed perception, that unequal mechanisms apply to the two parameters, or that multiple, contrasting effects compensate each other. Considering the disagreement with previous findings [9], our results imply that changes in contrast may be more relevant for speed perception than for TTC estimates. Hence, related measures must be accounted for individually when discussing the limitations of virtual environments. Since the expected TTC is critical to common street crossing tasks [3], it remains furthermore questionable if previous results bear the same relevance to pedestrian research as they do for driving scenarios, in which participants are supposed to maintain an appropriate speed. To clarify this issue, future research may extend the present results by exploring the role of diverse experimental tasks, differences between external and ego-motion, and interactions with further technological parameters such as the visual resolution.

Acknowledgments. This research was supported by the Deutsche Forschungsgemeinschaft (German Research Foundation/DFG, project number 317326196).

References

1. Ebner, A., Helmer, T., Samaha, R.R., Scullion, P.: Identifying and analyzing reference scenarios for the development and evaluation of active safety: application to preventive pedestrian safety. Int. J. Intell. Transp. Syst. Res. **9**(3), 128–138 (2011)
2. Feldstein, I.T.: Impending collision judgment from an egocentric perspective in real and virtual environments: a review. Perception **48**(9), 769–795 (2019)
3. Schneider, S., Bengler, K.: Virtually the same? Analysing pedestrian behaviour by means of virtual reality. Transp. Res. Part F: Traff. Psychol. Behav. **68**, 231–256 (2020)

4. Petzoldt, T.: On the relationship between pedestrian gap acceptance and time to arrival estimates. Accid. Anal. Prevent. **72**, 127–133 (2014)
5. Cavallo, V., Laurent, M.: Visual information and skill level in time-to-collision estimation. Perception **17**(5), 623–632 (1988)
6. Schneider, S., Maruhn, P., Dang, N.-T., Pala, P., Cavallo, V., Bengler, K.: Pedestrian crossing decisions in virtual environments: behavioral validity in CAVEs and head-mounted displays. Human factors (2021)
7. Petzoldt, T.: Size speed bias or size arrival effect-How judgments of vehicles' approach speed and time to arrival are influenced by the vehicles' size. Accid. Anal. Prevent. **95**(Pt A), 132–137 (2016)
8. Cavallo, V.: Perceptual distortions when driving in fog. In: Traffic and Transportation Studies. Proceedings of ICTTS 2002; July 23–25, 2002, Gui-lin, People's Republic of China. American Society of Civil Engineers, Reston, Va. 965–972 (2002)
9. Horswill, M.S., Plooy, A.M.: Reducing contrast makes speeds in a video-based driving simulator harder to discriminate as well as making them appear slower. Perception **37**(8), 1269–1275 (2008)
10. Snowden, R.J., Stimpson, N., Ruddle, R.A.: Speed perception fogs up as visibility drops. Nature **392**(6675), 450 (1998)
11. Stone, L.S., Thompson, P.: Human speed perception is contrast dependent. Vision Res. **32**(8), 1535–1549 (1992)
12. Owens, D.A., Wood, J., Carberry, T.: Perceived speed and driving behavior in foggy conditions [Abstract]. J. Vis. **2**(7), 631 (2002)
13. Pretto, P., Breciani, J.-P., Rainer, G., Bülthoff, H.H.: Foggy perception slows us down. eLife, 1–12 (2012)
14. Landwehr, K., Brendel, E., Hecht, H.: Luminance and contrast in visual perception of time to collision. Vision Res. **89**, 18–23 (2013)
15. UQO Cyberpsychology Lab: Presence Questionnaire, https://w3.uqo.ca/cyberpsy/en/index_en.htm. Accessed 27 Mar 2019 (2004)
16. Tageldin, A., Zaki, M.H., Sayed, T.: Examining pedestrian evasive actions as a potential indicator for traffic conflicts. IET Intell. Transp. Syst. **11**(5), 282–289 (2017)

Part V: Human Factors in Robotics (Edited by Sascha Wischniewski and Patricia H. Rosen)

Three-Stage Evaluation for Defining the Potential of an Industrial Exoskeleton in a Specific Job

Michiel de Looze[(✉)], Aijse de Vries, Frank Krause, and Saskia Baltrusch

TNO, Leiden, The Netherlands
michiel.delooze@tno.nl

Abstract. Determination of the effectivity, usability and acceptance of an exoskeleton for a specific job requires a three-stage approach in which we get a first impression of its usefulness and potential fit (field observation), in which we measure the work load reducing effect (controlled experiment), and in which we measure use and acceptance, performance, work load and fatigue during the working day in practice (field study). This approach is described and illustrated for the case of an arm-support exoskeleton in plastering. The field observation of plasterers and the subsequent controlled experiment showed promising results in terms of shoulder load reduction and reductions of perceived exertion. The outline of the study design for the (currently just started) field study on plasterers is presented.

Keywords: Heavy work · Exoskeletons · Work Load · Acceptance · Construction

1 Introduction

Many workers are still exposed to heavy work. Percentages of EU workers exposed to tiring or painful positions, handling heavy loads, and repetitive movements, for more than a quarter of their working time, are 43%, 32%, and 61% (Eurofound 2017). Heavy work may lead to discomfort and fatigue, which may limit productivity and job attractiveness. Heavy work is also associated with musculoskeletal injury, particularly in the low back and shoulders (Da Costa and Viera 2010, Van Rijn et al. 2010).

Industrial exoskeletons may form a new strategy to reduce the load in heavy work, particularly if other strategies like workstation configuration, re-organization of tasks, and robotization, are not feasible. Several passive (spring-based) exoskeletons, both back and arm-support devices, are currently finding their way into practice. It has been shown that these exoskeletons are effective in reducing the load on the low back and shoulders, but most evidence for this has been obtained from isolated near-static activities performed mainly in the lab (Vries and Looze 2019, Kermavnar et al. 2021, Theurel and Desbrosses 2019; McFarland and Fischer 2019). A real job however, involves multiple tasks while each task consists of multiple postures and movements. This may drastically lower the overall effectivity in load reduction.

N. L. Black et al. (Eds.): IEA 2021, LNNS 223, pp. 235–241, 2022.
https://doi.org/10.1007/978-3-030-74614-8_28

Moreover, for being usable and accepted in real work, an exoskeleton should not only reduce the workload significantly, but should also minimize negative side effects like movement limitation, hindrance, load shifts, heat stress, discomfort and pressure. These effects will depend on specific job and work context characteristics.

In fact, it holds for the effectivity, the usability as well as the acceptance of an exoskeleton, that these are all highly use-case specific. It also holds that the assessment of the load reducing effect in the low back and shoulder region for specific occupational tasks requires detailed measurements in a controlled environment. For these reasons we propose a three-stage approach for evaluating the effectivity, usability and acceptance of an exoskeleton for a specific job. By this approach we aim: (1) to estimate the potential fit of an exoskeleton in a specific context by observing the work and working context before implementing an exoskeleton (field observation), (2) to quantify the workload-reducing effects of the exoskeleton in simulated tasks (controlled experiment), and (3) to determine the effects on behaviour, usability, performance, work load and fatigue in the real work setting (field study). In this paper we describe the approach and its application on the job of plasterers.

2   Stage 1: Field Observation

The first step aims to define the usefulness and the potential fit of the exoskeleton for the job under consideration.

Hereto, the job content need to be analysed. Questions to be answered are: which tasks make part of the job, which body postures, movements and external forces are involved in each task, and how are these tasks organized over time (task durations, task frequency, task variation)? These questions could be answered by visual observation, through interviews or questionnaires, and can potentially be substantiated with motion recording. The outcome of this job analysis gives insight in the risks for developing low back and shoulder injury during the working day. Furthermore, the outcome should give an indication to what extent or to what proportion of time the exoskeleton could provide support or cause hindrance for the back and shoulder region. Also part of the first observation is the assessment of specific work context factors that may limit the usability or acceptance of an exoskeleton.

In case the results of the observations are promising regarding the usefulness and fit of a back or arm-support exoskeleton, it is meaningful to have the exoskeleton tested by a few workers (N = 3–5) in practice for about 30–120 min depending on the task variability within the job. Expert observation and interviews with the workers afterwards may bring forward (additional) benefits or drawbacks of exoskeleton use in the specific context.

The first step provides insight in the usefulness and fit of a specific exoskeleton in a specific work context. It does not provide evidence about the load and risk reduction that could be achieved by exoskeleton adoption. Particularly, where tasks consist of multiple movements and postures, the load reducing effect is not clear without further research.

We have evaluated the job of plasterers and the usefulness and potential fit of an exoskeleton in that population. On different locations the work of plasterers was observed and the tasks within the job were analysed by an expert in ergonomics.

Beside various secondary tasks, the primary tasks of the plasterers are the following: The first is applying the gypsum to the wall, by an upward movement, or ceiling, by a backwards backhand movement: for both wall and ceiling, this is done with the dominant arm, in the direction of the hand back, by external rotation and flexion of the shoulder while holding a trowel with a pronated wrist. The second task is screeding: the gypsum is spread and evened out over the surface. This task is mainly performed in an upward direction (wall), or backward direction (ceiling), with supinated wrists. The third task is finishing the wall or ceiling with a squeegee knife to create a smooth final surface. Movements in this task are highly variable. Generally, the tasks (both ceiling and wall) involve significant arm elevation, both in terms of degree and duration. According to ISO11228–3, the arm elevation levels observed can be associated with increased risks for developing shoulder injury. We decided that the testing of an arm-support exoskeleton could be valuable.

Therefore we asked four professional plasterers to test an arm-support exoskeleton (Skelex 360) in real-life. After instructions, they used the exoskeleton for 45–120 min. After testing, all plasterers indicated that they felt to be supported by the exoskeleton and that they would use this exoskeleton during certain activities (not the entire day). An ergonomist, after observing and interviewing the plasterers, concluded that the exoskeleton (in its current form without modification) could provide support for substantial time periods, mainly when plastering the ceiling, and that the chance for acceptance seems good despite some concerns (e.g. movement limitation in restricted areas, hindrance to carry loads on shoulder).

3   Stage 2: Controlled Experiment

The determination of the load-reducing effect that an exoskeleton may have in specific occupational tasks requires a controlled experiment in which tasks are performed without and with an exoskeleton by professional workers. Variables associated with the load on the back or shoulders should be obtained in both conditions and compared. These parameters may concern the required joint torques (to be generated by the worker), biomechanical estimates of internal compression or shear forces, subjective ratings of perceived load or exertion and the activation of muscles in the low back or shoulder region. When obtaining muscle activity, it is important to consider agonist muscles, which share the function of the exoskeleton (for arm support exoskeletons: lifting the arms), as well as antagonists, which oppose the function of the exoskeleton (for arm support exoskeletons: lowering the arm).

With regard to the job of plastering, we have performed a controlled experiment which has been described in detail by Vries et al. (2021). In short: Eleven plasterers performed their primary tasks of applying gypsum, smoothing and finishing, both on the ceiling and wall, with and without the exoskeleton (Skelex 360) in the national training center for plasterers in the Netherlands. The activity of four agonist muscles for arm elevation and two antagonists were recorded by EMG and plasterers rated their perceived exertion (RPE). RPE's were obtained after each task, EMG was obtained during the total duration of each task (which lasted about 2–6 min).

Figure 1 shows the muscle activity in both conditions for one of the tasks: finishing the ceiling. It shows that the EMG amplitudes of three agonist muscles, Trapezius and

Medial Deltoid, and Biceps Brachii, were lower when using the exoskeleton, while the activity of the antagonists (Triceps Brachii, Pectoralis Major) were not increased. The same statistically significant result was also obtained for the other tasks, while generally the positive effects were larger when working at the ceiling when compared to working on the wall. Additionally, the obtained subjective ratings of perceived exertion were lower when using the exoskeleton in all tasks, except for 'applying gypsum to the wall'. When asked whether they would wear the exoskeleton, during their work, all participants responded positively towards using it for particular tasks, but a high percentage responded negatively towards using the device for (almost) a whole work day. It was shown that especially work on the ceiling, with arms raised above the head, yielded positive results. For more detailed results we refer to the aforementioned paper (Vries et al. 2020 and 2021).

 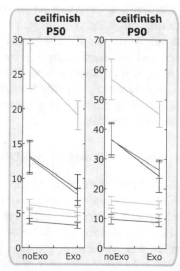

Fig. 1. Muscle activation levels (P50 and P90) expressed as percentage MVC and obtained during the task of finishing of the ceiling in the conditions without (noExo) and with the exoskeleton (Exo).

4   Stage 3: Field-Test

Will the exoskeleton be used in practice? In which tasks? For how long? Will exoskeleton use sustain over a longer period of time? How would the exoskeleton affect productivity? Does it lead to less discomfort and slower fatigue development over the working day? What is the experience of hindrance in real work, in which tasks? These questions can only be determined by doing a study in the practical field. The actual study design largely depends on the research questions to be answered.

For the plasterers we have set-up a field study with 45 participants. We formulated a set of eighteen questions addressing five themes, namely (1) usage, (2) behavior, (3) performance, (4) acceptance, and (5) work load an fatigue.

The design of the study is presented in Fig. 2. In a first meeting we will inform the participants about the study and they will be asked to fill in a questionnaire (Q1) on personal characteristics and their experience with exoskeletons. Participants will then work for a period of 1 week and will fill in a daily questionnaire (Q2) on the tasks they performed, task duration and the perceived exertion during these tasks. After this week they will be asked to fill in Q3, a questionnaire on their expectations regarding the exoskeleton and perceived local discomfort in different body areas during their work. Next, we organize a meeting with all participants where each participant gets his own exoskeleton, the exoskeleton will be introduced and properly adjusted to the participant's anthropometry. Subsequently, participants will use the exoskeleton at their work location for a period of 6 weeks. They can decide themselves for which tasks they use the exoskeleton. During these 6 weeks they will receive a daily questionnaire (Q4) and a weekly questionnaire (Q5). The daily questionnaire consists of questions regarding tasks they performed with the exoskeletons, how long they have been using the exoskeleton, their perceived working behavior due to the exoskeleton and their perceived effort. The weekly questionnaire will address reasons to use/not use the exoskeleton and perceived local discomfort. All questionnaires take about 1–2 min to complete. Participants who do not fill in the questionnaire will be reminded automatically. After the 6 weeks of monitoring we will visit the work location and participants will be asked for their perceptions during these 6 weeks. Any additional thoughts and opinions can be shared. In order to monitor the participation and to clarify any questions, we will also call each of the participants after week 1 and after week 3. At the time of writing this chapter results are not available yet.

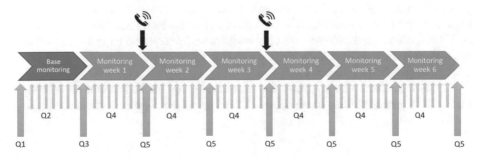

Fig. 2. Field study design

5 Discussion

Determining the effect of an exoskeleton on the back or shoulders in occupational tasks is a multifaceted challenge. It requires precise measurements under controlled conditions, which often cannot be realized in real working environments. Hereto we need to isolate, imitate, and study the tasks in a controlled (laboratory) environment. A preceding field observation to make a job and task analysis, is necessary: it provides us with an indication of usefulness and potential fit (which is useful to have before setting-up a larger experiment). It also enables us to properly imitate the tasks in the laboratory. Whether the effects which will be obtained in the laboratory will sustain in real work needs to be validated in practice. In practice, tasks and activities are not really isolated but make part of a set of primary, secondary, and sometime unexpected, tasks, which might affect the outcome in terms of work load and fatigue reduction. Moreover, other aspects, equally important for exoskeleton adoption, like usability and acceptance can only be measured in real day to day work. These are the main reasons behind the three-stage approach as proposed in this paper.

Our use case of plastering shows promising results obtained in the first two stages. In the first stage we found that an arm support exoskeleton had good potential based on the task and activity profiles, and that all participants (after short testing) would want to use the exoskeleton for certain, but not all of their plastering tasks. Results from the second stage show that activity levels of the main muscle groups involved in plastering are significantly reduced when the exo-skeleton is used, while the activity of antagonist muscles, potentially counteracted by the exoskeleton, was not increased. Ratings of perceived exertion were also significantly decreased. Most plasterers involved in the second stage were also quite convinced that they would use the exoskeletons in practice in certain activities. However, questions in terms of behaviour, use and usability, and productivity remains to be answered in the field study, to conclude on the acceptance of this exo-skeleton in the practice of the plasterer.

After finishing the third stage (field study), one will have a solid ground comprising effectivity, use and usability and acceptance data, on which one can decide to promote, implement and use exoskeletons.

Regarding effectivity, the three-stage evaluation provide evidence on the effects of exoskeleton on work load, local discomfort and fatigue reduction in a specific job. The approach will not provide scientific evidence that low back and shoulder injuries would really drop due to exoskeleton use. This would actually require a large long-term study including hundreds of people distributed across an experimental and control group. Such a study has not been performed yet.

To perform such a large, costly and time-consuming study, it might be wise to go through the proposed three-stage approach first, to get the right idea about such a large study.

References

Eurofound: Sixth European Working Conditions Survey – Overview report (2017). Publications Office of the European Union, Luxembourg. https://doi.org/10.2806/784968
Da Costa, B.R., Viera, E.R.: Risk factors for work-related musculoskeletal injuries. A systematic review of recent longitudinal studies. Am. J. Ind. Med. **53**(4), 285–323 (2010)
Van Rijn, R. M., Huisstede, B. M., Koes, B. W., Burdorf, A.: Associations between work-related factors and specific disorders of the shoulder - a systematic review of the literature. Scandinavian J. Work Environ. Health **36**(3), 189–201 (2010)

de Vries, A., de Looze, M.P.: The effect of arm support exoskeletons in realistic work activities: a review study. J. Ergon. **9**(4), 1–9 (2019)

Kermavnar, T., de Vries, A.W., de Looze, M.P., O'Sullivan, L.: Effects of industrial back-support exoskeletons on body loading and user experience: an updated systematic review. Ergonomics **16**, 1–27 (2021). https://doi.org/10.1080/00140139.2020.1870162

Theurel, J., Desbrosses, K.: Occupational exoskeletons: overview of their benefits and limitations in preventing work-related musculoskeletal disorders. IISE Trans. Occupat. Ergon. HF **7**, 264–280 (2019)

McFarland, T., Fischer, S.: Considerations for industrial use: a systematic review of the impact of active and passive upper limb exoskeletons on physical exposures. IISE Trans. Occupat. Ergon. HF **7**, 322–347 (2019)

de Vries, A., de Looze, M.P., Krause, F.: The effectivity of a passive arm support exoskeleton in reducing muscle activation and perceived exertion during plastering activities. Ergonomics **21**, 1–10 (2021). https://doi.org/10.1080/00140139.2020.1868581

de Vries, A., de Looze, M.P., Krause, F.: The experience of plasterers towards using an arm support exoskeleton. WeRob 2020. Biosystems & Biorobotics (in Press)

Human-Robot Collaboration During Assembly Tasks: The Cognitive Effects of Collaborative Assembly Workstation Features

Federico Fraboni[1](✉) ⓘ, Luca Gualtieri[2] ⓘ, Francesco Millo[1], Matteo De Marchi[2], Luca Pietrantoni[1] ⓘ, and Erwin Rauch[2] ⓘ

[1] Department of Psychology, Università di Bologna, Via Filippo Re 10, 40126 Bologna, Italy
Federico.fraboni3@unibo.it
[2] Industrial Engineering and Automation (IEA), Free University of Bozen-Bolzano, Piazza Università 1, 39100 Bolzano, Italy

Abstract. This experimental study is set out to explore the effects of collaborative robotic system features on Workers' perceived cognitive workload, usability and visual attention. This work's primary objective is to identify strategies for lowering workers' cognitive workload and increase usability when collaborating with robots in assembly tasks, ultimately fostering safety and performance. Perceived cognitive workload significantly decreased, and usability increased with the manipulation of workstation elements as well as the conditions of human interaction. Individual differences across participants suggest that robots should be capable of adjusting their behaviour according to the specific user.

Keyword: Collaborative robotics. Human-Factors and Ergonomics. Visual Attention. Cognitive workload

1 Introduction

Present-day industrial robotics is revolutionising many workplaces worldwide, and humans are increasingly finding themselves working in close relationship with robotic agents in so-called collaborative systems. It has been observed that collaborative robots, also called cobots, could help reduce negative work attributes and enhance positive ones, for instance, improving work conditions and easing work tasks (Welfare et al. 2019; Gualtieri et al. 2020). With modern advancements in human-machine systems, which became more complex and automated, the need to assess the operators' subjective mental workload and attention has become critical (Yagoda 2010).

2 Literature Review

Human-Robot Interaction (HRI) must be adequately designed to reduce risks for the human agent. Safety is a central issue in industrial robotic environments and is deeply influenced by psychological variables such as cognitive workload (Romero et al. 2018).

© The Author(s), under exclusive license to Springer Nature Switzerland AG 2022
N. L. Black et al. (Eds.): IEA 2021, LNNS 223, pp. 242–249, 2022.
https://doi.org/10.1007/978-3-030-74614-8_29

Visual attention can be considered an indicator of cognitive workload, and the two constructs have been considered by some authors as intertwined and ultimately connected to safety outcomes (Bhavsar et al. 2016; Evans and Fendley 2017). Authors showed that human-robot collaboration could increase productivity and make companies more flexible (Tsarouchi et al. 2016). Robots could help reduce negative work attributes and enhance positive ones, for instance, improving work conditions and easing work tasks (Welfare et al. 2019). With modern advancements in human-machine systems, which became more complex and automated, the need to assess the operators' subjective mental workload and attention has become critical (Yagoda 2010). Previous research has pinpointed the importance of addressing human operators' needs. Operators should be able to control and manage the robot according to their preferences to maximise effectiveness (Prewett et al. 2010).

Cognitive workload has been shown to have a significant relationship with safety and performance in human-robot collaboration (Villani et al. 2018). Previous research highlighted that various factors such as robot's low speed could reduce cognitive workload in human-robot interaction (Abd et al. 2017; Fujita et al. 2010). The effects of robots autonomy on human-machine collaboration have been studied extensively, and it has been concluded that it can reduce cognitive workload (Chen et al. 2014; Cummings et al. 2007). Authors found variable time delays in human teleoperation of a robot to increase cognitive workload (Yang and Dorneich 2019). Lohse et al. (2014) found that robot gestures increased user performance and decreased perceived workload in recall tasks.

Previous research has shown that visual attention strongly influences performance and safety in the interaction with automation technology (Kim et al. 2019). Authors investigated the connection between human-robot collaboration and visual-attention. They assessed the analysis of eye gaze patterns as recorded by a head-mounted eye-tracking system, showed that saccadic activation patterns increase and become more chaotic under the robot-assisted mode (Carlson and Demiris 2009). Camilli et al. (2008) showed that distributions of eye fixations are related to different levels of mental workload. Authors showed that the distribution of eye fixations appeared to be sensitive to variations in mental workload, being more dispersed when the workload is high, and more clustered when the workload is low (Camilli et al. 2008).

The present contribution aims at understanding how design features can increase safety and improve operators' experience, specifically examining the effect of different collaborative system features on operators' cognitive workload, visual attention, and perceived usability. Results could contribute to improving the design of human-robot collaborative systems in manufacturing environments. We hypothesised that manipulating system features and the conditions of HRI could affect cognitive workload, participants' visual attention and the workstation's perceived usability. Specifically, we tested the effect of autonomy and speed on users' perceived usability toward the system.

3 Methods

3.1 Procedure

The experiment took place at the Smart Mini Factory - Laboratory for Industry 4.0 of the Free University of Bozen-Bolzano. We adopted an experimental design in which participants were asked to work with a collaborative robot, model Universal Robot UR3, equipped with a Robotiq collaborative gripper. Participants had to sit in front of a workstation and complete a simplified manual task (i.e., a simplified assembly of an industrial pneumatic cylinder from Kuhnke). The workstation was equipped with multiple features: (a) boxes for storing and picking components; (b) assembly jigs to highlight relevant areas and components holders; (c) button array with an emergency button and three buttons for adjusting robot speed; (d) a virtual button for interacting with the robot; (e) an LCD screen for displaying instructions and information about the status of the robot system (i.e., mode and speed). Figure 1 shows a participant sitting at the workstation with the complete set-up. The workstation was also equipped with an AI-based 3D perception device (i.e. Smart Robots) for enabling gesture commands and collision avoidance capabilities.

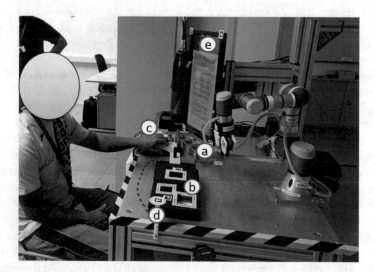

Fig. 1. The experimental setting. *Note:* letters indicate the workstation features.

3.2 Experimental Protocol

We enrolled 14 participants with no previous experience in collaborative robotics and minimal experience in performing manufacturing tasks. Upon arrival, participants were greeted and briefed by an experimenter which administered the informed consent and privacy form. Next, participants were introduced and trained to the assembly task in a replica of the workstation, where an experimenter was handing-over and holding components instead of the collaborative robot. Participants had the opportunity to try the assembly task until they felt confident in completing it without the assistance of the experimenter. After completing the training session, participants were guided in a different room, where the experimental workstation was set up. Participants were then asked to wear eye-tracker glasses and perform the same task in collaboration with the collaborative robot. The cobot mainly handed over and held components for participants. Participants were asked to perform the task sequence in three different Trials. After completing each Trial, participants were guided to the previous room and administered a survey. The time between each Trial was used by experimenters to re-arrange the features of the workstation.

In each Trial, we manipulated certain features of the robot (i.e., speed, acceleration and trajectories), features of the workstation (i.e., assembly gigs), conditions of human interaction with the robot (i.e., type of command and behaviour of the robot) and, information content (i.e., robot status and related speed). Next, the three Trials and related features will be described. We supposed that the results in terms of perceived cognitive workload, visual attention and usability should be better shifting from the first to the last Trial.

Trial 1 provides the lowest degree of interaction between the operator and the robot. Robot autonomy was very low, as the participant had to authorise almost every robot's movement by applying pressure on the gripper. Physical interaction with the manipulator was necessary. The collision-avoidance system was disabled, and the operator was not aware of the possibility of pausing the robot's motion thanks to the gesture control system. The LCD screen was not displaying information about robot status and speed. The robot speed was set to be slightly lower than the nominal value. Only necessary safety measures (i.e., arrest button and force feedback) were illustrated to participants.

In **Trial 2,** robot autonomy was slightly increased as the robot was allowed to switch between some tasks without needing input from participants. The LCD screen displayed information about the robot's status. The operator was informed about the possibility to stop the robot using gesture controls and was showed the functioning of the collision avoidance system. A different way of interacting with the robot was established through the activation of a virtual button. In this Trial, the participant does not physically and directly interact with the robot. Instead, she/he must use the virtual button in order to confirm the completion of a sub-task. Workstation layout was modified for increased clarity and safety (foam-protectors and highlighting rings/covers were added). The robot speed was set to be slightly higher than the nominal value.

In **Trial 3,** in addition to features in the previous Trial, the participant was allowed to set the robot's speed (i.e., nominal, slower, faster) by using the button array and choosing how to interact with the robot (physical pressure or virtual button). The robot speed was signalled on the LCD screen. The robot's movement patterns were reprogrammed to be more human-like using Minimum Jerk Trajectories (MJTs). Authors argued that this kind of motion patterns are more predictable and familiar compared to traditional trajectories (Rojas et al. 2019).

3.3 Measures

Visual Attention. Participants were asked to wear the Pupil Core eye-tracker glasses from Pupil Labs during each Trial. Recordings allowed to measure visual attention and gather an objective measure of cognitive workload by assessing the number, location and duration of fixations. Eye-tracker video recordings were also particularly useful to assess modifications in participants behaviour according to changes in interaction patterns and workstation features. Figure 2 shows a screenshot from the recordings. The yellow-circled green dot represents the gaze of the participant. The numbers next to it represent the observed fixation number.

Fig. 2. Point of view of a participant retrieving a component from the robot.

Cognitive Workload. Participants were asked to rate on a 5-point Likert-type scale (1 = very low to 5 = very high) a single item (i.e. "How mentally demanding was the task?") taken from the NASA-Task Load Index (NASA-TLX; Hart 2006).

Usability. Perceived usability has been measured using five items taken from the System Usability Scale (Lewis and Sauro 2017). Items were slightly re-adapted to address robotic systems. All items were rated on a 5-point Likert scale (1 = strongly disagree to 5 = strongly agree). Participants were asked to express their level of agreement with the following statements: (1) "I think I would like to use the robot frequently"; (2) "I found the robot's behaviour to be mostly predictable"; (3) "I found the various functions in the robot were well-integrated"; (4) "I found the robot to work appropriately."; (5) "I found that the robot could be operated and managed intuitively".

4   Results

To assess differences in participants' perceived cognitive workload and usability scores in each Trial, we carried out a repeated measure ANOVA using SPSS v23. The perceived cognitive workload was significantly affected by each Trial's different features, $F(2,26) = 5.02, p = .01$. Bonferroni post-hoc tests indicated that the mean score on perceived cognitive workload in Trial 3 was significantly lower than in Trial 2 ($p = .01$). Fig. 3 displays the estimated marginal means of perceived cognitive workload in the three Trials.

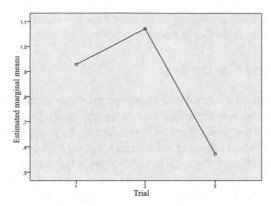

Fig. 3. Cognitive workload estimated marginal means in each Trial.

The perceived usability was also significantly affected by each Trial's different features, $F(2,26) = 4.24$, $p = .03$. Bonferroni post-hoc tests indicated that the mean usability score in Trial 3 was significantly higher than in Trial 1 ($p < .05$). Fig. 4 displays the estimated marginal means of perceived usability of the system in the three Trials.

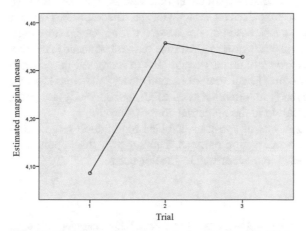

Fig. 4. Usability estimated marginal means in each Trial.

Preliminary analysis of eye-tracker video data highlighted visual attention patterns and scanning behaviour. Specifically, participants gazed significantly less to robot joints and gripper in the third Trial. In this case, participants also gazed more frequently to the components they needed to assemble to accomplish the sub-task. The number of fixations and fixations' duration was significantly higher when using physical pressure to command the robot instead of using the gesture-controlled virtual button.

When assessing eye-tracker video data, it was possible to note that, in Trial 2, participants often tried to reach out for the component before the robot completed its movement (only when the robot was programmed to lay the components directly on the workstation vs handling them to the participant). This behaviour activated the collision avoidance safety system resulting in delays in task completion.

5   Discussion and Conclusion

The present contribution illustrates an experimental study aiming to assess perceived workload, usability and visual attention by manipulating the workstation features and interaction patterns throughout three different Trials. In particular, results confirmed that introducing MJTs and allowing the human operator to set the pace of the robot as well choosing the preferred mode of interaction with the robot(i.e. physical pressure vs a virtual button) contributed to significantly lower levels of perceived workload and higher usability. Rojas et al. (2019) argued that the introduction of human-like MJTs in the robot movement patterns contributes to an increased sense of predictability and familiarity in participants. Higher predictability in Trial 3 is also reflected by results on perceived usability. This could imply that the human would use less cognitive resources to interact with the robot, thus lowering cognitive workload levels. Our results support this argument. Furthermore, the freedom of choosing the speed of the robot and the interaction channel were relevant features to achieve lower cognitive workload and higher perceive usability. This could find a possible explanation in the self-determination theory (Deci and Ryan 2000) which states that intrinsic motivation thrives mainly o three intertwined psychological needs. Among the three needs, there is autonomy, which comprises performing a task based on one's own volition. Our results suggest that allowing the operator to adjust the system's features (e.g. robot speed) and choosing interaction channels (e.g. type of command) could lead to increased perceived usability through increased motivation. The self-determination theory in HRIhas been recently used in the educational context (van Minkelen et al. 2020), and our study suggests that it could have favourable implication in the industrial context as well.

Qualitative analysis of eye-tracker video highlighted large individual differences across participants interaction patterns. This suggests that robots should be capable of adjusting their behaviour according to specific users.

References

Welfare, K. S., Hallowell, M. R., Shah, J. A., Riek, L.D.: Consider the human work experience when integrating robotics in the workplace. In *2019 14th ACM/IEEE International Conference on Human-Robot Interaction (HRI)* (pp. 75–84). IEEE, March 2019

Gualtieri, L., Palomba, I., Merati, F.A., Rauch, E., Vidoni, R.: Design of human-centered collaborative assembly workstations for the improvement of operators' physical ergonomics and production efficiency: a case study. Sustainability **12**(9), 3606 (2020)

Camilli, M., Nacchia, R., Terenzi, M., Di Nocera, F.: ASTEF: simple tool for examining fixations. Behav. Res. Meth. **40**(2), 373–382 (2008)

Abd, M., Gonzalez, I., Nojoumian, M., Engeberg, E.: Impacts of robot assistant performance on human trust, satisfaction, and frustration. RSS: Morality and Social Trust in Autonomous Robots (2017)

Bhavsar, P., Srinivasan, B., Srinivasan, R.: Pupillometry based real-time monitoring of operator's cognitive workload to prevent human error during abnormal situations. Ind. Eng. Chem. Res. **55**(12), 3372–3382 (2016)

Carlson, T., Demiris, Y.: Using visual attention to evaluate collaborative control architectures for human robot interaction. In: Proceedings of New Frontiers in Human-Robot Interaction: A symposium at the AISB 2009 Convention No. CONF, pp. 38–43. SSAISB (2009)

Chen, T., Campbell, D., Gonzalez, F., Coppin, G.: The effect of autonomy transparency in human-robot interactions: a preliminary study on operator cognitive workload and situation awareness in multiple heterogeneous UAV management. In: Proceedings of Australasian Conference on Robotics and Automation, pp. 1–10, December 2014

Cummings, M. L., Bruni, S., Mercier, S., Mitchell, P. J.: Automation architecture for single operator, multiple UAV command and control. Massachusetts Inst of Tech Cambridge (2007)

Evans, D.C., Fendley, M.: A multi-measure approach for connecting cognitive workload and automation. Int. J. Hum.-Comput. Stud. 97, 182–189 (2017)

Fujita, M., Kato, R., Tamio, A.: Assessment of operators' mental strain induced by hand-over motion of industrial robot manipulator. In: 19th International Symposium in Robot and Human Interactive Communication, pp. 361–366. IEEE (2010)

Yang, E., Dorneich, M.C.: The emotional, cognitive, physiological, and performance effects of variable time delay in robotic teleoperation. Int. J. Soc. Robot. 9(4), 491–508 (2017)

Lohse, M., Rothuis, R., Gallego-Pérez, J., Karreman, D.E., Evers, V.: Robot gestures make difficult tasks easier: the impact of gestures on perceived workload and task performance. In: Proceedings of the SIGCHI Conference on Human Factors in Computing Systems, pp. 1459–1466, April 2014

Prewett, M.S., Johnson, R.C., Saboe, K.N., Elliott, L.R., Coovert, M.D.: Managing workload in human–robot interaction: a review of empirical studies. Comput. Hum. Behav. 26(5), 840–856 (2010)

Romero, D., Mattsson, S., Fast-Berglund, Å., Wuest, T., Gorecky, D., Stahre, J.: Digitalising occupational health, safety and productivity for the operator 4.0. In: IFIP International Conference on Advances in Production Management Systems, pp. 473–481. Springer, Cham, August 2018

Tsarouchi, P., Makris, S., Chryssolouris, G.: Human–robot interaction review and challenges on task planning and programming. Int. J. Comput. Integrat. Manuf. 29(8), 916–931 (2016)

Lewis, J.J.R., Sauro, J.: Revisiting the factor structure of the system usability scale. J. Usabil. Stud. 12(4) (2017)

Villani, V., Pini, F., Leali, F., Secchi, C.: Survey on human–robot collaboration in industrial settings: safety, intuitive interfaces and applications. Mechatronics 55, 248–266 (2018)

Hart, S.G.: NASA-task load index (NASA-TLX); 20 years later. In: Proceedings of the Human Factors and Ergonomics Society Annual Meeting, vol. 50, no. 9, pp. 904–908. Sage publications, Los Angeles, October 2006

Yagoda, R.E.: Development of the human-robot interaction workload measurement tool (HRI-WM). In: Proceedings of the Human Factors and Ergonomics Society Annual Meeting, vol. 54, no. 4, pp. 304–308. SAGE Publications, Los Angeles, September 2010

Kim, H., Gabbard, J.L., Martin, S., Tawari, A., Misu, T.: Toward prediction of driver awareness of automotive hazards: driving-video-based simulation approach. In: Proceedings of the Human Factors and Ergonomics Society Annual Meeting, vol. 63, no. 1, pp. 2099–2103. SAGE Publications, Los Angeles, November 2019

Rojas, R.A., Garcia, M.A.R., Wehrle, E., Vidoni, R.: A variational approach to minimum-jerk trajectories for psychological safety in collaborative assembly stations. IEEE Robot. Autom. Lett. 4(2), 823–829 (2019)

Deci, E.L., Ryan, R.M.: The" what" and" why" of goal pursuits: Human needs and the self-determination of behavior. Psychol. Inqu. 11(4), 227–268 (2000)

van Minkelen, P., Gruson, C., van Hees, P., Willems, M., de Wit, J., Aarts, R., Vogt, P.: Using self-determination theory in social robots to increase motivation in L2 word learning. In: Proceedings of the 2020 ACM/IEEE International Conference on Human-Robot Interaction, pp. 369–377, March 2020

Evaluation of Physiological Costs Using Standardized Analysis Methods During Simulated Overhead Work with and Without Exoskeleton

Sandra Groos[(⊠)] [iD], Nils Darwin Abele [iD], Petra Fischer, Michael Hefferle [iD], and Karsten Kluth [iD]

Ergonomics Division, University of Siegen, Paul-Bonatz-Street 9-11, 57068 Siegen, Germany
groos@ergonomie.uni-siegen.de

Abstract. In spite of Industry 4.0 and the resulting increased automation of work processes, assembly activities in constrained postures, e.g. overhead work that cannot be performed by robots are still necessary. Here, the passive upper body exoskeleton Airframe® made by Levitate is intended to provide support for overhead work. Thus, it reduces the risk of musculoskeletal disorders of the shoulders, neck and upper back. The aim of this paper is to evaluate the physiological advantages and disadvantages of an exoskeleton during simulated overhead work under laboratory conditions. Twenty subjects, aged between 18 and 64 years, participated in the laboratory study. To determine the physiological costs under variable test conditions, the muscular activity of the muscles trapezius pars descendens, deltoideus pars clavicularis, deltoideus pars acromialis and latissimus dorsi (bilateral in each case) were continuously recorded by surface electromyography. In standardized test sequences, the test persons were asked to perform three partial tests with and without the exoskeleton. This procedure included plugging and screwing activities (by hand and using an electric screwdriver). After each run-through, the current physical condition was assessed using a simple body chart. In addition, a short survey on subjective perception was conducted after each partial test. The results show that the use of the exoskeleton Airframe® particularly favors a reduced muscular activity of the shoulder and neck muscles. The test person's subjective stress sensation also showed that the use of the exoskeleton had a positive effect on most activities, especially in the shoulder and neck area.

Keywords: Overhead-work · Exoskeleton · Electromyography · Muscular strain · Subjective perception

1 Introduction

In industrial manufacturing processes, robots can take on tasks that require great strength. However, the use of robots quickly reaches its limits in activities that require human skills, such as sensory perception, cognition, flexibility and learning ability. Unsuitable working environments, for example due to constructional conditions, can also complicate

N. L. Black et al. (Eds.): IEA 2021, LNNS 223, pp. 250–257, 2022.
https://doi.org/10.1007/978-3-030-74614-8_30

or even prevent their use. People still have to carry out activities that may involve forced postures and then have to be performed in physiologically unfavorable postures. This also includes overhead work, which often causes musculoskeletal disorders, especially in the shoulder and neck area [1]. Ergonomic workplace design is therefore imperative in order to preserve the employee's health and thus also their ability to work in the long term.

One support option for work-related overhead activities is the use of exoskeletons [2]. For overhead activities, upper torso exoskeletons are particularly suitable, which are intended to support the upper extremities and the back in favor of a load reduction of the shoulders and the back muscles in unfavorable postures. Due to the relatively young technology, there is still no experience in the long-term use of exoskeletons. Only short-term scientific studies can provide initial indications of both the benefits and the possible risks. Also because of the high product variance within the exoskeletons, only very few studies are available for selected models. The upper torso exoskeleton Airframe® from the manufacturer Levitate has been considered in a few studies so far [3–8]. Despite the paucity of scientifically based knowledge about the effects of exoskeletons in daily use, they are already frequently used in industry - especially in the automotive industry. For example, the Airframe® is already part of the mandatory safety equipment at Toyota's Woodstock plant (Canada), among others [9]. In order to further expand basic knowledge about the benefits and risks of industrial exoskeletons, the upper torso exoskeleton should be evaluated through a standardized laboratory study.

2 Methodology

2.1 Test Subjects

For a basic population of industrial workers, the subject collective should be selected as heterogeneously as possible. The height of the test subjects had to be between 160 cm and 190 cm, since the adjustment range of the exoskeleton is limited to these heights. Furthermore, the test subjects were not allowed to have any limitations or previous illnesses in the neck and shoulder area. The laboratory study was conducted with a subject collective of 20 adult volunteers in good health (Ø 3.3 ± 2.3 h sports per week) who had no experience using Levitate's Airframe® upper torso exoskeleton. The 9 men and 11 women who participated in the study were on average 31.9 ± 13.4 years old, 178 ± 7 cm tall and had a body mass of 79.6 ± 16.6 kg.

2.2 Test Performance

In the course of the experiment, the subjects completed simulated assembly tasks according to the test sequence shown in Fig. 1, which included a screwing activity by hand and with a cordless screwdriver as well as a plugging activity with Lego® building blocks, both with and without the exoskeleton. The experiments were supplemented by a drawing exercise in order to gain knowledge about the precision of the activity execution. However, this partial test is not considered further in the results section.

In order to prevent habit effects, the sub-tests were randomized among each other as well as the activities within the tests. Furthermore, the subjects were instructed to place the screws and Lego® bricks in a predefined time window according to an acoustically generated clock pulse. After each run, the current physical condition and the subjective perception, as described in 2.4, were queried during a recovery break.

A detailed description of the test procedure can be found in [10].

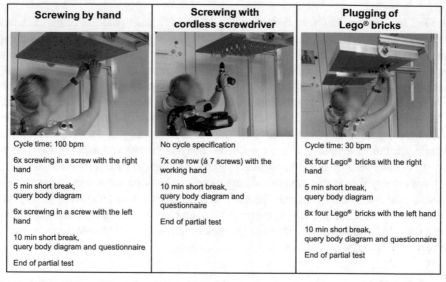

Screwing by hand	Screwing with cordless screwdriver	Plugging of Lego® bricks
Cycle time: 100 bpm	No cycle specification	Cycle time: 30 bpm
6x screwing in a screw with the right hand	7x one row (á 7 screws) with the working hand	8x four Lego® bricks with the right hand
5 min short break, query body diagram	10 min short break, query body diagram and questionnaire	5 min short break, query body diagram
6x screwing in a screw with the left hand	End of partial test	8x four Lego® bricks with the left hand
10 min short break, query body diagram and questionnaire		10 min short break, query body diagram and questionnaire
End of partial test		End of partial test

Fig. 1. Presentation of the three sub-tests (screwing by hand and with cordless screwdriver as well as plugging of Lego® bricks) with detailed description of the time allocation within a sub-test.

2.3 Electromyographic Measurements

The electromyographic activity (EA) of the trapezius muscle in the neck (m. trapezius p. descendens), the deltoid muscle in the shoulder (m. deltoideus p. clavicularis and m. deltoideus p. acromialis) and the large muscle of the back (m. latissimus dorsi) (both sides) was continuously recorded via bipolar electrodes on both halves of the body. The selection of the muscles to be recorded was made in the course of extensive pretesting, which is described in detail under [10]. Amplitude values of the myoelectric activity cannot be directly interpreted as strain data [11–13]. Therefore, reference values of the maximum exertions deliverable by a muscle were obtained by recording the EA during maximum voluntary contractions (MVCs). The MVCs in connection with the resting activity EA_0 allowed calculating standardized (normalized) electromyographic activities ($sEA = [(EA-EA_0)/(EA_{max}-EA_0)] * 100\%$) representing muscle strain in all working phases.

2.4 Subjective Methods

Before the start of the tests, the questionnaires and special aspects of the test's performance were explained first. This guaranteed a rapid answering of all questions during the individual test.

Subjective data collection consisted of standardized interviewing and observation. Observations of abnormalities during the trials were recorded directly. The standardized interview consisted of three parts, which is described in detail in [10]. This includes the assessment of the physical condition in individual body areas at different time points, the assessment of specific aspects of the individual sub-tests, and the assessment of the exoskeleton.

A simple body diagram, which divided the body into different areas, was used in combination with a rating scale to record the physical condition in individual body areas at different time points. The combination of two ordinal scales made it possible to distinguish level of impairment (0 'none' to 4 'very strong') and form of impairment (tension, numbness, pressure point). The assessment of individual sub-tests' specific aspects was mainly carried out by means of closed questions using an ordinal scale from -4 to $+4$ (for example 'very difficult' to 'very easy'). At the end of the tests, the test subjects were asked, among other things, about their assessment of the exoskeleton and how they used it. The questions were a mixture of open and closed questions. The familiar response scheme remained in place.

3 Results

3.1 Standardized Electromyographic Activity

The recorded muscular activity of the m. trapezius p. descendens, m. deltoideus p. clavicularis, m. deltoideus p. acromialis and m. latissimus dorsi muscles showed comparable values on both halves of the body. With the exception of the m. latissimus dorsi, a significant difference at a 0.1% error probability between the performance of the activity with and without the exoskeleton can be seen for the other muscle sites during the partial tests (cf. Tables 1 and 2). Overall, sEA was reduced by approximately four to six percent by the exoskeleton. The right-sided m. latissimus dorsi, on the other hand, as an antagonist of the three aforementioned muscles, showed no significant changes when working with and without the exoskeleton. For the left-sided m. latissimus dorsi, the differences were significant when screwing by hand (right and left hand), screwing with cordless screwdriver and plugging activity with the left hand. However, this muscle site had slightly lower values of one to two percent when working with the exoskeleton.

Table 1. Means (M), standard deviations (SD) and significances ($\alpha = 0.01$) of the standardized electromyography activity (sEA) in percent of the muscles recorded on the right side of the body and across all Ss (n = 20) for the sub tests screwing by hand and screwing with cordless screwdriver (working hand only) with the test variables with (A) and without (B) exoskeleton.

		Screwing by hand (right hand)		Screwing by hand (left hand)		Screwing with cordless screwdriver	
		A	B	A	B	A	B
m. trapezius	M	17.7	12.4	16.3	10.7	19.7	15.3
	SD	± 1.5	± 0.6	± 1.3	± 0.6	± 1.6	± 1.0
	α (0.01)	significant (*)		significant (*)		significant (*)	
m. delt. p. clav.	M	23.2	18.3	16.4	12.3	23.1	17.4
	SD	± 1.8	± 1.3	± 0.9	± 0.8	± 2.8	± 2.5
	α (0.01)	significant (*)		significant (*)		significant (*)	
m. delt. p. acro.	M	14.6	9.9	10.2	6.3	12.4	7.5
	SD	± 1.5	± 0.8	± 1.0	± 0.5	± 1.4	± 0.9
	α (0.01)	significant (*)		significant (*)		significant (*)	
m. latis- simus dorsi	M	7.1	6.8	4.6	4.9	6.6	6.4
	SD	± 1.2	± 1.3	± 0.7	± 0.6	± 2.1	± 1.4
	α (0.01)	not significant (-)		not significant (-)		not significant (-)	

Table 2. Means (M), standard deviations (SD) and significances ($\alpha = 0.01$) of the standardized electromyography activity (sEA) in percent of the muscles recorded on the right side of the body and across all Ss (n = 20) for the subtest plugging activity with the test variables with (A) and without (B) exoskeleton.

		Plugging activity (right hand)		Plugging activity (left hand)	
		A	B	A	B
m. trapezius	M	16.6	11.4	12.9	8.5
	SD	± 4.0	± 2.1	± 2.9	± 1.9
	α (0.01)	significant (*)		significant (*)	
m. delt. p. clav.	M	17.3	11.3	10.6	6.7
	SD	± 4.5	± 2.4	± 3.5	± 2.2
	α (0.01)	significant (*)		significant (*)	
m. delt. p. acro.	M	10.1	6.5	6.1	3.8
	SD	± 3.2	± 1.5	± 1.9	± 1.0
	α (0.01)	significant (*)		significant (*)	
m. latis- simus dorsi	M	4.9	5.2	5.1	5.2
	SD	± 1.4	± 1.1	± 0.9	± 0.9
	α (0.01)	not significant (-)		not significant (-)	

3.2 Subjective Assessments

The evaluation of the subjective data on the physiological condition shows that the test subjects experienced increased stress during the tests. The use of the exoskeleton had generally a stress-reducing effect on the shoulders, upper arms and lower back, with the exception of the sub-test 'plugging activity' with the right hand. For the upper back, tension was reported before the start of the test, but no longer afterwards. For the forearms, the test subjects in the sub-test 'screwing by hand' with exoskeleton indicated higher tensions in each case for the dynamically loaded half of the body. In the other sub-tests, the strains in the forearms and in the hands and fingers were reduced. The results for the complaints in the neck show in the data for the sub-tests'screwing with cordless screwdriver' and 'plugging activity' a higher strain when using the exoskeleton, whereas in the sub-test 'screwing by hand' no complaints are indicated when using the exoskeleton.

The assessment of working posture and muscular strain was consistently more positive after the subjects had performed the tests with the exoskeleton. The use of the exoskeleton had an effect in the working speed in that, for example, in the sub-test 'plugging activity', the speed without the exoskeleton was assessed by more subjects as 'too slow' compared to the performance with the exoskeleton. The situation was similar in the other tests. Overall, freedom of movement was rated neutrally. At the end of the tests, the exoskeleton was described as comfortable to wear, lightweight and good for working posture, and the possibilities for use in industry were rated highly. The confirmation of a majority of the test subjects to use the exoskeleton also in eight-hour shifts, depending on the task, confirmed the positive evaluation.

4 Discussion

The percentage relief of the shoulder-neck musculature examined varied depending on the activity to be performed. The trapezius muscle experienced the highest measured relief during the manual screwing activities. The questionnaires on the physical condition also showed an improvement in the complaints in the shoulder-neck area. In the comparison of the sEA for the left trapezius, the strain was highest during the screwing by left hand followed by the plugging by left hand. The evaluation of the sEA for the trapezius on the right shows the same tendencies. However, here the strain is highest during the screwing activity with the cordless screwdriver. During the plugging activities, the anterior deltoid muscles were unloaded the most in percentage terms. In this task, the clavicular part of the deltoid muscle was additionally challenged by pressing on the Lego® bricks. On the other hand, the evaluation of the sEA shows that the muscular strain during the screwing activities, both with and without exoskeleton, was significantly higher for the half of the body mainly performing the activity. The highest percentage reduction in the strain on the middle deltoid muscle occurred during the screwing activity with the cordless screwdriver. In comparison of the sEA, the results are very close to each other. The strain reduction during the screwing activity by hand is greatest for the m. deltoideus p. acromialis of the working side. The physical condition survey's results show that the subjects perceived a reduction in strain on the upper arms during the plugging tests. The perceived tension in the non-performing upper arm during the activities increased with the use of the exoskeleton. From the observations, it can be concluded that, on the one hand, the individual muscles are relieved to different degrees depending on their involvement in a task and, on the other hand, that the perceived strain does not converge with the measured strain.

In conclusion, the use of the exoskeleton during overhead work causes a significant reduction in muscular activity of the relevant shoulder and neck muscles. As shown by the investigations of [14], static forces in the range of more than 15% of the maximum force can already lead to local muscle fatigue and thus to a limitation of the possible exercise duration. By using the exoskeleton, values that were significantly above 15% could be reduced to values at or below 15%.

The originally suspected greater strain on the latissimus dorsi muscle when using the exoskeleton, especially when lowering the arms caudally against the support force of the exoskeleton, could not be proven. Thus, the use of the exoskeleton has no negative effects, at least with regard to the aforementioned muscle.

5   Limitations of the Study

On the basis of the present results, the exoskeleton examined can certainly be said to have a supportive and thus relieving effect, even though this was an initial investigation that also revealed some weak points.

The greatest challenge was the correct application of the OEMG electrodes, especially with regard to the m. trapezius p. descendens due to the position of the shoulder straps of the exoskeleton over the muscle. However, unfavorable physiological conditions of the test subjects, for example small and particularly slender persons, also made electromyographic measurements difficult when using the exoskeleton. Despite all efforts to standardize the tests with regard to body and hand posture as well as working speed, deviations were found between the test subjects but also during the measurements with one test subject for different test variables. Nevertheless, the present study is an initial guide to evaluate the benefits and possible limitations of industrial exoskeletons or upper torso exoskeletons, which are intended to relieve the strain on working people during overhead work.

Since the tests were conducted with a now technically outdated version of Levitate's Airframe®, it makes sense to repeat the tests with the most current model and a larger subject population. Likewise, a working length's variation and the use of other models of industrial upper torso exoskeletons to support the shoulder and neck muscles during overhead work would appear to be suitable for strengthening the validity of the findings obtained.

References

1. Frost, P., Bonde, J.P.E., Mikkelsen, S., Andersen, J.H., Fallentin, N., Kaergaard, A., Thomsen, J.F.: Risk of shoulder tendinitis in relation to shoulder loads in monotonous repetitive work. Am. J. Ind. Med. **41**(1), 11–18 (2002)
2. De Looze, M.P., Bosch, T., Krause, F., Stadler, K.S., O'Sullivan, L.W.: Exoskeletons for industrial application and their potential effects on physical work load. Ergonomics **59**(5), 671–681 (2016)

3. Butler, T., Gillette, J.C.: Exoskeletons: Used as PPE for injury prevention. Profess. Saf. **3**, 33–37 (2019)
4. Gillette, J.C., Stephenson, M.L.: EMG analysis of an upper body exoskeleton during automotive assembly. In: Conference Proceedings of the 42nd Annual Meeting of the American Society of Biomechanics. Rochester, MN (2018)
5. Kim, S., Nussbaum, M.A., Esfahani, M.I.M., Alemi, M.M., Alabdulkarim, S., Rashedi, E.: Assessing the influence of a passive, upper extremity exoskeletal vest for tasks requiring arm elevation: Part I-"Expected" effects on discomfort, shoulder muscle activity, and work task performance. Appl. Ergon. **70**, 315–322 (2018)
6. Kim, S., Nussbaum, M.A., Esfahani, M.I.M, Alemi, M.M., Jia, B., Rashedi, E.: Assessing the influence of a passice, upper extremity exoskeletal vest for tasks requiring arm elevation. Part II-"Unexpected" effects on shoulder motion, balance, and spine loading. Appl. Ergon. **70**, 323–330 (2018)
7. Liu, S., Hemming, D., Luo, R.B., Reynolds, J., Delong, J.C., Sandler, B.J., Jacobsen, G.R., Horgan, S.: Solving the surgeon ergonomic crisis with surgical exosuit. Surg. Endosc. **32**(1), 236–244 (2018)
8. Spada, S., Ghibaudo, L., Gilotta, S., Gastaldi, L., Cavatorta, M.P.: Investigation into the applicability of a passive upper-limb exoskeleton in automotive industry. Procedia Manuf. **11**, 1255–1262 (2017)
9. Marinov, B.: Toyota's Woodstock Plant Makes the Levitate AIRFRAME Exoskeleton Mandatory Personal Protective Equipment. Exoskeleton Report (2018). https://exoskeletonr eport.com/2019/02/toyotas-woodstock-plant-makes-the-levitate-airframe-exoskeleton-man datory-personal-protective-equipment/. Accessed 02 Mar 2021
10. Groos, S., Abele, N.D., Kruse, K., Fischer, P., Hefferle, M., Kluth, K.: Development of a multifunctional test station and a reproducible test design for the evaluation of stress and strain during overhead work with and without upper body exoskeletons. In: Proceedings of the 21st Triennial Congress of the International Ergonomics Association, Vancouver, Canada (2021)
11. Böhlemann, J., Kluth, K., Kotzbauer, K., Strasser, H.: Ergonomic assessment of handle design by means of electromyography and subjective rating. Appl. Ergon. **25**(6), 346–354 (1994)
12. Kluth, K., Böhlemann, J., Strasser, H.: A system for a strain oriented analysis of the layout of assembly workplaces. Ergonomics **37**(9), 1441–1448 (1994)
13. Kluth, K., Pauly, O., Keller, K. Strasser, H.: Assessment of the ergonomic quality of fire nozzles. In: Strasser, H. (ed.) Ergonomic quality of hand-held tools and computer input devices, pp. 239–254 (2007)
14. Rohmert, W.: Statische Haltearbeit des Menschen. Beuth Verlag, Berlin (1960)

Development of a Multifunctional Test Station and a Reproducible Test Design for the Evaluation of Stress and Strain During Overhead Work with and Without Upper Body Exoskeletons

Sandra Groos$^{(\boxtimes)}$ (iD), Nils Darwin Abele (iD), Kevin Kruse, Petra Fischer,
Michael Hefferle (iD), and Karsten Kluth (iD)

Ergonomics Division, University of Siegen, Paul-Bonatz-Street 9-11, 57068 Siegen, Germany
groos@ergonomie.uni-siegen.de

Abstract. There is a variety of upper body exoskeletons, which are featured by different characteristics. Their benefits, but also their limitations and possible dangers should be fundamentally scientifically investigated. For this, test conditions that are as close to reality as possible, but also reproducible and standardized are essential. A test station for objectification of stress and strain during overhead work was designed and built. The requirement was that the test station could be variably adapted to the height of the human body. Moreover, it allows the simulation of different activity scenarios. In addition to the test station, an experimental design was also developed consisting of two screwing tasks and one plugging task. Each partial test had a total duration of 5 to 10 min, whereby the working speed was partly determined by a certain beat. The developed test design was subsequently validated with an exoskeleton (Airframe® by Levitate) and some test persons. For this purpose, the necessary measurement technology for recording heart rate, muscular strain and energy expenditure was applied and tested. Furthermore, a standardized questionnaire was developed and tested.

Keywords: Overhead-work · Test station · Exoskeleton · Electromyography · Muscular strain · Hand-arm-shoulder system · Subjective assessment

1 Introduction

In industrial manufacturing processes, robots can take on tasks that require great forces. In addition to working environments that are unsuitable for robots – for example, due to constructional conditions – according to [1], the work task may also require human abilities that cannot yet be reproduced by robots. This situation means that humans still have to perform activities that may be carried out in forced postures and then in physiological unfavorable postures. Depending on the frequency, duration and intensity of the forced posture, such as overhead work, health consequences are foreseeable, which are often expressed by work-related musculoskeletal disorders (WMSD) [2]. Therefore,

N. L. Black et al. (Eds.): IEA 2021, LNNS 223, pp. 258–265, 2022.
https://doi.org/10.1007/978-3-030-74614-8_31

ergonomic workplace design is imperative in order to maintain the health of the employee and thus also their ability to work in the long term.

One support option is the use of industrial exoskeletons. Upper torso exoskeletons are particularly suitable for overhead activities. They are designed to support the upper extremities and the back in order to reduce the load on the shoulders, neck and back muscles in awkward postures.

2 Problem Statement and Research Question

There are already some commercially marketed exoskeletons designed to provide support – particularly to the shoulders, neck and back. However, this relatively new technology also means that the products are still changing very rapidly in technical terms. There is so far little scientific knowledge about the benefits, but also the possible dangers, of short- or long-term use.

In recent years, there has been increasing research in the field of industrial exoskeletons and, in particular, upper-body exoskeletons [cf. 1, 3–9]. However, the different experimental designs do not allow a comparison of the exoskeletons with each other. Furthermore, technical innovations of the exoskeletons, which may completely change the physiological and subjective experienced effects, are not explicitly considered in follow-up studies. This can lead to different scientific findings about an exoskeleton, which, however, can be justified in the product version.

The objective was to develop, build and validate a test station that allows reproducible results to be obtained for overhead work with and without an exoskeleton. The test station should be adapted to the anthropometric conditions of the test subjects (Ss). Furthermore, interchangeable work surfaces should allow different test designs and ensure continuous work without interruptions. Although the test station to be developed should be multifunctional, i.e. it should be usable for different tests to record physical stress and strain when working in variable postures and positions. A reproducible methodology for the simulation of realistic overhead work should be developed as well.

3 Multifunctional Test Station

For the development and construction of a multifunctional test station a list of requirements was first drawn up, which was continuously updated in the further course. On this basis, solution concepts were developed in an iterative process, which resulted in the final test station (see Fig. 1, left). Using aluminum profiles and some self-manufactured components, the test station was constructed as shown in Fig. 1 (right). Details on the construction of the test station can be found in [10].

Another key requirement of the test station was that it should be able to simulate typical industrial assembly activities. Screwing and clamping represents one of the main activities of overhead work. The screwing should be simulated by hand, but also with a cordless screwdriver, which represents an additional load due to its own weight. A total of 49 nuts with an M8 internal thread were hammered into a work plate in a 7×7 pattern, into which ling nuts M8 $\times$ 24 should be screwed in. The clips, clamps, plugs, etc., which are frequently used in the industrial sector, cannot usually be dismantled easily and, above all, without causing damage. Therefore, Lego® bricks were used to simulate such activities. For this purpose, a Lego® base plate was glued to another plate, onto which square and rectangular building blocks as well as cones and half-cones were to be mounted according to a specified pattern.

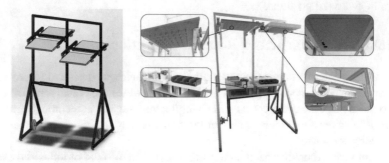

Fig. 1. 3D-CAD drawing of the designed test station (left) and completed test station (right) with enlarged threaded plate, base plate for plug-in test, angle adjustment and tray.

4 Development Reproducible Test Design

4.1 Test Performance

Figure 2 shows the typical test sequence. In the preparation phase, the body dimensions of the hand-arm system of the subjects as well as their gripping heights must be recorded. Based on these measurements, the test stand is set up and the working position is marked on the floor. This is followed by the application of the electrodes and measuring equipment (here: TELEmyo 2500T G2 from Noraxon) for the surface electromyographic (EMG) measurement and a causality test of the incoming signals. A mobile heart rate monitor (here: Polar V 800 with chest grill and transmitter unit H7) and/or an energy expenditure measurement system (here: MetaMax 3B from Cortex) can also be applied to record further stress and strain parameters.

It is essential to ensure that the large number of technical measurement applications on the body in conjunction with the geometry of the exoskeleton do not interfere with each other or even influence the measured values. In the present case, a reliable measurement of the muscular stress in the shoulder/neck area could not be guaranteed for all test subjects when the energy expenditure measurement system was used at the same time. The MetaMax 3B worn on the shoulder caused data artifacts during EMG measurement, especially while wearing the exoskeleton. For this reason, only muscular activity and heart rate were initially recorded in the subsequent follow-up study [11]. After the preparatory phase, a resting measurement was performed before the start of the actual tests. The individual sub-tests which are described in detail below, were followed by the maximum force measurement of the recorded muscles. In the follow-up phase, the subjects were finally asked about their subjective perceptions.

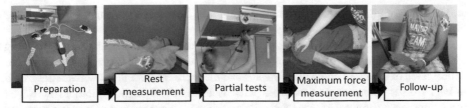

Preparation → Rest measurement → Partial tests → Maximum force measurement → Follow-up

Fig. 2. Sequence of a complete test run with one subject.

In order to prevent certain habituation effects but also an impairment of results due to possible muscular fatigue, the partial tests described below were performed in randomized order. Overhead work can only be tolerated for a few minutes, even with a low level of force. In a large number of preliminary tests, different time periods were tested and the final test duration was determined based on the findings obtained.

Screwing by Hand

The task is to screw in six screws one after the other by hand until they touch the threaded plate. The movement should be made from the wrist, as rotation from the fingers appears to be non-standardizable due to different finger dexterity. During the test, the test person stands at a marker one forearm's length away from the test stand. The free hand should remain at the same level as the working hand and therefore holds a small flashlight with which the screw is to be illuminated.

In the starting position, the subject stands facing the wall, arms hanging down beside the body, holding the flashlight in the free left hand. Screwing should be started on the left side of the given row so that the working hand is not restricted by screws that have already been screwed in. The individual work steps are shown and described in Fig. 3. After that, the work steps start again from the beginning. The 'screw in' process is guided by a metronome with a beat of 100 bpm. After the sixth screw the recording is stopped. Subsequently, the subject was asked about his physical condition before the test was performed again, but this time with the left hand as the working hand and working from right to left.

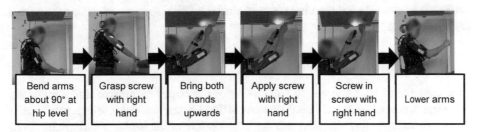

Bend arms about 90° at hip level → Grasp screw with right hand → Bring both hands upwards → Apply screw with right hand → Screw in screw with right hand → Lower arms

Fig. 3. Individual work steps during the screwing activity with the right hand.

Screwing with Cordless Screwdriver

In this part of the test, the subject is to screw in the screws that have already been applied with the aid of a cordless screwdriver. A fixed standing position is not prescribed. The free hand should be used at the subject's own discretion to stabilize the cordless screwdriver and must not hang down. Due to the different skill levels in handling the tool, a cycle time is not specified.

In the starting position, the test person stands facing the test station, arms hanging down beside the body, while holding the cordless screwdriver in the working hand. The subdivision of the work steps after the start of the measurement is shown and described in Fig. 4. After completing a row, a 5-s pause is taken before starting another row. Seven rows with seven screws each are processed in this way. After the test person has returned to the starting position, the measurement is stopped.

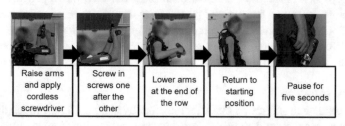

Fig. 4. Individual work steps during the screwing activity with the cordless screwdriver.

Plugging of Lego® Bricks

The plugging task is performed with the help of Lego® bricks. For this purpose, differently shaped Lego® bricks have to be plugged onto a base plate according to a given pattern. The work was done from a marked center line outwards, i.e. with the left hand from the center to the left and with the right hand from the center to the right. If necessary, the test person is told which Lego® bricks follow. The specified steps are accompanied by a metronome at 30 bpm. In the starting position, the test person stands facing the test station with his arms hanging down next to his body. The task is subdivided into the steps shown in Fig. 5. The subjects then starts again from the beginning and picks up the next four Lego® bricks. This sequence of operations is repeated until all of the specified 32 Lego® bricks have been inserted. After completing the measurement, the subject is briefly asked about his or her physical condition before performing the partial test again laterally reversed.

4.2 Electromyographic Measurements

The preliminary tests showed the activation of the trapezius muscle in the neck (m. trapezius p. descendens), the deltoid muscle in the shoulder (m. deltoideus p. clavicularis and m. deltoideus p. acromialis) and the large muscle of the back (m. latissimus dorsi) when performing the intended activities. Together with the findings from [1, 3, 4, 12–14] these facts confirmed the muscle selection as shown in Fig. 6. As previously described, the subjects' resting activity EA_0 and the maximum voluntary contractions (MVCs) were also recorded, which allowed calculating (normalized) electromyographic activities ($sEA = [(EA - EA_0)/(EA_{max} - EA_0)] * 100\%$) representing muscle strain in all working phases.

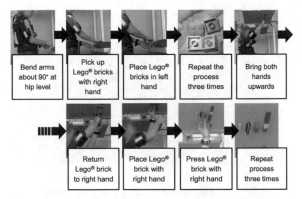

Fig. 5. Individual work steps during the plugging activity with Lego® bricks.

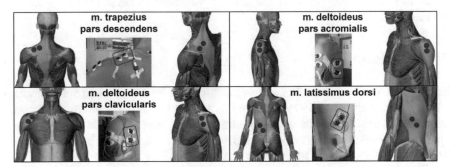

Fig. 6. Selection of the muscles and muscle parts for the electromyographic measurements.

4.3 Subjective Methods

The subjects current physical condition was queried by means of a body diagram, which divides the body into different segments (see Fig. 7). The combination of two ordinal scales made it possible to distinguish between form and intensity of impairment. Before the start of the test and after each measurement, the subjects indicated the area of their body in which they felt 'tension', 'pressure point' or 'numbness' and then assigned the impairment the level 'slight', 'moderate', 'strong' or 'very strong'. Otherwise, 'no impairment' was noted.

For each subtest, a question section was developed based on a standardized and well-proven questionnaire concept. The evaluation of the predominantly closed questions was to be answered using an ordinal scale with optical amplification. This means, the evaluation was done with a scale from -4 to $+4$ and the maximum ranges were adapted with a property to the question, i.e. for example 'very difficult' and 'very easy'. The questions focused, among other things, on the perceived muscular strain or the perceived working posture. Furthermore, there were questions that could only be answered at a certain point in time. For example, one question always referred to the choice between wearing or not wearing the exoskeleton during a similar task. This question could only be answered after performing the partial test with and without the exoskeleton. At the

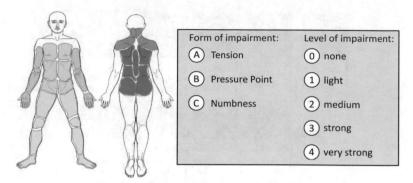

Fig. 7. Simple body diagram with rating scale to query the current physical condition.

end of the tests, the subjects were asked about their assessment of the exoskeleton and how they used it.

5 Discussion

The developed test station offers a high flexibility for further laboratory studies, especially due to the choice of aluminum profiles and the attachments and possible modifications. It is particularly suitable for the simulation of overhead work. By adjusting the height and swiveling of the worktops, various other hand, arm and body positions are also possible. Furthermore, the station theoretically allows interrupted work due to the 4 worktops.

The chosen experimental design is suitable for the evaluation of a passive exoskeleton and allows the reproducibility with products of other manufacturers. The developed subtests, their length and the developed questionnaire for recording subjective sensation also proved to be practicable, as shown by initial study results in [11].

6 Limitations of the Study

Due to the large number of different assembly activities in industry and the very individual body dimensions of humans, many variables had to be considered when developing the test station. Despite the developed standardized test procedure for the evaluation of upper body passive exoskeletons, the conditions must always be adjusted to the new test objects. This applies in particular to the type of activities, the working speed and the duration of the tests. Overhead work in particular causes high stress and strain, so the maximum possible test duration must be determined precisely. However, it must also be long enough to be able to obtain reliable results. The selection of muscles for recording muscular activity must also always be checked and, if necessary, adjusted due to the changed geometries of the individual exoskeletons. Because in this study, the main challenge was to apply the surface electromyography electrodes in a prescribed and correct manner, especially with regard to the m. trapezius p. descendens due to the position of the shoulder straps of the exoskeleton over the muscle. However, unfavorable physiological conditions of the subjects, for example small and particularly narrow persons, also complicate electromyographic measurements using the exoskeleton.

References

1. Schmalz, T., Schändlinger, J., Schuler, M., Bornmann, J., Schirrmeister, B., Kannenberg, A., Ernst, M.: Biomechanical and metabolic effectiveness of an industrial exoskeleton for overhead work. Int. J. Environ. Res. Public Health **16**(23), 4792 (2019)
2. Frost, P., Bonde, J.P.E., Mikkelsen, S., Andersen, J.H., Fallentin, N., Kaergaard, A., Thomsen, J.F.: Risk of shoulder tendinitis in relation to shoulder loads in monotonous repetitive work. Am. J. Ind. Med. **41**(1), 11–18 (2002)
3. Kim, S., Nussbaum, M.A., Esfahani, M.I.M., Alemi, M.M., Alabdulkarim, S., Rashedi, E.: Assessing the influence of a passive, upper extremity exoskeletal vest for tasks requiring arm elevation: part I-"Expected" effects on discomfort, shoulder muscle activity, and work task performance. Appl. Ergon. **70**, 315–322 (2018)
4. Kim, S., Nussbaum, M.A., Esfahani, M.I.M, Alemi, M.M., Jia, B., Rashedi, E.: Assessing the influence of a passice, upper extremity exoskeletal vest for tasks requiring arm elevation. Part II-"Unexpected" effects on shoulder motion, balance, and spine loading. Appl. Ergon. **70**, 323–330 (2018b).
5. Huysamen, K., Bosch, T.; de Looze, M., Stadler, K.S.; Graf, E., O´Sullivan, L.W.: Evaluation of a passive exoskeleton for static upper limb activities. Appl. Ergon. **70**, 148–155 (2018).
6. Maurice, P., Čamernik, J., Gorjan, D., Schirrmeister, B., Bornmann, J., Tagliapietra, L., Latella, C., Pucci, D., Fritzsche, L., Ivaldi, S., Babic, J.: Objective and subjective effects of a passive exoskeleton on overhead work. IEEE Trans. Neural Syst. Rehabil.n Eng.g **28**(1), 152–164 (2020)
7. van Engelhoven, L., Poon, N., Kazerooni, H., Barr, A., Rempel, D., Harris-Adamson, C.: Evaluation of an adjustable support shoulder exoskeleton on static and dynamic overhead tasks. Proc. Human Factors Ergon Society Annual Meet **62**, 804–808 (2018)
8. Rashedi, E., Kim, S., Nussbaum, M.A., Agnew, M.J.: Ergonomic evaluation of a wearable assistive device for overhead work. Ergonomics **57**(12), 1864–1874 (2014)
9. de Vries, A., Murphy, M., Könemann, R., Kingma, I., de Looze, M.: The amount of support provided by a passive arm support exoskeleton in a range of elevated arm postures. IISE Trans. Occup. Ergon. Human Factors **7**(3–4), 311–321 (2019)
10. Kruse, K.: Entwicklung und Evaluierung eines Versuchsstandes zur Objektivierung von Belastung und Beanspruchung während Überkopfarbeit mit und ohne Exoskelett. Bachelor thesis, University of Siegen (2019)
11. Groos, S., Abele, N.D., Fischer, P., Hefferle, M., Kluth, K.: Evaluation of the physiological benefits during simulated overhead work using standardized ergonomic analysis methods. In: Proceedings of the 21st Triennial Congress of the International Ergonomics Association, Vancouver, Canada (2021)
12. Butler, T., Gillette, J.C.: Exoskeletons: used as PPE for injury prevention. Prof Safety **3**, 33–37 (2019)
13. Gillette, J.C., Stephenson, M.L.: EMG analysis of an upper body exoskeleton during automotive assembly. In: Conference Proceedings of the 42nd Annual Meeting of the American Society of Biomechanics, Rochester, MN (2018)
14. Weston, E.B., Alizadeh, M., Knapik, G.G., Wang, X., Marras, W.S.: Biomechanical evaluation of exoskeleton use on loading of the lumbar spine. Appl. Ergon. **68**, 101–108 (2018)

Evaluation of Variables of Cognitive Ergonomics in Industrial Human-Robot Collaborative Assembly Systems

Luca Gualtieri[1]([⊠]), Federico Fraboni[2], Matteo De Marchi[1], and Erwin Rauch[1]

[1] Industrial Engineering and Automation (IEA), Free University of Bozen-Bolzano,
Piazza Università 1, 39100 Bolzano, Italy
lgualtieri@unibz.it
[2] Department of Psychology, Università di Bologna, Via Zamboni 33, 40126 Bologna, Italy

Abstract. In the context of Industry 4.0, a human-robot collaborative assembly system is an example of a cyber-physical production system, where operators and robots interact during assembly. Considering the growing market and the increasing use of industrial collaborative robotics, companies need support in the proper and profitable introduction of this technology in their production environment. From a design standpoint, it is necessary to develop safe and ergonomic interactions between the operator and the system, primarily focusing on operators' needs and characteristics of the robot. When designing collaborative systems and workstations, human-factors and cognitive requirements are often underestimated or ignored, even if they are crucial for the operator's wellbeing and production performances. Considering this gap, the present work aims to evaluate cognitive ergonomics variables in human-robot collaborative assembly systems. Three different scenarios of human-robot collaboration have been developed based on the analysis of the scientific literature. The effectiveness of the scenarios has been validated through multiple experiments based on a laboratory case-study where operators physically interacted with a low-payload collaborative robot for the joint assembly of a workpiece. Multiple cognitive variables have been identified and evaluated by gradually changing the workstation elements as well as the conditions of human interaction with the robot. Preliminary results showed the impact of each scenario in reducing the operator's stress and cognitive workload while improving the operator's trust, acceptance, and situation awareness.

Keywords: Human-robot interaction · Collaborative robotics · Human-factors and ergonomics · Collaborative assembly · Cognitive workload · Industry 4.0

1 Problem Statement

Human-robot collaboration is one of the key enabling technologies of Industry 4.0. Considering the continuous growth of the collaborative robotics market, one of the most interesting applications in the near future will be collaborative assembly. In this context, since prevention from mechanical hazards is justifiably perceived as the primary

N. L. Black et al. (Eds.): IEA 2021, LNNS 223, pp. 266–273, 2022.
https://doi.org/10.1007/978-3-030-74614-8_32

requirement [1], cognitive ergonomics and human factors are often overlooked [2], especially from an overall production system perspective. Cognitive ergonomics should be taken into account mainly in the design of automated, high-tech, or complex systems [3]. These aspects are strictly related to operators' safety, wellbeing and therefore, to the work-related performance [4]. Consequently, to develop efficient and effective Collaborative Assembly Systems (CASs), roboticists and companies have to take cognitive ergonomics aspects into account, and interdisciplinary research and approaches in the field are needed.

The work here presented has been conducted in the Smart Mini Factory (SMF) [5] lab in collaboration with experts in occupational human-factors and human-technology interaction from the "Human Factors, Risk and Safety Research Unit" of the University of Bologna [6]. This work aims to fill the identified research gaps in the context of cognitive ergonomics in industrial human-robot collaboration. Specifically, the study refers to the validation of variables for cognitive ergonomics in CASs. These are related to main cognitive risk factors: low levels of trust, low perceived usability, high frustration, low perceived enjoyment, low satisfaction, low acceptance high levels of stress, excessive cognitive/physical workload. Three experimental scenarios consider the implementation of different CAS features (i.e. workstation layout and elements, robot system features, robot system performance and organizational measures).

2 Methods

2.1 Variables of Cognitive Ergonomics

The main cognitive variables are here described according to the scientific literature:

- **Trust:** can be defined as the willingness to take the risk of being vulnerable to the actions of others regardless of the ability to control those actions [7]. Trust develops dynamically with knowledge and experience and is often addressed as a calibration process between the actual reliability of the system and the level of trust posed by the person interacting with it. Risk arises following a dysfunctional calibration, which can lead to over-trust or distrusts [8].
- **Usability:** refers to the extent to which a system, product or service can be used by specified users to achieve specified goals with effectiveness, efficiency and satisfaction in a specified context of use [9]. A lack of usability may represent a worker's risk factor.
- **Frustration:** is a psychological state derived from an unsatisfied need or unresolved problems. It can lead to an increased speed of performance and to increased errors, particularly in complex tasks and to a lesser extent in simple ones [11];
- **Perceived Enjoyment:** It is a feeling of joy or pleasure associated by the user with the use of the system. It has been studied in relation to robots acceptance and intention to use. Lack of perceived enjoyment can lead to lower levels of acceptance of the system.
- **Satisfaction:** refers to good feelings and self-motivation for workers in a job environment. Risks, such as occupational-stress, lower performances and higher turnover rates can arise in a condition of lack of worker's satisfaction [10];

- **Acceptance:** technology acceptance is the favorable reception of technology as a useful and practical tool [12]. Low level of technology acceptance may introduce a risk for workers;
- **Stress:** in general, it is defined as the human body's response to pressures from a situation or life event [13]. When this pressure exceeds certain limits, stress becomes a risk factor;
- **Cognitive workload:** refers to the cognitive effort that an individual shows during a task or to achieve a particular level of performance [14]. Assuming that cognitive resources of an individual are limited, the more effort is requested by a task the higher is the cognitive workload. It affects both safety and performances;
- **Physical workload:** refers to the physical effort that an individual requires during the completion of a task. Older studies showed its effects on risk perception and risk behaviour among the workers in different fields. Physical workload may impair the personnel's ability to avoid dangers [15].

2.2   Experimental Set-Up

The evaluation of variables for cognitive ergonomics is based on an experiment with three scenarios in a laboratory case-study. The main assumption to be tested is that it is possible to improve workers' experience by manipulating the system features and interaction patterns simulated in the three scenarios. In total, 14 participants with no previous experience with collaborative robotics and minimal experience in performing assembly activities interacted with a collaborative robot for the collaborative assembly of a workpiece. According to three different scenarios, features of the workstation and interaction modalities have been changed.

The main hardware components of the experimental set-up were the following:

- a collaborative robot model Universal Robot UR3 [17],
- a Robotiq collaborative gripper [18],
- an AI-based 3D perception device (Smart Robots [19]) for human-robot interaction (gesture recognition) and safety purposes (collision avoidance),
- an industrial electric screwdriver from Weber [20],
- a working table with assembly jigs, commands (button array and virtual button) for human-robot interaction, an emergency stop, some boxes for the storing and picking of assembly components, an LCD screen for displaying instructions and other information about the status of the robot systems (graphic user interface).

The product to be assembled was a simplified version of a common industrial pneumatic cylinder from Kuhnke (diameter of 32 mm and 50 mm stroke) with roughly 20 different components.

Figure 1 illustrates the main features related to the experimental set-up characterizing the scenarios to be tested.

In the following section, the three scenarios are briefly described.

Scenario 1: the first scenario provides the lowest degree of interaction between the operator and the robotic system. The operator has to authorize a large part of the robot's

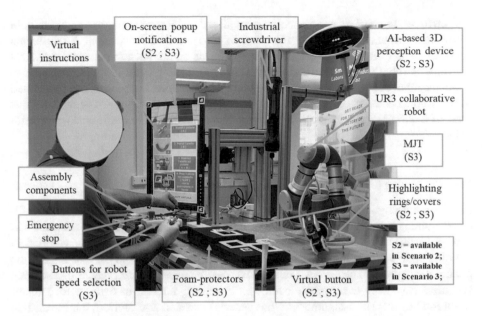

Fig. 1. Main features related to the experimental set-up that characterize the three scenarios.

task by applying pressure on the gripper, imposing therefore a physical interaction with the manipulator. The collision-avoidance system is disabled, and the operator is not aware of the possibility of pausing the robot's motion thanks to the gesture recognition system. The operator is not informed about the state of the workstation nor of the robotic arm. The robot speed is set to be slightly lower than the nominal value. Only the basic safety measures are introduced to the participants.

Scenario 2: the second scenario represents a compromise in terms of human-robot collaboration. The robot is allowed to perform more tasks without the confirmation of the operator. Even though this may be understood as a gain in robot's autonomy, it enhances the parallelization of operator's and manipulator's tasks, as well as improving the overall workflow with a consequent cycle-time reduction. The operator is now informed about workstation's and robot's state through on-screen popup notifications. Furthermore, the operator is aware of the possibility of pausing the motion of the robot thanks to the gesture recognition system provided by the AI-based 3D perception device, which also governs the collision avoidance feature, active in this case. A new human-to-system communication channel is established by implementing a virtual button (managed by the AI-based 3D perception device). In this scenario, the operator does not physically interact with the robotic arm. Instead, she/he has to use the virtual button in order to confirm the completion of a task. Finally, this scenario also foresees the introduction of features which aim at increasing the overall safety of the workstation (foam-protectors are applied around jigs and highlighting rings/covers are mounted on the robotic arm and around the main workstation elements). The robot speed is set to be slightly higher than the nominal value. The safety measures are explained in detail, and their effectiveness is demonstrated.

Scenario 3: the third scenario encompasses all the features of scenario number two. In addition, the operator is able to actively modify the speed of the manipulator through a set of three buttons and to freely chose the preferred communication channel (physical pressure on robot's end effector of a virtual button). The operator is now informed also about the robot's speed through on-screen popup notifications The robot is reprogrammed for the implementation of Minimum Jerk Trajectories (MJTs) since it is assumed that this kind of motion is more predictable and familiar with respect to traditional trajectories [21].

2.3   Procedure for Conducting the Experiments

Firstly, a training session (without the presence of the robot) was provided in a dedicated training workstation to prevent and reduce possible errors related to limited and heterogeneous knowledge of the product and the process. Later, participants were asked to collaborate with the low-payload collaborative robot to complete the assembly of the pneumatic cylinder. The task was repeated three times, one for each scenario. The three scenarios have been designed to include an increasing number of features for human-robot interaction. The assignment of the scenarios was non-randomized, this means that each participant started with scenario 1 and finished with scenario 3.

We hypothesized that the first scenario would be the worst one in terms of cognitive response, while scenario 2 and 3 were supposed to be gradually better. Three parallel approaches, based on qualitative and quantitative data, were used to measure participants' responses: questionnaires, video recordings, and semi-structured interviews. The questionnaire was composed of multiple scales aimed at assessing participants trust, perceived usability, acceptance, stress and cognitive workload. The same set of questions were repeated after the completion of each scenario. This allowed assessing cognitive risk factors. We further integrated data obtained from the survey with:

(a) Direct observations during the execution of the experiment: the testers observed the behaviours of participants during the experiments. The aim was to collect as much information as possible by noting particular events or situations;
(b) Video recording: all the experiments were recorded by using a camera system. The recordings were used to assess the number of errors, near miss and requests of clarification;
(c) Semi-structured interview: the testers asked open questions to participants at the end of the experiment. The aim was to collect further feedback on participants' feelings and preferences (e.g. particular comments that participants felt to share).

3   Results

In general, results confirmed our hypothesis and are in accordance with previous literature. Questionnaires, interviews and observations showed that:

(1) Trust increased, and frustration decreased with the enhancement of workstation features and interaction conditions by shifting from the various scenarios;

(2) Usability, perceived enjoyment, satisfaction and physical workload improved by shifting from scenario 1 to scenario 2 while they remained essentially unchanged changing from scenario 2 to scenario 3;

(3) Acceptance increased, and stress decreased considerably by shifting from scenario 2 to scenario 3 while they remained unchanged from scenario 1 to scenario 2;

(4) Cognitive Workload increased slightly in scenario 2 compared to scenario 1, while decreased considerably in scenario 3 compared to scenario 2. The increase of cognitive workload in the first transition is the only unexpected result of this analysis.

Figure 2 summarizes main results obtained from the experiments and especially from the survey (quantitative results). $\Delta1$ and $\Delta2$ represent the (percentual mean values) difference for each cognitive variable between Scenario 1 and Scenario 2 and between Scenario 2 and Scenario 3, respectively. The duration of each scenario mainly depended on the ability of the participants to deal with the specific assembly situation (i.e. ability to use the available tools, number of assembly errors, reasoning time according to various events etc.). On average, scenario 1 lasted 228.3 s for each participant (with a standard deviation of 17.5 s), scenario 2 lasted 221.2 s (with a standard deviation of 15.7 s), while scenario 3 lasted 213.0 s (with a standard deviation of 18.6 s). In addition, results showed that the number of critical assembly conditions (errors, near miss and requests of clarification related to the task) decreased mostly by shifting from scenario 1 to scenario 2 and even further in scenario 3.

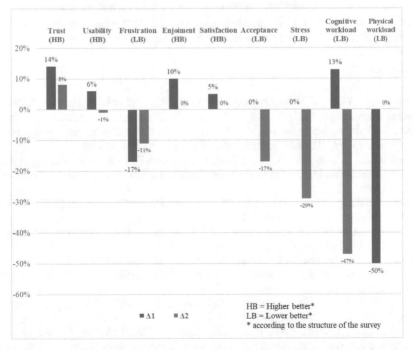

Fig. 2. Evaluation of cognitive variables according to different scenarios

4   Discussions and Conclusions

This work studied the role of cognitive ergonomics in industrial human-robot interaction. The aim of this study was to experimentally validate a set of variables of cognitive ergonomics in the design of human-robot CASs in industrial settings. These have been identified according to the analysis of the scientific literature. A laboratory case-study has been used for the validation of such variables. The final goal is to support designers in improving the wellbeing of workers in CASs also considering company's production performances.

Results confirmed that participants improved their cognitive experience of the collaborative assembly when applying the three scenarios with the enhancement of workstation features and interaction conditions. As expected, better results are related to scenario 3, which is the scenario with the highest number of features for human-robot interaction. Nevertheless, according to the quantitative and qualitative data, the most considerable improvement comes from the changes between scenario 1 and scenario 2. In particular, a higher robot autonomy, a better synchronization with the robot tasks, the possibility to have more control on the system and better awareness about workstation's and robot's state probably are the main contributions to this improvement.

Future studies should deeply explore the issue of cognitive ergonomics in industrial collaborative robotics from a system perspective. This will require a deeper analysis of different features for improving human-robot collaboration by summarizing them in a set of design guidelines for human-robot CASs. Furthermore, the implementation and validation of multiple case studies related to various conditions of human-robot interaction (i.e. by using different sizes of robots as well as testing different tasks) are needed. This will be crucial in increasing knowledge on the topic in order to limit as much as possible risks related to the collaboration between humans and robots.

References

1. Gualtieri, L., Palomba, I., Wehrle, E.J., Vidoni, R.: Potential and challenges in SME manufacturing automation through safety and ergonomics in human-robot collaboration. In: Matt, D.T., Modrak, V., Zsifkovits, H. (eds.) Industry 4.0 for SMEs Challenges, Opportunities and Requirements, pp. 105–144. Palgrave Macmillan, Basingstoke (2020)
2. Gualtieri, L., Rauch, E., Vidoni, R.: Emerging research fields in safety and ergonomics in industrial collaborative robotics: a systematic literature review. Robot. Comput. Integr. Manuf. **67**, 101998
3. International Ergonomics Association (IEA): Human Factors/Ergonomics (2020). https://iea.cc/what-is-ergonomics/. Accessed Dec 2020
4. Thorvald, P., Lindblom, J., Andreasson, R.: CLAM–A method for cognitive load assessment in manufacturing. In: Advances in Manufacturing Technology, vol. XXXI, pp. 114–119 (2017)
5. Smart Mini Factory (2020). https://smartminifactory.it/. Accessed Dec 2020
6. Human Factors, Risk and Safety – Research Unit (2020). https://site.unibo.it/hfrs/en. Accessed Nov 2020
7. Mayer, R.C., Davis, J.H., Schoorman, F.D.: An integrative model of organizational trust. Acad. Manage. Rev. **20**(3), 709–734 (1995)
8. De Visser, E.J., Peeters, M.M., Jung, M.F., Kohn, S., Shaw, T.H., Pak, R., Neerincx, M.A.: Towards a theory of longitudinal trust calibration in human–robot teams. Int. J. Soc. Robot. **12**(2), 459–478 (2020)

9. International Organization for Standardization (2018). ISO 9241-11 — Ergonomics of human-system interaction — Part 11: Usability: Definitions and concepts. (9241-11:2018). https://www.iso.org/standard/63500.html
10. Schwabe, H., Castellacci, F.: Automation, workers' skills and job satisfaction. Plos One **15**(11), e0242929 (2020)
11. Spector, P.E.: Organizational frustration: a model and review of the literature. Pers. Psychol. **31**(4), 815–829 (1978)
12. Davis, F.D.: Perceived usefulness, perceived ease of use, and user acceptance of information technology. MIS Q. 319–340 (1989)
13. Recipe for Stress (2020). https://humanstress.ca/stress/understand-your-stress/sources-of-stress. Accessed Dec 2020
14. Hart, S.G., Staveland, L.E.: Development of NASA-TLX (Task Load Index): results of empirical and theoretical research. In Advances in Psychology, vol. 52, pp. 139–183. North-Holland (1988)
15. Rundmo, T., Hestad, H., Ulleberg, P.: Organisational factors, safety attitudes and workload among offshore oil personnel. Safety Sci. **29**(2), 75–87 (1998)
16. Gualtieri, L., Rauch, E., Vidoni, R., Matt, D.T.: Safety, ergonomics and efficiency in human-robot collaborative assembly: design guidelines and requirements. Procedia CIRP **91**, 367–372 (2020)
17. Universal Robots (2020). https://www.universal-robots.com/. Accessed Dec 2020
18. Robotiq (2020). https://robotiq.com/. Accessed Dec 2020
19. Smart Robots (2020). https://smartrobots.it/. Accessed Dec 2020
20. Weber (2020). https://www.weber-online.com/en/. Accessed Dec 2020
21. Rojas, R.A., Garcia, M.A.R., Wehrle, E., Vidoni, R.: A variational approach to minimum-jerk trajectories for psychological safety in collaborative assembly stations. IEEE Robot. Autom. Lett. **4**(2), 823–829 (2019)

Optimizing Force Transfer in a Soft Exoskeleton Using Biomechanical Modeling

Christina M. Harbauer[(✉)] ⓘ, Martin Fleischerⓘ, Cerys E. M. Bandmann, and Klaus Benglerⓘ

Chair of Ergonomics, Technical University of Munich, 85748 Garching, Germany
christina.harbauer@tum.de

Abstract. A newly developed prototype of a soft cable-driven elbow exoskeleton for lifting and lowering of loads was developed. To identify potential harmful forces within the elbow joint, an analysis was conducted with biomechanical simulation. To analyze the effect of the exoskeleton on the human body, biomechanical simulations were conducted on the prototype to assess the joint reaction forces during a lifting task with and without the soft elbow exoskeleton. To reduce these forces, the optimal way to attach the cables for generating the moment around the elbow needs to be identified using biomechanical simulation. First results show that in average the load on the elbow joint is reduced while wearing the exoskeleton compared to lifting 5 kg without any assistance. A large distance between the lower arm and the attachment point in ventral direction is very beneficial, due to the introduction of another lever arm into the system. Especially if the elbow is fully stretched, whereas the pulling force vector would go parallel to the arm. With the implementation of the lever arm, the load on the elbow is lower for any position of the arm.

Keywords: Exoskeleton · Biomechanical simulation · Force optimization · Force analysis

1 Biomechanical Simulation in the Design of Exoskeletons

1.1 Motivation

The primary goal of exoskeletons for industrial applications is to reduce the load on the person using the system during physical straining tasks. Especially with active exoskeletons it is a concern that misalignments between the human biomechanics and the exoskeleton kinematic cause shearing forces and high loads in the human joints. This remarkably reduces their benefit and justification [1]. So in the design of exoskeletons those forces need to be considered and avoided in very early stages of the development [2]. These considerations are especially important for soft exoskeletons, since they do not contain rigid structures that can divert forces away from the human body.

Commonly used tools in literature for these early stage analyses are biomechanical simulations. They are used to investigate the muscular or joint load during specified movements to detect the intended reductions as well as unintended increase of strain on the human body. Similar to these approaches a new design for a soft cable-driven exoskeleton will be analyzed for efficiency and freedom from damaging forces.

Furthermore, a design optimization is performed to improve the force flow though the human body and identify the configuration with the minimal amount of strain on the joints.

1.2 Design of the Soft Exoskeleton

The design of the soft cable-driven exosuit is described in detail in [3]. Its intended use is the support of the flexion of the human elbow during lifting tasks. To do so, a cable is led through a tubing system along the lateral as well as the medial side of the upper and lower arm with a loop at the wrist [3]. The torque is induced around the elbow by the cable detaching shortly in front of and behind the elbow at the upper and lower arm. The motor for pulling the cable is located at the back of the exoskeleton. The course of the cable on the medial side is sketched in Fig. 1, the lateral side where the cable loops back is identical and therefore obscured in the figure.

A preliminary kinematic analysis shows a force vector pointing into the elbow and therefore potentially increasing the joint interaction forces which could lead to a damage in the joint with long term usage. The biomechanical simulation is needed to show, if these considerations are true or if a reduction of strain on the elbow joint can be achieved by the soft exoskeleton.

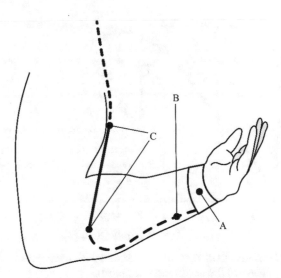

Fig. 1. Representation of the cable path running though the sleeve of the exoskeleton on the medial side. **A** represents the wrist cuff where the cable is looping though to the lateral side, **B** shows where the cable is lead through the tube; **C** are the two points where the cable leaves the tube on both sides of the arm.

2 Methodology

For this biomechanical optimization and analysis, the simulation software "OpenSim 4.0" made by SimTK was chosen.

Based on the method for simulating and modeling exoskeletons that are presented in [4] for the software "OpenSim" and the general approach for a model based optimization loop as described in [5], the simulation and optimization method is conducted in this project. In a similar way a similar exoskeleton but with rigid shells and spring-loaded actuation was optimized in [6].

The biomechanical model is based on the "Arm26" [7] model which was adapted to only include the muscles relevant to the elbow flexion and extension. It consists of triceps brachii modelled as three separate muscles, the biceps brachii, the brachialis anticus, anconeus muscle and the biceps brachioradialis.

The flexion movement was implemented in a way that only the elbow is flexed and extended from a fully stretched position at 0° to 145° and back. This represents the full range of movement in average for a person working in logistics [8]. The full movement takes 7.4 s with an average velocity of 39.14 °/s. The data was originally taken from a preliminary study published in [9] where loads were lifted in a similar setting as it is intended for the soft exoskeleton. It was adjusted to fit the whole movement of the arm with realistic accelerations, which results in an artificial dataset based on real life observations. The resulting curve for the degree of flexion over the time of movement is illustrated in Fig. 2.

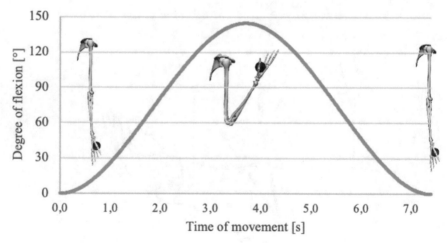

Fig. 2. Flexion angle of the elbow from 0° to 145° and back over movement duration of 7.4 s (artificial dataset based on real life observations from [9]).

For the first kinematic analysis in [3] two cable strands pulling lateral and medial at the lower arm were consolidated into one strand that it is applying the full force in the middle of the ventral side of the limb. So not the entire course of the cable is represented, only the part that is exposed between the two attachment points C as shown in Fig. 1.

The same approach is used in the biomechanical simulation to reduce the complexity of the optimization process. The target of the optimization is the minimization of the joint reaction forces by varying the attachment point on the forearm. The position of this attachment point is variated in two directions, along the arm and perpendicular to the surface. All iterations of these variables are tested for a lifting load of 5 kg with one arm and the optimal configurations are determined.

The tendon of the exoskeleton is simulated by a path actuator originating at the top of the humerus, is guided parallel to the bone of the humerus by a path point and in the end is connected to the forearm in a straight line.

The weight of the load is implemented with a simple ball geometry that is connected to the hand of the model and given the weight of 5 kg. Figure 3 is the final model for the biomechanical simulation.

Fig. 3. Green: tendon-driven exoskeleton represented as a path actuator, red: triceps brachii, biceps brachii, brachialis anticus, anconeus, biceps brachioradialis muscles, black: lifting load.

After the model is completed, the simulation is executed using static optimization (SO) tool by OpenSim which is based on inverse dynamics to generate movement. It calculates the muscle forces by minimizing the sum of squared muscle activations.

To calculate the joint reaction forces (JRF) OpenSim provides a joint reaction analysis (JRA) tool [10]. With the JRA the joint forces are calculated based on all loads acting on the model, which includes contributions by joint structures like cartilage contact and omitted ligaments.

For the optimization the attachment point was changed in discrete values of 2 mm along the y axis and 1 mm along the x axis resulting in 144 positions that run though the simulation and the JRF is calculated for. Of those 144 positions 45 are excluded, since they are not viable for designing the exoskeleton, since the attachment point would collide with the upper arm during the elbow flexion. The remaining attachment points are presented in Fig. 4.

For the analysis of the resulting datasets, first a baseline simulation without the exoskeleton was conducted.

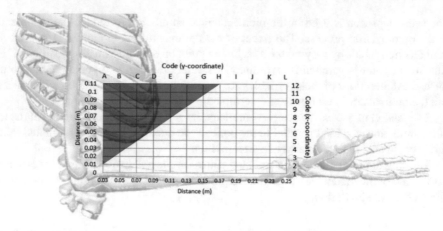

Fig. 4. Representation of the discrete attachment points used for the design optimization. The grey area marks the points that were removed from the dataset since they are not viable in a real exoskeleton.

3   Results

For the analysis of the exoskeleton the relevant output parameters of the JRA are the force x-, y-, and z- components of the JRF and their root-sum-of-squares (RSS), indicating the resulting force on the elbow. The co-moving coordinate system for the lower arm is shown in Fig. 5.

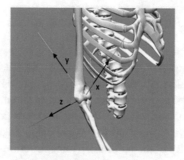

Fig. 5. The co-moving coordinate system for the lower arm.

In the case of the presented exoskeleton F_y is the potentially damaging force component, that may increase the compression of the joint tissue. Therefore, the RSS and the F_y are the two variables, that are compared for each variation of the attachment point and with the baseline.

The results for the baseline without the exoskeleton are for the largest peak in absolute values 419 N for F_y and 499 N for the RSS.

The results for the simulations with the different attachment points are clustered into two groups, one where the JRF are higher than the baseline and one group where the JRF are lower than the baseline. Those attachment points with lower forces than the baseline are clustered further, since they fulfill the minimum safety requirement that the forces are not increased by the exoskeleton usage. They are clustered into four areas of equal force ranges that are indicated in different shades in Fig. 6 and with ranges of 87 N for F_y and 106 N for the RSS. The absolute values for the thresholds between those areas are described in Table 1.

Table 1. Threshold forces for each cluster.

	C1 [N]	C2 [N]	C3 [N]	C4 [N]
Peak Fy	71–158	−245	−332	−419
Peak RSS	77–182	−288	−394	−499

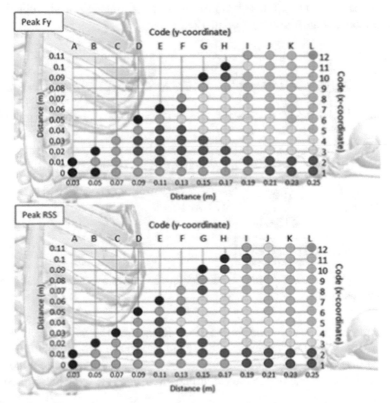

Fig. 6. Isometric force ranges for the F_y and the RSS peak forces. Black: higher than baseline, gray: C4; red: C3; yellow: C2; green: C1.

4 Discussion

The exoskeleton as described can decrease the joint load dramatically depending on the attachment point on the lower arm. There is a conflict between the optimal load and a feasible attachment point. To achieve the lowest joint reaction forces the attachment point needs to be as distal and ventral as possible. This results in a bulky construction that will find low acceptance with the users. To be convenient the attachment needs to be as proximal and as close to the arm as possible. Future studies need to evaluate where an optimum is, that satisfies both aspects sufficiently. However, there are only a few cases in Fig. 6, where the exoskeleton does not lower the joint load compared to lifting without exoskeleton.

While the reduction of joint reaction forces is a positive aspect, a second phenomenon manifests in the simulation. The direction of the RSS during the movement changes when wearing an exoskeleton compared to lifting without exoskeleton. This might damage the joint and it is to be evaluated in future studies if the reduction of the forces outweighs the change in directions. In Fig. 7 this phenomenon is demonstrated for the baseline without the exoskeleton and the attachment point 12K.

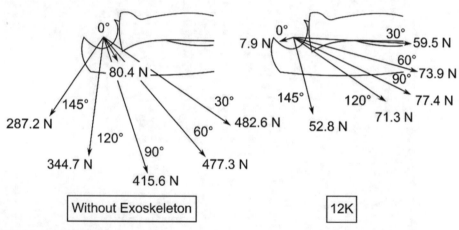

Fig. 7. Changing directions of the RSS vectors between the baseline without the exoskeleton and the attachment point 12K.

Limitation of the used model is the simplification of the bone structures in the forearm, which were consolidated into one rigid element, instead of ulna, radius and the hand separately. Also the gripping of the hand was not simulated and therefore a potential effect on the JRF due to the resulting muscle contraction in the forearm is not included.

In future work, similar to the presented method, a simulation and optimization of the attachment point of the upper arm needs to be done to achieve an optimization of the complete system.

Since simulation models are only an abstraction of the real word, the simulation results need to be validated. For that purpose, a test bench resembling the simulation setup will be constructed to validate the presented data.

References

1. Pons, J.L.: Wearable Robots. Biomechatronic Exoskeletons. Wiley, New York (2008)
2. Jarrasse, N., Morel, G.: Connecting a human limb to an exoskeleton. IEEE Trans. Robot. **28**, 697–709 (2011)
3. Harbauer, C.M., Fleischer, M., Nguyen, T., Bos, F., Bengler, K.: Too close to comfort? A new approach of designing a soft cable-driven exoskeleton for lifting tasks under ergonomic aspects. In: IRCE 2020. 2020 the 3rd International Conference on Intelligent Robotic and Control Engineering, Oxford, UK, 10–12 August 2020, pp. 105–109. IEEE, Piscataway (2020)
4. Khamar, M., Edrisi, M., Zahiri, M.: Human-exoskeleton control simulation, kinetic and kinematic modeling and parameters extraction. MethodsX **6**, 1838–1846 (2019)
5. Tröster, M., Wagner, D., Müller-Graf, F., Maufroy, C., Schneider, U., Bauernhansl, T.: Biomechanical model-based development of an active occupational upper-limb exoskeleton to support healthcare workers in the surgery waiting room. Int J Environ Res Public Health **17**, 5140 (2020)
6. Zhou, L., Bai, S., Andersen, M.S., Rasmussen, J.: Modeling and design of a spring-loaded, cable-driven, wearable exoskeleton for the upper extremity. MIC **36**, 167–177 (2015)
7. Holzbaur, K.R.S., Murray, W.M., Delp, S.L.: A model of the upper extremity for simulating musculoskeletal surgery and analyzing neuromuscular control. Ann. Biomed. Eng **33**, 829–840 (2005)
8. Kapandji, A.I., Rehart, S. (eds.): Funktionelle Anatomie der Gelenke. Schematisierte und kommentierte Zeichnungen zur menschlichen Biomechanik. Georg Thieme Verlag, Stuttgart, New York (2016)
9. Harbauer, C., Knott, V., Hergeth, L., Bengler, K.: Kinematische evaluation eines aktiven exoskeletts. In: 2019, Gesellschaft für Arbeitswissenschafst e. V. (GfA) (ed.) 65. Frühjahrkonferenz der GfA. Arbeit interdisziplinär analysieren - bewerten - gestalten, Beitrag B.4.4. GfA Press (2019)
10. Steele, K.M., Demers, M.S., Schwartz, M.H., Delp, S.L.: Compressive tibiofemoral force during crouch gait. Gait Posture **35**, 556–560 (2012)

How User Presence Impacts Perceptions and Operation Routines of Robotic Vacuum Cleaners – a 'Stay at Home' Experiment

Shanee Honig$^{(\boxtimes)}$ and Tal Oron-Gilad

Ben-Gurion University of the Negev, 84105 Be'er Sheva, Israel
shaneeh@post.bgu.ac.il

Abstract. For domestic service robots (DSRs) to be successful, their design must accommodate user needs and preferences when working from home. This study explores whether DSR usage patterns change when people spend more time at home and whether active observation of robotic behaviors (which is more likely to occur when working from home) impacts the perception of robotic characteristics. Thirty-one owners of robotic vacuum cleaners were provided with an interactive online questionnaire which guided them through a remote unmoderated experiment in their own home. Participants were asked to report their cleaning routines, before and during lockdown, and their perceptions of their robot, before and after they actively observed it clean and handle different obstacles. Advantages and disadvantages of this approach are discussed. Our results, while still preliminary, shed light on people's robot operation routines as they work from home. Even though most of our participants owned their robot for over a year, we found that active observation of the robot's work may impact the way in which robots are perceived. Our findings may have general implications to the design of controlled human-robot interaction experiments, which typically require active observation, unlike most interactions in naturalistic settings.

Keywords: Remote user studies · Human-robot interaction · User presence · Enhanced online questionnaires

1 Introduction

Affordable, commercially available robots for domestic use are becoming increasingly common. According to the International Federation of Robotics (2019), approximately 22.1 million domestic service robots (e.g. vacuum cleaners, lawn mowers and pool cleaners) were sold in 2019, 35% more than in 2018. As domestic service robots (DSRs) become more capable and affordable, and as the need for remote services increases due to COVID-19, the desire to own robots for different household tasks is likely to grow.

For DSRs to be successful, their design must accommodate user needs and preferences when working from home. Current estimates indicate that many people will continue to work from home long after COVID-19 is behind us [1, 2], suggesting a growing and continuous need to address this use case. Yet, little is known about how being at

N. L. Black et al. (Eds.): IEA 2021, LNNS 223, pp. 282–290, 2022.
https://doi.org/10.1007/978-3-030-74614-8_34

home impacts the way people use or perceive their DSRs. Such information matters for the design of future robots and raises concerns: assuming people have more opportunities to observe their DSRs in action, will this observation impact their perceptions of the robot's characteristics and abilities?

The influence of user presence on how robots are perceived and understood has been previously investigated [3, 4]. Most works compared among conditions in which participants actively observed and/or collaborated with the robot. However, in domestic settings, users decide for themselves when, how, and if to use or attend to their robots. This may lead to unique differences in the way people perceive robots in naturalistic settings as opposed to controlled experimental environments.

Few works studied patterns of use of DMRs in naturalistic settings. One exception is an ethnographic study which deployed nine iRobot Roombas for six months to different households [5, 6]. The researchers found that members of all nine households carefully observed how the Roomba moved around their homes when operating it for the first few times and most attempted to understand the logic behind the robot's path. Gaps in expectations led most households to be hesitant to let the robot clean when they were not at home. However, since the robot's vacuuming noise was disruptive to most people in the study, households that decided to continue to use the robot tended to activate it when leaving the home. These findings suggest that usage habits may change as people work more from home; however, conclusions cannot be drawn since user presence was not manipulated within the study.

We aim to explore two Research Questions (RQs): RQ1) Do DSRs usage patterns change when people spend more time at home? and RQ2) Does active observation of robotic behaviors impact the perception of robotic characteristics? As a first step towards these goals, an *interactive online questionnaire* was developed, which guides owners of domestic robots through a remote unmoderated experiment in their own home. We termed this methodology BYOB (Bring Your Own Bot). A pilot study was deployed to gain initial insights regarding the RQs and the BYOB methodology.

2 The BYOB (Bring Your Own Bot) Methodology

2.1 Overview

Thirty-one owners of robotic vacuum cleaners were provided with an interactive online questionnaire. Following consent, participants were asked for demographic information about themselves, their robot, and their household. Second, they were asked about their robot operational routines, before and after COVID-19 restrictions took place. They were then asked about their perceptions of their robot, how satisfied they are with it, and how they think it behaves in four situations: general cleaning, cleaning under a chair, cleaning around an obstacle (shoe), and carpet vacuuming. Following, they were asked to actively observe their robot while it cleaned and handled the four aforementioned situations, to record their experiences out loud on video and to upload the videos to the questionnaire. After they completed the activity, they were again asked about their perceptions of the robot, how satisfied they were, and how the robot behaved in each situation. Robotic vacuum cleaners were selected as the focus of the study because they are the most widely owned domestic service robot.

2.2 Participants

A convenience sample of participants were recruited via social media and word-of-mouth. All reside in Israel and own a robotic vacuum cleaner. The interactive questionnaire was distributed in April 2020, during the first COVID-19 lockdown. It was "marketed" as an activity for the entire family, to help pass time. No monetary compensation was offered for participation.

2.3 Interactive BYOB Online Questionnaire

The interactive questionnaire was implemented using Google Forms. It was divided into 6 sections.

Description and Consent Form. Participants were told the purpose of the study was to understand how they use and perceive their vacuum robot. All parts of the interactive questionnaire were described. Completion time was estimated at 30 min. Participants were encouraged to fill the survey on their mobile phones so that it would be easier to complete the activity and upload their videos.

Demographic Information. Questions about age, gender, profession, number of household members, how much time they have been under stay-at-home orders, their robot's brand and model, and how much time they have owned it.

Presence at Home and Robot Operational Routines. Participants were asked about their presence at home and robot operational routines, before and after the lockdown restrictions took place (see Appendix 4.1). This was done using a multiple-choice grid, where one row represented routines before restrictions and a second row represented routines after. Columns corresponded to possible responses.

Pre-observation Questions. Here we assessed how participants perceived their robot and the way it operates (see Appendix 4.2). Perceived competence and discomfort were measured using subscales from RoSAS [7], adjusted to a 5-point Likert Scale. Perceptions of the robot's safety were measured using the relevant subscale from the Godspeed Questionnaire [8]. Participants were also asked to rate how satisfied they are with their robot on a 5-point Likert Scale.

Active Observation of the Robot. At this point, participants were provided with written instructions for the activity portion of the questionnaire. They were asked to bring a rug, a shoe, and a chair to their surroundings, and state the number and age of those that will take part in the activity. Then, they were asked to turn their robotic vacuum cleaner on and actively watch it clean and respond to obstacles, while videorecording the robot and verbally describing their thoughts and experiences (think-aloud protocol [9]). They verbally described, as the robot operated, what strategy the robot used to clean, how many times it cleaned the same place, unexpected and/or incoherent behaviors, things that impressed them about the robot, and how the robot handled the obstacles that were placed for it. Participants were encouraged to invite other members of the household to participate in this activity, e.g., by helping to film, set up, reiterate questions, etc. Once the robot faced all obstacles, they were instructed to end the recording and return to the questionnaire.

Post-observation Questions. The concluding questionnaire included the same questions as in the pre-observation section. In addition, participants were asked to enter unexpected and unclear behaviors they had noticed, things that impressed them about the robot, and what they would have liked the robot to do differently. At the end, they were asked to upload their videorecording directly into the survey or by email.

2.4 Data Analysis

McNemar-Bowker tests were used to determine whether there is a significant change in usage habits after presence at home had changed. Paired t-tests were used to evaluate changes in usage frequency, and whether there was a difference in the robot's perceived safety, competence, and discomfort, before and after active observation of the robot. Spearmen's rank correlation coefficient test and a Wilcoxon Signed-Rank Test were performed to evaluate whether satisfaction with the robot changed after the active observation, and whether the perceived importance of the robot changed.

All videos were analyzed by two independent coders. Discrepancies in the analysis of the two coders were discussed and resolved between them. Objective measures regarding the robot's behavior were extracted, including how the robot handled each obstacle (chair, carpet, shoe), its cleaning path and how many times it cleaned the same area. Unexpected events and failures were recorded. Qualitative information regarding participants interactions with the robot and perceptions of it were extracted from their statements. A word-cloud was then generated based on the statements.

3   Results

3.1 Participants

Thirty-one participants (15 male, 16 female) completed the study. The pool was diverse, age ranged from 15 to 66 years old, from a wide variety of professions (8 students, 5 engineers, 3 soldiers, 3 lawyers, 2 project managers, 3 unemployed and 7 unspecified). Twenty-two (71%) of participants had two people living in their households, the remaining 9 participants had three or more household members. Most participants (24, 77%) completed the activity portion of the questionnaire on their own, 5 (16%) completed it together with another household member, and 2 (6%) completed it with two or more other household members. Twenty-three (74%) participants owned their robot for over one year. The most common robots were by iRobot (16, 52%) and Xiaomi (11, 35%), followed by ECOVACS (2), LG (1) and iLife (1).

3.2 Changes in Presence at Home

Before the lockdown, 23 (74%) participants spent most of their day outside their home, 5 (16%) stated the time they spent at home varied, and 3 (1%) spent most of their time at home. Twenty-five (81%) participants reported their presence at home increased due to the lockdown. Of these, 24 stated that at the time of the survey, they have been under restrictions for over a month. One participant was under restrictions for one to two weeks. The remaining 6 (19%) who had no increase in their time spent at home (i.e., essential workers), were removed from analyses of RQ1.

3.3 Impact of Increased Time at Home on Robot Usage Habits

No statistically significant differences were found in usage habits or in the robot's importance before and after the change in presence. Descriptive results are summarized in Table 1. Of the 25 participants that spent more time at home, most operated their robot at least once a week (20 before, 23 after), in the mornings or at no fixed hours (20 before, 19 after), and without direct supervision (20 before, 16 after). When operating the robot when no one is home (remote operation), more participants send the robot to clean the entire house (17) than specific regions (5). Regional cleaning is more common when people are home. Sixteen participants mentioned that the robot's sounds affected their activities and/or impacted where household members were located in the house. Most participants (29, 93%) reported performing preparations before operating their robot, primarily rearranging objects in the space (24/29, 83%).

Table 1. Change in robot usage habits for participants who had changed their presence at home

Aspect	Participants that changed habits	Greatest shift in usage
Supervision	17 (68%)	Remote operation → no direct supervision
Usage frequency	11 (44%)	At least 2–4 times a week → once a week
Timing	9 (36%)	Mornings → no fixed hours
Cleaning regions	6 (24%)	Varies → regional cleaning
Preparations	4 (16%)	No common shift

3.4 Impact of Active Observation on Robot Perception

The robots' perceived safety was significantly lower ($p = 0.02$) after active observation ($\bar{x} = 3.62$, $\sigma = 0.91$) than before ($\bar{x} = 3.42$, $\sigma = 0.91$). No significant change was found in the robot's competence ($\bar{x}_{before}$: 3.72, $\bar{x}_{after}$: 3.70, $p = 0.59$), discomfort ($\bar{x}_{before}$: 1.63, $\bar{x}_{after}$: 1.60, $p = 0.34$), and satisfaction ($\bar{x}_{before}$: 4.0, $\bar{x}_{after}$: 4.0, $p = 0.96$).

Twenty-six participants (84%) had at least one inaccurate perception regarding how their robot behaves. Most participants correctly predicted how it would handle cleaning around a chair (30/31), vacuuming a carpet (24/31) and its cleaning path (23/31). Less people correctly predicted how many times their robot cleans the same place (18/31). Most (18/31) participants incorrectly estimated how the robot will handle cleaning around a shoe.

Whereas all 31 participants reported completing the active observation, only 23 (74%) uploaded their video recording. The average recording time was 3 min, 55 s (SD = 3:02 min). Although participants were asked to observe the robot during the activity, 9 participants were seen helping their robot complete its tasks by either guiding it in the right direction or by moving obstacles from its way. Eight participants experienced technical robot failures during the activity (e.g. robot running into items, getting tangled, or getting stuck). Two participants named their robot and two spoke to it as it worked. The word-cloud indicated that the most common words retrieved from the videos were: loud, cleaned around the obstacle, learned the house, cleans randomly, pushed, stuck, handled it well.

Nineteen participants described, in writing or verbally in the video, things that the robot did that surprised them or were unclear. These statements were divided into positive surprises, where the robot exceeded expectations; neutral surprises, where the response was ambiguous; and negative surprises, where the robot failed to meet expectations. *Negative surprises* included: leaving a room too early, cleaning the same place too many times, moving items in the environment (e.g., folding a carpet, pushing a space heater), getting stuck, not cleaning where expected, going to areas where it shouldn't or where it is likely to get stuck (e.g. climbing the cat's litter box), moving in unexpected or inefficient ways, incorrect prioritization between regions, lack of learning abilities, and taking too much time to overcome obstacles. *Positive surprises* included: vacuuming better than expected, navigating better than expected, cleaning in areas participants thought it couldn't clean, picking up more dirt than expected, handling or recognizing obstacles better than expected, getting out of tight spaces, learning the environment, asking for human assistance with obstacles, not traversing the space randomly. *Neutral surprises* included traversing the space in unexpected ways, e.g., being able to move diagonally, or in a star-pattern.

Only three participants stated that there was nothing they wished their robot would do better. Others stated they wished their robots would be able to be better at: prioritizing areas that need cleaning, handling and avoiding obstacles, handling different types of flooring (e.g. carpets), learning the environment, cleaning the corners of the room. Participants also stated they wished the robot would work more quietly, traverse the space in a more predictable and/or intelligent way, have better suction, clean more efficiently or take less time to cover the space.

4 Discussion

This study acts as a preliminary investigation of how being at home impacts the way people use and perceive their DSRs, and how active observation impacts people's perceptions of its characteristics and abilities. With a convenience sample of 31 households, we cannot make definitive statements, however trends were found and insights regarding the BYOB methodology can be made.

From our results, it appears that the change to working-from-home may have had a limited impact on users' operation routines and the perceived importance of the robot. Possibly, this reflects our sample group, which consisted mainly of young couples without children (71%). It also may be a result of recollection biases [10], which likely influenced reported results relating to habits and perceptions before restrictions had taken place. In contrast to findings in [5, 6], which indicate hesitation to use robots when people are not home, many of our participants preferred to operate the robot in an empty house or without direct supervision. This may be a result of cultural differences between people in Israel and Switzerland, or a result of technological advances that have increased user trust over the past 7 years.

Most participants had at least one misperception regarding the way in which their robot handles various cleaning situations. This is consistent with the findings in [5, 6]. These misperceptions, however, did not impact the way they perceived the robot's competence, discomfort and satisfaction. Perhaps the end-result (cleanliness of the floors) is more impactful than the way in which the robot cleaned. In contrast, the robot's perceived safety was negatively impacted by the active observation. With growing opportunities to observe the robot in action when working from home, this is an issue of concern. Our analysis indicated that many participants were disappointed by how their robot responded to obstacles and traversed the space. They were also often uncomfortable with the noise their robots made. These unmet expectations could have negatively impacted the perceived safety of the robot [11]. To promote more positive perceptions, designers can try and isolate what aspects of the robots' behavior are perceived as unsafe during active observation and change them accordingly. Alternatively, they can encourage users to operate their DSRs remotely or while in another room.

Even though most of our participants owned their robot for over a year, we found that their perceptions of their robot and its abilities can change after active observation. Only four (13%) of our participants said there was nothing that surprised them about their robot's behavior during the activity. In naturalistic settings, people often multitask and operate their robots remotely, proximally but without direct supervision or with partial attention. This likely impacts the way they perceive their robot and its abilities. In contrast, in controlled experimental environments, active observation is frequently required. Researchers and designers should take this into consideration in the design of future studies; aiming to simulate more realistic settings, where participants split their attention between multiple goals and activities.

The BYOB idea to guide owners of DSRs through a remote unmoderated experiment in their own home has several strengths and limitations. On one hand, many insights relating to human-robot interaction can be extracted from this methodology, including information regarding people's perceptions and understanding of their robots, the types of failures their robots experience and how the robot objectively behaves in naturalistic environments. Having the experiment be self-guided from participants' homes provided naturalistic experimental settings, eliminated travel time, provided access to participants that cannot be in close proximity to the experimenters, and provided participants with complete flexibility regarding when to participate. The experiment being unmoderated reduced the amount of resources and time it took to complete, and eliminated operator-related biases (e.g. confirmation bias [12], the Hawthorne Effect [13]). The greatest limitation is that this method can only be applied to robots already in the market. In addition, participant experiences varied more than in controlled experiments, as we did not have complete control over the specific make of the robot, the time of day the activity was completed, the precise way participants executed the required tasks or the experimental environment. Our ability to obtain video-recordings of participant experiences was only partially successful, likely due to a lack of monetary incentives. The recordings we received varied more widely than in controlled experiments and were harder to analyze. Many alterations could be made to improve the BYOB methodology. For example, an instructional video can be added to detail how and in what conditions we would like participants to complete the interactive questionnaire. We hope that this preliminary investigation will open discussions on the extent to which remote, unmoderated experiments from participant homes should be used for evaluations of human-robot interactions.

Our results, while still preliminary, shed light on people's robot operation routines as they work from home and suggest that active observation of the robot's work may impact the way in which DSRs are perceived. Understanding how user presence impacts robot perceptions and how these perceptions could be evaluated remotely is important to being able to accommodate the changes brought upon us by COVID-19.

Appendix

4.1 Questions to Assess Presence at Home and Robot Operational Routines

1. How much time do you spend at home?
   (Mostly at home/not at home most of the day/variable presence)
2. How important is the robot to you?
   (Likert Scale; 1- not important at all, 5- very important)
3. How often do you operate your robot?
   (At least once a day, 2–4 times a week, once a week, once every two weeks, once a month or less)
4. What days do you operate your robot?
   (Multiple Choice (MC); No fixed days, fixed days during the work week, fixed days during weekends)
5. What times do you operate your robot?
   (MC; No fixed hours, mornings, afternoons, evenings, overnight)
6. What preparations do you make before operating your robot? (open question)
7. Under what conditions do you typically operate your robot?
8. What areas of the house do you ask the robot to clean,
   a) when people are at home, b) when no one is home?
   (only when someone can supervise, when people are home but without direct supervision, when no one is home, varies)
9. Does the robot's cleaning influence the types of activities members of the household engage in? (open question).

4.2 Questions to Assess Understanding of Robot Operation

10. How many times does the robot clean the same place?
    (I don't know, Once, Twice, More)
11. What strategy does the robot use to clean the floor?
    (I don't know, random path, back and forth, Warp and weft, outside in, inside out, other)
12. How does the robot handle a rug in its cleaning path?
    (MC; I don't know, goes on it and cleans to my satisfaction, goes on it but doesn't clean it well, goes around it, gets stuck, other)

13. How does the robot handle a shoe in its cleaning path?
    (MC; I don't know, pushes it, cleans around it, gets stuck on it, other)
14. How does the robot handle a chair in its cleaning path?
    (MC; I don't know, pushes it, cleans around it, cleans under it, gets stuck on it, other).

References

1. Thompson, C.: What If Working From Home Goes on…Forever?. New York Times (2020). https://www.nytimes.com/interactive/2020/06/09/magazine/remote-work-covid.html. Accessed 29 Jan 2021
2. PwC: It's time to reimagine where and how work will get done (2021). https://www.pwc.com/us/en/library/covid-19/us-remote-work-survey.html
3. Sheridan, T.B.: Human–robot interaction: status and challenges. Hum. Factors J. Hum. Factors Ergon. Soc. **58**, 525–532 (2016). SAGE Publications Sage CA: Los Angeles, CA. http://journals.sagepub.com/doi/10.1177/0018720816644364
4. Gittens, C.: Remote-HRI: a pilot study to evaluate a methodology for performing HRI research during the COVID-19 pandemic. In: Proceedings of the 54th Hawaii International Conference on System Science, p. 1878 (2021)
5. Vaussard, F., Fink, J., Bauwens, V., Rétornaz, P., Hamel, D., Dillenbourg, P., et al.: Lessons learned from robotic vacuum cleaners entering the home ecosystem. Rob. Auton. Syst. **62**, 376–391 (2014). Elsevier. https://linkinghub.elsevier.com/retrieve/pii/S0921889013001899
6. Fink, J., Bauwens, V., Kaplan, F., Dillenbourg, P.: Living with a vacuum cleaning robot. Int. J. Soc. Robot. **5**, 389–408 (2013). https://doi.org/10.1007/s12369-013-0190-2
7. Carpinella, C.M., Wyman, A.B., Perez, M.A., Stroessner, S.J.: The robotic social attributes scale (RoSAS). In: Proceedings of 2017 ACM/IEEE International Conference on Human-Robot Interaction, pp. 254–262. ACM, New York (2017). https://dl.acm.org/doi/10.1145/2909824.3020208
8. Bartneck, C., Kulić, D., Croft, E., Zoghbi, S.: Measurement instruments for the anthropomorphism, animacy, likeability, perceived intelligence, and perceived safety of robots. Int. J. Soc. Robot. **1**, 71–81 (2009). Springer. http://link.springer.com/10.1007/s12369-008-0001-3
9. Jääskeläinen, R.: Think-aloud protocol. Handb. Transl. Stud. **1**, 371–374 (2010). John Benjamins Publishing, Amsterdam/Philadelphia
10. Erdfelder, E., Brandt, M., Bröder, A.: Recollection biases in hindsight judgments. Soc. Cogn. Guilford Press **25**, 114–31 (2007)
11. Honig, S.S., Oron-Gilad, T., Zaichyk, H., Sarne-Fleischmann, V., Olatunji, S., Edan, Y.: Toward socially aware person-following robots. IEEE Trans. Cogn. Dev. Syst. **10**, 936–954 (2018). https://ieeexplore.ieee.org/document/8335753/
12. Nickerson, R.S.: Confirmation bias: a ubiquitous phenomenon in many guises. Rev. Gen. Psychol. **2**, 175 (1998). Educational Publishing Foundation
13. Jones, S.R.G.: Was there a Hawthorne effect? . Am. J. Soc. Univ. Chicago Press **98**, 451–68 (1992)

Evaluation of Different Degrees of Support in Human-Robot Cooperation at an Assembly Workstation Regarding Physiological Strain and Perceived Team Fluency

Verena Klaer[(✉)], Hendrik Groll, Jurij Wakula, and Tim Steinebach

Institute of Ergonomics and Human Factors, TU Darmstadt, D64287 Darmstadt, Germany
v.klaer@iad.tu-darmstadt.de

Abstract. This paper presents the results of an evaluation of two workflows for a human-robot collaboration at an assembly workstation at the Institute of Ergonomics and Human Factors. Using a skill-based task allocation, the first scenario (V1) is designed to achieve a time-efficient process design, while the other scenario (V2) emphasises more interaction between the collaborative robot and human as well as aiming to reduce the physical workload of the subject.

Two repetitions of each scenario are evaluated in a laboratory experiment with 11 participants. The total process assembly time, the active time portions of human and robot in the process, the physiological muscles strain of back, shoulders and upper extremities, and a subjective assessment of team fluency were measured.

The mean total cycle time was increased from 412.5 s (s = 95.3 s) for V1 to 455.1 s (s = 77.1 s) for V2, and the participants had more short breaks during the working process. While there were no significant differences between the two scenarios in terms of local physiological strain in the selected muscles and the subjective assessment, the concept of including physiological strain in the task allocation in a human robot dyad was overall successful for both scenarios. All in all, low local physiological strain was measured and the robot was assessed positively regarding teamwork, trust, robot attributes and team-success.

Keywords: Human robot cooperation · Small objects assembly · EMG · Team fluency · Task allocation

1 Introduction

Especially in flexible assembly lines, cooperative robots are used to maintain the versatility of humans while using the accurateness of robots. The goal to improve the ergonomic work situation of the workers while maintaining the process efficiency in production lines is among the most quoted reasons to introduce human robot cooperation [1]. This may well lead to conflicting goals, as a lower physiological strain does not necessarily lead to increased efficiency. Hence, these goals need to be incorporated early in the design processes of human-robot cooperation. In the early planning phase it is central to plan the

N. L. Black et al. (Eds.): IEA 2021, LNNS 223, pp. 291–299, 2022.
https://doi.org/10.1007/978-3-030-74614-8_35

task allocation between human and robot. The planning procedures that include human characteristics in the planning are mostly skill-based. However, by accessing the process in subtasks, these skill-based approach often does not take into account the ergonomics of the overall process for the human [2]. Also, in cooperation, the robot interacts with the worker and has therefore an impact on the workers and their work process [2]. Hence, the fluent transitions between the robot and human work process are often not considered in the allocation processes. Although many studies present the reduction of strain as a design goal, so far, there are only few examples of the evaluation of collaborative work stations with regard to the physiological strain of the participants [3].

This paper compares two scenarios based on a skill-based task allocation. According to the research gaps indicated above, the two scenarios are evaluated with regard to the time-efficiency of the process and the physiological strain of the participants. In addition, a subjective evaluation of the stress perception and an evaluation of the cooperation with regard to human-robot-team fluency is collected.

2   Task Allocation

The context of this study is the development of a workstation with a collaborative saywer robot for a small gearbox assembly (Fig. 1), which consists of eight components that are screwed together with 25 screws. Up to 16 variants of the gearbox can be built at the workstation with a total weight of 4.44 kg.

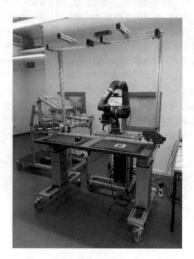

Fig. 1. Workstation for gear assembly.

The design of the station followed mainly the procedure of Schröter [4]. The criteria of the task allocation were extracted from literature, i.e. Malik and Bilberg [2, 5, 6]. The allocation criteria covered the properties of the used parts, the material supply, the attributes of the assembly process as well as a rating for the safety and the physical stress of the workers. With the help of these criteria, the automation potential of each subtask was calculated.

Based on the analysis of the automation potential the subtasks were allocated between the human and the robot. Due to technical limitations of the gripper, screwing processes was assigned to the human. The analysis showed high automation potentials to the tasks that included picking, transporting and placing of the parts.

Two different scenarios were derived from the task allocation. They included different levels of assistance and interaction. An extract of both work-processes can be seen in Fig. 2. V1 tested a low involvement of the robot by only picking and presenting large parts. This led to an efficient work design that included no planed idle time on the human side. In order to increase the robot involvement, V2 differed from V1 in two steps. Both steps included the handling and placing of assembly group 1 with a load about 2200 g, thus reducing the physical workload of the human.

Scenario 1 (V1)

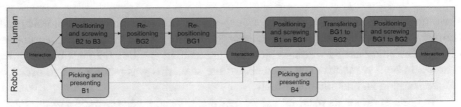

Scenario 2 (V2)

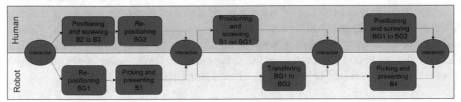

Fig. 2. Process flows for scenario V1 (top) and scenario V2 (bottom).

3 Methods and Study Design

3.1 Measurement Methods

The efficiency of the work process was evaluated using to the total process time (derived from the robot cycle time). In addition, the robot's control unit measured the time for each work step, which was used as an objective measurement for the team fluency according to the framework of Hoffmann [7]. Hence, the percentage of the total time of concurrent activity (C-ACT), the human's idle time (H-IDLE) and the robot's idle time (R-IDLE) were gathered.

The physiological strain - electrical activity (EA) - was measured with electromyography (EMG) following the AWMF guidelines. Since the task included mainly the handling of small weights and assembling tasks at the level of the upper body, the local physiological strain in the back and upper extremities, including shoulders, was assessed. The three muscles, m. deltoideus pars acromialis, m. bizeps brachii and m. extensor carpi ulnaris cover the upper extremities; m. erector spinae (trunci) covers the lower back. The electrical activity of each task was normalised with the maximum voluntary contraction and the mean static and dynamic EA throughout the two assembly processes was evaluated in each scenario. A 5 min long rest measurement was used as baseline.

The subjective perception of the workers was evaluated using the scales on team fluency [7]. It includes scales for the Human-Robot-team-fluency (TF), trust in the robot (TR), positive teammate traits (PT) and success of the team (EZ). All items were measured with a 7-point Likert scale. Furthermore, the subjective physiological exertion was evaluated also on a 7-point Likert scale.

3.2   Experiment Design

The study was carried out as a laboratory experiment at the Institute of Ergonomics and Human Factors of TU Darmstadt on the workstation for human robot collaboration (see Fig. 1). The study used a within-subject design, leading to all participants building the gearbox in both scenarios. The sequence of the scenarios was randomized in order to reduce learning and habituation effects.

First, the participants received safety instructions and a demonstration of the interaction possibilities with the robot. In addition, the EMG-system was installed and the maximal voluntary contraction of each muscle and rest measurement were gathered. Afterwards, a single gearbox was assembled as a test run to get to know the gearbox and the robot. Then, the gearbox was mounted twice in both versions (V1 and V2). The questionnaire was filled out after finishing each version in order to obtain an initial assessment of the subjective perception of the different characteristics.

3.3   Test Subjekts

Eleven subjects aged 18–29 (mean = 25.4) took part in the experiment. Four of them were female and seven male. All participants came from the TU Darmstadt.

The subjects participated voluntarily and were not compensated for their participation. One subject each stated that they had already assembled the gearbox once or had previous experience with collaborative robots. Furthermore, four subjects had experience in assembling and mounting.

4   Results

4.1   Process Efficiency

The mean total cycle time is 412.5 s (s = 95.3 s) for V1. For V2 the mean total cycle-time was 455.1 s (s = 77.1 s).

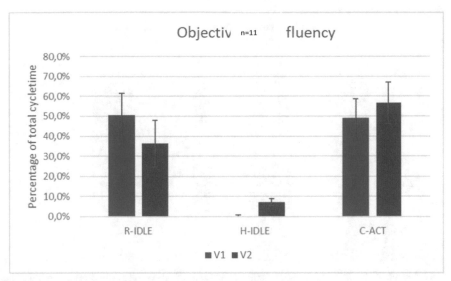

Fig. 3. Mean percentage active time portions for the human and robot: R-IDLE, H-IDLE and C-Act in percentage of the total cycle time in the versions V1 and V2

Regarding the active time portions of robot and human in the work process, the percentage shares of R-IDLE, C-ACT and H-IDLE in the total cycle time are calculated. These are plotted in Fig. 3. The mean R-IDLE was 50,6% ± 10,5% for V1 and 36% ± 12% for V2. One can see, that in V1 the percentage of H-IDLE nearly non-existent 0,2% ± 0,6%, while in V2 H-IDLE is taking 7% ± 2% of the total cycle time. C-ACT increased from 49% ± 9,6% of the total cycle time for V1 to 57% ± 10% for V2.

4.2 Subjective Assessment of Team Fluency

The subjective assessment of the team fluency was rated on a 7-point Likert scale. 1 indicates a negative inclination towards the robot and 7 points indicate a positive inclination towards the robot. The team fluency (TF) was rated with a mean of 5.91 ± 1,03 for V1 and 5.91 ± 0,79. Trust (TR) was rated with 6.14 ± 0.76 for V1 and 6.23 ± 0.42 for V2. The robot had positive teammate attributes (PT) with a mean of 5.58 ± 1.35 for V1 and 5.73 ± 1.31 for V2. The success was rated with 5.41 ± 0.75 and 5.61. ± 0.61. The physiological exertion was rated low with 1.91 ± 1.16 for V1 and 2 ± 1.28 for V2. T-test showed, that there is no significant difference (p > 0,05) between both scenarios (Fig. 4).

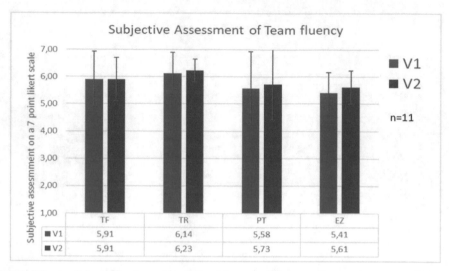

Fig. 4. Means of the subjective assessment of the team fluency scales rated on a 7-point Likert scale.

4.3 EMG

Dynamic and static EA-components in % MVC were evaluated and analysed for the scenario 1 and scenario 2. As can be seen in Table 1, the dynamic EA-component was similar for V1 and V2 in the muscles: m. biceps brachii, m. extensoe carpi ulnaris and m. erector spinae. There was a reduction of the dynamic EA in the m. deltoideus pars acromialis from 11.77% in V1 to 9.93% in V2. In the other muscles no reduction could be detected. The highest dynamic EA was measured for the m. extensor Carpi ulnaris with 18.29% MVC ± 16% and 18,79 ± 17%. However, as the high standard deviations indicate, these measures might result from single individuals.

5 Discussion

In this study, two different scenarios were compared regarding the efficiency of the process and the physiological strain of the participants. In addition, a subjective evaluation of the stress perception and an evaluation of the cooperation with regard to human-robot-team fluency are analysed.

As expected, the overall cycle time was lower for V1 compared to V2. Also, the human idle time was increased from V1 to V2. These short breaks could decrease the physiological, as well as the psychological strain of the worker in a full day's work. The physiological measurements are within the bounds of low risks of long-term damage. However, there only is a small difference in the mean dynamic EA-activity of the shoulder muscle. The forearm had the highest physiological strain. Hence, it could be feasible to enable the robot to take over some of the screwing activities, also to reduce the repetitivity for the work person.

The study does not indicate significant differences between the subjective assessment of the team fluency and the subjective assessment of the physiological strain. The

Table 1. Mean and Standard deviation of dynamic and static EA – components in % MVC for the Scenario 1 and Scenario 2 (n = 11)

	m. deltoideus pars acromialis		m. bizeps brachii		m. extensor Carpi ulnaris		m. erector spinae (trunci)	
	Mean	Standard deviation	Mean	Standard deviation	Mean	Standard deviation	Mean	Standard deviation
Dynamic EA in % MVC								
V1	11,77	±4,73	9,35	10	18,29	16	9,61	4
V2	9,93	±3,40	9,92	12	18,79	17	9,75	5
Static EA in % MVC								
V1	0,49	1,22	0,97	1	1,94	3	1,48	2
V2	0,20	0,83	0,81	1	1,11	1	1,45	2

subjective assessment is overall positive; especially trust in the robot and the human-robot team were rated highly. In addition, the participants rated the physiological strain of the work process moderately. These results are coherent with the study of Klaer et al., [8], in which the workstation and work process were assessed regarding the technology acceptance and received positive results.

The results of this study show that both scenarios would be feasible for the usage in an industrial environment. If the production time is crucial, V1 should be preferred.

The study is limited by the experience of the participants and by their small number. There are learning effects especially regarding the cycle time during the first three assembly processes. This should be taken into account by future studies, i.e. by extending the familiarisation phase. Also, the study was rather short with two repetitions for each scenario. More repetitions could lead to stronger effects, especially regarding the subjective assessment. Furthermore, the investigation of longterm effects of the imbalance of R-Idle and H-Idle would be interesting, especially whether the subjective assessment of the team fluency would align with the results of Hoffman [7].

Since the task is mainly using the upper extremities, further evaluations could focus on the m. extensor Carpi ulnaris und the m. deltoideus pars acromialis, if an increased efficiency is needed.

6 Conclusion

While there were no significant differences between the two scenarios in terms of local physiological strain, the concept of incorporating physiological strain in the analysis for the task allocation in a human robot dyad was overall successful. Thus low physiological strain shows both in the dynamic and static EMG as well as in the subjective assessment. All in all, the team fluency was also rated positively. The small differences between both scenarios show that both scenarios are feasible for a gear assembly and research on human robot cooperation, however, V1 should be preferred, if a smaller cycle-time is necessary. In order to achieve a more balanced workload in the dyad, a gripper enabling screwing for the robot could increase the overall performance of the work station.

References

1. Bauer, W., Bender, M., Braun, M., Rally, P., Scholtz, O.: Lightweight robots in manual assembly – best to start simply! Frauenhofer, Stuttgart (2016)
2. Buxbaum, H.-J.: Mensch-Roboter-Kollaboration. Springer Fachmedien Wiesbaden, Wiesbaden (2020)
3. Steidel, V., Gutzler, C.: Beanspruchungen durch die Mensch-Roboter-Kollaboration an industriellen Arbeitsplätzen: ein Überblick über den aktuellen Forschungsstand. In: Gesellschaft für Arbeitswissenschaft (ed.) Arbeit interdisziplinär, analysieren – bewerten – gestalten (2019)
4. Schröter, D.: Entwicklung einer Methodik zur Planung von Arbeitssystemen in Mensch-Roboter-Kooperation. Dissertation, Universität Stuttgart, Stuttgart (2017)
5. Malik, A., Bilberg, A.: Collaborative robots in assembly: a practical approach for tasks distribution. Procedia CIRP **81**, 665–670 (2019). https://doi.org/10.1016/j.procir.2019.03.173
6. Malik, A., Bilberg, A.: Complexity-based task allocation in human-robot collaborative assembly. In: IR 46 (4), pp. 471–480 (2019). https://doi.org/10.1108/IR-11-2018-0231

7. Hoffman, G.: Evaluating fluency in human-robot collaboration. IEEE Trans Hum. Mach. Syst. **49**(3), 209–218 (2019)
8. Klaer, V., Wakula, J.: Einfluss der Ausprägung des Handlungsspielraums in der Mensch-Roboter Kooperation bei einer Montageaufgabe auf die Akzeptanz der Arbeitsperson. Gesellschaft für Arbeitswissenschaft (ed.) Arbeit HumAIne gestalten

Field Study to Objectify the Stress and Strain on Male Workers During Car Wheel Changes in the Course of Using an Active Exoskeleton

Karsten Kluth$^{(\boxtimes)}$ ⓘ and Michael Hefferle ⓘ

Fachgebiet Arbeitswissenschaft/Ergonomie, Universität Siegen, Siegen, Germany
kluth@ergonomie.uni-siegen.de

Abstract. The aim of a field study was to prove whether the expected relief of the musculoskeletal system occurs when an active exoskeleton is used. For this purpose, the seasonal changing of car wheels was chosen as a work task. The active exoskeleton Cray X was used. The physical stress and strain of 10 professional workers during the wheel change was determined by measuring the heart rate, analyzing the work pulse and the energy expenditure. In addition, a survey was conducted with 20 employees to determine the physical stress in different body regions. When comparing the work performed with and without the exoskeleton, no significant difference was measured for the heart rate. The difference in the work pulses was only 2 beats per minute. The wheel change with active exoskeleton required an energy expenditure of 1073 kJ/h. When carried out without exoskeleton, only slightly reduced values for the energy expenditure (1066 kJ/h) were registered. However, the objectively undetectable relief is subjectively felt. The strongest differences of the different application scenarios are found for the lower and upper back (25% and 21% respectively) and for the lower and upper trunk (11% and 7% respectively) in favor of exoskeletal application. Nevertheless, it must be concluded, active exoskeletons cannot fundamentally protect the employee from medium and long-term musculoskeletal disorders by physically supporting the execution of movements.

Keywords: Manual material handling · Active exoskeleton · Ergospirometry · Heart rate · Subjective assessment

1 Introduction

In order to be able to make physically strenuous work in particular less stressful for the employee and thus hopefully also healthier, the use of active or passive exoskeletons is increasingly being evaluated in laboratory and field studies. Field studies on active exoskeletons are however still rare. Exoskeletons are supposed to relieve the hand-arm-shoulder system and the back, especially during handling procedures. Musculoskeletal complaints and diseases in these body regions represent a significant societal problem with a high burden for the health care systems, the economy and the affected persons themselves [1]. A causal relationship is hypothesized between, on the one hand, high and frequent force applications, repetitive activities, static muscle strains and, on the other hand, musculoskeletal complaints and diseases [2]. The passive and active support systems are now considered as an opportunity for prevention [3, 4]. The key operating principle of these assistive systems worn directly on the body is to transfer mechanical energy to the human body, thereby reducing physical stress on defined parts of the body [5].

Exoskeletons can be differentiated according to the type of energy supply, the body region supported, and the degree of fit to human anthropometry [6]. Already widely used are passive exoskeletons. These are usually a support frame that returns the energy absorbed and stored during a movement to the user for stabilization or movement support [6]. At the current state of the art, it is mainly passive exoskeletons that can be used for an industrial application. Here, there have been a variety of developments worldwide in recent years that have improved weight, wearing comfort and manageability.

In contrast, an exoskeleton is said to be "active" if it has one or more electrical and/or mechanical drive elements, pneumatic or hydraulic cylinders that enhance the performance of a user's joint system. Active systems are often still much heavier than passive systems and have yet to go through the development process of passive systems. However, development progress is readily apparent and the first systems are marketable, such as the "Cray X" from German Bionics used in the field study.

The current use case assembly or disassembly and storage or supply of car wheels represents work tasks that expose people to physical stress due to increased physical forces and unfavorable postures. In order to be able to evaluate such loads and stresses, a comparative field investigation was carried out during a car wheel change using the active exoskeleton "Cray X". The evaluation focused on the question of the physiological benefits but also the possible risks of the use of an active exoskeleton during car wheel changes under field conditions.

2 Methodology

As part of the objective and subjective analysis of working conditions with and without the use of an active "Cray X" exoskeleton, a field study was conducted in an automotive workshop. Only the use of the measurement technology and the simulated test environment or test conditions created an adapted laboratory "microcosm". The experiments were performed under a controlled condition, i.e. without exoskeleton, and under an intervened condition with the use of the "Cray X" exoskeleton. The starting test condition was changed in a controlled manner for each individual subject. The allocation of the subjects to the trials and thus to the start condition was randomized to prevent learning and sequence effects. The average age of the 20 male car mechanics was 24.9 ± 8.21 years with an average height of 178.4 ± 6.98 cm, a weight of 83.9 ± 16.09 kg and a BMI of 26.29 ± 4.17.

The mobile ergospirometry system "Cortex MetaMax 3B-R2" was used for the recording of the relevant physiological parameters. The spirometry device measures physical respiratory parameters using "Breath-by-Breath" or "Intra-Breath" measurement technique in- and expiratory oxygen uptake as well as respiratory flow delivery. The aim is to determine the energy expenditure under real working and environmental conditions. Furthermore, the system was coupled with the Polar® S810i heart rate measuring system.

The work task consisted of a typical wheel change on a working platform. The work phase consisted of the following work acts:

- unscrewing and removing of a total of four passenger car wheels with subsequent storage on the ground,
- storing or stacking four separate wheels, which were also on the ground, in a loading area at a height of 110 cm,
- mounting of the four wheels previously placed on the floor,
- tightening the individual wheel nuts,
- depositing the previously stacked wheels.

After the tests were conducted, the strain experience was evaluated using a modified body map [7] with the aid of the standardized scale from 0 "no stress" to 10 "maximum stress" and statistically analyzed [8]. The body map was used to evaluate both the front side of the body with a total of twelve different body parts and the back side of the body with six different body parts. A high degree of standardization was used to ensure the comparability of the responses of the different subjects. In addition, the degree of reliability of the results from standardized questionnaire surveys is always higher than with less standardized methods of a survey. The ordinal scaled data were analyzed using the non-parametric Wilcoxon signed rank sum test. Statistical significance was assumed from a significance value of 5%.

3 Results

In order to objectify the stress and strain of working with an exoskeleton, the assembly of motor vehicle wheels was analyzed from an occupational science perspective. In addition to body posture, the work-physiologically relevant parameters "heart rate", "work pulse" and "energy expenditure" were recorded. In the context of the objective presentation of results, an analytical statistical evaluation had to be omitted due to the small sample size of 10 subjects.

During the assembly tests, a near-optimal posture was ensured for a large proportion of the test subjects, regardless of whether the support system was used or not. In addition to an upright posture, a vertical downward upper arm position, an angular position between the upper and lower arm greater than 90°, and a gaze and head tilt of approx. 30–35° were also required. The test subjects also assumed a body position aligned "frontally" to the work task. The feet were about hip-width apart and turned slightly outward. This position formed a "relaxed, upright standing position." The position of the back and the position of the center of gravity of the load to be carried or lifted also have a significant influence on human stress and strain. If lifting and carrying is done with a straight back and close to the body, the resulting pressure is transmitted evenly to the intervertebral disc. There was an increased risk of incorrect stress on the intervertebral discs, particularly when picking up or putting down the wheels. Figure 1 shows by way of example that the test subjects differed in their posture or behavior during lifting and carrying. The manual handling of motor vehicle wheels corresponds to the handling of medium-heavy loads at an increased cycle frequency when the weight of a wheel of a BMW Mini is around 22 kg. If back complaints and movement pain occur as a result, e.g. due to a bent back posture (cf. Fig. 1, left), as is unavoidable when wearing the active exoskeleton, these lead to incorrect and relieving postures. This inevitably results in tension and further incorrect strain and damage to the intervertebral discs. Even with low load handling, it is important to reduce the prevailing compressive forces to a minimum with the aid of short lever arms, for example by lifting the wheels with the back or spine in a straight position from the knees, as can be seen in the right-hand illustration in Fig. 1.

Fig. 1. Body postures while picking up a wheel with (left) and without active exoskeleton "Cray X" (right).

The average time required to perform the work task is higher with the exoskeleton (37.85 s/work cycle) than without the support system (34.4 s/work cycle). The work pulse profiles measured in the tests show that both the storage and retrieval of the light alloy wheels weighing approx. 22 kg and the actual assembly and disassembly can be described as a physically demanding activity.

The average increase in heart rate without using the exoskeleton is 45 beats per minute (bpm). Although the heart rate "only" reaches 43 bpm when using the exoskeleton, both values are above the endurance level of 35 bpm compared to the resting heart rate measured in a sitting position. The average resting heart rate was 73 bpm (with and without exoskeleton). It should be kept in mind that the heart rate response to a given load depends on several influencing variables. In this context, it is important to note that every person experiences a decrease in maximum heart rate per year of life with increasing age. However, for the relatively young subject collective with an average age of 25.4 years, no problem with cardiac workload was yet to be expected. This is also shown by the calculations. The average heart rate was in relation to the maximum possible workload 61% when using the exoskeleton and 63% when not using the exoskeleton, and was therefore in the uncritical range.

After the presentation of the results of the work physiological parameter, which represents the strain side of the work, the energy expenditure represents the quantity with which the stress and thus the severity of the physical work can be characterized in a numerical value. The most important spirometric parameters include oxygen uptake, which averaged over all work subjects was 1.14 l/min when using the exoskeleton and 1.13 l/min without using the exoskeleton. The respiratory quotient was calculated from the oxygen uptake and the carbon dioxide output for both test scenarios in order to determine the energetic equivalent. The product of the energetic equivalent and the oxygen uptake per hour results in the gross energy expenditure.

In favor of a detailed comparison, gross energy expenditure must be broken down into basic energy expenditure and work energy expenditure, which depend on age, height and body mass. The latter represents the load experienced during work. The basal metabolic rate for an average age of 25.4 years and according to the Mifflin-St. Jeor formula [9] is 322 kJ/h or 89 W. Taking into account the efficiency of humans, which according to [10] is 5–10% in industrial activities, with a power input, i.e. work energy expenditure, of 1073 kJ/h or 298 W during the use of the "Cray X", at best 30 W were invested in the actual work task.

When the test was performed without an exoskeleton, only slightly reduced values were registered for the work energy expenditure (1066 kJ/h, 296 W). With just under 270 W, a considerable heat surplus was produced, assuming an average temperature or room temperature. With the help of respiratory parameters, different degrees of utilization of the entire cardiopulmonary system as a functional unit consisting of heart and lungs can be determined – similar to the degree of utilization of the heart for determining age-dependent strain. For this purpose, the oxygen uptake is set in relation to the maximum oxygen uptake, which defines the physical performance limit of the cardiopulmonary system [11]. The maximal oxygen uptake can then be calculated according to [12]. Thus, the subject collective can take up a maximum of about 3 l/min of oxygen. The degree of utilization of the cardiovascular system accordingly amounts to approx. 40% when using the exoskeleton, while a degree of utilization of 38% is recorded without support.

In order to be able to comparatively analyze the working conditions in the course of a motor vehicle wheel change when used with and without an exoskeleton, an important component of the holistic occupational science analysis was not only the objectification of the entire cardiopulmonary system, but also a personal statement by each individual test person regarding the subjectively perceived strain.

As the objective results already showed, the wheel change causes an increased physical strain. The assessment of the test subjects confirms this finding. The respondent collective now comprised 20 subjects with an average age of 24.9 years, whereby one subject had to be excluded due to missing information. In addition, individual subjects did not provide complete information, which reduced the sample for individual parameters. While only the neck and the buttocks caused a weak to moderate strain, the remaining parts of the body experienced a consistently increased strain. Upper and lower back, upper arms as well as knees and thighs experience a stronger (>6) and overall strongest strain on the scale from 0 to 10. The subjectively perceived additional strain is lower for the entire shoulder area, the trunk, the hips as well as for the back when using the "Cray X" than without its application. Only the upper extremities (with the exception of the elbow) as well as the neck and the feet register an additional strain during exoskeleton use, but these are marginal compared to use without support. The strongest differences of the different application scenarios are found for the lower and upper back (25% and 21% respectively) and for the lower and upper trunk (11% and 7% respectively) in favor of exoskeletal application (cp. Figure 2). The differences are significant for the upper (z = 2.79, p = 0.005, n = 17) and lower back (z = 2.82, p = 0.005, n = 18). While the activity without the use of the support system – especially for the lower back – is evaluated approximately as a very strong strain, the same task with the help of the exoskeleton is only "strenuous" from the subjects' point of view. If only the ten subjects from whom objective data were generated are considered in the context of the subjective feedback, the results are approximately confirmed in comparison to the entire collective.

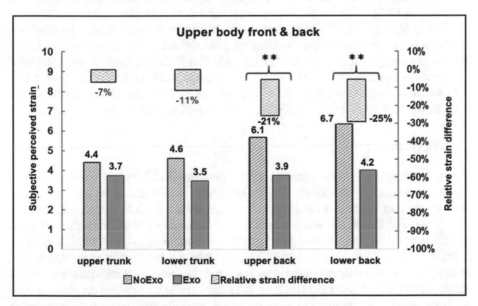

Fig. 2. Assessment of perceived strain in the upper and lower trunk as well as upper and lower back in the course of the work task. Mean values over 20 test subjects.

4   Discussion

The "Cray X" was specially designed to reduce the compression pressure in the lower back area when lifting heavy loads. If a manual handling with straight back is performed without exoskeleton and loads are lifted and carried close to the body, the pressure is evenly transferred to the intervertebral disc. In this case, the weight of the load and one's own body has only a relatively short lever arm to the spinal column. However, it has been shown that even basic ergonomically correct behavior, such as a straight back or lifting from the knees, is not fully maintained. When transporting the wheel, it is also difficult to carry the object, which weighs around 22 kg, close to the body due to its design, and postural work is therefore required. Overall, the partial processes can lead to compensatory hyperlordosis, i.e., discomfort in the back region or lumbar spine. Due to the increased demand for oxygen and the worsened blood circulation, the cardiovascular strain increases in addition to the muscular strain. All activities, including the assembly and disassembly of the wheels, are performed in a standing position. The employee is thus exposed to an increased energy expenditure during the entire work performance.

These findings are largely confirmed by the objective results. The work to be performed is individually connected with considerably less effort when using the "Cray X". However, the most expected support during the stacking or removal of the wheels with the help of the exoskeleton could only be proven to a limited extent. The objectively obtained data show slightly reduced values for the heart rate when using the exoskeleton. The energy expenditure is even marginally higher when using the "Cray X" than without. The weight of 8 kg of the exoskeleton contributes to this.

If a repetitive or high-frequency execution of the work task is assumed, the exoskeleton can thus generate physiological advantages for the user in the form of a reduction of the compression pressure in the lower back area. This finding is significantly confirmed by the subjectively perceived strain on the test persons, in particular by the fact that reduced strain on the back, trunk and hips was noted by using the active exoskeleton. In total, however, there is only a slight advantage in handling the wheels.

5 Conclusions

To what extent the activity analyzed here represents the fitting application scenario for an active-assistive exoskeleton is doubtful. After evaluation of the data, an overall view shows that only marginal differences were recorded. Only the pick-up and the setting down of the wheels was measurably and noticeably supported by the exoskeleton. However, this support is only really effective if the body posture without using an exoskeleton is not ergonomic, i.e. with legs stretched out and back bent. Irrespective of the application and implementation of such a support system, it seems sensible to inform employees about possible risks resulting from unfavorable postures and to provide them with comprehensive training in the areas of load handling and standing workplaces. A workplace analysis and an associated assessment of the implementation of exoskeletons are indispensable in order to generate efficient workplace conditions that minimize stress.

References

1. Burton, K., Kendall, N.: Musculoskeletal disorders. BMJ **348**, g1076 (2014)
2. Da Costa, B.R., Vieira, E.R.: Risk factors for work-related musculoskeletal disorders: a systematic review of recent longitudinal studies. Am. J. Ind. Med. **53**(3), 285–323 (2010)
3. De Looze, M.P., Bosch, T., Krause, F., Stadler, K.S., O'sullivan, L.W.: Exoskeletons for industrial application and their potential effects on physical work load. Ergonomics **59**(5), 671–681 (2016)

4. Epstein, S., Sparer, E.H., Tran, B.N., Ruan, Q.Z., Dennerlein, J.T., Singhal, D., Lee, B.T.: Prevalence of work-related musculoskeletal disorders among surgeons and interventionalists: a systematic review and meta-analysis. JAMA Surg. **153**(2), e174947 (2018)
5. Jezukaitis, P., Kapur, D.: Management of occupation-related musculoskeletal disorders. Best Pract. Res. Clin. Rheumatol. **25**(1), 117–29 (2011)
6. Huysamen, K., De Looze, M., Bosch, T., Ortiz, J., Toxiri, S., O'sullivan, L.W.: Assessment of an active industrial exoskeleton to aid dynamic lifting and lowering manual handling tasks. Appl. Ergon. **68**, 125–131 (2018)
7. Corlett, E.N., Bishop, R.P.: A technique for assessing postural discomfort. Ergonomics **19**(2), 175–182 (1976)
8. Borg, G.: Borg's perceived exertion and pain scales. Human Kinetics (1998)
9. Mifflin, M.D., St. Jeor, S.T., Hill, L.A., Scott, B.J., Daugherty, S.A., Koh, Y.O.: A new predictive equation for resting energy expenditure in healthy individuals. Am. J. Clin. Nutr. **51**(2), 241–247 (1990)
10. Strasser, H.: Physiologische Grundlagen zur Beurteilung menschlicher Arbeit – Belastung/Beanspruchung/Dauerleistung/Ermüdung/Streß. REFA-Nachrichten **39**(5), 18–29 (1986)
11. Wonisch, M., Fruhwald, F., Hödl, R., Hofmann, P., Klein, W., Kraxner, W., Maier, R., Pokan, R., Smekal, G., Watzinger, N.: Spirometrie in der Kardiologie – Grundlagen der Physiologie und Terminologie. Journal für Kardiologie Österreichische Zeitung für Herz-Kreislauferkrankungen **10**(9), 383–390 (2003)
12. Pothoff, G., Winter, U.J., Waßermann, K., Jäkel, D., Steinbach, M.: Ergospirometrische Normalkollektivuntersuchungen für ein Unsteadystate-Stufentestprogramm. Zeitschrift für Kardiologie **83**, 116–139 (1994)

Using Multimodal Data to Predict Surgeon Situation Awareness

Aurelien Lechappe[1,2,4], Mathieu Chollet[1,2], Jerome Rigaud[3],
and Caroline G. L. Cao[1,2,5(✉)]

[1] IMT Atlantique Bretagne-Pays de la Loire, Nantes, France
[2] Laboratoire des Sciences du Numérique de Nantes (LS2N), Nantes, France
[3] Centre Hospitalier Universitaire de Nantes, Nantes, France
[4] Université de Bretagne Occidentale (UBO), Brest, France
[5] Wright State University, Dayton, USA
`caroline.cao@wright.edu`

Abstract. The use of robotic surgical systems creates new team dynamics in operating rooms and constitutes a major challenge for the development of crucial non-technical skills such as situation awareness (SA). Techniques for assessing SA mostly rely on subjective assessments, observation or interviews; few utilize multimodal measures that combine physiological, behavioural, and subjective indicators. We proposed a conceptual model relating situation awareness with mental workload (MW), stress and communication. To validate this model, we collected subjective feedback, measurable behaviours and physiological signals from surgeons performing a robot-assisted radical prostatectomy procedure. Preliminary results suggest that subjective MW is a better indicator of SA than subjective stress. Physiological measures did not correlate with subjective measures of stress and MW. Results also suggest that some indicators of communication quality associated with various levels of SA tend to be linked with surgical complexity.

Keywords: Mental workload · Stress · Communication · Physiological signals · Robot-assisted surgery

1 Introduction

Many laparoscopic surgical procedures are increasingly performed with robotic assistance. Robot-assisted surgery (RAS) has many advantages for both patients and surgeons. However, the use of such devices creates new challenges inside the operating room. Unlike in traditional open surgery or laparoscopic surgery, the robot creates a physical barrier between the surgeon and the rest of the surgical team and the patient, leading to altered communication and team dynamics in the operating room (OR). In surgery, a lack of non-technical skills has been linked to a higher risk of surgical complications [1]. Non-technical skills such as communication, teamwork and decision-making are dependent on the operators' situation awareness (SA) [1]. In this complex environment, where distributed information is needed to perform the task, developing and maintaining SA can be difficult [2].

© The Author(s), under exclusive license to Springer Nature Switzerland AG 2022
N. L. Black et al. (Eds.): IEA 2021, LNNS 223, pp. 308–316, 2022.
https://doi.org/10.1007/978-3-030-74614-8_37

2   Situation Awareness: Definition and Assessment

2.1   Definition of Situation Awareness

Endsley [3] defines SA as "The perception of the elements in the environment within a volume of time and space, the comprehension of their meaning, and the projection of their status in the near future" (p. 36). Yule et al. [4] propose a similar definition applied to surgery: "developing and maintaining a dynamic awareness of the situation in the operating room, based on assembling data from the environment (patient, team, time, displays, equipment), understanding what they mean, and thinking ahead about what may happen next". Smith and Hancock [5] propose a definition considering the influence of other factors on SA and describes this concept as an "adaptive, externally directed consciousness directly related to stress, mental workload, and other energetic constructs that are facets of consciousness" (p. 138). Therefore, the influence of other cognitive factors have to be considered for assessing SA.

2.2   Assessment of Situation Awareness

Several techniques for assessing SA have been developed [6]. One of these, called "Freeze-probe technique" requires the operator to take a pause during the execution of a task to answer questions about the situation (e.g., Endsley's SAGAT survey [7]). This technique has not been applied to robotic surgery but has been applied in the medical area [2]. The "Real-time probe technique" is similar except that the questions are administered while the action is being performed without pause. Situation awareness can also be assessed using self-rating techniques such as the SART questionnaire [8]. Less intrusive techniques for assessing SA include observations by experts [6]. Some observation scales focus on assessing an individual operator (e.g., NOTSS [4], ICARS [9]), while others assess each team member and then derive an overall team score from individual assessments (e.g., OTAS [10], SPLINTS [11]). Performance measures can also be used to assess SA [12], as can psychophysiological indicators such as eye-tracking measures [13], EEG [14] and cardiac activity [15].

SA is a complex cognitive process functioning at a higher level, with underlying factors such as stress and MW [16]. Thus, an alternative technique for SA assessment would be to measure some of the factors underlying this development using psychophysiological and behavioural measures. Stress, MW and communication are measurable factors that we consider in our SA model since they are described as having an influence on SA [5, 17].

3   Model and Hypothesis

We proposed a novel framework for understanding SA in RAS contexts, and modeled SA and its relationship with measurable multimodal variables, such as communication, mental workload (MW), stress, heart rate and skin conductance [18]. In this model (Fig. 1), stress and MW influence each other [19], presumably varying in a similar way. Stress influences SA [20, 21]. In particular, stressed operators may still believe they have good SA, while their mental model of the situation actually diverges from reality, increasing operational risks. Mental workload influences SA, which may vary depending on the context [22]. Additionally, MW and stress have an influence on team communication quality [21]. Finally, communication quality influences SA [17, 23]. For example, low SA may be associated with repetitions, lack of action verbalization and the emergence of off-topic discussion in surgery, while high SA may be associated with numerous action verbalization, and with proximity to the operating table [24].

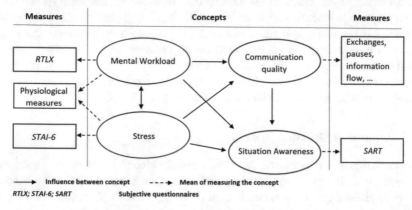

Fig. 1. Graphical representation of our SA model [18]

The main objective of this research is to validate the proposed model for assessing SA in RAS with multimodal data. We hypothesized the following:

- **H1** Physiological changes should be observed with variations in mental workload and stress levels.
- **H2** Situation awareness can be influenced by the mental workload level on the one hand, and stress on the other.
- **H3** Situation awareness is influenced by communication quality.

4 Method

To validate the model, we collected data from three surgeons of varying levels of experience, who collectively performed a total of seven radical prostatectomy procedures using a da Vinci Xi Robotic Surgical System.

4.1 Materials

Self-rating Questionnaires. STAI-6, RTLX and SART, which respectively measures stress, MW and SA, were used to gather subjective feedback from the surgeons at predefined interruption points during the surgery. The STAI-6 [25] is an effective scale for assessing perceived stress [6]. The RTLX [26] is a short version of the NASA-TLX, sensitive to variations in MW in laparoscopic surgery. We removed the "physical demand" subscale as it is less relevant to our context. Finally, the SART [8] measures an operator's subjective SA.

Physiological Measures. An Empatica E4 sensor was used to collect surgeons' physiological responses such as skin conductance (EDA), heart rate (HR), and heart rate variability (HRV) throughout the procedure [27]. HR is collected at a frequency of 1 Hz and EDA at a frequency of 4 Hz.

Communication Indicators. Transcriptions of the surgeons' verbalizations were recorded and annotated with a behaviour coding scheme. In this scheme, three types of exchanges related to the procedure: Requests for task execution, action verbalizations and teaching. Other exchanges can be related to surgical or robotic materials or irrelevant to the surgery. Total ratios for each exchange type were calculated for all phases of surgery to normalize the data since phases do not have the same duration. Communication indicators of SA, such as silences, interactions related to surgical task execution, action verbalization, teaching and irrelevant discussions, were noted [24].

4.2 Procedure

At the start of each surgical procedure, the surgical team was informed of the necessary interruptions to collect data. Four interruption points were selected based on consultation with expert surgeons to ensure minimal risk of distraction or surgical complications due to the interruption. During these breaks, the surgeon completed the three self-rating questionnaires on stress, MW and SA. Throughout the surgical procedure, audio-visual and Empatica recordings were continuous.

5 Results

Scores of each questionnaire for all interruption points were analysed using repeated measures ANOVA followed by a linear regression analysis. A similar analysis was performed on the physiological data, and the RTLX and STAI-6 questionnaires for correlations with MW or stress. In addition, each surgeon was asked to rank order the four surgical phases as a function of perceived difficulty (1: easiest; 2: easy; 3: complex; 4: most complex phase). Friedman-test and Wilcoxon test were performed to analyse differences in communication patterns across these surgical phases. In these preliminary analyses, we chose to set the p value at 0.1 [32].

5.1 Self-rating Questionnaires

There were no significant differences across surgical phases for the three questionnaires: SART ($F(3, 18) = 1.885$; $p = .17$); RTLX ($F(3, 18) = 1,887$; $p = .17$); STAI-6 ($F(3, 18) = 0.623$; $p = .61$). The analyses also showed no correlation between SA and stress level ($t(26) = -0.761, p = .45$), but a significant correlation between SA and MW level ($t(26) = 6.981, p < .001$). Mental workload and SA scores evolved similarly for each phase of the procedure.

5.2 Physiological Measures

Due to artefacts on the HR data, only three surgeries with valid HR and HRV data and seven with valid EDA data were analysed. While analysis showed significant differences between phases of the procedure for HR ($F(3, 6) = 7.224$; $p = .02$) and HRV measurements ($F(3, 6) = 8.014$; $p = .016$), pairwise comparisons showed no significant difference between each phase of the procedure for these physiological measurements. Skin conductance levels were not significant different between phases of the procedure ($F(3, 18) = 2.207$; $p = .12$). Pairwise comparisons showed similar results. Furthermore, analyses indicated no correlation between all physiological indicators and subjective measures of stress and MW.

5.3 Communication Indicators

We analysed the patterns of all communication indicators as a function of the complexity of the four surgical phases. The ratio of silent periods was not different between phases ($X2(3) = 0.429$, $p = .93$), neither was the ratio of verbal exchanges relative to the task execution, ($X2(3) = 5.914$, $p = .12$). However, one-tailed Wilcoxon tests showed significantly more interactions relative to the task execution in the most complex (4) and complex (3) phases than the easiest (1) phase (4-1: $Z = 25$, $p = .04$; 3-1: $Z = 25$, $p = .04$). There was significantly more interaction relative to task execution in the easy (2) phase than the easiest (1) phase (2-1: $Z = 22$, $p = .11$). Other tests showed no differences.

Analysis of action verbalization showed a significant difference between the phases ($X2(3) = 6.6$, $p = .09$). One-tailed Wilcoxon tests showed significantly more action verbalization exchanges in the most complex (4) phase than the easiest (1) ($Z = 24$, $p = .05$). They also showed more action verbalization exchanges in the most complex phase (4) than the complex phase (3) ($Z = 27$, $p = .016$).

No differences in teaching exchanges were found between the different phases ($X2(3) = 5.435$, $p = .14$). However, one-tailed Wilcoxon tests showed significantly more teaching exchanges in the easiest phase (1) than all other three phases (1-4: $Z = 2$, $p = .047$; 1-3: $Z = 25$, $p = .039$; 1-2: $Z = 27$, $p = .016$). Finally, analysis of irrelevant discussions showed no differences between the phases ($X2(3) = 1.258$, $p = .74$).

6 Discussion

6.1 Physiological Measures, Mental Workload and Stress

The results obtained do not support our first hypothesis (H1) that we should observe physiological changes related to changes in stress and MW. A first explanation of these results could be the limitations of the Empatica e4 sensor. Indeed, recent studies have shown that the data collected by this sensor could be strongly degraded due to its low recording frequency and the presence of artefacts related to the wrist-device's high sensitivity to movement [28]. These authors also discussed the validity of EDA and HRV measurements and their derived parameters measured by this sensor due to the limitations presented above. Other explanations include the small number of surgical procedures studied, as well as the large individual differences in physiological data.

We chose the Empatica e4 sensor for its ease of application and placement in the operating room, since environmental constraints severely limit the type of device that can be used. However, considering the difficulties to collect valid physiological data with this wrist-worn sensor, it would be prudent to consider the use of different measuring devices such as jackets with embedded physiological sensors instead. These alternate devices could be worn by all members of the surgical team without disrupting the sterile field in the operating environment.

6.2 Situation Awareness, Mental Workload and Stress

With regard to our second hypothesis (H2), results did not confirm the role of stress measured by questionnaire as an indicator of SA, but MW was. Although the STAI-6 scale has already been successfully used to assess stress associated with the execution of surgical tasks [6], it would appear that it is not suitable for repeated measurement of the stress felt by operators in a real surgical situation. Regarding MW and SA, our results showed that these two constructs evolved similarly for each phase of the procedure. Several hypotheses can explain these results. Endsley [29] questions the design of the SART questionnaire, which would evaluate cognitive processes close to MW. Another hypothesis supported by some authors [22, 30, 31] is that a high but reasonable MW would be necessary to achieve a high level of SA.

Future research could attempt to test our model using more appropriate measurement methods for assessment in a real surgical context. Research could be performed to find a more relevant stress measurement for this context. Future studies could also work on the design of an evaluation tool based on the SAGAT questionnaire [7], which would provide a more reliable measure of the operator's SA. The assessment tool should focus on items directly related to the situation.

6.3 Communication Quality, Task Complexity and Situation Awareness

To test H3, we analysed surgeons' communication patterns according to the complexity of the surgical phases in order to assess if some indicators associated with various SA levels are related to task complexity.

Silences and exchanges related to the task execution were analysed with the expectation that surgeons' communications decrease, and task execution exchanges increase, with task complexity, presumably due to increased MW and stress. Results showed that surgeons performed more task execution exchanges in the two complex (3,4) phases compared to the easiest (1) and tended to perform more task execution exchanges in the easy (2) phase than the easiest (1) phase. However, no differences in silence patterns were found between the phases of different complexity. According to the literature, these results about surgeons' verbalization and teaching exchanges would suggest better SA in more complex compared to easier phases. Indeed, high SA has been linked to increased verbalizations, and a lack of verbalizations with low SA [24]. Here, surgeons performed more verbalizations in the most complex (4) phase as compared to the complex (3) and the easiest (1) phases. Similarly, the emergence of off-topic exchanges such as teaching and irrelevant discussions has been linked to low SA [21]. Our results showed that surgeons performed more teaching exchanges in the easiest (1) phase than in other phases. Irrelevant discussions did not differ significantly across phases.

In general, most of the significant results regarding communication patterns were between the easiest and most complex phases. A potential explanation could be that the different phases of the prostatectomy procedure that we selected do not have large enough differences in terms of surgical complexity. This could also be directly due to the radical prostatectomy procedure, which could be an overly standardized procedure with small differences in complexity between each step of the procedure. This point could also explain why no significant differences were found between the different phases for the RTLX, and SART scores.

Other factors potentially influencing communication during surgery could include the number of operators in the operating room, their familiarity, or the level's experience of each operator in the considered surgery. While our results did not fully validate the hypothesis that surgeons' communication patterns are influenced by task complexity, and that communication quality influences SA, we observed some interesting results about action verbalization and teaching exchanges that can be linked with surgeons' SA. However, it should be noted that the interpretation of the data is to be moderated given the presence of some uncontrolled factors discussed above, and the small sample of surgeons studied. Nevertheless, these results may provide insights for preparing future studies in this field.

7 Conclusion

We presented an exploratory study where we collected preliminary data in order to validate a model of operators' situation awareness and its relationship with mental workload, stress and team communication. This study attests to the difficulty of developing a method to assess SA using multimodal parameters such as subjective, physiological and behavioural indicators. Contrary to our conceptual model, preliminary data did not support the role of stress as an indicator of SA, while MW was supported. The physiological data were noisy and thus inconclusive. Finally, the analysis of surgeons' communication patterns according to phase complexity raised potential trends of interest, but the presence of uncontrolled factors prevailed.

Future research to validate our model should involve a larger sample of surgeons, more reliable physiological sensors, different measures of stress and SA (e.g., SAGAT questionnaire), and perhaps with a surgical procedure with phases presenting larger differences in complexity. Finally, given the collaborative nature of the surgical team, it might be valuable to assess SA for the entire surgical team and not just the surgeon.

References

1. Pradarelli, J.C., Yule, S., Smink, D.S.: Evaluating non-technical skills in surgery. In: Dimick, J.B., Lubitz, C.C. (eds.) Health Services Research, pp. 125–135. Springer, Cham (2020). https://doi.org/10.1007/978-3-030-28357-5_12

2. Gardner, A.K., Kosemund, M., Martinez, J.: Examining the feasibility and predictive validity of the SAGAT tool to assess situation awareness among medical trainees. Simul. Healthc. **12**, 17–21 (2017). https://doi.org/10.1097/SIH.0000000000000181

3. Endsley, M.R.: Toward a theory of situation awareness in dynamic systems. Hum. Factors **37**, 32–64 (1995). https://doi.org/10.1518/001872095779049543

4. Yule, S., Flin, R., Paterson-Brown, S., Maran, N., Rowley, D.: Development of a rating system for surgeons' non-technical skills. Med. Educ. **40**, 1098–1104 (2006). https://doi.org/10.1111/j.1365-2929.2006.02610.x

5. Smith, K., Hancock, P.: Situation awareness is adaptive, externally directed consciousness. Hum. Factors: J. Hum. Factors Ergon. Soc. **37**, 137–148 (1995). https://doi.org/10.1518/001872095779049444

6. Anderson-Montoya, B.L., Scerbo, M.W.: Human factors psychology in surgery. In: Stefanidis, D., Korndorffer, J.R., Sweet, R. (eds.) Comprehensive Healthcare Simulation: Surgery and Surgical Subspecialties, pp. 153–167. Springer, Cham (2019). https://doi.org/10.1007/978-3-319-98276-2_14

7. Endsley, M.R.: Situation awareness global assessment technique (SAGAT). In: Proceedings of the IEEE 1988 National Aerospace and Electronics Conference, Dayton, OH, USA, pp. 789–795. IEEE (1988). https://doi.org/10.1109/NAECON.1988.195097

8. Selcon, S.J., Taylor, R.M.: Evaluation of the situational awareness rating technique (SART) as a tool for aircrew systems design. AGARD, Situational Awareness in Aerospace Operations 8 p (SEE N 90-28972 23-53) (1990)

9. Raison, N., Wood, T., Brunckhorst, O., Abe, T., Ross, T., Challacombe, B., Khan, M.S., Novara, G., Buffi, N., Van Der Poel, H., McIlhenny, C., Dasgupta, P., Ahmed, K.: Development and validation of a tool for non-technical skills evaluation in robotic surgery—the ICARS system. Surg. Endosc. **31**, 5403–5410 (2017). https://doi.org/10.1007/s00464-017-5622-x

10. Healey, A.N., Undre, S., Sevdalis, N., Koutantji, M., Vincent, C.A.: The complexity of measuring interprofessional teamwork in the operating theatre. J. Interprof. Care **20**, 485–495 (2006)

11. Mitchell, L., Flin, R., Yule, S., Mitchell, J., Coutts, K., Youngson, G.: Development of a behavioural marker system for scrub practitioners' non-technical skills (SPLINTS system): SPLINTS behavioural marker system. J. Eval. Clin. Pract. **19**, 317–323 (2013). https://doi.org/10.1111/j.1365-2753.2012.01825.x

12. Endsley, M.: Measurement of situation awareness in dynamic systems. Hum. Factors **37**, 65 (1995). https://doi.org/10.1518/001872095779049499

13. Tien, G., Atkins, M.S., Zheng, B., Swindells, C.: Measuring situation awareness of surgeons in laparoscopic training. In: Proceedings of the 2010 Symposium on Eye-Tracking Research & Applications, pp. 149–152 (2010)

14. Fernandez Rojas, R., Debie, E., Fidock, J., Barlow, M., Kasmarik, K., Anavatti, S.G., Garratt, M., Abbass, H.: Encephalographic assessment of situation awareness in teleoperation of human-swarm teaming. In: Gedeon, T., Wong, K.W., and Lee, M. (eds.) Neural Information Processing, pp. 530–539. Springer, Cham (2019). https://doi.org/10.1007/978-3-030-36808-1_58

15. Mehta, R.K., Peres, S.C., Shortz, A.E., Hoyle, W., Lee, M., Saini, G., Chan, H.-C., Pryor, M.W.: Operator situation awareness and physiological states during offshore well control scenarios. J. Loss Prev. Process Ind. **55**, 332–337 (2018). https://doi.org/10.1016/j.jlp.2018.07.010

16. Koester, T.: Situation awareness and situation dependent behaviour adjustment in the maritime work domain. Hum.-Centered Comput. Cogn. Soc. Ergon. Aspects. **3**, 255 (2019)

17. Nofi, A.A.: Defining and Measuring Shared Situational Awareness. Center for Naval Analyses, Alexandria (2000)

18. Lechappe, A., Chollet, M., Rigaud, J., Cao, C.G.L.: Assessment of situation awareness during robotic surgery using multimodal data. In: Companion Publication of the 2020 International Conference on Multimodal Interaction, pp. 412–416. Association for Computing Machinery, New York (2020) https://doi.org/10.1145/3395035.3425205

19. Karim, R.U.: The effect of stress on task capacity and situational awareness. Doctoral dissertation, North Dakota State University of Agriculture and Applied Science (2012)

20. Price, T., Tenan, M., Head, J., Maslin, W., LaFiandra, M.: Acute stress causes overconfidence in situation awareness. In: 2016 IEEE International Multi-Disciplinary Conference on Cognitive Methods in Situation Awareness and Decision Support (CogSIMA), pp. 1–6 (2016). https://doi.org/10.1109/COGSIMA.2016.7497778

21. Wheelock, A., Suliman, A., Wharton, R., Babu, E.D., Hull, L., Vincent, C., Sevdalis, N., Arora, S.: The impact of operating room distractions on stress, workload, and teamwork. Ann. Surg. **261**, 1079–1084 (2015). https://doi.org/10.1097/SLA.0000000000001051

22. Vidulich, M.A.: The relationship between mental workload and situation awareness. In: Proceedings of the Human Factors and Ergonomics Society Annual Meeting, vol. 44, pp. 3-460–3-463 (2000). https://doi.org/10.1177/154193120004402122

23. Parush, A., Kramer, C., Foster-Hunt, T., Momtahan, K., Hunter, A., Sohmer, B.: Communication and team situation awareness in the OR: implications for augmentative information display. J. Biomed. Inf. **44**, 477–485 (2011). https://doi.org/10.1016/j.jbi.2010.04.002

24. Randell, R., Honey, S., Hindmarsh, J., Alvarado, N., Greenhalgh, J., Pearman, A., Long, A., Cope, A., Gill, A., Gardner, P., Kotze, A., Wilkinson, D., Jayne, D., Croft, J., Dowding, D.: A realist process evaluation of robot-assisted surgery: integration into routine practice and impacts on communication, collaboration and decision-making. Health Serv. Deliv. Res. **5**, 1–140 (2017). https://doi.org/10.3310/hsdr05200

25. Marteau, T.M., Bekker, H.: The development of a six-item short-form of the state scale of the Spielberger State—Trait Anxiety Inventory (STAI). Br. J. Clin. Psychol. **31**, 301–306 (1992). https://doi.org/10.1111/j.2044-8260.1992.tb00997.x

26. Byers, J.C.: Traditional and raw task load index (TLX) correlations: Are paired comparisons necessary? Adv. Ind. Ergon. Saf. **1**, 481–485 (1989)

27. Echeverria, V., Martinez-Maldonado, R., Buckingham Shum, S.: Towards collaboration translucence: giving meaning to multimodal group data. In: Proceedings of the 2019 CHI Conference on Human Factors in Computing Systems, pp. 1–16 (2019)

28. Milstein, N., Gordon, I.: Validating measures of electrodermal activity and heart rate variability derived drom the Empatica E4 utilized in research settings that involve interactive dyadic states. Front. Behav. Neurosci. **14**, 148 (2020). https://doi.org/10.3389/fnbeh.2020.00148

29. Endsley, M.R.: The divergence of objective and subjective situation awareness: a meta-analysis. J. Cogn. Eng. Decis. Making **14**, 34–53 (2020). https://doi.org/10.1177/1555343419874248

30. Hendy, K.C.: Situation awareness and workload: Birds of a feather? Defence and Civil Institute of Environmental Medicine (1995)

31. Lee, Y.H., Jeon, J.-D., Choi, Y.-C.: Air traffic controllers' situation awareness and workload under dynamic air traffic situations. Transp. J. **51**, 338–352 (2012). https://doi.org/10.5325/transportationj.51.3.0338

32. Wasserstein, R.L., Schirm, A.L., Lazar, N.A.: Moving to a world beyond 'p < 0.05'. The American Statistician (2020). https://doi.org/10.1080/00031305.2019.1583913

Preliminary Requirements of a Soft Upper-Limb Exoskeleton for Industrial Overhead Tasks Based on Biomechanical Analysis

Dario Panariello[1,2]($\boxtimes$), Stanislao Grazioso[1], Teodorico Caporaso[1], Giuseppe Di Gironimo[1], and Antonio Lanzotti[1]

[1] Fraunhofer Joint Lab IDEAS, Department of Industrial Engineering, University of Naples Federico II, 80125 Napoli, Italy
[2] Department of Management, Information and Production Engineering, University of Bergamo, 24044 Dalmine, Italy
dario.panariello@unibg.it

Abstract. In this work we derive the requirements of a soft upper-limb exoskeletons starting from the biomechanical analysis of human workers while performing three different industrial overhead tasks in laboratory settings. The results of the work allow to define the degrees of freedom which need to be supported to reduce the biomechanical overloads, as well the dimensional characteristics, in terms of required lengths and forces, of the soft actuators of the wearable robot.

Keywords: Design · Biomechanics · Wearable robotics · Soft robotics · Soft exoskeleton · Industrial tasks

1 Introduction

Overhead tasks are considered as the most demanding tasks for the workers in assembly lines within the automotive industry [1]. These tasks are difficult to automate since they are really complex and usually involve the production of multiple variants of the same product; therefore, they are currently performed by workers alone [2].

In the last decade, wearable robots for upper limbs have been implemented in industrial practice to reduce the biomechanical overloading and fatigue of the worker during daily work. The most adopted technologies in industry are rigid exoskeletons, which include passive and active systems [3]. These systems are usually designed schematizing the shoulder as a 3 degrees of freedom (DOF) spherical joint, reproducing the behaviour of glenohumeral joint and neglecting the others articulations, i.e. scapulothoracic, sternoclavicular and acromioclavicular joints [4]. In the same way, the elbow joint is usually modeled as fixed joint; however, the natural elbow axis is not fixed but moves along the surface of a double conic frustum [5]. These hypotheses cause joint alignment problems [6]: it is recognized that the motion of rigid exoskeletons is perceived as non-natural for humans. Furthermore, rigid exoskeletons are invasive for the workers and, being bulky, in most of cases, they require a modification of workplaces.

N. L. Black et al. (Eds.): IEA 2021, LNNS 223, pp. 317–324, 2022.
https://doi.org/10.1007/978-3-030-74614-8_38

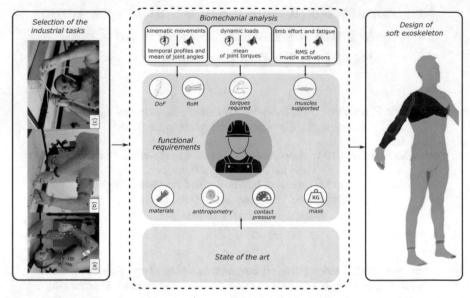

Fig. 1. The proposed biomechanical-based process to derive the functional requirements of a soft industrial exoskeleton.

Advancements in soft materials and bioinspired design have led to promising solutions for wearable robots. Soft exoskeletons have revolutionized the concept of motion assistance to human beings, in terms of invasiveness and natural human-robot interaction, as they are not related to a rigid structure but directly to human anatomy. The development of commercially available solutions of soft exoskeletons in the future might encouraging the widespread adoption of assistance devices in industry. The currently available actuation methods of soft wearable robots are based on [7]: (i) cable-driven systems, that generate the required movements and forces through cables (or tendons) [8]; (ii) fluid-driven soft actuators (or pneumatic actuators) [9], that generate specific movements and forces when pressurized, due to their particular design. They mimic the mechanisms of human muscles, and are usually based on fabric-based inflatables and textiles [9] or on pneumatic artificial muscles (PAM) [10].

Most of soft exoskeletons that have been designed and developed in the last years are intended to be used in assistive daily living tasks and rehabilitative applications, since they require lower forces than industrial applications. The recent developments of PAM and textiles able to generate ever higher forces could allow the use of soft wearable robots also in industrial settings [7].

In this work, we derive the functional requirement of a soft exoskeleton intended to assist human workers in performing overhead tasks. These requirements are derived by analysing the biomechanical behavior of human workers during the execution of such tasks in laboratory settings and from state-of-the-art considerations. The basic flowchart of the adopted methodology is illustrated in Fig. 1, which underlines the idea of developing user-centered wearable systems from understanding the human motor control [11].

2 Biomechanical Analysis of Overhead Tasks

Three different overhead tasks, i.e. drilling, leveraging and cabling tasks, are performed at ErgoS Lab, the Laboratory of Advanced Measures on Ergonomics and Shapes at CeSMA University of Naples Federico II.

2.1 Participants and Experimental Tasks

Participants. Four right-hand volunteer subjects (n = 4), mean age: 24 years (±5), weight: 84.9 kg (±8.5) and height: 182.5 cm (±6.8), were selected from the local population to participate in the study. All participants did not report any musculoskeletal disorders or problems over the past twelve months and they do not have or have limited experience with industrial work.

Task Setup. The experimental platform used to carry out the overhead tasks is composed by four circular section poles (height-adjustable), which support an overhead platform composed by a rectangular structure (square section).

Task Description. The overhead tasks selected for the experiments are tasks typically performed in the automotive industry. They were chosen in order to replicate tasks with different movements, weight of the tool and complexity [12]. The working heights selected to perform the tasks depend on the anthropometric characteristics of the subject, as defined in [13]. The description of the tasks are reported in the following. Drilling task (DT): the subjects were asked to drill a wooden beam (dimension: 70×70 mm) using a drill (weight: 1850 g) with a wood tip of diameter 10 mm, as illustrated in Fig. 1a; each trial consisted in three work cycles. Leveraging task (LT): the subjects were asked to clamp 3 bolts with 2 wrenches (weight: 70 g). The bolts were fixed on aluminum profile (dimension: $36 \times 36 \times 2$ mm), as shown in Fig. 1b; each trial consisted in three work cycles. Cabling task (CT): the subjects were asked to insert the cable inside a hole and finally to perform a knot with both hands, as illustrated in Fig. 1c; this task represents a simulated light assembly tasks where the subjects do not use a tool. For each trial the subjects carried out one work cycle. For all the tasks, two trials were conducted and the recovery time between two consecutive tests was chosen equal to 50% of the duration of the test.

2.2 Experimental Equipment and Measurement Protocols

Experimental Equipment. Ten infrared digital cameras, sampling frequency: 340 Hz (SMART DX 6000, BTS Bioengineering), are used as tracking system. Eight integrated force platforms, sampling frequency: 680 Hz (P-600, BTS Bioengineering), are used to measure the ground reaction forces. Six EMG sensors (FREEEMG 1000, BTS Bioengineering) are used to measure the muscle activations.

Measurements Protocols. An ad-hoc measurement protocol, composed of twelve markers placed on the upper body, was used in the experiments [14]. The identified markers allow to reconstruct the motion of the joint angles reported in Table 1. The EMG sensors, instead, were placed on the subjects' right upper limb according to [15] and following the indications given by the SENIAM project. In particular, the EMG sensors are placed on the muscles reported in Table 2.

2.3 Data Processing

The marker positions, the subject's forces exchanged with the ground and muscle activations during the task execution were acquired and processed using BTS SMART software (BTS Bioengineering). Then, the OpenSim software was used to reconstruct the joint angles and torques defined in Table 1. Firstly, the OpenSim model, *Full-Body Musculoskeletal Model* [16], was scaled in accordance with the anthropometric characteristics of the subject; subsequently the inverse kinematics and inverse dynamics were computed. The EMG signals, instead, were processed following the steps reported in [15].

2.4 Results

The results of joint angles and torques are reported in Table 1. The most loaded joints, for all tasks, are shoulder and elbow flexion-extension. The results of root mean square (RMS) of normalized muscle activations (NMA) are reported in Table 2. The results show that the most activated muscles, for the three selected tasks, are anterior deltoid for shoulder muscles and biceps brachii for elbow muscles.

Table 1. Mean values ± standard deviation of joint angles and torques for the selected tasks. DT: drilling task; LT: leveraging task; CT: cabling task.

	Joint angles [deg]			Joint torques [Nm]		
	DT	LT	CT	DT	LT	CT
Shoulder flexion-extension	54.9 (±4.0)	120.4 (±2.5)	107.7 (±11.5)	9.5 (±0.3)	7.5 (±0.5)	7.2 (±0.8)
Shoulder abduction-adduction	20.1 (±1.9)	10.5 (±1.2)	14.9 (±3.5)	0.7 (±0.1)	0.5 (±0.1)	0.4 (±0.3)
Shoulder rotation	7.9 (±1.2)	36.2 (±4.7)	37.4 (±10.6)	1.1 (±0.1)	0.8 (±0.2)	1.0 (±0.4)
Elbow flexion-extension	89.1 (±3.5)	57.0 (±3.6)	61.5 (±6.3)	2.0 (±0.1)	1.3 (±0.1)	1.2 (±0.2)

3 Functional Requirements

The results of the biomechanical analysis of the workers while performing industrial overhead tasks, illustrated in Sect. 2.4, are used here to derive the functional requirements of the soft exoskeleton for industrial overhead tasks.

Table 2. Mean values ± standard deviation of root mean square (RMS) of the normalized muscle activation (NMA) for the selected tasks. DT: drilling task; LT: leveraging task; CT: cabling task.

	RMS of NMA [-]		
	DT	LT	CT
Upper trapezium	0.33 (±0.07)	0.14 (±0.01)	0.12 (±0.04)
Anterior deltoid	0.53 (±0.13)	0.16 (±0.01)	0.14 (±0.02)
Medial deltoid	0.17 (±0.04)	0.09 (±0.01)	0.08 (±0.01)
Rear deltoid	0.07 (±0.02)	0.04 (±0.01)	0.05 (±0.02)
Biceps brachii	0.48 (±0.15)	0.18 (±0.01)	0.13 (±0.07)
Triceps brachii	0.13 (±0.04)	0.10 (±0.04)	0.11 (±0.02)

Movements and Muscles Supported. The most activated muscles, as reported in Table 2, are: anterior deltoid for shoulder movements and biceps brachii for elbow movements. Therefore, the soft exoskeleton should be able to support the shoulder and elbow flexion-extension, thus reducing fatigue to anterior deltoid and biceps brachii.

Table 3. Anthropometric data and measures for the involved subjects in the experiments, as obtained by using the model in [17].

Variable	Description	Length [mm]
l_{ua}	Length of upper arm	366
l_{fa}	Length of forearm	460
l_1	Distance from the elbow joint to anchor point of upper arm ($l_1 = 0.27\,l_{ua}$)	98.8
l_2	Distance from the elbow joint to anchor point of forearm ($l_2 = 0.21\,l_{fa}$)	96.6
l_{3x}, l_{3y}	Origin position at the shoulder joint	100
b	Distance between anchor point and the center of the upper arm	80

Kinematics and Dynamics. The kinematic and dynamic results, reported in Table 1, are used to estimate the required forces and lengths of ideal actuators able to support the arm during the task execution. To do this, we use the kinematic model and the equations which link the joint angles and torques with lengths and forces as derived in [17]; the anthropometric data of the subjects involved in this study and the characteristic measures of the exoskeleton are reported in Table 3. An example of the evolution of the joint angles, torques, required lengths and forces are shown in Fig. 2. The results for the most critical conditions are reported in the following: (i) for the shoulder, the maximum length occurs when the shoulder flexion-extension angle is equal to $0°$ ($l_{sh,max}$ ($\alpha = 0$) $=$ 350 mm), the minimum length occurs when the shoulder flexion-extension angle is equal to the maximum range of motion reported in Table 1 ($l_{sh,min}$ ($\alpha = 120.4$) $= 185.8$ mm), the maximum force occurs when the shoulder flexion-extension torque is equal to the maximum joint torque reported in Table 1 ($f_{sh,max}(\tau_1 = 9.5) = 75.0$ N); (ii) following the same approach for the elbow, we obtain $l_{el,max}$ ($\delta = 0$) $= 197.21$ mm, $l_{el,min}$ ($\delta =$ 89.1) $= 152.6$ mm, $f_{el,max}$ ($\tau_4 = 2.0$) $= 20.05$ N. Two ideal soft actuators (one for the shoulder and one for the elbow) should ensure the lengths and forces illustrated above to fully support the shoulder and elbow joints while performing industrial overhead tasks.

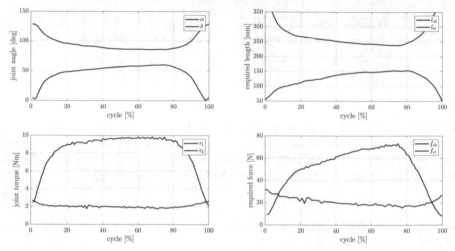

Fig. 2. Evolution of the joint angles, torques, required lengths and forces for drilling overhead tasks. α and τ_1: shoulder flexion-extension angle and torque; δ and τ_4: elbow flexion-extension angle and torque; l_{sh} and l_{el}: shoulder and elbow required lengths; f_{sh} and f_{el}: shoulder and elbow required forces.

Anthropometry. In order to realize a custom solution tailored for each worker, the exoskeleton suit should be designed on the external morphology of the worker. Furthermore, the parameters in Table 3 should be derived from real measurements taken on the worker's body, in particular for the anchor points for the actuators, whose position is decisive for the overall comfort of the worker and for obtaining the maximum force transmission between actuators and human joints. To develop custom and tailor made solutions, suitable 3D body scanners able to reconstruct the 3D body model and to extrapolate selective anthropometric characteristics should be used, as the INBODY - Instant Body Scan™ [18] from BeyondShape. An example of a custom and tailor made design of soft exoskeleton, developed on the real 3D body anatomy, is reported in Fig. 1.

In the following, indications from the literature are used to define the mass, materials and contact pressure of the soft wearable robot.

Mass and Materials. The current rigid exoskeletons used in industry define the mass limit, which is equal to 3.5 kg [3]. Soft systems are expected to weigh less, for instance pneumatic actuators are very light and the weight of the worn system can be estimated equal to 214 g [19]. The materials must be skin contact and stiff in order to guarantee the transfer of the forces due to the contraction of the actuator entirely to the arm. To do that, the exosuit composed by neoprene material, with thickness $\geq$ 1 mm (up to a maximum of 1.5 mm), can be an appropriate solution. Moreover, the anchor point can be reinforced using flexible plate as proposed in [9].

Contact Pressure. The limit of the contact pressure, defined as the pressure between the actuator and skin, is defined in such a way that it will not affect blood circulation. The literature sets the threshold value of the contact pressure to be equal to 10 kPa [20].

4 Conclusions

In this study, we have presented the derivation of functional requirements of a soft industrial exoskeleton from the biomechanical analysis of the workers and state-of-the-art considerations. The illustrated process allows to design custom solution to assist the workers in industrial overhead tasks. The results of this study will be used to develop a prototype of soft industrial exoskeleton.

References

1. Schneider, E., Irastorza, X.: Osh in figures: Work-related musculoskeletal disorders in the EU - facts and figures. European Agency for Safety and Health at Work (2010)
2. Maurice, P., Čamernik, J., Gorjan, D., Schirrmeister, B., Bornmann, J., Tagliapietra, L., Latella, C., Pucci, D., Fritzsche, L., Ivaldi, S., Babič, J.: Objective and subjective effects of a passive exoskeleton on overhead work. IEEE Trans. Neural Syst. Rehabil. Eng. **28**(1), 152–164 (2019)
3. De Looze, M.P., Bosch, T., Krause, F., Stadler, K.S., O'Sullivan, L.W.: Exoskeletons for industrial application and their potential effects on physical work load. Ergonomics **59**(5), 671–681 (2016)
4. Tondu, B.: Estimating shoulder-complex mobility. Appl. Bionics Biomech. **4**(1), 19–29 (2007)
5. Pennestri, E., Stefanelli, R., Valentini, P.P., Vita, L.: Virtual musculo-skeletal model for the biomechanical analysis of the upper limb. J. Biomech. **40**(6), 1350–1361 (2007)
6. Li, J., Zhang, Z., Tao, C., Ji, R.: A number synthesis method of the self-adapting upper-limb rehabilitation exoskeletons. Int. J. Adv. Robot. Syst. **14**(3), 1729881417710796 (2017)
7. Thalman, C., Artemiadis, P.: A review of soft wearable robots that provide active assistance: trends, common actuation methods, fabrication, and applications. Wearable Technol. **1** (2020)
8. Chiaradia, D., Xiloyannis, M., Antuvan, C.W., Frisoli, A., Masia, L.: Design and embedded control of a soft elbow exosuit. In: 2018 IEEE International Conference on Soft Robotics (RoboSoft), pp. 565–571. IEEE (2018)
9. O'Neill, C.T., Phipps, N.S., Cappello, L., Paganoni, S., Walsh, C.J.: A soft wearable robot for the shoulder: design, characterization, and preliminary testing. In: 2017 International Conference on Rehabilitation Robotics (ICORR), pp. 1672–1678. IEEE (2017)
10. Wehner, M., Quinlivan, B., Aubin, P.M., Martinez-Villalpando, E., Baumann, M., Stirling, L., Holt, K., Wood, R., Walsh, C.: A lightweight soft exosuit for gait assistance. In: 2013 IEEE International Conference on Robotics and Automation, pp. 3362–3369. IEEE (2013)
11. Caporaso, T., Grazioso, S., Panariello, D., Di Gironimo, G., Lanzotti, A.: Understanding the human motor control for user-centered design of custom wearable systems: case studies in sports, industry, rehabilitation. In: International Conference on Design, Simulation, Manufacturing: The Innovation Exchange, pp. 753–764. Springer, Cham (2019)

12. Spada, S., Ghibaudo, L., Gilotta, S., Gastaldi, L., Cavatorta, M.P.: Analysis of exoskeleton introduction in industrial reality: main issues and EAWS risk assessment. In: International Conference on Applied Human Factors and Ergonomics, pp. 236–244. Springer, Cham (2017)
13. Sood, D., Nussbaum, M.A., Hager, K.: Fatigue during prolonged intermittent overhead work: reliability of measures and effects of working height. Ergonomics **50**(4), 497–513 (2007)
14. Panariello, D., Grazioso, S., Caporaso, T., Palomba, A., Di Gironimo, G., Lanzotti, A.: Evaluation of human joint angles in industrial tasks using OpenSim. In: 2019 II Workshop on Metrology for Industry 4.0 and IoT (MetroInd4. 0&IoT), pp. 78–83. IEEE (2019)
15. Grazioso, S., Caporaso, T., Palomba, A., Nardella, S., Ostuni, B., Panariello, D., Di Gironimo, G., Lanzotti, A.: Assessment of upper limb muscle synergies for industrial overhead tasks: a preliminary study. In: 2019 II Workshop on Metrology for Industry 4.0 and IoT (MetroInd4. 0&IoT), pp. 89–92. IEEE (2019)
16. Rajagopal, A., Dembia, C.L., DeMers, M.S., Delp, D.D., Hicks, J.L., Delp, S.L.: Full-body musculoskeletal model for muscle-driven simulation of human gait. IEEE Trans. Biomed. Eng. **63**(10), 2068–2079 (2016)
17. Kim, Y.G., Little, K., Noronha, B., Xiloyannis, M., Masia, L., Accoto, D.: A voice activated biarticular exosuit for upper limb assistance during lifting tasks. Robot. Comput.-Integr. Manuf. **66**, 101995 (2020)
18. Grazioso, S., Selvaggio, M., Di Gironimo, G.: Design and development of a novel body scanning system for healthcare applications. Int. J. Interact. Des. Manuf. (IJIDeM) **12**(2), 611–620 (2018)
19. Das, S., Kurita, Y.: ForceArm: a wearable pneumatic gel muscle (PGM)-based assistive suit for the upper limb. IEEE Trans. Med. Robot. Bionics **2**(2), 269–281 (2020)
20. Ogata, K., Whiteside, L.A.: Effects of external compression on blood flow to muscle and skin. Clin. Orthopaedics Related Res.® **168**, 105–107 (1982)

A Pilot Study on Auditory Feedback for a Lower-Limb Exoskeleton to Increase Walking Safety

Jing Qiu[1], Yilin Wang[2(✉)], Hong Cheng[2], Lu Wang[1], and Xiao Yang[3]

[1] School of Mechanical and Electrical Engineering, University of Electronic Science and Technology of China, Chengdu, Sichuan, China
[2] School of Automation Engineering, University of Electronic Science and Technology of China, Chengdu, Sichuan, China
[3] Department of Orthopedics, Sichuan Provincial People's Hospital, Chengdu, Sichuan, China

Abstract. The ontological feedback is important to ensure the safety when walking. The current lower-limb exoskeleton (LLE) systems are developed widely to assist paraplegia patients without proprioception to stand and walk. Hence, the paraplegia patients can hardly perceive motions and states of their lower limbs. The feedback information from an LLE to the paraplegia wearer can remind the wearer current walking state. They do not need to stare at their feet using visual feedback when walking, which is important to walking safety and remain mental model of exoskeleton. What's more, visual feedback may result high workload and low safety during paraplegia patients' walking because they have to change their visual pattern to notice their feet and walking situations. Therefore, this paper conducted several auditory feedback experiments aiming to find out the most adaptive feedback method for the exoskeleton to improve walking safety. Ten healthy subjects were recruited from the University of Electronic Science and Technology of China. Firstly, voice- and music-prompt auditory feedback modes were compared and different prompt lengths/rhythms were set. Then, the advantageous mode was compared with no-feedback mode. In this procedure, different appearance time of the prompts was set in order to ensure the best effectiveness of auditory feedback. The accuracy, reaction time, and subjective assessments of these two auditory feedback modes were compared.

Keywords: Lower-limb exoskeleton · Spinal cord injury · Auditory feedback · Voice-prompt feedback mode · Music-prompt feedback mode

1 Introduction

1.1 A Subsection Sample

Lower-limb exoskeleton systems significantly improve the walking ability and quality of life of patients suffering from spinal cord injury (SCI). These wearable robots combine developments in fields such as wearable sensing, control engineering, electronics, biomedicine, and mechanics [1]. As gait-training and walking-assistance devices,

N. L. Black et al. (Eds.): IEA 2021, LNNS 223, pp. 325–334, 2022.
https://doi.org/10.1007/978-3-030-74614-8_39

lower-limb exoskeleton systems play an important role in patients' daily lives and have become widely used [2]. The ReWalk exoskeleton (ReWalk Bionics Inc., Israel) was the first such device approved by the U.S. Food and Drug Administration (FDA), in 2015. It was designed for patients with SCI to use all day at home and in the community [3]. The EksoNR (Ekso Bionics Inc., USA) robotic exoskeleton was the first device to obtain FDA clearance for use by patients with acquired brain injuries (ABI) [4]. The Hybrid Assistive Limb (HAL) exoskeleton (Cyberdyne Inc., Japan) makes possible the monitoring of muscle contractility through surface electromyography (EMG) at the extensor-flexor muscle region of the lower limbs [5]. REX (Rex Bionics Inc., New Zealand) is a hands-free, self-supporting exoskeleton that enables a person with mobility impairment to stand up and walk [6]. With the development of these systems, the recognition of human intent and the perception of the environment become increasingly important in human-exoskeleton interaction [7]. However, due to the lack of proprioception of the lower limbs, SCI patients do not know the motion states of their legs. Therefore, they do not have tactile feedback during heel contact. Thus, most patients stare at their feet to confirm the next state of the exoskeleton, which is cumbersome when walking outdoors. Therefore, a feedback system is important to prompt the motion state of an exoskeleton [8].

Vision, tactile sense, and auditory sense are the most important means for humans to gain information from the environment [9, 10]. Donati et al. employed eight patients with SCI receiving long-term gait-mode training based on bidirectional human-computer interaction, which combined virtual reality training, visual tactile feedback, and two electroencephalograph-controlled robotic actuators with the purpose of rehabilitating their motor nerves. After 12 months of training, all the subjects showed significant improvements in somatosensory and muscle control, which led to improvements in their walking performance [11]. Shokur et al. [12] used visual and tactile feedback to realize the perception of leg position and different ground conditions in virtual movements for patients with complete paraplegia. They proposed that tactile feedback is important to improve the acceptance and utilization rate of prostheses, as well as motor proficiency. Villiger et al. [13] improved the lower limb function and neuropathic pain of patients with chronic incomplete SCI through virtual reality, which combined visual feedback and leg training. Lieberman et al. [14] developed a wearable vibrotactile feedback suit for motor training, rehabilitation for neural injury, dance learning, and healthy posture retraining. The results indicated that the execution target accuracy had improved by 27%, and the accelerated learning rate by as much as 23%. Some researchers have worked on auditory feedback of human-computer systems. A control method of an anthropomorphic robot simulating continuous human speaking through auditory feedback was introduced [15], which was shown to help analyze the human voice mechanism and establish a new voice-generation system. The influence of auditory and tactile signals on the operational performance of a virtual reality hand rehabilitation system was evaluated [16]. The authors concluded that tactile sense is an important factor in improving the operational performance of subjects at a high level of difficulty, but auditory feedback was not significant at all difficulty levels. Zahariev et al. [17] argued that to provide auditory information while grasping virtual objects can improve movement speed, and auditory information improves spatial accuracy when tactile information is unavailable. Damiano et al. devised the ALEX II exoskeleton. Subjects who tested it with the combination of kinetic guidance and rhythmic cue modality were capable of improving gait symmetry after training, whereas people assigned kinetic and visual guidance modality were not [18].

SCI patients cannot constantly obtain the lower extremity movement status of the exoskeleton through visual-feedback when walking in complex environments. Lacking sensation in their lower limbs, they cannot receive feedback through tactile sense. An efficient feedback mode can guarantee the accuracy and effectiveness of information interaction between a subject and the exoskeleton. Few exoskeleton systems can provide an effective feedback mechanism to the wearer. An auditory feedback system may improve information reception and work efficiency.

To explore the most efficient auditory feedback mechanism and add such a system to an exoskeleton, we conducted a preliminary study to compare two auditory feedback modes. We also compared auditory feedback to no feedback to investigate the efficiency of an auditory feedback system.

2   Methods

2.1   Subjects

Ten healthy subjects (seven males and three females, of age 22.9 ± 2.0 years, height 168.8 ± 8.5 cm, and weight 59.7 ± 9.5 kg) were recruited from the University of Electronic Science and Technology of China. None suffered from any physiological or psychological disease, and they signed an informed consent before the experiment. This study was approved by the Civilian Ethics Committee of the School of Life and Science and Technology, University of Electronic Science and Technology of China.

2.2   Equipment and Materials

Three types of auditory feedback were compared in this study when the subjects performed the same tasks. These were voice feedback, musical feedback, and no feedback. In the voice feedback, three lengths of prompt voice commands were set as Table 1 shows. A female voice package from Iflytec Co. Ltd was used to perform the voice prompts. The voice speed was set to three Chinese words per second, which was the normal speaking speed. In Chinese, different broadcast scenes requires different speaking speed. The normal speaking speed is three words per second [19].

The software platform, including the user interface and data storage, was mainly based on Python. The music prompts were designed as shown in Table 1.

The longer line under the notes represents a beat, which lasts one second in the program, and the shorter line represents a half-beat. The falling tone, "533 (music tone is 'sol mi mi')," was associated with "from current state to previous state." If one is walking, then the previous state can only be to stop walking, and if one is standing, then the previous state is sitting. Therefore, the same prompt was used for "stop walking" and "from standing to sitting." Similarly, tone "335 (music tone is 'mi mi sol')" was associated with "from current state to next state." This design required subjects to remember

Table 1. Auditory feedback content based on voice.

Corresponding scenarios	Prompt commands		
	Length 1	Length 2	Length 3
Flat ground - up stairs	Go upstairs	Go upstairs, please	Begin to go upstairs
Flat ground - down stairs	Go downstairs	Go downstairs, please	Begin to go down stairs
Step over obstacles	Step over	Step over, please	Step over the obstacles
Bypass obstacles	Bypass it	Bypass it, please	Bypass the obstacle, please
Speed up	Speed up	Speed up, please	Begin to speed up
Slow down	Slow down	Slow down, please	Begin to slow down
Stop walking	Stop	Stop, please	Begin to stop walking
Standing- sitting	Sit down	Sit down, please	Begin to sit down
Standing- walking	Walk	Walk, please	Begin to walk
Sitting- standing up	Stand up	Stand up, please	Begin to stand up

less music prompts, which both reduced the workload and increased the accuracy. The duration of a beat was one second.

Subjects scored how well the voice/musical prompts matched the current action according to the Likert five-level scale [20]. The experiment used the scores of different tonal combinations as criteria to judge the sound as an important reference for the final tone feedback scheme. Information such as subject options and reaction time was recorded during the experiment.

After completing all the experiments, the subjects completed questionnaires for the two auditory feedback modes. The content of the questionnaire included "can judge directly," "do not need to remember deliberately," "widespread application," and "have good effects." The subjects scored each statement according to the Likert scale, where "1" indicates "strongly disagree" and "5" for "strongly agree."

2.3 Procedure

The subject randomly received any one of 10 voice prompts, determined the corresponding scene or state, and selected and confirmed the corresponding picture in the user interface, as shown in Fig. 1. A single experiment consisted of 40 trials. Each trial recorded information, such as subject options and reaction time, for a period of approximately 10 min. Subjects completed the trials within five days.

The subjects received musical prompts randomly (the music prompts were designed as Table 2 shows). Then they selected the corresponding picture in the experimental interface. A single experiment consisted of 32 trials, each of which recorded information such as subject options and reaction time for approximately eight minutes. Subjects

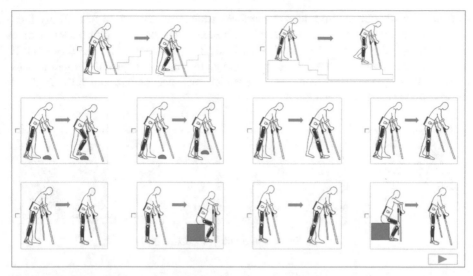

Fig. 1. A figure caption is always placed below the illustration. Short captions are centered, while long ones are justified. The macro button chooses the correct format automatically.

completed three trials within five days and completed questionnaires after completing the tasks.

Table 2. Music-based auditory feedback content.

Prompt numbers	Prompt commands	Corresponding scenarios
1	Flat ground- up stairs	1 4 7̇
2	Flat ground- Down stairs	7̇ 4 1
3	Step over obstacles	1 6̣ 1
4	Bypass obstacles	2 2 2
5	Speed up	3·̑ 4 5 6 7
6	Slow down	3 2 1
7	Stop walking	5 3 3
	From standing to sitting	5 3 3
8	From standing to walking	3 3 5
	From sitting to standing	3 3 5

The auditory feedback system and a system with no auditory feedback were compared on an AIDER exoskeleton (AssIstive Device for paRalyzed patients, University of Electronic Science and Technology, Chengdu, China). This experiment was divided into no-voice feedback and auditory feedback trials. The procedure of auditory feedback trial was shown in Fig. 2, and no-vioce feedback has the same process but without the prompts. Subjects were required to perform all the motions while wearing AIDER. In the auditory feedback trial, the exoskeleton automatically adjusted the gait according to environmental information, and the subject only needed to confirm the feedback information and continue walking.

Please stand up ⟶ Please walk ⟶ ... ⟶ Please step over/bypass ⟶ Please stop walking ⟶ Please sit down

Fig. 2. Process of auditory feedback trial.

2.4 Data Collection and Analysis

Before the experiment, the basic response time of each subject was collected as a baseline for subsequent experimental data. The experiment was videotaped to record its duration and the response of the subjects upon receiving feedback. After the experiment was completed, the subjective perception of the voice and musical feedback modes was collected by the self-made questionnaire. Information on subjects' options and reaction times was recorded during the experiment.

The parameters included the accuracy and reaction time after receiving the prompts, as well as the scores from questionnaires. IBM SPSS Statistics 22 was used to conduct the statistical analysis. We used paired t-test to analyze the statistical differences in reaction time between voice and musical auditory feedback. A Wilcoxon nonparametric test was used to analyze the statistical differences between the questionnaires on the two methods.

The completion time was recorded for the three methods. A paired t-test was used to analyze their statistical differences. A Wilcoxon nonparametric test was used to analyze the statistical differences in subjective feelings. The significant level was set on 5%.

3 Results

3.1 Comparison of Two Auditory Feedback Modes

In the comparison of voice and musical prompts as auditory feedback modes, subjects performed motions according to the prompts they received. The accuracy of those motions was recorded, as shown in Fig. 3. The accuracy rate for voice feedback was 100%, indicating that all subjects could receive information on the next motion solely by voice (Fig. 3(a)). The average accuracy rate based on the music-prompt feedback mode was 97.4%, with a median of 97.5%, indicating that most subjects were able to confirm the next movement of the exoskeleton through a musical prompt. The paired t-test results show significant differences between the two feedback modes (t = −3.122, P = 0.012).

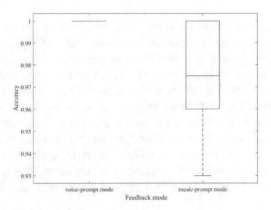

Fig. 3. Accuracy of two auditory feedback modes.

3.2 Comparison of Auditory Feedback System and No-Feedback System

In this trial, the subjects were required to complete walking tasks on an auditory feedback system and no-feedback system. In the auditory feedback system, two voice-prompt modes were used for comparison. In the first mode, the prompts appeared in the swing phase of the previous step when the subjects walked. In the second mode, the prompts appeared at the standing phase of the previous step. The result of the completion time was recorded and is shown in Fig. 4.

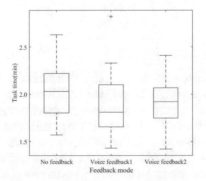

Fig. 4. Effect of no feedback and two kinds of voice-prompt feedback at different times in walking task.

The completion time of the walking task combined with the voice-prompt feedback was less than that with no feedback. A paired t-test showed a significant difference between the no-feedback mode and the two voice-prompt feedback modes (no-feedback mode and first voice-prompt feedback mode: t = 3.307, p = 0.0.004; no-feedback and second voice-prompt feedback mode: t = 2.56, p = 0.0.019). However, there was no significant difference between the two voice-prompt feedback modes (t = −0.392, p = 0.699).

The questionnaire about the subjects' subjective feelings about the voice-prompt feedback mode included "can perceive the next movement," "didn't interfere with normal walking," "can respond promptly in first voice-prompt mode," "can respond promptly in second voice-prompt mode," "feel more secure than no feedback," and "voice feedback is necessary." The results (Fig. 5) show that most subjects could clearly perceive the next movement state of the exoskeleton through voice feedback, and believed that voice feedback could make it safer to wear the exoskeleton. In the first voice feedback mode, the subject indicated that the feedback could prompt the next step in time. However, in the second voice feedback mode, most subjects were incapable of a timely response, and there is a significant difference between the subjective feelings toward the two voice-prompt modes according to the Wilcoxon nonparametric test (Z = −2.060, p = 0.039).

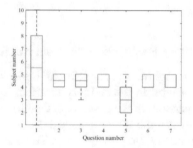

Fig. 5. Scores of each question

4   Conclusions

In this paper, the exoskeleton auditory feedback experiment was based on voice and music prompts. There is a significant difference between the two methods, and subjects scored voice feedback highly on the user-experience questionnaire. As such, voice prompt should be used as the feedback mode for the next movement state of the exoskeleton. To realize the application of voice feedback on an actual lower limb exoskeleton, we carried out a dynamic verification experiment of the exoskeleton system based on voice feedback. The feedback enables the subject to clearly perceive the next movement of the exoskeleton, and makes the exoskeleton more secure. When the voice feedback appears during the last swing phase, the subject is better able to perceive the feedback in time compared to feedback at the end of a standing period. Therefore, in the actual system, the next movement state of the exoskeleton will be fed back by voice at the previous swing period.

Acknowledgements. This research project is supported by the Open Funding Project of National Key Laboratory of Human Factors Engineering (6142222190308) and the Fundamental Research Funds for the Central Universities, University of Electronic Science and Technology of China (ZYGX2019Z010). We thank Letpub (www.letpub.com) for its linguistic assistance during the preparation of this manuscript.

References

1. Kazerooni, H., Steger, R.: The berkeley lower extremity exoskeleton. J. Dyn. Syst. Meas. Control **128**(1), 14–25 (2005)
2. Raab, K., Krakow, K., Tripp, F., Jung, M.: Effects of training with the ReWalk exoskeleton on quality of life in incomplete spinal cord injury: a single case study. Spinal Cord Series Cases **2**(1), 15025 (2015)
3. ReWalk Homepage: More Than walking. https://rewalk.com/rewalk-personal-3/. Accessed 02 July 2020
4. TheStreet. Ekso Stock Doubles – FDA Widens Marketing OK for Exoskeleton. https://www.thestreet.com/investing/ekso-gets-wider-fda-clearance-for-exoskeleton-device-for-brain-injury?utm_source=web&utm_medium=events&utm_campaign=20. Accessed 02 July 2020
5. Kubota, S., Nakata, Y., Eguchi, K., et al.: Feasibility of rehabilitation training with a newly developed wearable robot for patients with limited mobility. Arch. Phys. Med. Rehabil. **94**, 1080–7 (2013)
6. Contreras-Vidal, J.L, Grossman, R.G.: NeuroRex: a clinical neural interface roadmap for EEG-based brain machine interfaces to a lower body robotic exoskeleton. In: 35th Annual International Conference of the IEEE Engineering in Medicine and Biology Society, Osaka, pp. 1579–1582. IEEE (2013)
7. Smith, P., Terry, T.B.: The influence of active vision on the exoskeleton of intelligent agents. In: Proceedings on SPIE Smart Structures and Materials & Nondestructive Evaluation and Health Monitoring, Las Vegas, p. 979704, 1–7. SPIE (2016)
8. Leia, S., Ho, S., Eric, J., Kevin, D.: Human factors considerations for enabling functional use of exosystems in operational environments. IEEE Syst. J. **13**(1), 1–12 (2018)
9. Bouteraa, Y., Abdallah, I.B., Elmogy, A.M.: Training of hand rehabilitation using low cost exoskeleton and vision-based game interface. J. Intell. Robot. Syst. **96**, 31–47 (2019)
10. Dinh, H.Q., Walker, N., Hodges, L.F., et al.: Evaluating the importance of multi-sensory input on memory and the sense of presence in virtual environments. In: Proceedings on IEEE Virtual Reality, Orlando, pp. 222–228. IEEE (2002)
11. Donati, A.R., Shokur, S., Morya, E.: Long-term training with a brain-machine interface-based gait protocol induces partial neurological recovery in paraplegic patients. Sci. Rep. **79**(6), N13–N14 (2016)
12. Shokur, S., Gallo, S., Moioli, R.C., et al.: Assimilation of virtual legs and perception of floor texture by complete paraplegic patients receiving artificial tactile feedback. Sci. Rep. **6**(32293), 1–14 (2016)
13. Villiger, M., Bohli, D., Kiper, D., et al.: Virtual reality-augmented neurorehabilitation improves motor function and reduces neuropathic pain in patients with incomplete spinal cord injury. Neurorehabilit. Neural Repair **27**, 675–683 (2013)
14. Lieberman, J., Breazeal, C.: Development of a wearable vibrotactile feedback suit for accelerated human motor learning. In: Proceedings 2007 IEEE International Conference on Robotics and Automation, Rome, Italy, pp. 4001–4006. IEEE (2007)

15. Nishikawa, K., Kuwae, T., Takanobu, H., et al.: Mimicry of human voice sounds using an anthropomorphic talking robot by auditory feedback. In: IEEE/RSJ International Conference on Intelligent Robots and Systems, Sendai, pp. 272–278. IEEE/RSJ (2004)
16. Shing, C.Y., Fung, C.P., Chuang, T.Y., et al.: The study of auditory and haptic signals in a virtual reality-based hand rehabilitation system. Robotica 21(2), 211–218 (2003)
17. Zahariev, M.A., Mackenzie, C.L.: Auditory contact cues improve performance when grasping augmented and virtual objects with a tool. Exp. Brain Res. 186(4), 619–627 (2008)
18. Zanotto, D., Rosati, G., Avanzini, F., et al.: Robot-assisted gait training with complementary auditory feedback: results on short-term motor adaptation. In: 4th International Conference Proceeding on Biomedical Robotics and Biomechatronics, Rome, Italy pp. 1388–1393. IEEE RAS & EMBS (2012)
19. Zhang, X.: The application analysis of different types of program host's speaking speed. China Academic Journal Electronic Publishing House, pp. 192–193 (2020)
20. Gerhard, N.: Likert scale. Dictionary of Pharmaceutical Medicine, p. 106. Springer, Vienna (2009)

Human-Robot Collaboration (HRC) Technologies for Reducing Work-Related Musculoskeletal Diseases in Industry 4.0

Alberto Ranavolo[1]([⊠]), Giorgia Chini[1], Francesco Draicchio[1], Alessio Silvetti[1], Tiwana Varrecchia[1], Lorenzo Fiori[1], Antonella Tatarelli[1], Patricia Helen Rosen[2], Sascha Wischniewski[2], Philipp Albrecht[3], Lydia Vogt[3], Matteo Bianchi[4], Giuseppe Averta[4], Andrea Cherubini[5], Lars Fritzsche[6], Massimo Sartori[7], Bram Vanderborght[8], Renee Govaerts[8], and Arash Ajoudani[9]

[1] INAIL, Monte Porzio Catone, Italy
a.ranavolo@inail.it
[2] BAuA, Dortmund, Germany
[3] DIN, Berlin, Germany
[4] UNIPI, Pisa, Italy
[5] LIRMM, Univ. Montpellier, CNRS, Montpellier, France
[6] IMK Automotive, Chemnitz, Germany
[7] UT, Twente, The Netherlands
[8] VUB and Imec, Brussels, Belgium
[9] IIT, Genova, Italy

Abstract. The paper describes the activities of the European project SOPHIA, Socio-Physical Interaction Skills for Cooperative Human-Robot Systems in Agile Production. The consortium involves European partners from academia, research organizations and industry. The main goal of the project is to develop a new generation of CoBots and Wearbots and advanced instrumental-based biomechanical risk assessment tools in industrial scenarios to reduce work-related musculoskeletal disorders and to improve productivity in industry 4.0.

Further aim of the project is to create the basis for new ergonomic international Standards for manual handling activities.

Keywords: HRC · Biomechanical load · Workplace rehabilitation · Return to work · Ergonomic · WMSDs

1 Introduction

The new scenarios of a connected and digital world provide opportunities for the integration of new tools into everyday life and workplaces, the so-called Industry 4.0.

In the workplace, the use of sensor networks and human–robot collaboration (HRC) technologies are coming more and more to the fore as an opportunity for both biomechanical overload risk mitigation and for the adoption of new return-to-work strategies. On these grounds, the European Union's Horizon 2020 research and innovation program

N. L. Black et al. (Eds.): IEA 2021, LNNS 223, pp. 335–342, 2022.
https://doi.org/10.1007/978-3-030-74614-8_40

funded, under Grant Agreement No. 871237, the Socio-physical Interaction Skills for Cooperative Human-Robot Systems in Agile Production (SOPHIA) project with the aim to develop a new generation of HRC technologies and sensors networks.

Sensor networks, through the continuous and real-time monitoring of worker's physiological and biomechanical parameters (by measuring kinematic, kinetic and muscular activity, etc.), can be used to control the robots through specific interfaces, evaluate the efficacy of ergonomic interventions and provide vibro-tactile/acoustic/visual stimuli to the workers to execute the task in a less overloading way to reduce the risk of developing work-related musculoskeletal disorders (WMSDs).

HRC technologies include wearable assistive robots (WearBots, Exoskeletons) and collaborative robots (CoBots) able to act on the base of the real needs of the worker, support him during the working activity with the aim of minimize the biomechanical load and reduce the probability of WMSDs insurgence.

2   Wearable Sensors and Robotic Technologies: State of the Art

2.1   Wearable Sensors

Recently, commercial and research miniaturized wearable wireless sensors were introduced in the workplace to monitor workers during their activities.

These sensors include Inertial Measurement Units (IMUs) to measure bodies' kinematics, dynamometers to evaluate subjects' force and surface electromyography (sEMG) sensors to analyze the muscle behaviors.

Commonly used IMUs can be accelerometers (uni-/bi- or tri-axial), gyroscopes and magnetic sensors. Typically, the probes are equipped with three orthogonal accelerometers and three orthogonal gyroscopes to measure linear acceleration and angular velocity, respectively, along three orthogonal axes. These devices are particularly suitable for use in the workplace since they are portable, easy to wear for the users, monitored remotely and able to provide a direct feedback to the end-users [1–5].

The forces exchanged by workers with the environment can be measured by highly reliable [6], easy to use, portable and low-priced hand-held dynamometers. These devices are placed between a fixed point and the subject's body part to assess the isometric muscle (or muscle group) strength to investigate changes in the functional status of trunk, lower and upper limbs [7–11]. For a given hand size, forces are also recorded by superior grip dynamometers, by instrumented gloves (i.e., equipped by force sensitive resistors) or by force sensor mats applied to handles [12–18]. To adapt to a wide variety of handle sizes and geometries multi-dimensional grip dynamometers are a valid alternative. In the end, we can also mention the use of the haptic tools, physical bendable strips that enable the users to manipulate and apply deformations to digital surfaces and to move and rotate virtual objects [1].

sEMG sensors are used to investigate the muscle activity during the execution of manual handling activities. Single- or double differential bipolar recordings using wet electrodes are the most widely used sEMG measurement methods in the workplace, since in this case the probes do not interfere with the typical movements performed by workers thanks to the miniaturization process and wireless communication protocols.

2.2 Wearable Robotic Technologies

Exoskeletons are wearable devices that help people during the execution of specific tasks by applying forces and/or torques on one or more joints. They were first developed in the clinical setting for motor rehabilitation [19] and to support people with motor disabilities [20, 21], in military [22] and sport [23] fields.

More recently, the use of exoskeletons has also been extended to the industrial sector, as they can be an additional tool for reducing biomechanical risk in the workplace. The exoskeletons essentially differ based on how the torques/forces applied to the human joints are generated and therefore the first distinction is between active and passive exoskeletons.

Active exoskeletons are those that generate forces/torques with powered actuators, such as electric motors, pneumatic or battery-operated exoskeletons. The action of the exoskeleton is controlled by a computer program based on information acquired through a series of sensors applied to the body of the subject who uses it (e.g.: sEMG, accelerations, angular velocities). Since the functioning of these exoskeletons is based on the online processing of biomechanical parameters, these exoskeletons they follow the movement with greater precision than the passive ones for the tasks in which they can contribute. In addition, those with battery are also easier to move, and therefore more comfortable to use at workplace, than the tethered ones. On the other hand, however, these exoskeletons are heavier and less manageable than the passive ones [24].

Passive exoskeletons use elastic elements such as coil springs, compact rotational springs, integrated gas springs or elastic bands [24] for the generation of joint forces/torques.

Within each of these two macro categories, the exoskeletons are then divided into soft, rigid, or mixed.

2.3 Collaborative Robots (Cobots)

Collaborative robots, also called cobots [25] are robots based on HRC systems and represent a natural evolution of industrial robot, because they can solve existing challenges in industry, i.e., they can help workers to perform physically heavy tasks, thanks to the ability to physically interact with humans in a shared workspace; moreover, they are designed to be easily reprogrammed even by non-experts to be used for different roles [26]. Furthermore, the greater convenience of collaborative systems is their flexibility [27].

HRC systems were introduced primarily for occupational health (ergonomics and human factors) reasons [27]. The use of cobots can contribute to economic growth and the creation of better, healthier, and more attractive working environments for the future workforce since cobots can simultaneously increase productivity and reduce WMSDs, which represent the single largest category of work-related disease in industrial countries.

Anyhow, several technologies must be in place to enable humans and robots to work together to achieve shared goals.

So, it is important to distinguish the different ways of interaction. Müller et al. [28] proposed a classification for the different methodologies in which humans and robots can work together. They distinguish among: i) coexistence, when human and robot are in the same environment, but they do not interact, ii) synchronized if human and robot work in the same space at different time, iii) cooperation, when human and robot work in the same workspace at the same time, but they perform different tasks and iv) collaboration, when human and robot perform the task together.

Regardless of the type of the human-robot interaction, to make it effective, it is fundamental to ensure a correct information exchange between the operator and the cobot. This requires suitable interfaces that monitor human behavior—to properly plan the execution of the collaborative task—and strategies that increase the mutual awareness of the human–robot couple [29]. To this scope, as mentioned above, kinematic, kinetic and physiological sensors networks are available. In addition, other devices are also available that can enhance the sensory experience when using a cobot, such as wearable haptic systems to provide the user with the sense of touch [30], or augmented reality systems, in which components of the digital world may be superimposed upon or composed with the real world and used in teleoperation [31].

3   The SOPHIA Project Activities

3.1   Standardization

To provide definitions and guidelines for the safe and practical use of cobots in industry, several standards are already available [32–35]. Moreover, none of the ergonomics standards [36–41], neither the traditional methods listed within them cover the biomechanical risk detection when collaborative technologies are used. This gap, together with the need to strengthen the scientific basis upon which the standards are based [42], represents the reasons that existing standards should be supplemented or revised or, if necessary, that new standards should be developed [29].

Literature [43] already evidenced some critical issues such as: their observational nature, subjectivity, susceptibility to the restrictions of the equations and parameters, insufficient accuracy, precision and resolution, unclear choices of the preferred methods of risk assessment over others.

New sensor-based tools for biomechanical risk assessment will be used for quantitative "direct instrumental evaluations" to obtain the rating in standard methods, when applicable, to measure some parameters otherwise measured with poor precision and accuracy, necessary to obtain the level of risk.

In this light, SOPHIA is going to work on the need of a revision of current ergonomics standards to also include the use of these tools for biomechanical risk assessment.

3.2   Reduction of Biomechanical Risk

Bio-electrical activity, skeletal joint kinematics and kinetics data will be used to assess the worker motor capacity and how it varies over time thus providing a musculoskeletal model that can predict muscle fatigue and injury based on worker movements. Next step will be the investigation of the interaction between worker and external systems (wearable and robots) and to analyze how these impact on biomechanical load. These data could also be used to develop an online instrumental-based tool for monitoring and classifying the biomechanical risk in manual handling activities when standardized protocols cannot be used or for a confirmation of the rating of observational data with standard protocols. One more target is to develop wearable devices to monitor human-motor variables and to render haptic stimuli to specific areas of the worker's body (e.g. shoulder, lower back, ankle, knee, etc.) to inform the users about the inappropriateness of the posture adopted guiding them towards ergonomic postures and a safe action execution.

3.3 HRC in Work Environment

The European Union (EU) recognizes to HRC technologies a high relevance for the economic growth and for population health care. EU has planned a Strategic Research Agenda to provide a strategic overview and a technical guide aimed to identify medium term research and innovation goals [44, 45] and promotes standardization activities for a better market adoption and to develop a single digital market [46].

In this light, the SOPHIA project aims to achieve successful and robust HRC through the process of data from different sensors and to publish a software library and an open access dataset for benchmarking HRC solutions in collaborative scenarios. It will be also developed the overall cognitive decision frameworks allowing the human and robot to collaborate considering human and environment constraints, to guarantee health (ergonomics) and safety (collision avoidance). In this light it is critical to develop the social interaction principles (human-centered) to ensure a fluent communication between workers and HRC technologies.

To improve the flexibility of Fellow-Assistant robots, SOPHIA project includes activities focused on the development of stable hierarchical interaction controllers. This will enable CoBots to reconfigure the collaborative task frame, to simultaneously ensure human ergonomics and safety requirements and adapt task parameters by optimizing the required multi-task criteria. Multi-task and multi-person optimization will be central to the development of CoBot control framework in real environmental scenario.

4 HRC and Work Rehabilitation

SOPHIA project aims to validate the HRC technologies also in the healthcare sector and in return-to-work rehabilitation of neurological patients with motor disorders and to develop miniaturized wearable devices to monitor human-motor parameters and treat specific areas of the worker's body with tactile stimuli. To achieve these outcomes the European consortium is developing myoelectric HRC interfaces to study the interaction among hybrid work environments and workers with the aim to highlight their specific residual abilities and unfulfilled potential. Furthermore, the project aims to design training plans on sEMG based technique for broaden the audience of experienced professionals in multifactorial movement analysis.

Neurological disease patients can receive remarkable rehabilitation results from the use of HRC technologies. Ongoing monitoring of sEMG parameters such as muscle activation timing, amplitude and fatigue play a significant role in the design of innovative active exoskeleton controller systems. The main issue with using sEMG to control collaborative wearable trunk and upper limb devices designed to assist neurological patients, concerns the algorithms applied in human-robot interfaces. Just few years ago the application of these algorithms was limited due to their inaccuracy in recognizing the high subjective movement variability of neurological patients. But now, thanks to machine learning algorithms, these limits have been overcome and HRC technologies are enhanced and optimized also for people with severe upper and lower limb disabilities [53].

Hence, SOPHIA project will develop algorithms for the HRC to recognize specific movement pattern to predict patient's movement intention.

References

1. Ranavolo, A., et al.: Wearable monitoring devices for biomechanical risk assessment at work: current status and future challenges—a systematic review. Int. J. Environ. Res. Public Health **15**(9) (2018)
2. Wang, Q., et al.: Interactive wearable systems for upper body rehabilitation: a systematic review. J. NeuroEng. Rehabil. **14**(1), 20 (2017)
3. Cuesta-Vargas, A.I., Galán-Mercant, A., Williams, J.M.: The use of inertial sensors system for human motion analysis. Phys. Ther. Rev. **15**, 462–473 (2013)
4. Ullah, S., et al.: A comprehensive survey of wireless body area networks. J. Med. Syst. **36**, 1065–1094 (2012)
5. Patel, S., Park, H., Bonato, P., Chan, L., Rodgers, M.: A review of wearable sensors and systems with application in rehabilitation. J. NeuroEng. Rehabil. **9**, 1 (2012)
6. Holt, K.L., et al.: Hand-held dynamometry strength measures for internal and external rotation demonstrate superior reliability, lower minimal detectable change and higher correlation to isokinetic dynamometry than externally-fixed dynamometry of the shoulder. Phys. Ther. Sport **21**, 75–81 (2016)
7. Park, H.W., et al.: Reliability and Validity of a New Method for isometric back extensor strength evaluation using a hand-held dynamometer. Ann. Rehabil. Med. **41**, 793–800 (2017)
8. Jackson, S.M., Cheng, M.S., Smith, A.R., Kolber, M.J.: Intrarater reliability of handheld dynamometry in measuring lower extremity isometric strength using a portable stabilization device. Musculoskelet. Sci. Pract. **27**, 137–141 (2017)
9. Karthikbabu, S., et al.: Hand-held dynamometer is a reliable tool to measure trunk muscle strength in chronic stroke. J. Clin. Diagn. Res. **11**, YC09–YC12 (2017)
10. Andersen, K.S., et al.: Between-day reliability of a hand-held dynamometer and surface electromyography recordings during isometric submaximal contractions in different shoulder positions. J. Electromyogr. Kinesiol. **245**, 579–587 (2014)
11. Stark, T., et al.: Hand-held dynamometry correlation with the gold standard isokinetic dynamometry: a systematic review. PM R **3**, 472–479 (2011)
12. Kong, Y.K., Lowe, B.D.: Optimal cylindrical handle diameter for grip force tasks. Int. J. Ind. Ergon. **35**, 495–507 (2005)
13. Seo, N., et al.: The effect of torque direction and cylindrical handle diameter on the coupling between the hand and a cylindrical handle. J. Biomech. **40**, 3236–43 (2007)
14. Seo, N., Armstrong, T.: Investigation of grip force, normal force, contact area, hand size, and handle size for cylindrical handles. Hum. Factors **50**, 734–744 (2008)
15. Kong, Y.K., Freivalds, A., Kim, S.E.: Evaluation of handles in a maximum gripping task. Ergonomics **47**, 1350–1364 (2004)
16. Kong, Y.K., Freivalds, A.: Evaluation of meat-hook handle shapes. Int. J. Ind. Ergon. **32**, 13–23 (2003)

17. Hall, C.: External pressure at the hand during object handling and work with tools. Int. J. Ind. Ergon. **20**, 191–206 (1997)
18. Radwin, R.G., Oh, S., Jensen, T.R., Webster, J.G.: External finger forces in submaximal static prehension. Ergonomics **35**, 275–288 (1992)
19. Colombo, G., et al.: Treadmill training of paraplegic patients using a robotic orthosis. J. Rehabil. Res. Dev. **37**(6), 693–700 (2000)
20. Ortiz, J., Di Natali, C., Caldwell, D.G.: XoSoft-iterative design of a modular soft lower limb exoskeleton. Paper presented at International Symposium on Wearable Robotics, Pisa, Italy, pp. 351–355. Springer, Cham (2018)
21. XoSoft: XoSoft (2018). https://www.xosoft.eu
22. Kazerooni, H., Racine, J.L., Huang, L., Steger, R.: On the control of the Berkeley lower extremity exoskeleton (BLEEX). In: Proceedings of the 2005 IEEE International Conference on Robotics and Automation, pp. 4353–4360. IEEE (2005)
23. RoamRobotics (2018). https://www.roamrobotics.com
24. Toxiri, S., et al.: Back-support exoskeletons for occupational use: an overview of technological advances and trends. IISE Trans. Occup. Ergon. Hum. Factors. **7**(3–4), 237–249 (2019)
25. Colgate, J.E., et al.: Robots for collaboration with human operators. In: Proceedings of the 1996 ASME International Mechanical Engineering Congress and Exposition, Atlanta, GA, USA, pp. 433–439 (1996)
26. Guerin, K.R., et al.: A framework for end-user instruction of a robot assistant for manufacturing. In: Proceedings of the 2015 IEEE International Conference on Robotics and Automation (ICRA), Seattle, WA, USA, 26–30 May 2015, pp. 6167–6174 (2015)
27. Matheson, E., et al.: Human–robot collaboration in manufacturing applications: a review. Robotics **8**(4) (2019)
28. Müller, R., et al.: Skill-based dynamic task allocation in human-robot-cooperation with the example of welding application. Proc. Manuf. **11**, 13–21 (2017)
29. Ajoudani, A., et al.: Smart collaborative systems for enabling flexible and ergonomic work practices. IEEE Robot. Autom. **27**, 169–76 (2020)
30. Bianchi, M.: A fabric-based approach for wearable haptics. Electronics **5**(4), 44 (2016)
31. Andaluz, V.H., et al.: Transparency of a bilateral tele-operation scheme of a mobile manipulator robot. In: Proceedings of International Conference on Augmented Reality, Virtual Reality and Computer Graphics, pp. 228–245 (2016)
32. ISO 12100. Machine safety, general design principles, risk assessment, and risk reduction (2010)
33. ISO 10218-1. Robots and equipment for robots, Safety requirements for industrial robots, Part 1: Robots (2012)
34. ISO 10218-2. Robots and equipment for robots, Safety requirements for industrial robots, Part 2: Systems and integration of robots (2011)
35. ISO/TS 15066. Robots and robotic devices, Collaborative Robots (2016)
36. ISO/DIS 11228-1. Manual Handling Part 1: Lifting and Carrying (2003)
37. ISO 11228-2. Manual Handling Part 2: Pushing and Pulling (2007)
38. ISO/DIS 11228-3. Manual Handling Part 3: Handling of Low Loads at High Frequency (2007)
39. ISO/TR 12295. Application Document for ISO Standards on Manual Handling (ISO 11228-1/2/3) and Static Working Postures (ISO 11226) (2004)
40. ISO 11226. Evaluation of Static Working Postures (2000)
41. ISO/TR 12296. Manual Handling of People in the Healthcare Sector (2012)
42. Armstrong, T.J., et al.: Scientific basis of ISO standards on biomechanical risk factors. Scand. J. Work Environ. Health **44**(3), 323–329 (2018)
43. Alberto, R., et al.: Wearable monitoring devices for biomechanical risk assessment at work: current status and future challenges—a systematic review. Int. J. Environ. Res. Public Health **15**, 2569 (2018)

342   A. Ranavolo et al.

44. Multi-Annual Roadmap. https://ec.europa.eu/digital-single-market/en/news/multi-annualroa dmap- call-ict-24-robotics-now-available
45. Roadmap. https://www.eu-robotics.net/sparc/about/roadmap/index.html
46. Vanderborght, B.: Unlocking the Potential of Industrial Human–Robot Collaboration. A Vision on Industrial Collaborative Robots for Economy and Society; Publications Office of the EU, Luxembourg (2019)
47. Barbero, M., et al.: Atlas of Muscle Innervation Zones: Understanding Surface Electromyography and its Applications. Springer, New York (2012)
48. Merletti, R., Muceli, S.: Tutorial. Surface EMG detection in space and time: best practices. J. Electromyogr. Kinesiol. **49**, 102363 (2019)
49. Merletti, R., Cerone, G.L.: Tutorial. Surface EMG detection, conditioning and pre-processing: best practices. J. Electromyogr. Kinesiol. **54**, 102440 (2020)
50. Gao, B., et al.: Real-time evaluation of the signal processing of sEMG used in limb exoskeleton rehabilitation system. Appl. Bionics Biomech. **2018**, 1391032 (2018)

Results from the Third European Survey of Enterprises on New and Emerging Risks on Human-Robot Interaction

Sascha Wischniewski(✉), Eva Heinold, and Patricia Helen Rosen

German Federal Institute for Occupational Safety and Health (BAuA), Dortmund, Germany
wischniewski.sascha@baua.bund.de

Abstract. Representative data of the third European Survey of Enterprises on New and Emerging Risks (ESENER-3) shows that about 3.5% of the more than 45000 interviewed enterprises have implemented direct human-robot interaction (HRI). The distribution varies noticeably between countries and once the enterprises are separated according to their industry branches. This diverse landscape of direct HRI in Europe goes along with specific risks and challenges that are considered being linked to occupational safety and health: need for training, fear of jobs loss, flexibility requirements for employees regarding working time and work place as well as repetitive movements.

Keywords: Human-robot interaction · Survey of Enterprises · Diffusion of technology · Occupational safety and health

1 Introduction

New technologies are continuously emerging in the world of work. One of these are robotic systems that allow direct interactions with humans. Unclear however is, how much this technology is diffused in companies throughout Europe today and what kind of risks and challenges are associated with these systems in practice.

The European Survey of Enterprises on New and Emerging Risks (ESENER) is conducted in a five-year interval and focuses on the assessment and prediction of workplace related health and safety issues [1] and gives answers to this research questions in its third wave. The current ESENER-3 dataset of the European Agency for Safety and Health at Work (EU-OSHA) is therefore analysed to gain insights in the diffusion of this robotic technology in Europe and to learn more about risks and challenges associated with this kind of emerging technology.

2 Methodology

First, a descriptive analysis of the weighted source data set is performed to gain information on different aspects of the diffusion of this technology like country and branch. Second, since the enterprises were asked to name emerging technologies und risks and

© The Author(s), under exclusive license to Springer Nature Switzerland AG 2022
N. L. Black et al. (Eds.): IEA 2021, LNNS 223, pp. 343–346, 2022.
https://doi.org/10.1007/978-3-030-74614-8_41

challenges, logistic regressions with the unweighted complete data sets for all emerging technologies is performed since the risks are not associated to a specific technology class within the questionnaire. Eight logistic regressions are therefore performed for each of the given risk or challenge as outcome (need for continuous training, prolonged sitting, expected flexibility for employees in terms of place of work and working time, increased work intensity or time pressure, repetitive movements, information overload, blurring boundaries between work and private life and fear of job loss). Odd ratios (OR) are calculated and reported if significant for HRI. The other emerging technologies not further reported are

- personal computers at fix workplaces,
- laptops, tablets, smartphones or other mobile computer devices,
- machines, systems or computers determining the content or pace of work,
- machines, systems or computers monitoring workers performance and
- wearable devices such as smart watches, data glasses or other (embedded)
- sensors.

3 Results

On average 3.5% (n = 1611) of all interviewed enterprises reported using robots with direct interaction capabilities. The highest prevalence can be found in Slovakia (8.7%) followed by Denmark (6.9%) and the Czech Republic (6.7%). Noticeably below average lie Greece (1.6%), Cyprus (1.0%) and finally Serbia (0.9%) in last place (see also Fig. 1).

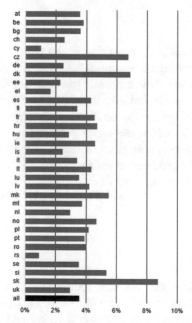

Fig. 1. Proportion of enterprises with HRI in Europe.

When sorted by branches there are two stand out sections making up about 47% of all reported human-robot interaction applications. In the manufacturing branch (C), 28% of enterprises report the use of robots with HRI, followed by wholesale and retail trade including repair of motor vehicles and motorcycles (G) with 19%. The lowest percentage is reported in the classes D (electricity, gas, steam and air conditioning supply) which accounts for 0.2% and B (mining and quarrying) accounting for 0.3%. Figure 2 shows the data for all branches.

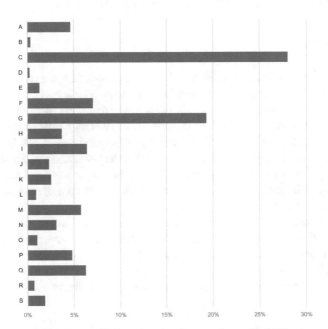

Fig. 2. NACE Rev. 2 code of enterprises with HRI.

Also worldwide, the automotive industry remains the largest industry with 30% of total robot installation, followed by electrical/electronics (25%), metal and machinery (10%) reported by the International Federation of Robotics in 2019 [2].

In the analysis regarding the discussion of possible risks and challenges through emerging technologies, only complete sets of data were included. Up to 11 679 establishments reported working with at least one emerging technology and answered discussing at least one risk related to it. The highest prevalence has prolonged sitting (11 679 times discussed), followed by need of training (11 664 times discussed) and repetitive movements (11 641 times discussed). Least reported, yet still at 11 531 and 11 483 accounts respectively, were blurring boundaries and increased work intensity.

In enterprises using HRI the fear of job loss seems to be discussed at a noticeably higher rate (31%) compared to those who don't use robots (23%). Similarly, the need for training is addressed most in establishments with HRI (87%) compared to any other technology. However, these descriptive findings might be biased since the risks and challenges were not asked for a specific technology. Therefore, to further investigate human-robot interaction and discussed related risks and challenges logistic regressions are performed. The results support the descriptive data and revealed four out of the eight risks have a significant interaction with HRI: if robots capable of direct interaction are introduced to the workplace, it becomes 1.45 more likely that the need for training as a potential challenge is discussed compared to non-HRI work environments. Second highest likelihood of discussion in an HRI environment is the fear of job loss (OR = 1.25). Third is employee's flexibility requirements with an OR of 1.18. Lastly, repetitive movements have a 1.14 higher likelihood to be discussed.

4 Discussion

While usage of robots throughout Europe is growing, robotic systems with direct interaction capabilities are not yet a wide spread technology. The level of distribution varies widely between European countries and branches. These results are in line with the prevalence and diffusion recorded by the IFR in 2019. The manufacturing and motor vehicle related sectors have the highest prevalence in using robots [2]. However, robot usage already shows a unique development related to the perceived and discussed impacts of their usage, significantly raising the likelihood for the need of training, fear of job loss, employee's flexibility requirements as well as repetitive movements as discussed risks and challenges in practice.

It has to be noted, that the strict selection process applied for the regression analysis reduces generalizability on a European level. Additionally some model estimates are rather low suggesting a more complex interaction than the input data is capable of depicting. However, these results provides a representative data based insight into the diffusion of HRI in Europe and the possible risks and challenges.

5 Conclusion

About 3.5% of the establishments interviewed in the ESENER-3 survey report the use of robotic systems with direct interaction capabilities. The usage throughout Europe varies between 1% and 9%. The manufacturing branch leads the field when it comes to utilizing these innovative systems. Enterprises using HRI more frequently discuss risks and challenges such as the need of training, fear of job loss, employee's flexibility requirements and repetitive movements compared to non-HRI environments.

References

1. Irastorza, X.: Third European Survey of Enterprises on New and Emerging Risks (ESENER-3). Publications Office of the European Union (2019)
2. International Federation of Robotics. Executive Summary World Robotics 2019 Industrial Robots. Frankfurt, IFR International Federation of Robotics (2019)

Part VI: Human Modelling and Simulation (Edited by Gunther Paul, Gregor Harih and Sofia Scataglini)

A Digital Human Modelling-Based Optimization Framework to Minimize Low Back Cumulative Loading During Design of Lifting Tasks

Sivan Almosnino$^{(\boxtimes)}$

Amazon.com, Inc., Seattle, WA 98109, USA

Abstract. Disproportionate exposure to low back cumulative loading (LBCL) has been implicated as a risk component for development of pain or injury during performance of lifting tasks. However, addressing LBCL during conceptual work design is challenging because of a lack of an established and widely accepted LBCL threshold value. We therefore propose to address the design challenge using an optimization framework aided by digital human modeling (DHM). We showcase our approach by simulation of a lifting-carrying-lowering task with 4 different relative weight handling frequencies. We further explore the effects of 4 LBCL integration calculation methods on design outputs. Our results show that the percentage agreement for the 4 different relative handling frequencies and integration methods ranged between 89.5% and 100%. Kendall's coefficient of concordance values ranged between 0.74 and 1.0 (all with p < 0.0001), showing good to perfect agreement amongst the solutions. Our proposed approach takes advantage of DHM task simulation capabilities to simulate proposed lifting scenarios and provide solution estimates at the conceptual design phase, a mainstay in optimal engineering practices.

Keywords: Digital human modeling · Ergonomics 4.0 · Optimization · Evolutionary algorithms · Artificial intelligence

1 Introduction

Disproportionate exposure to low back cumulative loading (LBCL) has been implicated as a risk component for development of pain or injury during performance of lifting tasks [1]. However, establishment of a threshold limit value (TLV) for LBCL has been curtailed because of various methodological reasons [1, 2].

To overcome the absence of an established LBCL TLV while understanding the potential LBCL risk contribution, we propose during conceptual design of lifting tasks to devise the problem using an optimization framework aided by digital human modeling (DHM). That is, for an allotted lifting task, we define an objective function to minimize LBCL given a set of productivity constraints. This approach has the benefits of not only circumventing the lack of a TLV but also provides confidence that an optimal (or near optimal) solution has not been ignored because of the non-trivial contributions of different task elements. In addition, the approach takes advantage of developments in

© The Author(s), under exclusive license to Springer Nature Switzerland AG 2022
N. L. Black et al. (Eds.): IEA 2021, LNNS 223, pp. 349–352, 2022.
https://doi.org/10.1007/978-3-030-74614-8_42

DHM technology, namely the ability to calculate low back compression *time-series* in a simulation environment.

Within this framework, the literature proposes several integration methods to calculate LBCL: Those assuming equal weighting to force and time entities, and those which weigh the contributions of the compressive force more heavily than the time component [2]. In practice, the use of different LBCL integration functions may end in different designs. Thus, it is important to assess whether and to what degree differing optimization inputs have on the final design output.

In this study, we showcase the use of an optimization framework for minimizing LBCL and compare different formulations of the objective functions based on different LBCL integration methods and assess their effect on the design outputs.

2 Methods

We used the task simulation builder module in Tecnomatix Jack digital human modeling software (Version 9.0, Siemens) to create a hypothetical lifting task involving the following elements: 1) Lifting a box from a 0.76 m fixed height conveyor, 2) Carrying and placing the box in one of 16 storage bin locations, and 3) Returning to the conveyor to grasp the next box. The aisle distance between the conveyor and storage locations was set to 1.2 m, and the storage locations were arranged in a 4×4 matrix with bins heights equally distributed between 0.07 m and 1.2 m. Box weights were set to 2 kg., 5 kg., 10 kg., and 15 kg., and 4 different relative handling frequencies were used for each weight category given a total of 250 lifts performed over an 8-h period (see example in Fig. 1). The simulations used a height and weight-scaled 50th percentile male based on the NHANES 2013–14 anthropometric database.

For each simulation iteration, we calculated compressive forces at the L4–L5 vertebrae level using a three-dimensional, static biomechanical model. Task performance times were estimated using MTM1 predetermined motion time system. The resulting compression-time series were integrated according to 4 suggested methods: 2 assuming equal weighting of force and time, and 2 in which the force values were raised to the 2nd and 4th power, respectively [2].

We devise our objective function per Eq. 1 [2]:

$$\min \sum (LBCL_{mi} \times Freq_i) \quad \text{for} \quad i = 1, n \tag{1}$$

Where $LBCL_{mi}$ is the integral for box weight category m for task i, $Freq_i$ is the frequency of task i and n are the number of different tasks performed. Our solution is subject to the constraints of a maximal handling rate of 250 boxes based on four relative handling distributions (e.g., Fig. 1), and a maximal number of boxes in each storage location equal to 16.

We solved the optimization problem using an evolutionary algorithm with the following parameter values: mutation rate $= 0.075$, convergence of 0.01%, and a population size of 100. We describe our results using percentage agreement of box weights allocation into specific storage locations for each of the four-relative weight distributions and LBCL integration methods. We further assess agreement across methods using Kendall's coefficient of concordance (W), with alpha preset at 0.05.

Relative Handling Frequency Condition: 80%-10%-6%-4%

	Integration Method # 1				Integration Method # 2				Integration Method # 3				Integration Method # 4			
	# of Boxes				# of Boxes				# of Boxes				# of Boxes			
2 kg	0	0	0	13	16	0	16	16	0	0	0	13	0	0	0	13
5 kg	0	6	16	3	0	16	0	0	0	6	16	3	0	6	16	3
10 kg	6	9	0	0	0	0	0	0	6	9	0	0	6	9	0	0
15 kg	10	0	0	0	0	0	0	0	10	0	0	0	10	0	0	0
2 kg	16	16	16	16	6	6	0	16	16	16	16	16	16	16	16	16
5 kg	0	0	0	0	9	0	0	0	0	0	0	0	0	0	0	0
10 kg	0	0	0	0	0	9	6	0	0	0	0	0	0	0	0	0
15 kg	0	0	0	0	0	0	10	0	0	0	0	0	0	0	0	0
2 kg	16	16	16	16	16	16	16	16	16	16	16	16	16	16	16	16
5 kg	0	0	0	0	0	0	0	0	0	0	0	0	0	0	0	0
10 kg	0	0	0	0	0	0	0	0	0	0	0	0	0	0	0	0
15 kg	0	0	0	0	0	0	0	0	0	0	0	0	0	0	0	0
2 kg	16	16	16	16	16	16	16	16	16	16	16	16	16	16	16	16
5 kg	0	0	0	0	0	0	0	0	0	0	0	0	0	0	0	0
10 kg	0	0	0	0	0	0	0	0	0	0	0	0	0	0	0	0
15 kg	0	0	0	0	0	0	0	0	0	0	0	0	0	0	0	0

Fig. 1. Box storage allocation solutions determined by each of the four LBCL integration methods for the one of the relative handling frequency scenarios, in which 2 kg boxes were handled 80% of the time, 5 kg boxes were handled 10% of the time, 10 kg boxes were handled 6% of the time, and 15 kg boxes were handled 4% of the time. For each storage location, the maximal number of boxes can be stored is 16. One storage location includes 1 column by 4 rows listing the number of boxes allocated for each weight category. The red-shade bin areas show a task exceeding NIOSH "Action Level" thresholds of low back compression forces >3400 N.

3   Results

Figure 1 shows an example solution obtained for one of the relative handling frequency simulations in terms of number of boxes per weight category allocated for storage in each of the 16 bin locations. For all 4 relative handling frequencies simulated, the percentage agreement in terms of the number and location of box allocations across the 4 integration methods ranged between 89.5% and 100%. Kendall's coefficient of concordance values, ranged between 0.74 and 1.0, showing good to perfect agreement amongst the unique solutions.

4   Discussion

Although there appears to be agreement amongst experts that weighting of the force component is warranted when quantifying LBCL via integration, there is no clear consensus on the validity of one method over the other [2]. Our results show that irrespective of the LBCL integration method used, the optimization solution is robust for the four relative weight handling frequencies simulated. In part, the results may be explained by the close maintenance of rank order amongst the different tasks irrespective of the integration method, which resulted in algorithm fitness score similarity.

In our study, we did not include additional ergonomic constraints because of our focus on examining the effects of different integration methods on the final design outcome. However, defining such constraints would be a necessity since one ergonomic measure alone is not likely to satisfy all injury or fatigue pathways. For example, in our study, several storage allocations exceeded NIOSH's recommendation of maintaining peak low back forces below 3400N (Fig. 1). Thus, users of our proposed method or using a similar optimization approach are encouraged in real design scenarios to identify all possible contributing factors to task physical demands (e.g., peak low back compression and shear, energy expenditure, psychophysical thresholds) and incorporate these into calculation procedures.

A limitation of our approach relates to inherent DHM technological challenges. In specifics, DHM inverse kinematics posture prediction algorithms differ from realistic postures adopted during performance of lifting and other tasks [3]. This presents a challenge in that variation amongst different workers are not considered in LBCL calculations. Currently, varying mannequin postures in DHM is a tedious, manual process which relies on expert judgement to reflect real world behaviors. Future work and DHM development should attempt to automate the posture adjustment process based on motor-control theory and empirical findings that would allow to incorporate variability between and within workers performing lifting tasks.

In conclusion, we present a practical solution to minimizing LBCL during conceptual design of lifting tasks using an optimization framework. The solution appears to be robust to the method of LBCL integration. The optimization method can aid engineers in addressing LBCL risk factors early in the design stage in the absence of an established TLV.

References

1. Waters, T., et al.: Cumulative spinal loading exposure methods for manual material handling tasks. Part 1: is cumulative spinal loading associated with lower back disorders? Theor. Issues Ergon. Sci. **7**(02), 113–130 (2006)
2. Waters, T., et al.: Cumulative spinal loading exposure methods for manual material handling tasks. Part 2: methodological issues and applicability for use in epidemiological studies. Theor. Issues Ergon. Sci. **7**(02), 131–148 (2006)
3. Cort, J.A., Devries, D.: Accuracy of postures predicted using a digital human model during four manual exertion tasks, and implications for ergonomic assessments. IISE Trans. Occup. Ergon. Hum. Factors **7**(1), 43–58 (2019)

Assessing the Efficiency of Industrial Exoskeletons with Biomechanical Modelling – Comparison of Experimental and Simulation Results

Lars Fritzsche[1]([⊠]), Christian Gärtner[1], Michael Spitzhirn[1], Pavel E. Galibarov[2], Michael Damsgaard[2], Pauline Maurice[3], and Jan Babič[4]

[1] imk Automotive GmbH, Amselgrund 30, 09128 Chemnitz, Germany
lars.fritzsche@imk-automotive.de
[2] AnyBody Technoloy A/S, Niels Jernes Vej 10, 9220 Aalborg, Denmark
[3] Université de Lorraine, CNRS, 54000 Inria, France
[4] Jožef Stefan Institute, Jamova cesta 39, 1000 Ljubljana, Slovenia

Abstract. Exoskeletons are currently introduced for several industrial applications, but in many cases the efficiency of such devices in supporting heavy physical work has not been fully proved yet. Biomechanical simulation could considerably contribute to determining the efficiency of exoskeletons in various use cases with different user populations. In this paper we present an approach to extent laboratory and field studies by using the software AnyBody Modelling System. The biomechanical simulation is applied to the "Paexo Shoulder", a commercial exoskeleton provided by Ottobock. Results show that the exoskeleton substantially reduces muscle activation and joint reaction forces in the shoulder and does not increase activation or forces in the lumbar spine. Comparison with laboratory measurements show very similar results. This indicates that the simulation framework could be used to evaluate changes in internal body loads as a result of wearing exoskeletons and thereby, supplements laboratory experiments and field tests during exoskeleton design and development.

Keywords: Musculoskeletal modelling · Exoskeleton · Biomechanical simulation · Industrial exoskeletons · AnyBody Modelling System · Paexo shoulder

1 Introduction

Industrial exoskeletons can potentially be used for supporting workers in heavy physical tasks that may be associated with high risks for developing musculoskeletal disorders (MSDs). Laboratory experiments and field studies are common approaches to evaluate feasibility and effects of industrial exoskeletons (de Looze et al. 2016). This kind of research is necessary to get valuable and real-world insights into objective measures as well as subjective comfort evaluation and acceptance. However, they often require complex sensor technologies like EMG electrodes that are difficult to use in practice.

© The Author(s), under exclusive license to Springer Nature Switzerland AG 2022
N. L. Black et al. (Eds.): IEA 2021, LNNS 223, pp. 353–357, 2022.
https://doi.org/10.1007/978-3-030-74614-8_43

They also do not allow conclusions about internal joint loads or compensatory mechanisms and they are costly or may disrupt ongoing work in field studies. Biomechanical simulations can tackle these challenges because they can be prepared on a computer and safely analyzed using digital human models. They also allow to calculate forces or joint moments inside the body and they can be used for investigating various use cases without expensive experimental set up.

In this paper we present an approach to extent laboratory and field studies by using the biomechanical software AnyBody Modelling System provided by AnyBody Technology A/S, Denmark. The simulation is applied to the "Paexo Shoulder", a commercially available exoskeleton provided by Ottobock SE & Co. KGaA, Germany. It weighs approx. 1.9 kg and is specifically designed to support overhead work. Detailed study results are published in Fritzsche et al. (in press).

2   Methods

This study applies the simulation framework firstly presented in Galibarov et al. (2019) using a set of data recorded at a laboratory experiment and compares simulation and experimental outcomes. The laboratory experiment included 12 participants (all male) performing an overhead drilling task with a hand-held tool (Fig. 1). Detailed descriptions are presented in Maurice et al. (2020), the data set is available on Zenodo (https://doi. org/10.5281/zenodo.1472214). All participants performed the task while wearing the Paexo Shoulder exoskeleton (WE), and without wearing it (NE). Whole body kinematics were retrieved using an Xsens MVN inertial motion tracking suit. Moreover, muscle activities of the right anterior deltoid and right erector spinae longissimus were recorded with Biometrics EMG system. Additionally, heart rate and oxygen consumption were measured as indicators of metabolic effort.

Using the motion capturing data that were recorded at the laboratory experiment, simulations were created and analyzed with AnyBody Modeling System v.7.3.2 (AMS). AMS uses a biomechanical human model comprised of most of the muscle elements, bones, and joints in the body. The system computes muscle activations, joint moments and reactions forces necessary to generate the specified motions by recruiting muscles in an optimal way (Damsgaard et al. 2006). In this study, a total of 2.880 trials (12 participants, 2 conditions NE/WE, 5 sets of 24 trials) were simulated and processed using a Python script (Lund et al. 2019). The processing model used anthropometric measurements available in the recorded Xsens files to scale corresponding model body parts to consistently represent body size of the participants (Fig. 2). Inverse dynamics analysis was then carried out to compute estimations of muscle activities and joint reaction forces.

Based on the repeated-measures design in the laboratory experiment, simulation data was grouped into two conditions "with exoskeleton" (WE) and "without exoskeleton" (NE). Data analysis was also done using a Python script to automatically analyze the 2.880 trials for each simulation variable. Single outlier values beyond three standard deviations above or below the mean were excluded. Descriptive data analysis included calculating box-plots and histograms for each variable. Wilcoxon signed-rank test was used to test for significant differences between the two conditions, since most of the

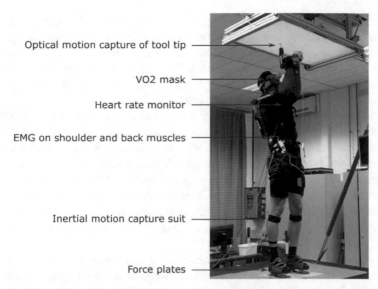

Fig. 1. Experimental set up at the laboratory experiment adapted from Maurice et al. (2020).

data was not normally distributed according to Kolmogorov-Smirnov-Test. Results were considered as statistically significant with $\alpha < .05$ (two-sided).

Fig. 2. AnyBody Model with "Paexo Shoulder" exoskeleton (left); application of Paexo Shoulder model in overhead drilling task (right) (adapted from Fritzsche et al. in press).

3 Results

Results of the AMS biomechanical simulation demonstrate that wearing the exoskeleton reduces muscle activation in the three deltoid shoulder muscles (anterior, posterior, lateral) by 74% to 87% compared to the baseline activation with no exoskeleton. Effects were stronger for the right deltoid muscles than for the left deltoid muscles because the drilling tool was used in the right hand, whereas the left hand was only needed to stabilize the body (Fig. 1). Similarly, infraspinatus muscle at the shoulder front showed a high baseline activation (NE) at the right side that is reduced by 42% while wearing the exoskeleton (WE). Other relevant muscles in the shoulder/arm area, such as triceps, biceps and trapezius, showed a very low baseline activation (<10% of maximal possible activation in both conditions on both sides). This indicates that these muscles were not very much involved in the overhead drilling task, although some of them also showed significant decreases of muscle activation on a low level.

Joint reaction forces in the shoulder were also analyzed by means of AMS simulation. The glenohumeral joint forces were reduced between 56% and 80% in all three force directions while wearing the exoskeleton. Similarly, forces in the acromioclavicular joint and in the sternoclavicular joint were reduced between 54% and 68% in all directions while wearing the exoskeleton, with one small opposite effect in the sternoclavicular medio-lateral force on a very low force level (4.5 N increase in WE condition). Overall, results on joint reaction forces are very consistent across different joints and force directions indicating that the exoskeleton is substantially reducing strain in the shoulder joints.

Finally, muscle activities and joint forces in the spine were analyzed with the simulation. Results showed a medium activation pattern in erector spinae muscles on left and right side (approx. 20%), but there were no significant differences with or without exoskeleton use. Moreover, compression forces in the L5/S1 disc area were unchanged in two directions or even slightly decreased (approx. 12%) while wearing the exoskeleton. Overall, wearing the exoskeleton did not significantly influence muscle activities or joint forces in the lumbar spine.

4   Discussion

Results of the AMS simulation study suggest that the Paexo Shoulder exoskeleton is an effective device to reduce biomechanical strain in overhead drilling tasks. Muscle activations of the shoulder complex are reduced, which should decrease the fatigue level of the workers. Similarly, it reduces reaction forces in the shoulder joint supposedly leading to a decrease in shoulder joint cartilage degeneration rates. The device does not redistribute the arm loads onto the lumbar spine, indicating that no adverse side effects for the lumbar spine have to be expected.

Results of the laboratory experiment and the simulation are quite similar for most parameters: (1) in the lab, measured EMG activity in the anterior deltoid muscle is decreased by 54% in average; in the simulation, the same muscle activity is reduced by 74% while wearing the exoskeleton. (2) Muscle activity of the erector spinae does not show any difference for with/without exoskeleton conditions in both laboratory measurement and simulation. (3) Metabolic parameters in the lab, such as decreased oxygen consumption (−33%) and heart rate (−19%), also confirmed that the use of the exoskeleton is related to reduced strain for the entire body.

In summary, these results are suggesting that the simulation framework is a valid approach for investigating the effects of exoskeletons supplementing experimental studies by providing insights into changes inside the human musculoskeletal system. This framework could be extended by analyzing a variety of basic movements/tasks wearing the exoskeleton with different human populations. It also allows investigating intended main effects as well as side effects of exoskeletons (and possibly other wearable devices). Such analysis can not only be used for product evaluation, but also for improving the design and functionalities of exoskeletons in the development phase.

Limitations include the exoskeleton fit to the body, because motion of the exoskeleton was not tracked during the experiment (virtual fitting of the exoskeleton was done for each participant according to the manufacturer's guidelines, but may contain some discrepancies with reality). Furthermore, experimental and simulation data can only be compared to some extent, because computed muscle activations represent a percentage of a maximum muscle force needed to perform motions and do not necessarily match EMG signals on an absolute scale.

Future research should take into account that the presented study and the simulation framework was developed based on the evaluation of passive exoskeletons with mechanical components (springs, etc.). It seems more difficult to apply for soft exoskeletons with mainly textile components and active exoskeletons with external power supply. Another field of future research is the question how biomechanical simulations can be prepared without any motion capturing data. AMS already allows to do that, but it still requires to a lot of expertise and effort to create realistic simulations. Other digital human models, such as ema Work Designer (Fritzsche et al. 2019) use algorithms for generating artificial motions with lower effort, which potentially could be used as an input for AnyBody biomechanical simulations in order to make such studies independent from lab recordings and allow evaluation of virtual prototypes.

References

Damsgaard, M., Rasmussen, J., Tørholm, S., Surma, E., de Zee, M.: Analysis of musculoskeletal systems in the AnyBody Modeling System. Sim. Model. Pract. Theory **14**, 1100–1111 (2006)

de Looze, M.P., Bosch, T., Krause, F., Stadler, K.S., O'Sullivan, L.W.: Exoskeletons for industrial application and their potential effects on physical work load. Ergonomics **59**, 671–681 (2016)

Fritzsche, L., et al.: Assessing the efficiency of exoskeletons in physical strain reduction by biomechanical simulation with AnyBody Modelling System. Wearable Technologies (in press).

Fritzsche, L., Ullmann, S., Bauer, S., Sylaja, V.J.: Task-based digital human simulation with editor for manual work activities – industrial applications in product design and production planning. In: Paul, G., Scataglini, S. (eds.) DHM and Posturography, pp. 569–575. Elsevier, London (2019)

Galibarov, P.E., Damsgaard, M., Spitzhirn, M., Gärtner, C., Fritzsche, L.: Application of a biomechanical simulation framework to assess effects of an exoskeleton on a human body. Presented at WearRAcon Europe (2019)

Lund, M.E., Rasmussen, J., Andersen, M.S.: AnyPyTools: a python package for reproducible research with the anybody modeling system. J. Open Source Softw. **4**(33), 1108 (2019). https://doi.org/10.21105/joss.01108

Maurice, P., et al.: Objective and subjective effects of a passive exoskeleton on overhead work. IEEE Trans. Neural Syst. Rehabil. Eng. **28**, 152–164 (2020)

Current Trends in Research and Application of Digital Human Modeling

Lars Hanson[1,2]([✉]) [iD], Dan Högberg[2] [iD], Erik Brolin[2] [iD], Erik Billing[3] [iD], Aitor Iriondo Pascual[2] [iD], and Maurice Lamb[3] [iD]

[1] Scania CV AB, Global Industrial Development, 151 32 Södertälje, Sweden
lars.hanson@scania.com
[2] School of Engineering Science, University of Skövde, 541 28 Skövde, Sweden
[3] School of Informatics, University of Skövde, 541 28 Skövde, Sweden

Abstract. The paper reports an investigation conducted during the DHM2020 Symposium regarding current trends in research and application of DHM in academia, software development, and industry. The results show that virtual reality (VR), augmented reality (AR), and digital twin are major current trends. Furthermore, results show that human diversity is considered in DHM using established methods. Results also show a shift from the assessment of static postures to assessment of sequences of actions, combined with a focus mainly on human well-being and only partly on system performance. Motion capture and motion algorithms are alternative technologies introduced to facilitate and improve DHM simulations. Results from the DHM simulations are mainly presented through pictures or animations.

Keywords: Digital Human Modeling · Trends · Research · Development · Application

1   Introduction

Manufacturing systems simulation provides quick, meaningful, low-cost, and low-risk analysis and insights when used in the process of designing manufacturing systems. In particular, manufacturing systems simulation can improve a designer's understanding of each component's influence in a manufacturing system without a physical prototype or implementation of the system (Mourtzis 2020). Digital human modeling (DHM) is one type of design and manufacturing simulation software that has been developed and used for decades. The software tools used for DHM incorporate results from research in fields such as anthropometry, ergonomics, and biomechanics, which, in some cases, are found in parallel with the software development process. Several anthologies and papers have been published over the years to document the ongoing activities and trends, e.g., *Digital Human Modeling for Vehicle and Workspace Design* (Chaffin 2001), *Future Applications of DHM in Ergonomic Design* (Bubb 2007), *Handbook of Digital Human Modeling* (Duffy 2008), *Ergonomic DHM systems: Limitations and trends - A review focused on the 'future of ergonomics'* (Alexander and Paul 2014), as well as *DHM and*

N. L. Black et al. (Eds.): IEA 2021, LNNS 223, pp. 358–366, 2022.
https://doi.org/10.1007/978-3-030-74614-8_44

Posturography (Scataglini and Paul 2019). Furthermore, Zhu et al. (2019) published a literature review specifying the applications and research trends of digital human models in manufacturing between 2014 and 2019. Zhu et al. conclude that human–robot collaboration, augmented reality, and motion planning are areas of focus.

This paper aims to contribute to the ongoing practice of investigating and reporting trends in DHM research and development, specifically by providing a unique window into the views of researchers and practitioners in DHM in 2020. The paper reports an investigation conducted during the DHM2020 Symposium regarding current trends in research and application of DHM in academia, software development, and industry.

2 Method

The IEA (International Ergonomics Association) Technical Committee on Digital Human Modeling and Simulation annually arranges a symposium in which researchers, developers, and industry stakeholders meet to present, demonstrate, and discuss the latest developments and results as well as anticipated needs in the field. Every third year the DHM symposium is integrated into the triennial IEA congress. The 6th International Digital Human Modeling Symposium 2020 (DHM2020) was hosted by University of Skövde in Sweden. The symposium was offered as a hybrid conference due to the COVID-19 pandemic. One hundred and fourteen participants (20 onsite and 94 online) from 14 countries were registered for the symposium. Sixty-one participants (54%) represented universities and research institutes. The remaining 53 participants (46%) were from companies. Sixteen percent of the participants had worked for more than 20 years in the field of DHM and 79% less than five years (based on the responses of 44 participants). During the symposium, an online tool provided by mentimeter.com was used to carry out polls among the participants. The results of these polls were presented in real time to the conference participants without any identifying information.

Three types of questions were used for the findings presented in this paper: open-ended questions, multiple-choice questions, and 100 points questions. Open-ended questions, such as "What are the current trends in digital human modelling?" allowed participants to freely provide a word or a short phrase (typically in English) in response to a prompt. Real-time results were presented as a word cloud. Multiple-choice questions offered a limited set of answers to choose from. Depending on the question, participants could select more than one answer. A final question type allowed users to split 100 points among several categories indicating the relative frequency or importance of the categories in the specified context. Real-time results from these question types were presented in the form of a bar graph. The poll questions presented here were related to the topics of the keynote speakers or the associated sessions and covered areas such as current trends, methods for considering diversity, techniques for controlling the manikins, factors evaluated in the simulations, and how results are visualized and presented. The questions also covered the majority of general steps in a DHM simulation process. The simulation process in DHM software typically includes five general steps: create the environment, create manikins, manipulate manikins, do assessments, and present and document results (Green 2000; Hanson et al. 2006). The following multiple-choice questions related to the process were used:

1. How do you represent human diversity? [boundary cases, company-specific families, percentiles, random samples, not considered]
2. How do you control/manipulate the manikin? [key frame, motion capture, model-driven, motion planning, motion synthesis]
3. What factors do you evaluate? [collision, company-specific methods, EAWS, forces on joints, length of walking, muscle activity, reach, RULA, vision, time to perform the task]
4. How do you visualize the results from the DHM analysis? [movies on desktop, experience in VR/HMD, graphs on objective numbers, pictures of results, tables with numbers, CAVE]

3 Results

Twenty-six attendees answered an open-ended question regarding current trends in digital human modeling; together they generated 49 keywords (Fig. 1). The most mentioned terms were virtual reality (VR) and augmented reality (AR). In total these technologies were mentioned 14 times. Digital twin or real-time fitting trials were mentioned five times. Usability and acceptance were mentioned four times as trend topics. Three times the respondents mentioned motion capture or motion modeling. Cognitive modeling, exoskeleton and wearables, dynamics, and safety were each mentioned twice. Keywords of trends mentioned once were scanning, cloud, machine learning, muscle strength, body deformation, posture, workplace design, ergonomics, CAD, data science, system integration, and performance. Three keywords were not understandable or not relevant.

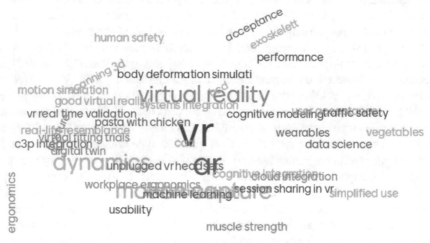

Fig. 1. Word cloud on the question about current trends in DHM.

Relating to general step 2 of the DHM simulation process, i.e., create manikins, 27 respondents, 18% of the registered participants, answered a 100 points question about how they represent human diversity when using DHM software. Respondents could indicate the relative importance of any of several methods (Fig. 2). The largest proportion of points (51.5%) was assigned to percentile methods, though only 37% of respondents assigned points to this method. Percentiles was the category most frequently assigned points by respondents using only one method. 57.1% of these respondents used percentiles. The most frequently selected method was random samples, which was assigned at least some points by 59.3% of the respondents, though it only received approximately 15% of the total points. For the remaining methods, 25.9% of participants assigned points to using boundary cases, and 11.1% of respondents use company-specific manikin families. 55% of the respondents use more than one method. In total, 70.4% of the respondents use an established method to consider diversity. 29.6% of the repondents stated that they did not consider diversity when using DHM tools.

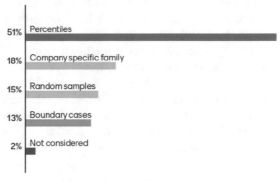

Fig. 2. Methods used for considering human diversity (percent of total responses rounded to nearest whole number).

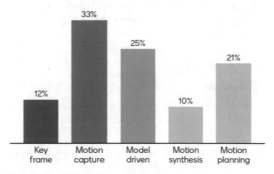

Fig. 3. Methods used for manipulating the manikins (percent of total responses rounded to nearest whole number).

Regarding the third step in the general process, 31 participants responded to a multiple-choice question about common methods for manipulating manikins (Fig. 3). Respondents could select multiple methods. Motion capture was reported as the most common way to manipulate the manikin, used by 54.8% of respondents. Model-driven (41.9%), motion planning (35.5%), key frame (19.4%), and motion synthesis (16.1%)

were also used. Notably, 87.1% of respondents indicated that they manipulate manikin motions using an algorithm, a mathematical model, or a test subject using motion capture. Only 12.1% of respondents indicated manual manipulation by the use of key frame as their sole method for manipulating manikins. The majority of respondents (61.3%) indicated using only a single method, 32.3% indicated two to three methods, and 6.4% indicated four to five methods.

Twenty-two participants responded to a 100 points question regarding which factors they evaluate in DHM software (Fig. 4.). Respondents could distribute points among multiple methods. The largest proportion of respondents assigned points to forces on joints and reach (both 68.2%), followed by collision (54.5%), muscle activity (50.0%), vision (50%), company-specific methods (36.4%), time to perform a task (36.4%), length of walking (22.3%), EAWS (18.2%), and RULA (18.2%). The majority of respondents (45.4%) indicated using two to three methods, 31.8% indicated four to six methods, 18.2% indicated seven or more methods and 4.5% indicated only using one method. 63.6% of the respondents used methods for both evaluation of human well-being, i.e., forces, reach, muscle activity, company-specific methods, vision, EAWS, RULA, and evaluation of system performance, i.e., collision, time to perform task, and length of walking. 36.4% of the respondents evaluated only human well-being. No respondents focus only on system performance. Participants were also asked a multiple-choice question about which cognitive and psychological aspects should be added to modern DHM software packages. 14 out of 21 (67%) respondents indicated a desire for the ability to analyse fatigue, task planning, and stress.

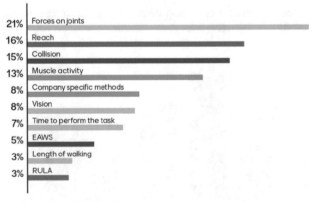

Fig. 4. Factors evaluated in DHM tools (percent of total responses rounded to nearest whole number).

Twenty-five respondents (17% of the registered participants) answered a multiple-choice question relating to how DHM results are formatted for presentation (Fig. 5). Respondents could select all the presentation formats that they use to present DHM results. Accordingly, 68% present simulations results in animations on desktop, 60% in pictures, 48% in graphs, 32% in tables, 28% in VR, and 4% in a CAVE environment. 88% of respondents indicated they use movies, pictures, or both as a presentation format for DHM data. 24% of respondents use four or more presentation methods, 52% two

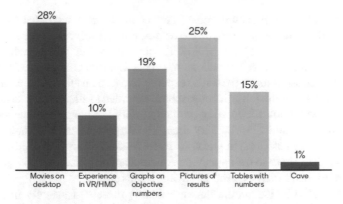

Fig. 5. How results from DHM analyses are presented (percent of total responses rounded to nearest whole number).

to three methods, and 24% indicated only one presentation method. In total, of the 67 responses, 66% stated that the DHM results are presented in visual format, and 34% of the responses indicated the use of objective formats, i.e., presented in graphs and tables. The majority of respondents (64%) indicated presenting their results using both objective and visualization formats. The rest of them use only one type of presentation format with 28% indicating only visualization formats and 8% only objective formats.

4 Discussion

The ability of DHM software to simulate diverse anthropometric manikins, typically grouped in "families", is in line with the industrial trend of mass customization. Mass customization is a production paradigm that focuses on making personalized products (Hu 2013). A higher degree of automation in the DHM software facilitates this personalization. Some DHM software tools can now handle several different manikins and make batch simulations based on task descriptions. The fact that nearly all respondents use established methods to consider human diversity indicates that researchers and users are making use of the ability of DHM to support inclusive design through diversity simulation methods. The most common diversity method is likely the traditional percentile method for defining manikins, as indicated by most of the respondents. The remaining respondents use more advanced mathematical methods or random samples, which also allows defining diverse manikin families.

The trend to assess a sequence of tasks and the motions in-between instead of a static posture is clear. These findings are also in agreement with those of Zhu et al. (2019). They also explain why motion capture and motion algorithms are the most common ways to manipulate the manikin, as opposed to manual methods. This is also in line with the industry's general trend to automate tasks that otherwise require significant human input (Siderska 2020).

DHM tools are continuously being developed and there is still much to do. Trend keywords include adding dynamics, body shapes, and cognitive aspects and were also previously mentioned by Alexander and Paul (2014). The addition of these kinds of functionalities and capabilities will most likely continue since the developer trend is to strive to make the manikin as human-like as possible. However, one challenge on this front remains the apparent uncanny valley. The uncanny valley was introduced by Mori (1970), who described people's reactions to robots that looked and acted almost like a human. He hypothesized that a person's response to a human-like robot would abruptly shift from empathy to revulsion as it approached, but failed to attain, a lifelike appearance. The discussion on the uncanny valley typically refers to the appearance and has been lively in the robotics and film industry area. The discussion is also important for the DHM community because trust in DHM software results requires realistic presentations of the results, related both to the appearance of the manikin and to its motions. Trust and acceptance were mentioned as trend keywords in this study.

Results from the DHM simulations are mainly presented visually in the form of animations or pictures. This is in agreement with the literature stating that the focus in DHM research and development is on visualization and rapidly developing technologies such as VR/AR (Zhu et al. 2019). VR and AR also appeared frequently in the current survey in response to the open question regarding current trends in DHM. However, only approximately a third of the respondents stated that they use these technologies to present their simulation results. There may be several reasons for the low usage of these technologies, such as the lack of additional objective information provided by VR/AR, the lack of multi-user VR/AR technologies, the slow integration of VR/AR features into DHM tools, the additional technical expertise required to run such a system, and/or the relative newness of most consumer VR/AR solutions. It may also be that while currently relatively few DHM tool users make use of VR/AR technology, many more do so than only a few years ago. Similar studies in the future may be able to more clearly indicate if there is an actual movement towards increased VR/AR adoption in the DHM community. While we cannot be certain of the reason for the apparent low adoption of VR/AR technologies, there may be a disconnect between researchers' expectations that VR/AR are a current trend in DHM and actual adoption of the technologies in the field. This suggests that while researchers see a clear benefit, more development is needed to convince the DHM community to adopt the technologies. Given the general sense that VR/AR tools can improve 3D design workflows and troubleshooting, further research on why AR/VR tools are not widely used is suggested to determine what is needed to make these technologies accessible to DHM tool users.

A parallel trend to VR/AR in the industry focuses on big data and a more data-driven approach for generating and presenting results (Tao et al. 2018). This trend is not currently visible in DHM. Big data or similar terms were not mentioned in response to the open question relating to trends in DHM. Today reach and vision analysis results tend to mainly be visualized. Muscle activity is evaluated, and results are presented in measures. Posture evaluation results are presented with both visualizations and objective measures. DHM users rely most on visualizations for presenting the results. In order to connect with the big data trend in industry, more objective measures for presenting analysis results should be introduced in DHM. Along with big data trends, it is also important to find the balance in DHM software between optimizing both human well-being and system performance, i.e., in correspondence with the aim of ergonomics according to the definition of ergonomics by IEA. Currently, most of the respondents use both human well-being and system performance in their evaluation. The number of evaluations may increase focus when the gap between the digital and physical world decreases.

Ignat (2017) states that linking the real-life factory with digital simulations will play an increasingly important role in global manufacturing. This form of digital and real links is referred to as a digital twin solution and has shown great promise for anticipating future design challenges and flaws. DHM simulation can play an important role in this trend towards using digital twins, providing a simulation of physical designs and the opportunity to simulate the users of those physical designs. In many ways, the DHM community appears to be working in line with the aims of digital twin solutions with their focus on diverse manikins, realistic motions, and robust simulation visualization tools.

5 Conclusions

The paper reports an investigation conducted during the DHM2020 Symposium regarding current trends in research and application of digital human modeling in academia, software development, and industry. Based on this investigation, we can say that in general, DHM tool users use percentiles to represent diversity, the majority use motion capture or mathematic algorithms to manipulate the manikin, and simulation results are mainly visualized through pictures and animations and consider both human well-being and system performance. Furthermore, the results show that there is a general trend to focus on VR/AR, digital twin and real-time fitting trails, and usability and acceptance.

Acknowledgement. This work was made possible thanks to the responses of the participants of the DHM2020 Symposium. We also want to thank for the support from the Knowledge Foundation and the associated INFINIT research environment at the University of Skövde in the Synergy Virtual Ergonomics (SVE) project and from the participating organizations. This support is gratefully acknowledged.

References

Alexander, T., Paul, G.: Ergonomic DHM systems – Limitations and trends – A review focused on the 'future of ergonomics'. Paper presented at the 3rd International Digital Human Modeling Symposium (DHM 2014), Tokyo, Japan, May 2014 (2014)

Bubb, H.: Future Applications of DHM in Ergonomic Design. In: Duffy, V.G. (ed.) Digital Human Modeling: First International Conference, ICDHM2007, Held as Part of HCI International 2007, Beijing, China, 22–27 July 2007, Proceedings, pp. 779–793 (2007)

Chaffin, D.B.: Digital Human Modeling for Vehicle and Workplace Design. SAE International, Warrendale (2001)

Duffy, V.G. (ed.): Handbook of Digital Human Modeling: Research for Applied Ergonomics and Human Factors Engineering. CRC Press, Boca Raton (2008)

Green, R.F.: A generic process for human model analysis. SAE Technical Paper 2000–01–2167. Society of Automotive Engineers, Warrendale, PA (2000)

Hanson, L., Blomé, M., Dukic, T., Högberg, D.: Guide and documentation system to support digital human modeling applications. Int. J. Ind. Ergon. **36**(1), 17–24 (2006)

Hu, S.J.: Evolving Paradigms of Manufacturing: From Mass Production to Mass Customization and Personalization. Procedia CIRP **7**, 3–8 (2013)

Ignat, V.: Digitalization and the global technology trends. IOP Conf. Ser. Mater. Sci. Eng. **227**(1), 012062 (2017)

Mourtzis, D.: Simulation in the design and operation of manufacturing systems: state of the art and new trends. Int. J. Prod. Res. **58**(7), 1927–1949 (2020)

Mori, M.: The uncanny valley. Energy **7**(4), 33–35 (1970)

Scataglini, S., Paul, G.: DHM and Posturography. Academic Press, Cambridge (2019)

Siderska, J.: Robotic Process Automation – a driver of digital transformation? Eng. Manag. Prod. Serv. **12**(2), 21–31 (2020)

Tao, F., Qi, Q., Liu, A., Kusiak, A.: Data-driven smart manufacturing. J. Manuf. Syst. **48**(Part C), 157–169 (2018)

Zhu, W., Fan, X., Zhang, Y.: Applications and research trends of digital human models in the manufacturing industry. Virtual Real. Intell. Hardware **1**(6), 558–579 (2019)

Validation of an Inverse Kinematic VR Manikin in Seated Tasks: Application in Ergonomics Training

Mohammad Homayounpour$^{(\boxtimes)}$, Dorien Butter, Saaransh Vasta, and Andrew Merryweather

University of Utah, Utah, SLC 84112, USA
m.homayounpour@utah.edu

Abstract. Lower back and neck pain are common musculoskeletal disorders (MSDs) among dentists and dentistry students. Increased awareness of ergonomics during job tasks could help to reduce MSDs. Virtual reality (VR) enhanced dentistry training programs are gaining popularity in academia. Quantifying inverse kinematics (IK) using VR manikins that mimic a user's body can inform ergonomic risk evaluations. We calibrated and investigated one of the IK manikins' accuracy compared to motion capture (MoCap) using a novel method. We show that posture estimation using VR is accurate to less than 10° in 81% of the seated pick and place tasks for the neck and trunk angles. These results suggest that an accurate estimation of posture in VR is achievable to inform real-time postural feedback. This postural feedback can be integrated into VR enhanced training for dental students to help reinforce ergonomic posture and safer movements.

Keywords: Posture estimation · Ergonomic training · Virtual reality · Inverse kinematic · Motion capture

1 Introduction

Musculoskeletal disorders (MSDs) negatively affect dentists worldwide and are even reported among dental students [1, 2]. The most prevalent regions for pain in dentists and dental students are the neck (19.8–85%) and back (36.3–60.1%) [2]. Awkward static postures and poor workplace practices are two main risk factors in developing MSDs in dentistry [2]. One strategy to reduce low back pain (LBP) and neck pain (NP) in dentistry students is providing just-in-time intervention (JITI) to reinforce proper ergonomic posture while learning a new skill. One crucial factor in helping people maintain a proper ergonomic posture and prevent MSDs is incorporating ergonomic principles into job training from the first day. Ergonomics training at the workplace shows higher behavioral translation levels and has lower musculoskeletal risk in an office environment [3]. Therefore, ergonomics training plays a critical role in preventing the risk for LBP and NP, and needs to be incorporated into dentistry curricula from the very beginning with the help of new technologies.

© The Author(s), under exclusive license to Springer Nature Switzerland AG 2022
N. L. Black et al. (Eds.): IEA 2021, LNNS 223, pp. 367–373, 2022.
https://doi.org/10.1007/978-3-030-74614-8_45

Virtual Reality (VR) is emerging as a new tool to train and educate workers and students across many disciplines [4]. VR training aims to create realistic and safe workplace experiences that allow users to learn how to avoid risks and apply ergonomics while working in demanding environments [5–7]. VR simulation and training have become a popular pre-clinical training tool in dentistry schools worldwide, and the results have been promising [8, 9]. Such training helps students develop their technical skills without the expenses and risks associated with dental models or patients.

VR systems are capable of solving for inverse kinematics (IK) using tracking data. Head-Mounted Displays (HMD), controllers, and Vive Trackers provide accurate position, orientation data, and latency are well within the margins of error compared to the data obtained from Mocap [10, 11]. The position and orientation data allow for developing a manikin inside VR by solving the IK to represent the user's movement and posture [12–14]. While increasing the number of trackers can improve the IK's accuracy, it will decrease user comfort and increase setup time and cost. Multiple groups have proposed IK manikins within VR [12–14], but the model's accuracy has only been validated qualitatively through questionnaires [12, 13] or by comparing the position and orientation of the end effector, not the joint angles [13]. To date, no methods have been proposed to validate these IK manikins quantitively using joint kinematics. Validation is critical to the further development and implementation of postural estimation in VR for ergonomics training.

Although MoCap systems can provide us with the most accurate kinematic tracking, its applications are mostly limited to research environments. In contrast, VR systems are not as accurate as MoCap but can solve for IK outside of research environments without the complexity and cost. This study aims to evaluate the IK manikin's accuracy in estimating the user's neck and trunk posture during sitting tasks. We propose a novel method to quantitatively measure the error in the estimated joint angles compared to a motion capture system (gold standard). Accurate posture estimation in VR would allow integrating postural feedback and ergonomics to VR training among dentistry students to encourage ergonomic behavior and identify hazardous movements.

2   Methods

Participants were recruited under the University of Utah Internal Review Board (IRB: 126927) protocol without any exclusion criteria.

2.1   Test Procedure

Participants were instrumented with 29 retroreflective MoCap markers to track the head, trunk, pelvis, and arms (Vicon, Nexus). Participants were also fitted with a Valve Index Head Mounted Display (HMD), two Valve Index controllers, three HTC VIVE Trackers, placed on the lumbar spine (hip), and both feet (Fig. 1). IK manikin using Final IK (ROOTMOTION) asset was used in Unity to mimic the participant posture. Virtual markers on the IK manikin modeled the MoCap markers on the IK manikin. The IK

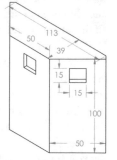

Fig. 1. Table dimensions in the setup.

manikin size was uniformly calibrated based on a participant's stature. Then the participant was asked to sit on the stool and look forward. The orientation of the head was corrected in this position. After that, the participant was asked to start neck flexion to adjust the hip tracker's position on the IK manikin. This adjustment was performed to achieve straight back on the IK manikin when they looked straight, and the hip was not lifted when they performed neck sagittal flexion visually.

After calibration, participants were instructed to pick up a virtual box ($10 \times 10 \times 10$ cm) from a shelf ($h = 150$ cm), and reach over a trapezoidal desk, Fig. 2, to place the box in one of three holes (right, middle, and left). Participants were instructed to only use their right hand. This task was repeated 15 times for each hole. This protocol was selected to maximize the range of motion (ROM) in the lower back and neck.

2.2 Data Analysis

Virtual marker data were converted to text files, mimicking MoCap file extension. The VR coordinate system was aligned with the MoCap's coordinate system, and the data were exported to Visual 3D (V3D) for kinematic analysis. A V3D model was created based on the markerset to calculate the neck and trunk angles. The same model was applied separately to both the virtual markers and MoCap markers for each participant. The trunk angles were calculated with respect to the lab coordinate system, and neck angles were calculated with respect to the trunk. "Pick" and "Place" events were defined for each trial based on markers' position. Pick event was the moment the subject grabbed

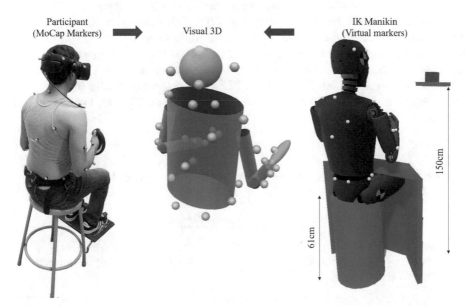

Fig. 2. Experimental setup. The upper body markerset was placed on the participant, and the same markerset was applied to the manikin in VR. Marker data from both the motion capture system and VR were imported to V3D to calculate the trunk and neck angles.

a new box and was defined as 90% of the maximum height of the right finger marker. Place event was the moment the subject placed the box in the designated hole, and was defined as the minimum height of the right finger marker. All trials were normalized from Pick to Place from 0 to 100%. MATLAB 2020a (MathWorks, Natick, MA, USA) software was used for statistical analysis and plots.

2.3 Statistics

Cross-correlation (Corr) and root mean square error (RMSE) were calculated on the normalized trials from Pick to Place, comparing the virtual markers (IK manikin) to the MoCap calculated angles. The trials were divided based on whether the box was placed in the right, middle, or left holes. Linear mixed models were used to estimate angles for neck and trunk at Pick and Place for each trial by assigning the source of the data, VR and Mocap, as the fixed factor and participant as the random factor.

3 Results

Six participants, four females and two males (age 24.9 ± 3.2 y.o (mean $\pm$ Std.), height 175.2 ± 8.2 cm, and weight 73.1 ± 7.2 kg) were tested. The neck and trunk maximum ROM, across all trials, were 45 and 54° in sagittal flexion, 34 and 89° in lateral flexion, and 46 and 90 for axial rotation, respectively. The IK manikin closely followed the movement trajectory of the participant in all the trials, Fig. 3. The mean (Std.) cross-correlation coefficient and the respective RMSE of all trials are reported in Table 1. The cross-correlation reported for the neck and trunk were higher than 0.88, and the mean RMSE was within 11.8° in all pains of motion. The neck and trunk angles at Pick and Place for the right, middle, and left trials are reported in Table 2. The VR system estimated the angles within 5° of error in 17 out of 36 reported events. The mentioned errors were within 5 to 10° in 12 out of 36 reported events and greater than 10° in just 7 events.

Table 1. Average of Cross-Correlation (Corr) and root mean square error (RMSE) values in degrees for the neck and trunk angles.

	Sagittal Extension		Lateral Flexion		Axial Rotation	
	Corr	RMSE	Corr	RMSE	Corr	RMSE
Neck	.90(.19)	6.7(3.9)	.91(.19)	6.6(5.1)	.93(.12)	11.8(10.7)
Trunk	.99(.03)	9.3(3.5)	.89(.25)	4.6(3.3)	.88(.20)	9.9(5.7)

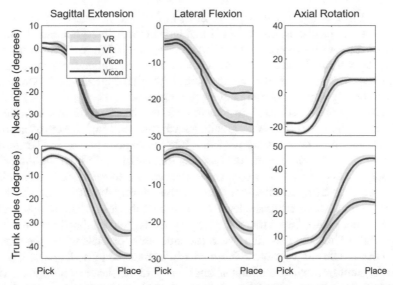

Fig. 3. The mean and Std. of neck and trunk angles from Pick to Place for the left trials.

Table 2. Neck and trunk angles (mean (SE)) measured with the VR system vs. MoCap (ground truth). The sagittal extension, lateral flexion and axial rotation are reported at the time of Pick and Place for the right, middle and left trials.

			Sagittal Ext.		Lateral Flex.		Axial Rot.	
			Pick	Place	Pick	Place	Pick	Place
Right	Neck	VR	-7.6(2.9)	-34.3(3.1)	1.6(1.7)	18.0(1.6)	-15.8(2.5)	-26.0(1.9)
		MoCap	-3.8(0.8)	-23.8(0.7)	4.0(0.5)	19.3(0.6)	-20.6(0.7)	-29.1(0.7)
	Trunk	VR	-1.1(0.7)	-26.1(1.8)	-2.6(0.8)	23.5(1.7)	-7.3(2.1)	-14.8(1.1)
		MoCap	-6.6(0.5)	-34.9(0.5)	-1.9(0.3)	31.6(0.4)	-3.5(0.4)	-18.2(0.6)
Middle	Neck	VR	-6.0(3.7)	-37.0(2.7)	-2.0(1.4)	-10.5(1.3)	-9.3(1.3)	5.0(1.9)
		MoCap	-4.0(0.8)	-30.8(0.6)	0.9(0.5)	-1.9(0.5)	-16.2(0.6)	-5.7(0.5)
	Trunk	VR	-0.7(0.9)	-37.9(3.0)	-3.5(0.6)	-3.4(0.9)	-5.3(1.6)	-1.7(1.6)
		MoCap	-6.2(0.5)	-49.3(0.7)	-2.5(0.2)	-1.6(0.6)	-0.7(0.4)	7.9(0.6)
Left	Neck	VR	-6.6(3.4)	-25.3(1.5)	-4.2(1.2)	-25.3(3.1)	-11.5(2.6)	31.1(2.0)
		MoCap	-4.0(0.8)	-26.5(0.8)	-1.0(0.6)	-17.3(1.7)	-17.7(1.9)	14.7(2.3)
	Trunk	VR	0.9(1.3)	-29.5(1.9)	-4.2(1.1)	-23.4(1.7)	-1.2(1.4)	16.2(2.5)
		MoCap	-5.2(0.4)	-40.6(0.8)	-3.2(0.3)	-30.1(0.9)	4.7(0.5)	38.5(0.6)

☐ Errors < 5 degrees
☐ 5 < Error < 10 degrees
☐ Error > 10 degrees

4   Discussion

We tested the accuracy of the IK manikin quantitatively using a novel method through V3D for estimating the neck and trunk angles in a sitting task. The IK manikin estimated the neck and trunk angles within 10° of error in 81% of the measured events across different tasks. It has been reported [15] that human error in ergonomic assessments, such as rapid upper limb assessment (RULA), was within 10° for neck and trunk angles; therefore, the reported IK manikin accuracy is within an acceptable range to be used for ergonomic assessments. The IK manikin could be integrated into dental VR training and warn the trainee if they do not maintain an ergonomic posture.

The accuracy of the estimated posture was variable based on the event. At the Place event, in trials where the errors were greater than 5°, the neck angles were overestimated in the IK manikin to compensate for trunk rotation underestimation. The motion of reaching over a table and placing the box required rotations in both the thoracic and lumbar spine. This study only used one tracker on the lower back to minimize the complexity and cost (the feet trackers were not used during the sitting tasks). Since we did not have a tracker at the thoracic level, the rotation at this level was not captured by the IK manikin. As a result, the IK manikin compensated for that rotation by overestimating the neck angle. This compensation was most noticeable for trials where the block was placed in the middle and left holes. This error can be reduced by adding a tracker on the thoracic segment or moving the lumbar tracker to a higher level of the spine. Also, in many of the trials, although the IK manikin closely followed the MoCap data, there was an offset between the two systems, which may be corrected by optimizing the virtual markers' placement on the IK manikin.

These results highlight the potential to integrate postural feedback based on ergonomic principles into VR training, an essential step in preventing MSDs [6]. Integrated postural feedback can reduce the required one-on-one time between an instructor and user and increase training consistency, which is especially beneficial for dentistry curricula, demanding many hours of training. Furthermore, integrating an accurate full-body IK manikin allows users to have the same proprioceptive and visual feedback on their body positioning and posture and more immersion in VR [16], further reinforcing a more ergonomic posture.

For future work, we propose improvements in the IK manikin's marker placement. This improvement can be made by minimizing the relative distances between the IK manikin markers and a MoCap markerset after the IK manikin is calibrated. This refined IK manikin may be used later as a tool to validate the other IK manikins in VR systems.

5   Conclusions

This study proposed a unique method to quantitatively test the accuracy of a VR IK manikin with integrated inverse kinematics based on joint angles. We created a virtual markerset on the IK manikin and used it as an input to V3D to compute the neck and trunk angles during seated tasks representative of dental procedures. These results suggest that posture estimation can be integrated into VR training, and users should benefit from real-time feedback to reinforce ergonomic posture.

Acknowledgment. This research was funded in part by grants from National Institute of Occupational Safety and Health (NIOSH) 5 T42OH008414–15-00 and R18HS025606 from the Agency for Healthcare Research and Quality (AHRQ). The content is solely the responsibility of the authors and does not necessarily represent the official views of the AHRQ or NIOSH.

References

1. Vijay, S., Ide, M.: Musculoskeletal neck and back pain in undergraduate dental students at a UK dental school-a cross-sectional study. British Dental J. **221**(5), 241–245 (2016). https://doi.org/10.1038/sj.bdj.2016.642
2. Hayes, M.J., Cockrell, D., Smith, D.R.: A systematic review of musculoskeletal disorders among dental professionals. Int. J. Dental Hyg. **7**(3), 159–165 (2009). https://doi.org/10.1111/j.1601-5037.2009.00395.x
3. Robertson, M., et al.: The effects of an office ergonomics training and chair intervention on worker knowledge, behavior and musculoskeletal risk. Appl. Ergon. **40**(1), 124–135 (2009). https://doi.org/10.1016/j.apergo.2007.12.009
4. Gasparevic, B.D.: Why Virtual - Reality Training for Employees Is Catching On, pp. 3–5 (2019)
5. Li, X., Yi, W., Chi, H.-L., Wang, X., Chan, A.P.C.: A critical review of virtual and augmented reality (VR/AR) applications in construction safety. Autom. Constr. **86**, 150–162 (2018). https://doi.org/10.1016/j.autcon.2017.11.003
6. Leskovský, R., Kučera, E., Haffner, O., Matišák, J., Rosinová, D., Stark, E.: A contribution to workplace ergonomics evaluation using multimedia tools and virtual reality. In: Presented at the Proceedings of the 2019 Federated Conference on Computer Science and Information Systems (2019)
7. Hu, B., Ma, L., Zhang, W., Salvendy, G., Chablat, D., Bennis, F.: Predicting real-world ergonomic measurements by simulation in a virtual environment. Int. J. Ind. Ergon. **41**(1), 64–71 (2011). https://doi.org/10.1016/j.ergon.2010.10.001
8. Mirghani, I., et al.: Capturing differences in dental training using a virtual reality simulator. Eur. J. Dental Educ. **22**(1), 67–71 (2018)
9. LeBlanc, V.R., Urbankova, A., Hadavi, F., Lichtenthal, R.M.: A preliminary study in using virtual reality to train dental students. J. Dental Educ. **68**(3), 378–383 (2004)
10. Niehorster, D.C., Li, L., Lappe, M.: The accuracy and precision of position and orientation tracking in the HTC vive virtual reality system for scientific research. Iperception **8**(3), 2041669517708205 (2017). https://doi.org/10.1177/2041669517708205
11. Choi, S.-W., et al.: P-195L: late-news poster: head position model-based latency measurement system for virtual reality head mounted display. In: SID Symposium Digest of Technical Papers, vol. 47, no. 1, pp. 1381–1384. Wiley Online Library (2016)
12. Caserman, P., Garcia-Agundez, A., Konrad, R., Göbel, S., Steinmetz, R.: Real-time body tracking in virtual reality using a Vive tracker. Virtual Real. **23**(2), 155–168 (2018). https://doi.org/10.1007/s10055-018-0374-z
13. Caserman, P., Achenbach, P., Göbel, S.: Analysis of inverse kinematics solutions for full-body reconstruction in virtual reality. In: 2019 IEEE 7th International Conference on Serious Games and Applications for Health (SeGAH), pp. 1–8. IEEE (2019)
14. Jiang, F., Yang, X., Feng, L.: Real-time full-body motion reconstruction and recognition for off-the-shelf VR devices. In: Presented at the Proceedings of the 15th ACM SIGGRAPH Conference on Virtual-Reality Continuum and Its Applications in Industry, vol. 1 (2016)
15. Golabchi, A., Han, S., Fayek, A.R., AbouRizk, S.: Stochastic modeling for assessment of human perception and motion sensing errors in ergonomic analysis. J. Comput. Civ. Eng. **31**(4) (2017). https://doi.org/10.1061/(asce)cp.1943-5487.0000655
16. Slater, M., Wilbur, S.: A framework for immersive virtual environments (FIVE): Speculations on the role of presence in virtual environments. Presence Teleoper. Virtual Environ. **6**(6), 603–616 (1997)

Multi-objective Optimization of Ergonomics and Productivity by Using an Optimization Framework

Aitor Iriondo Pascual[1](✉) ⓘ, Dan Högberg[1] ⓘ, Anna Syberfeldt[1] ⓘ, Erik Brolin[1] ⓘ, Estela Perez Luque[1] ⓘ, Lars Hanson[1,2] ⓘ, and Dan Lämkull[3] ⓘ

[1] School of Engineering Science, University of Skövde, 541 28 Skövde, Sweden
`aitor.iriondo.pascual@his.se`
[2] Scania CV AB, Global Industrial Development, 151 32 Södertälje, Sweden
[3] Advanced Manufacturing Engineering, Volvo Car Corporation, 405 31 Göteborg, Sweden

Abstract. Simulation technologies are widely used in industry as they enable efficient creation, testing, and optimization of the design of products and production systems in virtual worlds, rather than creating, testing, and optimizing prototypes in the physical world. In an industrial production context, simulation of productivity and ergonomics helps companies to find and realize optimized solutions that uphold profitability, output, quality, and worker well-being in their production facilities. However, these two types of simulations are typically carried out using separate software, used by different users, with different objectives. This easily causes silo effects, leading to slow development processes and sub-optimal solutions. This paper reports on research related to the realization of an optimization framework that enables the concurrent optimization of aspects relating to both ergonomics and productivity. The framework is meant to facilitate the inclusion of Ergonomics 4.0 in the Industry 4.0 revolution.

Keywords: Ergonomics · Digital human modeling · Productivity · Simulation · Optimization

1 Problem Statement

Simulation technologies are widely used in industry because they enable efficient creation, testing, and optimization of the design of products and production systems in virtual worlds, rather than creating, testing, and optimizing prototypes in the physical world. This saves time and money and facilitates more thorough investigation of the solution space. Thus, simulation is used to design workstations from a productivity perspective. Simulation is also used to assess ergonomics in the design of workstations by using digital human modeling (DHM) software [1]. However, these two types of simulations are typically carried out using separate software, used by different users, with different objectives. This can cause silo effects, leading to slow development processes and sub-optimal solutions.

N. L. Black et al. (Eds.): IEA 2021, LNNS 223, pp. 374–378, 2022.
https://doi.org/10.1007/978-3-030-74614-8_46

Research has shown that productivity and ergonomics often go hand in hand [2], since improving workers' conditions often improves productivity [3, 4]. Sometimes, however, productivity and ergonomics objectives may be in conflict. Companies need to find and realize solutions in their production facilities that uphold profitability, output, and quality, as well as worker well-being. Hence, companies need to consider both productivity and ergonomics when using simulation tools to improve factories. Previous studies have considered these aspects at the design level of a workstation [5]. However, there is a lack of frameworks that can handle an overall perspective, treat productivity and ergonomics within one tool, and assist production engineers and ergonomists to find optimal solutions taking both ergonomics and productivity into account. This paper reports on research related to the realization of an optimization framework that enables the concurrent optimization of ergonomics and productivity. The framework is meant to facilitate the inclusion of Ergonomics 4.0 in the Industry 4.0 revolution [6, 7].

2 Method

In information systems research, the design and creation methodology defines the steps involved in developing and evaluating an artifact, which may be a construct, model, method, instantiation, or framework [8]. In this paper, design and creation methodology is applied to the development of a framework to enable concurrent optimization of ergonomics and productivity using a simulation-based multi-objective optimization approach.

3 Results

The proposed framework (Fig. 1) presents a workflow to perform optimizations using DHM tools so that multi-objective simulation-based optimizations of ergonomics and productivity can be carried out. This workflow can be used both with manual optimization methods and automatic methods. The flow can be followed either by a user performing design improvements manually or with the support of optimization algorithms. The workflow of the framework can be divided into three parts: (1) problem definition and creation of the optimization model, (2) optimization process, and (3) presentation and selection of results.

3.1 Part 1 - Problem Definition and Creation of the Optimization Model

The first step in the workflow of the framework is to define the problem (Fig. 1). The problem can be either a productivity issue, an ergonomics issue, or both, and it must be capable of being represented in a DHM tool. After defining the problem, the requirements of the expected result are defined so that ergonomics and productivity targets are defined as well as the way to assess them and the conditions to end the optimization. These targets have to be measurable in the simulation results of the DHM tool, such as results from ergonomics evaluation methods and cycle times, and must represent the needs of the engineers/ergonomists.

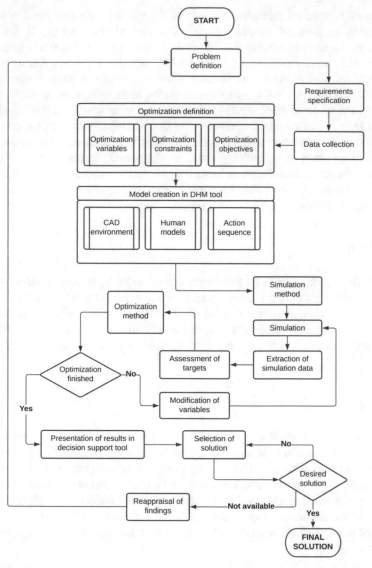

Fig. 1. Proposed optimization framework for optimization using DHM tools.

The next step is to collect data to define the optimization and create the model in the DHM tool. The optimization variables, constraints, and objectives of the ergonomics or productivity factors are defined based on the collected data. The DHM model containing the CAD environment, the human models, and the sequence of actions is then created. The CAD environment is made up of different elements depending on the case. For example, in an industrial case, the CAD environment can contain the factory layout, the resources/tools needed for production, and the product. The human models are defined so that diversity in the user group is represented. In the industrial case, this corresponds to representing diversity in the workforce. The action sequence represents the motions of the simulation. In an industrial case, the action sequence represents the actions that the workers perform to complete the tasks and other motions in the CAD environment, such as the motions of conveyor belts and robots.

3.2 Part 2 - Optimization Process

Once the model has been created, an iterative process is started to perform the optimization, following a circular generation-evaluation pattern. The simulation method defines the different settings for the subsequent simulations, such as collision avoidance and the motion generation solver (e.g., quasi-static or dynamic), and triggers the simulation (Fig. 1). The simulation data is extracted, and the targets are assessed by using the previously defined requirements. These requirements could be related to productivity (e.g., cycle time and other production metrics) and/or ergonomics (e.g., criteria of ergonomics evaluation methods). The assessed targets are input into the optimization method to calculate the optimization objectives. In manual optimizations, the optimization method and the requirements specification will define whether the optimization is finished; otherwise, only the optimization method (the optimization algorithm) will determine the end of the optimization. If the optimization has not met the requirements, the optimization method provides new variable values that modify the simulation input, and further iterations are run until the optimization is finished.

3.3 Part 3 - Presentation and Selection of Results

Once the optimization is finished, the results are presented (Fig. 1). The user then starts an iterative process of selecting solutions using a decision support tool and checking the solution results to evaluate whether the desired solution has been attained. The optimization objectives are displayed in the decision support tool to help obtain a good balance between ergonomics and productivity targets. Once a solution has been chosen, the optimization process is finished, and a final solution is defined as the result of the framework.

If no acceptable solution is available among the solutions, the findings need to be reappraised. This can lead to modifications of the previous steps, such as changes in the problem definition, requirements specification, data collection, optimization definition, or the model definition.

4 Discussion

The presented framework allows multi-objective optimizations of ergonomics and productivity using various DHM tools. The optimizations can be done by a user performing design improvements manually, or they can be done automatically using optimization algorithms. Using optimization algorithms to find optimized workstation designs allows exploring the solution space by performing a strategic search through feasible solutions without manually processing each of all possible configurations. However, results from the presented framework are sensitive to the accuracy of the virtual model. To obtain reliable results, the virtual model must appropriately represent the real world. Digitalization of the real-world industry and the workers could improve the accuracy of the simulation models. Such digitalization is one of the objectives of Industry 4.0 and Ergonomics 4.0. The most mature digitalization level is a digital twin of the factory, including both the environment and the workers. This digital twin could increase the accuracy of the results by creating more accurate models using new technologies, for example, motion capture systems could capture human motions and 3D scanning could capture the environment [9, 10].

Acknowledgment. This work has been supported by ITEA3 in the project MOSIM, the Knowledge Foundation and the associated INFINIT research environment at the University of Skövde, within the Virtual Factories with Knowledge-Driven Optimization (VF-KDO) research profile and the Synergy Virtual Ergonomics (SVE) project, and by the participating organizations. Their support is gratefully acknowledged.

References

1. Scataglini, S., Paul, G.: DHM and Posturography. Elsevier Academic Press, New York (2019)
2. Falck, A.-C., Örtengren, R., Högberg, D.: The impact of poor assembly ergonomics on product quality: A cost–benefit analysis in car manufacturing. Hum. Factors Ergon. Manuf. Serv. Ind. **20**, 24–41 (2010). https://doi.org/10.1002/hfm.20172
3. Vink, P., Koningsveld, E.A.P., Molenbroek, J.F.: Positive outcomes of participatory ergonomics in terms of greater comfort and higher productivity. Appl. Ergon. **37**, 537–546 (2006). https://doi.org/10.1016/j.apergo.2006.04.012
4. Widana, I.K., Sumetri, N.W., Sutapa, I.K.: Ergonomic work station design to improve workload quality and productivity of the craftsmen. J. Phys. Conf. Ser. **953**, 012091 (2018). https://doi.org/10.1088/1742-6596/953/1/012091
5. Battini, D., Faccio, M., Persona, A., Sgarbossa, F.: New methodological framework to improve productivity and ergonomics in assembly system design. Int. J. Ind. Ergon. **41**, 30–42 (2011). https://doi.org/10.1016/j.ergon.2010.12.001
6. Gašová, M., Gašo, M., Štefánik, A.: Advanced industrial tools of ergonomics based on Industry 4.0 Concept. Procedia Eng. **192**, 219–224 (2017). https://doi.org/10.1016/j.proeng.2017.06.038
7. Kadir, B.A., Broberg, O., Conceição, C.S.D.: Current research and future perspectives on human factors and ergonomics in Industry 4.0. Comput. Ind. Eng. **137**, 106004 (2019). https://doi.org/10.1016/j.cie.2019.106004
8. March, S.T., Smith, G.F.: Design and natural science research on information technology. Decis. Support Syst. **15**, 251–266 (1995). https://doi.org/10.1016/0167-9236(94)00041-2
9. Greco, A., Caterino, M., Fera, M., Gerbino, S.: Digital twin for monitoring ergonomics during manufacturing production. Appl. Sci. **10**, 7758 (2020). https://doi.org/10.3390/app10217758
10. Havard, V., Jeanne, B., Lacomblez, M., Baudry, D.: Digital twin and virtual reality: a co-simulation environment for design and assessment of industrial workstations. Prod. Manuf. Res. **7**, 472–489 (2019). https://doi.org/10.1080/21693277.2019.1660283

Demographic Effects on Mid-Air Gesture Preference for Control of Devices: Implications for Design

Haoyan Jiang[1,2], Mark Chignell[1], Sachi Mizobuchi[2(✉)], Farzin Farhadi Niaki[2],
Zhe Liu[2], Wei Zhou[2], and Wei Li[2]

[1] University of Toronto, 5 King's College Road, Toronto, ON M3S 3G8, Canada
chignell@mie.utoronto.ca
[2] Human-Machine Interaction Lab, Huawei, 19 Allstate Pkwy, Markham, ON L3R54, Canada
sachi.mizobuchi@huawei.com

Abstract. After eliciting 129 potential task-gesture combinations for 23 Smart TV tasks with a Canadian sample (N = 22), we then conducted studies that collected participant preference scores on mid-air bare-hand gestures for TV control in both Canada (N = 747) and China (N = 300), and we analyzed the effect of characteristics of individual participants on gesture preference scores. The results showed that age and cultural differences are important in determining task-gesture preferences. While exploratory, the present results indicate a need for more research in this area and suggest that one of two possible strategies may need to be adopted in designing future gesture interactions: 1) develop customized task-gesture combinations for different cultures and different age groups; 2) develop a core set of task-gesture combination possibilities and let users choose which gesture they want to use for each task.

Keywords: Mid-air/Bare-hand gesture design · Preference rating · Individual characteristics

1 Background

Early work on gesture-based interaction focused on table-top interfaces [1]. Gesture interaction with a TV was also considered, but it still required a hand-held controller [2]. Other contexts considered for gestural interaction have included driving [3] and gesturing with wearable devices [4]. In this paper we focus on mid-air gesturing, a natural interaction method that lets users control a system remotely without needing a special input device. With embedded cameras on Smart TVs, designers of electronic devices are considering the use of mid-air free hand interactions to control some of the major commands on devices such as Huawei's X65, the Hisense U7, and the Samsung F-series. While several researchers have proposed mid-air gesture designs for TV control [5–9], the input method is relatively new to most people and there is as yet no "standard" vocabulary of gestures. Thus it is difficult for UI designers to design gestures which will be widely accepted by users, and design recommendations are needed that will help UI designers choose the right gesture for different combinations of people and tasks.

© The Author(s), under exclusive license to Springer Nature Switzerland AG 2022
N. L. Black et al. (Eds.): IEA 2021, LNNS 223, pp. 379–386, 2022.
https://doi.org/10.1007/978-3-030-74614-8_47

2 Objective

Our objective in this research is to understand how the characteristics of individual users affect preference for gestures, focusing on cultural, age, and sex differences. This is a first step towards the development of evidence-based design recommendations concerning how to choose gestures for different groups of people to use when carrying out a particular interaction task.

3 Methodology

We ran two studies, one in Canada and one in China. The gestures used in the preference evaluation study were based on an earlier gesture elicitation study conducted in Canada (N = 22) using 23 TV control tasks (see Table 3 in appendix). The gesture elicitation identified 129 salient gesture-task combinations, or approximately six gestures per task on average. The Canadian study participants (N = 747) then used the same 23 tasks and 87 gestures, with gestures mapped to each task based on the suitability of the gesture for the task, as identified in the elicitation study, resulting in 129 task-gesture combinations. The participants in China (N = 300) rated their preference for a subset of 36 of the gestures matching with 12 of the tasks. Both the Chinese and Canadian participants used a 7-point Likert scale to rate how suitable each gesture was for carrying out/controlling the task that it was assigned to (Fig. 1). There were a total of 40 gesture-task combinations in the Chinese study, or a little over three gestures per task on average.

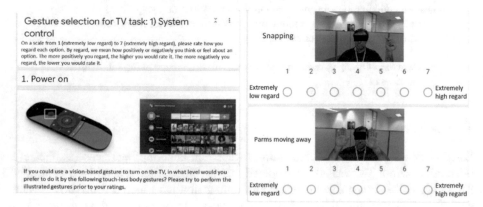

Fig. 1. Example of question and rating screen. The gesture image in this figure is an example frame from a GIF animation presented in the online questionnaire.

Across the two studies we addressed the following research questions:

- RQ1: Do preferred gestures, and gesture-task combinations differ according to the age of Canadian participants?
- RQ2: Do preferred gestures, and gesture-task combinations differ according to the age of Chinese participants?
- RQ3: Do Canadian and Chinese users differ in their preferred mappings of gestures to tasks?

4 Results

We began with an analysis of possible bias in use of the rating scale. Chinese participants tended to use higher ratings, and older people tended to use lower ratings. We ran one set of analyses assuming that absolute ratings were appropriate, and we used a second analysis where the ratings were transformed so as to reduce systematic differences in how participants used the rating scale (c.f. [10]). In this second analysis (reported in this paper), the rating scale data were transformed for each participant using a percentile transformation. Each person's set of rating data was converted to a uniform distribution between 0 and 1 by converting each rating point to a percentile equivalent and then dividing by 100.

Preliminary analysis showed that age effects were much stronger than sex effects in both the Canadian and Chinese samples and thus RQ1 focused on age. We used linear discriminant analysis (LDA) to identify a subset of task gesture combinations that differentiated between young (18–24) and older (65+) participants and plotted the corresponding distributions of normalized preferences as box plots (for the task gesture combinations having the highest LDA coefficients), first for the Canadian sample (Fig. 2) and then for the Chinese sample (RQ2, Fig. 3). Descriptions of the Task-Gesture combinations are provided in Table 1 where the first two columns refer to the Canadian sample and the rightmost two columns refer to the Chinese sample. For the Canadian sample, the medians for the older people on combinations T7G45, T22G50 and T12G58 are above the corresponding 75th percentiles for the 18–24 year olds. For the Chinese sample the medians for older people are similarly higher for T18G40, and perhaps T3G52 but are lower (the media is close to the 25th percentile for the young participants) for T22G48.

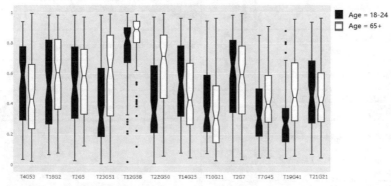

Fig. 2. Boxplot for age group normalized preference comparison (18–24 vs. 65+) among Canadian task-gesture combinations. Plot shows the top 12 (10%) of task gesture combinations ranked by size of discriminating function coefficient.

We then carried out Linear Discriminant Analysis (LDA) comparing normalized preferences for overlapping task-gesture combinations between the Chinese and Canadian samples. We conducted LDA and selected the eight gesture-task combinations that had the highest LDA Coefficients (Table 2), presenting the distributional differences as box plots (Fig. 4).

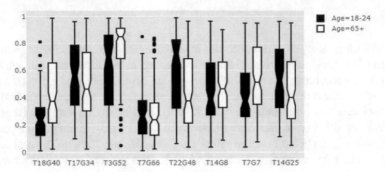

Fig. 3. Boxplot for age group normalized preference comparison among Chinese task-gesture combinations. Top 8 (20%) task gesture combinations ranked by LDA coefficient.

Table 1. Task-gesture combinations that most strongly differentiate young and old participants within the Canadian (leftmost two columns) and Chinese (rightmost two columns) samples along with a description of each combination.

Canadian Data Top 10%			Chinese Data Top 20%		
Code	Gestures x Task	Illustratoin	Code	Gestures x Task	Illustratoin
T4G53	Task: Unmute Gesture: Full hand pinch opening and closing ("blah blah")		T18G40	Task: Zoom in Gesture: Upright palm moving up	
T18G2	Task: Zoom in Gesture: Palms moving away.		T17G34	Task: Move backward Gesture: Upright fist moving left	
T2G5	Task: Power off Gesture: Waving		T3G52	Task: Mute Gesture: Index on lips (gesture for "shush").	
T23G51	Task: Volume down Gesture: Covering the ear with hand		T7G66	Task: Home Gesture: Index-middle roof sign	
T12G58	Task: Confirm (Yes) Gesture: Thumb up		T22G48	Task: Volume up Gesture: Turning a knob clockwise	
T22G50	Task: Volume up Gesture: Hand behind ear (sign of "listening")		T14G8	Task: Play Gesture: Opening to palm	
T14G25	Task: Play Gesture: Palm pushing		T7G7	Task: Home Gesture: Closing to fist	
T10G21	Task: Go to first Gesture: Rotated palm flicking left		T14G25	Task: Play Gesture: Palm pushing	
T2G7	Task: Power off Gesture: Closing to fist				
T7G45	Home Gesture: Splay closing to full hand pinch				
T19G41	Task: Zoom out Gesture: Upright palm moving down				
T21G21	Task: Previous Gesture: Rotated palm flicking left				

As shown in Fig. 4, the largest differences between the Canadian and Chinese samples were with respect to the T18G40, T22G48 and T18G44 combinations.

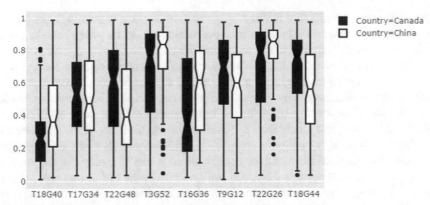

Fig. 4. Boxplot for age group preference comparison among Canadian and Chinese data task-gesture combinations. Plot shows the top 10% of task-gesture combinations ranked by LDA result.

Table 2. Top differentiating task gesture combinations between Canadian and Chinese preferences as determined by discriminant function coefficients.

Code	Gestures x Task	Illustration
T18G40	Task: Zoom in Gesture: Upright palm moving up	
T17G34	Task: Move backward Gesture: Upright fist moving left	
T22G48	Task: Volume up Gesture: Turning a knob clockwise	
T3G52	Task: Mute Gesture: Index on lips (gesture for "shush")	
T16G36	Task: Move forward Gesture: Pointing-index rotating clockwise	
T9G12	Task: Run/Select Gesture: Index tapping	
T22G26	Task: Volume up Gesture: Upward palm moving up	
T18G44	Task: Zoom in Gesture: Full hand pinch opening to splay	

5   Discussion

Our results show that demographic variables influence which gesture will work best for a particular task. Age and cultural differences seem to be important in determining task-gesture preferences (but not sex in our study). For the Canadian sample, the older people (65+) showed higher preferences on combinations T7G45, T22G50 and T12G58 as compared to the 18–24 year olds. T22G50 (cupping the Hand Behind the Ear for

Volume up) and T12G58 (the thumbs up gesture to confirm something) are gestures which occur quite frequently in in-person communication, so they may find the gesture familiar and natural. Cupping the hand behind the ear is also a strategy for effectively increasing the size of the ear and improving hearing in cases where a person (especially an older person) is having trouble hearing something. For younger people who have grown up with social media, thumbs up may more likely mean liking rather than confirmation, thus explaining their lower ratings for the task gesture combination. For T7G45 (the splayed hand closing to a pinch) may be familiar to some older people as a gesture used by orchestral conductors to signify completion, which could also be viewed as going Home. One feature of all three of these combinations is that they only use one hand and thus tend to use less energy than a two-handed gesture. For the Chinese sample, T22G48 (turning a knob clockwise to volume up) may have been less preferred because it puts more strain on the hand to make the relatively Fine movement. the largest differences between the Canadian and Chinese samples were with respect to the T18G40, T22G48 and T18G44 combinations. These effects may reflect cultural differences. For instance T18G40 (a gesture that moves the palm up to represent a zoom) does not seem natural to a Canadian. Interestingly the T22G48 (turning a knob clockwise to volume up) was less preferred by the Chinese sample perhaps reflecting the fact that the younger people in the Chinese sample were less familiar with that type of analogue technology. For a complete list of task-gesture combinations used in this research, see Table 3 in the Appendix.

6   Conclusions

Our results show that there is unlikely to be a "one size fits all" set of gestures that can be mapped to different tasks and that will work across groups of people with different demographics. We observed, even after adjusting scoring bias, cultural differences between Chinese and Canadian participants as well as demographic differences between young and old in both the Chinese and Canadian samples. Furthermore, the gestures that differentiated between young and old in Canada differed from those that differentiated young and old in the Chinese sample. We should note that the two studies that we carried out represent exploratory research and that further research is needed to find a comprehensive set of gesture task combinations that may work for different cultures and different demographics across, and within, cultures. While the present results are not comprehensive, they demonstrate significant problems for the one size fits all approach, with the best task gesture combinations depending on the type of person who will be using the system. This makes designing a common set of gestures that will suit everyone very challenging, if not impossible (see also [11]). One strategy for future mid-air gesture design may be to let people choose, from a small set of gestures, which one they want to use for a particular task. In this approach, designers will select a promising set of gestures that map well to a particular task and will then leave the final decision of which gesture to use to the user.

Acknowledgement. We thank Yanfang Liu and Yubo Zhang for their support in collecting Chinese data. We also thank Roger Luo for creating gesture illustrations.

Appendix

Table 3. List of the 129 Gesture Task Combinations used in the Canadian study. The overlapping subset of 36 combinations used in the Chinese study are highlighted with grey shading.

Task	Gesture	Code	Task	Gesture	Code
Power on	Snapping	T1G1	Play	Scissors sign	T14G23
	Palms moving away	T1G2		Snapping	T14G1
	Waving	T1G5		Closing to fist	T14G7
	Clapping	T1G4		Palm pushing	T14G25
	Index-middle knocking	T1G6		Thumb up	T14G58
	Pointing-index poking	T1G13		Clapping	T14G4
Power off	Palms getting closer	T2G3		Opening to palm	T14G8
	Snapping	T2G1		Upward palm moving up	T14G26
	Clapping	T2G4	Pause	Palm pushing	T15G25
	Waving	T2G5		Opening to palm	T15G8
	Index-middle knocking	T2G6		Victory sign	T15G24
	Closing to fist	T2G7		Timeout sign (both hands)	T15G28
	Pointing-index poking	T2G13		Snapping	T15G1
Mute	Index on lips (gesture for "shush")	T3G52		Clapping	T15G4
	Timeout sign (both hands)	T3G28		Closing to fist	T15G7
	Covering the ear with hand	T3G51		Downward palm moving down	T15G27
	Full hand pinch opening and closing (gesture for "blah blah")	T3G53	Move forward	Pinch moving right	T16G29
Unmute	Index on lips (gesture for "shush")	T4G52		Pointing-index rotating clockwise	T16G36
	Full hand pinch opening and closing (gesture for "blah blah")	T4G53		Upright palm moving right	T16G31
	Hand behind ear (sign of "listening")	T4G50		Upright fist moving right	T16G33
	Timeout sign (both hands)	T4G28		Index trigger moving right	T16G67
Back	Forehand slapping	T5G14		Scissors sign moving right	T16G69
	Thumb left moving left	T5G20	Move backward	Pinch moving left	T17G30
	Upright palm rotating left	T5G35		Upright palm moving left	T17G32
	Pointing-index swiping left	T5G54		Upright fist moving left	T17G34
	Index-middle knocking	T5G6		Pointing-index rotating counter-clockwise	T17G37
	Pointing-index rotating counter-clockwise	T5G37		Index trigger moving left	T17G68
Activate menu	Opening to palm	T6G8		Scissors sign moving left	T17G70
	Waving	T6G5	Zoom in	Camera fingers sign moving away	T18G46
	Full hand pinch opening to splay (hololenz gesture)	T6G44		Opening the hook-shape pinch to open thumb-index	T18G42
	Thumb up	T6G58		Full hand pinch opening to splay	T18G44
	Clapping	T6G4		Palms moving away	T18G2
	Index pinching	T6G11		Pinch moving up	T18G38
	Victory sign	T6G24		Upright palm moving up	T18G40
	Upright palm moving up	T6G40	Zoom out	Camera fingers sign Getting close	T19G47
	Closing to fist and hold it long	T6G55		Closing the hook-shape pinch to closed pinch	T19G43
	Flat four fingers (folded thumb)	T6G64		Splay closing to full hand pinch	T19G45
	Closing to fist	T6G7		Palms getting closer	T19G3
Home	Make a triangle with thumb and index finger with both hands	T7G56		Pinch moving down	T19G39
	Make a triangle with all fingers	T7G57		Upright palm moving down	T19G41
	Closing to fist	T7G7	Next	Backhand slapping	T20G17
	Splay closing to full hand pinch	T7G45		Rotated palm flicking right	T20G22
	Closing to fist and hold it long	T7G55		Upright palm moving right	T20G31
	Index-middle roof sign	T7G66	Previous	Forehand slapping	T21G14
Navigate	Index pointing	T8G9		Thumb left moving left	T21G20
	Upright index moving	T8G10		Rotated palm flicking left	T21G21
Run (Select)	Index pinching	T9G11		Upright palm moving left	T21G32
	Index tapping	T9G12	Volume up	Upward palm moving up	T22G26
	Pointing-index poking	T9G13		Turning a knob clockwise	T22G48
	Thumb up	T9G58		Pinch rotating clockwise	T22G62
	Closing to fist	T9G7		Pointing-index rotating clockwise	T22G36
	Index trigger	T9G65		Pinch moving up	T22G38
Go to first	Forehand slapping	T10G14		Upright palm moving up	T22G40
	Forehand slapping wide	T10G15		Hand behind ear (sign of "listening")	T22G50
	Long forehand slapping	T10G16		Side pinch moving up	T22G71
	Rotated palm flicking left	T10G21	Volume down	Downward palm moving down	T23G27
Go to last	Backhand slapping	T11G17		Turning a knob counter-clockwise	T23G49
	Backhand slapping wide	T11G18		Pinch rotating counter-clockwise	T23G63
	Long backhand slapping	T11G19		Pointing-index rotating counter-clockwise	T23G37
	Rotated palm flicking right	T11G22		Pinch moving down	T23G39
Confirm (Yes)	Thumb up	T12G58		Upright palm moving down	T23G41
	Nodding the head	T12G61		Covering the ear with hand	T23G51
	Index-middle knocking	T12G6		Side pinch moving down	T23G72
Reject (No)	Thumb down	T13G59			
	Shaking the head	T13G60			
	Waving	T13G5			

References

1. Epps, J., Lichman, S., Wu, M.: A study of hand shape use in tabletop gesture interaction. In: CHI 2006 Extended Abstracts on Human Factors in Computing Systems, pp. 748–753, April 2006
2. Kim, S.H., Ok, J., Kang, H.J., Kim, M.C., Kim, M.: An interaction and product design of gesture based TV remote control. In: CHI 2004 Extended Abstracts on Human Factors in Computing Systems, pp. 1548–1548 (2004)
3. Riener, A., Ferscha, A., Bachmair, F., Hagmüller, P., Lemme, A., Muttenthaler, D., Pühringer, D., Rogner, H., Tappe, A., Weger, F.: Standardization of the in-car gesture interaction space. In: Proceedings of the 5th International Conference on Automotive User Interfaces and Interactive Vehicular Applications, pp. 14–21 (2013)
4. Zeng, L.X., Jiang, X., Dai, C.Q.: Design principle of gesture interaction in the wearable device. Packag. Eng 36(20), 135–138 (2015)
5. Vatavu, R.D.: User-defined gestures for free-hand TV control. In: Proceedings of the 10th European Conference on Interactive Tv and Video, pp. 45–48 (2012)
6. Wu, H., Wang, J.: User-defined body gestures for TV-based applications. In: 2012 Fourth International Conference on Digital Home, pp. 415–420. IEEE (2012)
7. Dong, H., Danesh, A., Figueroa, N., El Saddik, A.: An elicitation study on gesture preferences and memorability toward a practical hand-gesture vocabulary for smart televisions. IEEE Access 3, 543–555 (2015)
8. Stec, K., Larsen, L.B.: Gestures for controlling a moveable tv. In: Proceedings of the 2018 ACM International Conference on Interactive Experiences for TV and Online Video, pp. 5–14 (2018)
9. Vatavu, R.D., Zaiti, I.A.: Leap gestures for TV: insights from an elicitation study. In: Proceedings of the ACM International Conference on Interactive Experiences for TV and Online Video, pp. 131–138 (2014)
10. Mansoury, M., Burke, R., Mobasher, B.: Flatter is better: percentile transformations for recommender systems. arXiv preprint arXiv:1907.07766 (2019)
11. Wu, H., Zhang, S., Liu, J., Qiu, J., Zhang, X.: The gesture disagreement problem in free-hand gesture interaction. Int. J. Hum. Comput. Interact. 35(12), 1102–1114 (2019)

A Human-Centered Design Procedure for Conceptualization Using Virtual Reality Prototyping Applied in an Inflight Lavatory

Meng Li[1,2]([✉]) [iD], Doris Aschenbrenner[1] [iD], Daniëlle van Tol[1] [iD], Daan van Eijk[1] [iD], and Peter Vink[1] [iD]

[1] The Faculty of Industrial Design Engineering, Delft University of Technology, 2628CE Delft, The Netherlands
`m-li.4@tudelft.nl`
[2] Mechanical Engineering School, Xi'an Jiaotong University, Xi'an 710049, People's Republic of China

Abstract. For designing large-scale products like an airplane, engaging end-users in the concept phase is difficult. However, early user evaluation is important to choose the path which fits the user's needs best. In particular, comfort-related assessments are difficult to conduct with digital models that are shown on a desktop PC application. Digital Human Modelling (DHM) plays a role in postural comfort analysis, while the subjective comfort feedback still largely relied on consulting with end-users.

This paper applies a human-centered design process and analyses the advantages and disadvantages of using VR prototypes for involving users during concept design. This study focused on using VR prototypes for concept selection and verification based on comfort assessment with potential end-users.

The design process started with an online questionnaire for identifying the quality of the design elements (Step 1 online study). Then, alternative concepts were implemented in VR, and users evaluated these concepts via a VR headset (Step 2 Selection study). Finally, the research team redesigned the final concept and assessed it with potential users via a VR headset (Step 3 Experience study).

Every design element contributed positively to the long-haul flight comfort, especially tap-basin height, storage, and facilities. The male and female participants had different preferences on posture, lighting, storage, and facilities. The final prototype showed a significantly higher comfort rate than the original prototypes.

The first-person immersion in VR headsets helps to identify the nuances between concepts, thus supports better decision-making via collecting richer and more reliable user feedback to make faster and more satisfying improvements.

Keywords: Virtual reality · Concept design · Human-centered Design · Virtual prototyping · First-person immersion

N. L. Black et al. (Eds.): IEA 2021, LNNS 223, pp. 387–393, 2022.
https://doi.org/10.1007/978-3-030-74614-8_48

1 Introduction

Designing a large-scale product like the Flying-V, the next-generation airplane, engaging end-users in the concept phase is difficult. However, early user evaluation is important in choosing the path which fits the user's needs best. In particular, comfort-related assessments are difficult to conduct with digital prototypes that are shown on a desktop PC application. Comfort is described as "a feeling of relief or encouragement", "contented well-being" and "a satisfying or enjoyable experience" by the Merriam-Webster Dictionary [1]. Despite the diverse perspectives on comfort-related experience, but most studied agree that "comfort is a subjective experience" [2]. Comfort plays an important role in boosting a traveler's well-being, especially during a long-haul flight. Hence, comfort is becoming increasingly significant in the interior design of transport systems like airplanes [2, 3]. Digital Human Modelling (DHM) took the advantages of various anthropometric parameters in postural comfort analysis for transport systems, while the subjective comfort feedback still largely relied on consulting with end-users [4]. Torkashvand reported that 'using the bathroom' is the second most important activity on board, influencing general satisfaction [5]. Yao and Vink found that reducing the waiting time for accessing lavatories and maintaining hygiene and refreshment are key points of improving long-haul flight comfort [6].

Understanding comfortable hygiene experiences in transportation systems is challenging, not only due to the privacy and safety issues but also due to the diverse demands of using public lavatories [7]. The co-creation sessions discovered that the activities around the basin, such as skin-caring, making-up, hair-styling, shaving, and washing face and hands are key to the comfortable hygiene experience during long-haul flights [6]. Considering the limited space of airplane lavatories, we found the following design elements relevant to the comfort of the long-haul flight: posture, lighting, the height of tap to the bottom of the basin, storage, and facilities.

The Human-Centered Design (HCD) methodology favors VR prototyping, as a tool to evaluate concepts in a cost-efficient, time-saving way. VR has been used in different stages of design processes, e.g. design reviewing with the CAVE (Cave Automatic Virtual Environment) systems [8, 9]. Virtual prototypes enhanced by tactile feedback have been used in the ergonomic evaluation of cockpit layout and car dashboard designs [10, 11]. A recent study showed that the VR prototype has the same level of confidence as the visual assessment of real products [12]. However, the suitability of VR prototypes for selecting design concepts regarding comfort remains unexplored. This suitability is heavily impacted by whether comfort-related elements like posture, lighting, height, storage space, and facilities are sufficiently conveyed via VR. This can be explored by testing which concepts are chosen by users when they are experiencing different VR prototypes.

1.1 Research Questions

The research aimed at answering how concept design could improve comfort from using VR and if it enabled potential users to better compare alternative concepts and possibly select a better solution. The research questions for this study are:

RQ1: Which design elements of the hygiene experience influence the comfort in long-haul flight?
RQ2: Which concepts are perceived more comfortable by end-users via showing them in VR prototyping?
RQ3: Whether VR prototyping helps to improve a comfortable experience?

2   Methodology

In this study, the design process started with an online questionnaire for identifying the quality of the design elements (Step 1 online study). Then, alternative concepts were implemented in VR and user evaluation of the selection process was carried out (Step 2 Selection study). Finally, the resulting concept was designed and assessed again by potential users via VR (Step 3 Experience study).

2.1   Step 1: Online Study

One hundred and one respondents (including 58 females and 43 males) took part in an online survey on ten design elements related to hygiene activities in a long-haul flight. A 7-point Likert scale was developed based on the Kano model [13]. On the scale, 1 means "very dissatisfied" while 7 means "very satisfied". The design elements included larger standing space, sitting in front of mirrors, storage, tap-basin space, warm lighting, easy-open door, the waiting-queue, open space, facilities, and changing room. These elements were categorized into five patterns: one-dimensional, must-be, indifferent, attractive, reverse [13]. The satisfaction differences between males and females were test via two-tailed T-tests.

2.2   Step 2: Selection Study

Twenty-eight students (including 12 males and 16 females) participated in the concept selection in the VR Lab of the Delft University of Technology. A 7-point Likert scale was used for collecting the comfort level (1 means "very uncomfortable", 7 means "very comfortable"). Ten concepts were evaluated regarding five design elements. The concepts were shown in an HTC Vive headset (1080×1200 per eye). A 1:1 cardboard enclosure provided the tactile feedback of the VR space. After filling in the informed consent, participants rated their comfort level when a concept was shown to them. Each concept was displayed for 40 s and was randomized for each participant. After the evaluation, the participants had an oral reflection session for collecting qualitative feedback. The means were calculated. Wilcoxon matched-pair signed-rank test was applied to compare the concepts.

2.3   Step 3: Experience Study

Thirty-three participants joined the final assessment of the lavatory concept at the same lab. A similar comfort questionnaire, a realistic questionnaire, and the Presence Questionnaire (PQ) were used for accessing the immersive experience. A predefined instruction asked participants to imagine that they were in a long-haul flight while seeking refreshment. They simulated refreshing activities in their preferred ways in the virtual environment. After the simulated usage, they filled in the questionnaires. The means and standard deviation were calculated.

3   Results

3.1   Step 1: Online Study

All elements are one-dimensional except open space and facilities while sitting posture and change room have more diverse distribution (Fig. 1a). Considering the gender differences, the males preferred sitting more and females liked larger standing space (Fig. 1b).

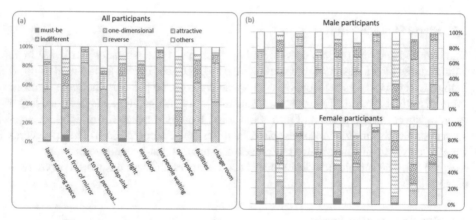

Fig. 1. (a) Design quality for the elements; and (b) for different genders.

3.2   Step 2: Selection Study

In general, lower tap-basin height, more available storage, and high-end facilities have significantly contributed to a more comfortable experience (Table 1). Warmer lighting was associated with better comfort. The comfort of females significantly depended on high-end facilities, while males would be more comfortable when standing pose and having more storage.

The participants thought tactile feedback created a believable perception of being inside the lavatory but did not influence their comfort level. The participants had vivid feedback, such as sharp edges, postures during turbulence, and bend angle when using the basin.

Table 1. The perceived comfort between the two concepts among different genders

	Male (12)		Female (16)		Total (28)	
	Mean (SD)	p value	Mean (SD)	p value	Mean (SD)	p value
With seat	3.83 (1.403)	0.077	3.87 (1.727)	0.309	3.85 (1.562)	0.056
No seat	4.75 (1.545)		4.56 (1.459)		4.64 (1.471)	
Light3000k	4.42 (1.621)	0.357	4.2 5(1.342)	0.070	4.32 (1.442)	0.053
Light3500k	4.75 (0.965)		4.00 (1.088)		4.82 (1.020)	
Tap-basin28cm	5.00 (1.279)	0.083	4.69 (1.448)	0.163	4.78 (1.368)	0.036*
Tap-basin24cm	5.58 (0.996)		5.27 (0.884)		5.41 (0.931)	
Storage shelves	5.08 (1.443)	0.055	4.69 (1.448)	0.171	4.86 (1.433)	0.021*
Storage box	4.08 (1.240)		4.06 (1.389)		4.07 (1.303)	
More facilities	5.58 (1.505)	0.224	5.69 (1.078)	0.004**	5.64 (1.254)	0.002**
Fewer facilities	4.75 (1.422)		4.25 (1.183)		4.46 (1.290)	

*indicates that p value < 0.05; **indicates that p value < 0.01.

3.3 Step 3: Experience Study

Participants rated every design element of the final prototype significantly higher than the prototypes in the selection study except the comfort of using water (Fig. 2a). The VR prototyping was realistic for the participants except using water and no significant differences between the people with or without VR experience (Fig. 2b). No significant simulation sickness symptoms were perceived by the participants.

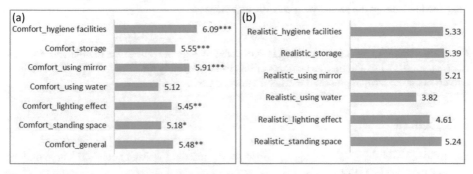

Fig. 2. (a) The comfort perception and (b) the realistic level of the final prototype. "*" indicates that p-value < 0.05; "**" indicates that p-value < 0.01; "***" indicates that p-value < 0.001.

4 Discussion and Conclusion

Regarding the research questions, every design element contributed positively to the long-hula flight comfort, especially tap-basin height, storage, and facilities. The male and female participants had different preferences, e.g. comfortable standing posture and storage are key for males, while high-end facilities and lighting are more critical to females. Lavatories provide a private bubble for many people during long-haul flights [6, 14], thus some participants wanted to remove the seat to limit the duration of each user. The shelves, providing more options for storing passengers' belongings were preferred. Kuijt-Evers also mentioned that storage space can be an element for improving the comfort of wheel loaders and excavators [15]. The basin improved comfort by providing sufficient space for cleaning hands and faces. This need is confirmed by a study showing the larger environments for washing hands increase user-friendliness [16].

The final prototype showed a significantly higher comfort rate than the first round. The first-person immersion provided by VR prototyping encouraged the participants to be more interactive and explorative during concept evaluation [11, 17]. The missing interaction of virtual objects like the tap might influence the perception of realism and thus alter the comfort perception, as we observed on the comfort of using water [18]. The knowledge on using a VR headset was mainly new to most of the participants, thus a formal practice session is needed [19]. The potential risk of prototyping using VR headset is some individuals might experience severe simulation sickness symptoms and quit the evaluation [20].

The first-person immersion in VR prototyping helps to identify the nuances between concepts, thus supports better decision-making via collecting richer and more reliable user feedback to make faster and more satisfying improvements. The next step of this study is comparing the VR prototyping with the physical prototyping within the Flying-V project to find out how to take advantage of both of them to create more effective and efficient human-centered design processes.

Acknowledgment. The authors wish to thank Ms. Xinhe Yao for her assistance in developing the VR prototyping and conducting the tests. The authors thank all the participants who shared their feedback about the prototyping and VR experience.

Funding. Meng Li's doctoral research is sponsored by a grant from China Scholarship Council (CSC) (No. 201706280020). The contents of this paper are solely the responsibility of the authors and do not necessarily represent the official views of CSC.

References

1. Merriam-Webster   Homepage.   https://www.merriam-webster.com/dictionary/comfort. Accessed 08 Feb 2021
2. Vink, P., Bazley, C., Kamp, I., Blok, M.: Possibilities to improve the aircraft interior comfort experience. Appl. Ergon. **43**(2), 354–359 (2012)
3. Richards, L.G.: On the psychology of passenger. Human Factors Transp. Res. **2**, 15–23 (1980)
4. Tao, Q., Kang, J., Sun, W., et al.: Digital evaluation of sitting posture comfort in a human-vehicle system under industry 4.0 framework. Chin. J. Mech. Eng. **29**, 1096–1103 (2016)
5. Torkashvand, G.: Optimization of cabin design for enhanced passenger experience(Doctoral dissertation). Florida Institute of Technology, Melbourne (2019)

6. Yao, X., Vink, P.: A survey and a co-creation session to evaluate passenger contentment on long-haul flight, with suggestions for possible design improvements to future aircraft interiors. In Proceedings of the International Comfort Congress. Delft University of Technology, Delft (2019)
7. van Eijk, D.J., Loth, M., Molenbroek, J.F.M.: Mock-up test of two train toilet modules. In: Ahram, T., Karwowski, W., Marek, T., (eds.) Proceedings of the 5th International Conference on Applied Human Factors and Ergonomics AHFE 2014, Louisville, KY, pp. 7575–7586 (2014)
8. Dunston, P.S., Arns, L.L., Mcglothlin, J.D., Lasker, G.C., Kushner, A.G.: An immersive virtual reality mock-up for design review of hospital patient rooms. In: Collaborative Design in Virtual Environments, pp. 167–176. Springer, Dordrecht (2011)
9. Majumdar, T., Fischer, M.A., Schwegler, B.R.: Conceptual design review with a virtual reality mock-up model. In: Joint International Conference on Computing and Decision Making in Civil and Building Engineering, pp. 2902–2911. Springer, Montréal (2006)
10. Bordegoni, M., Colombo, G., Formentini, L.: Haptic technologies for the conceptual and validation phases of product design. Comput. Graph. **30**(3), 377–390 (2006)
11. Ahmed, S., Zhang, J., Demirel, O.: Assessment of types of prototyping in human-centred product design. In International Conference on Digital Human Modeling and Applications in Health, Safety, Ergonomics and Risk Management, pp. 3–18. Springer, Cham, July 2018
12. Forbes, T., Barnes, H., Kinnell, P., Goh, Y.M.: A study into the influence of visual prototyping methods and immersive technologies on the perception of abstract product properties. In: Proceedings of NordDesign 2018. Linköping University, Linköping, Sweden (2018)
13. Kano, N.: Attractive quality and must-be quality. Hinshitsu (Quality J. Japan. Soc. Qual. Control) **14**, 39–48 (1984)
14. Reinhardt, R.: The outstanding jet pilot. Am. J. Psychiatry **127**(6), 732–736 (1970)
15. Kuijt-Evers, L.F.M., Krause, F., Vink, P.: Aspects to improve cabin comfort of wheel loaders and excavators according to operators. Appl. Ergon. **34**(3), 265–271 (2003)
16. Fukuizumi, M., Yamaguchi, T.: Automatic Faucet for Lavatory Unit of Aircraft. US; USOO7406722B2 (2006)
17. Li, M., Ganni, S., Ponten, J., Albayrak, A., Rutkowski, A.F., Jakimowicz, J. Analysing usability and presence of a virtual reality operating room (VOR) simulator during laparoscopic surgery training. In: 2020 IEEE Conference on Virtual Reality and 3D User Interfaces (VR), Atlanta, USA, pp. 566–572. IEEE, March 2020
18. Witmer, B.G., Jerome, C.J., Singer, M.J.: The factor structure of the presence questionnaire. Presence Teleop. Virtual Environ. **14**(3), 298–312 (2005)
19. Ihemedu-Steinke, Q.C., Erbach, R., Halady, P., Meixner, G., Weber, M.: Virtual reality driving simulator based on head-mounted displays. In: Automotive User Interfaces, pp. 401–428. Springer, Cham (2017)
20. Tregillus, S., Al Zayer, M., Folmer, E.: Handsfree omnidirectional VR navigation using head tilt. In: Proceedings of the 2017 CHI Conference on Human Factors in Computing Systems, New York, NY, USA, pp. 4063–4068. Association for Computing Machinery (2017)

Automated Segmentation of 3D Digital Human Model for Area and Volume Measurement

Flavia Cristine Hofstetter Pastura$^{(\boxtimes)}$ ⓘ, Tales Fernandes Costa ⓘ,
Gabriel de Aguiar Mendonça ⓘ, Thatiane dos Santos Lopes ⓘ,
and Maria Cristina Palmer Lima Zamberlan ⓘ

Laboratório de Ergonomia (LABER), Instituto Nacional de Tecnologia (INT),
Rio de Janeiro, RJ 20081-312, Brazil
`flavia.pastura@int.gov.br`

Abstract. Automated location of body landmarks and anthropometric measurements from 3D digital human models promote standardization of measurements, resulting in higher precision and consistence compared to traditional measurements. LABER has already developed a software tool to support automated body landmarks location and linear anthropometric measurements based on 3D digital human models. However, we have interest on area and body volume calculation, as these measurements are difficult to obtain by conventional methods. Considering this, we developed specialized algorithms for measurements of surface area, cross section area and volume based on automated segmentation of the digital human model into 13 body parts (trunk, upper arms, forearms, hands, thighs, calves, and feet).

Keywords: Anthropometry · Body landmark · 3D digital human model · Anthropometric characterization

1 Problem Statement

Traditional methods for collecting anthropometric data use tools to take physical measurements directly on the subject body. This usually requires experienced professionals that must follow extensive and laborious protocols that result in time-consuming and tiring measurement procedures for both subject and measurer. Evolution of 3D scanner technology and development of digital human models (DHM) make possible to collect anthropometric data with contactless measurement methods.

Some of the benefits that may be achieved using DHM [1, 2] are following:

- we can extract measurements that are difficult to get with conventional methods, such as surface areas, cross-section area and volumes.
- measurements can be taken without the individual's physical presence, allowing anthropometric measurements to be extracted at any time, either for new measurements not initially planned or for existing measurements to be retaken with new methods.

N. L. Black et al. (Eds.): IEA 2021, LNNS 223, pp. 394–402, 2022.
https://doi.org/10.1007/978-3-030-74614-8_49

– apply same standard automated measurement methods to all survey data, eliminating differences due to variation on measurement methods and measurers.

Anthropometric data can be manually extracted from DHM based on 3D point clouds (3DPC) or polygonal meshes by using commercial or opensource software tools such as Rhinoceros [3], Geomagic [4], Meshmixer [5] and CloudCompare [6]. Using such tools, a user can manually identify and locate anatomical body landmarks (ABL) and extract anthropometric measurements such as distance between landmarks, perimeters, surface areas and volumes. However, experience shows that manual extraction of anthropometric measurements from 3D images is not an easy task. Even if body landmarks previously marked on subjects can be visualized, it is difficult to locate the center of the landmarks on the DHM to extract distances between them. Moreover, for surface area and volume measurements specialized mesh processing is usually needed. So, specialized training is required for using the software tool and also to correctly locate and use the anatomical points as references for the measurements. Therefore, while it frees the subject from the measurement inconvenience, the measurer task may still be a laborious, time-consuming and error prone procedure [2].

Some commercial software tools offer automated anthropometric measurement, such as *Cyberware WBX* DigiSize and ScanWorX Anthroscan. But they also present some problems [7,8,9]:

– Tool may be for exclusive use with specific scanning equipment and may not be able to process DHM generated by other scanners.
– Acquisition costs may be too high for some research groups' budget.
– Technical specification, algorithms and procedures details used for measurements may be considered proprietary information, and not be available for the tool user.
– Measurements may be focused on specific industries needs and not be based on traditional anatomical landmarks
– Automated measurements may be restricted to specific posture or not be available for all measures needed.

Based in a long experience in traditional anthropometric surveys, LABER, identified the need for a software tool that allows for automated anthropometric measurements on 3D DHM. For this reason, we developed a software tool (SOOMA) for support of automated location of anatomical body landmarks (ABL) and calculation of linear anthropometric measurements [10]. This paper presents our work developing methods and algorithms for automated calculation of 3D measurements, such as body surface areas, cross section area and body volumes.

2   Methodology

Methods and algorithms presented here supports DHM positioned according to the CAE-SAR standing posture [11] as shown in Fig. 1. All DHM were created using *Cyberware WBX* scanner and its proprietary software *DigiSize* [12], generating a 3D triangular mesh binary file with Stanford Triangle Format (.ply) [13].

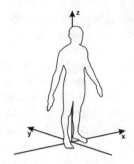

Fig. 1. CAESAR standing posture.

A typical DHM mesh contains about 700.000 vertices, where each vertex represents a point of reflected laser light detected by the scanner with vertical resolution of 2 mm.

For use by the segmentation and measurement algorithms, the triangular mesh is reduced to a 3DPC defined by the mesh vertices XYZ coordinates and three RGB based reflected colors. So, the algorithms do not depend on the mesh faces.

2.1 Body Segmentation

For body surface area and volume calculation, it is inconvenient to work with the DHM as a whole unit. When calculating the volume of an arm, the rest of the body does not matter, as this measurement, value is not affected by other body part presence, but they do affect the calculation effort. Considering this, our method for surface area and volume measurement starts by splitting the 3DPC in multiple body segments. At first, we performed manual segmentation based in planes parallel to the XYZ axes. However, we found out that results quality was too dependent on body physical characteristics. In many cases, this result in excessive cutting of the target segment or leftovers of other segments. After some experimentation, we found a better strategy using cutting planes defined by specific ABL references.

Cutting Plane Definition. To obtain each body segment, the 3DPC is divided into two parts by using cutting planes defined by a specific set of vectors created based on ABL coordinates previously located on the 3DPC [10]. Depending on the ABL references available for the body segment, we have three different options for defining the cutting plane: 1 - Three ABL on the cutting plane: a) create two vectors based on three ABL coordinates associated with the segment; b) define cutting plane based on these two vectors (Fig. 2).

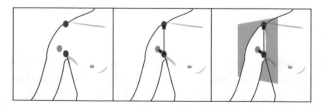

Fig. 2. Cutting plane definition for three ABL on the cutting plane.

2 - Two ABL on the cutting plane and a third ABL reference off the plane: a) create a vector based on the two ABL coordinates that will be on the plane; b) create a second vector based on one of these ABL and the third ABL off the plane; c) create a third vector that is orthogonal to first two vectors; d) define cutting plane based on first and third vectors (Fig. 3).

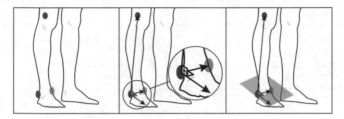

Fig. 3. Cutting plane definition for two ABL on the cutting plane and a third off.

3 - Two ABL reference on the cutting plane and two ABL off the plane: a) create a vector based on the two ABL coordinates that will be on the plane; b) create a second and third vectors based on one of the ABL above and two others ABL off the plane; c) create a fourth vector which is orthogonal to first and divides the angle between second and third vectors (2α) into two equal parts; d) define cutting plane based on first and fourth vector (Fig. 4).

For most segments, we need two cutting planes: top and bottom cutting planes. Exceptions are hands, feet, and head that need only one cutting plane. Table 1 presents the list of body segments currently considered in our segmentation method, with the ABL used as reference for cutting planes definition. Note the trunk segment is not listed in Table 1 because it does not need cutting planes. It is defined as the points left on the 3DPC after all other segments are removed. Also, as we are not currently working with ABL and measurements involving the human head, this segment is removed from the DHM for privacy reasons.

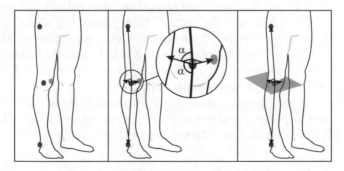

Fig. 4. Cutting plane definition for two ABL on the cutting plane and a two off.

Table 1. List of body segments and ABL references for cutting planes.

Body segment	Reference body landmarks ON the cut plane		Reference body landmarks OFF the cut plane	
	Top cut	Bottom cut	Top cut	Bottom cut
Hand (right/left)	- Ulnar Styloid - Radiale	-	- Distal Phalanx III - Lateral Humeral	-
Forearm (right/left)	- Humeral Epicondyle Lateral & Medial	- Ulnar Styloid - Radiale	- Ulnar Styloid - Acromion	- Distal Phalanx III - Lateral Humeral
Arm (right/left)	- Acromion - Axillar Anterior & Posterior	- Humeral Epicondyle Lateral & Medial	-	- Ulnar Styloid - Acromion
Foot (right/left)	- Malleolus Lateral & Medial	-	- Femur Lateral Epicondyle	-
Calf (right/left)	- Femur Epicondyle Lateral & Medial	- Malleolus Lateral & Medial	- Malleolus Lateral - Trochanterion	- Femur Lateral Epicondyle
Thigh (right/left)	- Trochanterions	- Femur Epicondyle Lateral & Medial	- Acromion	- Malleolus Lateral - Trochanterion
Head	-	- Cervicale	-	-

Segmentation Procedure. Some body segments such as feet, calves and hands may be separated using one or two cutting planes. However, for other segments these cutting planes may not be sufficient to fully isolate the target segment from other body parts that may also be cut by the same cutting plane. We present bellow our multiple cutting plane segmentation procedure, using as example the left arm segmentation shown on Fig. 5:

Step 1 – define horizontal lanes: 3DPC below Axillar ABL is divided in horizontal lanes of arbitrary width (sections 'B' and 'C' on Fig. 5).

Step 2 – define lane central point for wide spaces (section 'C'): on each lane from bottom up, 3DPC points are first ordered based on X axis and differences in X for neighboring pairs are calculated. The pair with highest X difference is identified and, if difference is higher than 1 cm, is defined as the pair delimiter. Midpoint between the pair delimiter is calculated and stored as the lane central point (see 'di' on Fig. 5). Repeat this step for next layer up the Z axis until highest X difference is equal or lower than 1 cm.

Step 3 – define lane central point for narrow spaces (section 'B'): for all lanes located between the Axillar ABL and last wide space lane, the central point is defined by interpolation of Axillar ABL with the last wide space lane central point.

Step 4 – select segment points based on stepped cutting planes: below Axillar ABL, 3DPC points are selected for the target segment if X coordinate is on the right side of the lane central point. Above Axillar ABL (section 'A'), points are selected if X coordinate is on the right side of the segment cutting plane (Fig. 5).

Step 5 – define 'top' and 'bottom' cutting borders: selected segment points within 5mm distance from cutting planes, are defined as belonging to segment sections identified as 'top' and 'bottom' cutting borders to be used by measurement functions.

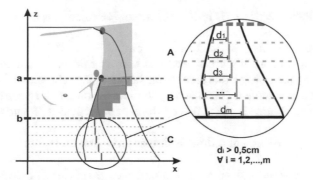

Fig. 5. Arm segmentation in the axillar region. Separation using cutting plane (A) and local cutting planes on narrow (B) and wide regions (C).

2.2 Measurements

Surface area and volume measurements are performed with largest segment dimension aligned with Z axis. For our standing posture, arms are rotated around Y axis based on calculation of their Z axis angle, while feet are first rotated 17° around Z axis and then 90° around Y axis [2, 11]. For all segments, measurement is based on sections defined in Fig. 6: top, middle, and bottom section.

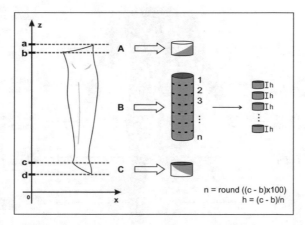

Fig. 6. Calf segment composed of three sections: top (A), middle (B) and bottom (C)

For A and C sections (see Fig. 6), a description of volume calculation follows:

a) Section is approximated by a regular cylinder based on previously selected points;
b) The cylinder cross-sectional area is calculated based on triangles defined by points on the top/bottom border perimeter and an estimated circumference center;
c) Cross-sectional area is multiplied by section height ('a-b' and 'c-d' in Fig. 6) and section volume is approximated as half this value to account for the inclined cut.

For the 'middle' section ('B' in Fig. 6), volume calculation is as follows:

a) Section is divided in equal height subsections;
b) For each subsection, the cross-sectional area is calculated and then volume is calculated by multiplying this area by the height of the subsection;
c) Middle section volume is calculated by the sum of subsections volume values;
d) Total segment volume is calculated by the sum of sections A, B and C values.

Surface area measurement follows a similar procedure except for:

– Instead of cross-sectional area, a circumference perimeter is calculated for each section, based on a perimeter method developed for SOOMA first version [10].
– Surface area is calculated multiplying this perimeter by section height.
– The value of cross-sectional areas that result from segment cutting are discounted from the segment total surface area. For example, cross-sectional area on the axillar region is discounted both from the arm and trunk surface area.

3 Results

Figure 7 shows surface area and volume calculated by SOOMA for 13 body segments.

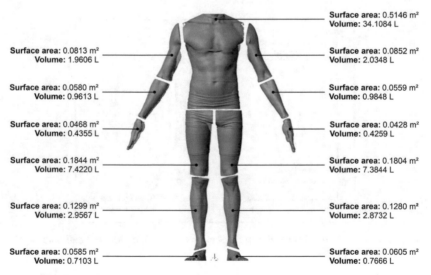

Surface area: 0.5146 m²
Volume: 34.1084 L

Surface area: 0.0813 m²
Volume: 1.9606 L

Surface area: 0.0852 m²
Volume: 2.0348 L

Surface area: 0.0580 m²
Volume: 0.9613 L

Surface area: 0.0559 m²
Volume: 0.9848 L

Surface area: 0.0468 m²
Volume: 0.4355 L

Surface area: 0.0428 m²
Volume: 0.4259 L

Surface area: 0.1844 m²
Volume: 7.4220 L

Surface area: 0.1804 m²
Volume: 7.3844 L

Surface area: 0.1299 m²
Volume: 2.9567 L

Surface area: 0.1280 m²
Volume: 2.8732 L

Surface area: 0.0585 m²
Volume: 0.7103 L

Surface area: 0.0605 m²
Volume: 0.7666 L

Fig. 7. Surface area and volume measurement results for body segments

Total measured elapsed time is 6.12 s for segmentation, 24.77 s for surface area measurements and 9.45 s for volume measurements on a Windows 10 desktop (i7 3.4 Ghz CPU, 16 GB RAM, 450 GB SSD) using R 4.0.3 [15].

4 Discussion

We compared our results against a regular solid built as a 3DPC cone section with following specification: height = 40 cm, larger radius = 9 cm, and smaller radius = 5 cm. This 3DPC was imported into RHINO [2], converted into an open mesh for surface area measurement and then manually converted into a closed mesh for both volume and surface area measurement. In addition, surface area and volume were calculated using known equations for a circular truncated cone [14]. Table 2 shows RHINO and SOOMA results compared to the regular solid equations values. Note that SOOMA and RHINO results differ from the Equations by less than 5%, except for the closed mesh, where RHINO adds the cone top/bottom circular surfaces to the surface area.

Table 2. Measurement comparison with regular solid.

Measurement tool		Regular cone section			
		Surface area (m2)	Difference (%)	Volume (Liter)	Difference (%)
RHINO	Open mesh	0,1849	4,55	---	---
	Closed mesh	0.2194	24.09	6.4268	1.61
SOOMA		0.1730	-2.18	6.1969	-2.03
Equations		0.1768		6.3251	

Table 3 shows results for a Left Calf segment compared to RHINO using different mesh processing options. Differences for open mesh surface area and volume are higher but still below the 10% and 5% range. Of note is RHINO's volume for the Meshmixer case where it differs from SOOMA by less than 0.5%.

Table 3. Measurement comparison for Calf segment.

Measurement tool		Left Calf			
	Mesh closing tool	Surface area (m2)	Difference (%)	Volume (Liter)	Difference (%)
	Open mesh	0.1374	7.33		
RHINO	Rhino	0.1452	13.43	2.7441	-4.49
	Cloud Compare	0.1498	17.01	2.9718	3.43
	Meshmixer	0.1532	19.64	2.8874	0.49
SOOMA		0.1280		2.8732	

5 Conclusions

Initial results show our automated segmentation and measurement method results in surface area and volume values close to those calculated using regular solid equation or specialized 3D mesh tools. However, additional tests with multiple DHM and different body segments still have to be performed. A search for additional measurements references for benchmarking is also being considered.

It should be noted that surface areas for open and closed meshes are distinct. Mesh closing necessarily increases the surface area by adding surface in regions where a hole existed. For a hole due to a flaw in the mesh this is not an issue, but when the hole is due to a segmentation cut, then the cover surface should not be counted as part of the segment surface area.

Specialized 3D tools used for DHM measurements may require considerable manual effort, in special for segmentation and closing of open meshes. As consequence, these complex manual actions decrease consistency and repeatability in measurement procedures. By using segment perimeter and cross-sectional area our method does not depend on closed meshes, a fully automated process is possible that results in consistent and repeatable measurement procedures.

References

1. Robinette, K.M., Vannier, M.W., Rioux, M., Jones, P.R.M.: AGARD Advisory Group For Aerospace Report 329, 3-D Surface Anthropometry: Review of Technologies (1997)
2. Pastura, F.C.H.: Extração Automática de Medidas Antropométricas a partir de Imagens Geradas por Digitalização a Laser e Câmeras CCD, UFRJ/COPPE, Rio de Janeiro (2017)
3. McNeel, R., and Associates. Rhinoceros, https://www.rhino3d.com. Accessed 19 Jan 2021
4. 3D Systems, Geomagic Wrap. https://www.3dsystems.com/software. Accessed 18 Jan 2021
5. Autodesk Meshmixer. https://www.meshmixer.com. Accessed 19 Jan 2021
6. CloudCompare. https://www.cloudcompare.org. Accessed 19 Jan 2021
7. Kuehnapfel, A., Ahnert, P., Loeffler, M., Scholz, M.: Body surface assessment with 3D laser-based anthropometry: Reliability, validation, and improvement of empirical surface formulae. Eur J Appl Physiol **117**, 371–380 (2017)
8. Kuehnapfel et al.: Reliability of 3D laser-based anthropometry and comparison with classical anthropometry, Scientific Reports (2016)
9. Glock, F., et al.: Validity and intraobserver reliability of three-dimensional scanning compared with conventional anthropometry for children and adolescents from a population-based cohort study. Pediatr. Res. **81**, 736–744 (2017)
10. Pastura, F.C.H., Costa, T.F., Mendonça, G.A., Zamberlan, M.C.P.L.: SOOMA - Software for Acquisition and Storage of Anthropometric Data Automatically Extracted from 3D Digital Human Models. In: Proceedings of 20th Congress of the International Ergonomics Association (IEA 2018), vol. IX, pp.472–481. Springer, Florence (2018)
11. Robinette, K.M., Blackwell, S., Hoeferlin, D., Fleming, S., Kelly, S., Burnsides, D.: Civilian American and European Surface Anthropometry Resource (CAESAR) Final Report, Volume I: Demographic and Measurement Descriptions. Hum. Factors 72 (2002)
12. WBX Cyberware whole body 3D color scanner, https://headus.com.au. Accessed 23 Jan 2021
13. Bourke, PPLY - Polygon File Format Also known as the Stanford Triangle Format. https://paulbourke.net/dataformats/ply/. Accessed 14 Dec 2020
14. Online Conical Frustum Calculator. https://www.calculatorsoup.com/calculators/geometry-solids/conicalfrustum.php. Accessed 23 Jan 2021
15. The R Project for Statistical Computing. https://www.r-project.org. Accessed 15 Dec 2020

A Conceptual Framework of DHM Enablers for Ergonomics 4.0

Gunther Paul[1,2](✉) and Leyde Briceno[1]

[1] Australian Institute of Tropical Health and Medicine (AITHM), Mackay, QLD, Australia
gunther.paul@jcu.edu.au
[2] James Cook University, Townsville, QLD, Australia

Abstract. Industry 4.0 lends itself to an ecosystem of human factors and ergonomics (HFE) related new concepts, such as Mining 4.0, Safety 4.0, Operator 4.0 and Ergonomics 4.0 which we studied here. Industry 4.0 refers to system elements such as Cyber-Physical Systems (CPS) and Augmented Reality/Virtual Reality (AR/VR), connections through the Internet of Things (IoT) and storage on Cloud Platforms (CP) to facilitate Cognitive Computing (CC) analysis and knowledge extraction. While the Industry 4.0 concept is centred around data, it also provides a platform to integrate the human operator with other elements of a system. Industry 4.0 and Ergonomics thus appear integrated and suggest the development of an Ergonomics 4.0 concept. This study searched and reviewed publications focusing on the enablers of Ergonomics 4.0. We identified their main elements and relationships with a focus on Digital Human Modelling (DHM). We systemized, clustered and synthesized the reviewed information and generated a taxonomy of Ergonomics 4.0 under the lens of digital human modelling using semantic analysis. We conclude that Ergonomics 4.0 is an essential part of Industry 4.0 and that DHM is a key enabler for Ergonomics 4.0.

Keywords: Ergonomics 4.0 · Industry 4.0 · Virtualization · Digital Twin · Digital Human Modeling (DHM)

1 Introduction

Industry 4.0 presents itself as an ecosystem; a collection of elements endowed with Cyber-Physical Systems (CPS) and Augmented Reality/Virtual Reality devices (AR/VR). These are connected through the Internet of Things (IoT) and uploaded to Cloud Platforms (CP) for analysis, knowledge extraction, and diagnostics through Cognitive Computing (CC) based on a large amount of data (Zidek et al. 2020). The concept is centred around data: creating data, sharing data, managing data, analysing data, and controlling data. Many factors influence this interconnected working environment, and for that reason planning and implementing a digital transformation implies many challenges at various abstraction levels. Industry 4.0 and Ergonomics are being integrated using a variety of tools and approaches (Zidek et al. 2020; Stern and Becker 2020; Sun et al. 2020; Hietanen et al. 2020), thus lending to the development of an Ergonomics

© The Author(s), under exclusive license to Springer Nature Switzerland AG 2022
N. L. Black et al. (Eds.): IEA 2021, LNNS 223, pp. 403–406, 2022.
https://doi.org/10.1007/978-3-030-74614-8_50

4.0 concept. This research reviews studies in the literature focusing on the enablers of Ergonomics 4.0, identifying the main elements and their interrelationship with a focus on Digital Human Modelling (DHM). We consider approaches such as Operator 4.0 (Sun et al. 2020) and Modelling and Simulation for Digital Twin Creation (Lim et al. 2020) which aim to accelerate the decision-making and adaptation processes inherent in a modern work environment.

2   Objective

The objective of this study is to review the most recent published articles in journals to identify the enablers of Ergonomics 4.0, while focusing on DHM, leading technologies, operations, and worker related aspects. We aim to identify a taxonomy of elements and relationships which form enablers of Ergonomics 4.0.

3   Hypothesis

We hypothesise that Ergonomics is integral to the Industry 4.0 concept, thus supporting the formulation of an Ergonomics 4.0 notion. We also hypothesise that DHM is an elementary component of such a construct for Ergonomics 4.0.

4   Methods

Literature was searched in JCU One Search, an integrative library search tool which access a large portion of the most common international publication databases. The search for 'Ergonomics 4.0' was limited to the most recently published articles in journals and ejournals published in English language in the years 2019 and 2020 with full texts available and yielded 1,230 results. The search was then refined to 'Ergonomics 4.0' AND 'DHM' which yielded 19 results. Ten publications were excluded after screening and a qualitative evaluation of nine publications was performed using semantic analysis.

The findings were then used to develop a theoretical taxonomy of enablers of Industry 4.0 and Ergonomics 4.0 based on various classifiers, which were structured and inter-linked in a topological illustration. While the taxonomy is intended to expose connections, it does not provide information on the origin or leading element of a relationship. Hence the quality of the relationships which were uncovered is not revealed or discussed.

5   Results

We identified five clusters which were categorized as Industry 4.0 technology (1: Industry 4.0), 2: Human Factors in Cyber-Physical Production Systems (CPPS), 3: Operator 4.0, 4: Human-Robot Collaboration (HRC) and Digital Twin and Digital Human Modelling (5: Operator as a Digital Twin).

The proposed conceptual framework for Ergonomics 4.0 describes processes, technology, information, and relationships which connect Industry 4.0 with Operator 4.0,

Human-Robot Collaboration, Operator as a Digital Twin, Digital Human Modelling and eventually define Ergonomics 4.0 (Fig. 1).

Human Cyber-Physical-Systems (H-CPS) emerges as a central concept within this framework which integrates Industry 4.0, Operator 4.0, Ergonomics 4.0 and Digital Twin/DHM.

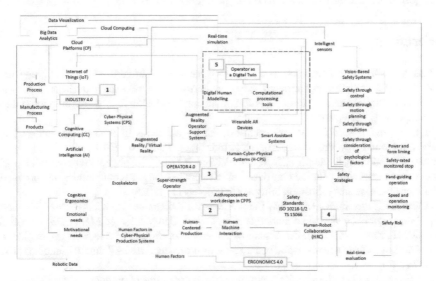

Fig. 1. Taxonomy of Ergonomics 4.0 in the context of Industry 4.0 and DHM.

6 Discussion

In the context of Industry 4.0, developments on Ergonomics are directed towards establishing real time evaluations and interventions in the production system, making the human factor once again the object of production research (Rauch et al. 2019).

On this basis the human worker assumes a bi-directional interactive role in the Industry 4.0 production system whilst making use of intelligent sensors, AR and VR technologies, collaborative robots, and exoskeletons (Hietanen et al. 2020). Ahmed et al. (2019) found that DHM enables ergonomic assessments and that it provides the means to visualize human product interactions, predict unexpected errors in the design process, and improve overall performance. Planning a human-centred workstation could thus be performed virtually from scratch (Gualtieri et al. 2020).

The basic problems in implementation of an Industry 4.0 concept are data acquisition and transmission of real-time production data from the manufacturing environment to a cloud platform (Caputo et al. 2019; Lim et al. 2020), as well as extraction of practical knowledge from heterogeneous data where cyber security issues can impact on operations (Lim et al. 2020). It is here where DHM simulation and the digital twin concept in a digital factory are expected to become crucial enablers to resolve the imminent issues.

7   Conclusion

This study proposes a conceptual framework for Ergonomics 4.0 and discusses DHM related aspects that are essential in the understanding of the role of Ergonomics, and integration of Ergonomics into Industry 4.0. In conclusion, we confirm the importance of Ergonomics in Industry 4.0, and the significance of DHM in Ergonomics 4.0.

References

Ahmed, S., Irshad, L., Demirel, O., Tumer, I.: Comparison of Virtual Reality and Digital Human Modeling for Proactive Ergonomics Design and Performance Assessment during an Emergency Situation. Digital Human Modeling and Applications in Health, Safety, Ergonomics and Risk Management, 1–19 (2019)

Caputo, F., Greco, A., Fera, M., Macchiaroli, R.: Digital twins to enhance the integration of ergonomics in the workplace design. Int. J. Ind. Ergon **71**, 20–31 (2019)

Gualtieri, L., Palomba, I., Merati, F., Rauch, E., Vidoni, R.: Design of human-centered collaborative assembly workstations for the improvement of operators' physical ergonomics and production efficiency: a case study. Sustainability **12**(3606), 89–111 (2020)

Hietanen, A.R., Pieters, R., Lanz, M., Latokartano, J., Kamarainen, J.-K.: AR-based interaction for human-robot collaborative manufacturing. Robot. Comput. Integr. Manuf. **63**, 1–9 (2020)

Lim, K.Y.H., Zheng, P., Chen, C.: A state-of-art survey of digital twin: techniques, engineering product lifecycle management and business innovation perspectives. J. Intell. Manuf. **31**, 1313–1337 (2020)

Rauch, E., Linder, C., Dallasega, P.: Anthropocentric perspective of production before and within Industry 4.0. Comput. Ind. Eng. **139**, 1–15 (2019)

Stern, H., Becker, T.: Concept and evaluation of a method for the integration of human factors into human-oriented work design in cyber-physical production systems. Sustainability **11**(4508), 233–265 (2020)

Sun, Sh., Zheng, X., Gong, B., Garcia-Paredes, J., Ordieres-Mere, J.: Healthy operator 4.0: a human cyber-physical system architecture for smart workplaces. Sensors, **20** 1–21 (2020)

Zidek, K., Pitel, J., Adamek, M., Lazorik, P., Hosovsky, A.: Digital twin of experimental smart manufacturing assembly system for industry 4.0 concept. Sustainability **12**, 3658, 39–54 (2020)

Characterizing Adaptive Display Interventions for Attentional Tunneling

Kayla Pedret[(✉)] and Greg A. Jamieson

Department of Mechanical and Industrial Engineering, University of Toronto, Toronto, Canada
kayla.pedret@mail.utoronto.ca

Abstract. The cognitive phenomenon wherein operators lock in on one source of information to the detriment of perceiving or processing others has been referenced using a variety of different names, including attentional tunneling. Unregulated and often used interchangeably, this list of terms makes cataloging research in this area unwieldy, and compiling existing literature on design interventions difficult. A search of relevant databases resulted in a review of literature on attentional tunneling and its variants. Terms and the contexts in which they are used are compared against a standard definition to organize the use of vocabulary. Next, a series of adaptive display interventions for attentional tunneling in the literature are summarized. A characterization is proposed to help organize and inform attentional tunneling literature for research planning and design.

Keywords: Attentional tunneling · Adaptive display · Cognitive countermeasure · Intervention

1 Introduction

As is the nature of cognitive/psychological state research, myriad different names have been used for *attentional tunneling*. Some are effectively interchangeable, yet others refer to peripherally related phenomena. The widely-accepted definition of attentional tunneling put forth by Wickens [24] is used in this paper to ground a shared understanding of the underlying phenomenon being referenced: "the allocation of attention to a particular channel of information, diagnostic hypothesis, or task goal, for a duration that is longer than optimal, given the expected cost of neglecting events on other channels, failing to consider other hypotheses, or failing to perform other tasks" (p. 812). The literature on attentional tunneling is spread across subspecialties in human factors, human-computer interaction, and psychology where terms are used inconsistently, often with little explanation. This causes difficulties when classifying and interpreting research as well as during the design process. If a consensus cannot be reached on the definition of a phenomenon, any resulting interventions designed to treat it will have likely been created using differing approaches, making comparison of multiple interventions difficult. This also creates a problem for researchers attempting to understand the scope of interventions and/or compare them. Compounding these issues is a lack of in-depth

© The Author(s), under exclusive license to Springer Nature Switzerland AG 2022
N. L. Black et al. (Eds.): IEA 2021, LNNS 223, pp. 407–414, 2022.
https://doi.org/10.1007/978-3-030-74614-8_51

explanation of existing interventions to attentional tunneling and the theoretical motivations behind their design. The objective in this paper is twofold. First, to summarize and classify the terminology used in the literature surrounding attentional tunneling. Second, to characterize the array of adaptive display interventions for attentional tunneling to support future research and design.

2   Methods

A review of the literature was conducted. First, terms relating to attentional tunneling were compiled and compared to differentiate the underlying phenomena and aspects of cognition being considered under those terms. There appears to be no controlled terminology for the concept of attentional tunneling, nor for any variant of the term. This makes it difficult to ensure a search has captured all the relevant literature in databases such as Scopus, Web of Science, Compendex, and PubMed. Even the same authors will use different terms across papers. For example, the term *cognitive tunneling* is used in [20, 23], but *attentional tunneling* is used in [24, 25]. Likewise, *Engineering Psychology and Human Performance* [26] uses multiple terms in different contexts. For example, the index entry for *cognitive tunneling* directs to the index entry for *attentional narrowing*, which then refers to sections in the text that use "attentional narrowing or tunneling" (p. 63), "engagement or cognitive tunneling" (p. 333), refers to *attentional narrowing* as a form of *selective attention* (p. 364), and *attentional tunneling* (p. 393).

Next, a review of interventions designed to combat the attentional/cognitive states referred by the aforementioned terms was conducted. The primary inclusion criterion was that the goal of the article was to design and/or test a display intervention to treat attentional tunneling (not necessarily exclusively). Interventions that relied on external factors, such as operator training (e.g., [16]) or mood-based interventions (e.g., [22]) were not included. Included papers came from domains such as aviation (e.g., [6, 8, 11, 23]), air traffic control (e.g., [9, 17]), military (e.g., [5, 20]), construction (e.g., [18]), and non-domain-specific research (e.g., [15]).

3   Results

Terms compiled included *attentional tunneling, attentional narrowing, cognitive tunneling, cognitive narrowing, perseveration syndrome, selective attention, inattentional blindness,* and *cognitive capture*. The definitions and contexts of use for the terms implies they were not always referencing the same phenomenon. Some terms refer to purely perceptual or information-processing occurrences, whereas others describe intentional focus or failures to engage attention elsewhere. Terms used to describe, for example, a failure to notice unexpected events or exclusively an inability to engage attention elsewhere are not attentional tunneling. Though similar, these perceptual or cognitive failures are not as encompassing as attentional tunneling, which involves a lock in on one source of information and an inhibition of processing others, regardless of whether or not there are unexpected events. However, from the review of literature, it appears that any variant of attentional or cognitive narrowing/tunneling does align with the definition proposed by Wickens [24] in this context.

Delineation between concepts became a bit murkier with terms such as *perseveration syndrome*, *cognitive capture*, and *inattentional blindness*. For example, one study directly equates attentional tunneling and inattentional blindness by saying "...salient but unexpected events can remain undetected even when presented in the foveal field... this inattentional blindness phenomenon also known as attentional tunneling" [17] (p. 1). Another study uses similar language to describe inattentional blindness as "...when an observer who is engaged in a resource-consuming task fails to notice an unexpected stimulus in front of their eyes" [16] (p. 513). Though the latter does not necessarily equate inattentional blindness to other concepts such as attentional tunneling, both definitions rely to some extent on the presence of an unexpected event. However, being in a state of attentional tunneling (or being inattentionally blind, for that matter) does not depend on the presence or absence of some external event or stimuli. One can be in a state of attentional tunneling when no unexpected event occurs. Kortschot & Jamieson [12] propose a modification to Wickens' [24] definition of attentional tunneling that bridges this gap. They propose that the definition should be "the allocation of attention... for a duration that is longer than optimal, given the *potential* (rather than *expected*) cost of neglecting events". If we are to say that attentional tunneling and inattentional blindness are the same thing, then we should revise the definitions to include the scenarios in which operators are attentionally tunneled with the potential to miss unexpected events.

This list of terms was then used to search for countermeasures to the respective phenomenon. Because terms are used inconsistently, all related terms were used to search for interventions in the literature. Only interventions adhering to the inclusion criteria were used. The search revealed interventions that seek to break attention tunnels, capture attention elsewhere, and create salient alarms, among other approaches. The design choices across interventions point to differences in how attentional tunneling is defined, differing in the information content shown, the behaviour it induces, the location of the intervention, and the approach it takes to capture or switch attention (see Fig. 1). Although the following sections outline examples for each design dimension, each intervention displays characteristics of all categories (e.g., a design can be a global display alert with forced action, motivated by bottom-up factors). There are successful interventions that span the whole range of design choices, and vice versa - there are unsuccessful interventions that span the range as well. That is to say that there is no one set of design choices that guarantee a successful intervention. Success, in this case, refers to whether or not the intervention had the intended result of breaking an attentional tunnel and improving operator performance (however this may have been defined for the given research paradigm).

3.1 Information Content

The information content dimension characterizes what the intervention alerts the operator to: the fact that there is a problem, or what to do about the problem. Display interventions act as a warning of an attentional tunnel, either notifying the operator of their state or providing an alert of high importance. Command interventions guide the operator to breaking their state and/or committing some prescribed action(s). Imbert et al. [9] provide an example of a display intervention wherein inward-radiating circles converge from one ATC icon to another, and Ververs & Wickens [23] describe a scene-linked

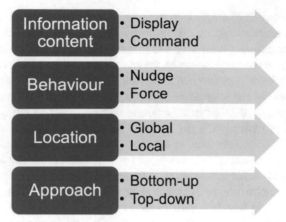

Fig. 1. Dimensions of design choices for interventions. Note that an intervention may have any combination of choices.

conformal symbology to guide flight path tracking. In contrast, Dehais et al. [6] tested a command intervention wherein the area of interest (AOI) likely being tunneled on was highlighted by a red circle, then replaced with a message to the operator (in this case, a pilot being instructed to "go back to Blagnac", the origin airport upon poor visibility conditions).

3.2 Behaviour

The behaviour dimension describes what level of behavioural modification the intervention spurs. Nudge interventions rely on choice architecture to alter an operator's behaviour. In contrast, forced interventions compel an operator to act a certain way. Sato et al. [18] designed an intervention that nudges operators to break an attentional tunnel by adding a secondary view on a teleoperation display that was landmarked to be consistent with the main view. The secondary view would vibrate at 5 Hz when it first appeared to attract attention. The addition of the secondary view (i.e., another channel of information) and the salient manner in which its presence is made known acts as a strong suggestion for operators to broaden or switch their attention but does not coerce any action. Dehais et al. [5] forced operator disengagement with a task to see a low battery warning by obscuring the AOI for 1 s, adding a warning message on the obscured area for 3 additional seconds, and then resuming the display with the warning message still overlaid for a final 3 s before returning to the original display. The removal of information as an intervention to attentional tunneling has been supported by previous results (e.g., [4]), and it is suggested that it helps relieve the inhibition that suppresses perception of information outside the attentional tunnel, forcing the operator to stop their search, allowing a saccade to a different AOI.

3.3 Location

Within the location dimension, global designs are those act on most – if not all – of the display. An example of this includes Red Alert, a system described by Saint-Lot et al. [17]

where the entire display is occluded by a red-orange filter for 300 ms at a 15% opacity such that the underlying field is still visible. Local interventions are those that are focused on a smaller region of the display, which often result in interventions dedicated solely to the space around a target AOI. Examples include alerts placed in specific areas of the display as in Dowell et al. [8], or highlighting alerts with blinking or moving borders, as in Dehais et al. [6] and Imbert et al. [9] with a box animation. In some cases, interventions have included both global and local aspects, such as a shadow mask in [9], where the entire background and irrelevant targets are faded (global), then the relevant target is animated to vibrate briefly (local). Another such design is the Trajectory Recovery System described in [11] where extraneous or task-irrelevant display information is cleared from the interface briefly (global), while a colour-coded bulls-eye appears to indicate current and target states to the operator (local).

3.4 Design Approach

Interventions can also be classified in terms of the design approach: whether they were created to capture attention from a bottom-up or top-down fashion, separating perceptually motivated and goal-directed interventions, respectively. Prinet [15] tested an intervention designed to capture attention with high saliency wherein a bright green border appears around the AOI being tunneled on, disappearing as another bright green border appears around the entire display. This is then repeated three times, resulting in the entire intervention taking 1800 ms. Top-down interventions are particularly prevalent in aviation head-up displays (e.g., [11, 23]), where the imposed symbology may not be designed to be particularly salient, but it is meant to provide high-value information where an operator expects to see it. Both approaches are valid design choices as long as they achieve the desired effect. Moreover, a design can incorporate both motivations by adding salient stimuli (e.g., movement, different colours, etc.) and goal-relevant adaptation(s).

4 Discussion

Where *attentional tunneling*, *attentional narrowing*, *cognitive tunneling*, and *cognitive narrowing* are mostly used in reference to the common phenomenon of an operator locking in on a source of information and inhibiting or locking out other sources, the other terms listed are not always as clear. Especially in the context of aviation psychology, *perseveration syndrome* is often used interchangeably with attentional tunneling, but it is worth noting that in clinical psychology, perseveration is used to describe an inability to switch focus. Though attentional tunneling does describe an inhibition of other sources of information, it is not inherently an inability to switch focus. *Inattentional blindness* is often used in this context as well. However, there are cases where it is used to refer to a failure of visual perception [13, 19], rather than encompassing attention and cognition. Likewise, it is often the case that the definition of inattentional blindness relies on the presence of some secondary (often unexpected) event (e.g., [13, 17, 19]). As stated in Sect. 3 and [12] attentional tunneling exists whether or not there is some additional event. *Selective attention* is used to describe a mechanism of attention that allows agents to direct their attention where it needs to be, implying intentionality, whereas attentional tunneling is an unintentional phenomenon. The term *selective attention* often involves a characterization of attention as a spotlight beam [10], independent of eye fixations. Though related to attentional tunneling, *selective attention* is often used to refer to a feature of attention, not the maladaptive state of attentional tunneling. *Cognitive capture* is used to describe seemingly diverse cognitive and attentional phenomena, each of which are similar, but not quite interchangeable with attentional tunneling (e.g., [2, 3, 21]).

Although there are several examples of successful interventions to break attentional tunneling, there are some examples in the literature in which the interventions were either not as effective as expected or resulted in worse operator performance than controls. In testing five different alert types, Imbert et al. [9] found that simply colouring a peripheral alert in red or causing it to blink does not sufficiently capture attention to break attentional tunneling. In Prinet [15] and Saint-Lot et al. [17], participants were not forewarned that display adaptations may occur or what they may mean, resulting in confusion. In both studies, participants misinterpreted the purpose of the adaptations, which confounds interpretation of performance data. In [15], this failure may have been compounded by the fact that the intervention (a blinking border around the area researchers assumed participants were tunneling on) was coloured in red. Red is often interpreted to signal an error or failure, and the author proposed that participants may have confused the alert to mean that the area required more attention, not less. Dowell et al. [8] point out that the placement of information on a display is also vital to its success or failure in breaking attentional tunneling. Not only does information in the centre of an out-the-window scene in an aircraft cockpit not break attentional tunneling, but it also induces it. In another study of cockpit information displays, Ververs and Wickens [23] found that not integrating with the outside scene so that pilots could appropriately sample both the display and the scene behind it led to performance degradation. These unsuccessful interventions are still informative, however, and help build general design guidelines for future work. Such guidelines include informing operators that display adaptations may occur and what they indicate, making sure the intervention is salient and large enough to be perceived even if in the periphery, and being judicious in the use of colour.

Future challenges include resolving operator habituation [17] to implemented intervention designs as well as ensuring automation etiquette and transparency [1, 7] when connecting interventions to classifiers and other imperfect automation. Because so many interventions rely on some degree of salience, habituation poses a unique challenge: the more an intervention is used the more operators will habituate to its presence and be able to tune it out. Some authors suggest only using interventions for attentional tunneling in safety-critical emergencies [5, 9], which would preserve the salience longer, but prevent use of the interventions in everyday operations. The second core issue with adaptive displays is that they rely on automation, which is rarely perfect. Even if an intervention was triggered by a classifier with an AUC value of 0.9 - a value generally considered to mean that the classifier has excellent discrimination - there is still a 10% chance that the classifier will incorrectly interpret the cognitive state of the operator [14]. That 10% chance could result in either the classifier not identifying a state of attentional tunneling (a miss), leaving the operator in a potentially dangerous state of attentional tunneling or the classifier identifies a state of attentional tunneling where one does not exist (false positive), triggering the intervention needlessly and interrupting and/or frustrating the operator. In either case, task performance would degrade. Balancing imperfect automation with the context that it will be integrated in is key to avoiding successful implementation of interventions on adaptive displays.

5 Conclusion

The characterizations provided can be used as a tool to organize and understand literature relating to attentional tunneling and the adaptive display interventions created to combat it. Synthesizing the divergence of terms used to describe attentional tunneling and the divergence of phenomena referenced by those terms is a step toward defining attentional tunneling as a cognitive state and establishing a shared understanding from which to build effective interventions. The characterizations of interventions used in previous research illuminates the range of alternatives available to display designers and informs their choices.

References

1. Amershi, S., et al.: Guidelines for human-AI interaction. In: Conference on Human Factors in Computing Systems - Proceedings. pp. 1–13 Association for Computing Machinery, New York, New York, USA (2019). https://doi.org/10.1145/3290605.3300233
2. Blanco, M., et al.: The impact of secondary task cognitive processing demand on driving performance. Accid. Anal. Prev. **38**(5), 895–906 (2006). https://doi.org/10.1016/j.aap.2006.02.015
3. Boston, B.N., Braun, C.C.: Clutter and display conformality: changes in cognitive capture. Proc. Hum. Factors Ergon. Soc. Annu. Meet. **40**(2), 57–61 (1996). https://doi.org/10.1177/154193129604000211
4. Dehais, F., et al.: GHOST: experimenting countermeasures for conflicts in the pilot's activity (2003)
5. Dehais, F., et al.: Mitigation of conflicts with automation: use of cognitive countermeasures. Hum. Factors J. Hum. Factors Ergon. Soc. **53**(5), 448–460 (2011). https://doi.org/10.1177/0018720811418635
6. Dehais, F., et al.: The perseveration syndrome in the pilot's activity: guidelines and cognitive countermeasures. In: Lecture Notes in Computer Science (including subseries Lecture Notes in Artificial Intelligence and Lecture Notes in Bioinformatics), pp. 68–80 (2010). https://doi.org/10.1007/978-3-642-11750-3_6
7. Dorneich, M.C., et al.: Considering etiquette in the design of an adaptive system. J. Cogn. Eng. Decis. Mak. **6**(2), 243–265 (2012). https://doi.org/10.1177/1555343412441001
8. Dowell, S.R., et al.: The effect of visual location on cognitive tunneling with superimposed hud symbology. Proc. Hum. Factors Ergon. Soc. Ann. Meet. **46**(1), 121–125 (2002). https://doi.org/10.1177/154193120204600125
9. Imbert, J.P., et al.: Attentional costs and failures in air traffic control notifications. Ergonomics. **57**(12), 1817–1832 (2014). https://doi.org/10.1080/00140139.2014.952680
10. Johnston, W.A., Dark, V.J.: Selective attention. Annu. Rev. Psychol. **37**(1), 43–75 (1986). https://doi.org/10.1146/annurev.ps.37.020186.000355

11. Kasdaglis, N., et al.: Trajectory recovery system: angle of attack guidance for inflight loss of control. In: Lecture Notes in Computer Science (including subseries Lecture Notes in Artificial Intelligence and Lecture Notes in Bioinformatics), pp. 397–408. Springer Verlag (2016). https://doi.org/10.1007/978-3-319-40030-3_39

12. Kortschot, S.W., Jamieson, G.A.: Classification of attentional tunneling through behavioral indices. Hum. Factors J. Hum. Factors Ergon. Soc. 001872081985726 (2019). https://doi.org/10.1177/0018720819857266

13. Mack, A.: Inattentional blindness. Curr. Dir. Psychol. Sci. 12(5), 180–184 (2003). https://doi.org/10.1111/1467-8721.01256

14. Mandrekar, J.N.: Receiver operating characteristic curve in diagnostic test assessment. J. Thorac. Oncol. 5(9), 1315–1316 (2010). https://doi.org/10.1097/JTO.0b013e3181ec173d

15. Prinet, J.: Attentional Narrowing: Triggering. University of Michigan, Detecting and Overcoming a Threat to Safety (2016)

16. Richards, A., et al.: Predicting and manipulating the incidence of inattentional blindness. Psychol. Res. 74(6), 513–523 (2010). https://doi.org/10.1007/s00426-009-0273-8

17. Saint-Lot, J., et al.: Red alert: a cognitive countermeasure to mitigate attentional tunneling. In: Proceedings of the SIGCHI Conference on Human Factors in Computing Systems, pp. 1–6 ACM, New York, NY, USA (2020). https://doi.org/10.1145/3313831.3376709

18. Sato, R., et al.: Cognitive untunneling multi-view system for teleoperators of heavy machines based on visual momentum and saliency. Autom. Constr. 110 (2020). https://doi.org/10.1016/j.autcon.2019.103047

19. Simons, D.J., Chabris, C.F.: Gorillas in our midst: sustained inattentional blindness for dynamic events. Perception 28(9), 1059–1074 (1999). https://doi.org/10.1068/p281059

20. Thomas, L.C., Wickens, C.D.: Visual displays and cognitive tunneling: frames of reference effects on spatial judgments and change detection. Proc. Hum. Factors Ergon. Soc. Annu. Meet. 45(4), 336–340 (2001). https://doi.org/10.1177/154193120104500415

21. Tönnis, M.: Time-critical supportive augmented reality issues on cognitive capture and perceptual tunneling (2007)

22. Vanlessen, N., et al.: Happy heart, smiling eyes: a systematic review of positive mood effects on broadening of visuospatial attention (2016). https://doi.org/10.1016/j.neubiorev.2016.07.001

23. Ververs, P.M., Wickens, C.D.: Designing head-up displays (HUDs) to support flight path guidance while minimizing effects of cognitive tunneling. Proc. Hum. Factors Ergon. Soc. Annu. Meet. 44(13), 45–48 (2000). https://doi.org/10.1177/154193120004401312

24. Wickens, C.: Attentional tunneling and task management. In: 2005 International Symposium on Aviation Psychology (2005)

25. Wickens, C., Alexander, A.: Attentional tunneling and task management in synthetic vision displays. Int. J. Aviat. Psychol. 19(2), 182–199 (2009). https://doi.org/10.1080/10508410902766549

26. Wickens, C.D., et al.: Engineering Psychology and Human Performance. Routledge, New York (2013)

Digital Production Planning of Manual and Semi-automatic Tasks in Industry Using the EMA Software Suite

Michael Spitzhirn[✉], Lars Fritzsche, and Sebastian Bauer

imk Automotive GmbH, Amselgrund 30, 09128 Chemnitz, Germany
Michael.Spitzhirn@imk-automotive.de

Abstract. The 3D planning software EMA offers a combined approach which takes into account the factory planning level and the detailed planning at the single work station level. Ema Work Designer supports digital production planning, prospective ergonomics and productivity assessment by providing a more efficient and accurate approach to 3D human simulation of manual and semi-automatic tasks at the micro level. Additionally, the new module EMA Plant Designer allows to include entire factories and production lines for evaluation of lead time, production costs, material flow, buffer position, space and layout at the macro level. An application example shows that ergonomic and productivity design don't contradict each other, if they are considered early in the design phase in one common software system. Many practical experiences suggest that this approach facilitates cooperation between different business units that are traditionally separated, such as factory/facility planning, manufacturing engineering, industrial engineering, production, and health & safety.

Keywords: Digital human modeling · Digital production planning · Digital factory · Ergonomic assessment · Productivity assessment

1 Introduction

The shortened product life cycle, market launch and innovation cycles require that work and production systems have to be planned and reconfigured faster and more frequently (Spath et al. 2017). When planning and designing products, factories and work processes - in addition to costs, times, quality, time-to-market and flexibility - the ergonomic design for the user group as well as the skill-based deployment of the workforce must be taken into account (Schenk et al. 2014; Schlick et al. 2018). However, especially small and medium enterprises have only limited possibilities to use cost-intensive and complex software systems due to a lack of qualification and financial resources. Moreover, many software systems are isolated and work as a monolith, but missing interfaces to other systems and business units in the same company lead to redundant and inconsistent data, which finally impairs efficiency.

Separate digital tools are used for the design of factories at macro level and for the detailed planning of work stations at micro level. These software systems differ, amongst

N. L. Black et al. (Eds.): IEA 2021, LNNS 223, pp. 415–419, 2022.
https://doi.org/10.1007/978-3-030-74614-8_52

others, in functional scope as well as in the software handling. A common data basis is not available or must be achieved through complex data conversions. This requires high effort at companies for finding suitable systems and providing sufficient expertise for the application. To improve the quality of results and to reduce the effort, it is necessary that systems from different areas, such as factory and workstation planning, can easily interact with each other. This paper presents a combined procedure to design manual and semiautomatic production processes at factory and workstation level by using EMA Work Designer (emaWD) and EMA Plant Designer (emaPD) software in the EMA Software Suite. This software is being developed and distributed by imk automotive GmbH, Germany.

2   Simulation Framework

In the planning phases before start of production, the holistic consideration of product, process and resource is required because there are interdependencies and iterative planning statuses between numerous planning disciplines (Dombrowski et al. 2018). In order to achieve an economical and ergonomic design of production, a combined approach to the planning and design of the factory and the individual workstations using the software systems emaPD and emaWD is be presented using the example of a washing machine production. The interaction of both systems between macro level of the factory and micro level of the individual workstations is illustrated in Fig. 1.

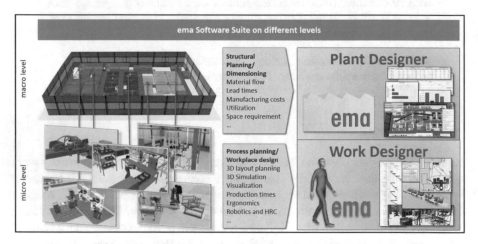

Fig. 1. EMA Software Suite on different levels of factory/production planning

In the presented case study, emaPD is used to plan and evaluate the production processes targeting a lean and highly efficient production system. emaPD enables computer-aided modelling, analysis and optimization of plants or production areas based on mathematical-analytical calculation methods such as queuing theory (Manitz 2008) and determine manufacturing and material flow costs, required space, lead time, and buffer positons needed. Bottlenecks and the critical path of the production can be identified and counter measures can be taken into account (e.g., adding a second machine or integrating a back-up strategy). The detailed output of results forms the basis for optimizing production including the operating resources, layout, and logistics with regard to lead times and manufacturing costs.

These results are applied for detailed planning and design at the workstation level with emaWD, which uses an algorithmic approach for self-initiated motion generation based on objective task descriptions (Fritzsche et al. 2019). It allows the graphical modelling of human work activities and the planning of assembly work stations involving human-robot collaboration (HRC) as well as the detailed evaluation of production times and ergonomic risks. The software provides a novel approach to simulate human work in an intuitive and efficient way. emaWD includes a library of predefined»tasks« that is used to create a parameterized job description solely by specifying the parameters pertaining to the job to be executed and the work environment (objects to be handled, target positions, etc.) (Fig. 2). This job description is subsequently evaluated geometrically by a simulation module for plausibility. emaWD also includes a library of various human models, lightweight and heavyweight robots (KUKA, Universal Robots, Yaskawa etc.) and other process-relevant objects such as tables, racks, tools, etc. Performance requirements of the human model, such as gender-specific percentilized body measurements (P05, P50, P95) and other characteristics (age) can be adjusted.

Fig. 2. Use case "washing machine production" simulated in EMA Work Designer

3   Simulation Results

The generated simulations are examined and optimized on the basis of industry standards such as MTM-UAS for production time estimation and Ergonomic Assessment

Worksheet (EAWS) for ergonomic risk assessment. Other ergonomic standard methods like NIOSH, RULA and OCRA might be included as well.

In the use case scenario different design alternatives were developed and evaluated with emaPD and emaWD. A preferred variant was selected according to economic key figures (time, costs, space requirements) while maintaining low ergonomic risks. Taking into account the required daily production rate, a capacity utilization of 90% was achieved in a 2-shift operation. At the level of emaWD, workplace design measures such as the introduction of handling devices and a collaborative robot ensured that the workplaces do not have ergonomically critical "red" workstations according to EAWS (Schaub et. al. 2012; Fig. 3). Before redesigning the washing machine production four red, two yellow and two green work places were included; after optimization no red, four yellow and four green work places are available. Furthermore, improvements in time and space requirements could be achieved through layout optimization.

	Werker_M50_Station 1R	Werker_M50_Station 1L	Werker_M50_Station 2R	Werker_M50_Station 2L	Werker_M50_Station 3L	Werker_M50_Station 4R
information	50th percentile, male, age group: 40, performance factor: 1	50th percentile, male, age group: 40, performance factor: 1	50th percentile, male, age group: 40, performance factor: 1	50th percentile, male, age group: 40, performance factor: 1	50th percentile, male, age group: 40, performance factor: 1	50th percentile, male, age group: 40, performance factor: 1
whole body [pts]	9.5	2	39.5	27.5	23.5	2
postures [pts]	2	2	2	2	2	2
trunk rotating [pts]	0	0	6	2.7	0	0
trunk bending [pts]	0	0	0	0	0	0
far reach [pts]	0	0	0	0	0	0
postures sum [pts]	2	2	8	5	2	2
17 finger forces [pts]	7.1	0	0	0	4.6	0
18 body forces [pts]	0	0	0	0	0	0
action forces [pts]	7.5	0	0	0	5	0
19 repositioning [pts]	0	0	31.2	22.5	16.3	0
19 holding [pts]	0	0	0	0	0	0
19 carrying [pts]	0	0	0	0	0	0
19 pushing & pulling [pts]	0	0	0	0	0	0
manual handling [pts]	0	0	31.5	22.5	16.5	0

Fig. 3. Example of ergonomic outcomes using EAWS in EMA Work Designer

4 Discussion

The combined use of emaPD and emaWD in the EMA Software Suit enables a systematic planning and dimensioning of the entire factory floor as well as a holistic process and workplace design. One advantage of the combined approach is that the planning at the factory level can be detailed using results from the work planning and vice versa. For example, the necessary assembly times in emaWD can be precisely determined using MTM-UAS and can be returned into emaPD to get more precise results regarding the number of required work stations and layout space, respectively. At the same time, the consideration of ergonomics at the factory planning level has great potential, which will become even more relevant for companies in the next years.

Furthermore, the presented approach offers a high potential for deeper cooperation between work planners and factory planners. In many large companies, these tasks are carried out by different people in different departments. Using the holistic EMA Software Suite may result in considerable cost and time savings not only at the shop floor, but also during the planning phase (e.g., by elimination of expensive corrective product and process changes due to misunderstandings between planning departments). The

3D visualization also supports communication and acceptance of the planned measures among production workers and other stakeholders.

References

Dombrowski, U., Karl, A., Ruping, L.: Herausforderungen der digitalen fabrik im kontext von industrie 4.0. ZWF Zeitschrift für wirtschaftlichen Fabrikbetrieb **113**(12), 845–849 (2018). https://doi.org/10.3139/104.112030

Fritzsche, L., Ullmann, S., Bauer, S., Sylaja, V.J.: Task-based digital human simulation with Editor for Manual Work Activities – Industrial applications in product design and production planning. In: Paul, G., Scataglini, S. (eds.) DHM and Posturography, pp. 569–575. Elsevier, London, UK (2019)

Manitz, M.: Queueing-model based analysis of assembly lines with finite buffers and general service times. Comput. Oper. Res. **35**, 2520–2536 (2008)

Schaub, K., Mühlstedt, J., Illmann, B., Bauer, S., Fritzsche, L., Wagner, T., Bullinger, A., Hoffmann, R.: Ergonomic assessment of automotive assembly tasks with digital human modelling and the "ergonomics assessment worksheet" (EAWS). International Journal of Human Factors Modelling and Simulation **3**(3/4), 398 (2012). https://doi.org/10.1504/IJHFMS.2012.051581

Schenk, M., Wirth, S., Müller, E.: Fabrikplanung und Fabrikbetrieb. Methoden für die wandlungsfähige, vernetzte und ressourceneffiziente Fabrik. 2., vollständig überarbeitete und erweiterte Auflage 2014. Berlin: Springer Vieweg (2014)

Schlick, C., Bruder, R., Luczak, H.: Arbeitswissenschaft. 4. Auflage. Berlin: Springer Vieweg (2018)

Spath, D., Westkämper, E., Bullinger, H.J., Warnecke, H.J.: Neue Entwicklungen in der Unternehmensorganisation. Berlin, Heidelberg: Vieweg (VDI-Buch Ser) (2017)

Probabilistic Human-System-Integration (HSI) Models: Review and Extension

Ephraim Suhir and Gunther Paul[(✉)]

James Cook University, Townsville, QLD, Australia

Abstract. Three probabilistic analytical ("mathematical") human-system-integration (HSI) models and their application in ergonomics engineering are addressed. The general concepts are illustrated by numerical examples. It is concluded that such models should always be considered, in addition to computer simulations, in every critical HSI effort.

Keywords: Probabilistic predictive modeling (PPM) · Human-in-the-loop (HITL) · Human factor (HF)

Acronyms: ASD = Assessed Sight Distance · DEPD = Double-Exponential-Probability-Distribution · HCF = Human Capacity Factor · HITL = Human in the Loop · HLS = Helicopter Landing Ship · HSI = Human-System-Integration · MWL = Mental Workload · PDF = Probability Distribution Function · PPM = Probabilistic Predictive Modeling

1 Introduction

By employing quantifiable and measurable ways of assessing the role and significance of critical uncertainties and treating the human-in-the-loop (HITL) as a part, often the most crucial part, of a complex man–instrumentation (both its hard- and software)–object-of-control–environment system, one could improve dramatically the state-of-the-art in ergonomics engineering, including its HSI aspect. In the analysis that follows several recently employed probabilistic HITL/HSI models are addressed. The models are based on the well-known general principles of applied probability (see, e.g., [1]) and can be and, actually, have been applied, when a human fulfils a challenging mission or encounters an extraordinary situation, and is expected to possess a high enough human capacity factor (HCF) to successfully cope with an elevated mental workload (MWL) [2]. The "object-of-control" could be, particularly, aerospace, automotive, railway or a maritime vehicle; another human, such as, e.g., medical patient or a business customer, particularly in the situations, when adequate trust is critical [3]. One cannot improve anything, if he/she does not quantify things. And since nobody and nothing is perfect, a physically meaningful and effective quantification should be done on the probabilistic basis. Probabilistic predictive modelling (PPM) is able predict, quantify and, if necessary and appropriate, even specify an adequate and never-zero probability of failure of an ergonomics undertaking of importance.

© The Author(s), under exclusive license to Springer Nature Switzerland AG 2022
N. L. Black et al. (Eds.): IEA 2021, LNNS 223, pp. 420–428, 2022.
https://doi.org/10.1007/978-3-030-74614-8_53

Tversky and Kahneman [4] seem to be the first ones who addressed, in application to decision making tasks in economics (2002 Nobel Prize in economics), various cognitive "heuristics and biases" with consideration of uncertainties in human psychology, but being top-notch, but still traditional, human psychologists, these authors discussed such problems from the qualitative viewpoint, while the importance of the probabilistic quantitative approach [5–28] that has been addressed and discussed here. It is noteworthy that the analytical PPM was used in all the referenced publications [8] and that the addressed ergonomics models originated from the models suggested and employed earlier in electronics and photonics reliability engineering (see, e.g., [6, 7]). The first attempt of doing so was undertaken in application to helicopter-landing-ship (HLS) situation [5]. It was shown that the likelihood that such landing would be successful and safe, i.e., the helicopter's undercarriage will not be damaged, if the probability that the anticipated random time of the calm "widow" in the sea state exceeds appreciably the sum of two random times: the actual time of landing and the times of the "go-non-go" decision making by the officer on shipboard and the helicopter pilot.

2 Analysis

As has been indicated, the **convolution model** was introduced and applied first in the HLS situation, and then employed in several other HSI problems [10–16]. Let us show, as a suitable example, how this model can be applied for the assessment of the probability of a head-on railway obstruction. Consider first a situation when the assessed sight distance (ASD) $\hat{S}$ determined by the system's radar and/or LIDAR is viewed as a non-random variable and assume that the random pre-deceleration constant speed distance S_0 and the subsequent constant deceleration distance S_1 (after the system and/or the machinist detected an obstacle) are random variables distributed in accordance with the Rayleigh law. Indeed, the most likely values of the breaking times and distances (modes) cannot be zero but cannot be very long (large) either. In addition, in emergency situations of the type in question, short times and small distances are much more likely than long times and large distances. Because of that, the modes of their probability density distribution functions (PDFs) should be heavily skewed towards short times and small distances. The Rayleigh distribution is the simplest distribution that possesses these features. The probability that the random distance $S = S_0 + S_1$ exceeds a certain non-random level $\hat{S}$ can be found as a convolution of the two Rayleigh distributed random variables S_0 and S_1 as follows:

$$P_S = 1 - \int_0^{\widehat{S}} \frac{s_0}{\sigma_0^2} \exp\left(-\frac{s_0^2}{2\sigma_0^2}\right)\left[1 - \exp\left(-\frac{(\hat{S} - s_0)^2}{2\sigma_1^2}\right)\right] ds_0 = \exp[-(1 + \eta^2)s^2] +$$

$$+ \exp(-s^2)\left(\frac{\exp\left(-\frac{s^2}{\eta^2}\right) - \exp(-\eta^2 s^2)}{1 + \frac{1}{\eta^2}} + \sqrt{\pi}\frac{s}{1 + \frac{1}{\eta}}\left[\Phi(\eta s) + \Phi\left(\frac{s}{\eta}\right)\right]\right).$$

$$(1)$$

Here $f(s_{0,1}) = \frac{s_{0,1}}{\sigma_{0,1}^2} \exp\left(-\frac{s_{0,1}^2}{2\sigma_{0,1}^2}\right)$ are the PDFs of the variables S_0 and S_1; $\sigma_{0,1}$ are their modes (most likely values); $s_{0,1} = \sqrt{\frac{\pi}{2}}\sigma_0$ and $\sqrt{D_{0,1}} = \sqrt{\frac{4-\pi}{2}}\sigma_{0,1}$ are their means and standard deviations, respectively; $s = \frac{\hat{s}}{\sqrt{2(\sigma_0^2+\sigma_1^2)}}$ and $\eta = \frac{\sigma_1}{\sigma_0}$ are the dimensionless parameters of the convolution (1); and $\Phi(\alpha) = \frac{2}{\sqrt{\pi}} \int_0^\alpha e^{-t^2} dt$ is the probability integral (Laplace function). If the probability (1) is small (how small is "small" should be determined, agreed upon and eventually included into the governing specifications), then there is reason to believe that the train will stop before hitting the obstacle, so that obstruction will be avoided. The calculated P_S values are shown in Table 1. As evident from the calculated data, the ASD parameter s plays the major role, while the ratio η of the most likely deceleration and the pre-deceleration distances is much less important.

Table 1. Calculated probabilities P_S of obstruction assuming non-random ASD

s/η	0	1.0	2.0	5.0	10.0	20.0
0	1.0000	1.0000	1.0000	1.0000	1.0000	1.0000
0.25	0.9394	0.9975	0.9962	0.9870	0.9719	0.9579
0.5	0.7788	0.9656	0.9515	0.8890	0.8413	0.8071
0.75	0.5698	0.8629	0.8232	0.7059	0.6424	0.6058
1.00	0.3679	0.6848	0.6259	0.5817	0.4324	0.3997
1.50	0.1054	0.2818	0.2399	0.2181	0.1344	0.1197
2.0	0.0183	0.0645	0.0534	0.0328	0.0253	0.0216
3.0	1.234E-4	6.562E-4	5.395E-4	2.852E-4	1.980E-4	1.577E-4
4.0	1.254E-7	1.064E-6	6.384E-7	2.673E-7	2.078E-7	1.125E-7
5.0	1.389E-11	1.231E-10	9.847E-11	4.853E-11	2.924E-11	2.085E-11

The role of the ASD variability could be accounted for based on the following reasoning. Assuming, based on the intuitively obvious physical considerations, that the ASD is a normally distributed random variable, the probability that this variable is below a certain level S is $P_A = \frac{1}{2}[1 - \Phi(s)]$. Obstruction will be avoided, when the random distance $S = S_0 + S_1$ is below a level $\hat{S}$ (the probability of this situation is $1 - P_s$) and, in addition, if the ASD distance is above this level (this probability is $1 - P_A$). Then the probability that the obstruction is avoided can be evaluated as $(1 - P_s)(1 - P_A)$, and the probability P_{SA} that obstruction will occur is therefore

$$P_{SA} = 1 - (1 - P_s)(1 - P_A) = P_A + P_s - P_A P_s = \frac{1}{2}[1 - \Phi(s) + P_s(1 + \Phi(s))]$$

(2)

The calculated P_{SA} values are shown in Table 2. As one could see by comparing the Tables 1 and 2 data, consideration of the variability of the ASD results in an insignificant

increase in the predicted probabilities of obstruction and this difference decreases with
the decrease in this probability. For very low probabilities of obstruction, consideration
of the ASD variability does not make any difference at all (see italic data in the last two
rows of Table 2). Intuitively, such a behaviour could be anticipated from (2). Indeed,
when the prediction of the ASD is absolutely accurate and, owing to that, the probability
P_A of obstruction caused by the inaccurate radar or a LIDAR measurements is zero
$(P_A = 0)$, then $P_{SA} = P_S$, and when P_S is low, P_{SA} is also low and is not different from
the P_S.

Table 2. Calculated probabilities P_{SA} of obstruction considering ASD variability

s/η	0	1.0	2.0	5.0	10.0	20.0
0	0.5000	0.5000	0.5000	0.5000	0.5000	0.5000
0.25	0.9613	0.9984	0.9976	0.9917	0.9821	0.9731
0.5	0.8318	0.9738	0.9631	0.9156	0.8793	0.8368
0.75	0.6319	0.8827	0.8487	0.7484	0.7281	0.6627
1.00	0.4176	0.7096	0.6553	0.6146	0.4770	0.4469
1.50	0.1206	0.2940	0.2528	0.2314	0.1491	0.1346
2.0	0.0201	0.0662	0.0551	0.0346	0.0271	0.0234
3.0	1.334E-4	6.662E-4	5.495E-4	2.952E-4	2.038E-4	1.677E-4
4.0	*1.254E-7*	*1.064E-6*	*6.384E-7*	*2.673E-7*	*2.078E-7*	*1.125E-7*
5.0	*1.389E-11*	*1.231E-10*	*9.847E-11*	*4.853E-11*	*2.924E-11*	*2.085E-11*

The **double-exponential-probability-distribution (DEPD) model** uses the DEPD
function. This function could be introduced in many ways, depending on a particular
problem of importance. In vehicular, such as, say, avionic engineering, if one intends
to evaluate the impact of the HCF F, the MWL G and the time t on the probability
$P^h(F, G, t)$ of the pilot's non-failure, this function can be sought in the form:

$$P^h(F, G, S_*) = P_0 \exp\left[-\left(\gamma_S S_* t + \frac{G^2}{G_0^2}\right) \exp\left(-\frac{F^2}{F_0^2}\right)\right]. \tag{3}$$

Here P_0 is the probability of human non-failure at the initial moment of time and/or in
the case of a very low MWL level G, but could be defined also as the level for the situation
when the HCF F is extraordinarily high, while the MWL G is still finite, and so is the
time t; S_* is the threshold (acceptable level) of the continuously monitored/measured
human health characteristic (symptom), such as, e.g., body temperature, arterial blood
pressure, etc.; γ_S is the sensitivity factor for the symptom S_*; $G \geq G_0$ is the actual
(elevated, off-normal) MWL; G_0 is the MWL in normal operation conditions; $F \geq F_0$
is the actual (off-normal) HCF exhibited or required in the extraordinary condition of
importance; F_0 is the most likely (normal, specified) HCF; γ_S is the sensitivity factor for
the governing symptom S_*. While measuring the MWL has become, for many years, a

key method of improving safety, HCF is a relatively new notion (see, e.g., [2, 3, 10, 11]) that plays with respect to the MWL more or less the same role as strength or capacity play with respect to stress or demand in structural analysis and in some economics problems. The function (3) makes physical sense. Indeed, when time t, and/or the level S_* of the governing symptom, and/or the level of the MWL G are significant, the probability of non-failure is always low, no matter how high the level of the HCF F is; when the level of the HCF is high, and the time t, and/or the level S_* of the governing symptom, and/or the level of the MWL G are finite, the probability $P^h(F, G, S_*)$ becomes close to the probability P_0; when the HCF F is on the ordinary level F_0 the formula (3) yields:

$$P^h(F, G, S_*) = P^h(G, S_*) = P_0 \exp\left[-\left(\gamma_S S_* t + \frac{G^2}{G_0^2}\right)\right], \tag{4}$$

and for a long time in operation ($t \to \infty$) and/or when the level S_* of the governing symptom is significant ($S_* \to \infty$) and/or when the level G of the MWL is high, the probability (4) of non-failure will be always low; at the initial moment of time ($t = 0$) and/or in the case of a very low S_* level ($S_* = 0$), the Eq. (4) yields: $P^h(F, G, S_*) = P^h(G) = P_0 \exp\left[-\left(\frac{G^2}{G_0^2}\right)\right]$; when the MWL G is high, this probability is low. In the function (3) there are two unknowns: the probability P_0 and the sensitivity factor γ_S. The probability P_0 could be determined by testing a group of highly qualified individuals. Let us show how the sensitivity factor γ_S can be determined. The Eq. (4) can be written as $\frac{-\ln \overline{P}}{\gamma_S S_* t + \frac{G^2}{G_0^2}} = \exp\left(-\frac{F^2}{F_0^2}\right)$. Let accelerated testing be conducted on a flight simulator for the same group of individuals with the same high HCF F/F_0 level (Captain Sullenberger [12] is a good example), but at two different elevated (off-normal) MWL conditions, G_1 and G_2. Let the governing symptom has reached its critical level S_* at the times t_1 and t_2 from the beginning of testing, respectively, and the percentages of the individuals that failed the tests were Q_1 and Q_2, so that the corresponding probabilities of non-failure were $\vec{P}_1$ and $\vec{P}_2$, respectively. Since the same group of individuals was tested, the right part of the above relationship should remain unchanged, and because of that the condition

$\frac{-\ln \overline{P}_1}{\gamma_S S_* t_1 + \frac{G_1^2}{G_0^2}} = \frac{-\ln \overline{P}_2}{\gamma_S S_* t_2 + \frac{G_2^2}{G_0^2}}$ should be fulfilled. This condition yields: $\gamma_S = \frac{1}{S_*} \frac{\frac{G_1^2}{G_0^2} - \frac{\ln \overline{P}_1}{\ln \overline{P}_2} \frac{G_2^2}{G_0^2}}{\frac{\ln \overline{P}_1}{\ln \overline{P}_2} t_2 - t_1}$.

After the sensitivity factor γ_S is determined, the probability $P^h(F, G, S_*)$ of human non-failure can be evaluated on the basis of the formula (3). Let the accelerated testing on a flight simulator was conducted twice for a group of individuals with high HCF $\frac{F}{F_0}$ levels at loading conditions, $\frac{G_1}{G_0} = 1.5$ and $\frac{G_2}{G_0} = 2.5$. The tests have indicated that the value of the symptom S of the critical magnitude of, say, $S_* = 180$, has been detected in 70% of individuals ($\overline{P}_1 = 0.3$) during testing under the loading condition of $\frac{G_1}{G_0} = 1.5$ after $t_1 = 2$ h of testing and in 90% of individuals ($\overline{P}_2 = 0.1$) during the second set of testing under the loading condition $\frac{G_2}{G_0} = 2.5$ after $t_2 = 1$ h. Then the sensitivity factor γ_S is as follows: $\gamma_S = \dfrac{1}{S_*} \dfrac{\frac{G_1^2}{G_0^2} - \frac{\ln \bar{P}_1}{\ln \bar{P}_2} \frac{G_2^2}{G_0^2}}{\frac{\ln \bar{P}_1}{\ln \bar{P}_2} t_2 - t_1} = \dfrac{1}{180} \dfrac{2.25 - \frac{-1.2040}{-2.3026} 6.25}{\frac{-1.2040}{-2.3026} - 2} = 3.8288 x 10^{-3} hr^{-1}$, and the Eq. (4)

results in the following probability of the human non-failure:

$$\bar{P} = \frac{P^h(F, G, S_*)}{P_0} = \exp\left[-\left(\gamma_S S_* t + \frac{G^2}{G_0^2}\right)\exp\left(-\frac{F^2}{F_0^2}\right)\right] = \exp\left[-\left(0.68918 t + \frac{G^2}{G_0^2}\right)\exp\left(-\frac{F^2}{F_0^2}\right)\right]$$

For a pilot of ordinary skills $\left(\frac{F}{F_0} = 1\right)$ (normal HCF) and for a normal MWL $\left(\frac{G}{G_0} = 1\right)$ this formula yields: $\bar{P} = \exp[-0.3679(0.68918t + 1)]$. In 10 h this probability will be only 5.48%. However, for an exceptionally highly qualified individual, like Captain Sullenberger, whose estimated HCF level is as high as $\frac{F}{F_0} = 3.14$ [12], the probability of the navigator's non-failure is considerably higher: $\bar{P} = \exp\left[-(0.68918t + 1)\exp(-9.8596)\right] = 0.9996$. For an individual with the HCF of, say, $\frac{F}{F_0} = 2.0$ this probability is significantly, by 13.5%, lower: $\bar{P} = \exp\left[-(0.68918t + 1)\exp(-4.0)\right] = 0.8654$. These results indicate particularly the importance of the HCF in the addressed HITL problem.

The probabilistic **segmentation model** [11, 15] was used to quantify a HSI related situation, when a vehicular mission of interest consists of a number of consecutive segments/phases characterized by different probabilities of occurrence of a particular harsh environment or and/by other extraordinary conditions during the particular segment of the mission, and/or by different durations of these segments/phases; and/or by different failure rates, of the equipment and instrumentation and/or the navigator(s). According to the probabilistic segmentation model, the probability of the mission non-failure can be calculated as the sum of the products of the likelihood q_i of the occurrence of a harsh environment of the given severity at each segment of the route, the probability $P_i^e(t_i)$ of non-failure of the equipment and the probability $P_i^h(t_i)$ of non-failure of the navigator(s). The probability of the mission failure can be determined as $Q = \sum_{i=1}^{n} q_i Q_i(t_i) = 1 - \sum_{i=1}^{n} q_i P_i^e(t_i) P_i^h(t_i)$. If at a certain segment of the fulfilment of the mission of interest the human performance is not critical, then the corresponding probability $P_i^h(t_i)$ of human non-failure should be put equal to one. On the other hand, if there is confidence that the equipment (instrumentation) failure is not critical, or if there is a reason to believe that the probability of the equipment non-failure is considerably higher than the probability of the human non-failure, then it is the probability $P_i^e(t_i)$ that should be put equal to one. Finally, if one is confident that a certain level of the harsh environment will be encountered during the fulfilment of the mission at the $i-$th segment of the route, then the corresponding probability q_i of encountering such an environment should be put equal to one. Let, for instance, the duration of a particular vehicular mission is 24 h, and the vehicle spends equal times at each of the six segments (so that $t_i = 4$ hours at the end of each segment), the failure rates of the equipment and the human performance are independent of the environmental conditions and are $\lambda = 8 x 10^{-4}$ 1/h, the shape parameter in the Weibull distribution in both cases is $\beta = 2$ (Rayleigh distribution), the HCF ratio is $\frac{F^2}{F_0^2} = 8 \left(\frac{F}{F_0} = 2.828\right)$, the probability of human non-failure at ordinary flight conditions is $P_0 = 0.9900$, and the MWL G_i/G_0 ratios are given vs. the probability q_i of occurrence of the environmental conditions in Table 3.

Table 3. Calculated probabilities of mission failure

i	1	2	3	4	5	6
q_i, %	95.30	3.99	0.50	0.10	0.06	0.05
G_i/G_0	1	1.414	1.732	2.000	2.236	2.4495
$\bar{P}_i$	1	0.9991	0.9982	0.9978	0.9964	0.9955
P_i^h	0.9900	0.9891	0.9882	0.9878	0.9864	0.9855
$P_i^e P_i^h$	0.9900	0.9891	0.9882	0.9878	0.9864	0.9856
$q_i P_i^e P_i^h$	0.9435	0.0395	0.0049	0.0010	0.0006	0.0005

The computations of the probabilities of interest yield:

$$P_i^e = \exp\left[-(\lambda t_i)^2\right] = \exp\left[-\left(8 \times 10^{-4} \times 4\right)^2\right] = 0.99999,$$

$$P_i^h = P_0 \bar{P}_i \exp\left[(\lambda t_i)^2\right] = 0.9900 \times 0.99999 \bar{P}_i = 0.99 \bar{P}_i$$

The probability of the mission's non-failure is $\sum_{i=1}^{n} q_i P_i^e(t_i) P_i^h(t_i) = 0.9900$, so that the probability of mission failure is $Q = 1 - \sum_{i=1}^{n} q_i P_i^e(t_i) P_i^h(t_i) = 1 - 0.990 = 0.01 = 1\%$.

3 Conclusion

A successful/safe outcome of an HSI related effort cannot be assured, nor even improved, if this outcome is not quantified. Since nobody and nothing is perfect, and the probability of failure is never zero, such a quantification should be done on the probabilistic basis, and the established never-zero probability of failure should be made adequate for a particular system, individual(s) and application. Analytical ("mathematical") predictive modelling should always be considered, in addition to computer simulations, in every critical HSI effort. These two types of models are based, as a rule, on different assumptions and use different calculation techniques, and if the predictions based on these models are in agreement, then there is a good reason to believe that the obtained data are both accurate and trustworthy.

References

1. Suhir, E.: Applied Probability for Engineers and Scientists. McGraw-Hill, New York (1997)

2. Suhir, E.: Mental workload (MWL) vs. human capacity factor (HCF): a way to quantify human performance. In: Bedny, Gregory, Inna (eds.), Applied and Systemic-Structural Activity Theory, CRC Press (2019)
3. Suhir, E.: Adequate trust, human-capacity-factor, probability-distribution-function of human non-failure and its entropy. Int. J. Human Factors Modelling and Simulation (IJHFMS) **7**(1) (2019)
4. Tversky, A., Kahneman, D.: Judgement under uncertainty: heuristics and biases. Science **185**(4157), 1124–1131 (1974)
5. Suhir, E.: Helicopter-landing-ship: undercarriage strength and the role of the human factor. ASME Offshore Mech. Arctic Eng. (OMAE) J. **132**(1) (2009)
6. Suhir, E.: Probabilistic design for reliability. Chip Scale Rev. **14**(6) (2010)
7. Salotti, J.-M., Suhir, E.: Manned missions to Mars: minimizing risks of failure. Acta Astronautica **93**, 148–161 (2014)
8. Suhir, E.: Analytical modelling occupies a special place in the modelling effort, short communication, J. Phys. Math. **7**(1) (2016)
9. Suhir E., Mogford, R.H.: Two men in a cockpit: probabilistic assessment of the likelihood of a casualty if one of the two navigators becomes incapacitated. J. Aircraft 48(4) (2011)
10. Suhir, E.: Likelihood of vehicular mission-success-and-safety. J. Aircraft **49**(1) (2012)
11. Suhir, E.: Human-in-the-Loop: Probabilistic Modeling of an Aerospace Mission Outcome. CRC Press (2018)
12. Suhir, E.: Miracle-on-the-Hudson: quantified aftermath. Int. J. of Human Factors Modeling and Simulation (IJHFMS), **4**(1) (2013)
13. Suhir, E., Lini, S., Bey, C., Salotti, J.-M., Hourlier, S., Claverie, B.: Probabilistic modelling of the concept of anticipation in aviation. Theor. Issues Ergon. Sci. (TIES) **16**(1), 69–85 (2015)
14. Suhir, E.: Human-in-the-loop: probabilistic predictive modelling, its role, attributes, challenges and applications. Theor. Issues Ergon. Sci. (TIES) **16**(2), 99–123 (2014)
15. Suhir, E.: Human-in-the-loop (HITL): probabilistic predictive modeling (PPM) of an aerospace mission/situation outcome. Aerospace **1**(3), 101–136 (2014)
16. Suhir, E.: Human-in-the-Loop: could predictive modelling improve human performance?. J. Phys. Math. **7**(1) (2015)
17. Suhir, E.: Human-in-the-loop: application of the double exponential probability distribution function enables one to quantify the role of the human factor. Int. J. Human Factor Modelling Simulation (IJHFMS) **5**(4) (2017)
18. Suhir, E.: Editorial, quantifying human factors: towards analytical human-in-the loop. Special Issue Int. J. Human Factors Modelling Simul. (IJHFMS) **6**(2/3) (2018)
19. Suhir, E.: Short note - assessment of the required human capacity factor using flight simulator as an appropriate accelerated test vehicle. Int. J. Human Factors Modelling Simul. (IJHFMS) **7**(1), 71–74 (2019)
20. Suhir, E.: Short note - adequate trust, human-capacity-factor, probability-distribution-function of human non-failure and its entropy. Int. J. Human Factors Modelling Simul. (IJHFMS) **7**(1), 75–83 (2019)
21. Suhir, E.: Failure-oriented-accelerated-testing and its possible application in ergonomics. Ergon. Int. J. **3**(2), 1–3 (2019). https://doi.org/10.23880/eoij-16000199
22. Suhir, E.: Head-on railway obstruction: a probabilistic model. Theoretical Issues in Ergonomics Science (TIES), (2020). https://doi.org/10.1080/1463922X.2020.1818867
23. Suhir, E., Scataglini S., Paul, G.: Extraordinary automated driving situations: probabilistic analytical modeling of human-systems-integration (HSI) and the role of trust. In: Cassenti D., Scataglini S., Rajulu S., Wright J. (eds.), Advances in Simulation and Digital Human Modelling, Proceedings of the AHFE 2020 Virtual Conferences on Human Factor and Simulation, and Digital Human Modelling and Applied Optimization, July 16–20, 2020, San-Diego, USA, Advances in Intelligent Systems and Computing, vol. 1206, Springer Nature (2020)

24. Suhir, E., Paul, G., Kaindl, H.: Towards probabilistic analysis of human-system integration in automated driving. In: Ahram, T., Karwowski, W., Vergnano, A., Leali, F., Taiar, R. (eds.), Advances in Intelligent Systems and Computing, Vol. 1131. Proc. of the 3rd Int. Conf. on Intelligent Human Systems Integration (IHSI 2020): Integrating People and Intelligent Systems, February 19–21, Modena, Italy. Springer Nature (2020)
25. Suhir E., Paul, G.: Avoiding collision in automated driving situation. Theoretical Issues in Ergonomics Science (TIES), (2020). https://doi.org/10.1080/1463922X.2020.1729895
26. Suhir, E.: Quantifying unquantifiable: the outcome of a clinical case must be quantified to make it successful. Global J. Med. Clin. Case Rep. 123–129 (2020). https://doi.org/10.17352/2455-5282.000115
27. Suhir, E.: Risk-analysis in aerospace human-factor-related tasks: review and extension. J. Aerosp. Eng. Mech. (JAEM) **4**(2) (2020)
28. Suhir, E.: Astronaut's performance vs. his/hers human-capacity-factor and state-of-health: application of double-exponential-probability-distribution function. Acta Astronautica **178**, 250–256 (2021)

Assessment of Biomechanical Risk Factors During Lifting Tasks in a Spacesuit Using Singular Value Decomposition

Linh Q. Vu[1]([✉]), Han K. Kim[2], and Sudhakar L. Rajulu[3]

[1] MEI Technologies, Houston, TX, USA
linh.q.vu@nasa.gov
[2] Leidos Inc., Houston, TX, USA
[3] NASA Johnson Space Center, Houston, TX, USA

Abstract. Spacesuits demonstrate unique motion patterns due to their mechanical design. These motion patterns may contribute to increased musculoskeletal stresses and injury risks for the astronaut and therefore it is important to understand how suited motion patterns correlate with injury risk. This study analyzed motions from manual material handling lifting tasks performed in the Mark-III spacesuit. The motion capture data were projected onto a reposable suit model for kinematic derivation of joint angles. Singular value decomposition (SVD) was performed on the time series of the joint angles, which identified the primitive motion patterns ("eigenpostures") across each task and their weightings as a function of time. The total joint displacement, low back moments, and postural stability were calculated as biomechanical risk metrics for each eigenposture. The eigenposture weightings were compared across tasks. Each eigenposture was associated with a different level of biomechanical stresses and some tasks, such as object pickup from the floor, had a higher composition of "risky" eigenpostures. The results of this work can be used to improve task and suit design to minimize risky movement patterns for injury mitigation.

Keywords: Ergonomics · Motion analysis · Manual material handling · NASA

1   Introduction

Future lunar surface missions will require astronauts to perform manual materials handling (e.g. lifting, pulling, dragging) and other tasks requiring forceful exertions (e.g. geological sampling) while wearing a pressurized planetary spacesuit. Since spacesuits have shown reduced range of motion and strength capabilities [1], there is an increased risk for musculoskeletal injuries. Furthermore, motion restrictions imposed by the spacesuit (e.g. suit pressurization and mechanical joints) result in unique movement patterns during extravehicular activity (EVA). Thus, EVA motions and the associated biomechanical stresses from wearing a spacesuit should be examined to define ergonomic guidelines and ensure safe spacesuit and mission design.

© The Author(s), under exclusive license to Springer Nature Switzerland AG 2022
N. L. Black et al. (Eds.): IEA 2021, LNNS 223, pp. 429–433, 2022.
https://doi.org/10.1007/978-3-030-74614-8_54

Traditionally, motions have been analyzed using individual joint angles. However, an alternative technique was considered to provide new insights and a different perspective into motion patterns previously unavailable. With this technique, a complex motion was decomposed into a weighted sum of primitive motions through a singular value decomposition (SVD) technique. Different studies have used SVD to decompose gait patterns into basic movements and evaluate subtle differences across different test conditions [2]. In this study, the unique motion patterns in suited lifting tasks were quantified using SVD. Each motion primitive was then quantified for the corresponding musculoskeletal loading and injury risks, which help in assessing the biomechanical risk factors for the astronauts performing EVA tasks.

2   Methods

Several different lifting motions were identified from a past IRB-approved study for a male subject performing simulated EVA tasks while wearing a Mark III Space Suit Technology Demonstrator (MK-III spacesuit). The subject had over three years of pressurized suited experience. Lifting tasks were varied, ranging from a $12 \times 12 \times 10$-inch crate pickup to one handed cross-body object transfer (Fig. 1). All lifted loads were under 5 lbs. The suit motions were recorded using a motion capture system (Vicon Motion Systems LTD UK), where markers were placed on the suit components and limbs (medial and lateral positions at the elbow, wrist, knee, ankle joints).

In order to extract the suit joint angles, the CAD models of individual suit components were incorporated into a 3D modeling environment. Mechanical configurations and motions of the spacesuit were represented in a Denavit-Hartenberg kinematic convention [3]. Virtual markers were placed onto the 3D suit component models that correspond with the physical placement of the retroreflective markers placed on the suit during the lifting task. The markers were linked to the suit components and inherited the 3D orientation of each suit component. For each frame of motion capture data, an iterative closest point (ICP) algorithm was performed to align the virtual markers to the physical markers. After the initial alignment from ICP, an optimization was performed to manipulate the suit joint angles to align the virtual markers on the limbs to the physical marker positions. A bound-constrained optimization was performed to minimize the distance between the two sets of markers. Mechanical joint range of motion limits were used as boundary conditions.

For each task, all joint angles were normalized to the corresponding angles at 100% task completion. The time series of joint angles across the different tasks were concatenated into one matrix. The SVD method was used to extract features from the joint angle time series, where the singular vectors were defined as eigenpostures (EP). Thus, progression of suited motion in each task was explained by a linear weighted combination of EPs, each of which the eigenvalue represents the relative contribution toward the overall motion. In this study, the three largest 3 EPs were considered, which combined to explain 59% of the total variance. All other EPs with smaller eigenvalues were not considered as they described only minor variations between arm and hand motions. The EP weightings were compared across all lifting task types.

Several metrics were also defined and measured to assess associated biomechanical loading for each EP, namely the total joint displacement, moments at the low back joint (about the flex ring pivot point), and total center of gravity (projected onto the ground) excursion. The moment and center of gravity were calculated using the suit joint kinematics and the documented component-wise weight distributions. For simplicity, human body segment masses were not incorporated into this calculation. These metrics were selected as they are assumed to be meaningfully associated with the musculoskeletal demands during lifting, thus enabling a structured analysis of EVA kinematics. These metrics were compared across different EPs and task types.

3 Results

The resulting EPs from the SVD analysis are illustrated in Fig. 1. Suited movements were stereotypical due to the idiosyncratic joint bearing rotations needed for movement actuation. The first eigenposture (EP1) was associated with hip and knee lifting motions and the second eigenposture (EP2) was more representative of arm motions. EP3 represented an isolated waist flexion/extension motion. The compositions of EPs were found to be different across the task types (Table 1). When compared across different task types, the relative weight of EP1 was largest with the object pickup from the floor task, while being the smallest with the cross-body pickup.

Each EP was associated with different levels of biomechanical demand metrics. For example, EP1 was associated with the largest joint angular displacement, low back moment, and center of gravity excursion (Table 1), compared to EP2 and EP3. Thus, EP1 was assumed to impose a larger biomechanical stress than other EPs. Conversely, EP2 which represents arm motions, had the lowest biomechanical stress.

Table 1. Cumulative weighting across tasks (top) and biomechanical stresses (bottom) for EP

Task Name	EP1	EP2	EP3
Static standing trial (baseline)	6	3	2
Crate pickup	600	116	54
Object pickup from floor	676	7	50
Cross-body pickup object from floor	396	42	139
Lateral-body object pickup	471	19	15
Total joint angular displacement (degrees)	701	321	345
Maximum low back moment (Nm)	641	361	480
Total center of gravity excursion(cm)	24.5	5.3	8.4

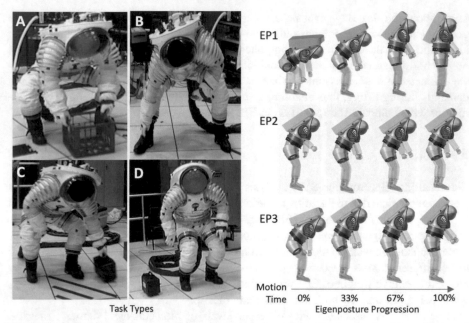

Task Types   Eigenposture Progression

Fig. 1. Left: Task Types A: crate pickup, B: pickup from floor, C: cross body pickup, D: lateral pickup. Right: Eigenposture progression with normalized motion time.

4   Discussion

In this study, EVA motions were decomposed into a weighted sum of primitive motions (i.e. EPs). Each observed EP was associated with different levels of biomechanical stress. The EVA tasks containing a higher proportion of EP with high biomechanical stress can be labeled as more risk-prone compared to the other tasks. For example, lifting an object from the floor had a higher composition of EP1, which had the greatest joint displacement and low back moment. Thus, these tasks may need interventions to mitigate biomechanical risk factors. In this case, if the object location were to be raised by redesigning the task or hardware, EP1 and EP3 scores can decrease. As mechanical moment about the waist ring was used to define the low back moment, muscular and spinal strain was not considered in this analysis. Adding load and body properties would enable stronger conclusions on low back muscular strain.

The results from this study and the developed methodology can be used to train astronauts to avoid specific risky movements. The risky suit postures may need to be monitored for the frequency and magnitudes during EVA. If a task can be achieved with different combinations of EPs, movement strategies can be investigated to identify alternative EP combinations which would minimize biomechanical risks. Such alternative movement strategies can be used as a reference for astronaut training. Suit engineers can also improve geometric and mechanical configurations of a spacesuit to reduce the risk-prone EP and improve overall movement patterns. EVA task designers can then incorporate these recommendations into the EVA concept of operations.

References

1. Carr, C.E., Newman, D.J.: Space suit bioenergetics: framework and analysis of unsuited and suited activity. Aviat. Space Environ. Med. **78**(11), 1013–1022 (2007)
2. Troje, N.F.: Decomposing biological motion: a framework for analysis and synthesis of human gait patterns. J. Vision **2**(5), 2 (2002)
3. Denavit, J., Hartenberg, R.S.: A kinematic notation for lower-pair mechanisms based on matrices. Trans. ASME J. Appl. Mech. **23**, 215–221 (1955)

A Preliminary Study on the Effects of Foam and Seat Pan Inclination on the Deformation of the Seated Buttocks Using MRI

Xuguang Wang$^{(\boxtimes)}$ ⓘ, Léo Savonnet ⓘ, and Sonia Duprey

Univ Lyon, Univ Gustave Eiffel, LBMC UMR_T9406, 69622 Lyon, France
xuguang.wang@univ-eiffel.fr

Abstract. The objective is to investigate the effects of foam and seat pan inclination on soft tissues deformation in the gluteal region using an open MRI. Four healthy male subjects, aged from 28 to 52 years old and BMI from 20 to 28 kg/m^2 participated in the experiment. A positional MRI scanner (Paramed® 0.5 T) was used. Each participant tested three seating configurations defined by varying the seat pan angle (A_SP) and cushion material while the back was fixed at 22° from the vertical: 1) A_SP = 7° without foam (Reference), 2) A_SP = 0° without foam (Shear), 3) A_SP = 7° with a 50 mm thick foam on the seat pan (Foam). In addition, one configuration (Unloaded) with the trunk-thigh angle about 105° and the buttock unloaded, was also scanned for comparison. After segmentation and 3D reconstruction, volumes of bone, gluteal muscle, fat, and other tissues in three regions of interest (ROIs) under the ITs were calculated. The largest tissue deformation was observed for Shear, while the smallest was found for Foam. Though these findings were expected, to our knowledge, this is the first time that the effect of shear force on tissue deformation was quantified directly, providing quantitative data needed for validating buttock-thigh finite element models. The findings of the present study also confirm that the tissue beneath their ITs was predominantly composed of fat and connective tissue and the gluteal muscles slid away from the IT.

Keywords: Seating comfort · Soft tissue · Deformation · Biomechanics · Human modeling

1 Introduction

Sitting for a long period is common in modern societies, either for leisure or occupational activities or due to mobility impairments. However, long-term sitting may lead to discomfort [1, 2], and even to pressure sores for people confined to a wheelchair [3]. Among biomechanical factors affecting seating discomfort, we can mention high peak pressure [1] and high shear force on the seat [4], which may lead to large deformation of soft tissues and reduction of blood flow. A full understanding of the soft tissues deformation particularly in the gluteal region in a seated position would be helpful for reducing discomfort and injury risk of seated people [5]. Thanks to recent development in medical

© The Author(s), under exclusive license to Springer Nature Switzerland AG 2022
N. L. Black et al. (Eds.): IEA 2021, LNNS 223, pp. 434–438, 2022.
https://doi.org/10.1007/978-3-030-74614-8_55

imaging, direct observation of soft-tissue strain under a realistic sitting loading condition is now possible using an open MRI. Recent MRI investigations by Sonnenblum et al. (2018) and Brienza et al. (2018) [6, 7] mainly focused on the effects of wheelchair cushion type on tissue deformation. To our knowledge, few researchers have investigated the effects of shear force and cushion type and their possible interaction on tissue deformation. The main objective is to investigate their effects on soft tissues deformation in the gluteal region using an open MRI.

2   Materials and Methods

2.1   Participants

Four healthy male subjects were recruited and their characteristics are summarized in Table 1. Université Gustave Eiffel (formerly French Institute of Science and Technology for Transport, Development and Networks – IFSTTAR) ethics committee approved the experimental protocol. Informed consent was obtained prior to experiment for all participants.

Table 1. Participant characteristics

Participant	1	2	3	4
Age (yrs)	28	52	35	31
Stature (cm)	173	163	169	187
BMI (kg/m^2)	20.3	25.9	27.6	23.6

2.2   Experimental Conditions

Participants were scanned in three seated and one unloaded positions in an upright MRI scanner (Paramed® 0.5 T (Fig. 1). The resolution of the scans was set to 3.1 mm slice thickness, and 3.1 mm slice gap. The field of view was adjusted to be $300 \times 300 \times 300$ mm in sagittal, coronal and transversal planes respectively. We used two wooden plates as for seat pan and backrest. Three seating conditions were defined by varying the seat pan angle (A_SP) and cushion material while the back was fixed at 22 degrees from the vertical: 1) A_SP $= 7°$ without foam (Reference), 2) A_SP $= 0°$ without foam (Shear), 3) A_SP $= 7°$ with a 50 mm thick foam on the seat pan (Foam). Compared to Reference, Shear had a shear force on the seat pan surface about 5% of body weight higher on average observed in our previous study [8], while Foam had a more uniform pressure distribution with a much lower peak pressure under the ischial tuberosities (ITs). For the unloaded position, we built a specific device so that participants could support their body by the arms, back, knees and feet while keeping the buttock and thighs unloaded. The backrest was reclined 50° from the vertical to support most of body weight. We controlled the back-thigh angle by a goniometer to be 105°, close to the reference seating position. The unloaded condition was tested the first, then followed the conditions Reference, Foam and Shear. Because of the limited field of view, two scans were needed to cover the buttocks and most part of the thighs. Each acquisition took about 8 min during which participants had to keep immobile.

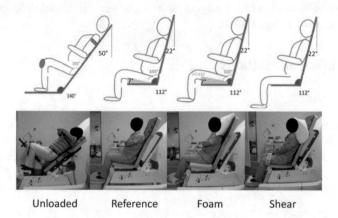

Fig. 1. Illustration of the four positions in the upright MRI scanner environment.

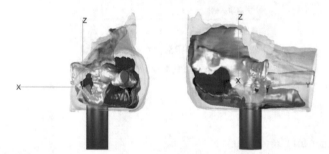

Fig. 2. Region of interest (ROI) characterized by a cylinder, illustrated for a Reference sitting condition. Three cylinders of 100 mm in length and 50, 20 and 10 mm in diameter were used. Their axis was perpendicular to the seat pan surface and centered at the ischium point which had the shortest distance to the seat. They were positioned so that the external circle of the upper surface was in contact with the ischium.

2.3   Data Processing

Raw DICOM data were imported into the open source software 3D Slicer (www.slicer.org) for segmenting the pelvis, femur, gluteus maximus and subcutaneous fat. Once segmented, 3D objects in two scans were merged and re-meshed using Meshlab. We defined three regions of interest (ROI) by three cylinders of 50, 20 and 10 mm in diameter. They were perpendicular to the seat pan surface and centered at the ischium point which had the shortest distance to the seat (Fig. 2). For the unloaded condition, which had no seat pan, the same ROIs as Reference were used by aligning the two pelvises. Volumes and average thicknesses of bone, gluteal muscle, fat, and other tissues inside the ROIs were calculated using a custom Matlab (R2020b) tool.

3 Results

For the three seating conditions Reference, Foam and Shear in case of ROI of 50 mm, tissue thicknesses reduced to 17.3, 19 and 15.9 mm on average respectively, representing a deformation of 65.5, 62.4 and 68.1% with respect to the unloaded condition (Table 2). The same trends were found for two other ROIs.

Table 2. Average thickness in mm of the soft tissues under the ischial tuberosity for the three cylindrical ROI of 50, 20 and 10 mm for the four conditions

Part.	Unloaded			Reference			Foam			Shear		
	50	20	10	50	20	10	50	20	10	50	20	10
1	49.3	43.8	42.9	13.9	11.3	9.3	15.8	11.3	10.5	14.8	7.7	6.8
2	61.2	59.8	59.2	15.6	12.8	12.1	18.6	15.6	15.7	15.2	12.1	11.1
3	48.0	44.5	43.8	19.6	12.8	11.9	20.5	16.6	17.0	15.8	10.7	9.9
4	46.5	39.2	38.0	20.3	12.6	11.6	21.0	15.6	14.8	18.5	11.2	10.6
M	51.2	46.8	46.0	17.3	12.4	11.2	19.0	14.8	14.5	16.1	10.4	9.6
SD	6.7	9.0	9.2	3.1	0.7	1.3	2.4	2.4	2.8	1.7	1.9	1.9

Table 3. % of gluteus maximus within the three cylindrical ROI of 50, 20 and 10 mm for the four conditions

Part.	Unloaded			Reference			Foam			Shear		
	50	20	10	50	20	10	50	20	10	50	20	10
1	55.1	71.0	72.8	10.2	0.0	0.0	2.1	0.0	0.0	5.3	0.0	0.0
2	13.4	4.3	0.2	0.0	0.0	0.0	0.0	0.0	0.0	0.1	0.0	0.0
3	8.4	0.0	0.0	0.0	0.0	0.0	4.9	0.0	0.0	3.3	0.0	0.0
4	27.1	33.6	37.2	0.0	0.0	0.0	5.7	0.0	0.0	0.6	0.0	0.0
M	26.0	27.2	27.5	2.6	0.0	0.0	3.2	0.0	0.0	2.3	0.0	0.0
SD	20.9	32.8	34.9	5.1	0.0	0.0	2.6	0.0	0.0	2.4	0.0	0.0

Regarding different composition of soft tissues in ROI, there were almost no gluteal muscles in the ROIs of 10 mm and 20 mm, while it was present in the ROI of 50 mm (Table 3), suggesting that the muscles slided away. Thus, only the fat tissues wrapped around the IT when seated.

There were large differences in soft tissue thickness and composition between the participants when looking at the unloaded condition. For the ROI of 50 mm, tissue thicknesses were 49.3, 61.2, 48.0, 46.5 mm and the percentages of gluteus maximus were 55.1, 13.4, 8.4, and 27.1% for the four participants.

4 Discussion and Conclusions

The largest tissue deformation was observed for Shear, while the smallest was found for Foam for all participants. Though these findings were expected, to our knowledge, this is the first time that the effect of shear force on tissue deformation was quantified directly, providing quantitative data needed for validating buttock-thigh finite element models [9]. The findings of the present study also confirm that the tissue beneath their ITs was predominantly composed of fat and connective tissue, suggesting that the gluteal muscles slide away from the IT area when seated. Muscle sliding in a sitting position has to be considered when performing simulation using FE models as already suggested by Sonenblum et al. (2018) [6].

References

1. De Looze, M.P., Kuijt-Evers, L.F.M., Van DieëN, J.: Sitting comfort and discomfort and the relationships with objective measures. Ergonomics **46**, 985–997 (2003)
2. Hiemstra-van Mastrigt, S., Groenesteijn, L., Vink, P., Kuijt-Evers, L.F.M.: Predicting passenger seat comfort and discomfort on the basis of human, context and seat characteristics: a literature review. Ergonomics **60**, 889–911 (2017)
3. Olesen, C.G., de Zee, M., Rasmussen, J.: Missing links in pressure ulcer research—an interdisciplinary overview. J. Appl. Physiol. **108**, 1458–1464 (2010)
4. Goossens, R.H., Zegers, R., Hoek van Dijke, G.A., Snijders, C.J.: Influence of shear on skin oxygen tension. Clin Physiol. Jan **14**(1), 111–118 (1994)
5. Al-Dirini, R., Nisyrios, J., Reed, M., Thewlis, D.: Quantifying the in vivo quasi-static response to loading of sub-dermal tissues in the human buttock using magnetic resonance imaging. Clin. Biomech. **50**, 70–77 (2017). https://doi.org/10.1016/j.clinbiomech.2017.09.017
6. Sonenblum, S.E., Ma, J., Sprigle, S.H., Hetzel, T.R., Cathcart, J.M.: Measuring the impact of cushion design on buttocks tissue deformation: an MRI approach. J. Tissue Viability **27**, 162–72 (2018). https://doi.org/10.1016/j.jtv.2018.04.001
7. Brienza, D., Vallely, J., Karg, P., Akins, J., Gefen, A.: An MRI investigation of the effects of user anatomy and wheelchair cushion type on tissue deformation. J. Tissue Viability **27**, 42–53 (2018). https://doi.org/10.1016/j.jtv.2017.04.001
8. Wang, X., Cardoso, M., Theodorakos, I., Beurier, G.: Seat/occupant contact forces and their relationship with perceived discomfort for economy class airplane seats. Ergonomics (2019). https://doi.org/10.1080/00140139.2019.1600050
9. Savonnet, L., Wang, X., Duprey, S.: Finite element models of the thigh-buttock complex for assessing static sitting discomfort and pressure sore risk: a literature review. Comput. Methods Biomech. Biomed. Eng. **21**(4), 379–388 (2018). https://doi.org/10.1080/10255842.2018.1466117

Tool Development for Ergonomic Design of Automated Vehicles

Hans-Joachim Wirsching[1]([✉]) and Martin Fleischer[2] [iD]

[1] Human Solutions GmbH, Europaallee 10, 67657 Kaiserslautern, Germany
hans-joachim.wirsching@human-solutions.com
[2] Chair of Ergonomics, Technical University of Munich, Munich, Germany
martin.fleischer@tum.de

Abstract. The ergonomic design of future automated vehicles will require new posture prediction features in digital human models to consider the large variety of non-driving related activities. This paper describes the experimental, modeling and implementation work to achieve new posture models for that kind of activities. In the experiment subject poses are measured while adopting a set of predefined sitting postures in a mock-up. These postures result from a pre-study which determined the most frequently observed postures for non-driving related activities. These poses are transferred to a digital human model and build the pool from which primary posture models are derived. Several methods are developed to create new secondary posture models out of them by joining upper and lower sub postures of significantly frequent posture combinations according to that pre-study. These methods and non-driving related posture models are implemented into a digital human model extending the standard posture prediction process. For simulating a desired activity in an automated vehicle design, a user can select the corresponding posture model taking into account the specific frequency rates.

Keywords: Digital human modelling · Automated driving · Ergonomic simulation

1 Introduction

With an increasing level of automation in future vehicles new concepts for interiors have to be developed due to the changing role of the driver. The number of non-driving related tasks will significantly increase which requires new concepts for the human-machine-interaction.

Current digital ergonomic design and validation tools have been established and applied for conventional vehicle concepts for decades [1]. But they hardly can be used to develop future automated driving concepts, since the corresponding occupant behavior cannot be properly simulated [2].

The goal of the presented study is the development of knowledge-based tools to simulate the occupant behavior in interiors of automated vehicles (SAE level 3 & 4) [3] by a 3D digital human model. The work splits up into the acquisition of appropriate

N. L. Black et al. (Eds.): IEA 2021, LNNS 223, pp. 439–446, 2022.
https://doi.org/10.1007/978-3-030-74614-8_56

posture data for non-driving related activities and the integration of the related methods and posture models into a digital human model.

The principal procedure is based on a former procedure of developing a simulation tool for the predict of manual driving postures consisting of experimental data collection and posture modelling [4]. The main difference is the large variety of potential non-driving related activities compared to the single well-defined conventional manual driving activity.

Hence the study focuses on the measurement of a reduced set of primary posture configurations which summarize the most frequently observed postures in important non-driving related tasks. Finally, several methods are developed to exploit these primary postures and generate new secondary postures for simulating a wide range of frequent non-driving related activities.

2 Methodology

2.1 Participant Study

From the findings of [5] eight postures were derived. These postures were chosen with regard to their occurrence probability. Figure 1 shows these postures which represent the combinations of lower and upper body postures deemed most significant.

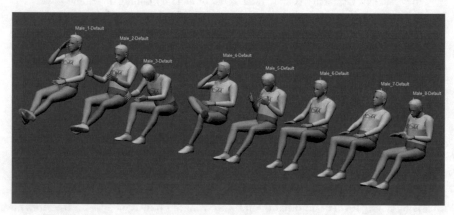

Fig. 1. Primary posture configurations 1 through 8 selected for the data pool

50 participants (average body height 175.3 cm, SD ± 8.8 cm) were recorded performing these postures using the Simi motion capturing system [6] portrayed in Fig. 2. Each posture was recorded three times in three different seat height configurations with H30 being 200 mm, 350 mm and 500 mm. This leads to nine recordings per posture and participant. With 50 participants, 8 postures, three H30s and three runs a total of 3600 recordings were gathered as a data pool for the posture modelling.

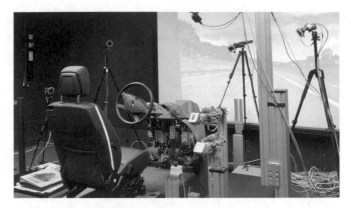

Fig. 2. Experiment setup

2.2 Data Transfer

The static motion capture recordings were processed to generate corresponding skeleton animations. These animations were transferred to the digital human model RAMSIS using the well-known bvh animation format (Fig. 3).

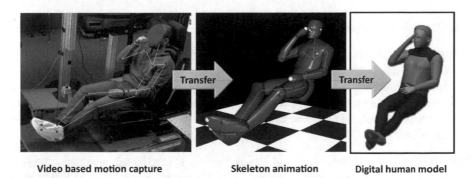

Video based motion capture   Skeleton animation   Digital human model

Fig. 3. Posture measure data transfer process

Since the skeleton structures of the Simi motion capture system and RAMSIS are not identical, a specific transfer method was implemented to match joint information (position and orientation) between the models and to fit the RAMSIS skeleton to the motion capture skeleton by an inverse kinematics solver.

2.3 Modeling

Following the approach in [4], for each posture and H30 configuration the corresponding 150 posture trials were statistically analyzed. In particular the frequency distribution was derived for each degree of freedom (DOF) in the kinematical human model.

These distributions were individually approximated by polynomial functions which have their maximum value of 1 at the DOF average and run to zero at the anatomical DOF limits (Fig. 4).

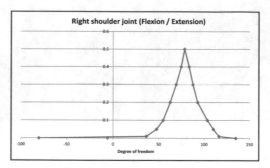

Fig. 4. Approximation of frequency distribution of right shoulder flexion/extension

All frequency distribution functions build the activity-specific posture model for the corresponding posture and H30 configuration. These 24 primary posture models are ready to be used in an optimization for calculating realistic task-specific postures.

2.4   Exploitation Methods

The generated 24 primary posture models build the basis to cover a wide range of non-driving related activities. Several methods were developed to automatically generate new secondary posture models taking into account important non-driving related activities, activity-depending torso angles and arbitrary H30 configurations. These methods and a corresponding graphical user interface were finally implemented into the digital human model system RAMSIS.

Non-driving Related Activities and Torso Angles. Using the sub posture occurrence frequency results in [5] the most important non-driving related activities (NDRA) were assigned to combinations of upper and lower body postures out of the measured primary posture configurations (Fig. 1). In addition, for each upper and lower sub posture a NDRA-specific occurrence frequency rate was calculated (Fig. 5), such that the total frequency of these composite posture models can be predicted.

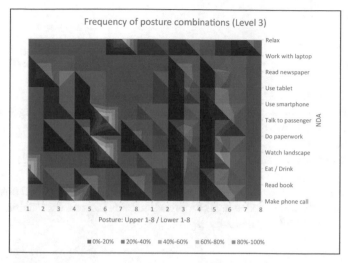

Fig. 5. Upper and lower sub posture frequency for non-driving related activities (level 3)

Furthermore, the preferred average torso angle was measured in a separate experiment and determined for each non-driving related activity [7].

Finally, a method was developed to split the primary posture models into their upper (torso and arms) and lower (legs) body part and to automatically recompose them to new secondary posture models while considering the NDRA specific torso angle (Fig. 6).

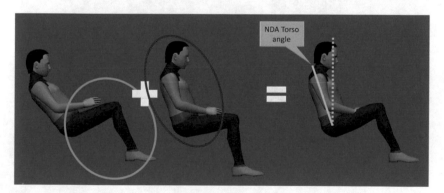

Fig. 6. Composing posture from upper and lower body and matching NDRA torso angle

First, the composed posture inherits all joint angles from the corresponding upper and lower body posture. Second, the torso is rotated to match the NDRA torso angle. Third, the hip joint angles are adjusted such that the thigh orientation fits to the given lower part and the chest rotation is adjusted such that it fits to the given upper body part.

H30 Configurations. A posture model for a given H30 value is generated by linear blending between posture models of neighbor measured H30 configurations.

3 Results

The graphical user interface developed for support an end-user defining a non-driving related posture model for a task analysis follows the subsequent process (Fig. 7):

1. The user selects the SAE level for automated driving (3 or 4).
2. Depending on the selected level, the user selects the non-driving activity (e.g. relaxing, using a smartphone).
3. In addition, the user defines the H30 value of the vehicle design.
4. For the selected level and activity, a list of the most frequent upper and lower postures and the corresponding frequency rates are displayed (see Fig. 5).
5. After the user selected the preferred upper and lower posture, the total posture model is automatically composed using the methods in Sect. 2.4, and the resulting combined occurrence probability rate is displayed.

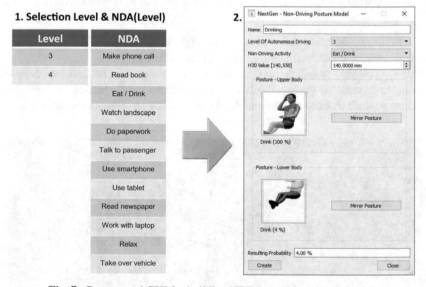

Fig. 7. Process and GUI for building NDRA specific posture models

This combined model can be used in a standard calculation process to predict a manikin posture subjected to user-defined restrictions (e.g. heels on floor, H-point on seating reference point) within an interior geometry of an automated vehicle (Fig. 8).

3D Environment

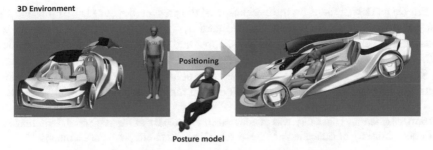

Positioning

Posture model

Fig. 8. Positioning manikins into an automated vehicle design

The resulting posture is the input for various ergonomic analyses such as reachability, visibility and space requirements.

4 Discussion

The presented method is suitable to provide flexible posture models for inverse kinematics based posture prediction and can be applied for future use cases. While this procedure was already validated for the manual driving use case, the validation for the variety of non-driving activities has not yet been completed.

The composition of postures is a possibility to generate additional probabilistic digital human models from recorded data. Considering the high effort required to generate data pools for such models, this provides a promising approach. Nevertheless, it still has to be proved that this methodology generates valid output. A major concern is the occurrence of unrealistically small angles between the torso and the legs. In the case presented these configurations do not occur as the probabilities of the upper and lower body postures generating such compositions are extremely low. For example, the leaned forward posture is only probable for NDRAs where a leg crossed posture is unlikely.

In addition, a challenge will be the comparison between real and simulated postures, because non-driving postures are less restricted by the interior (e.g. no contact to steering wheel and pedals). It might be necessary to divide the validation into smaller sub-validations to generate comparable data, e.g. validating the posture itself in relation to the H-Point and then validating the position of the H-Point in relation to the interior. This can compromise the validation and is thus to be discussed and tested in future work.

5 Conclusions

The presented approach applies a modelling method, which has been established in the ergonomic design of conventional manually controlled vehicles, to automated vehicles. The main difference is the larger posture variability. In order to handle this variability with limited resources, a method was introduced to compose postures from upper and lower sub postures. This gives end-users a maximum flexibility in simulating and assessing occupant behavior in automated vehicle concepts.

Future work will focus on the evaluation of the presented methods. Additionally, the posture simulation process has to be extended by the interaction of the occupant with movable geometrical objects (e.g. tablets, cups) and with own body parts (e.g. put hand on thigh) in order to cover important aspects of occupant behavior in automated vehicles.

Since nobody knows how occupants will definitely interact with future vehicle interiors, the presented approach should be open for new non-driving related tasks.

Acknowledgments. This study was conducted in the context of the project INSAA funded by the Federal Ministry of Education and Research of the Federal Republic of Germany.

References

1. Remlinger, W., Bengler, K.: RAMSIS kognitiv als Instrument zur Analyse und Auslegung von Sichtbedingungen. In: Bullinger-Hoffmann, A.C., Mühlstedt, J. (eds.) Homo Sapiens Digitalis - Virtuelle Ergonomie und digitale Menschmodelle, vol. 66, pp. 297–302. Springer, Heidelberg (2016)
2. Yang, Y., Fleischer, M., Bengler, K.: Chicken or egg problem? New challenges and proposals of digital human modeling and interior development of automated vehicles. In: Di Nicolantonio, M., Rossi, E., Alexander, T. (eds.) AHFE 2019. AISC, vol. 975, pp. 453–463. Springer, Cham (2020)
3. On-Road Automated Driving (ORAD) committee: Taxonomy and Definitions for Terms Related to Driving Automation Systems for On-Road Motor Vehicles. SAE International, 400 Commonwealth Drive, Warrendale, PA, United States (2018)
4. van der Meulen, P., Seidl, A.: Ramsis – the leading cad tool for ergonomic analysis of vehicles. In: Duffy, V.G. (ed.) ICDHM 2007. LNCS, vol. 4561, pp. 1008–1017. Springer, Heidelberg (2007)
5. Fleischer, M., Chen, S.: How do we sit when our car drives for us? In: Duffy, V.G. (ed.) HCII 2020. LNCS, vol. 12198, pp. 33–49. Springer, Cham (2020)
6. Simi markerless motion capture. http://www.simi.com/en/products/movement-analysis/markerless-motion-capture.html
7. Fleischer, M., Neth, S., Bengler, K.: Desirable backrest angles for non-driving related activities. In review for HCI International (2021)

Simplifying Ergonomic Assessment for Designers: A User-Product Interaction-Modelling Framework in CAD

Alexander Wolf[✉], Yvonne Wagner, Marius Oßwald, Jörg Miehling, and Sandro Wartzack

Friedrich-Alexander-Universität Erlangen-Nürnberg, Engineering Design, 91058 Erlangen, Germany
a.wolf@mfk.fau.de

Abstract. Digital human models have not yet reached their full potential for proactive virtual assessment of ergonomics in engineering and industrial design. Especially the modelling of interaction between user and product often is time demanding, cumbersome, unstandardized and embedded insufficiently in the computer-aided engineering environment. On the one hand, the interaction modelling needs to be applicable for a majority of products and shall contain as much a-priori knowledge regarding human behavior as possible. On the other hand, the method needs to be appropriate for designers, without special ergonomic expertise or human behavior training. In this contribution, we present an interaction-modelling framework based on the concept of affordances, which ought to resolve these partly contradictable demands. Hence, 31 elementary affordances, describing fundamental physical interaction possibilities between human end effectors and rudimental (product) geometries, were deduced using a classification method. The elementary affordances shall serve as a medium for interaction modeling. For this purpose, we introduce an interaction modelling routine, implemented in a CAD system, which makes use of the identified elementary affordances in terms of CAD-features. Those enable designers to apply interaction possibilities directly to a CAD-model in order to define the constraints for a DHM simulation.

Keywords: User product interaction · Digital human models · Affordance · CAD · Interaction modelling

1 Problem Statement

Digital human models (DHM) bear the potential for proactive virtual assessment of ergonomics in engineering and industrial design [1–3]. Usually simulated as a virtual mockup containing a virtual product model (e.g. CAD-model), a virtual environment and a human behavior model [4], DHM tools have not yet reached their full potential [5]. According to various publications, prevalent DHM tools are either cumbersome to use [6], unstandardized [7], time-demanding or not trustworthy [8]. Wolf et al. [4] deduced five requirements for interaction modelling approaches (utilizing DHM) to be suitable

© The Author(s), under exclusive license to Springer Nature Switzerland AG 2022
N. L. Black et al. (Eds.): IEA 2021, LNNS 223, pp. 447–452, 2022.
https://doi.org/10.1007/978-3-030-74614-8_57

for engineering design: According to their research, interaction modelling requires a (1) genuinely proactive/predictive and (2) a universally valid modelling approach as well as (3) a standardized, time-efficient and intuitive and (4) a comprehensible and straightforward modelling procedure. Additionally, the interaction modeling approach (5) should provide the opportunity of data consistent embedment in the computer-aided engineering environment. While the first two requirements deal with issues in human behavior-prediction the remaining requirements demand for a concept / framework, which enables designers to easily model the interaction between a chosen DHM and virtual product. The literature contains several examples of interaction modelling frameworks. Jung et al. [9] present a *Human-Product Constraint Management Function* to model interactions in CAD for vehicle interior design. Mardberg et al. [10] utilize a formal high-level language, composed of an *instruction grammar* and *extended finite automaton*. Bauer et al. [11] present a *task-based* method, where *tasks* represent definite human activities in terms of a movement satisfying kinematical constraints. Unfortunately, none of the frameworks prevalent in literature allows a universal application for DHM-Tools in engineering and industrial design. While the approaches of Bauer et al. [11] and Mardberg et al. [10] support the modelling of occupational processes, the approach of Jung et al. [9] is limited to a specific use case (vehicle interior design).

2 Research Objective

Our overall research aim is to develop a proactive virtual ergonomics tool for engineering design, consisting of a user-product interaction-modelling framework in CAD (frontend) which serves as an intuitive interface for a predictive DHM simulation tool (backend). In this contribution, we want to present the framework (method) for interaction modelling and its implementation. The identification and development of this method required the consideration of several demands derived from the above listed requirements. On the one hand, the method needs to be universally applicable (for a majority of products) and shall contain as much a-priori knowledge regarding human behavior as possible, in order to provide valid constraints for the predictive DHM simulation. On the other hand, the method needs to be appropriate for designers, without special ergonomic expertise or human behavior training, and needs to be intuitive, standardized, and time-efficient in use. The research question was to identify a way to resolve these partly contradictable demands.

3 Methodology

One key element for resolving this research question was using the concept of affordances. Affordances (artificial term for 'to afford something') describe the possibilities of interaction directly linked to physical objects, resulting from the abilities of the actor and the characteristics of the object. Originally introduced by Gibson [12] in psychology, the concept of affordances is now widely used in engineering [13] and industrial design [14]. In our framework, affordances serve as a medium for interaction modeling. Just as intuitively, as humans use affordances in their daily lives, designers shall use affordances to model user-product interactions. The basic hypothesis for our framework is, that many interaction concepts existing in technology can be reduced to a relatively small set of elementary affordances. This grants universal applicability while allowing for an intuitive, standardized, and time-efficient application. Another key element was the decision, to predict human behavior as a posture rather than a movement. The results of Wolf et al. [4] suggest that it is more likely to achieve a universal prediction of human behavior by predicting postures. Although posture evaluation is not sufficient for certain user-product interactions (because time-dependent factors such as inertia cannot be accounted for), they are easier to predict because the temporal dimension does not have to be modelled (e.g. maintaining dynamic balance). Hence, elementary affordances were defined as physical interaction possibilities existing between human end effectors (e.g. hand or foot) and rudimental geometries (e.g. surface, cylinder or cuboid). Additionally, elementary affordances shall be aim-independent, since the exclusion of interaction aims again removes a whole level of abstraction and thereby complexity. Based on the empirical data of Hu and Fadel [15] and Wolf et al. [16], we have developed a taxonomy of elementary affordances using a method introduced by Nickerson et al. [17]. With help of this taxonomy, elementary affordances were derived and described. Using feature technology [18], the identified elementary affordances were implemented as affordance-features in a CAD-System with an accompanying graphical user interface (GUI). The implementation was realized as a plugin for *Siemens NX*, which was developed using the *API OpenNX* and the *Block-UI-Styler*.

4   Results

The resulting taxonomy contains four dimensions – the rudimental interaction geometry, the end-effector posture, the kinematic minimal-dependency and the dynamic minimal-dependency –, each composed of different mutually exclusive but collectively exhaustive characteristics (see Fig. 1).

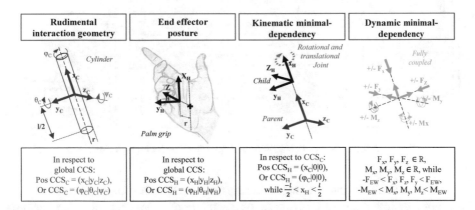

Fig. 1. Mechanical description of "hand grabs cylinder" (One of the 31 elementary affordances)

With help of the taxonomy, 31 elementary affordances were deduced from the empirical data. It turned out that a purely semantic description of the characteristics is advantageous for the development of the taxonomy, while for the resulting specification of elementary affordances a mechanical description of the characteristics seems to be more efficient. Figure 1 shows the mechanically described characteristics of one affordance "hand grabs cylinder". In this case, the *rudimental interaction geometry* includes information regarding the geometry's proportions in respect to the position and orientation of the local Cartesian coordinate system (CCS). The *end effector posture* includes the posture of the fingers (for illustrative purposes depicted as an opened hand in Fig. 1) and the local CCS position and orientation. In the example, the x-axis is oriented along the so-called thenar palmar crease, while the distance to the palm corresponds to the cylinder radius. The *kinematic minimal-dependency* is described via a mechanical joint definition (parent-child dependency), restricted by the proportions of the rudimental geometry. Lastly, the *dynamic minimal-dependency* contains possibilities of force transmission along the parent's CCS axes, restricted by threshold forces and moments resulting from the weight of the respective extremities. Each of the 31 elementary affordances is representable/expressible via a unique combination of such mechanical characteristics. The implementation of the elementary affordances as CAD-features was conducted as a plugin for *Siemens NX* but is based on a method/routine that may be implemented for any other CAD system as well (see Fig. 2).

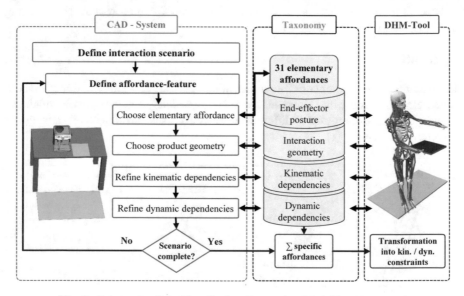

Fig. 2. Schematic of the User-Product Interaction-Modelling Framework

The method allows the designer to choose from the 31 elementary affordances (e.g. hand grabs cylinder) and to apply those to a geometry of a CAD-model (e.g. a handle). The abstraction of elaborate shapes to rudimental geometries (e.g. abstracting a fancy handle with a cylinder) is accomplished via a bounding volume function (implemented via the *ToolingBoxBuilder* in *Siemens NX*). In a next step, the designer can further refine the kinematic dependencies (e.g. the exact alignment of the end effector to the rudimental geometry). In the last step, the dynamic dependencies may be refined, by adding external forces or support forces in height and direction. Once an affordance is completely defined, it unites geometrical information about the interaction geometry – extracted from the CAD-System –, the end effector posture (stored in the taxonomy data) and kinematic and dynamic information (stored in the taxonomy-data and optionally further refined by the designer). Hereby, a sum off affordance-features describes an interaction scenario, which can be exported into a DHM tool as kinematic and dynamic constraints. As shown by many publications [3, 9], these can be used to predict postures using DHM tools.

5 Discussion

The developed interaction-modelling framework provides a universally applicable method, while keeping a comprehensible structure with a manageable amount of elementary affordances. The designer does not have to contribute with own a-priori knowledge regarding human behavior, since the provided mechanical descriptions solely need to be specified, instead of being modelled from scratch. The elementary affordances contain sufficient a-priori knowledge, enabling the distinct deduction of end-effector positions and orientations for a DHM posture prediction. The developed taxonomy shall not be understood as a comprehensive solution but rather than one possible solution, since there may be use cases, which were not considered during development. This is not problematic however, since extendibility is an important characteristic of a useful classification [17]. A validation of this method will be useful after researching and implementing the entire methodology. Therefore, the presented implementation of the taxonomy as an interaction-modelling framework in CAD provides all basic functionalities. Hence, this framework needs to be coupled with a predictive DHM simulation tool in a next step.

6 Conclusion

The presented framework demonstrates how the integration of user-product-interaction modelling into the computer-aided engineering environment, can be achieved in a comprehensible and straightforward way. The resulting simplicity and accessibility may constitute one key factor in order to exploit the potential of DHM simulation and proactive virtual assessment of ergonomics in engineering and industrial design.

Acknowledgements. The authors gratefully acknowledge the financial support of project WA 2913/31–1 by the German Research Foundation (DFG).

References

1. Ahmed, S., Irshad, L., Demirel, H.O., et al.: A comparison between virtual reality and digital human modeling for proactive ergonomic design. Lecture Notes in Computer Science (including subseries Lecture Notes in Artificial Intelligence and Lecture Notes in Bioinformatics) LNCS, vol. 11581, pp. 3–21 (2019)
2. Chaffin, D.B.: Improving digital human modelling for proactive ergonomics in design. Ergonomics **48**, 478–491 (2005)

3. Scataglini, S., Paul, G. (eds.): DHM and Posturography. Academic Press, London (2019)
4. Wolf, A., Miehling, J., Wartzack, S.: Challenges in interaction modelling with digital human models - a systematic literature review of interaction modelling approaches. Ergonomics 1–17 (2020)
5. Alexander, T., Paul, G.: Ergonomic DHM systems: limitations and trends - a literature review focused on the 'future of ergonomics'. In: International Digital Human Modeling Symposium (2014)
6. Ranger, F., Vezeau, S., Lortie, M.: Traditional product representations and new digital tools in the dimensioning activity: a designers' point of view on difficulties and needs. Des. J. **21**, 707–730 (2018)
7. Paul, G., Wischniewski, S.: Standardisation of digital human models. Ergonomics **55**, 1115–1118 (2012)
8. Perez, J., Neumann, W.P.: Ergonomists' and engineers' views on the utility of virtual human factors tools. Hum. Factors Man **25**, 279–293 (2015)
9. Jung, M., Cho, H., Roh, T., et al.: Integrated framework for vehicle interior design using digital human model. J. Comput. Sci. Technol. **24**, 1149–1161 (2009)
10. Mårdberg, P., Carlson, J.S., Bohlin, R., et al.: Using a formal high-level language and an automated manikin to automatically generate assembly instructions. IJHFMS **4**, 233 (2014)
11. Bauer, S., Sylaja, V.J., Fritzsche, L., et al.: Task-based digital human simulation with Editor for Manual work Activities - basic functionalities, applications, and future works. In: Scataglini, S., Paul, G. (eds.) DHM and posturography, pp. 57–62. Academic Press, London (2019)
12. Gibson, J.J.: The theory of affordances. In: Bornstein, M.H., Gibson, J.J. (eds.) The Ecological Approach to Visual Perception, pp. 127–137 (1979)
13. Maier, J.R.A., Fadel, G.M.: Affordance based design: a relational theory for design. Res Eng Design **20**, 13–27 (2009)
14. Norman, D.A.: The Design of Everyday Things. Revised and expanded edition. Basic Books, New York New York (2013)
15. Wolf, A., Miehling, J., Wartzack, S.: Elementary affordances: a study on physical user-product interactions. Procedia CIRP **91**, 621–626 (2020)
16. Hu, J., Fadel, G.M.: Categorizing affordances for product design. In: Proceedings of the ASME 2012 IDETC/CIE. American Society of Mechanical Engineers, New York, N.Y., pp. 325–339 (2012)
17. Nickerson, R.C., Varshney, U., Muntermann, J.: A method for taxonomy development and its application in information systems. Eur. J. Inf. Syst. **22**, 336–359 (2013)
18. Weber, C.: What is a feature and what is its use – results of DEMEX working group I. In: Proceedings of the 29th International Symposium on Automotive, Florenz, pp. 287–296 (1996)

Usability Study on a New Assembly of 3D Interactive Gestures for Human–Computer Interaction

Bohan Wu[1], Gang Zhang[2], Xuegang Zhang[2], Shibo Mei[2], Jinduo Wu[1], Hongting Li[1], and Zhen Yang[1(✉)]

[1] Department of Psychology, College of Science, Zhejiang Sci-Tech University, Jianggan District, Hangzhou, Zhejiang, China
yangzhen@zstu.edu.cn
[2] State Key Laboratory of Nuclear Power Safety Monitoring Technology and Equipment, China Nuclear Power Engineering Co., Ltd. Shenzhen of Guangdong Prov., Shenzhen 518172, China

Abstract. In 3D gesture interaction, people engage in contactless interaction with computers through arm and palm movements. The aim of this study was to develop and verify a reasonable evaluation scheme for 3D gesture usability through empirical methods and finally form an efficient, natural, and standard gesture library for 3D interaction. Two experiments were performed. In the first experiment, an evaluation scheme for 3D gestures with different weighted indexes of usability was developed, and then the ratings of the usability dimensions of 30 gestures within 10 operations in the 3D interaction were compared with one another. The purpose of this comparison was to summarize a set of 3D gestures with the highest usability. In the second experiment, the validity of the gesture set acquired in the first experiment was verified by comparing the usability differences between the high- and low-rated 3D gestures. An optimal set of 3D gestures was obtained by comparing the usability ratings of the different gestures and then verifying the superiority of the operation performance and users' satisfaction of this 3D gesture set in a real operation task.

Keywords: 3D gestures · Usability · Human–computer interaction

1 Introduction

Gesture interaction has gradually become a meritorious mode owing to its natural and efficient attributes and to the maturation of recognition technology. Meanwhile, 3D gesture interaction, also called gesture somatosensory interaction, refers to a new way in which people engage in contactless interactions with computers through arm and palm movements (Pallotta et al. 2007). In comparison with the 2D interactive mode, the current 3D gesture interaction mode is more adaptable and enables a more natural form of interaction with a machine. It can also reduce people's cognitive load because it is not limited to the form of hardware (Pantic et al. 2006).

© The Author(s), under exclusive license to Springer Nature Switzerland AG 2022
N. L. Black et al. (Eds.): IEA 2021, LNNS 223, pp. 453–461, 2022.
https://doi.org/10.1007/978-3-030-74614-8_58

Although new products or new recognition algorithms were used in previous studies for the design and evaluation of specific actions, most of them failed to include all the gestures that a platform may use. Considering the previous 3D gesture studies mentioned before, which mainly investigated the optimization of the gesture recognition algorithm or the usability for single or multiple gestures, it is necessary to use a reasonable multi-metric usability assessment method and obtain a set of gesture combinations with a high level of availability. Moreover, as the unified and effective evaluation criteria have not been formed yet, neither the specific index system of the evaluation of 3D gesture nor the weight of each index in the system is consistent. Thus, the existing standards or guidelines of 3D gesture design need to be improved to match the high requirement for human–machine interaction especially in complex tasks (Nielsen 2010).

The aim of this study was to develop and verify a reasonable evaluation scheme for 3D gesture usability through empirical methods and finally form an efficient, natural, and standard gesture library for 3D interaction. Two experiments were performed. In the first experiment, an evaluation scheme for 3D gestures with different weighted indexes of usability was developed, and 30 college students with minimal experience in using 3D interactive devices were recruited to rate the usability of 30 gestures within 10 operations by comparing with one another. The purpose of this comparison was to summarize a set of 3D gestures with the highest usability. In the second experiment, another 60 novices were recruited, and the validity of the gesture set acquired in the first experiment was verified by comparing the usability differences between the high- and low-rated 3D gestures. An optimal set of gestures was obtained by comparing the usability ratings of the different gestures and then verifying the superiority of the operation performance and users' satisfaction of this 3D gesture set in a real operation task.

2   Experiment 1

The aim of this experiment was to develop an optimal 3D gesture combination. The usability of 30 alternative gesture motions corresponding to 10 operations were compared with one another.

2.1   Method

Participants. A total of 30 Chinese undergraduates (mean age = 22.4 years, SD = 1.2 years) participated in this study, who have minimal experience in using 3D interactive devices, such as Leap Motion or Xbox.

Experiment Design. A within-subject design with one independent variable was conducted. The independent variable was the gesture motion for various operations, and each operation included three corresponding gesture motions. The dependent variable was the usability evaluation of gestures, which included four aspects, namely, learnability, metaphor, memorability, and comfort (Table 1). We presented the experimental materials randomly to avoid the order effect that may influence learning, evaluation, and recall of different gestures.

Table 1. Evaluation indexes of 3D gesture usability.

Index	Explanation	Operational definition
Learnability	Whether the gesture is easy to learn or not	The number of practice attempt when the gesture motion is completed twice correctly
Metaphor	Whether the gesture is consistent with users' intuition and expectation or conform to users' cognition in daily life	The result of assigning the gesture to one operation
Memorability	Whether the gesture is easy to remember	Accuracy of recognition task
Comfort	Whether the gesture can be effortlessly completed	Grade of subjective comfort

Material and Procedure. In order to determine the most frequently used gesture operations in 3D gesture interactions field, we first listed the gesture operations that exist on common 3D interactive devices (Leap Motion, Xbox and Kinect). Then, based on the 3D gesture interaction design principles proposed in previous studies, three expert users rated the listed gesture operations, considering their importance and frequency in actual use. Finally, the most typical 10 gesture operations and the most common three gesture motions for each operation were selected.

Experiment 1 consists of six tasks: evaluation task, learning task, practice task, gesture comfort rating task, recognition task, and index weight assignment task. All the materials for the tasks were presented with E-Prime in one Laptop except the material for the gesture motion practice task, which was presented with Leap Motion application in another Laptop. Figure 1 shows the entire procedure of this experiment.

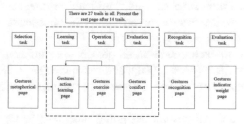

Fig. 1. Experiment 1: schematic diagram of experimental procedures.

2.2 Results

Outliers outside three standard deviations were removed for each experimental treatment, and the sifted data accounted for 1.18% of the total data.

Considering that the data of memorability was enumerative, we performed chi-square tests to test the differences in memorability among the three schemes. Table 2 shows the results. We used one-way ANOVA to compare the three schemes with respect to learnability, comfort, and metaphor for each gesture task (Table 3).

Table 2. Results of chi-square tests for memorability.

Operation	Gesture 1		Gesture 2		Gesture 3		χ^2
	True	False	True	False	True	False	
Left click	16	14	18	12	11	19	3.467
Right click	17	13	18	12	10	20	5.067
Page up/down	18	12	16	14	26	4	8.400*
Page left/right	25	5	25	5	26	4	0.180
Zoom	11	19	11	19	23	7	12.800**
Max/min	18	12	11	19	4	26	14.067**
Switch	27	3	29	1	1	29	70.048***
Volume control	25	5	8	22	20	10	21.020***
Double click	24	6	13	17	16	14	8.904*
Pause/start	17	13	23	7	29	1	13.260**

$^*p < 0.05$, $^{**}p < 0.01$, $^{***}p < 0.001$

The analysis of the three gestures of *Page up/down, Zoom, Max/min, Switch, Volume control, Double click, Pause/start* showed significant differences in memorability, but no difference in memorability was observed among the three gestures of *Left click, Right click* and *Page left/right* ($ps > 0.05$).

The three gestures of each operation all presented significant differences in learnability ($ps < 0.05$), comfort ($ps < 0.001$), and metaphor ($ps < 0.01$) except *Max/min, Right click* in learnability ($ps > 0.05$), *Switch* in comfort ($p > 0.05$) and *Page up/down* in metaphor ($p > 0.05$).

Table 4 shows 10 optimal gesture designing schemes (the highest overall score of the three gestures of each operation).

Table 3. Results of one-way ANOVA for learnability, comfort, and metaphor.

Operation	Gesture	Gesture evaluation dimension					
		Learnability		Comfort		Metaphor	
		Mean	D[a)]	Mean	D[a)]	Mean	D[a)]
Left click	1.1	.0676	A	.2945	B	−.6039	A
	1.2	−.2563	A	.4915	B	.9128	B
	1.3	1.8405	B	−1.1969	A	−.3006	A
	F	46.460***		35.988***		27.282***	
Right click	2.1	−.0858	A	.3508	B	−.5212	A
	2.2	.3404	A	.1820	B	.1682	B
	2.3	.3915	A	-.7466	A	−.3833	A
	F	2.124		14.289***		5.851**	
Page up/down	3.1	−.7166	A	.6041	B	.3888	A
	3.2	−.5290	A	.4915	B	.3613	A
	3.3	−.1369	B	−.9999	A	−.1075	A
	F	9.972***		37.162***		2.491	
Page left/right	4.1	−.4779	A	.6604	B	.4991	B
	4.2	−.5461	A	.7729	B	.9955	C
	4.3	.6813	B	−1.3657	A	−.5763	A
	F	29.882***		101.049***		37.418***	
Zoom	5.1	−.5461	A	.6322	B	.4716	B
	5.2	-.1710	A	−.0994	A	.4164	B
	5.3	.2040	B	−.2683	A	−.6867	A
	F	6.316**		10.630***		13.213***	
Max/min	6.1	−.3074	A	.7448	C	.6094	B
	6.2	.0506	A	.1257	B	−.4109	A
	6.3	−.1029	A	−.9436	A	−.4109	A
	F	1.363		32.373***		15.033***	
Switch	7.1	−.0347	A	−.0713	A	.6094	C
	7.2	1.2439	B	−.2683	A	.1131	B
	7.3	−.2904	A	.0131	A	−.7142	A
	F	23.986***		.780		23.916***	
Volume control	8.1	−.2733	B	−.4371	A	.6922	B

(*continued*)

458   B. Wu et al.

Table 3. (*continued*)

Operation	Gesture	Gesture evaluation dimension					
		Learnability		Comfort		Metaphor	
		Mean	D[a)]	Mean	D[a)]	Mean	D[a)]
	8.2	−.6995	A	.4352	B	−.3833	A
	8.3	−.6995	A	.3508	B	−.2454	A
	F	11.641***		14.541***		13.090***	
Double click	9.1	.5109	B	.3227	A	1.0507	B
	9.2	−.2222	A	.5197	B	−.5212	A
	9.3	1.5507	C	−.9155	B	−.3833	A
	F	22.447***		28.787***		29.746***	
Pause/start	10.1	−.3927	A	.8011	C	.1958	B
	10.2	−.3756	A	.2101	B	−.6867	A
	10.3	−.0176	B	−.6904	A	−.5488	A
	F	4.043*		34.164***		11.402***	

Note: D[a)], Duncan's multiple range test

Table 4. Gesture illustration and schematic of 10 optimal 3D gestures.

Task	Action description	Schematic
Left click	Open your palm, click downward with your index finger lightly	
Right click	Open your palm and turn it; bend your index finger, and then reverse it slowly	
Page up/down	Spread out your fingers, point upward to turn pages up, and point downward to turn pages down	
Page left/right	Slide your five fingers left and right	
Zoom	Extend five fingers to the screen (zoom in); shrink out five fingers off the screen (zoom out)	
Max/min	Open hand up /create a fist	
Switch	Turn the palm up and move upward	
Volume control	Point to the sound equipment, summon the menu, and move up or down to adjust	
Double click	Click twice with a single finger	
Pause/start	Supinate	

3   Experiment 2

The aim of this experiment was to verify the effectiveness and subjective satisfaction of gesture combinations developed in Experiment 1 in different operation tasks. The gesture combinations were compared with one another.

3.1   Method

Participants. A total of 60 Chinese undergraduates (mean age = 22.1 years, SD = 1.4 years) participated in this study, who have minimal experience in using 3D interactive devices, such as Leap Motion or Xbox.

Experiment Design. A between-subject design with one independent variable was conducted. The independent variable is the grade of gesture combination: high- and low-rated groups. The high-rated gesture combination was developed by the 10 optimal gesture motions that had been verified in Experiment 1. The low-rated gesture combination was composited by 10 gesture motions that were randomly selected from one of the other two gesture motions of each operation.

Material and Procedure. The material and procedure of Experiment 2 was simplified in comparison with Experiment 2. In this experiment, we developed only three sets of materials (gesture learning materials, gesture task program materials, and gesture subjective satisfaction rating materials) for three corresponding tasks (gesture learning, gesture operation, and subjective satisfaction rating). Gesture learning material and task were identical to those in Experiment 1.

Five simulated operation tasks that may be encountered in real-life context were designed. Each operation task required four gesture operations to complete and must be performed twice in each operation task. The participants were instructed to use the gestures recently learned to perform the actual operation in accordance with the requirements of actual situations. The time of accurately completing an operation task was recorded.

3.2   Results

Outliers outside three standard deviations were removed for each experimental treatment, and the sifted data accounted for 1.52% of the total data. Table 5 shows the descriptive data and the results of comparing two groups.

The high-rated group performed significantly better than the low-rated group among all five operation tasks: Task 1, $t_{(58)} = 2.291$, $p < 0.05$; Task 2, $t_{(58)} = 2.615$, $p < 0.05$; Task 3, $t_{(58)} = 2.912$, $p < 0.01$; Task 4, $t_{(58)} = 2.536$, $p < 0.05$; and Task 5, $t_{(58)} = 2.723$, $p < 0.01$.

For the subjective satisfaction, the high-rated group performed significantly better than the low-rated group in the four tasks (Task 1, $t_{(58)} = 2.541$, $p < 0.05$; Task 2, $t_{(58)} = 3.831$, $p < 0.001$; Task 4, $t_{(58)} = 2.435$, $p < 0.05$; and Task 5, $t_{(58)} = 3.307$, $p < 0.01$), except Task 3 ($t_{(58)} = 0.241$, $p = 0.810$).

These results suggest that the optimal gesture combinations that were developed in Experiment 1 indeed show operational advantage to cope with simulated operation scenarios.

Table 5. Operating performance and subjective satisfaction of high- and low-grade gestures.

Operating performance				Subjective satisfaction score		
Task	High grade group	Low grade group	t	High grade group	High grade group	t
1	20.28 ± 4.48	21.11 ± 4.90	2.291*	4.46 ± 1.04	3.81 ± 0.92	2.541*
2	26.50 ± 4.96	27.82 ± 4.70	2.615*	4.07 ± 0.96	3.13 ± 0.92	3.831***
3	20.55 ± 4.97	22.16 ± 4.45	2.912**	4.15 ± 0.93	4.09 ± 0.95	0.241
4	32.95 ± 6.42	35.54 ± 7.31	2.536*	3.59 ± 0.78	3.11 ± 0.70	2.435*
5	25.85 ± 5.92	27.99 ± 5.65	2.723**	3.93 ± 0.71	3.27 ± 0.80	3.307**

4 Discussion

Basing on previous studies and questionnaire surveys, we presented a comprehensive evaluation system, which included learnability, metaphor, comfort, and memorability as indicators with different weights for the 3D gesture design. In accordance with this comprehensive evaluation system, we conducted an optimal set of 3D gestures by comparing the usability of the different gestures and then verified the superiority of the operation performance and users' satisfaction of this 3D gesture set via a simulated operation task.

This study partially solves the lack of existing 3D gesture design proposed by (Norman 2010). First, the 3D gesture motions suggested by our study is natural and can be easily learned and memorized and also with a high level of availability. Second, high-rated gesture combinations suggested by our study had been proven to be effective in terms of usability and user satisfaction in complex operations.

This study had the following limitations and prospects. The usability data of all gestures proposed in this experiment were collected from college students. Given that gesture movements are affected by physiological and psychological factors, people with different ages and cultures may have different attitudes toward each gesture. In the future, exploring the preference differences on 3D gesture interaction among different age and cultural groups is necessary. Previous studies have suggested that as a result of the deterioration of the mobility of the elderly or the lack of athletic ability of some disabled people, 3D gesture interaction without actual touching is suitable for these special groups (Kobayashi et al. 2011; Leonardi et al. 2010; Murata and Iwase 2005). Moreover, using neurophysiological indicators, such as electroencephalogram or myoelectricity, may offer new insights into the design and usability test of 3D gestures.

References

Kobayashi, M., Hiyama, A., Miura, T., Ifukube, T.: Elderly user evaluation of mobile touchscreen interactions. In: International Conference on Human-Computer Interaction, vol. 6946, 83–99 (2011). https://doi.org/10.1007/978-3-642-23774-4_9
Leonardi, C., Albertini, A., Pianesi, F., Zancanaro, M.: An exploratory study of a touch-based gestural interface for elderly. In: Nordic Conference on Human-Computer Interaction, Reykjavik, Iceland, 16–20 October 2010. https://doi.org/10.1145/1868914.1869045

Murata, A., Iwase, H.: Usability of touch-panel interfaces for older adults. Hum. Factors **47**(4), 767–776 (2005). https://doi.org/10.1518/001872005775570952

Nielsen, J.: Kinect gestural ui: First impressions. Nielsen Norman Group, 27 December 2010. https://www.nngroup.com/articles/kinect-gestural-ui-first-impressions/

Norman, D.A.: Natural user interfaces are not natural. Interactions **17**(3), 6 (2010). https://doi.org/10.1145/1744161.1744163

Pallotta, V.: Kinetic user interfaces: physical embodied interaction with mobile pervasive computing systems. In: Kouadri-Mostefaoui, S. (ed.) Advances in Ubiquitous Computing: Future Paradigms and Directions, pp. 232–268. IGI (2007). doi: https://doi.org/10.4018/978-1-59904-840-6.ch008

Pantic, M., Pentland, A., Nijholt, A., Huang, T.S.: Human computing and machine understanding of human behavior: a survey. International Conference on Multimodal Interfaces **4451**, 239–248 (2006). https://doi.org/10.1007/978-3-540-72348-6_3

Combining a Wearable IMU Mocap System with REBA and RULA for Ergonomic Assessment of Container Lashing Teams

Sander Zelck[1]([✉]) [iD], Stijn Verwulgen[1] [iD], Lenie Denteneer[2] [iD],
Hanne Vanden Bossche[2] [iD], and Sofia Scataglini[1] [iD]

[1] Department of Product Development, Faculty of Design Sciences, University of Antwerp, Antwerp, Belgium
sander.zelck@uantwerpen.be

[2] Department of Rehabilitation Sciences and Physiotherapy, Faculty of Medicine and Health Sciences, University of Antwerp, Antwerp, Belgium

Abstract. Container lashing teams experience a number of repetitive and physically demanding tasks. These labor intensive tasks force container lashers into awkward postures which can lead to an increase of the biomechanical risk factors resulting in work related musculoskeletal disorders. An observation concluded that there is a knowledge gap between training and workplace practice. A comparison between the body posture of a dockworker instructor and a container lasher in the workplace should be examined. Conducting the ergonomic assessments requires a broader knowledge on how to implement the acquired observation tools in a port environment. A preliminary analysis of the container lashers lashing and de-lashing technique was created by applying recordings from a wearable inertial measurement units (IMU) mocap system, Xsens (MVN Awinda, Enschede, The Netherlands) to the rapid entire body assessment (REBA) and rapid upper limb assessment (RULA) tools. Representative ergonomic assessment scores for container lashers should include a broader interpretation of the load score and coupling score in RULA and REBA, as well as a detailed comparison of the anthropometric characteristics and the work experience of the container lashers.

Keywords: Maritime transportation · Container lashing · Ergonomic assessment · Wearable inertial mocap system · DHM

1 Introduction

1.1 Container Lashing in the Port of Antwerp

Dockworkers, otherwise known as riggers, stevedores or container lashers are indispensable in lashing and de-lashing of containers that enter the port facilities and use a lashing technique conform with the learned craftsmanship respecting the safety measurements and prevailing legislation [1]. Container lashing is one of the high-risk professions in maritime cargo [2, 3]. Hence the dockworkers (container lashers) in the port of Antwerp

N. L. Black et al. (Eds.): IEA 2021, LNNS 223, pp. 462–465, 2022.
https://doi.org/10.1007/978-3-030-74614-8_59

can suffer from chronic pain (neck, low back...) [4]. Due to the repetitive nature of lashing and de-lashing operations, the previously mentioned body parts obtain a rapidly increasing risk in musculoskeletal disorders (MSD) [5]. In Antwerp (Belgium), CEPA (employer's organization) [1] and OCHA (port labor training center) [6] are investing resources for training and prevention in order to build a dedicated training course on lifting techniques and ergonomic behavior to correctly lash containers [3].

1.2 Problem Statement

In the current setup, there is no comparison with the learned craftsmanship at the training center and the technique used when working on a ship. A comprehensive analysis of the observation constraints is required in order to correctly implement the innovative observation techniques within a port environment [7–9].

2 Materials and Methods

2.1 Setup of the Protocol

For this study participants demonstrate their regularly used lashing and de-lashing technique in the training center of OCHA. The training center possesses a simulation platform to help newly trained container lashers exercise the lashing technique in a safe environment. The training area consists of a container wall with a height of 5 containers and a width of 6 containers. In front of the container wall the platform is constructed. Participants are observed on top of the platform. As the observing researcher will not ascend the platform, participants are asked to perform the techniques from memory, thus actuating intuitive motions and gestures.

The container lashers will work in pairs, alternatingly performing the pre-determined lashing and de-lashing techniques while wearing an IMU wearable mocap system [10, 11]. Xsens Awinda (MVN Awinda, Enschede, The Netherlands) [11] is introduced to the pair of container lashers. Accurate body measurements are acquired, to generate a representative digital human model (DHM) of the participant. The container lasher wearing the mocap system [11] performs a calibration walk in front of the simulation platform. The observing researcher evaluates the successful calibration and requests the container lashing duo to ascend the platform. The recorded container lashing duo performs alternatingly a lashing and de-lashing task. On both sides of the platform video cameras are mounted to record the performed movements [12]. The recorded movements are converted by MVN Analyze [11] into kinematic datasheets (Excel).

2.2 Data Collection and Processing

The rapid entire body assessment tool (REBA) and the rapid upper limb assessment (RULA) [12–14] demand the kinematic data obtained by Xsens [11]. Inserting all provided joint angle data generates an ergonomic risk assessment score for the observed motions. The DHM assists in marking the relevant movements within the exported kinematic data to insert into the ergonomic assessment tools [13, 14].

3   Results

Due to the metal interference experienced in the port, the preliminary observations with Wearnotch [15] were rendered invalid. Xsens Awinda provided representative kinematic data [16]. In order to obtain a similar origin point for motion capturing [16], the calibration process was repeated up to six times to produce a good result in Xsens MVN Analyze. The use of video cameras deemed obsolete, rendering only the upper limbs and body parts of participants. Due to the high mass of container lashing rods and turnbuckles [17], the load score in REBA and RULA received for every participant the maximum value. The small operational floor of the platform, translates the coupling score in REBA to the maximum for every participant. The preliminary data analysis generated for all participants a score higher than the perceived maximum in REBA and RULA.

4   Discussion

The limited amount of voluntarily participants within container lasher profession resulted in a generalized population sample. Therefore, also rendering less representative results originating from REBA and RULA. A successive study needs to include detailed anthropometric data of the participant [18]. As work experience could have an effect on the performed lashing technique, the subsequential study requires a comparison between participants based on work experience [19]. The small operational space onto ships expects the use of a mocap system capable of recording biomechanical data in situations presenting severe occlusion [20].

5   Conclusion

The paper investigates the presented constraints while conducting a preliminary study between the taught and executed lashing technique performed by container lashers. The initial results from REBA and RULA do not differentiate between participants. In order to understand the biomechanical origin of musculoskeletal disorders within the container lashing profession, a detailed categorization of the population sample and more in depth comparison between participants needs to be considered. Future research should investigate the implementation of a rapid ergonomic assessment optimized for container lashing profession.

References

1. Cepa cvba Homepage. https://www.cepa.be/. Accessed 17 Dec 2019
2. Lima, E., Almeida, J., Alves, A., Pinto, M., Santos, F.: 362 Dockworkers musculoskeletal injury prevention program on a Brazilian terminal. BMJ, 269 (2018)
3. Zelck, S., Verwulgen, S., Denteneer, L., Scataglini, S.: Digital human modeling as a risk assessment tool for maritime workers. In: 6th International Digital Human Modeling Symposium, Svöde, Sweden, pp. 398–407. IOS Press BV (2020)

4. De Carvalho, M.P., Schmidt, L.G., Soares, M.C.F.: Musculoskeletal disorders and their influence on the quality of life of the dockworker: a cross-sectional study. Work 53, 805–812 (2016)
5. Gallagher, S., Heberger, J.R.: Examining the interaction of force and repetition on musculoskeletal disorder risk: a systematic literature review. Hum. Factors 55, 108–124 (2013)
6. OCHA Homepage. https://www.ocha.be/nl. Accessed 17 Dec 2019
7. Gómez-Galán, M., Callejón-Ferre, Á.J., Pérez-Alonso, J., Díaz-Pérez, M., Carrillo-Castrillo, J.A.: Musculoskeletal risks: RULA bibliometric review. Int. J. Environ. Res. Public Health 17, 1–52 (2020)
8. Hita-Gutiérrez, M., Gómez-Galán, M., Díaz-Pérez, M., Callejón-Ferre, Á.J.: An overview of REBA method applications in the world. Int. J. Environ. Res. Public Health 17, 2635 (2020)
9. Menolotto, M., Komaris, D.-S., Tedesco, S., O'Flynn, B., Walsh, M.: Motion capture technology in industrial applications: a systematic review. Sensors 20, 5687 (2020)
10. Alberto, R., Draicchio, F., Varrecchia, T., Silvetti, A., Iavicoli, S.: Wearable monitoring devices for biomechanical risk assessment at work: current status and future challenges—a systematic review. Int. J. Environ. Res. Public Health 15, 2001 (2018)
11. Xsens MTw Awinda. https://www.xsens.com/products/mtw-awinda. Accessed 22 Apr 2020
12. Vignais, N., Bernard, F., Touvenot, G., Sagot, J.C.: Physical risk factors identification based on body sensor network combined to videotaping. Appl. Ergon. 65, 410–417 (2017)
13. McAtamney, L., Nigel Corlett, E.: RULA: a survey method for the investigation of work-related upper limb disorders. Appl. Ergon. 24, 91–99 (1993)
14. McAtamney, L., Hignett, S.: Rapid entire body assessment. Appl. Ergon. 31, 201–205 (2000)
15. Wearnotch Homepage. https://wearnotch.com/. Accessed 30 Jan 2021
16. Ji, X., Piovesan, D.: Validation of inertial-magnetic wearable sensors for full-body motion tracking of automotive manufacturing operations. Int. J. Ind. Ergon. 79, 103005 (2020)
17. Container Technics N.V. LR-63 Lashing Rod. https://www.containertechnics.com/en/online-catalogue/loose-lashing/lr-63. Accessed 22 Apr 2020
18. Scataglini, S., Paul, G.: DHM and Posturography, 1st edn. Academic Press, London (2019)
19. Gonzalez, I., Morer, P.: Ergonomics for the inclusion of older workers in the knowledge workforce and a guidance tool for designers. Appl. Ergon. 53, 131–142 (2016)
20. Kim, W., Huang, C., Yun, D., Saakes, D., Xiong, S.: Comparison of joint angle measurements from three types of motion capture systems for ergonomic postural assessment. In: AHFE 2020 Virtual Conferences on Physical Ergonomics and Human Factors, Social & Occupational Ergonomics and Cross-Cultural Decision Making, USA, pp. 3–11. Springer (2020)

Development of Guidelines for the Ergonomic Evaluation of Human Work in Digital Factory Tools

Gert Zülch[✉]

ifab-Institute of Human and Industrial Engineering, Karlsruhe Institute of Technology, Karlsruhe, Germany
gert.zuelch@gefora-beratung.de

Abstract. For many years, the Association of German Engineers (VDI) has been issuing guidelines for simulating production and logistics systems as well as for Digital Factory tools. The target group encompasses experts from science, consulting institutions, industrial companies, interest groups and software houses. The guidelines represent the state of the art, but in individual cases can also be regarded as a preliminary stage of a standard. This opens up the possibility of publication without the topic already being viewed as capable of being standardized. An individual guideline can contain several guideline parts. In simulation software and Digital Factory tools, the working human is playing an increasing role. From this background, special guideline parts have already been published, which deal with the modeling of humans in production-logistic simulation and with ergonomic aspects in the Digital Factory. The last-mentioned guideline part deals with the work task and especially with related anthropometric and work-physiological aspects. A further guideline part is currently in the process of being published and regards the stresses and strains from the work environment. This guideline part with its close relation to Occupational Health and Safety is discussed in the following. It reveals that a large field of research and development issues still needs to be clarified in order to integrate these aspects into Digital Factory tools.

Keywords: VDI guidelines · Association of German Engineers (VDI) · Stress-strain concept · Occupational health and safety · Work task · Work environment

1 Objectives and Target Groups of VDI Guidelines

Since more than 20 years, the Association of German Engineers (VDI) has been dealing with questions relating to the simulation of production and logistics systems, including the planning of such systems with Digital Factory tools. The aim is, among others, to issue guidelines on related topics and to publish them as state of the art, at least for German-speaking countries.

A VDI guideline can include several parts that deal with a common main topic. The guidelines are not regarded as standards, but can - in individual cases - be viewed as their

N. L. Black et al. (Eds.): IEA 2021, LNNS 223, pp. 466–470, 2022.
https://doi.org/10.1007/978-3-030-74614-8_60

precursors. Thus, there is the option of already publishing the state of the art without the topic being already considered worthy of standardization.

The purpose of a guideline is to inform those interested in the topic about the level of knowledge that has been achieved. The guidelines therefore address planners of work systems, experts in ergonomic work design, occupational health and safety responsibles, plant physicians and company managers and works council members. The guidelines also aim at experts who are involved in the further development of simulation and Digital Factory tools.

2 Development Process

In order to develop a new guideline or a part of it, the initiating Technical Committee of the VDI appoints a Guideline Committee of experts for this purpose. The members of this Guideline Committee work on a voluntary unpaid basis. For example, the last Guideline Committee - VDI 4499 Part 5 - met up to the preliminary first version 17 times in face-to-face meetings and recently 8 times in web meetings. A total of 18 experts from science, consulting institutions, industrial companies and software houses took part in the development of this guideline part.

After editing by the VDI organization, there is a preliminary first version, the so-called green print, which will be put up for public discussion. Only after the possibly existing objections have been dealt with will the final version be published by Beuth (Berlin), in German and English.

3 Options for Ergonomic Evaluation

The guideline parts presented here are based on the well-known stress-strain concept and thus the influences on working humans from their work task and the work environment [1, 2]. They offer some possibilities for the ergonomic evaluation of work systems.

This development began in 2001 with the publication of Part 6 of VDI guideline 3633 [3]. It concentrated on the evaluation of work systems by means of production logistic criteria, which today can be regarded as generally available. This part of the guideline is currently being revised.

The macro-ergonomic evaluation criteria contained therein are primarily the effects of different skills and the workload of employees. In addition, the effects of different working time models are also considered.

A number of micro-ergonomic forecasting procedures in connection with the Digital Factory already exist. In Part 4 of VDI guideline 4499 [4], above all anthropometric and work-physiological aspects are considered. There are hardly any procedures with regard to occupational psychological and sociological aspects, as these are not regarded to be predictable.

Part 5 of VDI guideline 4499 [5] concentrates on the physical environmental influences in an indoor work space which the guideline committee has recognized as having priority. This part divides the environmental influences into the aspects of indoor work space, room air, mechanical vibrations and electromagnetic oscillations (Fig. 1). Work in negative and positive pressure, artificial optical rays (except for lighting) and radioactive corpuscular radiation are not dealt with. Chemical and biological factors that can occur during (tactile or ingestive) contact with work objects and materials are generally not dealt with. In this respect, the discussion is limited to the spread in the enclosed work area due to physical effects such as ventilation.

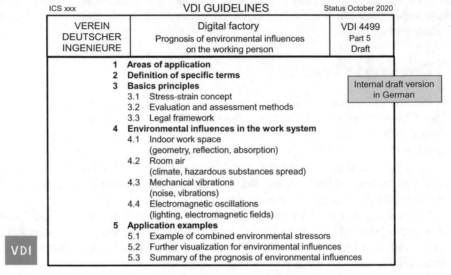

Fig. 1. VDI draft guideline 4499 part 5.

The exposure to the individual environmental influences is first evaluated and then assessed for compliance with existing normative specifications, for example from standards and directives. Evaluation methods relate on the one hand to point in time and period-related aspects, on the other hand to workplace and person-related ones. As far as a prognostic instrument is available, the strain on the working human is finally dealt with.

4   Discussion and Further Development Needs

The integration of procedures to forecast environmental influences in Digital Factory tools has proven to be particularly difficult. There are numerous software procedures for evaluating individual types of exposure, but these are for the most part isolated and not integrated into Digital Factory systems. In contrast, the assessment is easier, as there are many regulations from the field of Occupational Health and Safety that specify limit values for comparison. Only in a few cases are there already forecasting procedures for types of strain, i.e. for the effect of a type of stress on working humans. Furthermore, the connection to simulation procedures is still largely in the development phase, although this is necessary for the forecast of period-related stressors.

There is a certain need for research on the environmental influences, which are not dealt with in the VDI Guideline 4499 Part 5. This relates not only to stressors, but especially to the related strains, because there still exists a lack of appropriate research knowledge. The integrative evaluation of several environmental influences stays a long-known problem. Approaches to solving this problem using lexicographic order methods can only be a first approach [6].

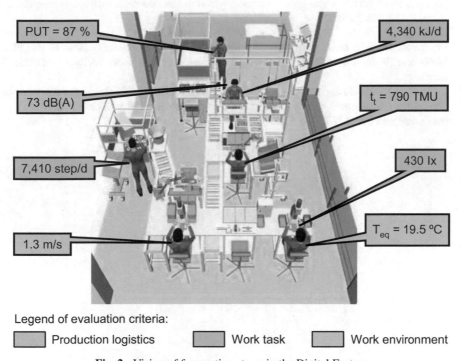

Legend of evaluation criteria:

◻ Production logistics   ◻ Work task   ◻ Work environment

Fig. 2. Vision of forecasting stress in the Digital Factory

Finally, to avoid multiple data entries a common database is required. Modeling based on the Industry Foundation Classes [7] could be a possible way. In summary, it can be stated that a wide field opens up for further research and development. Anyhow, there is still a long way to go in the future to arrive at the vision of predicting the production-logistical and ergonomic stress values in a common model (Fig. 2).

References

1. Rohmert, W.: Ergonomics: concept of work, stress and strain. Appl. Psychol. **35**(2), 159–181 (1986). https://iaap-journals.onlinelibrary.wiley.com/doi/abs/10.1111/j.1464-0597.1986.tb00911.x. Accessed 19 Dec 2020
2. Gervais, R.L.: Definition of work/job design (2020). https://oshwiki.eu/wiki/Definition_of_work/job_design. Accessed 17 Dec 2020
3. VDI 3633–6:2001–10. Simulation of systems in materials handling, logistics and production - representation of human resources in simulation models. Beuth, Berlin (2020). https://www.beuth.de/de/technische-regel/vdi-3633-blatt-6/44890290. Accessed 19 Dec 2020

4. VDI 4499–4:2015–03. Digital factory - Ergonomic representation of humans in the digital factory. Beuth, Berlin (2020). https://www.beuth.de/de/technische-regel/vdi-4499-blatt-4/222 813009. Accessed 19 Dec 2020
5. VDI 4499–5 - Projekt. Digitale Fabrik - Prognose von Umgebungseinflüssen auf den arbeitenden Menschen. Beuth, Berlin (2020). https://www.vdi.de/richtlinien/details/vdi-4499-blatt-5-digitale-fabrik-prognose-von-umgebungseinfluessen-auf-den-arbeitenden-menschen. Accessed 19 Dec 2020
6. Zülch, G., Zülch, M.: Ergonomic evaluation of a hybrid U-shaped assembly system. In: Lindgaard, G., Moore, D. (eds.) Proceedings of the 19th Triennial Congress of the IEA, Melbourne, 9–14 August 2015. International Ergonomics Association, Melbourne (2015). 8 pages
7. ISO 16739-1:2018-11 Industry Foundation Classes (IFC) for data sharing in the construction and facility management industries - Part 1: Data schema. Beuth, Berlin (2020). https://www.beuth.de/de/norm/iso-16739-1/299296219. Accessed 19 Dec 2020

Part VII: Neuroergonomics (Edited by Echezona Nelson Dominic Ekechukwu)

Cognitive Aspects in Control Rooms
Anticipated Response to Adverse Situations

Juan Alberto Castillo-M[1](✉) ⓘ and Maria Constanza Trillos Ch.[2] ⓘ

[1] ErgoMotion-lab, Universidad del Rosario, Bogotá, Colombia
Juan.castillom@urosario.edu.co
[2] GISCYT Research Group, Universidad del Rosario, Bogotá, Colombia

Abstract. The level of performance of a control console operator is associated with the speed of data processing, so that the contextual reconstruction of data, whether collaborative or individual, depends on aspects such as knowledge of the actual and effective technical operation, knowledge of the functional and operational history of the process units to be controlled; this is closely related to the physical, biomechanical and physiological availability. This study approaches the physiological aspects in two elements considering their relationship with neurological aspects that may affect the monitoring and control tasks. It also examines the relationship between professional experience and cognitive abilities bringing closer to the understanding of specific aspects of anticipation and their relationship with the elaboration of a knowledge base.

Keywords: Cognitive analysis · Neuro-musculoskeletal · Activity analysis · Control process · Knowledge architecture

1 Introduction

From an ergonomics and human factors point of view a control room is both a collaborative workspace and a decision center, in these scenarios experienced operators have extensive process knowledge, act appropriately in case of unexpected events, provided they have an excellent overview of the process status and are in the best physical and cognitive health conditions.

In the control room, the surveillance of a process is an activity, which is both focused and comprehensive. It is a focalized activity, because operators must concentrate their attention on the actions, they are carrying out in order to avoid errors, they must direct their perception to certain parts of the installations to apprehend certain phenomena in advance. At the same time, they must maintain an overall view in order not to overlook certain dysfunctions or to be able to recognize general changes in the process. The operator of a control room must not only identify deviations (be they positive or negative) from alarms or temporary status of the control units, he must also develop skills to achieve a comprehensive screening of the information that is in front of him, distributed in graphs, pages, data, values and projections; this implies understanding as a whole the meaning they carry in order to establish where, when and how to intervene to obtain the best results in the management and control of the components of its operating unit.

© The Author(s), under exclusive license to Springer Nature Switzerland AG 2022
N. L. Black et al. (Eds.): IEA 2021, LNNS 223, pp. 473–480, 2022.
https://doi.org/10.1007/978-3-030-74614-8_61

The cognitive aspects of control activities are composed of operational modes of action sequences, gestures, evidence search and information processing, communications, verbal or graphic identification, incidents or disturbances that characterize the actual task performed by the operator [1]. Several studies show that it is impossible to design automated systems that are reliable without human intervention, which increases the importance of operators to ensure the proper functioning of an industrial facility, being essential the participation of workers in the solution of production problems [2].

Mental activities depend on the availability of information related to the ongoing process of control and the use of memory for decision making. Appropriate design of a system's work prevents mental overloads, including loss or misinterpretation of signals, and facilitates quick and correct actions [3]. There was evidence in the literature that neural plasticity is experience-dependent and can be stimulated by both physical and mental practice to different degrees, depending on the content of the training and the skills to be tested. Compared to physical training, greater improvements in executive functions were observed after cognitive training. Cardiovascular and coordination training elicited differential changes in sensorimotor and visuospatial networks [4]. These observations are important for both cognitive improvements and motor learning.

In this order of ideas, a study was developed in 2019–2020, focused on understanding the human aspects (cognitive and physiological) associated with the anticipation of adverse events in the control room of the oil Refinery. The study was focused on establishing a health profile of the control room workers given the importance of understanding the relationship between physiological availability and the nature of the cognitive processes required for the proper development of supervision and control tasks. In addition, an analysis of ergonomic aspects was carried out, characterizing some workstations and defining worker profiles based on experience. At the same time, an analysis of workload perception and visual fatigue was carried out.

2   Methodological Aspects

This study was performed in the framework of the concepts developed by Bisseret and Enard, [5, 6], who found that the controller has in his memory a certain amount of data about the situation under his control and that he has a kind of "complementary device for the presentation of information that seems to increase his ability to control the situation". This temporary memory of current data has been described as "operational" to mean that it is organized and structured by working processes.

To understand this "complementary device" of the operators, the study is organized into five analytical dimensions; these comprise first a work session to address resources for activating collaboration; then using talk-aloud (self-reflective) processes, operational resources are identified from semi-directive interviews; the profile of the operators is completed through a risk profile questionnaire; the participants are then evaluated with a cognitive assessment battery for reasoning in order to identify the six key cognitive dimensions in the control processes (Perception, memory, reasoning, attention, coordination). Finally, a panel of experts led by the shift leaders is developed, where the essential aspects of the control task and the aspects of anticipation of events are analyzed. This panel is complemented with a questionnaire that examines the judgment skills of the experts.

2.1   Data Analysis

The development of the study involved a multi-method approach, which involved active observation, participatory observation, interviews, surveys, monitoring, physical evaluation and analysis of information processing sequences. For the control processes, content analysis of technical reports and validation with workers was used, including console operators, shift supervisors and other workers who interact and are involved in the control process.

In the first phase, a neuro-musculoskeletal analysis was performed, from which individual reports were produced for 96 workers; this information was consolidated into a database. Surveys of workload perception (NASAX method), of visual fatigue (INRS method), of physical activity (Stanford questionnaire) were also applied. In the second phase, 36 workers participated, 25 of whom were operators and board supervisors from the refinery's control center, who were selected based on the criteria of experience and operational function. Six shift supervisors also participated in the role of experts.

The data were analyzed in content and structure of the data obtained in the joint reflection and discussion sessions, the data from the questionnaires were analyzed according to the dimensions of these in qualitative terms, the battery was analyzed once normalized in a maximum scale of 800 points, where the participants are examined according to the scores achieved by classifying them into three risk zones.

Given the characteristics of the data collected, the treatments of these were carried out according to their function, i.e., the discussion derivatives are analyzed collectively and the questionnaires at the individual level.

2.2   Nature of the Activities

In the control room, the key actors in event management are the panel operator and the camp operator (together with the teams that interact in the control of the production units). The central interest of these interaction processes is to establish the functional and operational status of the different units. To achieve this, parallel actions are carried out that include strategies derived from the operating experience and those associated with the seasonal operation of the units.

This makes it possible to generate a knowledge base closely associated with the operation, variations and foreseeable effects of the possible events that occur. The latter results in the establishment of monitoring periods and specific strategies to define thresholds and operational limits linked to the behavior of the different units.

These elements constitute the cognitive reference base, since they imply the use of processes of identification, retrospective analysis and prospective estimates, which are based on individual and sometimes group experience and make possible the development of types of actions and interventions that facilitate the regulation or stabilization of the processes of each operational unit and therefore the integrity of the process. the question to be answered is: How can an organization strike a balance between, on the one hand, a level of anticipation that allows it to describe the most frequent responses to a wide range of situations and, on the other hand, leave front-line operators with a capacity to adapt when situations encountered fall outside the scope of anticipated situations? Figure 1 shows how the approach to answer this question has been performed.

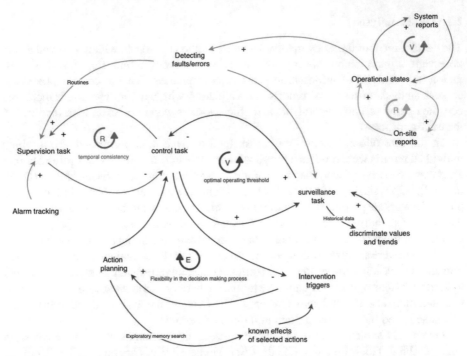

Fig. 1. Our methodological approach allows to identify from the activities of the control room operators, the differences in the tasks of surveillance, supervision and control, including actions of Data Retrieval [R], Validation data [V] and Options exploration [E].

3   Findings

3.1   Neuro-Musculoskeletal Evaluation

The purpose of the clinical neuro-musculoskeletal evaluation was to determine structural deficiencies that could represent a risk factor for suffering a musculoskeletal disorder that in turn could lead to a limitation in functional capacity. Its focus was given by quadrants, that is to say, the structural and functional interrelation from the spine to the upper and lower limbs was considered. This evaluation was oriented from two components: the first was subjective, supported by an interview with the worker about his general health condition and the presence or absence of symptomatology. The second component was objective, in which tests and measurements were applied that allowed the examiner to approach the deficiencies in the inert and contractile tissues.

96 workers were evaluated, 97% were men and 3% were women. Of those evaluated, 43% were in the 35 to 41 age range, followed by 33% in the 29 to 34 age range, 19% in the 42 to 48 age range and the remaining 5% in the 49 to 54 age range. 71% of the workers evaluated had specific experience in the job for 1 to 6 years, 27% for 7 to 12 years, 1% for 13 to 18 years and the remaining 1% for 19 to 24 years. 61% of the workers assessed where overweight, 24% obese and 15% within normal parameters.

72% of the workers evaluated presented some type of musculoskeletal symptom and 48% did not report any type of symptomatology. Among the segments involved, there was a greater manifestation of pain in the lumbar and cervical region. Concerning the duration of pain, they indicate that of the 48% of the workers with musculoskeletal pain, 37% have chronic pain, 6% have acute pain and 2% have both acute and chronic pain. 56% of the evaluated workers presented forward head position which is characterized by a flexion of the cervical spine in the lower sector, and an extension at the level of the upper cervical spine, this behavior is identified by the presence of a forward head, accompanied by a lower cervical rectification and a horizontal vision.

72% of the evaluated employees presented an increase in dorsal kyphosis, this behavior is usually accompanied by forward head. 41% of the workers evaluated presented lumbar hyper lordosis, which is characterized by an increase in lumbar lordosis. 56% of the evaluated employees present elevation of the right hemipelvis and 69% present pelvis rotation to the right.

3.1.1 Neuro-Musculoskeletal Conclusions

When the atlanto-occipital joint is in extension, the atlas approaches the occipital and can generate compression in the neurovascular structures in the suboccipital area. Keeping the cervical spine in an extension posture can compress the vertebral arteries and as a consequence can produce symptoms such as dizziness, vertigo, headaches, nausea, paresthesia, loss of balance and alterations of the myofascial system [7, 8].

Dorsal hyper kyphosis can produce alterations in both the form and function of the rib cage by increasing the anterior-posterior diameter, which can eventually affect the respiratory capacity [9].

3.2 Cognitive Analysis

The study of the activities of the controllers was focused on the cognitive components that play a central role not only in the control processes, but also in those associated with the structuring of a knowledge base based on the experience of each operator, it is very important to take into account that each of the analyses performed present a synthesis that seeks to integrate the greatest number of elements of the situation, However, it is not exhaustive given the inter-individual differences, for example, experiencing facts, events, emergencies provides a knowledge that helps the operator to find shorter routes to manage the changes, temporary variations or adjustments necessary to keep the units in operation.

It is also important to consider that the idea of operational normality differs greatly from the idea of operational optimum, which can be explained by the characteristic variables of a process that in its dynamics retains an operating interval with variations associated with multiple factors. Therefore, the results presented here tend to show through different elements how the state of balance between expected performance and obtained performance is achieved, with the purpose of identifying actions to maintain or guarantee the availability of cognitive resources that contribute to anticipate. In any case, throughout the process, operators in general, as well as shift managers, show a clear awareness of the unpredictability and uncertainties of the process, while showing confidence in their decision-making and cognitive skills and the role of prior and evolving knowledge of the processes and equipment with which they interact on a daily basis.

Age distribution of the population included in the study; the sample consisted of 96 COR console operators. The age curve indicates that an important part of the population is above the average age of 37 years; 76% of the sample is in the group over 36 years of age. In addition, in this group the accumulated work experience is 67.6 months on average.

It is not age as such that determines knowledge, but rather it is experience that provides the basis for understanding the positive correlations observed between advancing age and knowledge development (whether declarative or procedural knowledge). Consequently, subjects' experience can support and facilitate cognitive activity through knowledge acquired throughout the life course, which allows a person to apply compensatory strategies, such as adapting their activity and action patterns to maintain or increase their effectiveness.

There are three types of experience-related strategies: temporal strategies (anticipation, verification), strategies for building and using the collective (co-activity, cooperation) and control strategies.

When studying the risk behavior of the operators, it was found that the risk is taken through a concrete action before doing it to obtain a benefit, the way in which the possible development of the events could be controlled is examined, which shows an exercise of precaution when establishing the relationship between taking the action and effectively following its development, this is typical of the scenarios where uncertainty has a relevant weight when observing the possible effects of taking a risk through a concrete action.

Due to the scenarios that imply a dynamic situation, where unexpected and cyclical events may occur, the operators indicate that this is indeed the case since they must deal with the events immediately, however, the planning of the worst scenario divides opinions, this is due to the fact that the worst scenario is not completely plausible, this is evidently known, but the risk control taken does not always include the worst scenario, but rather by the accumulated experience and by the analogous situations dealt with, the possible outcome is visualized. For this reason, operators focus on having quality and sufficient information on the temporal status, define monitoring segments, and call on the field operator to complete the image of the variable set. Some examples are found in the shift reports.

a. Regarding a crude oil tank "...*vaporization continues to gradually decrease. once percentage normalization request occurs...*".
b. ..."*Follow up on the desalter level control...this is slow, and conditions are going very much at the lower and upper limit....*"

It can be observed that the current status is established, then the recorded behavior is stated and finally the focus of attention to be followed up is indicated, this same structure is generally found in the reports regarding the statuses identified by the operators; the indications imply the commitment to follow up and help to define the follow-up strategies to be taken up by the operator of the next shift. It is from these temporary states that operators search for data and locate information, formulating hypotheses that help them to identify the best solution path. An example allows to better understand the use of this hypothesis extracted from a report:

"... low water flow has been occurring during cooling, during the shift several actions were performed to improve this condition, although it is not ruled out that it is due to an obstruction in the veins of the drum, it is strange that it is repeated in all drums..."; "... it is presumed that the check in this line has a pass and is generating recirculation in the pumps and a decrease in the flow to the drums..."

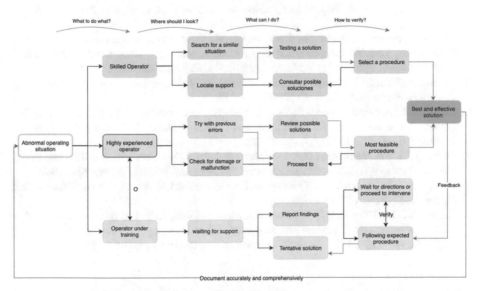

Fig. 2. This model shows the decision-action continuum paths for the three operator profiles identified in this study. In each case, the decision states explored by the operator are observed, which are also related to the speed required to find the most viable option to solve an operational or functional situation. This is also a way to refine the significance of alarms and signals associated with functional disturbances, which are useful for operators to develop quick access repertoires to perform control interventions. It is also presented how each operator profile approaches a functional problem.

The hypotheses are partly built on experience, also on information accumulated in dealing with similar situations, also included in these constructions of the operators include options for exploring causes (Fig. 2), that facilitate finding a solution, this also helps to establish how the operator can find temporary means of control and defines the aspects to be closely monitored.

The elaboration of these resources implies the availability of cognitive elements that help the operators to produce them, and they also contribute to the fact that together they can not only control the operation, but also help to understand the barriers that are presumed to be critical to anticipate events in the process. To understand the role of these cognitive elements, it is necessary to see if the operators have them, to study these elements and get an approach to this, the operators participating in the study were invited to complete a series of tests that allowed to obtain a record of the main elements using the cognitive assessment for reasoning, the results of this test will be presented below.

References

1. Antunes Lima, F.D.P.: Ergonomia, ciência do trabalho, ponto de vista do trabalho: a ciência do trabalho numa perspectiva histórica. Revista Ação ergonômica, vol. 1, no. 2, pp. 35–46 (2001)
2. Fassina, A.: L'analyse des aspects Cognitifs du Travail. In: Dadoy. Les Analyses du Travail. Enjeux et Formes. Paris: CEREQ, 1990. Author, F.: Article title. Journal **2**(5), 99–110 (2016)
3. Lida, I.: Ergonomics: Project and Production, 2nd edn. Blucher, São Paulo (2005). (in Portuguese)
4. Voelcker-Rehage, C., Godde, B., Staudinger, U.M.: Cardiovascular and coordination training differentially improve cognitive performance and neural processing in older adults. Front. Hum. Neurosci. **5**, 26 (2011). https://doi.org/10.3389/fnhum.2011.00026
5. Biseret, A., Enard, C.: Le probleme de la structuration de l'aprentisage d'un travail-complexe. Buletin de Psvchologie **XI**, 1–12 (1970)
6. Enard, C.-J.: Applications de la "Méthode d'interaction Constantes des Unités Programmées" (MICUP) à la formation des contrôleurs des centres réginaux de la Navigation Aérienne. Rapport IRIA C.0.72 11 C 17, 44 pp. (1972)
7. Hertling, D.: Management of Common Musculoskeletal Disorders: Physical Therapy. Principles and Methods (Edición: 4 ed). Lippincott Williams and Wilkins, Philadelphia (2005)
8. Cook, C.: Orthopedic Manual Therapy: An Evidence-Based Approach. Pearson/Prentice Hall, Upper Saddle River (2007)
9. Renno, A.C.M., Granito, R.N., Driusso, P., Costa, D., Oishi, J.: Effects of an exercise program on respiratory function, posture and on quality of life in osteoporotic women: a pilot study. Physiotherapy **91**(2), 113–118 (2005). https://doi.org/10.1016/j.physio.2004.09.020

Independent Driving Improved the Self-esteem and Health Related Quality of Life of a Polio Survivor

Olumide Olasunkanmi Dada[1,2(✉)] (iD), Femi Abolaji Ogundapo[2],
Olusegun Adeyemi Adejare[2], Chidozie Emmanuel Mbada[3],
and Echezona Nelson Dominic Ekechukwu[4,5,6] (iD)

[1] Department of Physiotherapy, College of Medicine, University of Ibadan, Ibadan, Nigeria
oo.dada@ui.edu.ng
[2] Department of Physiotherapy, University College Hospital, Ibadan, Ibadan, Nigeria
[3] Department of Medical Rehabilitation, College of Heath Sciences, Obafemi Awolowo University, Ile-Ife, Nigeria
[4] Department of Medical Rehabilitation, Faculty of Health Sciences and Technology, College of Medicine, University of Nigeria, Nsukka, Nigeria
[5] Environmental and Occupational Health Unit, Institute of Public Health, College of Medicine, University of Nigeria, Nsukka, Nigeria
[6] LANCET Physiotherapy Wellness and Research Centre, Enugu, Nigeria

Abstract. Outdoor mobility and access to transport modes are important for independence and an active life. Polio survivors often have impaired muscle function that can result in mobility problems including driving. This study sought to detail the modification of a vehicle for a polio survivor to achieve independent driving and investigate the impact of independent driving on the self-esteem and the health-related quality of life of the polio survivor with bilateral weakness of the lower limbs (paraparesis). This multi-level research utilized a mixed method combining quantitative and qualitative data collection. It is a case report of a polio survivor with inability to drive conventional vehicles. The Rosenberg self-esteem questionnaire and the SF-12 were administered and a direct interview was conducted to elicit qualitative responses on the self-perceived challenges of lack of independent mobility and consequence of modification of vehicle. The design and fabrication of a hand-powered pedal controls for modification of conventional vehicle was reported. Improvements were observed in the self-esteem and the HRQoL when current scores were compared to scores before driving. The narration has also changed with increased independence in several aspects of living especially mobility, with respect to driving achieved by modification of conventional vehicle. Independence in mobility-related activities such as driving can lead to improved self-esteem and HRQoL. Rehabilitation focus should be on simple and affordable modification of vehicles for persons with disability such as polio survivors to increase independence.

Keywords: Polio survivor · Mobility · Independent driving · Vehicle modification

© The Author(s), under exclusive license to Springer Nature Switzerland AG 2022
N. L. Black et al. (Eds.): IEA 2021, LNNS 223, pp. 481–486, 2022.
https://doi.org/10.1007/978-3-030-74614-8_62

1 Introduction

Poliomyelitis is a debilitating viral disease that attacks the brain and ventral horn of the spinal cord [1]. Damage to the lower motor neurons usually results in atrophy and weakness of muscle groups, perhaps paralysis and possibly deformity [2]. Many people who suffer from the late effects of polio have impaired walking ability due to reduced balance, muscle strength and pain, which impacts their daily life [4]. Polio survivors often have impaired muscle function that can result in mobility problems [5]. Community mobility may include walking, using mobility devices, using public transportation like buses or trains, using private transportation such as a ride from a friend or family member and driving a car. Independent mobility, i.e., having access to transportation, is critical for ensuring access to employment and education [6].

Mobility is of major importance for health, autonomy and wellbeing [5], and many different lifestyles and living patterns require transportation and mobility [7–9]. Being able to move independently from one place to another is essential for quality of life and for participation in many activities [7–10], especially for people with polio. It is particularly important to understand how polio survivors commute from one place to another and how the late effects of polio affect patients in their daily lives. While little emphasis has been placed on the state of mobility of people with disabilities in terms of ambulation, less emphasis is placed on the mode of transport and their ability to drive.

This study is a multi-level research which sought to investigate the mobility status of the participants, means of transportation and the ease of commuting. This report focuses on one of the participants whose vehicle was modified to allow him achieve independence in driving. The study utilized a mixed method combining quantitative and qualitative data collection incorporating direct interview.

2 Methods

The subject's demographics were obtained with a self-developed questionnaire and muscle oxford grading system was used to measure the muscle power. The participant was not able to drive initially because of the power in the lower limbs and lack of modified cars in the local market. With the challenges of independent mobility occasioned by the inability to drive in mind, the Rosenberg self-esteem questionnaire and the health related quality of life (HRQoL) were administered on the subject to obtain self-esteem and HRQoL. The current self-esteem and HRQoL scores (post self-driving) were assessed and recorded.

2.1 The Modification

The modification to the car was a product of necessity. He went for a ride in a friend's car which was converted into a specification for persons with disabilities (PwD) but we realized that the process of the conversion was cumbersome, costly and time-consuming.

The subject then ordered for a generic hand-powered pedal controls which he saw online. The cost was $ which was considered high in a country where the minimum wage is $50 per month. The product however took a very long time to be delivered which meant he had to continue relying on friends and family to drive him around. In the course of waiting for the imported product, we decided to design and fabricate a pair of metallic hand-powered pedal controls, as stop gaps.

The first step was for us to search for various specifications of hand driven cars both locally and internationally. So we decided to investigate deeper on YouTube and other relevant sites but could not get anything cheaper than the type we ordered for. The search however gave us an insight, as it became obvious to us that the technology required in the conversion of a conventional car into a modified car could be something very basic. It did not need to be highly technical. So we approached an artisan (known in our local parlance as a welder), described and drew what we wanted on a paper. When he delivered it was exactly what was described. This consists of two pairs metal plates with a hole drilled at each end (Fig. 1). The top plate was placed on the accelerator pedal of the car while the other plate was placed below the pedal. The two plates were connected (held) together with a pair of bolt and screw. The process was repeated for the brake pedal. Each of the top plates had a small cylindrical connecting rod in which a longer rod was inserted, thus allowing the driver to use his hand to move and stop the car whenever he pressed the accelerator and brake pedals respectively. The modification means he could drive any model of car with an automatic transmission without any form of restriction (Fig. 2).

We applied the hand-powered controls to the car pedals and checked with the automechanic to be sure that they were not an extra burden on the car, safe and would serve the function intended.

The car can be easily reverted to the default (factory) mode as the modification is removable, thus enabling others (including people without disability) drive it whenever they want. It cost less than $20 to produce the hand-powered pedal control which we have called the Ibadan Hand-Powered Pedal Control (IHPPC).

2.2 Direct Interview

A direct interview was conducted to elicit qualitative narration on the challenges of inability to drive and the benefits of being able to drive. It was intended to further elicit responses in line with the two thematic construct of self esteem and HRQOL and have a more qualitative description of the effects of non-driving and driving on his self esteem and quality of life. The subject was free to answer in any particular order as we avoided leading him into any preempted response. Some of the questions were:

1) "has driving made any impact on your life and wellbeing?" 2) "what were the advantages or otherwise of driving yourself?" 3) "when you were not driving yourself, did you encounter any challenge you would want to talk about?" 4) "would you say life is better compared to when you were nor driving."

The responses were recorded and transcribed by one of the researchers. The transcriptions were then sent to the subject to confirm whether they represented the true expressions of his thoughts.

3 Results

The subject is a 37 year old male polio survivor. The past medical history was consistent with the clinical presentation at the time of this study, the polio said to have occurred during the epidemic of the 80s. The bilateral lower limbs were affected presenting with paraplegia: the muscle power grades in the lower limbs were grossly 0 with no flicker of movements in the large muscles of the limbs, while the upper limb muscles grades were grossly 5 on the Oxford Muscle Grading System. For him to maintain upright standing and stability, the subject donned a pair of above-the-knee calipers. The calipers had hinges at the knee region to allowing flexion and extension movements at the knee. He also used a pair of elbow crutches for ambulation (four-point gait) adopting a bilateral waddling gait.

3.1 Self-esteem and HRQOL

The pre-driving self-esteem and Health Related Quality of Life (HRQOL) scores were lower compared to the respective post-driving self-esteem and HRQOL scores.

3.2 Direct Interview

The main purpose of the direct interview was to elicit qualitative narration on the challenges of inability to drive, the desire for driving and the perceived benefits of driving. Quoting the subject's direct response to some of the questions:

"… growing up I have come to accept the things I'm not able to do, although often times I might just find a way around. For example, I discovered that I won't be able to play with my legs so I decided to become a goalkeeper when I was pretty young". Nevertheless, I had always believed that activities like driving were beyond my reach. I considered myself a burden to those who had to take me around. Worst still, I must depend on others' schedule, having to fit my plans into theirs, since I required them to drive me around." The option of public transport was raised, and in his words *"Public transport was not safe and easy to come by: the experience of falling off a motorcycle was both demeaning and dangerous; cabs and taxis did not want to pick me because of the time it would take to board and alight from their vehicles".*

He, however, admitted that he had several loving people who were always ready to chauffeur him around.

The game changer was when he decided to undertake a postgraduate programme.

"I knew it would not 'blend' well with my friends' schedules and others who drove me around. We therefore decided, at that point, to look for a way out."

The need to drive was compelling in order to be able to attend classes and keep up with the rigour of the academic work required of him during the postgraduate programme. In his words.

"there was no one who would be able to keep up with the demands of driving me around except a paid driver. The schedule of lectures and clinical were flexible but unpredictable. I could not come to asking anyone to go through such trouble for me. It would have been insensitive on my part. And an affirmation that I am a burden on people."

With respect to the ability to drive on his own, "My joy knows no bound."

4 Discussion

The objective of this study was to describe the experience of outdoor mobility of an individual with late effects of polio living in Nigeria.

Unsurprisingly, the participant reported some kind of outdoor mobility problem which additionally affected his self-image, acceptance and overall quality of life. For example, he felt as though he was constantly struggling to fit in and be accepted. This is similar to what Gray et al. (2008) reported in their survey of environmental facilitators and barriers to participation by people with mobility impairments. They suggested that this group of people most often have mobility limitations [3].

Participant described one of the benefit of mobility as a facilitator rather than barrier for example he reported being able to take up additional money making opportunities. This partly agrees with the work [8] done among polio survivors in Sweden which assesses their outdoor mobility experiences. which reported that outdoor mobility could both be a facilitator and barrier For example, the use of mobility aids made both their disability and their decreased mobility function visible to others, something they experienced as harmful to their self-image. Similar perception was found in a recent study regarding mobility, where powered wheelchair users (different diagnoses) perceived the aid as an enabler for independence and activities but also that it impacted on their identity and self-esteem [9].

A theme that emerged in the interview of the participant is the importance of car in his live in order to maintain an active lifestyle with friends and family. Furthermore, by using a car, the participants felt less different from people without disabilities, which also increased their own self-esteem which confirms what has previously been reported [8–11].

Town planning in sub-saharan aimed at allowing citizen to move freely from one part to another with the appropriate transportation types or means requires modernization for people with physical disabilities to move freely like everyone else [10]. The participant reported some barriers ranging from difficulty in getting the appropriate means to individual refusing to stop and carry him, inaccessible bus stations and the level of acceptance of people with physical disability in the society. This is in tandem with the work of Sjodin et al. who recorded an interaction of human and environmental barriers as some of the barriers which are common in Europe [6, 12].

Strengths and Limitations
A strength of the present study was the use of a qualitative design which made it possible to enable a better understanding of outdoor mobility and the role of car in the life of polio survivors. However, the unavailability large sample size serves as weakness to this study.

5 Conclusions

Independent mobility is a major enabler for improved self esteem and being able to use a car increases the chances for integration into society for individual with late effects of polio. Driving can prevent involuntary isolation, facilitate participation and improve self esteem. An independent driving can improve the overall quality of life of individual with late effect of polio.

References

1. Bohlke, K., Davis, R.L., Marcy, S.M., Braun, M.M., DeStefano, F., Black, S.B., Mullooly, J.P., Thompson, R.S.: Risk of anaphylaxis after vaccination of children and adolescents. Pediatrics **112**, 815–820 (2003)
2. Cohen, J.I.: Enteroviruses and retroviruses. In: Kasper, D.L., Braunwald, E., Fauci, A.S. (eds.) Harrison's Principles of Internal Medicine, 16th edn, pp. 1144–1146. McGraw-Hill Professional, New York (2004)
3. Gray, D.B., Hollingsworth, H.H., Stark, S., Morgan, K.A.: A subjective measure of environmental facilitators and barriers to participation for people with mobility limitations. Disabil. Rehabil. **30**(6), 434–457 (2008). pmid: 17943511
4. Brogardh, C., Lexell, J.: How various self-reported impairments influence walking ability in persons with late effects of polio. NeuroRehabilitation **37**, 291–298 (2015)
5. Martha, T.M.: Rethinking equality and difference: disability discrimination in public transportation. Yale Law J. **97**, 863–880 (1988)
6. Oxley, J., Whelan, M.: It cannot be all about safety: the benefits of prolonged mobility. Traffic Inj. Prev. **9**(4), 367–378 (2008). pmid: 18696394
7. Stressel, D., Hegberg, A., Dickerson, A.E.: Driving for adults with acquired physical disabilities. Occup. Ther. Health Care **28**, 148–153 (2014)
8. Selander, H., Silva, I.S.T., Kjellgren, F., Sunnerhagen, K.S.: "The car is my extra legs" – experiences of outdoor mobility amongst immigrants in Sweden with late effects of polio, 31 October 2019. https://doi.org/10.1371/journal.pone.0224685
9. Labbé, D., Mortenson, B., Rushton, P.W., Demers, L., Miller, W.C.: Mobility and participation among ageing powered wheelchair users: using a lifecourse approach. Ageing Soc. 1–17 (2018)
10. Zeilig, G., Weingarden, H., Shemesh, Y.: Functional and environmental factors affecting work status in individuals with longstanding poliomyelitis. J. Spinal Cord Med. **35**, 22–27 (2012)
11. Agyemang, F., Morrison, N.: Recognising the barriers to securing affordable housing through the land use planning system in Sub-Saharan Africa: a perspective from Ghana. Urban Stud. **55**. 004209801772409 (2017). https://doi.org/10.1177/0042098017724092
12. Sjödin, L., Buchanan, A., Mundt, B., Karlsson, E., Falkmer, T.: Do vehicle grants and vehicle adaptations grants promote transport mobility and community access for children with disabilities in Sweden? Aust. Occup. Ther. J. **59**(1), 10–16 (2012). pmid: 22272878

Disability and Community Reintegration Among Community Dwelling Persons Living with Stroke, Spinal Cord Injury and Limb Amputation – A Comparative Study

Echezona Nelson Dominic Ekechukwu[1,2,3](✉) , Chinwendu Obi Nwokocha[1],
Blessing Chiagozikam Atuenyi[1], Antoninus Obinna Ezeukwu[1] ,
and Olumide Olasunkanmi Dada[4,5]

[1] Department of Medical Rehabilitation, Faculty of Health Sciences and Technology,
College of Medicine, University of Nigeria, Nsukka, Nigeria
nelson.ekechukwu@unn.edu.ng
[2] Occupational and Environmental Health Unit, Institute of Public Health, College of Medicine,
University of Nigeria, Nsukka, Nigeria
[3] LANCET Physiotherapy, Wellness and Research Centre, Enugu, Nigeria
[4] Department of Physiotherapy, Faculty of Clinical Sciences, College of Medicine,
University of Ibadan, Ibadan, Nigeria
[5] University College Hospital, Ibadan, Ibadan, Nigeria

Abstract. People living with disabilities (PLwD) experience limitations in their functional performance and reintegration into the community. Stroke survivors (SS), persons with spinal cord injuries (SCI) and amputees are the commonly encountered community dwelling persons with disabilities in Nigeria. There appear to be no study that has compared the functional potentials (FP) and community reintegration (CR) among community dwelling SS, SCI and limb amputees (LA). This study described and compared the level of functional potential and community reintegration among SS, SCI and amputees. Sixty (60) community dwelling PLwD (SS = 20, SCI = 20, LA = 20) participated in this study. Their functional potential (FP) and level of community reintegration (CR) were assessed using Barthel Index and Reintegration to Normal Living Index respectively. Data was analyzed descriptively, and with one way ANOVA. The level of significance was set at $\alpha = 0.05$. The participants' age ranged from 21 to 74 (51.25 ± 14.50) years, with mean scores of FP and CR of 58.83 ± 27.61 and 22.32 ± 3.98 respectively. There was a significant difference in FP (F = 107.80, p < 0.001) and CR (F = 8.03, p = 0.001) across the three groups. The pair-wise post-hoc comparison of FP revealed significant difference between SS > SCI (MD = 49.25, p < 0.001), LA > SCI (MD = 53.73, p < 0.0001) only. Similarly, the pair-wise post-hoc comparison of CR revealed significant SS > SCI (MD = 3.90, p = 0.003), significant LA > SCI (MD = 3.95, p = 0.003) only. PLWD (SS, SCI and LA) have a low FP and CR. Persons with SCI have the least FP and CR, while LA have the highest FP and CR among these cohorts.

Keywords: Disability · Community reintegration · Stroke · Spinal cord injury · Amputation

© The Author(s), under exclusive license to Springer Nature Switzerland AG 2022
N. L. Black et al. (Eds.): IEA 2021, LNNS 223, pp. 487–494, 2022.
https://doi.org/10.1007/978-3-030-74614-8_63

1 Introduction

According to World Health Organization [1], disability is the restriction in the ability to perform activities of daily living or inability to function independently in terms of basic activities of daily living or instrumental activities of daily living. There are different types of physical disabilities that affect an individual, common among which are spinal cord injuries, amputations, stroke and so forth. Research has shown that disability generally results in poor physical function, physical role performance and general health. Disability may impact negatively on mobility, emotion and social function. People with disability will experience a wide range of activity limitation and participation restriction which may affect their ability to participate in activities of daily living as well as their reintegration into the community.

One of the leading causes of disability is stroke [2]. Many people who have had a stroke live with physical and psychological problems and may also experience participation restriction [3]. This is also true for patients with spinal cord injury [4], and amputation [5]. Participation restriction is the problem an individual may experience in the involvement in life situations [6]. People with disability usually experience a wide range of activity limitation and participation restriction which may affect their ability to return to and maintain work, maintain social relationship, participate in leisure activities and be active member of the community; these collectively are regarded as community reintegration [7].

Research has shown that disability generally results in poor physical function, physical role performance and general health [8–10]. Disability may impact negatively on mobility and social function, thus people with disability may experience a wide range of activity limitation and participation restriction which may culminate in decreased functional potential and community reintegration [11]. It remains to be known, however, the level of functional potential and community reintegration of a mixed group of people with disability. We sought therefore, to assess and compare the level of functional potential and community reintegration among community dwelling persons living with stroke, spinal cord injury and limb amputation.

2 Methods

2.1 Participants

Community dwelling persons living with disabilities post stroke, spinal cord injury or limb amputation were recruited into this cross-sectional exploratory study using quota and snow-balling techniques. Community dwelling persons with multiple disabilities (e.g. a limb amputee with spinal cord injury) were excluded from the study.

2.2 Sample Size

Minimum Sample size was calculated using the population standard deviation effect. A minimum of 58 participants (stroke survivors = 19, persons with SCI = 19, limb amputee = 19) was derived from the calculation using a standard variate (Z) at 95% CI of 1.96, standard deviation (σ) of population estimated from Billinger et al. [12], of 3.9 and using a precision (e) of 2.21. However, a total of 60 participants (stroke survivors = 20, persons with SCI = 20, limb amputees = 20) completed this study.

2.3   Materials

2.3.1   Barthel Index [13]

The Barthel Index of Activities of Daily Living (BI) has been in use since 1955 [13]. It is used to quantify the ability of a patient with a neuromuscular or musculoskeletal disorder to care for him/herself (regardless of particular diagnostic designations). It is, perhaps, the most widely used measure of functional disability. The Barthel index is very simple, consisting of 10 common activities of daily living (ADL) activities, administered through direct observation. Eight of the ten items represent activities related to personal care; the remaining two are related to mobility. The index yields a total score out of 100 – the higher the score, the greater the degree of functional independence [14]. The Barthel index can take as little as 2–5 min to complete by self-report and up to 20 min by direct observation [15].

2.3.2   Reintegration to Normal Living Index (RNLI) [16]

RNLI was used to measure community reintegration of the participants. The RNLI is an 11-item instrument questionnaire developed to measure how people living with chronic conditions (like SCI) perceive and/or are satisfied with their participation in the society in terms of functional activities of daily life, social and recreational activities, and interactions with people. To score the RNLI, participants are asked to rate on a 4 point (1–4) scale how much they agreed with the various RNLI statements. The total scores range from 11–44. The scores for the items were reversed and summed, with higher scores indicating greater community reintegration.

2.3.3   Ethical Consideration

Ethical approval was sought and obtained from the Health Research Ethics Committee of the University of Nigeria Teaching Hospital, Enugu, Nigeria. Participants were informed about the research and duly signed informed consent obtained before their participation in the study.

2.3.4   Procedure

The study commenced after obtaining ethical approval from the Medical and Ethics Committee of the University of Nigeria Teaching Hospital. Informed consents of participants were obtained after ensuring that they have met the eligibility criteria. The participants' demographic details were recorded using a bio-data proforma. The various outcome measures as itemized above were then given randomly to the participants to so as to avoid data setting. The filled outcome measures were then retrieved from the participants. At the end of the data collection phase, all the filled outcome measures were prepared for data extraction and analysis.

2.3.5 Data Analysis

Data obtained were analysed descriptively using frequency and percentage, mean and standard deviation. Also, inferentially, one way ANOVA was used to compare functional potential and community reintegration across the groups while post-hoc Bonferoni test was performed to accentuate pair-wise comparisons in areas with significant difference. Level of statistical significance was set at $\alpha = 0.05$.

3 Results

A total of 60 community dwelling persons with physical disability participated in this study. They were equally distributed across the three groups of disability (20 amputees, 20 stroke survivors and 20 spinal cord injured patients). The participants' age ranged from 21 to 74 years, with a mean age of 51.25 ± 14.50 years.

The total mean scores of all the participants' functional potential and community reintegration were 58.83 ± 27.61 and 22.32 ± 3.98 respectively. The participants with limb amputation had higher levels of functional potential and community reintegration respectively (78.25 ± 9.36 & 23.65 ± 3.67) than the stroke survivors (73.75 ± 16.61 & 23.60 ± 4.38) and those with spinal cord injury (24.50 ± 11.46 & 19.70 ± 2.39). There was a significant difference in functional potential ($F = 107.80$, $p < 0.001$) and community reintegration ($F = 8.03$, $p = 0.001$) across the three groups as shown in Table 1.

The post-hoc analysis revealed that the significant difference in functional potential across the three groups laid in the pair-wise comparison between the groups with stroke and spinal cord injury ($MD = 49.25$, $p < 0.001$) as well as between the groups with spinal cord injury and limb amputation ($MD = -49.25$, $p < 0.001$). Also, the significant difference in community reintegration was found between the groups with stroke and spinal cord injury ($MD = 3.90$, $p = 0.003$) as well as between the groups with spinal cord injury and limb amputation ($MD = -3.95$, $p = 0.003$) as shown in Table 2.

Table 1. Comparison of Functional Potential and Community Reintegration of Community Dwelling Persons with Disability (N = 60)

Variables	Total (n = 60)	SS (n = 20)	SCI (n = 20)	LA (n = 20)	F	p
Functional Potential (x/100)	58.83 ± 27.61	$73.75 \pm 16,61$	24.50 ± 11.46	78.25 ± 9.36	107.80	<0.001*
Community Reintegration (x/44)	23.32 ± 3.98	23.60 ± 4.38	19.70 ± 2.39	23.65 ± 3.67	8.03	0.001*

Key: SS = Stroke Survivors; SCI = Spinal Cord Injury; LA = Limb Amputees; * = Significant

Table 2. Post-Hoc Pair-wise Comparison (Bonferoni) of Functional Potential and Community Reintegration across Groups (N = 60)

Variables	Types	MD	Significance
Functional potential	SS – SCI	49.25	<0.001*
	SS – LA	−4.5	0.818
	SCI – LA	−49.25	<0.001*
Community reintegration	SS – SCI	3.90	0.003*
	SS – LA	−0.05	0.965
	SCI – LA	−3.95	0.003*

Key: SS = Stroke Survivors; SCI = Spinal Cord Injury; LA = Limb Amputees; MD = Mean Difference; * = Significant

4 Discussion

Physical disability encumbers functional activities as well as social participation that may result in problems of reintegrating fully well into the society post injuries or ailments. Ergonomics plays a crucial role in the tertiary prevention of these problems in persons with disability through participatory ergonomics programme (PEP), inclusive designing, return to work/driving programme etc. An important element in PEP from the perspective of a neuroergonomist is the understanding that activity limitation and participation restriction differences exist when comparing heterogeneous groups of community dwelling individuals with physical disabilities [17]. Activity limitations and participation restriction as a result of neurological impairments such as spinal cord injury may differ markedly from those due to musculoskeletal impairment like limb amputation. This knowledge is therefore helpful in setting up both macro- and micro-ergonomics interventions for these cohorts. This study assessed and compared the functional potentials and community reintegration of community dwelling persons with limb amputation, spinal cord injury and stroke.

Generally, the participants in this study had reduced functional potential and community reintegration (about 50% of the expected maximum scores). The descriptive result however revealed that the participants with spinal cord injury had the least scores in these variables while those with limb amputation had the highest. The Sinoff's guidelines for the interpretation of the (Barthel index) used in this study to assess functional potential defined scores between 20 and 39 (reported among the participants with spinal cord injury) as being very dependent, while scores between 60 and 79 (reported among participants with spinal cord injury and stroke) are interpreted as being minimally dependent [18]. There was a significant difference in functional potential across the three groups; the participants with spinal cord injury had significantly lower functional potential than those with stroke and limb amputation but not between participants with stroke and those with limb amputation. Spinal cord injury is neurological condition that affects the sensory [19], motor [20], and autonomic nervous systems [21].

Sensory signals from the body is transmitted through peripheral sensory nerves to the spinal cord, where they are carried by ascending tracts (eg spinothalamic tracts or dorsal column – medial leminiscal pathway) in the spinal cord that also transverses the brainstem before reaching the thalamus (the ventro-postero-lateral nucleus) and fan out to the sensory cortex in the postcentral gyrus. The clinical significance of this is that an injury to the spinal cord eg a complete cord transaction or injury to the funniculi (dorsal or anterolateral), signals carried by the sensory nerve are abolished from getting to the sensory cortex and are therefore not interpreted (sensory loss). These sensory impairments reduce functional potential. For example proprioceptive or nociceptive impairments can result in joint or tissue damage. Although stroke is also a neurological disorder usually due to focal disruption of brain tissue perfusion, it rarely affects the sensory apparatus except in few cases of thalamic stroke or blood disruption to the post-central gyrus. Comparatively, in persons with limb amputation, only affects the peripheral sensory signals from the non-existing limb is lost, function can however be compensated for or carried out by the other limb(s).

Similarly, the motor impairments in spinal cord injury results mainly from the affectation of the descending tracts (eg corticospinal tract - CST) in cases of complete cord transaction or injury to the anterior horn. Also, the sensory loss (eg proprioception) contributes also to motor impairments as a result of perceptual deficits that ought to be relied upon for motor programming and execution. Motor impairments post-stroke usually present as hemiplegia or hemiparesis unlike SCI that can present with tetraplegia. Therefore, the unaffected side of a stroke survivor can be relied upon to compensate for the affected side, thus less functional disability compared to persons with SCI. Persons with limb amputation as explained above also have less functional limitation when compared with individuals with SCI; more so if it is a high level, complete cord transaction. Community dwelling persons with SCI rely heavily on assistive devices that are in reality not available especially in rural communities. Only 5–10% of persons with SCI in low and middle income countries like Nigeria have access to assistive devices [22]. This lack of assistive devices further compounds the functional disability of community dwelling persons with spinal cord injury.

The disruption of the interaction between supraspinal centres (eg brainstem) and the spinal autonomic components seen most traumatic spinal cord injuries result in several autonomic abnormalities such as compromised urinary, thermoregulatory, GIT, respiratory, cardiovascular and sexual activities [23]. Although autonomic dysreflexia may sometimes characterize certain types of stroke, its consequences are not as pronounced as in high level traumatic SCI. Limb amputation compared with the other two conditions appears to have the least autonomic consequences. It is pertinent to note that these autonomic dysregulation that characterizes most SCI have its psychological consequences such as anxiety, depression and emotional disturbances that further deteriorates functionality and quality of life in persons with SCI.

Community reintegration is a positively correlated with functional potential [24]. This may explain the significantly lower level of community reintegration seen in the group with spinal cord injury compared to the other two groups. Just as production is incomplete until the goods and services gets to the hands of the final consumers; so also, is neurological rehabilitation incomplete until the patient is reintegrated into the society. Therefore this finding poses a great challenge on rehabilitation of persons with disabilities, more so, those with spinal cord injury to improve their functional potential with a view to reintegrating them faster into their communities. Also, ergonomist especially neuroergonomists should be advocates for environmental accessibly, disability-friendly designs (inclusive design), system thinking etc.

5   Conclusion

The functional potential and community reintegration of stroke survivors, persons with limb amputation and spinal cord injury are low. Community dwelling persons with spinal cord injury suffer greater disabilities than stroke survivors and those with limb amputation. Efforts should be made at reducing these disabilities.

References

1. World Health Organization: What are the main risk factor for disability in old age and how can disability be prevented (2003)
2. Petrea, R.E., Beiser, A.S., Seshadri, S., Kelly-Hayes, M., Kase, C.S., Wolf, P.A.: Gender differences in stroke incidence and poststroke disability in the Framingham heart study. Stroke **40**(4), 1032–1037 (2009)
3. Hamzat, T.K., Ekechukwu, N.E., Olaleye, A.O.: Comparison of community reintegration and selected stroke specific characteristics in Nigerian male and female stroke survivors. Afr. J. Physiother. Rehabil. Sci. **6**(1–2), 27–31 (2014)
4. Ekechukwu, E.N., Ikrechero, J.O., Ezeukwu, A.O., Egwuonwu, A.V., Umar, L., Badaru, U.M.: Determinants of quality of life among community-dwelling persons with spinal cord injury: a path analysis. Nigerian J. Clin. Pract. **20**(2), 163–169 (2017)
5. Yu, T.W., Ennion, L.: Participation restrictions and vocational rehabilitation needs experienced by persons with a unilateral lower limb amputation in the Western Cape, South Africa. Afr. J. Disabil. (Online) **8**, 1–7 (2019)
6. World Health Organization. Towards a common language for functioning, disability and health ICF (2002). https://www.who.int/classifications/icf/icfbeginnersguide.pdf. Accessed Feb 2021
7. Belanger, P.: Community reintegration. Rehabil. Trauma. Brain Injury **24**, 255 (2018)
8. Hamzat, T.H., Ekechukwu, N.E.: Aerobic exercise training in stroke rehabilitation: any gap in knowledge. Nigerian J. Med. Rehabil. (2015)
9. Ekechukwu, E.N., Olowoyo, P., Nwankwo, K.O., Olaleye, O.A., Ogbodo, V.E., Hamzat, T.K., Owolabi, M.O.: Pragmatic solutions for stroke recovery and improved quality of life in low-and middle-income countries—a systematic review. Front. Neurol. **11**, 337 (2020)
10. dos Santos, P.D., Silva, F.C., Sousa, B.A., Pires, G.K., Iop, R.D., Ferreira, E.G., Silva, R.D.: Functionality and quality of life of children with disability. J. Hum. Growth Dev. **28**(2), 154–164 (2018)
11. Ekechukwu, N., Olaleye, O., Hamzat, T.: Clinical and psychosocial predictors of community reintegration of stroke survivors three months post in-hospital discharge. Ethiop. J. Health Sci. **27**(1), 27–34 (2017)
12. Billinger, S.A., Taylor, J.M., Quaney, B.M.: Cardiopulmonary response to exercise testing in people with chronic stroke: a retrospective study. Stroke Res. Treat. **2012** (2012)
13. Mahoney, F.I., Barthel, D.W.: Functional evaluation: the Barthel Index: a simple index of independence useful in scoring improvement in the rehabilitation of the chronically ill. Maryland State Med. J. (1965)

14. McDowell, I.: General health status and quality of life. Measuring Health: a guide to rating scales and questionnaires (1996)
15. Finch, E.: Physical rehabilitation outcome measures. A guide to enhanced clinical decision making, p. 64 (2002)
16. Stark, S.L., Edwards, D.F., Hollingsworth, H., Gray, D.B.: Validation of the reintegration to normal living index in a population of community-dwelling people with mobility limitations. Arch. Phys. Med. Rehabil. **86**(2), 344–345 (2005)
17. Dashner, J., Espin-Tello, S.M., Snyder, M., Hollingsworth, H., Keglovits, M., Campbell, M.L., Putnam, M., Stark, S.: Examination of community participation of adults with disabilities: comparing age and disability onset. J. Aging Health **31**(10_Suppl), 169S–194S (2019)
18. Sinoff, G., Ore, L.: The Barthel activities of daily living index: self-reporting versus actual performance in the old-old (≥75 years). J. Am. Geriatr. Soc. **45**(7), 832–836 (1997)
19. Zeilig, G., Enosh, S., Rubin-Asher, D., Lehr, B., Defrin, R.: The nature and course of sensory changes following spinal cord injury: predictive properties and implications on the mechanism of central pain. Brain **135**(2), 418–430 (2012)
20. Wrigley, P.J., Gustin, S.M., Macey, P.M., Nash, P.G., Gandevia, S.C., Macefield, V.G., Siddall, P.J., Henderson, L.A.: Anatomical changes in human motor cortex and motor pathways following complete thoracic spinal cord injury. Cereb. Cortex **19**(1), 224–232 (2009)
21. Taylor, J.A.: Autonomic consequences of spinal cord injury. Auton. Neurosci.: Basic Clin. **209**, 1–3 (2018)
22. World Health Organization: International Spinal Cord Society. International perspectives on spinal cord injury. World Health Organization (2013)
23. Hou, S., Rabchevsky, A.G.: Autonomic consequences of spinal cord injury. Compr. Physiol. **4**(4), 1419–1653 (2014)
24. Cohen, J.W., Ivanova, T.D., Brouwer, B., Miller, K.J., Bryant, D., Garland, S.J.: Do performance measures of strength, balance, and mobility predict quality of life and community reintegration after stroke? Arch. Phys. Med. Rehabil. **99**(4), 713–719 (2018)

Virtual Reality, a Neuroergonomic and Neurorehabilitation Tool for Promoting Neuroplasticity in Stroke Survivors: A Systematic Review with Meta-analysis

Echezona Nelson Dominic Ekechukwu[1,2,3](✉) (iD), Ikenna Collins Nzeakuba[1],
Olumide Olasunkanmi Dada[4] (iD), Kingsley Obumneme Nwankwo[5] (iD),
Paul Olowoyo[6] (iD), Victor Adimabua Utti[7] (iD), and Mayowa Ojo Owolabi[8,9,10] (iD)

[1] Department of Medical Rehabilitation, FHST, College of Medicine, University of Nigeria,
Nsukka, Nigeria
nelson.ekechukwu@unn.edu.ng
[2] Environmental and Occupational Health Unit, Institute of Public Health, College of Medicine,
University of Nigeria, Nsukka, Nigeria
[3] LANCET Physiotherapy Wellness and Research Centre, Enugu, Nigeria
[4] Department of Physiotherapy, Faculty of Clinical Sciences, College of Medicine,
University of Ibadan, Ibadan, Nigeria
[5] Stroke Control Innovations Initiative of Nigeria, Abuja, Nigeria
[6] Department of Medicine, Federal Teaching Hospital, Ido Ekiti, Nigeria
[7] University of Essex, Colchester, UK
[8] Center for Genomic and Precision Medicine, College of Medicine, University of Ibadan,
Ibadan, Nigeria
[9] University College Hospital, Ibadan, Ibadan, Nigeria
[10] Blossom Specialist Medical Centre, Ibadan, Nigeria

Abstract. Virtual Reality (VR) is an emerging neuroergonomics tool for stroke rehabilitation. It can be employed to promote post-stroke recovery during rehabilitation as a result of its neuroplasticity enhancing effects. This study systematically reviewed and meta-synthesised evidence on the effectiveness of virtual reality on selected markers of neuroplasticity among stroke survivors (SSv). The databases searched were PEDro, CINHAL, the Cochrane Library, and PUBMed using combinations of Medical subject heading (MeSH) terms and keywords in the titles, abstracts and text for the population, intervention and major outcome (PICO format). The studies included were randomized clinical trials that compared the effects VR among adult SSv. The PEDro scale was used for quality appraisal of the included studies. Forest plot (RevMan version 5.3) was used for the metasynthesis of the results, level of significance was set at $\alpha = 0.05$. A total of 6 studies were included in the meta-analysis (involving 441 stroke survivors). The pooled effects on the improvement in motor function (SMD $= -1.05$; CI $= -1.53, -0.56$, Z $= 4.22$, p < 0.0001, I2 $= 93\%$) and balance performance (SMD $= -3.06$; CI $= -3.80, -2.32$, Z $= 8.11$, p < 0.0001, I2 $= 94\%$) was significantly in the favour of VR. There is evidence that virtual reality is an effective neuroergonomics modality for encouraging neuroplasticity through its effects on the motor function, balance and muscle strength of stroke survivors.

© The Author(s), under exclusive license to Springer Nature Switzerland AG 2022
N. L. Black et al. (Eds.): IEA 2021, LNNS 223, pp. 495–508, 2022.
https://doi.org/10.1007/978-3-030-74614-8_64

Keywords: Virtual reality · Neuroergonomics · Neurorehabilitation · Neuroplasticity

1 Introduction

Stroke is the major cause of disability worldwide, with a high social-economic impact [1, 2]. One out of every four stroke cases is fatal and between 25 to 50% of the survivors requires a rehabilitative treatment [3, 4]. The World Health Organization reported that 15 million people globally experience a stroke annually [5]. Of these, 5 million die and another 5 million are left permanently disabled, placing a burden on family and community. Stroke affects about 62 million people worldwide [6], and is the second leading cause of death and the third leading contributor to burden of disease globally [6–8].

Stroke rehabilitation is complex, long lasting and expensive and its functional outcome is influenced not only by the brain lesion site and extension, but also by medical, demographic and neuropsychologic factors. Neurorehabilitation after a stroke is valued highly by patients, and studies have shown a strong evidence for its effectiveness [2, 9–11]. There are various models of neurorehabilitation techniques available for the management of stroke patients. The two conventional models commonly described are rehabilitation through facilitation like Bobath technique and the motor re-learning model [8]. There are other specific neurorehabilitation techniques for which systematic reviews are available, they include constraint induced movement therapy (in which the unaffected arm is immobilised for few hours each day in order to encourage learned use of the affected arm), body-weight supported treadmill training and other aerobic exercise training [7]. Stroke recovery and management requires neurorehabilitation techniques that enhances neuroplasticity. Current trend and studies have shown a transitioning from these conventional therapies to neuro-engineering models. Such emerging approaches to stroke rehabilitation include virtual reality, motor imagery and robotics [8].

Virtual reality is a new technology that simulates a three-dimensional virtual world on a computer and enables the generation of visual, audio, and haptic feedback for the full immersion of users [12]. Users of virtual reality can interact with and observe objects in three-dimensional visual space without limitation. Virtual reality is a neuroergonomic tool [13], capable of enhancing neuroplasticity/learning [14], thus supporting its use in neurorehabilitation. At present, virtual reality training has been widely used in rehabilitation of balance dysfunction [15]. When patients perform virtual reality training, the prefrontal, parietal cortical areas and other motor cortical networks are activated [16]. Growing evidence from clinical studies reveals that virtual reality training improves the neurological function of patients with spinal cord injury [17], cerebral palsy [18], and other neurological impairments [19–21]. These findings suggest that virtual reality training can activate the cerebral cortex and improve the spatial orientation capacity of patients, thus facilitating the cortical control on balance and improved motor functioning in stroke patients.

Literature appears unsettled with regards to the effects of virtual reality on the health outcomes of stroke survivors. While the study by Wang et al. reported significant beneficial effects of virtual reality in improving motor function of stroke survivors [22], the study by Brunner et al. reported a non-significant effect [23]. When literature becomes shrouded with conflicting reports from primary studies, systematic reviews can be used to provide superior evidence [24]. This study therefore systematically reviewed the evidences from randomised clinical trials on the effects of virtual reality in the rehabilitation of post-stroke patients.

2 Methods

2.1 Design

A systematic review with meta-analysis of randomized controlled trials on the effects of virtual reality on functional outcome of stroke survivors.

2.2 Inclusion Criteria

Types of Studies: Original research manuscripts in peer-reviewed journals published in English Language were included. Only randomized control trials that evaluated the effects of virtual reality on functional outcomes of stroke survivors were included.

Types of Participants: The participants in the primary studies were adults of any gender with a clinically diagnosed incidence of stroke.

Types of Intervention: Only studies whose primary aim was to determine the effects of virtual reality as an intervention for stroke rehabilitation were included.

Types of Outcome Measures: Studies involving any of post stroke functional outcome measures such as barthel index, functional independence measure, Fugl-Meyer assessment scale etc.

2.3 Information Sources

An extensive search strategy to recognize studies that can be used for the review was grouped into the search of bibliographic database and grey literature and eligibility criteria system of study inclusion. This procedure was created in accordance with the rules of the Cochrane Handbook of systematic reviews of intervention [25]. And advice for Healthcare review by the centre for reviews and dissemination [26].

Search Strategy: An extensive study strategy created to search bibliographic databases and grey literature that involved several combinations of search terms from Medical subject Heading (MeSH) terms and keywords in the titles, abstracts and text for the population, intervention and major outcome measures first in a pilot search to establish sensitivity and specificity of the search strategy. A host of commands which included the use of Boolean logic and search truncations was employed for the searches. There were modification of the strategy to suit the syntax and subject heading of the databases. The databases for the search were PEDro, CINHAL, the Cochrane Library, and PUBMed. Trial register and directory of open-access repository websites including https://www.clinicaltrial.gov, https://www.opendor.org and the web of science conference proceedings were also searched. Additionally, hand search was done from the reference list of identified studies and suggested articles.

Study Record and Data Management: Search results were exported to Ref works to check for duplication of studies. Bibliographic records were exported from Ref works into Microsoft Excel (Microsoft 2010) to facilitate articles inclusion and exclusion. On the basis of inclusion criteria, eligibility review questions and structures for the studies, considerations to the two levels of eligibility assessment were produced, piloted and refined when appropriate.

Selection Process: The eligibility criteria were liberally applied at the beginning to ensure that relevant studies were included and that no study was excluded without thorough evaluation. At the outset, studies were only excluded if they clearly met one or more of the exclusion criteria. Screening was conducted online simultaneously on the title and abstract by two reviewers to identify potentially relevant studies. Each reviewer cross-checked the initial screening results of the other. The two reviewers then read through the full text of selected studies for further screening (using the prior eligibility criteria). Differences of opinions occurring at any stage regarding inclusion or exclusion were resolved by discussion and reflection, in consultation with a third reviewer if warranted. When decision could not be made based on available information, study authors were contacted (to the maximum of three email attempts) to clarify issues of selection of any study. Studies were excluded and the reasons for exclusion were recorded when authors fail to respond to requests for clarifications on unclear issues regarding their reports. Details of the flow of studies throughout the process of assessment of eligibility and study selection were presented, along with the reasons for exclusion in a flow chart (PRISMA diagram).

2.4   Data Collection Processes

Quality Appraisal for Included Studies: The quality of the selected studies were assessed using the Physiotherapy Evidence Database (PEDro) quality appraisal tool. The PEDro is an eleven-item scale in which the first item relates to external validity and the other ten items assess the internal validity of a clinical trial. One point is given for each satisfied criterion (except for the first item) yielding a maximum score of 10. The higher the score, the better the quality of the study and the following grades were used: 9–10 (excellent); 6–8 (good); 4–5 (fair); <4 (poor). A point for a particular criterion was awarded only if the article explicitly reported that the criterion was met. A score of one was given for each yes answer and zero for no, unclear and not applicable (N/A) answers. The overall score was reported as a tally of all yes answers out of 10 based on the applicable answers for each study. Scores of individual items from the critical appraisal tool were added to present the total score.

Data Synthesis and Assessment of Heterogeneity: The Research question on the overall effects of virtual reality on the functional outcomes of stroke survivors were asked and answers attempted and appropriate statistical method was used. Given that the variables were on the ratio scale (continuous variable), weighted mean difference was used when outcomes were consistent or standard mean differences when there was the existence of variation in outcomes with a confidence interval of 95%. Meta-analysis was done whenever two or more studies existed that assessed similar outcomes using similar intervention. This was done to determine the pooled effect sizes across studies using a random effect model and relying on the level of heterogeneity of the outcomes. Assessment of heterogeneity was done via the Cochrane Chi-square test (10% significant level) and Higgins I^2 for which values of 25%, 50% and 75% were interpreted as low, medium and high heterogeneity respectively as stipulated by the guidance on the Cochrane Handbook for Systematic Reviews of interventions [25].

2.5 Data Analysis

Investigation and presentation of outcomes were made using the main outcome. Studies that were homogenous in study design, intervention and control were pooled together for meta-analysis using a random effect model [25]. Appropriate statistical techniques were used for each type of continuous (weighted mean differences if outcomes are consistent or standard mean difference if different outcomes were used, with 95% CI). Interpretation of studies that are heterogeneous was done by narrative synthesis following the guideline of the Centre for Reviews and Dissemination to investigate the relationship and findings within and between the included studies [26]. Data analysis (Meta-analysis) was done using RevMan 5.3 software.

3   Results

3.1   Flow of Studies through the Review

The initial searches identified a number of potential relevant papers. The flow of papers through the process of assessment of eligibility is represented with reasons for exclusion of papers at each stage of the process as in Fig. 1.

3.2   Characteristics of Included Trials

A total of 5,496 articles were generated from the aforementioned search strategy (Fig. 1) while 5,490 articles were eliminated after reading the abstracts and titles. Only six studies that contributed data for 441 stroke survivors were finally included in this review (see Table 1). All and none of the studies had random and concealed allocations respectively as shown in Tables 2 and 3. Considering both the PEDro ratings and sample size used, one study provided level-1 evidence whereas the others were considered as level 2 studies as shown in Table 3.

3.3 Methodological Quality Appraisal

The methodological quality of the included trials ranged from fair to good, with a average PEDro score of 7.9. Two trials had methodologically good quality with scores ≥ 6. The individual PEDro items satisfied by almost all the trials were random allocation to groups and point estimates and variability data as shown in Table 2.

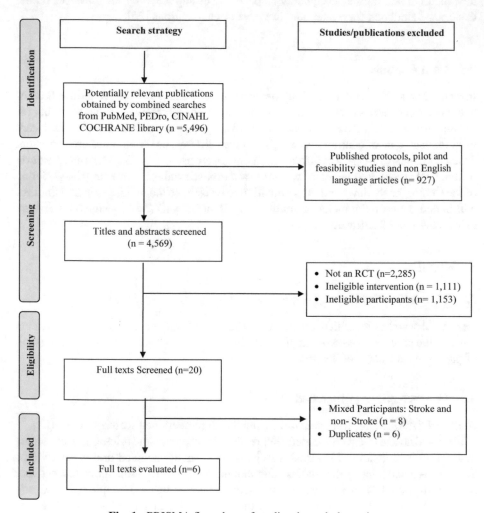

Fig. 1. PRISMA flow chart of studies through the review

3.4 Interventions

The major intervention used was exercise based virtual training. The most common exercise frequency and duration of time used was 3–5 days per week and 40–60 min per day, respectively. The most commonly prescribed treatment duration of the programme was ≥ 4 weeks as shown in Tables 1 and 4.

Table 1. Summary of study characteristics

| Study ID | n | Intervention | Intervention Parameters | | | Location | Outcome measures |
			Freq	Time	Duration		
Wang et al. [22]	26	VR	1 × 5	45 min	4wk	China	WMFT
Brunner et al. [23]	50	VR	1 × 5	60 min	4wk	Norway	ARAT
Kim et al. [27]	24	VR	1 × 3	40 min	4wk	korea	Balancia Software
Bang et al. [28]	40	VR	1 × 3	40 min	8wk	korea	Pedoscan
Park et al. [29]	30	VR	1 × 5	30 min	8wk	korea	BioRescue
Yang et al. [30]	14	VR	1 × 3	40 min	3wk	Taiwan	Footscan

Keys: n: number of participants, Freq: Frequency of treatment (session*days/week), VR: Virtual Reality, ARAT: Action reach arm test, WMFT: Wolf Motor Function Test

3.5 Outcome Measures

The Pedoscan, Biorescue, Footscan and Balancia Software were used to assess balance. Action reach arm test (ARAT) and Wolf motor function test (WMFT) were used in assessing motor function.

3.6 The Effect of Virtual Reality on Motor Function

The meta-analysis incorporated three trials that assessed motor function resulting in a total of 93 participants. There was a significant pooled effect ($Z = 4.22$, $p < 0.0001$) on motor function in favour of virtual reality group (SMD $= -1.05$; CI $= -1.53$, -0.56). The included studies were weakly homogenous ($X^2 = 27.63$, $I^2 = 93\%$) and a moderate risk of bias (42.8%). All the studies were however in favour of the experimental group as shown in Fig. 2.

3.7 The Effect of Virtual Reality on Balance Performance

The meta-analysis incorporated three trials that assessed balance performance resulting in a total of 87 participants. There was a significant pooled effect ($Z = 8.11$, $p < 0.0001$) on balance performance in favour of the virtual reality group (SMD $= -3.06$; CI $= -$ 3.80, -2.32). The included studies were strongly homogenous ($X^2 = 35.57$, $I^2 = 94\%$) and had a moderate risk of bias (57.1%). All the studies were in favour of virtual reality as shown in Fig. 3.

Table 2. Pedro quality appraisal of studies that investigated effect of aerobic exercise on diabetic health profile.

Study	Random allocation	Concealed allocation	Group similar at baseline	Participant blinding	Therapist blinding	Assessor blinding	<15% drop-outs	Intention to treat analysis	Between-group result reported	Point estimate & variability reported	Total
Wang et al. [22]	1	0	1	0	0	0	1	1	1	0	5
Brunner et al. [23]	1	0	1	0	0	0	1	1	1	1	6
Kim et al. [27]	1	0	1	0	0	0	0	1	1	0	4
Bang et al. [28]	1	0	0	0	0	0	1	1	1	0	4
Park et al. [29]	1	0	1	1	1	1	1	1	1	1	9
Yang et al. [30]	1	0	0	0	0	1	0	0	1	1	4

Key: 1 = yes; 2 = No

Table 3. Summary of quality and level of evidence of the studies

Methodological quality	Number of studies	%
Pedro rating criteria		
Random allocation to groups	6	100
Concealed allocation	0	0
Groups similar at baseline	4	66.7
Subject blinding	1	16.7
Therapist blinding	1	16.7
Assessor blinding	2	33.3
Less than 15% dropout	4	66.7
Intention to treat analysis	5	83.2
Btw groups statistics reported	6	100
Point estimates & variability data	2	33.3
Pedro total score		
Excellent (9–10)	1	16.7
Good (6–8)	1	16.7
Fair (4–5)	4	66.7
Poor (0–3)	0	0
Level of evidence		
Level 1	1	16.7
Level 2	5	83.3

Table 4. Summary of treatment protocols

Variables	Categories	N	%	Studies
Treatment time per session (mins)	<20	0	0	None
	21–30	2	33.3	27, 29
	31–40	1	16.7	28
	41–50	1	16.7	22
	51–60	2	33.3	23, 30
Number of treatment session per week	1–2	1	16.7	23
	3–5	6	100	22, 23, 27–30
	>5	0	0	None
Duration of treatment program (weeks)	1–3	1	16.7	30
	4–8	5	83.3	22, 23, 27–29

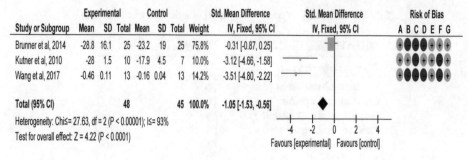

Study or Subgroup	Experimental Mean	SD	Total	Control Mean	SD	Total	Weight	Std. Mean Difference IV, Fixed, 95% CI
Brunner et al, 2014	-28.8	16.1	25	-23.2	19	25	75.8%	-0.31 [-0.87, 0.25]
Kutner et al, 2010	-28	1.5	10	-17.9	4.5	7	10.0%	-3.12 [-4.66, -1.58]
Wang et al, 2017	-0.46	0.11	13	-0.16	0.04	13	14.2%	-3.51 [-4.80, -2.22]
Total (95% CI)			48			45	100.0%	-1.05 [-1.53, -0.56]

Heterogeneity: Chi² = 27.63, df = 2 (P < 0.00001); I² = 93%
Test for overall effect: Z = 4.22 (P < 0.0001)

Risk of bias legend
(A) Random sequence generation (selection bias)
(B) Allocation concealment (selection bias)
(C) Blinding of participants and personnel (performance bias)
(D) Blinding of outcome assessment (detection bias)
(E) Incomplete outcome data (attrition bias)
(F) Selective reporting (reporting bias)
(G) Other bias

Fig. 2. Forest Plot for the Meta-analysis on the effects of Virtual Reality on Motor Function of stroke survivors

Study or Subgroup	Experimental Mean	SD	Total	Control Mean	SD	Total	Weight	Std. Mean Difference IV, Fixed, 95% CI
Bang et al, 2016	-5.8	1.35	20	-3.3	0.1	20	74.8%	-2.56 [-3.42, -1.70]
Kim et al, 2015	-0.13	0.07	10	0.08	0.05	7	22.7%	-3.18 [-4.73, -1.62]
Park et al, 2016	-78.7	0.1	15	-56.4	1.8	15	2.5%	-17.02 [-21.70, -12.34]
Total (95% CI)			45			42	100.0%	-3.06 [-3.80, -2.32]

Heterogeneity: Chi² = 35.57, df = 2 (P < 0.00001); I² = 94%
Test for overall effect: Z = 8.11 (P < 0.00001)

Risk of bias legend
(A) Random sequence generation (selection bias)
(B) Allocation concealment (selection bias)
(C) Blinding of participants and personnel (performance bias)
(D) Blinding of outcome assessment (detection bias)
(E) Incomplete outcome data (attrition bias)
(F) Selective reporting (reporting bias)
(G) Other bias

Fig. 3. Forest Plot for the Meta-analysis on the effects of Virtual Reality on Balance Performance of stroke survivors

4 Discussion

Virtual reality is an approach to user-computer interface that involves real-time simulation of an environment, scenario or activity that allows for user interaction via multiple sensory channels [31]. It creates sensory illusions that produce a more or less believable simulation of reality with the aim of fostering brain and behavioural responses in the virtual world that are analogous to those that occur in the real world [32]. VR simulations can be highly engaging, which provides crucial motivation for rehabilitative applications that require consistent, repetitive practice. Following damage to the brain as seen in stroke survivors, their ability to interact with the physical environment is diminished, thus compounding their disability. Virtual reality may potentially help reduce the burden of such physical limitations by providing an alternative, favourable environment in which to practice motor skills. It can be used to deliver meaningful and relevant stimulation to an individual's nervous system and thereby capitalise on the plasticity of the brain to promote motor learning and rehabilitation [33].

In this review, the use of virtual reality was found to be effective in promoting motor functional recovery among stroke survivors. It may be argued that motor plan is represented by the two premovement components [Negative Slope (NS) and Bereitschaft Potential (BP)] of the Motor Related Cortical Potential (MRCP) from an electroencephalogram (EEG) [34]. While the NS-wave (activity in the premotor area) which starts about 500 ms before the movement is believed to represent the urge to act, the BP (seen 1–3 s before the movement) is thought to reflect the early motor preparation (motor programme) in the supplementary motor (SM) area, as well as the superior and inferior parietal lobe [34–37]. Similar cerebral motor plans in the motor and pre-motor areas have been reported for real and virtual tasks actions [34]. It is therefore possible that virtual reality rehabilitation mimics the neural mechanisms of actual neurorehabilitation viz-a-viz the neuroplastic effects.

Virtual reality faccilitates the motor functional recovery of the paretic upper limb through neural reorganization. This can be clinically revealed by a functional magnetic resonance imaging (fMRI) scan that is capable of measuring the blood oxygen level dependent (BOLD) signal. Changes in both the location and level of the BOLD signal can reveal evidence of neuroplasticity [38]. In an RCT on the effects of Leap-Motion based virtual reality of motor functional recovery and cortical reorganization of subacute stroke survivors, Wang and his colleagues using an fMRI reported a shift in the activated motor area from the ipsilateral to contralateral motor area that was more obvious in the experimental groups [22]. This led to a significantly improved motor function compared with the control group that received conventional therapy. This change may be attributed to increased practice-induced neuroplasticity as a result of repetitive practice associated with virtual reality training and/or imitation-dependent neuroplasticity initiated in the virtual environment and carried out by the patient in the real world through mechanisms such as synaptic pruning, Hebbian mechanism, or long term potentiation (LTP) [37].

There was also a pooled significant improvement in the balance performance of stroke survivors in favour of virtual reality training [39]. The control of human balance is a comprehensive process relying on the integration of visual, vestibular and somatosensory inputs to the central nervous system. Balance performance can be therefore be affected by a dysfunction in the proprioceptors, muscle weakness, joint immobility and instability, pain or visual deficits; these impairments characterizes post-stroke morbidity. Balance as an outcome measure has been identified to be one of the key areas to be considered during stroke rehabilitation. About 70–80% of stroke patients experience a fall as a result of balance dysfunctions [30]. Virtual reality can be used to encourage long term potentiation of the vertibular cortext and its pathways for balance functioning through the visual feedback enhanced in a virtual environment; thus, "pathways that fire together, wire together". In an RCT to determine the effects of a community based virtual reality training on the balance performance of chronic stroke survivors, Kim et al. found that virtual reality significantly decreased the anterioposterior and total postural sway path lengths as well as the postural sway speed [27].

A major advantage of virtual reality training over conventional neurorehabilitation approach is adherence. Virtual reality is an entertaining, motivating and fun-therapy and thus encourages patient-participation, repetition, attention and enjoyment which are recipes for neuroplasticity. However, virtual reality is not without its own demerits. These include problems of availability, affordability, acceptability and adaptability especially in low and middle income countries where stroke morbidity and mortality is greatest.

5   Conclusion

Virtual reality is an effective neuroergonomic tool for the neurorehabilitation of stroke survivors by harnessing its neuroplastic effects.

References

1. Avan, A., Digaleh, H., Di Napoli, M., Stranges, S., Behrouz, R., Shojaeianbabaei, G., Amiri, A., Tabrizi, R., Mokhber, N., Spence, J.D., Azarpazhooh, M.R.: Socioeconomic status and stroke incidence, prevalence, mortality, and worldwide burden: an ecological analysis from the Global Burden of Disease Study 2017. BMC Med. **17**(1), 1–30 (2019)
2. Ekechukwu, E.N.D., Omotosho, I.O., Hamzat, T.K.: Comparative effects of interval and continuous aerobic training on haematological variables post-stroke–a randomized clinical trial. Afr. J. Physiother. Rehabil. Sci. **9**(1–2), 1–8 (2017)
3. Thrift, A.G., Thayabaranathan, T., Howard, G., Howard, V.J., Rothwell, P.M., Feigin, V.L., Norrving, B., Donnan, G.A., Cadilhac, D.A.: Global stroke statistics. Int. J. Stroke **12**(1), 13–32 (2017)
4. Ru, X., Dai, H., Jiang, B., Li, N., Zhao, X., Hong, Z., He, L., Wang, W.: Community-based rehabilitation to improve stroke survivors' rehabilitation participation and functional recovery. Am. J. Phys. Med. Rehabil. **96**(7), e123-9 (2017)
5. Someeh, N., Shamshirgaran, S.M., Farzipoor, F., Asghari-Jafarabadi, M.: The moderating role of underlying predictors of survival in patients with brain stroke: a statistical modeling. Sci. Rep. **10**(1), 1–9 (2020)
6. Queensland Brain Institute Stroke facts. https://qbi.uq.edu.au/brain/brain-diseases/stroke/stroke-facts. Accessed 04 Feb 2021
7. Ekechukwu, E.N.D., Olowoyo, P., Nwankwo, K.O., Olaleye, O.A., Ogbodo, V.E., Hamzat, T.K., Owolabi, M.O.: Pragmatic solutions for stroke recovery and improved quality of life in low-and middle-income countries—a systematic review. Front. Neurol. **25**(11), 337 (2020)

8. Owolabi, M.O., Platz, T., Good, D., Dobkin, B.H., Ekechukwu, E.N.D., Li, L.: Translating innovations in stroke rehabilitation to improve recovery and quality of life across the globe. Front. Neurol. **11** (2020)
9. Moradi, V., Hossein, M.A., Shariat, A., Cleland, J.A., Ansari, N.N., Savari, S.: Neurorehabilitation, the practical method of returning to work after stroke. Iranian J. Public Health (2021)
10. Lieshout, E.C.: Neurorehabilitation for upper limb recovery after stroke: the use of non-invasive brain stimulation (Doctoral dissertation, Utrecht University)
11. Anaya, M.A., Branscheidt, M.: Neurorehabilitation after stroke: from bedside to the laboratory and back. Stroke **50**(7), e180-2 (2019)
12. Gandhi, R.D., Patel, D.S.: Virtual reality–opportunities and challenges. Virtual Real. **5**(01) (2018)
13. Gramann, K., Fairclough, S.H., Zander, T.O., Ayaz, H.: Trends in neuroergonomics. Front. Hum. Neurosci. **5**(11), 165 (2017)
14. Eng, C.M., Calkosz, D.M., Yang, S.Y., Williams, N.C., Thiessen, E.D., Fisher, A.V.: Doctoral colloquium—enhancing brain plasticity and cognition utilizing immersive technology and virtual reality contexts for gameplay. In: 2020 6th International Conference of the Immersive Learning Research Network (iLRN), pp. 395–398. IEEE, 21 June 2020
15. Lei, C., Sunzi, K., Dai, F., Liu, X., Wang, Y., Zhang, B., He, L., Ju, M.: Effects of virtual reality rehabilitation training on gait and balance in patients with Parkinson's disease: a systematic review. PloS One **14**(11), e0224819 (2019)
16. Calabrò, R.S., Naro, A., Russo, M., Leo, A., De Luca, R., Balletta, T., Buda, A., La Rosa, G., Bramanti, A., Bramanti, P.: The role of virtual reality in improving motor performance as revealed by EEG: a randomized clinical trial. J. Neuroeng. Rehabil. **14**(1), 1–6 (2017)
17. Miguel-Rubio, D., Rubio, M.D., Salazar, A., Camacho, R., Lucena-Anton, D.: Effectiveness of virtual reality on functional performance after spinal cord injury: a systematic review and meta-analysis of randomized controlled trials. J. Clin. Med. **9**(7), 2065 (2020)
18. Ghai, S., Ghai, I.: Virtual reality enhances gait in cerebral palsy: a training dose-response meta-analysis. Front Neurol. **26**(10), 236 (2019)
19. Wang, B., Shen, M., Wang, Y.X., He, Z.W., Chi, S.Q., Yang, Z.H.: Effect of virtual reality on balance and gait ability in patients with Parkinson's disease: a systematic review and meta-analysis. Clin. Rehabil. **33**(7), 1130–1138 (2019)
20. Norouzi, E., Gerber, M., Pühse, U., Vaezmosavi, M., Brand, S.: Combined virtual reality and physical training improved the bimanual coordination of women with multiple sclerosis. Neuropsychol. Rehabil. **18**, 1–8 (2020)
21. Reynolds, L., Rodiek, S., Lininger, M., McCulley, M.A.: Can a virtual nature experience reduce anxiety and agitation in people with dementia? J. Housing Elderly **32**(2), 176–193 (2018)
22. Wang, Z.R., Wang, P., Xing, L., Mei, L.P., Zhao, J., Zhang, T.: Leap Motion-based virtual reality training for improving motor functional recovery of upper limbs and neural reorganization in subacute stroke patients. Neural Regeneration Res. **12**(11), 1823 (2017)
23. Brunner, I., Skouen, J.S., Hofstad, H., Aßmus, J., Becker, F., Sanders, A.M., Pallesen, H., Kristensen, L.Q., Michielsen, M., Thijs, L., Verheyden, G.: Virtual reality training for upper extremity in subacute stroke (VIRTUES): a multicenter RCT. Neurology **89**(24), 2413–2421 (2017)
24. Sylvester, R.J., Canfield, S.E., Lam, T.B., Marconi, L., MacLennan, S., Yuan, Y., MacLennan, G., Norrie, J., Omar, M.I., Bruins, H.M., Hernandez, V.: Conflict of evidence: resolving discrepancies when findings from randomized controlled trials and meta-analyses disagree. Eur. Urol. **71**(5), 811–819 (2017)
25. Higgins, J.P., Thomas, J., Chandler, J., Cumpston, M., Li, T., Page, M.J., Welch, V.A. (eds.) Cochrane Handbook for Systematic Reviews of Interventions. Wiley (2019)

26. Tacconelli, E.: Systematic reviews: CRD's guidance for undertaking reviews in health care. Lancet Infectious Dis. **10**(4), 226 (2010)
27. Kim, N., Park, Y., Lee, B.H.: Effects of community-based virtual reality treadmill training on balance ability in patients with chronic stroke. J. Phys. Ther. Sci. **27**(3), 655–658 (2015)
28. Bang, Y.S., Son, K.H., Kim, H.J.: Effects of virtual reality training using Nintendo Wii and treadmill walking exercise on balance and walking for stroke patients. J. Phys. Ther. Sci. **28**(11), 3112–3115 (2016)
29. Park, S.K., Yang, D.J., Uhm, Y.H., Heo, J.W., Kim, J.H.: The effect of virtual reality-based eccentric training on lower extremity muscle activation and balance in stroke patients. J. Phys. Ther. Sci. **28**(7), 2055–2058 (2016)
30. Yang, S., Hwang, W.H., Tsai, Y.C., Liu, F.K., Hsieh, L.F., Chern, J.S.: Improving balance skills in patients who had stroke through virtual reality treadmill training. Am. J. Phys. Med. Rehabil. **90**(12), 969–978 (2011)
31. Adamovich, S.V., Fluet, G.G., Tunik, E., Merians, A.S.: Sensorimotor training in virtual reality: a review. NeuroRehabilitation **25**(1), 29–44 (2009)
32. Bohil, C.J., Alicea, B., Biocca, F.A.: Virtual reality in neuroscience research and therapy. Nat. Rev. Neurosci. **12**(12), 752–762 (2011)
33. Weiss, P.L., Keshner, E.A., Levin, M.F. (eds.): Virtual Reality for Physical and Motor Rehabilitation. Springer, New York (2014)
34. Bozzacchi, C., Giusti, M.A., Pitzalis, S., Spinelli, D., Di Russo, F.: Similar cerebral motor plans for real and virtual actions. PLoS One **7**(10), e47783 (2012)
35. Bozzacchi, C., Giusti, M.A., Pitzalis, S., Spinelli, D., Di Russo, F.: Awareness affects motor planning for goal-oriented actions. Biol .Psychol. **89**(2), 503–514 (2012)
36. Shibasaki, H., Hallett, M.: What is the Bereitschaftspotential? Clin. Neurophysiol. **117**(11), 2341–2356 (2006)
37. Libet, B., Gleason, C.A., Wright, E.W., Pearl, D.K.: Time of conscious intention to act in relation to onset of cerebral activity (readiness-potential). In: Neurophysiology of Consciousness, pp. 249–268. Birkhäuser, Boston (1993)
38. Cheung, K.L., Tunik, E., Adamovich, S.V., Boyd, L.A.: Neuroplasticity and virtual reality. In: Virtual Reality for Physical and Motor Rehabilitation, pp. 5–24. Springer, New York (2014)
39. Gaerlan, M.G.: The role of visual, vestibular, and somatosensory systems in postural balance. UNLV theses, dissertations, Professional Papers, and Capstones, p. 357 (2010)

Are the Psychosocial and Physical Disabilities of Stroke Survivors Ageing Related?

Echezona Nelson Dominic Ekechukwu[1,2,3](✉) (iD), Nelson Okogba[1],
Kingsley Obumneme Nwankwo[4] (iD), Nmachukwu Ifeoma Ekechukwu[3],
Amaka Gloria Mgbeojedo[1], Olusegun Adeyemi Adejare[5],
Uchenna Prosper Okonkwo[6], and Victor Adimabua Utti[7] (iD)

[1] Department of Medical Rehabilitation, FHST, College of Medicine, University of Nigeria,
Nsukka, Nigeria
nelson.ekechukwu@unn.edu.ng
[2] Occupational and Environmental Health Unit, IPH, College of Medicine,
University of Nigeria, Nsukka, Nigeria
[3] LANCET Physiotherapy, Wellness and Research Centre, Enugu, Nigeria
[4] Stroke Control Innovations Initiative of Nigeria, FCT, Abuja, Nigeria
[5] Department of Physiotherapy, University College Hospital, Ibadan, Ibadan, Nigeria
[6] Department of Medicine Rehabilitation, FHST, Nnamdi Azikiwe University, Nnewi, Nigeria
[7] University of Essex, Colchester, UK

Abstract. Most stroke survivors, advanced in age are encumbered by physical
and psychosocial disabilities such as motor impairments, balance dysfunctions,
depression, activity limitation, participation restriction etc. These disabilities also
characterize ageing as seen among older adults. It is therefore not know if the
post-stroke disabilities are due to ageing or intrinsic neurological deficits. This
study sought to know if the physical and psychosocial disabilities of stroke survivors are due to ageing or stroke specific impairments. This cross-sectional study
with a matched design compared selected physical and psychosocial attributed
between stroke survivors (SS) and their age- and sex-matched apparently healthy
older adults (ASMAHOA). Physical attributes such as functional ability (FA),
participation, balance and motor function (MF) and psychosocial variables such
as depression, self-esteem, and self-efficacy were assessed using validated instruments. Data obtained were analysed using descriptive statics and paired t-test.
Level of significant was set at α = 0.05. A total of 34 SS and 34 ASAMAHOA
participated in this study, 19 (55.9%) males and 15 (44.1%) females in each group
with a mean age of 69.02 ± 5.55 years and 68.89 ± 5.40 years respectfully. Stroke
survivors had significantly (p < 0.05) lower scores compared to ASAMAHOA
(SS vs ASAMAHOAl) on FA (24.65 ± 8.57 vs 44.56 ± 8.36), MF [upper-limb
(68.62 ± 28.24 vs 97.09 ± 15.03), lower-limb (50.71 ± 25.14 vs 72.74 ± 8.40)],
self-esteem (63.18 ± 15.42 vs 77.94 ± 7.20) and self-efficacy (47.82 ± 25.48 vs
88.65 ± 17.94), but a significantly higher depressive symptoms (13.53 ± 8.23 vs
10.32 ± 4.30). Stroke survivors experience significantly greater disabilities than
their age- and sex-matched apparently healthy older adults. Therefore, post-stroke
disabilities are not primarily due to ageing.

Keywords: Stroke · Disability · Neuro-impairment · Ageing

1 Introduction

Stroke is a sudden neurological event that is usually followed by an abrupt onset of disability that might be life-long. Having a stroke often entails a major life-course disruption [1, 2]. The prevalence of fatigue after stroke is severe [3, 4], and physical performance is poor [5], due to the presence of disability and the experience of discontinuity in their lives. They are not only confronted with physical problems but also mental and psychosocial problems such as depression, anxiety, lower self esteem and poorer self-efficacy [6, 7].

Many of these impairments and disabilities such as motor disabilities, balance dysfunctions, gait abnormalities, lower self-efficay etc. have been reported to characterize normal ageing [8]. It is also a known fact that ageing is a risk factor of stroke [9]. And most stroke debilitations are commonly seen among the older cohorts [10]. It is therefore possible that these physical and psychosocial disabilities seen among older stroke survivors may be primarily due to ageing and not merely stroke specific impairments and disabilities. This study therefore set out to determine whether the physical and psychosocial impairments seen in older stroke survivors are primarily due to ageing or otherwise.

2 Methods

2.1 Participants

Only older adults ($\geq$60 years) with stroke and their age/sex-matched healthy counterparts were included in this exploratory study. Stroke survivors with additional neurological or disabling co-morbidities such as spinal cord injury, limb amputation, osteoarthritis etc. were excluded from the study.

2.2 Sample Size

Minimum Sample size was calculated using the population standard deviation effect. A minimum of 34 stroke survivors was derived from the calculation using a standard variate (Z) at 95% CI of 1.96, standard deviation (σ) of population estimated from Billinger et al. [11], of 3.9 and using a precision (e) of 1.2. These stroke participants ought to be matched equally by 34 apparently healthy older adults giving a total of 68 participants.

2.3 Materials

2.3.1 Geriatric Depression Scale (GDS) [12]

GDS was used to assess depression. The GDS is a self-rating scale comprised of 30 items. Questions require simple yes/no answers and were intended to be both non-threatening and age-appropriate. The respondent provided responses to each question with reference to the past week. One point is given for each "yes" response and the number of points is summed to provide a single score. Scores from 0 to 10 are considered normal, while scores 11 indicate the presence of depression. Depression can be further categorized into mild (11–20) and moderate-severe (21–30) depression [13].

2.3.2 Fugl-Meyer Assessment (FMA) [14, 15]

FMA was used to assess sensori-motor function. The scale comprises five domains; motor function (in the upper and lower extremities), sensory function, balance (both standing and sitting), joint range of motion and joint pain. Scale items are scored on the basis of ability to complete the item using a 3-point ordinal scale where $0 =$ cannot perform, $1 =$ performs partially and $2 =$ performs fully. The total possible scale score is 226. Points are divided among the domains as follows: 100 for motor function (66 upper & 34 lower extremity), 24 for sensation (light touch and position sense), 14 points for balance (6 sitting & 8 standing), 44 for joint range of motion & 44 for joint pain.

2.3.3 Berg Balance Scale (BBS) [16]

BBS was used to assess balance performance. The scale consists of 14 items requiring subjects to maintain positions or complete movement tasks of varying levels of difficulty. Administration of the scale is completed via direct observation of task completion. It requires a ruler, a stopwatch, chair, step or stool, room to turn 360° [16]. Items receive a score of 0–4 based on ability to meet the specific time and distance requirements of the test. A score of zero represents an inability to complete the item and a score of 4 represents the ability to complete the task independently. It is generally accepted that scores of less than 45 are indicative of balance impairment [17].

2.3.4 Frenchay Activities Index (FAI) [18]

FAI was used to assess activities of daily living. It contains 15 items or activities that can be separated into 3 factors; domestic chores, leisure/work and outdoor activities. The frequency with which each item or activity is undertaken (depending on the nature of the activity) is assigned a score of 1–4 where a score of 1 is indicative of the lowest level of activity. The scale provides a summed score from 15–60.

2.3.5 Reintegration to Normal Living Index (RNLI) [19, 20]

RNLI was used to assess participation. It has 11 declarative items, aach of the items are rated by the respondent on a 4-point categorical scoring systems, that yields a maximum score of 44.

2.3.6 State Self-esteem Scale (SSES) [21]

SSES was used to assess self-esteem. Determination of self-esteem state of participations is measured be filling the state self-esteem questionnaire which will provides information about what the individual is thinking at the moment. The state self-esteem scale is subdivided into three which include performance self-esteem, social self-esteem and appearance self-esteem. All items were answered using 5-point scale.

2.3.7 Fall Self-efficacy Scale (FSES) [22]

FSES was used to assess self-efficacy. Fall self-efficacy scale includes 13 activities rated from 0 (not confident at all) to 10 (completely confident), yielding a total score between 0 and 130. Higher scores indicate higher confidence in performing activities.

2.4 Ethical Consideration

Ethical approval was sought and obtained from the Health Research Ethics Committee of the University of Nigeria Teaching Hospital, Enugu, Nigeria. Participants were informed about the research and duly signed informed consent obtained before their participation in the study.

2.5 Procedure

After the ethical approval for this study was obtained, the informed consent of the participants was obtained after duly explaining the study objects and requirements to them. Thereafter the subject administered outcome measures (Geriatric Depression Scale, Frenchay activities index, State Self Esteem Scale, Fall Self Efficacy Scale and Reintegration to Normal Living Index) were administered randomly to avoid data setting. After ensuring that the outcome measures were properly filled by the participants, the filled instruments were retrieved. Subsequently, the researcher-administered outcome measures (Berg's Balance Scale and Fugyl Meyer) were administered by observing their performance of the required task/instruction.

2.6 Data Analysis

Data collected for this study was analyzed using SPSS for windows evaluation (version 20). Descriptive statistics of frequency, percentage, mean and standard deviation were used to summarize participant variables. Paired t-test was used to assess the difference in variable between stroke survivor and the age/sex matched apparently healthy participants. Level of significance was set at $\alpha = 0.05$.

3 Results

3.1 Demographic and Clinical Characteristics of the Participants

A total of 34 stroke survivors and 34 age/sex matched, normal subjects participated in this study, 19 males (55.9%) and 15 females (44.1%) in each group with a mean age of 69.02 ± 5.55 and 68.89 ± 5.40 years respectively for the stroke survivors and their matched participants. Among the stroke survivors, 63.7% had right sided hemiplegia while 36.3% had left sided hemiplegia. Most of the participants both for the stroke group (55.9%) and matched subjects (44.1%) were retirees as shown in the Table 1.

3.2   Comparison Between Stroke Survivors and Age/Sex Matched Normal Subject

There was no significant difference (t = 1.909, p = 0.065) between the mean age of stroke survivors (69.02 ± 5.55 years) and the matched participants (68.89 ± 5.40 years). However, there was a significant difference between the mean scores of the (upper limb and lower limb) sensori-motor function (t = −6.089, p < 0.001; and t = −5.537, p < 0.001) between the stroke survivors (70.67 ± 28.12 and 51.23 ± 24.27) and matched participants (98.38 ± 14.71 and 73.48 ± 8.18). There was also a significant difference (t = 2.20, p = 0.033) in the mean score of depression between the stroke survivors (13.30 ± 8.19) and the matched subjects participants (10.34 ± 4.33) as shown in Table 2. Table 2 also reveals that functional ability of the matched participants (42.00 ± 9.24) was significantly higher (t = −10.844, p < 0.0001) than those of the stroke survivors (25.45 ± 8.64). Similarly, the matched participants had significantly higher (t = 6.083, p < 0.001; and t = 6.083, p < 0.001) balance performance and participation (45.48 ± 8.27 and 35.30 ± 6.65) than the stroke survivors (26.57 ± 17.59 and 25.17 ± 9.94) respectively as shown in Table 2.

Table 1. Frequency distribution of participant variables (N = 68).

Variables	Categories	Frequency (%)	
		Stroke survivors (34)	Matched control (34)
Sex	Male	19 (55.9)	19 (55.9)
	Female	15 (44.1)	15 (44.1)
Occupation	Retirees	19 (55.9)	15 434.1)
	Business/Trading	8 (23.5)	11 (32.4)
	Lecturers	4 (11.8)	7 (20.6)
	Driver	0 (0.0)	1 (2.9)
	Clergy	3 (8.8)	0 (0.0)
Marital status	Married	26 (76.5)	27 (79.4)
	Widowed	6 (17.6)	7 (20.6)
	Divorces	2(5.9)	0(0.0)
Side of stroke	Left side	12 (35.3)	N/A
	Right side	22 (63.7)	N/A

Key: N/A = Not applicable

Table 2. Comparison of Measures of Disability between Stroke Survivors and their Matched Control (N = 68)

Variables	Mean ± SD		t	p
	SS (n = 34)	MC (n = 34)		
Age (years)	69.02 ± 5.55	68.89 ± 5.40	1.909	0.065
Depression (/30)	13.53 ± 8.23	10.32 ± 4.30	2.220	0.033*
Self Efficacy (/130)	47.82 ± 25.48	88.65 ± 17.94	−9.381	<0.001*
Functional Ability (/60)	24.65 ± 8.57	40.94 ± 9.06	−10.844	<0.001*
Participation (/44)	24.24 ± 9.92	34.71 ± 6.62	−6.083	<0.001*
State Self Esteem (/100)	63.18 ± 15.42	77.94 ± 7.20	−5.293	<0.001*
Balance (/56)	24.68 ± 17.08	44.56 ± 8.36	−7.123	<0.001*
SMF-UL (/136)	68.62 ± 28.24	97.09 ± 15.03	−6.089	<0.001*
SMF-LL (/96)	50.71 ± 25.14	72.74 ± 8.40	−5.537	<0.001*

Key: SS = Stroke survivors; MC = Matched control; SMF-UL = Upper limb sensorimotor function; SMF-LL = Lower limb sensomotor function; * = Significant

4 Discussion

There was a significant difference in functional ability and participation between stroke survivors and their age/sex matched normal counterparts. This may imply that stroke specific characteristics rather than ageing may be responsible for the decreased participation among stroke survivors. These results appear to be in line with other studies [23, 24], that revealed that participation restriction is generally high among stroke survivors. The low level reported has been fingered to be due to the failure to undergo home rehabilitation and follow up after discharge [24]. Therefore, follow up programmes to ensure successful reintegration of stroke survivors into their communities, families and return to work should be ensured by neurorehabilitation professionals involved in stroke rehabilitation.

The observed differences in motor function, balance, depression, self-esteem and self efficacy between stroke survivors and the matched subjects are corroborative pointers that the physical and psychological impairments seen among stroke survivors are not primarily due to ageing but are sequela of stroke pathology. Motor dysfunctions in stroke survivors are mainly as a result of the insult to the motor cortext and/or sub-cotical structures such as the basal ganglia, cerebellum and in very rare cases, the anterior horn of the spinal cord. This insult usually impedes the activities of the corticospinal tract and other descending tracts. Therefore neurological rehabilitation is targeted at encouraging neuroplsticity that will facilitate aborization of these tracts as well as synaptogenis. Also, stroke can be characterized by impaired cognitive functioning which may affect judgment and thus may have reflected in the significantly lower scores of self-esteem and self-efficacy compared to similarly matched apparently healthy older adults.

A major limitation of this study is that it cannot conclusively rule out the effects of ageing on post-stroke disability as the study was not designed to do so.

5 Conclusion

Older stroke survivors experience significantly greater disabilities than their age- and sex-matched apparently healthy persons. Therefore post-stroke disabilities are not primarily due to ageing.

References

1. Hawkins, R.J., Jowett, A., Godfrey, M., Mellish, K., Young, J., Farrin, A., Holloway, I., Hewison, J., Forster, A.: Poststroke trajectories: the process of recovery over the longer term following stroke. Glob. Qual. Nurs. Res. **4**, 2333393617730209 (2017)
2. Hamzat, T.K., Ekechukwu, N.E., Olaleye, A.O.: Comparison of community reintegration and selected stroke specific characteristics in Nigerian male and female stroke survivors. Afr. J. Physiother. Rehabil. Sci. **6**(1–2), 27–31 (2014)
3. Mahon, S., Theadom, A., Barker-Collo, S., Taylor, S., Krishnamurthi, R., Jones, K., Witt, E., Feigin, V.: The contribution of vascular risk factors in prevalence of fatigue four years following stroke: results from a population-based study. J. Stroke Cerebrovasc. Dis. **27**(8), 2192–2199 (2018)
4. Drummond, A., Hawkins, L., Sprigg, N., Ward, N.S., Mistri, A., Tyrrell, P., Mead, G.E., Worthington, E., Lincoln, N.B.: The Nottingham Fatigue after Stroke (NotFAST) study: factors associated with severity of fatigue in stroke patients without depression. Clin. Rehabil. **31**(10), 1406–1415 (2017)
5. Ekechukwu, E.N., Olowoyo, P., Nwankwo, K.O., Olaleye, O.A., Ogbodo, V.E., Hamzat, T.K., Owolabi, M.O.: Pragmatic solutions for stroke recovery and improved quality of life in low-and middle-income countries—a systematic review. Front. Neurol. **11**, 337 (2020)
6. Tsarkov, A., Petlovanyi, P.: Neuropsychiatric aspects of a common problem: stroke. Eur. J. Med. Health Sci. **1**(3) (2019)
7. Ekechukwu, N., Olaleye, O., Hamzat, T.: Clinical and psychosocial predictors of community reintegration of stroke survivors three months post in-hospital discharge. Ethiop. J. Health Sci. **27**(1), 27–34 (2017)
8. Webb, S.L., Birney, D.P., Loh, V., Walker, S., Lampit, A., Bahar-Fuchs, A.: Cognition-oriented treatments for older adults: a systematic review of the influence of depression and self-efficacy individual differences factors. Neuropsychol. Rehabil. 1–37 (2021)
9. Gorelick, P.B.: The global burden of stroke: persistent and disabling. Lancet Neurol. **18**(5), 417–418 (2019)
10. de Graaf, J.A., van Mierlo, M.L., Post, M.W., Achterberg, W.P., Kappelle, L.J., Visser-Meily, J.M.: Long-term restrictions in participation in stroke survivors under and over 70 years of age. Disabil. Rehabil. **40**(6), 637–645 (2018)
11. Billinger, S.A., Taylor, J.M., Quaney, B.M.: Cardiopulmonary response to exercise testing in people with chronic stroke: a retrospective study. Stroke Res. Treat. (2012)
12. Yesavage, J.A.: Geriatric depression scale. Psychopharmacol Bull. **24**(4), 709–711 (1988)
13. McDowell, I., Newell, C.: The index of independence in activities of daily living in measuring health: a guide to rating scales and questionnaires (1996)
14. Fugl-Meyer, A.R., Jääskö, L., Leyman, I., Olsson, S., Steglind, S.: The post-stroke hemiplegic patient. 1. A method for evaluation of physical performance. Scand. J. Rehabil. Med. **7**(1), 13–31 (1975)
15. Gladstone, D.J., Danells, C.J., Black, S.E.: The Fugl-Meyer assessment of motor recovery after stroke: a critical review of its measurement properties. Neurorehabil. Neural Repair **16**(3), 232–240 (2002)

16. Berg, K., Wood-Dauphine, S., Williams, J.I., Gayton, D.: Measuring balance in the elderly: preliminary development of an instrument. Physiother. Canada **41**(6), 304–311 (1989)
17. Berg, K.O., Maki, B.E., Williams, J.I., Holliday, P.J., Wood-Dauphinee, S.L.: Clinical and laboratory measures of postural balance in an elderly population. Arch. Phys. Med. Rehabil. **73**(11), 1073–1080 (1992)
18. Holbrook, M., Skilbeck, C.E.: An activities index for use with stroke patients. Age Ageing **12**(2), 166–170 (1983)
19. Wood-Dauphinee, S., Williams, J.I.: Reintegration to normal living as a proxy to quality of life. J. Chronic Dis. **40**(6), 491–499 (1987)
20. Wood-Dauphinee, S.L., Opzoomer, M.A., Williams, J.I., Marchand, B., Spitzer, W.O.: Assessment of global function: the reintegration to normal living index. Arch. Phys. Med. Rehabil. **69**(8), 583–590 (1988)
21. Heatherton, T.F., Polivy, J.: Development and validation of a scale for measuring state self-esteem. J. Pers. Soc. Psychol. **60**(6), 895 (1991)
22. Tinetti, M.E., Richman, D., Powell, L.: Falls efficacy as a measure of fear of falling. J. Gerontol. **45**(6), P239–P243 (1990)
23. Kossi, O.: Participation in community-dwelling stroke survivors in Africa (Doctoral dissertation, UCL-Université Catholique de Louvain) (2017)
24. Connolly, T., Mahoney, E.: Stroke survivors' experiences transitioning from hospital to home. J. Clin. Nurs. **27**(21–22), 3979–3987 (2018)

Analyzing the Effect of Visual Cue on Physiological Hand Tremor Using Wearable Accelerometer Sensors

Vishal Kannan[1], K. Adalarasu[2], Priyadarshini Natarajan[1], and Venkatesh Balasubramanian[1(✉)]

[1] RBG Labs, Department of Engineering Design, Indian Institute of Technology Madras, Chennai 600036, India
`chanakya@iitm.ac.in`
[2] Department of EIE, SEEE, SASTRA Deemed University, Thanjavur 613401, Tamil Nadu, India

Abstract. Physiological tremors are slight oscillations that are produced when head and limbs are left unsupported in healthy individuals. This study aims to verify the presence of neurogenic component in physiological hand tremor by appropriately choosing a neurophysiological parameter (i.e. visual cue – eyes open and eyes closed). The physiological hand tremor was recorded from eight subjects while performing three tasks – rest, postural and action under eyes open and eyes closed conditions. Accelerometer and EMG sensors were fixed at fingers, wrist, forearm, biceps and deltoid muscles. Consequently, time and frequency domain features were extracted from accelerometer and EMG data. One-way ANOVA was performed to evaluate the statistical difference ($p < 0.05$) between the two conditions. Our study concluded that visual cue had a significant effect on physiological hand tremor only during action task. Besides, the amplitude of the hand tremor was reduced during eyes open condition due to increase in voluntary muscle force, which showcased the positive influence of neurogenic component on physiological hand tremor.

Keywords: Tremor · Physiological · Neurogenic · Accelerometer · EMG

1 Introduction

1.1 Tremor

Tremor is an involuntary, rhythmic, oscillatory movement of a body part (Deuschl *et al.*, 1998). The new consensus criteria for classification of tremor are based on its clinical characteristics and etiology [1]. The clinical features include the historical features (onset age, temporal evolution and family history), tremor characteristics such as body distribution, activation condition & frequency and associated signs (neurological signs, signs of systemic illness). Based on these tremor characteristics, they are classified broadly as action or rest tremor, focal tremors, task and position specific tremors, orthostatic

N. L. Black et al. (Eds.): IEA 2021, LNNS 223, pp. 517–536, 2022.
https://doi.org/10.1007/978-3-030-74614-8_66

tremors, tremor with prominent additional signs and others such as functional and inter-mediate tremor [1]. On the other hand, etiological classification is based on whether it is genetic, acquired or idiopathic.

Any system that produces a periodic oscillation are technically termed as oscillators. The above notion forms the basis of pathophysiology of tremor studies, which narrows down the genesis of tremor into two factors namely mechanical and neurogenic origin [2]. From a biological perspective, an oscillator is not a single anatomical structure rather a collection of structures with a functional connectivity capable of producing rhythmic oscillations under certain conditions. This includes muscles in the case of mechanical origin and neuronal assemblies in case of neurological origin [3]. Human tremors are caused mainly by four factors namely the mechanical tremor of the extremity (mechanical component), activation of spinal reflex loop resulting in an oscillatory movement, central oscillations in the brain and finally oscillatory activity due to instability in any of the feedforward/backward loop involved in motor movement.

The simplest cause of tremor is the mechanical component generally termed as mechanical tremor of the extremity. Assuming our hand is being outstretched against the gravity parallel to the ground, the extensor muscles of the arm get stimulated and activates some of its muscle fibers causing it to vibrate at the resonant frequency of the hand. This ultimately leads to the hand oscillating at this resonant frequency, given by $F = \sqrt{K/I}$, where K is a constant denoting the muscle stiffness and I being the inertia of the oscillating hand. The second mechanism that causes tremor is mediated by the spinal reflex loops. The spinal reflex includes afferent signals from the muscle spindles to the alpha neurons in the spinal cord and vice-versa. The variable reflex gain and the conduction time latency during this reflex loop action produces oscillations in the periphery muscle, which may lead to a tremor [3]. The third factor that engenders tremors are the central oscillations, which include areas such as the motor cortex, thalamus and cerebellum (cerebello-thallamo- cortical pathway). The aberrant firing of the neurons due to lesions in any of these regions produce oscillations in the periphery where the time for excitatory inhibition or summation in different nuclei involved and asynchronous conduction time determine the frequency of the oscillation [3, 4]. The fourth mechanism is the malfunction of feed backward or forward loops within the CNS. For example, any movement requires an initiation by an agonist, termination by an antagonist and fine tuning by another agonist [5]. This feedforward activation requires perfect synchronism and it was observed that cerebellum acts as a control center for these pre – programmed movements [6, 7]. Any damage to cerebellum may lead to delay in any of these activations thereby introducing asynchronous conduction in the loop. This in turn produces oscillations in the periphery leading to a tremor [3].

1.2 Physiological Tremor

Physiological tremors are slight oscillations that are produced when head and limbs are left unsupported in healthy individuals [8]. This is usually asymptomatic, not visible and can be enhanced due to anxiety, stress and fatigue, producing a clinical condition termed as enhanced physiological tremor [1]. Physiological tremor consists of a strong mechanical component which is responsible for its main frequency component [9, 10]. Hand tremors due to intrinsic muscle property oscillate at 6–8 Hz. The mechanical component may be driven by resonant frequency of the muscle [11], cardio ballistic effects and the discontinuities of innervation [12]. The other component of the physiological tremor is the 8–12 Hz neurogenic component [3]. This component is believed to originate from various sources including olivocerebello-thalamo cortical pathways [13]. Many groups studied physiological tremor to validate the presence of mechanical and neurogenic component in it. Majority used a weight loading based experimentation and concluded the presence of strong mechanical component but were uncertain with the presence of any neurogenic component [14, 15].

1.3 Common Misdiagnosis and Tremor Analysis Techniques

Although there are many clinical features and pathophysiology, the major problem lies in the fact that similar clinical features and etiologies overlap and appear in multiple tremors and hence no tremor is completely understood [16]. For example, the tremor frequency of physiological and enhanced physiological tremor lies in the range of 6–12 Hz, ET lies between 4–12 Hz and PD has 3–6 Hz. Some of the other tremors include orthostatic tremor (13–18 Hz), neuropathic tremor (4–8 Hz), dystonic tremor (3–5 Hz) and cerebellar tremor (<5Hz) [4]. This has led to a lot of misdiagnosis in clinical conditions especially with essential and Parkinson's tremor. It has been reported that the misdiagnosis rate of ET ranges from 37%–50% [17, 18]. The early misdiagnosis rate of PD that shows hand tremors as the only symptom was as high as 25% [19].

Tremor analysis needs to provide an objective, reproducible and diagnostic information. This led to several approaches to analyze tremor namely questionnaire/score based, electrophysiological and imaging [4]. Scaling systems such as are used by clinicians to diagnose the level of tremor. Although scaling systems such as Unified Parkinson's Disease Rating Scale (UPDRS) score and Essential Tremor Rating Assessment Scale (TETRAS) are used for tremor assessment, all these scaling systems have a drawback of subjective variability as they are being graded by the individual clinicians [20]. Thus, there needs to be an objective assessment to reduce the manual error. This led to the rise in electrophysiological studies as it would not only provide information on tremor features such as frequency but also help the clinician to verify the presence of any mechanical and neurogenic component [21]. Most of the electrophysiological studies utilize accelerometer and EMG data which has been widely applied to investigate most of the tremors including physiological tremor, ET and Parkinson's tremor.

In the case of physiological tremor, though it is considered insignificant in clinical condition, ET has been commonly misattributed to enhanced physiological tremor [22]. Therefore, it poses a necessity to study physiological tremor and evaluate its distinguishable features from other pathological tremors.

1.4 Common Methods of Physiological Tremor Analysis and Its Limitations

The characterization of the tremor can be done by recording the movement of the tremor affected region and also the muscle movement that may be producing it [21]. Predominantly accelerometer has been used to record the movements while surface EMG has been utilized to study the underlying muscle force. Weight loading based investigations are common among a multitude of experimental methodology. These methods are commonly used to measure tremor, extract its clinical features and interpret the components producing it. On this context, several studies have shown that the physiological hand tremors (PT) are due to a strong mechanical component i.e., resonant frequency of the muscle wherein the advent of a neurogenic component in it is uncertain.

One study quantified the physiological finger and hand tremors using accelerometer and surface EMG sensors for a total of 117 healthy subjects [15]. In this study, the subjects were asked to keep their hands in an outstretched position (Postural position) with and without the weight loading. It was seen that tremor frequency reduced upon weight loading, indicating that mechanical component of the oscillating limb as the primary determinant of PT. Since only a third of the population showed EMG-EMG coherence, the indication of a central component in PT remained uncertain. On the same line, another study investigated PT in a population of normal subjects using a variable-reluctance accelerometer [23]. The objective of this work was to demonstrate the importance of 8–10 Hz band in normal physiological hand tremor and 15–20 Hz band in PT finger tremor using weight loading experiment. This study concluded that at least one frequency band was heavily influenced by the mechanical component while there is still possibility of a neural feedback producing a neural component as well. Another study aimed to determine the tremor-related motor unit entrainment in 200 elderly and young adults [24]. The hand tremor recorded using weight loading conditions witnessed reduction in tremor frequency with increase in inertial load (300 g) indicating a strong mechanical component in it. In addition, the EMG- acceleration pattern was reported to be varying among the population during mass loading and unloading conditions. From the different patterns, it was seen that 8% of the population produced an EMG-acceleration pattern that was similar to mild essential tremor conditions.

On the other hand, [25] opts for a different methodology to study the resonant component of PT. The vertical displacement of the hand was recorded using retro-reflective rangefinder laser and accelerometer was used to record the tremor simultaneously. The subjects were asked to adjust their position of the hand and match the spot on a computer display in front of them and the recordings were done during both postural and movement conditions. The findings showed an acceleration peak at 8 Hz with no EMG correlation indicating a strong a resonant component. In addition, when the voluntary movement were induced, the tremor size greatly increased and the tremor frequency reduced by 2 Hz (thixotropic effect). These results suggest that rhythm of hand tremor in postural and slow action rely on muscle and limb mechanics rather than a neural oscillator.

Electrophysiological approaches have been used to study other pathological tremors especially to distinguish Parkinson's (PD) from essential tremor (ET) and essential tremor from that of enhanced physiological tremor (EPT). One group aimed to distinguish PD from ET and EPT using a non-invasive approach [19]. Tremor was recorded at rest, postural and postural with weight loaded condition using accelerometer and EMG sensors. It was observed that the tremor frequency of ET patients at all the conditions were 5–8 Hz. EPT and PD patients had a frequency range of 6–12 Hz and 4–6 Hz respectively. This showed that there was a clear overlap in tremor frequency between the patients making the tremor frequency a poor variable for classification. It was the muscle contraction pattern observed from the EMG that acted as a distinguishable parameter.

Finally, on applying this parameter, PD and ET were distinguished by the latency and concentration effect whereas ET and EPT were distinguishable using weight loading effect.

On the contrary, [26] showed that tremor frequency was the only component that showcased a significant difference between PD and ET. Kinematic parameters such as RMS and sample entropy were only significantly different between control and ET patients. Another group applied empirical mode decomposition (EMD) and Hilbert Huang transform (HHT) to distinguish ET from PT [27]. Since the frequency characteristics of ET overlaps with PT, it was difficult to distinguish them using FFT based analysis. Accelerometers and EMG sensors were fixed at index finger and extensor carpi radialis forearm muscle respectively to record the tremor at the postural position. From the EMD-HHT analysis it was seen that a low frequency component of 3–5 Hz was present only in PT whereas the high frequency of 8 Hz was present in both PT and ET. Thus, this low frequency component of PT, which was derived from EMD-HHT analysis had an EMG-accelerometer correlation and was used to distinguish majority of ET patients from PT though few of ET patients did have a low frequency component.

Although, there are several electrophysiological approaches to extract the tremor characteristics to both unravel their origin and distinguish them from other movement disorders, it was clearly seen that there are many overlaps in the tremor characteristics, which makes it difficult to classify them. Adding to this, since there is no concrete evidence for any tremor etiology, it is suspected that a tremor might be of several etiological origins. Hence, it is important to design experiments to unravel the tremor components so as to get a better understanding of their corresponding features used in classification studies. Restricting our study to explore the physiological hand tremor, all the above studies pertaining to physiological hand tremor indicate that it includes a strong mechanical component and produce ambiguous reports on the neurogenic component.

Most of these studies are based on weight loading experimentation, which considers a constant stiffness of the muscle. Conversely, [28] reports that muscle stiffness is not constant and accelerometer-based tremor recording produces data that only reflects the information on the load applied and not any neurological phenomenon. The study recorded tremor with inertial loading (artificial mass) and in another condition where the force equivalent to the inertial loading was applied by increasing the 'g' using a human centrifuge. When the load was applied, the accelerometer tremor frequency reduced as expected indicating the resonant component. In the case of EMG, the reduction in frequency was insignificant during weight loading. This is because, as the mass increases, a feedback loop gets activated and increases the muscle force by activating more muscle fibers so as to hold the limb in the same position with the extra load. This ultimately leads to the increased muscle stiffness. Hence, the reduction in resonant frequency due to increased mass is counteracted by the increase in muscle stiffness producing an insignificant change in EMG frequency. Thus, the entire experimental design using weight loading to study the physiological tremor can give information only on the mechanical component of the tremor and not any neurogenic component in it.

Hence, it requires a neurophysiological variable in the experimental design to directly check the influence of any neurogenic component in physiological tremor. Based on this notion, the current study involves a visual cue (i.e., eyes open and closed), a neuro-physiological parameter as a variable to analyze the effect of neurogenic component on physiological tremor.

2   Materials and Methods

2.1   Data Acquisition

Subjects Summary. Eight healthy subjects (7 males, 1 female) within the age group of 22–28 years were recruited for the study. All subjects gave informed consent prior to the test and reported no physical or cognitive impairments. The exclusion criteria included any type of medication that might induce tremor, intake of any centrally acting drugs, the presence of orthopedic forearm and/or hand problem, and any neurological/systemic disease.

Data Acquisition System. Eight healthy subjects (7 males, 1 female) within the age group Hence, it requires a Hand and finger tremors were recorded in all subjects using accelerometer and EMG as a part of Delsys Trigno Avanti™ sensors (Fig. 1). This is a wireless biofeedback system consisting a total of sixteen sensors with a LED feedback indicating the status of the sensors. Each unit has an on board 4-channel EMG sensor, an inertial measurement unit that includes accelerometer and gyroscope sensors. The wireless communication is done through dual mode BLE-Base (Bluetooth Low Energy) communication with a transmission range of up to 20 m. Sensors contain a rechargeable lithium polymer battery with a performance time ranging from 4–8 h depending on the usage conditions.

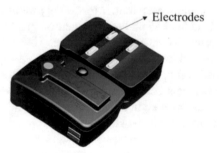

Fig. 1. Delsys Trigno Avanti™ sensor.

Electrode Placement. A total of ten sensors (S1–S10) were fixed among which five were placed each on one finger starting from thumb (S1) to record the finger tremors (Fig. 2A). Sixth sensor was fixed between 2nd and 3rd metacarpal region whereas the seventh and eighth sensors were fixed on the flexor and extensor carpi muscles of the forearm as these are the primary muscles involved in hand movement (Fig. 2A, B). The ninth and tenth sensors were placed on the biceps brachii muscle and deltoid muscle of the shoulder respectively to check if there is any onset of fatigue as the subjects perform the experimental tasks (Fig. 2C). The EMG was recorded from metacarpal region (S6), flexor (S7) and extensor carpi muscles (S8), biceps brachii (S9) and deltoid muscles (S10).

Fig. 2. A, B, C – Accelerometer /EMG sensor placements.

Experimental Protocol. Subjects were asked to perform three tasks namely rest, postural and action for both eyes closed and open conditions (Fig. 3). Figure 4 summarizes the various positions the subjects were asked to perform. In the case of rest, subjects were asked to be seated comfortably on an arm chair with their forearm rested on the arm rest and the hands hanging freely. For the postural task, the subjects were asked to hold their arm and hands in an upright position against the gravity with 0° to the ground. Finally, for the action task, they were asked to maintain the postural position with the hand part alone moving upward and downward in tandem with a metronome of 60 beats per minute. The data was recorded wirelessly for 20 s at a sampling frequency of 148 Hz for accelerometer and 1926 Hz for EMG with a relaxation time of one minute between each task.

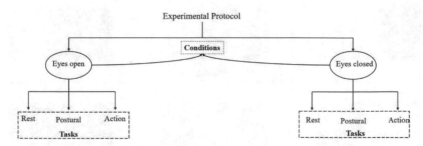

Fig. 3. Schematic representation of the experimental design.

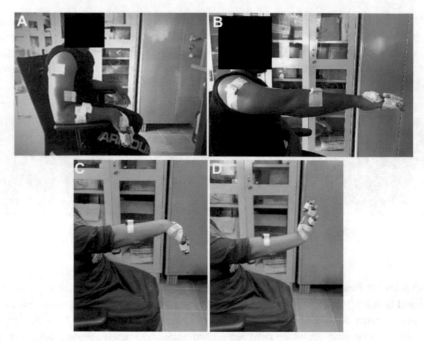

Fig. 4. Different positions the subjects were asked to perform. A - Rest position B - Postural position, C - Action downward, D - Action upward

2.2   Data Analysis

See Fig. 5.

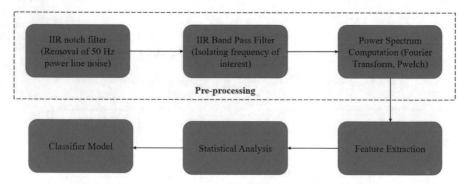

Fig. 5. Schematic representation of signal processing.

Pre-processing. The accelerometer signals were filtered using IIR notch filter of order 3 to remove the 50 Hz power line noise. The signals were then band pass filtered for 0.5–20 Hz to avoid any high frequency noise using IIR band pass filter with a filter order of 3. This was then subjected to secondary band pass filtering using the same IIR band pass filter of order 3 to isolate the physiological tremor frequency range of 6–12 Hz. Finally, Fourier Transform was performed on this 6–12 Hz signal and the respective features were obtained.

In the case of EMG, the power line noise of 50Hz was removed using IIR notch filter with a filter order of 3. Further, the signal was band pass filtered to 0.5–300 Hz using IIR band pass filter with an order of 3 to isolate the frequency with physiological importance. Finally, power spectral density was computed using a Pwelch method which includes an 50% overlapping Hanning window with a window length equal to the sampling frequency.

Feature Extraction. After taking spectrum of the accelerator signal, we extracted the six features for two experimental conditions (eyes open and closed) and its corresponding three tasks (rest, postural and action).

1. **Energy:** For a signal x of length N in a time series, energy of this signal in time domain is defined as:

$$E = \sum_{i=1}^{N} x_i^2 \tag{1}$$

2. **Total power:** For a signal x of length N in frequency domain having a power of x(w) for each frequency component, the total spectral power is defined as

$$P = \sum_{i=1}^{N} |x_i(w)|^2 \tag{2}$$

3. **Mean Power:** It represents the average value of power in the frequency domain which is defined as

$$\text{Mean Power} = \sum_{i=1}^{N} \frac{x_i(w)}{N} \tag{3}$$

4. **Median Power:** It represents the value of power above and below which there is exactly 50% distribution of rest of the power units.
5. **Peak Power:** The maximum power value obtained in the power spectral density.
6. **Peak Frequency:** It is defined as the frequency at which the peak power occurs. As it is difficult to locate the peak power and its respective frequency amidst all the discrete frequency components, the spectrum needs to be smoothened to increase the precision of the data without distorting the signal. Hence, a Savitzky–Golay filter with an order of 3 and window length of 95 was applied to smoothen the power spectrum. Savitzky–Golay filter is a digital filter that works based on the process of convolution which fits the adjacent points of our dataset with a linear polynomial using the method of linear least squares the result of which provides an averaged curve of our signal based on the window length and order. This was further used to extract the peak frequency.

In the case of EMG, three features were extracted for all the three tasks (rest, postural and action). In time domain, the features consist of root mean square (RMS), number of zero crossing while mean power frequency (MNF) was extracted from the frequency domain.

7. **Root Mean Square (RMS):** For a signal x of length N in a time series, energy of this signal in time domain is defined as:

$$RMS = \sqrt{\sum_{i=1}^{N} (x_i - \bar{x})^2} \tag{4}$$

8. **Zero Crossing (ZC):** It represents the number of times the amplitude of the signal in time domain crosses the value of zero from both negative and positive side.

9. **Mean Power Frequency (MNF):** For a signal of length N, it is defined as the sum of product of each power and frequency divided by the total sum of the power values in frequency domain.

$$MNF = \sum_{i=1}^{N} P_i F_i / \sum_{I=1}^{N} P_i \tag{5}$$

Statistical Analysis. One-way ANOVA was performed to validate the statistical significance in the feature set between the three experimental tasks (rest, postural, action). The confidence interval was set at 95% ($p < 0.05$). The groups (rest, postural and action) were used as independent parameters while the sensors were used as dependent parameters. The test was performed separately for both eyes closed and open conditions. Furthermore, one-way ANOVA was used to verify the statistical difference between eyes open and closed conditions within each task and thereby validate the effect of visual cue over physiological hand tremor. Here, the groups (eyes closed and eyes open) and each sensor value were set as independent and dependent parameters respectively.

3   Results

3.1   Eyes Closed Condition

Initially, the analysis was performed to check whether there was significant difference ($p < 0.05$) between the features extracted for each sensor between rest, postural and action tasks. In the case of accelerometer, it was seen that the features from action task were significantly high ($p < 0.05$) compared to that of rest and postural while the features from rest task were significantly low ($p < 0.05$) compared to postural and action. From the statistical results, it was seen that for the total spectral power and mean power, all the sensors except the seventh (flexor carpi muscle) had a significant difference between rest (R), postural (P) and action (A) tasks while the seventh sensor had only significant difference between rest and action tasks. In the case of median power, it was seen that sensors 1, 2, 3, 4, 5, 6 and 10 have a significant difference between rest and action tasks while 7th sensor showed a significant difference between rest and postural. All the ten sensors (S1–S10) showed a significant difference in peak power between the three tasks. Furthermore, sensors seven and nine showcased significant difference in peak frequency between rest and postural while the 8th sensor showed significance between all the three tasks.

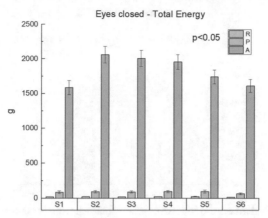

Fig. 6. Mean and standard error of the total energy value obtained from S1 – S6 sensors during eye closed condition.

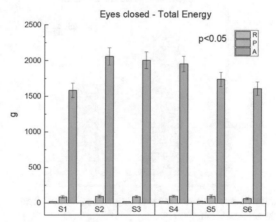

Fig. 7. Mean and standard error of the total energy value obtained from S7 – S10 sensors during eye closed condition.

From the Fig. 6 and Fig. 7, it can be seen that all the ten sensors show an increasing trend from rest to postural and postural to action with significant difference in total energy between rest, postural and action tasks.

In the case of EMG, only sixth sensor (metacarpal region) showed a significant difference in the features. It was seen that RMS for rest task was significantly lower than action task (Fig. 8) while there was no significant difference between rest and postural task.

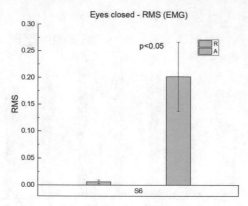

Fig. 8. Mean and standard error of the RMS value obtained from S6 sensor (metacarpal region) during eye closed condition.

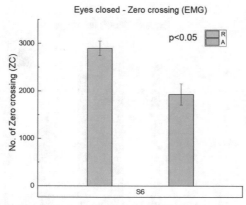

Fig. 9. Mean and standard error of the zero-crossing value obtained from S6 sensor (metacarpal region) during eye closed condition.

From the Fig. 9 and Fig. 10, the number of zero crossing (ZC) and the mean power frequency (MNF) was significantly ($p < 0.05$) low during action when compared to rest condition. Similar to the RMS, there was no significant difference between rest and postural for both ZC and MNF.

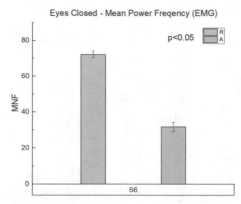

Fig. 10. Mean and standard error of the mean power frequency value obtained from S6 sensor (metacarpal region) during eye closed condition.

3.2 Eyes Open Condition

Similar to eyes closed condition, it can be seen that the accelerometer features from action task were significantly high ($p < 0.05$) compared to that of rest and postural while the features from rest task were significantly low ($p < 0.05$) compared to postural and action. It was seen that the total spectral power and median power extracted from all the sensors show a significant difference only between rest and action tasks whereas in the case of mean and peak power, all the ten sensors showcase a significant difference between rest, postural and action tasks. Furthermore, sensors seven and eight showed a significant difference in peak frequency between rest, postural and action while the 10th sensor established a significance only between rest and postural.

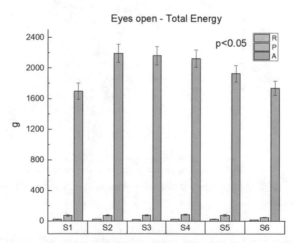

Fig. 11. Mean and standard error of the total energy value obtained from S1 – S6 sensors during eye open condition.

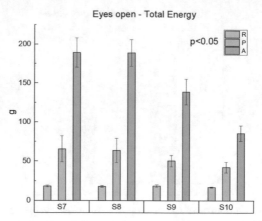

Fig. 12. Mean and standard error of the total energy value obtained from S7–S10 sensors during eye open condition.

From the Fig. 11 and Fig. 12, it can be seen that all the ten sensors show an increasing trend from rest to postural and postural to action with significant difference in total energy between rest, postural and action tasks.

In the case of EMG, similar to eyes closed condition, only sixth sensor (metacarpal region) showed a significant difference in the features. It was seen that RMS for action task (A) was significantly higher than rest (R) and postural task (P) (Fig. 13). There was no significant difference between rest and postural task.

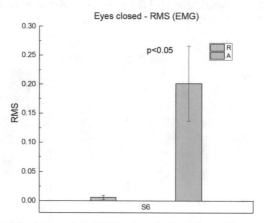

Fig. 13. Mean and standard error of the RMS value obtained from S6 sensor (metacarpal region) during eye open condition.

Similar to eyes closed condition, the number of zero crossing (ZC) and the mean power frequency (MNF) had a decreasing trend from rest to postural and from postural to action task with action task being significantly lower compared to rest task and postural

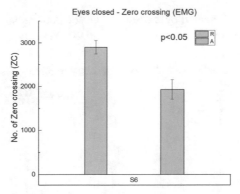

Fig. 14. Mean and standard error of the zero-crossing value obtained from S6 sensor (metacarpal region) during eye open condition.

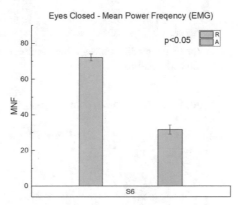

Fig. 15. Mean and standard error of the mean power frequency value obtained from S6 sensor (metacarpal region) during eye open condition.

task (Fig. 14, 17). There was no significant difference between rest and postural for both ZC and MNF.

3.3 Eyes Open Condition

Here, each task was analyzed separately to verify if there was a significant difference between the extracted features between two conditions (i.e., eyes closed (EC) and eyes open (EO) and thereby validate the effect of visual cue on physiological hand tremor. It was seen that visual cue did not show any influence on rest and postural tremor as there was no significant difference in the features between the two conditions. In the case of action task, median power extracted from sensors 1, 2, 3, 5, 6 and 10 showed a significant difference ($p < 0.05$) between eyes closed and eyes open. Furthermore, from the Fig. 16 and Fig. 17, it can be seen that median power at eyes closed condition was greater than that of eyes open condition. In the case of EMG analysis, none of the features showed a significant difference between eyes open and closed conditions for all the three tasks (i.e., rest, postural and action).

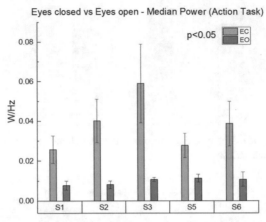

Fig. 16. .Mean and standard error of the median power value obtained from S1, S2, S3, S5 and S6 sensors during eye open and closed condition.

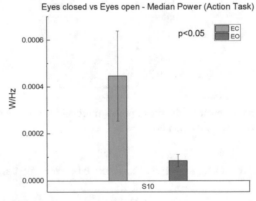

Fig. 17. Mean and standard error of the median power value obtained from S10 sensor during eye open and closed condition.

4   Discussion

The uncertainty surrounding the neurogenic component of physiological hand tremor is mainly attributed to studies with inadequate experimentation on validating it. Most of the studies take an indirect route using weight loading based experimentation and lack a neurophysiological variable to properly verify the presence of neurogenic component. Therefore, in the present study, we take visual cue as the neurophysiological parameter and analyze its effect on physiological hand tremor. Further, unlike EMG it is difficult to analyze tremors in time domain using accelerometers as it reflects only the peripheral movement and not any information on underlying muscle contraction. Hence, apart from EMG, we performed the spectral analysis for the accelerometer signal, which provides pertinent information on physiological hand tremor such as peak frequency, total power etc.

It can be seen from the results that the tremor amplitude increases almost 10 folds in postural position compared to that of rest position indicating the onset of postural tremor (Fig. 6, 7, 11, 12). This is mainly due to the fact that in postural position, the hand is unsupported and apart from the resonant vibration of the hand, there happens a process of tetanic contraction of muscles so as to maintain the position. Tetanic contraction is an outcome of repeated stimuli at short intervals such that the excited muscle fiber doesn't have time to fully relax before it is excited again. Moreover, for an actual muscle movement to take place, there needs to be activation of several muscle fibers. As the half relaxation time may vary across different muscle fibers, during tetanic contraction, there may be asynchronous excitation of different muscle fibers and consequently the possibility of a delay between muscle excitation and the actual muscle movement to hold the position, arises [29]. This delay in turn leads to intermittent oscillations in the muscles, which in the periphery is seen as physiological postural tremor. Furthermore, it was seen that the power of the tremor increases during action task compared to the postural tremor. This effect is attributed to the muscular thixotropy. Muscle thixotropy refers to the alteration in the stiffness of the muscles when they are lengthening or shortening (i.e., during movement) and when they are in a static position (i.e., postural task). Several studies reveal that the tremor size greatly increases and its frequency reduces at the onset of slow voluntary movements [25]. In our action task, as the voluntary movement begins, the muscle stiffness decreases but the inertial load on the hand is same as that of in postural task. This causes the decrease in tremor frequency as it is directly proportional to the muscle stiffness corresponding to the mechanical resonance origin. This was further evident from the Fig. 10 and Fig. 15 where the MNF was decreased in action task compared to rest task indicating a decrease in tremor frequency whereas the increase in the RMS of EMG supports the increase in tremor size. Also, the decrease in ZC during action task seen from the Fig. 11 and Fig. 14 indirectly denotes the reduced firing rate of the motor units corroborating the decrease in tremor frequency.

Furthermore, the eyes closed vs eyes open analysis shows that only median power from action task has a significant difference in sensors 1, 2, 3, 5, 6 and 10. Consequently, the median power for action task in eyes open condition is less compared to the eyes closed condition indicating a mild reduction in tremor size. This may be because during eyes open condition, the visual cue induces more voluntary effort to control the movement of the hand than in eyes closed condition. This increased voluntary effort imparts a mild resistance to muscle movement by increasing the stiffness of the muscle so as to control the unwanted shaking (tremor) during action task. Although, the resistance to movement is being increased, the action task is being continued making the muscle experience a condition similar to increased load. Thus, this increase in resistance to movement may have attributed to the decrease in tremor during eyes open condition indicating a positive effect of visual cue over physiological hand tremor. This can be considered only as a hypothesis as the RMS values did not show a statistical significance and the hypothesis is based only on the trend observed from the values.

Besides, the rest time of one minute between the tasks in the experimental design needs an optimization as muscle needs more time for relaxation and prevent it from fatigue. Also, the signal acquisition time of 20 s may not be sufficient enough to reveal the effect of visual cue on the physiological hand tremor. This may be because unlike EEG, which reflects the immediate changes in central activity, accelerometer only reflects the final peripheral movement. Consequently, accelerometer has a low sensitivity to biological changes compared to that of EEG and EMG and hence, in this case, it requires a profound change in muscle activity to get reflected in the accelerometer signal. Therefore, increase in acquisition time might produce more significant results for accelerometer features. In the case of EMG, there were contact issues which need to rectified by appropriately preparing the skin and electrode placements. In addition to this, the study needs to be carried out with a greater population to get a better statistical significance for both accelerometer and the EMG features.

5 Conclusion

In this study, we have proposed a new experimentation by using visual cue as a neurophysiological parameter to validate the presence of a neurogenic component in physiological hand tremor. Visual cue had a significant effect over physiological hand tremor only during action task. It was seen that the physiological hand tremor tends to reduce due to the increased voluntary muscle force during eyes open condition. This was clearly evident from the decrease in median power during eyes open condition showcasing the influence of a neurogenic component.

This methodology can be applied further to pathological tremors such as Parkinson's and Essential tremors with slight modification in the frequency range used for analysis. As these tremor patients are neurologically compromised, the varying effect of a neurophysiological parameter such as visual cue would provide drastic difference in their tremor characteristics. This visual cue-based methodology can be further developed as an assistive tool for objective diagnosis of neurological complications such as Parkinson's and Essential Tremors.

References

1. Bhatia, K.P., et al.: Consensus statement on the classification of tremors. from the task force on tremor of the international Parkinson and movement disorder society. Mov. Disord. 33(1), 75–87 (2018)
2. Manto, M.: Tremorgenesis: a new conceptual scheme using reciprocally innervated circuit of neurons. J. Transl. Med. 6, 1–6 (2008)
3. Deuschl, G., Raethjen, J., Lindemann, M., Krack, P.: The pathophysiology of tremor. Muscle Nerve 24, 716–735 (2001)
4. Saifee, T.A.: Tremor. Br. Med. Bull. 130(1), 51–63 (2019)
5. Hallett, M., Shahani, B.T., Young, R.R.: EMG analysis of stereotyped voluntary movements in man. J. Neurol. Neurosurg. Psychiatry 38, 1154–1162 (1975)

6. Homberg, V., Hefter, H., Reiners, K., Freund, H.J.: Differential effects of changes in mechanical limb properties on physiological and pathological tremor. J. Neurol. Neurosurg. Psychiatry **50**, 568–579 (1987)
7. Diener, H.C., Dichgans, J.: Pathophysiology of cerebellar ataxia. Mov. Disord. **7**, 95–106 (1992)
8. Schnitzler, A., Gross, J.: Normal and pathological oscillatory communication in the brain. Nat. Rev. Neurosci. **6**, 285–296 (2005)
9. Allum, J.H.J., Dietz, V., Freund, H.J.: Neuronal mechanisms underlying physiological tremor. J. Neurophysiol. **41**, 557–571 (1978)
10. Dietz, V.: Tremor, mechanical effect of the discharge behavior of motoneurones. Fortschr. Med. **96**, 215–219 (1978)
11. Timmer, J., Lauk, M., Pfleger, W., Deuschl, G.: Cross-spectral analysis of physiological tremor and muscle activity: I theory and application to unsynchronized electromyogram. Biol. Cybern. **78**, 349–357 (1998)
12. Freund, H.J.: Motor unit and muscle activity in voluntary motor control. Physiol. Rev. **63**, 387–436 (1983)
13. Raethjen, J., et al.: Corticomuscular coherence in the 6–15 Hz band: Is the cortex involved in the generation of physiologic tremor? Exp. Brain Res. **142**, 32–40 (2002)
14. McAuley, J.H.: Physiological and pathological tremors and rhythmic central motor control. Brain **123**(8), 1545–1567 (2000)
15. Raethjen, J., Pawlas, F., Lindemann, M., Wenzelburger, R., Deuschl, G.: Determinants of physiologic tremor in a large normal population. Clin. Neurophysiol. **111**(10), 1825–1837 (2000)
16. Elble, R.J.: Tremor: clinical features, pathophysiology, and treatment. Neurol. Clin. **27**(3), 679–695 (2009)
17. Jain, S., Lo, S.E., Louis, E.D.: Common misdiagnosis of a common neurological disorder: How are we misdiagnosing essential tremor? Arch. Neurol. **63**, 1100–1104 (2006)
18. Schrag, A., Münchau, A., Bhatia, K.P., Quinn, N.P., Marsden, C.D.: Essential tremor: an overdiagnosed condition? J. Neurol. **247**(12), 955–959 (2000)
19. Zhang, J., Xing, Y., Ma, X., Feng, L.: Differential diagnosis of Parkinson disease, essential tremor, and enhanced physiological tremor with the tremor analysis of EMG. Parkinsons. Dis. **2017**, 6–9 (2017)
20. Patrick, S.K., Denington, A.A., Gauthier, M.J.A., Gillard, D.M., Prochazka, A.: Quantification of the UPDRS rigidity scale. IEEE Trans. Neural Syst. Rehabil. Eng. **9**(1), 31–41 (2001)
21. Vial, F., Kassavetis, P., Merchant, S., Haubenberger, D., Hallett, M.: How to do an electrophysiological study of tremor. Clin. Neurophysiol. Pract. **4**, 134–142 (2019)
22. Elble, R.J.: Physiologic and essential tremor. Neurology **36**, 225 (1986)
23. Stiles, R.N., Randall, J.E.: Mechanical factors in human tremor frequency. J. Appl. Physiol. **23**(3), 324–330 (1967)
24. Elble, R.J.: Characteristics of physiologic tremor in young and elderly adults. Clin. Neurophysiol. **114**(4), 624–635 (2003)
25. Lakie, M., Vernooij, C.A., Osborne, T.M., Reynolds, R.F.: The resonant component of human physiological hand tremor is altered by slow voluntary movements. J. Physiol. **590**(10), 2471–2483 (2012)
26. Ruonala, V., Meigal, A., Rissanen, S.M., Airaksinen, O., Kankaanpää, M., Karjalainen, P.A.: EMG signal morphology and kinematic parameters in essential tremor and Parkinson's disease patients. J. Electromyogr. Kinesiol. **24**(2), 300–306 (2014)
27. Ayache, S.S., Al-ani, T., Lefaucheur, J.P.: Distinction between essential and physiological tremor using Hilbert-Huang transform. Neurophysiol. Clin. **44**(2), 203–212 (2014)

28. Lakie, M., Vernooij, C.A., Osler, C.J., Stevenson, A.T., Scott, J.P.R., Reynolds, R.F.: Increased gravitational force reveals the mechanical, resonant nature of physiological tremor. J. Physiol. **593**(19), 4411–4422 (2015)
29. Gallego, J.A., et al.: The phase difference between neural drives to antagonist muscles in essential tremor is associated with the relative strength of supraspinal and afferent input. J. Neurosci. **35**(23), 8925–8937 (2015)

Perceived Barriers and Facilitators of Return to Driving Among a Sample of Nigerian Stroke Survivors - A Qualitative Study

Kingsley Obumneme Nwankwo[1,2](✉) ⓘ, Olubukola Adebisi Olaleye[3] ⓘ,
Tal'hatu Kolapo Hamzat[3] ⓘ, and Echezona Nelson Dominic Ekechukwu[4,5,6] ⓘ

[1] Stroke Control Innovations Initiative of Nigeria, Abuja, Nigeria
[2] Fitness Global Consult Physiotherapy Clinic, Abuja, Nigeria
[3] Deptartmentof Physiotherapy, Faculty of Clinical Sciences, College of Medicine,
University of Ibadan, Ibadan, Nigeria
[4] Deptartment of Medical Rehabilitation, FHST, College of Medicine, University of Nigeria,
Nsukka, Nigeria
[5] Environmental and Occupational Health Unit, Institute of Public Health, College of Medicine,
University of Nigeria, Nsukka, Nigeria
[6] LANCET Physiotherapy Wellness and Research Centre, Enugu, Nigeria

Abstract. Stroke affects driving ability and as such impedes mobility, independence, freedom and quality of life. Return to driving after stroke serves as an integral part for community reintegration and improved quality of life. Driving is considered critical for continued independence, employment and recreation among stroke survivors. There was therefore the need to better understand the perceived facilitators and barriers to driving among stroke survivors with pre-stroke driving history. This study seeks to better understand the perceived facilitators of and barriers to return to driving after stroke so as to enable proper outcome in patient management and policy formulation. This is a qualitative phenomenological approach using in-depth focus group discussion (FGD) was employed. Six stroke survivors (5 males; 1 female) aged 58.0 ± 7.9 years participated in the FGD. Half (50%) of the participants had returned to driving. Seven themes were generated for the barriers as well as facilitators of return to driving after stroke. Findings from this study suggests that majority of the facilitators of return to driving are intrinsic factors. Majority of stroke survivors wish that they could be able to stop being dependent on their caregivers for their activities of daily living (ADL) which could invariably lead to activity limitation and participation restriction. Attention should be paid on the pre-morbid driving status of stroke survivors so as to enhance the facilitators of return to driving and minimize the barriers to return to driving after stroke.

Keywords: Return to driving · Stroke · Barriers · Facilitators

1 Introduction

Stroke affects driving ability [1], and as such impedes mobility, independence and freedom [2]. However, driving is a complex and dynamic task which requires a conscious activity level in novel situations and unconscious activity level in familiar situations [3]. People with stroke have reduced visual field, reduced visual scanning, attention deficit, decreased information processing speed, physical disabilities and impaired visuospatial skills which may influence their driving ability [4]. To effectively drive an automobile, a number of neurologic systems must be intact. These includes cognitive, vision and motor functions, intact coordination and good attention span [2]. Functional impairment in any of these domains can potentially lead to unsafe driving [2]. Neurological deficit or paroxysmal condition does not automatically exclude driving as fitness for driving is determined by the degree of deficit, frequency and type of event.

Inability to drive can result in a number of adverse consequences in mood, life satisfaction, identity [5], and social isolation [6]. Driving is an important contributor to quality of life after stroke. Finestone et al. [7] reported that driving is significantly associated with community integration after adjusting for health status in stroke patients. Several factors have been associated with the likelihood of returning to driving. These include younger age at stroke onset, lower level of disability, fewer cognitive deficits, being provided with advice and assessment related to driving as well as length of time after stroke [8–10]. Rate of return to driving after stroke ranged from 19% [11], to 30% [8], six months after admission to inpatient rehabilitation, up to 50% five years post rehabilitation [10]. Nonetheless, about 35% of stroke survivors will require driving-related rehabilitation before they can resume safe driving [1]. There is therefore the need to better understand the perceived facilitators of post stroke survivors who return to driving and the barriers preventing those who have not returned. This is to better understand the facilitators of and barriers to return to driving after stroke so as to enable proper outcome in patient management and policy formulation.

2 Method

2.1 Study Design

A qualitative phenomenological approach using in-depth focus group discussion (FGD) was employed to explore the facilitators of and barriers to return to driving among community dwelling stroke survivors with premorbid driving history.

2.2 Participants

Six stroke survivors with premorbid driving history of ≥ 2 years and with first incident stroke were purposively recruited. These were individuals with moderate disability but able to walk without assistance (≤3 on Modified Rankin Scale), not aphasic and with no cognitive impairment (≥24/30 on Mini Mental State Examination) or visual impairments (visual field or visual acuity). Stroke survivors with co-morbidities that can independently limit/impair mobility and/or quality of life (QoL) (e.g. psychiatric disorder, diabetes, AIDS, severe osteoarthritis) were also excluded from the study. The other members of the group were the researcher, moderator and a transcriptionist.

2.3 Data Collection Procedures

A focus guide was developed based on the study objective, literature and with the researcher's experience. Participants, who met the inclusion criteria and gave informed consent, were invited for a focus group discussion (FGD). The focus group was guided by a moderator, who is knowledgeable in FGD. The moderator used a focus guide consisting of semi-structured, open-ended questions to capture directly, the complexities of the participants' perception and probes were given where necessary. The participants were encouraged to talk freely and spontaneously. The researcher took field-notes along with the transcriptionist who was also present at the FGD. Furthermore, an audio tape recorder was used to record the discussion session. The discussion was carried out in English language. The FGD lasted three hours and data saturation was ensured.

2.4 Data Retrieval and Analysis

The audio taped information from the discussion was transcribed verbatim by a transcriptionist. The transcriptions were then read and compared to audio tape recordings and field notes several times to verify accuracy [1]. Themes from the FGD were generated using grounded theory analysis.

3 Results

Six stroke survivors (5 males; 1 female) aged 58.0 ± 7.9 years participated in the FGD. Half (50%) of the participants had returned to driving while the remaining half was yet to return. Seven themes were generated for the barriers as well as facilitators of return to driving after stroke. Severity of stroke was reportedly both a facilitator of and a barrier to return to driving after stroke. Desire to be independent and determination were leading facilitators while fear and environmental factors constitutes barriers to return to driving after stroke as shown in Table 1.

3.1 Perception of Participants to Return to Driving After Stroke

Narratives of respondents suggest common themes with respect to returning to driving after a stroke event. Though some participants were of the opinion that attempting to drive is helpful in overcoming fear of driving; others opined that it depends on factors such as degree of affectation and impairment:

> "…it will depend on the degree of stroke and the impairment that has taken place…it depends on the length or gravity of the stroke"

> (P1; Male, 52years, age at stroke - 50years, yet to return to driving).

> "Like myself now, on a certain day I wanted to go home…then I found out that the leg cannot press the pedal. And the motor cannot enter gear…

> '…But largely is a matter of determination. You are determined because you have this can-do-spirit within you. You are determined to do it; otherwise there are a thousand and one reasons why somebody may not attempt"

> (P2; Male, 63years, age at stroke – 59years, returned to driving)

Some participants perceived return to driving after stroke as initially strange and frustrating due to residual functional impairments.

"... the first time, starting driving will be strange to you ...because your hand is not straight as before. The first time, I hit my fence with the car but I didn't give up. OK.... Second day I tried it again ...I see that it's different."

(P4; Male, 55years, age at stroke – 55years, returned to driving)

"...Self-determination.... The 1st day I did it. They accompanied me to the church. The 2nd time, they also accompanied me, in the event there will be 'katakata' on the way ... but because of that strong determination within me that I should be able to do it..."

(P2; Male, 63years, age at stroke 59years, returned to driving)

3.2   Facilitators of Return to Driving After Stroke

According to the participants, factors that facilitate resumption of driving could be intrinsic or extrinsic. Intrinsic factors are factors related to the stroke survivors such as: the desire to be independent, perception of life, perception of driving, self-determination, severity of stroke and social isolation. Social expectations were identified as an extrinsic factor. Narratives that illustrate the intended meanings are as stated:

3.3   Desire to be Independent

One of the recurring facilitators of return to driving was the desire/urge to be independent so as to be able to function and carry out their activities without dependence on others. This is reflected in the statement of the participants quoted below:

"...what prompted me is that one day, I had an appointment in the hospital. I have to call... (The person who was to drive me) said he had an appointment....I said to myself how am I going to get to the hospital. I think is better I start driving this car so that I cannot be depending on anybody...I think is the urge or desire to be independent. I don't want to be dependent... It's not a normal life. I think it will be normal for one to go back and resume what he was doing before and that was giving you joy, comfort and normal pleasures of life."

(P4; Male, 55years, age at stroke 49years, returned to driving)

"...there's a time I wanted to go to work. I called one of my friends; he said he had no time. When I look at myself, I said how long will I depend on people like this... at least I can still drive now. ...urge to be independent"

(P6; Male, 55 years, age at stroke 55 years, returned to driving)

"...Like myself I can't sit down doing nothing. Even when I was admitted when I was on bed I told my doctor because if they don't discharge me I ran out of the bed because I'm not the type that will depend on..."

(P2; Male, 63years, age at stroke - 59years, returned to driving)

3.4 Perception of Life

Participants believed that an individual's perception of life events play a role in return to driving. He believed being a proactive and outgoing person can facilitate return to driving:

> "...*is the kind of person one is. Like myself I can't sit down doing nothing. I'm not the type that will...up until now and I don't see myself as a stroke man because they call it challenges because a challenge is not something permanent. I believe by exercising myself that challenge will wear off from me. So I always have in mind I can do it. I don't ever have 'NO' in my programmes in my life. So that is what prompted me to.*"
>
> (P4; Male, 55years, age at stroke 49years, returned to driving)

Another individual believed that the way he defined his condition was a factor that contributed to his ability to return to driving.

> "...*somebody like myself I've once said it. I don't ever look at myself as if I am a liability. And I think that one helped to work within the spasm. The moment I saw myself that I don't have any stroke I do perform very well on steering. Sir I don't have any challenge. I'm not even got a single...*"
>
> (P6; Male, 55 years, age at stroke 55 years, returned to driving)

3.5 Perception About Driving

One of the participants who is yet to return to driving but hopes to, believed perception of specific activities including driving as hobbies have the capacity to drive its resumption.

> "...*I don't enjoy myself by not driving because I'm used to driving as my hobby before the incident. So driving is my hobby...when I'm not driving, I'm not Ok. I must tell you that.*"
>
> (P3; Male, 52years, age at stroke 51years, yet to return to driving)

This position was further supported by another participant:

> "...*I see driving as a hobby. It's just like somebody who plays football*"
>
> (P2; Male, 63years, age at stroke - 59years, returned to driving)

3.6 Determination

Another perceived facilitator of return to driving after stroke as posited by some of the participants was courage and determination:

> "...*Courage and self-determination'*
>
> (P2; Male, 63years, age at stroke – 59years, returned to driving)

Indulging one's self in various forms of activities of daily living could further reduce participation restriction thus boosting the enthusiasm, courage and determination required to return to driving after stroke. The is as stated below.

...self-determination matters. And if you determine you going to do it, you are going to do it. ...there's improvement of every part of my body. ...but you start early in very small form...like closing my window and drawing curtain. Start it very little and then gradually you develop'

(P1; male, 65years, age at stroke - 64years, yet to return to driving)

'...with all that's been discussed I was determined to go back to the vehicle'

(P3; Male, 52years, age at stroke - 51years, yet to return to driving)

3.7 Social Isolation

Absence or reduced social interaction after a stroke could lead to boredom and loneliness. This situation prompted two of the participants to attempt resuming activities such as driving in a bid to assuage being lonely.

'... solitude, you are alone in the house.. At a stage the boredom will weigh you down and you will want to get out, take some fresh air. You know especially if you have always been the outgoing type. You have never being the indoor type'

(P3; Male, 52years, age at stroke - 51years, yet to return to driving)

'...I'm somebody who cannot sit down for one hour. So sit down looking at every-where. I had to stand up and walk round the house. One day I said I will go to work. When I get to the department, my HOD said who said you should come to work? I said I am tired of home. I don't tire of home. Nobody to play with. Children go to school...'

(P2; Male, 63years, age at stroke - 59years, returned to driving)

3.8 Severity of Stroke

According to some discussants, extent of the damage by the stroke and not just the length of driving prior to stroke serve as a contributory factor to returning to driving. He believes that individuals with less impairment will be able to return to driving as compared to their counterparts with a more severe impairment. The quotes below highlights the view of these participant.

'...that will be...that do not apply to everybody because it will depend on the degree of stroke and the impairment that has taken place.'

(P2; Male, 63years, age at stroke - 59years, returned to driving)

'...the length of the damage of the sickness'

(P3; Male, 52years, age at stroke - 51years, yet to return to driving)

3.9   Social Expectations

Work demands and the need to live up to expectation can drive return to driving after stroke. According to the participants men who are bread winners in their respective families and need to contribute to the financial upkeep of the families:

'...*you have people depending on you. You have to foot bills and even despite our conditions you have to manage to write some cheques that must be cashed...The urge to contribute financially towards the sustenance of a family may urge you to resume duty*'

(P2; Male, 63years, age at stroke - 59years, returned to driving)

The type of job one does and the need to reassure the management on the competency and capability of performing your duties without the impairment being a limitation. This, some participants said played a role in their return to driving.

'...*I earlier said that the kind of work one is doing*'

(P4; Male, 55years, age at stroke 49years, returned to driving)

'... *the nature of the job one is doing*'

(P2; Male, 63years, age at stroke - 59years, returned to driving)

3.10   Barriers to Return to Driving After Stroke

Intrinsic and extrinsic factors were identified as barriers to return to driving after stroke. The intrinsic factors identified were perceived fear, severity of stroke, temperament and driving competence prior to stroke as possible barriers to return to driving. They also opined that external factors such as environment (poor road network), unfriendly attitude of other road users, and lack of social support.

3.11   Fear

Fear of accident and possible death was highlighted as one of the discouraging factors. This was as stated in the quotes below by the participants.

'...*because when I want to think of driving, my fear is that what if I won't be able to turn to one road and hit another vehicle. They will damage me. That will make me die before my time.*'

(P5; Female, 72years, age at stroke – 70years, yet to return to driving)

'...*the fear of death can also hinder somebody... nobody wants to die*'

(P2; Male, 63years, age at stroke – 59years, returned to driving)

3.12   Severity of Stroke

The degree of impairment to the various parts of the body by stroke can undoubtedly limit attempting to resume driving according to a participant:

'The severity of the stroke... Yes if the limbs have been so badly affected...that will be like someone committing suicide, if the person decides to go and drive. In fact they will want you to go and write your will'

(P5; Female, 72years, age at stroke – 70years, yet to return to driving)

Similarly, the extent to which a stroke survivor recovers and resumes use of affected limbs will greatly determine his/her decision to attempt driving.

'...the extent of recovery from stroke.... because somebody should be careful too. The extent of recovery will guide your decision to say let me try again since you don't want to embarrass yourself'

(P4; Male, 55years, age at stroke - 49years, returned to driving)

3.13   Competence with Driving Prior to Stroke

Driving is a skill. The level of competence of a driver prior to stroke can limit return to driving.

'Dexterity before the illness, could be a factor ...because you want to... some probably lack the ability to drive as such.'

(P2; Male, 63years, age at stroke – 59years, returned to driving)

3.14   Temperament

Changes in temperament and mood are possible sequelae of stroke. Inability to effectively manage changes in mood may be a deterrent from resuming driving. Being angry and emotionally unstable could make informal caregivers to dissuade a stroke survivor from attempting driving:

"... Since the stroke started I know I am angrier. ...I know drivers outside will curse you. They can do anything and I decided I will cool it down. I'm a prison officer before I had the stroke. ...If anybody curse me, if anybody say get out, you better go and have another driver...I will not answer them"

(P3; Male, 52years, age at stroke - 51years, yet to return to driving)

"...so the ego of a person, headiness sometimes (Yoruba statement). You see you want to resist control, headiness and sometimes your wife will just do like this (demonstrates). In fact the one who does this is patient enough. In most cases they will start weeping. By the time they start screaming, are you helping? No you are not helping."

(P5; Female, 72years, age at stroke – 70years, yet to return to driving)

3.15   Environment

According to the stroke survivors, the environment is not enabling for return to driving with a disability. The poor road network, presence of obstruction such as bumps, potholes, cracks, uneven floors etc. on roads are critical to making a decision to resume driving. These environmental defects can greatly discourage/hinder driving.

"The condition of the roads could be a factor...For instance the type of environment where you live can hinder you sometimes. ...so you do not cause commotion within the neighbourhood. ...if the roads are not well laid and there is a ditch that is deep like a gorge... If the terrain is not conducive, you are likely to be hindered in a way"

(P4; Male, 55years, age at stroke - 49years, returned to driving)

3.16   Unfriendly Attitudes of Other Road Users

Certain attitudes displayed by other road users could limit attempting to drive after stroke. According to participant, poor driving habits of other road users can discourage return to driving after a stroke.

"...*even those who have not suffered a stroke sometime ...lose concentration on the road. ...they cannot keep to one lane. Some people have not mastered the art of driving...And when you are on the road, you wonder who gave this one a license...when you see people driving bumper to bumper it is either inexperienced or whatever"*

(P4; Male, 55years, age at stroke - 49years, returned to driving)

"... In Nigeria I have also observed that we don't have a very good road culture. When you see somebody who is driving slowly and has his hazards light on, do you know the way drivers will be cursing...go and die at home! ...Go and get a driver? It could be embarrassing."

(P6; Male, 55 years, age at stroke 55 years, returned to driving)

3.17   Lack of Social Support

Lack of adequate and proper social support can hinder recovery of lost functions and that will in the long term hinder resumption of driving. This was suggested by P2 below.

'*...Do you know if you have an uncooperative wife? If your wife is the impatient type who cannot bring herself to the level of appreciating the current situation this rickety man is into now. So if you don't have good family support... Your children, your wife, your friends who should ordinarily take it easy with you that could aggravate your situation.*'

(P2; Male, 63years, age at stroke – 59years, returned to driving)

The importance of social support was further emphasized by another participant as stated below.

'...that day I was about to come to the hospital. I told my wife lets go. You want to drive? and I said yes, with God all things are possible. I have nothing to fear... And the woman said, it is not, can't you see what I told you? And I said I will take it cool. And I take it cool from Ashi to Ojunrin. Before I got to Ojunrin she said you better park now. Let us call another man. We came down and call our mechanic who came and drove us to the hospital. The other day I called and I know that distance is nothing. I believe and I trust I can drive and I will drive'

(P3; Male, 52years, age at stroke - 51years, yet to return to driving)

4 Discussion

The study findings will be discussed under two sections which are facilitators of and barriers to return to driving after stroke with reference to relevant literature and the context of the study setting.

4.1 Perceived Facilitators to Return to Driving After Stroke

Findings from this study show that majority of the facilitators of return to driving are intrinsic factors. That is to say, they are factors which directly manifest from within the individual and can be influenced by the individual. The desire to be independent was shown to be a facilitator to return to driving after stroke as majority of stroke survivors wish that they could be able to stop being dependent on their caregivers for their activities of daily living (ADL) which could invariably lead to activity limitation and participation restriction. Driving is essential for traveling to work, completing everyday tasks like grocery shopping and going to doctors' appointments [10]. Driving as a symbol of independence and freedom [8, 12] could spur a stroke survivor who deems it necessary to be functionally independent to return to driving after stroke.

Perception of life was identified as a facilitator to return to driving among stroke survivors. The way a stroke survivor perceives life could have a great influence on his psyche. Stroke survivors who are more of positivists and who remains resolute and confident in their abilities may tend to return to driving more than their counterparts who are depressed. Mcnamara et al. [12] reported a relationship between confidence and driving behaviours post-stroke. Their study showed that stroke survivors with higher confidence will tend to return to driving than their counterparts with low confidence level. However, stroke survivors who do not have a positive perception about life may have psychological distress which will further make them functionally dependent and hence, not being able to return to driving. Driving as a functional task requires a certain degree of motor function to execute motor. Motor function has been reported to be an important component and predictor of driving after stroke [8, 13, 14]. Stroke survivors with psychological distress may remain functionally dependent as studies have shown an inverse relationship between psychological distress and motor functional recovery [15].

A stroke survivor's perception about driving could facilitate return to driving. Stroke survivors that see driving as a hobby and necessity towards meeting up with everyday demand may tend to return to driving due to self-motivation than individuals who do not

Table 1. Summary of findings from focus group discussion with stroke survivors

Name	Retirement status	Factors that encourage resuming driving		Factors that discourage driving		Consent from HCP	Type of car
		Intrinsic	Extrinsic	Intrinsic	Extrinsic		
P1	No	Urge to be independent					
P2	Yes	Urge to be independent, Driving dexterity, ego, headiness, functional recovery, economic considerations	Bad road culture, poor attitude of other drivers, possible distractions – use of mobile phones	Severity of stroke, incapacitation, degree of recovery	Poor driving habits,	Though necessary but may discourage taking positive steps	Both
P3	No	Urge to be independent, Mood swings, determination	Support from social networks		Excessive concern from carers		
P4	Yes	Driving as a hobby, societal demands		Self motivation, self-perception			Manual
P5	No			Fear, loss of confidence			
P6	Yes	Desire to be independent, Driving as a hobby	Availability of social support, boredom/loneliness			May deprive one from engaging in pleasurable activities	Automatic

*Both = Automatic and Manual gear system

see driving as a means to an end. This may also be related to their passion for driving as passion has been shown to have a relationship with motivation which invariably leads to achievement [16]. The study of Fuster et al. [16] showed that harmonious passion predicts higher levels of exploration, socialization, and achievement, while obsessive passion predicts higher levels of dissociation, achievement, and socialization. Stroke survivors who are self-motivated and determined to return to driving due to their passion for driving may be able achieve it as studies have shown (Geelen, R.J. and Soons, 1996; Maclean *et al.* 2000; Maclean et al. 2002; McKevitt *et al.* 2004; Holliday *et al.* 2005; Olofsson et al. 2005; Kwakkel, 2006; White *et al.* 2012) that motivation plays an important role in rehabilitation outcome of stroke survivors [5, 17, 18]. Determination to return to driving is also a facilitator to return to driving after stroke. Stroke survivors who will prioritize driving and is determined to actualize it, may likely return to driving than those who does not.

Stroke survivors are usually faced with the challenge of being functionally dependent on their caregivers due to the activity limitation and participation restriction associated with stroke. Participation restriction predisposes the individuals to social isolation and social isolation contributes to mortality and morbidity in patients with stroke [19]. In a bid to avoid social isolation, a stroke survivor may return to driving so as to enable the individual participate actively in ADL hence enable proper community reintegration [13].

Severity of stroke was also identified as an intrinsic factor to return to driving after stroke. Stroke survivors with minimal impairment from stroke would tend to return to driving than their counterparts with a more severe impairment. Stroke affects the function of multiple parts of the neuroligic system required for effective driving [4]. For effective driving, these parts of the neurologic system need to be intact. These includes cognitive, vision and motor functions, intact coordination and good attention span [2]. Therefore individuals with less affectation of this system (less impairment), will tend to return to driving after stroke than those with a more severe impairment.

Social expectation was identified in this study as an extrinsic facilitator of return to driving after stroke. Stroke survivors are most often within the middle aged range [20], who are still contributing to the upkeep of their families and also contributing to the growth of the national economy. These individuals are still within the active employment age and may want to return to work as working has been reported to have positive effect on the health of people with chronic conditions [21]. Some of the stroke survivors within this population own and drive a car and are dependent on their car for effective execution of their job description and earning of a living. The desire to meet up with their social expectations may have spurred them to return to driving after stroke.

4.2 Barriers to Return to Driving After Stroke

Barriers to return to driving after stoke identified from this study can be attributed to both intrinsic and extrinsic factors. Fear was a barrier to return to driving after stroke as participants insisted that the fear of death due to probable road traffic accident has made them not to have returned to driving. Stroke as the most feared cardiovascular event among healthy subjects and those with cardiovascular disease [22], is capable of affecting the psyche and instilling fear on the survivor. This may be attributed to the risk of harm rate of individuals with cerebrovascular disease while driving [23]. Fear to return to driving could also emanate from the degree of impairment and functional independence level.

Severity of stroke as a barrier to return to driving in this study could be attributed to the fact that individuals with more severe impairment may not be able to return to driving as compared to their counterparts with less impairment. Stroke affects multiple faculties of the neurologic system required for driving and these includes cognitive, vision and motor functions, intact coordination and good attention span [2]. For effective driving, these parts of the neurologic system need to be intact. So, for stroke survivors with a severe impairment in these areas would find it difficult returning to driving.

Pre-stroke driving experience was identified as a barrier to return to driving given that the individuals were not yet competent with driving prior to the stroke incidence. Driving just like every other task has to be learned and competence in the execution of this task is driven by experience dependent neural plasticity [24], which has principles that has to be followed so as to ensure effective learning. Learning is a process that involves changes in genes, synapses, neurons, and neuronal networks within specific brain areas [24–26]. Brain damage results in many changes in neurons and non-neuronal brain cells that can alter these learning processes. Therefore individuals with poor competence with driving prior to stroke may easily have the neuronal network specific to driving altered due to stroke hence affecting their confidence level towards driving as there is a relationship between competence and confidence [27].

Temperament was identified as one of the extrinsic barriers to return to driving after stroke. Stroke survivors are predisposed to myriads of psychological disorders [28] Post-stroke depression is the most studied psychological factor associated with stroke and has been reported to be negatively associated with functional recovery [28]. Driving is a task that requires a certain degree of functional independence to perform. Therefore, stroke survivors who are depressed or emotionally labile would most likely have a poor motor function and may consequently pose a barrier to return to driving.

Environmental factors pose a barrier to return to driving after stroke. This may not be unrelated with the poor state of roads in our study location (Nigeria) [29]. The state of road may not be favourable for stroke survivors who may want to return to driving given to the poorly maintained road network, pot-holes, bumps, paucity of traffic light, signage and traffic personnel. These factors are usually critical while trying to make decision on returning to driving after stroke. Bad road networks will require constant application of the break system, gear selection, steering control etc. Stroke survivors who belief that they cannot bear the rigours associated with carrying out these demands may likely not return to driven due to the aforementioned environmental factors.

Unfriendly attitude of other road users as identified from this study may pose a barrier to return to driving after stroke. The poor compliance to traffic rules by other road users may be thought to further predispose the stroke survivor who intends to return to driving to danger of accident. The lack of social support from concerned individuals and institutions may further discourage a premorbid driving stroke survivor from returning to driving. These social support could include retraining of premorbid driving individuals who have suffered a stroke on return to driving, providing a special speed limit lane for the physically challenged, providing adequate traffic signs and enforcing its compliance among others.

5 Conclusion

Attention should be paid on the driving status of stroke survivors with premorbid driving history so as to enhance the facilitators of return to driving and minimize the barriers to return to driving after stroke. This is to ensure improved quality of life, community and social reintegration among stroke survivors with premorbid driving history.

References

1. Akinwuntan, A.E., Feys, H., DeWeerdt, W., Pauwels, J., Baten, G., Strypstein, E.: Determinants of driving after stroke. Arch. Phys. Med. Rehabil. **83**, 334–341 (2002)
2. Drazkowski, J.F., Sirven, J.I.: Driving and neurologic disorders. Neurology. **76**, 44–49 (2011)
3. Akinwuntan, A.E., Wachtel, J., Rosen, P.N.: Driving simulation for evaluation and rehabilitation of driving after stroke. J. Stroke Cerebrovasc. Dis. **21**(6), 478–486 (2012)
4. Fisk, G.D., Owsley, C., Mennemeier, M.: Vision, attention, and self-reported driving behaviours in community dwelling stroke survivors. Arch. Phys. Med. Rehabil. **83**, 469–477 (2002)
5. White, G.N., Cordato, D.J., O'Rourke, F., Mendis, R.L., Ghia, D., Chan, D.K.Y.: Validation of the stroke rehabilitation motivation scale: a pilot study. Asian J. Gerontol. Geriatr. **7**, 80–87 (2012)
6. Dickerson, A.E., Molnar, L.J., Eby, D.W., Adler, G., Bedard, M., Berger-Weger, M., et al.: Transportation and aging: a research agenda for advancing safe mobility. Gerontologist. **47**, 578–590 (2007)
7. Finestone, H.M., Guo, M., O'Har, P., Greene-Finestone, L., Marshall, S.C., Hunt, L., et al.: Driving and reintegration into the community in patients after stroke. J. Phys. Med. Rehabil. **2**, 497–503 (2010)
8. Aufman, E.L., Bland, M.D., Barco, P.P., Carr, D.B., Land, C.E.: Predictors of return to driving after stroke. Am. J. Phys. Med. **92**, 1–8 (2013)
9. Marshall, S.C., Molnar, F., Man-Son-Hing, M., Blair, R., Brosseau, L., Finestone, H.M., Lamothe, C., Korner-Bitensky, N., Wilson, K.G.: Predictors of driving ability following stroke: a systematic review. Top. Stroke Rehabil. **14**(1), 98–114 (2007)
10. Fisk, G.D., Novack, T., Mennemeier, M., Roenker, D.: Useful field of view after traumatic brain injury. J. Head Trauma Rehabil. **17**, 16–25 (2002)
11. Allen, Z.A., Halbert, J., Huang, L.: Driving assessment and rehabilitation after stroke. Med. J. Aust. **10**, 599 (2007)
12. McNamara, A., Walker, R., Ratcliffe, J., George, S.: Perceived confidence relates to driving habits post-stroke. Disabil. Rehabil. **37**(14), 1228–1233 (2015)
13. Murie-Fenandez, M., Iturralde, S., Cenoz, M., Teasell, R.: Driving ability after a stroke: evaluation and recovery. Neurologia **29**, 161–167 (2014)
14. Devos, H., Akinwuntan, A.E., Nieuwboer, A., Ringoot, I., Van-Berghen, K., Tant, K., et al.: Effect of simulator training on fitness-to-drive after stroke: a 5-year follow-up of a randomized controlled trial. Neurorehabil. Neural Repair **24**, 843–850 (2010)
15. Koivunen, R.J., Harno, H., Tatlisumak, T., Putaala, J.: Depression, anxiety, and cognitive functioning after intracerebral hemorrhage. Acta Neurol. Scand. **132**, 179–184 (2015)

16. Fuster, H., Chamarro, A., Carbonell, X., Vallerand, R.J.: Relationship between passion and motivation for gaming in players of massively multiplayer online role-playing games. Cyberpsychol. Behav. Soc. Netw. **17**(5), 292–297 (2014)
17. Kwakkel, G.: Impact of intensity of practice after stroke: issues for consideration. Disabil. Rehabil. **28**, 823–830 (2006)
18. Olofsson, A., Andersson, S.O., Carlberg, B.: 'If only I manage to get home I'll get better'— interviews with stroke patients after emergency stay in hospital on their experiences and needs. Clin. Rehabil. **19**, 433–440 (2005)
19. O'Keefe, L.M., Doran, S.J., Mwilambwe-Tshilobo, L., Conti, L.H., Venna, V.R., McCullough, L.D.: Social isolation after stroke leads to depressive-like behavior and decreased BDNF levels in mice. Behav. Brain Res. **260**, 162–170 (2014)
20. Ekenze, O.S., Onwuekwe, I.O., Ezeala-Adikaibe, B.A.: Profile of neurological admissions at the University of Nigeria teaching hospital Enugu. Niger J. Med. **19**(4), 419–422 (2010)
21. Saka, O., McGuire, A., Wolfe, C.: Cost of stroke in the United Kingdom. Age Ageing **38**, 27–32 (2009)
22. Kinlay, S.: Changes in stroke epidemiology, prevention, and treatment. Circulation **124**, e494–e496 (2011)
23. Simpson, S., Ross, D., Dorian, P., et al.: CCS Consensus Conference 2003: assessment of the cardiac patient for fitness to drive and fly – Executive summary. Can. J. Cardiol. **20**(13), 1313–1323 (2009)
24. Kleim, J.A., Jones, T.A.: Principles of experience-dependent neural plasticity: implications for rehabilitation after brain damage. J Speech Lang. Hear Res. **51**, S225–S239 (2008)
25. Hosp, J., Luft, A.: Cortical plasticity during motor learning and recovery after ischemic stroke. Neural Plast. **2011**, 1–9 (2011)
26. Takeuchi, N., Izumi, S.: Maladaptive plasticity for motor recovery after stroke: mechanisms and approaches. Neural Plast. **9**, 1–9 (2012)
27. Clanton, J., Gardner, A., Cheung, M., Mellert, L., Evancho-Chapman, M., George, R.L.: The relationship between confidence and competence in the development of surgical skills. J. Surg. Educ. **71**(3), 405–412 (2014)
28. Huang, H.C., Huang, L.K., Hu, C.J., Chang, C.H., Lee, H.C., Chi, N.F., Shyu, M.L., Chang, H.J.: The mediating effect of psychological distress on functional dependence in stroke patients. J. Clin. Nurs. **23**, 3533–3543 (2014)
29. Ede, A.N.: Cumulative damage effects of truck overloads on Nigerian road pavement. IJCEE-IJENS **14**(1), 21–26 (2014)

VR Application for Vestibular System Training (Pilot Study)

Daria Plotnikova[1] ⓘ, Aleksandr Volosiuk[1,2](✉) ⓘ, Gleb Tikhonov[1] ⓘ,
Aleksandr Tsynchenko[3] ⓘ, Anastasiia Luneva[1] ⓘ, and Artem Smolin[1] ⓘ

[1] ITMO University, St. Petersburg, Russia
[2] St. Petersburg Electronical University, St. Petersburg, Russia
[3] First Pavlov State Medical University of St. Petersburg, R.M. Gorbacheva Research Institute of Paediatric Oncology, Haematology and Transplantation, St. Petersburg, Russia

Abstract. Nowadays, the most widespread methods for vestibular system training include physical activity and exercising on a specific training equipment. Even though these methods have their advantages, they do not directly affect the visual system. Thus, including the visual stimuli in vestibular system training seems to be a promising solution. Using a virtual reality headset allows to expand the area of influence on a person by creating a feeling of "complete immersion". Thus, based on the information studied from the medical side of the issue, as well as on the features of the VR headset, we propose developing an application for training the vestibular system. In the current study the authors present the initial design of the application and the experiment design to test the application efficacy in comparison to conventional vestibular system training.

Keywords: Virtual reality · Vestibular system · Motion sickness · Training application · HTC Vive

1 Introduction

A significant number of people suffer in one form or another from an insufficiently developed vestibular system [1]. The motion sickness effect occurs due to the conflict between the signals that the human brain receives from the vestibular apparatus and the visual organs. The conflict is especially noticeable in situations where the human body captures vibrations, while the eyes see static objects. Most often, "seasickness" arises from the discrepancy between the information received about the position of the body in space and the accelerations it experiences.

The current study is aimed to the development of a virtual reality (VR) application for training the vestibular system. The application is based on the existing set of exercises for the vestibular system development. The core application feature is to stimulate the user to perform actions that are exercises of the Cawthorne-Cooksey complex.

We present the following statement as the hypothesis of the study: The VR application, based on a set of Cawthorne-Cooksey exercises for the development of the vestibular system, supports the vestibular system development better than the conventional training without using specific equipment.

© The Author(s), under exclusive license to Springer Nature Switzerland AG 2022
N. L. Black et al. (Eds.): IEA 2021, LNNS 223, pp. 552–558, 2022.
https://doi.org/10.1007/978-3-030-74614-8_68

2 Methods

At the first stage, we launched a survey in order to find out how common the problem of poor development of the vestibular apparatus is. The majority of the respondents were students who fall into the age category of 18–25 years. The first part of the survey contained general questions, followed by a control question, in which a subject had to answer how much on a scale from 1 to 3 she rates her vestibular system. We complemented the scale with the following description:

1. I often gets seasick when traveling in public transport, by car and in other situations, I think that my vestibular system is rather poorly developed,
2. I rarely have problems with motion sickness, but I am familiar with it,
3. I have no problems with motion sickness as described above; I think that I have no issues with my vestibular system.

If a person had chosen the answer 1 or 2, the rest part of the question, asking about the details of the inconveniences experienced, opened for her. If a person had chosen answer 3, then the survey ended for him. 108 people took part in the survey. 77.8% of the respondents were people aged 18–25. The results (see Fig. 1) showed that 14.7% of the respondents suffer greatly from the poorly developed vestibular system. 56.9% have motion sickness problems that cause discomfort. As low as 28.4% of respondents have no problems with motion sickness. In general, it turns out that 78 out of 108 people mentioned problems with a poorly developed vestibular system. Of these, 87% answered that they would like to train their vestibular system.

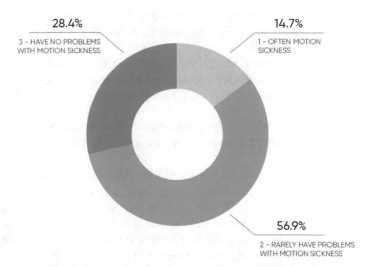

Fig. 1. The level of development of the vestibular system.

The survey results show that the vestibular system issues are relevant to 71.6% (77 people out of 100). Moreover, since most of the respondents were young adults, we can conclude that the problem of poor development of the vestibular system is common not only among children and the elderly but among young adults as well.

There already exist developed ways to improve the vestibular system. Most of these methods are based on a set of physical exercises involving specific equipment. However, now there are new technologies and capabilities that can be used to support the vestibular system improvement. One of these emerging technologies is virtual reality.

Recently, an application using Kinect technology for the vestibular system development was designed and tested. The researchers conducted several sessions with people suffering from Meniere's disease [2], who were asked to work in a game application using Kinect. The authors of the application used the Cawthorne-Cooksey set of exercises as the basis. The results of the study showed improvement of the vestibular system performance after a series of sessions. Thus, we can conclude that the vestibular system is amenable to development using virtual reality technology.

There are several different complexes for training the vestibular system. We reviewed the information on the available sets of exercises, and decided to use the Cawthorne-Cooksey exercise set, taking into account the results of the research [6]. The exercises from the complex forms the foundation of the application.

Currently, virtual reality technologies have broad development prospects. VR not only has a strong effect on the human visual organs, but also contributes to the creation of a "total immersion" effect. Accordingly, this technology is a promising tool for solving the problem of the vestibular system training.

However, it should be noted that a virtual reality headset has its own peculiarities [5]. For example, a person in a virtual reality helmet may feel nauseous. The following factors may support the nausea development:

- High latency (delay in the response of the program to user actions),
- Discrepancy between the scale of the physical world and the virtual,
- High sharpness of movement,
- Inadequate distortion of space, which the human eye is used to seeing,
- Gaze (camera) movement without the knowledge of the user (position and rotation of the camera is not well synchronized with the rotation and position of the observer's head),
- Insufficient accuracy of IMU sensors measuring the position of the device in space (however, we noted that HTC Vive performs better than the Oculus headset).

All of the above-mentioned factors should be considered when developing an application. We plan to solve some of them by optimizing the application.

The recently released ISO / IEC TR 23842-1: 2020 was also taken into account in the current study. The standard focuses on information technology for teaching, education and training; and provides Human Factors Guidelines for VR Content Creation.

We will take into account all the above-mentioned in order to minimize the possible side effects of the VR application usage.

Thus, we will design the VR application based on the gamification of the Cawthorne-Cooksey exercise set. For this, we analyzed a set of games in order to define general requirements for virtual reality headset applications.

We reviewed the following virtual reality headset applications:

- Beat Saber,
- Superhot,
- Half-Life: Alyx,
- Tilt Brush,
- OhShape.

The analysis mainly considered the core features and game mechanics, the essence of the application (is there a plot, what is it intended for, etc.), as well as the application rating (statistics were taken from digital distribution platforms of computer games and programs).

One can see the visualization of comparative data that represents the rating of the games in Fig. 2.

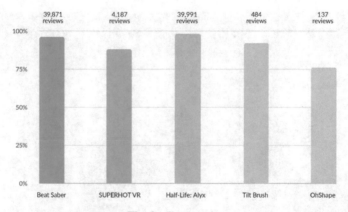

Fig. 2. Game rating

In order to design an application supporting the vestibular system development, we will use mechanics to stimulate user to perform coordination movements. The structure of these mechanics will consider the features of the reviewed games, helping in creating the most relevant and engaging content.

3   Results

At the moment, we did a pilot experiment which involved five people. Four of them were students with poorly developed vestibular system and the last person served as an example of the ideal performance of the exercises.

The purpose of the experiment was to reveal how well the virtual reality technologies are optimized and effective for performing exercises for the vestibular system development.

We decided to form two main groups: people who practice the excercises in a VR headset and people who practice without the headset. Each group had a person who worked with dynamic visualizations, when the rest of the group was working with the static ones (see Table 1).

Table 1. Pilot experiment

With VR	With video (performing Cawthorne-Cooksey exercises)	Without video (static visualization)
Without VR	With video (performing Cawthorne-Cooksey exercises)	Without video (static visualization)

The prototype test application has been developed using the Unreal Engine 4 (see Fig. 3). The user needs to perform a set of exercises that are demonstrated by the robot instructor in the application.

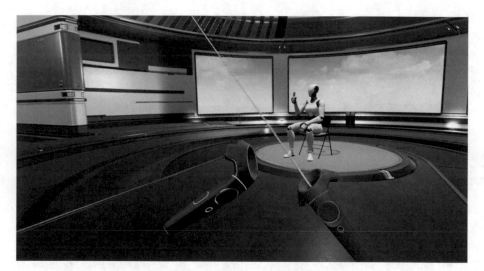

Fig. 3. Screenshot of the VR application (VR headset on)

All four participants worked in front of Kinect (see Fig. 4). All the data obtained was compared with the reference, which was the data record obtained from the fifth subject performing the exercises. These exercises were performed as technically and accurately as possible. In a pilot experiment, we compared the performance manually at a visual level. However, in the future, it is planned to automate this process using the Biovision Hierarchy technology which allows reading information about the angle of rotation of bones. Thus, the problem with different heights and proportions of people will be solved, since there will be compared information from key joints. We also plan to use OptiTrack technology, since it allows collecting information about approximately 50 joints, while Kinect allows you to initially collect 20 joints.

After analyzing the data obtained, it turned out that, while practicing in a VR headset, a person coordinates their movements more accurately.

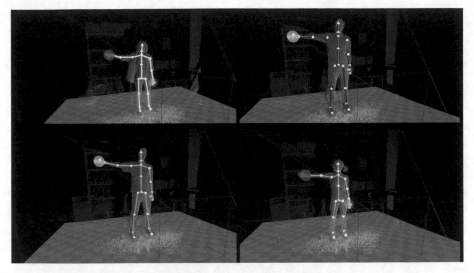

Fig. 4. Collecting data from Kinect

This experiment will be expanded and modified in the future to achieve more accurate and reliable results. The final experiment exercises will be performed in a full-fledged gamified VR application, which is currently in development.

Currently, we have developed the design of the experiment and it is planned to be carried out to test the resulting application. Three groups will be formed:

- control group,
- people who practice the Cawthorne-Cooksey exercises without the use of additional equipment using motion capture technology,
- people who are engaged in the application for a virtual reality headset using motion capture technology.

Each group will consist of approximately 10 people.

The whole experiment will be carried out during a month. There will be six sessions during which both groups will complete required test. In order to assess the degree of development of the vestibular system, there will be used existing assessment methods and force platform [3, 4]. Testing of all three groups will be carried out before the start of the experiment, as well as in the third group after the first lesson in a VR headset, since the first experience is often critical. Also, measurements will be made at the end of the experiment.

We will assess the technical performance of the exercises (based on the comparison of the experimental data with the "standard"). Information about this indicator will be obtained by processing the data obtained using motion capture technology, same as it was tested in the pilot experiment.

As a result, the indicators "before" and "after" will be taken into account to build the coefficient of the vestibular system development degree, as well as the coefficient of the exercises technical performance.

4 Discussion and Conclusions

The method of using VR technologies for training and developing of the vestibular system has broad prospects for further development. Using a virtual reality headset allows to expand the area of influence on a person by creating a feeling of "complete immersion". Thus, based on the information studied from the medical side of the issue, as well as on the peculiarities of the VR headset usage, we launched the development of an application for the vestibular system training. The prototype of the VR application has been tested in the experiment and confirmed it's possible efficiency. In the future, the application will be further tested and debugged. We also plan to create an additional progress assessment system to control the quality of the results obtained. In general, the topic appeared to be quite relevant, since many people have problems associated with poor development of the vestibular apparatus. Therefore, the problem requires further study.

References

1. Green, P.: Motion sickness and concerns for self-driving vehicles: a literature review (2016)
2. Hsu, S., Fang, T., Yeh, S., Su, M., Wang, P., Wang, V.Y.: Three-dimensional, virtual reality vestibular rehabilitation for chronic imbalance problem caused by Ménière's disease: a pilot study*. Disabil. Rehabil. **39**(16), 1601–1606 (2017). https://doi.org/10.1080/09638288.2016.1203027
3. Rine, R.M., Schubert, M.C., Whitney, S.L., Roberts, D., Redfern, M.S., Musolino, M.C., Slotkin, J.: Vestibular function assessment using the NIH toolbox. Neurology **80**(11 Suppl 3), S25–S31 (2013). https://doi.org/10.1212/wnl.0b013e3182872c6a
4. Nandi, R., Luxon, L.M.: Development and assessment of the vestibular system (2008)
5. Nausea in VR. https://vc.ru/flood/28637-toshnota-v-vr. Accessed 10 Nov 2020
6. Afrasiabifar, A., Karami, F., Najafi Doulatabad, S.: Comparing the effect of Cawthorne-Cooksey and frenkel exercises on balance in patients with multiple sclerosis: a randomized controlled trial. Clin. Rehabil. **32**(1), 57–65 (2018). https://doi.org/10.1177/0269215517714592

Determination of the Influence of Music on Working Memory Performance Using EEG Analysis

Minerva Rajendran, Tanya Malaiya, and Venkatesh Balasubramanian[✉]

Indian Institute of Technology, Chennai 600036, India
chanakya@iitm.ac.in

Abstract. Working memory forms an important component of the command centre of brain. Incoming information from all sensory modalities lasting from few seconds to several hours requires working memory for immediate storage before those information gets stored as long-term memory. Loading working memory with many information at one time can result in corrupted storage in long term memory. This could lead to less efficient recollection of information. This study aimed to investigate the efficiency of performance while loading the working memory with both primary and secondary task at the same time. Participants performed Backward Wechsler Digit Span test for digits from 3 to 7 as primary task in with-music and no-music condition. Behavioural parameters namely typing duration and accuracy, and electroencephalography (EEG) parameters namely theta, beta and alpha bands was collected for three stages: encode, maintenance and recall. Results revealed decrease in accuracy as size of digit sequence increased in the presence of music. Spectral power of theta band increased during with-music condition in comparison to no-music condition indicating strain on working memory due to music. The study results revealed that listening to favourite music during task, loads the working memory and hinders the task performance.

Keywords: Working memory · Music · Electroencephalography · Backward digit span memory test

1 Introduction

Working Memory (WM) refers to the limited capacity network (4 to 8 items/stimulus per unit time) for holding information in mind for several seconds in the context of cognitive activity (Baddeley and Hitch 1974). The Working memory and music are considered as an inevitable component of cognition and entertainment. Listening to music is a widely adapted secondary activities of humans. Research has shown background music to improve linguistic information processing (Angel et al. 2010), shielding from ambient noise, increasing task attention (Hargreaves and North 1997). However, the detailed interaction between music and memory on a physiological level needs further understanding about task performance. Baddeley & Hitch's working memory model (1974) bifurcated the working memory system into two subsystems: 1. Visuospatial sketchpad;

N. L. Black et al. (Eds.): IEA 2021, LNNS 223, pp. 559–565, 2022.
https://doi.org/10.1007/978-3-030-74614-8_69

2: Phonological loop. Processing and retaining visual and sound information were carried out in the sketch pad and phonological loop. Cocchini et al. (2001) and Salamé and Baddeley (1982) suggested the potential interference of auditory stimulus with the phonological loop, as the processing of acoustic info takes place in the loop. Salamé and Baddeley (1982) postulated that maintenance and rehearsal of verbal information took place in phonological loop. Listening to music during primary task will only result in the competition for phonological loop resources, resulting in corrupted memory and poor working memory performance. Thus, the current study hypothesized as follows:

H1: Background music will negatively impact working memory performance

However, to have more in-depth insights into the working memory function and its performance during musical interference, understanding the neural underpinnings using electrophysiological measurements becomes vital. Gevins et al. (1998) established the reliability of EEG as a tool to analyze working memory tasks. Therefore, this study utilized EEG to study working memory.

As Oberauer et al. (2004) suggested, the capacity of wm could be tested using tasks requiring memory and processing. Hence this study used backward digit span (BDS). Its prevalence in clinical psychology (Ramsay and Reynolds 1995) made BDS an appropriate task for the study. In BDS, subjects have to encode, process the encoded digits to invert, rehearse the digits in memory for efficient recollection. The task consisted of three stages, namely, encoding, maintenance, and recall of digits. The maintenance period was provided to utilize the rehearsing function of working memory. The performance of working memory relied on effective recall contingent on continuous rehearsing of digits. The frequency bands, namely theta, alpha, and beta, were studied. The paper is divided into 4 sections. Sections 2 elaborates on experimental methodology and acquisition of behavioral parameters and EEG signals, followed by results and inference in Sect. 3. Discussion and future direction are provided in Sect. 4.

2 Methodology

Six participants (26 ± 2.19 years old) with no history of mental illness were recruited for the study. All participants gave their informed consent. The study had two conditions: 1. With-music; 2. No-music and the choice of music was selected by the participants. The participants sat comfortably in a normally lit silent room, and the music was played in headphones at 60 db volume during with-music condition. Backward Wechsler Digit Span (BWDS) test was used in the study. All subjects participated in both the conditions in a counterbalanced fashion to reduce the bias. The digit stimuli were presented on the laptop using Paradigm Stimulation Presentation software (Perception Research Systems 2016). Behavioral parameters, namely accuracy and typing duration, along with electrophysiological signal electroencephalogram (EEG), were collected. Typing duration was defined as the period from the entry of the first digit till the last digit. Accuracy was the percentage of correct responses for each digit sequence.

EEG was collected using Emotiv 14 channel headset, and paradigm software recorded the typing duration and accuracy. EEG dataset was divided into two groups:

with and without music conditions. The bandpass filter of the range 0.5 Hz–30 Hz was used to filter the dataset. ICA was used to remove muscle artifacts, eye movements, and blinks. Each dataset was segmented into three epochs, namely encode, maintenance, and recall for each digit, theta, alpha, and beta spectral powers was calculated for each epoch for both conditions. Two subjects were removed from analysis due to excessive contamination of signals. All statistical analyses were performed in SPSS version 20.

2.1 Working Memory Task

The task had three stages: Encoding, Maintenance, and Recall. The encoding stage consisted of silent memorization of displayed digits. The maintenance phase consisted of holding the memorized digits in memory, and subjects typed the memorized digits backward during the recall phase. The sequence ranged from 3 to 7 digits, and each digit had five trials. For each trial, the digits were displayed individually on the center of the computer screen for 750 ms, followed by a black screen for 25 ms. The maintenance phase was a black screen with a duration of 4 s followed by recall phase. The methodology used in the experiment was shown in Fig. 1.

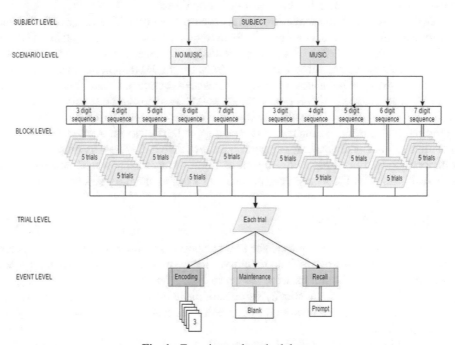

Fig. 1. Experimental methodology

3   Results

3.1   EEG Analysis

Spectral values were obtained for three frequency bands, namely theta (3–7.9 Hz), alpha (8–12.9 Hz), and beta (13–30 Hz) at all 14 sensor locations. Spectral values at pre-frontal, frontal, and parietal channels were averaged to obtain global theta, alpha, and beta spectral values. Two-way repeated measure ANOVA for factor Digits(5) X Stages (3) performed separately for two conditions did not yield significant results.

Digit 3 had a positive Pearson correlation between spectral values of alpha during recall and maintenance stages ($r = 0.993$, $p < 0.05$) and between spectral values of theta during encode and maintenance stage($r = 0.995$, $p < 0.05$) for with-music condition. Beta's spectral values during encoding and maintaining stages showed a strong positive Pearson correlation for digit 6 ($r = 0.999$, $p < 0.05$). Pearson correlation analysis of spectral values of beta showed strong positive association between encode and recall stages for digits 7 ($r = 0.991$, $p < 0.05$) and 6 ($r = 0.989$, $p < 0.05$); similar relationship was found between maintenance and recall stages for digits 7($r = 0.992$, $p < 0.05$) and 6 ($r = 0.988$, $p < 0.05$). All the p values were Bonferroni corrected. No correlation was found between stages and digits for no-music condition.

Two-way repeated-measures ANOVA for factors Condition (2) x Stages (3) revealed significant main effects for conditions in theta frequency band for digit 6 alone $F(1, 3) = 11.42$, $p < 0.05$, $\eta2 = 0.792$. The descriptive statistics showed that theta's mean spectral values in with-music condition were higher (mean $= 4.095$) than in no-music condition (mean $= 3.785$). Same analysis for digit 6 revealed significant main effect for stages in alpha band $F(2, 6) - 13.94$, $p < 0.05$, $\eta2 = 0.823$. A posthoc test using Bonferroni correction showed a statistically significant increase in mean spectral values during encoding than during the maintenance stage ($p < 0.05$). No interaction effects were significant in both the two-way repeated-measures ANOVA. Thus, as music competes with working memory during with-music condition, the spectral power of theta increases. This result suggests the interference of music in working memory task performance.

3.2   Behavioural Analysis

Typing duration and accuracy were the two behavioral parameters considered to determine music's influence on working memory. Mean typing duration and mean accuracy percentage for two conditions were shown in Fig. 2 and Fig. 3, respectively. Typing duration of digit 3 had a statistically significant mean difference between music (mean $= 1358.96 \pm 297.60$) and without music (mean $= 2126.42 \pm 491.27$) condition $t(3) = -6.89$, $p < 0.05$.

A paired t-test for accuracy, between with-music (mean $= 35 \pm 34.15$) and no-music (mean $= 60 \pm 36.51$) conditions revealed statistically significant mean difference in accuracy for digit 6 $t(3) = -5$, $p < 0.05$. This result indicates that the presence of music reduces the accuracy as working memory reaches its maximum capacity. Overall, as the digit sequence size increases, music competes for working memory resulting in reduced accuracy and larger typing duration.

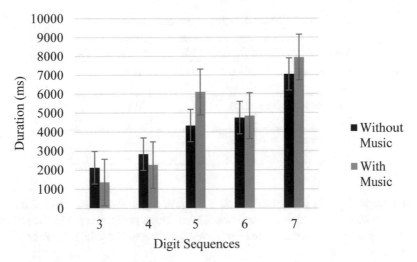

Fig. 2. Mean typing duration for two conditions. Error bars indicate standard errors.

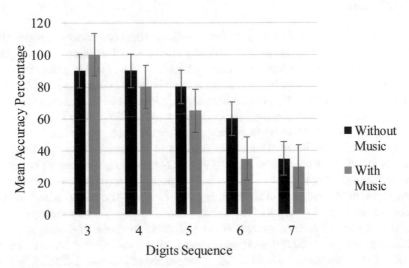

Fig. 3. Mean accuracy percentage for two conditions. Error bars indicate standard errors

3.3   Survey Analysis

A questionnaire survey was conducted to determine the preference of listening to music while engaging in low, medium, and high cognitively intensive tasks. 219 responses were obtained, and three answers were rejected due to duplication errors; thus, a total of 216 responses was considered for further analysis. Household chores, browsing social media were categorized as low-intensity tasks, reading a new novel and multi-texting as moderately intensive; driving, listening to lecture, studying were classified as high-intensity tasks. The results are shown in Table 1.

Table 1. Music listening preferences during tasks

Tasks intensity	Yes (%)	No (%)	Sometimes (%)
Low intensity tasks	62.6	31.0	6.4
Medium intensity tasks	22.6	47	30.6
High intensity tasks	34.7	36.5	28.8

On average, 39.96% preferred listening to music regularly, and 38.16% did not like music irrespective of the task's intensities. These results reveal the prevalence of music in day-to-day activities making music an essential factor to consider its role in affecting the task performance.

4 Discussion

High theta power during with-music condition indicated the occurrence of greater allocation of attentional resources as the task difficulty increases in the presence of background music. This result agrees with the research by Klimesch et al. (1997), where the authors reported an increase in theta with increasing task difficulty. An increase in alpha spectral power during encoding the digits in with-music condition revealed that more significant effort was needed to encode the digits in memory successfully. The alpha power was reported to reduce with increase in working memory load (Krause et al. 2000) during encoding. However, auditory stimulation resulted in increased alpha synchronization (Krause et al. 1997). Klimesch et al. (1999) also observed an increase in upper alpha power during encoding at central and parietal regions brain regions. As mentioned in existing research, the increase in alpha during encoding, despite being an unusual event, could be attributed to stimulation of the auditory cortex by music. The accuracy decreased as the size of digit sequences increased. The decrease in accuracy during with-music condition (mean $= 62 \pm 22.89$) was greater than during no-music condition (mean $= 72 \pm 15.06$). Typing duration showed an increasing trend as the task difficulty increased, which was in accordance with the Sternberg effect. The effect states an increase in recall time as the items held in working memory increases in size (Sternberg 1966). Thus, as the tasks begin to utilize the maximum capacity of working memory, music could only become a source of hindrance for efficient performance, as revealed by the study results. Although this study's sample size is limited, the study gave insight into the interaction between music, task difficulty, and working memory capacity. Nevertheless, the survey results showed music to be a preferred choice of the secondary task; the current study result indicated music negatively impacted the performance. The results recommended the disengagement from secondary tasks as the task difficulty increases.

As participants chose their preferred choice of music, music would have captured higher saliency (Gustavson 2014), demanding more attentional resources (Engle et al. 1999) and disrupting the task performance. Future research could manipulate the choice of music to study its impact on performance. In conclusion, music negatively impacted the working memory performance, and hence the hypothesis – music has a negative impact on working memory was accepted.

References

Baddeley, A.D., Hitch, G.: Working memory. In: Psychology of Learning and Motivation, vol. 8, pp. 47–89. Academic Press, Cambridge (1974)

Angel, L.A., Polzella, D.J., Elvers, G.C.: Background music and cognitive performance. Percept. Mot. Skills **110**(3_suppl), 1059–1064 (2010)

Hargreaves, D.J., North, A.: The Social Psychology of Music. Oxford University Press, Oxford (1997)

Cocchini, G., Beschin, N., Jehkonen, M.: The fluff test: a simple task to assess body representation neglect. Neuropsychol. Rehabil. **11**(1), 17–31 (2001)

Salame, P., Baddeley, A.: Disruption of short-term memory by unattended speech: implications for the structure of working memory. J. Verbal Learn. Verbal Behav. **21**(2), 150–164 (1982)

Gevins, A., Smith, M.E., Leong, H., McEvoy, L., Whitfield, S., Du, R., Rush, G.: Monitoring working memory load during computer-based tasks with EEG pattern recognition methods. Hum. Factors **40**(1), 79–91 (1998)

Oberauer, K., Lange, E., Engle, R.W.: Working memory capacity and resistance to interference. J. Mem. Lang. **51**(1), 80–96 (2004)

Ramsay, M.C., Reynolds, C.R.: Separate digits tests: a brief history, a literature review, and a reexamination of the factor structure of the test of memory and learning (TOMAL). Neuropsychol. Rev. **5**(3), 151–171 (1995)

Klimesch, W., Doppelmayr, M., Pachinger, T., Ripper, B.: Brain oscillations and human memory: EEG correlates in the upper alpha and theta band. Neurosci. Lett. **238**(1–2), 9–12 (1997)

Krause, C.M., Sillanmäki, L., Koivisto, M., Saarela, C., Häggqvist, A., Laine, M., Hämäläinen, H.: The effects of memory load on event-related EEG desynchronization and synchronization. Clin. Neurophysiol. **111**(11), 2071–2078 (2000)

Krause, C.M., Pörn, B., Lang, A.H., Laine, M.: Relative alpha desynchronization and synchronization during speech perception. Cogn. Brain Res. **5**(4), 295–299 (1997)

Klimesch, W., Doppelmayr, M., Schwaiger, J., Auinger, P., Winkler, T.H.: Paradoxical'alpha synchronization in a memory task. Cogn. Brain Res. **7**(4), 493–501 (1999)

Sternberg, S.: High-speed scanning in human memory. Science **153**(3736), 652–654 (1966)

Gustavson, A., Hanneken, K., Moldysz, A., Simon, B.: The effects of music on short-term memory and physiological arousal. J. Ass. Neuro. Wisc. Educ. Physiol. Dep. **435**, 1–8 (2014)

Engle, R.W., Tuholski, S.W., Laughlin, J.E., Conway, A.R.: Working memory, short-term memory, and general fluid intelligence: a latent-variable approach. J. Exp. Psychol. Gen. **128**(3), 309 (1999)

Part VIII: Working with Computer Systems (Edited by Nicole Jochems)

Empirical Comparison of the Effects of Symmetrical and Asymmetrical Video Game Console Controllers on Players Performance

Asma Alfargani and Ahamed Altaboli[✉]

Industrial and Manufacturing Systems Engineering Department, University of Benghazi,
Benghazi, Libya
ahmed.altaboli@uob.edu.ly

Abstract. This study utilized an experiment to evaluate the effect of video game console controllers, namely Sony PlayStation 3 (symmetrical type) and Xbox 360 (asymmetrical type), on players' performance. Twelve players were randomly chosen to perform tasks with both controllers. They were all males, their age ranged between 25 and 39 years with an average age of 30.75 years. All were right-handed. Each controller was tested when players were performing tasks consisting of playing selected levels of "Need for Speed" game. The first task is to complete a race on easy mode as a training task, and the second task is to complete a race on normal mode as the main experimental task. Player's completion time of the second race and the number of errors were used as performance measures. Errors were divided into two types: number of crashes and number of wrong turns. Result of the experiment showed that there were significant differences between the two types of console controllers in completion time and number of errors. The asymmetrical controller (the Xbox 360) resulted in better performance than the symmetrical controller (PlayStation 3) did.

Keywords: Video games controllers · Symmetrical and asymmetrical video game controllers · Video games players' performance

1 Introduction

Video games have grown immensely popular as both an entertainment medium and as a topic of scholarly inquiry. They comprise a large and profitable industry that continuing growing and expanding each year. In 2018, the total video game sales exceeded $43.4 billion and over 164 million adults in the United States play video games [1].

Video game controllers are often used for tasks other than gaming [5]. Thus, it is important to know how to evaluate and advance such technology. However, empirical studies that compare video game controllers are very rare. The authors of this study could not locate any empirical studies that compare symmetrical and asymmetrical types of video game console controllers.

One of the few studies concerned with comparing video game controllers that were found in the related literature included comparing video game controllers for point-select tasks using a Fitts' law task, as per ISO 9241-9 [5]. The compared controllers

N. L. Black et al. (Eds.): IEA 2021, LNNS 223, pp. 569–576, 2022.
https://doi.org/10.1007/978-3-030-74614-8_70

were the Nintendo Wii Remote for infrared pointing, the Nintendo Classic Controller for analogue stick pointing, and a standard mouse as a baseline condition.

Other published studies that involved video game controllers tested other types of controllers (than symmetrical and asymmetrical) and were mostly concerned with their interactions and effects on aspects of gaming other than player performance and usability. Types of controllers tested included Nintendo Wii vs PlayStation 2 [2, 4], traditional controller vs motion capturing controller [3, 6], and steering wheel vs traditional controller [7]. The studied aspects of gaming included presence and enjoyment [2, 3, 7], subjective experience [4] and frustration [6].

The controllers included in this current study are the Sony PlayStation 3 (PS3) controller and the Xbox 360 controller (see Fig. 1). The only significant design difference between the two is the positions of the analogue stick and directional pad. The PlayStation 3 has a symmetrical layout with the analogue stick on the right of the directional pad. While the Xbox 360 has an asymmetrical layout with the analogue stick on the left of the directional pad [5].

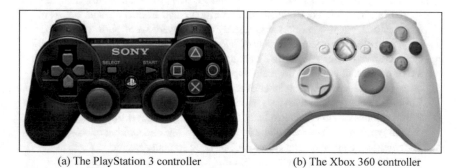

(a) The PlayStation 3 controller   (b) The Xbox 360 controller

Fig. 1. The two types of controllers included in the study.

This study utilized an experiment to evaluate the effect of video game consoles controller, namely Sony PlayStation 3 (symmetrical type) and Xbox 360 (asymmetrical type) on player's performance. The purpose of this study is to investigate and compare the effects of the selected two types of game consoles controllers (PS3 controller and Xbox 360 controller) on player's performance.

The main research questions that the study is trying to answer are: Does the type of video game console controller (symmetrical or asymmetrical) have an effect on players' performance? And if there is an effect, which type of controller gives better players' performance?

An experiment was designed and conducted to achieve the objective and answer the research questions.

2 Method

2.1 Design of the Experiment

An experiment was designed and performed to compare the difference between players' performance when using the two types of consoles controllers (PS3 and Xbox 360).

A counterbalanced between-participants design was utilized. The type of controller represents the main factor (independent variable) in the experiment. It has two levels: PS3 (symmetrical type) and Xbox 360 (asymmetrical type).

Players were instructed to perform the same tasks on the two consoles (two levels of the main factor) and two performance variables were measured: task's completion time and number of errors. These two variables were used as dependent variables (responses).

Paired t-tests were utilized to test the differences between the means of the performance variables under the two levels of the main factor (type of controller).

2.2 Participants

Twelve participants (players) performed the experiment. They were chosen randomly. They were all males, their age ranged between 25 and 39 years with an average age of 30.75 years. All participants had at least one year experience playing the PlayStation 3 and Xbox 360. All were right-handed.

2.3 Tasks and Procedure

The performed tasks in the experiment consist of playing selected levels of "Need for Speed" game. The first task is to complete a race on the easy mode as a training task, and the second task is to complete a race on the normal mode as the main experimental task.

Player's completion time and the number of errors of the second race were used as performance measures. Errors were divided into two types: type one is number of crashes and type two is number of wrong turns.

Prior to beginning, players were asked to complete a questionnaire. The questionnaire asked demographic questions such as age, gender, and frequency of use. After filling out the questionnaire, each player was asked to complete the first race on easy mode as a training trial, and then complete the second race on normal mode as the main task. Each player performed these tasks with both PS3 controller and Xbox 360 controller. The order with which they used the two types of controllers was counterbalanced; with half the participants using the PS3 first and the other half using Xbox 360 first.

The timing function on screen of the race game was used as record of the completion time. Numbers of errors was obtained by observing and recording the players' crashes and wrong turns.

3 Results

3.1 Results of Completion Time

Table 1 shows players' completion times and descriptive statistics for the two controllers. From the table, one can see that Xbox 360 has lower average completion time than PS3.

Table 1. Completion times (in minutes).

Player	PS3 Controller	Xbox 360 Controller
1	13.08	5.50
2	15.88	5.18
3	4.97	4.73
4	12.68	8.07
5	3.67	2.93
6	2.60	4.00
7	3.12	2.28
8	5.15	2.15
9	5.60	3.05
10	1.72	1.90
11	1.97	1.68
12	2.93	2.68
Average	**6.11**	**3.68**
Standard deviation	**4.9**	**1.9**

A paired t-test between the mean completion time of the two controllers was used to see if there were any statistically significant differences between them. Results of the test are shown in Table 2.

Table 2. Results of paired t-test between mean completion time of the two controllers

	PS3 Controller	Xbox 360 Controller
Mean	6.11	3.68
Variance	23.96	3.58
Degree of freedom	11	
t Statistic	2.35	
P-value	0.0382	

Statistically significant difference was found between the mean completion time of the two controller (p-value = 0.0382); the mean completion time of the Xbox 360 controller is significant lower than the mean completion time of the PS3 controller.

3.2   Results of Number of Errors

Number of Crashes

Table 3 shows number of crashes reordered in the second race. They are given per each player for PS3 controller and Xbox 360 controller. Descriptive statistics per each controller are also given in the table.

As with completion times, Xbox 360 has lower average number of crashes than PS3.

Results of paired t-test between mean number of crashes of the two controllers indicated that mean number of crashes of Xbox 360 is significantly lower than mean number of crashes of PS3, as shown in Table 4 with p-value = 0.032.

Table 3. Number of crashes.

Player	PS3 Controller	Xbox 360 Controller
1	63	25
2	60	23
3	27	21
4	73	37
5	30	26
6	33	22
7	22	17
8	17	15
9	18	14
10	5	13
11	63	25
12	60	23
Average	31.25	19.91
Standard deviation	22.13	7.28

Number of Wrong Turns

Table 5 shows number of wrong turns reordered in the second race. They are given per each player for PS3 controller and Xbox 360 controller. Descriptive statistics per each controller are also given in the table.

Table 4. Results of paired t-test between mean number of crashes of the two controllers

	PS3 Controller	Xbox 360 Controller
Mean	31.25	19.91
Variance	489.84	52.99
Degree of freedom	11	
t Stat	2.43	
P-value	0.032	

As with completion times and number of crashes, Xbox 360 has lower average number of wrong turns than PS3.

In this case too, mean number of wrong turns of Xbox 360 is significantly lower than mean number of wrong turns of PS3, as results of the paired t-test in Table 6 show, with p-value of 0.048.

Table 5. Number of wrong turns

Player	PS3 Controller	Xbox 360 Controller
1	17	19
2	11	9
3	9	12
4	54	18
5	20	6
6	18	8
7	8	0
8	13	5
9	15	10
10	2	0
11	4	2
12	3	4
Average	14.5	7.75
Standard deviation	13.8	6.28

Table 6. Results of paired t-test between mean number of wrong turns of the two controllers

	PS3 Controller	Xbox 360 Controller
Mean	14.5	7.75
Variance	190.45	39.47
Degree of freedom	11	
t Stat	2.216	
P-value	0.048	

4 Conclusions and Limitations

Results of the experiment showed significant differences in player's performance between the symmetrical PS3 controller and the asymmetrical Xbox 360 controller. Better players' performance in term of completion times and number of errors was recorded with the asymmetrical Xbox 360 controller compared to the symmetrical PS3 controller.

The main conclusion from this study is that the asymmetrical controller (Xbox 360) gives better performance than the symmetrical controller (PS3).

One limitation of this study is that all players participated in the experiment were males and right handed. This limits the results of this study to only right-handed male players. Another limitation is that the controllers were tested with relatively limited number of tasks that may not represent all the typical tasks players performed with the controllers.

In addition, in future work, it is recommended that the two types of controllers should be tested when used for tasks other than only playing games (e.g. media management).

References

1. Entertainment Software Association (ESA): 2019 Essential Facts (2019)
2. Limperos, A., Schmierbach, M., Kegerise, A., Dardis, F.: Gaming across different consoles: exploring the influence of control scheme on game-player enjoyment. Cyberpsychol. Behav. Soc. Netw. **14**(6), 345–350 (2011). https://doi.org/10.1089/cyber.2010.0146
3. McGloin, R., Krcmar, M.: The impact of controller naturalness on spatial presence, gamer enjoyment, and perceived realism in a tennis simulation video game. Presence: Teleoper. Virtual Environ. **20**(4), 309–324 (2011). https://doi.org/10.1162/PRES_a_00053
4. Nacke, L.: Wiimote vs. controller: electroencephalographic measurement of affective gameplay interaction. In: Proceedings of the International Academic Conference on the Future of Game Design and Technology (Futureplay 2010), pp. 159–166. Association for Computing Machinery, New York (2010). https://doi.org/10.1145/1920778.1920801
5. Natapov, D., Castellucci, S., MacKenzie, I.: ISO 9241-9 evaluation of video game controllers. In: Proceedings of Graphic Interface Conference 2009, pp. 223–230. Canadian Information Processing Society (2009)

6. Rogers, R., Bowman, N., Oliver, M.: It's not the model that doesn't fit, it's the controller! The role of cognitive skills in understanding the links between natural mapping, performance, and enjoyment of console video games. Comput. Human Behav. **49**, 588–596 (2015). https://doi.org/10.1016/j.chb.2015.03.027

7. Williams, K.: The effects of dissociation, game controllers, and 3D versus 2D on presence and enjoyment. Comput. Human Behav. **38**, 142–150 (2014). https://doi.org/10.1016/j.chb.2014.05.040

A Novel 3D Editor for Gesture Design Based on Labanotation

Kathleen Anderson, Börge Kordts$^{(\boxtimes)}$, and Andreas Schrader

University of Lübeck, Ratzeburger Allee 160, 23562 Lübeck, Germany
kordts@itm.uni-luebeck.de

Abstract. Applying the natural interaction paradigm to digital systems offers increased comfort to their users, but also poses new challenges to interaction designers, particularly for gesture-controlled systems. While the documentation of human movement has been a research topic for many years, its results have not yet been fully applied to the area of motion-controlled systems.

Labanotation, a motion notation language originating in theatre and dance, has been widely discussed as a promising candidate to overcome this issue. It has been argued that its major drawback is the effort required to learn how to use it.

In this paper, we contribute to the problem of a universally accepted standardized documentation method of human movement by presenting a novel 3D editor that reduces the hurdle to document gestures and transforms the cumbersome task of learning and using Labanotation into a simple and even enjoyable process. Notably, the editor allows learning the notation language via trial-and-error.

Keywords: Usability testing · Interaction design · Documentation · Labanotation · Natural user interface

1 Motivation

In the past decade, the natural interaction paradigm has been a strongly focused research topic in the human-computer interaction community, resulting in various contributions and insights. Consequently, the paradigm was largely adopted in practice and pervades our everyday lives, more recently also in novel AR and VR scenarios. Notably, whole-body gestures have been employed for interactions with ambient interactive systems.

The documentation of human movement has been a research topic for many years. In particular, the need for a standard machine and human-readable documentation method for natural interactions has been discussed [1]. However, its results have not yet been fully applied to the area of motion-controlled systems, which still faces the difficulty of conveying gestures without a unified description language. It has been argued that such a language and notation system would facilitate teaching and learning of movement styles, permit the writing of universally understood scores of movements, and provide a universal language through which specialists could communicate [2].

Labanotation, a graphical motion notation language, has been widely discussed as a promising candidate to overcome this issue. Despite its origin in theatre and dance,

N. L. Black et al. (Eds.): IEA 2021, LNNS 223, pp. 577–584, 2022.
https://doi.org/10.1007/978-3-030-74614-8_71

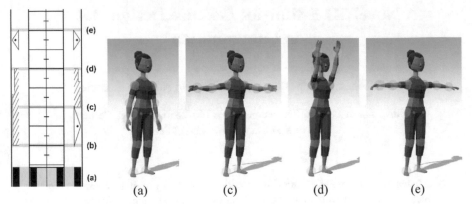

Fig. 1. An example of a very short Labanotation score and a visualization of the resulting positions. Note that in position (c), one arm is pointing forwards and the other arm directly to the side.

its creator, Rudolf Laban, specifically stated his intention of constructing a universal notation capable of capturing any kind of movement. Its graphical nature and basic design choices make it an accessible notation that still provides the flexibility to capture motion either roughly using only a few shapes or, if needed, in many small details. It has been argued that its major drawback is the effort required to learn how to use the notation.

Since the language was created as an adaptation of musical notes, it features a similar structure: symbols are positioned inside a staff, the distance to the beginning of the staff indicates the timing of a movement. Different from music sheets, the staff is oriented vertically and read from bottom to top. Every column defines the movement of one body part. The most elemental sign is the direction symbol, which expresses the horizontal direction (e.g., left, right, forward) through its shape and the vertical direction or level (high, middle or low) through its shading. While such a symbol is stretched so that its start and duration match the start and duration of the described movement, the symbol itself defines only the **final** position, which is reached after the movement.

Figure 1 demonstrates a very basic Labanotation score: we begin in (a), the neutral position with all body parts pointing downwards in a relaxed fashion. Starting in the position marked b, the left arm begins a very slow transition to a forward (symbol shape), high (symbol shading) direction, reflected by the long symbol in the leftmost column. As there are no further limitations given, the left arm is moved on the shortest route. The resulting position is displayed in image d. The right arm starts with a shorter movement to end up pointing directly to the side (right, middle) in position c. It then starts moving to ultimately have the same position as the left arm (forward, high) in d. After a short pause (in which the current position is simply held), the score defines a quick movement to the sides (right/left, middle) for both arms simultaneously, the same position that was already held by the right arm in c.

Once the concept is understood, creating basic Labanotation can be simple. However, matching the signs on a score to the movements of a person (and back) needs certain practice. Arguably, the effort required to learn how to use Labanotation is its major disadvantage [1].

In this paper, we present a 3D Labanotation editor that provides a supportive tool for interaction designers and novice users and fosters the usage of Labanotation to document motion and, in particular, gestures. To support the learning of Labanotation, the digital editor, on the one hand, directly transforms Labanotation symbols into the motion of an animated three-dimensional model. On the other hand, it features the calculation of the appropriate symbol for a position, after the user sets a joint angle on the same model. Hence, our editor presents an option to get used to Labanotation via a trial-and-error approach. It also offers a fast and interactive method of designing short animations, which are directly connected to the corresponding Labanotation.

2 Related Work

Due to the wide adoption of gesture control, there are by now many ways of documenting gestures. Besides the obvious solution of using a film, an image or a textual description, there are other, more inventive proposals. Gesture Cards, for example, represent a hybrid gesture notation mixing graphical and textual elements [3]. All approaches share the drawback of being subjective to the reader and not machine readable. The authors of GestIT [4] propose a solution based on the formulation of an expression using a set of ground terms and operators (such as *iterative* or *parallel*), following a complex set of rules.

We consider a visual representation an essential part of a gesture notation language if it is meant to be understood and used by both machines and humans. Instead of defining a new terminology, we examined existing gesture notation languages, of which Labanotation is the most popular candidate. However, as mentioned above, the clarity of Labanotation comes with the price of its complexity, especially for novices. Various software tackles this issue, but only a few allow the user to animate the motion in 3D. A thorough search of the relevant literature[1] yielded only LabanEditor3 [5] as a solution to manipulate Labanotation in 3D. The final version was released in 2010 and incorporates two components: a WYSIWYG editor for Labanotation and MotionViewer, the display of a 3D character animation.

While LabanEditor3 does resemble our editor, it does not allow the direct manipulation of limb angles to create a movement symbol, there is no visualization of the association from score column to body part, and the Labanotation score and the 3D animation cannot be viewed at the same time. While it can provide a useful tool to its main target group: dancers and choreographers, it is not sufficient for interaction designers, who are constructing and continuously changing a short movement, while, at the same time, getting used to the concept of Labanotation.

Any other tools to create animations for Labanotation are carried out by exporting a finished score from one application to a different one, which then renders an animation.

---

[1] Using, among others, Google Scholar, the IEEE Xplore Digital Library and the ACM Digital Library and combinations of the search terms "Labanotation", "3D", "editor" and "movement documentation" in April 2020.

An example of that practice is LabanWriter [6] (an editor for Labanotation scores), combined with LifeForms[2] to produce the animation.

All tools found in our research mainly focus on dance, and not specifically on gestures. Dance often means a movement through the whole room and results in the participants not only standing but also sitting or even lying on the ground. While the precise angles of some joints can be left open and will be defined by the movement of the remaining body, most gestures are explicitly timed to match the beats of the music. To utilize gestures as an input method for a system, the user usually stands in one place and is often required to face a camera. While the exact timing is generally not essential, a rather accurate angle of joints is needed for the software to recognize the gesture. This considerable difference necessitates a differentiation between the two applications of Labanotation, an editor meant solely to document dance cannot easily be used to notate gesture control movements.

3 Methodology

Loosely following a human-centred design process, first, an analysis was carried out covering related work, state of the art gesture controls, usage scenarios, and an examination of the target group, ultimately yielding in requirements for a 3D Labanotation editor that is supposed to support learning the notation language. Section 4 provides further insights into the results. Next, the editor was iteratively developed relying on the feedback of experts in the field of human-computer interaction and, in particular, user interface design.

A preliminary user study at the end of the process (see Sect. 6) was finally conducted to measure the editor's usability and to assess whether the tool is useful to notate gestures.

4 Analysis and Conception

To extract a set of gestures that need to be representable by our editor, we analysed many applications of human gestures used not only as part of common digital systems, but also in the real world[3]. Noticeably, an application tends to either include nothing but finger and hand movement, or full body motion with mostly undefined finger position. While both options could be useful when included into an editor, we decided to focus on full body movement by featuring an arbitrary rotation of the joints of the hip, knee, ankle, shoulder, elbow, wrist, and neck, while excluding the finger joints.

A simple approach to convey the direct association between a Labanotation column and a body part and respectively a symbol and a movement obligates the notation score and the human model to be visible at the same time. This further allows learning via trial

---

[2] https://www.credo-interactive.com/.

[3] The analysed utilizations include the American sign language and nonverbal communication in the context of both military (based on U.S. army commands [12]) and sports (referee signals for football games). Additionally, the Microsoft Kinect, the Samsung Smart TV, the Leap Motion, the Myo Armband, and the Microsoft Research Cambridge-12 Gesture Set [13–15] have been analysed.

and error: inputting a joint rotation on the three-dimensional model and immediately seeing the results in the expected symbol.

The user interaction required to set the joint positions in our application is exceedingly similar to the user input given while designing a three-dimensional scene or animation using software like Blender, AutoCAD and Unity3D[4]. An analysis of all three applications revealed many common points, which we integrated into our editor.

5 Realization

The editor was realized using Unity3D, an engine mainly used to create applications that combine a 3D component and a 2D user interface. The engine itself is implemented in C++, the code for this project is written in C#. To build a web application, Unity makes use of WebGL (Web Graphics Library)[5]. This JavaScript API renders interactive two- or three-dimensional graphics without the need for plug-ins and supports all common browsers. To save and load data, the gesture is translated to XML in a scheme [7] developed and already utilized for different applications [8].

Essentially, our editor consists of two parts: a 2D visualization of the Labanotation score and a 3D human model, animated to match the score. Both components are displayed next to each other (see Fig. 2a), however, the implementation is mostly separate. Apart from synchronizing state and time, both units function independently.

The 2D score display allows the manipulation or deletion of a symbol (via right click). Left click on a column highlights not only that column but also the corresponding joint of the model. The time cursor (blue line) indicates the position of the score that is currently seen in the 3D model. Following the standards of current 3D modelling software, configuration of a joint angle can be done either by selecting and dragging one of the three rotation rings (Fig. 2b) or by entering the desired Euler angles (bottom left in Fig. 2a).

Translating a basic movement symbol to a joint angle is fairly simple and can be done by matching both the shape (horizontal direction) and shading (vertical direction) of a symbol to an Euler rotation about the respective axis, which is then translated to Quaternions to avoid issues like Gimbal Lock. Due to the ambiguity of Euler angles, the reverse calculation from angle back to symbol is not directly based on a translation from Quaternion to Euler angles or a manual input of them.

Instead, the connection between the concerned joint and its directly subordinate parent[6] is translated to a vector and (in essence) projected into each of the three planes (xy, xz, yz) to find a consistent representation of the three axis rotations of Euler angles, which can then be converted to a Labanotation symbol using the inverse method of the opposite translation direction.

---

[4] https://www.blender.org/, https://www.autodesk.com/products/autocad/ and https://unity.com/ in January 2021.

[5] https://www.khronos.org/webgl/wiki/Main_Page in May 2019.

[6] The parent to the elbow is, for example, the shoulder, while the elbow itself is parent to the wrist.

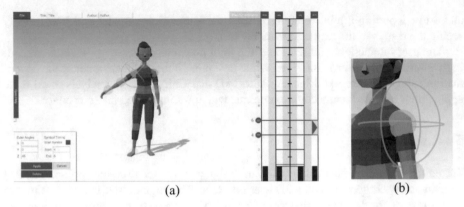

(a)

(b)

Fig. 2. The 3D Labanotation editor and the rotation rings.

6 User Study

A preliminary user study indicates that the resulting editor can convey Labanotation even to novice users and thus may reduce the initial hurdle to learn the notation language. We evaluated the usability based on the seven dialogue principles of ISO 9241-110 via an online survey. The testees where asked to perform two groups of tasks, including opening an existing file and creating a new one, editing the movement to create two gestures by moving symbols and by adding new ones, and saving the resulting gesture. Each subtask allowed direct feedback about potential problems or ideas. The tasks were followed by the standardized questionnaire ISONORM 9241/110-S [9].

The nine participants were aged between 20 and 30. None of them had worked with Labanotation before. They were either studying media computer science or working as developers and user interface designers in smaller companies. With a total score of approximately 113.89 of 147 (calculated by adding the means of all questions) and a mean of 5.42 from 7 (standard deviation 1.24), placing the result between "+" and "++" (good and very good), the usability of the software was considered agreeable by the survey participants, who pointed out that the usage of the 3D editor was easy and fast to learn. The testees also noted a few possible improvements that should be considered in future versions.

The main point of improvement was identified as the lack of options to individualize the application, like the decision whether to show or hide certain displays or menus and the option to change the colour scheme. Though relevant for future releases, this aspect carries less significance for our prototype. Two dialogue principles especially important to our objective are self-descriptiveness and suitability for learning: Labanotation is meant to be conveyed not by means of wordy descriptions but simply by using the software to input gestures. The self-descriptiveness was rated with a mean value of 5.15, suitability for learning with a mean of 6.04.

The result indicates that the implementation was able to meet the objective of conveying Labanotation to novice users, while at the same time presenting the activity of experimenting with gestures and Labanotation in an engaging and enjoyable fashion. All but one testee confirmed that they were able to understand the basics of the notation and now consider themselves able to utilise it (with the help of our software) to design gestures.

7 Conclusion

In this paper, we present a tool to support the documentation of motion and, in particular, gestures using Labanotation. Even though the description of human movement is a topic that has been researched as early as the fifteenth century [10, 11], scientists and designers implementing human gestures as a method to control digital systems have not yet established a standard approach to record gestures. Instead, descriptions are given as videos, images, or as natural language texts. All current options share the issue of being either too vague or including unwanted detail.

We believe Labanotation to be the most promising candidate for a unified motion documentation notation due to its flexibility and the representable and easily editable scores. Hence, our objective is to lower the initial hurdle users face when first confronted with Labanotation. We present an interactive illustration of the basic principles of the notation through the introduction of a three-dimensional component that is directly connected to the Labanotation score. Additionally, our editor is aimed to provide a fast and simple way to create movement descriptions for gestures.

The results of our evaluation strongly suggest that the goal was achieved. Using an interactive three-dimensional human model helps newcomers to understand and use Labanotation without necessitating extensive explanation, while at the same time transforming the labour of reading instructions and learning the meaning of symbols by heart into the entertaining activity of experimenting with movements and finding the matching symbol for a created gesture.

The basic functionalities of the software suffice to create simple movements. Although most of the advanced Labanotation symbols would make the first understanding of the language unnecessarily complicated, they would allow to describe a higher degree of detail of a gesture once understood. Future implementations of the editor could allow the user to include or exclude more complex Labanotation symbols and therefore adjust the system to his or her current skill level.

The *Movement Analysis Engine* [8] is able to calculate Labanotation based on motion capture data and to convert said Labanotation into the same XML scheme used in this work. Consequently, it is possible to indirectly use motion capture data from a depth camera stream as an input method. That option could be further extended by integrating the engine into our editor, which would allow the input of Labanotation symbols by performing them in front of a motion capture camera.

Implementing a tool to alleviate the initial hurdle of learning Labanotation presents an important step in the superordinate project of determining whether the language can replace other means of recording gestures. Further research is required to investigate the impact of a 3D Labanotation editor on the acceptance of the notation language as a standard tool for the documentation of natural interactions.

References

1. Altakrouri, B., Gröschner, J., Schrader, A.: Documenting natural interactions. In: CHI 2013 Extended Abstracts on Human Factors in Computing Systems, pp. 1173–1178. ACM (2013)
2. Kahol, K., Tripathi, P., Panchanathan, S.: Documenting motion sequences with a personalized annotation system. IEEE MultiMed. **13**, 37–45 (2006)
3. Hesenius, M., Gruhn, V.: GestureCards: a hybrid gesture notation. Association for computing machinery. Proc. ACM Hum.-Comput. Interact. **3**, 1–15 (2019)
4. Spano, L.D., et al.: GestIT: a declarative and compositional framework for multiplatform gesture definition. In: 5th ACM SIGCHI symposium on Engineering Interactive Computing Systems, pp. 187–196 (2013).
5. Choensawat, W., et al.: Description and reproduction of stylized traditional dance body motion by using labanotation. Trans. Virtual Reality Soc. Jpn. **15**, 379–388 (2010)
6. Fox, I., Ryman, R., Calvert, T.: Documenting dance for the 21st century: a translation interface between labanwriter and life forms. In: Twenty-Second Biennial Conference of the International Council of Kinetography Laban, pp. 193–205 (2001).
7. Altakrouri, B.: Ambient assisted living with dynamic interaction ensembles. Dissertation, University of Lübeck, Institute of Telematics (2014).
8. Kordts, B., Altakrouri, B., Schrader, A.: Capturing and analysing movement using depth sensors and labanotation. In: 7th ACM SIGCHI Symposium on Engineering Interactive Computing Systems, Duisburg, Germany, pp. 132–141 (2015)
9. Pataki, K., Prümper, J., Thüring, M.: Die Gewichtung von Usability-Aspekten anhand der "Analytic Hierarchy Process" - Methode von Saaty. In: Brau, H., Röse, K. (eds.), pp. 113–119. Fraunhofer Verlag, Stuttgart (2007)
10. Guest: Labanotation: the system of analyzing and recording movement. Routledge (2013)
11. Guest: Choreo-graphics: A Comparison of Dance Notation Systems from the Fifteenth Century to the Present. Psychology Press (1998)
12. US Army: Field Manual (FM 21-60): Visual Signals. Washington, DC (1987)
13. Fothergill, S., et al.: Instructing people for training gestural interactive systems. In: SIGCHI Conference on Human Factors in Computing Systems, pp. 1737–1746 (2012)
14. Hussein, M.E., et al.: Human action recognition using a temporal hierarchy of covariance descriptors on 3D joint locations. In: Twenty-Third International Joint Conference on Artificial Intelligence (2013)
15. Wang, P., et al.: Action recognition based on joint trajectory maps using convolutional neural networks. In: 24th ACM International Conference on Multimedia, pp. 102–106 (2016)

Advancing Towards Automated Ergonomic Assessment: A Panel of Perspectives

Daniel P. Armstrong[1], Christopher A. B. Moore[1], Lora A. Cavuoto[2], Sean Gallagher[3], SangHyun Lee[4], Michael W. Sonne[5], and Steven L. Fischer[1](✉)

[1] University of Waterloo, Waterloo, ON N2L 3G1, Canada
`steven.fischer@uwaterloo.ca`
[2] University at Buffalo, Buffalo, NY 14260, USA
[3] Auburn University, Auburn, AL 36849, USA
[4] University of Michigan, Ann Arbor, MI 48109, USA
[5] MyAbilities Technologies Inc., Burlington, ON, Canada

Abstract. Direct and continuous exposure measurement has posed challenges to human factors engineering (HFE) professionals when conducting risk assessments. However, emerging technologies have utility to automate elements of HFE assessment and strengthen opportunities for direct and continuous exposure measurement. Leading HFE researchers provide perspectives on how advances in technology and computing, including computer vision, machine learning and wearable sensors, can aid in the automation of exposure measurement to inform ergonomic assessment while also bolstering the opportunities for objective, data-driven insight. Drs. SangHyun Lee and Michael Sonne share perspectives on the development and validation of computer vision-based pose estimation approaches. Such pose estimation approaches allow HFE professions to record video data where software can convert video into a kinematic representation of a worker and then calculate corresponding joint angles without the need for any tedious posture matching, or additional post processing approaches. Dr. Cavuoto discusses how wearable technologies can unobtrusively measure kinematics in work, showcasing the potential of direct measurement, data-driven injury risk assessment. Finally, Dr. Gallagher showcases how data collected through automated approaches can be integrated with models to evaluate injury risk through a fatigue-failure injury mechanism pathway. In addition to showcasing how emerging technologies and approaches may enhance exposure and risk assessment in HFE, panelists also highlight anticipated challenges and barriers that need to be addressed to support more ubiquitous integration of such technologies into HFE assessment practice. The future for innovation and advancement in exposure measurement and assessment is bright.

Keywords: Ergonomic assessment · Physical ergonomics · Artificial intelligence · Risk assessment · Computer vision · Wearable technology

This session was submitted as part of the IEA Student/Early Career Researcher committee.

1 Introduction

Ergonomic assessments have relied on an ergonomist going out in the field to make measurements within the workplace primarily using a tape measure and a force gauge. Those measures can be used to inform risk assessment tools or biomechanical models to quantify exposures and ultimately assess the risk of work-related musculoskeletal disorders (WRMSDs) associated with the job. While this approach has been the standard in the field, there are limitations. For example, posture is an important risk factor where subjectivity or human error in the observation of a posture could influence the resultant risk assessment outcomes. Additionally, ergonomist can spend a lot of time taking detailed measurements which may take time away from learning more about the work from the workers who do the job, or from designing and implementing efficacious proactive ergonomics solutions. Given our reliance on time consuming measurement coupled with subjective, visual-based observation of postures, innovations that can both automate direct measurement and enhance objectivity of assessment are a necessary future direction.

Emerging technologies may have utility in automating ergonomic assessment. While force data remains more elusive, body worn wearable sensing technologies and video-based pose estimation provide approaches to directly and continuously measure posture and movement. In the near-term, access to such rich, objective time-series motion data may help to automate aspects of some existing assessment tools, providing HFE professional with insights more quickly. Over the longer term, availability and access to objectively and continuously measured motion data may support the development of new and innovative tools that were not possible in the absence of such data.

To achieve these overarching goals of automating ergonomic assessment, wearable technologies such as inertial motion units (IMUs), accelerometers or heart rate sensors can provide useful, direct measurement capabilities. IMU data can be used to describe worker kinematics, and heart rate data can inform understanding of the cardiovascular demands during work. Generally, these sensors are small in size and not overly cumbersome for workers to wear making them a potentially feasible solution. Additionally, they do not capture any potentially identifying information about the worker or workplace, an important contrast to video-based approaches. Examples of such technologies being used include the use of wristband heart rate sensors [1] or accelerometers [2, 3] being used in construction settings. While the use of wearable sensors has increased to measure exposure in the workplace, opportunities persist to develop algorithms that can relate or map direct, continuous measures on the biomechanical exposure measures related to MSD [4]. Pioneering efforts to evolve processing methods have included the use of machine learning to facilitate activity recognition [2] and fatigue detection [5–9]. Future innovations will surely continue to provide robust analytical frameworks to gain unique insights from wearable sensing technologies as necessary to inform ergonomic assessment.

The use of computer vision, and more specifically pose estimation approaches to quantify worker kinematics from 2D video data, is a second emerging technology with promise for the automation of ergonomic assessment. Pose estimation approaches enable machines to learn to identify the kinematic linkages of a human based on an image or series of images in the form of video [10]. From an ergonomics perspective, pose estimation-based methods permit body joint positions to be estimated in 2D or even in 3D space using a 2D image or video. The use of such computer vision solutions has shown good agreement between posture metrics measured with a computer vision-based approach and a gold-standard motion capture system where McKinnon et al., [11] showed an average of 75% agreement across ten simulated occupational tasks. Similar methods have been applied in the construction sector where the use of computer vision techniques have been used to quantify 3D body motion and then detect unsafe actions from the motion profiles [12–14]. Additionally, the quantification of motion data from computer vision-based methods have been shown to be of sufficient quality to conduct biomechanical analyses [15], which can provide further insight into risk assessment. While these computer vision approaches have shown utility, there are potential ethical drawbacks as they require video being collected from the workplace. However, these data may provide a more intuitive understanding to the ergonomist compared to the types of signals collected with wearable sensors such as IMUs.

Both wearable sensors and computer vision methods provide opportunities to objectively and directly collect continuous time-series data in the workplace, but there is a need for corresponding analytical methods to help glean insightful information. Concurrent advances in data science provide analytical approaches that may help yield greater insight for ergonomists to help identify and mitigate risks. For example, feature selection and classification methods have been applied to lifting motion data to identify unique movement strategy differences between lifters that significantly reduced their resultant biomechanical exposures relative to other lifers [16]. This insight was leveraged to develop a supervised machine learning model to classify lift motion strategy as having high exposure or low exposures [17], which in turn, can be used to provide more targeted movement coaching where appropriate. While these previous studies provide examples of how direct and continuously measured data can inform ergonomic assessment, relating accessible measures from wearable sensors or computer vision approaches to injury risk remains as an important consideration to maximize the impact of emerging technologies and data science methods.

One specific area where direct and continuous measurement may have great potential is the assessment of cumulative exposure. With several work tasks being repetitive in nature, the development of tools that infer cumulative injury risk is particularly important to provide insightful injury risk appraisal within automated ergonomic assessment approaches. The validity of such a risk assessment approach is supported by evidence suggesting that WRMSDs may result through a fatigue-failure injury pathway [18], where direct and continuous measurement may yield important insight. Recently, tools have been developed to appraise WRMSD risk through fatigue-failure pathways at the low back [19], shoulders [20] and distal upper extremity [21]. Automated methods may enhance the utility of emerging tools to provide more comprehensive injury risk assessments.

Advances in wearable technologies and data science methods, including computer vision will change ergonomic risk assessment. The goal of this panel discussion is to discuss emerging technological advances in more detail and to share insights about how these advancements may inform the automation of ergonomic assessment. However, these approaches do not provide a silver bullet to solve the MSD problem, so the barriers and limitation to the adoption and use of emerging technologies will be discussed. Panel speakers include: Dr. Lora Cavuoto, Dr. Sean Gallagher, Dr. SangHyun Lee and Dr. Michael Sonne, innovative leaders in HFE. Each speaker shares their unique perspectives on the potential for automating ergonomic assessment.

2 List of Speakers

2.1 Dr. SangHyun Lee

Dr. Lee is the founder and president of Kinetica Labs as well as a professor in the Department of Civil and Environmental Engineering at the University of Michigan. Kinetica Labs' "*Motion*Capture" application allows a user to record video data on their smartphone and generate corresponding posture data. The frequency, duration and severity of each posture are then calculated and can be used to inform ergonomic risk assessments.

> "*Ergonomic risk assessment involves time consuming, cumbersome, and subjective data preparation, which prevents the application of such necessary comprehensive evaluation in the field. Recent advancement in computer vision and deep learning have allowed for the development of rapid, easy-to use, and objective risk assessment solely using processing videos captured from a mobile device like a smartphone, and without attaching any sensors to workers and/or objects. I discuss how such technologies for the improvement of ergonomic risk assessment have been advanced and where they are heading next.*" – Dr. Lee.

2.2 Dr. Michael Sonne

Dr. Sonne is VP Innovations and Research at MyAbilities, co-founder of ProPlayAI and an adjunct professor at Brock University and Ontario Tech University. His work at MyAbilities helps create software to leverage artificial intelligence to perform ergonomics job analysis. Their software can be applied to video data to identify higher-risk work techniques and highlight high-risk body areas. Additionally, ProPlayAI uses computer vision methods to quantify kinematics in baseball pitching with the goal of improving performance through biomechanical insights.

> "*Ergonomics assessments have traditionally been completed by an ergonomist getting out their tape measure and force gauge, and surveying the plant floor. In the COVID era, access to facilities has been limited, making this traditional practice more and more difficult. Recent technological innovations in computer vision have made pose estimation in 3D, all from a cell phone video, more and more accessible. While these methods are not without fault, the ability to collect data remotely and through video has major implications for how ergonomists work. I identify the pros and cons of the approach, the current state of the art and where it is heading next.*" – Dr. Sonne.

2.3   Dr. Lora Cavuoto

Dr. Cavuoto is an associate professor in the Department of Industrial and Systems Engineering at the University at Buffalo. Dr. Cavuoto's research program aims to investigate workplace injury mechanisms, human capacity and physical performance while developing ergonomic controls and interventions. Her research program uses wearable sensors and machine learning techniques to quantify occupational fatigue.

"Sensor technology supports the feasibility of data collection, both in terms of accuracy and amount. Many existing ergonomics risk assessment tools are intended for short observations and have not been designed to consider cumulative or long-term risk for extended duration tasks. I discuss data-driven assessment to understand, model, and monitor changes in worker and task conditions for longer duration tasks." – Dr. Cavuoto.

2.4   Dr. Sean Gallagher

Dr. Gallagher is the Hal N. and Peggy S. Pennington professor in the Department of Industrial and Systems Engineering at Auburn University. Dr. Gallagher's research focuses on musculoskeletal disorder etiology and ergonomics. His recent work includes the development of tools to assess injury risk of the low back, distal upper extremity, and shoulders from a fatigue-failure perspective.

"The advent of techniques that allow continuous monitoring of MSD risk measures is an exciting advance in exposure assessment technology. However, with this advance comes with the complexity of determining exactly how such data should be analyzed, where these data may include a worker performing multiple tasks each having highly variable loading exposures. Fortunately, fatigue failure theory offers analysis techniques designed precisely for such situations and provide an assessment of the cumulative risk associated with highly variable load histories. I discuss potential benefits of fatigue failure techniques in automated MSD risk assessment, along with the challenges involved." – Dr. Gallagher.

3   Conclusion

Direct, objective, and continuous measurement coupled with analytical models based on strong theory (i.e., fatigue-failure) offer a promising direction in ergonomics, overcoming limitations such as subjectivity and time demands associated with current assessment practice. Panelists showcase emerging applications and discuss pitfalls and risks associated with the use of wearable technologies and computer vision techniques. Examples such as (near) real time, continuous postural analysis, fatigue prediction and cumulative failure risk offer new and unique opportunities to assess the demands of work, and ultimately overcome the MSD problem [22].

References

1. Hwang, S., Lee, S.: Wristband-type wearable health devices to measure construction workers' physical demands. Autom. Constr. **83**, 330–340 (2017)
2. Ryu, J., Seo, J., Jebelli, H., Lee, S.: Automated action recognition using an accelerometer-embedded wristband-type activity tracker. J. Constr. Eng. Manag. **145**(1), 04018114 (2019)
3. Jebelli, H., Choi, B., Lee, S.: Application of wearable biosensors to construction sites. II: assessing workers' physical demand. J. Constr. Eng. Manag. **145**(12), 04019080 (2019)
4. Lim, S., D'Souza, C.: A narrative review on contemporary and emerging uses of inertial sensing in occupational ergonomics. Int. J. Ind. Ergon. **76**, 102937 (2020)
5. Maman, Z.S., Chen, Y.J., Baghdadi, A., Lombardo, S., Cavuoto, L.A., Megahed, F.M.: A data analytic framework for physical fatigue management using wearable sensors. Expert Syst. Appl. **155**, 113405 (2020)
6. Maman, Z.S., Yazdi, M.A., Cavuoto, L.A., Megahed, F.M.: A data-driven approach to modeling physical fatigue in the workplace using wearable sensors. Appl. Ergon. **65**, 515–529 (2017)
7. Baghdadi, A., Megahed, F.M., Esfahani, E.T., Cavuoto, L.A.: A machine learning approach to detect changes in gait parameters following a fatiguing occupational task. Ergonomics **61**(8), 1116–1129 (2018)
8. Baghdadi, A., Cavuoto, L.A., Jones-Farmer, A., Rigdon, S.E., Esfahani, E.T., Megahed, F.M.: Monitoring worker fatigue using wearable devices: a case study to detect changes in gait parameters. J. Qual. Technol. **53**(1), 47–71 (2021)
9. Hajifar, S., Sun, H., Megahed, F.M., Jones-Farmer, L.A., Rashedi, E., Cavuoto, L.A.: A forecasting framework for predicting perceived fatigue: using time series methods to forecast ratings of perceived exertion with features from wearable sensors. Appl. Ergon. **90**, 103262 (2021)
10. Cao, Z., Hidalgo, G., Simon, T., Wei, S.E., Sheikh, Y.: OpenPose: realtime multi-person 2D pose estimation using Part Affinity Fields. IEEE Trans. Pattern Anal. Mach. Intell. **43**(1), 172–186 (2019)
11. McKinnon, C.D., Sonne, M.W., Keir, P.J.: Assessment of joint angle and reach envelope demands using a video-based physical demands description tool. Hum. Factors **10**, 0018720820951349 (2020)
12. Han, S., Lee, S.: A vision-based motion capture and recognition framework for behavior-based safety management. Autom. Constr. **35**, 131–141 (2013)
13. Seo, J., Starbuck, R., Han, S., Lee, S., Armstrong, T.J.: Motion data-driven biomechanical analysis during construction tasks on sites. J. Comput. Civ. Eng. **29**(4), B4014005 (2015)
14. Han, S., Lee, S., Peña-Mora, F.: Vision-based detection of unsafe actions of a construction worker: case study of ladder climbing. J. Comput. Civ. Eng. **27**(6), 635–644 (2013)
15. Seo, J., Han, S., Lee, S., Kim, H.: Computer vision techniques for construction safety and health monitoring. Adv. Eng. Inform. **29**(2), 239–251 (2015)
16. Armstrong, D.P., Budarick, A.R., Pegg, C.E., Graham, R.B., Fischer, S.L.: Feature detection and biomechanical analysis to objectively identify high exposure movement strategies when performing the EPIC lift capacity test. J. Occup. Rehabil. **4**, 1–3 (2020)
17. Armstrong, D.P., Ross, G.B., Graham, R.B., Fischer, S.L.: Considering movement competency within physical employment standards. Work **63**(4), 603–613 (2019)
18. Gallagher, S., Schall, M.C., Jr.: Musculoskeletal disorders as a fatigue failure process: evidence, implications and research needs. Ergonomics **60**(2), 255–269 (2017)
19. Gallagher, S., Sesek, R.F., Schall, M.C., Jr., Huangfu, R.: Development and validation of an easy-to-use risk assessment tool for cumulative low back loading: the Lifting Fatigue Failure Tool (LiFFT). Appl. Ergon. **63**, 142–150 (2017)

20. Bani Hani, D., Huangfu, R., Sesek, R., Schall, M.C., Jr., Davis, G.A., Gallagher, S.: Development and validation of a cumulative exposure shoulder risk assessment tool based on fatigue failure theory. Ergonomics **64**(1), 39–54 (2021)
21. Gallagher, S., Schall, M.C., Jr., Sesek, R.F., Huangfu, R.: An upper extremity risk assessment tool based on material fatigue failure theory: the distal upper extremity tool (DUET). Hum. Factors **60**(8), 1146–1162 (2018)
22. Wells, R.: Why have we not solved the MSD problem? Work **34**(1), 117–121 (2009)

From Globalization to Circular Economy, Which Issues for Health and Safety at Work?

Agnès Aublet-Cuvelier$^{(\boxtimes)}$, Michel Hery, and Marc Malenfer

INRS, Vandoeuvre les Nancy, France
`agnes.aublet-cuvelier@inrs.fr`

Abstract. Circular economy is presented as an alternative to promote sustainable and responsible development. This economic model involves deep organizational and production changes. INRS, the French institute for occupational safety and health, conducted a strategic foresight approach in order to assess its potential impact on working conditions and therefore, on health and safety at work. The aim was to anticipate future needs for the prevention of occupational risks by 2040. Indeed, if circular economy offers the opportunity for a better integration of prevention, this may cause also adverse effects on workers' safety and health. The first step of the study was to set up a 15-member team, associating OSH, foresight and circular economy experts who followed the exercise from start to finish. In association with partners outside the group, they identified the main key influencing drivers in the development of circular economy. Each of these drivers was then documented, in order to consider contrasted hypotheses of development in the future. Then, they built together global scenarios combining several hypotheses considering the drivers most likely to have an effect on working conditions and consequently on safety and health. They then drew up four stories, taking into account specific sectors and aspects of professional activity in order to make more concrete the potential consequences of different modes of circular economy development. OSH experts could translate them in terms of health and safety issues in order to reflect on the most relevant subjects to be taken into account in the future by INRS.

Keywords: 4.0 industry · Circular economy · Prevention · Occupational risk · Safety · Strategic foresight

1 Introduction

1.1 What About Circular Economy?

Circular economy appears as an alternative to promote sustainable and responsible development. It can be defined as an economic system of exchange and production, which aim is to increase the efficiency of use of resources at all stages [1, 2]. It includes a strong concern for the preservation of the environment, with a production life cycle geared towards the infinite reuse of all intermediate and final products. The well-being of individuals is also a main preoccupation to take into account in this economic model.

© The Author(s), under exclusive license to Springer Nature Switzerland AG 2022
N. L. Black et al. (Eds.): IEA 2021, LNNS 223, pp. 592–596, 2022.
https://doi.org/10.1007/978-3-030-74614-8_73

Its development seems to be unavoidable even if the transition to the circular economy model is progressive, partial and not ubiquitous. As it involves deep organizational and production changes, it is of main concern for occupational safety and health (OSH) professionals because of its potential impact on working conditions and consequently on safety and health at work.

1.2 A Challenge for Safety and Health at Work

The main studies devoted to the circular economy concern technological considerations regarding the reuse, remanufacturing, recycle of products, associated with the assessment of the sustainability of the process, through quantitative productive, economic and environmental indicators. However, the literature is poorer when it comes to the working conditions of the personnel involved in the production processes linked to the circular economy. It mainly focuses on toxicological risks, linked to the exposure to specific pollutants, especially in the de-construction sector. It also refers to mechanical risks, musculoskeletal disorders (waste sorting centers e.g.), and, to a lesser extend, to psychosocial risks, even if green jobs are more demanding in terms of cognitive and interpersonal skills, work experience and training. In order to anticipate the potential OSH consequences of this economic model, INRS carried out a strategic foresight study by 2040 [3]. This 20-year projection period was chosen in view of the gradual emergence of this economic model, in a context that is still very marked by mass production, difficult to reconcile with environmental issues. In order to think and integrate prevention as early as possible in the design of new production and services processes resulting from the transition to circular economy models, all types of risks (physical, biological, chemical, psychosocial, organizational…) have been taken into account in this study.

2   Material and Methods

The study was conducted in five stages. The first one was to set up a 15-member team, associating OSH, foresight and circular economy experts who followed the exercise from start to finish. During the second step, this team, with the help of partners from outside the group, identified the main key influencing drivers in the development of circular economy [4]. In the third step, each of these drivers was then documented by one of the members and presented to the whole team. It was discussed, with regard to its possible development in the future, from continuity trend to rupture hypothesis. Then, during the fourth step, using the "scenarios method", they built together global scenarios combining several hypotheses, considering the drivers most likely to have an effect on working conditions and consequently on safety and health. They then drew up four stories, taking into account specific sectors and specific aspects of professional activity in order to make more concrete the potential consequences of different modes of circular economy development. Finally, OSH issues were examined in light of the context described for each of the scenarios, to achieve the final aim to adjust the prevention policy to this challenge of the future.

3 Results

3.1 Global Scenarios

The project team built four contrasted scenarios describing a possible future in terms of working conditions and their potential consequences on OSH, based on the assumptions associated to the main drivers considered in the previous steps of the method.

The first one postulates for the general development of the circular economy, led by private actors from multinational corporations who are breaking with the previous model founded on a growing economy based on fossil fuels. They are the main investors for research and development for these innovations and this development is in phase with consumers' expectations.

The second one is based on the assumption of the localized development of circular economy in Northern and Western Europe, far ahead of other areas for different reasons, varying from one continent to the other (financial, political, ethical, perceptual,…). There's a good coordination from European to local level and the situation can be considered as stable by 2040.

In the third scenario, there is still a poor consideration for climate change and the linear economic model responds to the persistent needs of the consumers all over the world, especially from countries with the largest population development. This situation results in environmental, political, social and economic growing tensions. Public and private actors try to limit the impact by palliative and local solutions, that remain very insufficient.

The last scenario depicts an intermediate situation in which there is no real consensus on how to deal with climate changes in terms of economic model. In a context of severe socio-economic tensions. There are splits between citizens who adopt a frugal life style, more or less voluntarily, and those who continue to consume and waste. Some companies adopt some circular economy logics because of financial interests while others don't.

3.2 Application to Safety and Health at Work

From these scenarios, several stories were built up. They concern deconstruction activity, the re-use of raw materials and elements resulting from transformation, the maintenance and repair activity and finally the transport and logistics sector. Risks and opportunities for health and safety emerged through realistic situations described. They are briefly summarized above.

Potential Consequences in the Deconstruction Sector and Recycling Activities
These activities already imply exposure to various pollutants, mechanical risks and physical ones. In a future where recycling and deconstruction may be largely spread, because of the development of an economy supporting sustainable environment, this poly-exposure and other risks may increase…or not. It depends on the diversity and complexity of materials to be recycled/deconstructed, the status of the workers (self-employed workers vs employees), the degree of automation of the processes and the implication of private and public actors in the global socio-economic policy. All these variables may have an incidence on OSH. The responsibility of OSH, attributed to the activity provider or to

the individual, and then on the prevention means is an illustration. Another example concerns automation with robotics that may reduce specific physical, mechanical and chemical risks for workers but may conversely increase psychosocial risks induced by work intensification, supervisory tasks, increased psychological demands, and generate additional actions to compensate machine failures that can be stressful and dangerous.

Maintenance and Repair, What Perspectives?
Health and safety may be impacted by the expansion of this activity in a spread circular economy. The training conditions for these operations, the organization of maintenance (outsourced or not, geographically or technically sectored, made by independent workers or not) and the recruitment methods (social and solidarity economy, level of requirement in terms of technical expertise), but also technical and organizational means made available, may be the main determinants of working conditions. Concerning the weakening of OSH, self-employed workers for instance are supposed to implement measures to ensure their own safety in a context where they may have poor influence on the organization of their work, on prevention investments and no access to some adequate information about occupational risks and their prevention. Reversely, technical resources (drones, connected glasses, remotely controlled robots…) offered by high-performance companies, concerned about the well-being of their employees and supported by public policies for technological innovation could be an opportunity to protect workers in charge of maintenance from specific exposures, allowing them to have access to technical information quickly and to intervene at a distance while being protected from physical, mechanical or chemical risks.

The Future of Transport and Logistics
The complexity of transport flows at different stages of the life cycle of goods and products, the status of carriers more or less protective towards occupational risks, the mode of product grouping, the technology and the needs for traceability within the circular economy should be considered, depending on the scenarios. The circular economy could increase transport flows rather than reduce them, because of multiple operations of sorting, repairing, repackaging, deconstructing to recover parts that will be reused and recycling secondary raw materials. This situation could result in numerous occupational risks (manual handling, chemical, mechanical ones…), especially for operators involved in first-mile and last-mile stages for which standardization and automation of loading, unloading and transfer activities through "physical internet" are unrealistic. Technical solutions, such as industrial exoskeletons, should help reduce the difficulties encountered at these workstations [5].

4 Discussion and Conclusion

OSH issues may be integrated in the new processes and organizations, depending on the speed of development of the circular economy in the next two decades, but also on the technological and organizational maturity of companies whatever their size and their ability to implement prevention measures from the design stage onwards. The transition between a linear economic model to a circular one has to be done gradually if so. The new technologies (ICT, automation, cobotics, …) could play a major role in this evolution. They could be protective (reduction of chemical, mechanical and physical exposure). Conversely, they could step up work, increase information load and reduce the margin of manoeuver of operators involved in the processes. The approach should not be only technical but also take into account the organizational changes, the workers' status, new types of services, and their impact on safety and health at early stages of implementation.

References

1. Le Moigne, R.: L'économie circulaire: stratégie pour un monde durable, 1st edn. Dunod, Paris (2018)
2. Ministère de l'Environnement, de l'Energie et de la mer, Ademe Preventing waste, Overview (2016). https://www.ademe.fr/sites/default/files/assets/documents/preventing-waste_overvi ew2016_010312.pdf. Accessed 08 Feb 2021
3. Héry, M., Malenfer, M.: Development of a circular economy and evolution of working conditions and occupational risks—A strategic foresight study. Eur. J. Futures Res. **8**, 8 (2020). https://doi.org/10.1186/s40309-020-00168-7
4. Govindan, K., Hasanagic, M.: A systematic review on drivers, barriers, and practices towards circular economy: a supply chain perspective. Int. J. Prod. Res. (2018). https://doi.org/10.1080/ 00207543.2017.1402141
5. Héry, M., Devel, S.: Utilisation des robots d'assistance physique à l'horizon 2030 en France, 1st edn. INRS (2015) https://www.inrs.fr/inrs/prospective-quel-travail-demain.html#609a6630-6832-4b54-ab3a-d228382bc6f8. ISBN 978-2-7389-2217-5. Accessed 08 Feb 2021

Collaborative Robotics and Industry 4.0: An Engineering, Sociology and Activity-Centered Ergonomics Cross-Experience

Flore Barcellini[1(✉)], Willy Buchmann[1], Richard Béarée[2],
Tahar-Hakim Benchekroun[1], Mouad Bounouar[2,3], Gérard Dubey[4,5],
Caroline Moricot[5], Anne-Cecile Lafeuillade[1], Celine Rosselin-Bareille[5,6],
Marco Saraceno[5,7], and Ali Siadat[3]

[1] CRTD, Le Cnam, Paris, France
flore.barcellini@lecnam.net
[2] LIPSEN, Boulogne-Billancourt, France
[3] LCFC, Metz, France
[4] IMT, Business School, Évry-Courcouronnes, France
[5] Cetcopra, Université Paris 1, Paris, France
[6] Université d'Orléans, Orléans, France
[7] Université de Reims Champagne-Ardennes, Reims, France

Abstract. This communication aims to present a cross-perspective – robotics, industrial engineering, sociology and ergonomics – research project experience dealing with development of collaborative robotics in SMEs. Our conviction is that Industry 4.0 must imply: (1) "departitioning" of disciplines involved in the design of work situations and (2) construction of hybrid approaches for understanding and transforming work. In this communication, we propose to relate such an experience on the basis of a research project - funded by the French National Agency for Research (ANR), and focused on transformation of French Small and Middle Companies (SMC's) in relation to introduction of Collaborative Robotics. Collaborative Robotics is of particular interest for us as it embeds promises and pitfalls of articulation between technologies and work. However, these promises may be discussed and tempered by confronting them to actual design issues, work organization and transformation of work management.

Keywords: Collaborative robotics · Industry 4.0 · Ergonomics · Sociology · Industrial engineering

1 Problem Statement

This paper aims at present a cross-perspective – robotics, industrial engineering, sociology and ergonomics – research project experience dealing with development of collaborative robotics in Small and Medium French Companies (SME). Our research is set in the following context: according to "the factory of the future" – or Industry 4.0 - program in France, the globalisation of competition, coupled with the ageing of the working population and industrial facilities, makes it necessary for France to improve its production tool and competitiveness. Moreover, the COVID 19 crisis has increased awareness of the importance of preserving and developing a strong, innovative industrial activity that generates wealth and jobs. In order to achieve this, it would be necessary, again according to claims of the French Industry 4.0 program, to continue the modernisation of the production tool, in particular through the integration of collaborative robotics. In this context, our conviction is that an effective Industry 4.0 transition must overtake a pure techno-centered perspective and must imply: (1) "departinionning" of disciplines involved in the design of work situations and (2) construction of hybrid approaches for understanding and transforming work. In this communication, we propose to relate such an experience on the basis of a research project - funded by the French National Agency for Research (ANR), and focused on transformation of French Small and Middle Companies (SMC's) in relation to introduction of Collaborative Robotics. Collaborative Robotics is of particular interest for us as it embeds promises but also pitfalls of articulation between technologies and work. Among the "promises" made by proponents of this technology, we particularly note that:

- This technology is presented as "easy to implement and maintain"; "favouring productivity gains";
- It is also presented as virtuous on a societal level, by making certain workstations more attractive, or by contributing to the prevention of musculoskeletal disorders through the cobot's taking over repetitive or strenuous tasks;
- It is a model of potential non-substitutive technologies that may lead to a strong reification of what could/should be actual collaboration between workers and technologies [1].

However, it seems to us important and topical to confront these promises with real situations of design, work organisation and the transformation of work management.

2 Objective/Question

In this context, the main objectives of our interdisciplinary research project are to propose:

(1) An analysis of what is covered by the polysemic terminology of the research object "cobot".
(2) A work and activity approach related to organizational and socio-cultural transformation of work and activities of SMC's executive coping with the transformation of their companies;
(3) A socio-political and historical analysis of the French and German programmes related to the so-called "industry of the future" since the mid-70s in order to identify the evolution (or not) of the place of collaborative robotics in the history of robotics;

(4) Finally, based on the 3 previous points, a multidisciplinary approach to the management of design projects of companies engaged in the modernisation of their production tool (tools in the broad sense of the term, including: technical, organisational, social devices).

3 Methodology

This multidisciplinary research, carried out by 11 researchers, is based on the articulation between different research modalities specific to this project:

- a hybrid thesis in industrial engineering and ergonomics
- an action-research conducted in an SME by a researcher in sociology and a doctoral student in ergonomics.
- more than ten days of seminars between project researchers dealing with the exploration of cross concepts (collaboration/cooperation, work situation...) based on socio-political and historical work.

   In addition, specific methods were developed for each of the sub-objectives. More specifically, a state of the art on the evolution of robotics for (1), a multiple case study based on observations, interviews and analysis of company documents for (2) and the analysis of more than 400 documents and reports on "The industry 4.0" for (3).

4 Results

In order to meet the objectives announced above, we will present our results in 3 parts.

4.1 "Cobot", A Concept that is Still Under Debate and Still Evolving

If the definition of the industrial robot is precise and well framed in the robotics community, the notions of cobot and collaborative robot, frequently used when talking about Industry 4.0, are less so. It thus seems useful to go back over the history of this neologism: at the end of the 20th century, the word "cobot" designated mechanically compliant devices (COmpliantroBOT), intended to be used within the framework of haptic interfaces [8–10]. Later, the term "cobot" was used by robot manufacturers and industrialists to designate a new type of robot with sufficient safety features (mechanical and/or electronic properties) to be able to operate in the same workspace as humans. The word "cobot" has thus taken the other meaning of COllaborative-roBOT, cooperative or collaborative robots [9], cooperation or collaboration meaning, without further theoretical and/or practical details, the possibility to share the same workspace. Finally, the idea of co-manipulation, which refers to specific uses within the field of industrial robotics, has known in the last few years significant advances in order to increase the handling performances of workers. Cobots can interact (or not), with workers (perform movements in autonomy, share tasks, operate in the same workspace) but would no longer replace the human gesture in the strict sense of the word. Their function would rather be to guide or accompany it [3].

Thus, the meaning of "co" in cobot and the promise of collaboration, potential or actual, real or truncated, give rise to debates on two complementary levels:

- The notion of cooperation/collaboration between humans and robots is all the more difficult to stabilise as the notions of cooperation and collaboration between humans or between humans and machines [4] are controversial in the Social and Human Sciences.
- among specialists in technology, labour and industry in general, especially on the occasion of the (ongoing) revision of ISO 8373:2012, as some definitions are often outdated [8].

Faced with an evolving, sometimes protean definition, resulting both from the history of the development of so-called "manipulation" robotic systems and the conceptual evolutions produced by the interactions between Human and Social Sciences and Engineering Sciences, it seems reasonable to be on the lookout for new literature, to take a nuanced approach and to provide support to companies likely to be attracted by these tools.

4.2   SME Managers, Both Interested and Cautious About Cobots

The difficulties in stabilizing the functions covered by the "Cobot" tool described in the previous section raise questions about its actual integration in work situations. But more generally, in order to think about and carry out transformations likely to redraw the contours of the industrial landscape, executives and managers find themselves in the front line. And moreover, they are the guarantors of the decisions and methods of change management which will ultimately guarantee healthy and high-performance work. Thus, we were interested in the point of view of SME managers on the integration of cobots in their production facilities. We identified a contradiction on: on the one hand, the French "Industry 4.0" program presents collaborative robotics as a solution that is relatively easy to integrate and which would solve, among other things, problems related to physical wear and tear and work-related joint pain. We can add to this political will the strong technical progress making the cobots more and more easy to integrate, but also the rhetoric and marketing around these technologies which are pushing hard to seduce company managers. But on the other hand, a first exploratory part of our research showed that very few SMEs were really equipped with a working cobot (at least at the time of this research, 2018). Faced with this contradiction (large developments in the supply of cobots, but few SMEs equipped), we sought to understand through interviews with the managers of five volunteer SMEs, what are the expectations, the hopes, but also the points of vigilance or the obstacles to the integration of a cobot in a workstation.

The Managers Interviewed see the Cobot as a Potential Solution to Production and Occupational Health Problems

The Table 1 presents a summary of the results obtained. It should be noted in particular that the managers of 4 of the 5 SMEs surveyed are interested in cobot in order to limit biomechanical constraints, physical wear and tear, and the risk of occupational accidents or illness.

Table 1. Managers' interests in cobots

	SME1	SME2	SME3	SME4	SME5
…limit biomechanical stress, physical strain and wear and tear, the risk of accidents at work or occupational illness			X	X	X
…to alleviate the difficulties of recruiting for positions recognised as difficult		X			
…enriching the content of workers' work; mobilising them on "high added value" tasks	X			X	
…improve productivity, quality, better control of our production process	X			X	X
…to develop and offer new products			X	X	
…to convey the image of a company at the cutting edge of technology	X	X	X	X	

But Managers Measured Against the Promises Conveyed by the Cobots

The Table 2 presents a summary of the results obtained. It should be noted in particular that the managers are particularly concerned about the technical complexity of the cobot, and their ability to maintain it, and to protect themselves legally in the event of an accident. Several authors have already pointed out in the past [5] that the difficulties of designing cooperative systems are largely underestimated and that the promise of effective human-machine cooperation is not always kept.

There is also the question (line 4) of the capacity of this new technology to fit into the history, dynamics and know-how of the company. For the intention of managers is shaped by the history of the company, by experience of past successes and failures, and one of the challenges of change management is a compromise between rupture and continuity in strategic choices.

To conclude on this part of the results, despite the interest of the managers for the cobots, we noted a weak effective integration of this technology. This can be explained by technical difficulties in integrating a cobot into work situations (a simple technology, but one that reveals the complexity of work situations), but also by a certain vigilance on the part of managers, faced with "turnkey" technical solutions that would instantly respond to local health and productivity issues. This observation therefore calls for the techno-deterministic discourse as a solution to the current problems of work, which we will analyse in the following section.

4.3   Industry 4.0, Both in Continuity with and a Break from the Major Industrial Projects of the 1980s

Analysis of the literature describing the Industry 4.0 program [11] reveals elements of language very close to those used in the major plans of the 1980s in France, whose limits had already been identified [7]. The 1990s were marked by a relative discretion in the place of robots in industry reports. The rhetorical use of the robot in discourses

Table 2. Managers' points of vigilance toward cobots

	SME1	SME2	SME3	SME4	SME5
Lack of information on the potential and limits of the cobot, its integration process in production, solid experience feedback			X	X	
Complex and expensive tool to program and maintain (with liability issues in case of accident). Uncertainties about the time frame for the return on investment			X	X	X
The first studies of the workstation targeted in the company have revealed that the work is more complex than the managers imagined, and the cobot will not be able to do as well as the operator			X	X	
Fear of a break with the core business, with the company's culture	X	X			
...to develop and offer new products			X	X	
The operators concerned put on the brakes, arguing that by leaving the simple tasks to the cobot, the work for them will be intensified by only carrying out complex or unplanned tasks					X

on the industry of the future reappears in the 2010's in the form of the "collaborative robot" or "cobot". Continuity with past discourse is ensured by the place of the cobot in industrialisation (i.e. the cobot of 2019 is rhetorically part of the same discursive device as the robot of the 1980s: the idea is to make it a link between man and the automatic industrial process). The break with the past is ensured by "the passage from substitution to collaboration, which leads to the presentation of an industry using technical innovation to put man *"back at the heart"* ([11], p. 15).

Moreover, beyond these elements of language, the semantic analysis of the "Industry 4.0" program reveals a set of essentially techno-centric tools and methods and little room is left for real "engineering" of work transformations. In fact, it can be seen that in the program's promotional institutions in France, representatives of the human and labour sciences (ergonomics, occupational psychology, sociology of work, management and organisational sciences, adult education) occupy an extremely limited place. Technical rationality and political communication are predominant.

In order to lift this scientific lock, the doctoral work between robotics - industrial engineering and ergonomics carried out within the framework of our research project aims on the one hand to clarify the model of real collaboration between workers and robots and on the other hand to develop a hybrid management of the design process of collaborative robotics by articulating scientific and technical questions with a proposal of activity-centred management of the ergonomic design process [2]. We will come back to it in conclusion.

5 Discussion Conclusion

The ambition of our multidisciplinary project is to use developments in collaborative robotics to question and improve existing change management systems in industrial environments (and more specifically in SMEs). This project allows us on the one hand to re-discuss what is meant by "cobot" and to catch the issues of worker-machine-environment coupling (1), to understand the external (3) and internal context but also the stakes that weigh on SME managers (2).

Due to the multiplicity of issues (health, safety, work, employment, productivity, etc.) linked to the management of collaborative robotics projects, our research provides an opportunity for multidisciplinary discussions in order to co-develop new design methodologies, to remove certain identified obstacles: projects for the introduction of new technologies are driven by decision-making processes in which different logics (economic, production efficiency, quality, human resources management, safety, health, etc.) are confronted and therefore result from trade-offs between these different logics. However, the primacy of techno-deterministic approaches implies that technologies are often thought of as "remedies" to economic, competitiveness, production or risk factor problems, without questioning the "root causes", particularly the organisational causes of these problems, and the relevance of the technological solution alone. In the current context of strong political pressure to modernise, there is a potential risk of introducing heterogeneous technologies everywhere (cobotics and exoskeleton, additive manufacturing, big data and cloud, Internet of Things and RFID, augmented reality and virtual reality, etc.), without questioning their possible interactions (synergies or contradictions) or their consequences on real work.

These pitfalls reinforce the need to propose, upstream and throughout the projects accompanying the transformations of work towards an Industry 4.0, a model for change management:

- Participatory; between stakeholders (decision-makers, management, production, maintenance, designers, workers concerned, etc.) with different logics (economic, organisational, HR, health, safety, quality, production, work activities, staff representative bodies, etc.);
- Multiscalar: integrating micro, meso and macro issues, short, medium and long term temporalities, and different hierarchical levels;
- Based on real work in all its complexity and variability;
- Relying on methodological devices enabling stakeholders to draw on the experience of past successes and failures in order to understand the present and think about the future (for example, through projective methods of simulating future work and/or organisation) [4]. However, this model will have to be refined and replicated in other contexts in order to strengthen its methodological soundness.

References

1. Barcellini, F.: Conceptions of human-robot collaborative cooperation. A case of participation in a collaborative robot design process. Activités **17**(2), 1–29 (2020)

2. Bounouar, M., Bearee, R., Siadat, A., Benchekroun, T.-H.: On the role of human operators in the design process of cobotic systems. Cogn. Technol. Work (submit)
3. Bounouar, M., Bearee, R., Benchekroun, T.-H., Siadat, A.: Etat des lieux de la cobotique industrielle et de la conduite de projet associée. In: acte de: 16ème édition Smart colloque (AIP-Primeca), Les Karellis-France (2019). https://smart2019.event.univlorraine.fr/243184
4. Buchmann et Nascimento: Supporting the development of safety culture at the managerial level. In: Proceedings of the XXI IEA Congress, Vancouver, Canada (2021)
5. Hoc, J.M.: Towards a cognitive approach to human-machine cooperation in dynamic situations. Int. J. Hum.-Comput. Stud. **54**, 509–540 (2001)
6. Lafeuillade, A.C., Barcellini, F., Buchmann, W., Benchekroun, T.H.: Integrating collaborative robotics in work situations: the intentions of SME managers in the digital transformation of their companies. In: Bobillier-Chaumon, M.E. (ed.) Digital Transformations in the Challenge of Activity and Employees: Understanding and Supporting Emerging Technological Change. ISTE (2020)
7. Maire Brument, J.-M.: Conditions de travail et conduite de projet dans les industries de processus, Anact (1987)
8. Vicentini, F.: Collaborative robotics: a survey. J. Mech. Des. **143**, 040802 (2020)
9. Peshkin, M., Colgate, J.E.: Cobots. Ind. Robot: Int. J. **26**(5), 335–341 (1999)
10. Peshkin, M., Colgate, J.E., Moore, C.: Passive robots and haptic displays based on non-holonomic elements. In: Proceedings of IEEE International Conference on Robotics and Automation, vol. 1, pp. 551–556. IEEE, Minneapolis (1996)
11. Saraceno, M.: Human "at the heart". From robot to cobot, the myth of the "good automate" in Industry of the Futur mediatization (1978–2018). Communications **37**(1) (2020). https://doi.org/10.4000/communication.11293

Trade-offs of Users and Non-users of Life-Logging – Desire for Support vs. Potential Barriers

Laura Burbach[(⊠)] [iD], Chantal Lidynia, Philipp Brauner[iD], and Martina Ziefle [iD]

Human-Computer-Interaction-Center, RWTH Aachen University, Aachen, Germany
{burbach,lidynia,brauner,ziefle}@comm.rwth-aachen.de

Abstract. Understanding why (non-) users are motivated to use life-logging devices requires to consider wishes and concerns associated with life-logging as well as the influence of personality on usage motivation. We analyze whether the intention to use life-logging is more strongly influenced by the desire for support or by potential barriers with the first having a positive impact and the latter a negative one. Further, we investigate how some personality traits influence the desire for support and potential barriers. Our study shows that the desire for support is more important for the motivation to use life-logging, than potential barriers. Regarding personality traits, motives for physical activity showed the highest influence on the desire for support of users and non-users of life-logging. For users, their need for privacy also influences their desire for support. Barriers are primarily influenced by privacy concerns. In future, when introducing life-logging devices, the potential to support users to pursue goals and privacy concerns of potential users should be particularly considered.

Keywords: Life-logging · Life-logging devices · Motivation · Workplace · Pursue of goals · Privacy concerns

1 Introduction

The health of employees depends not only on the workplace itself (such as ergonomic infrastructure) but also on the behavior of employees. Instead of just sitting all day, employees should get up regularly and walk a few steps, drink enough water, and keep track of their nutritional intake. Life-logging technologies have high potential in motivating and supporting people in living a healthier life at home and at the workplace. Expected benefits of its use are large e.g. [1, 2], yet the number of users of life-logging is still limited.

1.1 Questions Addressed

To understand what *motivates people to use life-logging* technologies in their daily life or at work, we have looked at and compared the influence of the *desire for support* and the influence of *possible barriers*. We analyzed how strongly the *desire for support in*

N. L. Black et al. (Eds.): IEA 2021, LNNS 223, pp. 605–613, 2022.
https://doi.org/10.1007/978-3-030-74614-8_75

pursuing goals and *potential barriers* influence the *intention to use life-logging*. We also examined the influence of different personality traits (*technical self-efficacy, vitality, sports motivation, privacy concerns, need for privacy*) on the *desire for support* and on *potential barriers*. We addressed the following research questions:

1. How strongly does the desire for support influence the intention to use life-logging of users and non-users?
2. How strongly do potential barriers negatively influence the intention to use life-logging of users and non-users?
3. How strongly do various user-characteristics influence the desire for support?
4. How strongly do various user-characteristics influence potential barriers?

2   Related Work

In this study, we consider what factors influence whether individuals (want to) use a life-logging device and whether they (want to) change their behavior using it. Whether individuals use a product depends on technology acceptance [6] and can be described by models of behavior (change). According to the Theory of Reasoned Action (TRA) [7] the intention to perform a behavior strongly relates to what behavior a person actually performs. An individual's attitude and subjective norms toward the behavior influence what behavioral intention the individual displays. Similarly, the Planned Behavior Theory (TPB) [8] says that intention leads to behavior: Although other factors also affect intention, once the intention to perform a behavior is strong enough, it is very likely that a person will perform the behavior.

In addition to theoretical studies of technology acceptance (TAM) and behavior change (TRA, TPB), other studies looked at the use of wearables and fitness apps. They showed that many potential users had privacy concerns [9, 10] or felt that privacy was lacking [11]. Lidynia et al. found that there is a general interest in wearables. There was particularly strong interest in the data collected [12]. In contrast, they also showed that privacy concerns in particular discourage the use of lifelogging devices.

Considering life-logging in the workplace, company reward systems can also influence whether employees use a life-logging device to achieve self-imposed goals or goals set by the company. Reward systems can fundamentally motivate employees: If employees feel they are being rewarded for their good performance, they generally increase their work effort and performance as a result. If companies promote life-logging in the workplace through reward systems and employees feel thereby that the organization is interested in their well-being, they become more loyal to the company [18]. Besides, the potential rewards influence which company an individual chooses. Companies, that maintain and promote the health of their employees through life-logging can appear more attractive to potential employees [19]. Companies should have a great interest in ensuring that their employees remain or become healthy in the long term, as their workforce will then be retained for the long term.

3 Method

First, we introduce the structural equation model central to this study. Then, we describe the survey with which we collected the data for our structural equation model.

3.1 Structural Equation Model – Implementation and Evaluation

Implementation of Structural Equation Model: We implemented our model using the R package *SEMinR v.1.1.1* [14, 15]. To evaluate and describe the model, we used the *tidyverse* and *psych* packages [14, 16]. We bootstrapped our model for significance drawing 5,000 samples [13].

Evaluation of the Measurement Model: To evaluate the reflective measurement model, we evaluated the convergent validity using outer loadings ($\lambda \geq .40$). For discriminant validity, we looked at the heterotrait-monotrait ratio (1 not in the HTMT bootstrap confidence interval) [13]. We assessed the significance of loadings using two-tailed t-tests with the degrees of freedom (DF) being equal to the number of responses for each model ($t \geq 1.65$: 10% significance level, $t \geq 1.96$: 5% significance level, $t \geq 2.57$: 1% significance level). As significance levels for the t-value p, we used $p < .05$: 5% significance level, $p < 01$: 1% significance level, and $p < 001$: 0.1% significance level. According to the convention also accepted in smartpls we report loadings for mode a (correlation weights) composite constructs and weights for mode b (regression weights) composite constructs.

Evaluation of the Structural Model: We assessed the path coefficients of the structural model for their relevance and significance using two-tailed t tests, the bootstrapping confidence interval and p values as described above. For model predictiveness we looked at the coefficient of determination ($R2 \geq .19$: weak level of determination, $R2 \geq .33$: moderate level of determination, $R2 \geq .63$: substantial level of determination) and the adjusted coefficient of determination R2 adj for model comparison [17].

3.2 Online Survey

We based our online survey on 17 initial interviews with users and non-users of life-logging technologies in which we asked about goals for which (potential) users like support and barriers they might face. The online survey consists of three parts:

Firstly, we surveyed *demographic data, explanatory user factors* and participants' current *use of life-logging technologies*. Secondly, we asked which *goals* they might want to pursue using life-logging (e.g. *more active in daily life, increase overall well-being*) and thirdly which *potential barriers* (e.g., *constantly under surveillance, getting negative feedback*) would prevent them from using life-logging technologies.

Explanatory Variables: In the first section, we queried demographic data (*age, gender,* and *education*) as well as some user factors:

Subjective Vitality (VIT): To measure *subjective vitality,* we used 4 items taken from [20] and translated into German.

Motives for Physical Activity (MPAM-R): To survey *motivation for physical activity,* we used the scale of [21], which measures motivation on five dimensions: Perception of one's competence, appearance, fitness, pleasure, and social motives.

Self-efficacy in Interacting with Technology: Self-efficacy generally indicates which tasks an individual chooses to perform, their performance on those tasks, and their perseverance in the face of difficulty. Self-efficacy in the use of technologies influences how people interact with interactive systems. We measured the construct using 8 items based on a scale by Beier [22].

Privacy: For Privacy, we measured *Need for Privacy* and *Privacy Concerns* through 3 items each. *Need for Privacy* indicates participants' general attitudes toward information disclosure. *Privacy Concerns* refer specifically to concerns about the privacy of information in an online context.

Use of Life-Logging: As final explanatory user factor, we surveyed whether participants already *use life-logging* and in what ways they use it.

Dependent Variables

Desire for Support: Individuals can pursue different *goals using life-logging.* Through the initial interviews we created a list of 12 *possible goals.* To measure quantitatively, whether users and non-users can imagine that Life-Logging can support in reaching the objectives, we asked participants (on a 6-point Likert scale), whether they desire the support of a Life-Logging device in reaching the objective.

Perceived Barriers: We also asked, what prevents individuals from using life-logging devices. We identified 13 *potential barriers* through the interviews and surveyed them on 6-point Likert scales ranging from "do not agree at all" to "fully agree".

3.3 Statistical Procedures

To statistically analyze the results, we rescaled the items to 0 to 100% and aggregated the scales to arithmetic means. We used parametric and nonparametric methods to analyze the results. We calculated bivariate correlations (Pearson's r or Spearman's ρ) and simple and repeated multivariate and univariate analyses of variance (M/ANOVA). We set the type I error rate (significance level) at $\alpha = .05$. For the multivariate tests, we use the Pillai value. For arithmetic means, we report the standard deviations (denoted by $\pm$). We tested the scales used for internal reliability by calculating Cronbach's α. Cronbach's α was $> .60$ for all scales.

4 Results

In this section, we present the results of our study. After a brief presentation of our sample, we show the results of the conducted structural equation model.

4.1 Users and Non-users of Life-Logging

From the 412 survey participants, 225 (55%) were users of life-logging and 187 (45%) were non-users. The sample is balanced in terms of *gender*: 214 female (52%) and 198 male (48%) participants ended the survey. Participants are between 17 and 78 years old (mean 36.1 ± 12.2 years). Overall, we have a heterogeneous sample as *age* and *gender* are not correlated ($\rho = .061, p = .213 > .05$).

In our sample, the *use of life-logging technologies* did not relate to *age* ($F_{1,410} = .30, p = .863$), *privacy concerns* ($F_{1,410} = .409, p = .523$) and *vitality* ($F_{1,410} = 2.152, p = .143$). In contrast, users and non-users differ in *need for privacy* ($F_{1,410} = 7.327, p < .005$), *motivation for physical activity* ($F_{1,410} = 22.327, p < .001$), and *self-efficacy in interacting with technology* ($F_{1,410} = 26.421, p < .001$). While life-logging users show higher *motivation for physical activity* (users: 69 ± 14%; non-users: 62 ± 17%) and higher *self-efficacy in interacting with technology* (users: 80 ± 17%; non-users: 70 ± 22%), non-users have a higher *need for privacy* (users: 64 ± 20%; non-users: 69 ± 19%).

Some aspects associated with life-logging are perceived as stronger *barriers* than others. While respondents do not mind *negative feedback* and *reminders to exercise*, they perceive the *limited effectiveness*, the *perceived need to share one's activities on social networks* or *not knowing, what happens to the measured data negatively*.

4.2 Structural Equation Model – From the Initial to the Final Model

We hypothesized that both the *desire for support* and the *barriers* influence whether users and non-users of life-logging (*want to*) *use* a life-logging device. Besides, we hypothesized that five personality traits (*general motives for physical activity, vitality, self-efficacy in interacting with technology, Privacy Concerns* and *Need for Privacy*) influence how strongly individuals imagine that a *Life-Logging device can support them in reaching their objective* and how strongly they perceive *potential barriers* of life-logging. Thus, we calculated a structural equation model with the five named *personality traits* influencing *Goals support* and *Barriers*, which in turn influence the *motivation to use a life-logging device*.

The initial structural equation model did not comply with the quality criteria described above, so we had to amend the model. To obtain a good model (according to statistical criteria), we adjusted the initial model in two steps. First, we removed items from the measurement model with a t-value smaller than 1.65, with very small loadings/weights ($< .40$) and with change of sign in the bootstrapping confidence intervals. Second, we evaluated the structural model and removed all parts with path coefficients smaller than 0.01 as their influence is negligible. We further analyzed the discriminant validity of the constructs. Most constructs showed a HTMT bootstrap confidence clearly below 1 ($< .637$). Only the HTMT bootstrap confidence of *privacy concerns* and *need for privacy* was close to 1 (htmt = .862). Thus, the discriminant validity of both constructs is low, but since these are two well-established constructs in theory, the constructs are understandably similar in content and the value is still below 1, we retained the separation of the two constructs for our model.

4.3   Structural Equation Model – Structural Models

Figure 1 and 2 show the final structural models of users and non-users of life-logging. Contrary to what we expected only the *desire for support* affects the *willingness to use life-logging* of users (see Fig. 1, $\beta = .53$) and non-users (see Fig. 2, $\beta = .602$) and *potential barriers* do not influence the *willingness to use life-logging*.

Structural model of Users of life-logging

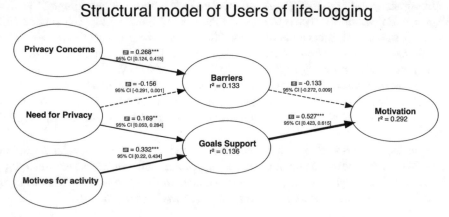

Fig. 1. Final structural model of **users** of life-logging. ** t $\geq$ 1.96 (5% significance level), *** t $\geq$ 2.57 (1% significance level)

For life-logging users (see Fig. 1), *Goals support* explained almost 30% of the variance of *motivation*. In turn, general *sport motivation* most strongly influenced the *desire for support* of users ($\beta = .331$). Users with a higher *need for privacy* also showed a higher *desire for support* ($\beta = .174$). Users with higher privacy concerns evaluated *potential barriers* more negatively ($\beta = .263$).

Structural model of Non-Users of life-logging

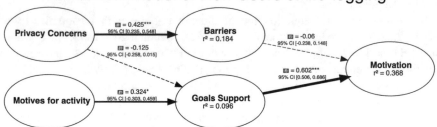

Fig. 2. Final structural model of **non-users** of life-logging. * t $\geq$ 1.65 (10% significance level), *** t $\geq$ 2.57 (1% significance level).

For non-users of life-logging (see Fig. 2), *Goals support* explained almost 37% of the variance of *motivation*. As with users, motivation for physical activity has the greatest influence on the *desire for support* of non-users ($\beta = .328$). Non-users with higher *privacy concerns*, also perceived *potential barriers* more negative ($\beta = .425$). Contrary to users, we did not find an influence of *need for privacy* on *goals support* for non-users.

5   Discussion

Our study shows that the intention to use life-logging technologies strongly depends on the desire for support of users and non-users. Thus, it is important that (potential) users have concrete goals and can imagine life-logging helping them to pursue these goals. (Potential) barriers showed no influence on the intention to use life-logging devices. Although the previous analysis of barriers showed that participants rated some barriers as very negative when asked about them, this showed no influence on the motivation to use life-logging. Nevertheless, even people, who already use life-logging rated some barriers very negative. Therefore, we still assume that barriers although they do not prevent people from using a life-logging device, are at least perceived as annoying during use. Therefore, it is still useful to know which barriers particularly disturb life-logging users and to avoid them if possible, if the goal is that individuals use life-logging for a long time. Besides, privacy concerns particularly influence how strongly (potential) users of life-logging technologies show the desire for support and how strongly they perceive potential barriers. Thus, to motivate people to use life-logging technologies, privacy concerns regarding such technologies need to be taken into account. When introducing life-logging technologies, potential objectives and privacy concerns of (potential) users should be addressed.

Using life-logging in the workplace also brings with it the concern of who has access to the data. The importance of concerns associated with data is also undelined by the fact that participants were particularly negative about the barriers of not knowing what happens to the data and having to show the data to others on social media. In addition to the concerns of (potential) life-logging users, ethical and data privacy concerns must also be considered when the workplace has access to the life-logging data of its employees. Therefore, it is probably easier to achieve that more people use a life-logging device privately than in a professional context in the future. If life-logging should be used in the workplace, it must be clearly communicated to employees what happens to the data.

6   Conclusion

When trying to motivate employees at the workplace to move regularly (e.g., a couple hundred steps every hour) using life-logging devices, it must be taken into account that people are only motivated to use a life-logging device if they consider the device to be helpful in achieving a goal they want to achieve. Potential barriers are less important for motivation than the assessment that the device can help to achieve goals. Nevertheless, barriers should also be considered, especially if people are already using a device. It should also be considered that (potential) users of life-logging devices are different as in they bring different premises but also requirements and should not be lumped together into a single entity.

Acknowledgements. I like to thank Lilian Kojan for her assistance in creating and implementing the structural equation model.

Parts of this work have been funded by the German Ministry of Education and Research (BMBF) under project No. KIS1DSD045 "myneData" and V5JPI004 "PAAL."

References

1. Warburton, D.E.R., Nicol, C.W., Bredin, S.S.D.: Health benefits of physical activity: the evidence. CMAJ **174**, 801–809 (2006)
2. Lee, I.-M., Shiroma, E.J., Lobelo, F., Puska, P., Blair, S.N., Katzmarzyk, P.T., Alkandari, J.R., Bo Andersen, L., Bauman, A., Brownson, R.C., Bull, F.C., Craig, C.L., Ekelund, U., Goenka, S., Guthold, R., Hallal, P.C., Haskell, W.L., Heath, G.W., Inoue, S., Kahlmeier, S., Kohl III, H.W., Lambert, V., Leetongin, G., Loos, R., Marcus, B. Davis, F.D., Bagozzi, R.P., Warshaw, P.R.: User acceptance of computer technology: a comparison of two theoretical models. Manag. Sci. **35**, 982–1003 (1989)
3. Fishbein, M., Ajzen, I.: Belief, Attitude, Intention and Behavior: An Introduction to Theory and Research. Addison-Wesley Publishing Company Inc., Reading (1975)
4. Ajzen, I.: The theory of planned behavior. Organ. Behav. Hum. Decis. Process. **50**, 79–211 (1991)
5. Bansal, G., Zahedi, F.M., Gefen, D.: The impact of personal dispositions on information sensitivity, privacy concern and trust in disclosing health information online. Decis. Support Syst. **49**, 138–150 (2010)
6. Motti, V.G., Caine, K.: Users' privacy concerns about wearables. In: Brenner, M., et al. (eds.) FC 2015 Workshops, pp. 231–244. International Financial Cryptography Association (2015)
7. Wieneke, A., Lehrer, C., Zeder, R., Jung, R.: Privacy-related decision-making in the context of wearable use. In: PACIS 2016 Proceedings Paper 67 (2016)
8. Lidynia, C., Brauner, P., Ziefle, M.: A Step in the right direction – understanding privacy concerns and perceived sensitivity of fitness trackers. In: Ahram, T., Falcão, C. (eds.) Advances in Intelligent Systems and Computing - Advances in Human Factors in Wearable Technologies and Game Design. Springer, Cham (2018)
9. Hair, J.F., Hult, G.T.M., Ringle, C.M., Sarstedt, M.: A Primer on Partial Least Squares Structural Equation Modeling (PLS-SEM), 2nd edn. Sage, Los Angeles (2017)
10. R Core Team: R: A Language and Environment for Statistical Computing. Vienna, Austria: R Foundation for Statistical Computing (2020). https://www.R-project.org/
11. Ray, S., Danks, N.P., Estrada, J.M.V.: seminr: Domain-Specific Language for Building PLS Structural Equation Models, Mai 2020. Accessed 08 July 2020
12. Wickham, H., Averick, M., Bryan, J., Chang, W., McGowan, L.D., François, R., Yutani, H.: Welcome to the tidyverse. J. Open Source Softw. **4**(43), 1686 (2019). https://doi.org/10.21105/joss.01686
13. Davcik, N.S.: The Use and misuse of structural equation modeling in management research: a review and critique. SSRN Electron. J. (2014). https://www.ssrn.com/abstract=2196120. https://doi.org/10.2139/ssrn.219612. Accessed 06 Feb 2021
14. Mowday, R.T., Porter, L.W., Steers, R.M.: Employee-Organization Linkages: The Psychology of Employee Commitment, Absenteeism, and Turnover. Academic Press, New York (1982)
15. Reward Systems in Organizations. In: Performance Appraisal and Rewards. https://opente xtbc.ca/organizationalbehavioropenstax/chapter/reward-systems-in-organizations/#ch08rf in-9. Accessed 06 Feb 2021
16. Ryan, R.M., Frederick, C.: On energy, personality and health: subjective vitality as a dynamic reflection of well-being. J. Pers. **65**, 529–565 (1997)

17. Ryan, R.M., Fredrick, C.M., Lepes, D., Rubio, N., Sheldon, K.M.: Intrinsic motivation and exercise adherence. Int. J. Sport Psychol. **28**, 335–354 (1997)
18. Beier, G.: Kontrollüberzeugungen im Umgang mit Technik [Locus of control when interacting with technology]. Rep. Psychol. **24**, 684–693 (1999)

Enabling Collaborative Situations in 4.0 Industry: Multiple Case Study

Nathan Compan[1]([✉]), Fabien Coutarel[1], Daniel Brissaud[2], and Géraldine Rix-Lièvre[1]

[1] Université Clermont Auvergne, ACTé, 63000 Clermont-Ferrand, France
`nathan.compan@uca.fr`
[2] Univ. Grenoble Alpes, CNRS, Laboratoire G-SCOP, Grenoble, France

Abstract. The clinic of use [1] carries the idea that technology is the operator's partner in his activity. However, it is not uncommon, within 4.0 industry, to observe technologies that don't allow operators to develop their skills and capacities for action. It happens that some technologies are "technopush" implemented, which may explain the disappointing results of some projects with high technological goals. Our works objective is therefore to define criteria for an Human-Technology enabling collaborative situation (ECS), in order to guide conception projects at an early stage. The study of scientific literature leads us to define the ECS according to 3 criteria. These characteristics are considered essential from the point of view of the operator's activity deployment: learn a new and more efficient way of doing things, increase the available possibilities and ways of doing things, and adjust the Human-Machine couple attributes according to the evolution of situations over time. We present here the results of a multiple case study of innovation projects. This case study is designed to confront the criteria of the ECS with the actors feelings (success or failure). These initial results suggest that the ECS would be an interesting way to understand the contrasted reality of projects, beyond the general positive feelings received in both cases. We hope that the ECS criteria will allows to guide more precisely and in a more demanding way the industrialists in their technological implementation projects.

Keywords: 4.0 Industry · New technologies · HMI · Enabling situations · Human-technology collaborations

1 Introduction

In ergonomics and related theoretical and disciplinary fields, many authors [2, 3] have highlighted on the developmental relationships between technology and individuals. These authors invite the designers to ensure that the new technology and the new service promote the development of the operators/users' activity and, above all, do not constrain it. Inspired by the instrumental approach [4] and Falzon's work on enabling environments [5, 6], we propose a definition of an enabling collaborative situation (ECS) in order to understand how technology can promote the human activity deployment and, in particular, human's capacity for action on his Milieu [7]. Thus, an ECS when using a technology would be a situation with three characteristics.

N. L. Black et al. (Eds.): IEA 2021, LNNS 223, pp. 614–620, 2022.
https://doi.org/10.1007/978-3-030-74614-8_76

Learn a New and More Efficient Way of Doing Things. Performance is an essential factor in work activity, both for the operator and his organization, and therefore conditions the technological acceptance [8]. An ecological assessment of performance (and therefore very close to real-life situations of use) is then necessary to identify the relevant performance criteria. With these criteria, we associate the dimensions of utility [9], affects, emotions and moods [10, 11], and sensemaking [12].

Increase the Available Possibilities and Ways of Doing Things. Gestural diversity constitutes a resource for the activity: facing the variability of work, a wide range of available ways of doing things constitutes a situational leeway [13] which is essential for the preservation of performance and health building. Collaboration with technology should thus make it possible to increase the range of capacities that can be expressed in situations.

Adjust the Human-Machine Couple Attributes According to the Evolution of Situations Over Time. Confronted with changing work situations (his condition, skills, trade-offs, etc.), the operator may feel the need to vary his relationship to technology. The instrumental genisis [4], must be supported. To do so, he must have the appropriate skills and authorizations or call upon the collective and organization for help in the day-to-day running of the organization. It is thus desirable that the operator can, by himself, modify the machine characteristics. The operational transparency [4] of the technology, and the non-overflow of the operator [5] should allow him to take his own activity as an object of analysis in order to be able to carry out continuous design in use [14]. Some contexts imply that change cannot happen quickly and require broader organizational support. Thus, in order to allow continuous design in use, space for work debate and times for collective regulation should be included in the day-to-day running of the organization [5, 15]. An enabling management [16] is therefore also desirable.

2   Material and Method

A multiple case study [17, 18] was conducted to compare two technology implementation projects, using a holistic, in depth [19] and context sensitive [17] approach. The history of each project was thus formalized in a monograph, based on multiple data sources [20]: recorded interviews, observations of work situations and organizations, and consultation of documents (job descriptions, etc.). We have identified in this data what was, on the one hand, a global appreciation of the project by the different actors (managers, engineers, team leaders or operators), and, on the other hand, what, in the description of the project, could be found among the 3 characteristics of an ECS that we are trying to validate.

The two projects studied here are those of two international companies (automotive suppliers): the first (A) introduced a cobot in an assembly line. The second (B) introduced an augmented reality system in a maintenance department.

3   Results

We were therefore able to extract from our monographs analysis several points about the different ECS characteristics (see in Table 1).

Table 1. Overall synthesis, taking into account all actors, of the results by characteristic of an ECS.

Enabling collaborative situation (ECS) characteristics	Case A	Case B
Learn a new and more efficient way of doing things	The cobot is unanimously considered useful. It allows a better rate of production and reduces the error rate, by performing a visual control	Operators consider the system to be almost useless for their work. It doesn't allow them to go faster because they already know the locations. It does not appear to reduce the error rate either
Increase the available possibilities and ways of doing things	Operators have a lack of situational leeway to complete their tasks. Despite a few improvised regulations, they have only one way to accomplish their tasks	Depending on the scenario, operators may have more or less situational leeway. Indeed, this will depend on the way the scenario is designed and the flexibility it leaves to the operator
Adjust the Human-Machine couple attributes according to the evolution of situations over time	The technology is understood by the different actors. The glass cage allows the operators to see the progress of the cobot and the visual interface gives them an overview of the entire process (number of parts made, etc.) Operators are not overwhelmed by their tasks The debates times are quick (before the service takes place) and not all actors are present (especially the Methods team) Operators are autonomous and empowered Some operators feel they are not being listened to	Actors seem to understand how the device works (despite some use difficulties related to the "air tap" mechanism). The glasses are not always intuitive to handle and the instructions are not always clearly transmitted (especially the points of interest location) Operators are not overwhelmed by their tasks The debates times are regular (25–30 min before the service takes place) but not all actors are present (especially technology integrators) Operators are autonomous and empowered Scenarios are designed by the operators who are currently masters of the tool

For case A, the actors consider that the integration of the cobot is a success. From the ECS point of view (see in Table 1), this case has a positive balance on the first characteristic but the technical staff wants a more efficient cobot because they know its potential. In addition, this new and more efficient way of doing things is maintained over time despite operator rotations. The situation has a negative balance on the second characteristic because there is a lack of situational leeway. Although operators have little situational leeway by being able to prepare parts in advance, they are still extremely dependent on the cobot and its speed. Indeed, there is only one possible operating mode, with a predefined sequencing, and a maximum speed also predefined by the cobot. Regarding the third characteristic, we can see a contrasted balance. We can see a good operational transparency, because the operators understand how the cobot works and therefore have the possibility to anticipate its behavior. They can therefore adapt they behaviour by assembling some parts in advance in order to feed the cobot. On the other hand, they do not have the possibility to transform the characteristics of the technology or to vary their interaction modes. Their local capacities of intervention on one of the elements of the Human-Machine couple are very limited. Operators still have the possibility to contact the Methods department and their own leader in order to report informations (breakdowns, suggestions, etc.). However, this seems rather anecdotal in reality because the changes are very technocentric (production speed, error rate, etc.). Some operators feel they are not being listened to. The debate times do not involve all the actors, and in particular the Methods department. This absence does not make it possible to have a time for collective exchanges about the work between engineers and operators that would allow a debate more efficient and potentially better feedback from the operators.

Regarding the second case (B), the actors also consider that the integration of augmented reality glasses is a success. Regarding the ECS criteria (see in Table 1), this case has a negative balance on the first characteristic. The system is not used by operators who are experts and who consider the technology not very useful for their work. Indeed, if we can observe the learning of a new and more efficient way of doing things (according to the chosen criteria), it concerns rather novice operators. Case B has a contrasted balance on the second characteristic: depending on the scenario, the operators fear a loss of situational leeway and autonomy, but the leaders and the integrators are rather optimistic about it. Operators are therefore afraid that their management will dictate, depending on the situation, a unique way of working. Indeed, the situational leeway is very dependent on the context and the scenario. Tasks may vary from one intervention to another (different machines, different intervention duration, etc.). It is therefore possible to have a very linear prescribed scenario in the form of consecutive steps or a more evasive one that leaves more freedom to the operator. Regarding the third characteristic, we find a positive balance, a majority of the criteria are positive, the balance is contrasted about the level of operative transparency and times for work debate, but this is not a significant concern in this case. It's the operators themselves who build the operating mode (potentially several) and the interface according to the scenarios, so they have the possibility to adjust the Human-Machine couple attributes according to the evolution of the situations over time. Even more, the operators remain «masters of the tool» (they control the augmented reality glasses) and a «personal space» is under consideration for each operator in the device. We can note that there is indeed a time to discuss the work every morning (lasting about 25–30 min) in the presence of working site managers and operators. The leader is also regularly present. Although not all the actors are present (especially the technology integrators), this time allows feedbacks from the field and work discussions. Operators report that they have time to think about their activity during their work, which makes this meeting time more effective. We can also see that management is moving towards an enabling management where it is consistent to leave autonomy, trust and responsability to operators. Finally, operational transparency is a leader's desire, and all the actors seem to understand, in its majority, how the system works and what it expect from them. Nevertheless, we note some difficulties of use as orientation difficulties and use of the «air tap» mechanism.

In a transversal approach, we can therefore note that:

- The different actors of a project can give a positive opinion about it, even if there is no obvious improvement in the work situation. For example, the integration of augmented reality glasses is not an enough amelioration from a performance point of view for the operators (expert) in case B.
- The collaboration level varies greatly depending on the technology and the task type. Cobots are designed as a collaborative tool but may have, in fact, only a low level of collaboration with humans (and even being used autonomously). According to the different classifications, we would be, here, in a situation of cooperation or weak collaboration between the human and the cobot [21–24]. On the contrary, according to some classifications, the augmented reality glasses (case B) has the system directly placed on the operator and has a high level of collaboration.
- Each type of actor does not underline the same subjects and does not provide the same opinions of the project.
- In these two projects, the characteristic of increasing the available possibilities and ways of doing things is not present.
- In both cases, there is no optimal time for debates about work because specialists in technology (cobot or augmented reality) are not present.

4   Discussion

Our project is to test the value of the enabling collaborative situation (ECS) in order to analyze technology implementation projects. Further results will have to be produced to confirm or qualify these initial results. The scientific literature identifies many other factors for a successful technology implementation that can be evaluated in the use situation (safety for example). Some criteria of a project management are also important: the way in wich uses and users are integrated into the conception [25, 26] conditions the quality of the future ECS.

We have chosen to leave them aside for this presentation to focus on the ECS interest. Our initial results seem to confirm the relevance of continuing along this path: the actors' positive overall experience in their project hide significant differences on several criteria that appear to us to be decisive.

These initial results also show that the second characteristic is not satisfactorily met in either case. Despite of this, actors evaluate the projects overall positively. Several interpretations can be made at this stage: 1. This characteristic from the literature is not relevant; 2. This characteristic is more difficult to meet today in project management; 3. The concerned operators do not experience negatively the absence of a broadening of their way to do things, because they are accustomed to not having this freedom.

Future results will therefore have to answer these questions, to support the ambition to assist the designers. Our objective is to give to designers of future technological devices some more precise and demanding criteria.

Our approach to use of technology by the ECS does not take into account the nature of the technology. We consider that the criteria relative to the activity deployment are fundamental, and therefore not dependent on specific technologies properties. From techniques anthropology by Marcel Mauss [27] to contemporary authors in activity ergonomics [28] fundamental questions remained present, althought renewed because of the properties of the new tools. It gives our proposal a transversal and longitudinal validity made necessary by the speed of contemporary technological changes. However, it has the disadvantage to potentially mask important differences in what different technologies can do. But it also allows us to propose a macro view and free this project from the everchanging specific properties of new technologies. In our 2 case studies, we compare a situation of interaction between an user and a cobot, with a situation of interaction between an user and augmented reality glasses. It would be interesting to be able to map the different potentialities offered by the ECS with the many technologies associated with 4.0 Industry.

5 Conclusion

It is now classic to assert that the Human must be very much taken into account, also in the 4.0 industry field. However, it is often found that technological implementation is not associated with an enrichment of human work, especially from the operator point of view. The ECS aims to provide more demanding critera for the technology use that can guide design processes. The results presented here remain insufficients from this point of view and deserve to be confronted with new case studies and other more experimental works.

References

1. Bobillier Chaumon, M.E., Clot, Y.: Clinique de l'usage : Les artefacts technologiques comme développement de l'activité: Synthèse Introductive au dossier. Activités **13**(2) (2016). https://doi.org/10.4000/activites.2897
2. Rabardel, P., Beguin, P.: Instrument mediated activity: from subject development to anthropocentric design. Theoret. Issues Ergon. Sci. **6**(5), 429–461 (2005)
3. Clot, Y.: Travail et pouvoir d'agir. PUF, Paris (2008)
4. Rabardel, P.: Les hommes et les technologies; approche cognitive des instruments contemporains, p. 195 (1995)
5. Falzon, P.: Ergonomics, knowledge development and the design of enabling environments, p. 8 (2005)
6. Falzon, P.: Enabling environments, enabling organizations, p. 4 (2014)
7. Canguilhem, G.: The living and its milieu. Grey Room, pp. 7–31 (2001)
8. Bobillier-Chaumon, M., Dubois, M.: Technology acceptance and acceptability in organizations. Le travail humain **72**(4), 355–382 (2009)
9. Nielsen, J.: Usability Engineering. Morgan Kaufmann, Burlington (1994)

10. Hassenzahl, M.: The thing and I: understanding the relationship between the user and the product. In: Blythe, M.A., Monk, A.F., Overbeeke, K., Wright, P. (eds.) Funology: From Usability to Enjoyment, pp. 31–42. Kluwer Academic Publishers Netherlands (2003)
11. Lallemand, C., Gronier, G.: Méthodes de design UX: 30 méthodes fondamentales pour concevoir et évaluer les systèmes interactifs. Editions Eyrolles (2016)
12. Récopé, M., Fache, H., Beaujouan, J., Coutarel, F., Rix-Lièvre, G.: A study of the individual activity of professional volleyball players: situation assessment and sensemaking under time pressure. Appl. Ergon. **80**, 226–237 (2019)
13. Coutarel, F., Caroly, S., Vézina, N., Daniellou, F.: Marge de manœuvre situationnelle et pouvoir d'agir: Des concepts à l'intervention ergonomique. Le travail humain **78**(1), 9 (2015). https://doi.org/10.3917/th.781.0009
14. Rabardel, P., Pastré, P.: Modèles du sujet pour la conception: dialectiques, activités, développement, p. 260. Octarès, Toulouse (2005)
15. Rocha, R., Mollo, V., Daniellou, F.: Le débat sur le travail fondé sur la subsidiarité: Un outil pour développer un environnement capacitant. Activités **14**(2) (2017). https://doi.org/10.4000/activites.2999
16. Yahia, N.A., Courcy, F., Montani, F., Lauzier, M., Boudrias, J.-S.: Promouvoir le leadership habilitant du supérieur pour contrer les méfaits du stress au travail et optimiser l'innovation et la performance, p. 139 (2019)
17. Yin, R.K.: Validity and generalization in future case study evaluations. Evaluation **19**(3), 321–332 (2013). https://doi.org/10.1177/1356389013497081
18. Flyvbjerg, B.: Five misunderstandings about case-study research. Qual. Inq. **12**(2), 219–245 (2006). https://doi.org/10.1177/1077800405284363
19. Feagin, J., Orum, A., Sjoberg, G.: A Case for Case Study. University of North Carolina Press, Chapel Hill (1991)
20. Tellis, W.M.: Application of a case study methodology. Qual. Rep. **3**(3), 1–19 (1997). https://nsuworks.nova.edu/tqr/vol3/iss3/1
21. Bdiwi, M., Pfeifer, M., Sterzing, A.: A new strategy for ensuring human safety during various levels of interaction with industrial robots. CIRP Ann. **66**(1), 453–456 (2017). https://doi.org/10.1016/j.cirp.2017.04.009
22. Kolbeinsson, A., Lagerstedt, E., Lindblom, J.: Classification of collaboration levels for human-robot cooperation in manufacturing. Advances in Transdisciplinary Engineering, pp. 151–156 (2018). https://doi.org/10.3233/978-1-61499-902-7-151
23. Morais, A.: Impact sur les conditions de travail de l'utilisation de la robotique dans l'industrie automobile (2018)
24. Jansen, A., van Middelaar, J.: Ministry of Social Affairs and Employment, p. 79 (2018)
25. Daniellou, F., Garrigou, A.: Participatory approach to future work activity, case-studies in the printing industry. In: Karwowski, W., Rahimi, H. (eds.) Human Aspects of Hybrid Automated Systems II, pp. 493–500 (1990)
26. Garrigou, A., Daniellou, F., Carballeda, G., Ruaud, S.: Activity analysis in participatory design and analysis of participatory design activity. Int. J. Ind. Ergon. **15**(5), 311–327 (1995)
27. Mauss, M.: Les techniques du corps. Journal de psychologie **32**(3–4), 271–293 (1936)
28. Daniellou, F., Rabardel, P.: Activity-oriented approaches to ergonomics: some traditions and communities. Theoret. Issues Ergon. Sci. **6**(5), 353–357 (2005)

The Impact of Expertise on Query Formulation Strategies During Complex Learning Task Solving: A Study with Students in Medicine and Computer Science

Cheyenne Dosso[1]([✉]), Lynda Tamine[2], Pierre-Vincent Paubel[1], and Aline Chevalier[1]

[1] University of Toulouse, CLLE-CNRS, 05 Allée Antonio Machado, 31058 Toulouse, France
cheyenne.dosso@univ-tlse2.fr
[2] University of Toulouse, IRIT-CNRS, 118 Route de Narbonne, 31062 Toulouse, France
lynda.lechani@irit.fr

Abstract. This study focus on queries formulation strategies when expert users in a medical or computer science domain solved complex tasks. Ten medical students and ten computer science students had to perform four fact-finding search tasks (two simple tasks and two inferential tasks) and six learning tasks (two exploratory, two decision-making and two problem solving tasks) in these two domains. Results showed that non-experts used more terms from task statement to build their queries than experts did. Experts often produced new keywords than non-experts did. Specifically, computer science experts used more keywords not specific to the domain knowledge whereas medical experts used specific domain keywords to formulate queries. These results are a beginning to better understand how users are searching to learn when they are using Internet but further ergonomics studies have to more explore this subject to create search systems adapted to Search as Learning activity.

Keywords: Search as learning · Task complexity · Expertise domain · Query strategies

1 Introduction

When users are engaging in information search (IS) activity with a search engine, they are often faced with a lot of information they have to with regard to their objectives, prior knowledge to achieve their search goals. (Sharit et al. 2015). Recently, many researchers have emphasized the importance of improving current search systems in a learning context because users often pursue an overall objective of acquiring new knowledge (Gwizdka et al. 2016). To develop systems that fit users' learning objectives, it is important to consider user's individual characteristics involve in this activity. Among them, the level of prior domain knowledge play a central role. If many studies focused on the role of prior domain knowledge on IS (Monchaux et al. 2015; Sanchiz et al. 2017a), in the Searching as Learning approach the impact of this variable need a better

N. L. Black et al. (Eds.): IEA 2021, LNNS 223, pp. 621–627, 2022.
https://doi.org/10.1007/978-3-030-74614-8_77

understanding specifically on users' search behavior when they are solving complex learning tasks. To this end, in the present study, we focus on query formulation strategies with regard to the level of prior domain knowledge of users (i.e. experts vs non-experts) and the type of search tasks to be performed (fact-finding vs learning tasks). First, we present related work concerning the information search activity, particularly concerning query formulations and the expertise effects. In the second part, we present the method used to study formulation strategies of users. Then the results are presented and we finish on the discussion with limits and the perspectives of further researches.

2   Related Work

The cognitive model of IS initially developed by Sharit et al. (2015) describe IS into three main stages: 1. *Planning:* users have to build a mental representation of the search goal from task statement and their prior domain knowledge. 2. *Evaluation of information:* users have to compare their search goal stored in working memory with information from Search Engine Results Pages (SERPs). 3. *Depth processing and navigation:* From links selected just before, users access to information content (i.e. web pages, PDF...). They may decide to process information more precisely by comparing their goal with content or to navigate within several web pages. To plan the activity, to evaluate and to process information content, prior domain knowledge allows building a more consistent mental representation of the search problem, to be more relevant in the select of links from SERPs and for analyzing the web pages content (Sanchiz et al. 2020). At the level of query formulation strategies during IS, expert users are more efficient than non-expert ones. They formulate more queries (Monchaux et al. 2015; Sanchiz et al. 2017a) and longer ones than non-experts do (Hembrooke et al. 2005; Tamine and Chouquet 2017). They also produce more new keywords (Monchaux et al. 2015; Sanchiz et al. 2017b) linked to domain vocabulary (Sanchiz et al. 2017a; Tamine and Chouquet 2017; O'Brien et al. 2020), than non-experts, who need to use the task statement to build their queries (Sanchiz et al. 2017a, b). This is a major problem for non-expert users because they have to get to relevant content to be able to learn new knowledge, but search engine results pages depend on queries content (Vakkari 2016). In this way, the activity of search as learning should be more critical for users without prior domain knowledge because they do not have specific vocabulary to formulate queries allowing to get new information.

In addition, the information search activity depends on characteristics of tasks to be performed. For instance, complexity of search task is often manipulated at the level of task goal (e.g., Monchaux et al. 2015; Sanchiz et al. 2017a, b). For learning tasks, literature describes several complexity level. Firstly, the exploratory learning tasks, allowing users to gain knowledge about a topic (Marchionini 2006). These tasks are open-ended because several sub-goals may be carried on by users. Then, there were decision-making tasks, in which the final goal is to select the better solution among several possibilities and make the better decision (Campbell 1988). The sub goals consist to compare a set of information leading to decision-making. This task is also open-ended, because several answer are acceptable. To make choice, users have to define criteria related to the goal to be achieve with regard to their level of knowledge. Finally, there is problem-solving task, which needs the elaboration and the creation of a new set of information. Users have find the better path to achieve the goal, which is clearly specified (Campbell 1988) and they have to re-use retrieved information.

The objective of this study is to better understanding how users formulate queries depending on their level of prior domain knowledge according to the search and learning task complexity.

3 Method

3.1 Variables

Independents Variables. *IV1-Prior domain knowledge level* (experts vs non-experts) as between-subject factor. *IV2-Task type* (simple, exploratory learning, decision-making, problem solving, inferential) as within-subject factor. *IV3-Task domain* (medical vs computer science) as within-subject factor.

Dependents Variables. All dependents variables were recorded per search session (i.e. to complete one task, user have to do one search session from the first query produced to the close of navigator).

DV1a-Total number of new queries produced and DV1b-Query length: DV1a corresponds to the total number of new queries submitted to the search box. If user submitted the same query during his/her search session, only first production was computed. For DV1b, query length was calculated as a mean of all queries produced divided by all keywords produced per search session.

DV2-Total number of keywords used from tasks corresponds to the total number of keywords used, which were terms contained in the task statement per search session.

DV3a-Total number of new keywords produced by users from not specific vocabulary and DV3b-Total number of new keywords produced by users from specific vocabulary. DV3a corresponds to the total new keywords not related to medical or computer science domain produced by users per search session. DV3b corresponds to the total new keywords related to medical or computer science produced by users per search session.

3.2 Participants

Twenty participants performed the experience: ten in computer science (6 males, 4 females) and ten in medical (5 males, 5 females). The age of participant was ranging from 20 to 32 years old (M = 24.6 SD = 3.3), for computer science (M = 23.8 SD = 3.2) and for medical (M = 25.4 SD = 3.4). All of them were students in master degree, five for computer science and two for medical, or were PhD students, five in computer science and 8 in medical. We selected students with similar level of information search to avoid its influences on information search activity (Sanchiz et al. 2020). We controlled this variable through pre-test online distributed from Qualtrics XM plateform, which contained a self-efficacy scale in information search (Rodon and Meyer 2018). The total score was calculated from the ten items proposed with a 4-point likert scale. There were no significant differences between two groups ($t(18)$ = 1.24, $p >$ .05, computer science students (M = 33.5 SD = 5) and medical students (M = 30.8 SD = 4.83). We also controlled the level of prior domain knowledge, through a self-report 5-point Likert scale of prior domain knowledge. There was a significant difference for the computer science knowledge self-report ($t(18) = 5.5, p < .001$), where computer science students reported to have higher knowledge (M = 4.2 SD = 0.42) than medical students (M = 2 SD = 1.2). The reverse was obtained for medical knowledge ($t(18) = -11.5, p < .001$), for which medical students indicated to have higher knowledge (M = 4.2 SD = 0.6) than computer science students (M = 1.3 SD = 0.5). Participants also had to complete a knowledge questionnaire in the two domains, with ten questions for each domain and 5 possible answers per question (one right, three wrongs and one "I do not know"). Concerning the computer science knowledge test (α = .94), computer science students obtained better score (M = 6.8 SD = 2.2) than medical students (M = 0.5 SD = 0.7) ($t(18) = 8.8, p < .001$). We also found a significant difference ($t(18) = -12.1, p < .001$) for the medical knowledge test (α = .84): medical students (M = 5 SD = 0.7) had better scores than computer science students (M = 0.5 SD = 1).

3.3 Procedure

The study was in two stages. First, participants received a first mail containing a link to the pre-test online (i.e. demographic information, age, level and domain of studies, knowledge self-report scale, ten question tests, self-efficacy scale in information search). Participants had to sign a free and informed consent. Second, given COVID-19 crisis, we scheduled an appointment with each participant to provide him/her the experimental material (i.e. general instructions, USB key containing the software for experiment that allowed retrieving logs during search session and the instructions with task statements).

Table 1. Examples of task statements per domain.

Task type	Examples of task statement
Simple	*Medical* - What is the value of severe hyponatremia?
Exploratory	*Computer science* - You want to learn more about "Big Data"
Decision-making	*Medical* - An 83-year-old woman had an unremitting stroke 5 months ago. On the stroke assessment, atrial fibrillation was discovered. She has fallen 3 times in the last two months. Should anticoagulant treatment be started? After evaluating the risk-benefit ratio of starting anticoagulant treatment or not, select the management that seems best for you and justify your choices
Problem solving	*Computer science* - As part of your job interview, you will be asked to create a resource that allows you to transcribe a text written in textos language into a text written in a well-trained language. With information collected on the internet, propose a general but precise methodology that shows your assets and motivates the employer to hire you
Inferential	*Medical* - A very young person comes in for consultation and presents a sudden and transient onset dermatitis. By observing the lesions, we note the presence of papules. At the rest of the clinical examination, adenopathy are found. In your opinion, what does this patient suffer from?

At the end of the experiment, all participants received a gift-card of 15 euros. During search sessions, participants solved ten tasks: 4 fact-finding search tasks (i.e. simple task and inferential task in each domain, computer science and medical domain), and 6 learning search tasks (i.e. exploratory learning, decision-making and problem solving task in each domain too). Some examples of task statements per domain are introduced in Table 1.

4 Results

For each dependents variables, we performed an ANOVA (repeated measures) on three independents variables: 1. Prior domain knowledge level (experts vs non-experts) as between-subject factor; 2. Task type (simple, exploratory learning, decision-making, problem solving, inferential) as within-subject factor; 3. Task domain (medical vs computer science) as within-subject factor. When ANOVA was significant, we performed Scheffe post-hoc. All results with means and standard deviations are presented below.

Concerning the total number of new queries produced and their length, none significant effect appeared ($ps > .05$).

For the number of keywords from task statement, the ANOVA was not significant for the expertise ($p > .05$) nor the interaction between expertise and the task type ($p > .05$). But, the ANOVA was significant for the interaction between expertise and task domain ($F(1,18) = 37$, $p < .001$, $\eta_p^2 = 0.70$). Computer science experts used more keywords from the statement for medicine tasks (M = 4.3 SD = 3.1) than computer science tasks (M = 3.04 SD = 3.1) with $p < .001$. On the contrary, medical experts used more keywords from the statement for computer science tasks (M = 4.22 SD = 2.73) than medical tasks (M = 2.8 SD = 2.8) with $p < .001$. The interaction between expertise and task type and domain was significant ($F(4,72) = 12.4$, $p < .001$, $\eta_p^2 = 0.41$). For decision-making tasks, medical experts used more keywords from statement in computer science (M = 7.4 SD = 2.8) than for medicine decision-task (M = 1.9 SD = 1), with $p < .001$. In addition, medicine experts used more keywords from statement in computer science than computer science experts (M = 3.8 SD = 2.44; $p < .05$). For the decision-making task in medicine, computer science experts used more keywords from the statement (M = 5.7 SD = 3.3) than medical experts ($p < .001$). For problem solving task in medicine, experts in computer science (M = 8.3 SD = 3.43) and medicine (M = 6.1 SD = 2.3) use more keywords from the statement than when solving the computer science task, with experts (M = 2.8 SD = 1.6) and medical experts (M = 2.8 SD = 0.8) using $p < .001$ for both comparisons. For the inferential task in computer science, medical experts used more keywords from the statement (M = 7.1 SD = 1.9) than they did for the inferential task in medicine (M = 2.6 SD = 1.6), with $p < .001$.

For the number of not specific new keywords, the ANOVA did not reveal any significant effect of expertise, nor interaction between expertise and task type ($p < .05$). The ANOVA was significant for expertise × task domain interaction ($F(1,18) = 6.43$, $p < .05$, $\eta_p^2 = 0.3$): Computer science experts produced more not specific keywords ($p = .001$) in computer science tasks (M = 2.9 SD = 2.8) than in medical tasks (M = 1.12 SD = 2.8). They also produced more not specific keywords ($p < .05$) than medical experts did in computer science tasks (M = 1.5 SD = 1.8) and in medical tasks (M = 1.10 SD = 1.8) with, $p < .05$.

For the interaction between expertise, type and domain, ANOVA indicated a significant effect ($F(4,72) = 2.8, p < .05, \eta_p^2 = 0.13$). Post-hoc analysis showed that for inferential tasks only, computer science experts produced more not specific keywords (M = 5.6 SD = 3.53) than they did in the medicine task (M = 1.10 SD = 1), with $p < .001$. Finally, computer science experts produced more not specific keywords in the inferential computer science task than did medical experts in the inferential medicine task (M = 1.2 SD = 1.5), with $p < .001$.

Concerning the main effect of expertise on the number of specific keywords, the ANOVA was significant ($F(1,18) = 7.11, p < .05, \eta_p^2 = 0.30$). Medical experts produced more specific keywords (M = 1.2 SD = 1.71) than computer science experts (M = 0.6 SD = 1.21). The ANOVA was not significant for expertise $\times$ task type interaction ($p > .05$). The interaction between expertise and task domain was significant ($F(1,18) = 23.8, p < .001, \eta_p^2 = 0.57$): Medical experts formulated more specific domain keywords ($p < .05$) in medical tasks (M = 1.90 SD = 1.80) than computer science experts in their task domain (M = 0.80 SD = 1.20). They also formulated more ($p < .001$) than when solving computer science tasks (M = 0.54 SD = 1.71) and more ($p < .001$) than computer science experts completing medical tasks (M = 0.44 SD = 1.26).

5 Discussion and Perspectives

The present experiment did not show any significant effect of expertise on number of queries and their length. In contrast, significant differences appeared concerning the keywords produced. Non-experts used more task statement words when these ones were not from their domain, whereas experts when solving tasks in their domain used fewer keywords from task statements. This effect was particularly true for decision-making and inferential tasks. In addition, computer science experts tended to produce more not specific new keywords (i.e. common language) in computer science than in medical tasks. In contrast, medical experts tended to formulate more queries with more domain specific words related to a high vocabulary in medicine when solving tasks in medicine than the non-experts. Results showed that experts users translated easier learning task goals to others terms, whereas non-experts needed to rely on statements. However, the generation of new keywords tended to be more not specific in computer science and more specific in medicine. This difference may be explained by the fact that computer science vocabulary (e.g. software, programming…) are words fallen in the everyday language whereas medicine words are more specific to this domain.

One main limit of this study is the sample size. Currently, we are retrieving more data from more participants in computer science and medicine. In addition, to study only query formulation strategies is not enough to understand relationships between search behavior and learning. To bring deepen result interpretations, we will analyze the relevance of the outcomes (answers) provided as well as variables from questionnaires completed before and after each tasks (e.g. expected and perceived difficulty, self-perception of answer quality). Finally, further studies should investigate the expertise domain on search abilities during search as learning. The aim is to link search and learning variables to determine difficulties experienced by no-experts users and how experts users do to perform better than no-experts users during complex learning tasks? These studies will allow proposing new web navigational supports for users who are searching complex information out of their domain of knowledge.

Acknowledgments. The French National Research Agency (ANR), CoST-Modelling Complex Search Tasks (ANR-18-CE23-0016), supported this research.

References

Campbell, D.J.: Task complexity: a review and analysis. Acad. Manag. Rev. **13**(1), 40–52 (1988). https://doi.org/10.5465/amr.1988.4306775

Gwizdka, J., Hansen, P., Hauff, C., He, J., Kando, N.: Search as learning (SAL) workshop 2016. In: Proceedings of the 39th International ACM SIGIR conference on Research and Development in Information Retrieval, pp. 1249–1250 (2016). https://doi.org/10.1145/2911451.2917766

Hembrooke, H.A., Granka, L.A., Gay, G.K., Liddy, E.D.: The effects of expertise and feedback on search term selection and subsequent learning. J. Am. Soc. Inf. Sci. Technol. **56**(8), 861–871 (2005). https://doi.org/10.1002/asi.20180

Marchionini, G.: Exploratory search: from finding to understanding. Commun. ACM **49**(4), 41–46 (2006). https://doi.org/10.1145/1121949.1121979

Monchaux, S., Amadieu, F., Chevalier, A., Mariné, C.: Query strategies during information searching: effects of prior domain knowledge and complexity of the information problems to be solved. Inf. Process. Manag. **51**(5), 557–569 (2015). https://doi.org/10.1016/j.ipm.2015.05.004

O'Brien, H.L., Kampen, A., Cole, A.W., Brennan, K.: The role of domain knowledge in search as learning. In: Proceedings of the 2020 Conference on Human Information Interaction and Retrieval, pp. 313–317, Mars 2020. https://doi.org/10.1145/3343413.3377989

Rodon, C., Meyer, T.: Self-efficacy about information retrieval on the web across all domains: a short measure in French and English. Behav. Inf. Technol. **37**(5), 430–444 (2018). https://doi.org/10.1080/0144929x.2018.1449252

Sanchiz, M., Amadieu, F., Chevalier, A.: An evolving perspective to capture individual differences related to fluid and crystallized abilities in information searching with a search engine. In: Fu, W.T., van Oostendorp, H. (eds.) Understanding and Improving Information Search, Human–Computer Interaction Series, pp. 71–96. Springer, Cham (2020). https://doi.org/10.1007/978-3-030-38825-6_5

Sanchiz, M., Chin, J., Chevalier, A., Fu, W.T., Amadieu, F., He, J.: Searching for information on the web: impact of cognitive aging, prior domain knowledge and complexity of the search problems. Inf. Process. Manag. **53**(1), 281–294(2017a).https://doi.org/10.1016/j.ipm.2016.09.003

Sanchiz, M., Chevalier, A., Amadieu, F.: How do older and young adults start searching for information? Impact of age, domain knowledge and problem complexity on the different steps of information searching. Comput. Hum. Behav. **72**, 67–78 (2017b).https://doi.org/10.1016/j.chb.2017.02.038

Sharit, J., Taha, J., Berkowsky, R.W., Profita, H., Czaja, S.J.: Online information search performance and search strategies in a health problem-solving scenario. J. Cogn. Eng. Decis. Making **9**(3), 211–228 (2015). https://doi.org/10.1177/1555343415583747

Tamine, L., Chouquet, C.: On the impact of domain expertise on query formulation, relevance assessment and retrieval performance in clinical settings. Inf. Process. Manag. **53**(2), 332–350 (2017). https://doi.org/10.1016/j.ipm.2016.11.004

Vakkari, P.: Searching as learning: a systematization based on literature. J. Inf. Sci. **42**(1), 7–18 (2016). https://doi.org/10.1177/0165551515615833

Artificial Intelligence (AI) in the Workplace: A Study of Stakeholders' Views on Benefits, Issues and Challenges of AI Systems

Tamari Gamkrelidze[1,2]([✉]), Moustafa Zouinar[1,2], and Flore Barcellini[2]

[1] Orange Labs, 44 avenue de la République, 92320 Châtillon, France
moustafa.zouinar@orange.com
[2] Le CNAM - Center for Research On Work and Development (CRTD), 41 rue Gay Lussac, 75005 Paris, France
{tamari.gamkrelidze.auditeur,flore.barcellini}@lecnam.net

Abstract. This paper aims to discuss issues raised by Artificial Intelligence/Machine Learning (AI/ML) in work situations, in the light of literature and an ongoing empirical study. Based on semi-structured interviews with 21 workers and 15 designers, this study explores stakeholders' viewpoints and experiences of AI systems. The preliminary findings show the place and the use of AI systems by workers in different situations, the issues of explainability and trust, the preoccupations of workers about the introduction of AI systems in work activities and the transformations that it may cause. Finally, we discuss about an analytical framework for analyzing and anticipating the consequences of AI systems on work activities and for designing these systems through a Human-Centered approach.

Keywords: Artificial Intelligence · Machine learning · Ergonomics · Work transformation · Analytical framework

1 Introduction

Our societies have been experiencing fast and significant technological advances for many years now. Among the latest technological advances, we are witnessing an increase both in computational power of computers and the generation and availability of huge sets of data (so-called "Big Data"). These advances have opened a new era for Artificial Intelligence (AI), particularly the field of Machine Learning (ML) which has become dominant in AI. An AI system can be defined as a "set of algorithms, machines and more broadly technologies in various forms (software, robotics, etc.) that are inspired by or aim to imitate human cognitive faculties such as the perception, production and understanding of natural language, the representation of knowledge, or reasoning" [11, p.73].

Progress made in ML, particularly Deep learning techniques, have increased computers' performance in various areas such as image classification, object recognition, natural language understanding and robotics. This progress have raised questions about their consequences on human activity at work, and, more broadly, on work. However, the majority of discourses on these issues remains mainly speculative as they does not rely on empirical studies of the actual or potential consequences of "new" AI systems on workers' activities.

The empirical study presented in this paper aims at filling this gap in analyzing stakeholders' (workers, decision makers, managers, designers) point of view on consequences, risks and benefits of AI systems in work situations in France. It also aims at defining an activity-centered framework which may help to explore the consequences of AI systems on human activities and work organization, and to support the design of AI systems for the workplace.

2 Literature Review: Current Issues and Challenges Around Artificial Intelligence

Current AI systems offer several functionalities for work situations, for instance in terms of information search, diagnosis, prediction, recommendations or "autonomous" execution of actions [11]. Many professional sectors, for example, health, justice, education, defense and security, finance, transport etc., are concerned by the development and use of these systems. For instance, AI systems can be used in the legal field to predict the possible outcomes of a case before a court [5] or in radiology for the interpretation of medical images [25].

The (potential) deployment of these systems in the workplace has generated the discussion of different themes and issues, which can be summarized as follow.

Firstly, there is fear of a generalized replacement of workers by AI systems, associated with a new era of automation [7] or substitution [8]. Some studies have contributed to this fear with statistical forecasting about the automation of jobs through AI in the USA. It has been supposed that this automation may cause massive unemployment [10]. However, other studies have shown that the consequence of the new era of automation will be rather the evolution and transformation of jobs than their disappearance [2].

Consequently, new transformations in organizations and work situations are announced, for example in terms of the evolution of jobs [19], new forms of allocation of tasks between humans and AI systems [20] and the creation of "new" jobs, for instance in the design of AI systems [31]. As an illustration, in radiology, the use of AI is supposed to transform the radiologist profession to data clinician profession [22]. With the use of AI systems which take over "repetitive" tasks, the radiologist might be able to concentrate on the more interesting tasks, the patient relational and the care tasks [16, 22]. Delegating "repetitive" tasks to AI systems which would therefore help humans to save time and use the saved time to develop social and relational skills [12, 21, 29] is a popular idea in the sense that it is also described as a potential benefit for other work settings. For Mcafee and Brynjolfsson [20], all tasks that can be automated should be delegated to machines. In this way, the machines would make decisions in the well-known situation and the humans would take control of the decisions in new situations. However some previous studies on automation show that leaving the human out of the loop with the role of applying machines' decisions is problematic [3, 24, 27, 28, 30].

Another theme discussed in the literature has to do with the "relationship" between human workers and AI systems. It is supposed that they could "collaborate" like "partners" [6, 23]. But current AI systems are not able yet to support a real human type collaboration [4, 33]. "Collaboration" or "partnership" are at best metaphors for human-AI interaction. Another approach consists in seeing AI systems as tools which augment human capabilities and in return, human can also "augment" AI system by developing and training it [6, 15, 19].

Finally, the use of ML techniques and especially Deep Learning raise the problem of explainability [33] and the issue of trust [17] in AI systems. Indeed, Deep Learning uses multi-layer artificial neural networks to build "learning" models [13]. These models are trained with training data (many examples prepared by a human), so they aren't explicitly programmed. Some concepts and operations based on these techniques are so complex that they can be considered as a black box [26] which raises the problem of a lack of explainability or opacity. That means that it is difficult for humans to understand how these AI systems work and produce their outputs. This lack of explainability can have important consequences in work situations, while these outputs can affect humans' decisions, behaviors and uses of the systems [33]. Lack of explainaibility can also challenge the trust in AI systems which becomes an important element for the design and the use of these systems [1].

While all the discourses that point out these issues are important contributions for reflecting on the (potential) use and consequences of AI systems on work, there is a lack of empirical studies that give an understanding of these issues from the point of view of stakeholders involved in the design of or concerned by these systems (e.g. workers, designers, managers, decision makers). To fill this gap, we have conducted a study that aims to understand and analyze stakeholders' visions and experiences about the use of AI systems, the risks, benefits and transformations of work situations. The next sections present respectively the method and then the first results of this study.

3   Method

We conducted in France semi-structured interviews with 21 workers (radiologist, radiology technician, radiology secretary coordinator, health manager, digital law lawyer, innovation project manager, etc.) and 15 designers of AI systems (computer scientists, representatives and managers of companies from the legal field, industry, medical imaging and telecommunications that develop and commercialize AI systems). They have participated to this study on a voluntary basis. As AI is progressively introduced through different tools in radiology and law, these fields appeared as relevant for our study.

The collected data was subjected to a thematic analysis. The preliminary results are guided both by this thematic analysis and the themes extracted from the literature: the general understanding of what AI is; functionalities, uses, potential benefits and risks of AI systems; the allocation of tasks between Human(s)-AI; AI systems' potential consequences on workplaces and their transformations; preoccupations about the deployment and use of AI systems.

4 Preliminary Results

In contrast to what speculative discourse disseminates about AI's capacities, the interviewees show a "realistic" conception of AI. The interviewees consider AI systems as a tool, not as a "partner" or "collaborator", which would be useful in terms of analysis, sorting, synthesis or detection of meaningful information: *"Artificial Intelligence is a tool, a tool like any other but a very powerful tool"* (Radiologist 1). They appear to be aware of the limits of AI (for instance, its performance may be not enough for complex tasks) and consider delegating to AI systems "simple" and "repetitive" tasks (for example, classifications tasks such as filtering requests of medical examination) or tasks that humans cannot perform (for example, analyzing big databases to extract important information). This view is aligned with what is commonly expected from the application of AI in work settings.

For some interviewees, the benefits of using AI systems can be multiple: saving time, improving the quality of work or developing new skills: *"It [AI system used in the legal field] saves me time, and especially this time that I save, I can also invest it in the search for an amicable agreement"* (Lawyer of the family law). Some even talk about "augmentation" provided by AI systems that would enable them to be more efficient: *"It's really something (…) that will allow me to augment in that it will bring to me or predigest everything that today with my own brain I am not able to do"* (Innovation Project Manager - telecommunications field). For others, AI systems could respond to organizational problems, e.g. large volume of radiological examinations to be interpreted or the overloading of the courts with cases that could be settled without going before a judge: *"It takes time to read an exam properly, and the number of exams means there is no time to do it. I think artificial intelligence would save a lot of time on a pile of boring exams"* (Radiologist 7). However, there is no consensus on the benefits of AI. Some workers identify a gap between their real needs and the functionalities of promoted AI systems. For example, the following radiologist explains that he would be more interested by an AI system that helps him in the task of managing medical imaging examination requests than an AI system which assists him for the interpretation of medical images:

> *"In AI today, there are few people who are interested by this aspect, that is to say, what happens before the acquisition of the images (…) before someone explains to me that there are things that will interpret the images better than me and that it will save me time, for a start, save me time on this* [the task of classifying / filtering requests of medical examination before the acquisition of the medical images]" (Radiologist 3).

For others – e.g. in the legal field – this system may remain a "gadget" if it does not bring new relevant information and if it isn't able to take into account the specific features and singularities of legal cases. For instance, the following lawyer tried an AI system which is supposed to estimate the success rate of a legal case. He explains that this system's performance isn't enough for his work: *"We do case-by-case, it is* [the AI system] *not precise enough (…) the analysis is absolutely not enough discerning. In fact, it is a rather crude analysis i.e. they* [this kind of systems] *are telling us what we already know. We have absolutely no added value"* (Lawyer of the physical injury law).

Several preoccupations about the consequences of allocating tasks to AI systems and their use also appeared in the interviews. Four types of consequences emerged:

- intensification and complexification of work: "*If you take away all your repetitive and easy tasks, you are left with only the difficult tasks*" (Radiologist 2);
- questioning of the professional's expertise. For example, according to the interviewees, the professional may be accountable and liable if he/she follows the machine's recommendations which produces unreliable outputs and his/her expertise can be questioned: "*In cases where the machine will say there is a 100% chance* [of winning], *the lawyer loses, can a client seek the lawyer's liability?*" (Lawyer - digital law field); "*If I say I think it's cancer and the algorithm says no, no, don't worry, it's not cancer, I wasn't sure I'm going to believe it, and later it turns out it's cancer, what happens? We'll say the radiologist, he is ba*d [incompetent]" (Radiologist 3);
- reconfiguration of skills and professions following the deployment of AI systems. For example, according to this radiology technician, the use of AI could increase his/her value and enrich his/her occupation: "*That* [AI as a diagnostic aid] *would open us the door to the private practice* [in France]" (Radiology technician 1). In this way, the idea of using AI system as a diagnosis aid by paramedics is emerging.
- the replacement of workers. The interviewees mentioned two types of possible replacement. The first one is the replacement of some workers by other professional categories. For instance, in the medical imaging, if an AI system carries out radiology technicians' technical tasks, radiology technicians mention the possibility of being replaced by nurses or nursing assistants for care tasks: "*It's never just a simple tool, if one day the MRI* [Magnetic Resonance Imagery] *is able to work on its own without the radiology technician, he/she* [radiology technician] *can be replaced by a nursing assistant or a nurse*" (Radiology technician 2). The second one is the possible replacement of worker who would not use AI systems by those who use AI systems: "*Those who do not do it today* [use AI], *the colleagues who work the old-fashioned way, tomorrow will no longer have a firm, no more clients.*" (Family Law Lawyer).

Finally, the majority of interviewees consider the possibility to work with AI systems on condition that the outputs provided by these systems are reliable and relevant. If not, they could question the usefulness of the system and may have less confidence in it: "*From the first error, we are going to discredit the machine much more than we would have discredited a human because error is human, we do not accept that the machine makes a mistake, we would say I would use the machine only if it is perfect.*" (Lawyer - digital law field). For some interviewees, the reliability and the capacity of explainability of an AI system seem to participate in the building of trust in those systems. The explainability of AI systems' outputs and the control of its functioning seem also to be essential because AI systems aren't considered as perfect machines: "*They* [AI systems] *make huge mistakes (…) and if you don't have a doctor behind to say it's nonsense… you always get a result that's what's terrible with the machine learning.*" (Radiologist 1). Moreover, in some situations, the use of an AI system can lead to a phenomenon of over-trust in which the degree of workers' expertise seem to be important. For instance, the following radiologist explain this kind of phenomenon:

"The problem is that as soon as there was a very small variation in comparison to the norm, it [the system] *was labelling for example circumflex* [an artery] *the right coronary or the opposite, and there are people who have made diagnoses (...) with what the Automatic Coronary Detection System was saying, some people just took what it* [the system] *was saying at face value and that led to inappropriate treatment (...) in good hands it's no problem, but... in inexperienced hands that can't criticize, it led to disasters (...) we trust blindly, we don't know* [human] *anatomy and we say, well if the machine says it must be this and* [in reality] *it's."* (Radiologist 1).

5 Discussion - Conclusion

The aim of this paper was to bring to light and discuss the issues raised by AI systems in the context of work situations, from the stakeholders' perspective. The first results of our study outline various stakeholders' preoccupations that echo – more or less - what we can find both in the recent literature on AI and in past, Human factors/ergonomics literature on automation and the design of socio-technical systems. For example, opacity of automation, task allocation, trust, human-machine "cooperation" or augmented cognition through computers have been studied since at least the 60s [9, 14, 18, 24, 32].

One of the first results from our interviews echoes the widely idea of the division of tasks between human and AI by delegating "simple" and "repetitive" tasks to the system. If in some well-known situations, using an AI system may be interesting (for example, to save time), for specific and new situations, some AI systems seem not to be yet efficient enough. The idea of a collaborative relationship between humans and AI systems is growing in the literature. But in our interviews, AI is considered as a tool which can augment human capabilities and not as an entity with which humans should/could collaborate. The AI systems' explainability seems important according to the interviewees in order to understand the outputs produced by the system and to trust it. As we have seen, this trust also seems to depend on the level of expertise of the worker and the risks that the use of the system involves for him/her. Finally, the interviewees are aware of possible transformations that may be generated by the introduction of AI systems in their work. Thus, they also reveal some preoccupations about their replacement, whether by AI systems or by other professional categories.

Finally, these findings from our study and the literature review has led us to outline an analytical framework which includes several dimensions that seem to us important to take into account in the design and integration of AI systems in work settings through a Human-Centered approach:

- Place and usage of AI/ML systems in work systems: the functionalities of an AI system, their usefulness and uses in work situations, the tasks allocation between humans and AI system;
- Type of "relationships" between AI/ML systems and workers: how can workers and AI system work "together"? What they can bring to each other?
- Explainability of AI/ML systems: the capacity of explainaibility of an AI system, the type and the precision of explanations provided by the system;

– Worker's trust in AI/ML systems: the level of workers' trust in an AI system and its consequences on use of the system and on "relationship" between the system and workers;
– Work transformations: what are the transformations in the organization and for the different professions caused by the deployment and the use of an AI system?

The next step of our research is to consolidate this framework by an in-depth analysis of new data, understanding the role of AI project management and a social and organizational context and testing this framework by mobilizing it in the context of the design and the deployment of an AI system.

To conclude, some limitations of this study should be mentioned. It is limited to the French context and is based for the moment only on interviews. It could then be interesting to extend the study to other contexts in other countries where the AI systems and their uses could be different, and mobilize other methods such as observation of work activities to better understand and analyze work transformations in real situations.

References

1. AI HLEG: Ethics Guidelines for Trustworthy AI (2019)
2. Arntz, M., et al.: The Risk of automation for jobs in OECD countries. OECD Social, Employment and Migration Working Papers 189 (2016). https://doi.org/10.1787/5jlz9h56dvq7-en
3. Billings, C.E.: Human-Centered Aircraft Automation: A Concept and Guidelines (1991).https://doi.org/10.1207/s15327108ijap0104_1
4. Van Den Bosch, K., Bronkhorst, A.: Human-AI Cooperation to Benefit Military Decision Making, pp. 1–12. STO (2018)
5. Buat-Ménard, É.: La justice dite «prédictive»: prérequis, risques et attentes - l'expérience française. Les Cah. la Justice. N° 2, 2, 269 (2019). https://doi.org/10.3917/cdlj.1902.0269
6. Daugherty, P.R., Wilson, J.: Humans + Machine: Reimagining Work in the Age of AI. Harvard Business Review Press, Boston (2018)
7. Davenport, T.H., Kirby, J.: Beyond automation. Harvard Bus. Rev. **93**, 58–65 (2015)
8. Dekker, S.-W.-A., Woods, D.D.: MABA-MABA or Abracadabra? Progress on human-automation co-ordination. Cogn. Technol. Work **4**(4), 240–244 (2003). https://doi.org/10.1007/s101110200022
9. Engelbart, D.C.: Augmenting human intellect : a conceptual framework, SRI Summary Report AFOSR-322 (1962)
10. Frey, C.B., Osborne, M.A.: The Future of Employment: How Susceptible are Jobs to Computerisation? University of Oxford, Oxford (2013)
11. Gamkrelidze, T., et al.: The "old" issues of the "new" artificial intelligence systems in professional activities. In: Bobillier Chaumon, M.-E. (éd.) Digital Transformations in the Challenge of Activity and Work: Understanding and Supporting Technological Changes, pp. 71–86. Wiley-ISTE (2021)
12. Giblas, D., et al.: Intelligence artificielle et capital humain. Quels défis pour les entreprises ?, Malakoff Médéric; Boston Consulting Group (2018)
13. Goodfellow, I., et al.: Deep Learning. The MIT Press, Cambridge (2016)
14. Hoc, J.-M.: Coopération humaine et systèmes coopératifs. In: Boy, G. (éd.) Ingénierie cognitive. IHM et cognition, pp. 139–187. Hermès, Paris (2003)

15. Jarrahi, M.H.: Artificial intelligence and the future of work: human-AI symbiosis in organizational decision making. Bus. Horiz. **61**(4), 577–586 (2018). https://doi.org/10.1016/j.bus hor.2018.03.007
16. King, B.F.: Artificial intelligence and radiology: what will the future hold? J. Am. Coll. Radiol. **15**(3), 501–503 (2018). https://doi.org/10.1016/j.jacr.2017.11.017
17. Lee, J.D., See, K.A.: Trust automation : designing for appropriate reliance. Hum. Factors **46**(1), 50–80 (2004)
18. Licklider, J.C.R.: Man-computer symbiosis. IRE Trans. Hum. Factors Electron. **HFE-1**, 4–11 (1960). https://doi.org/10.1109/THFE2.1960.4503259.
19. Lincoln, C.M., et al.: Augmented radiology: looking over the horizon. Radiol. Artif. Intell. **1**, 1 (2019). https://doi.org/10.1148/ryai.2019180039
20. Mcafee, A., Brynjolfsson, E.: Machine Platform Crowd: Harnessing Our Digital Future. W.W. Norton and Company, New York (2017)
21. McIntosh, S.: AI and automation: The benefits for business and industry (2018). https://www.sage.com/en-gb/blog/ai-and-automation-business/
22. Moehrle, A.: "Radiology" is going away… and that's okay: titles change, a profession evolves. J. Am. Coll. Radiol. **15**(3), 499–500 (2018). https://doi.org/10.1016/j.jacr.2018.01.018
23. Norman, D.: Design, business models, and human-technology teamwork. Res. Manag. **60**(1), 26–30 (2017)
24. Parasuraman, R., Wickens, C.D.: Humans: still vital after all these years of automation. Hum. Factors **50**(3), 511–520 (2008). https://doi.org/10.4324/9781315095080-14
25. Pesapane, F., et al.: Artificial intelligence in medical imaging: threat or opportunity? Radiologists again at the forefront of innovation in medicine. Eur. Radiol. Exp. **2**, 1 (2018). https://doi.org/10.1186/s41747-018-0061-6
26. Rudin, C.: Stop explaining black box machine learning models for high stakes decisions and use interpretable models instead. Nat. Mach. Intell. **1**(5), 206–215 (2019). https://doi.org/10.1038/s42256-019-0048-x
27. Sarter, N.B., et al.: Automation surprises. In: Handbook of Human Factors and Ergonomics, pp. 29–31 (1997). https://doi.org/10.1109/VTSA.2003.1252543
28. De Terssac, G., et al.: Systèmes experts et transferts d'expertise. Sociol. Trav. **3**, 461–477 (1988)
29. Villani, C.: Donner un sens à l'intelligence artificielle (2018)
30. Wiener, E.L., Curry, R.E.: Flight-Deck Automation: Promises and Problems. Ames Research Center, California (1980)
31. Wilson, H.J., et al.: The jobs that artificial intelligence will create. Mit Sloan Manag. Rev. **58**(4), 14–16 (2017). https://doi.org/10.1016/j.trf.2006.08.002
32. Woods, D.D., et al.: Explorations in joint human-machine cognitive systems. In: Human-Machine Cognitive Systems, pp. 123–158 (1990). https://doi.org/10.1108/jd.2008.27864f ae.001
33. Zouinar, M.: Evolutions de l'Intelligence Artificielle et travail : Quels enjeux pour l'activité humaine et la relation Humain-Machine ? Activités **17**, 1 (2020)

The Remanufacturing Activity: Skills to Develop and Productive Organizations to Rethink

Kevin Guelle[1,2(✉)], Sandrine Caroly[1], and Aurélie Landry[2]

[1] Institute of Political Studies (PACTE), University of Grenoble-Alpes, Grenoble, France
kevin.guelle@univ-grenoble-alpes.fr
[2] Inter-University Psychology Laboratory (LIP), University of Grenoble-Alpes, Grenoble, France

Abstract. The circular industry is increasingly at the heart of today's preoccupations, both through savings in raw materials and the development of a different production method. This mode of production, which is more respectful of the environment, questions us in ergonomics area. Remanufacturing is one of these production methods, by its specificity of producing new products guaranteed as «like-new condition» from used products. From an organizational point of view, this activity takes root from a product in a variable state of wear and having already lived a first life, before its reuse and its (re)valorization in a second life. In order to understand this activity, the -industrial- request was oriented around the question of mobilized skills by operators, treated here on the basis of individual and collective operative regulations. This communication presents the results of an intervention lasting several months on the skills mobilized by operators during the appraisal -expertise- phases of the specific industrial remanufacturing process. Our results show a plurality of sensory skills, developed through experience and knowledge around the "potential" of each part and/or product. Based on these results, a debate on the means proposed by the Industry of the Future is proposed in order to consider the remanufacturing of tomorrow.

Keywords: Skills · Remanufacturing · Railway company · Operative regulations

1 Context and Interests of This Study

In a context where global industry is well aware of the multiple interests of undertaking a circular mode of production, the right balance is pointed out between the reuse of raw materials and the need to perpetuate innovation. Nowadays, several processes (e.g., recycling, reconditioning, remanufacturing, etc.) have emerged. This current research fits fully into this context. As part of a project of the University of Grenoble (IDEX CDP CIRCULAR), the objective is the analysis -by several disciplines- of these circular processes. This project contributes to the transformation of used products into products with high added value, viewing at the same time considering their development in Industry 4.0.

From the point of view of ergonomics, these new circular production processes question us: on the one hand, on the organization of the work activity, on the other hand

N. L. Black et al. (Eds.): IEA 2021, LNNS 223, pp. 636–642, 2022.
https://doi.org/10.1007/978-3-030-74614-8_79

on the activity actually carried out and the skills mobilized by operators, to achieve «like-new condition» products performance targets. Several elements are at the origin of our thinking:

- Independently the line of business, companies are changing their production paradigm by incorporating more circular ways of reusing their products and components, while conserving the necessary energy and manpower [1].
- These processes are little studied from an activity point of view; consideration should be given to these new and uncertain situations [2, 3], especially for remanufacturing which falls within the scope of activities little studied until now in ergonomics [4].
- Few operators are trained and competent to respond the circular objectives pursued by industrial players and their skills deserve to be studied [5, 6].

At that point, our research aims to capture the specificities of the remanufacturing activity [7]. There are also questions about the integration of digital tools, piloted management or even cobotics, but which will not be the subject of this communication.

The results of an intervention carried out on the remanufacturing activity in a large French Railway company will be presented. Based on an analysis of the regulations of operators, treated here as a mode of expression of skills, this research proposes to report on this activity and to debate (in the discussion section) the possible integration of the precepts of Industry 4.0 in this specific activity.

2 Theoretical Consideration: From a Little-Known Process to Skills

2.1 From the Scarcity of Resources to the Production of «Like-New» Products: Remanufacturing, a Process of the Future

Remanufacturing is a circular economy process whose originality lies in extending the useful life of products, through secondary use or diverted use of the original function, using as raw material components of end-of-life products [5]. In the world's first article presenting its concept [8], the term remanufacturing is reserved for products recovered after user use, restored to «like-new condition». The work of Ijomah & Chiodo (2010) [9] makes it possible to differentiate more specifically remanufacturing from other circular processes, which we can simplify at one such position: the guarantees granted to remanufactured products are considerable and extend to all parts, the original identity of the product may be lost in favor of another identity (eg, a given product becomes another product by reusing parts of the given product), as much as upgrading is allowed for remanufacturing. In that way, it is today considered to be the ultimate form of preservation of the added value of products, in the sense that it allows a product to be given a second life before considering possible recycling of materials [10]. Since it pursues the objective of intervening down to the room level, it also has a known process (Fig. 1) [11]:

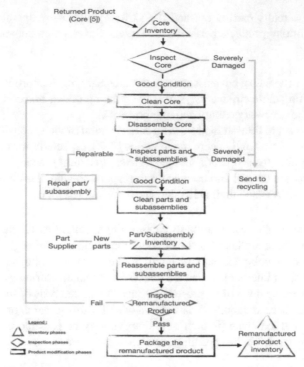

Fig. 1. The remanufacturing process (adapted from [11], p. 9)

2.2 From a Product with Variable Wear and Tear to a Remanufacturing Activity

By its process, remanufacturing takes place until the complete disassembly of the product, from the main carcass (namely core, Fig. 1) to the part [7]. For ergonomists, the recovery and expertise of returned products whose state of wear is variable changes the activity and organization of production. Whether it is the dismantling of the entire product and its sub-assemblies, its cleaning, its refurbishment and the combination of remanufactured parts and new parts, the work activity prove to be specific. Indeed, as this activity is still little understood, the scientific community highlights a crucial lack of available operators with the skills to do so [6, 12]. In addition, the current literature is scarce on the skills of operators. On the one hand, specific skills should be considered in the processing of cores (p. 59) [13]. Other authors consider that these would not be specific skills, but qualifications required at each phase [14]. Other works support their analysis around skills in the dismantling and repair of cores [15]. Also, experience and know-how would be a prerequisite for carrying out the activity [16]. The work of Andrew-Munot & Ibrahim (2013) highlights that the reduction of disassembly times could be improved from the introduction of a highly qualified workforce (understood here from the introduction of robots) [17]. Finally, problem-solving skills would also be developed (p. 13) [18].

2.3 Operative Regulations as a Way of Expressing Skills

To study the remanufacturing activity, we will approach it by means of the skills mobilized by the operators, specifically by the operative regulations developed in the activity in the work situation [19]. The concept of operative regulation can be defined as the implementation of specific activities aimed at maintaining work performance, despite the appearance of variability in working conditions or in the condition of the operator [20]. Firstly, skills «include logical rules, including rules of causation and inference, which end up constituting a kind of science, but localized to a restricted technical field» (p. 15) [21]. On another note, the operator complements his competence by inventing the ignored knowledge he needs to increase the information he perceives and the responses he adapts to it, for example by re-drafting the rules [22]. We situate our research within the framework of individual and collective regulations [22].

The research problem is as follows: how do operators diagnose what is recoverable with a view to the possible remanufacturing of a product with varying wear and tear? From our analysis, the question of improving possible human-machine interactions is discussed with a view to possible learning situations integrating interactive machines that we will keep under discussion (e.g., cobotic).

3   Methodology

Based on an industrial request on remanufacturing skills, this communication proposes to present the results of a five-month intervention carried out with a French Railway maintenance company. The request queries the skills of operators in different phases of the activity, including dismantling, reassembly and expertise. This communication proposes to deal specifically with the expertise phases; anticipated expertise, at the start of the process, during the process and at the end of the process. To analyze operator strategies and communications as part of an analysis of three areas of this business (bogies, axles and transformers), we performed a total of 16 open observation sessions. Subsequently, we carried out 44 systematic observation sessions equipped with analysis grids on 18 male operators. The criteria used are the following: actions on the equipment, visual and gestural exploratory strategies, type of object, movements and communications. Finally, these observations were fed by the following 11 self-confrontation interviews on the observations made.

4   Results of This Study

The expertise phases of the remanufacturing activity reveal fine analysis skills at different sensory, material and cognitive levels, making it possible to classify the different states and possible re-uses (i.e., maintained or diverted use). Indeed, based on our systematic observations sessions, the use of tactile, visual and auditory senses by operators reflects their experience on specific parts of the train in terms of wear but also knowledge of product development. It appears that the expertise at the start of the process makes it possible to carry out a general diagnosis by making decisions by the operators as to whether or not to carry out the general dismantling of the train or subassemblies. These

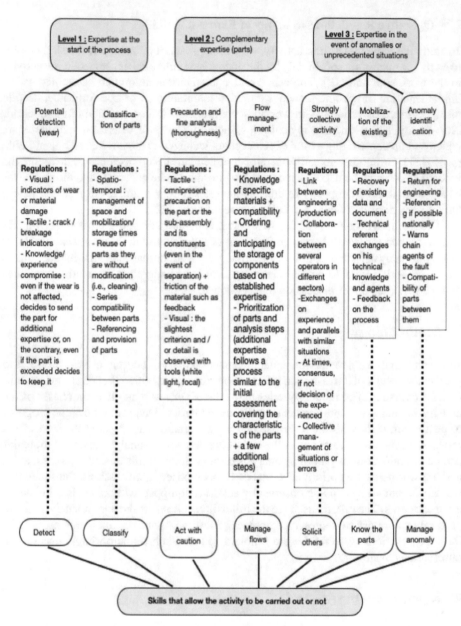

Fig. 2. The skills developed during the expertise phases of the remanufacturing activity

expertises also make it possible to orient the activity towards maintaining or diverting the original use of the part. This is a real skill of operators to know how to use different parts of trains or to substitute a part from one sector to another. It appears that the expertise phases are based on a collective activity between the operators assigned to the reassembly phases and the operators carrying out the expertise phases around the possible remanufacturing and an association between new parts and reconditioned used parts. The data analysis made it possible to schematize our results (Fig. 2), in which we propose to expose the skills mobilized by the operators at three levels of expertise: input expertise, additional expertise (at part level) and expertises in the event of anomaly(s) or unprecedented situation(s). In this figure, we can read for example that at the input of the process, tactile regulations by the sense of touch (e.g., the operator rubs, touches, presses, etc.) make it possible to have indicators of wear or material damage with the aim to decide on further treatment.

5   Discussion and Perspectives

Although some similarities appear with other processes such as maintenance activities, skills are specific to remanufacturing due to the high aspect of «potential» for salvage. Each part has a potential that the operator exploits through its regulations in the activity. This potential character, established from the fine analysis by the operator of the potentially reusable state of core, leads to very fine decision-making skills. These regulations are the result of knowledge acquired through reflective activity and through action, which make it possible to mobilize skills that are finer than the initial task. On the one hand, the collective dimension in the activity appears during collective decisions around the remanufacturing carried out (i.e., keeping the identity, diverting the use of the product or even disassembling it to explode the parts). On the other hand, the operator with expertise through his experience makes a diagnosis and an extremely detailed analysis of the entire product based on known usage criteria in order to formalize and transmit his knowledge.

Based on the analysis of the skills of the operators in this expertise activity for parts to be remanufactured, a gradual integration of Industry 4.0 tools can be envisaged in certain forms. On the one hand and by way of example, digitized tools could be a support to the operator's activity to manage input and output information data of the core and new parts to consider. They can also facilitate manager-guided between operators at different workstations (e.g., disassembly, reassembly, etc.). The integration of 3D technology in the framework of the modeling of cores can also be a tool for facilitating exchanges, and learning to allow more efficient management over time. On the other hand, considering the extreme variability in the condition of a product arriving before remanufacturing, it does not seem wise to focus on tools for managing a product line. In addition, any form of integration of remote or autonomous control tools, without possible sensory expertise at the visual, tactile and auditory levels is to be avoided.

Considering the scarcity of available resources, remanufacturing is understood as a circular production process of the future. It makes it possible, through the activity of operators with multiple skills, to give a used product a second life either by becoming the same product again or by reintegrating into another product. This research work opens up perspectives for ergonomic studies of the reference situations of the remanufacturing activity for its future design. The gradual integration of digitalization and industrial computerization raises questions about the development of expert skills made by operators hitherto practiced in the absence of these new tools. It appears important to consider training programs and to design suitable work organizations so that the remanufacturing technologies in the industry of the future are resources for the development of operator skills.

References

1. The Ellen MacArthur Fondation. Towards a Circular Economy - Economic and Business Rationale for an Accelerated Transition. Green Energy Management International (2012)
2. De la Garza, C., Weill-Fassina, A.: Les modalités de gestion collective des risques ferroviaires sur des chantiers d'entretien des voies. Recherche Transports Sécurité **49**, 78–83 (1995)
3. Grusenmeyer, C.: Interactions maintenance-exploitation et sécurité. Exploratory Study. Cahiers de Notes Documentaires Hygiène et Sécurité du Travail (186), 53–66 (2002)
4. Barcellini, F., Van Belleghem, L., Daniellou, F.: Les projets de conception comme opportunité de développement des activités. Ergonomie Constructive, 191–206 (2013)
5. Lund, R.T.: Remanufacturing: the experience of the United States and implications for developing countries. WBT (31) (1984a)
6. The Golisano Institute for Sustainability. Technology Roadmap for Remanufacturing in the Circular Economy. Rochester Institue of Technology, pp. 1–60 (2017)
7. Guelle, K., Caroly, S., Landry, A., Nasse, C., Boudoin, O.: Les régulations développées dans l'activité de remanufacturing: premiers résultats d'une intervention menée sur les bogies de trains. Communication for the SELF Congress, pp. 1–6 (2020)
8. Kutta, R.M., Lund, R.T.: Remanufacturing: A Preliminary Assessment. Center for Policy Alternatives, MIT (1978)
9. Ijomah, W.L., Chiodo, J.D.: Application of active disassembly to extend profitable remanufacturing in small electrical and electronic products. Int. J. Sustain. Eng. (3), 246–257 (2010)
10. Zwolinski, P. Conception intégrée de produits durables: de l'éco-conception aux nouveaux paradigmes de production et de consommation. Marché et organisations, pp. 17–29 (2013)
11. Ali Ilgin, M., Gupta, S.: CRC Press, Boca Raton (2012)
12. Barquet, A.P., Rozenfeld, H., Forcellini, A.: An integrated approach to remanufacturing: model of a remanufacturing system. J. Remanuf. **3**, 1–11 (2013)
13. Ferrer, G., Clay Whybark, D.: From garbage to goods: successful remanufacturing systems and skills. Bus. Horiz. **43**(6), 55–64 (2000)
14. Jacobsson, N.: Emerging products strategies: selling services of remanufacturing products (Licenciate Dissertation). Lund University Sweden (2000)
15. Guide, V.D.R., Jayraman, V., Srivastava, R., Benton, W.C.: Supply chain management for recoverable manufacturing systems. Interfaces **30**, 125–142 (2000)
16. Freiberger, S.: Remanufacturing of Mechatronics and Electronics. APRA Mechatronics and Electronics Division (2006)
17. Andrew, M., Ibrahim, R.N.: Remanufacturing process and its challenges. J. Mech. Eng. Sci. **4**, 488–495 (2013)
18. Xing, B., Gao, W.J.: Computational Intelligence in Remanufacturing. AEEGT (2014)
19. Leplat, J.: Compétences individuelles, compétences collectives. Psychologie du travail et des organisations **6**, 47–73 (2000)
20. Vézina, N., Chatigny, C., Calvet, B.: L'intervention ergonomique: que fait-on des caractéristiques personnelles comme le sexe et le genre? Perspectives interdisciplinaires sur le travail et la santé 18(2) (2016)
21. De Montmollin, M., Leplat, J.: Les compétences en ergonomie. Octares (2010)
22. Caroly, S.: Activité collective et réélaboration des règles: des enjeux pour la santé au travail. HDR (2010)

Steady Hands - An Evaluation on the Use of Hand Tracking in Virtual Reality Training in Nursing

Tino Hentschel[(✉)] and Jan A. Neuhöfer

Hamburg University of Applied Sciences, Finkenau 35, 22081 Hamburg, Germany
{Tino.Hentschel,Jan.Neuhoefer}@HAW-Hamburg.de

Abstract. Our paper describes the setup and the results of an empirical study on comparison of usability and performance while using two different input methods for training of nursing procedures in virtual reality: hand-held controller input and markerless hand tracking. As part of a research project funded by the German Ministry of Health, our study features the aseptic wound cleansing with tweezers and swabs. Our results indicate that the input method could have no significant impact on performance, but ratings on usability show a trend in favor of controller input.

Keywords: Virtual reality training · Hand tracking · Nursing

1 Introduction

Training of nursing personnel requires trainees to adopt a wide range of fine motor skills for various tasks, such as the aseptic cleansing of a wound during the change of a dressing. As even slight inaccuracies in performing these tasks bear a risk for the patients' as well as the trainees' safety, these procedures need extensive training. As prequalification for physical training in a skills lab [1], Virtual Reality (VR) is already under examination in a variety of research projects [2].

Our research is part of a project funded by the German Federal Ministry of Health, focusing on digital prequalification for nursing trainees with migration background. The solution pursued in this project will feature an overall range of 24 interactive, web-based E-learning modules. A selection of these modules will come with an additional implementation in virtual reality to allow practice of motoric aspects of the particular procedure.

As input method, most VR systems usually include a pair of hand-held controllers. These controllers act as physical "mediators" between the trainees' real hands and their virtual representations and so add an extra layer of abstraction. In addition, the physical hand pose of the trainee does mostly not match the displayed pose of the virtual hand in the simulation. Thus, this way of interaction might not be ideal for training of tasks where fine motor skills are essential.

N. L. Black et al. (Eds.): IEA 2021, LNNS 223, pp. 643–649, 2022.
https://doi.org/10.1007/978-3-030-74614-8_80

Some VR Systems, for example the Oculus Quest [3], provide camera-based, markerless hand tracking as an alternative input method. This is in many use cases robust enough to allow the user to hold an object like a pair of tweezers. By doing so, trainees could take up the same hand postures that are required in reality. Consequently, our research focuses on the question whether there is a difference between hand-held input and markerless tracking input especially concerning usability and performance.

2   Related Work

Virtual Reality is receiving increasing attention as a technology to complement classic education and training in the field of nursing, as it enables students to train critical procedures in realistic, repeatable interactive 3D scenarios without any risk to actual patients [4]. While many established solutions use hand-held controllers as input devices, recent studies present camera-based, markerless hand tracking as a promising alternative that could provide a more direct and immersive input method [5]. In this context, a study within the project "Virtual Skills Lab" [6] compares the usability of HTC Vive controllers with Leap Motion hand tracking. The study shows no significant difference in the usability of the two input methods, but it points out that participants need significant less time to complete a specific training task when using hand tracking compared to hand-held controller input.

A more recent study indicated a better performance and a lesser perceived difficulty of the HTC Vive Controllers compared to Leap Motion hand tracking when used for general interactions in virtual environments like gabbing, stacking and sorting small objects [7].

3   Our VR Training Module for Wound Cleansing

Our virtual reality module for wound cleansing allows the user to practice the procedure of an aseptic wound dressing change with all object as detailed, virtual replications of real nursing equipment.

3.1   Training Scenario and Procedure

The module is set in the middle of a nursing room, as shown in Fig. 1.

To clean the wound, the user must grab the tweezers to pick up a swab, turn to the patient and carefully move the swab over the surface of the wound. Movements must happen unidirectional alongside the wound, to avoid touching the same part of the wound twice, as this can lead to a wound infection. If the user deviates from this trajectory, cleansing must start from the beginning. Multiple cleansing strikes must be performed, and after each strike, the swab must be disposed into the cardboard tray, so for each strike, the user needs to pick up a new swab. During the process, the user can monitor the overall progress as well as errors above the wound in graphical overlay. At the end of the process, the user must dispose the tweezers into the waste container to end the training.

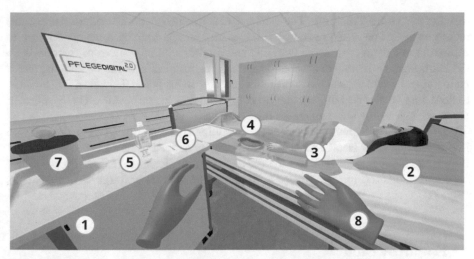

Fig. 1. The user starts in front of a dressing trolley (1) next to a bed with a patient (2). One arm of the patient is exposed and has an oblong-shaped wound of about 5 cm of length (3). Next to the wound, a cardboard tray (4) is used to dispose used dressing material. The materials needed in the following are set on top of the dressing trolley, including disinfected sterile ball swabs (5), sterile tweezers (6) and a waste container (7). During the scenario, the user is wearing non-sterile gloves (8).

3.2 Input Methods

Hand-Held Controller. The Oculus Quest uses two ergonomic controllers that are tracked by multiple infrared sensors in the cameras in front of the head-mounted display (HMD) [8]. The tracking supports 6 degrees of freedom (6DOF) to project the position and rotation of the controllers in real time onto 3D hand models. Users can grab virtual objects by pushing and holding the grip button (Fig. 2A).

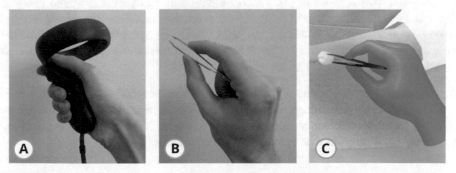

Fig. 2. The Oculus Controller with button pressed (A) and markerless hand tracking with a pair of real tweezers (B). Both input methods lead to the same posture of the virtual hand (C).

Markerless Hand Tracking. The Oculus Quest's camera captures both (left and right) hand postures. The resulting image is interpreted in real-time by a neural network to estimate the state of two correlating 3D hand models with 26 degrees of freedom each [9]. Although working with acceptable stability under ideal conditions, tracking might be lost if real world objects block the cameras view on the hands. However, it is possible to hold small real-world objects that do not occlude the hands posture. The tweezers in the wound cleansing scenario match this criterion.

The Oculus Integration Framework for Unity [10] supports gesture detection to implement input for Hand Tracking. One of the predefined gestures is the pinching of thumb and index finger to select and hold an object in VR. Since real tweezers are also held with a pinch (Fig. 2B), this gesture is used as input to grab the virtual tweezers (Fig. 2C).

4 Empirical Study

On January 21, 2021, we conducted an empirical study to test controller input and hand tracking in our VR module on training of aseptic wound cleansing regarding usability and influence on the performance of trainees during task execution.

4.1 Research Questions

1. Is there a significant difference in the perceived usability of the input methods Controller Input and Hand Tracking in a VR training module for nursing?
2. Does the input method have a significant influence on the performance of trainees while task execution (execution time, error rate)?

4.2 Test Design

We compared two versions of the VR module on training of aseptic wound dressing: The first version used hand-held controllers as input device and the second version used markerless hand tracking, holding a real pair of tweezers. Apart from the input method, the two modules were identical. The order of the two modules was switched for each user. The study was executed under laboratory conditions.

Participants. The sample comprised eight participants (4 female, 4 male) between 28 and 37 years of age with no experience in nursing. Six participants had low to moderate experience with virtual reality; one participant was using VR on a regular basis. Three participants had experience with markerless hand tracking.

Procedure. The procedure of the study consisted for each participant of a pre-test and two tests in virtual reality, each finalized by a questionnaire on usability. Participants started the pre-test by filling out a questionnaire regarding their demographic data and previous experience and running a test on visual acuity and stereopsis. After the pre-test, Participants received instructions about the wound cleansing task and on how to use the VR headset and the two respective input methods. They started with either the hand-held controller input or markerless hand tracking. During execution, for both methods, time to completion and number of errors were recorded for performance tracking. After each run, participants filled out the System Usability Scale (SUS) questionnaire [11] to assess the usability of the input method. Additionally, participants had the opportunity to give free text feedback for each of the input methods. The study lasted 62 min on average.

4.3 Results

Performance. The means and standard deviations for the time needed to complete the VR module and the number of errors made during the training are reported in Table 1. The Shapiro-Wilk Test indicated a normal distribution for all four data sets, so a paired samples t-Test was used for comparison. However, no significant difference between the execution times or the error counts can be detected.

Table 1. Means and standard deviations of the time to complete the VR module and the number of errors made during the task for controller input and hand tracking.

	Controller input		Hand tracking	
	Mean	SD	Mean	SD
Execution Time (s)	46.34	19.58	86.60	52.94
Number of Errors	0.25	0.46	1.38	2.77

Usability. Figure 3 shows a boxplot of the usability scores for both input methods. According to the mean SUS scores grading system [12], the hand-held controller input was rated with the grade A ($M = 83.75$, $SD = 8.02$) and markerless hand tracking was rated with the grade C ($M = 70.94$, $SD = 11.18$). The Shapiro-Wilk Test indicated a normal distribution for both data sets, so we conducted a paired samples t-Test. It reported a significant difference between the two input methods with a strong effect size ($t(7) = 4.26$, $p < 0.0037$, $r = 0.85$).

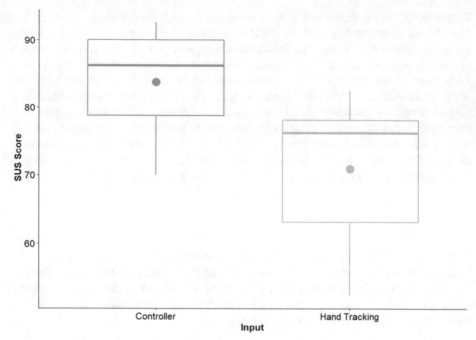

Fig. 3. Boxplot diagram of the SUS scores with the mean (large dot), median (vertical line), interquartile range (box) and minimum and maximum values (end of horizontal lines) for the hand-held controller input method (blue) and markerless hand tracking method (yellow).

4.4 Discussion

The difference in performance is not significant, but it indicates that the VR training scenario takes less time and participants make fewer errors with the hand-held controller. Still, this hypothesis needs verification with a larger sample size.

The SUS scores for the perceived usability show a statistically significant difference between the two input methods in the selected VR training scenario. A cause for this could be the more stable and precise tracking of the hand-held controllers in comparison to the markerless hand tracking.

Another cause could be the divergence between the haptics and the visual perception of the tweezers when using markerless tracking with real tweezers. Some participants reported they felt the real tweezers in a slightly different position in their hand in comparison to the virtual tweezers' position. In consequence, they occasionally confused the position of the tweezers and deviated from the trajectory. Further studies with larger sample sizes should investigate this assumption.

5 Outlook

In the future, we plan extended investigations on the value and effects of virtual reality on training in nursing. Apart from the input method, coming studies include further parameters of design space, like realistic ambient sound or the interaction virtual patients. To examine the effectivity of the VR modules as a pre-qualification for skills lab training, samples with also comprise actual nursing students. Additionally, we will investigate the quality of the VR modules' user interface design with eye tracking technology.

This project is funded by the German Ministry of Health.

References

1. Strand, I., Nåden, D., Slettebø, Å.: Students learning in a skills laboratory. Nord. J. Nurs. Res. **29**(3), 18–22 (2009)
2. Jenson, C.E., Forsyth, D.M.: Virtual reality simulation - using three-dimensional technology to teach nursing students. CIN Comput. Inform. Nurs. **30**(6), 312–318 (2012)
3. Using deep neural networks for accurate hand-tracking on Oculus Quest. https://ai.facebook. com/blog/hand-tracking-deep-neuralnetworks. Accessed 28 Feb 2021
4. Chen, F.-Q., Leng, Y.-F., Ge, J.-F., Wang, D.-W., Li, C., Chen, B., Sun, Z.-L.: Effectiveness of virtual reality in nursing education: meta-analysis. J. Med. Internet Res. **22**(9), e18290 (2020)
5. Han, S., Liu, B., Cabezas, R., Twigg, C.D., Zhang, P., Petkau, J., Yu, T.-H., Tai, C.-J., Akbay, M., Wang, Z., Nitzan, A., Dong, G., Ye, Y., Tao, L., Wan, C., Wang, R.: MEgATrack: monochrome egocentric articulated hand-tracking for virtual reality. ACM Trans. Graph. **39**(4) (2020). Article 87
6. Meyer, L., Pfeifer, T.: Vergleich von Leap Motion Hand-Interaktion mit den HTC-Vive MotionControllern in einer VR-Trainingssimulation für manuelle Arbeiten. In: Dörner, R., Kruse, R., Mohler, B., Weller, R. (eds.) Berichte aus der Informatik. Virtuelle und Erweiterte Realität - 14. Workshop der GI-Fachgruppe VR/AR, pp. 91–102 . Shaker Verlag, Aachen (2017)
7. Caggianese, G., Gallo, L., Neroni, P.: The vive controllers vs. leap motion for interactions in virtual environments: a comparative evaluation. Smart Innovation, Systems and Technologies, pp. 24–33 (2018)
8. Powered by AI: Oculus Insight. https://ai.facebook.com/blog/powered-by-ai-oculus-insight. Accessed 08 Feb 2021
9. Using deep neural networks for accurate hand-tracking on Oculus Quest. https://ai.facebook. com/blog/hand-tracking-deep-neural-networks. Accessed 08 Feb 2021
10. Hand Tracking in Unity. https://developer.oculus.com/documentation/unity/unity-handtr acking. Accessed 08 Feb 2021
11. Brooke, J.: SUS: a "quick and dirty" usability scale. In: Jordan, P.W., Thomas, B., Weerd-meester, B.A., McClelland, A.L. (eds.) Usability Evaluation in Industry, pp. 189–194. Taylor and Francis, London (1996)
12. Sauro, J.: A Practical Guide to the System Usability Scale: Background, Benchmarks, & Best Practices. Measuring Usability LLC, Denver CO (2011)

Supporting Pain Management for Mechanically Ventilated Intensive Care Patients Using a Novel Communication Tool

Jan Patrick Kopetz$^{(\boxtimes)}$ and Nicole Jochems

Institute for Multimedia and Interactive Systems, Universität zu Lübeck, Ratzeburger Allee 160, 23562 Lübeck, Germany
{kopetz,jochems}@imis.uni-luebeck.de

Abstract. Intensive care patients that are weaned from mechanical ventilation are facing substantial communication problems due to their limited ability to communicate verbally. This can lead to stress, misunderstandings, prolonged healing processes and a delirium. This paper describes the development of an application supporting the management of pain which is part of a larger system supporting patient needs. In a Human-centred design process, we analyzed both state of the art and context to narrow down and specify requirements, before we iteratively developed a high-fidelity prototype allowing patients to select and express their pain parameters like intensity and location, helping medical staff to initiate appropriate pain management.

The prototype was rated positively in an evaluation conducted with 10 nursing and usability experts. Their qualitative feedback also showed some minor usability issues to be addressed. Building on these positive results, planning processes for studies with former and actual weaning patients can be intensified.

Keywords: Mechanical ventilation · Weaning · Intensive Care Unit · Human-centred design · Human-computer interaction · Augmentative and alternative communication

1 Introduction

Patients in intensive care units (ICU) are often mechanically ventilated through an endotracheal tube. They are connected to several lifesaving and monitoring devices through intravenous lines, feeding tubes, drains, catheters and more. When awaking from unconsciousness, many patients experience severe difficulties communicating even their basic needs to healthcare staff and relatives, causing stress for everyone involved. Research results indicate that the communication taking place is often insufficient and, as a result, care-relevant patient needs are insufficiently recognized by the healthcare staff [1].

In the project ACTIVATE[1], researchers determine solutions to improve the situation of weaning patients by addressing the problems described above. The primary goal of the

---

[1] https://projekt-activate.de; funded by the German Federal Ministry of Education and Research.

N. L. Black et al. (Eds.): IEA 2021, LNNS 223, pp. 650–657, 2022.
https://doi.org/10.1007/978-3-030-74614-8_81

ACTIVATE project is to develop an interactive system supporting patient communication [2]. Patients interact with the system using an innovative, ball-shaped interaction device called "BIRDY" [3], which is developed within the project and explicitly designed for the ICU context. The built-in movement sensor technology allows detecting gestures like tilt left/right and squeeze which were designed to be easily performed by ICU patients lying in bed.

A main feature of the interactive system is the communicator application. It is intended to compensate for the lack of the patients' verbal communication skills and allows them to communicate with healthcare staff or visiting relatives through predefined statements and questions. Although this method is suitable for general communications, the requirements for pain management differ and several methods for assessment of pain to rely on are already established. Puntillo [4] describes that pain of non-verbal patients is typically assessed externally by healthcare staff using observation-based pain scales, while insufficiently treated pain is one of the most frequently reported strains [5]. Tools supporting self-assessment of pain could provide a real benefit. This led to the development of a specific sub-module supporting self-assessing pain management that is described in this paper.

2 State of the Art

Before starting the actual development, it is important to know the state of the art and related work. Two domains were reviewed as a preparation for the development: established pain assessment instruments (PAI) in Germany and digital tools to support pain management for patients.

Pain assessment instruments include scales to assess pain intensity. They allow systemizing the subjective data of the affected patients. As the application should be used in German intensive care units, the focus lay on German pain assessment instruments. Depending on cognitive and communication skills, two types of assessment are used: self-assessment and external assessment.

The pain visual analogue scale (pain VAS) is a measure of pain intensity based on a 100 mm long line between *no pain* and *unbearable pain*, where patients mark their perceived pain value. The evaluation is performed by measuring the specified section length in millimetres [6]. The numeric rating scale (NRS) extends the VAS with intervals marked with numbers from 0–10 (or sometimes 0–20) with equal spacing [6]. The verbal rating scale (VRS) uses 6 points based on the verbal description (nil, mild, moderate, severe, very severe, unbearable). The smiley analogue scale (SAS) consists of 5–6 smiley faces, where the pain corresponds to the facial expression [7]. All of them are unidimensional measures and established scales. The German pain questionnaire is a multidimensional pain measurement scale and is standardized to assess chronic pain. It includes a body sketch to locate the pain [7]. Another multidimensional instrument is the pain diary where pain can be documented over a period [7]. The pain of weaning patients is due to cognitive and communication deficits typically externally assessed, thus we also reviewed established, experimental, and other currently used instruments like for instance the behavior pain scale (BPS), Dolophus, Zurich Observation Pain Assessment (ZOPA) [7–9]. When discussing the existing instruments, we agreed to consider as many aspects as possible of the reviewed self-assessment scales, while the external assessment scales did not provide any aspects to rely on.

Furthermore, several approaches for compensating communication deficits and offering pain management are described in the literature, using touch gestures, buttons, or eye movements. Approaches on assisting communication not explicitly specified on pain communication were reviewed earlier [3]. Using smartphones and tablets has been investigated, but still seems not suitable for everyday usage in critical care settings [10]. The app stores offer several pain management apps (i.e. [11, 12]). In many reviewed cases, medical experts were not involved in development [13]. Tests with the Vida-Talk iPad application showed promising results [12]. LifeVoice [14] showed promising results in a pilot study testing their universal communication system on a monitor attached next to the bed, that can be controlled using touch gestures, physical buttons or eye-tracking as input methods.

Most approaches focusing on pain communication combine different scales uniting their advantages [11, 12, 14]. Several of them provided valuable insights for our development, including choosing the intensity and location of the pain, and probably also the quality. These aspects now had to be adapted to our system based on specific interactions consisting of using BIRDY gestures to navigate and select [3].

3 Methodology

Following the Human-centred design approach described in ISO 9241-210 [15], expert interviews were conducted with experienced ICU nurses and nursing researchers (n = 3) to gather information about the context and design implications. Combined with data from our literature analysis (see Sect. 2) requirements were specified that led to the design of a first low-fidelity prototype. It was formatively evaluated by six usability and four nursing experts (10 in total) and the insights led to a redesigned high-fidelity prototype. Again, it was tested in a usability evaluation by seven usability experts and three nursing experts.

3.1 Requirements

The context and literature analysis led to the following set of requirements with different priorities: Patients must be able to select their pain intensity (R1) and their pain location (R2). Selecting pain quality (R3) is optional. Patients must be able to edit their choices (R4). The application must be integrable into the overall ACTIVATE interaction concept (R5), where the preferred interaction gestures should be tilt left/right to navigate and press to select (R6a). Tilt upwards/downwards should be avoided (R6b), as they might be perceived as uncomfortable. Additional requirements were derived from health status and situation of the user group described in the expert interviews. Previous and current selections must be displayed clearly understandable (R7). Interactions should be as simple as possible (R8), and the interaction costs must be as low as possible (R9), as the patients are actively perceiving pain. Also, each aspect of the application must be easily understandable (R10) as the attention might be limited.

3.2 Development of Design Solutions

Several iterations were passed to design and evaluate different concepts. The resulting prototypes are described below.

The first prototype (see Fig. 1) was designed when the interaction device BIRDY was still in an early phase of development, meaning the set of potential interaction gestures were not finally discussed and selected. The prototype based on a 4-step guided process with questions about the specific pain location, the pain intensity, the pain type, and a summary page.

Users were able to select front, back, or whole body and then navigate through a body map to select the specific body part. A pain scale combining benefits from smiley pain scale, numerical rating and visual analogue scale allowed them to select the pain among different complexities of pain assessment on the next view. The pain type page (borrowing items from the German pain questionnaire) allowed to select a characterization of the pain. The summary view showed a visual summary of the selection and provided options to edit or finally confirm the choices. Also, after each single process step, the user was able to edit the choices.

The results of the formative evaluation were mixed. The overall process with its steps results in a broad description of the pain, which is valuable information for nurses and doctors. Still, the whole application seemed to be to complex (even for experts) and especially the interaction design was rated improvable. Some participants were not able to complete each given task. Especially navigating vertically through the body map using the given horizontal interaction gestures (left/right) had a confusing effect on some participants. Considering the target user group having pain, we decided to focus on easy usage and low complexity, remove some functionality and redesign the application.

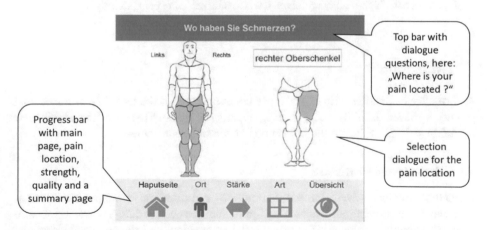

Fig. 1. Interface of the first prototype, where patients select their pain location on a body map.

The second prototype was designed with the intention to reduce complexity by hiding elements when they are not needed. When starting the application, clear instructions are displayed ("Choose your pain level first and then your pain location"). The presentation of the pain level picker was visually improved (see Fig. 2.) and unobtrusive animations were added. The choice of pain location was simplified, as the body map was replaced by simple buttons and the number of choices was reduced from 52 to 13. The second prototype allows to choose between head, upper body, arms, legs (each time right, left or both sides) and everywhere. We discussed these design decisions with our advising nurses, and they stated that an approximate location would be sufficient. After choosing the location, selections are displayed, and a simple context menu is displayed where users can select to confirm or to edit their choices (this reopens the corresponding dialogue). After editing pain level, users reconfirm the pre-selected pain location to get to the summarizing screen.

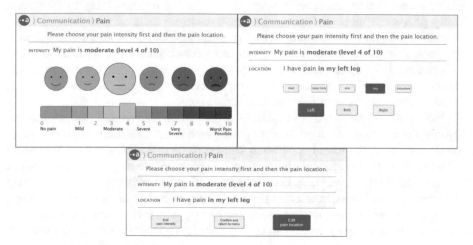

Fig. 2. Second high-fidelity prototype interfaces for selecting pain intensity and location.

4   Evaluation

A formative evaluation with experts was conducted to test the usability of the second prototype. Seven usability and 3 nursing experts (60% male) between 25 and 55 (M = 32.1, SD = 8.42) evaluated the prototype in a remote usability test.

4.1   Methods and Procedure

First, the participants were informed about the procedure and demographic informa- tion was filled in using an instance of the online survey tool *Limesurvey*. They were instructed about the scope of the project, the application, and the controls. Normally, BIRDY would be used to control the prototype; due to the remote situation, the alter- native controls were the enter and arrow keys left and right. We used the *think-aloud* protocol to get precise information about potential usability problems the participants experience. They performed two tasks: first, they had to select pain intensity *mild* on *level 2* located in the *left leg*. In the second task, they had to edit their pain intensity to *level 4*. When they had finished the tasks, they completed a comprehensive questionnaire (based on [16]) with various questions about interaction design (dialogue principles described in ISO 9241-110 [17]) and information design (principles for the presentation of information described in ISO 9241-112 [18], each principle includes up to 10 items). Further questions were related to feedback about the specific user interface elements and how (un)obtrusive animations were perceived.

4.2 Results

All participants solved the given tasks without any problems. Overall, the interaction design principles were rated as fulfilled. 100% of the participants rated suitability for learning (1 answer rated it as not verifiable), suitability for the task, conformity with user expectations, self-descriptiveness, and error tolerance as fulfilled. Controllability was rated as fulfilled by 77,8% of the participants (rated not verifiable by 1 participant). Suitability for individualization was rated as not verifiable by 9 out of 10 answers (1 answer stated it was not fulfilled). Principles for the presentation of information were also mostly rated as fulfilled (see Table 1). 80% of the participants rated the usage of animations as about right (one participant each wanted to have more/fewer animations). Three principles (design of text input fields, input prompts and error messages) were discussed as not applicable and were therefore rated consistently as not verifiable.

Table 1. Principles for the presentation with the corresponding mean value (M) and standard deviation (SD) of the fulfillment ratio (FR); values $< .33 =$ insufficient, $\leq .66 =$ satisfactory, $> .66 =$ good– excellent.

Principle	M_FR	SD_FR
Interface layout	1	0
Use of colors	.98	.08
Labelling of interface elements	.96	.07
Menus	.96	.13
Textual content	.95	.10
Grouping of interface elements	.94	.13

Five Participants did not like that they had to reconfirm pain location after editing the pain intensity. They would prefer to be directed straight to the context menu. Furthermore, five participants recommended using graphics supporting the choice of pain location. Three participants discussed the order (pain level or pain location first), two of them would prefer to select pain location first, one of them approved our choice selecting pain level first. Further comments suggested slight improvements in labelling, wording, pre-selections, button order and size, icons, and other design-related issues. Also, topics like selecting multiple pain locations with different pain levels, offering more potential pain locations (for instance belly, breast, back, wound pain).

5 Discussion and Further Research

In this paper, we described the development of an application for the ACTIVATE-system supporting pain management for mechanically ventilated and verbally impaired intensive care patients. It is a part of a larger application supporting communication processes in this context. In a Human-centred design process, we iteratively developed a high-fidelity prototype allowing users to select their pain intensity and pain location, which is necessary and sufficient information for medical staff to initiate appropriate pain management. Experienced nurses as well as usability experts were involved during the whole design process of two prototypes and contributed valuable feedback, most recently in the expert evaluation described in Sect. 4. Interaction design and information design were rated positively. The suggested improvements for both the redirection after editing pain intensity and using graphics supporting the choice of pain location are plausible and will be discussed. Extending the main management process to allow choosing multiple pain locations might also be a potential useful improvement. Next steps are to implement several suggested improvements and test the application with users. A two-step approach is planned for this. First, former weaning patients test the application in a laboratory test. After that, a clinical trial should provide evidence, if actual weaning patients can use the system and if communication processes can be improved by the system.

Acknowledgements. We would like to thank Raul Kakkar for his contribution of the first prototype in his bachelor thesis, all colleagues of the ACTIVATE project and all participants of our evaluations.

References

1. Schindler, A.W., Schindler, N., Enz, F., Lueck, A., Olderog, T., Vagts, D.A.: ICU personnel have inaccurate perceptions of their patients' experiences. Acta Anaesthesiol Scand. **57**, 1032–1040 (2013). https://doi.org/10.1111/aas.12148
2. Kordts, B., Kopetz, J.P., Balzer, K., Jochems, N.: Requirements for a System Supporting Patient Communication in Intensive Care in Germany. Presented at the Clusterkonferenz "Zukunft der Pflege", Oldenburg (2018)
3. Kordts, B., Kopetz, J.P., Henkel, A., Schrader, A., Jochems, N.: Requirements and interaction patterns for a novel interaction device for patients in intensive care. i-com **18**, 67–78 (2019). https://doi.org/10.1515/icom-2019-0004
4. Puntillo, K.: Pain Assessment and Management for Intensive Care Unit Patients: Seeking Best Practices. ICU Manage. Pract. **16**, 233–236 (2016)
5. Bohrer, T., Koller, M., Neubert, T., Moldzio, A., Beaujean, O., Hellinger, A., Lorenz, W., Rothmund, M.: Wie erleben allgemeinchirurgische Patienten die Intensivstation? Ergebnisse einer prospektiven Beobachtungsstudie. Der Chirurg. **73**, 443–450 (2002)
6. Downie, W.W., Leatham, P.A., Rhind, V.M., Wright, V., Branco, J.A., Anderson, J.A.: Studies with pain rating scales. Ann. Rheum. Dis. **37**, 378–381 (1978). https://doi.org/10.1136/ard.37.4.378
7. Thomm, M.: Schmerzanamnese, Methoden zur Schmerzerfassung und Dokumentation. In: Thomm, M. (ed.) Schmerzmanagement in der Pflege, pp. 11–22. Springer, Heidelberg (2016). https://doi.org/10.1007/978-3-662-45414-5_2

8. Gerhard, C.: Praxiswissen Palliativmedizin. Thieme Verlag (2015). https://doi.org/10.1055/b-002-101345

9. Sellinger, J.J., Wallio, S.C., Clark, E.A., Kerns, R.D.: Comprehensive pain assessment: the integration of biopsychosocial principles. In: Ebert, M.H., Kerns, R.D. (eds.) Behavioral and Psychopharmacologic Pain Management, pp. 44–66. Cambridge University Press, Cambridge (2010). https://doi.org/10.1017/CBO9780511781445.004

10. Attri, J.P., Khetarpal, R., Chatrath, V., Kaur, J.: Concerns about usage of smartphones in operating room and critical care scenario. Saudi J. Anaesthesia **10**, 87 (2016). https://doi.org/10.4103/1658-354X.169483

11. Patient Communicator - Apps on Google Play. Accessed 08 Feb 2021. https://play.google.com/store/apps/details?id=com.sccm.thumbsup

12. Happ, M.B., Walaszek, L., Von Visger, T., Weber, M., Vermillion, B., Chipps, E., Traughber, B., Patak, L.: Usability and acceptability testing of an ipad communication application in the intensive care unit. Critical Care Med. **42**, A1505 (2014). https://doi.org/10.1097/01.ccm.0000458100.13793.0c

13. Rosser, B.A., Eccleston, C.: Smartphone applications for pain management. J. Telemed. Telecare **17**, 308–312 (2011). https://doi.org/10.1258/jtt.2011.101102

14. Miglietta, M.A., Bochicchio, G., Scalea, T.M.: Computer-assisted communication for critically ill patients: a pilot study. J. Trauma Acute Care Surg. **57**, 488 (2004). https://doi.org/10.1097/01.TA.0000141025.67192.D9

15. ISO 9241-210:2019 - Ergonomics of human-system interaction - Part 210: Human-centred design for interactive systems. Beuth Verlag GmbH. https://doi.org/10.31030/3104744

16. Simply usable – questionnaire for expert evaluations. https://www.simply-usable.de/methode/expertenevaluation/. Accessed 08 Feb 2021

17. ISO 9241-110:2020 - Ergonomics of human-system interaction - Part 110: Interaction principles. Beuth Verlag GmbH. https://doi.org/10.31030/3147467

18. ISO 9241-112:2017 - Ergonomics of human-system interaction - Part 112: Principles for the presentation of information. Beuth Verlag GmbH. https://doi.org/10.31030/2580439

Users' Error Recovery Strategies in the Interaction with Voice Assistants (VAs)

Isabela Motta$^{(\boxtimes)}$ ⓘ and Manuela Quaresma ⓘ

LEUI, Laboratory of Ergodesign and Usability of Interfaces, Department of Arts and Design,
PUC-Rio University, Rio de Janeiro, Brazil
isabelamotta@aluno.puc-rio.br, mquaresma@puc-rio.br

Abstract. Errors in interactions with Voice Assistants (VAs) are still recurrent, but evidence shows that users try to repair interactions by applying error recovery strategies and that such tactics are affected by VA responses. Although previous studies have addressed this matter in voice-based interfaces, VAs have specific characteristics that demand new investigations. Thus, this study aimed to understand the relationship between different types of VA responses and users' error recovery strategies. We conducted usability tests followed by debriefing sessions with VA users and identified categories of VA responses and user behavior. Our findings echo previous studies that pointed to VA responses as a source of understanding about the VA. While speech recognition issues were dealt with changes in pronunciation and repetition, participants approached unintended feature execution with exploratory behavior. Finally, when users received instructions on how to proceed, they followed recovery paths, indicating the importance of support for error handling. However, our findings show that HF/E specialists need to carefully design such guidance to accommodate users' preferences and achieve successful recoveries.

Keywords: Voice assistants · Voice interfaces · Error recovery ·
Human-computer interaction · Usability

1 Introduction

Voice Assistants (VAs), such as Siri and Google Assistant, are artificial intelligence-powered virtual agents that can perform a range of tasks in a system, which users interact through a voice interface that may be supported by a visual display [15]. Although increasingly popular, users' interactions with VAs are not free from errors: the literature shows that communication failures are recurrent, as VA misrecognize queries [3], struggle to understand accents and foreign languages [3, 8], and are unable to bear contextual references of time or space [8, 9].

Despite facing failures, evidence shows that users apply error handling strategies to continue interacting with VAs. Beneteau et al. [1] analyzed users' interactions with Alexa and showed that users try to repair communication by repeating requests, adjusting a command's meaning, wording or structure, and modifying pronunciation (i.e.,

N. L. Black et al. (Eds.): IEA 2021, LNNS 223, pp. 658–666, 2022.
https://doi.org/10.1007/978-3-030-74614-8_82

sound, volume, and rhythm). Likewise, Yarosh et al. [13] and Cheng et al. [2] observed children's interactions with voice interfaces and identified that children employed repair strategies as changing pronunciation, repeating commands, replacing words [2, 13], adding information [13], and speaking louder [2].

However, users do not randomly employ such tactics. Instead, the way voice interactions are designed may be significant for users' choice of repair strategies. Porcheron and colleagues [11, 12] observed users' interactions with conversational agents and showed that VAs' responses were indicators for failures, serving as resources for users to understand trouble sources [12]. The authors argued that users tend to reason and interpret VAs' outputs to identify errors and reformulate commands [11]. Accordingly, Kim et al. [6] conducted a simulated driving experiment and observed a significant effect of a voice interface's responses on participants' understanding of error sources and behavior. Similarly, Myers et al. [10] showed a relationship between obstacle types and error handling tactics by participants using a voice-based calendar.

Although the literature indicates that error recovery behavior is related to voice interface responses, VAs, by design, are remarkably different from other speech interfaces. Firstly, since VAs can perform several tasks, a wide range of responses may be provided for users. Moreover, VAs support natural language, increasing the number of words and phrase structures users may apply, as remembering pre-programmed commands is unnecessary. Due to these characteristics, examining the relationship between VA responses and users' error handling strategies is still needed. This study aims to understand the relationship between different types of VA responses and users' error recovery strategies. To this end, we created three research questions (RQ):

- **RQ1:** What are the types of responses provided by VAs?
- **RQ2:** Which strategies VA users apply to handle errors?
- **RQ3:** How are VA response types related to users' error handling strategies?

2   Method

To answer these RQs, we conducted usability tests followed by debriefing sessions. This method allowed us to observe both users' error handling behavior and real VA responses. Rather than pre-defining types of VA outputs, this exploratory observation was needed due to VAs' unique interactional features mentioned above.

The participants (n = 20) were Brazilian smartphone users who used at least one VA – Siri and/or Google Assistant (GA) – at least once a month. We chose Siri and GA since these were the most commonly used VAs among respondents of a previously conducted survey. Users were recruited by social media and chat apps.

The usability tests had a within-subject design in which participants had to perform six tasks using Siri and GA on a smartphone. In this paper, we only considered for analysis the task with the higher incidence of errors: adding an appointment to a calendar. The task revolved around the scenario of a musical concert that users were hypothetically interested in attending. A Motorola G4 Play running Android 7.1.1. OS was used for GA and an iPhone XR running iOS 12.4.1. for Siri. We recorded users in video and audio and used apps to capture the smartphones' screens. Moreover, for users to express emotional responses, we employed the emocards [see 4].

The usability tests were arranged in three parts: 1) introduction, 2) two rounds of task performance, and 3) debriefing session. In the introduction, participants read and signed a term of consent and filled a digital form to gather profile data. The moderator provided an oral explanation concerning the experiment's goal and procedure.

Users performed tasks through Siri and GA. Independently of their previous experience with VAs, each round started with guidance, a training session on VA activation, and a trial task (ask for a joke). This preparation aimed to get participants familiarized with the VAs so that learnability would not affect the results. To mitigate order presentation bias, half of the users started the test with Siri and half with GA.

For the calendar task, users were instructed to add an appointment to the calendar with a title, date, time, and place. The moderator orally guided users through a previously scripted instruction and provided cards with the event's details, as exemplified: *"You will attend Sandy and Junior's concert and decide to add an appointment to your calendar with this title, date, time, and place* [points to the card]." Thereafter, participants chose an emocard [4] to illustrate their feelings towards the task.

In the debriefing sessions, the moderator asked users about the reasons behind their emotional responses and whether they utilized a VA to perform the tasks in their routines. The tests were conducted from September to November 2019, and sessions lasted around 45 min. The procedure was validated through pilot testing.

For the data analysis, the video recordings were reviewed for analysis, and users' queries and VA responses were transcribed into a table sheet. Thereafter, we followed three steps to address the RQs. Firstly, we coded all VA responses that presented or proceeded an error using a bottom-up approach to identify VA response types (RQ1). The same procedure was applied to commands uttered by users in response to VA outputs, therefore unfolding user strategies (RQ2). We excluded system outputs and user commands that preceded errors from the analysis as this study focuses on error recovery. VA responses or user queries recurrently fell into more than one category and were coded as belonging to all relevant categories. As for RQ3, we counted how many times each strategy was applied immediately after each response type (Fig. 1). Moreover, the debriefing interviews were transcribed, and statements that explained user behavior or displayed their understanding about VA actions were identified.

3   Results

3.1   Response Types and User Behavior

Eight types of VA responses were identified in the analysis (Table 1). Instructions were the most common response types (51,7%) since they comprised not only explicit directions but also questions and confirmations, which were frequently necessary steps to complete the task. The other 48.3% of the responses were caused by errors (1–7). Speech recognition issues (3–5) accounted for 38.4% of such mistakes, although a misrecognition error was the least frequent. As a consequence, these issues led to Wrong Information errors (21.9%), but VAs also added wrong details despite failures in speech recognition. Different Task were recurrent among errors (26.5%) and included tasks unrelated to managing the calendar (e.g., web search) and unrequested calendar features (e.g., showing scheduled appointments). Error Messages (7.3%) and Request for Manual Interaction (6%) were infrequent failures.

Table 1. VA response types.

Response type	Description
1- Different task (n = 40)	The VA perform an activity or task other than the task required
2- Wrong information (n = 33)	The VA adds the wrong details to the appointment
3- Input failure (n = 27)	The VA does not capture *any* part of the user's command
4- Interruption (n = 19)	The VA stops to capture input halfway through users' command
5- Misrecognition (n = 12)	The VA misrecognizes one or more words in the input
6- Request for manual interaction (n = 9)	The VA asks the user to interact manually to add information, save, or cancel events. This was considered an error type as users consider requests for manual interaction as a nuisance [3, 9]
7- Error messages (n = 11)	The VA explicitly tells the user that an error has occurred (e.g., "Sorry, I didn't understand") or that it cannot perform the task
8- Instructions (n = 178)	The VA explicitly tells the user how to proceed in case of error or offer directions to move the interaction forwards (e.g., "Say 'yes' to save"). Questions (e.g., "What is the event's title?") and confirmations (e.g., "I created the event") were considered indirect instructions as they provide cues to advance interactions. We considered for analysis instructions that were provided *after* or *along* with an error or that preceded changes of approach

Table 2 shows the detailed descriptions for user strategies. Users Changing Prosody in response to VAs' outputs were the most recurrent strategy (34.6%). Changing Approach (18.1%), Adding or Removing Information (17.7%), and Repeating a Command (16%) had a similar frequency of observations. Referencing a Past Interaction (9.5%) and Touching the Screen (4.1%) were the least preferred strategies.

Table 2. User strategies.

User strategies	Description
Repeating a command (n = 39)	The user repeats the command to the VA exactly or similarly to the previously uttered command, maintaining the query's meaning (e.g., "Edit event" becomes "Modify event")
Changing prosody (n = 84)	The user adjusts their command by changing phrase prosody: "the rhythmic pattern that results from the relative durations and relative stress levels of its syllables" [5, p. 371]. Speaking faster or hyperarticulation (i.e., "speaking more slowly, more loudly, and more clearly"; [14, p. 2]) were considered changes in prosody
Touching the screen (n = 10)	The user touches the screen to add the appointment's details or answer VAs' confirmation request (i.e., click "save" or "cancel")
Referencing a past interaction (n = 23)	The user mentions a past interactional turn to complete the task. References were explicit (e.g., "alter the *last* event created") or implicit (e.g., "add a place in *the event* [I just created]")
Varying information amount (n = 43)	The user changes their commands by adding or removing entities (e.g., verbs, nouns) to commands in the same approach. For example, users *add* information by changing "add an event to the calendar" to "add 'Show Sandy & Junior' to the calendar on November 9th at 9 pm at Parque Olímpico") when *starting over*
Changing the approach (n = 44)	Users varied how they approached the task after an error, i.e., took different completion *paths* to overcome obstacles. Four approaches were identified: Starting Over (restarting the task from zero), Editing (editing an incorrect appointment), Opening the Calendar (opening the calendar to view events), and Giving Up. Figure 2 shows the percentage for each approach applied after each VA response. However, we observed that users also Changed their Approach as a way to handle failures, and thus considered it a recovery strategy

3.2   Relationship Between VA Responses and User Strategies

Participants seem to have varied their strategies for different system responses (Fig. 1). We also observed that users followed approaches differently when faced with varied response types (Fig. 2). To facilitate visualization, we grouped Interruptions, Input Failures, and Misrecognition as they are results of Speech Recognition Issues.

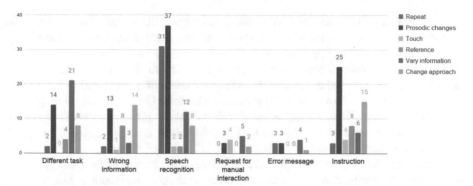

Fig. 1. Number of User Strategies employed after each category of VA response.

Firstly, users frequently Varied Information Amount from their queries and Changed Prosody and Approach when faced with Different Task errors (Fig. 1). As observed in the debriefing sessions, varying information amounts may be an indicator of exploratory behavior, that is, changing their queries to understand how to speak. Users reported that there is a "right way" to speak with the system and had to change the way they posed queries: "*I'm speaking wrongly. I'd even try to speak better to check if it returns* [an appropriate result]. *(…) Did I try to reformulate?*" (P19). Nevertheless, some of them were unsure about how to speak: "*I feel like I don't understand how* [the VA] *was developed, how it thinks*" (P15). Results in Fig. 2 strengthen the possibility that users were uncertain about how to approach these outputs: Starting Over had the higher percentage, but Editing and Opening calendar were also recurrent, suggesting that Different Task may not lead to an obvious recovery path.

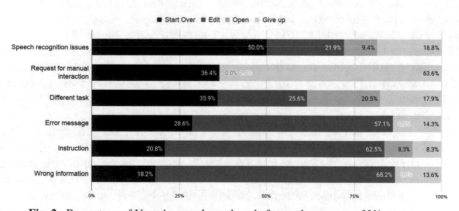

Fig. 2. Percentage of User Approach employed after each category of VA response.

Although prosodic changes were common for Different Task, they were recurrent for all response types, as participants seemed to have employed this tactic independent of system responses. However, this strategy was persistent for Speech Recognition Issues (39.8%) and Instructions (41.7%). We believe that such a high number of prosodic changes in Instructions were not related to these outputs alone but rather by errors in precedent turns. Accordingly, if only Instructions that proceeded error-free turns were considered, the number of prosodic changes would lower to nine (20.5%).

Differently, Speech Recognition Issues may be more determinant for prosodic changes as they are caused by input capture failures. Users may apply tactics to be *heard* when faced with such errors since Repetition and Starting Over were highly employed. Consistently, two participants explained that they changed prosody to meet the system design: *"I had to speak really fast so* [the VA] *could catch everything. And If I stopped just for a bit to think, it considered that I had finish talking."* (P9).

Similar results were found for Wrong Information errors, Error Messages, and Instructions, probably due to Instructions often accompanying these errors (e.g., an error message containing an instruction: "I did not understand. Say "yes" to save"). Referencing Past Interactions and Changing Approach were the leading tactics employed by participants for Wrong Information and Instructions. After these outputs, participants preferred to Edit failed results (Fig. 2) on most occasions. This preference may be due to Instructions' characteristics, which offered cues and requested users' confirmation to advance interactions. As a result, participants employed the Reference tactic, probably attempting to explain to the VA which event to alter. The low count of variations on information amount, an exploratory tactic, reinforces this idea.

Thus, opposite to Different Task errors, explicit or implicit directions on how to alter details may not only decrease abandonment rates (as Instructions had the lowest Give Up rate) but also users guide users to a particular path (Edit). Corroborating this possibility, users' statements showed that instructions helped them editing unsuccessful outcomes: *"At least Siri gave me a clue. It asked me if I wanted to edit, which was wonderful because I wanted to edit and just had to say 'edit.'"* (P8). Furthermore, six users liked VAs instructions: *"I was so happy that Siri asked me everything. (…) I think it's fun and very pleasant."* (P5). Nevertheless, seven participants complained that such responses were insufficient to complete the task: *"Damn, why did you* [the VA] *not asked me the appointment's title?!"* (P16). *"It didn't show the option I wanted* [to edit] *(…) This made me kind of desperate because I couldn't change"* (P18). Likewise, insufficient information caused confusion on five participants regarding the reasons for a failure: *"I didn't understand. [The VA] put 20:30 but I said 21:30"* (P2). Moreover, two participants did not like the step-by-step nature of some instructions: *"I had to say topic by topic (…) Google* [Assistant] *was so dumb and slow."* (P15).

Few Requests for Manual Interaction were observed (9), but participants either Started Over or Gave Up (i.e., touch the screen or abandon the task) on all occurrences. Users Touched the Screen and Added or Removed information in their queries for Requests for Manual Interaction, and also varied information for Error Messages. However, as these responses were rare, no definitive conclusions can be drawn.

4   Discussion and Conclusion

Evidence in the literature shows that users try to repair interactions by applying error recovery strategies, and that these strategies are affected by different error types. However, an examination of VAs was still needed due to characteristics that distinguish VAs from other voice interfaces. This study aimed to understand the relationship between different types of VA responses and users' error recovery strategies. To achieve this goal, we conducted usability tests and debriefing sessions with VA users.

Our findings showed that speech recognition issues were frequent errors in user - VA interaction, echoing previous studies [3, 8, 9]. Unlike other voice-based interfaces [6, 10], we identified recurrent Different Task errors. Our results were similar to the literature showing that hyperarticulation is the most common error handling strategy [2, 10, 13], as well as repeating queries, variating a command's information amount [1, 2, 6, 10, 13], and adding references [9]. However, users seem to approach the interaction differently to find completion paths, for example, by starting over or editing.

As previously indicated [10–12], our results suggest that VA responses may impact users' comprehension of why errors happen, leading to behavioral changes that aim to diagnose and solve problems. In line with previous studies, Speech recognition Issues were dealt with a particularly high number of changes in prosody [6, 10] and repetition [6], suggesting users' attempts to be successfully *heard*. On the other hand, strategies such as varying information amounts and restarting have shown to be exploratory [10] and were used for Different Task errors. For these outputs, participants seemed to iterate commands to be correctly *interpretated,* as they employed exploratory strategies, had a less standardized approach pattern, and reported confusion during the debriefing. Hence, we believe that such responses may provide little support for users to identify and correct trouble sources, probably due to these responses not being a computational error [12], and therefore lacking "awareness" of a mistake. To approach this issue, interaction designers may consider increasing system transparency [12] by displaying to users the rationale behind VA outputs. This information may facilitate error recovery and improve users' mental models of VAs entirely [9].

Conversely, Instructions and Wrong Information responses led users to recovery behaviors and paths (i.e., editing on past interactions), which was welcomed by most participants, and reinforce the idea that providing instructions may increase performance [7]. Notwithstanding, we observed that the instructions evaluated for the calendar task are still not appropriate, as there was missing guidance for some steps. HF/E specialists may consider increasing instructions when designing VAs but should understand all of the task's characteristics and subtasks to provide adequate support. Additionally, as users perceive features to have different complexity levels [9], designers should be careful when presenting guidance. Excessive instructions may slow down interactions [7] and may be disliked, especially for simple activities. Users' preferences should be considered for guidance design.

Our results are limited to the calendar task, and therefore further examinations are needed to encompass other response types that may surface in other features. Moreover, as we employed an exploratory approach to identify VA responses and user behavior, we did not control response types in isolation, and most VA outputs comprised more than one response category. Hence, although debriefing corroborated our results, additional studies are needed to control for response type and guarantee causality between each response type and user behavior.

Acknowledgements. This study was financed in part by the Coordenação de Aperfeiçoamento de Pessoal de Nível Superior - Brasil (CAPES) - Finance Code 001.

References

1. Beneteau, E., Richards, O.K., Zhang, M., et al.: Communication breakdowns between families and Alexa. In: Conference on Human Factors in Computing Systems- Proceedings, pp. 1–13. Association for Computing Machinery, Glasgow (2019). https://doi.org/10.1145/3290605. 3300473
2. Cheng, Y., Yen, K., Chen, Y., et al.: Why doesn't it work? Voice-driven interfaces and young children's communication repair strategies. In: IDC 2018 - Proceedings of the 2018 ACM Conference on Interaction Design and Children, pp. 337–348. ACM, Trondheim, Norway (2018)
3. Cowan, B.R., Pantidi, N., Coyle, D., et al.: "What Can i Help You with?": infrequent users' experiences of intelligent personal assistants. In: Proceedings of the 19th International Conference on Human-Computer Interaction with Mobile Devices and Services, pp. 1–12. Association for Computing Machinery, Vienna (2017)
4. Desmet, P., Overbeeke, K., Tax, S.: Designing products with added emotional value: development and application of an approach for research through design. Des. J. **4**(1), 32–47 (2001). https://doi.org/10.2752/146069201789378496
5. Freund, A.: Word and phrase recognition in speech processing. In: Massaro, W.D. (ed.) Understanding Language - An information-Processing Analysis of Speech Perception, Reading, and Psycholinguistics, pp. 357–390. Academic Press, New York, NY, USA (1975)
6. Kim, J., Jeong, M., Lee, S.C.: "Why did this voice agent not understand me?": error recovery strategy for in-vehicle voice user interface. In: Adjunct Proceedings - 11th International ACM Conference on Automotive User Interfaces and Interactive Vehicular Applications, AutomotiveUI 2019, pp. 146–150. ACM, Utrecht (2019)
7. Kirschthaler, P., Porcheron, M., Fischer, J.E.: What Can I Say? In: Proceedings of the 2nd Conference on Conversational User Interfaces, Bilbao, Spain, pp. 1–9 (2020). https://doi.org/10.1145/3405755.3406119
8. Lopatovska, I., Griffin, A.L., Gallagher, K., et al.: User recommendations for intelligent personal assistants. J. Librarianship Inf. Sci. **52**(2), 577–591 (2020). https://doi.org/10.1177/0961000619841107
9. Luger, E., Sellen, A.: "Like Having a Really Bad PA": the gulf between user expectation and experience of conversational agents. In: Proceedings of the 2016 CHI Conference on Human Factors in Computing Systems, pp. 5286–5297. Association for Computing Machinery, San Jose (2016)
10. Myers, C., Furqan, A., Nebolsky, J., et al.: Patterns for how users overcome obstacles in voice user interfaces. In: Proceedings of the 2018 CHI Conference on Human Factors in Computing Systems, pp. 1–7. ACM, Montréal (2018)
11. Porcheron, M., Fischer, J.E., Sharples, S.: "Do Animals Have Accents?" In: Proceedings of the 2017 ACM Conference on Computer Supported Cooperative Work and Social Computing, pp. 207–219. ACM, Portland (2017)
12. Porcheron, M., Fischer, J.E., Reeves, S., Sharples, S.: Voice interfaces in everyday life. In: Conference on Human Factors in Computing Systems – Proceedings, pp. 1–12. ACM, Montréal (2018)
13. Yarosh, S., Thompson, S., Watson, K., et al.: Children asking questions: speech interface reformulations and personification preferences. In: Proceedings of the 17th ACM Conference on Interaction Design and Children, pp. 300–312. ACM, Trondheim (2018)
14. Stent, A.J., Huffman, M.K., Brennan, S.E.: Adapting speaking after evidence of misrecognition: local and global hyperarticulation. Speech Commun. **50**, 163–178 (2008). https://doi.org/10.1016/j.specom.2007.07.005
15. UNESCO Digital Library. https://unesdoc.unesco.org/ark:/48223/pf0000367416.page=1. Accessed 08 Feb 2021

User Needs for Digital Creativity Support Systems in an Occupational Context

Lorenz Prasch$^{(\boxtimes)}$ (iD), Lena aus dem Bruch, and Klaus Bengler

Chair of Ergonomics, Technical University of Munich, Munich, Germany
lorenz.prasch@tum.de

Abstract. In a two-step study, an interview followed by an online questionnaire , we investigated the potential and user needs for systems that can support humans in the context of creative work. We found that participants usually follow a general creative process in problem identification, preparation, idea generation and idea evaluation, while frequently jumping and iterating between those phases. Interviewees as well as survey participants had greater difficulties in divergent thinking as opposed to convergent thinking and used convergent thinking more often in their daily work. Since advice from colleagues was most frequently sought out during the idea generation phase, this phase provides the greatest opportunity for a creativity support system. Most participants work primarily using computers and digital tools, both alone as well as in teams. It was mentioned that especially information research can be very time consuming. Therefore, from a user's point of view, development of an inspirational assistant that can facilitate research as well as collaboration in a digital way seems to be the most promising approach for creativity support systems for creative workers.

Keywords: Creativity support systems · User needs · New work · Human machine interaction

1 Introduction

Work is – and always has been – changing. Automation has resulted in a tremendous shift from manual labour towards cognitive tasks such as monitoring, planning, and creating. Following continuous advancements in artificial intelligence, software is used to solve numerous cognitive tasks automatically [1]. Human work will gradually develop towards creative generation [2]. As such, there is an increased need and potential for human factors/ergonomics to contribute to creative work [3–5] and new work in general.

Despite the fact that there is still some controversy about what creativity is [6], the generation of ideas and products that are considered novel as well as useful appears especially to be a final frontier of human capability and a major challenge for artificial intelligence [7]. When assuming that computer systems will not in fact render humans superfluous for the creative act, it is important to determine *where* and *how* humans can be supported. Algorithms appear capable of such an endeavour, especially since in the past, several computational systems have already shown potential to assist humans

N. L. Black et al. (Eds.): IEA 2021, LNNS 223, pp. 667–674, 2022.
https://doi.org/10.1007/978-3-030-74614-8_83

with specific tasks. For example, automated driving or AI-based diagnosis systems seem capable of augmenting human intelligence in a meaningful way.

The augmentation and support of creativity and specific configuration of an assistance system are the key objectives of this research. When transferring the idea of cognitive support systems to the creative domain, how exactly could an artificial assistance system support humans in their means to generate truly creative solutions at work?

2   State of the Art

Scientific interest in systems that stimulate or document creative processes, or *creativity support systems* [8, 9], has been growing, but research is still incomplete [10, 11]. Recent reviews focusing on group [12] and individual [13] creativity support systems respectively, shed light on current approaches and state of the art. Lubart indicates that "computers may facilitate (a) the management of creative work, (b) communication between individuals collaborating on creative projects, (c) the use of creativity enhancement techniques, and (d) the creative act through integrated human-computer cooperation during idea production" [14]. Group support systems typically focus on tele-cooperation and support of the creative process by information exchange. On the individual level, there are some systems that support the entire creative process (e.g. [15, 16]), the majority, however, supports at least one of four phases associated with being part of the creative process [17, 18]. Those phases are *problem identification* or problem finding, *preparation* or information research/finding, *idea generation* or idea finding, and *idea evaluation*, including iteration [19–23] (c.f. Fig. 1). The amount of systems that support a certain phase, however, varies. This is shown by a recent review examining 48 existing support systems: problem identification (7), preparation (19), idea generation (42), and evaluation (20) [13]. While most systems support multiple phases of the process, single phase support is only available for preparation (information research) and idea generation, suggesting these two as the easiest to amplify in a standalone environment.

Creative cognition is generally divided into divergent and convergent thinking, with divergent thinking as a generative process, and convergent thinking as an evaluative process. Development of creativity support systems has primarily focused on stimulation of divergent thinking [24]. Ideally, however, both types of thinking should be supported to enable the production of both novel and useful solutions [25]. The design and development of these tools is usually based on theoretical frameworks [24–26], but lacks empirical evidence of where and how exactly users of those systems would like to be supported. Consequently, this paper examines the need for creativity support systems with a user-centred approach, using a combination of interviews and an online survey.

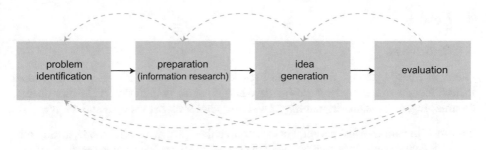

Fig. 1. Four phases commonly assumed to be part of the creative process (including jumps and loops between phases) and used as a model process for interviews and survey in this paper.

3 Methods

3.1 Interviews

We conducted semi-standardised interviews with people from creative professions. The professions were classified as creative according to Guilford's definition, which lists *inventing*, *designing*, *contriving*, *composing*, and *planning* amongst creative patterns [27]. Due to the COVID-19 pandemic, all interviews were conducted remotely using the open-source video conferencing tool BigBlueButton[1], hosted on a server at the university. Audio was recorded during the interviews.

Prior to the start of the interview, informed consent was obtained from all participants. The interview guideline contained demographics as well as questions regarding the current modus operandi, the application of the creative process and visions of the future application of creativity amplification in the participant's jobs.

The interviews were evaluated using qualitative content analysis [28]. For this purpose, the interviews were first transcribed, followed by paraphrasing and generalisation of the participant's statements by three individual raters. Interrater reliability shows a Krippendorff's alpha of $\alpha = .976$ and reliable consensus of the ratings [29].

3.2 Online Survey

Additionally, we conducted an online survey amongst people working creatively. The questionnaire was presented using LimeSurvey[2], an online survey tool, hosted on a server at the university. As an incentive to participate, five Amazon vouchers were raffled amongst participants.

After participants gave their informed consent, the first part of the survey contained some demographic questions to assign participants to creative professions and get an overview of the sample. Subsequently, participants were asked to answer questions similar to those in the interview, but in a closed question format.

---

[1] https://bigbluebutton.org/.
[2] https://www.limesurvey.org/.

4 Results

4.1 Interviews

Our $N = 7$ participants (5 female; ages between 24 and 41; $M = 30$, $SD = 4.78$) worked in architecture, user experience design (two participants), graphic design, fashion design, engineering, and theatre dramaturgy. The interviews took between 18 and 38 min.

Modus Operandi. Most participants stated that they primarily work alone, asking others for feedback only at certain points in the process. All participants do this from offices with 2 to 20 co-workers as well as from home using laptops or computers. Four participants stressed that they used analogue tools like pen and paper as well. The goals to be met can be distinguished into two categories, namely economic requirements (selling products, quality, and meeting deadlines), and social aspects (social critics, sustaina-bility, and looking for new horizons). Four participants use convergent thinking more often, three use both types of thinking to the same extent. All but one participant mentioned that convergent thinking was easier for them.

Creative Process. Five participants indicated that they follow a process similar to the one presented in Fig. 1, while stressing the importance of the non-linearity of the process. Two participants said they were only responsible for particular steps of the process within their organi-sations. All participants exchange ideas with colleagues. Five actively request feed-back when needed, two stated that such discussions are organised through regular meetings at their workplaces.

Vision of Creativity Amplification. One participant stated that there was no need for work support and was reluctant to hand over parts of his work. The remaining participants would use support systems, especially if they saved time or could be used for research. The system ideas men-tioned can be roughly divided into four areas of application: data management & research (5), particular task support (3), workflow & organisation (2) and inspiration (2).

4.2 Online Survey

A total of $N = 110$ people participated in the survey. The link to the survey was distributed via social and career networks. Prior to statistical analysis, we excluded incomplete datasets (33), datasets that indicated participants did not work in creative domains (10) or not full time (7), as well as one dataset whose participant stated they worked primarily manually, since the study was aimed at knowledge workers. This resulted in $n = 59$ datasets that were included in the analysis. 41 participants were female, 18 male and the overall sample was relatively young ($M = 27.89$, $SD = 6.05$).

Modus Operandi. Of our participants, 96.6% indicated that their work consisted of both teamwork and working alone with varying ratios (27.1% more alone, 25.4% more team, 44.1% balanced). Convergent thinking was predominant in most of our participant's daily work and was easier for the majority when compared to divergent thinking (see Table 1).

Table 1. Answers of $n = 59$ participants regarding which types of thinking they used more often in their daily work, as well as which one was easier for them.

	Convergent thinking	Divergent thinking	Equal
Used more often	55.9%	6.8%	37.3%
Easier	69.5%	23.7%	6.8%

Reasons for finding convergent thinking easier were the limited number of possible solutions as well as the required logical or inferential thinking based on real-world criteria. Participants who preferred divergent thinking did so because in that case no decision had to be made and no evaluation took place. The majority of participants reported using digital tools at least in part (33.9% worked digitally only, 50.8% both digitally and analogue). Only 15.3% of respondents said they worked exclusively analogue.

Creative Process. Of the 59 respondents, 55 (93.2%) stated that the process depicted in Fig. 1 corresponds to their usual procedure when working on their professional tasks. The other four stated that they did not have a fixed procedure, that creativity was not a linear process for them or that tasks were identified rather than problems and only one solution was developed, which was then checked by the team. Participants felt uncer-tain about their competence mostly in idea generation (35.6%), followed by prepara-tion (22%), evaluation (18.6%) and problem identification (15.3%). Similar results can be observed in terms of a need for assistance. We asked participants how often they requested help from their colleagues in the respective phases (see Fig. 2). For idea generation, 58.2% stated that they often or always sought advice from colleagues.

Vision of Creative Amplification. A majority of respondents (69.5%) indicated that they would use a creativity support system at work if one were available to them. The remaining 30.5% said they would not use such a system for the following reasons:

- Doubts about the capabilities of the system (10 mentions)
- Implementation not conceivable (2 mentions)
- Social exchange too important (6 mentions)

Of those who would use a creativity support system, preferred would be one that assists in preparation or information research.

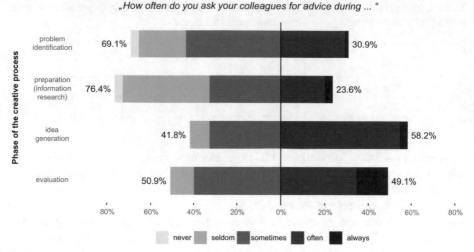

Fig. 2. Descriptive data of $n = 59$ participants answering the question how often they asked colleagues for advice in the respective phases of the creative process.

5   Discussion

In general, a clear connection between the respondents' preferred way of thinking and the most problematic process steps can be observed. Convergent thinking is easier for a large proportion of respondents and more widely used. The point at which ideas are generated is the phase at which uncertainty is greatest and support or advice are sought most often. Coincidentally, this is also the phase most commonly associated with divergent thinking [30]. It is understandable that people who are better at convergent thinking have difficulties at this point.

Interview participants stated that information research can be very time-consuming, and therefore suggested the most support systems for this phase. This is in line with data from the interviews, where participants preferred a system that would assist with data management & research.

These results are in line with current development, seeing that dedicated creativity support systems are available solely for the two phases preparation and idea generation [13]. However, while current systems have clearly identified the need for support in idea generation, for example via guidance through several creativity techniques, support in data management & research still lacks prominence in creativity research.

Overall, results show a need for and a willingness to use creativity support systems in daily work, which makes continued development of such systems a promising endeavour.

6   Limitations and Future Research

Considering the two-step approach of the study, with first an interview followed by an online questionnaire, we are confident that the results are well founded. Yet, one could argue that due to the small sample size in the interviews, it is difficult to differentiate between domain vs. individual differences. However, the alignment in results between interviews and the online questionnaire is promising. Unfortunately, the distribution of domains was skewed towards engineering (20 participants), so the results from the online survey might not be applicable to the general population. However, there was no significant relationship between domain and modus operandi (team vs. solo work: $\chi^2(60) = 59.63, p = 0.49$; divergent vs. convergent thinking: $\chi^2(30) = 25.97, p = 0.68$), and nearly all participants agreed to the proposed creative process.

When implementing strategic support systems for creative workers, we should aim for digital support systems that facilitate research and provide inspiration during the divergent thinking process or idea generation and support a way to easily share the progress of one's work amongst colleagues.

References

1. Acemoglu, D., Restrepo, P.: Artificial Intelligence, Automation and Work. University of Chicago Press, Cambridge, MA (2018)
2. Prasch, L., Maruhn, P., Brünn, M., Bengler, K.: Creativity assessment via novelty and usefulness (CANU) - approach to an easy to use objective test tool. In: Proceedings of the Sixth International Conference on Design Creativity (ICDC 2020), pp. 019–026, no. 1914 (2020)
3. Dul, J., Ceylan, C.: Work environments for employee creativity. Ergonomics **0139**(January), 1–25 (2011)
4. Dul, J., et al.: A strategy for human factors/ergonomics: developing the discipline and profession. Ergonomics **55**(4), 377–395 (2012)
5. Prasch, L., Bengler, K.: Ergonomics in the age of creative knowledge workers – define, assess, optimize. Adv. Intell. Syst. Comput. **821**, 349–357 (2019)
6. Batey, M.: The measurement of creativity: from definitional consensus to the introduction of a new heuristic framework. Creat. Res. J. **24**(1), 95–104 (2012)
7. Colton, S., Wiggins, G.A.: Computational creativity: the final frontier? In: Proceedings of the 20th European Conference on Artificial Intelligence, vol. 242, pp. 21–26 (2012)
8. Massetti, B.: An empirical examination of the value of creativity support systems on idea generation. MIS Q. **20**(1), 83 (1996)
9. Wierenga, B., van Bruggen, G.H.: The dependent variable in research into the effects of creativity support systems: quality and quantity of ideas. MIS Q. **22**(1), 81 (1998)
10. Bonnardel, N., Zenasni, F.: The impact of technology on creativity in design: an enhancement? Creat. Innov. Manage. **19**(2), 180–191 (2010)
11. Shneiderman, B.: Accelerating discovery and innovation. Commun. ACM **50**(12), 20–32 (2007)
12. Gabriel, A., Monticolo, D., Camargo, M., Bourgault, M.: Creativity support systems: a systematic mapping study. Think. Ski. Creat. **21**, 109–122 (2016)
13. Wang, K., Nickerson, J.V.: A literature review on individual creativity support systems. Comput. Hum. Behav. **74**, 139–151 (2017)
14. Lubart, T.I.: How can computers be partners in the creative process: classification and commentary on the special issue. Int. J. Hum. Comput. Stud. **63**(4–5), 365–369 (2005). SPEC. ISS.
15. Forgionne, G., Newman, J.: An experiment on the effectiveness of creativity enhancing decision-making support systems. Decis. Support Syst. **42**(4), 2126–2136 (2007)
16. Marakas, G.M., Elam, J.J.: Creativity enhancement in problem solving: through software or process? Manage. Sci. **43**(8), 1136–1146 (1997)

17. Amabile, T.M.: Creativity in Context: Update to the Social Psychology of Creativity. Routledge (2018)
18. Lubart, T.I.: Models of the creative process: past, present and future. Creat. Res. J. **13**(3–4), 295–308 (2001)
19. Howard, T.J., Culley, S.J., Dekoninck, E.: Describing the creative design process by the integration of engineering design and cognitive psychology literature. Des. Stud. **29**(2), 160–180 (2008)
20. Gero, S., Kannengiesser, U.: The situated function-behaviour-structure framework. Des. Stud. **25**(4), 373–391 (2004)
21. Amabile, T.M.: The social psychology of creativity: a componential conceptualization. J. Pers. Soc. Psychol. **45**(2), 357–376 (1983)
22. Amabile, T.M.: A model of creativity and innovation in organizations. Res. Organ. Behav. **10**(1), 123–167 (1988)
23. Olszak, C.M., Kisielnicki, J.: A conceptual framework of information systems for organizational creativity support. lessons from empirical investigations. Inf. Syst. Manage. **35**(1), 29–48 (2018)
24. Althuizen, N., Reichel, A.: The effects of IT-enabled cognitive stimulation tools on creative problem solving: a dual pathway to creativity. J. Manage. Inf. Syst. **33**(1), 11–44 (2016)
25. Müller-Wienbergen, F., Müller, O., Seidel, S., Becker, J.: Leaving the beaten tracks in creative work - a design theory for systems that support convergent and divergent thinking. J. Assoc. Inf. Syst. **12**(11), 714–740 (2011)
26. Yamamoto, Y., Nakakoji, K.: Interaction design of tools for fostering creativity in the early stages of information design. Int. J. Hum. Comput. Stud. **63**(4–5), pp. 513–535 (2005). SPEC. ISS.
27. Guilford, J.P.: Creativity. Am. Psychol. **5**(9), 444–54 (1950)
28. Mayring, P.: Qualitative content analysis. Companion Qual. Res. **1**(2004), 159–176 (2004)
29. Krippendorff, K.: Content Analysis: An Introduction to its Methodology. Sage publications (2018)
30. Runco, M.A., Acar, S.: Divergent thinking as an indicator of creative potential. Creat. Res. J. **24**(1), 66–75 (2012)

An Empirical Study on Automation Transparency (i.e., seeing-into) of an Automated Decision Aid System for Condition-Based Maintenance

Fahimeh Rajabiyazdi[(⊠)], Greg A. Jamieson, and David Quispe Guanolusia

Department of Mechanical and Industrial Engineering,
University of Toronto, Toronto M5S 3G8, Canada
fahimeh.rajabiyazdi@mail.utoronto.ca

Abstract. Prior studies have shown conflicting results about the impact of information disclosure on human performance– often referred to as transparency (i.e., seeing-into) studies. We conducted an experiment to investigate whether transparency manipulations predicted whether participants could identify whether features and their relative weights of a decision aid guided by a Machine Learning model were consistent with stated best practices for making maintenance decisions. We had insignificant results on state estimation, automation reliance, trust, workload, and self-confidence. This study shows that disclosing information about the decision aid rationale does not necessarily impact operator performance.

Keywords: Automation transparency · Decision aids · Maintenance

1 Introduction

In Machine Learning (ML)-based decision aid systems, human oversight may be required to check that the ML rationale aligns with end-user goals and metrics. Furthermore, the end-user may need to verify that the training and validation data are representative of real-world conditions. Thus, the ML rationale may have to be disclosed to the end-user. However, the effective presentation of this rationale for these end-user tasks is still an ongoing research question.

Doshi-Velez and Kim [1] distinguished between *local* and *global* explanations to end-users for ML algorithms. A global explanation is one that offers information on the logic of an ML algorithm as a whole. A local explanation discloses the logic of an ML algorithm that led to a specific decision. Human Factors researchers have evaluated the impacts of information disclosure about automation logic on end-user performance under the notion of *transparency*. For instance, Seong and Bisantz [2] and Mercado et al. [3] reported that disclosing information about automation had a positive impact on human task performance and trust calibration. In contrast, Adhikari et al. [4] reported that participants objectively performed the worst when presented with any amount and type of information. However, participants self-reported a better understanding of the ML-based Decision Support System rationale with greater information disclosure. Similarly, Skraaning and Jamieson [5] reported that participants performed worst but calibrated trust with information disclosure as automation capabilities increased. Given these inconsistent and, at times, conflicting results, there is a need to conduct more empirical studies on transparency to establish the effective type and amount of information disclosure that positively impacts human performance.

As suggested by [1], we anticipate that local explanations will support participants to assess the correctness of a specific decision made by the ML algorithm. Thus, our research question is: What are the effects of disclosing the rationale that led to an automated decision through Feature Weight (also known as Feature Importance) and the Decision Rules on human performance (including reliance decisions, trust, task efficacy, and workload)?

2   Method

2.1   Participants

We recruited 24 (14 female, 10 male) chemical engineering undergraduate and graduate students from the University of Toronto who had completed courses in process engineering and statistics. Participants were between the ages of 18 and 30 ($M = 25$, $SD = 3.17$). Ten participants indicated prior work experience in the process operation industry ($M = 23$ months, $SD = 25$). Eleven participants stated moderate familiarity with ML (i.e., had completed ML courses or self-taught ML concepts). Participants were paid $15/hour rounded to the nearest 20 min. To incentivize participants, they were entered into a draw for an extra $25 after study completion. To motivate participants to follow the instructions, we told them to imagine that a company hired them as a consultant to perform this task.

2.2   Apparatus

A machine learning-based micro-world platform for condition-based maintenance named Automated Reliability Decision Aid System (ARDAS) was used for this experiment [6]. The architecture of ARDAS comprises the ML algorithm and the user interface. In ARDAS, a supervised ML algorithm is trained to generate models that predict the states of four hydraulic components. The models were trained using multi-sensor time-series and historical event data to classify sensor measurements [7].

The original ML model in ARDAS used a random forest algorithm trained with sixty-eight features and composed of thousands of trees. These features are extracted from the statistical moments (including mean, kurtosis, skewness, and variance) of seventeen sensors data. Due to the complexity of the ML model, it was necessary to reduce the number of features to employ this ML model while fulfilling the constraints of a controlled experiment. The constraint for our experiment was that participants must be able to complete the experimental task (i.e., estimate the hydraulic component's state) in every experimental condition while avoiding learning effects in trials.

To meet this constraint, we simplified the model. First, we obtained the global feature weights of each components using sixty-eight features. Then, we selected five features for each component imposing the following constraints: First, select features that deemed most influential by the original ML model. Second, select only features that represent the mean of the sensors data. Third, select only features that adhered to process engineering principles about the hydraulic system.

This process resulted in five different global influential features in determining each hydraulic component's states. At this stage we employed Wizard of Oz technique [8]. We used the same five features specific for each component in each trial but assigned a unique local weight to each feature. Using engineering principles, the feature's weights were calculated based on how far the value of the feature is into the threshold as a function of the threshold's size. Finally, we estimated a component's state based on the weighted average of the estimated probabilities. These probabilities were guided by the thresholds of the different decision trees within the ML model.

The user interface of ARDAS (Fig. 1) included a hydraulic process diagram (top-left), three mean sensor data graphs (top-right), and a confidence probabilities table (bottom-right). Depending on the experimental condition, the user interface also included the Local Feature Weights (Fig. 1, dashed red box), the Decision Rules (Fig. 1, solid green box), or both. The Feature Weights and Decision Rules presented the automation rationale that led to a particular state estimation.

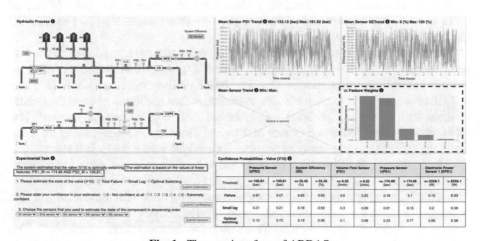

Fig. 1. The user interface of ARDAS

Hydraulic Process Diagram

The top left section in Fig. 1 shows the hydraulic process diagram that includes the positions of the components in the yellow rectangles (Valve (V10), Pump (MP1), Cooler (C1)), and seventeen sensors in blue squares and circles. Each hydraulic component has three states (normal functioning, minor malfunctioning, failure).

Mean Sensor Value Graphs

The top right section in Fig. 1 displays up to three-line graphs of mean sensor values over a 12-h period. The minimum and maximum mean sensor values are written at the top of each graph. If a fourth sensor is selected, the earliest line graph will be replaced by the newly selected sensor's mean graph. In this experiment, the point of interest is the sensor value at the current time.

Confidence Probabilities Table
The bottom right section in Fig. 1 shows a confidence probabilities table. For each component, probabilities are shown for each state, given the thresholds for each feature. Each feature's value is compared against a threshold for determining each state's probability for given component.

2.3 Experimental Design

A 2×2 within-subject design was employed, with Local Feature Weights (displayed, not displayed) and Decision Rules (displayed, not displayed) as factors. The result is four levels of Display: none [baseline], Local Feature Weights, Decision Rules, and Combined (Local Feature Weights and Decision Rules). Each level was presented in a separate block of twelve independent trials. Each participant completed all four blocks.

We used the method proposed by Zeelenberg and Pecher [9] to counterbalance the order of the four experimental conditions, and the assignment of trial sets 1–4 to these conditions. This method systematically identifies 8 block-condition orders (a pair of Latin squares) that balance the immediate and remote sequence effects. The order of trials within a set was not randomized.

We created a total of 48 independent trial stimuli by selecting three unique hydraulic components (Valve (V10), Pump (MP1), Cooler (C1)), each with three states. The state of each hydraulic component was generated based on five features. Each feature was assigned a unique value in each trial. Furthermore, in the conditions wherein the feature weights were disclosed, the feature weights and their orders were randomized. The 48 stimuli were divided into four sets of 12 trials, labelled 1–4, each having the three hydraulic components appear four times but with unique values for each feature.

The automated decisions were manipulated to produce incorrect estimates in 8 out of 48 trials (83.3% reliability). We challenged participants to identify whether the decision aid's features, and their relative weights were consistent with the company's best practices. Thus, we simulated incorrect automated decisions due to incorrect features (4 trials) and incorrect weights (4 trials). There were two incorrect trials in each block. The order of these eight incorrect trials was randomized throughout the blocks.

The company's best practice was to estimate the state of each component using the five designated features. If the decision aid system used any other features, then its decision should deem incorrect (i.e., incorrect features error trial). Furthermore, there is a chance of noisy measurement readings in virtual sensors (i.e., cooling efficiency and system efficiency) since their values are computed based on multiple sensors. Thus, the company practice is that if these virtual sensors' feature values are at or within $\pm 0.5\%$ higher or lower than the threshold, the least weight should be associated with it. If that is not the case, then the automated decision is incorrect (i.e., incorrect weights error trial).

2.4   Experimental Task

Participants estimated the state of a hydraulic component given three possible states. In all trials, the state estimation for that component was given. To estimate the state of a hydraulic component and assess whether they agreed with the decision aid system's state estimation, the participants were expected to compare the automated estimation against their domain knowledge. However, participants' domain knowledge may differ. To minimize the effect of prior domain knowledge on subjects' assessment of the automation rationale, were trained participants on what information to incorporate in their decisions. Participants were trained to complete the task in the following steps: First, determine the value for each of the five designated features at the current time using the mean sensor value graphs. Second, compare the values against the designated threshold given in the confidence probabilities table to determine each state's probability. Finally, calculate the average of the probabilities for each of the three states. The state with the highest probability is the company's desired estimation. Participants were told to use ML's rationale as appropriate.

Transparency Conditions

Local Feature Weight Graph
The feature weights represent the amount that each feature contributed to the final prediction. The local feature weight graph (Fig. 1, dashed red box) presents the weights of the five most prominent features used to estimate the hydraulic component state. In each trial, each feature of a component is assigned a weight by the automation. The sum of the five weights is one.

Decision Rules
The decision rules present the IF-THEN rules (solid green box, Fig. 1) guided by the decision trees within the ML algorithm to estimate the hydraulic component condition. The decision rule condition statement included the features weighted more than or equal to 0.2 and the threshold that the feature value was compared against.

Combined (Local Feature Weight Graph+Decision Rules)
In this condition, both the local feature weight and the decision rules were presented.

2.5   Procedure

The experiment was conducted online with the experimenter present. The protocol was executed over two consecutive days, and on average, participants took 4 and a half hours to complete the study. At the start of the first day, participants signed a consent form and completed a demographic questionnaire. They then watched a video explaining the platform and experiment task. Afterwards, participants were given three practice trials where they were encouraged to think-aloud before proceeding with the experiment.

In each trial, after submitting their state estimation, participants were asked to state their confidence on a scale of whole numbers between 0 and 5 inclusively with 0 = "not confident at all" and 5 = "extremely confident". After each trial, the participants were asked to indicate the sensor data that they used to arrive at a state estimation for the component (in descending order of influence). This question was asked to ensure that participants were not randomly choosing a state but rather were using the sensors to estimate the components' states. After each block, participants rated their mental workload on the NASA-TLX questionnaire modified to a seven-point scale [10]. They rated their trust in the automated estimation on a modified trust questionnaire designed by [11]. After the final block, participants completed the relative weighting portion of the NASA-TLX questionnaire as it applied to all the experimental tasks throughout the blocks. Finally, we conducted a semi-structured interview asking participants about their experience using the platform and their strategies in estimating component states.

3   Results

For the analysis below, trial data was aggregated by block' (N = 96). State estimation, correct automation usage, correct automation rejection, were treated as proportion data. Respectively, that is the number of correct estimations out of 12 trials, the number of correct automation usage event out of 10 trials, and the number of correct automation rejections out of 2 error trials in each block.

We used the *glmer()* function from the lme4 package to build a generalized linear mixed model with a binomial distribution for state estimation, correct automation usage, and correct automation rejection. First, we built a baseline model from only the intercept. Then, we added Display as a predictor to our model. We specified a random part to our model. The random effect was specified as the Display nested within participant ID to account for our data dependency. For each of these dependent variables, we compared the baseline to the main model with the Display predictor.

3.1   State Estimation

The state estimation is categorical with either correct or incorrect estimation. The correct estimation is the most probable state among three states. Display was not a significant predictor of correctly estimating a state, $X^2(3) = 5.27$, Pr (> *Chisq*) = 0.15. Non-orthogonal contrasts revealed that state estimations were not significantly more correct for Feature Weight compared to Baseline, $B(SE) = 0.42(0.22)$, $z = 1.91, p = 0.06$, odds ratio = 1.52, or between Decision Rules or Baseline, $B(SE) = -0.03(0.21)$, $z = -0.16$, $p = 0.88$, odds ratio = 0.96, or between Combined or Baseline, $B(SE) = 0.21(0.22)$, z = 0.97, $p = 0.33$, odds ratio = 1.23.

3.2   Correct Automation Usage

The correct automation usage is categorical with two categories of yes or no. Display was not a significant predictor of correctly using automation, $X^2(3) = 5.90$, Pr (> *Chisq*) = 0.12. Non-orthogonal contrasts revealed that automation usage was not significantly more correct for Feature Weight compared to Baseline, $B(SE) = 0.47(0.26)$, $z = 1.83, p = 0.07$, odds ratio = 1.61, or between Decision Rules or Baseline, $B(SE) = -0.12(0.24)$, z = -0.5, $p = 0.60$, odds ratio = 0.88, or between Combined or Baseline, $B(SE) = 0.17(0.25)$, $z = 0.70$, $p = 0.48$, odds ratio = 0.17.

3.3 Correct Automation Rejection

The correct automation rejection is categorical with two categories of yes or no. Display was not a significant predictor of correctly rejecting automation, $X^2(3) = 0.88$, Pr ($>$ $Chisq$) $= 0.83$. Non-orthogonal contrasts revealed that automation usage was not significantly more correct for Feature Weight compared to Baseline, $B(SE) = 0.35(0.44)$, $z = 0.80, p = 0.42$, odds ratio $= 1.43$, or between Decision Rules or Baseline, $B(SE) = 0.26(0.44)$, $z = 0.60$, $p = 0.55$, odds ratio $= 1.30$, or between Combined or Baseline, $B(SE) = 0.35(0.44)$, $z = 0.80$, $p = 0.42$, odds ratio $= 1.43$.

3.4 Mean Confidence, Mean Trust, Workload, Mean Response Time

We calculated workload scores using the method advised by [10]. We scaled the workload scores and the first 10 questions in the modified trust questionnaire to 0 to 100 (inclusive) for the analysis.

According to Levene's test, the homogeneity of variance assumption was met for mean confidence F $(3, 92) = 0.11$, Pr ($>$F) $= 0.96$, mean trust F $(3,92) = 2.21$, Pr ($>$F) $= 0.09$, and workload F $(3,92) = 0.36$, Pr ($>$F) $= 0.78$. According to Shapiro-Wilk test, mean confidence ($W = 0.99, p = 0.50$), mean trust ($W = 0.97, p = 0.06$), and workload ($W = 0.98, p = 0.40$) met the assumption of normality.

We conducted ezANOVA on these variables with orthogonal contrasts. Mauchly's test indicated that the assumption of sphericity had been met for mean confidence ($W = 0.91, p = 0.85$), mean trust ($W = 0.72, p = 0.21$), and workload ($W = 0.73, p = 0.24$). The results showed that mean confidence F $(3, 69) = 2.56$, p $= 0.66$, $\eta^2 = 0.02$, mean trust F $(3,69) = 0.43$, $p = 0.73$, $\eta^2 = 0.01$, and workload F $(3,69) = 0.40$, $p = 0.75$, $\eta^2 = 0.01$ were not significantly affected by the type of Display.

According to Levene's test, the homogeneity of variance assumption was met for mean response time, F $(3, 92) = 0.13$, Pr ($>$F) $= 0.94$. However, according to Shapiro-Wilk test, the assumption of normality has been violated for mean response time ($W = 0.94$, $p < 0.05$). Log transformation was used after which it met the assumption of normality ($W = 0.99$, $p = 0.82$). We conducted ezANOVA on mean response time. Mauchly's test indicated that the assumption of sphericity had been violated for mean response time ($W = 0.33, p < .05$), therefore, degrees of freedom were corrected using Huynh-Feld estimates of sphericity ($\varepsilon = 0.74$). The results showed that mean response time was not significantly affected by the type of display, F $(2.21, 50.85) = 0.67$, $p = 0.53$, $\eta^2 = 0.01$.

4 Discussion and Conclusion

We found no evidence to corroborate the common belief that presenting a rationale for a decision aid's conclusion will positively impact automation reliance and efficacy. Disclosing information about the decision process in the form of local feature weights, decision rules or both combined did not predict performance on state estimation, automation reliance, trust or self-confidence, workload, or mean response time.

One of many limitations is the constraints that we imposed on the ML features (see Sect. 2.2). It is possible that, had we not restricted the ML features in the described manner, participants may have benefitted more from the rationale disclosure. However, it is also possible that the complex nature of ML models may not lend itself to controlled experimental traditions that characterize human factors and ergonomics research.

References

1. Doshi-Velez, F., Kim, B.: Towards a rigorous science of interpretable machine learning. arXiv preprint arXiv:1702.08608 (2017)
2. Seong, Y., Bisantz, A.M.: The impact of cognitive feedback on judgment performance and trust with decision aids. Int. J. Ind. Ergon. **38**(7–8), 608–625 (2008)
3. Mercado, J.E., Rupp, M.A., Chen, J.Y.C., Barnes, M.J., Barber, D., Procci, K.: Intelligent agent transparency in human-agent teaming for multi-UxV management. Hum. Factors **58**(3), 401–415 (2016)
4. Adhikari, A., Tax, D.M.: LEAFAGE: example-based and feature importance-based explanations for black-box ML models. In: 2019 IEEE International Conference on Fuzzy Systems (FUZZ-IEEE), pp. 1–7. IEEE (2019)
5. Skraaning, G., Jamieson, G.A.: Human performance benefits of the automation transparency design principle: validation and variation. Hum. Factors. **63**(3), 379–401 (2021)
6. Quispe, D., Rajabiyazdi, F., Jamieson, G.A.: A Machine learning-based micro-world platform for condition-based maintenance. In: 2020 IEEE International Conference on Systems, Man, and Cybernetics (SMC), pp. 288–295. IEEE (2020)
7. Helwig, N., Pignanelli, E., Schutze, A.: Condition monitoring of a complex hydraulic system using multivariate statistics. In: IEEE International Instrumentation and Measurement Technology Conference (I2MTC) Proceedings, pp. 210–215. IEEE (2015)
8. Stanton, N.A., Salmon, P.M., Rafferty, L.A., Walker, G.H., Baber, C., Jenkins, D.P.: Human Factors Methods. In Human Factors Methods. Ashgate Publishing, Ltd. (2013)
9. Zeelenberg, R., Pecher, D.: A method for simultaneously counterbalancing condition order and assignment of stimulus materials to conditions. Behav. Res. Methods **47**(1), 127–133 (2015)
10. Hart, S.G., Staveland, L.E.: Development of NASA-TLX (Task Load Index): results of empirical and theoretical research. Adv. Psychol. **53**, 139–183 (1988)
11. Jian, J.Y., Bisantz, A.M., Dury, C.G.: Foundations for an empirically determined scale of trust in automated systems. Int. J. Cognit. Ergon. **4**(1), 53–71 (2000)

A User Study to Evaluate the Customization of Automatically Generated GUIs

David Raneburger[1] ⓘ, Roman Popp[2] ⓘ, and Hermann Kaindl[3](✉) ⓘ

[1] Lienz, Austria
[2] Purgstall an der Erlauf, Austria
[3] Institute of Computer Technology, TU Wien, Vienna, Austria
`kaindl@ict.tuwien.ac.at`

Abstract. Graphical User Interface (GUI) development is time-consuming and error-prone. Hence, automated GUI generation from higher-level interaction design models may become more and more important . In particular, auto-mated generation can help with interface design prototyping. The usability of fully-automatically generated GUIs is considered unsatisfactory, however. Manual changes to the generated GUI itself would need to be made persistent. Hence, we proposed *customization rules* on a higher level of abstraction, and changes of style sheets. This paper presents a new user study on whether this kind of customization can actually improve generated GUIs. This study achieved statistically significant results that the *adjusted task time* of the customized version is less than that of the fully-automatically generated one. The subjective results indicated that attractiveness and wording were improved through customization.

Keywords: User study · Automated GUI generation · Interface design prototyping · Interaction design · Usability

1 Introduction

Previously, we devised and implemented a unique approach to automated GUI generation based on *communicative acts* [1] (as abstractions from speech acts), which can model basic building blocks of communication, like a question or an answer. Based on communicative acts, we defined high-level interaction design models, which contain *discourse models* for specifying all the possible discourses in the sense of dialogues [2]. The automated GUI generation is based on model-transformation rules according to the model-driven architecture [3, 4]. Based on this technology, we created a specific transformation engine [5] and, on top of it, a tool for automated GUI generation [6]. Based on AI optimization techniques, it tailors GUIs automatically to a device such as a smartphone according to a given device specification [7].

David Raneburger and Roman Popp did this work when they were with the Institute of Computer Technology at TU Wien.

N. L. Black et al. (Eds.): IEA 2021, LNNS 223, pp. 683–690, 2022.
https://doi.org/10.1007/978-3-030-74614-8_85

Already some time ago, we studied *end-user modeling* of interaction design based on our approach [8]. Later, we defined a process for facilitating interaction design through automated GUI generation using our tool support [9].

Still, the general problem has persisted that the usability of fully-automatically generated GUIs is not satisfactory. There are certain inherent problems that require *customization*, which we supported both through *custom widgets* [10] and *customization rules* [11].

The concrete research question of this paper is whether *customization rules* as a specific approach to customization can actually improve generated GUIs. We designed and performed a user study along the lines of our own previous user studies, which compared GUIs generated according to differently tailoring strategies and for different devices, see e.g., [12, 13].

The remainder of this paper is organized in the following manner. First, we explain the user study design. Based on it, we present the results of the user study. Finally, we provide a short conclusion.

2 User Study Design

We combined quantitative data (task completion time) with subjective data (user questionnaires and interviews) [14, 15]. In particular, we designed this user study as an experiment similarly to [16], where touchscreen usability (via hyperlink clicks) was investigated.

2.1 Setup

We compared two different versions of a GUI with the same overall layout, tailored for a small smartphone. The first version was generated fully-automatically (GUI-A). For this GUI, a heuristic evaluation of the automatically generated screens had been performed. It revealed a specific usability problem that we addressed later by a *customization rule*. The second version was essentially the same as GUI-A, but customized through this *customization* rule, and a different style sheet given as a CSS file, (GUI-C). Both GUIs were presented using the standard Web browser.

The application was a simplified bike-rental scenario consisting of five GUI screens listed and explained in Table 1. Figures 1 and 2 show screenshots of the two versions of Screen 3 as compared.[1] For GUI-A, a heuristic evaluation of the automatically generated screens had been performed in the course of a project. It revealed for this particular screen shown in Fig. 1 that too much information is given in the course of saying "Hello", actually everything available in the Domain-of-Discourse model [6]. This was addressed later by a *customization* rule for reducing this information, where Fig. 2 shows the result of automated generation employing this rule.

---

[1] At the time of this user study, the *Final User Interface* was implemented using HTML 4.0, CSS and JavaScript.

Table 1. List of Screens for Bike-rental.

Screen 1	presents a login dialog and a button leading to registration as a new user.
Screen 2	presents a form for registration of a new user.
Screen 3	says Hello and requests the user to select one of the bikes.
Screen 4	requests confirmation of the rental.
Screen 5	asks whether the user wants to return the bike rent.

Fig. 1. Screen 3 of GUI-A   **Fig. 2.** Screen 3 of GUI-C

Our user study investigated the *correlation* between the time a user needed for a given task on a given screen on the GUI version used. In addition, we collected *subjective opinions* on several usability-related questions through a questionnaire and, sometimes, a brief and informal interview.

2.2 Participants

We hired 47 participants of about the same age and about the same level of education (students). All participants had to perform the given task twice, once with each of the two GUI versions. We split the participants into two groups, however, reversing the order according to a *within-subject design*.

2.3 Procedure

At the beginning of each trial, we informed the participant about the content of the study and the procedure. We emphasized that the point was to test the GUIs, not the skill of the participants. We asked each participant to fill in some background data and to give consent to recording the voice and filming the hands operating the smartphone (for subsequent video annotation). We fixed the smartphone to the table in portrait mode, since the Web GUI used has actually been tailored for this mode. Filming and video annotation would have been difficult if the participants were holding the device.

Before starting the video camera, we explained the following scenario, leaving a print-out version in front of the participant, so that s(he) did not have to remember the data:

You are at Salzburg train station. You want to rent a bike at the terminal in front of the station with your smartphone to explore the city. To do so you:
Register yourself (you are Thomas Huber, username Huber, password huber75, phone number 0123456) with your MASTERCARD (number 1234 5678 9012 4567, valid thru 12/21) and rent out Bike5. Finally you log out and head towards the city center.

We especially emphasized the urgency of the task, so that the participant would concentrate on the task and finish it as quickly as possible. The task specification contained all the information that needed to be entered during the task to avoid bias through different data.

After each participant completed the given task twice, according to the group assigned, we collected the subjective opinion on several usability-related issues through a questionnaire and finally asked for any further comments, if provided, in a brief interview.

2.4 Analysis

For our analysis, we were primarily interested in the *correlations* between task time and the GUI version. An independent variable for our statistical analysis was the GUI with the two different values GUI-A and GUI-C. This variable is dichotomous, as we only compared two GUIs. A second independent variable was the order of presenting the GUIs to the participants, i.e., GUI-A first and then GUI-C, or vice versa. The dependent variable was *(adjusted) task completion time.* For the (adjusted) task completion analysis, we measured the total time a test participant spent on a screen for solving the given task. In addition, we measured the time needed for text input (on the keyboard), the time for loading the screen and submitting information, and the time for validation and error messages, since these are independent of the specific GUI version used and may bias the results due to irrelevant random effects. Therefore, we subtracted all these times from the total time, resulting in adjusted task time, which includes orientation on the screen, widget selection with fingers, and value selection from widgets.

As the type of GUI is dichotomous and the calculated time is on an interval scale, we calculated the *point-biserial Pearson correlation coefficients.* Our tests also showed that the variables are nearly normally distributed and, thus, satisfy the prerequisites of the point-biserial Pearson correlation. Note the difference to the more common *t-test*, which deals with differences of means.

The corresponding *null hypothesis* is a *correlation hypothesis* as follows:

NH_{AC}: *There is no statistically significant correlation (p-value = 0.05) between the adjusted task time and the type of Web GUI: GUI-A and GUI-C.*

All tests were taped on video to facilitate the data extraction. We used the video-annotation tool Anvil[2] to precisely extract the task completion time, which we subsequently converted to Comma Separated Value (CSV) lists and put into SPSS to perform the statistical analysis.

The participants were also given a *subjective usability questionnaire* for collecting information on how they perceived usability. With some adaptations, our definition of usability was based on [17], which synthesizes the best-known usability definitions in the literature at the time. We discarded those usability characteristics that were irrelevant for the Web GUIs compared, and tried to phrase the usability criteria as short and self-explanatory questions, for which we also consulted the USE Questionnaire[3], the W3C's WAI[4], the Software Usability Measurement Inventory[5] (SUMI) and the Cognitive Dimensions framework [18]. Table 2 shows the questions that we selected for use in our questionnaire.

Table 2. Questions of the questionnaire with subjective results.

	GUI-A extremely	GUI-A strongly	GUI-A moderately	Equal	GUI-C moderately	GUI-C strongly	GUI-C extremely
Which interface is visually more attractive?	0	4	11	6	15	9	2
Which interface makes interaction more intuitive?	0	2	11	21	6	7	0
Which interface makes it easier to figure out what to do next?	0	5	11	17	7	6	1
Which interface makes it clearer how to use it?	0	4	8	24	5	6	0
Which interface demands less time from you?	2	1	7	26	8	3	0
Which interface is easier to handle errors on?	0	1	5	35	5	0	1
Which interface uses a more natural wording?	0	2	5	28	8	3	1
Overall, which interface would you use to rent a bike?	1	2	10	12	11	8	3

For each question, the participant had to state the preferred GUI version on a Likert scale with preference being "extreme", "strong", "moderate", and "equal". The participants were explicitly asked to focus on the differences between the versions of the Web GUI, rather than evaluate the usability of each version independently. The reason is that for our study, which compares different versions, their difference is relevant. Measuring usability on an absolute scale is more difficult and not necessary for our study.

---

[2] https://www.anvil-software.org/.

[3] https://www.stcsig.org/usability/newsletter/0110_measuring_with_use.html.

[4] https://www.w3.org/WAI/EO/Drafts/UCD/questions.html.

[5] https://sumi.ucc.ie/en/.

3   User Study Results

The results of our study consist of the statistical analyses of adjusted task time together with a brief evaluation of the subjective questionnaires.

3.1   Adjusted Task Time Analysis

Table 3 summarizes the statistical results for the adjusted task time analysis. The negative correlations in this table indicate that the performance using GUI-C is better than the performance using GUI-A, with statistically significant results. The performance on Screen 1 is an exception here, and this result is not statistically significant. In fact, this screen was visible upfront, so that the times measured for it can actually not be taken into account. Hence, the null hypothesis NH_{AC} can be rejected for this experiment for Screens 2, 3, 4 and 5.

Table 3.   Correlation between adjusted task time on a screen and its version.

	Pearson Corr.	Sig. (1-tailed)	*GUI-A* av. time	*GUI-C* av. time
Time Screen1 × GUI	+0.078	0.318	18.71s	29.84s
Time Screen2 × GUI	**−0.421**	0.004	47.65s	49.25s
Time Screen3 × GUI	**−0.612**	0.000	11.10s	8.49s
Time Screen4 × GUI	**−0.563**	0.000	9.06s	5.04s
Time Screen5 × GUI	**−0.325**	0.043	6.90s	5.03 s

3.2   Subjective Results

Table 2 summarizes the subjective results, where the numbers of participants are listed that selected the corresponding answer on the Likert scale of the questionnaire. A remarkable result is that subjectively the time demand was slightly judged less for GUI-A than for GUI-C by the participants, while the measured data contradict this. The measured result is statistically significant, but this subjective result may well come from chance fluctuation. When comparing the two versions as exemplified through Screen 3 in Figs. 1 and 2, the changes through CSS and the customization rule are reflected in the subjective results about attractiveness and wording. Overall, the participants seem to have slightly preferred GUI-C over GUI-A.

In the final interviews, the majority of statements were in favor of GUI-C, the customized version. For instance, a participant said that the customized Web GUI is more intuitive and logical. Another participant indicated that she finds both GUIs easy to use, but she prefers the customized one. And yet another one said that both GUIs are more or less the same but she prefers the customized one.

With regard to potentially using this bike rental application in real life, the participants actually did not distinguish between the two versions. On participant said that she finds the bike rental application OK and would use it in real life, another one would use the bike rental application in real life, if this would be a product of a known company. Actually, several participants took this prototype so seriously as to worry about giving credit their card number without any security systems, or found it strange that you do not need to fill in the MasterCard CCV number. Another participant said that he is having a second thought about using this application in real life, because there are not written any terms of use and he misses signs of internet protection.

4 Conclusion

Since the usability of fully-automatically generated GUIs generally is not satisfactory because of inherent problems, we previously enhanced our approach and tool support with *customization*, which we supported both through custom widgets [10] and customization rules [11]. In this paper, we report on a user study on the question of whether *customization rules* as a specific approach to customization can actually improve generated GUIs.

The statistically significant experimental results of our study and subjective opinions collected suggest that customization on a higher level of an interaction design using *customization rules* can improve generated GUIs. As another promising approach to improving usability even for users with low-vision accessibility, we more recently proposed a combination with *responsive design* [19].

References

1. Falb, J., Popp, R., Röck, T., Jelinek, H., Arnautovic, E., Kaindl, H.: Using communicative acts in interface design specifications for automated synthesis of user interfaces. In: Proceedings of the 21st IEEE/ACM International Conference on Automated Software Engineering, pp. 261–264 (2006)
2. Bogdan, C., Falb, J., Kaindl, H., Kavaldjian, S., Popp, R., Horacek, H., Arnautovic, E., Szep, A.: Generating an abstract user interface from a discourse model inspired by human communication. In: Proceedings of the 41st Hawaii International Conference on System Sciences. IEEE, Waikoloa (2008)
3. Kavaldjian, S., Bogdan, C., Falb, J., Kaindl, H.: Transforming discourse models to structural user interface models, models in software engineering. In: MoDELS 2007 Workshops, LNCS 5002, pp. 77–88. Springer-Verlag, Berlin-Heidelberg (invited) (2008)
4. Raneburger, D., Popp, R., Kaindl, H., Falb, J., Ertl, D.: Automated generation of device-specific WIMP-UIs: weaving of structural and behavioral models. In: Proceedings of the 2011 SIGCHI Symposium on Engineering Interactive Computing Systems (eics'11), 2011.
5. Popp, R., Falb, J., Raneburger, D., Kaindl, H.: A transformation engine for model-driven UI generation. In: Proceedings of the 4th ACM SIGCHI Symposium on Engineering Interactive Computing Systems (eics´12), Copenhagen, Denmark (2012)
6. Popp, R., Raneburger, D., Kaindl, H.: Tool support for automated multi-device GUI Generation from discourse-based communication models. In: Proceedins of the ACM SIGCHI Symposium on Engineering Interactive Computing Systems (eics'13) (2013)
7. Raneburger, D., Kaindl, H., Popp, R.: Strategies for automated GUI tailoring for multiple devices. In: Proceedings of the 48st Annual Hawaii International Conference on System Sciences (HICSS-48) (2015)

690   D. Raneburger et al.

8. Bogdan, C., Kaindl, H., Falb, J., Popp, R.: Modeling of interaction design by end users through discourse modeling. In: Proceedings of the 2008 ACM International Conference on Intelligent User Interfaces (IUI'08), Maspalomas, Gran Canaria. ACM Press, Spain (2008)
9. Raneburger, D., Kaindl, H., Popp, R., Šajatovic, V., Armbruster, A.: A process for facilitating interaction design through automated GUI generation. In: Proceedings of the 29th ACM/SIGAPP Symposium on Applied Computing (SAC'14) (2014)
10. Rathfux, T., Popp, R., Kaindl, H.: Adding custom widgets to model-driven GUI generation. In: Proceedings of the 8th ACM SIGCHI Symposium on Engineering Interactive Computing Systems (eics'16), Brussels, Belgium (2016)
11. Raneburger, D., Kaindl, H., Popp, R.: Model Transformation rules for customization of multi-device graphical user interfaces. In: Proceedings of the 7th ACM SIGCHI Symposium on Engineering Interactive Computing Systems (eics'15), pp. 100–109 (2015)
12. Raneburger, D., Alonso-Ríos, D., Popp, R., Kaindl, H., Falb, J.: A user study with GUIs tailored for smartphones. In: Human-Computer Interaction – INTERACT 2013 (Heidelberg) (Lecture Notes in Computer Science), vol. 8118. pp. 505–512. Springer (2013)
13. Raneburger, D., Popp, R., Alonso-Ríos, D., Kaindl, H., Falb, J: A user study with GUIs tailored for smartphones and tablet PCs. In: Proceedings of the 2013 IEEE International Conference on Systems, Man and Cybernetics (SMC'13), pp. 3727–3732 (2013)
14. Buchanan, G., Farrant, S., Jones, M., Thimbleby, H., Marsden, G., Pazzani, M.: Improving mobile internet usability. In Proceedings of the 10th international conference on World Wide Web (Hong Kong, Hong Kong) (WWW '01), pp. 673–680. ACM, New York (2001)
15. Jones, M., Marsden, G., Mohd-Nasir, N., Boone, K., Buchanan, G.: Improving Web interaction on small displays. Comput. Netw. 31, 1, 1129–1137 (1999). 1–16 (May 1999)
16. Watanabe, W.M., Pontin de Mattos Fortes, R., da Graça Campos Pimentel, M.: The link-offset-scale mechanism for improving the usability of touch screen displays on the web. In: Proceedings of the 13th IFIP TC 13 International Conference on Human-Computer Interaction - Volume Part III (Lisbon, Portugal) (INTERACT'11), pp. 356–372. Springer-Verlag, Heidelberg (2011)
17. Alonso-Ríos, D., Vázquez-García, A., Mosqueira-Rey, E., Moret-Bonillo, V.: Usability: a critical analysis and a taxonomy. Int. J. Hum. Comput. Interact. 26(1), 53–74 (2010)
18. Blackwell, A.F., Britton, C., Cox, A., Green, T.R.G., Gurr, C., Kadoda, G., Kutar, M.S., Loomes, M., Nehaniv, C.L., Petre, M., Roast, C., Roe, C., Wong, A., Young, R.M.: cognitive dimensions of notations: design tools for cognitive technology. In: Beynon, M., Nehaniv, C., Dautenhahn, K. (eds.) Cognitive Technology: Instruments of Mind. Lecture Notes in Computer Science, vol. 2117, pp. 325–341. Springer, Heidelberg (2001)
19. Rathfux, T., Thöner, H., Popp, K.R.: Combining design-time generation of web-pages with responsive design for improving low-vision accessibility. In: Proceedings of the ACM SIGCHI Symposium on Engineering Interactive Computing Systems (eics'18), Paris (2018)

A Framework for Future Navigation Aids

Adam J. Reiner[1]($\boxtimes$), Greg A. Jamieson[1], and Justin G. Hollands[2]

[1] University of Toronto, Toronto, Canada
adam.reiner@mail.utoronto.ca
[2] Defence Research and Development Canada, Toronto, Canada

Abstract. We have developed a new framework for navigation aids that focuses on how spatial information can be presented with advances in display technology. Our framework focuses on the relationship between the navigator and spatial information within an aid in two ways, i) perspective or scene-dependence of the aid's presentation, and ii) the aid's ability to sense and adapt to the navigator's context. Examples of aids in each category are provided and their effect on navigation tasks is discussed.

Keywords: Navigation · Wayfinding · Map · GPS · Augmented Reality

1 Introduction

Advances in display and information technology have changed humans' relationship with their environment. These technologies can determine the user's location, through Global Positioning Systems (GPS), and provide contextually relevant cues directly over their view of the environment, through Augmented Reality (AR) displays. The knowledge required to navigate an unfamiliar environment has been greatly reduced as many of the planning and decision-making tasks can be supplanted by smart devices. However, this availability of spatial information may negatively affect spatial abilities without an aid [8]. To characterize the benefits and limitations of current and future navigation aids, a new framework for discussing navigation aids is described. This framework takes into account the ability of the aid to collect and display spatial information, and its relationship with the user.

2 Navigation

Navigation is "coordinated and goal-directed movement through the environment" ([12], p. 257). This definition of navigation incorporates both *wayfinding,* the goal-directed planning of movement through an environment, and *locomotion,* the physical act of moving through a directly perceptible environment. Locomotion in this chapter will primarily be considered in its relationship to wayfinding. As new information becomes available, a navigator may need to re-orient and re-plan. Possible routes will be affected by method of locomotion, including travel speed and affordances.

© The Author(s), under exclusive license to Springer Nature Switzerland AG 2022
N. L. Black et al. (Eds.): IEA 2021, LNNS 223, pp. 691–698, 2022.
https://doi.org/10.1007/978-3-030-74614-8_86

Wayfinding and Spatial Knowledge. Given its goal-directed nature, navigation generally relates to reaching a destination. As the environment becomes more complicated (e.g., greater distances, no direct access, lack of visibility), more information about the environment is required for wayfinding. This information can be internal (i.e., existing as spatial knowledge) or external (i.e., provided by an aid) to the navigator. While much of the rest of this chapter focuses on the external, the internal representation is also important and is briefly considered first.

Internal spatial knowledge develops from both direct environmental experience and by studying external representations [19]. Spatial information and knowledge can be considered *scene-dependent* (SD) or *scene-independent* (SI) [26]. SD spatial information relies on self-to-object relations, commonly referred to as egocentric, and changes with the navigator's position and orientation within the environment. SI spatial information relies on the relative positions of objects to each other, referred to as allocentric, regardless of the navigator's position within (or outside of) an environment. *Survey information*—the topographic layout of a given environment—is commonly conflated with an SI perspective since that is how it is often presented (e.g., paper maps).

2.1 Aids for Navigation

A navigation aid is an external representation of spatial information separate from the environment. Navigation aids may either support or supplant some aspects of, or the entirety of, a navigation task or set of tasks. Spatial visualization and information access tasks are performed when using aids.

Spatial Visualization. Spatial information acquired from an aid must be translated into the navigator's own frame of reference (FOR), and vice versa, through spatial visualization [10]. Spatial visualization is the mental manipulation, rotation, twisting, or inversion of two- or three-dimensional pictorially presented visual stimuli [5]. In navigation, this is a continuous process of imagining and translating information or cues from one source to another. Examples include relating a marker on a map to the environment or recognizing cues in the environment that relate to the next turn depicted by an aid. As the difference between two FORs increases, comparing information between them becomes more difficult, negatively affecting accuracy, response time, and/or mental workload [22].

Information Access. Information access cost (IAC) [23] refers to the expenditure of resources (predominantly physical effort, increasing from eye to head to body movement) to acquire information from a navigation aid or the environment. Increases in IAC have been shown to affect both information-seeking behaviour and performance, resulting in greater reliance on more error-prone knowledge in the head, rather than knowledge in the world as IAC increases [6].

2.2 Navigation Tasks

Wiener et al. [24] developed a taxonomy of unaided wayfinding tasks using Montello's [12] definition of navigation. Wiener et al. categorized tasks according to the spatial knowledge of the navigator using Siegel and White's [18] framework of landmark, route, and survey knowledge. Wiener et al. define landmark and route knowledge as knowledge about the destination (they do not consider other landmarks) and the path to the destination, respectively, whereas survey knowledge is described as 'cognitive-map-like' integrated knowledge of the environment.

Wayfinding Tasks. Wiener et al.'s [24] taxonomy of unaided wayfinding presents a framework based on existing spatial knowledge. Other researchers have employed sequential or hierarchical descriptions of the required tasks. Passini [15] describes wayfinding as a process of spatial problem solving, where navigators continuously develop a hierarchical decision plan to accomplish the goal of reaching a destination. Farr et al. [4] break wayfinding down into four subtasks: 1) orientation, 2) route planning, 3) route control (which requires locomotion), and 4) destination recognition. These wayfinding subtasks serve as the basis for the discussion of navigation tasks.

Orientation is the task of understanding location and heading with respect to a relative or absolute reference point (e.g., a landmark) or within an absolute coordinate system (e.g., latitude and longitude). A navigator may keep track of a reference point as they locomote through the environment to update their understanding of relative position.

Route planning is the task of determining a path through an environment; that is, a set of sequential actions for travel between two locations. If the destination is visible or its relative direction known, then the route may be as simple as a straight line towards the destination until a turn is required. Spatial information like directional cues through signs or survey information through maps can further support route planning.

Route control necessitates locomotion with the additional cognitive tasks of confirming that the navigator is on the planned route and that the route is still viable, (e.g., not obstructed). If the navigator finds themselves off route or the route is non-viable, the plan will need to be updated, returning to route planning.

Destination Recognition. During route control, the navigator will need to relate information about the destination to what is visible in the environment to determine when they have reached the destination. Relating cues in the environment to those held by the navigator (internally or externally) is also an aspect of spatial visualization.

Spatial Learning. Spatial knowledge can be gained through direct experience and/or studying survey information [19, 26]. Intentional spatial learning can fit within the definition of navigation (i.e., goal-directed movement could be a means to gain spatial knowledge), although incidental learning can also occur while navigating.

Current Descriptions of Navigation Aids. As with tasks in Wiener et al.'s [24] unaided wayfinding taxonomy, descriptions of navigation aids have commonly been based on Siegel and White's [18] model of spatial knowledge. While the landmark-route-survey hierarchy may be suited to describing more traditional aids, (e.g., SD directions and SI paper maps), new technology has enabled new presentations of spatial information. Smartphones present survey maps with turn-by-turn directions, changing the interaction and knowledge required to navigate. AR displays that can overlay spatial information onto the navigator's direct view may further change this relationship. A framework that accounts for an aid's capabilities and perspectives should better assist the understanding of how and when navigation aids work than those based on spatial knowledge development alone. The information available for a given task will change how that task is performed, so this framework should be able to better describe how navigation tasks are supported by each category of aid.

3   A Framework for Navigation Aids

Table 1 categorizes navigation aids by their perspective on spatial information, or scene-dependence, and context adaptability, as static or dynamic. Scene-dependence is continuous, as aids may have both SD and SI features or the ability to change perspective. A paper map's SI perspective is fixed, whereas directions are SD and will depend on a navigator's position and orientation in the environment. Electronic maps are primarily SI, though commonly include some SD features such as centering on the navigator's position and track-up rotation. Perspective differs from whether route or survey information is presented. For example, route directions are SD (e.g., turn left), but a route could be described in SI terms (e.g., as a set of geographic coordinates).

For context adaptability, moving from left to right in Table 1 reflects advances in technology from paper, to screens, to head worn AR. Dynamic aids can also sense navigator context, from position and heading to environment depth and shape. By considering how aids from each general category support navigation, the effects of technological advances in the presentation of spatial information can be investigated and used to consider the viability of future navigation aids. In particular, the presentation of survey information has trended towards adopting more SD features as technology can sense context and continuously update its presentation.

Table 1.   Framework for navigation aids.

Perspective on Spatial Information	Context Adaptability		
	Static	Dynamic	
		Screen-based Aids Senses: **Position, Heading** Display: **Screen**	Augmenting Aids Senses: **Environment** Display: **AR**
Scene-Independent	*Paper Map* *You-Are-Here Maps*	*Electronic Map*	*Virtual Window Map*
Scene-Dependent	*Directions*	*Route GPS*	*SkyMap* *Landmark/Route Cues*

3.1   Static Aids

For static aids, content must be set in advance and designed for a purpose. As a result, static aids commonly fit into the distinction of SI as survey and SD as route information. Although it is possible to present survey information from an SD perspective, such as in some You-Are-Here maps, survey information is predominantly SI. A considerable literature exists regarding human factors issues with static aids [2, 13].

Paper Maps. Spatial visualization with a paper map requires the translation of cues between the map's 2D SI FOR and the navigator's 3D SD FOR. Paper maps commonly have a north-up presentation, so the navigator will need to align the map's FOR with their own by physically or cognitively rotating the paper map or their position. These alignments increase IAC and spatial visualization effort, respectively, with degree of misalignment [13]. Error and workload also increase with misalignment [1, 22]. A navigator will need to relate 2D distances on the map to 3D depth in their own FOR, which will be affected by the map's scale.

Paper maps support wayfinding in unfamiliar environments by providing survey information. Orientation with a paper map requires the use of environmental cues to determine their position and heading relative to the map. Route planning with a map allows a navigator to view the possible routes between two points where an appropriate path can then be determined. Paper maps may present other valuable information for planning, such as one-way streets, although cannot adapt to changing conditions. Route control requires the navigator to reach a point on the planned route and then periodically update their position in the environment relative to the paper map to determine whether they are on course.

Paper maps support navigation tasks by presenting the underlying SI spatial structure of an environment, providing the flexibility to decide how to operate within that structure [20]. Directions can supplant the cognitively effortful task of route planning but rely on navigators to follow them correctly. If an error is made, directions are no longer useful unless the navigator can recover from that error.

3.2 Dynamic Aids: Screen-Based Displays

As smartphones become more ubiquitous, paper maps and static direction lists are increasingly being replaced by dynamic aids that (if working as intended) have the flexibility and convenience of both types of aid. Screen-based displays can provide the navigator with relevant spatial cues. Electronic maps often allow the navigator to switch between north-up or track-up map presentation and adjust scale. Spatial visualization with electronic maps requires similar cognitive transformations as with a paper map. Some transformations, like rotation, can be performed on demand or automatically by the aid, while others, particularly scaling distances, still need to be performed by the navigator. The IAC of an electronic map is like a paper one; it needs to be held and brought into view through some combination of arm and head movements. Interacting with the survey information directly (e.g., zooming or scrolling) differs considerably between paper and screen-based presentations.

Electronic maps have changed the knowledge and effort required for most wayfinding subtasks. For orientation, position is determined through geolocation and a self-marker is placed on the electronic map. Searching for a destination can be completed by typing in a name or address and the aid can then supplant route planning by generating a route from the navigator's position to the destination. Turn-by-turn directions are provided and automatically updated if a mistake is made. Some situational information, like traffic patterns and road closures, can also be shown. With electronic maps, most wayfinding subtasks can be supplanted with other actions, requiring less prior knowledge or effort.

In general, electronic aids have shown faster completion time and lower mental workload than paper maps on route control tasks [3, 16].

Some screen-based aids can change their presentation of survey information from SI to SD during route control to provide the navigator with perspective on the environment. The viewpoint for this type of SD survey map is commonly above and behind the navigator, tethered to a self-marker [7], adapting with the navigator's speed to provide more context or detail. This SD survey information may be closer to a navigator's own FOR and support spatial visualization better than SI perspectives.

There is evidence that navigators using electronic maps can be less engaged with or aware of their surroundings [21]. Reduced environment engagement can prevent the development of spatial knowledge [8, 14]. Current electronic maps are also bound by the limitations of the device including screen space, IAC, and limited understanding of the navigator's direct surroundings. Device limitations also include need for a network connection (e.g., cell reception), processing speed, and battery life.

3.3 Dynamic Aids: Augmented Reality Displays

AR displays superimpose virtual imagery over the environment, either on a lens or screen. This can include any smart device that acquires information from the environment and presents an augmented version of it. Using continuous input of the environment and device orientation, AR displays create the appearance of interaction with the navigator's surrounding. Virtual spatial information appears at the intended depth and orientation, updating as the navigator moves through the environment.

Although augmenting aids are SD by nature, they may offer improved presentations of SI survey information. An SI 2D map could be presented in a virtual window not subject to the physical limits of a screen. Figure 1 depicts **three kinds of** augmenting aids (in purple), including virtual landmark and route cues overlaid on the environment, **an** SI virtual windowed map, and SkyMap [9]. Current augmenting aids are largely limited to overlaying route and landmark cues in the navigator's view of the environment [11]. Overlaid cues (e.g., highlighting a landmark or marking the next turn) can reduce spatial visualization and IAC but their overuse can increase display clutter [25].

Few concepts for presenting survey information from an SD perspective in augmenting aids have been considered, though SkyMap (Fig. 1, top) is one of the first. SkyMap presents large scale SD survey information aligned with the environment from a navigator's perspective. Alignment, amongst other features, makes SkyMap's support for navigation tasks characteristically different from any previously discussed aids and has showed some promising initial results for spatial visualization [17].

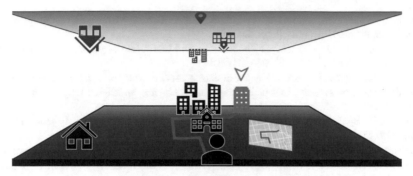

Fig. 1. Augmenting aids

4 Conclusion

A new framework to describe and characterize how current and future navigation aids may support navigation tasks was introduced. Building on frameworks for characterizing spatial knowledge [24], our framework considers the perspective and context adaptability of an aid and how that aid may support various navigation tasks. Examples from different aid categories within the framework are then described to highlight how this framework may be used to discuss navigation aids in the future.

References

1. Aretz, A.J.: The design of electronic map displays. Hum. Factors **33**(1), 85–101 (1991)
2. Castro, C., Horberry, T.: The Human Factors of Transport Signs. CRC Press (2004)
3. de Waard, D., Westerhuis, F., Joling, D., Weiland, S., Stadtbäumer, R., Kaltofen, L.: Visual map and instruction-based bicycle navigation: a comparison of effects on behaviour. Ergonomics **60**(9), 1283–1296 (2017)
4. Farr, A.C., Kleinschmidt, T., Yarlagadda, P., Mengersen, K.: Wayfinding: a simple concept, a complex process. Transp. Rev. **32**(6), 715–743 (2012)
5. Golledge, R.G., Dougherty, V., Bell, S.: Acquiring spatial knowledge: survey versus route-based knowledge in unfamiliar environments. Ann. Assoc. Am. Geogr. **85**(1), 134–158 (1995)
6. Gray, W.D., Fu, W.: Soft constraints in interactive behavior: the case of ignoring perfect knowledge in-the-world for imperfect knowledge in-the-head. Cogn. Sci. **28**(3), 359–382 (2004)
7. Hollands, J.G., Lamb, M.: Viewpoint tethering for remotely operated vehicles: effects on complex terrain navigation and spatial awareness. Hum. Factors **53**(2), 154–167 (2011)
8. Ishikawa, T.: Satellite navigation and geospatial awareness: long-term effects of using navigation tools on wayfinding and spatial orientation. Prof. Geogr. **71**(2), 197–209 (2019)
9. Kapler, T., King, R., Segura, D.: "SkyMap": world-scale immersive spatial display. In: Symposium on Spatial User Interaction, pp. 1–3 (2019)
10. Lobben, A.K.: Tasks, strategies, and cognitive processes associated with navigational map reading: a review perspective. Prof. Geogr. **56**(2), 270–281 (2004)
11. Medenica, Z., Kun, A.L., Paek, T., Palinko, O.: Augmented reality vs. street views. In: Proceedings of the 13th International Conference on Human Computer Interaction with Mobile Devices and Services - MobileHCI 2011, p. 265 (2011)

12. Montello, D.R.: Navigation. In: The Cambridge Handbook of Visuospatial Thinking, pp. 257–294. Cambridge University Press (2005)
13. Montello, D.R.: You are where? The function and frustration of you-are-here (YAH) maps. Spat. Cogn. Comput. **10**(2–3), 94–104 (2010)
14. Parush, A., Ahuvia, S., Erev, I.: Degradation in spatial knowledge acquisition when using automatic navigation systems. In: Spatial Information Theory, pp. 238–254. Springer, Heidelberg (2007)
15. Passini, R.: Spatial representations, a wayfinding perspective. J. Environ. Psychol. **4**(2), 153–164 (1984)
16. Rehman, U., Cao, S.: Augmented-reality-based indoor navigation: a comparative analysis of handheld devices versus Google glass. IEEE Trans. Hum.-Mach. Syst. **47**(1), 1–12 (2016)
17. Reiner, A.J., Hollands, J.G., Jamieson, G.A., Boustila, S.: A mirror in the sky: assessment of an augmented reality method for depicting navigational information. Ergonomics **63**(5), 548–562 (2020)
18. Siegel, A.W., White, S.H.: The development of spatial representations of large-scale environments. In: Advances in child development and behavior, vol. 10, pp. 9–55 (1975)
19. Thorndyke, P.W., Hayes-Roth, B.: Differences in spatial knowledge acquired and navigation from maps. Cogn. Psychol. **589**(14), 560–589 (1982)
20. Vicente, K.J.: Cognitive Work Analysis. CRC Press (1999)
21. Waters, W., Winter, S.: A wayfinding aid to increase navigator independence. J. Spat. Inf. Sci. **3**(3), 103–122 (2011)
22. Wickens, C.D., Keller, J.W., Small, R.L.: Left. No, right! Development of the frame of reference transformation tool (FORT). In: Proceedings of the Human Factors and Ergonomics Society Annual Meeting, vol. 54, no. 13, pp. 1022–1026 (2010)
23. Wickens, C.D., McCarley, J.: Applied attention theory. In: Applied Attention Theory. CRC Press (2007)
24. Wiener, J.M., Büchner, S.J., Hölscher, C.: Taxonomy of human wayfinding tasks: a knowledge-based approach. Spat. Cogn. Comput. **9**(2), 152–165 (2009)
25. Yeh, M., Merlo, J.L., Wickens, C.D., Brandenburg, D.L.: Head up versus head down: the costs of imprecision, unreliability, and visual clutter on cue effectiveness for display signaling. Hum. Factors **45**(3), 390–407 (2003)
26. Zhang, H., Zherdeva, K., Ekstrom, A.D.: Different "routes" to a cognitive map: dissociable forms of spatial knowledge derived from route and cartographic map learning. Mem. Cogn. **42**(7), 1106–1117 (2014)

Explainable AI for Entertainment: Issues on Video on Demand Platforms

Cinthia Ruiz$^{(\boxtimes)}$ ⓘ and Manuela Quaresma ⓘ

LEUI, Laboratory of Ergodesign and Usability of Interfaces, PUC-Rio, Rio de Janeiro, Brazil
cinthiaruiz@aluno.puc-rio.br, mquaresma@puc-rio.br

Abstract. With the proliferation of Artificial Intelligence-based systems, several questions arise involving ethical principles. In addition, the human-centered approach takes the focus on the user experience with these systems and studies user needs. A growing issue is the relationship between the transparency of these systems and the trust of users, since most systems are considered black-boxes. In this scenario, the Explainable Artificial Intelligence (XAI) emerges, with the proposal to explain the rationale of the decision making of the algorithms. XAI then starts to gain space in systems that involve high risk, such as health. Our research aims to discuss the importance of transparency to improve the user experience with recommendation mechanisms for entertainment, such as Video on Demand (VoD) platforms. In addition, we intent to raise the adjacent consequences of including XAI, such as improving the control and trust of VoD platforms. For this, we conducted an exploratory research method named Directed Storytelling. The study was conducted with thirty-one participants, all users of VoD platforms, regardless of time and frequency of use of this kind of systems. We note that people understand that there is an automated mechanism making recommendations for content in a personalized way for them, based on their browsing history, but the rules are not explicit. Thus, many users are suspicious of being manipulated by the system's recommendations and resort to external recommendations, such as tips from third parties or Internet searches through specialized channels.

Keywords: Explainable AI (XAI) · Artificial Intelligence (AI) · User Experience (UX) · Machine Learning (ML) · Video on Demand (VoD) platform

1 Introduction

Artificial Intelligence (AI) is increasingly present in our lives, through several digital systems. Machine Learning (ML), a branch of AI, offers recommendations for the daily decisions of a very diverse audience. AI has become popular again thanks to ML advances [1, 2]. AI is evolving in sophistication, complexity and autonomy, which opens up opportunities for transformation for business and society [2]. As a result, questions arise as to how to take advantage of its potential and what are the risks of AI, crossing the issue of trust, which makes explainability increasingly critical.

Machine learning is based on the idea that systems can learn from data, identify patterns and make decisions with minimal human intervention. Although algorithms

N. L. Black et al. (Eds.): IEA 2021, LNNS 223, pp. 699–707, 2022.
https://doi.org/10.1007/978-3-030-74614-8_87

are programmed by humans, they can find relationships between data and create their own logic. As a result, we have predictions based on logic that are not understandable to humans. That is to say, neither the development of the system, nor the end-user, know the rationale followed by ML to arrive at the result. The field of Explainable AI (XAI) attracts more and more attention, as it proposes precisely the development of methods with which the results are transparent: traceable, explainable and understandable. However, the best performing ML algorithms are usually a black-box, since they do not inform the rationale of their predictions [1, 3]. The studies [1, 2, 4–7] strongly point out the need for XAI when it involves risk, but we believe that it can be well used in the entertainment industry, as a way to increase trust and consequent user engagement with the systems. We seek to understand whether the lack of transparency in AI-based VoD (Video on Demand) platforms undermines the users' experience, as it shakes their confidence in personalized recommendations.

This research aims to discuss the validity of investing in transparency in the recommender mechanisms for entertainment, such as VoD platforms, in order to improve the user experience. In addition, we want to raise the adjacent consequences of including XAI, such as improving the control and trust of VoD platforms.

The way they are designed today, the recommendations of VoD platforms are not transparent, as they do not explain their rationale. However, users understand that there is an automated mechanism that makes content recommendations in a personalized way for them, based on their browsing history, but they are not clear about the rules and combination of factors. Thus, many users are suspicious of the system's recommendations and resort to external recommendations, such as tips from third parties or Internet searches through specialized channels.

2 Recommender System of VoD Platforms

The recommender systems of VoD platforms (e.g., Netflix and Amazon Prime) aim to select and classify films and series, in order to offer a list of recommendations in a personalized way to each user. Its objective is to streamline, facilitate and guide the choice of each user, according to their profile, amidst the large volume of content available through the platforms. ML algorithms enable customization, based on the analysis of large volumes of data at high speed.

The recommender systems of VoD platforms use some types of filters such as content-based and collaborative [8]. The content-based filter compares new content with the user's preferences to recommend it. The collaborative, on the other hand, identifies affinity between users, evaluating their interests and comparing similarities. There are also hybrid recommendations, which combine two or more techniques to overcome individual limits by combining strategies [6].

However, most recommender systems based on ML act as black-boxes, not clarifying the system logic or justification of the recommendations to the user. Thus, they run the risk of losing users' trust and not being accepted, therefore, Samih el al. [6] defend explainability. Unfortunately, the explainability of a ML model is generally inverse to its forecasting accuracy, that is, the higher the forecasting accuracy, the lower the model's explainability [7].

In the early 1990s, with the rapid expansion of the Internet, recommender systems based on collaborative filtering were invented to help users make choices in the medium of information overload. Since then, great technological advances have led to the proliferation of digital systems enhanced by the functionality of the recommendation. In this scenario, new evaluation metrics have emerged, largely based on the increase and success rates of the systems, but the accuracy of the recommender system does not guarantee user satisfaction [9].

The recommendation best evaluated by standard metrics are sometimes not the most useful for users [10]. Evaluation metrics should be user-centered and take into account the factors that impact their satisfaction [6]. Thus, there is an increase in evaluation metrics for user-centered recommender systems [11].

Some factors that increase users' confidence in a recommender system are: precision of the algorithm, transparency and the possibility of interaction with recommender systems. Transparency does not necessarily have to be a justification for the recommendation. Sometimes, a more detailed explanation of the recommended item is enough for the user to understand its logic. These explanations improve the user's trust and loyalty, consequently, increasing satisfaction, since they speed up and facilitate the choice. In addition, the explanations help in accepting unexpected news and items [11].

Transparency collaborates with users' confidence in the recommendation because they understand the reasons behind it [12]. In addition to bringing benefits such as engagement and understanding of the operation of the system, to know its limits and capabilities. From the user's perspective, transparency inspires confidence in the recommender system, as they clearly understand the inputs and outputs [13]. Gedikle, et al. [14] consider satisfaction a prerequisite for trust and their study shows that the transparency perceived by the user is a highly important factor for user satisfaction.

3 Explainable Artificial Intelligence (XAI)

XAI is as an area focused on designing intelligent systems, capable of explaining its results to a human being [15]. One of the objectives of XAI is to provide explanations about the rationale for ML algorithm recommendations [16], thus helping the user to understand and trust the system. XAI allows the system to be transparent, providing explanations of its decisions with some level of detail [17]. XAI can create models capable of summarizing the reasons for the behavior of the neural network, gaining the trust of users or producing perceptions about the causes of their decisions [17].

Oxborought et al. [2] reports that over the past 30 years, the evolution of AI has been interrupted at various times by technological limitations. However, the current technological advance is conducive to its development, since it allows the construction of increasingly powerful tools, but gaining the trust of society can be a new barrier for the evolution of AI. For this reason, the authors [2] defend the need for explainable AI. Ribera and Lapedriza [3] searched the literature for the concept of explainability and found a relationship with transparency, interpretability, trust, fairness and accountability.

An important aspect of human intelligence is our ability to explain the rationale of our decisions to other people. Explaining their decisions is an important factor in social interactions and, often, a prerequisite for establishing a trusting relationship between people, like a doctor explaining the treatment decision to his/her patient [4].

It is easy to see the importance of XAI when there is a high risk involved, as in the medical field, for example. An ML-based system can assist in the diagnosis of patients and recommend treatment, but the vision of a specialist doctor is indispensable for the final decision. The transparency of this system is vital for confidence in its predictions. In turn, trust is essential for engaging in the use of the system. In these critical decision-making tasks, the explainability in the recommender system is important for users to understand, trust and manage the results [6].

As machines begin to replace humans in their decisions, it becomes necessary for these mechanisms to explain themselves. Despite achieving success in several areas, there is a general suspicion about their results, a problem that could be solved with explainability [17]. In contrast, Oxborought et al. [2] point out that when referring to recommender systems, most users trust the results, without the need for transparency of the ML algorithm, since there would be easy understanding and low risk. We believe that even for entertainment, transparency brings gains to the user experience. Bharadhwaj and Joshi [18], for defending the explainability of the recommendations, proposed a model and tested it with the Netflix dataset, demonstrating the effectiveness of the prediction accuracy and explainability. The authors describe a framework for explainable temporal recommendations in a Deep Learning model, considering a neighborhood based scheme for generating explanations.

For the XAI behavior of a system to be adequate to the needs and expectations of users, at the right time and format, one must consider who will receive the explanation, why the explanation is necessary and the context in which the explanation will be presented [19]. To ensure a good user experience, it is essential to apply the knowledge of UX (User Experience) Design in projects with XAI, focusing on people's needs and understanding how AI can impact human decisions. Ferreira and Monteiro [19] comment that although there are publications favoring the UI (User Interface) and UX aspects of XAI, they do not find any publication with the word "user" in the title. The conclusion is that they are very focused on technology and that practical AI applications do not communicate effectively with their users.

There are commercial benefits for companies to invest in XAI, such as: pressures for regulation and good practices regarding responsibility and ethics, in addition to building trust, as XAI systems provide greater visibility into unknown vulnerabilities and flaws [2]. Holziger [1] also warns that current privacy trends require greater transparency from AI systems.

Another issue that favors XAI is related to the level of control. ML-based systems make decisions and present options to users to help their decisions. XAI can increase the level of control of users [2], as they will not be limited to choose among the options presented. From the moment they understand the rationale of predictions, they can question how the machine options and through new inputs, achieve greater assertiveness.

Although there has been progress in recent years in relation to XAI, the explanation methods developed today focus on solutions for AI specialists, while they should focus on end users [20]. Therefore, recent XAI approaches do not meet the needs of the end user [16].

4 Methodology

To understand how transparency is handled in the AI area, we studied several lists of AI principles [21–27]. According to BAAI [21], developing AI systems with an ethical approach is fundamental to making the systems trustworthy. For that, one must invest in transparency, explainability and predictability, making the systems more traceable, auditable and accountable. For MIC [22], transparency allows the verifiability of the inputs and outputs of the AI systems and the explainability of their judgments. Google PAIR [23] also links transparency to explainability, which in turn, is directly linked to trust. For FLI [24], Microsoft [25] and OECD [26], transparency brings an understanding of why. EGE [27] sees transparency in a different scenario, relating it to autonomy. Only with transparency and predictability, humans would be able to choose whether, when and how to delegate decisions and actions to AI systems. We conclude that transparency is strongly linked to the explainability of the AI-based system, a fundamental concept for users to understand how it works to control it and trust its predictions.

Then, we conducted an exploratory research method named Directed Storytelling [28], to analyze the user experience with VoD platforms. The process is to explore participants' memories to reveal patterns in people's experiences. We chose this method because it allows us to collect good qualitative data remotely, since we were in a period of social isolation by COVID-19. In addition, the method proved to be very suitable for exploring various memories of experiences lived by the participants.

Participants were initially recruited using a screening questionnaire posted on social media platforms and we used the snowball method to expand the sample. The recruitment criterion was that each participant was a user of at least one AI-based VoD platform, regardless the time and frequency of use of the platforms. The study was conducted in July 2020, with thirty-one Brazilian participants, resident or not in Brazil. We seek to cover all age groups from eighteen to over sixty-five, regardless of gender, in a balanced way. The use and preference of users for Netflix as a VoD platform was massive, so most of the comments were focused based on it.

The participants' responses were then analyzed using an affinity diagram, which seeks to group similar behaviors, to identify common patterns. In this way, we were able to relate the participants' perceptions and behaviors in relation to the issues surrounding transparency.

5 Results

The principle of AI transparency suggests that there must be clarity for users about the inputs and outputs of the interaction with the AI system, as well as the rationale of the system's decision making, so that people understand and trust the predictions. Its absence generates fragility in the users' mental model, hindering the interaction with VoD platforms, as users do not understand how the content is organized, to orient themselves. Furthermore, it undermines the rationale and confidence in the system's predictions, as they do not understand the logic of the selection offered to it. Users must be able to apply their own judgments to make their choices.

The VoD platforms used by the participants do not explain their rules of operation to users. The most transparent we found were some categories that make the relationship with the user's history more explicit, such as "because you watched certain content" or with the collaboration between users, "whoever saw certain content also saw it". We then tried to understand the participants' understanding of the rules of interaction and evaluate their behaviors.

We found three critical issues for the users' experience, which could be solved with the application of Explainable AI:

Because They Do Not Know the Rules and the Level of Customization of the System, Users Do Not form the Appropriate Mental Model for Their Use and Do Not Know How to Teach ML to Improve Recommendations. Most participants (26) identify that there is a relationship between the content offered and their consumption history, but they do not know how much each category of recommendation has a personalization, randomness, influence of popularity of the content or promotional interest. It is not clear which and how much the categories are personalized or common to all users, covering titles and ordering, as well as images displayed. Eight participants do not understand the logic of categorizing some content, as they think that the categories present mixed content or that they are not related. Categories with more explicit titles, such as "because you watched certain content" or "for you", are more successful. Netflix is successful in these categories, as it helps users understand which of their actions were taken into account by the recommender system [29]. The "like", direct feedback, goes unnoticed, being mentioned by only one of the participants. In general, they do not know which of their actions influence the recommendations and supposed that could be: the use of the search tool, watch the preview of trailers or even their navigation data in other systems connected to the internet, as well as the relationship between the users' profiles.

Personalized Recommendations, Which are the Great Innovation of ML Systems, are Often Overlooked by Users Due to Lack of Confidence. Twenty participants demonstrate that they resort to external recommendations more than those of the system, since they prioritize the choice of content by indication of other people, social media searches or categories clearly influenced by other users such as those that take into account the popularity and ranking of views. Seven participants even commented that some content did not seem interesting being recommended by the platform, but that they were convinced to watch it when it was recommended by other people. Five participants even comment that the platforms make recommendations for commercial interests, which reduces the credibility of the recommender system from theis point of view. We believe that if there were more transparency in the recommendations, users would understand the rationale and trust the results of the system's predictions, contributing to the engagement.

Misaligned Recommendations to the Novice User Profile Can Accustom it to Do its Always Choices with Search Tool. As the ML algorithm needs time to learn from the use of people, the first interactions of a new user do not bring recommendations so aligned with the user profile. User actions are not reflected immediately. Therefore, some people get used to not browsing the recommended content categories, bringing external tips and always using the search tool. Three participants never check the system's recommendations, as their first contacts did not represent a good experience. Konstan [9] warn of the problem of not being able to personalize recommendations for new users.

Greater transparency could increase the tolerance of these people and motivate them to continue investing in the recommender system.

6 Conclusion

Although the principle of transparency is recommended in all the lists of AI principles we have studied, adding to all publications that advocate the use of XAI with a focus on the end-user, VoD platforms still do not fully employ the explainability of their recommendations well. A great failure for this to happen, may be the worst performance of the explainable algorithms, compared to the black-box models. Another limiting reason may be the commercial interests of innovative systems not opening their logic to competition completely.

XAI, like ML, is evolving. Human factor studies are also gaining importance within this area. Therefore, we believe that we will still experience many evolutions in human interaction with AI, minimizing or even eliminating the problems we encounter with our study.

We found that most of the participants involved are aware that there is an automatic mechanism, but it is not clear how it works and the level of customization to make the most of its capacity. Working with AI transparency is essential to gain trust and improve users' experience with the recommender system.

We argue that VoD platforms should invest in finding ways to make the operating rules of ML-based VoD platforms clearer to users, aiming at a better experience. Ahmad et al. [30] point out that the type of explanation to be provided depends on some issues related to the system user, such as cognitive capacity and experience time, and the level of detail of the explanation may vary.

Acknowledgments. This study was financed in part by the Coordenação de Aperfeiçoamento de Pessoal de Nível Superior – Brasil (CAPES) – Finance Code 001.

References

1. Holzinger, A.: From machine learning to explainable AI. In: DISA 2018 - IEEE World Symposium on Intelligence for Systems and Machines Proceedings, pp. 55–66 (2018)
2. Oxborought, C., Cameron, E., Rao, A., Wetermann, C.: Explainable AI: driving business value throught greater understanding. PwC-UK (2018)
3. Ribera, M., Lapedriza, A.: Can we do better explanations? A proposal of user-centered explainable AI. In: Joint Proceedings of the ACM IUI 2019 Workshops, Los Angeles, USA, 20 March, p. 7. ACM, New York (2019)
4. Samek, W., Wiegand, T., Müller, K.-R.: Explainable artificial intelligence: understanding, visualizing and interpreting deep learning models (2017)
5. Gade, K., Geyik, S., Kenthapadi, K., et al.: Explainable AI in industry: practical challenges and lessons learned. In: Companion Proceedings of the Web Conference 2020, pp. 303–304. ACM, New York (2020)
6. Samih, A., Adadi, A., Berrada, M.: Towards a knowledge based explainable recommender systems. In: ACM International Conference on Proceeding Series (2019)

7. Xu, F., Uszkoreit, H., Du, Y., et al.: Explainable AI: a brief survey on history, research areas, approaches and challenges. In: Tang, J., Kan, M.-Y., Zhao, D., et al. (eds.) Natural Language Processing and Chinese Computing: 8th CCF International Conference, NLPCC 2019 Dunhuang, China, 9–14 October 2019 Proceedings, Part II, pp. 563–574. Springer, Dunhuang (2019)
8. Aggarwal, C.C.: Recommender Systems: The Textbook. Springer, Yorktown Heights (2016)
9. Konstan, J.A., Riedl, J.: Recommender systems: from algorithms to user experience. User Model User-Adapt Interact **22**, 101–123 (2012)
10. McNee, S.M., Riedl, J., Konstan, J.A.: Being accurate is not enough: how accuracy metrics have hurt recommender systems. In: Conference on Human Factors in Computing Systems – Proceedings, pp. 1097–1101 (2006)
11. Tintarev, N., Masthoff, J.: Explaining recommendations: design and evaluation. In: Recommender Systems Handbook, pp 353–382. Springer, Boston (2015)
12. Herlocker, J.L., Konstan, J.A., Riedl, J.: Explaining collaborative filtering recommendations. In: Proceedings of ACM Conference on Computer Support Coop Work, pp. 241–250 (2000)
13. Swearingen, K., Sinha, R.: Interaction design for recommender systems. In: Designing Interactive Systems, pp. 1–10 (2002)
14. Gedikli, F., Jannach, D., Ge, M.: How should I explain? A comparison of different explanation types for recommender systems. Int J Hum Comput Stud **72**, 367–382 (2014)
15. Lamy, J.B., Sekar, B., Guezennec, G., et al.: Explainable artificial intelligence for breast cancer: a visual case-based reasoning approach. Artif Intell Med **94**, 42–53 (2019)
16. Weitz, K., Schiller, D., Schlagowski, R., et al.: "Let me explain!": exploring the potential of virtual agents in explainable AI interaction design. J Multimodal User Interfaces (2020). https://link.springer.com/article/10.1007/s12193-020-00332-0#citeas
17. Gilpin, L.H., Bau, D., Yuan, B.Z., et al.: Explaining explanations: an overview of interpretability of machine learning. In: Proceeding - 2018 IEEE 5th International Conference on Data Science and Advanced Analytics, DSAA 2018, pp. 80–89 (2019)
18. Bharadhwaj, H., Joshi, S.: Explanations for temporal recommendations. KI - Kunstl Intelligenz **32**, 267–272 (2018)
19. Ferreira, J.J., Monteiro, M.S.: What are people doing about XAI user experience? A survey on AI explainability research and practice. In: Marcus, A., Rosenzweig, E. (eds.) Design, User Experience, and Usability. Design for Contemporary Interactive Environments. HCII 2020. Lecture Notes in Computer Science, vol. 12201. Springer, Cham (2020)
20. Miller, T., Howe, P., Sonenberg, L.: Explainable AI: beware of inmates running the asylum or: how I learnt to stop worrying and love the social and behavioural sciences (2017)
21. BAAI: Beijing AI Principles (2019). https://www.baai.ac.cn/news/beijing-ai-principles-en.html. Accessed 07 May 2020
22. Ministry of Internal Affairs and Communications (MIC) the G of J.: AI R&D Principles (2017)
23. Google PAIR: People + AI Guidebook (2019). https://pair.withgoogle.com/. Accessed 07 May 2020
24. Future of Life Institute (FLI): Asilomar AI Principles (2017). https://futureoflife.org/ai-principles/. Accessed 07 May 2020
25. Microsoft: Microsoft AI Principles (2018). https://www.microsoft.com/en-us/ai/our-approach-to-ai. Accessed 07 May 2020
26. OECD Council Recommendation on Artificial Intelligence: OECD Principles on AI (2019). https://www.oecd.org/going-digital/ai/principles/. Accessed 07 May 2020
27. European Group on Ethics in Science and New Technologies (EGE), European Commission Statement on artificial intelligence, robotics and "autonomous" systems : Brussels (2018)
28. Evenson, S.: Directed storytelling: interpreting experience for design. In: Bennett, A. (ed.) Design Studies, pp. 231–240. Princeton Architectural Press, New York (2006)

29. Budiu, R.: Can users control and understand a UI driven by machine learning? (2018). https://www.nngroup.com/articles/machine-learning-ux/. Accessed 22 Nov 2020
30. Ahmad, M.A., Eckert, C., Teredesai, A.: Interpretable machine learning in healthcare. In: Proceedings of the 2018 ACM International Conference on Bioinformatics, Computational Biology, and Health Informatics, pp 559–560. ACM, New York (2018)

Reliability of Heuristic Evaluation During Usability Analysis

Thomas J. Smith[(⊠)] [iD] and Cindy Kheng[iD]

University of Minnesota, Minneapolis, MN 55455, USA
{smith293,kheng005}@umn.edu

Abstract. Scientific reliability—the degree to which a research method produces stable and consistent results—represents a major linchpin of tenable scientific research. A number of different studies support the conclusion that usability testing of software interfaces lacks scientific reliability (Jacobsen et al., 1998; Jordan, 2017). The present report augments this conclusion with findings that heuristic evaluation, the second major pillar of usability analysis, also lacks reliability. We conclude that a key priority of "usability science" should be to initiate a systematic program of inquiry to investigate the degree to which this term has meaning.

Keywords: Reliability · Heuristics · Heuristic evaluation · Usability · Usability testing

1 Introduction and Background

There is a broad consensus that scientific reliability—an experimental procedure yielding comparable results across successive trials—represents a major linchpin of tenable scientific research. From this perspective, a number of different studies support the conclusion that usability testing of software interfaces lacks scientific reliability [1–5]. The statement of Jacobsen and colleagues [2] embodies this conclusion:

> "…both selection of usability problems and selection of the most severe problems are subject to considerable individual variability."

The recurrent problematic issues identified by these studies include: 1) the number of problems contained in a given interface; 2) the difficulty in detecting a given problem; and 3) the number of users recruited to test the usability of the interface. Collectively, these issues affect the probability that a problem will be detected by a usability test.

In addition to usability testing, the second major methodological domain of usability analysis is heuristic evaluation. Heuristic evaluation—informed judgment about the key design features of an interface—dates back to the origins of the usability field. In his seminal chapter on how to design usable systems, Gould [6] includes a section on interface design considerations. Heuristic evaluation as one of the basic methods of evaluating interface design is addressed by Nielsen [7] and by Mandel [8], and in the more recent book by Kortum [9].

© The Author(s), under exclusive license to Springer Nature Switzerland AG 2022
N. L. Black et al. (Eds.): IEA 2021, LNNS 223, pp. 708–714, 2022.
https://doi.org/10.1007/978-3-030-74614-8_88

A limited number of past studies have explored the reliability of heuristic evaluation. Georgsson and colleagues [10] studied a heuristic evaluation by three raters of an mHealth (the use of mobile and wireless devices to improve health outcomes) self-management interface for diabetes patients. To prepare the raters in advance for the evaluation, they first were introduced to the interface by means of: 1) a short demonstration video; 2) a guide with common interface interaction scenarios; and 3) tasks representing patients' typical interface use. Using a statistic called Krippendorff's alpha, this study found an extremely low alpha of .0815, denoting low inter-rater reliability [11]. Similarly, White and colleagues [12] report findings documenting weak inter-rater reliability in heuristic evaluation of video games.

The present report provides an analysis of results from heuristic evaluations of four selected social networking sites—Facebook, YouTube, Instagram, and Snapchat—by two independent groups of raters. Raters were asked to judge the level of excellence for different design features of these sites by rating the quality of heuristics relevant to the sites. Results are contained in term reports submitted by different teams of upper level undergraduate and graduate students enrolled in a University of Minnesota (UM) human-centered design course over a nine-year period (2010–2018). Over this period, the Instructor for this course is the first author of the present report.

The analysis presented here, pertaining to the reliability of heuristic evaluation, differs from those cited above [10, 12] in three major respects: 1) the number of raters; 2) the span of time covered by the analysis; and 3) comparison of paired heuristic quality rating results from multiple paired independent groups of raters.

2 Method

During fall semesters for the years covered by this report (2010–2018), the first author of this report taught an upper level course through the UM School of Kinesiology (KIN) entitled Human-Centered Design (aimed at assessing the usability of different types of systems). In these classes, for purposes of this report, each team of two or three students was required to: (1) carry out an in-depth usability analysis of a selected social networking web site; and (2) prepare a term report summarizing the background, method, results and conclusions of the analysis. Selection of the web site to analyze by a given team was up to the team members themselves. A Wikipedia search in June, 2019, documented close to 200 such sites—it is likely that, over the years covered by this report, there were an ample number of sites to choose from. The report by Smith [13] provides further details about this class.

As part of their usability analysis, each team carried out a heuristic evaluation of relevant design features of the site selected. Five years, 2010 and 2015 through 2018, provided acceptable data for the analysis presented here. For the heuristic evaluations, the explicit instructions specified that each team should: 1) carry out their own heuristic evaluation of their selected site—however, provision of numeric ratings for selected heuristics by each team member was optional; and 2) recruit a separate set of users (two or more) to complete a perceptual survey, soliciting numeric ratings for a series of heuristics relevant to the selected site. With the numeric ratings, each group member (team or recruited users) was asked to use a Likert scale to rate the quality of each of a set of heuristics relevant to design features for the web site selected.

Suggestive, but not explicit, guidance for the teams was provided as to selection of appropriate heuristics for the heuristic evaluations. These include: 1) six design heuristics specifically relevant to interface design [6], namely the quality of site navigation, functionality, interactivity, content, visual design and consistency; 2) four more general design heuristics cited by Norman [14], namely that the interface design should provide a good conceptual model, make things visible, support behavioral mapping, and provide feedback; and 3) 15 other heuristics variously cited by Gould [6], Mandel [8], and Kortum [9].

The general outcome of this guidance was that the set of heuristics selected by each team was distinct. The rationale for this approach is inherent to the definition of the term itself: "A heuristic is any approach to problem solving or self-discovery that employs a practical method, not guaranteed to be optimal, perfect, logical, or rational, but instead sufficient for reaching an immediate goal" (https://en.wikipedia.org/wiki/Heuristic, last accessed, 2019/6/10).

Summarizing the heuristic evaluation approach outlined above: 1) four social networking sites—Facebook, YouTube, Instagram, and Snapchat—were selected for analysis by two or more groups, with at least one survey group and one team group; and 2) across these four sites, 4 to 9 heuristics were selected for evaluation by both team and survey group members. Outcomes of this analysis are provided in the next section.

3   Results

Findings from two different analytical approaches are summarized to support the conclusion that heuristic evaluation lack reliability: correlation analysis, and calculation of Krippendorff's alpha.

Correlation Analysis. Table 1 summarizes quality rating results for a series of different heuristics for four different social networking sites, as outlined above. Specified in the table, starting with the leftmost column, are: (1) the social networking site; (2) the numbers of female ($\female$) and male ($\male$) subjects (team members plus recruited survey subjects) that rated the quality of different heuristics for each of the four specified social networking sites, across the years 2010 through 2018; (3) the age ranges of heuristic quality rating subjects, across both team and survey group members; (4) the heuristic whose quality is rated; and (5 and 6) average quality ratings based on 1–5 Likert rating scales (1 = lowest quality rating, 5 = highest quality rating), categorized by social networking site and by heuristic, for both team members and survey group members.

In the two rightmost columns in Table 1, only paired heuristic quality rating averages are listed. That is, for each heuristic specified in the table, at least two independent groups provided quality ratings for the same heuristic.

Figure 1 shows a scatter plot of the paired average heuristic quality ratings by team members (plotted on abscissa) vs. survey group members (plotted on ordinate). The trend line on the plot is the regression line, for which the correlation coefficient (r) is 0.37. For 25 paired values (Table 1), the degrees of freedom (DOF) value is 23. At a DOF = 23, an r value of 0.37 is statistically non-significant [15, p. 557].

Table 1. Reliability of heuristic evaluation of selected social networking sites, based on quality ratings of selected heuristics

Site	Gender Numbers ♂ ♀	Age Range	Heuristic	Average Team Member Ratings	Average Survey Group Ratings
Facebook	17 19	15-88	Layout	4.0	3.7
			Ease of Navigation	4.2	3.8
			Content	4.0	3.3
			Site Privacy/Security	3.5	3.5
			Visual Design	4.2	3.6
			Functionality	4.3	4.4
			Interactivity	4.1	4.5
			Overall Quality	2.7	4.1
YouTube	4 4	Average 24	Ease of Navigation	4.3	4.6
			Content	5.0	3.2
			Functionality	4.3	4.6
			Interactivity	3.3	3.2
Instagram	44 20	18-73	Ease of Navigation	3.4	4.0
			Content	3.4	3.8
			Readability	4.6	4.6
			Visual Design	3.4	4.0
			Functionality	4.2	4.1
			Interactivity	4.1	4.3
			Ease of Use	4.0	3.9
			Provides Feedback	3.3	4.6
			Overall Quality	3.4	4.1
Snapchat	11 8	19-60	Ease of Navigation	1.0	2.6
			Content	3.6	3.1
			Visual Design	4.5	3.1
			Overall Quality	3.3	3.5

Krippendorff's alpha (Kalpha, or α) is a statistic used to provide reliability estimates for independent judgments of the same set of data—Kalpha may be considered to represent the litmus test of reliability analysis [10, 11, 16, 17]. Kalpha values range from 0 to 1, where 0 is perfect disagreement and 1 is perfect agreement. Krippendorff [17, p. 241] suggests, "It is customary to require $\alpha \geq .800$ (for statistically significant reliability). Where tentative conclusions are still acceptable, $\alpha \geq .667$ is the lowest conceivable limit".

Table 2 lists Kalpha values calculated (rightmost column) for each social networking site, based on inter-rater agreement on quality ratings for each heuristic, plus the value calculated for all rating pairs combined. All Kalpha values are well under 0.8, associated with low inter-rater reliability [17]. This finding supports the conclusion that heuristic evaluation by independent groups of raters, documented in this report, lacks reliability.

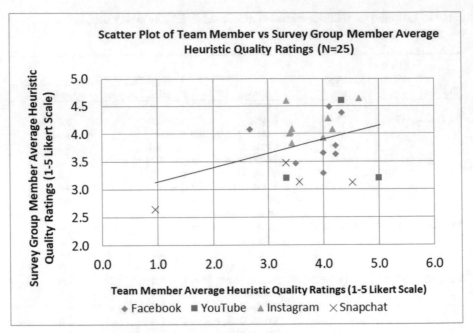

Fig. 1. Scatter plot of paired average heuristic quality ratings by team members vs. survey group members (see Table 1).

Table 2. Kalpha values – individual site data and combined data

Site	Number of rating groups	Number of heuristics	Kalpha
Facebook	7	11	0.03
YouTube	2	4	0.33
Instagram	9	11	0.10
Snapchat	4	7	0.03
Combined	22	12	0.12

4 Limitations

The central limitation of the analysis offered here is that there is no precedent, and no standards, governing the presence or lack of reliability in heuristic quality judgments of interface design. Is it reasonable to expect a high reliability of such judgments, or does a lack of reliability represent a more reasonable, or even desirable, expectation? If the latter, what is an acceptable level of reliability in judgments of heuristic quality for a given interface design? The results in Fig. 1 and Table 2 support the conclusion that heuristic evaluation is not reliable, but do not provide an answer to these questions.

The source of the data in Table 1 represents another limitation. These data derive from an unstructured and uncontrolled set of field observations. For example, for both team and survey group members, no guidance was provided as to which social networking site to analyze. Moreover, since the choice of heuristics for analysis likewise was not explicitly specified, only eleven distinct heuristics for these four sites yielded rating results acceptable for analysis.

A further limitation is that the Likert scale used for heuristic quality rating analysis likewise was not explicitly specified. Consequently, some teams used a 1–5 rating scale, whereas others used a 1–7 scale. To address this discrepancy, all rating results based on the 1–7 scale were normalized to the 1–5 scale.

5 Conclusions

This study extends prior research on usability testing by exploring the reliability of heuristic evaluation, the second scientific pillar of usability analysis. Two sets of results are described: 1) lack of significant correlation of paired independent quality ratings, across four different social networking sites, for selected heuristics by team members vs. survey group members; and 2) computation of Krippendorff's alpha values, all less than the minimum level of 0.8 for significant inter-rater reliability. These results, showing a lack of reliability in between two independent groups of individual raters of the quality of different heuristics for a selected number of web sites, complement earlier research showing a comparable lack of reliability with usability testing (Introduction). It thus appears that usability testing and heuristic evaluation, the two empirical foundations of usability analysis, both lack reliability.

Of course, the observation of some level of variance in how different groups rate the quality of different heuristics for a given web site is not surprising. The key question, as noted above, is what degree of variance is acceptable in terms of establishing a standard for reliability for heuristic evaluation as an essential component of usability analysis (thereby mitigating the harsh conclusion noted above)? Additional research will be required to provide insight into this question?

In summary, the analysis in this report addresses the following major questions and conclusions: 1) does a lack of reliability in ratings of heuristic quality represent a reasonable, or even desirable, expectation? 2) what is an acceptable level of variability in judgments of heuristic quality for a given interface design? and 3) given that prior research on usability testing, coupled with the evaluation of heuristic quality ratings presented in this report, both point to a lack of reliability in these empirical pillars of usability analysis, a reasonable conclusion is that the scientific validity of usability analysis is open to question. Given this conclusion, a key priority of "usability science" should be to initiate a systematic program of inquiry to investigate the degree to which this term has meaning.

References

1. Bevan, N., Butler, S., Curson, I., Kindlund, E., Kirakowski, J, Miller, D., Molich, R.: Comparative evaluation of usability tests. In: Proceedings of the Usability Professionals Association 1998 Conference, pp. 1–12. Usability Professionals Association, Washington, D.C. (1998)

2. Jacobsen, N.E., Hertzum, M., John, B.E.: The evaluator effect in usability studies: problem detection and severity judgments. In: Proceedings of the Human Factors and Ergonomics Society 42nd Annual Meeting, pp. 1336–1339. Human Factors and Ergonomics Society, Washington, D.C. (1998)

3. Jordan, C.: Reliability and generalizability of usability testing. https://medium.com/@courtn eyjordan/reliability-and-generalizability-of-usability-testing-8c6e1837ed2f. Accessed 9 June 2019

4. Hughes, M.: Reliability and dependability in usability testing. https://www.uxmatters.com/mt/archives/2011/06/reliability-and-dependability-in-usability-testing.php. Accessed 2 Feb 2021

5. Molich, R.: Are usability evaluations reproducible? https://interactions.acm.org/archive/view/november-december-2018/are-usability-evaluations-reproducible. Accessed 2 Feb 2021

6. Gould, J.D.: How to design usable systems. In: Helander, M. (ed.) Handbook of Human-Computer Interaction, pp. 757–789. Elsevier, Amsterdam (1988)

7. Nielsen, J.: Heuristic evaluation. In: Mack, R.L., Nielsen, J. (eds.) Usability Inspection Methods, pp. 25–62. Wiley, New York (1994)

8. Mandel, T.: Elements of User Interface Design. Wiley, New York (1997)

9. Kortum, P.: Usability assessment: how to measure the usability of products, services, and systems. Human Factors and Ergonomics Society, Washington, D.C. (2016)

10. Georgsson, M., Weir, C.R., Staggers, N.: Revisiting heuristic evaluation methods to improve the reliability of findings. In: Lovis, C., Séroussi, B., Hasman, A. Pape-Haugaard, L., Saka, O., Andersen, S.K. (eds.). E-health - for Continuity of Care. Proceedings of the 25th European Medical Informatics Conference – MIE 2014, pp. 930–934. IOS Press, Amsterdam (2014). https://bth.diva-portal.org/smash/get/diva2:834138/FULLTEXT01.pdf. Accessed 11 Jan 2021

11. Hayes, A.F., Krippendorff, K.: Answering the call for a standard reliability measure for coding data. Commun. Methods Meas. **1**, 77–89 (2007). https://www.statisticshowto.com/krippendo rffs-alpha/. Accessed 19 Dec 2020

12. White, G.R., Mirza-Babaei, P., McAllister, G., Good, J.: Weak inter-rater reliability in heuristic evaluation of video games. In: Proceedings of the 29th Annual CHI Conference on Human Factors in Computing Systems. CHI 2011 Extended Abstracts on Human Factors in Computing Systems, pp. 1441–1446. Association of Computing Machinery, New York (2011)

13. Smith, T.J.: Observer perceptions of overall system quality – the Lake Wobegon effect. In: Proceedings of the Human Factors and Ergonomics Society 59th Annual Meeting, pp. 1769–1773. Human Factors and Ergonomics Society, Washington D.C. (2015)

14. Norman, D.A.: The Design of Everyday Things. Doubleday, New York (1988)

15. Snedecor, G.W., Cochran, W.G.: Statistical Methods. 6th edn. The Iowa State University Press, Ames (1967)

16. Krippendorff, K.: Bootstrapping distributions for Krippendorff's alpha. https://scholar.goo gle.com/scholar?q=Bootstrapping+distributions+for+Krippendorff%E2%80%99s+alpha&hl=en&as_sdt=0&as_vis=1&oi=scholar. Accessed 5 Feb 2021

17. Krippendorff, K.: Content Analysis: An Introduction to Its Methodology. Sage, Thousand Oaks (2004)

Clinical Usability Studies – Clash of Cultures? Study Design Proposal from Lessons Learned

Thomas Stüdeli[1]([⊠]) and Limor Hochberg[2]

[1] F. Hoffmann-La Roche Ltd., Grenzacherstrasse 124, 4070 Basel, Switzerland
thomas.stuedeli@roche.com
[2] Bose Corporation, 80 Guest Street, Boston, MA 02135, USA

Abstract. We can recently see an increased interest in real-world usability data from various global regulatory bodies for medical devices (MDs) and Software as a Medical Device (SaMD). Notably, the new European Medical Device Regulations from 2017 emphasizes the importance of clinical evaluation of the usability of MDs.

As promising as the combination of clinical trials in a real-world setting and usability tests in simulated use can be, it is challenging in practice to combine these well-established methodologies. This paper discusses the challenges around important "cultural" differences and reports on lessons learned. It highlights the opportunities and strengths that both worlds offer and provides guidance for an appropriate selection or combination of user centered design methodologies. The analysis of the user experience and usability research questions and their translation into a clinical protocol is a key element.

In most cases, the usability of an MD or SaMD can be sufficiently assessed with a human factors engineering evaluation (e.g., a simulated-use usability test), which can provide evidence of safe and effective use from an interactive perspective. However, some cases (e.g., for certain clinical claims) may require assessing use within a real-world environment, requiring the integration of methods from the human factors and clinical worlds. For such demanding cases, we propose a framework for a study design: a proposal on how to consider and integrate usability tests into a clinical trial.

Keywords: Clinical trial · Usability study · Medical device · eHealth application

1 Usability Tests for MD and SaMDs and Clinical Studies

In the last decades, the development processes of MD and SaMD have been highly regulated. Alongside guidance on risk management and design control, the application of Human Factors Engineering (HFE) to medical device development has become established and became a state-of-the-art in the product development in the field of healthcare. The HFE process comprises the user-centered design activities in all stages of the product life cycle and contributes to the desired safe and effective use of these products. US FDA laid the groundwork with local HFE guidelines, and in 2007 the HFE process was, for the first time, described in an international process standard [1, 2] that established

© The Author(s), under exclusive license to Springer Nature Switzerland AG 2022
N. L. Black et al. (Eds.): IEA 2021, LNNS 223, pp. 715–724, 2022.
https://doi.org/10.1007/978-3-030-74614-8_89

the activities needed to develop product designs that are aligned to the needs and capabilities of their users. Ultimately, applying HFE enables manufacturers to create robust and efficient designs [1–3].

Today most local guidelines and regulations distinguish between two kinds of usability studies for MDs and SaMDs: formative studies and human factors validation studies. **Formative usability studies** aim to inform the design during the device development process. Formative studies, depending on the stage of development and study goals, can have more flexible, exploratory methods. They are not typically mandatory, but are considered best practice for patient centricity and ensuring readiness for validation studies and for the market from a commercial perspective. In contrast, **human factors validation studies** (summative studies) aim to validate the design, establishing safe and effective use in the intended use environment and by the intended users, from an interactive perspective [1–3]. Notably, both types of usability tests are typically simulated use studies, often occurring a lab environment rather than actual use environments, and often utilizing simulated rather than actual delivery of the medical device therapy. The tests are in representative and simulated use environments and with representative devices and with a relatively small number of representative participants. As such, HFE often takes a qualitative rather than quantitative perspective. Such usability tests, conducted in a controlled and safe environment, allow a window into the actual user interactions, primarily based on simulated, first-time use. Early formative tests, in particular, help the manufacturer understand how users will benefit from the product and utilize its features to achieve their goals and helps to design and communicate the intended use. Notably, these tests are led by a moderator and rely on in-depth follow-up interviews to uncover the root causes of any use related problems. In interpreting participant responses and interactions, the moderator can consider the clinical context for a particular patient (e.g., whether the patient is having a "good" or "bad" day in the course of her chronic illness, pain, tremors). Data derived from such tests are important for the assessment of the use-related risks. Having a solid understanding of user interactions, as well as the associated risks, is a prerequisite for the use of a MD or a SaMD in real-world settings. In most cases, the performance of a human factors validation study is a prerequisite for the use of MD or a SaMD in a real-world setting, as in a clinical study. By conducting tests in a simulated, moderated environment, the manufacturer can ensure that the product is robust with respect to use-related risks before providing it for less-supervised or unsupervised use in a clinical trial. After market introduction, the HFE process includes monitoring and addressing of use problems encountered by device users, within the framework of post-market surveillance activities. Notably, this is the only context in which the medical HFE standard [1] requires manufacturers to apply human factors engineering to real-world data. In summary, human factors engineering plays an important role in medical device development, but it focuses primarily on assessing simulated use in controlled environments, typically for a relatively short window of time. However, when usability data from real patients over an extended period of time is necessary, a different type of study is needed: one that combines aspects of both clinical trials and typical, in-lab usability tests. We call this type of study a **clinical usability study**, and we describe this study type and its benefits in the following section. Notably, conducting this type of study requires merging two well-established, highly regulated, and scientific test cultures. That said, merging the cultures is not a simple task, given the complexity of the typical clinical trial framework. Since the mid 20th century, clinical trial methods have included certain hallmarks, such as informed consent, single- or double-blind design, and ethics considerations related to conducting randomized controlled trials. Clinical trial set-ups are driven by statistics and follow standards and guidelines of the International Council for Harmonisation of Technical Requirements for Pharmaceuticals for Human Use, as well as Good Clinical Practice, which have been developed over the past several decades. According to [4], for the eHealth challenges ahead of us, clinical trials "lack a well-coordinated pragmatic trial extension to our system of development of medical interventions." We propose a typology of studies involving the intended user population, across the human factors engineering and clinical disciplines that both seek to collect and analyze data directly from the user (Table 1). Certain types focus only on a single discipline, while Types 3 and 4 merge both disciplines. Our paper will focus on Type 4: **the clinical usability study**.

Table 1. Types of user tests as part of the user centered design activities and patient centricity within the Human Factors Engineering process of a Medical Device (MD) or a Software as a Medical Device (SaMD).

Study type	Description
Type 0	Clinical trials, focused on drug/medical claims unrelated to usability [4]
Type 1	Usability test for exploration, to inform the design
Type 2	Usability test for validation, a summative evaluation [1–3]
Type 3	Clinical trials with usability endpoints, including device-related questions
Type 4	Clinical usability studies that combine medical claims that are dependent on the use and the usability of the MD and the SaMD [5]

2   The Clinical Usability Study: What, When, and Why

A **clinical usability study** is a study that combines both clinical and human factors engineering methods to provide a broad view of patient interactions with a device, in the context of a real world setting and over an extended duration. An early example of such might be [5]. Such a study seeks to collect data towards both usability and clinical endpoints, and to understand how such endpoints are related. Here are some examples of questions that a clinical usability study is best suited to answer:

- Does product A's enhanced ease-of-use, as compared to predecessor product B, help patients achieve better clinical outcomes?
- If an interactive application is added to work in concert with a medical device, will using this application increase patient adherence?

- Are patients satisfied with a software developed to enhance coordination with health-care personnel on their clinical care team? How does this software shape their experience and recovery?

What are the objectives of a clinical usability study? Clinical usability studies may be designed to support the following types of objectives:

- **Support clinical usability claims**, such as those related to feasibility of long-term treatment, level of engagement, and satisfaction and user experience,
- **Determine opportunities for design improvement,** particularly those that require an assessment of real-world use,
- **Investigate research questions that pertain to extended product use,** such as those regarding adoption and compliance as inputs to clinical outcomes.

3 Study Design for Clinical Usability Studies

3.1 High-Level Study Design

The study design for a clinical usability study must be tailored to its objectives. That said, we expect that study design will be longitudinal, meaning that the study will occur over an extended period of time, so as to gather information about the product in a real-world use setting. We propose the following structure:

- **Initial laboratory-based test session.** The study may start with an initial, traditional laboratory-based test session during which users work with the device for the first time under moderator observation. Such a study may be limited to a typical "out of the box" discovery and first use. Or, it may include tasks based on specialized use cases, if (a) there is a need for early feedback on such a scenario, (b) when this should be evaluated with a first-time, naive user, or (c) when there is a desire to exposure the user to a feature early during the study. Otherwise, specialized use cases may be evaluated in the final laboratory-based test session.
- **Extended usage (longitudinal portion).** The study participants will use the product over a period of time, which may be as little as a week or as long as a year. During this usage period, the study may employ a variety of research activity types, such as surveys, individual phone interviews, group interviews, direct observations, and diary entries.
- **Final laboratory-based test session.** The study may include a final, laboratory-based test session for controlled observation of the users' interaction with the device after extended usage. This test session would give insights in a learned steady use in contrast to the first time use and may also include a follow-up interview with pre-prepared questions based on the participant's individual usage patterns (e.g., automatically collected by an app) and independent research activities (e.g., diary entries).
- **Debrief.** At the study conclusion, the researchers should debrief with the participants, as is typical for a clinical trial. Such debriefs may include assessments of various clinical aspects, such as regarding disease development (e.g., clinical questionnaire), as well as patient satisfaction with the treatment.

Note that this study framework is quite different from the typical randomized, double-blind, placebo-controlled clinical trial. As needed, the study investigators may choose to employ one or more of these elements, if possible and important for their particularly study's research questions and design.

3.2 Study Method

Here, we provide practical guidance on specifics of the study method in the clinical usability context:

- **Sample size.** The sample size for a clinical usability study will vary based on its objectives. The sample size will typically be larger than a human factors validation test, given the clinical objectives of interest and variability in the users and user environments, but smaller than a typical clinical trial.
- **Sample selection (user groups):** Consider including representatives from each user group, as described in the indications for use and as per a typical human factors validation test.
- **Recruitment criteria.** Recruitment criteria must consider factors affecting usability, with a view toward user characteristics, as well as clinical factors, with a view towards disease characteristics and progression. In particular, consider whether recruitment should include clinical subgroups (e.g., stage of the condition), and how differences in user characteristics related to disease progression may affect usability.
- **Site selection.** As for clinical trials, collecting data from sites representing the diversity of the intended user population will enhance the study's generalizability. As relevant to the study objectives, consider the following factors: geography, demographics, differences in healthcare delivery (e.g., among systems or countries), and local cultural characteristics.
- **Training.** In a clinical usability study, the desire to provide representative training must be balanced against participant safety and the research questions. We propose the following strategy for a clinical usability study:

  1. Provide representative training at the start of the initial lab-based test session, as is typical for a usability test. This might be training for all users, some users, or no users.
  2. Conduct the usability test session.
  3. Provide additional training before the longitudinal portion of the study, given (a) the need to ensure participant safety, and (b) any specific study research questions, such as how training affects behavior.

Importantly, the study design must consider the effects of such additional, non-representative training on the study results, balancing the additional intervention of non-representative training against the study goals, while ensuring participant safety.

3.3   Study Measures

Collaborative Selection of Measures. The particular measures selected will depend on the study's research questions, and may represent a mix of traditional HFE measures, clinical measures, and device usage data. Importantly, the clinical measures must be developed in close collaboration with clinical partners, and the frequency of their collection may depend on the speed of disease progression. Similarly, the usage data should be selected in partnership with supportive functions and technology. Software engineering and data science collaborators should ensure that (a) clinical partner can support the collection of this data and (b) the technology is ready to specifically collect this data during the study, ideally on an ongoing basis (e.g., remotely by the MD or the SaMD itself).

Consideration of Data Types. Table 2 below shows the variety of data types that may be collected in a clinical usability study, which may be useful during the study planning phase. Usability metrics may include objective measures, subjective measures, and a combination of both. In order to support the desired claims, a set of quality-of-life, wellbeing and usability questionnaires, interviews and focus group discussions, along with other typical clinical trials endpoints, might need to be considered. The clinical measures will be specific to the device indications for use, and as such, are represented generically.

Table 2. Data types in a clinical usability study across multiple dimensions.

	Subjective	Objective
Qualitative	• Individual interview or focus group question responses • Observations during initial and final lab-based test sessions • Root causes of use errors • Diary entries - unstructured data • Survey/questionnaire responses	• Demographic data about users • Descriptive usage data, such as the type of device used to access a platform • Clinical measures
Quantitative	• Interview question responses - rating scales • Diary entries - structured data, such as rating scales • Survey/questionnaire responses • Trends in use-related root causes	• Pass/fail ratings and use errors during the test sessions • Usage data, such as frequency of device use, duration of session, etc. • Clinical measures

Linking Measures to Research Questions. After developing this basic Table 2, we suggest that researchers develop a matrix connecting each of the main research questions to the appropriate data, to consider (a) what types of data might be used in considering each question and (b) opportunities for integrating data during analysis. The example matrix (Table 3) below shows how typical research questions might be considered from multiple perspectives.

For example, ease of use might be considered through the lens of initial lab-based test session performance, participant responses in follow-up interviews during the test sessions, and diary entries. Frequency of device use might be answered empirically by analyzing usage data, while an associated root cause analysis of the frequency patterns might rely on diary entry and follow-up interviews.

Endpoint Selection. If the study will use a traditional clinical trial framework for its protocol and report, each row of the Table 2 above can then be used to select primary and secondary endpoints for each research question.

Table 3. A sample framework for considering how research questions (RQs) are related to the data collected during various stages of the study. The table depicts a simplified example, rather than a comprehensive template.

Data type	Initial test session			Extended usage period		Final test session
	Task pass/fail ratings	Use errors	Interview question responses	Usage data	Diary entries	Interview question responses
RQ 1 (ease of use)	X	X	X		X	X
RQ 2 (frequency of use)				X	X	X

3.4 Practical Considerations/Specific for Clinical Usability Studies

Consider the following practical and logistical considerations in study planning:

- **Regulation.** Work with clinical and regulatory partners to determine whether the clinical usability study must or should follow clinical trial regulations. Consider both ethical obligations as well as the ability to support and clinical or marketing claims.
- **Adverse event collection.** Consider how the study will collect adverse event data, and how the study will train any study administrators to collect such data. Resource clinical staff as part of the adverse event data collection and monitoring effort, particularly during the extended usage period.
- **Compensation.** Provide sufficient compensation to motivate participants to complete the study. However, consider that overly generous compensation might bias certain study measures, such as regarding engagement and/or frequency of use.

4   Discussion

Although the framework provided is general and may be applied to any type of technology, it is particularly useful for handling the complexities related to integrating qualitative data from speaking to users, objective clinical data, and automatically-generated usage data collected by devices, as is becoming more prevalent in the Internet of Things (IoT) era. Connected medical devices, artificial intelligence technology, and big data are pushing the classical simulated-use studies for SaMDs and MDs to their limit as there is more and different relevant data to capture and the traditional methods may not be good enough on their own to do the most robust evaluation. Additionally, there are an increased emphasis on post-market surveillance and the desire to incorporate insights from long-term use patterns into device design.

We suggest this clinical usability study framework to support the necessary interdisciplinary collaboration between HFE specialists and these associated fields [9]. In some cases, medical device usability is not just a nice-to-have, but rather an integral part of the clinical claim, requiring the integration of usability endpoints into clinical trials.

That said, at the outset of planning a user study, the manufacturer must consider which of user study types are best suited, and most efficient, for answering the research questions at hand. When simulated-use studies are sufficient to generate the desired evidence, do not run a clinical usability study! A simulated-use study's controlled environment will be safer and offer a more consistent experimental setting; moreover, the study will be faster and cheaper to conduct than a clinical usability study. Reserve the resources necessary for a clinical usability study for cases in which its unique advantages are needed.

What is the real benefit of combining both? Clinical usability studies have several unique advantages. They enable the assessment of compliance and/or adoption in a naturalistic environment. They allow for the investigation of product usability over time, in the context of disease progression, health beliefs, or other stratifications. Finally, they facilitate the investigation of root causes associated with product use, such as understanding the reasons for particular usage patterns that occur in a real-world setting.

4.1   Biases and Limitations

As with any type of research, biases and limitations of the clinical usability format must be considered during planning. Perhaps the greatest tension in such a format is the extent of interventions during the course of the study. Specifically, the desire to collect "pure", unmanipulated real-world data from actual patients – to enable a view into important questions such as adherence – lies in contrast to the necessary, periodic interactions of the study staff with the participants, so as to discuss patients' experiences with them directly and understand the motivations behind their behavior.

For example, participants will likely need to complete additional (i.e., non-representative) training so they may safely use the product at home. Consequently, this additional training must be considered when interpreting the study data. For example, questions regarding initial discovery of certain features over time cannot be answered if they're introduced in training. However, sustained use of such features may be investigated. Additionally, the timing of interviews with participants must be selected carefully, because including such interviews during the extended usage period may influence their behavior in variable ways. Some participants' adoption, or adherence, may increase due to this intervention, while other participants may be demotivated. Interview questions and data analyses might be included to determine the extent to which such interventions affect usage patterns.

Ultimately, we propose to follow the credo: "Collecting as much relevant data as possible and at the same time as little as necessary". This guideline helps to limit possible bias related to moderator activities where moderator-participant interactions may create unwanted effects on the outcome of the study.

4.2 Applying the Framework to Product Development Strategy

In many cases, the two key disciplines generating insights directly from users – clinical and HFE – are siloed. Each discipline develops a research plan for the course of product development (e.g., the usability engineering plan and a clinical evaluation plan). Both of these are nicely documented in the product's design history file, and the work of each discipline proceeds. We propose that, in some cases, it is best to develop an overall user study research strategy, in which the clinical and the HFE groups meet at the outset of product development and identify the number and types of studies (see Table 1) that will be conducted by each group, and how insights may be shared as inputs to each others' study designs and data interpretation. In the course of such planning, the clinical and HFE groups can then also determine whether a clinical usability study is a beneficial method for answering complex, cross-disciplinary research questions.

Consider also, how to provide insights generated from the clinical usability study as it progresses, to inform product development, particularly in agile environments. For example, consider utilizing a phased reporting structure or cross-disciplinary review meetings at predetermined checkpoints. Importantly, consult with the regulatory affairs group to determine which regulations might apply to the specific clinical usability study under design. Include representatives from data science and software engineering for studies that integrate large amounts of usage data.

4.3 Conclusion

Notably, regulatory bodies have shown increased interest in patient preference and satisfaction as an input to risk-benefit calculations, increasing the need to understand how product design affects users' behavior and motivations in support of improved clinical outcomes. The here provided typology of user studies, the design framework of a clinical usability study, and the discussion of key considerations for protocol development and cross-disciplinary collaboration aim to facilitate the communication with the health authorities and the internal decision making. Although they require close interdisciplinary collaboration, clinical usability studies offer unique advantages and circumstances, particularly as automatically generated usage data collected by devices becomes more prevalent in the IoT era.

References

1. International Electrotechnical Commission: 62366-1 Medical devices - Part 1: Application of usability engineering to medical devices. IEC/ISO Standard No. 62366-1:AMD2020 (2020)

2. International Electrotechnical Commission: 62366-2 Medical devices - Part 2: Guidance on the application of usability engineering to medical devices. IEC/ISO Technical Report No. 62366-2 (2016)
3. U.S. Department of Health and Human Services, Food and Drug Administration: Applying Human Factors and Usability Engineering to Medical Devices, Guidance for Industry and Food and Drug Administration Staff, February 3, 2016 (supersedes "Medical Device Use-Safety: Incorporating Human Factors Engineering into Risk Management" issued July 18, 2000)
4. Antman, E.M., Bierer, B.E.: Standards for clinical research: keeping pace with the technology of the future. Circulation **133**(9), 823–825 (2016)
5. Stone, A.A., Saul Shiffman, S., Schwartz, J.E., Broderick, J.E., Hufford, M.R.: Patient compliance with paper and electronic diaries. Control. Clin. Trials **24**(2003), 182–199 (2003)
6. Vincent, C.J., Li, Y., Blandford, A.: Integration of human factors and ergonomics during medical device design and development: it's all about communication. Appl. Ergon. **45**(3), 413–419 (2014)

Collaborating with Communities in Participatory System Development

Torben Volkmann[✉], Michael Sengpiel, and Nicole Jochems

Institute for Multimedia and Interactive Systems, Universität zu Lübeck, Ratzeburger Allee 160, 23562 Lübeck, Germany

{volkmann,sengpiel,jochems}@imis.uni-luebeck.de

Abstract. Designing information and communication technology for older adults has been identified as one of the grand challenges of HCI. HCD+ is a Participatory Design framework based on Human Centered Design, aiming to provide practical guidelines to improve older adults' participation in systems development. This paper describes a study evaluating these guidelines with 19 older adults aged between 60 and 77 years and 12 younger systems developers.

Results indicate three main factors of concern for working with older adults: (1) the commitment of a trusted person in a group, (2) the atmosphere and social interaction, and (3) reciprocity of the engagement. Furthermore, results show benefits for everyone: (younger) participants as developers gained a better understanding of the potential user group and their mental models and thus felt more secure in finding appropriate design solutions.

Keywords: Human-centered computing · Older adults · Aging · Participatory design · User studies

1 Introduction

As our society is ageing, new information and communication technology (ICT) emerges, which could aid social inclusion and positive ageing. Yet too often the needs and abilities of older adults are ignored. Especially young software developers often struggle to take the perspective of a diverse older user group [1, 2]. Designing ICT for the well-being of our ageing population has been identified as one of the grand challenges of HCI, to nurture the human potential and strengthen mental health [3]. Participatory Design (PD) can build a bridge between developers and potential users. This requires including older adults in all phases of technology development to accommodate their requirements, fears and needs [4]. Hence, their participation, responsibilities and resources have to be organized [5]. The HCD+ approach focuses on the participatory development of ICT, considering special user characteristics of older adults. It provides seven general guidelines for working with older adults in terms of recruitment, atmosphere, and methods in an HCI context [6]. See [6] for an overview of the guidelines and respective descriptions.

© The Author(s), under exclusive license to Springer Nature Switzerland AG 2022
N. L. Black et al. (Eds.): IEA 2021, LNNS 223, pp. 725–734, 2022.
https://doi.org/10.1007/978-3-030-74614-8_90

This paper addresses the evaluation of participatory activities using HCD+ guidelines in a community context inferred from our experience with older participants from the German Association of RuralWomen and the German Women's Circle.

Besides, this paper emphasizes the developers involved in the project and focuses specifically on their personal experiences with the Participatory Design methods and the lasting effects on well-being.

The cooperation with these stakeholders is embedded in the Historytelling project, a social networking service for writing and sharing personal life stories.

1.1 Participatory Design

Participatory design (PD) describes a mindset democratizing the design process and integrating various stakeholders into all phases of product development [4]. It can be defined as "a process of investigating, understanding, reflecting upon, establishing, developing and supporting mutual learning between multiple participants in collective 'reflection-in-action'" [7]. Participants typically fulfill the two principal roles of users and designers, where the designers strive to learn about the users' situation, while the users strive to articulate their desired aims and to learn appropriate technological means to obtain them [7]. Thus, PD promises a better understanding between users and system developers as well as better products and services [8, 9].

While PD can in general provide a platform to advocate the needs of marginalized individuals and to get better insights into user needs for future product development [4], PD with older adults can improve their safety and quality of life as well as the usability of products and services they use [5, 10]. In particular, "previous research suggests that older adults are valuable as co-designers of innovative technology concepts and there is potential benefit in co-designers having prior interaction with the technology of interest to aid in the design ideation process" [4]. Also, the structure and methods of PD including collaborative feedback work best when informed by an understanding of the community of interest [4].

1.2 Participatory Design in Communities

Even though Participatory Design (PD) has increasingly been used in non-classical work contexts, most of the published studies and projects are still in a work domain with clear hierarchies and clear context [7, 11, 12]. Typically, they share two main goals: (1) development and evaluation of design practices that foster cooperation between designers and developers within the organization and (2) development and evaluation of work systems that support work activities.

Besides its traditional field of application, PD in communities offers new challenges and opportunities for practitioners and society [7, 13]. Communities mostly relate to geographical structures and are thus tied to a specific location such as neighborhood, city, or region. At the same time, however, they share a certain common identity [7]. Communities are social, heterogeneous structures, some of which are fluid and unclear. They often share a passion or concern on a particular topic and want to learn about it. Members are often intrinsically motivated rather than by external factors such as money, favoring collaboration if ICT supports communities' goals. This makes it difficult to apply a

"one-size-fits-all" design strategy. Instead, community-based PD projects need pluralistic approaches that meet the different challenges and contexts of communities [7]. At
the same time, PD in communities can help to find and support creative talents in large
groups, making them more sustainable over time and within the community [7, 11].

1.3 The Historytelling Project

To conduct ongoing research on PD with older adults, we were looking for ICT context
that could provide sufficient value to (intrinsically) motivate older adults to use it and
that plays to their strengths rather than just compensates their weaknesses. Thus, the idea
to the Historytelling project (HT) was born and has not disappointed since. This might in
large part be attributable to its components of social networking services (SNS), which
can provide great benefits for older adults. While SNS use is associated with increased
social capital and reduced loneliness [14, 15], direct communication is important to
facilitate and maintain friendships, making it important to have both: a diverse set of
weak ties and the communication context to take advantage of them [14]. A detailed
introduction to the HT project can be found in [16].

The existing collaboration with various stakeholders allowed us to create guidelines for working with older people (HCD+ guidelines), based on the literature and the
experience gained during the HT activities and other projects involving older adults [6],
including guidelines for user interface design created in special parts of HT [17]. In addition to the development of individual components, a style guide was created providing
general design guidance to improve the usability of interfaces for older people [18]. The
current state of development can be found on the HT project website [19].

2 Method

This paper describes the questionnaire study of two stakeholder groups within the participatory process. The first stakeholder group were older adults as potential users of
HT, recruited to validate the HCD+ guidelines (see Table 1) [6]. The second stakeholder
group were former HT developers. They filled in a questionnaire focused on the personal
experience with PD methods and subsequent effects on the project's development.

To validate the HCD+ guidelines on working with older adults in HCI contexts, a
questionnaire and interview study was conducted. The questionnaire was completed by
21 older adults, 2 of them were excluded from the analysis because they were too young
(aged below 60 years). The remaining 19 participants were aged between 60 and 77 years
($M = 67.7$; $SD = 5.1$). The participants who were members of the German Association
of RuralWomen ($N = 17$) were recruited by the chairwoman of the local chapter of
the Association of RuralWomen. The remaining participants ($N = 4$), members of the
German Women's Circle, were recruited by email.

11 of them completed the questionnaire in a café, 3 in a RuralWomen member's
home and 7 in their own home.

To assess the personal experiences of the (former) developers and the lasting effects
on their well-being, an online questionnaire was completed by 12 participants. They
were former students that had participated in the HT project in the course of thesis and
project work between 2016 and 2020.

Table 1. HCD+ guidelines developed for working with older adults in an HCI context. For a in-depth description see [6]

Category	Guideline
Recruitment	Group Leader Engagement (R1)
	Emphasize reciprocity when recruiting (R2)
Atmosphere and procedure	Cultivate socializing atmosphere (AP1)
	Schedule more time (AP2)
Methods	Accommodate participants' wishes (M1)
	Establish Fallbacks (M2)
	Use abstract descriptions of technology (M3)

2.1 Results on Evaluation of Participatory HCD+ Guidelines

Table 2 provides an overview of the questionnaire results for older adults. Since participants varied in prior experience with HT activities, results in are split by frequency of prior participation to indicate alteration over time: four women had never participated in HT activities, 5 had participated in one activity, 3 women in two activities, and 7 women in three or more activities. The column marked ">0" shows means for all 15 respondents who had participated in one or more HT activities before.

Answers to open questions were categorized post hoc and varied in frequency: 18 concerned reasons for future participation, 15 incentives for future participation, 15 reasons for first participation, and 8 for atmosphere. The results are described below.

Recruitment and Participation. For older adults, responses confirmed the importance of being approached for HT participation by known persons, such as the local chapter chairwoman or a well-known member of the HT project team (M = 7.5). A known person should also be present during the HT activity, which increases the likelihood of workshop attendance (M = 6.7). In general, the willingness to participate increased if people had participated in previous workshops and if a known person was present. Two participants also stated in the free text responses, that an invitation from the chairperson was their reason to participate in the first HT activity.

Emphasis on Reciprocity. Responses revealed that learning something new (M = 8.9) and receiving results from previous activities (M = 8.2) were important motivators for participation, as was mirrored in the free text comments: Older adults mentioned learning new things and curiosity as reasons for first and future participation (7) as well as interest in the project (5), support for their organization (3), and curiosity about the project progress (3). Even when asked about incentives for further participation, they mentioned the importance of learning something new every time (6), especially regarding technology use and methods. Participants also focused on personal interest and a positive atmosphere (2).

Cultivate a Socializing Atmosphere and Accommodate Participants' Wishes. Older adults emphasized the importance of good atmosphere and social interaction (M = 8.8),

Table 2. Mean importance ratings for HCD+ guideline categories, on a scale from 1 (low) to 10 (high), split by frequency of respondents prior to participation in HT activities, with column " >0" showing means for all 15 respondents who had participated in HT activities before, N = 19.

HCD+ guideline category	Frequency of participations					
	All	0	>0	1	2	≥3
N	19	4	15	5	3	7
Importance to be recruited by known people	7.5	8.8	7.2	6.0	9.0	7.3
Importance of presence of a known person	6.7	8.3	6.3	6.2	8.7	5.3
Probability of participation if no known person is present	6.5	5.3	6.9	5.8	6.7	7.7
Probability of participation if recruited by unknown person	4.4	3.0	4.8	3.8	7.0	4.6
Importance of learning something new	8.9	8.5	9.1	9.4	8.3	9.1
Importance of being informed about results of former activities	8.2	7.8	8.3	8.4	8.7	8.1
Importance of atmosphere and social interaction	8.8	9.5	8.6	9.3	8.0	8.4

as was mirrored again in the free text comments in the older adult's questionnaire. They focused on the interaction with the interviewer as well as with other participants, and the fruitful exchange between young and old. Four people also gave advice on improving the atmosphere through better task explanation and prototype preparation.

2.2 Results on Developers' Experience

There were 12, 11 and 8 answers to the three free text questions regarding the expectations of the HT project (initial expectations/fulfilled expectations/unfulfilled expectations). Table 3 summarizes effects of active user involvement on the development process and results and describes the subjective personal experience on reciprocity as well as the importance of social interaction and atmosphere for (former) HT developers.

Initial and (Un)fulfilled Expectations. Participants in this questionnaire study cited a general interest in both, the user group (8) and the topic (6) as initial reasons for deciding to work on HT. Other reasons included the supervisor (4), the participatory development process (4), the desire to make a contribution (2), and the technology being used (1).

A total of 11 responses concerning fulfilled expectations included the following topics: cooperation with older adults was good (7), as was the iterative approach to the project (3) and the practical experience gained through the implementation of the project (3). Also, research in the field of HT was seen as important (2) and academic support as good as expected (2). Working in a dynamic iterative HCD process can be hard and lead to unfulfilled expectations, of which 8 were described in detail: Collaboration with the target group was more difficult than expected (2) and no final product could be handed in at the end of the work (2). Developed subsystems did not work equally well for everyone in the summative evaluation (1), project setup and programming was more difficult than expected (1), project was more labor-intensive than expected (1) and work was not carried out across generations (1).

Table 3. Overview of questionnaire responses for (former) HT developers regarding personal benefits, Efficacy of User Involvement, as well as reciprocity and enjoyment. The scale ranges from 1 (low) to 10 (high), N = 12.

Efficacy of user involvement	M	SD
I felt safer in system development	8.6	1.2
I got new ideas for HT development	9.0	0.8
I got valuable feedback on the current state of my work	8.6	1.6
I iterated quicker	6.3	2.0
Reciprocity and enjoyment	M	SD
I learned something new through participatory system development	9.4	0.8
Participants learned something new through participatory system development	8.6	0.9
I enjoyed sharing my experience with others	9.0	1.0
I enjoyed learning from the experience of others	9.1	0.9
The atmosphere and social interaction were very important to me personally	9.8	0.4
Personal benefits	M	SD
I established a connection to the user group	9.3	0.9
I understood the mental model of the user (group) better	9.6	0.6

Experiences on Reciprocity in Learning and Enjoyment. Participant developers stated they could learn something new by the participatory way of working (M = 9.4), giving them joy (M = 9.1), and that they were able to pass on their experience (M = 8.6), which again gave them great joy (M = 9.0). This indicates that reciprocity and learning worked within the HT framework and that there was mutual benefit in the relationship. Further HT activities should focus on maintaining and strengthening opportunities to learn from one another. The high importance ratings for social atmosphere also show the developers' appreciation for the user group and might emphasize perceived importance of the project and its general topic.

Former developers emphasized the importance of good atmosphere and social interaction (M = 9.8). The high importance ratings for social atmosphere also show the developers' appreciation for the user group and might emphasize perceived importance of the project and its general topic.

Efficacy of User Involvement. Participant developers were asked to what extent active user involvement helped them in the development, addressing whether their involvement helped to better understand the user group and whether it helped with the comprehensibility of development process itself. They reported that they felt more secure overall during development (M = 8.6) while maintaining a high quality of user involvement, ensuring that new ideas were developed (M = 9.6) and feedback on the current status could be obtained (M = 8.6). Finally, involving users always takes time that could be used otherwise, e.g., in analysis or further project development, and there was considerably less agreement whether the active involvement of the user group helped with fast iteration (M = 6.3).

Personal Benefits. Results show that developers could establish a connection to the user group during the development process (M = 9.3), and that they better understood the user mental models (M = 9.6).

Also, aspects of personal well-being were measured. For these items, the scale ranged from −5 (decreased) to 5 (improved) with no neutral option.

Above all, their self-confidence (M = 3.3) and satisfaction (M = 3.0) had increased through development with the target group, as had the zest for life (M = 2.6), the perceived importance of their own life (M = 2.3), and the quality of life (M = 2.1).

3 Discussion

Three factors have proven to be particularly important for participatory development in the Historytelling project: (1) commitment of the chairperson (especially for the Rural-Women Berkenthin), (2) atmosphere and social interaction in joint HT activities, and (3) reciprocity of engagement in HT. Without the interest and dedication of the chairperson, most participants would not have joined HT activities. She acted as an important peer in the project, who understood the user group, was trusted, and could motivate them. From the initial contact, a relationship between participants and researchers could develop, creating a basis for mutual trust.

During HT activities, it was important for participants to have a pleasant working atmosphere with extra time for social interaction, e.g., during a meal before the actual workshop or extended coffee breaks. However, participants did not take part in HT just for pleasure. Mutual learning was an important motivator for them, especially regarding the use of new technologies. Guided by intrinsic motives, older adults desire to preserve and shape something for posterity, society, and their community. The results of their participation were important to them, which is in accord with the literature, showing that it is especially important for older people to spend their time sensibly [20].

Within the participatory design approach, HT system developers were able to gain a better understanding of the older user group and to establish a connection with them, which had positive impact on the developers and the product they developed. Changes in well-being for participant developers should be addressed more thoroughly in future research. Also, the issue of self-selection in the research sample should be addressed better in the future: interviewed participants are likely to be more active people in their communities, yet the HT project might also interest more withdrawn people who could thus become more socially integrated, which is in turn associated with higher well-being.

Overall, the HT-project has proven to be very suitable for cross-generational and intergenerational research. Here, older adults can learn about software, hardware and development methods while supporting their communities and younger people can learn about historical events, older users' mental models and participatory development while creating their own prototypes and strengthening their self-confidence.

4   Conclusion and Future Work

This paper describes the evaluation of participatory design processes in the Historytelling project within a local RuralWomen community and the German Women's Circle based on guidelines described in [6]. This HCD+ approach extends the Human Centered Design (HCD) process by focusing specifically on user characteristics and their influence on the development process and results. The evaluation is based on 31 interviews with older adults as potential users (N = 19) and younger developers (N = 12). Results indicate that especially the recruitment of participants and empahsis on reciprocity are peculiar for communities. Without the dedication of the chairpersons, a lot of participants would not have joined our participatory activities. Also, supporting their communities was an important factor for them. Besides, results show that the social atmosphere at the conducted workshops were important and that the participatory development had positive impact on the developed product and the experience of participant users and developers. Involving older adults in the development process added value for both groups, and a trusting relationship was established.

This study marks a first step to reflect on the results on the product and on the underlying process of participatory design in the Historytelling project, especially for local communities. The existing HCD+ guidelines will be iteratively improved over time and new guidelines will be added to foster the cooperation with older adults.

Simultaneously, further system components will be developed for HT and existing components will be improved iteratively in a PD process with older adults. Also, the cooperation with the RuralWomen is extended to support them in their anniversary of the local association chapter and cooperation with RuralWomen at the state level and with other entities, such as museums, is actively pursued.

One caveat for this study lies in the participants' gender: cooperation so far relies heavily on organizations in which women are dominant. However, the initial contact and the work during HT activities might conceivably change with the involvement of male-dominated organizations. Finally, it will be essential to test the validity of the HCD+ guidelines with more communities and to extend cooperation with other organizations.

Acknowledgements. We would like to thank all participants of the Historytelling project, especially the German Association of RuralWomen of Berkenthin and surrounding. Without them, this research could not be done.

References

1. Lindsay, S., Jackson, D., Schofield, G., Olivier, P.: Engaging older people using participatory design. In: Proceedings of the SIGCHI Conference on Human Factors in Computing Systems, pp. 1199–1208. ACM, New York (2012). https://doi.org/10.1145/2207676.2208570

2. Coleman, G.W., Gibson, L., Hanson, V.L., Bobrowicz, A., McKay, A.: Engaging the disengaged: how do we design technology for digitally excluded older adults? In: Proceedings of the 8th ACM Conference on Designing Interactive Systems, pp. 175–178. ACM, New York (2010). https://doi.org/10.1145/1858171.1858202
3. Stephanidis, C., Salvendy, G., Antona, M., Chen, J.Y.C., Dong, J., Duffy, V.G., Fang, X., Fidopiastis, C., Fragomeni, G., Fu, L.P., Guo, Y., Harris, D., Ioannou, A., Jeong, K., Konomi, S., Krömker, H., Kurosu, M., Lewis, J.R., Marcus, A., Meiselwitz, G., Moallem, A., Mori, H., Fui-Hoon Nah, F., Ntoa, S., Rau, P.-L.P., Schmorrow, D., Siau, K., Streitz, N., Wang, W., Yamamoto, S., Zaphiris, P., Zhou, J.: Seven HCI grand challenges. Int. J. Hum.–Comput. Interact. 1–41 (2019). https://doi.org/10.1080/10447318.2019.1619259
4. Harrington, C.N., Wilcox, L., Connelly, K., Rogers, W., Sanford, J.: Designing health and fitness apps with older adults: examining the value of experience-based co-design. In: Proceedings of the 12th EAI International Conference on Pervasive Computing Technologies for Healthcare – Pervasive Health 2018, pp. 15–24. ACM Press, New York (2018). https://doi.org/10.1145/3240925.3240929
5. Demirbilek, O., Demirkan, H.: Universal product design involving elderly users: a participatory design model. Appl. Ergon. **35**, 361–370 (2004). https://doi.org/10.1016/j.apergo.2004.03.003
6. Sengpiel, M., Volkmann, T., Jochems, N.: Considering older adults throughout the development process – the HCD+ approach. In: Proceedings of the Human Factors and Ergonomics Society Europe Chapter 2018 Annual Conference, Berlin (2019)
7. Simonsen, J., Robertson, T. (eds): Routledge International Handbook of Participatory Design. Routledge (2012). https://doi.org/10.4324/9780203108543
8. Kensing, F., Munk-Madsen, A.: PD: structure in the toolbox. Commun. ACM. **36**, 78–85 (1993). https://doi.org/10.1145/153571.163278
9. Kopeć, W., Nielek, R., Wierzbicki, A.: Guidelines towards better participation of older adults in software development processes using a new SPIRAL method and participatory approach. In: Proceedings of the 11th International Workshop on Cooperative and Human Aspects of Software Engineering, pp. 49–56. Association for Computing Machinery, New York (2018). https://doi.org/10.1145/3195836.3195840
10. Newell, A.F.: Design and the digital divide: insights from 40 years in computer support for older and disabled people. In: Design and the Digital Divide: Insights from 40 Years in Computer Support for Older and Disabled People. Morgan & Claypool (2011)
11. Halskov, K., Hansen, N.B.: The diversity of participatory design research practice at PDC 2002–2012. Int. J. Hum.-Comput. Stud. **74**, 81–92 (2015). https://doi.org/10.1016/j.ijhcs.2014.09.003
12. Carroll, J.M., Rosson, M.B.: Participatory design in community informatics. Design stud. **28**, 243–261 (2007)
13. Voorberg, W.H., Bekkers, V.J.J.M., Tummers, L.G.: A systematic review of co-creation and co-production: embarking on the social innovation journey. Public Manage. Rev. **17**, 1333–1357 (2015). https://doi.org/10.1080/14719037.2014.930505
14. Burke, M., Marlow, C., Lento, T.: Social network activity and social well-being. In: Proceedings of the SIGCHI Conference on Human Factors in Computing Systems, pp. 1909–1912. ACM, New York (2010). https://doi.org/10.1145/1753326.1753613.
15. Deters, F.G., Mehl, M.R.: Does posting Facebook status updates increase or decrease loneliness? An online social networking experiment. Soc. Psychol. Pers. Sci. **4**, 579–586 (2013). https://doi.org/10.1177/1948550612469233
16. Volkmann, T., Sengpiel, M., Jochems, N.: Historytelling: a website for the elderly a human-centered design approach. In: Proceedings of the 9th Nordic Conference on Human-Computer Interaction, pp. 100:1–100:6. ACM, New York (2016). https://doi.org/10.1145/2971485.2996735

17. Volkmann, T., Grosche, D., Sengpiel, M., Jochems, N.: What can i say?: Presenting stimulus material to support storytelling for older adults. In: Proceedings of the 10th Nordic Conference on Human-Computer Interaction, pp. 696–700. ACM, New York (2018). https://doi.org/10.1145/3240167.3240256
18. Volkmann, T., Unger, A., Sengpiel, M., Jochems, N.: Development of an age-appropriate style guide within the historytelling project. In: Zhou, J., Salvendy, G. (eds.) Human Aspects of IT for the Aged Population. Design for the Elderly and Technology Acceptance, pp. 84–97. Springer, Cham (2019).
19. Universität zu Lübeck: Historytelling. (2019)
20. Ellis, R.D., Kurniawan, S.H.: Increasing the usability of online information for older users: a case study in participatory design. Int. J. Hum.-Comput. Interact. **12**, 263–276 (2000). https://doi.org/10.1207/S15327590IJHC1202_6

Making Tax eForms Less Taxing—Comparing Evaluation Measures of User-Experience, Usability, and Acceptance in Public Sector eForms

Mourad Zoubir[(✉)], Daniel Wessel, Tim Schrills, Thomas Franke, and Moreen Heine

Institute for Multimedia and Interactive Systems, University of Lübeck, Lübeck, Germany
zoubir@imis.uni-luebeck.de

Abstract. eForms have become a means to decrease workload and processing speed in the public sector. As eForms go beyond simply "digitally replacing" analogue systems, their potential is not yet exhausted. However, to systematically improve eForms, appropriate tools to tailor eForms to user needs and evaluate their usability are required. The objective of this paper is to develop and evaluate a user experience questionnaire for eForms. We introduce the eForms User Experience Scale (EFUXS), which is based on the psychological needs aspect of Self-Determination Theory and its three facets (competence, autonomy, and relatedness). To assess the validity of EFUXS, its results were compared with well-known usability (System Usability Scale; Brooke, 1996) and acceptance (simple acceptance scale, van der Laan, 1997) measures. In an online study with a randomized within-subject design, university students ($N = 60$) evaluated their experience with two versions of the same registration form. These forms were designed to implement the best practices from a governmental guide on eForms or their inverse ("worst practices"). All three scales were able to differentiate between "good" and "bad" tax-form versions. The item-analysis of the EFUXS showed acceptable to excellent internal consistency, item difficulty, and discrimination. The scale correlated with the two comparison measures, indicating convergent validity, while offering additional insights into psychological need fulfilment. This study suggests the viability of the EFUXS as a user experience measure and highlights advantages in its use to improve eForms.

Keywords: eGovernment · Self-determination theory · eForms · User experience

1 Introduction

Governmental electronic Forms (eForms) are used in the exchange of information between a private (e.g., citizen or company employee) and public (e.g., a governmental agency) entity. They often convey information relevant to decision making (e.g., eligibility for a service) or the implementation of decisions (e.g., banking details for the transfer of social services). Studies on eForms have shown that such tools can decrease

© The Author(s), under exclusive license to Springer Nature Switzerland AG 2022
N. L. Black et al. (Eds.): IEA 2021, LNNS 223, pp. 735–745, 2022.
https://doi.org/10.1007/978-3-030-74614-8_91

completion time and reduce error rates (cf. e.g. [1]), thus bringing advantages to both users of these forms and governments processing them.

One common example of a legally mandated transaction is tax-filing. In Germany approximately 192.7 million filings on income tax have been conducted since the establishment of the service in 2011 [2]. Globally, the number of countries offering online interaction is increasing (e.g., by 16% between 2018 and 2020), particularly for services such as registering a business, applying for a birth/marriage certificate, a driver's license, or for a personal identity card [3]. At the same time, permeation within certain countries has not been maximized, and in cases such as Germany, use of eGovernmental services have declined [4].

One explanation for the non-use of e-government services is poor *usability* (i.e. completion in an efficient, effective, and satisfying manner [5]) - this has been confirmed in various studies [6, 7]. Therefore, it is essential that eForms demonstrate adequate usability, so that eForms e.g. do not cause frustration (cf. e.g. [8]). However, while improving usability may support the adoption of eGovernment services, this is a "lesser of two evils approach" – with eForms only being selected for being easier than paper forms. Instead, governments should consider increasing intrinsic motivation, i.e. choosing to use digital services because of the internal, positive reaction it elicits.

In other words, eForms should also enhance *user experience* (UX). UX includes aspects of usability, as well as users' emotions, beliefs, preferences etc. before, during and after system usage [9]). Good UX has been shown to facilitate the adoption of new technologies (e.g. [10]), which can support the digital transformation of eGovernment. Furthermore, good UX can shape positive experiences in situations that are not always voluntary (which has been shown in non-eGovernment contexts, e.g. medical adherence [11]). This is crucial in government interactions in which citizens depend on services based on information they provide (e.g., welfare benefits) or when they have to fulfill their legal obligations (e.g. tax filing).

At the same time, forms represent laws. This must be considered in their design and reveals a central challenge between conformity with the law and UX [12]. For example, legal terms must be translated into understandable language without distorting content. Furthermore, laws often also allow for discretionary decisions. All information relevant to the decision must be available and potentially requested in the form (if it has not already been collected and transmitted elsewhere in the sense of the once-only principle).

So that eForms can overcome this challenge and provide excellent user experience, benchmarking tools are needed. These tools must enable non-specialized practitioners to evaluate and tailor their eForms to suit the wide variety of user's needs and create an experience that fosters the relationship between citizen and government. Yet, empirical research on UX for eForm development in the public sector is lacking.

Due to the heterogenous user base of eForms, benchmarking tools must address basic psychological needs inherent in all individuals. One applicable and well-established framework is that of the basic psychological needs, which is one of six mini theories encompassing self-determination theory (referred to here as SDT for brevity; [13, 14]). SDT asserts three basic needs: competence (sense of efficacy), autonomy (sense of volition), and relatedness (sense of belonging or being cared for). High levels of need fulfillment are associated with increased performance and intrinsic motivation, and a system which fulfills these needs can increase feelings of well-being and growth. While many self-report measures on SDT exist (cf. e.g. [15]), and previous research has applied it in the field of Human Computer Interaction (for a review, cf. e.g. [16] or [17]) or eGovernment (e.g. [18]), SDT has not yet been applied as a UX measure in this specific context.

The objective of this paper was to develop a scale to specifically assess user experience of eForms, and to appraise its suitability by a) conducting an item analysis of the scale, b) assessing its ability differentiate between electronic tax forms of different quality and comparing its performance with measures of usability and acceptance, and c) exploring correlations with other measure for construct validity.

2   EFUXS Scale Development

The development process of the eForms User Experience Scale (EFUXS) adapts the first four phases of the scale development process described by Boateng et al. [19]. The first three phases are described in this section, while the fourth is described in Sects. 3 and 4.

Identification of Domain and Item Generation. The dimensions of the scale were based on the three facets of SDT: *Competence*, encompassed a feeling of efficacy in (universal) eForm completion; *Autonomy*, the sense of volition and sovereignty afforded by the eForms; and *Relatedness*, the feeling of being taken care of (here: to what extent the agency was supporting the user through the eForm process). Item were generated in two manners: either based on previous work of the SDT facets (i.e. converting items from existing SDT measures to the current context; referred to as "classification from above" [19]) and expert interviews with psychologists, who generated potential items based on their expert knowledge of the SDT facets ("classification from below"). Items were consolidated by the authors in multiple iterations.

Content Validity. The content validity of the respective versions was evaluated in multiple focus group of expert researchers in the field of eGovernment (backgrounds in politics, psychology, or media and computer science, $N = 6$). Three reviews were carried out by this panel to select items that were appropriate, accurate, and could be interpreted. Items were accepted, rejected, or modified until a consensus was reached.

Pre-testing of Questions. The scale was pre-tested with a heterogeneous user group ($N = 4$) of differing age (young adult, middle aged, senior) and levels of education (high-school diploma, apprenticeship, university education). Cognitive interviews were used, during which participants verbalized mental processes while completing an eForm and the EFUXS. The results were used to iteratively improve the comprehensibility of item wording. Participants were also asked to group similar EFUXS items, which were then compared with the underlying domain. Grouping corresponded strongly with the respective domains (45 of 48 grouped correctly). The final version of the EFUXS is shown in Table 1.

Table 1. Analysis of EFUXS items, relative to their subscales ($n = 120$).

Item	This form was designed in such a way that…	M (SD)	Item-total	Difficulty	Discrim.	α if removed
C1	…I feel like I can complete it well	4.58 (1.5)	.91	.76	.83	.88
C2	…I feel incompetent while working on it. (I)	4.94 (1.3)	.71	.82[a]	.71	.94[c]
C3	…I can complete it competently	4.59 (1.3)	.90	.78	.83	.88
C4	…I feel like I could complete similar forms well	4.58 (1.4)	.89	.78	.86	.88
				Subscale Cronbach's α =		.92
A1	…I can express my wishes clearly	4.55 (1.3)	.64	.76	.64	.67
A2	…my decision-making options were unclear. (I)	4.19 (1.5)	.40	.70	.40[b]	.79[c]
A3	…it was clear why a question had to be answered	4.07 (1.7)	.65	.68	.65	.65
A4	…I could complete the form in a self-determined manner	4.41 (1.4)	.58	.74	.58	.70
				Subscale Cronbach's α =		.76
R1	…I felt I was supported	3.82 (1.5)	.93	.64	.83	.94
R2	…I felt my wishes were not really understood. (I)	3.18 (1,5)	.93	.64	.90	.94
R3	…I felt I was being taken care of	3.76 (1.5)	.88	.63	.81	.95
R4	…it was clear, they were concerned with me	3.67 (1.6)	.85	.61	.78	.96
				Subscale Cronbach's α =		.96
				EFUXS Cronbach's α =		**.95**

Note: Original German Language Items in Appendix. C1–C4: competency subscale, A1–A4: autonomy subscale, R1–R4: relatedness

3   Method

3.1   Participants

Participants ($N = 60$) were recruited via student mailing-lists (35 *female*, 20 *male*, 1 *diverse*; 4 without answer; age $M = 23.2$, $SD = 3.13$). As compensation, participants could take part in a raffle of ten 10€ cash prizes.

3.2   Material

User Experience. The final iteration of the pre-tested EFUXS measure was used (see Table 1).

Usability. We used the established 10-item System Usability Scale [20], which has been widely applied to evaluate usability and is considered by some researchers to be the gold standard [21]. As the SUS uses a neutral middle, we adapted its response scale from a 5-point to a 6-point Likert scale to increase consistency with the UX measure. Nouns of the items were adapted to the eGovernment context. For example, "system" was replaced with "form". The internal consistency in the study was excellent ($\alpha = .96$), as interpreted according to George and Mallery (2003).

Acceptance. As measure of user-acceptance and to assess convergent validity, the van der Laan simple acceptance scale [22] was included. The scale consists of two subscales: usefulness and satisfaction and assess these constructs with a 6-point semantic differential. The satisfaction ($\alpha = .93$) and usefulness ($\alpha = .90$) subscales both showed good internal consistency.

eForms. Two sets of eForms were created, which were based upon paper registration forms for municipal dog license fees in a German city. Registration for dog license fees was selected as students (i.e. young adults with possibly transient living situations) were assumed not to be overly familiar with this form, while at the same time having the potential to be relevant for them in the future.

To create a best-practice version of this form, the best-practice guide "Improving and Reviewing Government Forms" [23]) was applied. Specifically, we made changes to increase the pragmatic and hedonic quality the original form. For example, we applied the guideline suggesting that forms should use the second person "you", rather than the third person 'the applicant'. To create a worst practice version as contrast, the opposite of the suggested best practice was applied. For example, for the guideline suggesting simplified sentence structure, we connected multiple sentences with a conjunction. In total, 25 changes in each of the two versions were made to the original form.

Participants were provided with fictional personal information to be entered for each version of the eForm. These included identification and insurance cards, as well as "post-it" notes for other necessary information, e.g., the date of birth of the dog.

3.3 Procedure

Participants were randomly assigned to the best or worst practice version. They completed the first form and evaluated it, then repeated the process for the other version. After completing both conditions, demographic information was assessed. The study was conducted in LimeSurvey [24]. Statistical analysis of the results was conducted with R [25] in RStudio [26]. Where applicable, results were calculated with non-parametric tests, as Shapiro-Wilk tests indicated non-normal distributions in all measures.

4   Results

4.1   Item Analysis of EFUXS

Items of both within-groups were evaluated together on item-total correlation, item difficulty, item discrimination and internal consistency (see Table 1). Groups were combined to allow for a greater sample size thus allowing for the detection of smaller effect sizes and to balance out sequence effects ($n = 2 \times 60 = 120$).

Internal consistency of EFUXS and the subscales can be interpreted as excellent (i.e. >= .9, according to [27]), except for the autonomy subscale, which was acceptable (i.e. > = .7). Further analysis indicated two inverted items, C2 and A2, would improve internal consistency if removed, making them candidates for removal or reversal. These results suggest a strong reliability of the scale, baring the mentioned items.

4.2 Differentiation

A Wilcoxon Signed-Rank Test indicated that EFUXS scores of the best practice eForm were significantly higher than on the worst practice eForm ($W = 374$, $p < .001$, large effect size: $r = .69$). Similarly, the SUS showed a statistically significant differences between both eForms ($W = 347.5, p < .001$; strong effect: $r = .70$). Acceptance measures also indicated that the values of the usefulness ($W = 547.5$, $p < .001$, $r = .61$) and satisfaction subscales ($W = 391.5$, $p = .001$, $r = .68$) were higher on the best practice than the worst practice eForm, with large effect-sizes each. These results suggest that our UX scale was able to successfully classify our best-practice stimuli similarly well as established measures. See Fig. 1 for a comparison of boxplots.

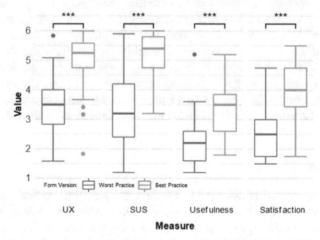

Fig. 1. Comparison of scale values between versions of test-forms ($n = 120$). Note: ***: $p <$ .001.

4.3 Convergent Validity

Spearman correlations between the EFUXS and its subscales, and the other measures (see Table 2) showed a strong correlation in general with the SUS and a moderate correlation with the acceptance measures (as interpreted by Cohen, 1998). The Autonomy subscale had a stronger correlation with the Usefulness than the overall measure. However, Fischer's z tests showed that this was not significant ($z = 0.314, p = .37$).

Table 2. Correlation of EFUXS and its subscales to other measures. ($n = 120$).

	SUS	Acceptance (usefulness)	Acceptance (satisfaction)
EFUXS (competence subscale)	.88 ***	.37 ***	.41 ***
EFUXS (autonomy subscale)	.82 ***	.39 ***	.39 ***
EFUXS (relatedness subscale)	.84 ***	.35 ***	.37 ***
EXFS (overall)	.91 ***	.38 ***	.41 ***

Note: Correlations between subscales or between non-EFUXS measures are excluded for clarity. ***: p < .001

5 Discussion

This study was a first step in creating a UX-measure to specifically assess eForms in the public sector eForms: EFUXS. In an iterative development process, the facets of SDT were used in a bottom-up and top-down item generation process. The items were evaluated by experts in focus group discussions and by users in cognitive interviews. The final iteration was tested in a field study, with participants completing contrasting best- and worst-practice eForms and evaluating them with the EFUXS, SUS and the simple acceptance scale. Item analysis suggested that the EFUXS differentiated similarly well to other measures, although it could be improved by the removal of two inverted items. Correlations of the scale and individual subscales to other measures imply convergence with the properties of these measures.

Based on the results of the present research we see first evidence to support the EFUXS as a promising tool to quantify UX in the context of eForms. It can discriminate between forms based on how well these forms support basic psychological needs. Thus, in contrast to the general usability and acceptance scales, the EFUXS specifically measures the fulfillment of the underlying basic needs (SDT), and thus indicates which steps must be taken to improve the user experience of the eForm. Furthermore, this study lays the groundwork for the additional use of SDT in eGovernment.

In particular, the EFUXS allows practitioners to understand the effects eForm design on autonomy and relatedness. Autonomy and relatedness are heavily influenced by the nature of user-government transactions, i.e. the often-non-voluntary nature of eForms (such as tax filing) suppresses feelings of autonomy (e.g. "I don't have a choice, I have to do it") and relatedness (e.g. "They don't care about me, they simply need the information"). Here we were successful in creating a measure which can assess how well an agency has successfully overcome these limitations specific to the context of eGovernment. Similarly, and perhaps more importantly - it is useful in ascertaining if an eForm encroaches upon user's feeling of autonomy or relatedness, which reduces user's intrinsic motivation, making the use of (potentially more costly) extrinsic motivators necessary.

Regarding the final facet of SDT, fulling the need for competence has previously been associated with usability (e.g. in eHealth [29]). Therefore, we argue that the EFUXS competence subscale can give a reliable indication of usability with four items. This underlines the advantage of using the EFUXS instead of the SUS, as the EFUXS offers more utilizable information with a similar number of items.

The presented scale of twelve items is reliable and economical. Future work can further expand upon the latter. A confirmatory factor analysis, preferably in a sample including at least 300 observations (cf. [30]) could offer additional support to the validity of the subscales by categorizing these items as factors. Further analysis could also identify potential candidates for removal.

One limitation of this study is that discriminate validity was not established, i.e. while the SDT approach was valid and novel, the data gathered here cannot yet argue for the variance to other measures. This could be due to two reasons.

Firstly, the very high EFUXS-SUS correlation suggests that the test material may have been too similar in pragmatic and hedonic value. In other words, the applied best- and worst-practices affected both usability and user experience similarly. Test stimuli which differs exclusively in hedonic elements (e.g. wording with similar readability or comparison of corporate designs) could be used to better assess the discriminative power of the EFUXS.

Secondly, the current study does not contain a pure UX measure. While usability and user-acceptance have a strong theoretical overlap with UX (in that usability contributes to UX, while acceptance is a possible consequence of UX and usability, cf. e.g. [31]), a correlation study with a holistic UX measures, such as the User Experience Question-naire, which contains a subscale for usability [32] could further provide insights into convergent or discriminate validity.

Nevertheless, the content validity and reliability established here shows the great potential for the EFUXS to help create eForms which support user's basic psychological needs.

6 Conclusion

The interaction between a government and its citizens or organizations is often over-shadowed by its compulsory nature. However, with the right methods, these transactions can still fulfill basic psychological needs for competence, autonomy, and relatedness, which provide a positive user experience and may increase the likelihood of timely and motivated completion. With the EFUXS, we present a first benchmarking tool to support everyday practitioners in creating eForms that are not only usable but make filling them out a positive experience for users.

Appendix

The Original German Language EFUXS

Im Folgendem geht es darum, das soeben ausgefühlte Formular zu bewerten.						
Bitte geben Sie Ihr Grad der Zustimmung an. Dieses Formular ist so gestaltet, dass...	stimmt gar nicht	stimmt weitgehend nicht	stimmt eher nicht	stimmt eher	stimmt weitgehend	stimmt völlig
a …ich mein Anliegen klar ausdrücken konnte.	☐	☐	☐	☐	☐	☐
b ...ich es selbstbestimmt ausfüllen kann.	☐	☐	☐	☐	☐	☐
c ...ich den Eindruck habe, dass man sich um mich kümmert.	☐	☐	☐	☐	☐	☐
d ...ich das Gefühl habe, unterstützt zu werden.	☐	☐	☐	☐	☐	☐
e ...ich es kompetent ausfüllen kann.	☐	☐	☐	☐	☐	☐
f ...ich das Gefühl habe, auch andere ähnliche Formulare gut ausfüllen zu können.	☐	☐	☐	☐	☐	☐
g ...klar wird, dass man sich Gedanken um mich macht.	☐	☐	☐	☐	☐	☐
h ...ich das Gefühl habe, dass ich es gut ausfüllen kann.	☐	☐	☐	☐	☐	☐
i ...ich mich bei der Bearbeitung unfähig fühle.	☐	☐	☐	☐	☐	☐
j ...meine Entscheidungsoptionen unklar bleiben.	☐	☐	☐	☐	☐	☐
k ...deutlich ist, warum diese Fragen beantwortet werden müssen.	☐	☐	☐	☐	☐	☐
l ...ich den Eindruck habe, dass mein Anliegen nicht wirklich verstanden wurde.	☐	☐	☐	☐	☐	☐

References

1. Wroblewski, L.: Web Form Design: Filling in the Blanks. Rosenfeld Media (2008)
2. ELSTER - Presse. https://www.elster.de/eportal/infoseite/presse. Accessed 05 Feb 2021
3. UN E-Government Survey 2020. UN DESA, New York (2020)
4. Krcmar, H., Akkaya, C., Müller, L.-S., Dietrich, S., Boberach, M., Exel, S.: eGovernment MONITOR 2017. Bundesministerium des Innern (2017)
5. ISO 9241–11:2018(en), Ergonomics of human-system interaction—Part 11: usability: definitions and concepts. https://www.iso.org/obp/ui/#iso:std:iso:9241:-11:ed-2:v1:en. Accessed 05 Feb 2021
6. Chen, L., Aklikokou, A.K.: Determinants of E-government adoption: testing the mediating effects of perceived usefulness and perceived ease of use. Int. J. Public Adm. **43**, 850–865 (2020). https://doi.org/10.1080/01900692.2019.1660989
7. Ozen, A.O., Pourmousa, H., Alıpourc, N.: Investigation of the critical factors affecting e-government acceptance: a systematic review and a conceptual model. Innov. J. Bus. Manage. **7**, 77–84 (2018)
8. Bruun, A., Law, E.L.-C., Heintz, M., Alkly, L.H.A.: Understanding the relationship between frustration and the severity of usability problems: what can psychophysiological data (not) tell us? In: Proceedings of the 2016 CHI Conference on Human Factors in Computing Systems, pp. 3975–3987. Association for Computing Machinery, New York (2016)
9. ISO 9241–210:2010(en), Ergonomics of human-system interaction—Part 210: Human-centred design for interactive systems, https://www.iso.org/obp/ui/#iso:std:iso:9241:-210:ed-1:v1:en. Accessed 05 Feb 2021
10. Fehnert, B., Kosagowsky, A.: Measuring user experience: complementing qualitative and quantitative assessment. In: Proceedings of the 10th International Conference on Human Computer Interaction with Mobile Devices and Services, pp. 383–386. Association for Computing Machinery, New York (2008). https://doi.org/10.1145/1409240.1409294
11. Gloyd, D.M.: Positive user experience and medical adherence. In: Proceedings of the 2003 International Conference on Designing Pleasurable Products and Interfaces, pp. 17–21. Association for Computing Machinery, New York (2003). https://doi.org/10.1145/782896. 782902
12. Scholta, H., Balta, D., Räckers, M., Becker, J., Krcmar, H.: Standardization of forms in governments. Bus. Inf. Syst. Eng. **62**, 535–560 (2020). https://doi.org/10.1007/s12599-019-00623-1
13. Ryan, R.M., Deci, E.L.: Intrinsic and extrinsic motivation from a self-determination theory perspective: Definitions, theory, practices, and future directions. Contemp. Educ. Psychol. **61**, 101860 (2020). https://doi.org/10.1016/j.cedpsych.2020.101860
14. Deci, E.L., Ryan, R.M.: The general causality orientations scale: self-determination in personality. J. Res. Pers. **19**, 109–134 (1985). https://doi.org/10.1016/0092-6566(85)90023-6
15. Metrics & Methods: Questionnaires – selfdeterminationtheory.org. https://selfdeterminationtheory.org/questionnaires/. Accessed 08 Feb 2021
16. Huang, Y.-C., Backman, S.J., Backman, K.F., McGuire, F.A., Moore, D.: An investigation of motivation and experience in virtual learning environments: a self-determination theory. Educ. Inf. Technol. **24**, 591–611 (2019). https://doi.org/10.1007/s10639-018-9784-5
17. Tyack, A., Mekler, E.D.: Self-determination theory in HCI games research: current uses and open questions. In: Proceedings of the 2020 CHI Conference on Human Factors in Computing Systems, pp. 1–22. Association for Computing Machinery, New York (2020). https://doi.org/ 10.1145/3313831.3376723
18. Cupido, K., Ophoff, J.: A model of fundamental components for an e-government crowd-sourcing platform. Electron. J. e-Govern. **12**, 142–157 (2014)

19. Boateng, G.O., Neilands, T.B., Frongillo, E.A., Melgar-Quiñonez, H.R., Young, S.L.: Best practices for developing and validating scales for health, social, and behavioral research: a primer. Front. Public Health. **6** (2018). https://doi.org/10.3389/fpubh.2018.00149
20. Brooke, J.: SUS: a "quick and dirty" usability scale. In: Usability Evaluation in Industry, pp. 207–212. CRC Press, London (1996). https://doi.org/10.1201/9781498710411-35
21. Lewis, J.R.: The system usability scale: past, present, and future. Int. J. Hum.-Comput. Interact. **34**, 577–590 (2018). https://doi.org/10.1080/10447318.2018.1455307
22. Van Der Laan, J.D., Heino, A., De Waard, D.: A simple procedure for the assessment of acceptance of advanced transport telematics. Transp. Res. Part C: Emerg. Technol. **5**, 1–10 (1997). https://doi.org/10.1016/S0968-090X(96)00025-3
23. Dunleavy, P., Davies, M., O'Farrell, H.: Improving and reviewing government forms: a practical guide. National Audit Office (2013)
24. Schmitz, C.: LimeSurvey: an open source survey tool. LimeSurvey Project, Hamburg, Germany (2020)
25. R Core Team: R: A language and environment for statistical computing. R Foundation for Statistical Computing, Vienna, Austria (2020)
26. RStudio Team: RStudio: integrated development environment for R. Boston, MA (2020)
27. George, D., Mallery, P.: Reliability analysis. SPSS for Windows, step by step: a simple guide and reference, p. 222, 232. Allyn & Bacon, Boston (2003)
28. DeVellis, R.F.: Scale Development: Theory and Applications. SAGE Publications (2016)
29. Fu, H.N., Konstan, J.A., Wolfson, J.A., Adam, T.J., Clancy, T.R., Wyman, J.F.: Influence of patient characteristics and psychological needs on diabetes mobile app usability in adults with type 1 or type 2 diabetes: crossover randomized trial. JMIR Diabetes **4**, e11462 (2019)
30. Clark, L.A., Watson, D.: Constructing validity: basic issues in objective scale development. American Psychological Association, Washington (2016). https://doi.org/10.1037/14805-012
31. Hassenzahl, M.: The thing and i: understanding the relationship between user and product. In: Blythe, M.A., Overbeeke, K., Monk, A.F., and Wright, P.C. (eds.) Funology: From Usability to Enjoyment, pp. 31–42. Springer, Dordrecht (2004). https://doi.org/10.1007/1-4020-2967-5_4
32. Laugwitz, B., Held, T., Schrepp, M.: Construction and evaluation of a user experience questionnaire. In: Holzinger, A. (ed.) HCI and Usability for Education and Work, pp. 63–76. Springer, Heidelberg (2008). https://doi.org/10.1007/978-3-540-89350-9_6

Part IX: Ergonomic Work Analysis and Training (EWAT) – *Addendum* (Edited by Catherine Delgoulet and Marta Santos)

Learning Scenarios for the Improvement of Operating Safety of Machine Tools

Leif Goldhahn$^{(\boxtimes)}$ and Robert Eckardt

Faculty Engineering Sciences, InnArbeit – Centre of Innovative Process Planning and Ergonomics, University of Applied Sciences Mittweida, Technikumplatz 17, 09648 Mittweida, Germany

`{Goldhahn,Eckardt}@hs-mittweida.de`

Abstract. Virtual Reality (VR) unveils adequate possibilities in the context of demand-oriented qualification of employees. This state-of-the-art technology represents especially for employees an attractive and effective opportunity for the acquisition and transfer of knowledge relating to processes and products [1]. The guiding principle for the application of VR technology in the context of employee qualification consists in a more substantial and sustainable knowledge development if experienced and not abstractly learned using classic learning methods. Virtual learning scenarios, such as for the commissioning or the setting-up of a machine tool, are oriented towards the sensomotoric knowledge development and therefore support the transfer of procedural and action related skills in a virtual training environment. The embedding of learning scenarios in a virtual learning environment, which represents an accessible and realistic depiction of the real work environment as well as the respective work tasks including operating actions, an improved orientation within the real work environment based on the experiences of the virtual world is expected.

Apart from a methodological approach for the development of virtual learning scenarios, two defined and developed types of learning scenarios related to the commissioning of a machine tool as well as considering different learning requirements of employee qualification are introduced in this contribution.

Keywords: Virtual reality · Learning scenarios · Work process · Virtual training systems · Training tool · Method

1 Introduction

The increasing flexibilisation of work tasks, the handling of complex products, high consequential costs in case of misconduct or dynamic product variations within the manufacturing are physically and psychologically demanding for the human being and require innovative technical and organizational aids [2, 3]. In order to fulfill these requirements, digital technologies such as virtual reality introduce novel potentials and approaches for self-regulated and self-organized learning processes in the context of employee qualification. In mechanical and plant engineering, one of Germany's largest industrial sectors,

N. L. Black et al. (Eds.): IEA 2021, LNNS 223, pp. 749–757, 2022.
https://doi.org/10.1007/978-3-030-74614-8_92

the secure operation and utilization of machine tools is considered as a success criteria in employee qualification. This includes tasks of maintenance and repair [1, 5, 6].

Digital technologies represent novel potentials and approaches for the qualification of employees (knowledge transfer) in the context of learning for these areas of responsibility.

Among other things, the usage of VR technology in civil pilot training reduces error rates but also the training efforts in real operation considerably [8].

For machine tools and their specific operating actions within the process, there is currently only a very limited availability of simulations based on VR [1]. Though the damage potential for humans, machines or tools in case of accidents or operating errors within the process can be enormous. Furthermore, unproductive downtimes of machine tools are to be reduced. These result for instance in case of insecure operation, operating errors or even training processes themselves.

The virtual learning scenarios introduced in this contribution focus on the approach of the VR-based pilot training and correspondingly transfer it to the demands for the utilization of machine tools to potentially eliminate misconduct or operating errors on the machine. Exemplary use cases on machine tools were analyzed, structured and methodologically processed.

2 Background

2.1 Employee Qualification

Current learning applications such as e-learning or blended learning support a fundamental qualification, knowledge building and expansion or the development of competences.

Substantial disadvantage of these learning applications consists in the fact that practical skills and abilities are oftentimes only communicable on the real object. The essential additional value of VR based technologies "consists in the temporal and spatial flexibility of the learning processes" [9].

VR enables, in dependence of the respective VR system (hardware) utilized and the VR application (software) developed, a substantially realistic depiction of the work environment as well as the therein appearing work tasks including operating actions. This supports practice on the virtually real object [9, 10].

2.2 Virtual Reality and Virtual Operating Actions

Literature describes virtual reality as the "visual depiction and manipulation of three-dimensional data in real time" [7].

In general, virtual reality addresses the visual, acoustic and tactile senses of humans. The visualization and perspective modifications ensure a depth impression close to reality [11]. Describe that the VR systems available on the market (e.g. Head Mounted Display (HMD)) can be differentiated by the degree of separation of the user from the real world as well as the embedding in a virtual environment.

VR based operating action describes a holistic virtual operating process for the initiation, implementation and completion of a function on a virtual technical facility which can have an impact on the virtual technical facility immediately and within multiple stages. An HMD such as the HTC vive pro with a high degree of immersion [13] enables the free interaction with both hands by means of controllers on a virtual workplace to specifically and repeatedly practice work tasks including operating actions. For this purpose, virtual learning scenarios have to be developed.

3 Virtual Learning Scenarios

3.1 General Facts

Within a virtual learning scenario, a preferably wide range of action situations in the context of problem solving and action strategies is provided [14]. Literature refers to a high level of practical relevance and "good results with regard to effectiveness of learning" in the context of the usage of VR in learning scenarios (also "learning-related interactivity") [1, 15].

Virtual learning scenarios support the transfer of procedural and action-related skills and at the same time provide accessible environments (training worlds) close to reality which serve the orientation in the real space and increase learning motivation and acceptance [16].

The virtual learning scenarios are based on the operating states of the machine tools (for example normal operation, starting and shutdown (shift-related), commissioning and decommissioning) and the activities needed for the component-specific processing (such as setting-up, insertion and operational activities) [12, 17]. Work tasks such as the commissioning of a machine can be depicted in a virtual learning scenario and subsequently trained within a virtual learning environment [1, 4]. This decreases the quantity and severity of errors occurring within the real commissioning, potentially threatening humans as well as a real machine.

Within preliminary works, three types of virtual learning scenarios related to the commissioning of a milling machine were defined and developed for training with a HTC vive pro, also including varying demands of learning. The employee qualification was conducted utilizing VR glasses HTC vive pro (hardware) and an in-house development of the University of Applied Sciences Mittweida.

3.2 Methodological Approach for the Development of Virtual Learning Scenarios

One of the prerequisites for the acceptance of a virtual learning scenario consists in a user experience adequate to the expectation of the user. This means that there should be a high degree of recognition of the virtual environment in comparison to the real environment as well as a signal or a change.

It is therefore essential to evaluate the user experience. First trials with the virtual learning scenarios developed showed that in the first place, it was not the implementation of the operating actions required causing problems for the users but the handling within the fully immersive VR technology itself.

8 out of 10 users (employees and students of the University of Applied Sciences Mittweida) were not able to cope with the steering and navigation within the virtual

learning environment. Therefore the training within the virtual learning scenario was not carried out because the test persons showed a high level of frustration.

In order to eliminate problems within the acceptance based on steering and navigating difficulties in the future, a questionnaire for detecting prior knowledge of the test persons in regards to the usage of VR technology was developed.

A training scenario was additionally developed and enables the test persons to practice steering and navigation as well as specific operating actions in the context of a successful handling of the VR hardware and the characteristic tasks on machine tools.

The exercise scenario was designed similarly to the virtual learning environment, which lead to a high degree of recognition. The initial technical trials related to feasibility and acceptance are conducted therewith.

The two users (2 of 10) which had little or no issues with the navigation and control within the virtual learning environment were able to complete the virtual learning scenario in accordance with set aims. They were provided with a questionnaire based on the User Experience Questionnaire [18] in order to document the user experience and subsequently refine the virtual learning scenario. A quality criterion for the assessment of the implementation of a particular operating action consisted in how good or bad the test person was able to implement the respective operating action (e.g. the virtual turning of a main switch for the securing of the energy supply).

The test persons had seven different response possibilities within the questions mentioned (ranging from very good until very bad).

For the virtualization of the learning environment, the flexible manufacturing system "training plant 4.0" is utilized, which is available as laboratory equipment of the institute InnArbeit – Centre of Innovative Process Planning and Ergonomics of the University of Applied Sciences Mittweida.

The virtual learning environment including the integrated learning scenarios were created as a detailed three-dimensional model in order to enable the user to virtually experience and use it in the first person view (FPV) (see also Fig. 1).

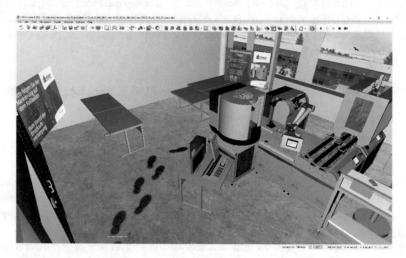

Fig. 1. Virtual learning environment with elements for orientation (footprints)

For the specification of demand-oriented learning contents of the virtual learning scenarios, the usage of a competence profile based on the approach according to [4] is expedient. In this process, the respective work tasks and the operating actions necessary substantially define the requirements for the executing employee. Based on the sum of requirements for the respective employee (competences necessary) and the tasks to be carried out, a corresponding competence profile is derived.

In the course of this, a comparison of the level of qualification required after completing the virtual learning scenario and the level of qualification actually being present for the employee is conducted. This emphasizes the extent of qualification demand and the respective qualification contents as well as the need for the support within an appropriate and user-oriented learning scenario.

3.3 Approach for the Development of a Virtual Learning Scenario

With an methodic approach (including 12 steps an 1 optional step), the development of virtual learning scenarios based on dynamic three-dimensional models for the qualification of users for operating and implementing actions on machine tools can be realized. The real testing environment, which is what the virtual learning scenarios are developed for, was modeled on a data-related basis using the CAD software SolidWorks and transferred into the VR software using exchange format. In order to define the virtual learning scenarios necessary for the qualification of employees, the approach according to [4] is expedient. The learning scenarios are expected to provide adequate learning contents for various levels of competences needed and existing for respective employees using a multi-stage model (see Table 1). The operating complexity (OC) and the operating level (OL) included in the multi-stage model were defined within three stages. This is necessary in order to integrate and therefore to classify the complexity of each individual learning scenario. In this context, the operating complexity includes the degrees of freedom and dependencies of the respective learning scenario within the learning environment. The operating level includes the quantity of information provided for the successful implementation of the learning scenario needing to be entered by the user.

Table 1. Multi-stage model of VR based operating actions for the classification of learning scenarios

OL = Operating level								
Increase in information provided for the respective operating action	level	3	OC	1	OC	2	OC	3
			OL	3	OL	3	OL	3
		2	OC	1	OC	2	OC	3
			OL	2	OL	2	OL	2
		1	OC	1	OC	2	OC	3
			OL	1	OL	1	OL	1
			1		2		3	
			OC= Operating complexity Increase in degrees of freedom and number of decisions					

On the basis of the approach according to [4] as well as the multi-stage model developed, three types of learning scenarios with varying learning requirements were defined. These were conceptualized for the operating actions necessary for the start of a milling machine within the learning environment training plant 4.0:

Learning scenario 1: Fully guided operating actions → visual observation without individual actions (OC1/OL1)
Learning scenario 2: Informationally guided operating actions → visually and acoustically supported operating actions (OC2/OL2)
Learning scenario 3: Fully autonomous operating actions → possibilities for failures and feedback for the user (OC3/OL3)

The virtual learning scenarios are described in detail in the following section. Focus is especially set on the increase of complexity of learning contents and the independent action of the user within the learning environment.

3.4   Exemplary Virtual Learning Scenarios

The **first** learning scenario includes a fully guided tour in which all operating actions for the commissioning of a milling machine are virtually shown to the user. In this process, the user does not have any influence on the implementation of the operating actions or the movement within the learning scenario. Selected advantages and disadvantages for the user as well as the instructor are listed below:

(+) Learning of functioning of the controllers for navigating not necessary (useful for employees which have not yet worked with a VR system)
(+) Standardized verbal description of operating actions demonstrated by the instructor
(-) High effort when adapting contents to new technical conditions

The **second** learning scenario comprises informationally (visually, acoustically and haptically supported) guided operating actions. In this scenario, the user navigates him-/herself through the learning environment and virtually works through the respective operating actions in a predefined order. Errors within the order of operating actions are not possible, which ensures the successful completion of the scenario.

(+) User can get used to the learning environment (here: training factory 4.0)
(-) Learning from errors within the operating order is not included within learning scenario two
(+) low effort in explaining the operating actions to be conducted
(-) occasional support of the user during learning of virtually depicted operating actions (e.g. turning of a switch) necessary

Figure 2 shows the test person while performing the second virtual learning scenario.
Within the virtual learning environment, she is depicted as an avatar and has the task to follow the footsteps shown on the floor. These provide guidance and function as navigation to the next operating action to be conducted. The figure furthermore shows information boards, which are provided for the test person and contain instructions for the operating action to be conducted (What has to be done? Why? How?).

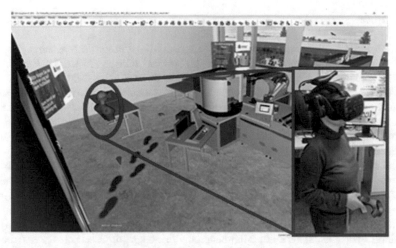

Fig. 2. Scene of the VR-based learning scenario 2 – informationally guided operating actions

4 Summary

Virtual learning scenarios are expedient for learning essential operating actions on milling tools when using an appropriate VR technology. The "moving" in the virtual environment, but also the implementation of operating actions were strongly impeded within the first trials, which was caused by operating errors of the VR technology. This clearly reduced the learning success desired as well as the acceptance for the technology. It can therefore be concluded, that there is a need to initially and specifically demonstrate the user handling of the HMD technology as well as interacting with the VR software environment. The existing state of work in regards to the methodological approach has to be supplemented by questionnaires in the future, which specify demand-oriented learning contents and detect training requirements in regards to the fundamental VR usage if necessary. Additionally, the development of the virtual learning scenario 3 with components of autonomous implementation of operating actions is intended. In this learning scenario, the user is able to make errors and receive the respective error information through the learning environment. An appropriate method-based tool will thus be established, which is expected to improve the learning success and subsequently the qualification of employees as well as generate a robust learning outcome in the context of learning from mistakes. In general, the learning success is to be verified by means of a multimedia questionnaire perspectively. This includes for instance the spatial orientation within the real environment as a learning outcome from navigating within the virtual environment. In addition and for the quantification of the learning outcome, questions regarding the functions of respective components and their handling (e. g. pressing the reference drive button) are being asked in the form of multiple choice questions (e.g. Why does a reference drive have to be performed?). The time and correctness of the operating in real trial can be used for measuring the learning success as well.

References

1. Hirt, C., Spahni, M., Kompis, Y., Jetter, D., Kunz, A.: Alles rund um die Maschine – Begehbare virtuelle Schulung an Werkzeugmaschinen. In: Putz, M., Klimant, P., Klimat, F. (eds.) VAR^2 2019 – Realität erweitern, Chemnitz, pp. 43–58 (2019). ISBN 978-3-00-064420-7
2. DIN EN ISO 6385, Grundsätze der Ergonomie für die Gestaltung von Arbeitssystemen (2016)
3. Bundesministerium für Arbeit und Soziales; Digitalisierung am Arbeitsplatz, p. 16, Zugang am Jan 08, 2020 (2016). https://www.bmas.de/SharedDocs/Downloads/DE/PDF-Publik ationen/a875-monitor-digitalisierung-am-arbeitsplatz.pdf;jsessionid=7C4EB42D0C7F765 A2D22B10EF1832359?__blob=publicationFile&v=3
4. Goldhahn, L., Eckardt, R., Pietschmann, C., Roch, S.: Competency profiles as a means of employee advancement for a resource-efficient chipping production. In: Karwowski, W., Trzcielinski, S., Mrugalska, B. (eds.) AHFE 2019. AISC, vol. 971, pp. 146–157. Springer, Cham (2020). https://doi.org/10.1007/978-3-030-20494-5_14
5. Goldhahn, L., Eckardt, R., Pietschmann, C., Roch, S.: Lernszenarien und Virtual Reality-basierte Bedienhandlungen zur Mitarbeiterqualifizierung. In: Gesellschaft für Arbeitswissenschaft e. V. (Hrsg.): Digitaler Wandel, digitale Arbeit, digitaler Mensch? Bericht zum 66. Arbeitswissenschaftlichen Kongress vom 16–18 März 2020, B1.1, pp. 1–6. GfA Press, Dortmund (2020). ISBN 978-3-936804-27-0
6. FOERST GmbH, Effiziente Fahrsimulatoren für Pkw, Lkw und Busse (2020). https://www.fahrsimulatoren.eu/de/. Accessed 7 Jan 2020
7. Dörner, R., Broll, W., Jung, B., Grimm, P., Göbel, M.: Einführung in virtual und augmented reality. In: Dörner, R., Broll, W., Grimm, P., Jung, B. (eds.) Virtual und Augmented Reality (VR/AR), pp. 1–42. Springer, Heidelberg (2019). https://doi.org/10.1007/978-3-662-588 61-1_1
8. Bauer, M.: Einsatzmöglichkeiten heutiger Virtual-Reality-Technologie im zivilen Pilotentraining am Beispiel zweier Szenarien im Rahmen einer Studie. Masterthesis. Technische Universität Darmstadt, Darmstadt. Institut für Flugsysteme und Regelungstechnik (FSR) (2010). https://tuprints.ulb.tu-darmstadt.de/2043/1/master_arbeit_V_2_0.pdf. Accessed 15 Dec 2020
9. Thomas, O., Metzger, D., Niegemann, H. (Hg.): Digitalisierung in der Aus- und Weiterbildung. Springer, Heidelberg (2018). https://doi.org/10.1007/978-3-662-56551-3
10. Bues, M., Schulze, T.: Training und Ausbildung mit Virtual Reality. In: WerkstattsTechnik 2020 (7/8), p. 572 (2020). https://www.ingenieur.de/fachmedien/wt-werkstattstechnik/fraunh ofer-gesellschaft/neue-wege-zur-qualifikation/. Accessed 15 Dec 2020
11. Klimant, P., Klimant, F., Putz, M., Allmacher, C.: Trends der virtuellen und erweiterten Realität mit dem Fokus auf virtueller Inbetriebnahme. In: Reimund Neugebauer, Matthias Putz et Phillip Klimant, coord.: VAR2 2019 – Realität erweitern. Tagungsband. 5. Fachkonferenz zu VR/AR-Technologien in Anwendung und Forschung an der Professur Werkzeugmaschinen und Umformtechnik. Chemnitz, pp. 7–26 (2019)
12. VDI/VDE Richtlinie 3699 – Prozessführung mit Bildschirmen. Berlin, Beuth
13. Engel, B.: Immersion oder Versinken in der virtuellen Realität – auch ein Thema für die Arbeitsmedizin? In: Zeitschrift für medizinische Prävention, vol. 54, no. 09, pp. 604–607 (2019). https://www.asu-arbeitsmedizin.com/node/30413/print
14. Hirschle, T.: Lernszenario, Zugang, 07 January 2020 (2020). https://bildungsserver.berlin-brandenburg.de/fileadmin/bbb/unterricht/faecher/gesellschaftswissenschaften/ethik/Lernsz enario.pdf
15. Wannemacher, K., Jungermann, I., Scholz, J., Tercabli, H., von Villiez, A.: Digitale Lernszenarien im Hochschulbereich, p. 16, Zugang Jan 7, 2020 (2016). https://hochschulforumd igitalisierung.de/sites/default/files/dateien/HFD%20AP%20Nr%2015_Digitale%20Lernsze narien.pdf

16. Schwan, S., Buder, J.: Virtuelle Realität und E-Learning, pp. 7–9, Zugang Jan 7, 2020 (2006). https://www.e-teaching.org/didaktik/gestaltung/vr/vr.pdf
17. Zühlke, D.: Nutzergerechte Entwicklung von Mensch-Maschine-Systemen: Useware-Engineering für technische Systeme, 2nd edn. Springer, Berlin (2012)
18. Laugwitz, B., Schrepp, M., Held, T.: Konstruktion eines Fragebogens zur Messung der User-Experience von Softwareprodukten. In: Heinecke, A.M., Paul, H. (eds.) Mensch & Computer 2006- Mensch und Computer im Strukturwandel. Oldenbourg Verlag, pp. 125–134 (2006)

Developing a Training Action for Primary School Teachers by Doubly Considering (Their) Work

Ana Rodrigues$^{(\boxtimes)}$, Maria Cadilhe⊙, Filipa Ferreira, Cláudia Pereira⊙, and Marta Santos⊙

Faculty of Psychology and Education Sciences, University of Porto, 4200-135 Porto, Portugal

```
{anarodrigues,mariacadilhe,filipa_ferreira,cpereira,
                    marta}@fpce.up.pt
```

Abstract. This paper aims to describe the development of a training action for primary school teachers, considering and respecting their real work activity, with the purpose of discuss with them the relevance of integrating into their teaching activity with their students a reflection about work, considering issues of gender, age, and health in the work contexts. This study was developed in the scope of an action-research project, in partnership with Porto City Council, and involved the development and pilot implementation of an in-person training action, with 4 primary teachers within 2 different public schools in Portugal. Customized tools were built with the purpose of bringing teachers' work activity to be discussed in the training action.

The teachers involved evaluated the training' contents and tools as being very appropriate; felt that their work activity was respected and that the training action was well articulated with what was foreseen. These results point towards the benefit of discussing with teachers the contents to be developed with children and to how this process can be done. At the same time, having this discussion about work for teachers to explore the topic with their students resulted in a reflection about their own work activity and the conditions for its realisation.

This project constituted a practical application of doubly considering the work activity of primary school teachers as the starting point to the design of a contextualized training action.

Keywords: Training · Development · Primary school teachers · Work analysis

1 Introduction

1.1 Contextualization

It is generally recognized that career development occurs in a lifelong perspective, with childhood assuming a growing importance [1] in both career research and practice. Previous studies have shown that career interventions in the school environment (e.g., career education lessons; exposure to non-traditional workers) play an important role

N. L. Black et al. (Eds.): IEA 2021, LNNS 223, pp. 758–763, 2022.
https://doi.org/10.1007/978-3-030-74614-8_93

in broadening children's knowledge about work [2], and have the potential to promote other important benefits, such as a better perception of the relationship between school and work [2] and reduction in occupational gender stereotyping [3].

With this background, and studies demonstrating how critical the exploration developed during childhood is for later vocational exploration [4], researchers conducted a project, in partnership with a City Council, that aimed to develop a practical approach to broad the knowledge about different types of work activities and their conditions in children aged 6–10 years old. This project intended to bring into the classrooms the discussion and reflection about real work dimensions (e.g., working conditions; constraints of the activities), considering where different professionals work, at what times, with what equipment, and for what purpose. Considering the important role of school and teachers as key agents of early intervention in vocational development [4], the project consisted of developing a training action with primary school teachers to discuss with them the relevance of integrating into their teaching activity with their students a reflection about work, considering issues of gender, age, and health in the work contexts.

Thereby, this paper will focus on the training development and implementation process, assuming the tradition that considers the work analysis as a means to conceiving a training action [5], successively updated, and enriched by different contexts and geographies [6].

1.2 Teachers' Work Activity

When one thinks about the work carried out by teachers, it is quickly associated with the act of teaching, sometimes disregarding the other tasks (e.g., meetings with parents/guardians; meetings with other teachers; homework correction; preparation of classes; preparation of study visits) and demands that characterize this activity (e.g., multiplicity of tasks; time pressures; bureaucratization of processes; rigidity of educational programs; individuality of each student) [7, 8]. In itself, and in the Portuguese context, teachers' work activity underlies a set of requirements, such as compliance with official instructions (prescriptions) which include, in particular, the educational policy guidelines and requirements of the national curriculum in force, and also the school's educational project [9]. This compliance is demanding for teachers, namely on the classes' preparation and restructuring they need to make (considering variables such as the characteristics of the students, time, and resources available, among others) and can be seen as a constraint, since it is a prescription in which many teachers do not participate, and which leads to a need to change the working procedures [5]. When we talk about primary school teachers in the context of the Portuguese educational system, we are referring to professionals that teach the first four years of schooling, in a monodocency regime, in classes of about 24 to 26 children [10]. As far as the content of the expected learning is concerned, the 1st and 3rd year of schooling are described by teachers as being strongly related to the acquisition of knowledge (of Portuguese language, mathematics, and study of the social environment) and the 2nd and 4th year are typically described as being related with the consolidation of the acquired knowledge. This justifies the decision taken by the research team of addressing this project to the 2nd and 4th year.

Primary school teachers, in the Portuguese context, have 25 hours per week scheduled for teaching, in which another 10 weekly hours are reserved for non-teaching activities (such as preparation of classes and evaluation of the teaching-learning process, participation in meetings and training actions, among others) [9].

2 Methodology

2.1 Objective

In the scope of the action-research project "growing I Lifelong Career Guidance", this study aims to address the way teachers evaluated the approach developed to discuss with them the relevance of integrating into their teaching activity with their students a reflection about work, that sought to consider and respect components of their work activity, such as the initiatives they already provide in their real context, the curriculum they have to comply with, as well as the communication channels they have to guarantee with different interlocutors (e.g. parents/guardians).

2.2 Participants

The study was requested by the Economy Department of the local Municipality (Porto City Council) and it was implemented by the research team with the support and involvement of the Educational Department, which maintains a close relationship with local schools. This department was responsible for identifying two different Primary Schools to be involved in the project, considering schools that were available to host this project and that were diverse in terms of socio-economic background.

To guarantee that the choice about which teachers to involve would be taken on a voluntary basis, a briefing session was held within each of the two schools to present the project to the school' coordinators and teachers. Through this session, a higher number of volunteer teachers was obtained than the vacancies that were previously defined for this phase of implementation. Nevertheless, the decision on who would participate was taken by the teachers' collective and 4 teachers were identified to participate in the project (two teachers from each school), where two of them were currently teaching the 2nd year of schooling and the other two the 4th class.

2.3 Procedures

Data Collection. Once it was not possible to make observations of teachers' activity, due to time constraints, we decided to "bring the work activity" to the training action [11], by creating tools, who have assumed the role of symbolic mediators [12], to promote the reflection and discussion, which will be detailed below. It should also be noted that for the development of this approach we have relied on an advisor teacher, who helped the research team to understand some of the issues about the teachers' work activity, documents that should be analyzed, among others.

Knowing that teachers' work activity is strongly linked with the established Curriculum, an analysis of the contents planned for the curricular years in question (2nd and 4th) was carried out by the researchers, considering the Curricular Plan in force and the Essential Learnings' Standards, established through the Decree-Law 55/2018. This analysis was carried out with the intention of understanding when and how was planned to address the subject of the professions in the classroom and supported the development of a "Linking Tool", in an infographic format, that highlighted the links between the established learning contents and the professions. This tool was used in the training action to promote 1) the discussion about whether or not that (predicted) content was close to what is actually being explored in their classrooms and how this exploration is done; 2) the reflection about what kinds of work activities can be intentionally explored in each part of the programme; and 3) the identification of work dimensions that are usually discussed with children.

Another tool was developed that presupposed the completion of a chronological timeline, in which every teacher was asked to identify the various actions already planned for the current school year (e.g., projects, field trips, schoolwork, curriculum content highlighted in the previous tool), and that could be intentionalised to explore the thematic, without increasing the workload or the number of initiatives to be developed. This tool was developed to support teachers to recover their own activity and reflect on it, ensuring that the singularities of each specific case were considered when exploring and reflecting about the subject under analysis.

Alongside the training development, an evaluation model on teachers' perceptions about the relevance, coherence, effectiveness, and sustainability of the approach, adapted from a pre-existing evaluation model [13], was also developed. Some of the questions that were addressed were about the importance of the thematic (relevance); appropriateness of the approach (coherence); about whether the proposed approach was effective for promoting the discussion on work activities (effectiveness) and also about if the approach was likely to be incorporated into their activity (sustainability). This data was collected through a questionnaire developed for this purpose, answered by teachers at the end of the training, and through the consideration of their verbalizations during training crossing quantitative indicators with qualitative data.

Developed Activities. An in-person training action lasting 4 hours was carried out for each of the schools involved. It was carried out in pairs composed by the two teachers from the same school. Both tools (Linking Tool and Chronological Timeline) were used in the training action as the starting point for discussing their adequacy and adherence to their real work scenario and for discussing and planning possible situations to explore the work activities in the course of the school year.

It should be also stated that several decisions regarding the project implementation (e.g., project timeline and scheduling of activities, feedback on the materials) were decided together with the teachers in the training action, to consider their activity and tacit experience about their professional context.

Those elements (tools and shared decision making) offered the possibility for the teachers involved to be actors and actively participate in their own formation, recognizing them as being the specialists in their own activity.

Also, knowing that the teachers would have to make the project known to the parents/guardians of the children in the classes involved, the research team, in order not to overload the teachers, planned and made a small presentation of the project in a meeting that was already scheduled in the school calendar.

3   Results and Discussion

The discussion and collective construction made it possible to strengthen the importance of intentionalizing the topic with children and of promoting the discussion of the professions in the classroom beyond their understanding as an economic activity (as foreseen in the curriculum). In this scope, teachers identified the approach «*as being able to promote a new knowledge of the world of work*» (Teacher 1, School 2), as they felt it was an alternative approach to the subject that makes it possible to make a wider range of professions known to children and help them understand that «*they [the professions] all have their role and are important for the functioning of society*» (Teacher 1, School 1). It also made it possible to value some dimensions that are related to work and that are important to consider when exploring the work activities with children, namely the issues of gender, age, and health in the work contexts.

The tools that were developed and used in the training action allowed the activity to be brought into the discussion, enabling the confrontation with different ways of bringing this topic into the classroom. In qualitative notes left by the participants, we could understand their contentment about the fact that «*what was worked on crossed with the contents of the curriculum of the disciplines*» (Teacher 1, School 1). This allowed the sessions to be held with the children not to be perceived as separate and out of context from what was planned or as an overload compared to what they have already planned to do.

Also, the tools built to work on these issues with children, which considered their inputs, were considered relevant and useful in such a way that the teachers involved consider the possibility of continuing to use them. Since these tools have been built so that they can be used not only in the classroom, but also in the family context, they were seen as facilitators of the home-school integration, involving families in the contribution they can make to the knowledge of working contexts.

Finally, it was also mentioned that the proposed approach, for the way it brought their work activity to be discussed in the training action, allowed teachers to reflect on their own work activity and on the conditions for its realisation. In fact, they referred that no other project to be implemented in the school has foreseen a formative moment to discuss these issues and that this was a much-appreciated differentiating factor.

4   Conclusion

The results reinforce the importance of taking teachers' activity into account when considering changes to it, first of all, by trying to understand if they consider the contents as relevant to be worked on with the children and then how they can be worked on without overloading or profoundly altering the ways in which their activity is carried out. They also point to the training as being itself a developmental awareness-raising factor about their own work activity [14] and regarding the importance of talking about work, its conditions, and instruments with children from an early age.

References

1. Patton, W., Porfeli, E.: Career exploration for children and adolescents. In: Skorikov, V., Patton, W. (eds.) Career Development in Childhood and Adolescence, pp. 47–69. Sense Publishers, Rotterdam (2007)
2. Gillies, R., McMahon, M., Carroll, J.: Evaluating a career education intervention in the upper elementary school. J. Career Dev. **24**, 267–287 (1998)
3. Bailey, B., Nihlen, A.: Effect of experience with nontraditional workers on psychological and social dimensions of occupational sex-role stereotyping by elementary school children. Psychol. Rep. **66**(3), 1273–1282 (1990)
4. Taveira, M.: Early Intervention and Career Development. Psicologia: Teoria Investigação e Prática **4**(1), 173–189 (1999)
5. Leplat, J.: Psychologie de la formation. Jalons et perspectives. Choix de textes (1955–2002). Octarès Éditions, Toulouse (2002)
6. Teiger, C., Lacomblez, M.: (Se) Former pour transformer le travail – Dynamiques de constructions d'une analyse critique du travail. Presses de l'Université Laval/PUL/ l'European Trade Union Institute/ETUI, Québec/Bruxelles (2013)
7. Pereira, C., Santos, M.: The regulatory process of the visual and technological education teachers' activity: analysis of the impact of the 2012 curricular restructure in Portugal. Laboreal **13**(2), 24–38 (2007)
8. Cau-Bareille, D.: L'intensification du travail dans les milieux enseignants. In: Motard, M.H. (Coord.) Apprendre à écouter le travail: une experience de «travail sur le travail», pp.80–83. FSU Poitou-Charentes/Institut de recherché de la FSU (2013)
9. Decree-Law No 41/2012 of the Portuguese Ministry of Education and Science. Diário da República, II series, No 37 (2012)
10. Regulatory Dispatch n° 10-A/2018 of the Portuguese Offices of the Deputy Secretary of State for Education and of the Portuguese Secretary of State for Education. Diário da Republica II series, No 116 (2018)
11. Teiger, C., Laville, A.: L'apprentissage de l'analyse ergonomique du travail, outil d'une formation pour l'action. Travail et Emploi **47**, 53–62 (1991)
12. Rabardel, P.: Les hommes et les technologies: approche cognitive des instruments contemporains. Armand Colin (1995)
13. Institute for Cooperation and Language (Camões, I.P.): Evaluation guide, 3rd edn. Department of Foreign Affairs: Lisboa (2014)
14. Lacomblez, M., Teiger, C.: Ergonomia, formações e transformações. In: Falzon, P. (ed.) Ergonomia, pp. 587–602. Edgard Blücher, São Paulo (2006)

Part X: HF/E Education and Professional Certification Development – *Addendum* (Edited by Chien-Chi (Max) Chang and Maggie Graf)

Applications and Implications of the Brazilian Ergonomics Regulatory Standard (NR17)

Lia Buarque de Macedo Guimarães[1]([envelope]) [iD], Marcia Gemari Derenevich[2] [iD], and Rosimeire Sedrez Bitencourt[2] [iD]

[1] CNPq/Universidade Federal do Rio Grande do Sul, Porto Alegre, Brazil
lia.buarque@pq.cnpq.br
[2] Pontifícia Universidade Católica do Paraná, Curitiba, Brazil

Abstract. This article presents an analysis of the Brazilian Ergonomics Regulatory Standard - NR17 and its application. The association of the NR17guidelines with the domains of ergonomics specialization showed that it stresses the physical domain (50.7% of the guidelines, two of them related to people with disabilities – PwDs), while 41.5% are related to the organizational and 7.8% to the cognitive domain. This unbalance is reflected in published studies on the application of NR17, since all of them stress physical changes in the workplace, approximately half consider organizational issues and 15% address cognitive issues. Brazilian companies usually perform ergonomic interventions to comply with NR17, therefore its updates should consider increasing the number of guidelines related to cognitive issues and PwDs needs, and include macroergonomics guidelines for orienting the application of ergonomics under a systemic approach in order to guarantee higher quality of work and improve overall system performance.

Keywords: Brazilian Ergonomics Regulatory Standard · NR17 · Ergonomics domains of specialization · Applications of NR17 · Guidelines

1 Introduction

In Brazil, the discipline of Ergonomics was introduced in the years 1960 in undergraduate courses in Engineering, Medicine and Psychology [1], but its practice gained force in the 1970s, mainly after 1978 with the publication of the Brazilian Ergonomics Regulatory Standard NR17 (revised in 1990, 2007 and 2018). NR17 (2007) "aims to establish parameters that allow the adaptation of working conditions to the psychophysiological characteristics of workers, in order to provide maximum comfort, safety and efficient performance" [2] and applies to all companies that have employees contracted under the Consolidation of Labor Laws (CLT) [3], which governs labor relations in Brazil since 1943. Therefore, basically all Brazilian companies must comply with the NR17. Although other countries such as Australia, Canada, European Union, Mexico, Singapore, South Africa, Sweden, United Kingdom and the US have ergonomics standards and guidelines (see [4] for a list) NR17 (2017) explicitly demands an EWA, which should follow the guidelines and comply with what is stated in the items of the standard.

N. L. Black et al. (Eds.): IEA 2021, LNNS 223, pp. 767–774, 2022.
https://doi.org/10.1007/978-3-030-74614-8_94

Considering that EWA is mandatory, this study evaluated how the NR17 parameters are being addressed by Brazilian companies, how well they fit into the physical, cognitive and organizational domains of ergonomics specialization, and whether NR17 meets the ergonomics goals: "to optimize human well-being and overall system performance" [5].

2 Brazilian Ergonomics Regulatory Standard NR17

The first version of NR 17 (1978) did not present the objectives of the standard, addressing only the lifting, transport and unloading of materials; countertops, tables, desks and panels; and adjustable seat. In 1986, representatives of the Union of Employees in a Data Processing Company in the State of São Paulo - SINDPD/SP sought the Regional Labor Office of the State de São Paulo - DRT/SP, in order to seek solutions to reduce the number of work-related musculoskeletal disorders (WMSD) among the typists of companies in this segment. This initiated a debate among doctors, engineers, employees, employers, and other stakeholders, also aiming at WMSD that reached other professions in the country [6], resulting in the review of the standard. The NR17 of 1990 included aspects related to lifting, transport and unloading of materials, furniture, equipment, environmental conditions of the workplace, work postures and work organization. In 2007, NR17 underwent another edition [2] with Annex I specific for the work of checkout operators and Annex II for the work in tele-assistance/telemarketing. Item 8.4 of Annex II states that "it is up to the employer to carry out the Ergonomic Work Analysis (EWA), which must address, at a minimum, working conditions as established in this Regulatory Standard" [2] including:

a) description of the characteristics of the workstations with regard to furniture, utensils, tools, physical space for carrying out the work and conditions for positioning and moving body segments;

b) assessment of work organization including: 1) real work and prescribed work; 2) description of production in relation to the time allocated for the tasks; 3) daily, weekly and monthly variations in the service load, including seasonal variations and more frequent technical-operational complications; 4) number of work cycles and their description, including shift work and night work; 5) occurrence of inter-cycle breaks; 6) explanation of the production rules, the time requirements, the determination of the time content, the work rate and the content of the tasks performed; 7) monthly history of overtime hours worked each year; 8) explanation of the existence of static or dynamic overloads of the musculoskeletal system;

c) statistical report on the incidence of complaints of health problems collected by Occupational Medicine in medical records;

d) reports of assessments of job satisfaction and organizational climate, if carried out within the company;

e) registration and analysis of impressions and suggestions from workers in relation to the aspects of the previous items;

f) ergonomic recommendations expressed in clear and objective plans and proposals, with definition of implementation dates.

EWA report should include the following stages: a) explanation of the demand for the study; b) analysis of tasks, activities and work situations; c) discussion and return of results to the workers involved; d) specific ergonomic recommendations for the evaluated workstations; e) evaluation and review of interventions carried out with the participation of workers, supervisors and managers; f) evaluation of the efficiency of the recommendations.

In another revision in 2018 [7], the items related to workplace lighting were removed from the body of the standard, and the ones related to the deadlines for adequacy to the standard were removed from the annexes. In August 2019, a proposal of revision [8] was submitted for public consultation and is under analysis.

3 Method

The objectives of the study are twofold: 1) analysis of the NR17 in order to – in the interest of - understand how it contemplates the ergonomics goals and the issues related to the physical, cognitive and organizational domains; 2) evaluation of published articles with application of the NR17.

As the latest version (2018) of NR17 presents few changes compared to the previous edition (2007) and was approved and made available on the Ministry of Labor website when this research had already started, this study focused the 2007 version. Analysis of NR17 (2007) considered its structure, formulation and specificities. The standard items and paragraphs were categorized into 'guideline' (referring to the procedures for contemplating the standard), 'term' (related to the definition/meaning of the terms used in the standard) or 'other' (items that were neither a guideline nor a term). The guidelines were analyzed and associated with the three domains of ergonomics specialization.

Research on applications of the NR17 considered published academic studies from 2007 (year of publication of the 2007 version of NR17) up to 2018. In May 2019, a search for the terms "NR17", "NR-17", "NR 17" and "Ergonomics Regulatory Standard 17" was carried out in the national proceedings of the Brazilian Association of Production Engineering (ABEPRO) and in the journal Ação Ergonômica, which publishes the articles of the congresses promoted by the Brazilian Association of Ergonomics (ABERGO). The abstracts were analyzed and the ones related to the application of NR17 were read in full. Of the 60 articles resulting from the search, only 13 reported an application of NR17 and they were selected for analysis. On July 18, 2020, a search was made in the Brazilian Digital Library of Theses and Dissertations [9] for publications with application of NR17, returning 18 studies for analysis.

4 Results and Discussion

4.1 Analysis of the NR17

NR17 (2007) has three parts: the first is the body or generic part, with no specific indication of the work environment or profession, provides for the lifting, transport and individual discharge of materials, workstation furniture and equipment, environmental conditions, and work postures. The second part is Annex I, specific for the work of check-out operators and the third is Annex II, for the work in call center/telemarketing, which brings the item work organization, contemplating aspects of organizational ergonomics and the minimum requirements and mandatory items for an Ergonomic Work Analysis (EWA) (NR17, 2007). The training and qualification of employees is only exposed in Annex I and Annex II of the NR17, what can lead to the understanding that workers who are not included in the two specific groups do not need training. Since the annexes were added after the promulgation of NR17, they bring the deadlines for companies to make the necessary adaptations to comply with the standard. NR17 also defines the terms adopted in the standard. For example, there is a difference between manual load transport and regular manual load transport.

In each of the three parts of NR17, items were classified as guidelines, terms or others. Annex II has the largest number of guidelines (83), followed by the body of the standard (60), and Annex I (54). Most guidelines (66.7%) from the body part aimed at the physical environment, 26.7% deals with the organizational domain and only 6.6% of the guidelines refer to cognitive issues. In Annex I of the standard, more than half (55.6%) of the guidelines refer to the physical domain, 1.8% to the cognitive, 38.8% to the organizational and 3.7% to the three domains. Annex II includes guidelines referring mostly to the organizational domain (53%), followed by the physical domain (34.9%), the three domains (8.4%) and the cognitive domain (3.6%). Considering the total number of NR17 guidelines (197), 50.7% deal with physical issues (with two guidelines related to people with disabilities – PwDs), 41.5% are related to organizational issues, and 7.8% address the cognitive ones. Figure 1 presents the proportion of guidelines, terms and others in each of the three parts of the NR17 (2007).

In 2019, a proposal for revision of the NR17 was submitted to public evaluation and is now with a tripartite committee (composed of government, employers and employees representatives), for review and approval. The positive points of this proposal in comparison to the current NR17 are clarity of language and ease of reading and interpreting the standard, and the increased number of items. Negative aspects are the removal of items related to work journey duration and breaks, and the exempt of micro and small companies from EWA, unless their activity category rank as high risk). A comparison between all items in the body part of NR17 (2007) and the one in the 2019 proposal is shown in Fig. 2. It is observed that the 2019 proposal includes new items, and that the number of items related to the organizational domain increased. However, its main focus remains predominantly physical, with fewer items related to the cognitive domain, which should be increased. A more systemic (sociotechnical) approach to ergonomics was also expected to be considered in the 2019 proposal, since legislation should follow the scientific advances for improving the quality of work and overall system performance. By expanding NR17 with macroergonomics guidelines, the application of the standard might result in better outcomes for humans, organizations and the whole society.

Another important criticism about the proposed revision is that by dispensing small and micro-sized companies from an EWA, most Brazilians will not have the guarantee of an adequate work environment, not to mention the ones (about 35% of the work force) who work in the informal sector. Just because a company activity category is listed as low risk (therefore, it is exempted from the EWA), it is not possible to prove that it is risk

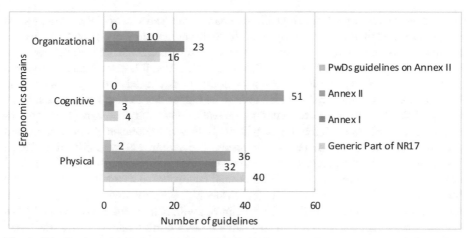

Fig. 1. Distribution of the NR17 (version 2007) guidelines according the domains of ergonomics specialization

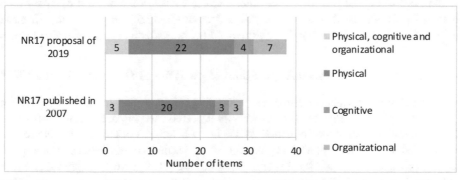

Fig. 2. Distribution of NR17 items in the 2007 version and in the 2019 proposal considering the domains of ergonomics specialization

free without performing an EWA, which is probably the only available instrument for giving a minimum orientation for improving work in Brazilian companies. Micro and small businesses represent 99% of all companies in the country, the small ones being responsible for 54% of formal jobs [10]. The risk of serious accidents in small industrial companies (no matter the activity category) is about 3.77 times that of large companies, and 1.96 times that of medium companies [11] therefore they should be encouraged to keep ergonomics programs with complete EWAs to prevent illnesses, injuries, accidents and deaths. However, most of these companies do not hire ergonomics consultancy (usually considered expensive, regardless of price), and often ask the safety technician (with no training in ergonomics) to solve the "problem" of the mandatory EWA, just to comply with NR17 [12] and not necessarily to improve the work system.

Considering that a possible reason for dispensing companies from the EWA is that they do not want to bear the cost of hiring a professional ergonomist, a solution could be keeping the mandatory EWA to be paid with part of the National Social Security (NSS) compulsory contribution tax. Companies (formally registered workers and employers) pay this tax as an insurance to cover a range of compensation benefits including accidents, injuries, occupational diseases, illnesses and deaths. It is calculated according to activity risk level (very low, low, medium or high) and not based on company's working conditions and associated risks, which tend to be higher due to poor ergonomics. Lowering the NSS tax due to risk reduction as a result of mandatory subsidized ergonomics programs, carried out by ergonomists, will not only benefit companies and workers but also all society as it will be paying for hazard prevention, safety, and health instead of paying for accident compensation (which cannot ever be compensated for by any money). In 2018, there were over 576 thousand occupational accidents in Brazil and 2 thousand deaths [13], the country ranking fifth and fourth, respectively, in the International Labour Organization's (ILO) list of countries with more accidents and work related deaths. However, besides a possible 80%–90% underreporting rate, statistics was based only on data from employees with a formal contract [14], therefore the number of cases might be seven times greater [15]. A conservative evaluation [16] estimated the annual costs of accidents at over U$ 42 billion (U$ 24.3 paid by the companies + U$ 8.3 paid by the NSS + U$ 9.4 paid by the families), which is 9% of the amount of salary paid in Brazil [16], almost the national health budget of U$ 45.5 billion [17] and all these unacceptable figures more than justify the need for immediate prevention effort [16].

4.2 Evaluation of Published Applications of the EWA as Demanded by the NR17

From the search for papers on Brazilian proceedings and journals, of the 13 articles with applications of NR17 selected for analysis, all reported carrying out an EWA: 46.2% in the Northeast, 30.7% in the South and 23.1% in the Southeast of the country. No results were found for the North or Midwest regions. All 13 articles commented and/or applied physical changes in the workplace, approximately half dealt with organizational issues and a small portion (15%) addressed issues in the cognitive domain. Two articles report on improvement of system performance.

The search in the Brazilian Digital Library of Theses and Dissertations [9], identified 18 studies related to the NR17, and three are relevant to this study: one proposes a model for industrial ergonomics management and the other proposes a guide for the application of work safety in chemistry teaching laboratories, but only physical issues (biomechanics, environmental factors and satisfaction with these factors) were addressed, reflecting the physical bias of NR17. A third dissertation proposes changes in NR17, stressing the insertion of aspects for selection and application of materials for products and environment.

5 Conclusion

Considering that the Brazilian Standard of Ergonomics - NR17 is, in Brazil, a way of inserting ergonomics (in its physical, cognitive and organizational domains) in most industrial, commercial and service companies, this research aimed to analyze NR17 and its applications. The results show an unbalance in the distribution of NR17 items related to the ergonomics domains, the focus being the physical one (lifting, transport and handling loads, adopted postures, furniture and environmental conditions), in detriment to the cognitive domain. This ends up reflecting on the studies related to the application of the NR17 (2007) which focus on biomechanical, anthropometric and environmental aspects, all 13 articles commenting and/or proposing physical changes in the workplace, approximately half dealing with organizational issues and only 15% addressing the cognitive ones. Improvement of system performance, which is an ergonomics goal, is not included in the studies.

The focus on the physical ergonomics domain persists in the proposed revision of NR17 (2019). It should have more cognitive items, and those to address exceptional cases (i.e., people with disabilities-PwDs, and people with abnormal anthropometric dimensions), since in Brazil it is mandatory the inclusion of PwDs in companies with more than 100 employees, in addition to being a social commitment. It is necessary to make it clear, in the body of the standard, what is expected from an ergonomic work analysis - EWA, which should be kept mandatory (and subsidized by the National Social Security compulsory contribution tax) for all activities under study.

In order to reach the objectives of ergonomics, it is recommended a revision of the NR17 from a systemic (macroergonomic) perspective, therefore NR17 can contribute to more effective work systems analysis and design, promoting safety, quality of work life, social well-being, competitiveness and sustainability of Brazilian companies.

Acknowledgements. This study was supported by the Brazilian Coordenação de Aperfeiçoamento de Pessoal de Nível Superior – CAPES (finance code 001) and the Conselho Nacional de Desenvolvimento Científico e Tecnológico – CNPq.

References

1. Moraes, A., Soares, M.M.: Ergonomia no Brasil e no mundo: um quadro, uma fotografia. ABERGO, Rio de Janeiro (1989)
2. Brasil, Ministério do Trabalho e Emprego: NR 17 - Ergonomia. Ministério do Trabalho e Emprego, Brasília (2007). http://www.guiatrabalhista.com.br/legislacao/nr/nr17.htm. Accessed 30 Jan 2020
3. Brasil: Decreto-Lei 5.452 de 1° de maio de 1943. Consolidação das leis do trabalho, Brasília (2017)
4. Budnick, P.: Ergonomics standards and guidelines (2019). https://ergoweb.com/ergonomics-standards-and-guidelines/. Accessed 23 Jan 2021
5. IEA Homepage. https://iea.cc/definition-and-domains-of-ergonomics/. Accessed 23 Jan 2021
6. Brasil, Ministério do Trabalho: Manual de aplicação da norma regulamentadora n°17. 2 ed. Ministério do Trabalho e Emprego, Brasília (2002)
7. Brasil, Ministério do Trabalho e Emprego: NR 17 - Ergonomia. Ministério do Trabalho e Emprego, Brasília (2018). https://www.trt02.gov.br/geral/tribunal2/LEGIS/CLT/NRs/NR_17.html. Accessed 13 Sept 2020
8. Brasil, Secretaria de Trabalho: Norma regulamentadora 17 – NR17. Brasília: Ministério do Trabalho e Emprego (2019). https://enit.trabalho.gov.br/portal/images/Arquivos_SST/SST_NR/consulta-publica/NR17---consulta-pblica.pdf. Accessed 13 Sept 2020
9. Capes: Catálago de teses e dissertações (2018). https://catalogodeteses.capes.gov.br/catalogo-teses/#!/. Accessed 18 July 2020

10. Sebrae: Pequenos negócios em números (2016). https://www.sebrae.com.br/sites/Portal Sebrae/ufs/sp/sebraeaz/pequenos-negocios-em-numeros,12e8794363447510VgnVCM10 00004c00210aRCRD#:~:text=No%20Brasil%20existem%206%2C4,MEI%20(dezembro% 2F2013). Accessed 20 Sept 2020
11. Mendes, R.: Importance of small factories in occupational accidents in S. Paulo, Brazil Rev. Saúde Pública **10**(4), 315–325 (1976)
12. Silva, P.S.S.: As perspectivas de consultoria: uma apreciação crítica do participante profissional de ergonomia em atividade consultiva. Ph.D. thesis, Rio de Janeiro: COPPE, Universidade Federal do Rio de Janeiro (2007)
13. Brasil: Anuário estatístico de acidentes do trabalho: AEAT. Ministério da Fazenda, Brasília (2009)
14. CESTEH: Brasil é um dos países com maior número de mortes e acidentes de trabalho no mundo. Será o trabalhador brasileiro superprotegido? (2019). http://www.cesteh.ensp. fiocruz.br/noticias/brasil-e-um-dos-paises-com-maior-numero-de-mortes-e-acidentes-de-tra balho-no-mundo-sera-o. Accessed 23 Jan 2021
15. Fundacentro: Accidents at work in Brazil in 2013: comparison between selected within two data sources: IBGE National Household Health Survey and Statistical Yearbook of the Social Security by Ministry of Social Welfare (2015). http://biblioteca.cofen.gov.br/wp-content/upl oads/2015/08/Acidentes-de-trabalho-no-Brasil-em-2013.pdf. Accessed 27 Jan 2021
16. Pastore, J.: O custo dos acidentes e doenças do trabalho no Brasil. Lecture given to the Tribunal Superior do Trabalho (2011). http://www.josepastore.com.br/artigos/rt/rt_320.htm. Accessed 13 Jan 2021
17. Sinpait: Custo humano e econômico dos acidentes de trabalho (2016). https://sinpait.org.br/ 2016/05/estudossinpait29/. Accessed 13 Jan 2021

Part XI: Organisation Design and Management (ODAM) – *Addendum*
(Edited by Laerte Idal Sznelwar)

Occupational Safety and Protection Against Infection in Times of the Pandemic: Challenges for Human Factors and Regulation

Thomas Alexander[✉], Lars Adolph, and Stefan Voss

Federal Institute for Occupational Safety and Health (BAuA), 44149 Dortmund, Germany
Alexander.Thomas@baua.bund.de

Abstract. The SARS-CoV-2 pandemic had a tremendous impact on societies, economies and individuals. The increased spreading of the virus in the society led to new challenges for occupational safety and health, and, thus, for fast reactions. In Germany federal regulations and technical rules for health care and activities within the scope of the biological agents ordinance were in place already, but companies in other domains, e.g. production and services, implemented only own solutions to the best of their knowledge. This led to confusion and uncertainty. Soon it became clear that official standards and mandatory federal technical rules were required to identify suitable protective methods and means. Moreover, they were required for legal certainty. This led to the early publication of the German SARS-CoV-2 Occupational Safety Standard and the subsequent development of sectoral rules of the German Social Accident Insurance. Soon afterwards, the mandatory SARS-CoV-2 Occupational Safety Technical Rule provided further details about background of the pandemic, central aspects and definitions, protective technical means and methods, and preventive occupational healthcare. The development was coordinated by the Federal Institute for Occupational Safety and Health (BAuA) and elaborated by the Advisory Committees of the Federal Ministry of Labour and Social Affairs (BMAS). The committees have a pluralistic composition, which ensure that the relevant groups in society have a good specialist representation. This has been very important for acceptance and compliance in the working environment.

Keywords: Occupational safety · Federal regulation · Technical, Organizational and individual protection

1 Occupational Safety and Health in Times of the Pandemic

Occupational safety and health (OSH) are of high importance for a successful economy. Therefore, there is a well-established system of laws, federal regulation, standards and rules in place. The system includes different actors with clear responsibilities. This has been a solid base for the challenges of the pandemic. However, it required adjustments to consider the risk of infection within this system.

© The Author(s), under exclusive license to Springer Nature Switzerland AG 2022
N. L. Black et al. (Eds.): IEA 2021, LNNS 223, pp. 777–782, 2022.
https://doi.org/10.1007/978-3-030-74614-8_95

1.1 Occupational Safety and Health Regulation in Germany

In Germany, public (federal, state, regional) and insurance regulations and institutions form a dual system for occupational safety and health (OSH) [1]. On the one hand, the state adopts laws, which are substantiated by ordinances, which are specified further by technical rules. Federal committees of the Federal Ministry of Labour and Social Affairs (BMAS) develop these technical rules in a consensus-based process. The committees include representatives of the social partners (e.g. federal and private employers, and unions), experts from OSH and scientific experts. The regulation is also based on regulation and guidelines of the European Union. The statutory accident insurance institutions, the BGs and the public-sector accident insurers, form the second half of the system. They publish DGUV regulations, rules and principles to support occupational safety. Furthermore, standards and publications to special topics complete the OSH-system. The total system is hierarchically organized and spans from from laws to standards and publications as referrenced scientific evidence. It forms a self-consistent and unambiguous system of OSH-rules and regulation.

1.2 Regulation in Times of the Pandemic

The development of a technical rule, including research of relevant results, discussing and finding a consensus between parties with different interests and formulating the legal text is usually a time-consuming process. In times of the pandemic, there was a vast need for dynamic and fast adaptation to a developing amount of scientific knowledge about the infection. There was only little time to transfer last-minute scientific results, findings from practice at work and new requirements to practice. It became obvious early, that employers and companies were eager to take protective means and measures, but were unsure about the suitable, correct measure [2].

At the beginning in February/March 2020, a drastic step was a lockdown of large parts of the German society. However, an effective infection protection was crucial for the society, individuals and, thus, for work and workplaces. After decisions to liberate the lockdown, the BMAS published the SARS-CoV-2 Occupational Safety and Health Standard which provided general recommendations for disease control at work, including aspects like distance, hygiene and protective masks [3]. But a further specification was required to guarantee safe and healthy work during the pandemic and to provide more detailed information. Moreover, the specifications had to fit to the established OSH system. The Federal Institute for Occupational Health and Safety was assigned to develop a technical rule together with the federal committees. The technical rule is de-facto mandatory because, legally, it reflects the state-of-the-art of OSH. This ensures legal compliance for employers in times of the pandemic if they abide the rule [4]. The technical rule was published in August 2020 [5].

The change of scientific knowledge and validity of protective measures required new and fast ways to adopt the development of the technical rule. This was only possible because all participating parties agreed upon the importance of the success of the activity.

This publication addresses the development of the SARS-CoV-2 Occupational Safety Technical Rule. The accident insurance institutions developed SARS-CoV-2 Occupational Safety Standards and practical information for different industrial sectors. While doing so, contents, criteria and objectives of the two regulation domains were continuously communicated, discussed and adjusted between experts from the different institutions.

2 SARS-CoV-2 Occupational Safety Technical Rule

Unlike other technical rules, the scope of the SARS-CoV-2 Occupational Safety Technical Rule is very broad and not limited to single aspects of work. Therefore, all federal committees of the BMAS were involved to a varying extend. The technical rule also had to fit into the existing OSH-system and reference other regulation. Because of the pandemic it extends existing requirements and protective measures.

2.1 General Structure

The general structure of the SARS-CoV-2 Technical Rule is similar to the structure of comparable technical rules: Scope and purpose of the rule are described in the beginning, followed by definitions in greater detail and background information about the SARS-CoV-2 pandemic and COVID-19. This is required for a general understanding of the relevance of the protective measures and the need for correct behavior and compliance. The following chapter deals with the central element of risk assessment and the need to update the risk assessment for infections and diseases.

The main part describes specific protective measures. They follow the basic TOP principle. According to this, technical measures are prioritized against organizational measures and person-related/individual measures. The following chapters describe basic aspects of infection protection during the pandemic: Reducing the number of contacts between people, requirements for minimum distance, hygiene issues and general code of conducts.

The next chapter refers to occupational health and prevention topics. This includes the role of the occupational physicians at work. It also refers to preventive occupational health care, evaluations of infections among employees, the handling of particularly vulnerable employees and those returning after infection.

The appendix addresses workplaces of special interest. These are construction sites, agriculture and forestry, outdoor and delivery services as well as collective accommodation.

2.2 General Protective Means and Measures

The main part of the technical rule refers to protective measures. The general notion is to reduce the risk of infection for employees and workers by a set of different technical, organizational and personal measures.

In accordance with the WHO, the German Federal Ministry of Health published the general "AHA formula" (Abstand, Hygiene, Alltagsmaske: German for distance, hygiene, community mask) at an early stage [6]. In autumn, the German government added the "L" for ventilation [7]. These four aspects serve as a cross-term baseline for protective measures.

2.3 Distance

Close contact between persons is one of the main factors for infection. Therefore, reducing contact between persons is essential. Maintaining a minimum distance of 1.5 m between employees or between employees and other persons significantly reduces the infection risk. The technical rule also stresses, that larger distances are required for certain activities when an increased aerosol emission is likely. Short-term contacts between persons, which take less than 15 min cumulatively for the entire day, result into a low risk of infection so that no minimum distance is required. This is important for short-term contacts in doorways.

In principle, the occupational health and safety guidelines (ASR) are still applicable for workplaces during the pandemic. They specify the dimensions of workplace and movement areas (ASR A1.2), doorways (ASR A1.8), sanitary rooms (ASR A4.1), break rooms and areas (ASR A4.2) and for collective accommodation of workers (ASR A4.4). Additional marks can highlight required distance between persons.

If the required minimum distances is not possible at workplaces, further technical measures such as physical barriers or separators are required. This is also the case for contacts with other persons or with customers. The separators have to cover a certain height in order to provide sufficient protection while sitting or standing.

Furthermore, a set of organizational measures might have to be considered in order to reduce the number of employees at the workplace. This includes home office, adjusting working hours, re-scheduling breaks or shift schedules to enable working in fixed teams. However, this can also increase stress and has to be considered in a risk assessment. Home office as a form of mobile work is another possibility for reducing the number of employees in the company and, thus, the number of personal contacts. However, the technical rule stresses that it also requires a risk assessment and instructions for home office. The instructions have to addresses, among other things, ergonomic workplace design, the use of work equipment, correct and changing sitting postures, and movement breaks.

2.4 Hygiene

In order to avoid smear infections, compliance with hygiene rules is another key element of infection risk reduction. Consequently, the employer has to provide hygienic equipment and installations for employees. This includes easily accessible washing facilities with running water, sufficient liquid soap, and facilities for drying hands in sanitary areas. The sanitary rooms have to be cleaned several times on a working day, at least once.

Work equipment/tools, PPE and work clothing should only be used by a single person. If this is not possible, they have to be cleaned with a commercial (household) detergent before passing them to another person. This also applies to surfaces of workplaces, e.g. table tops, IT equipment, telephone handsets, steering wheels, etc.

2.5 Protective Mask

Protective masks are individual measures that are only required if technical and organizational measures are insufficient. This is the case if the minimum distance is not guaranteed, e.g. if two or more workers work together at production plants.

The technical rule first describes the different protective masks and their protection levels: Community masks (MNB), medical masks (MNS), filtering face pieces (FFP), respirators and face shields. MNB and MNS are sufficient for many workplaces. A filtering face piece (FFP2, N95 or comparable) is only required if the risk assessment reveals an increased risk of infection. This is the case when a close contact to persons without protective masks is expected. Face shields do not replace masks, but might decrease infection risk when used in addition to a mask.

2.6 Ventilation

First infection hotspots in special industrial branches revealed that the dispersion of infective aerosols is likely to increase the risk of infection. Therefore, ventilation became a relevant measure to reduce the risk of infection (Bundesregierung, 2020). This became very important during autumn and winter, when daily life shifted from outdoor to indoor activities. Ventilation allows for an effective removal or reduction of the virus dispersion. Ventilation subsumes free ventilation (if possible, shock ventilation) through windows and doors as well as technical ventilation systems. With reference to ASR A3.6, the technical rule recommends ventilation with a duration of 3–10 min for meeting rooms after 20 min and for offices after 60 min.

In case of technical ventilation systems, different measures reduce the risk of infection: The amount of fresh air from the outside should be increased to a maximum. Regular and thorough maintenance (e.g., by changing filters) also contribute. Finally, upgrading existing systems can also help, e.g. by the installation of additional, high-performance filters or disinfection modules.

3 Results and Conclusion

Reliable means and measures for occupational safety and health has always been a crucial topic. It has become even more important with the pandemic. However, the broad spectrum of available information from different sources has led to uncertainty for employers and employees. There was a vast need for valid and reliable information about risks of infection and protective means and measures.

The development of the SARS-CoV-2 Technical Rule provided information, jointly with publications of other OSH-actors. Moreover, the technical rule matches with the well-established legal system of German technical rules. Consequently, it guarantees legal certainty. If the employer takes measures specified in the technical rule, the employer has legal certainty. The Occupational Safety and Health inspectorate would not record deficits. As a consequence, the SARS-CoV-2-Technical Rule is considered to be mandatory.

Our first evaluation studies reveal that the companies know and follow the regulation well. Infection control has top priority, most frequently positioned at the highest management. However, it has also shown that increased infection rate in the general population results into further lockdowns for businesses.

The continuously expanding knowledge about the pandemic development, the virus dispersion and protective means and measures, requires a continuously update of the Technical Rule. Consequently, the technical rule is being monitored by the federal institute for occupational safety and health and the responsible committees. The goal is to update information as soon as a significant gain in scientific knowledge or a significant change of environmental factors occur. This led to more detail for ventilation and for an alignment with other standards and rules at the beginning of 2021.

Further details are given by the framework of sector-specific rules and information, for example from the statutory accident insurance institutions or, due to the highly dynamics, very often also in the form of Frequently Asked Questions (FAQs) of the different OSH institutions. Such a way of information dispersion was found practical and useful for the public.

However, the overall intent is to provide valid and reliable information at a steady and stable level. This is very important in a very dynamic surrounding with the pandemic. So far, responses from practice were positive.

References

1. WHO Region Office for Europe: Country Profile of Occupational Health System in Germany (2012). https://www.euro.who.int/__data/assets/pdf_file/0010/178957/OSH-Profile-Germany.pdf. Accessed 08 Feb 2021
2. baua: Aktuell 2/2020: Corona-Pandemie (German). BAuA, Dortmund. https://www.baua.de/DE/Angebote/Publikationen/Aktuell/2-2020.pdf?__blob=publicationFile&v=5. Accessed 08 Feb 2021
3. BMAS: SARS-CoV-2 Occupational Safety and Health Standard. GMBI. 2020, p. 303 (2020)
4. baua: Aktuell 3/2020: SARS-CoV-2 Arbeitsschutzregel (German). BAuA, Dortmund. https://www.baua.de/DE/Angebote/Publikationen/Aktuell/3-2020.html. Accessed 08 Feb 2021
5. German Government: Press release (2020). https://wwww.bundesregierung.de/breg-de/themen/coronavirus/bund-laender-beschluss-1744224. Accessed 08 Feb 2021
6. BMAS: SARS-CoV-2 Occupational Safety and Health Technical Rule. GMBl 2020, pp. 484–495 (2020)
7. BMAS: Press release: Recommendations for correct ventilation (2020). https://www.bmas.de/DE/Service/Presse/Pressemitteilungen/2020/empfehlungen-zum-infektionsschutzgerechten-lueften.html. Accessed 08 Feb 2021

Presenteeism and Voice: Ergonomic Factors for Sports Coaches

Katie Buckley[1,2]($\boxtimes$) (iD), Jennifer Oates[1] (iD), Paul O'Halloran[1],
Mandy Ruddock-Hudson[1] (iD), and Lindsay Carey[1]

[1] La Trobe University, Melbourne, Australia
Katie.Buckley@unimelb.edu.au
[2] The University of Melbourne, Melbourne, Australia

Abstract. Sports coaches are vocally reliant, with recognized occupational risk factors affecting their voice use and vocal health. Limited prior research has cooperatively explored coaches' experiences of vocal ergonomic factors during coaching participation. Further, no research has explored coaches vocal or broader presenteeism experiences. As part of a broader action inquiry, coaches (n = 28) in nine professional basketball teams were asked about their vocal and broader health experiences relative to coaching participation. In seven teams, inquiry dialogue with coaches explored coaches' experiences of presenteeism, including the contributions of vocal ergonomic factors. These factors were present at various levels of coaches' work systems, including personal factors, work activity demands, team culture, club-based factors, and sport-related factors. These discussions also revealed how gender and adverse vocal health were associated with coaches' beliefs regarding presenteeism behaviors. Findings from this inquiry provide innovative contributions to the broader academic narrative regarding presenteeism.

Keywords: Presenteeism · Vocal ergonomics · Participatory ergonomics · Sports coaches

1 Introduction

Workers increasingly rely on their voices for workplace activities and participation [1, 2]. Across international labour forces, at least 25% to 33% of workers' voices are affected by attributes of their jobs [1–5]. Examples of vocally reliant occupations include educators [6], call-centre operators [7], performers [8], and sports coaches [9, 10].

Across labour forces, critical vocal reliance increases workers likelihood of poor vocal health [2, 4, 11]. This poor vocal health includes experiencing adverse voice symptoms and voice problems [2, 4, 11]. Workers' poor vocal health is also associated with: diminished work capacities [6, 12], increased workload demands [6, 12], reduced psychosocial wellbeing [6, 12], challenges to occupational participation (e.g. absenteeism, limited career trajectory) [12], broader health problems (e.g. WMSDs [13] and mental health disorders [12]). However, research with vocally reliant workers does not typically consider presenteeism.

N. L. Black et al. (Eds.): IEA 2021, LNNS 223, pp. 783–790, 2022.
https://doi.org/10.1007/978-3-030-74614-8_96

Presenteeism occurs when a worker continues to engage in work activities and participation, despite experiencing poor health status [5, 14]. Presenteeism can negatively affect productivity [15–17], workers' long-term health and wellbeing [18], and workplace economy [15]. Further, workers may engage in presenteeism despite recognising that their health status warrants leave taking [14, 16]. Alternatively, they may perceive their health condition as illegitimate for health recovery withdrawal [19].

Sports coaches are a highly vocally reliant occupational group [9, 10]. Occupational risk factors are recognised as affect coaches' voice use and vocal health [9, 10]. However, there is paucity regarding coaches health behaviours in the presence of these factors. This includes coaches' experiences of system participation relative to presenteeism.

1.1 Research Objectives

This research aimed to collaboratively explore vocal ergonomics with, by, and for sports coaches. This included identifying and addressing vocal ergonomic factors. Vocal ergonomics investigates people's use and experience of voice within systems [1, 3, 9]. Through applying HFE approaches and principles [20, 21], vocal ergonomics identifies factors and (re)designs systems to optimize voice users' activities and system participation [9].

2 Methodology

The methodology of this research aligned with cooperative action inquiry [22] and longitudinal, dialectic, multicase study [23]. Cooperative action inquiry explores development of contextually-anchored knowledge [22–24] with local experts [25, 26].

Participants cooperatively undertake meaning and decision making [22], to facilitate considered actions and context-anchored inquiry [26].

Cooperative action inquiry applied to Human Factors/Ergonomics (HFE) sits within the umbrella of participatory ergonomics. This includes an ergonomist (subject matter expert) *actively participating with* system participants (local experts) [9, 25]. HFE action inquiry aims to deeply understand system participation and develop localised actions [9, 25].

2.1 Participants

In the current research, an ergonomist (and the lead author) collaborated with 28 coaches from nine professional basketball teams. Each team had 2–4 coaches, who coached squads of 10–16 (semi)professional athletes. All coaches in all teams participated in the research. Each team was considered one context for coaching participation, and thus a case unit.

2.2 Overall Action Inquiry

The overall action inquiry in each team used a four-stage research approach (please see [9] for further details of this approach). Various methods of data collection, generation, and analyses were engaged across the research. This paper will only report on methods and findings pertinent to the presenteeism inquiry.

2.3 Inquiry in Presenteeism

Aligned with this action inquiry approach [22, 26], participants developed avenues of investigation as the action inquiry was undertaken with their team. All coaches in all teams were asked about their vocal and broader health experiences relative to coaching participation. These discussions occurred in: (1) the preliminary stage, during 1:1 semi-structured interviews between each coach and the ergonomist; (2) the development stage, within search conferences held at each team [27]; and (3) the evaluation stage, during evaluation focus groups [1] held with each team. A discussion guide provided probes for vocal ergonomic factors during each discussion. However, coaches' lead heavily influenced the nature of all interactions. Across seven teams, presenteeism formed part of discussions.

In each case, categorical aggregation and direct interpretation [28] were undertaken at the end of each action inquiry stage (please see [9] for further details). This facilitated actions and inquiry undertaken in subsequent stages. Beyond field analysis also included reflexive thematic analysis [29] and cross-case analysis [23]. This generated a coherent inquiry dialogue across teams. Findings from this analysis related to the presenteeism inquiry are reported in the results for this paper.

3 Results

Presenteeism was part of the inquiry dialogue within seven teams. Coaches shared that that their engagement in presenteeism behaviours was influenced by personal factors, coaching activity demands, team culture, club-based factors, and sport-related factors.

3.1 Personal Factors

Coaches identified engaging in presenteeism behaviours because they held expectations of not yielding to illness. They also expected themselves not to engage in absence for health recovery. Coaches shared specifically preserving with coaching activities when experiencing adverse vocal health. They shared that views regarding the inevitability of experiencing voice symptoms and problems while coaching influenced their presenteeism behaviours. This included their decisions to "suck it up" and continue to coach, rather than engaging in preventative or recovery behaviours for voice.

Coaches also highlighted that positive personal outcomes from coaching motivated their continued participation when unwell. These outcomes included strongly enjoying coaching participation, beingly highly satisfied by undertaking coaching particularly with others, high levels of personal satisfaction from pursuing excellence, and feeling personally passionate about coaching participation.

3.2 Coaching Activity Demands

Coaches discussed that the nature of undertaking coaching activities influenced their presenteeism behaviours. Heavy workloads were linked to persevering with coaching participation, even when they recognised the need for imminent withdrawal for health recovery.

Coaches shared they were particularly likely to ignore voice symptoms and problems. However, coaches also reflected on the effects of this vocal presenteeism behaviour on their voices and vocally reliant coaching. Coaches recognised that persevering with coaching when experiencing adverse vocal health increased: their overall coaching workloads, vocal effort, and vocal demands. They specifically highlighted having to talk more and engage in lengthier vocally reliant tasks when experiencing adverse vocal health. This was due to impaired voice performance and diminished speech intelligibility.

3.3   Team Culture, Shared Beliefs, and the Perceptions of Others

Team culture was associated with presenteeism. Coaches reported being more likely to engage in presenteeism when a team held shared beliefs that team-member presence marked commitment.

Coaches also noted that the perceptions of others influenced their presenteeism behaviours. This included being seen as committed and having grit. Coaches highlighted the potential for sickness withdrawal to be perceived as weakness, lack of dedication, or lack of abilities to cope with the demands of top-level sport. Avoiding these perceptions from others motivated coaches' presenteeism.

Female coaches shared specifically wanting to avoid gender-based assumptions associated with recovery withdrawal. These assumptions included the negative gender stereotypes of female coaches being less capable than their male colleagues. Female coaches noted engaging in presenteeism behaviours to show their comparable skills and because they "had a point to prove".

3.4   Club-Based Factors

Coaches recognised that club-based factors influenced their continued engagement in coaching when unwell. Coaches highlighted the disparity in resource access across teams in their leagues. When teams lacked adequate resources (e.g. playing facilities, time with players), coaches were more likely to engage in presenteeism. Coaches also noted that their appointment precariousness influenced their health behaviours, as negative perceptions of their capabilities may affect their ongoing employment. Further, coaches noted that club-based performance expectations motivated their engagement in presenteeism. This included persevering with coaching when unwell due to club-based pressures for wins.

3.5   Sport-Related Factors

Coaches highlighted the impact of sport-related factors on their presenteeism behaviours. They discussed that *playing while hurt* was a commonly held belief schema across professional basketball. Coaches detailed that playing while hurt was generally seen as being a good teammate and committed athlete. This shared cultural narrative reinforced coaches' presenteeism behaviours in service of their teams. Coaches also recognised that the competitive nature of coaching appointments motivated their presenteeism behaviours.

4 Discussion

Presenteeism has not been extensively explored for coaches. Further, voice-related presenteeism within extant research focuses only on workers with medically diagnosed voice disorders (e.g. spasmodic dysphonia) [17]. As such, the results of this inquiry provide novel insights for both coach-specific research, and for broader presenteeism literature. Within this inquiry, no coaches discussed factors that supported their engagement in recovery behaviors. However, coaches highlighted various contributory factors to their presenteeism. The following sections discussing these factors.

4.1 Personal Factors

The influence of personal beliefs on presenteeism demonstrated in this inquiry mirror broader research [8, 30]. Performing artist often persist with work despite illness due, at least in part, to beliefs that the 'show must go on' [8]. Strong work engagement also facilitated coaches presenteeism. This has also been found in academics [30]. Work enjoyment enhanced wellbeing but increased work undertaken for both occupations.

4.2 Coaching Activity Demands

Workload is recognized as contributing to presenteeism via wok engagement [30] and reduced productivity [15–17]. Coaches in this inquiry specifically recognized that adverse vocal health increased their coaching workloads and vocal effort. Given that coaches' performance influences the team's performance overall, research should further explore the coaches' presenteeism in light of workload factors.

4.3 Team Culture, Shared Beliefs, and the Perceptions of Others

Culture describes peoples' shared beliefs, norms, language, perspectives, attitudes, priorities, customs, and behaviors [31]. Culture is recognized as contributing to presenteeism, as situationally anchored patterns of behavior are reinforced by social contexts [32, 33].

The social theories of hegemonic masculinity theory [34, 35] and stigma theory [36] may also assist in explaining how and why culture affects coaches' presenteeism behaviors. Hegemonic masculinity theory considers how peoples' actions and beliefs ascribe to notions of dominant power roles within systems, as they relate to gender [35]. Stigma theory explores individuals management of others' impressions, through the concealment of personal attributes that are stigmatized [36].

Both theories explore the role of performance to align with idealized or socially accepted norms. Performative masculinity explains how an individual chooses actions to demonstrate idealized masculine characteristics (e.g. excellence, grit, strength) [34, 35]. Stigma theory asserts that concealment acts are performative, as they aim to align with desired perceptions from others [36].

Neither theory has previously been applied to coaches' presenteeism behaviors. However, basketball coaching is strongly masculinized, due to the nature of sport, organizational structures, and male role dominance [37]. Further, *playing while hurt* is recognized as performatively masculine behavior [35]. Stigma theory has been used to explain athletes' persistence with playing when injured rather than help-seek [34]. Stigma is also associated with broader presenteeism behaviors for workers experiencing mental health disorders [19], vulnerable workers such as Roma [38], and male farm-workers [39].

Within the current inquiry, these two social theories may help to explain some aspects of coaches' engagement in presenteeism. For example, coaches discussed engaging in presenteeism behaviors as demonstrate of their strength, capabilities, commitment, willingness to take risks, and want of excellence. These demonstrations appear to align with performative masculinity. Coaches also detailed using presenteeism behaviors are markers to manage the perceptions of others, including gender-based concerns, and where perceptions may influence precarious appointments status. Both masculinity theory and stigma theory provide contexts for unpacking these discussions. Further exploration of this is warranted.

4.4 Club-Based Factors

Psychosocial factors associated with organizational structures contribute to workers presenteeism behaviors [40]. Studies vary regarding the influence of resource access on presenteeism behaviors. Research has found that resourceful work (e.g. high decision latitude, reward) both motivates [41] and discourages [30] presenteeism. Research with police has also found that resource limitations (e.g. time-pressures) and staffing issues are associated with sickness presenteeism [40].

4.5 Sport-Related Factors

Playing while hurt is a sport-specific and pervasive presenteeism problem, particularly in elite sport [42]. Given the career pathways form high-level athletes to high performance coaching, ongoing presenteeism behaviors are anticipated for sports coaches working in other sports. Further demographic and prevalence on data coaches' presenteeism behaviors should be more fully explored.

5   Conclusions

Coaches are a vocally reliant occupational group who engage in presenteeism. Findings from this inquiry suggest that coaches' presenteeism behaviours are influenced by factors anchored across their work systems. Future research with vocally reliant workers should further explore these considerations to optimize vocally reliant system participation. Further, a systems lens should be applied when considering broader, and voice-specific, presenteeism for sports coaches.

References

1. Vilkman, E.: A survey on the occupational safety and health arrangement for voice and speech professionals in Europe. In: Dejonckere, P.H. (ed.) Occupational Voice: Care and Cure, pp. 129–137. Kugler, The Hague (2001)

2. Verdolini, K., Ramig, L.O.: Review: occupational risks for voice problems. Logop. Phoniatr. Vocology **26**(1), 37–46 (2001)
3. Vilkman, E.: Occupational safety and health aspects of voice and speech professions. Folia Phoniatr. Logop. **56**(4), 220–253 (2004)
4. Titze, I.R., Lemke, J., Montequin, D.: Populations in the U.S. workforce who rely on voice as a primary tool of trade: a preliminary report. J. Voice **11**(3), 254–259 (1997)
5. Eurofound: Working Conditions and Workers' Health. Publications Office of the European Union, Luxembourg (2019)
6. Antunes Rezende, B., Natali Silva Abreu, M., Avila Assunção, A., Mesquita de Medeiros, A.: Factors associated with the limitation at work because of the voice: study with teachers of basic education in Brazil. J. Voice 13 (forthcoming)
7. Fuentes-López, E., Fuente, A., Contreras, K.V.: Inadequate vocal hygiene habits associated with the presence of self-reported voice symptoms in telemarketers. Logop. Phoniatr. Vocology **44**(3), 105–114 (2019)
8. McHenry, M., Evans, J., Powitzky, E.: Vocal assessment before, after, and the day after opera performance. J. Voice **30**(2), 186–191 (2016)
9. Buckley, K., Oates, J., O'Halloran, P., Ruddock-Hudson, M.: Action inquiry and vocal ergonomics: a pilot study with sports coaches. Work (forthcoming)
10. Penteado, R.Z., da Silva, N.B., de Lima Montebello, M.I.: Voice, stress, work and quality of life of soccer coaches and physical trainers. CoDAS **27**(6), 588–597 (2015)
11. Morawska, J., Niebudek-Bogusz, E.: Risk factors and prevalence of voice disorders in different occupational groups–a review of literature. Otorynolaryngologia **16**(3), 94–102 (2017)
12. da Rocha, L.M., de Lima Bach, S., do Amaral, P.L., Behlau, M., de Mattos Souza, L.D.: Risk factors for the incidence of perceived voice disorders in elementary and middle school teachers. J. Voice **31**(2), 258.e7–258.e 12 (2017)
13. Rantala, L., Sala, E., Kankare, E.: Teachers' working postures and their effects on the voice. Folia Phoniatr. Logop. **70**, 24–36 (2018)
14. Aronsson, G., Gustafsson, K.: Sickness presenteeism: prevalence, attendance-pressure factors, and an outline of a model for research. J. Occup. Environ. Med. **47**(9), 958–966 (2005)
15. Hemp, P.: Presenteeism: at work - but out of it. Harvard Bus. Rev. 1–9 (2004)
16. Koopman, C., Pelletier, K.R., Murray, J.F., et al.: Stanford presenteeism scale: health status and employee productivity. Occup. Env. Med. **44**(1), 14–20 (2002)
17. Meyer, T.K., Hu, A., Hillel, A.D.: Voice disorders in the workplace: productivity in spasmodic dysphonia and the impact of botulinum toxin. Laryngoscope **123**(Suppl. 6), 1–14 (2013)
18. Demerouti, E., Le Blanc, P.M., Bakker, A.B., Schaufeli, W.B., Hox, J.: Present but sick: A three-wave study on job demands, presenteeism and burnout. Career Dev. Int. **14**(1), 50–68 (2019)
19. Kendall, E., Muenchberger, H.: Stressors and supports across work and non-work domains: the impact on mental health and the workplace. Work **32**, 27–37 (2009)
20. Bridger, R.S.: Introduction to Ergonomics. McGraw-Hill; New York (1995)
21. International Ergonomics Association. Human factors/ergonomics (HF/E) definition and applications [Internet]. IEA, Geneava, Switzerland (2020). http://iea.cc/whats/index.html. Accessed 20 Oct 2020
22. Heron, J., Reason, P.: A participatory inquiry paradigm. Qual. Inq. **3**(3), 274–294 (1997)
23. Stake, R.E.: Multiple Case Study Method. The Guilford Press, New York (2006)
24. Braun, V., Clarke, V.: One size fits all? What counts as quality practice in (reflexive) thematic analysis? Qual. Res. Psychol. 11 (2020)
25. Burgess-Limerick, R.: Participatory ergonomics: Evidence and implementation lessons. Appl. Ergon. **68**, 289–293 (2018)

26. McNiff, J., Whitehead, J.: All You Need to Know about Action Research, 2nd edn. Sage, London (2012)
27. Varney, H., Rumbold, B., Sampson, A.: Evidence in a different form: the search conference process. J. Appl. Arts Heal. **5**(2), 169–178 (2014)
28. Stake, R.E.: The Art of Case Study Research. Sage, Thoasand Oakes (1995)
29. Braun, V., Clarke, V.: Reflecting on reflexive thematic analysis. Qual. Res. Sport Exerc. Heal. **11**(4), 589–597 (2019)
30. Kinman, G., Wray, S.: Presenteeism in academic employees - occupational and individual factors. Occup. Med. **68**, 46–50 (2018)
31. Kahn, J.S.: The 'culture' in multiculturalism: a view from anthropology. Meanjin **50**, 48–52 (1991)
32. Cooper, C.L., Lu, L.: Presenteeism as a global phenomenon. Cross Cult. Strateg. Manag. **23**(2), 216–231 (2016)
33. Krane, L., Ladekjær Larsen, E., Vinther Nielsen, C., Malmose Stapelfeldt, C., Johnsen, R., Bech Risør, M.: Attitudes towards sickness absence and sickness presenteeism in health and care sectors in Norway and Denmark: a qualitative study. BMC Public Health **14**(880), 13 (2014)
34. Gucciardi, D., Hanton, S., Fleming, S.: Are mental toughness and mental health contradictory concepts in elite sport? A narrative review of theory and evidence. J. Sci. Med. Sport **20**(3), 307–311 (2017)
35. Connell, R.W., Messerschmidt, J.W.: Hegemonic masculinity: rethinking the concept. Gend. Soc. **19**(6), 829–859 (2005)
36. Goffman, E.: Selections from stigma. In: Davis, L.J. (ed.) The Disability Studies Reader, 5th edn, pp. 133–144. Routledge, New York (2006)
37. Walker, N.A., Sartore-Baldwin, M.L.: Hegemonic masculinity and the institutionalized bias toward women in men's collegiate basketball: What do men think? J. Sport Manag. **27**, 303–315 (2013)
38. Collins, H., Barry, S., Dzuga, P.: Working while feeling awful is normal": one Roma's experience of presenteeism. Work Employ. Soc. (forthcoming)
39. Roy, P., Tremblay, G., Robertson, S.: Help-seeking among male farmers: connecting masculinities and mental health. Eur. Soc. Rural Sociol. Sociol. Rural **54**(4), 460–476 (2014)
40. Taloyan, M., Kecklund, G., Thörn, L., et al.: Sickness presence in the Swedish Police in 2007 and in 2010: associations with demographic factors, job characteristics, and health. Work **54**, 379–387 (2016)
41. d'Errico, A., Ardito, C., Leombruni, R.: Work organization, exposure to workplace hazards and sickness presenteeism in the European employed population. Am. J. Ind. Med. **59**(1), 57–72 (2016)
42. Mayer, J., Thiel, A.: Presenteeism in the elite sports workplace: the willingness to compete hurt among German elite handball and track and field athletes. Int. Rev. Sociol. Sport **53**(1), 49–68 (2018)

Ergo@Large: Collaborating for the Benefits of HF/E

Jeanne Guérin[✉]

Ergonovix Inc., Blainville J7C 6B3, Québec, Canada
ergo@jeanneguerin-ccpe.com

Abstract. Ergo@Large is a group of passionate and caring people collaborating on a journey to improve health and wellness through a unique Human Factors/Ergonomics collaborative and inclusive approach opened at large to the many professions involving humans at work in Canada. A group of professors, students and experts came together and formed a sub-committee of the Association of Canadian Ergonomist (ACE) to explore the current state and future of Ergonomics. The committee aims at inspiring new approaches and to encourage discoveries. This article explains the creative approach through four different programs: 1 - Student Projects, 2 - Monitoring/Analyzing, 3 - Survey/Tendencies and 4 - Redaction/Publishing and steps taken since the creation of the Ergo@Large committee with plans for the next five years. The committee operates virtually facilitating an innovative operation structure based on a hockey team organization to avoid silos and divisions per province but rather regroup the pan Canadian group members in teams regardless of their geographic locations to foster inclusion and collaboration.

Keywords: Human factors · Ergonomics · Collaboration · University outreach · Field experts · Student projects

1 Problem Statement

1.1 Understanding Human Factors/Ergonomics (HF/E)

The profession of Ergonomics is at the cross roads. The world has seen unprecedent events in the last year that accelerated the transformation of our work system. Industry 4.0, Robotics, Artificial Intelligence, 5G, are now part of a common vocabulary at work where human tasks are being refocused. The pandemic COVID-19 pushed the work into our homes and proved that people performances are not at stake, however mental and social impacts are still unknown.

The world is changing and at the same time, the relation between humans and work can benefit from new perspectives. Human Factors/Ergonomics (HF/E) is important for multiple academic specialization. HF/E is the branch of science that plays a central role in any discipline where humans, and especially humans at work, are concerned. With the advent of transformative innovations in the workplace and other settings, it is important to stay at the forefront of the emerging technologies and processes in each specific field. This is where having a good understanding of HF/E is critical to human wellbeing and overall system performance.

© The Author(s), under exclusive license to Springer Nature Switzerland AG 2022
N. L. Black et al. (Eds.): IEA 2021, LNNS 223, pp. 791–796, 2022.
https://doi.org/10.1007/978-3-030-74614-8_97

2   Objectives

2.1   Ergo@Large Goals and Mission

The Ergo@Large team is a sub-committee of the Association of Canadian Ergonomists (ACE).

The goal of the working committee is to find ways to react at the transformations we are currently experiencing in the world by expanding the boundary of traditional ergonomics. The group is composed of professors, experts and students located across Canada and specializing in various fields aiming at improving Human Factors/Ergonomics (HFE) for people in the society and in the industry.

The group's mission is to strengthen the position of the Human Factors/Ergonomics (HFE) profession in Canada to gain recognition as a fundamental discipline for human well-being, especially in this time of industry 4.0 revolution.

The long-term vision includes the development of a replicable model to be implemented in developing countries, a grant program to help multidisciplinary student projects come to fruition, cutting-edge multidisciplinary collaborative projects, constant and sustained efforts to promote ergonomics at all levels.

3   Methodology

3.1   Creation of Ergo@Large

Ergo@Large is taking its first steps. A University and a Field Experts outreach was conducted across Canada in 2020. We are still recruiting and promoting the concept to each academic discipline to bring as many professional, students and professors together with the common vision of expanding the field of Human Factors/Ergonomics (HFE) and benefiting from exceptional collaboration.

3.2   Ergo@Large the Hockey Team

The group has entered a structuration phase in early 2021 and is operating according to the organization structure of a hockey team. (see Fig. 1). This organization was preferred to a regional division structure to help promote collaboration and team work. This system was feasible due to the virtual nature of the committee.

A hockey team organization structure involves:

1. A General Director
2. A head coach
3. An assistant coach for defense
4. An assistant coach for offense
5. A goalie
6. Two sets of defensive players including an assistant captain
7. Four trios of offensive players including a team captain and an assistant captain
8. Fans

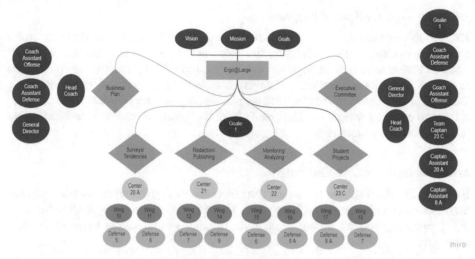

Fig. 1. Organization structure of Ergo@Large according to one of a hockey team.

3.3 Task Assignments

The following six sub-committees were formed to tackle this huge task of anchoring HFE as a fundamental discipline focusing on the wellbeing of humans in the society and in the industry in Canada.

The Business Plan team was formed first to establish the baseline and structure of the group. The nature of this group is transitional and will be dissolved as the group matures and its tasks included in those of the executive committee. At first, The Business Plan group will also be part of the Executive Committee along with the captain, assistant captains and goalie. Their first mandate is to establish the foundations and the permanence of the committee for a period of two years. Thereafter, an election will be planned to elect new executive members.

The four main working groups: 1-Surveys/Tendencies, 2-Redaction/Publishing, 3-Monitoring/Analysis and 4-Student Projects were staffed with offensive players. The two sets of defense team members were assigned two offensive trios each. The goalie was assigned the role of a go to person for the four trios and liaison to the General Director. The roles and responsibilities for the players was decided by each trio. For example, the center of each trio arbors a leadership role. The center and the wings are taking actions such as writing articles, analyzing the state of Ergonomics through the social medias and technology, developing surveys and the defense player's role is to review the projects before publishing, ensuring the projects are aligned with the mission of Ergo@Large and the artistic and content quality are at an exceptional level.

3.4 Ergo@Large Programs

The four main programs of Ergo@Large are described below:

3.4.1 Surveys/Tendencies Program

This group's function is to examine the fundamental questions affecting the ergonomics profession in Canada. This sub-committee looks at the perception of ergonomics in all strata of Canadian society through surveys. For example, The perception of ergonomics in companies, among consumers, at government level, in unions and associations etc. The goal of this section is to understand the place of ergonomics in order to take concrete actions to change perceptions. The results from this group are expected to be effective in the short and medium term.

3.4.2 Redaction/Publishing Program

Based on the efforts of the three programs involved in Ergo@Large: Survey Program, Students Projects Program and Monitoring Program, the group is responsible for writing, publicizing and promoting ergonomics through various media targeting specific segments.

3.4.3 Monitoring Program

This program is responsible for monitoring HFE news, social medias, literature, technologies, processes, working methods, developments in science, other groups similar to Ergo@Large, university disciplines related to ergonomics and ergonomics in industrialized and developing countries. It is important to understand and be attentive to the evolution of the world of work to ensure that the discipline of ergonomics can keep up with and even anticipate the progress in these fields so as to be recognized as a fundamental discipline for the human well-being.

3.4.4 Student Projects Program

Student projects are supported by a multidisciplinary team. For example, students can be collaborating from various disciplines such as engineering, industrial design, ergonomics and agriculture to develop a tool to avoid back pain during harvesting. Pilot projects and grants are planned to help students complete their efforts.

In this section, professors, experts and students collaborate for cutting-edge results in the disciplines involved. The goal is to instill in the various fields involved, the rudiments of ergonomics so that the newly graduated professionals are able to recognize the problems in their professional life and thus do business with ergonomists. This component tackles the recognition of ergonomics at the long-term multidisciplinary level. This level works on the basis, the foundation of the integration of ergonomics in companies in the future.

4   Results

4.1   Where We Are

Ergo@Large is taking its first steps. So far, the team was created and became a sub-committee of ACE, members were recruited, the team organized and assigned roles and responsibilities, a student's project identified, two papers written and a panel created for the International Ergonomics Association (IEA) triennial congress 2021.

In the future, the expectations are for the Student Projects Program to include pilot projects, presentations on different formats, product development, program inclusion in the industry etc. depending on the discipline, projects and involvement level, according to different timelines corresponding to the academic calendars. The end goal of this effort is to enhance the understanding of human/work systems and to integrate the newly gained knowledge in the work field. The young professionals will be cognizant of HFE when entering the market, therefore well-positioned to influence the improvement of human/machine system in their respective organizations.

The Survey and Monitoring Programs will identify elements with the greatest impact on HFE awareness in Canada at large. This committee is supported by the Redaction/Publishing Program and results will be published as papers, pilot projects, lectures, conferences, methods, tools etc.

4.2 Next Steps

The next steps of the committee are to continue recruiting from various academic's disciplines to grow the collaborative exchange, develop content through the sub-committees, to coach the student's projects by supporting, guiding and reviewing the projects as they are progressing and finally to continue to expand the recognition of Human Factors/Ergonomics in Canada at large.

The following Ergo@Large five years' timeline diagram shown (see Fig. 2), explains the main steps of the committee from creation to replication as a model to be used for other similar organizations and developing countries.

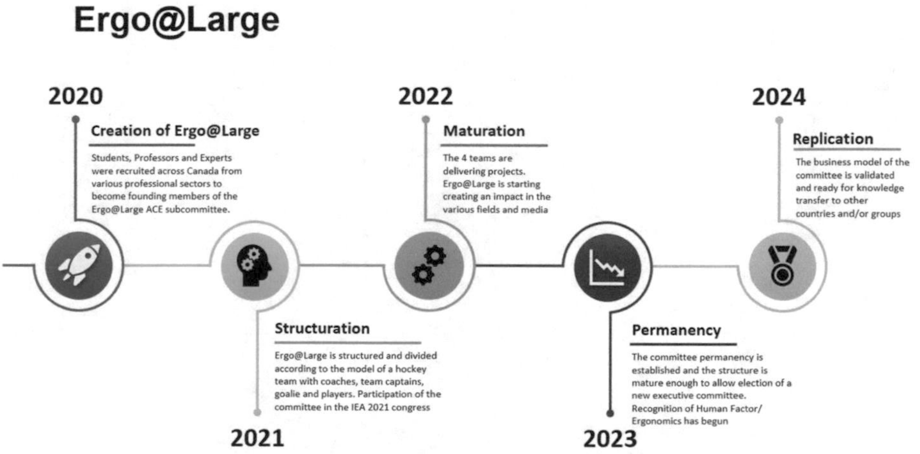

Fig. 2. Ergo@Large 5 years' timeline.

5 Conclusion

5.1 2021 Goals

Ergo@Large promotes an open, creative and collaborative approach. The benefits of joining the group are numerous from satisfaction of leading the future of ergonomics to networking and recognition by taking action in a topic that you care about. Everyone is welcomed to contribute.

The group's goals for the year 2021 are:

1. To be present at the International Ergonomics Association triennial congress and beyond with papers and a panel to promote ergonomics.
2. Keep promoting HFE through ACE and in Canada at large
3. Supporting students' projects

A Synthesis of Subjective Scales Which Assess Worker Fatigue: Building a Simple, Reliable, and Effective Evaluative Instrument

Gabriella M. Hancock[1]([⊠]), Mira Gruber[2], Uyen D. Bui[1], Jessica Blay-Moreira[1], Yvette Apatiga[1], Christian E. Schmitz[1], and Peter A. Hancock[2]

[1] California State University Long Beach, Long Beach, CA 90840, USA
Gabriella.Hancock@csulb.edu
[2] University of Central Florida, Orlando, FL 32816, USA

Abstract. The accurate assessment of operator fatigue has bedeviled ergonomics since before the field was formally constituted. From the archives of the British Industrial Fatigue Research Board in the pre-World-War I era, to Muscio's (1921) famous inquiry "is a fatigue test possible?' [1], the question of assessment has been a perpetual challenge. The lack of accurate assessment is allied to a ready recognition that fatigue plays a critical role in many large-scale disasters as well as errors and incidents of less social prominence, but which are nevertheless equally problematic. In recent decades, in our 24-7-365 world, the issue of operator fatigue continues to impact multiple millions of workers around the world; a propensity that the COVID-19 pandemic has only exacerbated. Yet all is not doom and gloom. Most especially in the 21st century, a number of promising methods and techniques have been offered to provide reliable, quantitative values which specify fatigue levels. Very much like the allied concern for workload assessment [2], the three primary methods of assessment concern primary task performance, physiological assessment approaches, and subjective evaluations. The present work is focused on the latter mode, being arguably the most useful for the prospective projection of future fatigue levels. In short, the issue of fatigue is a large and growing one, its assessment is a crucial ergonomic concern, synthesized subjective assessment techniques promise to provide a vital answer.

Keywords: Fatigue · Subjective assessment · Questionnaire development · Psychometrics

1 Introduction

Fatigue has been and continues to be a ubiquitous issue concerning human performance and safety whose influence is felt across operators, tasks, domains, and time. One study found that 20% of National Transportation Safety Board investigations identified fatigue as a contributing cause to safety incidents across domains (surface transportation, flight and marine operations, etc.) [3]. Research conducted on medical professionals attests to their fatigue-inducing working conditions (regular 24–36 on-duty shifts), their feelings

© The Author(s), under exclusive license to Springer Nature Switzerland AG 2022
N. L. Black et al. (Eds.): IEA 2021, LNNS 223, pp. 797–803, 2022.
https://doi.org/10.1007/978-3-030-74614-8_98

of fatigue affecting their work, and the fact that it puts them and their patients at greater risk of harm [4]. Fatigue has been shown to slow response times, impair judgment, and compromise decision-making skills [5]. These tendencies would typically hamper performance across any task but would be particularly detrimental to those reliant on effective vigilance and efficient attentional allocation such as driving a semi-autonomous vehicle, baggage screening, medical diagnostic screening, anesthesia monitoring, and air traffic control. Understanding, measuring, and designing to effectively alleviate fatigue is critical to the successful operation and safety of human-machine systems across the world.

Yet despite its pervasive nature and influence, a single, agreed-upon operational definition and scheme of quantification and measurement remain elusive. This work examines these issues and seeks to create a unified, coherent, reliable, valid, and easily applicable trans-domain subjective fatigue assessment instrument.

1.1 Definitions

Defining fatigue becomes problematic as theorists disagree even upon its fundamental nature. Some consider fatigue an emotion, a subjective feeling; others a behavioral pattern, a performance outcome, or a moderator/mediator of stress. Still others would characterize it as its own unique stressor unto itself. Though the debate rages on in some academic circles, the authors would like to put forth their position on these contentions. Firstly, fatigue is a construct, a feature of the operator, not merely their behavior or a performance outcome. Secondly, performance decrements and fatigue are not wholly commensurate with one another. Fatigue may cause performance decrements, but performance decrements alone are not sufficient for prescribing a fatigue state. Thirdly, there is a pervasive tendency to equate fatigue and sleepiness. Though these states are related to each other, they are not the same. Sleepiness is the urge or tendency to fall asleep, while fatigue is more multidimensional and see Sect. 1.2 [6].

Though there are many competing operational definitions of fatigue, Soames-Job and Dalziel's is arguably the most accurate and comprehensive. They define fatigue as "the state of an organism's muscles, viscera, or central nervous system, in which prior physical activity and/or mental processing, in the absence of sufficient rest, results in insufficient cellular capacity or system-wide energy to maintain the original level of activity and/or processing by using normal resources" [7]. This definition clearly specifies the cause of fatigue in prior physical or mental activity, reflecting one of the key dimensions of fatigue's nature which will be discussed shortly. The caveat specifying that fatigue manifests 'in the absence of sufficient rest' accurately conveys how operators can be in a fatigued state at the onset of performance as well as accounting for the demonstrable benefit of rest breaks [8]. Moreover, by specifying 'insufficient cellular capacity or system-wide energy', not only does this characterization encapsulate physiological processing, but it also thereby overcomes the circular reasoning inherent to most competing definitions. Finally, the last clause concerning the inability to maintain performance using the typical reserve of resources acknowledges the imbalance of existing physical or mental resources and task demands [9] and implies performance decrements without making them synonymous with the fatigue state.

1.2 Dimensions

Fatigue is a complex and multi-dimensional construct. When examining the literature, it is possible to find works that explain the theoretical distinctions between such dimensions and empirical works that demonstrate their effects. However, no subjective assessment tool yet identified has addressed all of the following dimensions. It is the intention of this project to create a psychometric instrument capable of quantifying and being sensitive to the levels of these different types of fatigue.

Active versus Passive Fatigue

Dependent on the type of task, fatigue may manifest from either active or passive activity. Active fatigue is the result of prolonged task performance necessitating continuous effortful processing and motoric execution [10]. Passive fatigue, on the other hand, results from prolonged monitoring performance (which taxes limited attentional resources) wherein operators are rarely, if ever, required to provide an overt response [10].

Cognitive versus Physical Fatigue

Cognitive fatigue is characterized as a deficit in mental resources (namely, attention) due to their expenditure on task performance, and the consequent inability to maintain performance [11]. Physical fatigue, in contrast, is an inability to continue physical work or performance to a required level due to prolonged use of the muscles [12, 13].

Acute versus Chronic Fatigue

Acute fatigue is characterized as a transient and temporary state experienced by healthy operators as the direct result of taking part in effortful work [14, 15]. In contrast, chronic fatigue is a long-term condition (or even illness) that persists as a feeling and influence on performance despite adequate rest [16].

1.3 Types of Response

Just as there are diverse dimensions and sources (task, environment, etc.) of fatigue, so too are the responses many and varied. In nature, these responses may be categorized as objective or subjective responses to the fatigue experience. Both types hold significant implications for performance outcomes as well as operators' state, health, and well-being. Ideally then, the proposed psychometric assessment method attempts to gauge both such responses.

Objective Responses

Objective indicators of a fatigued state include sleepiness, alertness, activity level, muscle tension, and muscular capacity. Polysomnography can objectively measure physiological correlates of restful sleep that can be predictive of operator state [17]. Activity trackers can record activity and inactivity levels over time in an easy, non-intrusive fashion [18]. Such actiwatches can also track unintended sleep. Finally, researchers have established a battery of muscular strength measures to gauge physical fatigue [19].

Subjective Responses

Subjective responses to fatigue include various cognitive and affective reactions. A representative though inexhaustive list of such responses include perceived tiredness, sleepiness, lethargy, and exhaustion [20]. Operators' subjective experiences of fatigue are commonly measured via visual analog scales and/or valid and reliable questionnaires using Likert-type items. Typically, however, the psychometric options address only a single dimension or symptom of fatigue; for example, the Karolinska Sleepiness Scale [21]. As a result, the goal of the present project is to generate a valid, reliable, and widely applicable subjective fatigue assessment instrument capable of assessing the many causes, dimensions, and responses of fatigue.

2 Methodology

From the survey of all extant subjective fatigue assessment scales, commonalities were distilled in terms of concepts addressed (e.g., feelings of lassitude), subjective symptomatology (e.g., 'heavy' eyes), and subjective performance degradation (e.g., metacognitive recognition of increased error rate), as well as specific interrogatories and queries. This procedure took the form of assessing 1,033 identified articles derived from keyword searches and reference list searches from all the major scientific databases. The extension beyond the typical human factors and ergonomic databases was necessary as fatigue assessment is practiced in highly disparate constituencies (e.g., airspace operations, clinical psychological assessments, etc.). For the key terms, exclusionary terms, and modifiers, please see Table 1.

From this survey, 89 key subconstructs were identified that contribute to the latent construct of 'fatigue', which were embodied in 1,698 questionnaire items. These collective identifications have been summated into an extended survey instrument in order to conduct critical factor identification. This inquiry is currently in progress and will form the foundation of an accompanying meta-analytic study of fatigue effects and assessment.

3 Results

From the above elicited data, the authors identified 90 currently developed scales which provide substantive assessments of subjective fatigue state. Eighty-nine subconstructs related to fatigue embedded within these 90 identified scales were reviewed. The results compare and contrast the validity, reliability, and applicability of such scales alongside recommendations for practitioners who employ them. Moreover, the subconstructs for fatigue were analyzed and categorized to reflect its multifaceted nature in the construction of the more comprehensive proposed scale. The dimensions of the authors' own developing scale include i) active versus passive fatigue; ii) acute versus chronic fatigue; iii) subjective versus objective responses (mental, physical, and emotional dimensions), as well as iv) the contributions of diverse other sources of fatigue (i.e., task, environment, etc.).

Next steps include analyzing the 1,698 items to remove duplicates, re-phrasing items to allow for maximum applicability in terms of administration and use (i.e., generic or specifiable system terms), assessing internal consistency, and determining the nature of responses (i.e., visual analog scale versus Likert-type scale). Items must also be generated

Table 1. Key terms, exclusionary terms, and modifiers.

Database	Key terms	Exclusionary terms*	Modifiers**
Google Scholar	Fatigue	Material, metal, respiratory, anemia, mitochondrial, structural, weld, blade, steel, chronic	acute, chronic, active, passive, mental,
	Assessment	Weld, cycle, frame, train, material, metal, turbine, welds, vessel, production, rig	physical, central, peripheral,
	Questionnaire	Material, metal, respiratory, anemia, mitochondrial, structural, weld, blade, steel, chronic	cognitive, driver, pilot, trucker,
	Tiredness	Material, metal, respiratory, anemia, mitochondrial, structural, weld, blade, steel, chronic	medical, and workplace
	Lassitude	Metal, material, recovery, cell, sickness	
	Sleepiness	Rats, mice, pain, metal	
	Sleep deprivation	Rats, mice, pain, metal	
	Boredom	Rats, mice, pain, metal	
	Task disengagement	Metal, material, rats	
	Ennui	Metal, material, rats	
	Fatigued	Metal, material, rats, + only English articles	
	Burnout	Metal, material, rats, pigs, + only English articles	
	Exhaustion	Metal, material, recovery, cell	
	Weary	Metal, material, recovery, cell, cows, calves	
	Weariness	Metal, material, recovery, cell	
	Lethargy	Metal, material, recovery, cell	
	Dullness	Metal, material, rats, cell, infection	
	Languor	Metal, material, rats, cell, infection	
	Listlessness	Metal, material, rats, cell, infection	

*Some modified key terms had different exclusionary terms. The most common are listed.
**Each keyword was modified with the same 14 modifiers.

if an acceptable exemplar cannot be identified or refined from existing scales. This latter process may need to occur multiple times given the dearth of existing scales addressing some of the key dimensions of fatigue.

Assuming a Likert-type scale, items will be positively worded with some being reverse-coded to ensure the integrity of responses. A selection of items will therefore be determined for each dimension of fatigue. Each of these subsections will then be amalgamated into the complete battery for fatigue assessment. This completed questionnaire will then undergo multiple validation studies to ensure the internal consistency of all items, and that each item loads onto its proposed sub-construct associated with the latent construct of fatigue.

4 Discussion

Creating an effective worker fatigue assessment instrument does not only consist of item identification, selection, grouping, administration and verification of validity and reliability. There are also ergonomic issues involved with its administration. In the present project, the authors have created a fatigue 'app' which employs minimalist interface design principles to garner both objective (e.g., time-of-day of administration) and subjective (e.g., specific item response levels), in order to produce a fatigue ratio scale ranging from 0–100. These anchors connote no discernible presence of fatigue and the ceiling being intolerable fatigue. Some present concerns involve questions as to whether individuals can effectively respond at the 100 level, or whether increasing levels on the ratio scale actually inhibit accurate responding. Efforts are also underway in the process of identifying salient thresholds on the scale; that is, providing easily recognized cognitive anchors for meaningful values (e.g., 50).

5 Conclusions

Subjective assessment of fatigue holds important promise for ergonomic applications. Yet, current methods, derived from multiple disciplines and domains, provide no simple unified scale that is easily applicable in real-world circumstances. Here, the authors provide a roadmap to such scale development and report on the progress of this effort thus far.

To date, the authors have combed the relevant literature from multiple disciplines, including human factors/ergonomics, to establish what psychometric instruments are currently in use for the dynamic assessment of operator fatigue. Herein, the strengths and limitations of those instruments have been discussed as well as propositions for their improvement, particularly with regard to their utility to practitioners. Given the nature of evolving human-machine systems and ever more autonomous adaptive automation, fatigue may well be one of, if not the, most pressing human performance issue of the future. The successful quantitative assessment of fatigue's effects on performance and operators' cognitive and affective states is therefore not only integral to the design of future human-machine systems; it is also critical for determining the efficacy of targeted countermeasures. A valid, reliable, and flexible instrument for the subjective assessment of fatigue across multiple tasks, environments, and operational domains is therefore desperately needed, and this work represents the first steps in the construction and validation of this valuable psychometric instrument.

References

1. Muscio, B.: Is a fatigue test possible? Br. J. Psychol. **12**(1), 31 (1921)
2. Hancock, P.A., Matthews, G.: Workload and performance: associations, insensitivities, and dissociations. Hum. Factors **61**(3), 374–392 (2019)

3. Marcus, J.H., Rosekind, M.R.: Fatigue in transportation: NTSB investigations and safety recommendations. Injury Prev. **23**(4), 232–238 (2017)
4. Gaba, D.M., Howard, S.K.: Fatigue among clinicians and the safety of patients. N. Engl. J. Med. **347**, 1249–1255 (2002)
5. Duffy, J.F., Zitting, K.-M., Czeisler, C.A.: The case for addressing operator fatigue. Rev. Hum. Factors Ergon. **10**(1), 29–78 (2015)
6. Lerman, S.E., et al.: Fatigue risk management in the workplace. J. Occup. Environ. Med. **54**(2), 231–258 (2012)
7. Soames-Job, R.F., Dalziel, J.: Defining fatigue as a condition of the organism and distinguishing it from habituation, adaptation and boredom. In: Hancock, P.A., Desmond, P.A. (eds.) Stress, Workload, and Fatigue. CRC Press, New York (2001)
8. Tucker, P.: The impact of rest breaks upon accident risk, fatigue and performance: a review. Work Stress **17**(2), 123–137 (2003)
9. Hancock, P.A., Warm, J.S.: A dynamic model of stress and sustained attention. Hum. Factors **31**(5), 519–537 (1989)
10. Desmond, P.A., Hancock, P.A.: Active and passive fatigue states. In: Hancock, P.A., Desmond, P.A. (eds.) Stress, Workload, and Fatigue. CRC Press, New York (2001)
11. Pattyn, N., Neyt, X., Henderickx, D., Soetens, E.: Psychophysiological investigation of vigilance decrement: Boredom or cognitive fatigue? Physiol. Behav. **93**(1–2), 369–378 (2008)
12. Latash, M.L., Danion, F., Bonnard, M.: Effects of transcranial magnetic stimulation on muscle activation patterns and joint kinematics within a two-joint motor synergy. Brain Res. **961**, 229–242 (2003)
13. Mehta, R.K., Parasuraman, R.: Effects of mental fatigue on the development of physical fatigue: a neuroergonomic approach. Hum. Factors **56**(4), 645–656 (2014)
14. Aaronson, L.S., Pallikkathayil, L., Crighton, F.: A qualitative investigation of fatigue among healthy working adults. West. J. Nurs. Res. **25**(4), 419–433 (2003)
15. Barker, L.M., Nussbaum, M.A.: Fatigue, performance and the work environment: a survey of registered nurses. J. Adv. Nurs. **67**(6), 1370–1382 (2011)
16. Cameron, C.: A theory of fatigue. Ergonomics **16**(5), 633–648 (1973)
17. Ingram, D.G., Crane, S.C.M., Halbower, A.C.: Polysomnography. In: Accardo, J.A. (ed.) Sleep in Children with Neurodevelopmental Disabilities, pp. 27–43. Springer, Cham (2019). https://doi.org/10.1007/978-3-319-98414-8_3
18. Kim, E., Lovera, J., Schaben, L., Melara, J., Bourdette, D., Whitham, R.: Novel method of measurement of fatigue in multiple sclerosis: real-time digital fatigue score. J. Rehabil. Res. Dev. **47**(5), 477–484 (2010)
19. Earle-Richardson, G., Jenkins, P.L., Strogatz, D., Bell, E.M., May, J.J.: Developmental and initial assessment of objective fatigue measures for apple harvest work. Appl. Ergon. **37**(6), 719–727 (2006)
20. Rogers, A.E.: The effects of fatigue and sleepiness on nurse performance and patient safety. In: Hughes, R.G. (ed.) Patient Safety and Quality: an Evidence-Based Handbook for Nurses. Agency for Healthcare Research and Quality, Washington DC (2008)
21. Shahid, A., Wilkinson, K., Marcu, S., Shapiro, C.M.: Karolinska sleepiness scale (KSS). In: Stop, That and One Hundred Other Sleep Scales. Springer, New York (2011)

Heat Stress Management in the Construction Industry: A Socio-technical Systems Perspective

Damithri Gayashini Melagoda$^{(\boxtimes)}$ and Steve Rowlinson

The University of Hong Kong, Pokfulam, Hong Kong SAR
damithri_melagoda@hku.hk

Abstract. Due to heavy physical outdoor work construction workers' safety is compromised by climatic heat stress. Heat stress in construction consists of environmental, organizational, technological, and personal elements. Administrative controls, environmental engineering controls, and personal engineering controls are safety interventions in the construction industry adopted to cope with heat stress. Numerous indices, models, and protective guidelines are introduced to measure and manage heat stress. Wet-bulb globe temperature (WBGT), Humidex, thermal work limit (TWL), predicted heat strain (PHS) are common indices used to measure heat stress. Imposing mandatory work-rest regimens is done through regulations as well as organizational work systems. Self-pacing, an alternative method of heat stress management, can be optimized by work system design using self-regulating worker groups. Because of the pragmatic and loosely-coupled nature of the construction industry, the design of self-regulating worker groups needs to be addressed in a socio-technical approach. It would comprise of consultative and substantive worker participation to optimize the work system for the benefit of individual and organization.

Keywords: Construction safety · Heat stress · Socio-technical systems · Self-regulating worker groups · Worker participation

1 Introduction

Excessive heat exposure poses significant risks to workers in hot climates. When people perform physical activities in hot environments, they are at risk of an increase in deep body temperature, a decrease in physical work capacity, and mental capacity. The reduced mental performance induces speed of response, reasoning ability, visual perception, associative learning, and mental alertness negatively which are reported to be the possible causations of fatal accidents [1]. Heat stress influences work performance and productivity as well. In warm areas of the world, it is estimated to occur an 11–27% of productivity decline [2]. Construction is often classified as a high-risk industry for its significant injury rates. It involves complicated processes, changing work locations, and complex work environments. Less standardized worker behaviors provoke extra attention for site safety measures. Further, heavy physical outdoor work exposes construction workers to regular occupational heat stress.

Heat stress intervention in the construction industry encapsulates administrative controls: assigned or rescheduled work practices and policies; environmental engineering controls: mitigate workers exposure through heat stress monitoring; and personal engineering controls: offering personal protective equipment [3]. Administrative controls are rescheduling of work rotation and self-regulation of workers to cope with heat stress. Thus, environmental engineering controls and personal engineering can assist to design work rotation and self-regulating work systems. In this discipline, most studies are focused on quantifying heat stress and its consequences. This article proposes self-regulating work group design as a heat stress management practice in the construction industry from a socio-technical perspective.

2 Method

To present a novel perspective for heat stress management practices in the construction industry, an integrative literature review is undertaken. An integrative literature review is defined as "a form of research that reviews, critiques, and synthesizes representative literature on a topic in an integrated way such that new frameworks and perspectives on the topic are generated" [4]. Various databases were used to access literature on heat stress management in construction and socio-technical systems. These include PubMed, Google Scholar, Scopus, EBSCO, Web of Science, PROQUEST, etc. Using keyword search containing "heat stress" and "construction"; "socio-technical systems"; "socio-technical systems" and "safety" in each database, pertinent literature were identified and duplicates were removed after abstract screenings. Important articles to the study were then recognized based on the content of each identified paper. Finally, relevant arguments and findings from the articles were summarized, synthesized, and integrated as appropriate to develop the proposition of this study.

3 Heat Stress and the Construction Industry

Construction is one of the most affected industries by heat stress that seconds only to agriculture [5]. In the United States (US), 36.8% of heat-related fatalities are accounted for by the construction industry [6]. Hong Kong construction industry reported 43 heat-related accidents including 11 fatalities from 2007 to 2011 [7]. Further to a study conducted in the US, cement masons face ten times elevated risk of heat-related death than the average construction worker while roofers and helpers were seven times more likely; brick masons three times, and construction laborers two times [8]. Countries have implemented policies and regulations to prevent heat-related injuries. For example, the U.S. Occupational Safety and Health Administration (OSHA) recommended preventive measures providing rest, shade, and water; limiting physical activities when the heat index increases as a guideline for employers [9]. Similar guidelines were issued in the United Kingdom [10], Hong Kong (particular to the construction industry) [11], and Australia [12]. As recommendations and guidelines are not enforceable and did not bring about expected results, countries introduced educational campaigns to improve the awareness of heat stress prevention practices among workers [13].

Workers have to face physiological as well as psychological health issues, safety problems by continuous exposure to extremely hot environments. It also reduces the productivity of workers due to fatigue [14]. Heat stress in construction consists of environmental, organizational, technological, and personal elements. Prominent risk factors are identified as climatic heat caused by lack of wind, humidity, and solar radiant heat; workplace heat; clothing effect due to personal protective equipment; metabolic heat generated by workload, work pace, and continuous work time; and personal factors such as ethnicity, aging, acclimatization, fatigue, personal health and lifestyle, dehydration, risk perception, job skills, mindfulness and psychological stress [15]. Three ways of managing heat stress risk in the construction industry are introduced: (1) control of environmental heat stress exposure through the use of an action-triggering threshold system, (2) control of continuous work time referred by maximum allowable exposure duration with mandatory work-rest regimens and (3) enabling self-paced working through the empowerment of employees [16].

3.1 Control of Environmental Heat Stress Exposure Through the Use of an Action-Triggering Threshold System

Action-triggering threshold systems encapsulate heat strain indices, models, and protective guidelines to protect workers from heat exposure. Wet Bulb Globe Temperature (WBGT) is the most widely used index. It is a combination of the natural wet bulb temperature, the global temperature, and the air temperature [17]. It also serves as the metric for ISO 7243: heat stress standard which determines ergonomic effects of the thermal environment [18]. Using air temperature and relative humidity, Humidex describes the degree of comfort of an average person [19]. The thermal work limit (TWL) uses a combined measure of dry bulb and wet bulb temperatures, radiant heat, and wind speed to predict the safe limit of work a worker should carry out [20]. Based on TWL Abu Dhabi Occupational Safety and Health Centre defined working zones for control interventions and rest-work and hydration schedules [21]. While these indices are based on environmental measures, the physiological strain index (PSI) rates the bodily strain of humans using rectal temperature and heart rate [22]. In 1989, the International Organization for Standardization espoused the required sweat rate model to determine and interpret thermal stress which was then revised by adopting the predicted heat strain (PHS) model in 2004. The PHS model is based on the thermal equilibrium of the human body. It indicates the maximum allowable exposure time of a human by assessing the heat stress that can lead to excessive core temperature and water loss [23]. Later a heart rate-based PHS model is introduced to predict individual heat stress in dynamic working environments [24]. A Fatigue Assessment Scale for Construction Workers (FASCW) was developed to assist in taking possible actions for fatigue regulation and heat stress management by understanding the fatigue symptoms among construction workers [25]. Sensing technologies and smart wearables such as wrist-worn temperature sensors [26], thermal cameras [27] can make use of a multitude of thermal comfort data of workers. It enables real-time information on worker conditions to manage them safely and effectively.

3.2 Control of Continuous Work Time Referred by Maximum Allowable Exposure Duration with Mandatory Work-Rest Regimens

Construction work is labor-intensive and comprises heavy physical outdoor work. Continuous exposure to heat causes physiological disorders due to heat accumulation in the human body. Maximum allowable exposure duration (D_{lim}) gives reference values to determine the continuous exposure time of workers. According to ISO 7933, D_{lim} is the combination of environmental and metabolic heat stress and clothing effect [16]. Limiting working hours during the summer is enabled as a regulation in several Middle Eastern countries such as the United Arab Emirates [28] and Qatar [29]. Based on a study with rebar workers during the summer in Beijing, China, 14:00–15:00 h are identified as the most hazardous and 07:00–09:00 as the least hazardous working hours [30].

3.3 Enabling Self-paced Working Through the Empowerment of Employees

Self-pacing: workers reducing their work pace to avoid accumulating excessive heat, is suggested as an effective measure for heat stress management [32]. Thus, in the normal course of work, workers have to deal with conflicts between espoused and enacted priorities [17]. In the construction industry self-pacing for safety is constrained by influences such as time pressure; financial incentives; peer pressure and self-perception of effectiveness; awareness and knowledge of heat stress; individual and biological differences [33].

4 Socio-technical Systems Perspective

A sociotechnical system is defined as "the synergistic combination of humans, machines, environments, work activities and organizational structures and processes that comprise a given enterprise" [31]. The construction project itself is a complex socio-technical system where the worker performs multiple tasks using different tools and technologies in a physical environment under organizational conditions. All these elements are inter-related and difficult to distinguish from each other. Decision making in construction projects is characterized by complex inter-organizational relationships, sub-clustering, information dependencies, and considerable division of labor. Decisions related to health and safety on construction sites cannot easily be traced to a single project participant acting in isolation [32]. The socio-technical systems approach to risk management believes accidents are caused not only by human errors or physical events but as a result of organizational settings and the environment it operates in [33]. This proposes a holistic approach to consider both social and technical influences on occupational safety within a working system.

Physical tasks in construction demand different skill levels, technology requirements, and continuity requirements. For example, concreting is an intensive task that needs to be conducted continuously until completion when the pouring is started. Whereas steel bending is conducted freely, thus, it is highly disciplined teamwork [34]. Design of work system to suit all tasks in a construction project, therefore, becomes complicated and absurd. In that case, self-regulating work group (also referred to as self-managing or autonomous groups) is a promising alternative to traditional forms of work design. In contrast to Scientific Management, socio-technical systems proposed to ease the job control or autonomy to improve the work system based on semi-autonomous groups [31]. These workgroups include a relatively whole task; workers' freedom of choice to decide the method of work and task schedules [35]. There are three contemporary approaches to safe work system design and assessment consistent with sociotechnical principles, namely, human-systems integration (HSI), macroeconomics, and safety climate [36]. Here, HSI is a framework, macroergonomics is a method, and safety climate is the outcome of the process [37]. HIS considers workers as a critical element in a working system and adopts a human-centric approach in work system design to increase both productivity and safety [38]. Maroergonomics is portrayed as a method that emphasizes the critical impact of social and organizational factors on the design of safe and effective work systems, processes, and equipment. Work system deals with the scheduling of work: work-rest schedules, hours of work and shift work; job design: the complexity of tasks, skill and effort required, and degree of worker control; interpersonal aspects of work: relationships with supervisors and co-workers; management style: participatory management practices and teamwork; and organizational characteristics: climate, culture, and communications [39].

In any work setting, workers are the experts in the practical sense. They are the most suitable agents to analyze a problem and come up with a solution that serves both productivity and safety goals which will also be accepted by those who are affected. Thus, workers need to be empowered with adequate knowledge, skills, tools, resources, and encouragement [40]. Based on this assumption, participatory ergonomics is the active participation of workers "in planning and controlling a significant amount of their work activities" to boost productivity and reduce health and safety risks [41]. This approach gives room for improvement of climatic heat-related safety practices in construction, basically, self-regulating worker group approaches.

5 Conclusion

Workers play the central role in the conceptualization of socio-technical systems where occupational health and safety is considered to be an emergent attribute. Empowering self-regulating worker groups with participative ergonomics approach in health and safety in work procedures is assumed to manage the risk of heat stress in the construction industry. Thus, this proposition needs to be analyzed through a practical application with different worker groups who are exposed to different heat stresses, involve in varying tasks in the construction industry.

References

1. Chi, C., Chang, T., Ting, H.: Accident patterns and prevention measures for fatal occupational falls in the construction industry. Appl. Ergon. **36**(4), 391–400 (2005)
2. Zander, K.K., Botzen, W.J., Oppermann, E., Kjellstrom, T., Garnett, S.T.: Heat stress causes substantial labour productivity loss in Australia. Nat. Climate Change **5**(7), 647–651 (2015)

3. Yang, Y., Chan, A.P.: Heat stress intervention research in construction: gaps and recommendations. Ind. Health **55**(3), 201–209 (2017)
4. Torraco, R.J.: Writing integrative literature reviews: guidelines and examples. Hum. Resour. Dev. Rev. **4**(3), 356–367 (2005)
5. Xiang, J., Bi, P., Pisaniello, D., Hansen, A., Sullivan, T.: Association between high temperature and work-related injuries in Adelaide, South Australia, 2001–2010. Occup. Environ. Med. **71**(4), 246–252 (2014)
6. Gubernot, D.M., Anderson, G.B., Hunting, K.L.: Characterizing occupational heat-related mortality in the United States, 2000–2010: an analysis using the census of fatal occupational injuries database. Am. J. Ind. Med. **58**(2), 203–211 (2015)
7. Chan, A.P.: From heat tolerance time to optimal recovery time-a heat stress model for construction workers in Hong Kong (2012)
8. Dong, X.S., West, G.H., Holloway-Beth, A., Wang, X., Sokas, R.K.: Heat-related deaths among construction workers in the United States. Am. J. Ind. Med. **62**(12), 1047–1057 (2019)
9. Using the Heat Index: A Guide for Employers. https://www.osha.gov/SLTC/heatillness/heat_index/pdfs/all_in_one.pdf. Accesses 02 Jan 2021
10. Heat stress in the workplace: A brief guide, https://www.hse.gov.uk/pubns/indg451.pdf. Accesses 02 Jan 2021
11. Guidelines on site safety measures for working in the hot weather, http://www.cic.hk/cic_data/pdf/about_cic/publications/eng/V10_6_e_V00_Guidelines%20on%20Site%20Safety%20Measures%20for%20Working%20in%20Hot%20Weather.pdf. Accesses 02 Jan 2021
12. Managing the risks of working in heat: Guidance material. https://www.safeworkaustralia.gov.au/system/files/documents/1902/guide_for_managing_the_risks_of_working_in_heat_1.pdf. Accesses 02 Jan 2021
13. Acharya, P., Boggess, B., Zhang, K.: Assessing heat stress and health among construction workers in a changing climate: a review. Int. J. Environ. Res. Public Health **15**(2), 247 (2018)
14. Habibi, P., Momeni, R., Dehghan, H.: Relationship of environmental, physiological, and perceptual heat stress indices in Iranian Men. Int. J. Prevent. Med. **6** (2015)
15. Jia, Y.A., Rowlinson, S., Ciccarelli, M.: Climatic and psychosocial risks of heat illness incidents on construction site. Appl. Ergon. **53**, 25–35 (2016)
16. Rowlinson, S., YunyanJia, A., Li, B., ChuanjingJu, C.: Management of climatic heat stress risk in construction: a review of practices, methodologies, and future research. Accid. Anal. Prev. **66**, 187–198 (2014)
17. Budd, G.M.: Wet-bulb globe temperature (WBGT)—its history and its limitations. J. Sci. Med. Sport **11**(1), 20–32 (2007)
18. Parsons, K.: Heat stress standard ISO 7243 and its global application. Ind. Health **44**(3), 368–379 (2006)
19. Rana, R., Kusy, B., Jurdak, R., Wall, J., Hu, W.: Feasibility analysis of using humidex as an indoor thermal comfort predictor. Energy Build. **64**, 17–25 (2013)
20. Miller, V.S., Bates, G.P.: The thermal work limit is a simple reliable heat index for the protection of workers in thermally stressful environments. Ann. Occup. Hyg. **51**(6), 553–561 (2007)
21. Safety in Heat. https://www.oshad.ae/safetyinheat/documentPDFs/ThermalWorkLimit-WorkingZones/Drink_Water_Technical_Info_Eng.pdf. Accesses 04 Feb 2021
22. Moran, D.S., Shitzer, A., Pandolf, K.B.: A physiological strain index to evaluate heat stress. Am. J. Physiol. Regul. Integr. Comp. Physiol. **275**(1), R129–R134 (1998)
23. Du, C., Li, B., Li, Y., Xu, M., Yao, R.: Modification of the Predicted Heat Strain (PHS) model in predicting human thermal responses for Chinese workers in hot environments. Build. Environ. **165**, 106349 (2019)

24. Yao, R., Li, Y., Du, C., Li, B.: A 'heart rate'-based model (PHSHR) for predicting personal heat stress in dynamic working environments. Build. Environ. **135**, 318–329 (2018)
25. Zhang, M., et al.: Development and validation of a fatigue assessment scale for US construction workers. Am. J. Ind. Med. **58**(2), 220–228 (2015)
26. Aryal, A., Becerik-Gerber, B.: A comparative study of predicting individual thermal sensation and satisfaction using wrist-worn temperature sensor, thermal camera and ambient temperature sensor. Build. Environ. **160**, 106223 (2019)
27. Cosma, A.C., Simha, R.: Using the contrast within a single face heat map to assess personal thermal comfort. Build. Environ. **160**, 106163 (2019)
28. UAE regulates work hours to limit labourers' sun exposure. https://www.ioshmagazine.com/uae-regulates-work-hours-limit-labourers-sun-exposure. Accesses 01 Feb 2021
29. Qatar: Take Urgent Action to Protect Construction Workers. https://www.hrw.org/news/2017/09/27/qatar-take-urgent-action-protect-construction-workers. Accesses 01 Feb 2021
30. Li, X., Chow, K.H., Zhu, Y., Lin, Y.: Evaluating the impacts of high-temperature outdoor working environments on construction labor productivity in China: a case study of rebar workers. Build. Environ. **95**, 42–52 (2016)
31. Carayon, P., Hancock, P., Leveson, N., Noy, I., Sznelwar, L., Van Hootegem, G.: Advancing a sociotechnical systems approach to workplace safety–developing the conceptual framework. Ergonomics **58**(4), 548–564 (2015)
32. Lingard, H., Cooke, T., Blismas, N., Kleiner, B.: A socio-technical systems analysis of OSH decision-making in the early stages of construction projects. In: Proceedings, CIB W, pp. 1–16 (2011)
33. Leveson, N.: A systems approach to risk management through leading safety indicators. Reliab. Eng. Syst. Saf. **136**, 17–34 (2015)
34. Rowlinson, S., Jia, Y.A.: Application of the predicted heat strain model in development of localized, threshold-based heat stress management guidelines for the construction industry. Ann. Occup. Hyg. **58**(3), 326–339 (2014)
35. Cummings, T.G.: Self-regulating work groups: a socio-technical synthesis. Acad. Manag. Rev. **3**(3), 625–634 (1978)
36. Kleiner, B.M., Hettinger, L.J., DeJoy, D.M., Huang, Y.-H., Love, P.E.: Sociotechnical attributes of safe and unsafe work systems. Ergonomics **58**(4), 635–649 (2015)
37. Waterson, P., Robertson, M.M., Cooke, N.J., Militello, L., Roth, E., Stanton, N.A.: Defining the methodological challenges and opportunities for an effective science of sociotechnical systems and safety. Ergonomics **58**(4), 565–599 (2015)
38. Tvaryanas, A.P.: Human systems integration in remotely piloted aircraft operations. Aviat. Space Environ. Med. **77**(12), 1278–1282 (2006)
39. Carayon, P., Smith, M.J.: Work organization and ergonomics. Appl. Ergon. **31**(6), 649–662 (2000)
40. Stanton, N.A., Hedge, A., Brookhuis, K., Salas, E., Hendrick, H.W.: Handbook of Human Factors and Ergonomics Methods. CRC Press, Boca Raton (2004)
41. Corlett, E.N., Wilson, J.R., Corlett, N.: Evaluation of Human Work. CRC Press, Boca Raton (1995)

Attitude Towards Artificial Intelligence in a Leadership Role

Deborah Petrat[✉]

Institute for Human Factors and Ergonomics, Technical University of Darmstadt, Darmstadt, Germany
deborah.petrat@tu-darmstadt.de

Abstract. The current development of AI technologies shows that in the future it will be possible to help people with certain problems by analyzing data sets but also to support them with more complex tasks. For example, AI has already been implemented in some companies to take over routine tasks in the HR department or to assist managers with administrative tasks so that they can focus on essential tasks. Thus, this interview study was designed to answer the main research question of what attitudes people have toward AI as a manager. N = 32 subjects from different industries participated in the interview *(16 male and 16 female; mean age 36.74, SD = 12.42)*, of which 14 had leadership responsibilities and 18 had no employee responsibilities. It was found that tech-savvy individuals find it difficult to envision AI technologies in both work context and leadership. If it ever comes to that, the subjects want a transparent application that supports them and gives them space for interpersonal interactions with a human supervisor. Further research in this area is needed.

Keywords: Artificial intelligence · Leadership · Expectations

1 Introduction

Due to the advancing development of digitalization, artificial intelligence (AI) is no longer a future version. Through various methods, such as machine learning, it is now already possible to work with a large amount of data. The goal of AI development is to provide the best possible support for people in both professional and private context (Buxmann and Schmidt 2018). This development has an impact on the organization, employees and work processes (Work 4.0) and consequently on managers (Leadership 4.0) (Offensive Mittelstand 2018). The aim of this paper is to capture attitudes towards AI as a leader by means of an interview study in order to preempt initial insights into requirements of such AI as well as potential implementation problems.

2 Background

First, the terms artificial intelligence and leadership are defined before both research areas are merged. The chapter concludes with the research questions of this study.

© The Author(s), under exclusive license to Springer Nature Switzerland AG 2022
N. L. Black et al. (Eds.): IEA 2021, LNNS 223, pp. 811–819, 2022.
https://doi.org/10.1007/978-3-030-74614-8_100

2.1 Definition of Artificial Intelligence

The term AI is not new. The research discipline of AI was founded at the Dartmouth Conference in New Hampshire in 1956 (Dartmouth College 1956). Since then, this technology has become a relevant application in academia as well as in private and work contexts (Agrawal et al. 2018; Varian 2018). There is no universal definition for AI, nor is there one for human intelligence. Thus, there are some approaches in research for a unified understanding of this technology. For example, one approach is to distinguish between strong and weak AI (Buxmann and Schmid 2018; Mainzer 2016). Weak AI refers to targeted algorithms for specific, delimited problems, such as data analysis. Strong AI, in turn, refers to all approaches that attempt to map and mimic humans or the processes in the brain (Pennachin and Goertzel 2007; Searle 1980). This definition is difficult for current research, because strong AI technologies do not yet exist and such development must be awaited (Buxmann and Schmidt 2018). In addition to approaches to defining AI, methods can contribute to a unified understanding of this technology. Machine learning encompasses all methods that use learning processes to identify relationships in existing data sets and make predictions based on them (Murphy 2012). Another method based on machine learning is deep learning. Here, artificial neural network approaches are used as a basis to capture more complex relationships and solve problems (Buxmann and Schmid 2018; Krizhevsky et al. 2012). For this interview study, the author did not limit this study to one method or understanding of AI.

2.2 Definition of Leadership

In science, many different theories, styles and models regarding leadership activities have emerged since the Great Man Theory by William James (1882) (compare Lippmann et al. 2018). For this thesis, situational leadership according to Hersey and Blanchard (1988) was chosen to create the interview. This theory assumes that the leader adapts to the capabilities of the employees by taking one of the four roles: directing, training, supporting, or delegating. This is how a task goal is to be successfully achieved. On the one hand, this theory includes leadership styles that are picked up in transactional and transformational leadership, but can be easily distinguished from each other based on the time course of the situational model. Second, situational leadership is still a favored leadership theory in management literature today (Berger 2018).

2.3 Artificial Intelligence and Leadership

According to a Gartner survey, 37% of the world's companies have implemented AI in any form, which represents a 270% increase over the last four years (Costello 2019). Especially faster-growing companies want to make greater use of AI, particularly for leadership tasks (Kiehne 2019). The time that human managers save, will be invested in motivating and inspiring their employees, identifying new market opportunities, and setting the right goals. Moreover, a Bain outlook predicts most teams will be self-managed by 2027, making many traditional manager positions obsolete (Allen et al. 2017). The authors add that instead of having a permanent superior, most employees will have some kind of career supporter or mentor, supporting a profound change in the perception of leadership and leadership roles.

Some companies are already using AI technologies for certain management tasks. Klick, a company from Canada, has automatized most of its management and administrative processes to such an extent that it does not rely on a human resources department any longer (Moulds 2018). Yet, Klick's associate Goldman affirms that the AI is not managing but supporting. In another use case, the startup B12 builds websites with the help of an AI called Orchestra (Kessler 2017). As soon as clients place an order, Orchestra coordinates the project's whole workflow by generating chat groups, identifying both available and suitable team members, and assigning the work accordingly in the right order. Further, it creates a hierarchy of team members who can provide feedback for each other. The human workers are relieved of coordination and regular management tasks; thus, they can dedicate themselves to the technical side of the business. Other organizations use AI in the recruiting process which allows them to select the ideal candidate in an objective, non-discriminatory fashion (dpa 2020).

It turns out that most integrated AI solutions are so supportive that they are well suited to perform routine tasks. Given the above predictions, we can expect the implementation of even more far-reaching AI applications in leadership. What is notable about all of these application examples is that the focus is mostly on the function of AI, with little or no mention of the impact on the workforce or the path to implementation. Instead, performance improvements and efficiency gains are mostly communicated. A first study in the field was conducted by Fügener et al. (2019). They showed that the best end results in delegation tasks are achieved when AI takes over the role of the delegator, because humans assess themselves significantly better. Therefore, this interview study aims to answer the research question, what are people's attitudes towards an AI as a leader? In addition, it will be answered whether other factors, such as affinity for technology or the current position in the company, have an influence on this attitude.

3 Method

In order to be able to answer the research question, a semi-structured interview was designed which basically consisted of three parts. The first part starts with welcoming the participant, explaining the goal of the interview and give an overview of the various AI definitions. For a better understanding of AI and its possibilities, practical examples are given, such as X-ray analysis to support cancer diagnosis, chatbots and knowledge butlers. Part one ends with questions about the following personal data: Age, gender, job title, position in the company, industry of the company and current main tasks in the company. The second part of the interview focuses on the interview partner. Thus, technology affinity is first surveyed using the TA-EG questionnaire by Karrer et al. (2009). After the affinity question, the subject is asked to list the main tasks of their leader. This listing served as mental preparation for assessing potential leadership tasks that an AI could take on. Subsequently, subjects were asked to read through five descriptions of leaders and assign their leader to one of these descriptions. The five leaders present the four leadership styles in situational leadership according to Hersey and Blanchard (1988). The fifth leadership style as well as all the descriptions of the styles for the interviewees go back to the "Grid – Tableau" of Blake and Mouton (1968). Already at that time, they related the behavior of a leader to the consideration of the person as well as his or her performance and introduced a "normal" leadership behavior as an amalgamation of the remaining four leadership styles (Baumgarten 1977). The second part of the survey is concluded with the assessment of current job satisfaction using a 5-point Likert scale (1 = very satisfied to 5 = very dissatisfied). Thus, job satisfaction can be contrasted with the prevailing leadership style and the attitude toward an AI as a leader. The third and final part of the interview deals with AI as a leader. Here, the following questions about expectations and attitudes are asked in an open response format:

- Can you imagine an AI taking over tasks of a manager in the future or replacing a full manager or can you imagine having an AI as a supervisor?
- Which of your executive's tasks could an AI fully or partially take over?
- Which of your manage's tasks should an AI definitely not take over as a manager?

For the first question, a 5-point Likert scale was first provided as a response format as a classification, and then the opportunity was given to elaborate on the answers. Since this interview study is a pilot study, no pre-existing measurement instruments could be used. To conclude the third part as well as the entire interview, questions are asked about the acceptance of AI as a leader. Introducing this topic, the open-ended question is asked: What conditions must exist so that you accept AI as a leader? Since existing acceptance questionnaires are limited to existing products or things and there is currently no AI that takes on leadership tasks in the true sense, the Bochum Inventory for Leadership Description (BIF) (Schardien 2013) was used as the basis for the acceptance subscale. The BIF describes leadership with 13 scales, which in turn can be grouped into relationship quality, organization, interaction behavior and appreciation, and willingness to change. Thus, one question was formulated per scale, each of which could be introduced with "I would like it if an AI with leadership tasks…" and answered by means of a 5-point Likert scale (see Table 1).

The semi-structured interview was conducted from July 20 to August 18, 2020. The online meeting tools Zoom and Skype had to be used due to Corona restrictions in Germany. An interview lasted 25 min on average. The sample consists of N = 32 subjects *(16 male and 16 female; mean age = 36.74, sd = 12.42)*, of which 14 had management responsibility and 18 had no employee responsibility. In selecting the sample, care was taken to ensure that many different industries were represented (e.g., wholesale, retail, education, and aviation). The open-ended responses were analyzed using a Qualitative Content Analysis according to Mayring (2010). SPSS was used for the statistical analysis.

4   Results

First, the results of the subscales, such as technology affinity and job satisfaction, are presented. Then, the attitudes of the test persons regarding AI as a manager are presented and combined with the results of the subscales. The results section ends with the responses in the acceptance section. The interpretation of all results follows in the discussion. Since all subjects completed the interview with the author in full, all results are presented and to be interpreted with N = 32 subjects.

4.1 Results of the Subscales

Technology affinity was assessed using the TA-EG questionnaire by Karrer et al. (2009). This questionnaire is composed of the scales enthusiasm *(mean = 3.39; sd = .83)*, positive attitude *(mean = 3.87; sd = .49)*, negative attitude *(mean = 2.75; sd = .73)*, and competence *(mean = 3.77; sd = .74)*. Based on the average scale means, it can be stated that the sample tends to be more tech-savvy.

When assessing the leadership style using the five descriptions according to Blake and Mouton (1968), 68% of the subjects indicated that their managers mainly live out the participative leadership style. This is followed by the normal leadership style with 13%. The familial as well as the authoritarian leadership style were each selected by 6%. One respondent indicated that the supervisor practiced a laissez-faire leadership style.

Job satisfaction was reported with a mean of 4.29 *(sd = .90)*, which represents very high job satisfaction.

4.2 Results of Attitudes Toward AI as a Leader

77% of respondents cannot imagine or can only partially imagine AI taking over leadership tasks in the future, while 22% can. When asked what supervisor tasks AI could support or completely take over, 54% said that supervisory and support activities would be possible, 25% think of administrative activities, and 16% don't recognize any possibility or deny it completely. In contrast, 32% say that AI could theoretically take over all the tasks of a manager (multiple answers possible). When asked which tasks AI should definitely not take on as a manager, 78% stated interpersonal tasks. The respondents understood this to mean interaction between supervisor and employee involving empathy, negotiation and creativity. The remaining 22% could not give any information on this or made it dependent on the technique. A t -test with an $\alpha = .05$ revealed no significant differences between the attitudes of those with and those without managerial responsibilities. The male subjects *(mean = 2.75, sd = 1.07, n = 16)* are more likely to imagine an AI as a leader than the female subjects *(mean = 1.73, sd = .80, n = 16)*, $t(29) = -2.991, p = .006$. The Cohen (1992) effect size is $r = .49$, corresponding to a medium effect. Simple linear regression revealed no significant effect regarding age on attitude *(F(1, 29) = .089, p = .767)*. A calculation of group differences and correlations in relation to the subscales job satisfaction as well as current leadership style could not be calculated due to the small group size and the non-heterogeneous distribution of the sample.

4.3 Results of Acceptance of AI as a Leader

When asked what requirements must be met for respondents to accept an AI as a leader (multiple answers possible), 35% stated that such technology must be transparent and comprehensible. For 26% of the respondents, it was also important to have a control authority or a monitoring level for an AI. 22% also wanted an empathetic and sympathetic AI. For a further 22%, it was also important for an AI to relieve the workload of managers and support employees. For the 13 items based on the questionnaire BIF (Schardien 2013), which could be answered with a 5-point Likert scale, the mean is 3.97 $(sd = .65)$, which can be classified in a high range. Thus, all given leadership tasks of AI were checked with "neutral" to "strongly agree" (see Table 1). A difference between male subjects $(mean = 3.93, sd = 8.3, n = 16)$ and female subjects $(mean = 4.00, sd = .39, n = 16)$ could not be found, $t(29) = .284, p = .778$. A simple linear regression revealed no significant influence regarding age on the acceptance items $(F(1, 29) = .078, p = .782)$. A calculation of group differences and correlations in relation to the subscales job satisfaction as well as current leadership style could not be calculated due to the small group sizes and the non-heterogeneous distribution of the sample.

Table 1. Items based on BIF and its descriptive values. The 5-point Likert scale ranges from 1 = strongly disagree to 5 = strongly agree.

I would like to have an AI with leadership tasks…	N	Mean	Sd	Min	Max
That would assist in the distribution of tasks	32	3.94	.89	1	5
That would take over coordination tasks	32	3.94	1.12	1	5
That would be responsible for time management in my department	32	3.58	.96	1	5
That would be employed in my department	32	3.35	1.20	1	5
that would support me professionally	32	3.97	1.17	1	5
That would give me feedback	32	3.84	1.04	1	5
That would share information within the company	32	3.45	1.12	1	5
That would be kind and polite to me	32	3.97	1.25	1	5
That is fair or would make decisions transparent	32	4.35	1.02	1	5
That would be reliable	32	4.71	.78	1	5
That would be secretive about personal information	32	4.42	.96	1	5
That would trust me	32	3.87	1.41	1	5
That would respect me	32	4.16	1.19	1	5

5   Discussion

A semi-structured interview was conducted with N = 32 individuals who showed a high affinity for technology and job satisfaction. The results show that most people (77%) have difficulty imagining AI applications being able to take over leadership tasks in the near future, and if so, then only partially and not completely. The other 23% can well imagine AI as a leader. Regardless of what tasks such technology may or may not be able to take over in the future, 78% of the interviewees agree that interpersonal tasks should not be taken over by any system. And in terms of digitization, the Corona pandemic in particular shows that these tasks are more important than ever. The interviewees understood interpersonal tasks to be, for example, employee or annual appraisals in which personal performance is assessed, settling disputes, resolving conflicts, and creative brainstorming. This desire is not surprising in terms of leadership research. As early as 1955, leadership research focused on the skills that leaders should bring to the table. These were initially divided into technical, conceptual as well as social skills (Katz 1955). Until today, the skills have been repeatedly expanded and adapted (Mumford et al. 2000; Stippler et al. 2014). Currently, charismatic leadership is discussed in science, which is a part of transformational leadership (Bass 2008; Stippler et al. 2014; Yukl 2013). Thus, the leader should be a role model for employees, act courageously and decisively, lead sacrificially, convey enthusiasm, and act with integrity. Transformational leadership also focuses on individualized care of employees, their motivation, and intellectual stimulation. These are all factors based on social skills or interpersonal tasks/interactions/communication and, based on the interview results, are important to both managers and employees.

In research, the topic of acceptance is mainly focused on the technology acceptance model of Davis (1985), which has been further developed in recent years by Davis and colleagues to TAM 2 and TAM 3 (Davis 1985; Venkatesh and Davis 2000; Venkatesh and Bala 2008). These three models include, among others, the factors "perceived ease of use" and "actual use," which can only be tested on an existing product or prototype. Other measurement tools, such as the Service User Technology Acceptability Questionnaire (SUTAQ) by Hirani et al. (2016), have been developed for specific application areas, such as telemedicine health applications for patients. With the approach presented in the methodology section for testing acceptance regarding AI as a leader, a first proposal for measurement has been made. Items were formulated for each of the thirteen subscales of the Bochum Inventory for Leadership Description (BIF) (Schardien, 2013) and presented to the subjects using a 5-point Likert scale. The results do not represent valid statements, but give the tendency that employees are open-minded for AI - applications that are used supportively in the company, polite and reliable.

The interview study has some limitations. It must be pointed out that the semi-structured interview consists of some self-generated and non-validated items. Especially with regard to the acceptance towards AI as a leader, the results should be interpreted with caution. In the future, a valid instrument for measuring acceptance of future products or technologies would be desirable in order to address the needs of customers and/or users before the actual development of these. In addition to that the author did not limit this study to one method or understanding of AI. This may have an impact on how the interview questions are answered.

6 Conclusion

This pilot study in the form of a semi-structured interview explores the question of what attitudes people have towards AI as a leader. It has been shown that for tech-savvy people, AI technologies are still very abstract and for many it is not conceivable that AI will be able to take over leadership tasks in the future. If it should ever come to that, the test persons would like to have a transparent application that supports them and gives them room for interpersonal interactions with a human superior. Further research should be sought to ensure a smooth implementation of AI applications to relieve the burden on supervisors, among other things.

References

Agrawal, A.K., Gans, J.S., Goldfarb, A.: Economic Policy for Artificial Intelligence. In: Lerner, J., Stern, S. (eds.) Innovation Policy and the Economy, pp.139–159. University of Chicago Press, Chicago (2018)

Allen, J., Root, J., Schwedel, A.: The Firm of the Future. Boston, United States: Bain & Company Inc. Retrieved from Bain & Company Inc. website (2017). https://www.bain.com/insights/firm-of-the-future

Baumgarten, R.: Führungsstile und Führungstechniken. Walter de Gruyter, Berlin (1977)

Bass, B.M.: The bass handbook of leadership: theory, research, & managerial applications, vol.4. Free Press, New York (2008)

Berger, P.: Wie es dazu kam–Die Entstehung von Führung als Resultat gesellschaftlicher Entwicklung. In: Praxiswissen Führung, pp. 3–41. Springer Gabler, Heidelberg (2018)

Blake, R., Mouton, J.S.: Verhaltenspsychologie im Betrieb. Das Verhaltensgitter, eine Methode zur optimalen Führung in Wirtschaft und Verwaltung. Düsseldorf, Wien (1968)

Buxmann, P., Schmidt, H., (eds.): Künstliche Intelligenz: Mit Algorithmen zum wirtschaftlichen Erfolg. Springer (2018)

Costello, K.: Gartner Survey Shows 37 Percent of Organizations Have Implemented AI in Some Form [Press Releases] (2019). Gartner website: https://www.gartner.com/en/newsroom/press-releases/2019-01-21-gartner-survey-shows-37-percent-of-organizations-have. Accessed 21 Oct 2020

Dartmouth College. Summer research project on artificial intelligence (Vox of Dartmouth) (1956)

Davis, F.D.: A Technology Acceptance Model for empirically testing new end-user information systems; theory and results, Massachusetts Institute of Technology, pp. 1–291, Massachusetts USA (1985)

dpa. Ersetzt Künstliche Intelligenz bald den Jobvermittler? [Newspaper] (2020) from Zeit Online website: https://www.zeit.de/news/2020-03/03/ersetzt-kuenstliche-intelligenz-bald-den-jobvermittler?utm_referrer=https%3A%2F%2Fwww.google.com%2F. Accessed 21 Oct 2020

Fügener, A., Grahl, J., Gupta, A., Ketter, W.: Collaboration and delegation between humans and AI: an experimental investigation of the future of work. In: ERIM Report Series Research in Management (2019)

Hersey, P., Blanchard, K.: Management of Organizational Behaviour. Prentice Hall, Englewood Cliffs (1988)

Hersey, P.H., Blanchard, K.H., Dewey, E.J.: Management of Organizational Behavior: Leading Human Resources, 10th edn. Prentice-Hall, London (2013)

Hirani, S.P., et al.: Quantifying beliefs regarding telehealth: development of the whole systems demonstrator service user technology acceptability questionnaire. J. Telemed. Telecare 23(4), 460–469 (2016)

James, W.: Great men, great thoughts, and their environment. Atlantic Monthly 46, 441–559 (1882)

Karrer, K., Glaser, C., Clemens, C., Bruder, C.: Technikaffinität erfassen–der Fragebogen TA-EG. Der Mensch im Mittelpunkt technischer Systeme 8, 196–201 (2009)

Katz, T.L.: Skills of an effective administrator. Harvard Bus. Rev. 33(1), 33–42 (1955)

Kessler, S.: Robots are replacing managers, too (2017). Quartz website: https://qz.com/1039981/robots-are-replacing-managers-too/. Accessed 21 Oct 2020

Kiehne, A.: Microsoft-Studie zu KI & Leadership: Künstliche Intelligenz verändert Führung in Unternehmen (2019). Microsoft website: https://news.microsoft.com/de-de/microsoft-studie-ki-leadership/. Accessed 19 Oct 2020

Krizhevsky, A., Sutskever, I., Hinton, G.E.: ImageNet classification with deep convolutional neural networks. In: Neural Information Processing Systems (NIPS), Proceeding. NIPS 2012 Proceedings of the 25th International Conference on Neural Information Processing Systems – Volume 1 (S. 1097–1105). Nevada, Lake Tahoe (2012)

Lippmann, E., Pfister, A., Jörg, U., (eds.): Handbuch Angewandte Psychologie für Führungskräfte: Führungskompetenz und Führungswissen. Springer (2018)

Mainzer, K.: Künstliche Intelligenz-Wann übernehmen die Maschinen? Springer, Heidelberg (2016). https://doi.org/10.1007/978-3-662-48453-1

Mayring, P.: Qualitative inhaltsanalyse. In Handbuch qualitative Forschung in der Psychologie, pp. 601–613. VS Verlag für Sozialwissenschaften (2010)

Moulds, J.: Robot managers: The future of work or a step too far? [Newspaper] (2018). from The Guardian website: https://www.theguardian.com/business-to-business/2018/apr/06/robot-managers-how-a-firm-automated. Accessed 21 Oct 2020

Mumford, M.D., Zaccaro, S.J., Connelly, M.S., Marks, M.A.: Leadershipskills: conclusions and future directions. Leadersh. Quar. **11**, 155–170 (2000)

Murphy, K. P.: Machine learning: A probabilistic perspective. Cambridge, MA: MIT Press. (2012)

Offensive Mittelstand. Verbundprojekt Prävention 4.0. Umsetzungshilfe 1.2.1 Führung und 4.0 Prozesse. Heidelberg (2018)

Pennachin, C., Goertzel, B.: Contemporary approaches to artificial general intelligence. In: Goertzel, B., Pennachin, C. (eds.) Artificial General Intelligence: AGIRI – Artificial General Intelligence Research Institute (S. 1–28). Springer, Berlin (2007)

Schardien, P.: Zufrieden mit dem Chef? Der Einfluss der Mitarbeiterpersönlichkeit auf die Zufriedenheit des Mitarbeiters auf Basis der Theorie kognitiver Dissonanz. Dissertation, Ruhr-Universität Bochum (2013)

Searle, J.R.: Minds, brains, and programs. Behav. Brain Sci. **3**, 417–457 (1980)

Stippler, M., Moore, S., Rosenthal, S., Dörffer, T.: Führung - Überblick über Ansätze, Entwicklungen, Trends. Verlag Bertelsmann Stiftung, Gütersloh (2014)

Varian, H.: Artificial Intelligence, Economics, and Industrial Organization, Cambridge (2018)

Venkatesh, V., Bala, H.: Technology acceptance model 3 and a research agenda on interventions. Decis. Sci. **39**(2), 273–315 (2008)

Venkatesh, V., Davis, F.D.: Atheoretical extension of the Technology Acceptance Model: Four longitudinal field studies. Manag. Sci. **46**(2), 186–204 (2000)

Yukl, G.: Leadership in organizations, vol. 8. Pearson, Harlow (2013)

Macroergonomics-Based Approach for a Management Trainee Program in the Utilities Industry

Yogi Tri Prasetyo[✉] and Johnamae Khow

Mapúa University, Manila, Philippines
ytprasetyo@mapua.edu.ph

Abstract. The purpose of this study was to help companies to design a better management trainee program using macroergonomics-based approach. The study used observation and focus group discussion to gather data and assess the management trainee program of a company in the utilities industry in order to propose a new job design for management trainees that might boost employee retention and satisfaction among the program graduates even after program graduation. Through qualitative data gathering, this study identified which factors play an important role in keeping management trainees engaged and motivated. With a successful management trainee program, companies might be able to attract high-caliber graduates and train them into becoming future leaders in a more effective and efficient way. The study found that in order to improve the management trainee program, the company should focus on training for individual holistic development, job rotation within the critical functions, mentorship and feedback for continuous improvement, ownership and responsibility, performance evaluation, job enrichment, and job enlargement.

Keywords: Macroergonomics · Management trainee program · Graduate trainee program · Training

1 Introduction

The new generation of job seekers, particularly, recent graduates, are found to have higher demands and expect more from employers and the job, thus, they tend to hop from one job to another when their needs are not met (as cited in Timisjärvi 2009). With this, companies have been trying to come up with ways to attract the selective talented jobseekers. Management trainee programs, also known as graduate trainee or future leaders' programs, have been a popular choice for employment among fresh graduates as a starting point for their career. This is because most management trainee programs, or graduate trainee programs provide the notion of accelerated career growth and abundant learning opportunities. These management trainee programs usually entail rotation among many job functions to train individuals in the different key areas of the business, so that in the future, when a need arises, the individual can fill the specific role

© The Author(s), under exclusive license to Springer Nature Switzerland AG 2022
N. L. Black et al. (Eds.): IEA 2021, LNNS 223, pp. 820–826, 2022.
https://doi.org/10.1007/978-3-030-74614-8_101

by being equipped with the necessary skills and knowledge, as well as a certain level of loyalty and motivation (as cited in Wapakala 2016).

As a response to the increase in demands and expectations from jobseekers, companies create and offer competitive management trainee programs in order to pique the interest of top-notch young jobseekers and increase the retention rate among the talents by keeping them engaged and excited about their role. Training programs are one of the most critical and strategic techniques to get talented employees to enter and stay in the organization (Karasar and Öztürk 2014). In turn, companies would be able to ensure continuity when it comes to human resources. Furthermore, management trainee programs are considered as a long-term technique of preparing high-potential graduates by honing their leadership skills (Gama and Edoun 2020).

Macroergonomics can be applied in this research as it is the branch of ergonomics that is a large system approach emphasizing integration and organizational design (Kleiner 2006). Designing a better management trainee program would be beneficial for both the company and the recent graduates, and a well-designed program can increase retention rate among program graduates. As discussed by Demerouti (2014), modifying and tailoring of tasks and interactions according to what is beneficial for both the company and the employees are part of designing a job, which is a dynamic way of sustaining the level of engagement and motivation of employees. Moreover, since this study aims to find a better design for a management trainee program, macroergonomics is applicable because it can be used in studying various research areas such as both physical and cognitive ergonomics, organizational psychology, sociotechnical systems, social psychology, and system engineering (Murphy et al. 2014).

The purpose of this study was to help companies to design a better management trainee program. With a successful management trainee program, companies might be able to attract high-caliber graduates and train them into becoming future leaders in a more effective and efficient way. Through qualitative data gathering, this study aims to collect information from management trainee program graduates and identify which factors play an important role in keeping them engaged and motivated to stay in the program and in the company even after graduating from the program.

2 Methodology

Mixed methods research was conducted in this study. This research utilized observation and focus group discussion in order to propose a new job design for management trainees that might boost employee retention and satisfaction among the program graduates.

Hall (2010) conducted a similar study on graduate trainees to assess job rotation as a learning tool. The said study used a survey on 14 participants and a semi-structured group interview wherein both current and former graduate trainees were involved. Since there has only been one batch of management trainees with 10 trainees in the company that was studied for this research, using a survey is not suitable. Following Hall's (2010) research, the researcher opted to conduct a focus group discussion.

As a graduate of a management trainee program, the researcher studied observations on the job design of the 12-month management trainee. In addition, a focus group discussion was conducted to gain more insights from other program attendees about the current job design of the management trainee program and understand what factors could be modified to increase retention rate and satisfaction among program graduates.

The focus group discussion consisted of seven (7) participants aged 23 to 25 years old. All participants were part of the batch 2018 Apprenticeship Program for Excellence (APEx), a management trainee program for high potential fresh graduates, launched in November 2018. Five out of the seven participants are still with the company, while two are no longer with the company. Overall, the discussion was semi-structured, containing open-ended questions, and follow-up questions were asked. The focus group discussion lasted for 1 h and 54 min.

3   Results

Figure 1 shows the framework of the management trainee program as the researcher observed when she was part of the program. The 12-month program entails two major parts: 1) classroom training and workshops, and 2) job rotation. For the first part, the classroom training sessions only included lectures about the company's history, its products and services, and its organizational structure. As for the job rotation, the management trainee was only rotated within the same department. This means that he/she just focused on the sub-functions of one department. Additionally, monthly group mentoring sessions were also held throughout the duration of the program wherein one mentor gathered all management trainees in one batch then assessed their performance. After 12 months into the program, the management trainees graduated. After graduation from the program, the trainees were assigned to a permanent position which were within the same level that they entered the organization. The selection of the permanent position was solely based on the mentor's discretion.

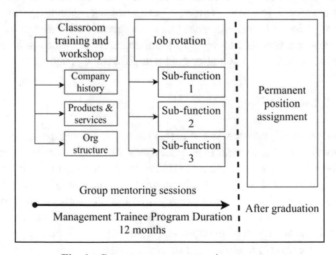

Fig. 1. Current management trainee program

During the focus group discussion, all participants expressed similar thoughts on the topic. The primary factors that made them accept the program offer were the promise of accelerated career growth, training opportunities, rotation among the different functions of the company, and mentoring and coaching during the entire program. However, 6 out of 7 participants initially wanted to quit the 12-month program before it ended because of the following reasons: 1) The job rotations were only within one department, which they found unengaging and boring; 2) the classroom sessions only focused everything about the company, while no new skills were being developed; and 3) there was not enough feedback from the mentors regarding the trainees' performance. Generally, the level of engagement was low because of the reasons stated.

Figure 2 shows the modified program which incorporated the factors that could be modified or added to the program that could increase retention rate, as shared by the participants. Knowledge and skills training should involve sessions that will hone leadership and management skills, finance acumen, decision making skills, negotiation and communication skills, and planning and execution skills. Meanwhile, the job rotation should have rotations to other departments and job functions within the company so that the trainees would have a holistic view on the company's operations, instead of just learning about one function.

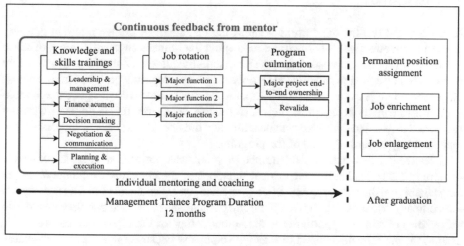

Fig. 2. Proposed management trainee program

Moreover, there should be a culminating activity by the end of the program such as a major project assigned to the trainee and a *revalida* exam that includes everything they have learned in order to gauge what function suits them best to avoid job mismatch. These culminating activities would create a sense of fulfillment among the program graduates and the permanent position assignment would be data driven.

In addition, the participants highlighted the importance of getting feedback from their mentor to enable them to strive for continual improvement. Knowing what they are good at and what to improve on motivates them to work harder. Also, the participants prefer to have individual mentoring and coaching sessions compared to having group mentoring sessions. This is because they were not able to fully express their concerns during those sessions.

All participants finished the 12-month program, but two of them left the company after graduating from the program because they were offered a permanent position within the same level that they entered the organization. The remaining five who are still with the company also expressed their desire to leave the company if they come across an opportunity with another company. All participants expressed that after graduating from the program, there should be job enrichment and enlargement if they meet the required criteria. Going back to the same job level and function after the program did not motivate them to excel in their permanent positions since job enlargement and enrichment were promised during the offer.

From this, the researchers deduce that the current program lacks opportunities for professional development and opportunities for continuous improvement. The current program would meet these needs by providing the trainees with adequate training for individual holistic development, job rotation within the critical functions, mentorship and feedback for continuous improvement, experience in leading projects, performance evaluation.

4 Discussion

As seen in the results, the current setup of the management trainee program that was studied is not effective when it comes to keeping the trainees engaged. Six out of seven participants (85.7%) expressed their desire to initially quit the 12-month program before it ended because the job rotations were only within one department, the training courses only focused on lectures about the company, and the trainees did not get enough feedback from the mentors regarding their performance. Moreover, the participants were not motivated to excel in their role also because they did not have a sense of ownership and responsibility towards the end of the program.

Meanwhile, the management trainee program was not able to meet its objective of honing future leaders for the critical functions of the company. Although all seven participants finished the program, after graduation, two participants (28.6%) already left the company. Meanwhile, all five remaining participants expressed that they would also quit if they obtain an opportunity with another company. On top of the reasons stated earlier, the participants wanted to leave the company because there was no evaluation for possible job enrichment and job enlargement after graduating from the program, which was promised during the job offer. Instead, the participants were assigned to a permanent position in the same level that they came in. To aggravate the situation, five out of seven participants (71.4%) expressed discontent with their permanent assignment because they feel like their skills do not match the position.

The gaps are seen throughout the duration of the program, as well as in what happens upon its completion. Training and development opportunities were not adequate during the program, while job enlargement and job enrichment were not available after the program. Furthermore, the researchers found that the participants' disappointment toward the program could have stemmed from the high expectations that were set during the job offer, prior to the start of the program.

In conclusion, to improve the management trainee program, the company should focus on the following:

1. Training for individual holistic development
2. Job rotation within the critical functions
3. Mentorship and feedback for continuous improvement
4. Project ownership and responsibility
5. Performance evaluation
6. Job enrichment and job enlargement upon program graduation

Similarly and Ozkeser (2019) found that training activities should be given importance because it increases loyalty and contribution. Ozkeser (2019) further states that training sessions should be for the individual development of the employee and not just for job-specific topics. Nawaz et al. (2014) also found that human resource practices like training and empowerment have a positive and supportive relationship with employee engagement. Meanwhile, Hall (2010) found that job rotation promotes the learning and motivation of employees. With regard to performance evaluation, Sanyal and Biswas (2014) found that performance appraisal has a positive effect on employee motivation. They also discussed that during performance appraisal, it is important to highlight self-development and empowerment instead of just measuring their performance levels in order to keep employees committed and engaged. Furthermore, Saleem et al. (2012) substantiates that job enlargement and job enrichment has a direct impact on employee satisfaction.

This research is limited to only one company in the utilities industry and only one 12-month management trainee program was studied. To improve this research, future researchers could gather more participants from various companies or industries and use a mixture of quantitative and qualitative research methods. By getting more participants for the study, using a survey will be suitable unlike in this study wherein there were only seven participants. Statistical analyses could also be used to obtain more compelling data- driven results and to avoid bias. Furthermore, researchers could also study a wider scope within macroergonomics, for example, by incorporating the technology and tools that the trainees use.

Acknowledgement. The authors would like to thank Mapua University DRIVE for supporting this study.

References

Demerouti, E.: Design your own job through job crafting. Eur. Psychol. **19**(4), 237–247 (2014). https://doi.org/10.1027/1016-9040/a000188
Gama, L.Z., Edoun, E.L.: The relationship between the graduate trainee programme and talent management in corporate organisations in Eswatini. SA J. Hum. Resour. Manag. **18**(1), 1–6 (2020). https://doi.org/10.4102/sajhrm.v18i0.1249
Hall, L.W.: All change: job rotations as a workplace learning tool in the flinders university library graduate trainee librarian program. In: World Library and Information Congress: 76th IFLA General Conference and Assembly. Gothenberg (2010). https://www.ifla.org/past-wlic/2010/
Idowu, A.: Effectiveness of performance appraisal system and its effect on employee motivation. Nile J. Bus. Econ. **3**(5), 15 (2017). https://doi.org/10.20321/nilejbe.v3i5.88

Karasar, S., Öztürk, Ö.F.: Management trainee program of turkish airlines: global distance education. Turk. Online J. Educ. Technol. **13**(2), 111–120 (2014)

Kleiner, B.M.: Macroergonomics: analysis and design of work systems. Appl. Ergon. **37**(1), 81–89 (2006). https://doi.org/10.1016/j.apergo.2005.07.006

Murphy, L.A., Robertson, M.M., Carayon, P.: The next generation of macroergonomics: integrating safety climate. Accid. Anal. Prev. **68**, 16–24 (2014). https://doi.org/10.1016/j.aap.2013.11.011

Nawaz, M.S., Hassan, M., Hassan, S., Shaukat, S., Asadullah, M.: Impact of employee training and empowerment on employee creativity through employee engagement: empirical evidence from the manufacturing sector of Pakistan. Middle-East J. Sci. Res. **19**(4), 593–601 (2014). https://doi.org/10.5829/idosi.mejsr.2014.19.4.13618

Ozkeser, B.: Impact of training on employee motivation in human resources management. Procedia Comput. Sci. **158**, 802–810 (2019). https://doi.org/10.1016/j.procs.2019.09.117

Saleem, S., Shaheen, W.A., Saleem, R.: The impact of job enrichment and job enlargement on employee satisfaction keeping employee performance as intervening variable: a correlational study from Pakistan. Kuwait Chapter Arab. J. Bus. Manag. Rev. **1**(9), 145–165 (2012)

Sanyal, M.K., Biswas, S.B.: Employee motivation from performance appraisal implications: test of a theory in the software industry in west bengal (India). Procedia Econ. Finan. **11**, 182–196 (2014). https://doi.org/10.1016/s2212-5671(14)00187-7

Timisjärvi, N.: Attracting Future Talent through Graduate Trainee Programs (thesis) (2009). https://pdfs.semanticscholar.org/58b4/d52eb63cef92b1453959cc1564e78e62d467.pdf. unpublished

Wapakala, A.W.: Influence of Graduate Trainee Programs on Employee Performance: A Case Study of Nokia Networks Kenya (thesis) (2016). https://pdfs.semanticscholar.org/cdda/c37be2809d4be7ca6ba6b48e1c0a10dd4fc6.pdf. unpublished

Part XII: Systems HF/E – *Addendum* (Edited by Paul M. Salmon)

Human Factors Effects on a Human-Robot Collaboration System: A Modelling Approach

Guilherme Deola Borges$^{(\boxtimes)}$, Paula Carneiro, and Pedro Arezes

University of Minho, Guimaraes, Portugal

Abstract. This work introduces a system dynamics-based model for designing feedback mechanisms related to the physical and mental workload in Human-Robot Collaboration (HRC) systems. As a dynamic and non-linear system, HRC workplaces challenges ergonomic operations in the medium and long terms, and it is crucial to understand the whole system in order to increase reliability in decision-making about ergonomic interventions. The aim of this paper is to define which variables are to be considered and how they interact to predict the behavior of the HRC system over time. The method applied in the work follows four phases: literature review to systematic search for case studies and theoretical literature embracing the objectives of this work; summary of factors in HRC systems and their relationships obtained through the review of previous studies; definition of variables for the model gathered in a way they became the variables to be modeled; design of the Causal Loop Diagram (CLD) as a qualitative model developed from the variables, which formalizes and delimits the context to be analyzed. This paper proposes the conceptual definition by considering both physical and mental overload as cause of Work-related Musculoskeletal Disorders (WMSD) and influence on productivity. The work shows both subsystems, how they are connected, and reinforce the importance of looking at ergonomic problems with a systemic approach. Modeling the whole system is key to solve ergonomic problems in industry. The qualitative model CLD provided through the literature review is useful in understanding HRC systems.

Keywords: Human-Robot collaboration · System dynamics · Ergonomics

1 Introduction

The development of Human-Robot Collaboration (HRC) workstations is already a need for the industry. Despite their rise in popularity, integrating a collaborative robot into a work process poses many challenges and variables. Production time, quality, efficiency, and minimization of safety risks are often used as criteria for assessing the performance of HRC. Recent works have also considered ergonomic consequences of task allocation and schedule in order to maximize global reward while minimizing cost, i.e. by considering both production time and physical stress when generating human-robot task plans [1]. However, prior research on HRC workstations does not offer a flexible and operational solution for quantifying the variables involved or exploring their tradeoffs and behavior

© The Author(s), under exclusive license to Springer Nature Switzerland AG 2022
N. L. Black et al. (Eds.): IEA 2021, LNNS 223, pp. 829–838, 2022.
https://doi.org/10.1007/978-3-030-74614-8_102

along a time horizon. As a dynamic and non-linear system, HRC workplaces challenges ergonomic operations in the medium and long terms resulting in difficulties to predict their future behavior [2], particularly when involving ergonomics [3]. Therefore, the aim of this paper is to define which variables are to be considered and how they interact to predict the behavior of the HRC system over time.

2 Theoretical Background

2.1 HRC Workstation

An effective collaboration between human and robot means a combination of their skills: precision, speed and fatigue free operation of the robot with cognitive of the human. There are different Levels of Collaboration (LoC) between the worker and the robot depending on the technology available and what is needed for completing the task. As presented in Fig. 1, these levels are: Level 0 (cell), Level 1 (coexistence), Level 2 (synchronized), Level 3 (cooperation), and Level 4 (collaboration).

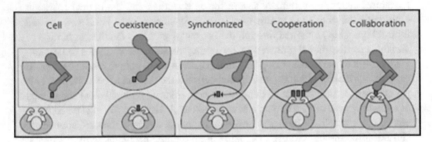

Fig. 1. Levels of collaboration in HRC systems. Source: [4].

2.2 System Thinking in HRC

A human-machine system exists in an environment within boundaries. It is characterized by its structure, and elements that interact to achieve the goals of a system [5]. For a successful implementation of a HRC system, ergonomics need to be considered [6], with the three dimensions of ergonomics - physical, cognitive and organizational [7]. By not considering ergonomics, the HRC system may present undesired effects, such as fatigue, monotony, and performance decrements [8]. Regarding the risk factors to develop WMSD, [9] states that they can be physical, biomechanical, individual, organizational, psychosocial, and they often work in combination.

3 Method

The method applied in this work follows four phases as represented in Fig. 2.

Fig. 2. Method used in the development of this work.

Phase 1 (Literature review) - a review following the Systematic Search Flow method [10] has been established as a research plan for three systematic searches embracing the objectives of this work. The databases were search on August 27, 2020 with the following queries: ("ergonomic*" OR "human factor*") AND ("dynamic*system*" OR "system*dynamic*"); ("ergonomic*" OR "human factor*") AND ("human*robot" OR HRC); ("dynamic*system*" OR "system*dynamic*") AND ("human*robot" OR HRC). The process is shown in Table 1.

Table 1. Articles in the portfolio.

Database	Number of articles
Scopus	354
Web of knowledge	199
Total	553
After excluding duplicates	420
After excluding out of scope articles	16

Phase 2 (Factors in HRC systems) - The contributing factors and their relationships were summarized in the column labeled "comments" in Table 2.

Phase 3 (Variables definition for the model) - The factors gathered were grouped in a way they became the variables to be modeled. Some factors are presented in more than one ergonomic domain, which means they influence the system in different ways.

Phase 4 (CLD design) - The construction of the qualitative model was developed from the variables found in Phase 3. The conceptual model CLD formalizes and delimits the context to be analyzed. This diagram outlines the relationships among variables of the system using a system of lines and arrows, where the arrows indicate the direction of causality.

4   Results

4.1   Ergonomic Factors in HRC

Table 2, Table 3 and Table 4 show the results of the analysis for the surveyed literature regarding ergonomics factors that influences HRC. Although different terms have been used to label factors to consider in HRC system, for the model of this work they have been grouped into a representative variable. In the comments' column, the words in italics inside parentheses are the different expressions found in the literature for a given factor.

Table 2. List of physical variables.

Physical		
Workplace environment	[11–15]	Physical characteristics of the workplace that impose itself over the worker (*light, temperature, noise, vibration*) or physical characteristics of the workplace that impose to the worker the way to behave (*layout, working postures*)
Repetitive movements	[3, 12, 15–19]	Physical overload caused by repetition (*stereotyped movements, fatigue*)
Work-related musculoskeletal disorder - WMSD	[3, 15–17, 19]	WMSD caused by physical and mental overload (*biomechanical stress, illness*)
Cycle time	[3, 19]	Time between the beginning and the end of a process (*cycle time*) or the speed a process has to occur depending on the demand (*takt time*)
Recovering time	[3, 19]	Time to rest and to reduce physical overload and is related to the shift length. Recently considered in models as a way to reduce physiological factors
Individual characteristics	[11, 14, 15, 17, 19]	Physical characteristics of an individual (*anthropometric measurements, height, weight, sex, age*) or measures over the effort when working (*magnitude of the load, contact forces, body segments position*)
Level of collaboration (LoC)	[11, 15, 17, 20]	Effects of the robot collaboration on physical workload (*level of collaboration, predictability, and interface*).
*Health and safety climate, circadian rhythm	[14–16]	Very peculiar characteristic of the worker that can vary a lot and are difficult to measure, but were considered to influence a socio-technical system

Although different terms were used, they were grouped into a single term represented by the first column. The criteria for inclusion in the CLD was decided by the authors as the model has to be as simple as possible, and some variables brings too much uncertainty to be simulated afterwards.

Table 3. List of cognitive variables.

Cognitive		
Workplace environment	[11, 14, 15, 17, 20, 21]	Mental characteristics of the workplace that impose itself over the worker (*layout, field of view*) or environmental factors (*noise, illumination, temperature*)
Performance pressure	[11, 12, 15, 16, 21, 22]	Cognitive factors related to performance pressure (*strain, stress, fatigue*)
Task complexity	[14, 17]	Cognition or mental complexity of the task that result in mental workload.
Training	[11, 14–16]	Importance of training in the resulting mental workload (*knowledge, skill, competence, awareness, safety climate, experience, expertise*)
Individual characteristics	[14, 15, 22]	Mental characteristics of an individual (*self-confidence, personality, attentional capacity, and attitude*) in the presence of a robot (*comfort towards robots*)
Trust in the robot	[6, 23]	Mental impact of the robot on the individual (*reliability, safe co-operation, motion speed, predictability, exterior design, appearance*)
*Self-recompensing	[11, 14, 16]	Mental comfort for fulfilling the work (*motivation, satisfaction, feeling of competence*)
*Self-punishment	[11, 15]	Mental discomfort for not fulfilling the work (*human error*)
*Absenteeism	[21]	Mental workload for doing work of an absent worker

Table 4. List of cognitive variables.

Organizational		
Workplace environment	[11, 14, 15, 17, 20, 21]	Organizational characteristics of the workplace (*layout, risk level, field of view*) and environment factors (*noise, illumination, temperature*) that impose itself over the system
*Participatory implementation	[6, 15, 21, 24]	Ergonomic interventions are more efficient when workers take part in decisions and ideas (*participatory in designing and implementing changes in the workplace*)
*Top management support	[6, 15, 16, 24]	Efficacy of a manager (*communication, supervisor's effectiveness*)
*Design of working times	[3, 14–16, 19, 21]	To plan the overall production (*shift length, working hours, cycle time, takt time, recovering*)
*Empowerment of the workforce	[6, 12, 16, 25]	To keep worker in a position to make decisions, especially in the presence of a robot (*worker's control over work*)
*Team work	[15, 16, 21]	Friendly team (*team work, co-worker's support*)
*Procedures	[11, 15]	Organizational importance of procedures (*safe methods, procedures*)
Task complexity	[12, 15]	Organizational impact of the task complexity (*task complexity, difficulty, multi-tasking requirement*)
Recovering time	[12, 14]	Organizational caution over worker's recovering (*recovery, break*)
Absenteeism	[3, 19]	Organizational problems caused by absence (*absenteeism*)
Training	[3, 6]	Organizational gains by knowledge of the workforce (*training workforce, task knowledge*)

* Factors that are not considered in the model due to irrelevance in the present study.

4.2 Design of the Causal Loop Diagram

To facilitate the understanding of the CLD, it was divided in two subsystems: physical workload and mental workload. These cycles are respectively identified by the green and red boundaries in Fig. 3, which are individually discussed in Sect. 5.

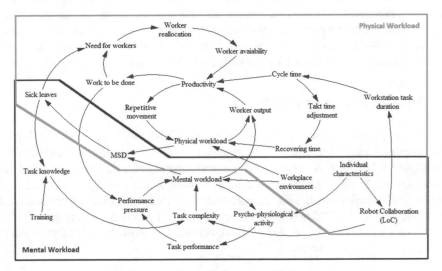

Fig. 3. Causal loop diagram in a HRC system.

5 Discussion

In order to discuss the dynamic of this HRC system, it is divided in Subsystem Physical Workload and Subsystem Mental Workload. When teaming a human with a robot, workers' physical variables to be taken into account and used to inform the robot are anthropometric measures, postures, and ranges [12, 14, 15, 26], while cognitive variables are attention capacity, reliability, personality traits, and attitude towards robots [14, 15, 22]. Therefore, this work reinforce the importance of looking at ergonomic problems with a systemic approach. Both physical and mental workloads are to be considered in a HRC system.

5.1 Subsystem Physical Workload

Physical overload results in fatigue and WMSD, leading to sick leaves and impacting production [3, 12, 15–19]. In this subsystem the physical workload is indirectly affected by the productivity through repetitive movements, as well as by the cycle time taken into account the recovering time. This is less obvious, but still very intuitive, and also confirmed by literature. WMSD evolve to sick leaves and ultimately affects productivity, which affects physical overload. LoC influences the cycle time, which very much impact productivity and, finally, affects physical overload.

5.2 Subsystem Mental Workload

Mental workload is a response that depends on physiologically active mechanisms, where the worker output can be expressed in physiological feedbacks [27, 28]. In this subsystem mental workload is directly influenced by workplace environment and task complexity. It is also indirectly affected by productivity as it increases performance pressure. When mental workload exceeds workers' mental limits it is called mental overload, which is in a cycle that increases performance pressure, as it burns psycho-physiological activity. WMSD is a direct consequence of mental overload. As already discussed, sick leaves affects productivity, but also task knowledge, which increases task complexity.

6 Conclusion and Future Work

This paper proposes a model to enable the design of HRC workstation considering it as a complex system and providing insights using a qualitative model. Modeling the whole system where ergonomics are involved is key to solve ergonomic problems in industry. The represented HRC system includes the three main aspects of ergonomics: physical, mental, and organizational. This qualitative model is useful for computer simulations regarding workstations with HRC. As future work, it is planned to develop the following phases of the system dynamic analysis, namely, the structural description and the quantification and prospection.

Acknowledgement. This work has been supported by FCT – Fundação para a Ciência e Tecnologia within the R&D Units Project Scope: UIDB/00319/2020.

References

1. Pearce, M., Mutlu, B., Shah, J., Radwin, R.: Optimizing makespan and ergonomics in integrating collaborative robots into manufacturing processes. IEEE Trans. Autom. Sci. Eng. **15**, 1772–1784 (2018)
2. Saurin, T.A., Gonzalez, S.S.: Assessing the compatibility of the management of standardized procedures with the complexity of a sociotechnical system: case study of a control room in an oil refinery. Appl. Ergon. **44**, 811–823 (2013)
3. Mattos, D.L.D., Ariente Neto, R., Merino, E.A.D., Forcellini, F.A.: Simulating the influence of physical overload on assembly line performance: a case study in an automotive electrical component plant. Appl. Ergon. **79**, 107–121 (2019)
4. Bauer, W., Bender, M., Braun, M., Rally, P., Sholtz, O.: Lightweight robots in manual assembly – best to start simply! Fraunhofer Institute for Industrial Engineering IAO (2016)
5. Salvendy, G.: Handbook of Human Factors. John Wiley & Sons Location, New Jersey (2012)
6. Charalambous, G., Fletcher, S., Webb, P.: Identifying the key organisational human factors for introducing human-robot collaboration in industry: an exploratory study. Int. J. Adv. Manuf. Technol. **81**, 2143–2155 (2015)
7. Ender, J., Wagner, J.C., Kunert, G., Larek, R., Pawletta, T., Guo, F.B.: Design of an assisting workplace cell for human-robot collaboration. In: International Interdisciplinary PhD Workshop, pp. 51–56. Institute of Electrical and Electronics Engineers Inc., Wismar, Germany (2019)

8. Green, S.A., Billinghurst, M., Chen, X., Chase, J.G.: Human-robot collaboration: a literature review and augmented reality approach in design. Int. J. Adv. Robot. Syst. **5**, 1–18 (2008)
9. EU-OSHA: Musculoskeletal disorders (2020). https://osha.europa.eu/en/themes/musculosk eletal-disorders
10. Ferenhof, H.A., Fernandes, R.F.: Demystifying the literature review as basis for scientific writing: SSF method. Rev. ABC. **21**, 550–563 (2016)
11. di Nardo, M., Gallo, M., Madonna, M., Santillo, L.C.: A conceptual model of human behaviour in socio-technical systems (2015)
12. Abaeian, H., Inyang, N., Moselhi, O., Al-Hussein, M., El-Rich, M.: Ergonomic assessment of residential construction tasks using system dynamics. In: 33rd International Symposium on Automation and Robotics in Construction, ISARC 2016, pp. 258–266. International Association for Automation and Robotics in Construction I.A.A.R.C) (2016)
13. Pini, F., Ansaloni, M., Leali, F.: Evaluation of operator relief for an effective design of HRC workcells. In: 21st IEEE International Conference on Emerging Technologies and Factory Automation. Institute of Electrical and Electronics Engineers Inc. (2016)
14. Fruggiero, F., Fera, M., Iannone, R., Lambiase, A.: Revealing a frame to incorporate safe human behaviour in assembly processes. IFAC-PapersOnLine **51**, 661–668 (2018)
15. Rücker, D., Hornfeck, R., Paetzold, K.: Investigating ergonomics in the context of human-robot collaboration as a sociotechnical system (2019)
16. Abaeian, H., Al-Hussein, M., Moselhi, O.: Evidence-based evaluation of psychosocial risk factors and the interaction of their stressors using system dynamics. In: Francesco, L., Michael, A., Miquel Angel, P., Agostino, G.B., Emilio, J. (eds.) 29th European Modeling and Simulation Symposium, EMSS 2017, pp. 166–175. CAL-TEK S.r.l (2017)
17. Pini, F., Ansaloni, M., Leali, F.: Evaluation of operator relief for an effective design of HRC workcells. In: 2016 IEEE 21ST International Conference on Emerging Technologies and Factory Automation (ETFA). IEEE (2016)
18. Lorenzini, M., Kim, W., Momi, E.D., Ajoudani, A.: A new overloading fatigue model for ergonomic risk assessment with application to human-robot collaboration. In: 2019 International Conference on Robotics and Automation, pp. 1962–1968. Institute of Electrical and Electronics Engineers Inc. (2019)
19. Farid, M., Neumann, W.P.: Modelling the effects of employee injury risks on injury, productivity and production quality using system dynamics. International Journal of Production Research, pp. 1–15 (2019)
20. Ranz, F., Komenda, T., Reisinger, G., Hold, P., Hummel, V., Sihn, W.: A morphology of human robot collaboration systems for industrial assembly. In: 51st CIRP Conference on Manufacturing Systems, CIRP CMS 2018, pp. 99–104. Elsevier B.V., Vienna, Austria (2018)
21. Neubauer, M., Krenn, F., Majoe, D.: Towards an architecture for human-aware modeling and execution of production processes. In: 15th IFAC Symposium on Information Control Problems in Manufacturing (INCOM 2015), vol. 28, pp. 294–299 (2015)
22. Jafari, M.-J., Zaeri, F., Jafari, A.H., Najafabadi, A.T.P., Hassanzadeh-Rangi, N.: Human-based dynamics of mental workload in complicated systems. EXCLI J. **18**, 501–512 (2019)
23. Koppenborg, M., Nickel, P., Naber, B., Lungfiel, A., Huelke, M.: Effects of movement speed and predictability in human–robot collaboration. Hum. Factors Ergon. Manuf. **27**, 197–209 (2017)
24. Chavalitsakulchai, P., Ohkubo, T., Shahnavaz, H.: A model of ergonomics intervention in industry: case study in Japan. J. Hum. Ergol. (Tokyo) **23**, 7–26 (1994)
25. Challenger, R., Leach, D.J., Stride, C.B., Clegg, C.W.: A new model of job design: Initial evidence and implications for future research. Hum. Factors Ergon. Manuf. **22**, 197–212 (2012)

26. Pini, F., Ansaloni, M., Leali, F.: Evaluation of operator relief for an effective design of HRC workcells. In: IEEE 21st International Conference on Emerging Technologies and Factory Automation, pp. 1–6. IEEE (2016)
27. Ryu, K., Myung, R.: Evaluation of mental workload with a combined measure based on physiological indices during a dual task of tracking and mental arithmetic. Int. J. Ind. Ergon. **35**, 991–1009 (2005)
28. Mehler, B., Reimer, B., Coughlin, J.F., Dusek, J.A.: Impact of incremental increases in cognitive workload on physiological arousal and performance in young adult drivers. Transp. Res. Rec. **2138**, 6–12 (2009)

Part XIII: Slips, Trips and Falls – *Addendum* (Edited by Richard Bowman)

The Future of Footwear Friction

Kurt E. Beschorner[1]([✉]) [iD], Yue (Sophia) Li[2] [iD], Takeshi Yamaguchi[3], William Ells[4], and Richard Bowman[5]

[1] University of Pittsburgh, Pittsburgh, PA 15260, USA
beschorn@pitt.edu
[2] KITE, Toronto Rehabilitation Institute, University Health Network, Toronto, Canada
[3] Graduate School of Engineering and Graduate School of Biomedical Engineering, Tohoku University, Sendai Miyagi 980-8577, Japan
[4] Vibram Corporation, North Brookfield, MA 01535, USA
[5] Intertile Research Pty Ltd., Brighton East, Victoria 3187, Australia

Abstract. New technologies that enhance our understanding of shoe-floor mechanics have opened opportunities to address slip and fall accidents. Footwear has been identified as one critical factor capable of reducing an individual's risk. Thus, this moment is ripe for reducing the burden of slips, trips, and fall events. New technology can be broadly categorized into: 1) new modeling methods for predicting footwear friction performance; 2) new experimental methods for characterizing friction mechanics; and 3) new human-centred methods for characterizing interactions between the footwear and the user. These emerging technologies have the potential to elevate friction and traction performance of footwear and enhance the information available to ergonomics professionals to match appropriate footwear to applications. However, the deployment of these technologies is only beginning to guide footwear design and consumer behaviors. Thus, the footwear manufacturers' perspective in implementing new technology will also be presented. In this workshop, we will A) present information regarding emerging technologies in addition to their benefits and limitations; and B) survey the audience, disaggregated by industry sector, to obtain new data on the potential for these technologies to be accepted and implemented by professionals.

Keywords: Slip, trip and fall · Slip-resistant · Traction · Footwear · New technology

1 Introduction

Footwear is known to be a powerful tool to improve safety during ambulation. Slip-resistant footwear is associated with a reduction of 50–67% of slips in slippery workplace environments [1, 2]. The founding of the Vibram company was inspired by a mountaineering accident which lead to the loss of lives in 1935 [3]. Furthermore, footwear friction has an influence on performance (an effect sometimes referred to as "traction"), especially when performing activities that involve rapid acceleration, direction changes, or highly sloped surfaces [4–6]. Slip and fall accidents persist as one of the leading causes of public health and occupational hazards [7–11]. While the causal factors of falls vary across population, occupation, and initiating event; footwear is a critical tool in limiting injuries especially for falls caused by slips.

The friction performance of footwear is closely linked to the shoe's outsole design and the materials used. The friction performance of footwear is commonly measured by robotic devices or human-centred approaches [12, 13]. Robotic devices commonly measure the ground reaction forces during forced sliding. The ratio of friction to normal forces is the available coefficient of friction (COF). Measuring the slip outcome of individuals while ambulating on an inclined surface is a common human-centred approach to measuring friction performance [14, 15]. In these tests, the maximum angle that the individual can ambulate without a slip becomes the performance metric. COF has been shown to be a valid metric for predicting slip outcome [6, 12, 16].

Many shoe outsole parameters have been found to influence friction performance, in broad categories of: geometry of the drainage channels, geometry of the contact region, shoe surface topography, and material properties. The presence of tread channels, their dimensions, and the distribution of channels across the surface (i.e., the space separating them) influence the shoe's friction performance, especially in the presence of high viscosity fluids [17–21]. Several geometric tread features have been shown to influence friction performance, including the overall contact area, the shape of the heel, the height of the tread, and tread dimensions [17, 22–26]. Some studies have indicated that sole roughness influences friction performance in the presence of liquids, while others have not found such a trend [22, 23, 27]. In the presence of ice, sole roughness has been associated with improved friction [28–30]. Lastly, the material has an important role in friction. Material properties can influence the deformability of the surface, which can change the contact region and subsequently alter friction performance [22, 31]. Shoe materials also vary by their chemical composition, which influences their interaction with fluids (e.g., hydrophobicity) and with walking surfaces (e.g., adhesion formed between dry surfaces) [32–35]. Some materials with embedded abrasive particles or fibers have been shown to be effective at generating plowing friction on ice surfaces [36–38]. Therefore, many design features can influence friction across different use conditions.

Barriers exist for implementing modern technologies for improving the friction performance of footwear. One challenge is the complex nature of shoe-floor friction. Specifically, multiple mechanisms are relevant to friction performance, which can lead to nonlinear responses to design changes. For example, increasing the height of tread channels can be beneficial or detrimental depending on the operating conditions [18, 24, 39]. Thus, the effects of design changes are context dependent. This challenge is especially relevant because footwear is often expected to operate in multiple operating conditions (dry, wet, muddy, snowy). Design choices that optimize its performance in one set of conditions may not translate well to other use conditions. Lastly, footwear is an extension of the human user. Thus, human factors of footwear must be considered. This might include the interdependency of human biomechanics and footwear friction. To understand this interdependency, testing methods have been developed to assess footwear paired with the human in simulated laboratory conditions or outside the lab "in the wild". Emerging methods may address these barriers by: 1) providing tools that identify the causal factors of low footwear friction; and 2) assess footwear across a range of operating conditions using human participants.

The purpose of this chapter is to outline these emergent technologies, which will be presented in a special workshop session, The Future of Footwear Friction, at the 2021 International Ergonomics Association Triennial Congress. This work will be presented in 5 sections: 1) finite element analysis as a design tool for shoe tread; 2) use of fluid pressure sensors for assessing tread drainage; 3) use of human-centred testing with in-shoe force measurement for assessing friction requirements across the outsole; 4) using human-centred methods to assess footwear across a range of walking surfaces; and 5) using human-centred methods to determine footwear friction performance on different wintery surfaces with different user groups.

2   Modeling Mechanics of Footwear Friction: Finite Element Analysis of Shoe-Floor Friction

2.1   Motivation and Theoretical Foundation

Shoe-floor friction in the presence of a fluid contaminant is highly dependent on a type of friction known as hysteresis [40, 41]. Hysteresis friction is caused by energy loss in the outsole material as it slides against a rough floor surface [42, 43]. In particular, the periodicity of rough surfaces causes the sliding shoe material to experience load cycling and energy is lost in each of these cycles. The mechanical basis for this phenomenon makes it well positioned to be simulated by finite element analysis. Another strategy to improve friction is removing or displacing boundary lubricants (molecules of fluid that coat the floor surface). High contact pressures can remove these lubricants and enable better contact between the tread and the walking surface. These tread features are commonly referred to as "wipers" in shoe design and their effectiveness is dependent on the generated pressures.

The footwear design process makes it well positioned to benefit from FEA modeling. First, 3D models, a key input for FEA modeling, of footwear are typically developed early in the design process. Second, footwear prototyping can be expensive and time-consuming. Given the narrow margins and tight timelines, finite element analysis provides the opportunity for identifying and correcting design flaws early in the process. Lastly, finite element analysis can further be utilized to optimize friction performance for shoes where friction performance is a critical priority.

2.2   Technology

Finite element analysis simulates the shoe's mechanical response to the loads from stepping [25, 44]. The response can include material deformation, stresses within the material, contact pressures, and friction due to hysteresis. The loading conditions can be defined to simulate the under-shoe conditions during walking or slipping. Multiscale models have been developed where: a) the microscopic model simulates the shoe material interacting with rough flooring to predict COF as a function of contact pressure [45]; and b) the macroscopic, whole-shoe, model combines information from the microscopic model and contact pressures determined from the whole-shoe model to map coefficient of friction across the shoe surface (Fig. 1) [44].

Fig. 1. Example of the multiscale model where microscopic model simulates the sliding of rough surfaces and a whole-shoe (macroscopic models) maps the results of the microscopic model to the shoe.

2.3   Prior Applications and Potential for Future Footwear

These models have been validated against experimental shoe-floor COF to determine the impact of tread design features on COF [44]. Multiscale models have determined that reduced contact pressure can enhance friction performance. Tread features that reduced these contact pressures include removing texturing and beveling the heel [44, 46]. Furthermore, models can generate heat maps of friction, which can be used to identify tread regions in need of a redesign (e.g., lowering tread heights). Interestingly, models on the wiper region interpret that *higher* pressures are beneficial for friction. Smaller tread blocks were found to produce higher wiper pressures [25].

For shoes that perform multiple prototyping iterations, FEA may offer opportunities to reduce design costs and enhance the quality of information that is received. FEA simulations can be completed in 0.5–3 weeks, provide an estimate for the overall shoe performance, and provide heat maps of the regions of the shoe contributing to friction, and give information about the efficacy of wiper designs. Thus, these simulations provide richer information beyond just an overall COF value. Lastly, these models enable the independent variation of tread geometry and material properties, which could enable footwear to be optimized across multiple design parameters.

3   Experimental Mechanics of Footwear Friction: Under-Shoe Fluid Pressures During Shoe Sliding

3.1   Motivation and Theoretical Foundation

To achieve adequate shoe-floor-liquid friction performance, it has long been presumed that shoe tread needs to enable drainage [47, 48]. Failure to adequately drain the fluid enhances its lubricity and reduces friction performance [49, 50]. A combination of the squeeze-film effect (i.e., the fluids resistance to being drained) and the wedge effect (i.e., dynamic effects of the fluid flowing through the narrow heel region during shoe sliding) can contribute to these lubricating effects. Indicators that lubricating effects are present include increased fluid pressures (indicating that the fluid is supporting the shoe instead of shoe-floor contact), which is accompanied by increased film thickness separating the surfaces (i.e., indicating that the shoe and floor surfaces have separated) [51]. Thus, measurement of fluid pressures can reveal whether a failure to drain fluid is causing reduced friction performance in the shoe.

3.2 Technology

Fluid pressure sensors embedded in the floor surface (Fig. 2) have been developed to detect the presence of fluid pressures during friction measurement tests [18, 19, 52, 53] and human slipping [54, 55]. Prior to its use with footwear, these methods had been used to measure fluid pressures in other engineering contexts, such as chemical mechanical polishing [56]. Using multiple sensors, multiple trials, or multiple data points within a trial, fluid pressures can be mapped across the whole shoe surface [53]. This mapping method provides detailed information regarding the outsole locations associated with the greatest fluid pressure. This mapping also enables fluid pressures to be integrated over the area to calculate the net fluid force, which provides an overall assessment of the shoe's drainage capacity.

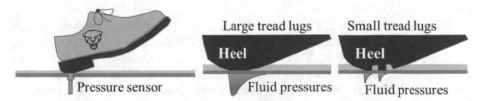

Fig. 2. Shoe sliding across wet floor instrumented with a fluid pressure sensor (left). Fluid pressures are higher (red shading) for large tread lugs (center) and worn shoes than for shoes with smaller tread lugs (light blue shading, right).

3.3 Prior Applications and Potential for Future Footwear

Fluid pressure technology has been used to assess the impact of tread design and wear on the shoe's drainage capacity. Fluid pressures were determined to be most relevant in the presence of high viscosity fluids (biofluids, oils, etc.) and across a range of flooring [53, 57]. Previous research has indicated that non-slip-resistant shoes have greater fluid pressures than their slip-resistant counterparts, which is explained by larger tread features [55]. Other research confirms that fluid pressures can be high for new shoes when these shoes have large tread features [58] (Fig. 1). This technology has demonstrated that the drainage capacity of shoes is substantially inhibited as they become worn and that this increase in fluid pressures is associated with reduced friction and increased slip risk [19, 54, 55].

This new technology has the opportunity to improve future footwear through three pathways: 1) findings from research involving this technology can be used to develop design guidelines; 2) this technology offers the opportunity to diagnose the cause of low friction in poorly performing footwear; and 3) future developments using this technology could guide durable footwear that has friction performance that is more robust to wear. Existing research suggests that smaller tread features, especially those with dimensions below 15 mm, are likely to reduce the presence of fluid pressures [58, 59]. This information could be used by designers to limit the size of tread elements. In cases where shoes are not meeting the desired level of wet friction, this technology can be used to determine if drainage is the reason for that poor performance and to identify the tread location in need of a redesign.

4 Localized 3 Degree of Freedom (DOF) Force Measurement for Tread-Level Force Distribution and Its Application

Ground reaction forces (GRFs) during walking are typically measured using a force plate. However, GRFs are caused due to the local 3 degree of freedom (3DOF) forces that are acting in the entire contact area between the shoe sole and force plate. Thus, obtaining distributions of local 3DOF forces in the entire contact area between the shoe and floor with a force plate is difficult. Recently, the sensor shoes with miniature triaxial force sensors have been developed to measure the local 3DOF force distribution for each individual tread [60–63].

Moriyasu et al. [60, 61] developed a shoe that was mounted with miniature triaxial force sensors on the shoe outsole. They measured 3DOF forces and traction coefficient, i.e., the ratio of the horizontal force to the vertical force, at 19 local positions in the shoe sole area while running. This tread-level force distribution provided information about the location in the contact area where and in which direction large friction is needed to prevent local slips during running. Moreover, this was used to develop a high-grip shoe sole tread pattern for running shoes. Yamaguchi [63] measured 3DOF forces at 52 local positions in the region of the shoe sole during straight walking and investigated the local traction coefficient at each location (Fig. 3). Yamaguchi also found that the locally required coefficient of friction (RCOF) values at the lateral rearfoot and toe area (> 0.6) were much higher compared with the RCOF values calculated from the resultant GRFs (0.18).

The sensor shoe technology mentioned above is prospective in the investigation of (1) the local 3DOF force distribution during various gait task (e.g., turning and pivoting, and so on); (2) individual difference in 3DOF force distribution during walking; (3) 3DOF force distribution in the real-life environment (occupational place, home, and so on); and (4) tread-level 3DOF force distribution on multisurfaces. Furthermore, the sensor shoe will also be promising in the on-site friction measurement of shoes under actual contact conditions during walking (e.g. outdoor ice surfaces).

5 A Balanced Approach to Laboratory Machine and Human Subject Testing of Footwear When Considering the Needs of Slip Resistance and Traction

The needs and balance of both design and function are often the major drivers for footwear designers, developers and product engineers. The needs and desires of the

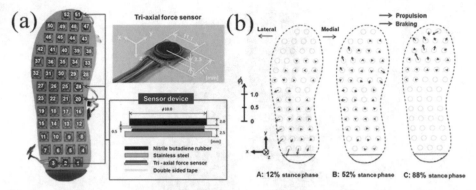

Fig. 3. (a) Sensored shoe with miniature triaxial force sensors and (b) the magnitude of the local traction coefficient and direction of the horizontal force at each stance phase [63]. The length of the arrow in (b) indicates the magnitude of the local traction coefficient at each position. *Red* and *blue arrows* correspond to braking and propulsion, respectively.

intended final consumer have a dramatic influence on the final product, as well as the materials used and construction of the footwear. As it relates to outsole design and materials, for example, a casual shoe intended for everyday wear around town. Then consider the needs of those who work in the foodservice/restaurant industry or warehouse distribution centers. Now imagine the needs of a construction worker or those in law enforcement as well as those who serve in the military. The needs of the public in general, as well as those whose work environment often require different levels of "slip resistance" and or the need for "traction". Those needs require creating different approaches to measuring both the "slip resistance" and "traction" of footwear.

This presentation will inform and educate the audience on the need for a practical and multi-disciplined approach to testing footwear. We will compare and contrast the materials which influence the user's experience, the differences in testing methodologies (machine Vs human factor), the effect of the floor surface on the needs of the footwear and the results of the testing. For example, see Fig. 4.

Using a skilled "Tester Team", the tester evaluates the **traction** of the footwear over a series of paths, which include sand, gravel, wood, lava rock, stone, stainless steel and other surfaces—both wet and dry, as shown in Fig. 5. To gauge and compare the **slip resistance** of the footwear, testing is performed using articulating ramps, static load cells, both using the same tester used for traction testing, along with machine testing. The data from three slip test methods are then combined with the traction test results to obtain a complete evaluation of the footwear as it relates to its intended user category.

6 Human-Centred Assessment Approaches

Slip-resistant footwear can be effective for preventing falls due to slips. However, the current standard mechanical tests for measuring slip resistance of footwear in slippery condition, especially in winter conditions is inadequate and have poor biofidelity [38].

Fig. 4. The sole on the right was designed firstly for "traction" and then "slip resistance" (for Military and industrial use). The sole on the left was specifically designed for "slip resistance" (for work service).

Footwear kinematics in friction testing standards exhibit differences with footwear kinematics during actual slips [64]. The lack of an accurate measurement method makes it difficult for footwear designers and manufacturers to optimize the slip resistance properties of winter footwear and appropriately inform consumers of footwear performance.

Slipping occurs when the friction between the foot or footwear sole and the walking surface provides insufficient resistance to counteract the forward or rearward forces that occur during the stepping process, i.e. interaction between human (foot or footwear sole) and walking surfaces. Factors such as walking surfaces and contaminations (Fig. 6), lighting, ambient temperatures, individual characteristics, footwear styles and sole materials (Fig. 7), and tread pattern are all important factors that will affect the footwear-floor coefficient of friction [65]. In the slip resistance testing service industry, there is a need to provide accurate footwear testing on a range of walking surfaces (including snow and ice). There is a need to select the best footwear for the human behaviour and walking surfaces that exist at the particular sites of investigation. There is also a need to provide accurate flooring material testing with a range of footwear and users to help select the best flooring materials that provide the safest walking surfaces.

The solution to the problem could be developing a method that could test the slip resistance of footwear on different surfaces with different user groups. The testing could involve having young, old, even people with mobility impairments wearing the test footwear, walking on the surfaces that paved with the specific material and contaminant that needs to be tested. Examples of surfaces include vinyl, marble, tiles, concrete, snow, and ice depends on the function of the footwear. The test could be firstly done in the lab with simulated walking surfaces (Fig. 8) and then validate the results in the real world. Using the human-centred three-dimensional footwear slip resistance assessment approaches to investigate the slip resistance properties of footwear and walking surfaces could provide a valuable knowledge base to reduce slip and fall accidents.

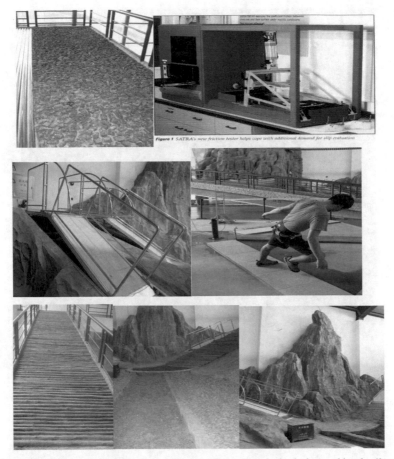

Fig. 5. Various surfaces are used in the evaluation of traction. Articulating and load cell apparatus along with bench top equipment used for slip testing.

7 Toward the Future of Footwear Friction

This chapter covers several emerging technologies in footwear assessment that has the potential to guide a future in footwear. Realizing this potential will enhance human performance and promote human safety. Emerging technologies provide a basis for enhancing friction performance of contacting regions (Sect. 2) and enhancing tread design to ensure adequate drainage (Sect. 3). New methods for measuring shoe tread forces enable footwear manufacturers to prioritize regions of the shoe relevant to specific gait activities like walking and running (Sect. 4). The generalizability of shoe design performance across multiple operating conditions can be determined (Sect. 5). Tread design and materials that are specifically targeted to icy conditions have been enabled through other advances in human-centred methods (Sect. 6). Collectively, these emerging methods offer the potential to improve the safety and versatility of footwear across several contexts.

Fig. 6. Examples of different walking surfaces and contaminations.

The availability of this new science and technology does not make improved footwear tread designs inevitable. Several barriers exist that may impede footwear from achieving its potential. The authors debated these barriers with the intent that identifying the barriers may guide efforts to overcome them. One barrier is that friction performance is one only of several critical features of footwear. Other priorities include comfort, cost, aesthetics, and other desired functionality (water-proof, etc.). Footwear brands that value these other priorities more than friction performance may not have the bandwidth to learn and implement best practices to improve friction performance. Another barrier is a lack of friction knowledge among shoe designers. Footwear tread designers do not typically have an engineering background and may have a limited understanding of friction mechanics. Thus, their ability to utilize engineering tools to enhance footwear friction is limited in many cases. Another challenge surrounds the economics and logistics of footwear production. Footwear is developed on a tight timeline and with narrow profit margins. Thus, opportunities and resources available for testing and redesign are limited. Lastly, the generalizability of test results across members of the population, especially clinical

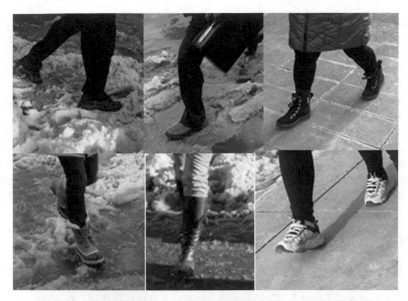

Fig. 7. Examples of different footwear that people wear in winters.

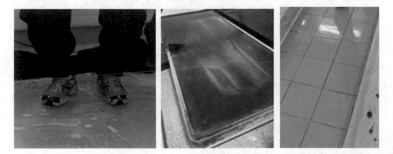

Fig. 8. Examples of different walking surfaces that can be simulated in the laboratories.

populations, is not fully understood. Thus, the benefits of footwear that performs well in these tests to various aspects of the population are unknown.

Despite the many barriers that may impede progress for future footwear, there are strategies that are capable of overcoming these barriers. For example, the development of outsole design guidelines based on research utilizing these technologies may improve footwear design without requiring shoe companies to use the technologies. This approach may need to be coupled with improved education for designers so that best design practices could be implemented from the initial conception instead of during a redesign iteration. Government intervention may lead to improved prioritization of footwear friction. Forms of government intervention could include supportive measures (incentivizing shoe designs with good friction or subsidize resources for improving tread design) and coercive methods (a regulation that mandates certain friction performance or increased liability). Furthermore, research that expands our flexibility for applying testing and good design to clinical applications is still needed despite calls for this research existing for at least two decades [66]. Better coordination between medical researchers (who are commonly focused on clinical populations), experts in friction performance (who have traditionally focused on fall risk in non-clinical populations), and their funders may be needed to overcome this barrier.

In conclusion, the potential to create a generation of footwear that dramatically reduces slip and fall risk is within reach. A new wave of technology has emerged in the past ten years, expanding our capacity to improve the connections between footwear design, friction performance, and human safety. However, the degree to which this potential is realized depends on our ability to anticipate and respond to implementation barriers. The benefits of success are profound and worthy of the efforts needed to overcome these barriers.

References

1. Bell, J.L., Collins, J.W., Chiou, S.: Effectiveness of a no-cost-to-workers, slip-resistant footwear program for reducing slipping-related injuries in food service workers: a cluster randomized trial. Scand. J. Work Environ. Health **45**(2), 194–202 (2019)
2. Verma, S.K., et al.: A prospective study of floor surface, shoes, floor cleaning and slipping in US limited-service restaurant workers. Occup. Environ. Med. **68**(4), 279–285 (2011)
3. Wikipedia. Vibram (2020). [cited 2/5/2021]. https://en.wikipedia.org/wiki/Vibram
4. Frederick, E.: Optimal frictional properties for sport shoes and sport surfaces. In: ISBS-Conference Proceedings Archive (1993)
5. Van Groningen, D.J.: Effects of outsole shoe patterns on athletic performance (2016)
6. Hanson, J.P., Redfern, M.S., Mazumdar, M.: Predicting slips and falls considering required and available friction. Ergonomics **42**(12), 1619–1633 (1999)
7. U.S. Department of Labor-Bureau of Labor Statistics, Nonfatal cases involving days away from work: selected characteristics (2011 forward) Series ID: CSUE4X00000063000, CSU00X00000063000: Washington, D.C. (2020)
8. Welfare, M.O.H.L.A.: Vital statistics of Japan Final data General mortality, V. Statistics, Editor: Shinjuku-ku, Japan (2020)
9. Canadian Institute for Health Information, Exercise caution: Canadians frequently injured in falls (2017)
10. U.S. Department of Labor-Bureau of Labor Statistics, Nonfatal cases involving days away from work: selected characteristics (2011 forward) Series ID: CSUAFS422XXX6E100, CSUAFS42XXXX6E100: Washington, D.C. (2020)
11. Nachreiner, N.M., Findorff, M.J., Wyman, J.F., Mccarthy, T.C.: Circumstances and consequences of falls in community-dwelling older women. J. Women's Health **16**(10), 1437–1446 (2007)
12. Iraqi, A., Cham, R., Redfern, M.S., Beschorner, K.E.: Coefficient of friction testing parameters influence the prediction of human slips. Appl. Ergon. **70**, 118–126 (2018)
13. Chang, W.R., et al.: The role of friction in the measurement of slipperiness, Part 2: survey of friction measurement devices. Ergon **44**(13), 1233–1261 (2001)
14. Grönqvist, R., et al.: Human-centred approaches in slipperiness measurement. Ergonomics **44**(13), 1167–1199 (2001)
15. Hsu, J., et al.: Slip resistance of winter footwear on snow and ice measured using maximum achievable incline. Ergonomics **59**(5), 717–728 (2016)

16. Beschorner, K.E., Iraqi, A., Redfern, M.S., Cham, R., Li, Y.: Predicting slips based on the STM 603 whole-footwear tribometer under different coefficient of friction testing conditions. Ergonomics **62**(5), 668–681 (2019)
17. Blanchette, M.G., Powers, C.M.: The influence of footwear tread groove parameters on available friction. Appl. Ergon. **50**, 237–241 (2015)
18. Hemler, S., et al.: Changes in under-shoe traction and fluid drainage for progressively worn shoe tread. Appl. Ergon. **80**, 35–42 (2019)
19. Hemler, S.L., Pliner, E.M., Redfern, M.S., Haight, J.M., Beschorner, K.E.: Traction performance across the life of slip-resistant footwear: preliminary results from a longitudinal study. J. Saf. Res. **74**, 219–225 (2020)
20. Li, K., Chen, C.: The effect of shoe soling tread groove width on the coefficient of friction with different sole materials, floors, and contaminants. Appl. Ergon. **35**, 499–507 (2004)
21. Li, K.W., Chen, C.J.: Effects of tread groove orientation and width of the footwear pads on measured friction coefficients. Saf. Sci. **43**(7), 391–405 (2005)
22. Iraqi, A., Vidic, N.S., Redfern, M.S., Beschorner, K.E.: Prediction of coefficient of friction based on footwear outsole features. Appl. Ergon. **82**, 102963 (2020)
23. Jones, T.G., Iraqi, A., Beschorner, K.E.: Performance testing of work shoes labeled as slip resistant. Appl. Ergon. **68**, 304–312 (2018)
24. Yamaguchi, T., Katsurashima, Y., Hokkirigawa, K.: Effect of rubber block height and orientation on the coefficients of friction against smooth steel surface lubricated with glycerol solution. Tribol. Int. **110**, 96–102 (2017)
25. Hale, J., O'connell, A., Lewis, R., Carré, M., Rongong, J.: An evaluation of shoe tread parameters using FEM. Tribol. Int. **153**, 106570 (2021)
26. Moriyasu, K., Nishiwaki, T., Shibata, K., Yamaguchi, T., Hokkirigawa, K.: Friction control of a resin foam/rubber laminated block material. Trib. Int. **136**, 548–555 (2019)
27. Yamaguchi, T., et al.: Development of new footwear sole surface pattern for prevention of slip-related falls. Saf. Sci. **50**(4), 986–994 (2012)
28. Gao, C., Abeysekera, J., Hirvonen, M., Aschan, C.: The effect of footwear sole abrasion on the coefficient of friction on melting and hard ice. Int. J. Ind. Ergon. **31**(5), 323–330 (2003)
29. Gao, C., Abeysekera, J., Hirvonen, M., Grönqvist, R.: Slip resistant properties of footwear on ice. Ergonomics **47**(6), 710–716 (2004)
30. Yamaguchi, T., Hsu, J., Li, Y., Maki, B.E.: Efficacy of a rubber outsole with a hybrid surface pattern for preventing slips on icy surfaces. Appl. Ergon. **51**, 9–17 (2015)
31. Tsai, Y.J., Powers, C.M.: The influence of footwear sole hardness on slip initiation in young adults*. J. Forensic Sci. **53**(4), 884–888 (2008)
32. Kietzig, A.M., Hatzikiriakos, S., Englezos, P.: Ice friction: the effects of surface roughness, structure, and hydrophobicity. J. Appl. Phys. **106**(2), 024303 (2009)
33. Shibata, K., et al.: Effect of groove width and depth and urethane coating on slip resistance of vinyl flooring sheet in glycerol solution. Tribol. Int. **135**, 89–95 (2019)
34. Nishi, T., Moriyasu, K., Harano, K., Nishiwaki, T.: Influence of dewettability on rubber friction properties with different surface roughness under water/ethanol/glycerol lubricated conditions. Tribol. Online **11**(5), 601–607 (2016)
35. Sato, S., et al.: Dry sliding friction and Wear behavior of thermoplastic polyurethane against abrasive paper. Biotribology **23**, 100130 (2020)
36. Bagheri, Z.S., Anwer, A.O., Fernie, G., Naguib, H.E., Dutta, T.: Effects of multi-functional surface-texturing on the ice friction and abrasion characteristics of hybrid composite materials for footwear. Wear **418**, 253–264 (2019)
37. Rizvi, R., Naguib, H., Fernie, G., Dutta, T.: High friction on ice provided by elastomeric fiber composites with textured surfaces. Appl. Phys. Lett. **106**(11), 111601 (2015)

38. Roshan Fekr, A., et al.: Evaluation of winter footwear: comparison of test methods to determine footwear slip resistance on ice surfaces. Int. J. Environ. Res. Publ. Health **18**(2), 405 (2021)
39. Li, K., Wu, H., Lin, Y.: The effect of shoe sole tread groove depth on the friction coefficient with different tread groove widths, floors and contaminants. Appl. Ergon. **37**, 743–8 (2006)
40. Moore, D.F.: The Friction and Lubrication of Elastomers, International Series of Monographs on Material Science and Technology. Pergamon Press, Oxford (1972)
41. Strobel, C.M., Menezes, P.L., Lovell, M.R., Beschorner, K.E.: Analysis of the contribution of adhesion and hysteresis to shoe–floor lubricated friction in the boundary lubrication regime. Tribol. Lett. **47**(3), 341–347 (2012)
42. Heinrich, G., Klüppel, M., Vilgis, T.A.: Evaluation of self-affine surfaces and their implication for frictional dynamics as illustrated with a Rouse material. Comput. Theor. Polym. Sci. **10**(1–2), 53–61 (2000)
43. Persson, B.N.: Theory of rubber friction and contact mechanics. J. Chem. Phys. **115**(8), 3840–3861 (2001)
44. Moghaddam, S., Acharya, A., Redfern, M., Beschorner, K.: Predictive multiscale computational model of shoe-floor coefficient of friction. J. Biomech. **66**, 145–152 (2018)
45. Moghaddam, S.R.M., Redfern, M., Beschorner, K.: A microscopic finite element model of shoe-floor hysteresis and adhesion friction. Tribol. Lett. **59**(3), 1–10 (2015)
46. Moghaddam, S.R., Beschorner, K.E.: Sensitivity of a multiscale model of shoe-floor-contaminant friction to normal force and shoe-floor contact angle. In: Society of Tribologists and Lubrication Engineers 2017, Atlanta, GA (2017)
47. Strandberg, L.: The effect of conditions underfoot on falling and overexertion accidents. Ergonomics **28**(1), 131–47 (1985)
48. Tisserand, M.: Progress in the prevention of falls caused by slipping. Ergonomics **28**, 1027–1042 (1985)
49. Beschorner, K., Lovell, M., Higgs, C., Redfern, M.: Modeling mixed-lubrication of a shoe-floor interface applied to a pin-on-disk apparatus. Tribol. Trans. **52**(4), 560–568 (2009)
50. Chang, W.R., et al.: The role of friction in the measurement of slipperiness, Part 1: friction mechanisms and definition of test conditions. Ergonomics **44**(13), 1217–32 (2001)
51. Hamrock, B.J., Schmid, S.R., Jacobson, B.O.: Fundamentals of Fluid Film Lubrication. CRC Press, Boca Raton (2004)
52. Hemler, S., Charbonneau, D., Beschorner, K.: Predicting hydrodynamic conditions under worn shoes using the tapered-wedge solution of Reynolds equation. Trib. Int. **145**, 106161 (2020)
53. Singh, G., Beschorner, K.E.: A method for measuring fluid pressures in the shoe-floor-fluid interface: application to shoe tread evaluation. IIE Trans. Occup. Ergon. Hum. Factors **2**(2), 53–59 (2014)
54. Beschorner, K.E., Albert, D.A., Chambers, A.J., Redfern, M.R.: Fluid pressures at the shoe-floor-contaminant interface during slips: effects of tread & implications on slip severity. J. Biomech. **47**(2), 458–463 (2014)
55. Sundaram, V., Hemler, S.L., Chanda, A., Haight, J.M., Redfern, M.S., Beschorner, K.E.: Worn region size of shoe soles impacts human slips: testing a mechanistic model. J. Biomech. **105**, 109797 (2020)
56. Shan, L., Levert, J., Meade, L., Tichy, J., Danyluk, S.: Interfacial fluid mechanics and pressure prediction in chemical mechanical polishing. J. Trib. **122**(3), 539–543 (2000)
57. Iraqi, A.: Comparison of interfacial fluid pressures generated across common shoe-floor friction testing apparatuses. In: Department of Mechanical Engineering. Blekinge Institute of Technology, Karlskrona, Sweden (2013)
58. Walter, P., Tushak, C., Hemler, S., Beschorner, K.: Effect of tread design and hardness on interfacial fluid force and friction in artificially worn shoes. Footwear Sci., in review (2021)

59. Beschorner, K.E., et al.: An observational ergonomic tool for assessing the worn condition of slip-resistant shoes. Appl. Ergon. **88**, 103140 (2020)
60. Moriyasu, K., Nishiwaki, T., Yamaguchi, T., Hokkirigawa, K.: New technique of three directional ground reaction force distributions. Footwear Sci. **2**(2), 57–64 (2010)
61. Moriyasu, K., Nishiwaki, T., Yamaguchi, T., Hokkirigawa, K.: Experimental analysis of the distribution of traction coefficient in the shoe-ground contact area during running. Tribol. Online **7**(4), 267–273 (2012)
62. Niwa, E., et al.: Load vector sensors using strain-sensitive cr-n thin films and their applications. Electron. Commun. Jpn. **99**(4), 58–67 (2016)
63. Yamaguchi, T.: Distribution of the local required coefficient of friction in the shoe–floor contact area during straight walking: a pilot study. Biotribology **19**, 100101 (2019)
64. Albert, D.L., Moyer, B., Beschorner, K.E.: Three-dimensional shoe kinematics during unexpected slips: implications for shoe-floor friction testing. IIE Trans. Occup. Ergon. Hum. Factors **5**(1), 1–11 (2017)
65. Chang, W.-R., Leclercq, S., Lockhart, T.E., Haslam, R.: State of science: occupational slips, trips and falls on the same level. Ergonomics **59**(7), 861–883 (2016)
66. Chang, W.R., Courtney, T.K., Gronqvist, R., Redfern, M.S.: Measuring slipperiness- discussions on the state of the art and future research. In: Chang, W.R., Courtney, T.K. (eds.) Measuring Slipperiness: Human Locomotion and Surface Factors. Taylor & Francis, London, New York (2003)

Effects of Foot–Floor Friction on Trip-Induced Falls During Shuffling Gait: A Simulation Study

Takeshi Yamaguchi[1]([⊠]), Kenichi Nakatani[1], Tomoki Hirose[1], Takashi Yoshida[2], and Kei Masani[3,4]

[1] Graduate School of Engineering, Tohoku University, Sendai Miyagi 980-8579, Japan
takeshi.yamaguchi.c8@tohoku.ac.jp
[2] University Medical Center Göttingen, 37075 Göttingen, Germany
[3] KITE Research Institute–University Health Network, Toronto M4G 3V9, Canada
[4] Institute of Biomedical Engineering, University of Toronto, Toronto M5S 3V9, Canada

Abstract. Tripping while walking has been identified as the most common cause of falls among the elderly as they tend to utilize a shuffling gait while walking, which increases the risk of falling. Since tripping occurs when toes make unexpected contact with objects on the floor, a number of studies have investigated the impact of foot clearance on the risk of tripping. However, only a few studies have examined the effects of foot–floor friction on the risk of tripping. Thus, in this current study, we investigated the effect of foot–floor friction on the probability of trip-induced falls during normal and shuffling gaits in a computational simulation study. We used a computational model with neural rhythm generators and neuromusculoskeletal systems to simulate gait in a self-organized manner. By changing the parameters of the neural rhythm generator, gait parameters such as step length, cadence, and foot clearance were automatically reduced, which simulated the shuffling gait. To alter the foot–floor friction, we changed the spring coefficient ratio of the floor in horizontal and vertical directions. As per our results, it was determined that slip-induced falls occurred under low foot–floor friction conditions in both normal and shuffling gaits, whereas trip-induced falls occurred under high foot–floor friction conditions only with a shuffling gait. These results suggest that optimal foot–floor friction may prevent trip- and slip-induced falls among the elderly.

Keywords: Shuffling gait · Friction · Trip-induced fall · Neuromusculoskeletal model

1 Introduction

Falling accidents impede long healthy life spans among the elderly. Falls often lead to serious injuries, such as hip fractures and head traumas, which can only deteriorate mobility and reduce independence. The most common cause of falls in the elderly is tripping while walking, which results in a loss of balance in the forward direction [1].

Age-related gait changes reduce gait speed, step length, hip and knee extension, and ankle dorsiflexion angle at heel strike, as well as the clearance between the foot and

N. L. Black et al. (Eds.): IEA 2021, LNNS 223, pp. 856–860, 2022.
https://doi.org/10.1007/978-3-030-74614-8_104

floor surface; i.e., foot clearance [2]. As a result, the elderly tend to exhibit a gait that is similar to a shuffling gait [3]. This increases the chance of collision between foot and objects on the floor during walking, which often results in tripping. Therefore, a number of studies have investigated the influence of foot clearance on the risk of tripping [4, 5].

In developing barrier-free environments, many researchers have focused on floor friction-induced falls. A few studies have indicated that excessive slip resistance between feet and the floor could lead to tripping [6]. Although many studies investigated the effects of foot–floor friction on slipping [7–9], studies examining the effects of foot–floor friction on the risk of trip-induced falls during walking remain scarce. Therefore, this current study aimed to investigate the effect of foot–floor friction on the probability of trip-induced falls during normal and shuffling gaits simulated using a neuromusculoskeletal model.

2 Methods

The neuromusculoskeletal model used in this study is presented in Fig. 1. Based on Taga's model [10], it is used to simulate normal and shuffling gaits. By changing the positive constant for torque generation at each joint, a shuffling gait was simulated, which resulted in a reduction of step length, cadence, and foot clearance (0.60 m, 102 steps/min, 0.02 m, respectively, in the shuffling gait compared with 0.68 m, 120 steps/min, 0.14 m, respectively, in the normal gait).

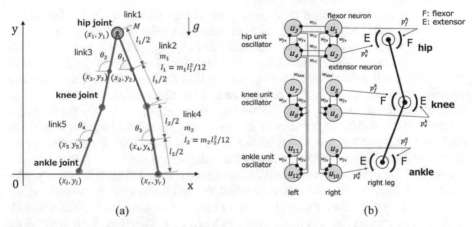

(a)   (b)

Fig. 1. Neuromusculoskeletal model [10]. (a) Musculoskeletal system. Mass of the upper body, thigh, and shank were determined to be 48.0, 7.0, and 4.0 kg, respectively. Length of the thigh and shank are 0.5 and 0.6 m, respectively. (b) Neural rhythm generator. p_f^h, p_e^h, p_f^k, p_e^k, p_f^a, and p_e^a values for normal gait were 15, 85, 15, 15, 100, and 75, respectively. p_f^h, p_e^h, p_f^k, p_e^k, p_f^a, and p_e^a values for shuffling gait were 8, 48, 1, 2, 55, and 27.5, respectively.

To alter the foot–floor friction, we changed the ratio of the spring coefficient of the floor in the horizontal (k_{gx}) and vertical (k_{gy}) directions (k_{gx}/k_{gy}). The horizontal movement of the foot increased with the decreasing k_{gx}/k_{gy} values, which could simulate a slip resulting from a low horizontal ground reaction force (i.e., friction force). In contrast, a high k_{gx}/k_{gy} value was found to cause a large horizontal ground reaction force, thereby simulating a high foot–floor friction condition. The length of the level walkway was 12 m. The k_{gx}/k_{gy} value of the walkway surface for 0–4 m was 0.02, but it changed after 4 m. White noise was then set to u_0 which is an external input in the differential equations of the neural rhythm generator for each condition. For the identical k_{gx}/k_{gy} value condition, 100 trials were conducted. A fall was identified based on the height of the body's center of mass. Slip-induced falls were recognized as those in which the foot moved in the horizontal direction and a fall occurred in the opposite direction to the movement of the foot. Meanwhile, trip-induced falls were identified as those in which the fall occurred in the forward direction after the feet made contact and stopped. The probability of falls for each k_{gx}/k_{gy} value condition was calculated based on the number of fall trials in 100 trials on normal and shuffling gaits.

3   Results and Discussion

Figure 2 shows the representative simulation results of a shuffling gait with different k_{gx}/k_{gy} values. As shown in Fig. 2(a), due to the reduction in the k_{gx}/k_{gy} value from 0.02 to 0.0004, the leading foot slid forward, and a backward fall then occurred. No fall occurred when the k_{gx}/k_{gy} value changed from 0.02 to 0.03, as shown in Fig. 2(b). On the other hand, when the k_{gx}/k_{gy} value increased from 0.02 to 0.65, the trailing foot slid forward but stopped due to high friction (Fig. 2(c)). Consequently, a forward fall occurred due to the friction-induced trip.

Figure 3 shows the effect of the k_{gx}/k_{gy} value on the probability of a fall for normal and shuffling gaits. When walking with a normal gait (Fig. 3(a)), slip-induced falls were noted to occur under low-friction conditions ($k_{gx}/k_{gy} < 0.02$). Moreover, there were no trip-induced falls, which means that high foot–floor friction is desirable to prevent falls when walking with a normal gait. However, when walking with a shuffling gait (Fig. 3(b)), slip-induced falls occurred under low-friction conditions, whereas trip-induced falls occurred under high-friction conditions ($k_{gx}/k_{gy} > 0.04$). These results indicate that a trip-induced fall is unlikely to occur in normal walking but is likely to occur in shuffling gait across a high-friction floor. This means that the shuffling gait is more sensitive to foot–floor friction compared to the normal gait.

Our results provide new insight into the footwear and floor design for the elderly, who tend to walk in a shuffling gait. Excessive high friction in the shoe–floor combination might be inappropriate for the elderly in terms of preventing trip-induced falls, although excessive low friction can also result in slip-induced falls. Therefore, there must be an optimal range for a friction coefficient between foot and floor contact in order to reduce the risk of trip- and slip-induced falls for people who walk with a shuffling gait. As these hypotheses are based on purely theoretical approaches, further experimental research is needed to identify the optimal range for a friction coefficient.

4   Conclusions

Using a computational simulation, we were able to demonstrate that trip-induced falls occur under high foot–floor friction conditions when walking with a shuffling gait,

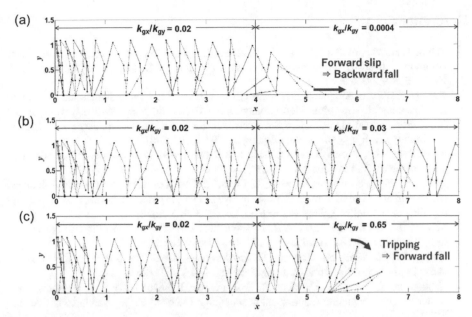

Fig. 2. Representative simulation results (stick diagram) of shuffling gait. (a) Slip-induced fall; (b) no-fall; (c) trip-induced fall.

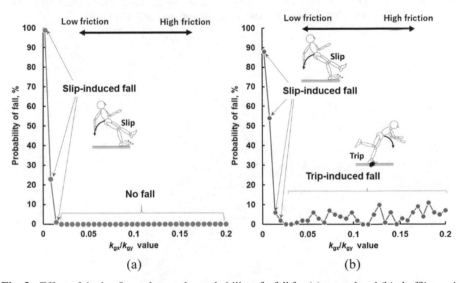

Fig. 3. Effect of the k_{gx}/k_{gy} value on the probability of a fall for (a) normal and (b) shuffling gait.

whereas slip-induced falls occur under low foot–floor friction conditions in a normal gait. These results suggest that an optimal foot–floor friction may exist in terms of preventing both trip- and slip-induced falls for individuals who walk with a shuffling gait, including the elderly.

References

1. Talbot, L.A., Musiol, R.J., Witham, E.K., Metter, E.J.: Falls in young, middle-aged and older community dwelling adults: perceived cause, environmental factors and injury. BMC Publ. Health 5(86), 1–9 (2005)
2. Kim, H., et al.: Are gait parameters related to knee pain, urinary incontinence and a history of falls in community-dwelling elderly women? Jpn. J. Geriatr. 50, 528–535 (2013). (in Japanese)
3. Lord, S.R., Lloyd, D.G., Li, S.K.: Sensori-motor function, gait patterns and falls in community-dwelling women. Age Ageing 25, 292–299 (1996)
4. McKenzie, N.C., Brown, L.A.: Obstacle negotiation kinematics: age-dependent effects of postural threat. Gait Posture 19(226–234), 20 (2004)
5. Wang, Y., Wang, S., Bolton, R., Kaur, T., Bhatt, T.: Effects of task-specific obstacle-induced trip-perturbation training: proactive and reactive adaptation to reduce fall-risk in community-dwelling older adults. Aging Clin. Exp. Res. 32, 893–905 (2020)
6. Menz, H.B., Morris, M.E., Lord, S.R.: Footwear characteristics and risk of indoor and outdoor falls in older people. Gerontology 52, 174–180 (2006)
7. Yamaguchi, T., Yano, M., Onodera, H., Hokkirigawa, K.: Effect of turning angle on falls caused by induced slips during turning. J. Biomech. 45, 2624–2629 (2012)
8. Yamaguchi, T., Yano, M., Onodera, H., Hokkirigawa, K.: Kinematic of center of mass and center of pressure predict requirement at shoe–floor interface during walking. Gait Posture 38(2), 209–214 (2013)
9. Chang, W.-R., Leclercq, S., Lockhart, T.E., Haslam, R.: State of science: occupational slips, trips and falls on the same level. Ergonomics 59, 861–883 (2016)
10. Taga, G., Yamaguchi, Y., Shimizu, H.: Self-organized control of bipedal locomotion by neural oscillators in unpredictable environment. Biol. Cybern. 65, 147–159 (1991)

Correction to: Proceedings of the 21st Congress of the International Ergonomics Association (IEA 2021)

Nancy L. Black, W. Patrick Neumann, and Ian Noy

Correction to:
N. L. Black et al. (Eds.): *Proceedings of the 21st Congress*
of the International Ergonomics Association (IEA 2021),
LNNS 223, https://doi.org/10.1007/978-3-030-74614-8

In the original version of the book, the following belated corrections have been incorporated: The author name "Yue (Sophia) Li" has been changed to "Sofia Scataglini" in the part VI.

The updated version of the book can be found at
https://doi.org/10.1007/978-3-030-74614-8

Author Index

A

Abele, Nils Darwin, 250, 258
Adalarasu, K., 517
Adejare, Olusegun Adeyemi, 481, 509
Adolph, Lars, 777
Aguwa, Emmanuel Nwabueze, 81
Ajoudani, Arash, 335
Albrecht, Philipp, 335
Alexander, Thomas, 777
Alfargani, Asma, 569
Almosnino, Sivan, 131, 349
Altaboli, Ahamed, 569
Anderson, Kathleen, 577
Anyaene, Chiamaka Chinyere, 81
Apatiga, Yvette, 797
Aprilin Asikin, Dwilita, 39
Arezes, Pedro, 829
Arinze-Onyia, Susan U., 81
Armstrong, Daniel P., 585
Aschenbrenner, Doris, 387
Ashdown, Susan P., 105
Atuenyi, Blessing Chiagozikam, 487
Aublet-Cuvelier, Agnès, 592
Averta, Giuseppe, 335
Avila Chaurand, Rosalio, 96

B

Babapour, Maral, 3
Babič, Jan, 353
Baker, Michael, 45
Balasubramanian, Venkatesh, 517, 559
Baltrusch, Saskia, 235
Bandmann, Cerys E. M., 274
Barcellini, Flore, 597, 628

Barrero, Lope H., 206
Bauer, Sebastian, 415
Béarée, Richard, 597
Benchekroun, Tahar-Hakim, 597
Bengler, Klaus, 274, 667
Beschorner, Kurt E., 841
Bianchi, Matteo, 335
Billing, Erik, 358
Bitencourt, Rosimeire Sedrez, 767
Blake, Josie, 200
Blay-Moreira, Jessica, 797
Boldt, Rachel S., 105
Boos, Annika, 224
Borges, Guilherme Deola, 829
Bortolotti, Sara, 162
Bounouar, Mouad, 597
Bowman, Richard, 841
Brauner, Philipp, 605
Briceno, Leyde, 403
Brissaud, Daniel, 614
Brolin, Erik, 358, 374
Bruch, Lena aus dem, 667
Buchmann, Willy, 597
Buckley, Katie, 783
Bui, Uyen D., 797
Burbach, Laura, 605
Butter, Dorien, 367

C

Cadilhe, Maria, 758
Cao, Caroline G. L., 308
Caporaso, Teodorico, 317
Cappelletto, Jessica, 131
Carey, Lindsay, 783

Carneiro, Paula, 829
Caroly, Sandrine, 636
Carvalho, Miguel A. F., 105
Castillo-M, Juan Alberto, 473
Castillo-Ortega, Rafael, 114
Cavuoto, Lora A., 585
Cheng, Hong, 325
Cherubini, Andrea, 335
Chevalier, Aline, 621
Chignell, Mark, 379
Chini, Giorgia, 335
Chollet, Mathieu, 308
Cobaleda-Cordero, Antonio, 3
Colosio, Claudio, 162
Compan, Nathan, 614
Costa, Tales Fernandes, 394
Coutarel, Fabien, 614
Covarrubias Cruz, Julieta María, 54
Cupar, Andrej, 148

D

Dada, Olumide Olasunkanmi, 481, 487, 495
Damsgaard, Michael, 353
de Aguiar Mendonça, Gabriel, 394
De La Rocha Barbosa, María Fernanda, 54
De la Vega-Bustillos, Enrique Javier, 122
de Looze, Michiel, 235
de Macedo Guimarães, Lia Buarque, 767
De Marchi, Matteo, 242, 266
de Paulo, Beatriz, 12
de Vries, Aijse, 235
Denteneer, Lenie, 462
Derenevich, Marcia Gemari, 767
Desbrosses, Kévin, 175
Détienne, Françoise, 45
Di Gironimo, Giuseppe, 317
Ditchen, Dirk, 206
Dolšak, Bojan, 148
dos Santos Lopes, Thatiane, 394
Dosso, Cheyenne, 621
Douwes, Marjolein, 175
Draicchio, Francesco, 175, 191, 335
Dubey, Gérard, 597
Duprey, Sonia, 434
Dy, Arvidas Kio, 20

E

Eckardt, Robert, 749
Ekechukwu, Echezona Nelson Dominic, 81, 481,
　　487, 495, 509, 537
Ekechukwu, Nmachukwu Ifeoma, 509
Ellegast, Rolf, 139, 175, 206
Ells, William, 841
Enquist, Henrik, 175
Ezeukwu, Antoninus Obinna, 487

F

Farhadi Niaki, Farzin, 379
Ferreira, Fernando B. N., 105
Ferreira, Filipa, 758
Fiori, Lorenzo, 191, 335
Fischer, Matthias Sebastian, 31
Fischer, Petra, 250, 258
Fischer, Steven L., 585
Fleischer, Martin, 274, 439
Forsman, Mikael, 175
Fraboni, Federico, 242, 266
Franke, Thomas, 735
Fritzsche, Lars, 335, 353, 415

G

Galibarov, Pavel E., 353
Gallagher, Sean, 585
Gamkrelidze, Tamari, 628
Ganguli, Anindya K., 183
Gärtner, Christian, 353
Giorgianni, Concetto Mario, 162
Goldhahn, Leif, 749
González-Muñoz, Elvia Luz, 96
Govaerts, Renee, 335
Grazioso, Stanislao, 317
Griffin, Linsey, 105
Groll, Hendrik, 291
Groos, Sandra, 250, 258
Gruber, Mira, 797
Gualtieri, Luca, 242, 266
Guérin, Jeanne, 791
Guelle, Kevin, 636
Gundel, Katharina, 224
Gupta, Nidhi, 175

H

Hadi Kusumo, Argo, 39
Hamzat, Tal'hatu Kolapo, 537
Hancock, Gabriella M., 797
Hancock, Peter A., 797
Hanson, Lars, 358, 374
Harbauer, Christina M., 274
Harih, Gregor, 148
Hartono, Markus, 39
Hauqui Tonin, Paulo Eduardo, 62
Hefferle, Michael, 250, 258, 300
Heine, Moreen, 735
Heinold, Eva, 343
Heinrich, Kai, 139, 206
Hentschel, Tino, 643
Hermanns-Truxius, Ingo, 139, 175, 206
Hernández-Grageda, Pilar, 54, 71
Héron, Robin, 45
Hery, Michel, 592
Heßling, Stefan, 175

Hiranai, Kazuki, 155
Hirose, Tomoki, 856
Hochberg, Limor, 715
Hoehne-Hückstädt, Ulrike, 206
Högberg, Dan, 358, 374
Holder, Daniel, 31
Hollands, Justin G., 691
Holtermann, Andreas, 175
Homayounpour, Mohammad, 367
Honig, Shanee, 282
Huangfu, Rong, 131
Hurst, Simon, 215

I

Ibarra Caballero, María Inés, 71
Ibarra Mejia, Gabriel, 96
Ikefuna, Ogechukwu, 81
Iriondo Pascual, Aitor, 374
Iroezindu, Israel Chijioke, 81

J

Jäger, Matthias, 206
Jamieson, Greg A., 407, 675, 691
Jiang, Haoyan, 379
Jochems, Nicole, 650, 725

K

Kaindl, Hermann, 683
Kaljun, Jasmin, 148
Kannan, Vishal, 517
Kato, Macky, 171
Kheng, Cindy, 708
Khow, Johnamae, 820
Kim, Han K., 429
Klaer, Verena, 291
Kluth, Karsten, 250, 258, 300
Konemann, Reinier, 175
Kopetz, Jan Patrick, 650
Kordts, Börge, 577
Krause, Frank, 235
Kruse, Kevin, 258

L

Lafeuillade, Anne-Cecile, 597
Lamb, Maurice, 358
Lämkull, Dan, 374
Landry, Aurélie, 636
Lanzotti, Antonio, 317
Lazo, Margarita, 20
Lechappe, Aurelien, 308
Lechner, Norbert, 175
Lee, SangHyun, 585
Li, Hongting, 453
Li, Meng, 387
Li, Wei, 379

Li, Yue (Sophia), 841
Lidynia, Chantal, 605
Liu, Zhe, 379
Loewis, Peter, 175
Luneva, Anastasiia, 552

M

Maier, Thomas, 31
Malaiya, Tanya, 559
Malenfer, Marc, 592
Mänttäri, Satu, 175
Maruhn, Philipp, 215
Masani, Kei, 856
Masci, Federica, 162
Mathiassen, Svend Erik, 175
Maurice, Pauline, 353
Mbada, Chidozie Emmanuel, 481
Mei, Shibo, 453
Melagoda, Damithri Gayashini, 804
Merryweather, Andrew, 367
Mgbeojedo, Amaka Gloria, 509
Miehling, Jörg, 447
Millo, Francesco, 242
Mizobuchi, Sachi, 379
Moore, Christopher A. B., 585
Moraes, Anna S. P., 105
Moricot, Caroline, 597
Motta, Isabela, 658
Murano, Ryota, 171

N

Nakajima, Kimie, 171
Nakajima, Mizuki, 171
Nakatani, Kenichi, 856
Natarajan, Priyadarshini, 517
Neuhöfer, Jan A., 643
Nwankwo, Kingsley Obumneme, 495, 509, 537
Nwokocha, Chinwendu Obi, 487
Nzeakuba, Ikenna Collins, 495

O

O'Halloran, Paul, 783
Oates, Jennifer, 783
Ogundapo, Femi Abolaji, 481
Okeke, Theodora A., 81
Okogba, Nelson, 509
Okonkwo, Uchenna Prosper, 509
Olaleye, Olubukola Adebisi, 537
Olivares Jiménez, Ana Sofía, 71
Olowoyo, Paul, 495
Oron-Gilad, Tal, 282

Oßwald, Marius, 447
Owolabi, Mayowa Ojo, 495

P

Panariello, Dario, 317
Pascual, Aitor Iriondo, 358
Pastura, Flavia Cristine Hofstetter, 394
Paubel, Pierre-Vincent, 621
Paul, Gunther, 403, 420
Pedret, Kayla, 407
Pereira, Cláudia, 758
Perez Luque, Estela, 374
Petrat, Deborah, 811
Pietrantoni, Luca, 242
Pinder, Andrew, 175
Plotnikova, Daria, 552
Popp, Roman, 683
Prasch, Lorenz, 667
Prasetyo, Yogi Tri, 820

Q

Qiu, Jing, 325
Quaresma, Manuela, 12, 658, 699
Quispe Guanolusia, David, 675

R

Rajabiyazdi, Fahimeh, 675
Rajendran, Minerva, 559
Rajulu, Sudhakar L., 429
Ranavolo, Alberto, 191, 335
Raneburger, David, 683
Rauch, Erwin, 242, 266
Reiner, Adam J., 691
Rey Galindo, John A., 96
Rigaud, Jerome, 308
Rix-Lièvre, Géraldine, 614
Rodrigues, Ana, 758
Rodríguez-Vega, Dora Aydee, 114, 122
Rodríguez-Vega, Graciela, 114, 122
Rosecrance, John, 162
Rosen, Patricia Helen, 335, 343
Rosselin-Bareille, Celine, 597
Rowlinson, Steve, 804
Ruddock-Hudson, Mandy, 783
Ruiz, Cinthia, 699

S

Safin, Stéphane, 45
Salloum, Mariam, 224
Santos Rivera, Fernanda, 54
Santos, Andreana Gabrielle, 20
Santos, Marta, 758
Saraceno, Marco, 597
Sartori, Massimo, 335
Sato, Takeshi, 171

Savonnet, Léo, 434
Scataglini, Sofia, 462
Schams, Peter, 175
Schellewald, Vera, 175
Schiefer, Christoph, 139, 175
Schmitz, Christian E., 797
Schneider, Sonja, 224
Schrader, Andreas, 577
Schrills, Tim, 735
Schust, Marianne, 175
Seidel, David H., 206
Sengpiel, Michael, 725
Seo, Akihiko, 155
Seva, Rosemary, 20
Sharma, Neelesh K., 183
Siadat, Ali, 597
Silvetti, Alessio, 191, 335
Smith, Thomas J., 708
Smolin, Artem, 552
Sonne, Michael W., 585
Spatari, Giovanna, 162
Spitzhirn, Michael, 353, 415
Steinebach, Tim, 291
Strebl, Michaela, 175
Stüdeli, Thomas, 715
Suhir, Ephraim, 420
Syberfeldt, Anna, 374

T

Tamine, Lynda, 621
Tatarelli, Antonella, 191, 335
Taylor, Carrie, 200
Thakur, Atul, 183
Tikhonov, Gleb, 552
Tiwari, Mayank, 183
Trillos Ch., Maria Constanza, 473
Tsynchenko, Aleksandr, 552

U

Urías Dueñas, Lilia Atziri, 71
Utti, Victor Adimabua, 495, 509

V

van Eijk, Daan, 387
van Tol, Daniëlle, 387
Vanden Bossche, Hanne, 462
Vanderborght, Bram, 335
Varrecchia, Tiwana, 335
Vasta, Saaransh, 367
Veiersted, Kaj Bo, 175
Verwulgen, Stijn, 462
Vink, Peter, 387
Vogt, Lydia, 335
Volkmann, Torben, 725
Volosiuk, Aleksandr, 552

Voss, Stefan, 777
Vu, Linh Q., 429

W

Wagner, Yvonne, 447
Wakula, Jurij, 291
Wang, Lu, 325
Wang, Xuguang, 434
Wang, Yilin, 325
Wartzack, Sandro, 447
Weber, Britta, 139, 175, 206
Wessel, Daniel, 735
Wirsching, Hans-Joachim, 439
Wischniewski, Sascha, 335, 343
Wolf, Alexander, 447
Wu, Bohan, 453
Wu, Jinduo, 453

Y

Yaji, Miho, 155
Yamaguchi, Takeshi, 841, 856
Yang, Xiao, 325
Yang, Zhen, 453
Yoshida, Takashi, 856

Z

Zaldívar-Colado, Ulises, 114, 122
Zaldívar-Colado, Xiomara Penelope, 114, 122
Zamberlan, Maria Cristina Palmer Lima, 394
Zelck, Sander, 462
Zhang, Gang, 453
Zhang, Xuegang, 453
Zhou, Wei, 379
Ziefle, Martina, 605
Zoubir, Mourad, 735
Zouinar, Moustafa, 628
Zülch, Gert, 466

Printed in the United States
by Baker & Taylor Publisher Services